"Our world is shrinking." Modern means of travel and communication have shortened distance and time to an astounding degree and facilitated contacts between people and nations. This "shrinking" is placing renewed emphasis on the value of foreign-language learning for a deeper appreciation of other cultures and a more rewarding experience in communication.

This dictionary will be a valuable aid in the study of German and English. Its more than 40,000 entries have been carefully and scientifically selected on the basis of frequency and with a view to its greatest usefulness for both students and travelers. Besides accurate meanings in various synonymous and semantic shadings of the listed words, a large number of the entries include derivations and compounds of the words and illustrate their use in many idiomatic phrases. Thus the German word *Glocke* is interpreted by three English words: "bell; (glass) shade; clock." This is followed by the phrase *etwas an die grosse Glocke hängen*, with its meaning: "to make a big fuss about something." Seven compounds with their equivalents in English complete the entry. The same procedure is followed for English words. In this way the book becomes a most useful tool not only for the interpretation of material written in either of the two languages, but also for guidance in correct and enriched expression in speaking and writing.

With respect to the manner of listing it should be noted that both compounds and derivatives are listed under their first element. German nouns derived from adjectives or participles are given in the form required for the nominative when preceded by the definite article.

A feature which definitely enhances the value of this dictionary is the listing and interpretation of many modern expressions like *aerial, airborne, feedback, filter-tip, intercom, long-playing, overdrive, photo finish, picture window, striptease,* and many quite recent terms that have come from the area of science and the international scene, such as *air lift, antimissile, antimissile missile, countdown, cyclotron,* ICBM, IRBM, *microgroove, spaceship, summit conference, tranquilizer, turbojet.*

World-wide
GERMAN
DICTIONARY

German-English   *English-German*
(AMERICAN ENGLISH)

COMPILED BY
PAUL H. GLUCKSMAN, Ph.D.

EDITED BY
HERBERT RODEK, Ph.D.
AND
T. C. APPELT, Ph.D.

FAWCETT PREMIER • NEW YORK

CONTENTS

GERMAN PRONUNCIATION

A proper pronunciation of foreign words is best acquired by imitation. The following statements will be helpful for German.

VOWELS AND DIPHTHONGS

Vowels are either long or short. A vowel is long when followed by a single consonant, when doubled, or when followed by *h*. Examples: *sagen, Haar, Jahr*. A vowel is short when followed by more than one consonant. Ex.: *Mann, Kappe, wenn*. In some short words the vowel is short even if followed by only one consonant: *in, am, um, mit, das*.

a, aa, ah long, like *a* in *father*. Examples: *Vater, Aal, Jahr*.
a short, like *a* in *artistic*, but shorter. Ex.: *Mann, Land, Park*.
ä, äh long, like *ai* in *air*. Ex.: *Mädchen, mähen, Mähne*.
ä short, like *e* in *let*. Ex.: *Kälte, Bälle*.
e, ee, eh long, like *ay* in *gay*. Ex.: *den, See, sehr*.
e short, like *e* in *let*. Ex.: *Bett, nett, Emma*.
e in unaccented syllables, like the slurred *e* in *open*. Ex.: *Frage, Glocke*.
i, ie, ih long, like *ee* in *meet*. Ex.: *wir, Bier, Wien, ihr*.
i short, like *i* in *it*. Ex.: *mit, Finger, Wind*.
o, oo, oh long, like *o* in *note*. Ex.: *oder, wo, Grossvater*.
o short, like *u* in *fun*. Ex.: *Gott, kommt*.
ö, öh long, like the vowel sound in *her* or *hurt*. Ex.: *hören, Röhre*.
ö short, like the vowel sound in unaccented *-ter* in *Walter*, but quite
    short. Ex.: *können, zwölf*.
u, uh long, like *oo* in *boot*. Ex.: *gut, rufen, Schuh*.
u short, like *oo* in *foot*. Ex.: *Butter, Busch, und*.
ü, üh long, like *ee* with lips rounded for long *oo* (in *boot*). Ex.: *Mühle,
    über*.
ü short, like short *i* with lips rounded for short *oo* (in *foot*). Ex.:
    Rücken, Glück.
y is pronounced like *ü*.
au like *ou* in *out*. Ex.: *Haus, laufen*.
ei, ai, ay, ey like *y* in *my*. Ex.: *Ei, mein, Mai, Bayern, Mayer, Meyer*.
eu, äu like *oi* in *oil*. Ex.: *heute, Deutschland, Fräulein*.

CONSONANTS

b, d, f, g, h, m, n, p, ph, t, and *x* are pronounced as in English. When
    b, d, and *g* are in final position they are pronounced like *p, t, k*.
    Ex.: *gab* (like *gap*), *Kind* (like *Kint*), *Tag* (like *Tak*). *g* before
    a vowel is always pronounced hard as in English *go*, never soft
    as in *gem*. In the final syllables *-ig, -igst -igt* the *g* is pronounced
    like *ch*. Ex.: *ewig, billigst, verewigt*.

c is retained only in words of foreign origin. It is pronounced like *ts* before *e*, *ä*, *i*, *y*, otherwise like *k*.

ch like the *h* when whispering English *huge*. Ex.: *ich, weich, euch.* When preceded by *a, o, u, au*, it is produced by forcing the breath between the tongue and the uvula. Ex.: *ach, doch, Tuch, auch.* In some words of Greek origin *ch* is pronounced like *k*. Ex.: *Chor, Christus.*

chs like *ks* or *x*. Ex.: *Fuchs, Sachsen.*

j like *y* in *yes*, never like English *j*. Ex.: *ja, jung.*

kn like *k* followed by *n;* the *k* is pronounced; not like English *knee*. Ex.: *Knie.*

l not like English *l*. The tip of the tongue is placed at the base of the upper teeth. Ex.: *leben, lang.*

ng like the *ng* in *sing*, not like *finger*. Ex.: *singen, Finger.*

pf like *p* followed by *f;* both *p* and *f* are pronounced. Ex.: *Pferd, Pfund.*

ps like *p* followed by *s*, not like *ps* in English *psalm*. Ex.: *Psalm, Psychologie.*

qu like *qv*. Ex.: *Quelle, quitt.*

r is produced either by the uvula vibrating against the tongue, or by trilling with the tip of the tongue. The latter is easier.

s like *z* in *zone*. Ex.: *sagen, Sonne*. At the end of a word or syllable, *s* is pronounced like *s* in *son*. Ex.: *das, was, Gras, Wasser.*

ss or *sz* like *s* in *son*. Ex.: *gross* or *grosz.*

sch like *sh* in *shine*. Ex.: *schon, scheinen.*

sp and *st* at the beginning of a word or syllable sound like *shp* and *sht*. Ex.: *sprechen, stehen.*

th like *t*, never like English *th*. Ex.: *Theke, Thomas, Goethe.*

z, tz like *ts* in *fits*. Ex.: *zu, zeigen, sitzen*. *z* is never pronounced like English *z*.

v like *f* in *father*. Ex.: *Vater, von.*

w like *v* in *very*. Ex.: *wer, wo, wie, was.*

THE GLOTTAL STOP

In English there is a tendency to permit words to "run together," as when *not at all* is spoken as *notatall;* the glottis or opening between the vocal chords remains open. In German the glottis is closed before a word or syllable beginning with an accented vowel; every word or syllable of this type is enunciated separately. Ex.: *Wo ist er?* In English this may also occur in emphatic expressions, as e.g. "It's awful!"

ACCENT

German words are accented on the stem syllable; generally, this is the first syllable: *le'ben, Fräu'lein*. In words compounded with prefixes (syllables placed before the stem) the prefix is accented except for the following: *be-, emp-, ent-, er-, ge-, ver-, zer-*. These prefixes are never stressed. Ex.: *ge'hen, aus'gehen, bege'hen, verge'hen, zerge'hen.*

The end-syllable (suffix) *-ei* is always stressed. Ex.: *Fischerei'.*

Words of foreign origin are generally accented on the last syllable: *Student', Papier'*. In some foreign words the accent is on the next-to-last syllable: *Charak'ter.*

ABBREVIATIONS

abbr.	abbreviation	*m.*	masculine
adj.	adjective	math.	mathematics
adv.	adverb	mech.	mechanics
avi.	aviation	med.	medicine
agr.	agriculture	mil.	military
anat.	anatomy	min.	mining, minerals
arch.	architecture	mus.	music
art.	article	*n.*	noun
ast.	astronomy	naut.	nautical
auto.	automobile	*neu.*	neuter
bibl.	biblical	opt.	optical
biol.	biology	orn.	ornithology
bot.	botany	phil.	philosophy
chem.	chemistry	phot.	photography
coll.	colloquial	phy.	physics
com.	commerce	physiol.	physiology
conj.	conjunction	*pl.*	plural
dent.	dentistry	poet.	poetry
dial.	dialectal	pol.	politics
eccl.	ecclesiastic	*p.p.*	past participle
educ.	education	*prep.*	preposition
elec.	electricity	*pron.*	pronoun
ent.	entomology	rad.	radio
f.	feminine	rail.	railway
fig.	figurative (ly)	rel.	religion
geog.	geography	rhet.	rhetoric
geol.	geology	*sing.*	singular
geom.	geometry	sl.	slang
gram.	grammar	theat.	theater
hort.	horticulture	TV	television
ichth.	ichthyology	typ.	typography
interj.	interjection	*v.*	verb
interr.	interrogative	zool.	zoology
lit.	literature		

GERMAN — ENGLISH

A

Aachen *neu.* Aix-la-Chapelle
Aal *m.* eel
aalglatt *adj.* elusive, slippery
Aar *m.* (poet.) eagle
Aas *neu.* carcass, carrion; bait, lure
ab *adv.* away, down, from, off; — **und zu**
to and fro, now and then; **von nun** —
henceforth
abändern *v.* to alter, to modify; to amend
Abänderung *f.* alteration; modification
Abart *f.* variety
Abbau *m.* cutting down, reduction; discharge; (min.) working; exhaustion;
demolition
abbauen *v.* to cut down, to reduce; to discharge; (min.) to work; to demolish
abbekommen *v.* to get a share of; to get
hurt
abberufen *v.* to recall; to call away
abbestellen *v.* to countermand; to cancel
abbiegen *v.* to bend off; to branch off
Abbild *neu.* copy, image, likeness
abbilden *v.* to copy, to portray, to delineate
Abbildung *f.* picture, illustration
abbinden *v.* to untie, to tie off
Abbitte *f.* apology
abbitten *v.* to apologize for; to beg off
abblasen *v.* to blow off (*oder* away); to
sound retreat; to cancel, to call off
abblättern *v.* to strip off (leaves); to shed
(leaves); to exfoliate, to peel off
abblenden *v.* to dim, to screen, to shade
abblühen *v.* to cease blooming; to fade,
to wither
abbrechen *v.* to break off; to tear down,
to interrupt suddenly; to cut short; to
drop (a subject)
abbrennen *v.* to burn down; to fire off
abbringen *v.* to lead away; to dissuade
Abbruch *m.* breaking off; rupture, demolition; — **tun** to damage, to injure, to
disparage; **auf** — **verkaufen** to sell as
scrap
abbruchreif *adj.* dilapidated
abbüssen *v.* to atone for, to expiate; (law)
to serve a sentence
abdachen *v.* to slope, to slant
abdämmen *v.* to dam off; to embank
abdampfen *v.* to cease to evaporate; (coll.)
to depart, to steam away

abdanken *v.* to resign, to abdicate; to discharge; (mil.) to cashier
abdecken *v.* to flay, to skin; to turn down
(bed); to clear (table); to pay (debts)
abdienen *v.* to pay in service
abdrehen *v.* to switch (*oder* turn, twist)
off
abdrosseln *v.* (mech.) to throttle, to choke
Abdruck *m.* copy; impression, print; cast,
mark, stamp; —**srecht** *neu.* copyright
abdrucken *v.* to print, to imprint, to
stamp
Abend *m.* evening, night; **am** — in the
evening, at night; **gestern** — yesterday
evening, last night; **heute** — this evening, tonight; **es wird** — it's getting
dark; —**andacht** *f.* evening prayer;
—**anzug** *m.* full dress; —**blatt** *neu.* evening
paper; —**brot** *neu.*, —**essen** *neu.* supper;
—**dämmerung** *f.* dusk, evening twilight;
—**land** *neu.* occident; West; —**mahl** *neu.*
Lord's Supper; —**röte** *f.* sunset glow;
—**schule** *f.* evening classes; —**sonne** *f.*
setting sun; —**stern** *m.* evening star
Abenteuer *neu.* adventure
Abenteurer *m.* adventurer
aber *adv.* again; — *conj.* but, yet; however; —**mals** *adv.* once more; —**malig** *adj.*
repeated
Aberglaube *m.* superstition
abergläubisch *adj.* superstitious
abfahren *v.* to depart; to start; (skiing)
to glissade; to sever by driving over;
to wear out by driving; — **lassen** to
snub
Abfahrt *f.* departure; (skiing) glissade
Abfall *m.* falling off; slope, declivity;
refuse, garbage; (fig.) revolt, apostasy
abfallen *v.* to fall off, to slope; to lose
(weight); to apostatize; to be wasted;
to fail; to be snubbed
abfällig *adj.* sloping; adverse; disparaging
abfangen *v.* to intercept; to snatch, to
catch
abfärben *v.* to lose color; to stain; — **auf**
to influence
abfassen *v.* to draw up; to compose, to
write; (coll.) to catch, to arrest
abfertigen *v.* to dispatch; to forward;
(coll.) to snub
abfeuern *v.* to fire off, to discharge

11

abfinden v. to compensate; to pay off; to satisfy; **sich — mit** to come to terms with; to resign oneself to (*oder* with)

abflachen v. to flatten, to level

Abflug m. (avi.) take-off, start

Abfluss m. flowing off; discharge; **-graben** m. drain; **-rohr** neu. drain pipe

abfragen v. to interrogate, to examine, to inquire of

abfressen v. to eat off, to consume

Abfuhr f. removal, carting off; rebuff

abführen v. to lead (*oder* carry) away; (med.) to purge

Abführmittel neu. laxative, purgative

Abgabe f. delivery; duty, tax; **-n** pl. fees

Abgang m. departure; exit; retirement; loss, offal; **-sprüfung** f. final examination

Abgas neu. exhaust (*oder* waste) gas

abgeben v. to deliver; to share (*oder* deal) with; **sich — mit** to occupy oneself with

abgebrannt adj. burned down; (fig.) stone-broke

abgebrüht adj. scalded; (fig.) callous

abgedroschen adj. trite, hackneyed, commonplace

abgegriffen adj. thumbed; worn out by handling

abgehen v. to depart; to deviate; to retire; to exit; to branch off; to be missing; to relinquish; (med.) to be discharged; **gut —** to end well; **sich nichts — lassen** to deny oneself nothing

abgelebt adj. decrepit, worn out

abgelegen adj. remote, distant

abgemacht adj. settled; **— interj.** agreed! all right!

abgemessen adj. measured; slow; formal

abgeneigt adj. disinclined; averse to

Abgeordnete(r) m. representative, deputy

abgerechnet adv. deducted; **— davon** aside from

abgerissen adj. ragged, shabby; torn off; abrupt, disjointed

Abgesandte(r) m. delegate, messenger; ambassador, envoy

abgeschieden adj. secluded; deceased

abgeschmackt adj. in bad taste; absurd, silly

abgesehen prep. apart from, without regard to

abgespannt adj. exhausted, tired

abgestumpft adj. blunted; dull, indifferent

abgewöhnen v. to wean from; **sich etwas — to** give up the habit of something

Abglanz m. reflection

Abgott m. idol

Abgötterei f. idolatry

abgrenzen v. to mark off, to demarcate; to define

Abgrund m. abyss; precipice

Abguss m. cast, copy

abhalten v. to hold (*oder* keep) off; to hinder, to restrain; **Versammlung —** to hold a meeting

abhandeln v. to get (by bargaining); to discuss, to debate

abhanden adv. missing, lost; **-kommen** to get lost

Abhandlung f. treatise, essay

Abhang m. slope, declivity

abhängen v. to take off; **— von** to depend on

Abhängigkeit f. dependence

abhärmen v. **sich —** to languish, to pine away

abhärten v. to harden; to toughen

abhaspeln v. to reel off

abhauen v. to chop off; (sl.) to scram

abheben v. to lift off; to withdraw; to cut (cards); **sich — von** to contrast with

abhelfen v. to help, to remedy, to redress

abhold adj. ill-disposed, disinclined

abholen v. to pick up, to call for; to collect

abhören v. to overhear; to hear (lesson)

abirren v. to deviate; to go astray

abjagen v. to override, to overdrive; to snatch away

abkanzeln v. (coll.) to rebuke, to scold

abkaufen v. to buy from

abkehren v. to sweep from; to turn away; **sich — von** to withdraw assistance

Abklatsch m. stereotype plate, proof; (fig.) poor imitation

abknappen, abknapsen v. to stint, to curtail

abknöpfen v. to unbutton; **jemand etwas — to** do someone out of something

abkommandieren v. (mil.) to detach, to detail, to order away

Abkomme, Abkömmling m. descendant; derivative

Abkommen neu. agreement; origin; decline

abkommen v. to deviate, to digress; to drop; to get off (*oder* away); to become obsolete

abkratzen v. to scratch off; (sl.) to kick the bucket

abkühlen v. to cool, to chill, to refrigerate

Abkunft f. descent, origin, extraction

abkürzen v. to shorten, to abbreviate; to curtail

abladen v. to unload, to discharge

ablagern v. to deposit, to store; to season, to mature

Ablass m. (eccl.) indulgence

ablassen v. to drain off; to cease, to desist; to reduce (prices)

Ablauf m. running off; course; expiration; start; sink; (com.) maturity

ablaufen v. to run off (*oder* down); to expire; to start; to wear out; **gut — to** pass off well

ableben v. to die

ablegen v. to put away; to file; to render (account); to make (confession); to pass (examination); to take (oath); to bear (witness)

Ableger m. (bot.) slip, shot; (fig.) branch

ablehnen v. to decline, to refuse

Ablehnung f. refusal, rejection

ableiten v. to turn aside, to divert; to drain; to derive

ablenken v. to distract; to deflect; to avert; to diffract; to divert

ablesen v. to read off; to pick off, to gather

ableugnen v. to deny, to disclaim

abliefern v. to deliver, to hand over

ablösen v. to loosen; to remove, to detach; (mil.) to change (*oder* relieve) guards

abmachen v. to undo, to remove, to detach; to settle, to arrange for

Abmachung f. arrangement, settlement; agreement

abmagern v. to reduce (*oder* lose) weight

Abmarsch m. marching off; start

abmelden v. to give notice of departure

abmessen v. to measure, to gauge, to survey; **seine Worte —** to weigh one's words

abmühen v. **sich —** to exert oneself

Abnahme f. taking off; sale; decrease, decline; loss (in weight); (astr.) wane

abnehmen v. to lose weight; to take off; to decrease, to diminish; to subside; to gather; to buy; to cut (cards); (astr.) to wane

Abnehmer m. buyer, customer

Abneigung f. aversion, dislike; antipathy

abnutzen, abnützen v. to wear out, to use up

Abnutzung f. wear and tear; attrition

Abonnement neu. subscription

Abonnent m. subscriber

abonnieren v. to subscribe for

abordnen v. to delegate, to deputize

Abort m. toilet, latrine; (med.) abortion

abpassen v. to watch for; to measure; to lie in wait for

abplacken, abplagen v. **sich —** to drudge

abprallen v. to rebound, to recoil; (mil.) to ricochet; to glance off

abputzen v. to clean, to polish; to rough-cast

abquälen v. to torment; **sich —** to worry oneself; to toil

abraten v. to dissuade; to warn (against)

abräumen v. to take (*oder* clear) away; to remove

abrechnen v. to deduct; to settle

Abrechnungsstelle f. clearing house

Abrede f. agreement; **in — stellen** to deny, to dispute

abreden v. to dissuade (from)

abreiben v. to rub off (*oder* down); to scour

Abreise f. departure

abreisen v. to depart; to leave (for)

abreissen v. to tear off; to pull down, to demolish; to wear out

abrichten v. to train, to break in (animals)

Abriss m. sketch, draft; summary, abstract

abrollen v. to roll off; to unwind (film)

abrücken v. to move off (*oder* away); (mil.) to march off; to depart

abrufen v. to call off (*oder* away); (rail.) to call out

abrunden v. to round off; to make round

Abrüstung f. disarmament

absägen v. to saw off; (coll.) to discharge

Absatz m. paragraph; pause, stop; heel; sale, circulation; (stairs) landing; **-gebiet** neu. market

abschaffen v. to do away with; to abolish

abschätzen v. to evaluate, to appraise

Abschaum m. scum

abscheiden v. to separate; to refine; **von**

der Welt — to die

Abscheu m. aversion; loathing; abhorrence

abscheulich adj. abominable, atrocious

abschicken v. to send off, to dispatch

abschieben v. to deport; to shove (*oder* move) off; (coll.) to back out of

Abschied m. parting; dismissal; **— nehmen** to take leave, to say goodbye; **seinen — bekommen** to be dismissed; **seinen — nehmen** to resign; **-sbesuch** m. farewell visit

abschiessen v. to fire; to shoot off; (*oder* down); **den Vogel —** to take the cake

abschinden v. to skin (bargain); to drudge

Abschlag m. fall (in price); **auf — by** installments, on account

abschlagen v. to beat (*oder* knock) off; to refuse, to deny; (mil.) to repel

abschlägig adj. negative

abschleifen v. to grind, to polish

abschleppen v. to drag off; to tow away; (fig.) to tire oneself out

abschliessen v. to lock up; to balance (account); to strike (bargain); to finish (work); **sich —** to seclude oneself; **-d** adj. conclusive, definitive, final

Abschluss m. conclusion; settlement; balancing (account); **-prüfung** f. final examination

abschmieren v. (mech.) to lubricate, to grease; (coll.) to copy carelessly

abschminken v. to remove make-up; (sl.) to desist from

abschneiden v. to cut off (*oder* short), to clip; **gut —** to come off well

Abschnitt m. cut; division; period; (com.) coupon; (lit.) part, paragraph, chapter

abschrecken v. to deter, to dishearten

Abschreckung f. deterrence; **-swaffe** f. deterrent weapon

abschreiben v. to copy; to plagiarize; (com.) to deduct; (educ.) to crib

abschreiten v. to pace

Abschrift f. copy, duplicate, transcript

abschüssig adj. steep, precipitous

Abschusstisch, Abschussturm m. launching pad

abschwächen v. to weaken, to diminish, to soften

abschweifen v. to stray; to digress

abschwören v. to deny upon oath; to recant

absehbar adj. within sight; **in -er Zeit** before long

absehen v. to learn by observation; to copy; **— von** to desist from; to disregard; **es — auf** to aim at

abseits adv. and prep. apart, aside, away from; (sport) offside

absenden v. to send off (*oder* away); to dispatch, to forward

Absender m. sender, shipper

absetzen v. to put down, to deposit; to depose; to remove; to sell; to pause; to deduct

Absicht f. intention, purpose; **in böser —** with malice; **in der —** with the intention; **mit — on purpose

absichtlich adj. intentional; **— adv. on

purpose

absitzen v. to dismount; to serve (sentence)

absolvieren v. to absolve, to acquit, to finish (studies)

absondern v. to detach, to isolate; to secrete; **sich —** to seclude oneself

abspannen v. to unbend, to unharness, to uncock; to relax

abspenstig adj. disloyal; **— machen to** alienate, to estrange

absperren v. to bar, to lock; to shut off; to block; to isolate, to separate

abspielen v. **sich —** to take place; **vom Blatt —** to play at sight

abspringen v. to jump (oder leap) off, to crack off; (avi.) to bail out; (coll.) to digress

Absprung m. jump; (avi.) parachute jump

abstammen v. to descend; to be derived (from)

Abstand m. distance; interval; difference, contrast; **— nehmen von** to desist from; **-geld** neu., **-ssumme** f. indemnity, compensation

abstatten v. to make, to give, to render; to return (thanks); to pay (visit)

abstechen v. to pierce, to stab; to trump; **— von** to contrast with, to stand out against

Abstecher m. excursion, side-trip; digression

abstecken v. to unpin; to trace, to stake out

absteigen v. to descend; to dismount; to alight; to put up (at a hotel)

abstellen v. to put down; to stop, to turn off; to park; to abolish; to redress, to remedy

absterben v. to die away (oder out) to fade

Abstieg m. descent

abstimmen v. to tune (in); to vote; **— lassen** to put to a vote

abstossen v. to knock (oder push, rub) off; to repel; **-d** adj. repellent, repulsive

abstrahieren v. to abstract

abstreichen v. to strike off; to cancel

abstreiten v. to deny; to dispute

Abstufung f. gradation; shading

abstumpfen v. to blunt; to dull; **sich — gegen** to become insensible to

Absturz m. crash; precipice; **zum — bringen** to bring (oder shoot) down

abstürzen v. to fall precipitately; (avi.) to crash

absuchen v. to search; to scour

Abt m. abbot; **-ei** f. abbey

Abteil neu. compartment

abteilen v. to divide; to partition off; to separate

Abteilung f. department, section; (med.) ward; (mil.) detachment

abtragen v. to wear out; to carry (oder clear) away; to pull down; to level

abtreiben v. to drive away (oder off); to dispossess; (med.) to cause abortion; (avi.) to yaw

abtrennen v. to detach, to separate; to rip off

abtreten v. to resign; to retire; to abdicate; to exit; to yield; to tread off

Abtritt m. toilet; (theat.) exit

abtrudeln v. (avi.) to auger

abtrünnig adj. apostate; disloyal; faithless

abwägen v. to weigh; to consider carefully

abwälzen v. to roll away (oder down, off); to shirk (responsibility), to shift (blame)

Abwandlung f. (gram.) declension; conjugation

abwarten v. to await; to wait and see

abwärts adv. and prep. down, downward(s)

abwechselnd adj. alternating, intermittent; **— adv.** alternately; by turns

Abwechslung f. change, variety; alternation; **zur — for** a change

Abweg m. wrong way; **auf -e geraten to** go astray

abwehren v. to keep off; to defend; to parry

Abwehrgeschoss neu. anti-missile

Abwehrrakete f. interceptor missile

abweichen v. to deviate; to differ

abweisen v. to refuse, to reject; to repulse; (law) to dismiss; (mil.) to repel

abwenden v. to avert, to prevent; to turn away

abwendig adj. alienated; **— machen to** estrange

abwerfen v. to throw (oder cast) off; to shed; (avi.) to drop (bombs); to yield (profit)

abwesend adj. absent; (fig.) absent-minded

abwickeln v. to unwind; (fig.) to finish

abzahlen v. to pay off; to pay by installments

abzehren v. to waste (away); to consume

Abzeichen neu. badge; stripe; **— pl.** insignia

abzeichnen v. to copy, to draw; **sich — to** stand out against

Abziehbild neu. decalcomania

abziehen v. to take off; to strip; to skin; to strop; to draw off; to distill; to print; to subtract, to deduct; (sl.) to move off

Abzug m. departure, retreat; outlet; (com.) allowance, deduction, discount, rebate; (mech.) trigger; (phot.) print; (typ.) proof; **-skanal** m. drain, sewer, culvert

ach! interj. ah! oh! alas! **— so!** I see! **— was! — wo!** nonsense! not at all!

Achse f. axle; axis

Achsel f. shoulder; **auf die leichte — nehmen** to take it easy; **die -n zucken** to shrug one's shoulders; **über die — ansehen** to look down on; **-höhle** f. armpit

Achte f. eighth; **-eck** neu. octagon; **-el** neu. eighth; **-elnote** f. quaver; **-er** m. eighth

Acht f. attention, care; ban; **ausser — lassen** to disregard; **in die — erklären** to outlaw; **sich in — nehmen** to beware

acht adj. eight; **heute in — Tagen** a week from today; **-mal** adv. eight times; **-zehn** adj. eighteen; **-zig** adj. eighty

acht: **-bar** *adj.* respectable; **-en** *v.* to esteem, to regard, to respect; **-geben** (*or* **-haben**) *v.* to pay attention, to take care; **-los** *adj.* careless, negligent; **-sam** *adj.* attentive, careful

Achtung *f.* esteem, regard; **—!** *interj.* attention! beware! look out!

achtungsvoll *adj.* respectful

ächzen *v.* to groan, to moan

Acker *m.* field, soil; acre; **-bau** *m.* agriculture; **-bestellung** *f.* tillage; **-boden** *m.* arable soil; **-gerät** *neu.* agricultural implement; **-knecht** *m.* farmhand; **-smann** *m.* farmer

ackern *v.* to plow, to till

addieren *v.* to add (*oder* sum) up

Ade! *neu.* (coll.) adieu! goodbye! farewell!

Adel *m.* aristocracy, **-stand** *m.* nobility; in den **-stand erheben** to ennoble

Adelbert *m.* Ethelbert

Adelheid *f.* Adelaide

ad(e)lig *adj.* noble, titled; blueblooded

Ader *f.* vein; (min.) lode, seam; (wood) grain

Adler *m.* eagle; **-nase** *f.* aquiline nose

Adress: **-at** *m.* addressee; (com.) consignee; **-buch** *neu.* directory; **-e** *f.* address; **per —e** care of

adressieren *v.* to address

Adria *f.* Adriatic Sea

Aerodynamik *f.* aerodynamics

Affe *m.* ape, monkey

Affekt *m.* affection, passion, impulse

äffen *v.* to mock, to mimic: to fool

After *m.* anus, posterior, behind; **-kritiker** *m.* would-be critic, **-miete** *f.* subletting; **-weisheit** *f.* sophistry

Agentur *f.* agency

Ägypten *neu.* Egypt

Ahle *f.* awl

Ahn, Ahnherr *m.* ancestor, forefather; **-frau** *f.* ancestress

ahnen *v.* to anticipate, to foresee

ähnlich *adj.* resembling, similar

Ahnung *f.* presentiment, foreboding; **er hatte keine —** he had no idea

ahnungslos *adj.* unsuspecting; without misgivings

ahnungsvoll *adj.* full of foreboding; ominous

Ahorn *m.* maple

Ähre *f.* (bot.) spike; ear

Akademiker *m.* academician

akademisch *adj.* academic(al)

Akazie *f.* acacia

Akkord *m.* agreement, contract; (mus.) chord; **-arbeit** *f.* piece work

Akt *m.* action; act; (art) nude; **-en** *pl.* deeds, documents, records, files; **zu den -en legen** to pigeonhole; **-enmappe** *f.* brief case

Aktie *f.* share, stock; **-ngesellschaft** *f.* stock company

Aktionär *m.* shareholder

Aktiva *neu. pl.* assets

aktivieren *v.* to activate

Akustik *f.* acoustics

Alarm *m.* alarm; **blinder —** false alarm; **-bereitschaft** *f.* (mil.) alert; **-start** (mil.) scramble

albern *adj.* foolish, silly

Albrecht *m.* Albert

Aleutischen Inseln *f. pl.* Aleutian Islands

Alge *f.* seaweed

Algerien *neu.* Algeria

Alimente *neu. pl.* alimony

Alkohol *m.* alcohol; **-iker** *m.* alcoholic, drunkard; **-schmuggler** *m.* bootlegger

alkoholfrei *adj.* nonalcoholic

all *adj.* all, entire, whole; each, every, any; **-e Tage** every day; **-e Welt** everybody; **auf -e Fälle** in any case; **in -er Eile** in great hurry; **ohne -en Grund** for no reason at all; **trotz -em** in spite of everything; **vor -em** above all; **-bekannt** *adj.* notorious; **-enfalls** *adv.* possibly, perhaps, if need be; **-esamt** *adv.* altogether; **-gegenwärtig** *adj.* omnipresent; **-gemein** *adj.* universal; general; **in -em** in general; **-jährlich** *adj.* annual, yearly; every year; **-mächtig** *adj.* omnipotent; **-mählich** *adj.* gradual; **-mählich** *adv.* gradually, by degrees; **-seitig** *adj.* all-round; universal; **-täglich** *adj.* daily, everyday; commonplace, trivial; **-überall** *adv.* everywhere; **-wissend** *adj.* omniscient; **-zu(viel)** *adj.* too (much); too much by far; **-zeit** *adv.* at all time, always

All *neu.* universe; **-gemeinheit** *f.* generality, universality; **-heilmittel** *neu.* panacea, universal remedy; **-macht** *f.* omnipotence; **-tag** *m.* working day; daily life

Allee *f.* avenue, parkway

allein *adj.* alone, apart, single; solitary; **—** *adv.* by oneself; **—** *conj.* but, however; **von —** without assistance, of one's own account; **-ig** *adj.* exclusive, sole; **-stehend** *adj.* detached; isolate; single

Allein: **-besitz** *m.* sole ownership; **-betrieb** *m.* sole management; **-handel** *m.* monopoly; **-herrschaft** *f.* absolutism, autocracy; **-sein** *neu.* loneliness, solitude

aller: **-dings** *adv.* certainly, to be sure; **-hand** *adj.* of all kinds (*oder* sorts); **-lei** *adj.* diverse, of all kinds; **-liebst** *adj.* most charming

Allergie *f.* allergy

Allerlei *neu.* hodge-podge; miscellany; medley

Allerweltskerl *m.* smart fellow

Alliierte *m.* ally

allumfassend *adj.* omnibus

Alm *f.* Alpine meadow (*oder* pasture)

Almosen *neu. pl.* alms; **-büchse** *f.* poor box; **-empfänger** *m.* pauper

Alp *f.* mountain (meadow); **-en** *pl.* Alps; **-englühen** *neu.* alpenglow; **-enveilchen** *neu.* cyclamen

Alpen *pl.* Alps

alphabetisch *adj.* alphabetic(al)

als *conj.* as, but, than, when, like; for; **— ob as if** (*oder* though); **kein and(e)rer — none** other than; **sobald —** as soon as; **sowohl —** as well as; **-bald** *adv.* at once, forthwith; **-dann** *adv.* then, thereupon

also *adv.* thus, so; **—** *conj.* therefore,

hence, consequently

alt *adj.* old; ancient; stale; worn; **alles beim -en lassen** to leave things as they were; — **angesessen** long-established; **-backen** *adj.* stale; (fig.) old-fashioned; **-bewährt** *adj.* of long standing; **-ern** *v.* to age, to grow old; to decline; **-erschwach** *adj.* decrepit, senile; **-ertümlich** *adj.* antique; archaic; **-hergebracht** *adj.* customary, traditional; **-klug** *adj.* precocious; **-modisch** *adj.* old-fashioned

Alt *m.* (mus.) alto; **-istin** *f.* alto singer

Alteisen *neu.* scrap iron

Alter *neu.* age; epoch; **bibilisches —** a great age; **blühendes -er** prime of life; **-sgenosse** *m.* one of the same age, contemporary; **-sgrenze** *f.* age limit; **-sschwäche** *f.* senility; **-sversorgung** *f.* old age insurance; **-tum** *neu.* antiquity; **-tumsforschung** *f.* archeology

älter *adj.* older; elder, senior

Altpapier *neu.* waste paper

Altwaren *f. pl.* Secondhand goods

am: an dem *prep.* at (*oder* by, in, on) the

Amateurrennwagen *m.* hot-rod

Amboss *m.* anvil

Ameise *f.* ant; **-nsäure** *f.* formic acid

Amme *f.* wet nurse

amputieren *v.* to amputate

Amsel *f.* blackbird

Amt *neu.* office, charge, employment; post, appointment; duty; board; **seines -es walten** to officiate; **von -s wegen** officially; **-salter** *neu.* seniority; **-sbefugnis** *f.* competence; **-sbereich** *m.* jurisdiction, **-sbewerber** *m.* candidate; **-sgeheimnis** *neu.* official secret; **-shandlung** *f.* official act; **-sgericht** *neu.* district court; **-sniederlegung** *f.* resignation; **-sschimmel** *m.* red tape

amtieren *v.* to officiate

amtlich *adj.* official

amüsant *adj.* amusing

amüsieren *v.* to amuse; to enjoy oneself

an *prep.* at, by, in, on; along, near: up to; about; against; — **der Arbeit sein** to be at work; **es ist — mir** it is my turn; — *adv.* onward, upward; **von nun —** henceforth

analog *adj.* analogous

Analphabet *m.* illiterate

Analyse *f.* analysis

analysieren *v.* to analyze

Analytiker *m.* analyst

analytisch *adj.* analytic(al)

Ananas *f.* pineapple

anbahnen *v.* to pave the way for; to initiate

Anbau *m.* (agr.) cultivation; (arch.) annex, wing

anbauen *v.* (agr.) to cultivate, to grow, to till; (arch.) to build on

anbei *adv.* herewith, enclosed

anbeissen *v.* to bite into; (coll.) to take the bait

anberaumen *v.* to appoint (day *oder* time)

anbeten *v.* to adore; to worship; to idolize

Anbetracht, Anbetreff *m.* concern; in — der Lage considering the situation

anbieten *v.* to offer

anbinden *v.* to tie to; (coll.) to pick a quarrel with; **kurz angebunden sein** to be blunt (*oder* curt)

Anblick *m.* sight, view

anbrechen *v.* to commence; to open; **der Tag bricht an** the day is dawning

anbrennen *v.* to kindle; to catch fire; to burn

anbringen *v.* to bring in; to fix; to make; to settle; to sell, to dispose of; **gut angebracht** appropriate, suitable; **schlecht angebracht** out of place, unsuitable

Anbruch *m.* beginning, opening; — **des Tages** daybreak; — **der Nacht** nightfall

Andacht *f.* devotion; prayers

andächtig *adj.* devout, pious; (fig.) attentive

Anden *pl.* Andes

Andenken *neu.* remembrance; souvenir, keepsake; **zum — an** in memory of, as a souvenir of

ander *adj. and pron.* (an)other; different; **am —en Morgen** next morning; **-er Meinung sein** to be of a different opinion; **ein -es Mal** another time; **ums-e Mal** repeatedly; **etwas -s** somewhat different; **nichts -es als** nothing but; **unter -em** among other things; **-nfalls** *adv.* or else, otherwise; **-nteils** *adv.* on the other hand; **-wärts, -weit** *adv.* elsewhere; **-weitig** *adj.* from another quarter

ändern *v.* to alter, to change

anders *adv.* otherwise; differently; else; — **sein als** to be different from; — **werden** to change; **-denkend** *adj.* dissenting; **-gesinnt** *adj.* of a different mind; **-gläubig** *adj.* of a different faith; **-wo** *adv.* elsewhere; **-woher** *adv.* from elsewhere; **-wohin** *adv.* to some other place

anderthalb *adj.* one and a half

andeuten *v.* to indicate, to intimate, to hint

Andrang *m.* pressing forward, rush; congestion

andrängen, andringen *v.* to crowd, to press against

Andreas *m.* Andrew

andrehen *v.* to turn on; (mech.) to cause to start; (sl.) to trick, to hoax

aneignen *v.* to adopt, to appropriate

aneinander *adv.* together; against one another; — **geraten** to come to blows

anekeln *v.* to disgust

Anerbieten *neu.* offer, proposal

anerkennen *v.* to acknowledge, to admit; to appreciate; to honor (a bill); to recognize

anfachen *v.* to blow (into a flame); to kindle; (fig.) to stimulate, to incite

anfahren *v.* to drive (*oder* bring) up to; to collide, to run into; (naut.) to call (at a port); (coll.) to address gruffly

Anfall *m.* assault; (med.) fit

anfallen *v.* to assail, to attack

Anfang *m.* beginning, start; **von — an** from the very beginning; **-sbuchstabe** *m.* initial letter; **-sgründe** *m. pl.* fundamental principles (*oder* elements); rudiments

anfangen r. to begin; to do; to contrive

Anfänger m. beginner

anfänglich adj. initial, incipient; — adv. in the beginning, at first

anfassen v. to handle, to touch; to take hold of; to set to work; **mit** — to lend a hand

anfechten r. to contest, to dispute; (law) to attack; (rel.) to tempt; to trouble

Anfeindung f. hostility, persecution

anfertigen v. to make, to manufacture

anfeuchten v. to dampen, to moisten

anfeuern v. to inflame; to encourage

anflehen r. to implore

anfliegen (Flugplatz) v. to make a pass

Anflug m. (avi.) incoming flight; (fig.) tinge, touch, trace; **-splatz** m. (avi.) landing field

Anforderung f. claim, demand; **grosse -en stellen** to expect great things

anfragen v. to inquire; to question; **bei einem** — to ask someone

anfressen v. to gnaw (oder nibble) at; to corrode, to decay

anführen v. to lead, to command; to cite, to quote; to cheat, to trick

Angabe f. assertion, declaration, statement; instruction; boast; **nach seinen -n** according to him; **nähere -n** particulars

angängig adj. feasible, permissible

angeben v. to state, to indicate, to specify; to declare; to denounce; to boast; **Ton** — to set the fashion; to give the keynote; (cards) to deal first

Angeber m. informer, spy; **zum — werden** to turn state's evidence; **-ei** f. denunciation

angeblich adj. ostensible, alleged

angeboren adj. congenital; innate

Angebot neu. bid, offer, tender; **— und Nachfrage** supply and demand

Angegriffenheit f. nervous (oder delicate) state of health; physical exhaustion, strain

angehen v. to concern, to apply to, to ask for; to be feasible; **das geht nicht an** that will not do; **-d** adj. beginning, incipient

angehörig adj. belonging to; related to

Angehörige m. relative, next of kin

Angeklagte m. the accused, the defendant

Angel f. fishing-rod; (mech.) hinge

Angelegenheit f. affair, concern

angeln v. to angle, to fish; (coll.) to hook

angeloben v. to promise solemnly; to vow

angemessen adj. adequate, appropriate; suitable; **der Zeit nicht —** out of season, untimely

angenehm adj. acceptable, agreeable; **du bist mir immer —** you are always welcome; **sehr —!** pleased to meet you!

angesäuselt adj. (coll.) tipsy

angeschlagen adj. groggy; knocked out

angesehen adj. esteemed; respected

Angesicht neu. face; **dem Tod ins — schauen** to face death; **im Schweisse deines -s** in the sweat of thy brow; **von — zu —** face to face

angesichts prep. in view of, considering

angestammt adj. hereditary

Angestellte m. employee

angewachsen adj. increased; grown together; rooted; **wie —** rooted to the ground

angewandt adj. applied

angewiesen adj. assigned; **— auf** dependent on

angewöhnen v. to accustom; **sich etwas — to** get in the habit of something

Angewohnheit f. habit, custom

angleichen v. to assimilate

angreifbar adj. assailable, vulnerable

angreifen r. to take hold of, to seize; to undertake; to attack; to affect; to exhaust; **-d** adj. exhausting, trying

Angreifer m. aggressor, assailant; invader

angrenzen v. to border on, **-d** adj. adjacent

Angriff m. attack; **in — nehmen** to begin, to take in hand; **zum — vorgehen** to take the offensive; **-skrieg** m. offensive war

angriffslustig adj. agressive

Angst f. anguish, anxiety; fear; **-hase, -meier** m. coward; **-schweiss** m. cold sweat

ängstigen r. to distress; to frighten; **sich — to** feel anxious, to worry; **sich — vor** to be afraid of

ängstlich adj. afraid, frightened

anhaben r. to have on, to wear; **einem etwas — to** accuse (oder harm) someone

anhaften v. to stick, to cling to

Anhalt m. support; foothold; **-spunkt** m. clue; proof, evidence

anhalten r. to stop; to spur on; **— um** to propose to; **-d** adj. continuous

Anhang m. appendix, supplement; adherents, followers; (sport) fans

anhangen r. to adhere, to stick to

anhängen r. to add, to append; to hang on; (tel.) to hang up; **jemand etwas —** to slander someone

Anhänger m. disciple, follower; partisan; (auto.) trailer; (jewelry) pendant

anhänglich adj. attached; faithful

anhäufen v. to accumulate; to hoard

anheben v. to lift, to raise; (fig.) to begin

anheimeln v. to remind one of home; **-d** adj. cozy, snug

anheimfallen v. to pass into possession of

anheimstellen v. to leave (oder submit) to

Anhöhe f. elevation, hill, rising ground

anhören v. to listen to; **sich — wie** to sound like

Anis m. anise; **-samen** m. aniseed

Ankara neu. Angora

Ankauf m. acquisition; purchase

Anker m. anchor; **vor — gehen** to anchor; **vor — liegen** to ride at anchor; **-mast** m. mooring mast; **-winde** f. windlass, capstan

ankern r. to anchor, to moor

Anklage f. accusation; indictment; impeachment; **eine — erheben** to bring (oder make) a charge; **-bank** f. dock; **-schrift** f. indictment

anklagen v. to accuse; to indict; to impeach

Ankläger *m.* accuser; prosecutor

Anklang *m.* reminiscence; (mus.) accord; —**finden** to meet with approval

ankleben *v.* to glue (paste, *oder* stick) on; to adhere (*oder* cling) to; -**d** *adj.* adhesive

ankleiden *v.* to attire, to dress

anklingeln *v.* to ring (doorbell); (tel.) to call

anknüpfen *v.* to fasten (*oder* tie) to; **eine Bekanntschaft** — to strike up an acquaintance; **Verbindungen** — to establish connections

ankommen *v.* to arrive; **darauf** — to depend on; **darauf soll es nicht** —**!** never mind that! **es darauf** — **lassen** to chance (*oder* risk) it; **gut** — to be well received

Ankömmling *m.* newcomer; stranger

ankünd(ig)en *v.* to announce, to advertise

Ankunft *f.* arrival, coming

ankurbeln *v.* to start, to stimulate; to boost

Anlage *f.* grounds, park; plant, works, installation; investment; (letter) enclosure; talent; tendency; -**kapital** *neu.* stock, funds

anlangen *v.* to arrive; to concern

Anlass *m.* cause, occasion; **ohne allen** — for no reason at all

anlassen *v.* to leave on; to start; to turn on (water); to temper (metal); to rebuke, to snub; **sich gut** — to promise well

Anlasser *m.* (auto.) starter

Anlauf *m.* run, start; attack, onset; (avi.) take-off run; **einen** — **nehmen to take a running start**

anlegen *v.* to apply; to put on; to establish; to lay out (*oder* against); to take in hand; to invest; (dog) to tie up; (gun) to aim; (naut.) to moor; **Fesseln** — to put in chains; **Feuer** — to commit arson; **Trauer** — to go into mourning

anlehnen *v.* to lean against; to find support in; **Tür** — to leave the door ajar

Anlehnung *f.* imitation; **in** — **an** in imitation of, with reference to

Anleihe *f.* loan

anleiten *v.* to guide; to instruct

Anliegen *neu.* request; desire; concern

anliegend *adj.* adjacent, adjoining; neighboring; — *adv.* enclosed (in a letter)

anlocken *v.* to allure, to entice

anmachen *v.* to attach; to fix; to mix (*oder* dress salad); to light (fire)

anmassen *v.* **sich** — to arrogate; to presume; to pretend; -**d** *adj.* arrogant; presumptuous

anmelden *v.* to announce; to notify; to register

anmerken *v.* to jot down; to perceive

Anmut *f.* charm, grace; (fig.) sweetness

anmutig *adj.* charming, graceful

Anna *f.* Ann

annähern *v.* to approximate; to approach

Annahme *f.* acceptance; assumption, hypothesis

Ännchen *n.* Nancy

annehmbar *adj.* acceptable

annehmen *v.* to accept, to receive; to assume; to suppose; to adopt; to contract (habit)

Annehmlichkeit *f.* amenity, comfort

Annonce *f.* advertisement

annoncieren *v.* to advertise

anordnen *v.* to direct; to arrange; to regulate

anpacken *v.* to grasp, to seize

anpassen *v.* to (make) fit; to suit; **sich** — to adapt oneself to

Anpassungsvermögen *n.* adaptability

anpflanzen *v.* to plant, to cultivate

Anprall *m.* collision; impact

anpreisen *v.* to commend, to praise; to extol

anprob(ier)en *v.* to fit (*oder* try) on

anraten *v.* to advise, to recommend; **dringend** — to urge

anrechnen *v.* to charge; **hoch** — to value greatly; **zuviel** — to overcharge

Anrecht *neu.* claim, title; — **haben auf** to be entitled to

anreden *v.* to address, to accost

anregen *v.* to incite, to stimulate; to suggest; -**d** *adj.* interesting, stimulating

anreihen *v.* to add to; to rank with; to join; **sich** — to stand in line

Anreiz *m.* incitement; stimulus; incentive

anrichten *v.* to prepare; to serve up; to cause

anrüchig *adj.* disreputable

anrücken *v.* to draw near; to approach

Anruf *m.* appeal; shout; (tel.) call

anrufen *v.* to appeal to; to hail; (tel.) to call

anrühren *v.* to touch, to mix, to stir

ansagen *v.* to announce; (cards) to bid

Ansager *m.* (rad.) announcer; (cards) bidder

ansammeln *v.* to accumulate; to collect

ansässig *adj.* resident; settled

Ansatz *m.* start; tendency; incrustation; (math.) statement; (mus.) mouthpiece

anschaffen *v.* to buy; to provide, to procure

anschauen *v.* to look at; to contemplate

anschaulich *adj.* descriptive; graphic

Anschauung *f.* view; perception; contemplation

Anschein *m.* appearance; den — **erwecken** to make believe; **es hat den** — it seems as if; **sich den** — **geben** to pretend that

anscheinend *adj.* apparent, seeming

anschicken *v.* **sich** — to prepare, to set about

Anschlag *m.* poster, placard; stroke; plot; (com.) estimate; (law) assault; (mus.) touch; **in** — **bringen** to take into account; (gun) aim; -**brett** *neu.* bulletin board; -**geschwindigkeit** *f.* impact velocity

anschlagen *v.* to affix, to post; to take effect; (orn.) to sing; (zool.) to bark; **einen anderen Ton** — to change tone

anschliessen *v.* to annex; to chain; to join; to follow, to accompany; to fit close; (mil.) to close ranks; -**d** *adj.* following

Anschluss m. annexation; joining; supply; connection; — **suchen** to seek company; **-dose** f. (elec.) junction box

anschmieren v. to smear, to daub; (coll.) to cheat

anschnauben, anschnauzen v. to snub, to snort at

anschneiden v. to begin to carve (oder cut); (fig.) to broach a subject

Anschnitt m. first cut (oder slice)

anschreiben v. to write down; to charge; to score; to chalk up; — **lassen** to take on credit; **bei jemand gut angeschrieben sein** to stand high in a person's favor

Anschrift f. (letter) address

anschuldigen v. to charge with, to accuse of

anschwärzen v. to blacken; (coll.) to slander

anschwellen v. to swell; to increase

anschwemmen v. to wash up (oder ashore)

Anschwemmung f. alluvium

anschwindeln v. to swindle; to bamboozle

ansehen neu. to look at; to take for; to esteem

Ansehen neu. appearance; authority; esteem; **dem — nach** to all appearance; **ohne — der Person** without respect of persons; **sich ein — geben** to give oneself airs; **von — kennen** to know by sight

ansehnlich adj. considerable; imposing

Ansicht f. sight, view; opinion; **nach meiner —** in my opinion; **zur —** on approval; **-skarte** f. picture postcard

ansiedeln v. to colonize, to settle

anspannen v. to stretch; to harness; to strain

anspielen v. to begin to play; (cards) to have the lead; (tennis) to serve; — **auf** to hint at, to allude to

anspitzen v. to point, to sharpen

Ansporn m. spur, stimulus

anspornen v. to spur on, to stimulate

Ansprache f. address, speech

ansprechen v. to speak to; to accost; to appeal to, to please; **-d** adj. attractive

anspringen v. to jump at; (motor) to start

Anspruch m. claim, demand; — **haben auf** to be entitled to; — **machen auf** to lay claim to; **in — nehmen** to take up (time)

anspruchslos adj. modest, unassuming

anspruchsvoll adj. fastidious; presumptious

anstacheln v. to spur on; to incite; to stimulate

Anstalt f. establishment, institution; institute; **-en treffen** to make arrangements

Anstand m. decency; decorum; — **nehmen** to doubt, to hesitate; **ohne —** without hesitation; **-sbesuch** m. formal call; **-sgefühl** neu. tact

anständig adj. decent, respectable; proper

anstatt conj. and prep. instead of

anstechen v. to prick; to tap

anstecken v. to fasten to, to pin on; to light, to kindle; (med.) to contaminate, to infect; **-d** adj. catching, contagious

anstellen v. to place against; to appoint, to employ; to draw (comparison); to undertake; (mech.) to start; (rad.) to turn on; **sich —** to behave; to feign; to make a fuss

anstellig adj. able, handy

Anstieg m. ascent

anstiften v. to cause, to incite to; to plot

Anstifter m. instigator

anstimmen v. to begin to sing; to strike up

Anstoss m. collision; impulse; (football) kickoff; — **erregen** to offend, to shock; — **nehmen** to take offense; **ohne —** fluently; without delay; **Stein des —es** stumbling block

anstossen v. to bump (oder knock) against; to nudge; to stammer; to clink (glasses); to adjoin, to border on; **-d** adj. adjacent

anstössig adj. improper, obnoxious, offensive

anstreichen v. to score; to paint; **jemand etwas —** to make someone pay for something; **weiss —** to whitewash

Anstreicher m. house painter

anstrengen v. to exert, to strain; **Prozess — to bring action against**

Anstrich m. paint; color; appearance; tinge

anstürmen v. to assail, to rush headlong

Anteil m. portion; share; — **nehmen** to sympathize (with), to take an interest (in)

Antenne f. aerial; antenna

Antike f. antiquity

Antiquar m. dealer in antiques (oder secondhand books)

Antlitz neu. face; countenance

Anton m. Anthony

Antrag m. proposal, proposition; motion; **einen — stellen** to make a motion

antreten v. to start, to take possession of

Antrieb m. impulse; impetus; stimulus; incentive, motive; drive, propulsion

Antriebsrakete f. booster rocket

Antritt m. accession; **-srede** inaugural address

antun v. to put on; to do, to inflict; to harm; **es einem — to bewitch someone**

Antwerpen neu. Antwerp

Antwort f. answer, reply

antworten v. to answer, to reply

anvertrauen v. to confide in, to entrust with

anverwandt adj. related to

anwachsen v. to grow on (to); to take root; to rise, to swell; to augment, to increase

Anwalt m. attorney; counsel

Anwandlung f. attack, fit; touch (of pity)

anweisen v. to direct; to instruct, to assign

Anweisung f. direction; instruction; order

anwendbar adj. applicable; practicable

anwenden v. to apply; to employ, to use

anwerben v. to recruit (troops); to enlist

anwerfen v. (motor) to start

Anwesen neu. estate; **-den** m. pl. those

present; **–heit** f. presence
anwesend adj. present
anwidern v. to disgust
Anzahl f. number; quantity; **–ung** f. payment on account
anzapfen v. to tap
Anzeichen neu. indication, sign, symptom; omen
Anzeige f. advertisement; announcement; notice; (law) denunciation
anzeigen v. to advertise; to announce; to notify; to inform against, to denounce
anzetteln v. to plot, to scheme
anziehen v. to draw; to tighten; to absorb; to dress, to put on; to quote; to rise; to approach; to attract, to interest; (chess) to move first; **–d** adj. attractive
Anzug m. dress; suit; (chess) opening move; **im — sein** to approach; to be imminent; **Raum–** space suit
anzünden v. to light; to kindle
Anzünder m. lighter
apart adj. uncommon, distinctive
apathisch adj. apathetic(al)
Apfel m. apple; **in den sauren — beissen** to swallow a bitter pill; **–mus** neu. applesauce; **–wein** m. cider
Apfelsine f. orange
Apotheke f. pharmacy; **–r** m. pharmacist
Apparat m. apparatus, appliance; instrument; telephone; (coll.) camera; **am — bleiben** (tel.) to hold the line
Appell m. (mil.) roll-call; (fig.) appeal
appellieren v. to appeal (to); to move for a new trial
appetitlich adj. appetizing; dainty
Aprikose f. apricot
Aquarell neu. aquarelle, water color painting
Äquator m. equator
Ära f. era
Arabien neu. Arabia
Arbeit f. work, job; **–geber** m. employer; **–nehmer** m. employee; **–samt** neu. employment bureau; **–seinstellung** f. strike; **–sfeld** neu. sphere of action, province; **–slohn** m. wages; **–slosenunterstützung** f. unemployment compensation; **–slosigkeit** f. unemployment; **–ssperre** f. lockout; **–szeit** f. working hours; **–szeug** neu. tools
arbeiten v. to work; to make; (agr.) to cultivate
Arbeiter m. worker, laborer; **geistiger —** brainworker; **–bund** m., **–gewerkschaft** f. labor union; **–mangel** m. labor shortage; **–schaft** f. working class
arbeitsam adj. diligent, industrious
arbeitsfähig adj. able-bodied
arbeitslos adj. unemployed
arbeitsunfähig adj. disabled, unfit for work
Arche f. ark
Archipel m. archipelago
Archiv neu. archives, public records; **–ar** m. archivist
arg adj. bad, evil; mischievous, severe; (coll.) awful, very; **–es Versehen** gross mistake; **–listig** adj. crafty, cunning; **–los** adj. harmless, unsuspecting; **–willig**

adj. malevolent; **–wöhnen** v. to suspect; **–wöhnisch** adj. suspicious
Argentinien neu. Argentine
Ärger m. anger; vexation; **–nis** neu. annoyance, vexation; scandalous behavior
ärgerlich adj. angry, annoying, provoking
ärgern v. to make angry, to vex, to annoy
Arie f. (mus.) air, aria
aristokratisch adj. aristocratic(al)
arktisch adj. arctic
arm adj. poor; indigent; needy; piteous; **–selig** adj. beggarly, miserable, wretched
Arm m. arm; branch; **die –e frei haben** to have elbowroom; **unter die –e greifen** to give a lift; **–band** neu. bracelet; **–banduhr** f. wrist watch; **–binde** f. badge; (med.) sling; **–höhle** f. armpit; **–leuchter** m. chandelier; **–sessel** m., **–stuhl** m. armchair, easy chair
Armee f. army; **–befehl** m. army order
Ärmel m. sleeve; **aus dem — schütteln** to do easily; **–aufschlag** m. cuff
Ärmelkanal m. English Channel
Armen m. pl. (the) poor; **–anstalt** f. poorhouse; **–viertel** neu. slum
Armesündergesicht neu. hangdog look
ärmlich adj. miserable, needy, shabby
Armut f. poverty; **— schändet nicht** poverty is no disgrace; **–szeugnis** neu. sich **ein –szeugnis ausstellen** to show one's incapacity
arretieren v. to arrest
Art f. manner, mode; kind, sort; race, breed; species; way; **aus der — schlagen** to vary from type; **einzig in seiner — unique**
arten v. **— nach** to take after, to resemble
Arterie f. artery; **–nverkalkung** f. arteriosclerosis
artig adj. well-behaved; gallant; pretty
Artikel m. article; commodity
Arznei f., **Arzneimittel** neu. medicine, drug; **–kunde** f. pharmacology; **–verschreibung** f. prescription
Arzt m. physician, doctor
ärztlich adj. medical
As neu. ace; (mus.) A flat
Asche f. ash(es); **in — legen** to burn down; **in — verwandeln** to reduce to ashes, to incinerate; **–nbecher** m. ash tray; **–nbrödel** neu. scullion; Cinderella
asch: **–fahl** adj., **–farben** adj., **–farbig** adj., **–grau** adj. ash-colored, ash gray
Aschermittwoch m. Ash Wednesday
Asien neu. Asia
Ast m. branch; **–loch** neu. knothole; **–werk** neu. branches, boughs
ästhetisch adj. aesthetic(al)
Astrobiologie f. astrobiology
Astrolog m. astrologer; **–ie** f. astrology
Astronom m. astronomer; **–ie** f. astronomy
Astronaut m. astronaut
Astrophysik f. astrophysics
Asyl neu. asylum, refuge, shelter
Atelier neu. studio
Atem m. breath; **— anhalten** to hold one's breath; **— holen** to breathe; **bis zum letzten –zug** to one's last breath
Äther m. ether; celestial space; **mit —**

betäuben to put under ether, to etherize

ätherisch *adj.* ethereal; (rad.) etheric(al)

Äthyl *neu.* (chem.) ethyl

Atlas *m.* atlas; (fabric) satin

atmen *v.* to breathe

Atmungsapparat *m.* resuscitator

Atom *neu.* (phys.) atom; **—bombe** *f.* atom(ic) bomb, A-bomb; **—gewicht** *neu.* atomic weight; **—kern** *m.* nucleus; **—krieg** *m.* atomic war; nuclear war; **—säule** *f.* atomic pile; **—zertrümmerer** *m.* atom smasher

atomisch *adj.* atomic(al)

atomisieren *v.* to atomize

Attentat *neu.* assault, assassination

Attrappe *f.* mock-up

auch *conj.* also, too; likewise; even; **— nicht einer** not a single one

Audionröhre *f.* detector tube

auf *prep.* on, upon; at; in; for; to, towards; — *adv.* up, upwards; aloft; **alle bis — einen** all but one; **— Dein Wohl** here's to you; **— dem Meere** at sea; **— dem nächsten Wege** by the nearest way; **— der Stelle** on the spot; **— der Strasse** on the street; **— Deutsch** in German; **— einen Augenblick** for a moment; **— einmal** suddenly; **— Erden** on earth; **— jeden Fall** in any case; **— meine Bitte** at my request; **— und davon laufen** to run away, to make off; **es geht — neun** it is getting on to nine; **von klein —** from childhood on

aufarbeiten *v.* to work open; to use up; to finish; to refurbish

aufatmen *v.* to breathe again; to feel relieved

aufbahren *v.* to put on the bier

Aufbahrung *f.* lying in state

Aufbau *m.* erection; construction; plot

aufbäumen *v.* to rear, to prance; to rebel

aufbekommen *v.* to get open; (educ.) to be assigned; to eat up

aufbessern *v.* to mend; to improve; to raise

aufbewahren *v.* to keep; to preserve; to store

aufbieten *v.* to cite, to summon; to publish (banns); (mil.) to call up; **alles — to** make every possible effort

aufbinden *v.* to untie; to tie on; to impose on; **er lässt sich alles —** he swallows everything; **jemand einen Bären —** to hoax someone

aufblähen *v.* to swell, to puff up; to inflate

aufblasen *v.* to inflate; to raise (dust)

aufbleiben *v.* to remain open; **spät — to** stay up late

aufblicken *v.* to look up; to raise the eyes

aufblühen *v.* to begin to blossom; to flourish

aufbrauchen *v.* to use up; to consume

aufbrausen *v.* to bubble up; to effervesce; to roar; to flare up

aufbrechen *v.* to break (*oder* burst) open; to crack; to depart, to set out

aufbringen *v.* to get open; to rear; to raise; to provoke, to irritate

Aufbruch *m.* break-up, departure

aufdecken *v.* to uncover; to disclose; (cards) to show one's hand

aufdrängen *v.* to push open; to obtrude upon

aufdrehen *v.* to unravel; to unscrew; to wind up; to turn on

aufdringlich *adj.* importunate; obtrusive

aufdrücken *v.* to press on (*oder* open)

aufeinander *adv.* one upon (*oder* after) another; successively

Aufeinanderfolge *f.* succession; series

Aufenthalt *m.* sojourn, residence; delay, stop

auferlegen *v.* to inflict; to impose; to enjoin

Auferstehung *f.* resurrection

auffädeln *v.* to thread, to string

auffahren *v.* to ascend, to rise; to jump up; to flare up; to run aground

Auffahrt *f.* ascent; ramp

auffallend, auffällig *adj.* striking, remarkable; conspicuous, showy

auffangen *v.* to catch; to intercept; to parry

auffassen *v.* to catch; to apprehend; **falsch — to** misconceive; **leicht — to** be quick-witted

Auffassung *f.* comprehension; conception, view; interpretation; **—sgabe** *f.* perceptive faculty

auffliegen *v.* to fly up (*oder* open); to explode

auffordern *v.* to call upon; to demand; to invite; to challenge, to summon

auffrischen *v.* to freshen up; to revive; to renew; (art) to touch up; (coll.) to brush up on

aufführen *v.* to erect; to behave; (theat.) to act, to perform; **einzeln — to** itemize

Aufgabe *f.* duty, task; problem; resignation; posting; **—schein** *m.* receipt of delivery

Aufgang *m.* ascent; stairs; (sun) rising

aufgeben *v.* to give up, to abandon; to resign; to post; to set (task)

Aufgebot *neu.* public notice; banns of marriage; levy; **mit — aller Kräfte** with might and main

aufgebracht *adj.* angry, furious

aufgeh(e)n *v.* to come up; to open; to get loose; to rise; to break up; to take root; to be spent; (math.) to leave no remainder; **—in** to be absorbed in; **die Augen gehen mir auf** it dawns on me

aufgeklärt *adj.* enlightened

aufgeknöpft *adj.* unbuttoned; (coll.) approachable

aufgeräumt *adj.* high-spirited

aufgeweckt *adj.* awake; alert, intelligent

aufgiessen *v.* to pour upon; to infuse; **Tee — to** make tea

aufgreifen *v.* to catch; to snatch up

aufhaben *v.* to have open, to wear (hat); **wir haben zuviel auf** we have too much homework

aufhalten *v.* to hold open; to stop; to delay, to retard; **den Strom — to** stem the tide; **sich — to** stay; to find fault; **sich unnütz — to** waste one's time

aufhängen *v.* to hang up; **jemandem**

etwas — (coll.) to play a trick on someone
aufhäufen v. to heap up; to accumulate
aufheben v. to lift, to pick up; to preserve; to annul; to cancel; **die Tafel —** to rise from the table; **ein Urteil —** to quash a sentence; **eine Belagerung —** to break a siege; **eine Sitzung —** to adjourn a meeting; **eine Verlobung —** to break an engagement to marry; **Handelsgenossenschaft —** to dissolve partnership; **gut aufgehoben** well taken care of
aufheitern v. to cheer up; to clear up
aufhelfen v. to help up; to aid
aufhellen v. to brighten, to clear up
aufhören v. to cease, to stop; to discontinue; **da hört sich alles auf!** that's the limit!
aufkaufen v. to buy up, to forestall
aufklappen v. to open
aufklären v. to clear up; to clarify; (mil.) to reconnoiter; to enlighten; to solve (mystery)
Aufklärungsflug m. reconnaissance flight
aufkommen v. to come (oder get) up; to approach; to rise; (med.) to recover; **— für** to be responsible for; **nicht — gegen** to be no match for
aufkündigen v. to give notice; to retract; to renounce; **Freundschaft —** to break (oder sever) friendship; **Gehorsam —** to refuse obedience; **Hypothek —** to call in a mortgage
aufladen v. to load; to charge; **sich Verantwortung —** to take responsibility
Auflage f. edition; duty, tax
auflassen v. to let rise; to leave open
auflauern v. to lie in wait (oder ambush)
Auflauf m. mob; commotion; riot; soufflé
aufleben v. to revive
auflegen v. to lay on, to apply; to publish; to inflict; **gut aufgelegt** in a good mood; **Karten —** to spread one's cards
auflehnen v. to lean against; **sich —** to rebel
auflesen v. to pick up, to gather; to glean
aufliegen v. to lie (oder lean) on; to be on show; to be exposed; to develop bedsores
auflockern v. to loosen
auflösbar adj. (dis)soluble; solvable
auflösen v. to loosen; to undo; to analyze; to dissolve; to solve; to disband
Auflösung f. (dis)solution; dispersal; (mil.) disbandment; **-szeichen** neu. (mus.) natural
aufmachen v. to open; to undo; to set out
aufmerken v. to pay attention to; to heed
aufmerksam adj. attentive; polite
aufmuntern v. to cheer up; to encourage
Aufnahme f. admission, enrollment; reception; photograph; **— von Geld** loaning
aufnehmen v. to take up; to receive; to admit; to take (picture); to absorb; (law) to draw up; (geog.) to map out; **als Beleidigung** (or **Scherz**) **—** to take as an insult (oder joke); **Arbeit wieder —** to resume work; **es — mit** to cope

with; **Geld —** to borrow money
aufopfern v. to sacrifice; to devote
aufpassen v. to adapt; to be attentive, to watch
aufpeitschen v. to whip up; to stimulate
aufpflanzen v. to fix (oder set) up; to plant
aufprallen v. to bounce against, to rebound
aufputzen v. to polish; (coll.) to spruce up
aufraffen v. to snatch up; **sich —** to pull oneself together; (med.) to recover from
aufragen v. to tower up. to stand up
aufräumen v. to clear away; to tidy up; to set in order; (coll.) to make a clean sweep of
aufrecht adj. erect, upright; **-erhalten** v. to keep up, to maintain, to preserve
aufregen v. to excite; to arouse
Aufregung f. excitement, agitation
aufreiben v. to rub open; to chafe; (mil.) to annihilate; **sich —** to wear oneself out
aufreissen v. to burst (oder tear) open; to open wide, **den Mund —** to gape; **eine alte Wunde —** to reopen old sores
aufreizen v. to incite, to provoke, to stir up
aufrichten v. to raise, to set up; to comfort; to erect; **sich —** to sit upright; **sich wieder —** to recover from
aufrichtig adj. frank, sincere; candid
Aufriss m. draft, sketch; (arch.) elevation
aufrollen v. to roll up; to coil; to unroll; to raise (curtain); to broach (question)
Aufruf m. call; proclamation; (law) appeal, summons
aufrufen v. to call up (oder upon); **namentlich —** (mil.) to call the roll
Aufruhr m. rebellion, insurrection, mutiny, riot; uproar; **in hellem —** in open revolt
aufrühren v. to stir up; to inflame; **alte Geschichten wieder —** to rake up old grievances; **Erinnerungen —** to revive memories
Aufrührer m. insurgent, mutineer, rebel, rioter; agitator
Aufrüstung f. rearmament
aufrütteln v. to shake; to rouse
aufsagen v. to recite; **Dienst —** to give notice to quit a position (oder job)
aufsässig adj. hostile; rebellious
Aufsatz m. composition, essay, article; treatise; centerpiece, head-piece, crest
aufsaugen v. to absorb, to suck up
aufscheuchen v. to scare up, to startle
aufschieben v. to push open; to defer, to postpone; to adjourn
Aufschlag m. bounce; (cloth) facing, revers; (price) advance; (tennis) service; **-geschwindigkeit** f. impact velocity
aufschlagen v. to break open; to bounce, to rebound; to open (eyes, books); to advance (prices); to pitch (tent); (tennis) to serve
Aufschluss m. disclosure, explanation; **— geben** to throw light on; **— erbitten** to ask for full particulars
aufschneiden v. to cut open, to carve; to boast, to brag; to exaggerate

Aufschneider *m.* boaster, braggart

Aufschnitt *m.* (act of) cutting open; (med.) incision; **kalter —** cold cut (meat)

aufschrecken *v.* to startle; to frighten

Aufschrei *m.* scream, shriek; outcry

aufschreiben *v.* to write down; (cards) to score; (com.) to enter, to charge

Aufschrift *f.* address; inscription; epitaph

Aufschub *m.* delay, deferment; postponement

aufschwatzen *v.* **jemand etwas —** to talk a person into a thing

Aufschwung *m.* upswing; soaring; progress; prosperity; **plötzlicher —** (com.) boom

Aufsehen *neu.* surprise; scandal, sensation; **wenig — machen** to attract little attention

Aufseher *m.* custodian; foreman, inspector

aufsetzen *v.* to put on, to set up; to draw up; to make out (account); **seinen Kopf —** to be obstinate

Aufsicht *f.* supervision; guardianship; custody; **-srat** *m.* board of directors

aufsitzen *v.* to sit up(on); to mount (horse)

aufspannen *v.* to stretch; to mount; to open (umbrella); to spread (sails); (mus.) to string

aufsperren *v.* to unlock; to open wide

aufspielen *v.* to strike up (tune); **sich —** to pose as, to swagger, to put on airs

aufspiessen *v.* to impale; to gore

aufspringen *v.* to jump up; to chap, to crack

aufspüren *v.* to trace, to track down

aufstacheln *v.* to goad; to spur on; to incite

Aufstand *m.* insurrection, rebellion; uproar

aufstechen *v.* to prick open; (med.) to lance

aufstecken *v.* to stick on; to pin up; **jemand ein Licht —** to enlighten a person

aufstehen *v.* to get up; to arise; to stand open; **— gegen** to rebel

aufsteigen *v.* to ascend; to rise; to climb

aufstellen *v.* to set up; to expose; to erect; (pol.) to nominate; (mil.) to activate

Aufstieg *m.* ascent; rise

Aufstiegmessgerät *n.* (avi.) climb indicator

aufstossen *v.* to push open; to belch

aufstreichen *v.* to spread on; (mus.) to start to play

aufsuchen *v.* to seek for; to look up; to visit

auftauchen *v.* to emerge, to appear suddenly

auftauen *v.* to thaw; to become communicative

auftischen *v.* to serve up; to regale with; **alte Geschichten —** to warm up old tales

Auftrag *m.* commission; charge, mission, order; **im — von** by order of, in behalf of; **-geber** *m.* consignor; employer;

customer

auftragen *v.* to serve up; to commission; to wear out; **dick —** to lay it on thick, to exaggerate

auftreiben *v.* to drive upward; to rouse (game); to obtain with difficulty; (med.) to distend

auftrennen *v.* to ravel out

auftreten *v.* to appear; to behave; to open by stepping on

Auftritt *m.* appearance; (theat.) scene

auftrumpfen *v.* to stamp; to trump

auftun *v.* to open; to disclose

auftürmen *v.* to pile up, to rise aloft

aufwachen *v.* to awake, to wake up

aufwachsen *v.* to grow up

aufwärmen *v.* to warm up; (coll.) to rehash

aufwarten *v.* to wait on; to serve; to visit

Aufwärterin *f.* waitress, stewardess

aufwärts *adv.* upwards; uphill

aufwecken *v.* to rouse, to wake up

aufweichen *v.* to soften; to soak

aufweisen *v.* to exhibit; to show

aufwenden *v.* to spend upon

aufwerfen *v.* to throw open (*oder* up); **aufgeworfene Lippe** pouting lip; **aufgeworfene Nase** turned-up nose

aufwiegeln *v.* to incite, to stir up

aufwiegen *v.* to counterbalance; to compensate

aufwieglerisch *adj.* inflammatory, seditious

aufwinden *v.* to reel; to hoist (with windlass); to untwist; to weigh (anchor)

aufwirbeln *v.* to whirl up; **Staub —** to raise dust; to make a great stir

aufwühlen *v.* to root (*oder* stir) up; to agitate

aufzählen *v.* to count up; to enumerate

aufzäumen *v.* to bridle

aufzehren *v.* to consume; to use up

aufzeichnen *v.* to note down; to sketch; to record

aufziehen *v.* to pull up (*oder* open); to wind up (watch); to stretch on; to approach; to string; to rear; to cultivate, to breed; (coll.) to tease; **andere Seiten —** to adopt a different tone

Aufzug *m.* attire; pageant; parade; crane; elevator; (theat.) act

Augapfel *m.* eyeball; (poet.) darling

Auge *neu.* eye; (bot.) bud; (cards) spot; sight; **aus den -n verlieren** to lose sight of; **ein — zudrücken** to connive; **ganz — sein** to be all eyes; **im — behalten** to keep in mind; **kein — zutun** to sleep not a wink; **mit blossem —** with the naked eye; **unter seinen -n** under his very eyes; **unter vier -n** privately; **-narzt** *m.* oculist, optometrist; **-nblick** *m.* moment; **-nbraue** *f.* eyebrow; **-nhöhle** *f.* eye socket; **-nlicht** *neu.* eyesight; **-nmass** *neu.* **ein gutes -nmass** a sure eye; **-nmerk** *neu.* attention; **-nschein** *m.* in **-nschein nehmen** to inspect; **-ntäuschung** *f.* optical illusion; **-nweide** *f.* welcome sight; **-nwimper** *f.* eyelash; **-nzeuge** *m.* eyewitness

augen: -blicklich *adj.* instantaneous; momentary, at present; **−fällig** *adj.*, **−scheinlich** *adj.* apparent, obvious, evident

Aula *f.* hall

aus *prep.* by, for, from, of, out of; in, on, on account of, upon; — *adv.* over, finished; — **dem Deutschen** from the German; — **dem Kopfe** by heart; — **freier Wahl** by free choice; — **Furcht vor** for fear of; — **Gold** made of gold; — **Neugier** out of curiosity; — **Unwissenheit** through sheer ignorance; **die Kirche ist** — church is over; **mit ihm ist es** — he is done for; **von Grund** — thoroughly; **von mir** — for my part

ausarbeiten *v.* to work out; to elaborate

ausarten *v.* to degenerate

ausatmen *v.* to breathe out, to exhale

Ausbau *m.* extension; completion

ausbauen *v.* to complete, to develop; to enlarge

ausbedingen *v.* to stipulate; to reserve (right)

ausbessern *v.* to mend, to repair; to correct

Ausbeute *f.* gain; profit, yield

ausbeuten *v.* to exploit; to take advantage of

ausbieten *v.* to offer for sale; to hawk (wares)

ausbilden *v.* to educate; to develop; to drill, to train; **sich** — to improve one's mind

ausbitten *v.*, **sich** — to ask (*oder* beg) for; to insist on

ausblasen *v.* to blow out; **das Lebenslicht** — **to kill**

ausbleiben *v.* to stay away; to fail to appear (*oder* take place)

Ausblick *m.* outlook, view; prospect

ausbrechen *v.* to break out; to escape; (med.) to vomit; **in Lachen** — to burst out laughing

ausbreiten *v.* to spread; to extend; to display; to promulgate; to propagate

ausbrennen *v.* to burn out; (med.) to cauterize

ausbringen *v.* to bring out, to get off; (naut.) to hoist out; **Gesundheit** — to toast

Ausbruch *m.* outburst; eruption; escape

ausbrüten *v.* to hatch out; to brood on; to plot

ausdauern *v.* to hold out; to persevere

ausdehnen *v.* to expand, to extend; to stretch

ausdenken *v.* to think through; to contrive; to devise; **sich etwas** — to imagine; to invent

ausdrehen *v.* to switch (*oder* turn) off

Ausdruck *m.* expression; phrase, term

ausdrücken *v.* to press (*oder* squeeze) out; to express; **sich klar** — to speak clearly; **sich kurz** — to be brief

ausdrücklich *adj.* explicit; strict

ausdruckslos *adj.* inexpressive, blank

ausdrucksvoll *adj.* expressive

ausdunsten, ausdünsten *v.* to sweat out, to exhale; to evaporate

auseinander *adv.* apart, separately; **−brin−**

gen *v.* to separate; **−fliegen** *v.* to fly in different directions; **−gehen** *v.* to part company, to disband, to diverge; **−halten** *v.* to keep separate, to distinguish; **−nehmen** *v.* to take to pieces, to dismount; **−setzen** *v.* to set apart; to explain; to analyse; to discuss

auser: −koren *adj.* selected, elect; **−lesen** *adj.* choice, exquisite; **−sehen** *v.* to choose, to select; **−wählen** *v.* to single out, to destine

ausfahren *v.* to go (*oder* take, drive) out; (min.) to ascend; (naut.) to put to sea

Ausfahrt *f.* drive, excursion; gateway

ausfallen *v.* to fall out; to be deducted (*oder* omitted); (mil.) to attack, to make a sally; to fail to take place; **gut** — to turn out well; **−d** *adj.* aggressive; insulting

ausfertigen *v.* to draw up, to make out; to issue

Ausfertigung *f.* execution; issue; **in zweifacher** — in duplicate

ausfinden, ausfindig machen *v.* to find out, to discover

ausfliegen *v.* to fly out; to leave home; to make a trip; to escape

ausfliessen *v.* to flow out; to emanate

Ausflucht *f.* loophole; excuse; evasion; pretext

Ausflug *m.* excursion, outing

Ausflügler *m.* excursionist; hiker

ausforschen *v.* to investigate, to inquire into; to sound out

ausfragen *v.* to quiz; to question closely; (coll.) to pump

ausfressen *v.* to corrode; (coll.) to eat up; to make mischief

Ausfuhr *f.* export

ausführ: −bar *adj.* exportable; feasible, practicable; **−en** *v.* to lead out; to export; to execute; to perform; to finish; to explain; **−lich** *adj.* detailed, full

Ausführung *f.* execution, performance; statement

ausfüllen *v.* to fill up (*oder* in); to pad

Ausgabe *f.* expenditure, expense; outlay; edition, issue; delivery

Ausgang *m.* going out; outlet; exit; result, upshot; day off; **−spunkt** *m.* starting point

ausgeben *v.* to give out; to issue; to spend; (cards) to deal; to distribute; **sich** — **für** to pretend to be

ausgeh(e)n *v.* to go out; to come (*oder* fall) out; to fade; to run short; to end, to terminate; **— auf** to aim at; **leer** — to get nothing, to be left out in the cold

ausgelassen *adj.* exuberant, frolicsome

ausgemacht *adj.* agreed on; settled; **ein −er Gauner** a complete scoundrel; **eine −e Sache** an established fact

ausgenommen *adv.* except, save; with the exception of; **niemand** — bar none

ausgeprägt *adj.* pronounced, distinctive

ausgerechnet *adv.* precisely; that very

ausgeschlossen *adj.* locked out; excluded; impossible; out of the question

ausgeschnitten *adj.* cut out; low-necked (dress)

ausgesprochen *adj.* pronounced; decided, marked; — *adv.* especially

ausgestalten *v.* to shape; to develop; to arrange; to elaborate

ausgesucht *adj.* choice, select, exquisite

ausgezeichnet *adj.* excellent; distinguished

ausgiebig *adj.* abundant; plentiful; rich

ausgiessen *v.* to pour out; to vent; to diffuse

Ausgleich *m.* agreement; settlement; compromise; equalization; (com.) balance; (tennis) deuce

ausgleichen *v.* to equalize; to compromise, to settle; to compensate; to balance; **sich — mit** to become reconciled with

ausgleiten, ausglitschen *v.* to slip, to slide

ausgraben *v.* to dig out; to excavate; to disinter; **Leiche —** to exhume

ausgreifen *v.* to take long strides; **-d** *adj.* far-reaching

Ausguck *m.* lookout; watch

Ausguss *m.* outpouring; gutter; sink; spout

aushalten *v.* to hold out, to last, to bear, to endure; **nicht zum —** beyond endurance

aushändigen *v.* to hand over; to deliver up

Aushang *m.* display; placard; notice

aushängen *v.* to hang out; to unhinge; to post

Aushängeschild *neu.* signboard; best product; pretense

ausharren *v.* to hold out; to persevere

aushauchen *v.* to exhale; **die Seele —** to expire, to die

aushauen *v.* to hew out; to excavate; to carve out; to thin (forest); to flog

ausheben *v.* to lift out; to unhinge; (mil.) to draft; (police) to raid; **sich die Schulter —** to dislocate one's shoulder

aushecken *v.* to hatch; to concoct, to plot

ausheilen *v.* to heal up; to cure completely

Aushilfe *f.* temporary aid; stopgap

aushöhlen *v.* to hollow out; to excavate

ausholen *v.* to raise the arm (for striking, throwing); to sound out; to spar; **weit — to** be circumstantial; **zum Sprung —** to take a running start to jump

aushorchen *v.* to sound out; to pump

aushungern *v.* to famish, to starve out

aushusten *v.* to expectorate

auskennen *v.* **sich — to** be well qualified; to know what's what; **sich nicht — to** be at wit's end

auskleiden *v.* to undress; to line, to coat

Auskleideakt *m.* striptease

ausklopfen *v.* to beat out, to dust

ausklügeln *v.* to puzzle out

auskneifen *v.* (coll.) to slip off; to run away

auskochen *v.* to extract by boiling; to scald; (coll.) to plot

auskommen *v.* to come (*oder* break) out; to escape; to manage with; to become public; **gut (*or* schlecht) — to** be on good (*oder* poor) terms

Auskommen *neu.* livelihood; subsistence; **es ist kein — mit ihm** nobody can get along with him

auskosten *v.* to taste thoroughly; to enjoy

auskratzen *v.* to scratch (*oder* scrape) out; (coll.) to run off; (med.) to curette

auskundschaften *v.* to explore; (mil.) to reconnoiter; (coll.) to discover, to spy out

Auskunft *f.* information; **-sbüro** *neu.*, **-sstelle** *f.* information office; **nähere —** particulars

auskuppeln *v.* to throw out of gear

auslachen *v.* to laugh at

ausladen *v.* to unload; to lighten (ship); to disembark; (arch.) to project; **-de Geste** sweeping gesture

Auslage *f.* (com.) advance; disbursement, outlay; (show window) display

Ausland *neu.* foreign country; **im Inland und — at** home and abroad

Ausländer *m.* foreigner, alien

ausländisch *adj.* foreign, alien; outlandish

auslassen *v.* to let (*oder* leave) out; to omit; (cooking) to render; **sich — to** explain oneself; to give vent to

auslaufen *v.* to run (*oder* set) out; to end; to diverge; to clear (*oder* leave) port; to leak

Ausläufer *m.* errand boy; (bot.) runner, sucker; (geol.) spur; (fig.) branch

ausleeren *v.* to empty; to drink up; to clear out; to drain; (med.) to purge

auslegen *v.* to lay (*oder* spread) out; to display, to expose for sale; to advance, to pay; to inlay, to tile; to expound, to interpret

ausleihen *v.* to lend out, to loan; **sich etwas — to** borrow something from

auslernen *v.* to finish learning (*oder* studying)

Auslese *f.* selection; choice wine

auslesen *v.* to choose, to select; to sort; to pick out, to cull; to finish reading

ausliefern *v.* to hand over; to deliver up; to give up; to surrender, to extradite

auslöffeln *v.* to spoon (*oder* ladle) out; **etwas — to** pay for one's mistake

auslosen *v.* to draw lots for; to raffle

auslöschen *v.* to put (*oder* blot) out, to extinguish; to erase

auslösen *v.* to loosen; to ransom; to cause

Auslöser *m.* (phot.) release, trigger

ausmachen *v.* to constitute, to make up; to extinguish; to take out; to husk, to shell; to agree on, to decide, to settle; **nichts — it** does not matter

ausmalen *v.* to paint; to color, to emblazon, to illuminate; to imagine (in detail)

Ausmass *neu.* degree, extent

ausmerzen *v.* to eliminate; to expurgate

ausmessen *v.* to measure, to survey

ausmisten *v.* (agr.) to clear of manure; to clean up a mess

Ausnahme *f.* exception; **-fall** *m.* exceptional case; **-zustand** *m.* state of emergency

ausnahmsweise *adv.* exceptionally

ausnehmen *v.* to take out; to draw (fowl); to exempt; to except; **sich gut — to** look well; **-d** *adj.* exceptional; **-d** *adv.*

exceedingly

ausnutzen, ausnützen v. to wear out, to utilize; to make the most of; to exploit

auspfeifen v. to hiss; to catcall, to condemn

ausplaudern v. to divulge, to blab

ausprägen v. to coin, to impress

auspressen, ausquetschen v. to squeeze out; to extort

ausprob(ier)en v. to test, to try; to taste

Auspuff m. exhaust; **–klappe** f. exhaust valve; **–rohr** neu. exhaust pipe; **–topf** m. muffler

auspumpen v. to pump out (oder dry); to exhaust; to produce a vacuum

ausquartieren v. to dislodge; to quarter out

ausradieren v. to erase

ausräuchern v. to smoke out; to fumigate

ausräumen v. to clear away, to empty

ausrechnen v. to calculate, to compute; **falsch —** to miscalculate

Ausrede f. excuse, pretext; evasion; **faule — bad excuse**

ausreden v. to finish speaking; to speak freely; to dissuade, to argue (oder talk) out of; to exculpate; (coll.) to wriggle out of

ausreichen v. to suffice; **–d** adj. sufficient

Ausreise f. departure; journey abroad

ausreissen v. to tear out; to pull up; to burst; (coll.) to bolt, to desert

ausrenken v. to dislocate

ausrichten v. to straighten out; to execute; to accomplish, to perform; **Grüsse — to give regards to; nichts —** to fail

ausringen v. to wring out; **er hat ausgerungen** his struggles are over; he is dead

ausroden v. to root out; to grub up; to clear

ausrotten v. to eradicate, to exterminate

ausrücken v. to march off; to decamp; to throw out of gear

Ausruf m. outcry, shout; exclamation; proclamation; **–ungszeichen** neu. exclamation mark

ausrufen v. to call (oder cry) out; to ejaculate; to exclaim; to proclaim

ausruhen v. to rest; to repose; to relax

ausrüsten v. to equip, to fit out; to endow

ausrutschen v. to slide, to slip, to skid

aussäen v. to sow; to disseminate

Aussage f. assertion, declaration, statement; (law) deposition; (gram.) predicate

aussagen v. to state, to give evidence

Aussatz m. leprosy, Hansen's disease

Aussätzige m. leper

aussaugen v. to suck dry (oder out); to drain, to exhaust; to bleed; to impoverish

ausschachten v. to deepen, to excavate, to sink

ausschalten v. to switch off; to disconnect; to eliminate, to remove

Ausschank m. retailing of liquor; bar, tavern

Ausschau f. lookout; **— halten** to watch for

ausscheiden v. to separate; to resign; to eliminate; to excrete, to secrete

ausschelten v. to scold, to abuse

ausschenken v. to pour out; to retail liquor

ausschiffen v. to put to sea, to set sail; to land, to disembark; to unload; to discharge

ausschimpfen v. to revile, to cuss out

ausschlachten v. to cut up (for sale); (fig.) to broaden

ausschlafen v. to sleep amply; **Rausch — to sober up**

Ausschlag m. (mech.) amplitude, deflection; (med.) eruption, rash; (fig.) issue (of events), **einer Sache den — geben** to clinch the matter

ausschlagen v. to beat (oder thrash) soundly; to knock out; to trim, to line; (bot.) to bud, to sprout; (mech.) to deflect, to turn; (med.) to erupt; (fig.) to decline, to refuse

ausschliessen v. to lock out; to exclude; to disqualify

ausschliesslich adj. exclusive

Ausschluss m. exclusion; disqualification; (typ.) justification; **mit (or unter) — der Öffentlichkeit** behind closed doors

ausschmücken v. to adorn, to decorate; to embellish; (coll.) to deck out

Ausschnitt m. cut(ting) out; clipping; (arch.) bay; (dress) low neck; (math.) sector

ausschöpfen v. to bail, to scoop; to exhaust

ausschreiben v. to write out; to copy; to announce, to proclaim, to advertise; (tax) to impose

ausschreien v. to shout out; to proclaim; **sich die Kehle —** to strain one's voice

ausschreiten v. to step out; to go too far

Ausschuss m. board, committee; refuse; wastepaper; **–sitzung** f. committee meeting; **–waren** f. pl. damaged goods, remnants

ausschütten v. to pout out; **Dividende — to distribute dividends; sich vor Lachen — to split one's sides with laughing**

ausschweifen v. to digress, to ramble; to lead a dissolute life; **–d** adj. dissolute

ausschwitzen v. to exude; to sweat out

aussehen v. to appear; to look out; **gesund —** to look well; **nach Regen — to look like rain**

Aussehen neu. appearance, aspect, look

aussen adv. outside; out-of-doors; **nach — outward; von — betrachten** to judge from the outside

Aussen: –bordmotor m. outboard motor; **–dienst** m. foreign (oder outdoor) service; **–handel** m. export trade, **–minister** m. Minister for Foreign Affairs; **–politik** f. foreign policy; **–seite** f. outside; surface; **–seiter** m. outsider; **–stände** m. pl. outstanding claims; **–welt** f. external (oder visible) world

ausser prep. beside(s), outside of; out of; beyond; except; **— acht lassen** to neglect, to overlook; **— sich sein** to be beside oneself; **— Bereich** beyond reach; — **der Zeit** out of season, at the wrong time; — **Dienst** off duty; out of employment; — **Frage** beyond all doubt; — **Kurs setzen** to withdraw from circulation; — **Landes gehen** to go abroad; — *conj.* but, except, save, unless; — **dass** except that; **–amtlich** *adj.*, **–dienstlich** *adj.* unofficial, private; **–dem** *adv.* moreover; **–ehelich** *adj.* illegitimate; **–gerichtlich** *adj.* extrajudicial; **–gesetzlich** *adj.* unlawful; **–gewöhnlich** *adj.* extraordinary, unusual; **–halb** *prep.* outside; **–ordentlich** *adj.* extraordinary, amazing; **–stande** *adv.* unable (to)

äusser: –e *adj.* outer, outward; external, exterior; **–lich** *adj.* external; superficial; **–n** to manifest; to show; to express, to utter; **–st** *adv.* extremely, exceedingly; **–ste** *adj.* outermost, ut(ter)most

Aussicht *f.* view; prospect; expectation

aussichtslos *adj.* hopeless; without prospects

aussöhnen *v.* to reconcile

aussondern, aussortieren *v.* to select, to single out; to sort out; to cull

ausspannen *v.* to unharness; to extend, to stretch; to relax, to rest

aussperren *v.* to lock (*oder* shut) out; (typ.) to space out

ausspielen *v.* to play to the end; to play for (prize); (cards) to lead; **einen gegen den andern** — to play off one against the other

ausspionieren *v.* to ferret (*oder* spy) out

Aussprache *f.* pronunciation; articulation; brogue, accent; discussion, talk

aussprechen *v.* to finish speaking; to pronounce; to articulate; to declare; to express; **Urteil** — to pass a sentence

Australien *neu.* Australia

Ausspruch *m.* utterance; remark; (law) decision, finding, sentence, verdict

ausspülen *v.* to rinse out; to wash away

ausspüren *v.* to trace; to track down

ausstaffieren *v.* to equip, to fit out; to trim

Ausstand *m.* outstanding debt; strike

ausständig *adj.* outstanding (debt); in arrears; on strike

ausstatten *v.* to equip, to fit out; to establish, to set up; to give (dowry); to endow

aussteh(e)n *v.* to be exposed (for sale); to stand out; to bear, to endure; **nicht — können** to be unable to stand

aussteigen *v.* to get out, to alight from; (naut.) to land; (rail.) to leave (train)

ausstellen *v.* to exhibit; to display; — **an** to find fault with; to issue

Ausstellung *f.* exhibition, show; **–en machen** to raise objections, to find fault

aussterben *v.* to die out, to become extinct (*oder* desolate)

Aussteuer *f.* dowry; trousseau; endowment

ausstopfen *v.* to stuff; to pad, to wad

ausstossen *v.* to push out; to expel; to eject, to oust; to banish, to excommunicate; (gram.) to drop, to elide; (med.)

to excrete; **Fluch** — to swear; **Schrei** — to scream, to yell; **Worte** — to ejaculate, to utter

ausstrahlen *v.* to radiate, to emit rays

ausstreichen *v.* to cross (*oder* strike) out; to cancel; to smooth out; to obliterate

ausstreuen *v.* to scatter, to disseminate; to circulate

ausströmen *v.* to flow, to stream forth; (phys.) to emanate, to escape

aussuchen *v.* to pick out, to select

austauschen *v.* to barter, to exchange

austeilen *v.* to dole out; to distribute; to allot; (eccl.) to administer; **Befehle — to give orders**

Auster *f.* oyster; **–nbank** *f.* oyster bed; **–nfang** *m.* oyster catching (*oder* dredging)

austilgen *v.* to obliterate; to exterminate; to eradicate; to wipe out (guilt, debt)

austoben *v.* **sich** — to sow one's wild oats; to cease raging; **Jugend muss sich — youth** must have its fling

austreiben *v.* to drive out; to eject; to dislodge; to evict; to cast out, to exorcise

austreten *v.* to step out; to withdraw; to resign; to wear out by treading; (mil.) to fall out; to overflow; to go to the toilet

austrinken *v.* to drink up, to empty

Austritt *m.* resignation, withdrawal; inundation, overflow; emergence

ausüben *v.* to exercise (authority); to practice; to commit (crime)

Ausverkauf *m.* clearance sale

ausverkaufen *v.* to sell out; to clear of stock

Auswahl *f.* selection; assortment; anthology

auswählen *v.* to choose, to select; to pick out

auswandern *v.* to emigrate

auswärtig *adj.* foreign; abroad

auswärts *adv.* outward(s); outside of

auswechseln *v.* to change for; to exchange

Ausweg *m.* way out; evasion, loophole; **keinen — mehr wissen** to be at wits' end

ausweichen *v.* to make way for, to turn aside; to evade, to elude

ausweinen *v.* to have a good cry; **sich die Augen —** to cry one's eyes out

Ausweis *m.* proof of identity; certification

ausweisen *v.* to expel, to deport; to show, to prove; **sich —** to identify oneself

ausweiten *v.* to widen, to stretch; to scoop out

auswendig *adj.* outward, external; by heart

auswerfen *v.* to throw out (*oder* overboard); to eject; to vomit; to allow, to grant

auswerten *v.* to evaluate; to make full use of

auswirken *v.* to work out; to effect; to obtain; to procure

Auswuchs *m.* excrescence; (med.) hump; tumor; **Auswüchse** *pl.* abuses

Auswurf m. scum, refuse; garbage, rubbish; (med.) expectoration, discharge; **— der Menschheit** dregs of humanity

auszacken v. to indent; to notch; to scallop

auszahlen v. to pay out; to disburse

auszählen v. to count out; to score

Auszehrung f. wasting away; (med.) phthisis

auszeichnen v. to mark out; to decorate; (com.) to label, to ticket

ausziehen v. to draw out, to take off; to disrobe; to extract; to move away; to stretch

Auszug m. moving out; departure; emigration; summary; extract; quintessence; abstract; (rel.) exodus

Auto neu. auto(mobile), (motor) car; **-bahn** f. freeway; **-biographie** f. autobiography; **-didakt** m. self-taught person; **-droschke** f. taxi-(cab); **-falle** f. police trap; **-gramm** neu. autograph; **-heber** m. jack; **-mat** m. automat

Autor m. author, writer; **-enschaft** f. authorship; **-ität** f. authority

autorisieren v. to authorize; to license

Avancen machen v. to make a pass

Axt f. ax, hatchet

B

Bach m. brook, creek; **-stelze** f. wagtail

Back: **-fisch** m. fried fish; teen-age girl; bobby-soxer; **-obst** neu. dried fruit; **-ofen** m. oven; **-pulver** neu. baking powder; **-stein** m. brick

Back: **-e** f. cheek; **-enbart** m. side whiskers; **-enknochen** m. jawbone; **-enzahn** m. molar; **-pfeife** f., **-enstreich** m. box on the ear

backen v. to bake

Bäcker m. baker; **-ei** f. bakery; pastries; **-laden** m. bakery

Bad neu. bath; spa, health resort; **-anstalt** f. baths; bathing establishment: **-anzug** m. swim suit; **-ekur** f. treatment at medicinal springs; **-emantel** m. bathrobe; **-er** m. barber; (lit.) surgeon; **-estrand** m. beach; **-ewanne** f. bathtub; **-ezimmer** neu. bathroom

baden v. to bathe

Bagage f. luggage; baggage; (coll.) rabble

Bagger m. dredger

baggern v. to dredge

Bahn f. road, track, way; course; career; railway; orbit; **-brecher** m. pioneer; **-g(e)leis(e)** neu. railway track; **-hof** m. station, terminal; **-linie** f. line; **-netz** neu. railway system; **-steig** m. train platform; **-übergang** m. railway crossing

bahnbrechend adj. pioneering; epoch-making

bahnen v. to open up (path); to pioneer; to prepare; **einen Weg —** to force one's way

Bahre f. stretcher; **von der Wiege bis zur — from** the cradle to the grave

Bai f. bay

Bakkalaureus m. bachelor (B.A., B.S., etc.)

Bakteri: **-e** f. bacterium; **-ologie** f., **-enforschung** f., **-enkunde** f. bacteriology

Balance f. balance; equilibrium

bald adr. soon; presently; almost

Baldachin m. canopy

Balg m. skin; slough; bellows; (coll.) brat

balgen v. to scuffle, to wrestle, to tussle

Balken m. beam, rafter; joist; girder

Balkon m. balcony; **-tür(e)** f. French window(s)

Ball m. ball; globe; dance; **-anzug** m. full dress; **-kleid** neu. evening dress; **-saal** m. ballroom; **-schläger** m. racket; bat; batter

Ballen m. bale; packet, bundle; (anat.) bunion

ballen v. to form a ball; to bale; to conglomerate; **die Faust —** to clench one's fist

Ballon m. balloon; **-korb** m. nacelle

balsamieren v. to embalm

Bambus m. bamboo

banal adj. banal; commonplace

Banane f. banana

Band neu. band, ribbon; tape; ligament; fetters; (mech.) hoop; link, bond, tie; **laufendes —** conveyor belt; **-eisen** neu. hoop (oder strap) iron; **-erole** f. revenue stamp; **-mass** neu. tape measure; **-säge** f. band saw; **-wurm** m. tapeworm

Band f. binding, cover; volume

Bande f. band; gang, pack; (billiards) cushion; **-nkrieg** m. guerrilla warfare

bändigen v. to subdue, to tame; to break in

bange adj. alarmed, anxious, frightened; **-n** v. to be afraid, to tremble for, to worry about

Bank f. bench, seat; pew; reef; **auf die lange —** schieben to put off, to delay

Bank f. bank; **die — sprengen** to break the bank; **-abschluss** m. balance sheet; **-beamte** m. bank clerk; **-ier** m. banker; **-konto** neu. bank account

Bänkelsänger m. ballad singer, rhymester

Bankett neu. banquet

bankrott adj. bankrupt

Bann m. ban; constraint; spell; excommunication; **-fluch** m. anathema; **-kreis** m., **-meile** f. sphere of influence, spell; **-ware** f. contraband

bannen v. to fascinate; to conjure; to banish; to exorcise; to excommunicate

Banner neu. banner, flag, standard; **-träger** m. standard bearer

bar adj. bare, naked; devoid of; pure, unmixed; **— bezahlen** to pay in cash; **-e Münze** face value; **-er Unsinn** sheer nonsense; **-es Geld** ready cash

Bär m. bear; **Grosser —** (ast.) Big Dipper; **-in** f. female bear

Baracke f. barrack

Barbar m. barbarian; **-ismus** m. barbarism

barbarisch adj. barbaric

Barbier m. barber

barbieren v. to shave; (coll.) to cheat

Barett neu. beret, biretta

barfuss, barfüssig adj. barefoot(ed)

barhäuptig *adj.* bareheaded

barmherzig *adj.* merciful; charitable; compassionate; — **Samariter** good Samaritan

Baron *m.* baron; —esse *f.*, —in *f.* baroness

Barriere *f.* barrier

Barsch *m.* (ichth.) perch

barsch *adj.* gruff, rude, tart

Bart *m.* beard; whiskers; wattle; (key) bit; in den — brummen to mutter to oneself; jemanden um den — gehen to flatter someone

bärtig *adj.* bearded, whiskered; barbed

Base *f.* female cousin; (chem.) base, alkali

Basis *f.* base, basis; foundation

Bass *m.* (mus.) bass; —geige *f.* bass viol; —ist *m.* bass singer

Bassin *neu.* basin; reservoir

Bast *m.* bast, inner bark

basta! *interj.* that will do! that's enough!

basteln *v.* to put together; to work at a hobby; to potter

Batterie *f.* battery

Bau *m.* building, construction; structure; build; (agr.) cultivation; (min.) working; (zool.) lair; den; burrow; —art *f.* style of architecture; —fach *neu.* architecture, building trade; —gerüst *neu.* scaffold(ing); —holz *neu.* timber; —kasten *m.* set of building blocks; —meister *m.* architect; —platz *m.* —stelle *f.* building lot (*oder* site)

Bauch *m.* belly, abdomen; —fellentzündung *f.* peritonitis; —landung *f.* (avi.) bellylanding; —redner *m.* ventriloquist; —speicheldrüse *f.* pancreas; —weh *neu.* (coll.) belly-ache; colic

bauen *v.* to build, to construct; (agr.) to cultivate; (min.) to work; to rely (*oder* count) on

Bauer *neu.* bird cage, aviary

Bauer *m.* builder, constructor; farmer; peasant, rustic; yokel, boor; (cards) knave, jack; (chess) pawn; —nbursche *m.* country lad; —ndirne *f.* country girl; —nfänger *m.* swindler; crook; —nhof *m.* farm

Bäuerin *f.* peasant woman; farmer's wife

bäuerlich *adj.* rural, rustic; (fig.) boorish

baufällig *adj.* dilapidated

Baum *m.* tree; beam; boom; —schule *f.* tree nursery; —stamm *m.* trunk; —wolle *f.* cotton

bäumen *v.* to prance; (horse) to rear

Bayern *neu.* Bavaria

Bazillus *m.* bacillus; germ

beabsichtigen *v.* to intend; to mean to do

beacht: —en *v.* to take notice; to observe; —enswert *adj.*, —lich *adj.* noteworthy, remarkable

Beamte *m.*, Beamtin *f.* official; public officer; officeholder; —nherrschaft *f.* bureaucracy; —nschaft *f.*, —ntum *neu.* civil service; officialdom; —wirtschaft *f.* redtape methods

bean: —spruchen *v.* to claim, to demand; Zeit —spruchen to take up time; —standen to demur; to object, to contest; —tragen to move, to propose; to apply; —worten to answer, to reply

beängstigen *v.* to make anxious; to alarm

bearbeiten *v.* to work (on); to fashion; (agr.) to cultivate; (lit.) to adapt; to revise; to rewrite; **jemanden —** to belabor someone

beaufsichtigen *v.* to supervise; to control; to inspect

beauftragen *v.* to charge (with), to commission, to empower

bebauen *v.* to build (up)on; (agr.) to cultivate

beben *v.* to quiver, to quake, to tremble

Beben *neu.* quivering; earthquake

Becher *m.* cup, goblet; beaker; mug, tumbler; dice-box; calyx

Becken *neu.* basin, bowl; (anat.) pelvis; (mus.) cymbal

bedacht *adj.* thoughtful, wary; intent on; —sam considerate; (coll.) a bit slow

bedächtig *adj.* considerate, circumspect

Bedarf *m.* need, requirement; —sartikel *m.* requisites, utensils

bedauerlich *adj.* deplorable, regrettable

bedauern *v.* to pity, to deplore; to regret

Bedauern *neu.* pity; sympathy; regret

bedecken *v.* to cover, to screen; to protect; to escort; der Himmel ist bedeckt the sky is overcast

bedenken *v.* to consider, to mind; to provide; sich anders — to change one's mind; sich — to hesitate

Bedenken *neu.* doubt, scruple; hesitation

bedenklich *adj.* doubtful, serious; critical

Bedenkzeit *f.* time for reflection; respite

bedeut: —en *v.* to mean, to signify; to indicate; es hat nichts zu —en it is of no consequence; —end *adj.* significant; notable; —end *adv.* by far, considerable; —sam *adj.* significant, meaningful

Bedien: —stete *m.* employee; —te *m.* servant; footman; —ung *f.* service; attendance, servants

bedienen *v.* to attend, to serve; to wait on; (mech.) to operate; (cards) to follow suit; sich — to help oneself

Bedienungsturm *m.* (Rakete) gantry

bedingen *v.* to stipulate; to involve

bedingt *adj.* conditional; limited; qualified

Bedingung *f.* condition; restriction; terms

bedrängen *v.* to press hard; to oppress; to vex

bedrohen *v.* to menace, to threaten

bedrücken *v.* to press upon; to depress

bedürfen *v.* to need; to be in want of

Bedürfnis *neu.* need, want; necessity; —anstalt *f.* comfort station

bedürftig *adj.* needy, poor

beeiden *v.* to confirm by oath; to swear

beeilen *v.* to hasten, to hurry; to hustle

beeinflussen *v.* to influence

beeinträchtigen *v.* to impair; to injure

beend(ig)en *v.* to end, to finish; to terminate

beerben *v.* to inherit, to be heir to

Beerdigung *f.* burial, interment; funeral

Beere *f.* berry

Beet *neu.* (agr.) bed, border

befähigen *v.* to enable; to qualify

befähigt *adj.* capable, talented; fit

befallen *v.* to befall, to happen (to); to attack

befangen *adj.* shy; biased, prejudiced; embarrassed, confused

befassen *v.* to touch, to handle; **sich — mit** to concern (*oder* occupy) oneself with

Befehl *m.* command; order; decree; **zu — stehen** to be at the service of

befehlen *v.* to command; to order; to decree

Befehlsausgabe *f.* briefing

befehlshaberisch *adj.* imperious; dictatorial

befestigen *v.* to attach, to fasten, to fix; to stiffen, to harden; to fortify

befeuchten *v.* to moisten, to wet

befinden *v.* to deem, to consider; **sich —** to be present; to feel (ill, well, etc.)

Befinden *neu.* opinion; condition; health

beflecken *v.* to soil, to spot, to stain; to contaminate, to pollute; to sully

befleiss(ig)en *v.* **sich —** to apply oneself to; to take great pains to

beflissen *adj.* diligent; zealous

beflügeln *v.* to add wings to; to accelerate

befolgen *v.* to follow, to obey; to observe

befördern *v.* to forward, to transport; to convey; further, to promote; to favor

befragen *v.* to interrogate; to consult

befreien *v.* to liberate; to release; to free

befremdend, befremdlich *adj.* odd, strange

befreunden *v.* **sich — mit** to befriend, to become friends; to reconcile oneself to

befrieden *v.* to pacify; to bring peace to

befriedigen *v.* to satisfy; to gratify; to appease; **schwer zu —** hard to please; **-d** *adj.* satisfactory

befruchten *v.* to fructify, to impregnate; to fecundate, to fertilize

Befugnis *f.* authority; warrant; competence

befühlen *v.* to feel, to finger, to touch

Befund *m.* finding; condition, state; diagnosis

befürchten *v.* to fear, to dread; to suspect

befürworten *v.* to recommend; to advocate; to back, to support

begabt *adj.* gifted, talented

Begabung *f.* gift, talent; capacity, endowment

Begebenheit *f.* event, occurrence; happening

begegnen *v.* to meet, to come upon, to run across; to happen; to obviate

begeh(e)n *v.* to walk (tracks); to celebrate, to commemorate; to commit, to perpetrate

begehren *v.* to desire, to covet, to crave; to demand, to request; **-swert** *adj.* desirable

begeistern *v.* to inspire; to fill with enthusiasm

Begier(de) *f.* longing, eagerness; desire; lust; appetite; cupidity

begierig *adj.* eager, desirous; lustful; covetous; **— zu erfahren** anxious to learn

begiessen *v.* to water, to wet; to baste

Beginn *m.* beginning; commencement; origin; **-en** *neu.* undertaking, enterprise

beginnen *v.* to begin, to commence

beglaubigen *v.* to attest, to certify; to authenticate; to accredit

Begleit: -er *m.* companion; attendant; accompanist; (ast.) satellite; **-erscheinungen** *f. pl.* circumstances, symptoms; **-ung** *f.* accompaniment; attendants, suite; escort, convoy

begleiten *v.* to accompany; to escort

beglückwünschen *v.* to congratulate

begnad(ig)en *v.* to pardon; to amnesty

begnügen *v.* **sich — mit** to be content (*oder* satisfied) with

Begräbnis *neu.* burial, interment; funeral; **-platz** *m.* burial ground

begreifen *v.* to finger, to handle, to touch; to comprehend, to grasp; **das Haus ist im Bau begriffen** the house is being built; **im Anmarsch begriffen** to be on the way; **nicht zu —** incomprehensible, inconceivable

begreiflich *adj.* comprehensible, conceivable; **-erweise** *adv.* understandably, naturally

begrenzen *v.* to bound, to limit; to confine

Begriff *m.* concept, idea; abstraction; **im — sein** to be about (*oder* on the point of); **schwer von — sein** to be slow of comprehension; **-sbestimmung** *f.* definition; **-svermögen** *neu.* intellectual capacity, comprehension

begründen *v.* to base (*oder* found); to establish; to prove, to substantiate

begrüssen *v.* to greet, to welcome; to salute

begünstigen *v.* to favor; to promote

Begünstigte *m.* favorite; protégé

begutachten *v.* to give an opinion on; to judge

begütert *adj.* rich, wealthy

begütigen *v.* to appease, to placate, to soothe

behaart *adj.* hairy; hirsute

behäbig *adj.* corpulent; easy, comfortable

behaftet *adj.* afflicted with; subject to

behagen *v.* to please, to suit

behaglich *adj.* comfortable, cozy, snug; **es sich — machen** to feel at home (*oder* at ease)

behalten *v.* to keep, to retain; to maintain; to remember; **für sich —** to keep secret

Behälter *m.* container, reservoir; box; tank

behandeln *v.* to handle; to deal with; to manage; (med.) to treat, to dress

beharren *v.* to persevere, to persist; to insist (*oder* hold) on, to continue

beharrlich *adj.* persevering, constant, tenacious

behaupten *v.* to assert, to affirm; to maintain; **sich —** to hold one's own (*oder* out)

Behausung *f.* lodging; home, dwelling

Behelf *m.* expedient, shift; device

behelfen *v.* **sich —** to make shift; sich mit

wenigem — to get along with a minimum

behelligen *v.* to annoy, to bother, to importune

behend(e) *adj.* agile, nimble

beherbergen *v.* to harbor, to shelter, to lodge; to accomodate

beherrschen *v.* to govern, to rule; to dominate; to master; to sway; **sich —** to control (*oder* restrain) oneself

beherzigen *v.* to take to heart; to consider well; to heed

behexen *v.* to bewitch; to charm, to enchant

behilflich *adj.* helpful; serviceable; **— sein** to lend a hand; to render assistance

Behörde *f.* governmental authorities

behutsam *adj.* careful, cautious; wary

bei *prep.* at, by, near; amid, among; in, on; to, with; in connection with; upon; **— alledem** for all that; **— Gelegenheit** on occasion; **— gutem Wetter** if the weather permits; **— guter Gesundheit** in good health; **— hellem Tage** in broad daylight; **— seinen Lebzeiten** during his lifetime; **— sich behalten** to keep to oneself; **— Sicht** on presentation; **— weitem nicht** far from it; **dicht —** close to; **nicht — Geld sein** to be short of cash

Beiblatt *neu.* supplement; extra sheet

beibringen *v.* to bring forward; to produce; to adduce; to inflict; to teach, to impart

Beicht: -e *f.* confession; **-vater** *m.* father confessor; **-kind** *neu.* penitent; confessor

beichten *v.* to confess

beide *adj.* and *pron.* both; either; **alle —** both of them; **wir —** we two; **-mal** *adv.* both times; **-rlei** *adj.* both kinds, of either sort; **-rseitig, -rseits** *adv.* on both sides; mutually, reciprocally

beieinander *adv.* together

Beifall *m.* assent; approbation; applause

beifolgend *adj.* enclosed; herewith

beifügen *v.* to add; to append; to enclose

Beigabe *f.* something added; supplement

beigeben *v.* to add

beikommen *v.* to come (*oder* get) at; to equal; **jemandem —** to get hold of somebody; **sich — lassen** to take into one's head; to dare

Beil *neu.* hatchet; axe

Beilage *f.* enclosure; supplement; side dish

beiläufig *adj.* incidental; approximate; **— *adv.*** incidentally; by the way

beilegen *v.* to add, to enclose; to ascribe to, to impute; to confer; to settle; (naut.) to heave to; **sich —** to assume (name)

beiliegen *v.* to be enclosed; (naut.) to lie to

beimengen, beimischen *v.* to add to, to admix

beimessen *v.* to ascribe, to attribute, to impute

Bein *neu.* leg; bone; **auf die -e bringen**

to get (*oder* set) going; **das — stellen** to trip up; **die -e in die Hand nehmen** to take to one's heels; **es geht durch Mark und — it** sends thrills through one; **immer auf den -en sein** to be always on the go; **sich auf die -e machen** to leave; **sich kein — ausreissen** to take one's time; **wieder auf die -e kommen** to convalesce; **-kleider** *neu. pl.* trousers, pants

beinahe *adv.* almost, all but; nearly; **— umkommen** to have a narrow escape

Beiname *m.* surname; nickname; epithet

beiordnen *v.* to co-ordinate; to adjoin

beipflichten *v.* to agree, to assent; to espouse

beisammen *adv.* together; **dicht —** close to each other; **seine Gedanken — haben** to have one's wits about one

Beischlaf *m.* cohabitation

Beisein *neu.* presence

beiseite *adv.* apart, aside; **-bringen** *v.* to purloin; to spirit away

Beispiel *neu.* example; instance; **als — anführen** to quote as a precedent; **zum — for example**

beispiellos *adj.* unprecedented, unheard of

beispringen *v.* to run to assist; to give aid

beissen *v.* to bite; to burn; to prick (conscience); **in den sauren Apfel —** to swallow the bitter pill; **ins Gras —** to bite the dust, to die; **-d** *adj.* mordant; sarcastic, pungent

Beistand *m.* support; assistance; aid, help; assistant; **— vor Gericht** legal counsel

beistehen *v.* to render aid; to back up, to side with; to plead (*oder* speak) for; to comfort; **Gott stehe ihm bei** God help him!

Beisteuer *f.* contribution; subsidy; collection

beistimmen *v.* to agree to (*oder* with); to concur (with); to accede to

Beitrag *m.* contribution; quota, share; premium

beitragen *v.* to contribute to(wards); to be instrumental in; to promote

beitreten *v.* to join (club, etc.); to assent to; to concur (with): to espouse

Beitritt *m.* joining (club, etc.); accession to

Beiwagen *m.* sidecar

Beiwerk *neu.* accessories

beiwohnen *v.* to attend; to be inherent; to cohabit

beizeiten *adv.* betimes, early; in good time

beizen *v.* to corrode; to tan; to etch (copper); to stain; to cauterize

bejahen *v.* to affirm; to assent to, to accept; **-d** *adj.* (in the) affirmative

bejahrt *adj.* aged; elderly

bejammern *v.* to deplore, to lament

bekämpfen *v.* to combat, to resist; to strive against; to oppose; to overcome

bekannt *adj.* (well-)known, renowned; familiar (with); **-lich** *adv.* as everybody knows: **-machen** to advertise, to publish; to announce; **sich -machen** to acquaint one of (oder with)

Bekanntschaft f. acquaintance

bekehren v. to convert, to evangelize

bekennen v. to admit, to confess, to acknowledge; (law) to plead guilty; (tel.) to profess; **Farbe —** (cards) to follow suit

Bekenntnis neu. confession; (rel.) denomination; **-schule** f. denominational school

beklagen v. to lament, to deplore; to commiserate; to regret; **sich —** to complain about; **-swert** adj. deplorable, pitiable

Beklagte m. accused; defendant

beklatschen v. to applaud, to clap; to gossip

bekleben v. to paste on (oder over); **mit Zettel —** to label

bekleckern, beklecksen v. to bespatter, to spot

bekleiden v. to clothe, to dress; to cover, to drape; to face, to line; to veneer, to wainscot; **ein Amt —** to hold office

beklommen adj. anxious, uneasy; depressed

bekommen v. to get, to receive; to obtain; **einen Korb —** to meet with a rebuff (oder refusal); **einen Schnupfen —** to catch cold; **es fertig —** to bring about; **es wird ihm schlecht —** he will fare badly with it

beköstigen v. to board, to feed

bekräftigen v. to confirm, to corroborate

bekränzen v. to wreathe; **mit Lorbeer —** to crown with laurel

bekreuz(ig)en v. (rel.) to make the sign of the cross upon; to cross oneself

bekritteln r. to criticize, to carp at

bekümmern v. to grieve, to trouble; to afflict; **sich — um** to concern oneself with, to meddle with

bekunden v. to depose, to state; to manifest

beladen v. to burden (oder load) with; — adj. encumbered, weighed down, burdened

Belag m. anything laid on (oder upon); sandwich meat; coating; film (teeth)

belagern v. to beleaguer, to besiege

Belang m. importance; **von —** important; **nicht von —** of no consequence

belang: -en v. to concern; (law) to sue; to prosecute; **-los** adj. insignificant. of no consequence; **-reich** adj. important

belasten v. to burden, to load; to accuse, to incriminate; to debit

belästigen v. to bother, to importune, to molest

Belastung f. burden(ing); load; debit, charge; **-szeuge** m. witness for the prosecution

belaufen v. **sich —** to amount (oder come up) to

belauschen v. to overhear; to spy out

beleben v. to animate, to enliven; to cheer

belebt adj. animated, lively; crowded

Belebungsmittel neu. restorative

Beleg m. proof; document; voucher; **-schaft** f. personnel, staff; (min.) gang; **-stelle** f. quotation, authoritative passage

belehren v. to inform, to instruct; **eines Besseren —** to set right, to correct

beleibt adj. corpulent, stout; portly, plump

beleidigen v. to affront, to insult, to offend; **tätlich —** to assault; **-d** adj. offensive

beleuchten v. to light up, to illuminate; to elucidate, to examine

Beleuchtung f. illumination; elucidation; **-skörper** m. lighting fixture

Belgien neu. Belgium

belichten v. (phot.) to expose to light

belieb: -en v. to be pleasing; to condescend; **-ig** adj. optional; anything, no matter what; **-t** adj. liked, popular; beloved; favorite; **sich -t machen** to ingratiate oneself (with); **wie -t?** what did you say?

bellen v. to bark, to bay; to yelp

Belobigung f. commendation, praise

belohnen v. to recompense, to reward; to remunerate; **-swert** adj. deserving a reward

belustigen v. to amuse, to entertain

bemächtigen v. **sich —** to seize; to take over by force

bemalen v. to paint (oder daub) over

bemannen v. to man

bemerkbar adj. observable, perceptible

bemerken v. to notice, to observe, to perceive; to note; to mention, to remark

bemitleiden v. to pity; to be sorry for

bemittelt adj. prosperous, wealthy; well-to-do

bemoost adj. mossy; **-es Haupt** old stager

bemühen v. to trouble; **sich — um** to take pains; to endeavor, to strive; to seek to promote

benach: -bart adj. neighboring; adjacent **-richtigen** to advise (oder inform) of; to notify; **-teiligen** to prejudice; to damage; to injure; to put at a disadvantage

benebelt adj. foggy, cloudy; tipsy

benehmen v. to take away from; to make impossible; **sich —** to behave (oder conduct) oneself

Benehmen neu. behavior, conduct; bearing; **feines —** good manners

beneiden v. to envy, to begrudge; **-swert** adj. enviable

Bengel m. (coll.) rude fellow; rascal

benommen adj. benumbed, giddy

benutzen v. to use, to utilize; to employ; to profit by, to take advantage of

Benzin neu. benzine; gasoline

beobachten v. to observe, to watch; to shadow

Beobachtung f. observation; observance

bequem adj. comfortable; convenient; easygoing

Bequemlichkeit f. comfort(ableness); convenience; ease

beraten v. to advise; to settle by conference; **sich —** to deliberate; **-d** adj. consultative

Beratung f. advice; consultation; conference

berauben v. to rob; to deprive of; **des Augenlichts beraubt** (poet.) blind

berauschen v. to intoxicate; to enchant

berechnen v. to calculate, to compute; to charge; to estimate; **-d** adj. calculating; scheming

berechtigen v. to authorize; to entitle

bereden v. to persuade, to talk over; to gossip

Beredsamkeit f. eloquence

Bereich m. and neu. range, sphere; province

bereichern v. to enrich; to enlarge

bereit adj. prepared, ready; disposed (to); **-en** v. to get (oder make) ready; to prepare, to ride over, to inspect on horseback; to break in (horse); **-s** adv. already; previously; **-willig** adj. ready (oder willing) to do

bereuen v. to regret, to repent; to be sorry

Berg m. mountain; hill; **das Haar stand ihm zu -e** his hair stood on end; **er ist über alle -e** he took to his heels; **goldene -e versprechen** to promise pie in the sky; **hinter dem — halten** to keep in the dark; **über den — sein** to be out of the woods; **-ahorn** m. sycamore, maple; **-arbeit** f. mining; **-arbeiter** m. miner; **-bau** m. mining; **-bewohner** m. highlander, mountaineer; **-geist** m. gnome; **-gewerkschaft** f. miner's union; **-gipfel** m. mountain top; **-kessel** m. gorge, **-kette** f. mountain range; **-knappe** m. miner, pitman; **-kristall** m. rock crystal; **-land** neu. highland; **-mann** m. miner; mountaineer; **-predigt** f. Sermon on the Mount; **-rutsch** m. landslide; **-schlucht** f. ravine; **-spitze** f. peak, summit; **-steiger** m. mountain climber; **-stock** m. alpenstock; **-wand** f. mountain side; **-werk** neu. mine

berg: -ab adv. downhill; **-an** adv. uphill; **-en** v. to save, to salvage; **-ig** adj. mountainous

Bericht m. account, report; (rad.) commentary; **-erstatter** m. reporter, correspondent; (rad.) commentator

berichten v. to report, to inform, **falsch —** to misinform

berichtigen v. to adjust, to correct, to rectify; to settle

Beringstrasse f. Bering Strait

Bernstein m. amber; **schwarzer —** jet

bersten v. to burst; to split; to crack

berüchtigt adj. notorious

berück: -en v. to enchant, to fascinate; **-end** adj. fascinating, bewitching; **-sichtigen** to consider, to regard; to take into account

Beruf m. occupation, profession, business; vocation; **-sberatung** f. vocational guidance; **-sspieler** m. (sports) professional; **-ung** f. appointment, call; (law) appeal; **unter -ung auf** with reference to

beruf: -en v. to call; to appoint; to convoke; to convene; (law) to appeal, to summon; **sich -en auf** to cite a precedent, to refer to; **-en** adj. competent; celebrated; **-lich** adj. professional; **-stätig** adj. employed

beruhen v. to be based (oder rest) on; **etwas auf sich — lassen** to let it pass

beruhigen v. to calm, to pacify

Beruhigungsmittel neu. (med.) sedative; tranquilizer

berühmt adj. celebrated, famous

berühren v. to touch; to come in contact with

besänftigen v. to assuage, to soothe, to appease

Besatzung f. garrison; crew; **-sheer** neu. occupation army

beschädigen v. to damage, to injure

beschaffen v. to procure, to supply; — adj. conditioned; qualified

Beschaffenheit f. condition; constitution; character, disposition

beschäftigen v. to engage, to employ; to occupy

beschämen v. to put to shame, to make ashamed; **-d** adj. disgraceful

beschauen v. to look at; to examine, to inspect; to contemplate

Beschauer m. looker-on, spectator; inspector

Bescheid m. answer; decision, information; **abschlägiger —** negative reply, refusal; **— geben** to inform; (coll.) to give a piece of one's mind; **bis auf weiteren —** until further notice; **über alles — wissen** to know what's what

bescheiden v. to allot; to inform, to instruct; **sich —** to resign oneself; **zu sich — to send for; —** adj. modest, unassuming; backward

bescheinigen v. to attest, to certify; **Empfang — to acknowledge receipt**

beschenken v. to present

bescheren v. to distribute gifts; to bestow

Bescherung f. distribution of gifts; **das ist eine schöne —!** what a mess!

beschimpfen v. to insult, to revile, to abuse

beschirmen v. to protect, to shield; to defend

beschlafen v. to sleep on; to consider over night

Beschlag m. (glass) moisture; (horse) shoe; (mech.) mounting, fittings; **in — nehmen, mit — belegen** to confiscate, to seize; **-nahme** f. confiscation, seizure

beschleunigen v. to accelerate; to speed up

Beschleunigungsmesser m. accelerometer

beschliessen v. to conclude; to resolve

Beschluss m. conclusion; decree; resolution

beschmutzen v. to soil, to dirty; to pollute

beschneiden v. to clip; to prune; to circumcise

beschönigen v. to gloss over; to extenuate

beschränken v. to confine, to limit, to restrict; to curb; to curtail

beschränkt adj. dull; weak-minded; limited

beschreiben v. to describe; to write upon

beschreiten v. to walk on; to step over into; **den Rechtsweg —** to go to court beschuldigen *v.* to accuse, to charge (with)

beschützen *v.* to protect, to defend

Beschwerde *f.* grievance; complaint

beschweren *v.* to burden, to charge; sich — to complain of

beschwerlich *adj.* troublesome; — fallen to be a burden (*oder* trouble)

beschwichtigen *v.* to appease; to allay; sein Gewissen — to silence one's conscience

beseh(e)n *v.* to look at; to examine, to inspect

beseitigen *v.* to eliminate; to remove

Besen *m.* broom; -stiel *m.* broomstick

besessen *adj.* possessed, fanatic; raving

besetzen *v.* to occupy, to garrison, to border; to people; (naut.) to man; to distribute; to edge, to trim (cloth); to garnish; to engage, to fill; to reserve

Besetzung *f.* occupation; (theat.) casting

besichtigen *v.* to inspect; to view

besiedeln *v.* to settle, to colonize

besiegeln *v.* to seal

besiegen *v.* to defeat, to conquer

besinnen *v.* to consider, to reflect on; sich eines anderen — to change one's mind; sich auf etwas — to recollect

Besinnung *f.* consciousness; jemand zur — bringen to bring one to his senses; zur — kommen to recover consciousness

besinnungslos *adj.* senseless; unconscious

Besitz *m.* possession, property; estate; -er *m.* owner, proprietor; -ergreifung *f.* seizure; occupation, usurpation; -recht *neu.* legal possession; -tum *neu.*, -ung *f.* property

besitzen *v.* to possess; to own

besoffen *adj.* (coll.) drunk, tipsy

besohlen *v.* to sole

besolden *v.* to pay wages, to remunerate

besondere *adj.* particular; peculiar; separate

besonders *adv.* especially; exceptionally; separately

besonnen *adj.* prudent, considerate, thoughtful

besorgen *v.* to take care of; to manage; to procure; to fear

besorgt *adj.* alarmed, apprehensive; anxious

besprechen *v.* to discuss; to talk over; to review; to conjure; sich — mit to confer with

Besprechung *f.* conference; discussion; review

besser *adj.* better; umso — so much the better

bessern *v.* to improve; to correct; to reform; to advance; nicht zu — incorrigible

Besserungsanstalt *f* reformatory

Bestand *m.* continuation, duration; amount (*oder* stock) on hand; -(s)aufnahme *f.* inventory; -teil *m.* ingredient; component

beständig *adj.* constant, steady, continual

bestärken *v.* to confirm; to fortify

bestätigen *v.* to confirm; to okay; to ratify; to verify; sich — to prove true

bestatten *v.* to bury, to inter

bestauben, bestäuben *v.* to cover with dust, to spray; (bot.) to pollinate

beste *adj.* best; auf das — in the best way; etwas zum -n geben to treat, to entertain with; zum -n haben to tease; -nfalls *adv.* at best, at most; -ns *adv.* as well as possible

Beste *neu.* (the) best; der erste — the firstcomer; zu Ihrem -n in your interest

bestechen *v.* to bribe, to corrupt

bestehen *v.* to undergo; to stand; to overcome; to exist; to subsist, to continue; to pass (examination); — auf to insist on; — aus to consist of; nicht — to fail

bestehlen *v.* to steal from; to plagiarize

besteigen *v.* to ascend; to mount; (naut.) to board

bestellen *v.* to order, to send for; to appoint; to set in order; to deliver (greetings); (agr.) to till; es ist schlecht mit ihm bestellt he is in a sad plight

besteuern *v.* to tax

Bestie *f.* beast; brute

bestimmen *v.* to determine; to appoint; to define; to evaluate; to analyze; jemand — etwas zu tun to induce a person to do something; über etwas — to dispose of

bestimmt *adj.* decided; certain; definite; — nach bound for; — sein für to be destined for

Bestimmung *f.* determination; destiny, vocation; definition; evaluation; amtliche -en regulations

bestrafen *v.* to punish

bestrebt *adj.* endeavored; — sein to exert oneself, to strive

bestreichen *v.* to spread over, to smear, to butter; (mil.) to sweep

bestreiten *v.* to contest; to deny, to pay for

bestricken *v.* to ensnare

bestürmen *v.* to storm, to assail, to importune

bestürzt *adj.* dismayed; amazed; confused

Besuch *m.* call, visit; visitor(s); attendance

besuchen *v.* to visit; to attend; to frequent

betagt *adj.* aged, elderly

betätigen *v.* to practise, to put in action; sich — to be busy, to take active part in

betäuben *v.* to deafen; to stun; to anesthetize; to stupefy

beteiligen *v.* to give a share (*oder* interest) in; sich — to take part in

beten *v.* to pray, to say one's prayer

beteuern *v.* to assert; to swear to

Beton *m.* concrete

betonen *v.* to stress, to accent, to emphasize

Betracht *m.* account, consideration, respect; in — ziehen to take into account

betrachten *v.* to consider, to regard; to reflect on; Dinge im rosigen Lichte — to look at things through rose-colored glasses

beträchtlich *adj.* considerable

Betrag *m.* amount

betragen *v.* to amount to; **sich —** to behave

betrauen *v* to entrust with

betrauern *v.* to mourn for, to deplore

Betreff *m.* reference; **in — ·with** regard to, in respect of, concerning

betreffen *v.* to concern, to affect; to fall upon; **-d** *adj.* concerning, concerned

betreiben *v.* ·to carry (*oder* urge) on; to pursue

betreten *v.* to set foot on, to enter, to mount; **—** *adj.* perplexed, embarrassed

betreuen *v.* to take care of; to attend to

Betrieb *m.* factory, plan; workshop; business; **in — setzen** to set in motion; **-sjahr** *neu.* fiscal year; **-skapital** *neu.* working capital; **-skosten** *f.* *pl.* operating expenses; **-sleiter** *m.* manager, superintendent; **-sstockung** *f.*, **-sstörung** *f.* breakdown

betrieb: **-sam** *adj.* active, industrious; **-sfertig** *adj.* ready for service; **-ssicher** *adj.* foolproof

betrübt *adj.* sad, dejected

Betrug *m.* fraud, deceit; swindle

betrügen *v.* to cheat, to deceive, to defraud

Betrüger *m.* cheat, deceiver; swindler

Bett *neu.* bed; **das — hüten** to be confined to bed; **-decke** *f.* coverlet; blanket; **-laken** *neu.*, **-tuch** *neu.* sheet; **-stelle** *f.* bedstead; **-wäsche** *f.* bed linen

betteln *v.* to beg; to plead continuously

bettlägerig *adj.* bedridden

Bettler *m.* beggar; **-sprache** *f.* beggars' argot

beugen *v.* to bend; to lower; (gram.) to inflect; **sich —** to humble oneself, to submit

Beule *f.* boss, bump; boil, tumor, lump

beunruhigen *v.* to alarm, to disquiet; to harass

beurlauben *v.* to give leave, to furlough; **sich —** to withdraw, to take leave

beurteilen *v.* to judge, to criticize; to review

Beute *f.* booty, prey; **auf — ausgehen** to go plundering; **-macher** *m.* looter

Beutel *m.* bag, pouch; purse; **-ratte** *f.* opossum; **-schneider** *m.* cutpurse, pickpocket

bevölkern *v.* to populate; to people

Bevölkerung *f.* population, people, inhabitants

bevollmächtigen *v.* to empower; to authorize

bevor *conj.* before; **—** *adv.* beforehand; **-munden** to act as guardian; to prevent autonomous action; **-zugen** to favor

bewachen *v.* to watch over; to guard; to shadow

bewaffnen *v.* to arm

bewahren *v.* to keep, to preserve; **— vor** to guard against; to protect from; **Gott soll mich —!** Heaven forbid!

bewähren *v.*, **sich —** to stand the test, to prove true

bewandert *adj.* versed, skilled

bewässern *v* to irrigate

beweg: -en *v.* to move, to keep in motion; to agitate, to excite; to induce; **sich —** to move; **sich um etwas —** to revolve round; **-end** *adj.* moving; **-lich** *adj.* mobile, agile

Beweggrund *m.* motive

Bewegung *f.* motion, movement; stir; agitation; emotion

beweinen *v.* to deplore

Beweis *m.* proof; sign, evidence; **-führung** *f.* demonstration

beweisen *v.* to prove; to show, to demonstrate

bewerben *v.* **sich —** to apply for; to compete, to solicit; to court, to woo

bewerkstelligen *v.* to accomplish, to effect

bewilligen *v.* to grant, to concede

bewirken *v.* to bring out; to cause; to effect

bewirten *v.* to entertain, to regale, to treat

bewohnen *v.* to inhabit, to occupy; to reside in

bewölkt *adj.* cloudy, overcast

bewundern *v.* to admire; **-swert** *adj.* admirable

bewusst *adj.* conscious; known; intentional; **die -e Sache** the matter in question; **sich — sein** to be aware of; **-los** *adj.* unconscious

Bewusst: -heit *f.* consciousness, knowledge; **-losigkeit** *f.* unconsciousness, insensibility; **-sein** *neu.* consciousness, awareness

bezahlen *v.* to pay; to compensate for; **mit gleicher Münze —** to give tit for tat

bezähmen *v.* to tame; **sich —** to control (*oder* restrain) oneself

bezaubern *v.* to bewitch, to charm; **-d** *adj.* charming, enchanting

bezeichnen *v.* to designate; to mark; to indicate; **-d** *adj.* characteristic, significant

bezeugen *v.* to testify; to bear witness

beziehen *v.* to cover; to occupy; to draw, to receive, to obtain, to get; to procure; (bed) to change; (mus.) to string; **Lager — to** encamp; **sich — to** become cloudy; **sich — auf** to relate to

Beziehung *f.* relation; **in dieser —** in this respect; **in freundschaftlichen -en stehen** to be on good terms

beziehungsweise *adv.* respectively

Bezirk *m.* district

Bezug *m.* cover(ing); supply; reference, relation; (mus.) set of strings; **Bezüge** *pl.* income, salary; **— nehmen auf** to refer to; **in — auf** in regard to

bezweifeln *v.* to doubt, to question

bezwingen *v.* to overcome, to subdue; to master; **sich —** to control (*oder* restrain) oneself

Bianca *f.* Blanche

Bibel *f.* Bible

Biber *m.* beaver

Bibliothek *f.* library

biblisch *adj.* biblical

biegen *v.* to bend, to bow; to decline, to inflect; **um die Ecke —** to turn the corner

biegsam *adj.* flexible; yielding

Biene *f.* bee; **–könignin** *f.* queen bee; **–nkorb** *m.*, **–nstock** *m.* beehive; **–nzüchter** *m.* beekeeper

Bier *neu.* beer; **helles —** ale; **–bass** *m.* beery voice; **–brauerei** *f.* brewery; **–fass** *neu.* beer barrel; (coll.) paunch; **–hefe** *f.* yeast; **–idee** *f.* stupid idea; **–krug** *m.*, **–seidel** *m.* beer mug

bieten *v.* to offer; to bid; **das lässt sich niemand —** nobody can swallow that; **dem Glück die Hand —** to try one's good luck; **sich alles — lassen** to put up with everything

Bild *neu.* picture, portrait, illustration, representation; view; idea; symbol; metaphor; **auf der –fläche erscheinen** to come into view; **im –e sein** to understand: **lebendes —** tableau; **–erschrift** *f.* hieroglyphs; **–hauer** *m.* sculptor; **–nis** *neu.* portrait, likeness; **–seite** *f.* (coin) face; **–ung** *f.* education, culture; formation

bilden *v.* to form, to shape; to constitute; to educate, to cultivate; to fashion **–de Künste** fine arts

bildlich *adj.* figurative

Billet *neu.* ticket; note

billig *adj.* cheap; fair, just; moderate

billigen *v.* to approve, to sanction

Billion *f.* billion; (Am.) trillion

Binde *f.* band; bandage; (neck)tie; (arm) sling; **–gewebe** *neu.* connective tissue; **–glied** *neu.* connecting link; **–strich** *m.* hyphen, dash; **–wort** *neu.* conjunction

binden *v.* to bind; to fasten, to tie; to hoop (cask); (cooking) to thicken; **–d** *adj.* obligatory

Bindfaden *m.* string, twine; **es regnet —** (coll.) it is raining cats and dogs

Binnen: –gewässer *neu.* inland water(s); **–handel** *m.* domestic trade; **–land** *neu.* interior; **–meer** *neu.* inland sea

Birke *f.* birch

Birne *f.* pear; (elec.) bulb

bis *prep.* as far as, down (*oder* up) to; till, until; (even) to; **— conj.** till, until; **alle — auf einen** all but one

Bisam *m.* musk

Bischof *m.* bishop; **–shut** *m.*, **–smütze** *f.* mitre; **–ssitz** *m.* episcopal see; **–sstab** *m.* crosier; **–sstuhl** *m.* episcopate

Biss *m.* bite, sting; **–en** *m.* mouthful; snack, morsel; **guter –en** tidbit

bissig *adj.* biting, snappish; sharp, sarcastic

Bistum *neu.* bishopric, diocese

Bitt: –e *f.* request, petition; supplication; entreaty; **–e!** *interj.* please! you're welcome! **–gang** *m.* pilgrimage; **–schrift** *f.* petition; **–steller** *m.* petitioner, supplicant

bitten *v.* to ask; to beg; to entreat; to invite; to request; **darf ich Sie —?** may I trouble you? **für jemanden —** to plead for someone; **um Aufträge —** to solicit orders; **wie bitte?** what did you say?

bitter *adj.* bitter; (fig.) severe, grievous; **–böse** *adj.* very angry (*oder* wicked)

blähen *v.* to inflate, to swell; **sich —** to swell; to boast; **–d** *adj.* flatulent

blamieren *v.* to expose, to ridicule; **sich —** to disgrace oneself

blank *adj.* bright, polished, shining; bare

Blas: –e *f.* bubble; bladder; flaw (in metal, glass); (sl.) gang, lot; **–ebalg** *m.* bellows; **–instrument** *neu.* wind instrument; **–rohr** *neu.* blow pipe

blasen *v.* to blow; (mus.) to sound

blass *adj.* pale

Blatt *neu.* leaf; sheet; blade; newspaper; (cards) hand; **das — hat sich gewendet** the tide has turned; **das steht auf einem anderen —** that's another matter; **ein neues — beginnen** to turn over a new leaf; **vom — singen** (*or* spielen) to sing (*oder* play) at sight

Blattern *f. pl.* smallpox

blättern *v.* to turn over the leaves; to leaf

blau *adj.* blue; **— machen** (coll.) to stay away from work; **–e Bohne** *f.* (coll.) bullet; **–e Jungs** *m. pl.* sailors; **–geschlagenes Auge** black eye; **der –e Rock** military service

Blau *neu.*, **Bläue** *f.* color, dye; **das –e vom Himmel herunterreden** to talk a blue streak; **Fahrt ins –e** a trip to an unknown destination; **–papier** *neu.* carbon paper; **–stift** *m.* blue pencil

bläulich *adj.* bluish

Blech *neu.* sheet-metal, tin plate; (coll.) nonsense; **–instrument** *neu.* brass instrument; **–kanne** *f.* tin can; **–schmied** *m.* tinsmith

blechen *v.* (coll.) to pay, to fork out

blechern *adj.* tin

blecken *v.* **Zähne —** to show one's teeth

Blei *neu.* lead; plummet; **–kugel** *f.* bullet; **–stift** *m.* pencil; **–stiftanspitzer** *m.* pencil sharpener

bleiben *v.* to remain, to stay; to fall (in battle); **— lassen** to let alone; **dabei muss es —** there the matter must rest; **es bleibt dabei** agreed; **–d** *adj.* permanent, lasting

bleich *adj.* pale; **–en** *v.* to bleach

Bleichsucht *f.* chloremia

blenden *v.* to blind; to dazzle

Blick *m.* look; glance, view

blicken *v.* to look; **sich - lassen** to appear

blind *adj.* blind; dull; blank; **–anflug** *m.* instrument approach

Blind: –darm *m.* appendix; **–darmentzündung** *f.* appendicitis; **–darmoperation** *f.* appendectomy; **–ekuh** *f.* blindman's buff; **–enanstalt** *f.* home for the blind; **–flug** *m.* instrument flight

blinke(r)n *v.* to gleam, to glitter, to twinkle; (naut.) to signal with lights

Blinkfeuer *neu.* blinker; intermittent light

blinzeln *v.* to blink, to wink

Blitz *m.* lightning, flash; **–ableiter** *m.* lightning rod; **–funk** *m.* radiotelegraphy; **–licht** *neu.* (photo.) flashlight; **–lichtlampe** *f.* flash bulb; **–schlag** *m.* stroke of lightning; **–strahl** *m.* flash of lightning; **–zug** *m.* (rail.) flyer

blitz: –blank *adj.* spick and span; **–en** *v.* to lighten, to flash, to sparkle; **–sauber** *adj.* very pretty; **–schnell** *adj.* quick as a lightning

Block *m.* block; log; pad; stocks; (pol.) bloc; **-haus** *neu.* log cabin

blöde *adj.* imbecile, stupid

Blödsinn *m.* imbecility; nonsense

blond *adj.* blond(e), fair

bloss *adj.* bare, naked; plain, simple; mere; — *adv.* barely, merely, only; **-legen** *v.* to lay bare; **-stellen** *v.* to expose, to compromise

Blösse *f.* bareness, nakedness; weak point

Blosstellung *f.* exposure

blühen *v.* to bloom, to blossom; to flourish; **-d** *adj.* blooming; flourishing

Blume *f.* flower; aroma, bouquet, flavor; **durch die — sprechen** to speak in metaphors; **-nbeet** *neu.* flower-bed; **-nblatt** *neu.* petal; **-nerde** *f.* gardenmold; **-händler** *m.* florist; **-nkohl** *m.* cauliflower; **-nstrauss** *m.* bouquet; **-nzucht** *f.* floriculture

Bluse *f.* blouse

Blut *neu.* blood; lineage, race; **böses — machen** to arouse angry feelings; **das liegt im -(e)** it runs in the blood; **-ader** *f.* blood vessel; **-armut** *f.* anemia; **-bad** *neu.* massacre; **-druck** *m.* blood pressure; **-egel** *m.* leech; **-erguss** *m.* hemorrhage; **-schande** *f.* incest; **-sturz** *m.* violent hemorrhage; **-sverwandtschaft** *f.* blood relationship; **-vergiessen** *neu.* bloodshed; **-vergiftung** *f.* blood poisoning; **-wasser** *neu.* lymph, serum; **-zeuge** *m.* martyr

blut-: -arm *adj.* anemic; very poor; **-durstig, -rünstig** *adj.* bloodthirsty; **-en** *v.* to bleed; to suffer; **-ig** *adj.* bloody; **-jung** *adj.* very young; **-wenig** *adj.* very little

Blüte *f.* blossom, bud; bloom; prime of life; **-nstaub** *m.* pollen

Bock *m.* ram, he-goat; (coachman's) box; (gym.) horse; (mech.) jack; **den — zum Gärtner machen** to set the wolf to mind the sheep; **einen — schiessen** to blunder, to slip; **-springen** *neu.* leapfrog; **-sprung** *m.* caper, gambol

bock-: -(bein)ig *adj.* obstinate, stubborn; **-en** to butt, to prance; (coll.) to sulk

Boden *m.* ground, soil; base, floor, bottom; attic, loft; **-radarpeilung** *f.* ground control; **-satz** *m.* grounds, dregs, sediment

bodenlos *adj.* bottomless; (coll.) enormous

Bodensee *m.* Lake of Constance

bodenständig *adj.* deeply rooted, indigenous

Bogen *m.* bow, bend; curve; arc(h); sheet (of paper); **-gang** *m.* arcade; **-lampe** *f.* arc lamp; **-schütze** *m.* archer

Böhmen *neu.* Bohemia

Bohne *f.* bean; **blaue —** (coll.) bullet; **keine — no idea**; **keine — wert** not worth a straw; **-nkaffee** *m.* pure coffee

bohnen *v.* to polish, to wax

bohren *v.* to bore, to drill

Bohrer *m.* borer, drill, gimlet

Boje *f.* (naut.) buoy

Bolzen *m.* bolt; pin; rivet; heater (of an iron)

bomb(ardier)en *v.* to bomb(ard), to shell

Bombe *f.* bomb, shell; bombshell; **-nerfolg** *m.* (theat.) hit, huge success; **-nflugzeug** *neu.* bomber; **-zielgerät** *n.* bombsight

bombensicher *adj.* bombproof; quite certain

Bonze *m.* (coll.) big shot; bigwig

Boot *neu.* boat; **-sanlegestelle** *f.*, **-shafen** *m.* marina; **-smann** *m.* boatswain

Bord *m.* border, edge, rim; (naut.) board; **über — werfen** to jettison; **-buch** *neu.* logbook; **-funker** *m.* (avi. *und* naut.) radio operator; **-schwelle** *f.* curb

borgen *v.* to borrow

Borke *f.* bark, rind

borniert *adj.* narrow-minded; conceited

Börse *f.* purse; stock exchange; **-nkurs** *m.* rate of exchange; **-nmakler** *m.* stockbroker

börsenfähig *adj.* negotiable, marketable

Borste *f.* bristle

Borte *f.* border, braid, lace

bösartig *adj.* malicious, malignant, virulent

böse *adj.* bad, evil, wicked; angry, sore (wound); **er meint es nicht — he means no harm; in -n Ruf bringen** to bring into disrepute

Böse *m.* devil, fiend; **— neu.** evil; **-wicht** *m.* villain

boshaft *adj.* malicious

Botanik *f.* botany; **-er** *m.* botanist

botanisch *adj.* botanic(al)

Bote *m.* messenger; **-ngang** *m.* errand

Botschaft *f.* message; embassy; **-er** *m.* ambassador

Böttcher *m.* cooper; **-ei** *f.* cooperage

Bottich *m.* tub, vat; barrel

Bowle *f.* bowl; spiced wine

boxen *v.* to box

Brand *m.* burning; fire(brand); (bot.) blight, mildew; (med.) gangrene; ardor; **in — geraten** to catch fire; **in — setzen** (*or* stecken) to set on fire, to commit arson; **-blase** *f.* blister; **-bombe** *f.* incendiary bomb; **-mal** *neu.* brand, scar; stigma; **-mauer** *f.* fireproof wall; **-sohle** *f.* inner sole; **-stifter** *m.* arsonist; **-stiftung** *f.* arson

Brandung *f.* surf

Branntwein *m.* brandy, whisky; **-brennerei** *f.* distillery

Brasilien *neu.* Brazil

Brat: -en *m.* roast meat; **den -en riechen** to smell a rat; **-enwender** *m.*, **-spiess** *m.* turnspit; **-fisch** *m.* fried fish; **-huhn** *neu.* roast chicken; **-kartoffeln** *f. pl.* fried potatoes; **-pfanne** *f.* frying pan, skillet; **-wurst** *f.* sausage for frying

braten *v.* to fry, to grill, to roast

Bräu, Gebräu *m.* and *neu.* brew

Brauch *m.* custom, usage; use

brauchbar *adj.* serviceable, useful

brauchen *v.* to use; to need, to require

Braue *f.* eyebrow

brauen *v.* to brew

Brauer *m.* brewer; **-ei** *f.* brewery

braun *adj.* brown; tanned; tawny

bräunlich *adj.* brownish
Braunschweig *neu.* Brunswick
brausen *v.* to bluster, to rage, to storm; to roar, to rush; to shower; to effervesce
Braut *f.* bride; fiancée; **–ausstattung** *f.* trousseau; **–führer** *m.* best man; **–jungfer** *f.* bridesmaid; **–kleid** *neu.* wedding dress; **–paar** *neu.* engaged couple; **–schatz** *m.* dowry; **–schleier** *m.* bridal veil
Bräutigam *m.* bridegroom; fiancé
brav *adj.* honest; good, well-behaved
brechen *v.* to break, to fracture; to quarry; to fold; to violate; to vomit; (flower) to pick; (phy.) to refract
Brei *m.* mush, porridge; **–masse** *f.* pulp
breit *adj.* broad; wide; **–beinig** *adj.* straddle-legged; **–schlagen** (coll.) to induce; **–treten** (coll.) to dilate upon
Breite *f.* breadth, width; diffuseness; **–ngrad** *m.* degree of latitude
Brems: **–e** *f.* gadfly; brake; **–fallschirm** *m.* drag chute, drogue; **–klappe** *f.* (avi.) flap; **–klotz** *m.* brake block; **–rakete** *f.* retro-rocket; **–schuh** *m.* brake shoe (*oder* block)
bremsen *v.* to brake, to put the brake on
Brenn: **–er** *m.* burner; distiller; **–holz** *neu.* firewood; **–kammer** *f.* combustion chamber; **–kraftmotor** *m.* combustion engine; **–material** *neu.* fuel; **–ofen** *m.* kiln; **–punkt** *m.* focus
brennen *v.* to burn; to brand; (bricks) to bake; (chem.) to distill; (coffee) to roast; (hair) to wave; (med.) to cauterize; (wounds) to sting
Bretagne *f.* Brittany
Brett *neu.* board, plank; **am schwarzen — on the bulletin board; die –er betreten** to go on the stage; **mit –ern vernagelt** that's the end of it; **–er** *pl.* ski; **–erbude** *f.* shed
Bre(t)zel *neu.* pretzel
Brief *m.* letter; **eingeschriebener —** registered letter; **–beschwerer** *m.* paper weight; **–bote** *m.*, **–träger** *m.* letter carrier, mailman; **–einwurf** *m.*, **–kasten** *m.* mailbox; **–fach** *neu.* pigeonhole; **–geheimnis** *neu.* privacy of correspondence; **–marke** *f.* postage stamp; **–ordner** *m.* letter file; **–papier** *neu.* writing paper; **–porto** *neu.* postage; **–post** *f.* first-class mail; **–tasche** *f.* billfold, pocketbook, wallet; **–taube** *f.* carrier pigeon; **–umschlag** *m.* envelope; **–waage** *f.* postage scale; **–wechsel** *m.* correspondence
brieflich *adj.* and *adv.* by letter
brillant *adj.* brilliant; diamond
Brille *f.* glasses, spectacles; goggles; **–nschlange** *f.* cobra
bringen *v.* to bring, to convey; to escort; **an sich —** to acquire; **es mit sich —** to involve; **es zu etwas —** to achieve something; **Gewinn —** to yield profit; **nach Hause —** to see one home; **Opfer — to make sacrifices; Schaden —** to cause injury; **um etwas —** to deprive of; **ums Leben —** to murder; **Zinsen —** to bear interest; **zu Fall —** to ruin;

zu Papier — to put (*oder* write) down; **zustande —** to bring about, to accomplish
Brise *f.* breeze
Britannien *neu.* Britain
Brokat *m.* brocade
bröck(e)lig *adj.* crumbly, friable
bröckeln *v.* to crumble
Brocken *m.* crumb; fragment; scrap
Brom *neu.* bromine; **–beere** *f.* blackberry
Brosam *m.*, **–e** *f.* (poet.) crumb
Brosche *f.* brooch
broschiert *adj.* paper-bound
Broschüre *f.* brochure, pamphlet
Brot *neu.* bread; loaf; (fig.) livelihood; **sein — verdienen** to earn one's living; **–aufstrich** *m.* spread; **–erwerb** *m.* making a living; **–herr** *m.* employer; **–korb** *m.* **dem –korb höher hängen** to keep (one) on short rations; **–röster** *m.* toaster; **–studium** *neu.* professional study
Brötchen *neu.* roll; **belegtes —** sandwich
Bruch *m.* breach, break; fold, crease; (law) violation; (math.) fraction; (med.) fracture, rupture; **in die Brüche gehen** to come to naught; **–band** *neu.* truss; **–landung** *f.* crash landing; **–strich** *m.* division (*oder* fraction) sign; **–stück** *neu.* fragment; **–teil** *m.* fraction
Brücke *f.* bridge; dental arch; small rug
Bruder *m.* brother; friar
brüderlich *adj.* brotherly, fraternal
Brüderschaft *f.* brotherhood; **— trinken** to hobnob
Brühe *f.* broth; sauce; gravy
brühen *v.* to scald
Brügge *neu.* Bruges
brüllen *v.* to roar; to bellow; to low; to howl
brummen *v.* to growl, to grumble; to snarl; (sl.) to be in jail; **in den Bart —** to mutter; **mir brummt der Kopf** my head whirls
Brunnen *m.* fountain, spring, well; spa
Brunst *f.* ardor, lust, rut; **–schrei** *m.* bell; **–zeit** *f.* rutting season
brünstig *adj.* ardent; lustful; (zool.) in heat
Brüssel *neu.* Brussels
Brust *f.* breast, chest; **sich in die — werfen** to put on airs; **–bonbon** *m.* cough drop; **–fellentzündung** *f.* pleurisy; **–schwimmen** *neu.* breast stroke; **–warze** *f.* nipple
brüsten *v.* **sich —** to boast, to brag
Brut *f.* brood; (ichth.) fry, spawn; **–apparat** *m.* incubator; **–henne** *f.* sitting hen; **–stätte** breeding place; hotbed
brüten *v.* to brood, to hatch
Brutto: **–betrag** *m.* gross amount; **–einnahme** *f.*, **–ertrag** *m.* gross receipts (*oder* earnings); **–gewicht** *neu.* gross weight
BTU (britische Wärmeeinheit) *f.* British Thermal Unit, BTU
Bube *m.* boy; (cards) jack; (coll.) rascal; **–nstreich** *m.* knavish trick
Buch *neu.* book; **ein — herausgeben** (*or* **verlegen**) to edit (*oder* publish) a book; **–binder** *m.* bookbinder; **–deckel** *m.*

book cover; **-druck** *m.* printing, typography; **-halter** *m.* bookkeeper; **-führung** *f.*, **-haltung** *f.* bookkeeping; **-handel** *m.* book trade; **-handlung** *f.* bookshop; **-stabe** *m.* letter (of alphabet); type; **-umschlag** *m.* jacket; **-ung** *f.* entry

Buch: **-e** *f.* beech; **-ecker** *f.*, **-el** *f.* beechnut; **-weizen** *m.* buckwheat

buchen *v.* to enter, to book

Bücher *neu. pl.* books; **-abschluss** *m.* balancing (*oder* closing) of books; **-brett** *neu.* bookshelf; **-ei** *f.* library; **-freund** *m.* bibliophile; **-kunde** *f.* bibliography; **-revisor** *m.* auditor; **-schrank** *m.* bookcase

Buchsbaum *m.* boxtree; **-holz** *neu.* boxwood

Büchse *f.* box, case; can; rifle; **-nfleisch** *neu.* canned meat; **-nöffner** *m.* can opener; **-nschütze** *m.* rifleman

buchstabieren *v.* to spell; **falsch —** to misspell

buchstäblich *adj.* literal, verbal, exact

Bucht *f.* bay, creek, inlet

Buckel *m.* hump(back); buckle, boss, stud

buck(e)lig *adj.* humpbacked

bücken *v.* to stoop; to bow; to incline

Bückling *m.* smoked herring; bow. curtsy

Bude *f.* booth, stall; den

Büffel *m.* buffalo

büffeln *v.* to drudge, to slave; (coll.) to cram

Büf(f)ett *neu.* sideboard; bar, counter

Bug *m.* bow (of a ship)

Bügel *m.* handle; coat hanger; **-brett** *neu.* ironing board; **-eisen** *neu.* flatiron; **-falte** *f.* crease

bügeln *v.* to iron; to press

bugsieren *v.* to tow, to take in tow

buhlen *v.* to make love; to strive (for); to vie (with)

Bühne *f.* stage; platform; **-nanweisung** *f.* stage direction; **-nausstattung** *f.* scenery; **-nbild** *neu.* stage background; **-dichter** *m.* playwright, dramatist; **-nleiter** *m.* stage manager

Bull: **-auge** *neu.* porthole; **-e** *m.* (zool.) bull; **—** *f.* (rel.) bull; **päpstliche —** papal bull

Bumm: **-el** *m.* stroll; **-elei** *f.* loafing, laziness; **-elzug** *m.* slow train; **-ler** *m.* bum, tramp

Bund *m.* alliance; band; **—** *neu.* bundle; **-esgenosse** *m.* ally; **-eslade** *f.* Ark of the Covenant; **-estag** *m.* Federal Diet

Bündel *neu.* bundle

bündig *adj.* concise; convincing; **sich kurz und — ausdrücken** to speak to the point

Bündnis *neu.* alliance, union

bunt *adj.* many-colored; motley; mixed; stained; topsy-turvy; gay; **er treibt es zu —** he goes too far; **-gefleckt, -gesprenkelt** *adj.* speckled, spotted

Bürde *f.* burden, load

Burg *f.* castle, citadel; (fig.) refuge

Bürge *m.* guarantor; bailsman

bürgen *v.* to guarantee; to furnish bail

Bürger *m.* citizen, commoner; **-krieg** *m.*

civil war; **-kunde** *f.* civics; **-meister** *m.* mayor; **-steig** *m.* sidewalk; **-wehr** *f.* militia

bürgerlich *adj.* civic, civil; middle-class; **-es Gesetzbuch** code of civil law

Bürgschaft *f.* bail; surety; guaranty

Bursche *m.* lad, fellow; (coll.) guy

Bürste *f.* brush; **-nbinder** *m.* brushmaker; **-nabzug** *m.* (typ.) galley

bürsten *v.* to brush

Busch *m.* bush; **auf den — klopfen** to beat about the bush; **hinter dem -e halten** to hesitate; **sich seitwärts in die Büsche schlagen** to slip away; **-werk** *neu.* shrubbery

Büschel *neu.* bunch, tuft

buschig *adj.* bushy, shaggy

Busen *m.* bosom, breast; heart; bay, gulf

Busse *f.* penance; atonement

büssen *v.* to atone for; to expiate

Büsser *m.* penitent

bussfertig *adj.* penitent, repentant, contrite

Büste *f.* bust; **-nhalter** *m.* brassiere

Büttel *m.* beadle, bailiff, jailer

Butter *f.* butter; **-blume** *f.* buttercup; **-brot** *neu.* (slice of) bread and butter; **für ein -brot kaufen** to buy for a song; **-fass** *neu.* churn

C

Chaiselongue *f. and neu.* couch, long chair

Champagner *m.* champagne

Champignon *m.* champignon, edible mushroom

chaotisch *adj.* chaotic(al)

Character *m.* character; type; **-istik** *f.* characterization; **-losigkeit** *f.* lack of principles; **-zug** *m.* characteristic

characterisieren *v.* to characterize

characteristisch *adj.* characteristic

Chaussee *f.* highway; **-graben** *m.* roadside ditch

Chef *m.* chief; head; (coll.) boss; **-redakteur** *m.* editor-in-chief

Chemi: **-e** *f.* chemistry; **-ker** *m.* chemist; **-kalien** *f. pl.* chemicals

chemisch *adj.* chemical

Chemosphäre (Luftschicht 32–50 km über der Erde) *f.* chemosphere

Chiffre *f.* cipher, numeral; code

Chinin *neu.* quinine

Chirurg *m.* surgeon; **-ie** *f.* surgery

Chlor *neu.* chlorine

chloroformieren *v.* to chloroform

cholerisch *adj.* choleric

cholesterin *neu.* cholesterol

Chor *m.* choir, chorus; **-gang** *m.* aisle; **-hemd** *neu.* surplice; **-herr** *m.* canon; **-stuhl** *m.* stall

Christ *m.* Christian; **Christ(us)** *m.* Christ; **-abend** *m.* Christmas Eve; **-baum** *m.* Christmas tree; **-enheit** *f.* Christendom; **-entum** *neu.* Christianity; **-fest** *neu.* Christmas

christlich *adj.* Christian

Chrom *neu.* chrome, chromium

Chronik *f.* chronicle

chronisch *adj.* (med.) chronic(al)

Chronist *m.* chronicler

conferencier *m.* master-of-ceremonies

Coupé *neu.* (rail.) compartment; two-door automobile

Creme *f.* cream, cosmetic cream; high society

Cypern *neu.* Cyprus

D

da *adv.* here, there; in existence, present; in that case, this being so, then; — *conj.* as, when, while; because, since; — **haben wir's** there we are; — **sein** to be at hand; **von — an** (*or* ab) from that time, since then; **–behalten** *v.* to retain; **–bleiben** *v.* to stay

dabei *adv.* near, nearby; therewith; besides, moreover; but; as well, at the same time; — **kommt nichts heraus** nothing can be gained by it; — **sein** to be present, to take part; **ich bin —** agreed; I'll go along; **was ist —?** what does that matter? **–bleiben** *v.* to persist in

Dach *neu.* roof, shelter; **–balken** *m.* rafter; **–boden** *m.* loft; **–decker** *m.* roofer; **–fenster** *neu.* attic window; **–first** *m.* ridge (of roof); **–geschoss** *neu.* attic; **–rinne** *f.* gutter

Dachs *m.* badger; **ein frecher —** a fresh guy

dadurch *adv.* through it; thereby; by this means

dafür *adv.* for it (*oder* that); instead of it; **ich kann nichts —** I can't help it; **–halten** *v.* to be of the opinion

dagegen *adv.* and *conj.* against; in comparison with; on the contrary; on the other hand; in exchange (*oder* return) for; nichts; **–haben** to have no objection to; **–halten** *v.* to compare; to put side by side

daher *adv.* thence, from that place; — *conj.* therefore, hence, accordingly, consequently

dahin *adv.* to that place (*oder* time); so far that; along, away; gone; past; (poet.) thither; **bis —** until then; **–bringen** *v.* to manage to; to induce; **–geben** *v.* to give up, to sacrifice; **–stehen** *v.* to be uncertain

dahinten *adv.* behind there

dahinter *adv.* behind it (*oder* that); **–kommen** to find out, to get to the bottom of; **es steckt nichts —** there is nothing in it

Dakron *neu.* dacron

damals *adv.* then; at that time

Damast *m.* (fabric) damask

Dame *f.* lady; dame; (cards, chess) queen; (checkers) king; **–brett** *neu.* checkerboard; **–nheld** *m.* ladies' man; **–nsattel** *f.* side-saddle

damit *adv.* and *conj.* therewith; with it (*oder* that); by it (*oder* that); **es ist nichts —** it is useless; **er ist — einverstanden** he agrees to it; **es ist — aus** it is all over; — **ist mir nicht gedient** that won't help me; — *conj.* in order

to; — **nicht** lest

dämlich *adj.* stupid, dull

Damm *m.* dam, dike; mole, pier; embankment; barrier; **auf dem — sein** to be okay

dämmen *v.* to dam up; to restrain, to stop

dämmerig *adj.* dusky, dim; uncertain; dreamy

Dämmerung *f.*, **Dämmerlicht** *neu.* twilight, dawn

Dämon *m.* demon

dämonisch *adj.* demoniac(al)

Dampf *m.* steam, vapor; **–bad** *neu.* steam bath; **–boot** *neu.* steamboat; **–druck** *m.* steam pressure; **–er** *m.* steamer; **–fleisch** *neu.* stew; **–kessel** *m.* boiler; **–kochtopf** *m.* pressure cooker; **–maschine** *f.* steam engine; **–walze** *f.* steamroller

dampfen *v.* to steam

dämpfen *v.* to dampen, to subdue; to stew

danach *adv.* after it (*oder* that); accordingly; **er sieht — aus** he quite looks it; **ich frage nicht —** I don't care

daneben *adv.* near it, next to it, close by; — *conj.* besides, also; **–gehen** *v.* to go amiss; **–treffen** *v.* to miss one's mark

Dänemark *neu.* Denmark

danieder *adv.* down; on the ground; **–liegen** *v.* to be prostrate; to be depressed

Dank *m.* thanks; reward; **— wissen** to be grateful; **zu — verpflichten** to oblige

dankbar *adj.* grateful, thankful; profitable

danken *v.* to thank; **danke!** *interj.* thank you!

dann *adv.* then, moreover; thereupon

d(a)ran *adv.* at (*oder* by, in, on, to) it (*oder* that); near it; in regard to it; **gut — sein** to be well off; **was liegt —?** what does it matter? **wir sind —** it's our turn; **–geh(e)n** *v.* to set to work; **–setzen** *v.* to risk

d(a)rauf *adv.* (up)on it, after that; **gleich —** directly afterwards; **–dringen** *v.* to demand; **–geh(e)n** *v.* to be lost; **–hin** *adv.* thereupon

d(a)raus *adv.* from it (*oder* that); **ich mache mir nichts —** I don't care

darben *v.* to suffer, to want

darbieten *v.* to offer, to present

Darbietung *f.* offering; performance

d(a)rein *adv.* into it; **–finden** *v.* **–fügen** *v.* to put up with; **–reden** *v.* to interfere; **–willigen** *v.* to consent

d(a)rin(nen) *adv.* in it; inside, within

darlegen *v.* to explain, to expose

Darleh(e)n *neu.* loan

Darm *m.* intestine, bowel, gut; **–saite** *f.* (mus.) catgut string; **–verschluss** *m.* (med.) enteritis

Darre *f.* kiln-drying, drying oven

darstellen *v.* to describe, to represent; to exhibit; to act. to perform

Darsteller *m.* actor

dartun *v.* to demonstrate, to prove

d(a)rum *adv.* around; therefore; **er weiss — he** is aware of it; **es ist mir nur —** **zu tun** my only object is; **–bringen** to deprive of; **–kommen** *v.* to lose

das *art.* *neu.* the; — *pron.* that, which

Dasein *neu.* existence; life; presence; **-skampf** *m.* struggle for existence

dass *conj.* that; **auf —** in order that; **ausser —** except that; **es sei denn —** unless

datieren *v.* to date

Dattel *f.* (bot.) date

Datum *neu.* (time) date

Daube *f.* stave (barrel, vessel etc.)

Dauer *f.* duration; continuance; **auf die —** in the long run; **-flug** *m.* nonstop flight; **-karte** *f.* season-ticket; **-lauf** *m.* endurance run; **-welle** *f.* permanent wave; **-wurst** *f.* hard sausage

dauer: -haft *adj.* durable, lasting; **-n** *v.* to continue, to last; **es -t mich** I am sorry for it; **-nd** *adj.* enduring, lasting

Daumen *m.* thumb; **den — halten** to keep one's fingers crossed

davon *adv.* of it; away; off; by that; **das kommt —** that's the result; **sie sind auf und —** they left in a hurry; **-bleiben** *v.* to keep off, to leave alone; **-kommen** *v.* to escape; **-laufen** *v.* to take to one's heels; to desert; **-machen, sich -machen** *v.* to steal away, to abscond; **-tragen** *v.* to carry off; to win

davor *adv.* in front of; before; against it

dawider *adv.* against it

dazu *adv.* for (*oder* to) something; for the purpose of; in addition to that; **ich komme nie —** I can never find time for that; **-geben** *v.* to contribute to; **-gehören** *v.* to belong to; **-kommen** *v.* to come across

dazwischen *adv.* among, in the midst of; between (times); **-kommen** *v.* to intervene; **-liegend** *adj.* intermediate; **-treten** *v.* to interpose

Deck *neu.* deck; **-adresse** *f.* "in care of" address; **-blatt** *neu.* (bot.) bract; (cigar) wrapper; **-e** *f.* blanket, cover; ceiling; **sich nach der -e strecken** to adapt oneself to circumstances; **unter einer -e strecken** to conspire together; **-el** *m.* cover, lid; (coll.) hat; **-mantel** *m.* (fig.) cloak, pretense; **-name** *m.* pseudonym, nome de plume; **-offizier** *m.* (naut.) warrant officer

decken *v.* to cover, to protect, to secure; to reimburse; **den Tisch —** to set the table; **sich —** to coincide; to be identical (with)

defekt *adj.* defective, imperfect

Defekt *m.* defect, imperfection

definieren *v.* to define

definitiv *adj.* definite; final

Degen *m.* sword

dehnen *v.* to extend; to stretch; to drawl

dehnbar *adj.* elastic; vague

Deich *m.* dike

dein *pron.* and *adj.* your; (bibl.) thy, thine; **-erseits** *adv.* on your part; **-esgleichen** *adj.* and *pron.* such as you, thy like, your equal; **-ethalben** *adv.*, **-etwegen** *adj.*, **-etwillen** *adv.* for your sake, on your account

Dekan *m.* dean

deklamieren *v.* to recite, to declaim

deklinieren *v.* (gram.) to decline, to inflect; (ast.) to deviate

Dekoration *f.* decoration; ornament; (theat.) scenery; **-smaler** *m.* scene painter

Dekret *neu.* decree

delikat *adj.* delicate; delicious; dainty;

Delphin *m.* dolphin

dem *art.* to the; **— conj.** whom; **-entsprechend**, **-gemäss**, **-nach** *adv.*, **-zufolge** *adv.* accordingly; **-nächst** *adv.* shortly, soon; **-ungeachtet** *conj.* notwithstanding, nevertheless

Dementi *neu.* denial

dementieren *v.* to deny

demolieren *v.* to demolish

demonstrieren *v.* to demonstrate

demontieren *v.* to dismantle

Demut *f.* humility

demütig *adj.* humble; **-en** *v.* to humiliate

Denk: -er *m.* thinker; **-mal** *neu.* memorial, monument; **-zettel** *m.* reminder; punishment

denk: -bar *adj.* conceivable; **-en** *v.* to think; to reflect, to contemplate; to believe; to intend; **auf Mittel und Wege -en** to devise ways and means; **-en an** to remember, to think of; **sich -en** to imagine; **-würdig** *adj.* memorable

denn *adv.* and *conj.* because, for then; **es sei —** unless, provided that; **-(n)och** *conj.* nevertheless, still, though

Depesche *f.* telegram

deponieren *v.* to deposit; (law) to depose

Deputierte *m.* deputy

der *art. m.* the; **— pron.** that, who, which; **-art** *adv.* in such a manner; **-artig** *adj.* of such kind; **-(mal)einst** *adv.* some day, in the future; **-einstig** *adj.* future; **-enthalben** *adv.*, **-entwegen** *adv.*, **-entwillen** *adv.* on her (*oder* their, whose) account; **-gestalt**, **-massen** *adv.* in such manner; **-gleichen** *adv.* such; **-zeit** *adv.* at present; **-zeitig** *adj.* present

derb *adj.* solid, sturdy; rough, clumsy; blunt

des: -gleichen *adv.* likewise; **-halb** *prep.*, **-wegen** *prep.* therefore; **-to** *adv.* the; **-to besser** all the better

Deserteur *m.* deserter

desertieren *v.* to desert

desinfizieren *v.* to disinfect

destillieren *v.* to distill

Detail *neu.* detail; retail

deut: -eln *v.* to twist (meaning); **-en** *v.* to point (at); to explain, to construe, to interpret; **-lich** *adj.* distinct, clear; intelligible

deutsch *adj.* German

Deutschland *neu.* Germany

Devise *f.* device, motto; **-n** *pl.* foreign money

Dezember *m.* December

dezimal *adj.* decimal

dezimieren *v.* to decimate

Diagnose *f.* diagnosis

Dialog *m.* dialogue

Diamant *m.* diamond

Diät *f.* diet; daily allowance

dicht *adj.* dense, thick, compact; tight, close; **-en** *v.* to tighten, to caulk dichten *v.* (lit.) to write; (coll.) to dream up

Dichter *m.* poet; **–ling** *m.* rhymester, poetaster

Dichtung *f.* poem, poetry; poetical work; fiction

dick *adj.* thick; corpulent, fat; **–e Freunde** intimate friends; **er hat es — hinter den Ohren** he is not as simple as he looks; **etwas — haben** to be fed up with; **sich — tun** to boast, to brag; **–bäckig** *adj.* chubby; **–bäuchig** *adj.* pot-bellied; **–blütig** *adj.* thick-blooded; **–fellig** *adj.* thick-skinned; callous; **–flüssig** *adj.* viscous; **–köpfig** *adj.* obstinate, blockheaded; **–leibig** *adj.* corpulent

die *art. f.* the; **—** *pron.* that, who, which

Dieb *m.* thief, crook; **–stahl** *m.* theft

diebisch *adj.* thievish

Dietrich *m.* Theodore

Diele *f.* board, plank; floor; hall

dienen *v.* to serve; **womit kann ich —?** may I help you? **zu nichts —** to be of no use

Diener *m.* domestic, servant; bow; curtsy; **–schaft** *f.* servants, domestics

dienlich *adj.* serviceable, useful

Dienst *m.* service; duty; employment, post; good turn; **ausser — off** duty; retired; **im — in** service, on duty; **in — treten** to enter service; (mil.) to enlist; **–ablösung** *f.* relief; **–abzeichen** *neu.* service badge, stripe; **–alter** *neu.* seniority; **–bote** *m.* domestic, servant; **–grad** *m.* rank; **–kleidung** *f.* livery; uniform; **–mädchen** *neu.* servant girl, maid; **–mann** *m.* porter, messenger; handyman; **–pflicht** *f.* official duty; **–stelle** *f.* headquarters; center, administrative department; **–stunden** *f. pl.* official (*oder* business) hours; **–weg** *m.* official channel, (coll.) red tape; **–wohnung** *f.* official residence; **–zeugnis** *neu.* reference (for employment); **–zwang** *m.* compulsory (*oder* military) service

Dienstag *m.* Tuesday

dies: **–bezüglich** *adj.* referring to this; **–e** *pron.*, **–er** *pron.*, **–es** *pron.* this; **–jährig** *adj.* of this year; **–mal** *adv.* this time; **–seitig** *adj.* on this side: **–seits** *adv.* and *prep.* on this side, here

Diktat *neu.* dictation; **–or** *m.* dictator; **–ur** *f.* dictatorship

diktieren *v.* to dictate

Diktiermaschine *f.* dictaphone

Dilettant *m.* amateur, layman

Ding *neu.* thing; matter; object; **das dumme —** the silly girl; **ein — der Unmöglichkeit** an impossibility; **guter –e sein** to be in high spirits; **vor allen –en** above all

ding: **–en** *v.* to hire; **–fest** *adv.*, **–fest machen** to arrest; **–lich** *adj.* real, judicial

Diözese *f.* diocese

Diplom *neu.* diploma; certificate; **–at** *m.* diplomat; **–atie** *f.* diplomacy

dir *pron.* to you, to thee

direkt *adj.* direct; **— beziehen** to buy direct (from manufacturer); **–er Zug** through train

Direktion *f.*, Direktorium *neu.* management; board of directors

Direktor *m.* headmaster, principal; manager

Dirigent *m.* conductor, band leader

dirigieren *v.* to conduct; to direct, to manage

Dirnd(e)l *neu.* dirndl; (dial.) girl, lass

Dirne *f.* girl; (coll.) hussy, prostitute

Diskant *m.* descant; treble, soprano; **–schlüssel** *m.* treble clef

Diskont(o) *m.* discount

diskret *adj.* discreet, tactful

Diskretion *f.* discretion

Diskurs *m.* discourse, conversation

diskutieren *v.* to discuss, to debate

Dispens *m.* dispensation; special license

dispensieren *v.* to release; to dispense

disputieren *v.* to dispute; to debate

Distanz *f.* distance

Distel *f.* thistle; **–fink** *m.* goldfinch

distinguiert *adj.* distinguished

Disziplin *f.* discipline; branch of knowledge; organized study

disziplinarisch *adj.* disciplinary

disziplinieren *v.* to discipline; to train

dividieren *v.* to divide

Diwan *m.* couch, divan, sofa

doch *conj.* and *adv.* however, nevertheless; after all; though; but, still, yet; **ja — but** of course; **nicht —!** certainly not! don't!

Docht *m.* wick

Dock *neu.* dock (yard)

Docke *f.* baluster; skein; (dial.) doll; sheaf of grain; straw torch

Dogge *f.* bulldog; **deutsch — great Dane**

Dohle *f.* jackdaw

Doktor *m.* doctor; physician, surgeon; **den — machen** to confer a doctor's degree; **–at** *neu.* doctorate, doctor's degree

dokumentieren *v.* to document

Dolch *m.* dagger; **–messer** *neu.* bowieknife; **–stich** *m.* dagger wound; **–stoss** *m.* stab

dolmetschen *v.* to interpret

Dom *m.* cathedral; dome, cupola

Domäne *f.* domain; province

Domino *m.* domino

Dompfaff *m.* bullfinch

Donau *f.* Danube

Donner *m.* thunder; **–keil** *m.* thunderbolt; **–schlag** *m.* thunderclap; **–stag** *m.* Thursday; **–wetter** *neu.* thunderstorm; (coll.) scolding; **–wetter! interj.** confound it!

donnern *v.* to thunder; (gun) to boom; to fulminate; to roar

Doppel *neu.* double; duplicate; **–boden** *m.* false bottom; **–bruch** *m.* compound fracture (*oder* rupture); **–decker** *m.* biplane; **–ehe** *f.* bigamy; **–fehler** *m.* (tennis) double fault; **–flinte** *f.* double-barreled gun; **–gänger** *m.* double, second self; **–laut** *m.* diphthong; **–leben** *neu.* double life; **–punkt** *m.* (gram.) colon; **–rolle** *f.* (theat.) double part;

-sinn *m.* double meaning; ambiguity; -spiel *neu.* (tennis) double; double-dealing; -steuerung *f.* (avi.) dual control; -währung *f.* (currency) double standard

doppel: läufig *adj.* double-barreled; -n *v.* to double; -reihig *adj.* double-breasted; -sinnig *adj.* ambiguous; -t *adj.* double, twofold; -te Buchführung double-entry bookkeeping; -t *adv.* doubly, twice; -züngig *adj.* double-dealing

Dorf *neu.* village, hamlet; -bewohner *m.* villager; -gemeinde *f.* rural parish; -krug *m.*, -schenke *f.* country inn; -leute *f.* village folk; -schulze *m.* village magistrate

Dorn *m.* thorn, prickle, spine; mandrel; ein — im Auge a thorn in the side; -röschen *neu.* Sleeping Beauty

dorren *v.* to become dry; to wither

dörren *v.* to desiccate, to parch; to kiln-dry

Dörrobst *neu.* dried fruit

dort *adv.* yonder; in that place, (over) there; bis -hin as far as that place; — herum thereabouts; -her *adv.* from there; -ig *adj.* of that place; -zulande *adv.* in that country

Dose *f.* box; can; -nöffner *m.* can opener

dösen *v.* to doze, to be drowsy

Dosis *f.* dose

Dotter *m.* and *neu.* yolk; -blume *f.* marsh marigold, buttercup

Dozent *m.* university teacher (*oder* lecturer); -ur *f.* (German university) right to teach

Drache(n) *m.* dragon; serpent; kite; (coll.) termagant; -nkopf *m.* (arch.) gargoyle

Dragoner *m.* dragoon; (coll.) virago

Draht *m.* cable, wire; line; -anschrift *f.* telegraphic address; -antwort *f.* telegraphic reply; -geflecht *neu.* wire netting; -hindernis *neu.*, -verhau *neu.* wire entanglement; -nachricht *f.* wire, telegram; -puppe *f.* marionette; -seilbahn *f.* cable railroad, funicular railway; -stift *m.* wire nail; -zaun *m.* wire fence

drall *adj.* tight; firm, robust; buxom

Drama *neu.* drama; -tiker *m.* playwright; -turg *m.* producer

dramatisch *adj.* dramatic

dramatisieren *v.* to dramatize

Drang *m.* pressure; distress; impulse; craving; hurry; -sal *f.*, *neu.* affliction, distress

dränge(l)n *v.* to crowd, to press, to push, to shove; to urge, to hurry; sich durch die Menge — to elbow (*oder* force) one's way through the crowd; sich in eine Ecke — to crouch in a corner

drangsalieren *v.* to oppress; to vex, to harass

drapieren *v.* to drape

drastisch *adj.* drastic

Draufgänger *m.* daredevil; -tum *neu.* recklessness

Drauflosfahren *neu.* reckless driving

draussen *adv.* outside, abroad

drechseln *v.* to turn on a lathe

Drechsler *m.* turner; -ei *f.* turner's craft (*oder* workshop)

Dreck *m.* dirt, filth, mud; dung, excrement; rubbish, trash; -fink *m.* filthy fellow

dreckig *adj.* dirty, filthy, muddy; nasty

Dreh: -bank *f.* turning lathe; -brücke *f.* swing bridge; -buch *neu.* (film) scenario; -bühne *f.* revolving stage; -er *m.* turner; -kran *m.* derrick; -kreuz *neu.* turnstile; -orgel *f.* barrel organ; -punkt *m.* pivot; -ring *m.* swivel; -scheibe *f.* (potter's) wheel; turntable; -tür *f.* revolving door

drehbar *adj.* rotary

drehen *v.* to revolve, to turn; to twist; (avi.) to spin; (film) to shoot; es dreht sich darum the point is

drei *adj.* three; -eckig *adj.* triangular; -erlei *adj.* of three kinds; auf -erlei Art in three (different) ways; -fach *adj.* threefold, treble, triple; -jährig *adj.* three years old; -kantig *adj.* three-edged; -mal *adv.* three times; -malig *adj.* occurring three times; -monatlich *adj.* quarterly, every three months; -saitig *adj.* three-stringed; -seitig *adj.* three-sided, trilateral; -ssig *adj.* thirty; -stellig *adj.* (math.) of three places; -stündig *adj.* of three hours (duration); -teilig *adj.* in three parts; -winklig *adj.* triangular; -zehn *adj.* thirteen

Drei *f.* three; -bund *m.* Triple Alliance; -eck *neu.* triangle; -eckslehre *f.* trigonometry; -einigkeit *f.* Trinity; -fuss *m.* tripod; -käsehoch *m.* (coll.) toddler; -königsabend *m.* Twelfth-night; -königsfest *neu.* Epiphany; -rad *neu.* tricycle; -sprung *m.* hop, skip, and jump; -zack *m.* trident; -zahl *f.* triad

dreist *adj.* bold, daring, audacious; impudent

Dresch: -e *v.* (sl.) good beating; -en *neu.* threshing; -er *m.* thresher; -flegel *m.* (agr.) flail; -maschine *f.* threshing machine, combine

dreschen *v.* to thresh; (sl.) to beat up, to thrash

dressieren *v.* to tame, to train, to break in; to coach, to drill

Drill *m.* (mil.) drill(ing); -bohrer *m.* crankshaft; -säge *f.* hack saw

Drilling *m.* triplet; lantern pinion; three-barrelled gun

dring: -en *v.* to press forward; to urge, to compel; to penetrate; -end *adj.* pressing, urgent; -lich *adj.* urgently

dritt: -e *adj.* third; -ens *adv.* thirdly

Drittel *neu.* third

droben *adv.* above, on high, up there

Drog: -e *f.* drug; -erie *f.* pharmacy; -ist *m.* druggist

Drohbrief *m.* threatening (blackmail) letter

drohen *v.* to threaten, to menace

Drohne *f.* (ent.) drone; (coll.) idler

dröhnen *v.* to roar, to rumble; to boom

drollig *adj.* droll, funny, comical

Dromedar *neu.* dromedary; (coll.) blockhead

Droschke f. cab; taxi; **-nlenker** m. cab driver

Drossel f. (orn.) thrush; (mech.) throttle

drosseln v. to throttle

drüben adv. over there, yonder

Druck m. compression, pressure; weight; oppression; (typ.) print(ing); impression; **kleiner** (or **grosser**) — small (oder large) type; **-er** m. printer, typographer; **-erei** f. printing; print shop; **-erlaubnis** f. imprimatur; **-erpresse** f. printing press; **-erschwärze** f. printer's ink; **-fehler** m. misprint, typographical error; **-jahr** neu. year of issue; **-kabine** f. pressurized cabin; **-knopf** m. snap fastener; **-kombination** f. pressure suit; **-luft** f. compressed air; **-probe** f. printer's proof; **-sache** f. printed matter; **-schrift** f. publication

drucken v. to print, to impress

drücken v. to press; to grip, to squeeze; to pinch; to lower; to bring down (prices); to depress; to oppress; **sich —** (coll.) to sneak off, to steal away; **-d** adj. heavy, sultry

Drücker m. latch; (gun) trigger

drunten adv. below, down there

Drüse f. gland; **-nentzündung** f. adenitis

Dschungel neu. jungle

du pron. thou, you; **auf — und — stehen** to be on intimate terms

Dublette f. duplicate; doublet

ducken v. to duck, to stoop; to bow; to humble

Duckmäuser m. coward; sneak; soft-pedaler

Dudelei f. monotonous (oder poor) music

Dudelsack m. bagpipe

Duell neu. duel

duellieren v. to fight a duel

Duett neu. duet

Duft m. fragrance, scent

duft: -en v. to be fragrant, to smell sweetly; **-end** adj., **-ig** adj. fragrant; airy, light

Dukaten m. ducat

duld: -bar adj. tolerable, endurable; **-en** v. to tolerate; to suffer, to endure; **-sam** adj. tolerant; patient; long-suffering

dumm adj. stupid; foolish, silly; **-dreist** adj. impertinent; **-stolz** adj. conceited

Dummkopf m. blockhead

dumpf adj. damp, muggy, stuffy; hollow-sounding; oppressive; vague; **-ig** adj. damp, musty

Düne f. dune

Dung, Dünger m. dung, manure

düngen v. to fertilize, to manure

dunkel adj. dark, dim; sombre; suspicious; **-n** v. to grow dark (oder dim)

Dünkel m. conceit, arrogance

dünkelhaft adj. conceited, arrogant

Dunkelkammer f. (photo.) darkroom

dünken v. to appear; to look, to seem

dünn adj. thin, fine; slender; sparse; diluted, weak; rare; **-bäckig** adj. hollow-cheeked; **-beinig** adj. spiderlegged

Dunst m. exhalation; vapor; fume; haze;

false appearance; **jemand blauen — vormachen** to bamboozle (oder humbug) a person; **-gebilde** neu. phantom; **-kreis** m. atmosphere

dunsten v. to evaporate, to steam; to exhale

dunstig adj. vaporous; hazy, misty; damp

Duplikat neu. duplicate

durch adv. and prep. through; across; by (means of); because of; during; throughout; — **die Finger sehen** to overlook (someone's blunder); — **die Post** by mail; — **und —** thoroughly; — **und — nass** drenched to the skin; — **Zufall** by chance

durcharbeiten v. to work through; to study thoroughly; to elaborate

durchaus adv. thoroughly; throughout; in every way; quite; absolutely, positively; by all means; — **nicht** not at all

durchbilden v. to educate (oder develop) thoroughly

durchblättern v. to leaf (oder skim) through

Durchblick m. vista, view; penetration

durchblicken v. to look through; to appear; — **lassen** to hint, to give to understand

durchbohren v. to bore through; to pierce; to perforate

durchbrechen v. to break through; to pierce

durchbrennen v. to burn through; (elec.) to fuse; (coll.) to abscond, to flee

durchbringen v. to carry through; to rear; to enact (law); to dissipate, to squander; **sich —** to subsist

Durchbruch m. (act of) breaking through; eruption; rupture; (teeth) cutting; gap

durchdenken v. to think through; to ponder

durchdrängen v. to force through; **sich —** to elbow one's way through

durchdring: -en v. to permeate; to penetrate; to prevail, to succeed; **-end** adj. penetrating; shrill, keen; **-lich** adj. penetrable

durcheinander adv. confusedly; promiscuously; pell-mell, topsy-turvy

Durcheinander neu. confusion, disorder; jumble

durchfahren v. to drive (oder pass) through; to traverse; to wear out by driving

Durchfahrt f. thoroughfare, passage; driving (oder passing) through; gateway; channel

Durchfall m. falling through; (med.) diarrhea; failure, rejection

durchfallen v. to fall through; to fail, to be rejected; to fall flat

durchfechten v. to fight it out (oder one's way through)

durchfeilen v. to file through; (fig.) to polish; to give the finishing touches

durchfinden v. **sich —** to find one's way through

durchfliegen v. to fly (oder rush) through, to skim over

Durchflug m. flight through; nonstop

flight

durchforschen v. to search through; to examine closely; to investigate

durchfressen v. (zool.) to eat through; to corrode; (sl.) to struggle through; to sponge on

durchfrieren v. to freeze completely; to chill to the bone

Durchfuhr f. transit; **-handel** m. transit trade; **-zoll** m. transit duty

durchführbar adj. practicable, feasible

durchführen v. to convey (oder lead) through; to accomplish, to execute; (mus.) to develop

Durchgang m. passing through; passage, thoroughfare; defile; transit; gateway; **-sgüter** neu. pl. goods in transit; **-srecht** neu. right of way; **-swagen** m. (rail.) through car

Durchgänger m. bolting horse; absconder

durchgängig adj. throughout, without exception

durchgehen v. to go through; to pass; to penetrate; to escape, to abscond; to examine, to peruse, to work through; (horse) to bolt

durchgeistigt adj. spiritual, intellectual

durchgiessen v. to filter, to pour through

durchglühen v. to heat red hot; (chem.) to calcine; (mech.) to anneal; to inflame

durchgreifen v. to put one's hand through; to proceed vigorously, to act decisively; **-d** adj. decisive, sweeping, vigorous, thorough

durchhalten v. to hold out; to carry through

durchhauen v. to cut through; to cleave

durchhecheln v. to heckle, to criticize

durchkauen v. to chew through; (coll.) to repeat

durchkommen v. to get through; to pass; to succeed; to escape; to recover

durchkreuzen v. to cross, to traverse; to thwart

durchlassen v. to let through, to allow to pass; (phy.) to transmit

durchlässig adj. pervious, penetrable

durchlaufen v. to filter; to go through; to wear out (shoes)

durchleuchten v. to shine through; to flood with light; to irradiate; to X-ray

durchliegen v. to become bedsore

durchlochen, durchlöchern v. to perforate; to punch; to puncture; (coll.) to badger

durchmachen v. to go (oder pass) through; to experience; to suffer

Durchmarsch m. march(ing) through; (cards) grand slam

durchmessen v. to measure through; to traverse

Durchmesser m. diameter; (mil.) caliber; (opt.) aperture

durchmustern v. to review; to search through, to examine, to inspect, to scrutinize

durchnässen v. to wet through; to soak

durchnehmen v. to go over; to analyze; to explain; to criticise

durchpeitschen v. to flog (oder whip)

soundly; to dispatch quickly

durchprügeln v. to beat (oder thrash) soundly

durchreiben v. to rub through; to wear out by friction; to chafe

Durchreise f. journey through, passage, transit

durchschauen v. to look through; to penetrate; to detect, to discover

durchscheinen v. to shine through; **-d** adj. transparent, translucent; diaphanous

durchschiessen v. to shoot through; to dash through; to interleave; (typ.) to lead

Durchschlag m. colander, strainer; carbon copy

durchschlagen v. to beat (oder punch) through; to penetrate; to strain, to filter; to beat soundly; to blot; to be effective; **Sicherungen —** to cause a short-circuit

durchschlüpfen v. to slip through; to have a narrow escape

durchschneiden v. to cut through; to cross, to traverse; to intersect

Durchschnitt m. cut(ting) through; intersection; cross-section; section, profile; average

durchschnittlich adj. average, of medium size (oder quality); **—** adv. on an average, ordinarily speaking

durchsehen v. to see (oder look) through; to scrutinize; to proofread; to revise

durchseihen v. to filter, to strain

durchsetzen v. to carry through; to make one's way; to succeed; to intersperse

Durchsicht f. vista, correction, revision

durchsichtig adj. transparent; clear

durchsickern v. to trickle (oder ooze) through; to percolate

durchsieben v. to sift, to bolt, to screen

durchsprechen v. to talk over; to discuss

durchstechen v. to pierce through; to cut; to transfix; to perforate; to prick

durchstöbern v. to rummage through; to ransack

durchstossen v. to push (oder knock) through; to pierce, to stab

durchstreichen v. to strike out; to cancel; to roam through; (orn.) to pass through

durchstreifen v. to range (oder roam) through

durchsuchen v. to search; to examine closely

durchtreten v. to wear (oder step) through

durchtrieben adj. crafty, cunning, sly

durchwachsen adj. (meat) marbled; streaked

durchweben v. to interweave; to interlace

Durchweg m. through-passage; thoroughfare

durchweg adv. throughout; without exception

durchwirken v. to interweave; to have effect

durchwühlen v. to root up; to burrow; to rummage

durchzeichnen v. to trace (through paper)

durchziehen v. to draw (oder pass) through; to thread; to soak; (coll.) to criticize

durchzucken v. to flash through; to realize suddenly; to convulse

Durchzug m. passing (oder drawing) through; through draft

dürfen v. to be allowed (oder permitted); **darf ich?** may I?

dürftig adj. indigent, needy; shabby; scanty

dürr adj. parched, arid; withered; lean; skinny; bare, **mit –en Worten** in plain language

Dürre f. dryness, aridity; drought; leanness

Durst m. thirst

dursten, dürsten v. to be thirsty, to thirst

Dusche f. shower bath

Düse f. nozzle, jet; **–nbomber** m. jet bomber; **–nflugzeug** n. jet plane; (coll.) blowtorch; **–nstrahl** m. jet stream

Dusel m. (coll.) pure luck, windfall

duselig adj. dreamy, drowsy; dizzy

düster adj. dark, dusky, sombre, gloomy; sad

Dutzend neu. dozen; **–gesicht** neu. ordinary face; **–mensch** m. commonplace person

dutzendweise adv. by the dozen

duzen v. to address familiarly

dynamisch adj. dynamic(al)

D-Zug m. express train

E

Ebbe f. ebb tide; **–n** v. to ebb

eben adj. even, level; smooth; plane; **zu –er Erde** on the ground floor; — adv. just, quite; namely, exactly; evenly; — **erst** just now; **–bürtig** adj. equal (in birth); **–da** adv. at the same place; **–falls** adv. likewise, also; **–mässig** adj. proportionate; **–so** adv. just so; **–sowohl** adv. just as well

Eben: **–bild** neu. exact likeness, image; **–e** f. plain; level ground; plane; **in gleicher –e** on a level with; **schiefe –e** gradient, inclined plane; (coll.) skid row; **–mass** neu. symmetry, right proportion

Ebenholz neu. ebony

Eber m. wild boar

ebnen v. to make level, to smooth; **die Bahn** — to pave the way

echt adj. genuine, authentic, unadulterated, pure; real, original; fast (color)

Eck neu. (dial.) corner, angle, edge; **–brett** neu. corner shelf; **–chen** neu. nook; **–e** f. angle, corner; (arch.) quoin; **an allen –en und Enden** everywhere; **um die –e bringen** (sl.) to murder; **um die –e gehen** to turn the corner; **–stein** m. cornerstone; (cards) diamond; **–zahn** m. eye tooth

edel adj. noble, genteel, benevolent; precious, superior, refined; **–e Teile** vital parts; **–gesinnt** adj. high-minded, magnanimous

Edel: **–frau** f. titled lady; **–knabe** m. page; **–mann** m. nobleman; **–metall** neu. precious metal; **–mut** m. generosity,

magnanimity; noble-mindedness; **–rost** m. patina; **–stein** m. precious stone, jewel; **–wild** neu. deer

Edikt neu. edict

Efeu m. ivy

Effekt m. effect; **–en** pl. movable goods; (com.) securities; **–enbörse** f. stock exchange; **–enhändler** m. stockbroker; **–hascherei** f. sensationalism, playing to the gallery

egal adj. equal; alike, same; **das ist mir ganz** — it's all the same to me

Egel m. (zool.) leech

Egge f. (agr.) harrow

Egoismus m. egoism; selfishness

egozentrisch adj. self-centered

ehe adv. before, until; **–dem** adv. before this; **–malig** adj. former; **–mals** adv. formerly, of old; **–r** adv. earlier, sooner; rather, more easily; **je –r je lieber** the sooner the better; **–stens** adv. as soon as possible

Ehe f. matrimony, marriage; **wilde** — common-law marriage; **–bett** neu. marriage bed; **–brecher** m. adulterer; **–bruch** m. adultery; **–bund** m. matrimony; **–hälfte** f. one's "better half"; **–kreuz** neu. (coll.) termagant; **–krüppel** m. (coll.) hen-pecked husband; **–leute** pl. married couple; **–mann** m. husband; **–paar** neu. married couple; **–pflicht** f. conjugal duty; **–recht** neu. matrimonial law; **–scheidung** f. divorce; **–schliessung** f. contracting of marriage; **–stand** m. married life; **–stifter** m. matchmaker; **–versprechen** neu. promise of marriage; **–vertrag** m. marriage contract

ehelich adj. conjugal, matrimonial; (child) legitimate; **–lichen** to marry

ehelos adj. unmarried, single

Ehr: **–abschneider** m. slanderer; **–e** f. honor, praise; credit; distinction; **–furcht** f. awe, veneration; **–gefühl** neu. sense of honor; self-respect; **–geiz** m. ambition; **–ung** f. honors; **–verlust** m. loss of civil rights; **–würden** f. Reverend; Reverence

ehr: **–bar** adj. honorable, respectable; decent, decorous; reputable; **–erbietig** adj. respectful, reverential; **–fürchtig** adj. awe-inspiring, reverential; **–lich** adj. honest, fair dealing, loyal, true; **–los** adj. dishonorable; **–sam** adj. decent, worthy, respectable; **–vergessen** adj. unprincipled, base-minded; **–widrig** adj. disgraceful, discreditable; **–würdig** adj. reverent, venerable

ehren v. to honor; to esteem; to revere; **–amtlich** adj. honorary; **–haft** adj. honorable, high-principled; **–halber** prep. for honor's sake; **–rührig** adj. defamatory, libelous; **–voll** adj. honorable; **–wert** adj. respectable

Ehren: **–amt** neu. honorary office; position of honor (oder trust); **–bezeugung** f. ovation; proof of esteem; (mil.) salute; **–bürger** m. honorary citizen; **–dame** f. maid of honor; **–doktor** m. honorary doctor; **–erklärung** f., **–ret**

tung *f.* reparation of honor; rehabilitation; **-gast** *m.* guest of honor; **-geleit** *neu.* honorary escort; **-halle** *f.* hall of fame; **-handel** *m.* affair of honor; **-klage** *f.* libel suit; **-kränkung** *f.* affront, insult, libel; **-mitglied** *neu.* honorary member; **-raub** *m.* dishonoring; **-sache** *f.* unquestionable duty; duel; **-sold** *m.* honorarium, donation; **-tag** *m.* anniversary; **-titel** *m.* honorary title; **-trunk** *m.* toast; **-wache** *f.* guard of honor; **-wort** *neu.* word of honor; (law) parole; **-zeichen** *neu.* decoration, medal

Ei *neu.* egg; **hartes —** hard-boiled egg; **kaum aus dem — gekrochen** just out of the shell; (coll.) a greenhorn; **verlorenes —** poached egg; **wie aus dem — gepellt** (*or* **geschält**) spic and span; **-dotter, -gelb** *neu.* yolk; **-erkuchen** *m.* omelet; **-erschnee** *m.* whipped white of eggs; **-erstock** *m.* ovary; **-weiss** *neu.* white of egg, albumin; **-weisstoff** *m.* protein

Eich: **-e** *f.* oak; **-el** *f.* acorn; (cards) clubs; **-horn** *neu.*, **-hörnchen** *neu.*, **-katze** *f.* squirrel

eichen *v.* to calibrate

Eichung (Gradeinteilung) *f.* calibration

Eid *m.* oath; **-brecher** *m.*, **-brüchige** *m.* perjurer; **-bruch** *m.* perjury; **-esabnahme** *f.* taking an oath; **-genosse** *m.* confederate

Eidechse *f.* lizard

eif: **-ern** *v.* to show zeal, to display ardor; to emulate, to vie (with); **-ern gegen** to inveigh against; **-ersüchtig** *adj.* jealous; **-rig** *adj.* eager, zealous, ardent

Eifer *m.* zeal, ardor, fervor, emulation; **-er** *m.* zealot; **-sucht** *f.* jealousy; **-süchtelei** *f.* petty jealousy

eigen *adj.* own, proper, individual; particular, special, separate; exact; peculiar; odd, strange; **sich zu — machen** to adopt; to appropriate; **-artig** *adj.* peculiar; **-händig** *adj.* with (*oder* in) one's own hand; **-mächtig** *adj.* on one's own authority; arbitrary; **-nützig** *adj.* selfish, self-interested; **-s** *adv.* expressly, purposely; **-sinnig** *adj.* stubborn, obstinate; capricious; **-tlich** *adj.* real, true; proper; intrinsic; **-tlich** *adv.* properly, exactly, really; **-tümlich** *adj.* real, proper, specific; peculiar; characteristic; **-willig** *adj.* willful, self-willed

Eigen: **-art** *f.* peculiarity; **-bericht** *m.* (newspaper) special report; **-brödler** *m.*, **-brötler** *m.* quaint fellow, introvert; **-gewicht** *neu.* net weight; **-liebe** *f.* self-love, egotism; **-lob** *neu.* self-praise; **-nutz** *m.* self-interest, selfishness; **-peilung** *f.* (avi.) homing; **-schaft** *f.* attribute, property; quality; characteristic; **-schaftswort** *neu.* adjective; **-sinn** *m.* willfulness; obstinacy; **-tum** *neu.* property; ownership; **-tümer** *m.* proprietor, owner; **-tumsrecht** *neu.* proprietorship; copyright; **-tumssteuer** *f.* property tax; **-wille** *m.* willfulness

eignen *v.* **sich — für** to be suited for

Eignung *f.* qualification; aptitude; **-sprü-**

fung *f.* aptitude test

Eil: **-brief** *m.* special delivery letter; **-bote** *m.* courier; special-delivery mailman; **-e** *f.* haste, hurry; speed; **-fracht** *f.*, **-gut** *neu.* express freight; **-marsch** *m.* forced march; **-zug** *m.* express train

eil: **-en** *v.* to hasten, to hurry; **-ends** *adv.* hastily, quickly; **-fertig** *adj.* precipitate; hasty; **-ig** *adj.* urgent; quick, speedy

Eimer *m.* pail; bucket

eimerweise *adv.* by buckets, in pailfuls

ein *art.* a(n); **—** *adj.* one; **— für alle Mal** once and for all; **— ums andere Mal** alternatively; **in -em fort** continuously; **um -s** at one o'clock; **—** *pron.* a, one, some; **— jeder** each one; **-er von beiden** either one; **— und derselbe** the very same; **—** *adv.* in; **— und aus gehen** to frequent; **-ander** *pron.* one another, each other; **-armig** *adj.* one-armed; single-branched; **-äugig** *adj.* one-eyed, monocular; **-bändig** *adj.* in one volume; **-deutig** *adj.* having but one meaning, unequivocal; **-erlei** *adj.* of one kind, monotonous; **-erseits, -esteils** *adv.* on the one hand; **-fach** *adj.* simple; single; plain; frugal; (math.) indivisible; **-fache Buchführung** single entry bookkeeping; **-fältig** *adj.* silly, simpleminded; **-farbig** *adj.* one-colored, plain; monochromic; **-förmig** *adj.* uniform, monotonous; **-geboren** *adj.* native; (rel.) only begotten; **-händig** *adj.* one-handed; **-heitlich** *adj.* uniform, homogenous, centralized; **-hellig** *adj.* unanimous; **-ig** *adj.* in agreement; united; **-ige** *adj.* some; **-(ig)en** *v.* to unify, to unite; to conciliate; **sich -igen** to agree, to come to terms; **-jährig** *adj.* one-year-old; annual; **-mal** *adv.* once; formerly; at some future time; **-malig** *adj.* happening but once, one-time, unique; **-mütig** *adj.* unanimous; **-reihig** *adj.* single-breasted; **-sam** *adj.* solitary; lonely; **-seitig** *adj.* **-silbig** *adj.* monosyllabic; taciturn; **-sitzig** *adj.* singleseated; **-spurig** *adj.* single-railed; **-stimmig** *adj.* unanimous; of (*oder* for) one voice; solo; **-stöckig** *adj.* onestoried; **-tägig** *adj.* lasting one day, ephemeral; **-tönig** *adj.* monotonous; tedious; **-trächtig** *adj.* harmonious; united; **-zellig** *adj.* one-celled; **-zig** *adj.* only, single, sole; unique; **-zigartig** *adj.* unique, matchless

Ein: **-bahnstrasse** *f.* one-way street; **-decker** *m.* monoplane; **-ehe** *f.* monogamy; **-er** *m.* any number under ten; **-erlei** *neu.* uniformity, monotony, sameness; **-falt** *f.* simplicity; artlessness, silliness; **-faltspinsel** *m.* simpleton; **-geborene** *m.* native; **-glas** *neu.* monocle; **-heit** *f.* unity; unit; **-klang** *m.* harmony; accord, unison; **-maleins** *neu.* multiplication table; **-siedler** *m.* hermit; recluse; **-tracht** *f.* harmony, concord, union

einarbeiten *v.* to train; **sich —** to familiarize oneself (with) einäschern v. to reduce to ashes, to incinerate; to calcine

einatmen v. to inhale

einbalsamieren v. to embalm

Einband m. (book) binding

einbe: −dingen v. to include (in a bargain); −griffen adj. included; −halten to detain; −rufen v. (mil.) to call up (oder out); to convene; to convoke; to summon

einbiegen v. to bend inward; to turn into

einbilden f. to fancy (oder imagine); sich etwas — to be conceited

Einbildungskraft f. power of imagination; poetic fancy; fantasy

einblasen v. to blow (oder breathe) into; to insinuate, to prompt

einbläuen v. to blue; to inculcate

Einblick m. insight, glance into

Einbrecher m. housebreaker, burglar

einbrennen v. to burn into; to brand; (cooking) to thicken; to fumigate; to cauterize

einbringen v. to bring in; to yield (profits); etwas wieder — to make good, to retrieve

einbrocken v. to crumble into; sich etwas — to get into trouble

Einbruch m. housebreaking, burglary

einbürgern v. to naturalize; to enfranchise

eindecken v. to provide with; to store up

eindeutschen v. to Germanize

eindrängen v. to push in; sich — to intrude

eindringen v. to enter forcibly; to penetrate; to infiltrate

eindringlich adj. penetrating; impressive, touching; affecting, forcible

Eindringling m. interloper, intruder

Eindruck m. impression; imprint

eindrücken v. to crush; to imprint; to impress

eindrucksvoll adj. emphatic, impressive

einebnen v. to flatten, to level, to smooth

einengen v. to confine, to narrow, to limit

einernten v. to reap, to harvest; to gain

einexerzieren v. to drill, to train

einfädeln v. to thread; to contrive

einfahren v. to drive in(to); to carry (oder bring) in; to enter; (horse) to break in; (min.) to descend

Einfahrt f. (act of) driving in; entry, gateway, inlet; (min.) descent

Einfall m. invasion; sudden idea, notion; (phys.) incidence

einfallen v. to fall in, to ruin; to interrupt; to occur; to invade; (mus.) to join in

einfangen v. to catch, to seize

einfassen v. to border, to edge, to trim; to enclose, to frame

einfetten v. to grease, to lubricate

einfinden v. sich — to appear, to arrive, to turn up

einflössen v. to instill, to inspire; to imbue

Einflug m. (act of) flying in

Einfluss m. influx; influence

einflussreich adj. influential

einflüstern v. to whisper to; to insinuate

einfordern v. to call in, to demand

einfrieren v. to freeze in; to be icebound

einfügen v. to insert; to dovetail; sich — to adapt oneself to; to fit in

Einfuhr f. import(ation); −sperre f. embargo on imports; −zoll m. import duty

einführen v. to import; to introduce; to install; to inaugurate; to bring in

Einführung f. introduction; elementary guidance

Eingabe f. petition; presentation; memorial

Eingang m. (act of) entering, entry; arrival; access; (anat.) passage; (geog.) inlet, mouth; (lit.) preface, introduction; kein — no admission; nach — on receipt

eingeben v. to prompt; to inspire; to give, to hand in; (med.) to administer

eingebildet adj. imaginary, fanciful, conceited

eingedenk prep. mindful of, remembering

eingefallen adj. sunken (eye), hollow (cheek)

eingefleischt adj. incarnate; inveterate

eingehen v. to go in; to arrive; to enter; to decay; to cease; to die; to shrink; — lassen to give up, to leave off; to drop; Vergleich — to come to terms; Wette — to wager; −d adj. thorough, exhaustive, in detail

Eingemachte neu. preserves; jam; pickles

eingemeinden v. to merge, to incorporate

eingenommen adj. prepossessed, biased, partial

Eingesandt neu. letter to the editor

eingeschränkt adj. limited, confined

eingeschrieben adj. registered

Eingeständnis neu. avowal, confession

eingestehen v. to avow, to confess; to concede

Eingeweide neu. pl. bowels, entrails, intestines

Eingeweihte m. initiated person; adept

eingewöhnen v. sich — to accustom oneself; to get used to

eingewurzelt adj. deep-rooted, inveterate

eingezogen adj. retired, secluded; confiscated; (mil.) drafted

eingittern v. to fence in; to rail off

eingliedern v. to incorporate; to embody

eingraben v. to dig in; to bury; to entrench; to engrave

eingravieren v. to engrave

eingreifen v. (mech.) to catch; to interlock; to gear together; (fig.) to encroach, to interfere; to intervene

Eingriff m. intervention; interference; encroachment; (med.) operation

einhaken v. to hook into; sich — to link arms

Einhalt m. stop, check; impediment, prohibition

einhalten v. to observe, to fulfill, to keep; to pause, to stop; to restrain; to hem

einhändigen v. to hand over; to deliver

einhauchen v. to breathe into; to inspire

einhauen v. to hew in, to cut into; (mil.) to attack, to charge; (coll.) to dig in

einheimisch adj. native; indigenous; homemade

einheimsen v. to get in, to house; (coll.) to

reap; to rake in, to pocket

einher adv. along; **–stolzieren** v. to strut

einholen v. to bring in, to collect, to gather; to overtake; to seek; to apply for, to shop; (naut.) to haul (oder take) in

einhüllen v. to wrap up; to envelop

einimpfen v. to inoculate, to vaccinate; (fig.) to implant, to inculcate

einkassieren r. to cash; to collect

Einkauf m. (act of) buying; purchase; **–spreis** m. cost price

einkaufen v. to buy, to purchase; to shop

Einkäufer m. buyer

Einkehr f. short rest (oder stay); **—** bei sich selbst contemplation; remorse

einkehren v. to turn in, to enter; to stop at (an inn); to call at

einkellern v. to cellar; to store, to lay up

einkerkern v. to incarcerate; to imprison

einkitten v. to fix with cement (oder putty)

einklammern v. to fasten with clamps; to put in brackets (oder parentheses)

einkleiden v. to clothe; to accouter; (mil.) to provide with uniforms; (eccl.) to veil

einknicken v. to fold; to bend in. to double up; to give way, to break down

einkochen v. to boil down; to put up (preserves)

Einkommen neu. income; revenue; emoluments; **–steuer** f. income tax

einkreisen v. to encircle, to encompass, to surround

Einkünfte f. pl. income, revenue

einkuppeln v. to throw into gear

einladen v. to invite; to load in; to freight; **–d** adj. inviting; attractive

Einlage f. enclosure; insertion; deposit; (gaming) stake; (med.) arch support

einlagern v. to store

Einlass m. entrance, admission; inlet; **–ventil** neu. intake valve

einlassen v. to admit, to let in; **sich auf** (oder in, mit) etwas **—** to engage in (oder meddle) with something

einlaufen v. to arrive, to come in; to shrink; to enter (harbor); **jemandem das Haus —** to pester someone

einleben v. **sich —** to become used to; to familiarize oneself with

einlegen v. to put in, to enclose; to inlay; to insert; (com.) to deposit; (cooking) to preserve, to pickle; **Berufung —** to appeal; **Ehre —** to gain honor; **ein gutes Wort —** to intercede

einleiten v. to begin, to initiate; to introduce; (law) to institute

Einleitung f. introduction; preamble, preface; (mus.) prelude, overture

einlenken v. to turn in; to lead into; to give in; to be reasonable

einlernen v. to teach, to train

einleuchten v. to be clear (oder intelligible); **–d** adj. evident, obvious

einliefern v. to deliver up; to hand over

einliegend adj. enclosed

einlösen v. to redeem; to honor (bill, check)

einmachen v. to preserve, to pickle, to can

Einmarsch m. entry (of troops); marching in

einmarschieren v. to march in

einmauern v. to wall in; to immure

einmeisseln v. to chisel in

einmengen, einmischen v. to intermix, to mingle (oder meddle) with; to interfere

einmieten v. to engage lodgings; to pit (potatoes)

Einnahme f. (act of) receiving, receipt; revenue, proceeds; capture; **–quelle** f. source of revenue

einnehmen v. to take in; to receive; to collect; to capture, to occupy; to fascinate; to influence, to prejudice; **–d** adj. captivating, charming

einnicken v. to fall asleep; to nod

einnisten v. to nest(le); to establish firmly; **sich —** to insinuate oneself

Einöde f. desert

einordnen v. to put in proper order; to arrange, to classify, to file

einpacken v. to pack (oder wrap) up; (coll.) to give way

einpassen v. to fit in; to adjust

einpauken v. to drum into; to cram

einpflanzen v. to plant in; to implant

einpfropfen v. to cork up; to cram in; to engraft

einpökeln v. to pickle; to cure, to salt

einprägen v. to impress, to imprint

einpuppen v., **sich —** to change into a chrysalis (oder pupa); (coll.) to buy new clothes

einquartieren v. (mil.) to billet (oder quarter)

einrahmen v. to frame

einrammen v. to ram in

einräumen v. to put away; to store; to give up; to concede; to furnish (rooms)

Einrede f. objection, protest, remonstrance

einreden v. to make (one) believe; to urge, to persuade; to convince; to object

einreiben v. to rub in

einreichen v. to hand in, to deliver; to present

einreihen v. to arrange in a line (oder row) to range, to rank; to insert

Einreise f. entry into a country; **–erlaubnis** f. entry permit

einreissen v. to pull down, to demolish; to tear; (fig.) to gain ground, to spread

einrenken v. to set (bones oder joints)

einrennen v. to ram open, to batter into

einrichten v. to arrange; to establish; to furnish; to set (bone); **sich —** to prepare for; to economize

einrosten v. to become rusty; to rust in; to become stupid (oder dull) by inactivity

einrücken v. to enter, to march into; to insert; to advertise, to announce (in newspapers); (mil.) to join the ranks; (typ.) to indent

eins adj. one; **—** adv. the same; **— A** (coll.) A one; excellent; **— werden** to agree, to come to terms; **es kommt auf — hinaus** it amounts to the same thing;

mit — all at once

einsacken r. to put into sacks, to pocket

einsalben r. to anoint

einsalzen r. to salt, to pickle

einsammeln r. to gather, to glean; to collect; (coll.) to pass the hat

Einsatz m. insertion; stake; attachable (oder interchangeable) part; (mus.) cue; **-besprechung** (mil.) briefing (Lagebesprechung)

einsäuern r. to leaven; to pickle (in vinegar)

einsaugen r. to suck in; to absorb

einschachteln r. to put into a box; to encase

einschalten r. to insert; to put in; to interpolate; to intercalate (leap-year); to engage (gears); (elec.) to switch on

einschärfen v. to impress upon; to inculcate

einscharren r. to bury; to scrape in

einschätzen r. to assess, to estimate, to evaluate

einschenken v. to pour in; **reinen Wein — to tell the plain truth**

einschieben v. to shove in; to insert; to intercalate; to interpolate

einschiessen r. to test (gun); to shoot in; (com.) to deposit, to contribute; **sich — to practice shooting**

einschiffen r. to embark; to take on board

einschlafen r. to fall asleep; to become numbed (oder dormant); to die

einschläfern v. to lull to sleep (oder security); to narcotize

Einschlag m. impact; (bomb) burst; (com.) handshake; woof; wrapper, cover, envelope; **-papier** neu. wrapping paper

einschlägig adj. relative to; competent

einschleichen v. **sich — to sneak (oder steal) in**

einschliessen v. to lock up; to enclose; to encircle; to include, to comprise

einschliesslich adj. inclusive

Einschluss m. inclusion; enclosure

einschmeicheln v. **sich — to insinuate oneself (into); to ingratiate oneself (with); -d** adj. engaging, winning

einschmelzen v. to melt down

einschmieren v. to grease, to oil

einschneiden r. to cut into; to notch; **-d** adj. incisive

Einschnitt m. incision; cut; notch, indentation; turning point; (math.) segment

einschnüren v. to cord; to lace (oder tie) up

einschränken v. to restrict; to limit, to check; to confine; to reduce; **sich — to economize, to retrench**

einschreiben v. to write in (oder down); to inscribe; to enter; to register; to enroll

einschreiten v. to step in; to interfere, to intervene; to proceed against

einschrumpfen, (coll.) **einschrumpeln** v. to shrink, to shrivel up

Einschub m. insertion; interpolation

einschüchtern v. to abash; to intimidate

Einschuss m. capital advanced, share;

woof; admixture; (bullet) point of entry

einsegnen v. to consecrate, to bless; to confirm

einsehen v. to look into; to comprehend to realize, to understand

einseifen v. to soap, to lather; (sl.) to humbug, to take in

Einsender m. sender, transmitter, contributor

einsetzen v. to put (oder set) in; to insert to employ, to use; to appoint, to install to begin; to plant; to risk; **sich — für to stand up for; to side with**

Einsicht f. inspection, examination; view insight, understanding, judgment

einsichtig adj. sensible, prudent, judicious

einsickern r. to trickle in; to soak into; to infiltrate

einspannen v. to stretch; to yoke, to harness; to enlist (help)

einsperren v. to lock up; to imprison

einsprechen v. to influence, to persuade to inspire; **bei jemanden — to drop in for a visit; Mut — to encourage**

einspringen r. to pump (oder leap) in; to catch, to snap; to substitute

einspritzen r. to give a shot; to inject

Einspritzpumpe f. injection pump

Einspritzung f. injection, (coll.) shot

Einspruch m. objection, protest; **— erheben** to protest, to oppose, to interrupt

einst adv. in days past, at some future time; **-weilen** adv. meanwhile, for the time being; temporarily; **-weilig** adj temporary, provisional

einstechen v. to dig in; to puncture; to prick

einstecken v. to put (oder stick) in; to pocket; to sheathe; **Beleidigungen — to swallow insults; jemanden —** (coll.) to clap someone into jail

einstehen r. to substitute; to answer (oder be responsible) for

einsteigen v. to get in; to embark; to break into (a house); **—! interj.** all aboard!

einstellen v. to put in; to adjust; to focus to engage; to stop; to suspend; to set in; (mil.) to enlist; (rad.) to tune in **Arbeit — to strike; Betrieb — to close down; sich — to appear**

Einstellung f. adjustment; hiring (workers); cessation; strike; shut-down (mil.) enlistment; tuning-in; attitude opinion

einstimmen v. to join in; to agree with, to consent to; to harmonize

einstossen v. to push (oder smash) in

einstreichen v. to pocket, to rake in (money)

einstudieren v. to study; to rehearse

einstürmen v. to assail; to rush upon

Einsturz m. collapse; cave-in

einstürzen v. to collapse; to tumble down

Eintänzer m. gigolo

eintauchen r. to dip in; to immerse

eintauschen v. to exchange, to get in exchange

einteilen r. to divide; to distribute; to classify; to calibrate; to budget

Eintrag *m.* earnings, proceeds, gain; damage, detriment; **-ung** *f.* entry; registration

eintragen *v.* to carry in; to enter, to register; to yield

einträglich *adj.* lucrative, profitable

eintränken *v.* to steep, to impregnate

eintreffen *v.* to arrive; to coincide; to happen, to be fulfilled

eintreiben *v.* to drive in (*oder* home); to collect (debts); to exact (payment)

eintreten *v.* to enter, to step in; to join; to occur, to take place; to intercede (for); to act as substitute; to kick in

Eintritt *m.* entering, entry; entrance, admission; commencement; setting in; (mil.) enlistment; **-skarte** *f.* admission ticket

eintrocknen *v.* to dry in (*oder* up)

eintunken *v.* to dip in; to sop; to dunk

einüben *v.* to practice; to exercise; to drill

einverleiben *v.* to incorporate, to embody

Einvernehmen *neu.* understanding; agreement; **sich ins — setzen** to bring to an understanding

einverstanden! *interj.* agreed! — **sein** to agree

Einwand *m.* objection, protest

Einwanderer *m.* immigrant

einwandern *v.* to immigrate

Einwanderung *f.* immigration

einwärts *adv.* inward(s)

einwechseln *v.* to change; to cash

einweichen *v.* to soak, to steep

einweihen *v.* to initiate; to ordain; to consecrate; to inaugurate

einwenden *v.* to object, to demur

einwerfen *v.* to throw in; to interject, to object

einwickeln *v.* to wrap up; to envelop; to curl (hair); (coll.) to cause to believe

einwilligen *v.* to consent; to agree; to acquiesce

einwirken *v.* to interweave; to influence

einwohnen *v.* to lodge with; **sich —** to begin to feel at home

Einwohnerschaft *f.* inhabitants; population

einzahlen *v.* to pay in, to deposit

einzäunen *v.* to fence in; to enclose

einzeichnen *v.* to draw (*oder* mark) in; **sich —** to enter one's name; to subscribe

Einzel: **-fall** *m.* individual case; **-haft** *f.* solitary confinement; **-handel** *m.* retail trade (*oder* sale); **-heit** *f.* singularity; detail; **-heiten** *f. pl.* particulars; **-spiel** *neu.* (tennis) singles; **-wesen** *neu.* individual being

einzeln *adj.* odd, single; individual

einziehen *v.* to draw (*oder* pull) in; to move (*oder* march) into; to call in; to collect; to confiscate, to seize; (naut.) to furl; to absorb, to soak

Einzug *m.* solemn entrance; moving

Eis *neu.* ice, ice cream; (mus.) E sharp; **-bahn** *f.* skating-rink; **-bär** *m.* polar bear; **-bein** *neu.* pig's knuckles; **-decke** *f.* sheet of ice; **-gang** *m.* drift (clear break up) of ice; **-händler** *m.* iceman;

-lauf *m.*, **-laufen** *neu.* skating; **-läufer** *m.* skater; **-maschine** *f.* freezer; **-meer** *neu.* polar sea; **-picke** *f.* ice pick; **-regen** *m.* sleet; **-scholle** *f.* floe; **-schrank** *m.* refrigerator; **-strom** *m.* glacier; **-zacken** *m.*, **-zapfen** *m.* icicle

eis: **-en** *v.* to turn into ice; **-grau** *adj.* hoary with age; **-ig** *adj.* icy, covered with (*oder* cold as) ice; **-laufen** to skate

Eisen *neu.* iron; iron instrument; **Not bricht —** necessity knows no law; **zum alten —** werfen to scrap; **-abfälle** *m. pl.* scrap iron; **-beton** *m.* reinforced concrete; **-blech** *neu.* sheet-iron; **-erz** *neu.* iron ore; **-fresser** *m.* (coll.) braggart, bully; **-guss** *m.* iron casting; **-hammer** *m.* sledge hammer; **-hütte** *f.* iron works; forge; **-walzwerk** *neu.* iron rolling mill; **-ware** *f.* hardware

Eisenbahn *f.* railroad; **-abteil** *neu.* railroad compartment; **-er** *m.* railroad man; **-fahrt** *f.* railroad trip; **-netz** *neu.* railroad system; **-schwellen** *f. pl.* sleepers; **-übergang** *m.* railway crossing; **-zug** *m.* train

eisern *adj.* iron; hard, stern; **-e Lunge** *f.* iron lung; **-er Bestand** reserve for emergencies

eitel *adj.* vain; conceited; futile, empty

Eiter *m.* pus, matter; **-beule** *f.* abcess

eitern *v.* to fester, to suppurate, to ulcerate

Ekel *m.* nausea, disgust; (coll.) nasty fellow

ekelhaft *adj.* nauseous; disgusting, loathsome

ekeln *v.* to nauseate; to loathe; **es ekelt mich** I am nauseated

Eklipse *f.* eclipse

Ekstase *f.* ecstasy

Ekzem *neu.* eczema

Elastizität *f.* elasticity

Elch *m.* elk

Elefant *m.* elephant; **-enrüssel** *m.* elephant's trunk; **-enzahn** *m.* elephant's tusk

Eleganz *f.* elegance

Elegie *f.* elegy

Elektriker *m.* electrician

elektrisch *adj.* electric(al)

elektrisieren *v.* to electrify; to thrill

Elektrizität *f.* electricity

Elektro: **-lyse** *f.* electrolysis; **-technik** *f.* electrical engineering

Elektronenbeschleuniger *m.* cyclotron; **-gehirn** *neu.* Univac

Element *neu.* element; (elec.) cell

Elementar: **-buch** *neu.* primer; **-schule** *f.* elementary school

Elend *neu.* misery, distress, want; **graues —** (coll.) the blues; **-er** *m.* wretch

elend *adj.* miserable, forlorn; wretched; in distress; indigent; despicable; ill

Elf *f.*, **Elfer** *m.* eleven; **-tel** *neu.* eleventh part

elf *adj.* eleven

Elfenbein *neu.* ivory

elfenbeinern *adj.* ivory

Elle *f.* ell (seventh part of yard); ulna

Ell(en)bogen *m.* elbow

Elsasz neu. Alsace

Elster f. magpie

elterlich adj. parental

Eltern pl. parents

elternlos adj. orphaned

Email neu. enamel

emanzipieren v. to emancipate

Emigrant m. emigrant

Empfang m. reception; receipt; **–sapparat** m. receiver; **–sdame** f. receptionist; **–sschein** m. receipt; **–störung** f. (rad.) interference

empfangen v. to receive; to welcome; to conceive; to become pregnant

Empfänger m. receiver; recipient; consignee; acceptor; payee; receiving instrument

Empfängnis f. conception

empfehlen v. to commend; to give regards (to); **es empfiehlt sich** it is advisable; **sich –** to take leave; to offer one's services; **–swert** adj. commendable; worthy of recommendation

Empfehlung f. recommendation; compliments; **–sschreiben** neu. letter of introduction

empfind: **–en** v. to experience; to feel; to perceive; **übel –en** to take as an offense; **–lich** adj. sensitive; painful, touchy; **–sam** adj. sentimental, sensitive, delicate; **–ungslos** adj. unfeeling, apathetic

Empfindung f. feeling; perception, sensation; sentiment; **–slosigkeit** f. apathy, callousness

empor adv. up, upward(s); on high; aloft; **–blicken** to look up; **–ragen** to tower; **–streben** to strive upwards; to aspire

Empore f. (arch.) gallery, choir

empören v. to enrage, to excite; to rouse to anger; **sich –** to become furious; to rebel

Empörer m. rebel, insurgent

Emporkömmling m. upstart

Empörung f. insurrection; indignation

emsig adj. assiduous, industrious; active, busy

End: **–bahnhof** m. (rail.) terminal; **–e** neu. end; conclusion; aim; finale; death; (antler) point; **–ergebnis** neu. final result; **–ung** f. ending, termination; **–ziel** neu. final aim; **–zweck** m. ultimate object, main design

end: **–gültig** adj. conclusive, final, definite; **–(ig)en** v. to end, to finish; to cease; to terminate; to conclude; to expire, to die; **–lich** adj. finite; final; **–lich** adv. at last; finally; **–los** adj. endless, infinite

Energie f. energy, vigor

energisch adj. energetic, vigorous

eng adj. narrow; tight, close; intimate; im **–eren Sinne** strictly speaking; **–anschliessend** adj. tight-fitting; **–befreundet** adj. very intimate; **–brüstig** adj. asthmatic; **–herzig** adj. narrow-minded; straitlaced; **–maschig** adj. close-meshed; **–spurig** adj. (rail.) narrow-gauge

Enge f. narrowness, tightness; defile; strait; **in die – treiben** to corner

Engel m. angel; **–schar** f. host of angels; **–sgruss** m. (rel.) Hail Mary

engelhaft adj. angelic

Engländer m. Englishman; monkey wrench

englisch adj. English; **–e Krankheit** rickets

Engpass m. narrow pass, defile, strait

en gros adv. wholesale

Enkel m. grandson; **–in** f. granddaughter; **–kind** neu. grandchild

enorm adj. enormous

entarten v. to degenerate, to deteriorate

entäussern v. **sich –** to part with; to discard; to divest oneself of

entbehren v. to do without; to miss, to lack; **ich kann ihn nicht –** I cannot spare him

entbehrlich adj. dispensable; superfluous

Entbehrung f. privation, want

entbieten v. to send for, to summon; to offer, to present

entbinden v. to unbind, to untie; to release, to disengage, to absolve; to give birth

Entbindung f. dispensation; release; childbirth; **–sanstalt** f. maternity hospital

entblättern v. to strip of leaves; to defoliate

entblössen v. to bare, to uncover; to unsheathe

Entblössung f. deprivation, destitution

entbrennen v. to catch fire, to blaze up; to be inflamed

entdecken v. to discover, to explore; to find out, to detect; **sich –** to disclose (oder reveal) oneself

Ente f. duck; (coll.) hoax

entehren v. to dishonor; to degrade, to disgrace; to deflower

enteilen v. to hurry away; to slip away

enteisen v. to de-ice

enterben v. to disinherit

Enterhaken m. (naut.) grappling iron

Enterich m. drake

entfachen v. to inflame; to kindle

entfahren v. to escape from; to slip out of

entfallen v. to fall out of; to slip from (memory); **– auf** to fall to (as share)

entfalten v. to unfold, to unfurl; to burst into bloom; to develop; to display

entfärben v. to discolor; **sich –** to change color; to grow pale

entfernen v. to remove; to take away; to alienate; **sich –** to go away, to withdraw, to depart, to slip away; to deviate (from)

entfernt adj. far away; remote, distant

Entfernung f. distance, range; withdrawal; removal; **–smesser** m. rangefinder

entfesseln v. to unchain; to set free

entflammen v. to inflame; to kindle

entfliehen v. to flee; to escape; to pass (time)

entfremden v. to alienate; to estrange

entführen v. to carry off; to elope (with); to kidnap

entgegen adv. and prep. towards; opposed to; against; contrary to; **–arbeiten** to

work against; to counteract; **–blicken**
to look towards (*oder* forward to);
–geh(e)n to go to meet; to face (danger); **–gesetzt** *prep.* and *adj.* opposite,
contrary; **–halten** to hold toward; to
object to; to contrast with; **–kommen**
v. to come to meet; to meet halfway;
to obviate; **–kommend** *adj.* obliging,
accommodating; **–laufen** *v.* to run towards; to oppose; to clash with; **–nehmen** *v.* to accept, to receive; **–rücken**
to push towards, to march against;
–sehen to look forward to; to expect;
–setzen *v.* to oppose; to contrast with;
–steh(e)n *v.* to face; to be opposed to;
–stellen *v.* to set against; to contrast
with; to oppose; **–wirken** *v.* to counteract; to check; (med.) to repel; **–ziehen**
v. to advance, to march towards
entgegnen *v.* to answer, to reply; to retort
entgeh(e)n *v.* to escape, to elude
entgelt *neu.* and *m.* remuneration; recompense, compensation
entgelten *v.* to pay (*oder* atone) for
entgleisen *v.* to derail; to make a slip
(*oder* mistake)
entgleiten *v.* to slip away, to escape from
entgräten *v.* to bone (fish)
enthalten *v.* to contain, to hold; to comprise, to include; **sich —** to abstain
from
enthaltsam *adj.* abstemious; continent;
–keit *f.* abstinence
enthaupten *v.* to behead, to decapitate
entheben *v.* to remove (from office)
entheiligen *v.* to desecrate, to profane
enthüllen *v.* to unveil; to reveal, to disclose
enthusiasmus *m.* enthusiasm
enthusiastisch *adj.* enthusiastic
entkleiden *v.* to undress, to disrobe; to
deprive (*oder* divest) of
entkleideakt *m.* striptease
entkommen *v.* to escape
entkorken *v.* to uncork
entkräften *v.* to debilitate, to enervate;
to exhaust; to invalidate; to refute
entladen *v.* to unload; to explode, to discharge
entlang *adv.* along; by the side of
entlassen *v.* to discharge, to dismiss
entlasten *v.* to unburden; to relieve; to
exonerate
entlastung *f.* relief; exoneration; (com.)
crediting; **–szeuge** *m.* witness for the
defense
entlaufen *v.* to run away; to desert
entlausen *v.* to delouse
entledigen *v.* **sich —** to get rid of; **sich
eines Auftrages —** to execute one's
commission; **sich eines Versprechens
—** to keep one's word
entleeren *v.* to empty; to evacuate; to
void
entlegen *adj.* distant, remote
entlehnen *v.* to borrow; to lend; to plagiarize
entleiben *v.* **sich —** to commit suicide
entlocken *v.* to draw, to elicit, to wheedle
entmannen *v.* to castrate; to emasculate

entmenscht *adj.* inhuman; brutal
entmutigen *v.* to discourage, to dishearten
entnehmen *v.* to take out; to understand
entpuppen *v.*, **sich —** to burst from the
cocoon; to reveal as; to turn out to be
entraffen *v.* to snatch from; **sich —** to disengage oneself from
enträtseln *v.* to decipher; to solve
entreissen *v.* to snatch from; to rescue
entrichten *v.* to pay
entrinnen *v.* to run (*oder* slip) away; to
escape
entrollen *v.* to roll down (*oder* away); to
unroll
entrücken *v.* to remove from (sight); to
put beyond the reach of; to enrapture
entrüsten *v.* to make indignant; **sich —** to
become angry
entsagen *v.* to renounce; to waive; to
relinquish, to abdicate
entschädigen *v.* to compensate, to indemnify; to reimburse
entscheiden *v.* to decide; to arbitrate; to
pass sentence; **–d** *adj.* decisive; final;
critical
entschieden *adj.* decided; determined,
resolute
entschlafen *v.* to fall asleep; to pass away,
to die
entschliessen *v.* to decide, to determine;
sich — to make up one's mind
entschlossen *adj.* determined, resolute
entschlummern *v.* to fall asleep; to doze
off; to die (gently)
Entschluss *m.* resolution; determination
entschuldigen *v.* to excuse; **sich —** to
apologize; **— Sie!** I beg your pardon!
entschwinden *v.* to disappear, to vanish
entseelt *adj.* dead, lifeless
entsetzen *v.* to dismiss; to depose; to
relieve; **sich —** to be horrified (*oder*
terrified)
Entsetzen *neu.* terror; horror; dismissal,
relief
entsetzlich *adj.* frightful, horrible, shocking
entsinnen *v.* **sich —** to recollect, to remember
Entspannung *f.* relaxation, easement; rest,
recreation
entspinnen *v.* **sich —** to begin; to develop
entsprechen *v.* to correspond to, to be
analogous to; **–d** *adj.* adequate, appropriate; corresponding; pertinent
entspringen *v.* to spring (*oder* arise) from;
to descend from, to originate in; to
escape
entstammen *v.* to descend from
entsteh(e)n *v.* to arise; to originate; to
result from; to break out (fire, etc.)
entstellen *v.* to disfigure, to deform; to
distort, to misrepresent, to garble
entsühnen *v.* to absolve
enttäuschen *v.* to disappoint, to disillusion
entvölkern *v.* to depopulate
entwachsen *v.* to outgrow
Entwaffnung *f.* disarmament
Entwarnung *f.* all-clear signal
entweder *conj.* either; **— oder** either . . .
or

entweichen v. to escape; to flee; to vanish
entweihen v. to desecrate, to profane
entwenden v. to misappropriate, to embezzle
entwerfen v. to draft; to sketch; to outline
entwickeln v. to develop; to evolve; (mil.) to deploy; to explain
Entwickler m. (phot.) developer
Entwicklungszeit f. adolescence
entwinden v. to wrest from; sich — to extricate oneself
entwischen v. to slip away, to escape
entwöhnen v. to wean; to disaccustom
Entwurf m. draft; design, plan; project
entwurzeln v. to uproot
entziehen v. to withhold, to deprive of; sich — to shun, to withdraw from
Entziehung f. deprivation; withholding; -skur f. treatment (for drug addicts, etc.)
entziffern v. to decode, to decipher
entzücken v. to enchant, to delight; to enrapture
Entzücken neu. rapture, delight; ecstasy
entzünden v. to kindle; sich — to catch fire; (med.) to become inflamed
Entzündung f. ignition; inflammation
entzwei adv. in two, asunder; broken, torn; -en v. to disunite, to estrange; sich -en to quarrel; to become alienated; -geh(e)n v. to break; to go to pieces; -schlagen v. to smash
Epidemie f. epidemic
Epik f. epic poetry; -er m. epic poet
epileptisch adj. epileptic
Epistel neu. and f. epistle
Epoche f. epoch
er pron. he; — selbst he himself
erachten v. to consider, to deem; meines -s in my opinion
Erb: -adel m. hereditary nobility; -begräbnis neu. family lot in a cemetery; -e m. heir; successor; -e neu. heritage, inheritance; -feind m. sworn foe; (fig.) devil; -folge f. hereditary succession; -krankheit f. hereditary disease; -lasser m. testator; -recht neu. right of succession; -schaft f. inheritance, legacy; -schaftsgericht neu. probate court; -stück neu. heirloom; -sünde original sin; -teil neu. share of an inheritance
erb: -en v. to inherit; -eigen adj., -lich adj. hereditary
erbarmen v. sich — to pity; to have mercy
Erbarmen neu. compassion, pity; mercy
erbärmlich adj. miserable; contemptible
erbarmungslos adj. pitiless, merciless
erbauen v. to build, to erect; (fig.) to edify
erbeben v. to tremble
erbieten v. to offer; to volunteer
erbitten v. to beg (oder ask) for; to solicit
erbittern v. to embitter; to exasperate
erblassen, erbleichen v. to grow pale; to fade, (poet.) to die
erblicken v. to see; to catch sight of
erblinden v. to grow blind
Erbse f. pea
Erd: -apfel m. (dial., poet.) potato; -arbeit f. excavation, digging; -ball

m. globe; -beben neu. earthquake; -beere f. strawberry; -boden m. soil; ground; -ferne (höchster Punkt der Raketenflugbahn) f. apogee; -gas neu. natural gas; -geist m. gnome; -geschoss neu. ground floor; -kreisbahn f. orbit; -kunde f. geography; -leitung f. earth connection; ground wire; -nuss f. peanut; -öl neu. petroleum; -reich neu. earth; (bibl.) Earthly Kingdom; -rinde f. earth's crust; -rutsch m. landslide; -schluss m. (elec.) ground; -scholle clod; -teil m. continent
erdenken v. to conceive; to devise, to invent
erdenklich adj. conceivable, imaginable
erdichten v. to invent, to imagine
erdolchen v. to stab to death
erdrosseln v. to strangle; to throttle
erdrücken v. to crush; to overwhelm
erdulden v. to endure, to suffer
ereignen v. sich — to happen, to come to pass
Ereignis neu. event, occurrence
ereilen v. to catch up with; to overtake
Eremit m. hermit
erfahren v. to hear, to learn; to experience; — adj. experienced; expert
Erfahrung f. experience; empirical knowledge; in — bringen to ascertain, to hear, to learn
erfahrungsgemäss adv. from experience
erfassen v. to seize, to take hold of; to comprehend
erfinden to invent; to think out, to conceive
erfinderisch adj. inventive; resourceful, creative; Not macht — necessity is the mother of invention
Erfindung f. invention; fiction
erflehen v. to implore for; to entreat
Erfolg m. result, outcome; success
erfolgen v. to ensue; to follow (from); to result; to take place
erfolgreich adj. successful, effective
erforderlich adj. necessary, requisite
erfordern v. to require; to demand
Erfordernis neu. requirement, presupposition
erforschen v. to explore; to search into
erfragen v. to find out by questioning
erfrechen v. sich — to have the impudence
erfreuen v. to delight, to gladden; to cheer; sich — to rejoice, to enjoy oneself
erfreulich adj. gratifying; delightful, pleasing; -erweise adv. fortunately
erfrieren v. to freeze to death
Erfrierung f. frost-bite
erfrischen v. to refresh; to recreate
erfüllen v. to fulfill, to perform; to fill up, to imbue, to accomplish, to keep (promise); sich — to be realized (oder fulfilled)
ergänzen v. to complete; to supplement; to replenish; to restore
Ergeb: -enheit f. devotion; resignation; -nis neu. result; outcome; -ung f. surrender

geben v. to yield, to prove; **sich —** submit; to surrender; to result from; to devote oneself to; to indulge in; to be resigned (to)

geh(e)n v. to fare (well oder ill); to be issued (oder promulgated); **sich —** to stroll; to indulge in

giebig adj. productive; abundant; lucrative

giessen v. to pour forth (oder out); **sich — to** discharge; to flow into

götzen v. to entertain, to delight; **sich — to** enjoy oneself

götzlich adj. amusing, diverting, droll

greifen v. to seize; to arrest; to take (up); to choose (profession); to touch; **-d** adj. touching; gripping

griffen adj. moved (oder touched)

griffenheit f. emotion

grimmen v. to become angry (oder furious)

gründen v. to fathom; to get to the bottom of

guss m. discharge; effusion; gush

haben adj. elevated; in relief; eminent; exalted; sublime; **sich — fühlen über etwas** to feel above (oder superior) to something

halten v. to obtain, to receive; to preserve, to maintain, to support; **gut —** in good condition (oder repair); **sich — von** to subsist on

hängen v. to hang; **sich —** to hang oneself

härten v. to harden; to confirm, to corroborate

haschen v. to catch, to seize, to snatch

heben v. to lift up, to heave; to elevate; to raise; to bring (suit); to collect (taxes); to extol, to praise; **sich — to** ise; to arise; to rebel

eblich adj. considerable; important; weighty

eitern v. to amuse, to cheer

ellen v. to illuminate; to elucidate; to become clear (oder evident)

itzen v. to heat; to inflame; **sich —** to become heated; to fly into a passion

hen v. to raise, to elevate; to increase; to exalt; (mus.) to raise by a sharp

olen v. **sich —** to recover, to improve; om.) to rally

olung f. recovery, recreation, relaxa-

iren v. to give ear; to hear, to grant

a f. heather

nern v. to remind; **sich —** to recollect, remember

nerung f. recollection, remembrance; miniscence; **zur — an** in memory of

lten v. to grow cold

lten v. to chill; **sich —** to catch a cold

ufen v. to buy; to bribe

nn: **-tnis** f. cognition; knowledge, rception, understanding; (law) ver-et; **-ung** f. recognition; (bibl.) carnal owledge; **-ungsmarke** f. identification badge; **-ungswort** neu. watchword ennen v. to recognize; to perceive; to ealize; to understand; (com.) to credit;

(law) to judge; (med.) to diagnose

erkenntlich adj. recognizable; grateful

Erker m. bay window

erklären v. to explain; to expound, to interpret; to comment; to proclaim, to declare; **sich —** to avow; to propose (marriage)

Erklärung f. explanation; elucidation, interpretation, commentary; manifesto; proposal

erklecklich adj. sufficient; considerable

erklettern, erklimmen v. to climb; to clamber up; to scale; to ascend to the top

erkoren adj. chosen, selected

erkundigen v. **sich — (nach)** to inquire about

Erkundigung f. inquiry

erlangen v. to attain, to achieve; to obtain

Erlass m. dispensation, indulgence; remission; exemption, deduction; writ; decree, edict

erlassen v. to decree, to publish; to remit, to abate; to release; to exempt (from)

erlauben v. to allow, to permit, to license; **sich —** to dare, to presume

Erlaubnis f. permission; leave; dispensation; license; **-schein** m. permit

erläutern v. to explain, to elucidate; to illustrate; to comment

Erle f. alder

erleben v. to live to see; to experience

Erlebnis neu. experience; event; adventure

erledigen v. to settle, to finish; to carry through; to dispatch, to execute

erlegen v. to kill; to lay down; to deposit

erleichtern v. to facilitate, to ease; to lighten; to alleviate, to relieve; (coll.) to steal (from)

erleiden v. to suffer; to bear, to endure

erlernen v. to learn, to acquire, to master

erlesen v. to choose, to select; **—** adj. chosen; select, exquisite, choice

erleuchten v. to light up; to illuminate; to enlighten, to inspire

erliegen v. to be defeated; to succumb, to die

erlogen adj. fabricated, false, untrue; acquired by lying

Erlös m. proceeds; **-er** m. deliverer, liberator; Redeemer; **-ung** f. deliverance; redemption

erlöschen v. to go out, to expire; to cease; to die (oder fade) away; to lapse

erlösen v. to deliver, to free; to redeem

ermächtigen v. to authorize, to empower

ermahnen v. to admonish, to exhort, to warn

ermangeln v. to be deficient (oder lacking)

ermannen v. **sich —** to summon up courage

ermässigen v. to moderate; to abate; to reduce

ermatten v. to fatigue; to become weary

ermessen v. to judge; to consider; to gauge

ermöglichen v. to make possible (oder feasible)

ermorden v. to murder, to assassinate

ermüden *v.* to tire, to weary; to become tired (*oder* weary)

ermuntern *v.* to wake (*oder* cheer) up; to encourage, to rouse, to incite

ermutigen *v.* to encourage; to summon up courage

ernähren *v.* to nourish; to maintain, to support; **sich —** to subsist on; to make a living

ernennen *v.* to appoint, to nominate

erneue(r)n *v.* to renew, to renovate; to revive

erniedrigen *v.* to lower; to degrade, to humble; to humiliate; (mus.) to flatten

Ernst *m.* seriousness; gravity; sternness

ernst(haft) *adj.* earnest, serious; grave, stern

Ernte *f.* harvest; crop; (fig.) reward; **-dankfest** *neu.* thanksgiving; **-monat** *m.* August

ernten *v.* to harvest; to gather in; to reap

ernüchtern *v.* to make sober; to disillusion; **sich —** to sober up

erobern *v.* to conquer, to capture, to captivate

eröffnen *v.* to open; to inaugurate; to begin; to disclose; to inform

erörtern *v.* to consider; to discuss thoroughly

erotisch *adj.* erotic

erpicht *adj.* intent (upon); eager (for)

erpressen *v.* to blackmail, to extort

erproben *v.* to test, to try

erquicken *v.* to refresh, to revive, to quicken

erquicklich *adj.* refreshing; invigorating

erraten *v.* to guess, to conjecture; to solve

Erreg: **-er** *m.* exciter, agitator; (med.) germ; (phys.) agent; **-theit** *f.* excitement; irritation; **-ung** *f.* excitation, provocation

erregbar *adj.* excitable, irritable; sensitive

erregen *v.* to excite, to provoke; to agitate; to stir up; **-des Mittel** (med.) stimulant

erreichen *v.* to reach; to attain; to accomplish; to catch (train)

erretten *v.* to rescue, to save; to redeem

errichten *v.* to erect, to establish, to found

erringen *v.* to obtain by struggling (*oder* wrestling); to gain, to win; to achieve

erröten *v.* to blush

Errungenschaft *f.* achievement; acquisition

Ersatz *m.* reparation; compensation; substitute; replacement, reserve; **-mann** *m.* substitute, proxy; **-rad** *neu.* spare wheel (*oder* tire); **-stoff** *m.* substitute; **-stück** *neu.*, **-teil** *neu.* spare part; **-wahl** *f.* by election

ersaufen *v.* (coll.) to be drowned; to flood

ersäufen *v.* (coll.) to drown

erschaffen *v.* to create; to produce, to make

erschallen *v.* to resound; **— lassen** to spread

erschau(d)ern *v.* to shudder, to tremble (with horror)

erscheinen *v.* to appear; to be published; to seem

Erscheinung *f.* appearance; phenomeno vision; apparition; publication; sym tom

erschiessen *v.* to shoot (dead)

erschlaffen *v.* to languish; to slacken; enervate; to relax

erschlagen *v.* to slay, to kill, to murd

erschliessen *v.* to unlock; to open; to d close; to make accessible

erschöpfen *v.* to exhaust; (fig.) to dra

erschrecken *v.* to frighten, to alarm, startle

erschüttern *v.* to shake; to convulse; affect deeply, to shock

Erschütterung *f.* shaking, shock; (mee concussion

erschweren *v.* to render difficult; to a gravate; to obstruct

erschwingen *v.* to attain with difficult to manage, to afford

ersehen *v.* to see; to observe, to learn; choose, to select

ersehnen *v.* to long (*oder* yearn) for; desire

ersetz: **-bar** *adj.*, **-setzlich** *adj.* reparabl **nicht -bar** irreparable; **-en** *v.* to replac to make amends; to reimburse; to **i** deunify; to repair, to restore

ersichtlich *adj.* evident; obvious; clea plain

ersinnen *v.* to think out; to contrive, devise

ersparen *v.* to save, to spare, to economi

Ersparnis *f.*, Ersparung *f.* saving(economy

erspriesslich *adj.* profitable; beneficial

erst *adv.* (at) first; above all; just; n till; only; **-e** *adj.* first; foremost, prin leading, der **-ere** the former; **eben** just now; **— recht** all the more; **fürs** for the present; **-ens** *adv.* in the fir place. to begin with; **-genannt a** aforementioned; **-klassig** *adj.* fi class; **-malig** *adj.* first-time; **-mals a** for the first time

erstarren *v.* to stiffen; to congeal, to free

erstatten *v.* to restore, to replace; to co pensate, to recompense; Bericht **—** make a report; wieder **—** to refu

erstaunen *v.* to astonish; to amaze; to amazed (*oder* astonished)

Erstaunen *neu.* amazement, astonishme

erstaunlich *adj.* amazing, astonishing

erstechen *v.* to stab to death

ersteigen *v.* to ascend, to climb, to mou

ersticken *v.* to suffocate; to choke; stifle; to suppress; im Keime **—** to n in the bud

Erstickung *f.* asphyxiation

erstreben *v.* to aspire; to strive f **-swert** *adj.* desirable

erstrecken *v.* to extend; to reach, stretch

erstürmen *v.* to take by storm (*oder* sault)

ersuchen *v.* to beseech, to implore; request

ertappen *v.* to catch, to detect, to surpr

erteilen *v.* to bestow on; to grant; to gi to impart; (rel.) to administer, to **d** pense

ertönen v. to (re)sound

ertöten v. to deaden; to mortify

Ertrag m. yield; -sfähigkeit f. productivity

Erträgnis neu. produce; proceeds; profit

ertragen v. to bear, to endure, to tolerate

erträglich adj. bearable, endurable, tolerable

ertränken v. to drown

ertrinken v. to be drowned

ertrotzen v. to get by obstinacy (oder under duress)

erübrigen v. to save, to lay (oder put) by; sich — to be superfluous (oder unnecessary)

erwachen v. to awake; to arise (to new life)

erwachsen v. to grow up; to spring (from); to arise, to accrue from; — adj. adult, grown-up

erwägen v. to ponder; to consider; to discuss

erwählen v. to choose, to select; to elect

erwähnen v. to mention; to call to notice

erwärmen v. to warm, to heat; sich — für to take a lively interest in

erwarten v. to await; to expect

erwecken v. to awaken, to rouse; to resuscitate; to stir up, to arouse

erwehren v. sich — to defend oneself (against); to restrain (tears), ich kann mich des Lachens nicht — I cannot help laughing

erweichen v. to soften; to move, to touch

erweisen v. to render, to show; jemandem einen Gefallen — to do someone a favor; sich — to prove, to turn out

erweitern v. to enlarge, to widen; to expand, to extend, to amplify

Erwerb m. acquisition; gain; earnings; -slosenunterstützung f. unemployment compensation

erwerben v. to acquire, to earn, to gain

erwidern v. to reply, to retort; to requite; to reciprocate; to return

erwiesenermassen adv. as has been proved

erwirken v. to effect; to bring about; to procure

erwischen v. (coll.) to catch, to detect

erwünscht adj. desired; agreeable, welcome

erwürgen v. to strangle, to throttle

Erz neu. metal; ore, bronze, brass; -ader f. vein of ore; -förderung f. output of ore; -giesserei f. brass (oder bronze) foundry; -grube f. mine; -hütte f. smeltery; -kunde f. metallurgy, minéralogy

Erz-: -betrüger m., -gauner m. extraordinary scoundrel; -bischof m. archbishop; -bistum neu. archbishopric; -engel m. archangel; -herzog m. archduke; -kämmerer m., -kanzler m. Lord High Chamberlain (oder Chancellor); -tugend f. cardinal virtue

erzählen v. to relate; to report; to narrate; (coll.) to make believe

Erzähler m. narrator; novelist; writer;

story teller

erzeigen v. to show, to render; to prove

erzeugen v. to beget, to procreate; to manufacture, to produce; to generate; to breed

Erzeuger m. creator, father; producer

Erzeugnis neu. produce; product; production

erziehen v. to educate; to rear; to train

Erzieher m. educator; teacher, tutor

Erziehungsanstalt f. educational establishment

erzielen v. to obtain; to realize (profit)

erzürnen v. to anger, sich — to become angry

erzwingen v. to force, to extort (from)

erzwungen adj. forced, feigned, simulated

es pron. it; er sagt — he says so; — gibt there is

Esche f. ash (tree)

Esel m. donkey, ass; (coll.) blockhead, dunce; -ei f. stupid blunder, stupidity; -sbrücke f. pony (students); -sgeschrei neu. braying; -sohr neu. (book) dog-ear

Espe f. aspen (tree)

Ess-: -en neu. food; meal; dish; -gelage neu. banquet, feast; -gier f. gluttony; -löffel m. tablespoon; -lust f. appetite; -waren f. pl. eatables, provisions

essbar adj. edible

Esse f. chimney, flue; forge

essen v. to eat, to dine; (mil.) to mess

Essig m. vinegar; -gurke f. pickled cucumber; -säure f. acetic acid

Estland neu. Esthonia

Estrade f. platform

Estrich m. plaster (oder clay, cement) floor

etablieren v. to establish, to set up

Etage f. floor, story; -re f. bookshelf, whatnot

Etat m. budget, estimate; financial statement; -sjahr neu. financial year

Ethik f. ethics

ethisch adj. ethical

Etikette f. etiquette; — neu. label, ticket

etliche pron. some, a few; several

etwa adv. about, nearly; perhaps; -ig adj. eventual; contingent

etwas pron. something; — adj. some, any; — adv. somewhat; a little

Etzel m. Attila

euch pron. pl. (to) you

euer adj. pl. your; — adv. yours

Eule f. owl; -nspiegelei f. tomfoolery; practical joke

eur-: -esgleichen pron. like you, of your kind; -ethalben adv., -etwegen adv., -etwillen adv. for your sake, on your account; -ig pron. yours

Europa neu. Europe

Euter neu. udder

e.V. (eingetragener Verein) m. Inc. (Incorporated)

evangelisch adj. evangelical, protestant

Evangelium neu. (rel.) gospel

eventuell adj. possible; — adv. possibly, perhaps; under certain circumstances

ewig adj. eternal; endless, perpetual; (coll.) very long; auf — forevermore;

der —e Jude the wandering Jew; **immer und —** for ever and ever

Examen *neu.* examination

examinieren *v.* to examine

Exempel *neu.* example; problem, sum

exemplarisch *adj.* exemplary; excellent

exerzieren *v.* (mil.) to drill, to train

Exerzitium *neu.* (educ.) homework; (rel.) devotional exercise, meditation

Exil *neu.* exile

existieren *v.* to exist, to subsist, to be

exkommunizieren *v.* to excommunicate

expedieren *v.* to dispatch, to forward

Expedition *f.* expedition; dispatching, forwarding; shipping department

Experiment *neu.* experiment

experimentieren *v.* to experiment

exportieren *v.* to export

Extrablatt *neu.* special edition, supplement

Extremitäten *f. pl.* (anat.) extremities

exzentrisch *adj.* eccentric

Exzess *m.* excess

F

Fabel *f.* fable; (lit.) plot; tale, fiction

fabelhaft *adj.* fabulous; incredible, marvelous

Fabrik *f.* factory, mill, plant; **—ant** *m.* manufacturer; **—at** *neu.* manufactured product; **—ation** *f.* manufacturing; **—zeichen** *neu.* trade-mark

fabrizieren *v.* to manufacture, to fabricate

Facette *f.* facet

Fach *neu.* compartment, drawer, pigeonhole; branch, department, speciality; subject; line, profession, trade; **—ausdruck** *m.* technical term; **—gelehrte** *m.* specialist; **—mann** *m.* expert; **—ordnung** *f.* classification; **—schule** *f.* professional school; **—simpelei** *f.* shop talk; **—studium** *neu.* professional study; **—werk** *neu.* (arch.) framework; **—wissenschaft** *f.* technical knowledge; **—zeitschrift** *f.* technical journal

fach: **—kundig** *adj.*, **—männisch** *adj.* competent, expert; **—simpeln** *v.* to talk shop

fächeln *v.* to fan

Fächer *m.* fan; **—palme** *f.* fan palm

Fackel *f.* torch; **—zug** *m.* torchlight procession

fackeln *v.* to flicker; to hesitate

Façon, Fasson *f.* fashion, manner, pattern

fad(e) *adj.* insipid; stale; dull, flat

Faden *m.* thread; string, twine; filament; fiber; (naut.) fathom; **keinen trockenen — am Leibe haben** to be wet to the skin; **—nudeln** *f. pl.* vermicelli

fadenscheinig *adj.* threadbare, shabby

Fagott *neu.* bassoon

fähig *adj.* able, capable; gifted; competent

fahl *adj.* pale, faded

Fahne *f.* flag, banner; ensign, standard, colors; vane; (feather) barbs; (typ.) galley proof; **—neid** *m.* oath of allegiance; **—nflucht** *f.* desertion; **—nflüchtige** *m.* deserter; **—nstange** *f.* flagstaff; **—nträger** *m.* standard bearer

Fähnrich *m.* (mil.) ensign; (naut.) midshipman

Fahr: **—bahn** *f.*, **—damm** *m.* roadway; **—betrieb** *m.* traffic; **—dienst** *m.* railroading; **—dienstleiter** *m.* station master; **—er** *m.* driver; **—gast** *m.* passenger; **—geld** *neu.* fare; **—gelegenheit** *f.* conveyance; **—gestell** *neu.* undercarriage; chassis; **—karte** *f.* ticket; **—kartenschalter** *m.* ticket office; **—p an** *m.* timetable; **—rad** *neu.* bicycle; **—strahl** *m.* (avi.) gunsight beam; **—strasse** *f.* highway; **—stuhl** *m.* elevator; **—t** *f.* journey, trip, drive, ride; **—wasser** *neu.* (naut.) wake; (fig.) element; **—zeug** *neu.* vehicle

fahr: **—bar** *adj.* passable, navigable; **—en** *v.* to drive, to ride, to go (by train, etc.); to convey; to fare (ill, well); **aus der Haut —en** (coll.) to hit the ceiling; **—ig** *adj.* fickle, re. —; **—lässig** *adj.* negligent, careless; **—plänmässig** *adj.* on schedule, regular

Fährte *f.* scent, track, trail; **auf falscher — sein** to be . the wrong track (*oder* at fault)

faktisch *adj.* actual, real, founded on facts

Faktotum *neu.* factotum; Jack-of-all-trades

Faktura *f.* invoice

Falke *m.* falcon; **—nbeize** *f.* falconry

Fall *m.* fall; waterfall; ruin; seduction; case, instance; **auf jeden —** in any event; **auf keinen —** on no account; **gesetzt den —** supposing that; **im —e** in case; **zu — bringen** to ruin; **zu — kommen** to be ruined; **—beil** *neu.* guillotine; **—e** *f.* trap; **—ensteller** *m.* trapper; **—gesetz** *neu.* law of gravitation; **—grube** *f.* pitfall; **—obst** *neu.* fallen fruit; **—reep** *neu.* (naut.) rope ladder, gangway; **—schirm** *m.* parachute; **—schirm-Sanitäts-personal** *m.* paramedics; **—schirmtruppen** *f. pl.* paratroopers; **—schirmspringer** *m.* parachutist; **—strick** *m.* snare, noose; **—sucht** *f.* epilepsy; **—tür** *f.* trapdoor

fall: **—en** *v.* to fall; to drop; to decrease, to go down; to be ruined (*oder* seduced); to die (in battle); **aus allen Wolken —en** to be thunderstruck; **in den Rücken —en** to attack from behind; to deceive; **in die Augen —en** to catch the eye; **in die Rede —en** to interrupt; **in Ohnmacht —en** to faint; **leicht** (*or* **schwer**) **—en** to be easy; (*oder* difficult); **—ieren** *v.* to fail; to become bankrupt; **—s** *adv.* if; in case; provided

fällen *v.* to cut, to fell; to pronounce (judgment); (chem.) to precipitate; to draw (perpendicular); to lower (bayonet); **Entscheidungen —** to make decisions

fällig *adj.* due; payable

falsch *adj.* wrong; false; incorrect; artificial; counterfeit, forged; perfidious, deceitful; **— anführen** to misquote; **— aussprechen** to mispronounce; **— schreiben** to misspell; **— schwören** to perjure; **— singen** to sing out of tune; **—e Würfel** loaded dice; **—klingend** *adj.*

dissonant, discordant

Falsch *neu.* (poet.) falsehood; **ohne —** guileless; **–heit** *f.* falsity, perfidiousness, deceit(fulness); **–münzer** *m.* forger, counterfeiter; **–spieler** *m.* cheat, cardsharp

fälschen *v.* to falsify; to adulterate; to forge; to counterfeit

Fälscher *m.* forger

fälschlicherweise *adj.* erroneously; by mistake

Falsett *neu.* falsetto

Falt: –boot *neu.* collapsible boat; **–e** *f.* fold; pleat; crease; wrinkle; **die Stirne in –en ziehen** to knit one's brow; **–enrock** *m.* pleated skirt; **–enwurf** *m.* arrangement (of draperies)

falten *v.* to fold; to crease; to wrinkle; to pleat; to clasp (hands)

Falter *m.* butterfly, moth

faltig *adj.* pleated; wrinkled

Falz *m.* fold; groove, channel, rabbet; **–bein** *neu.* paper knife (*oder* folder)

Familie *f.* family; tribe; **–nname** *m.* family name, surname

famos *adj.* famous; fine, grand, great

Fanal *neu.* beacon; signal

Fanatiker *m.* fanatic

fanatisch *adj.* fanatic(al)

Fanatismus *m.* fanaticism

fangen *v.* to catch, to capture; to seize; to hook, to trap, to snare; **sich —** to be caught (*oder* entangled); to regain security

Farb: –band *neu.* typewriter ribbon; **–e** *f.* color, tint, shade; dye, paint, stain; complexion; (cards) suit; **die –e wechseln** to change sides; **–e bekennen** (cards) to follow suit; (fig.) to show one's true colors; **–ige** *m.* nonwhite person, Negro; **–stift** *m.* colored pencil; **–ton** *m.* tint, shade

farbecht *adj.* fast, fadeless

färben *v.* to color; to stain; to dye

farbig *adj.* colored; stained

Färbung *f.* dyeing; hue, tinge; touch, shading

Farn *m.*, **Farnkraut** *neu.* fern

Fasan *m.* pheasant

Faschismus *m.* fascism

faseln *v.* to talk nonsense; to fuss

Faser *f.* fiber, filament; thread

fasern *v.* to fray, to ravel

Fass *neu.* barrel, cask; butt, tun; tub, vat; (coll.) potbelly; **das schlägt dem — den Boden aus!** that's the last straw! **frisch vom —** on draught; **–bier** *neu.* draught beer; **–binder** *m.* cooper; **–daube** *f.* stave; **–hahn** *m.* spigot; **–reifen** *m.* hoop; **–spund** *m.* bung

fass: –en *v.* to seize, to catch, to take hold; to comprise, to contain; to mount, to set; to comprehend; to grasp; **eine Meinung –en** to form an opinion; **einen Gedanken –en** to conceive an idea; **einen Vorsatz –en** to resolve; **sich kurz –en** to be brief; **Wurzel –en** to take root; **–lich** *adj.* conceivable;

comprehensible, intelligible

Fassung *f.* setting, mounting; wording; composure, self-control; **aus der — bringen** to upset, to disconcert; **–sgabe** *f.*, **–skraft** *f.*, **–svermögen** *neu.* power of comprehension

fassweise *adj.* by the barrel

fast *adv.* almost, nearly, all but

Fast: –en *neu.* fasting, abstention; **–enzeit** *f.* Lent; **–nacht** *f.* Shrove Tuesday

fasten *v.* to fast; to abstain (from food)

faszinieren *v.* to fascinate

fatal *adj.* disagreeable, annoying, unfortunate

faul *adj.* rotten, putrid; mouldering; uncertain, unreliable; idle, lazy; **–en** *v.* to rot, to putrefy; **–enzen** *v.* to be idle; to loiter

Faul: –heit *f.* idleness, laziness; **–pelz** *m.* lazybones, sluggard; **–tier** *neu.* sloth

Fäule, Fäulnis *f.* rottenness; putrefaction

Faust *f.* fist; **auf eigene —** on one's own responsibility; **sich ins Fäustchen lachen** to laugh in one's sleeve; **–kampf** *m.* boxing match; (coll.) fisticuff; **–kämpfer** *m.* boxer; **–recht** *neu.* club law; government by violence

Faxe *f.* tomfoolery; **–nmacher** *m.* buffoon

Fazit *neu.* final sum (*oder* result)

Februar *m.* February

fechten *v.* to fence; to fight with foil (*oder* rapier, sword); (coll.) to beg

Feder *f.* feather; pen, nib; spring; **in die –n gehen** (coll.) to go to bed; **–ball** *m.* badminton; **–busch** *m.* tuft of feathers, plume; (orn.) crest; **–fuchser** *m.* scribbler, ink slinger; **–kiel** *m.* quill; **–kleid** *neu.* (orn.) plumage; **–kraft** *f.* elasticity; **–messer** *neu.* penknife; **–vieh** *neu.* poultry; **–wisch** *m.* feather duster; **–wolke** *f.* cirrus (cloud); **–zug** *m.* stroke of the pen; signature

feder: –(art)ig *adj.* feathered, feathery; **–n** *v.* to moult; to be springy (*oder* elastic); **–nd** *adj.* elastic, springy

Fee *f.* fairy

feenhaft *adj.* fairylike; marvelous, magical

Fegefeuer *neu.* purgatory

fegen *v.* to sweep, to clean; (coll.) to scamper

Fehl *m.* fault, blemish; **–bestand** *m.* deficiency, shortage; **–betrag** *m.* deficit; **–druck** *m.* misprint; **–er** *m.* blemish, defect, flaw; fault, error, mistake; (mech.) *m.* abort; **–farbe** *f.* off shade; (cards) renounce; **–geburt** *f.* abortion, miscarriage; **–griff** *m.* failure, disappointment; **–schluss** *m.* wrong conclusion; **–tritt** *m.* false step, slip; moral lapse; **–zündung** *f.* (mech.) misfire, backfire

fehl *adv.* amiss, wrongly; in vain; **–bar** *adj.* fallible; **–en** *v.* to miss; to err; to fail, to lack; to sin; to be absent (*oder* missing, wanting); **–erhaft** *adj.* faulty, defective

Feier *f.* celebration; festival; solemnity ceremony; rest; **–abend** *m.* cessation of work; hours of leisure; **–lichkeit** *f.* solemnity, ceremony; **–tag** *m.* day of rest, holiday

feierlich *adj.* solemn, festive

feiern *v.* to celebrate, to commemorate; to rest, to cease working

feig(e) *adj.* cowardly; faint-hearted

Feige *f.* fig

Feigheit *f.* cowardice; poltroonery

Feigling *m.* coward

feil *adj.* for sale; venal; **–bieten** to offer for sale; to auction; **–schen** to bargain, to haggle

feilen *v.* to file (*oder* rub); to elaborate

fein *adj.* fine, thin, delicate; subtle; elegant, refined; **–fühlig** *adj.* sensitive; **–hörig** *adj.* sharp of hearing; **–körnig** *adj.* fine-grained

Fein: **–bäckerei** *f.* fancy (*oder* pastry) bakery; confectioner's shop; **–gefühl** *neu.* delicacy; **–gehalt** *m.* fineness, standard; **–kosthandlung** *f.* delicatessen; **–schmecker** *m.* gourmet, epicure; **–sliebchen** *neu.* (poet.) sweetheart

Feind *m.* enemy, foe; adversary, opponent; (bibl.) devil; **–schaft** *f.* enmity; hostility; hatred; **–seligkeit** *f.* hostility; **–seligkeiten** *f.* war

feindlich *adj.* hostile; inimical

feist *adj.* fat, well-fed, plump

Feld *neu.* field; ground; plain; locale of war; sphere of action; (arch.) panel; (chess) square; das — behaupten to hold a position; das — räumen to quit a position; ins — rücken to take a position; **–arbeit** *f.* agricultural labor; **–arzt** *m.* army surgeon; **–bett** *neu.* camp-bed; **–blume** *f.* wild flower; **–dienst** *m.* (mil.) active service; **–flasche** *f.* canteen; **–funksprecher** *m.* walkie-talkie; **–geschrei** *neu.* war cry; **–herr** *m.* warrior, strategist; **–herrnkunst** *f.* strategy; **–hospital**, **–lazarett** *neu.* field hospital; **–lager** *neu.* camp; **–messer** *m.* surveyor; **–messkunst** *f.* art of surveying; **–prediger** *m.* army chaplain; **–schlacht** *f.* battle; **–spat** *m.* feldspar; **–stecher** *m.* field glasses, binoculars; **–stuhl** *m.* folding chair; **–webel** *m.* sergeant; **–webelleutnant** *m.* warrant officer; **–zeichen** *neu.* military flag; **–zeugmeister** *m.* quartermaster; **–zug** *m.* campaign, crusade

Fell *neu.* hide, skin; fur; (anat.) film, ein dickes — haben to be thick-skinned; jemandem das — gerben to thrash someone; jemandem das — über die Ohren ziehen to fleece (*oder* cheat) someone; **–eisen** *neu.* knapsack, carpetbag

Fels, Felsen *m.* rock; cliff; crag; **–block** *m.* boulder; **–enhöhle** *f.* grotto; **–enriff** *neu.* reef; **–(en)wand** *f.* precipice

Felsengebirge *neu.* Rocky Mountains

Fenster *neu.* window; hotbed; **–bogen** *m.* window arch; **–brett** *neu.*, **–sims** *neu.* window sill; **–brüstung** *f.* window ledge; parapet; **–flügel** *m.* casement; **–gitter** *neu.* window lattice; **–jalousien** *f. pl.* Venetian blinds; **–kitt** *m.* putty; **–laden** *m.* window shutter; **–rahmen** *m.* window frame; **–riegel** *m.* window catch;

–scheibe *f.* window pane

Ferien *pl.* vacation; (law) recess; **–kolonie** *f.* vacation camp

Ferkel *neu.* suckling pig; (coll.) dirty person

fern *adj.* far distant, remote; das sei — von mir! far be it from me! **–er** *adv.* further; besides, moreover; **–erhin** *adv.* furthermore, henceforth; **–liegen** *v.* to be out of one's line; **–mündlich** *adj.* by telephone; **–stehen** *v.* to be a stranger (to)

Fern: **–e** *f.* distance, remoteness; **–gespräch** *neu.* long distance call; **–glas** *neu.*, **–rohr** *neu.* telescope; **–sehen** *neu.* television, video; **–sicht** *f.* prospect; vista; **–sprecher** *m.* telephone; **–sprechzelle** *f.* telephone booth; **–steuerung** *f.* remote control; **–verkehr** *m.* long distance traffic; **–zug** *m.* mainline train

Fernlenkgeschoss mittlerer Reichweite *neu.* intermediate range ballistic missile (IRBM)

Fernlenkung *f.* space command

Fernsehgrossprogramm *neu.* spectacular

Ferse *f.* heel

fertig *adj.* ready; accomplished; finished; ready-made; er ist — he is ruined, he is done for; sich **–machen** to get ready; **–bringen** *v.* to accomplish, to bring about; **–en** *v.* to make, to manufacture; **–stellen** *v.* to complete, to get ready; to terminate

Fertig: **–fabrikat** *neu.*, **–ware** *f.* manufactured (*oder* ready-made) goods; **–keit** *f.* dexterity; skill, **–stellung** *f.* completion

Fes *m.* and *neu.* fez

fesch *adj.* fashionable; stylish, smart

Fessel *f.* fetter, shackle; (anat.) pastern; **–ballon** *m.* captive balloon

fesseln *v.* to chain, to fetter, to shackle; to fascinate

fest *adj.* solid, firm; tight; fast, fixed; constant; permanent; strong, safe; **–e Nahrung** solid food; **–er Platz** fortress, stronghold; **–er Schlaf** sound sleep; **–fahren** *v.* to run aground; **–halten** *v.* to hold fast; to detain; to arrest; to portray; to write down; to adhere (*oder* cling, stick) to; **–igen** *v.* to secure; to consolidate; **–legen** *v.* to invest (money); to drop anchor; **–liegen** *v.* to be set fast (*oder* fixed to); **–machen** *v.* to fasten; to tighten; to fortify; to settle; **–nehmen** *v.* to arrest, to seize; **–setzen** *v.* to fix; to establish; to arrest; to stipulate; sich **–setzen** *v.* to gain a footing; **–sitzen** *v.* to be stuck, to be firmly fixed; **–steh(e)n** *v.* to stand firm; to be certain; **–stellbar** *adj.* capable of proof; **–stellen** *v.* to ascertain, to establish, to determine, to identify

Fest *neu.* festival; feast; holiday; **–essen** *neu.* gala dinner, banquet; **–halle** *f.* banquet hall; **–lichkeit** *f.* festivity, solemnity; **–spiel** *neu.* festival performance; **–tag** *m.* holiday, festival day

Fest: **–e** *f.* citadel; (bibl.) firmament; **–igkeitsgrenze** *f.* breaking-point; **–land**

neu. continent; **–nahme** *f.* seizure; arrest

festlich *adj.* festive; solemn; splendid

Festung *f.* fortress; **–sbau** *m.* fortification; **–swerk** *neu.* fortification

fett *adj.* fat; stout; greasy, rich; (agr.) fertile; lucrative; (typ.) bold-faced; **–bäuchig** *adj.* paunch-bellied; **–(halt)ig** *adj.* fatty; greasy, oily; **–leibig** *adj.* corpulent; **–wanstig** *adj.* paunchy

Fett *neu.* fat; grease; lard; **–darm** *m.* straight intestine; **–fleck** *m.* grease spot

Fetzen *m.* shred, tatter; rag, scrap

feucht *adj.* moist; damp; humid; **noch — hinter den Ohren** still wet behind the ears, inexperienced; **–emesser** (für Atmosphären) *m.* psychrometer

Feuchtigkeit *f.* moisture; dampness, humidity; **–smesser** *m.* humidistat; hygrostat

Feuer *neu.* fire; firing, bombardment; brilliance, ardor; **— fangen** to catch fire; **— und Flamme sein** to be very enthusiastic; **–bestattung** *f.* cremation; **–eifer** *m.* ardent zeal; **–haken** *m.* poker; **–leiter** *f.* fire escape; **–löschapparat** *m.*, **–löscher** *m.*, **–löschgerät** *neu.* fire extinguisher; **–mal** *neu.* birthmark; mole; scar (of burn); **–melder** *m.* fire alarm; **–sbrunst** *f.* conflagration; **–schiff** *neu.* lightship; **–stein** *m.* flint; **–ung** *f.* firing; fuel; heating; **–versicherung** *f.* fire insurance; **–wache** *f.* fire station; **–waffe** *f.* firearm; gun; **–wehr** *f.* fire department; **–wehrleiter** *f.* snorkel; **–werk** *neu.* fireworks; **–werkerei** *f.* pyrotechnics; **–zange** *f.* fire tongs; **–zeug** *neu.* lighter

feuer: **–fangend** *adj.* inflammable; combustible; **–fest** *adj.* fireproof; **–gefährlich** *adj.* inflammable; **–n** *v.* to burn fuel; to fire

Fiasko *neu.* fiasco, failure, break-down

Fibel *f.* primer; tibula

Fiber *f.* fiber

Fichte *f.* spruce (tree)

fidel *adj.* jolly, jovial; merry

Fieber *neu.* fever; **— messen** to take (someone's) temperature; **vom — befallen** fever-stricken; **–phantasie** *f.* delirium; **–thermometer** *neu.* clinical thermometer

fieber: **–haft** *adj.*, **–ig** *adj.* feverish; **–n** *v.* to be feverish (*oder* delirious, agitated)

Fiedel *f.* fiddle; **–bogen** *m.* fiddle bow

Figur *f.* figure; shape, form; image; diagram; (cards) picture card; (chess) piece

figürlich *adj.* figurative

Filet *neu.* network; netting; (meat) fillet

Filiale *f.* branch (establishment)

Filigran *neu.* filigree, filigrane

Film *m.* film; movie; **–atelier** *neu.* motion picture studio; **–aufnahme** *f.* filming, shooting; **–rolle** *f.*, **–streifen** *m.* reel; film strip; **–verleih** *m.* film exchange

Filz *m.* felt; (coll.) hat

filzig *adj.* of felt, feltlike; stingy, mean

Finanz *f.*, **–en** *pl.* finance(s); **–amt** *neu.* tax office; **–ausschuss** *m.* finance committee; **–jahr** *neu.* fiscal year; **–mann**

m. financier; **–minister** *m.* minister of finance; secretary of the treasury

finanzieren *v.* to finance; to support

Findelkind *neu.*, **Findling** *m.* foundling

finden *v.* to find; to discover; to meet; to consider; to deem; **sich — in** to resign oneself to; **wie — Sie es?** How do you like it?

Finger *m.* finger; **jemandem auf die — sehen** to keep strict watch on someone; **lange — machen** to steal; **sich etwas aus den –n saugen** to imagine something; **–abdruck** *m.* finger print; **–fertigkeit** *f.* manual skill, easy (*oder* rapid) fingering; **–hut** *m.* thimble; (bot.) foxglove; **–satz** *m.* (mus.) fingering; **–spitze** *f.* finger tip; **–zeig** *m.* hint, tip

Fink *m.* finch

Finne *f.* fin; claw (of hammer); pimple, acne

finster *adj.* dark, gloomy; obscure

Finsternis *f.* darkness, gloom; obscurity; (ast.) eclipse; (bibl.) hell

Finte *f.* feint; trick; excuse; deception

Firm: **–a** *f.* firm, business; **–enbuch** *neu.*, **–enregister** *neu.* commercial (*oder* trade) directory

Firmelung *f.* (Catholic) confirmation

Firn *m.* mountain snow; **–is** *m.* varnish

firnissen *v.* to varnish

First *m.* ridge, roof

Fisch *m.* fish; **–adler** *m.* osprey, sea eagle; **–bein** *neu.* whalebone; **–brut** *f.*, **–laich** *m.* fry, spawn; **–er** *m.* fisherman; **–erei** *f.* fishing, fishery; **–ereigerät** *neu.* fishing tackle; **–gräte** *f.* fish bone; **–händler** *m.* fishmonger; **–kunde** *f.* ichthyology; **–leim** *m.* fish glue, isinglass; **–reiher** *m.* heron; **–rogen** *m.* roe; **–schuppe** *f.* scale; **–tran** *m.* fish (*oder* train) oil; **–zucht** *f* pisciculture; **–zug** *m* catch (*oder* haul) of fish

fisch: **–blütig** *adj.* cold-blooded; **–en** *v.* to fish; **im Trüben –en** to fish in trouble waters; **–ig** *adj.* fishy

Fiskus *m.* state treasury

Fistel *f.* (med.) fistula; **–stimme** *f.* falsetto

Fix: **–ierbad** *neu.* (phot.) fixing bath; **–iermittel** *neu.* fixing agent; **–ierung** *f.* fixation; **–stern** *m.* fixed star; **–um** *neu.* fixed salary

flach *adj.* flat, level; shallow; insipid, dull, unoriginal; **–gedrückt** *adj.* flattened

Flach: **–ball** *m.* (tennis) drive; **–glas** *neu.* plate glass; **–land** *neu.* low country; **–relief** *neu.* bas relief

Fläche *f.* surface; level, plain; **–ninhalt** *m.* area; **–nmass** *neu.* square (*oder* plane) measure

Flachs *m.* flax; **–brechen** *neu.* flax dressing; **–hechel** *f.* flax comb; **–samen** *m.* linseed

flachsen, flächsern *adj.* flaxen

flackern *v.* to flicker; to flare

Fladen *m.* flat, thin cake

Flagge *f.* flag; colors; **die — aufziehen** (*or* hissen) to hoist the flag; **die — streichen** to strike (*oder* haul down) the flag

flaggen *v.* to (display the) flag

Flak f. anti-aircraft battery (*oder* fire)

Flakon *neu.* phial; scent bottle

Flamme f. flame; blaze; (coll.) sweetheart; **–nwerfer** m. flame thrower

flammen v. to flame, to blaze; to flash; **–d** adj. aflame, blazing, flaming

Flanke f. flank; (tennis) side

flankieren v. to flank; (mil.) to enfilade

Flasche f. bottle; flask; **auf –n ziehen** to bottle; **–nbier** neu. bottled beer; **–nhals** m. bottleneck; **–nzug** m. block and tackle

flatterhaft adj. fickle, inconstant

flattern v. to flutter, to dangle; to wave

flau adj. feeble, weak; faint; slack; insipid

Flaum m. down, fluff; **–bart** m. downy beard

Flaus(ch) m. tuft of hair; fleecy woolen cloth

Flause f. fib; evasion; humbug

Flaute f. calm weather; poor business

Flechse f. sinew, tendon

Flecht: –e f. braid, plait, tress; (bot.) lichen; (med.) tetter, ringworm; **–er** m. braider, basket maker; **–werk** neu. wickerwork

flechten v. to braid, to plait; to interweave

Fleck m. blot, stain; place, spot; blemish, flaw; **sich nicht vom –e rühren** not to budge an inch; **–en** m. market town, village; **–enwasser** neu. stain remover

Fledermaus f. (zool.) bat

Flederwisch m. feather duster

Flegel m. flail; (coll.) boor; **–ei** f. rudeness; insolence; **–jahre** neu. pl. teens

flegelhaft adj. rude; boorish

flehen v. to implore; to beseech, to entreat

Fleisch neu. flesh; meat; pulp; (bibl.) man, humanity; **sich ins eigene — schneiden** to injure oneself; **wildes —** proud flesh; **–beschau** f. meat inspection; **–brühe** f. meat broth; **–er** m. butcher; **–eslust** f. carnal desire; **–fresser** m. carnivore; **–gift** neu. ptomaine; **–kloss** m. meatball; **–konserve** f. canned meat; **–pastete** f. meatpie; **–ton** m. flesh tint; **–werdung** f. (rel.) incarnation; **–wolf** m. meat grinder

fleisch: –farben, adj., **–farbig** adj. flesh-colored; **–fressend** adj. carnivorous; **–geworden** adj. (rel.) incarnate; **–ig** adj. fleshy; pulpy; **–lich** adj. fleshly, carnal, sensual

Fleiss m. diligence; application; industry; **mit —** (coll.) intentionally; on purpose

fleissig adj. diligent, industrious; regular

fletschen v. **die Zähne —** to show one's teeth

Flick: –arbeit f. patchwork; **–en** m. patch; **–schneider** m. job tailor; **–schuster** m. cobbler; **–wort** neu. expletive

flicken v. to mend, to repair, to patch; to botch; to cobble, to vamp; to darn; **jemand etwas am Zeuge —** to find fault with someone

Flieder m. lilac; elder (tree)

Fliege f. fly; bow tie; **–n** neu. flight, soaring; **–nfenster** neu. window screen; **–nklatsche** f. fly swatter; **–npilz** m. toadstool

fliegen v. to fly; (coll.) to be fired; **–d** adj. airborne; **–des Blatt** fly leaf

Flieger m. aviator, pilot; **–abwehr** f. anti-aircraft; **–alarm** m. alert; **–einsatz** m. sortie; (unvollständig) abort; **–in** f. aviatrix; **–station** f. air station

fliehen v. to flee; to retreat; to avoid

Fliehkraft f. centrifugal force; (der Erde) G-force

Fliess neu. fleece; **–band** neu. conveyor belt; **–papier** neu. blotting paper

fliessen v. to flow; to stream; to run, to rush; **–d sprechen** to speak fluently

flimmern v. to glimmer, to glitter; to flicker; to sparkle; **–de Sterne** twinkling stars

flink adj. brisk, nimble; agile, alert

Flinte f. gun, rifle; **die — ins Korn werfen** to throw in the sponge

flirren v. to flit about; (air) to vibrate

Flirt m. flirtation

flirten v. to flirt

Flitter m. tinsel; spangle; frippery; **–glanz** m. false splendor, hollow pomp; **–gold** neu. tinsel; leaf gold; **–kram** m. cheap trinkets; **–wochen** f. pl. honeymoon

flitzen v. to dash (*oder* flit, shoot) along

Flocke f. flake; flock

Floh m. flea

Flor m. bloom, blossom; flourishing condition; crape, gauze; veil; bevy

florieren v. to flourish, to prosper

Floss neu. float, raft; **–e** f. fin; **–brücke** f. floating bridge; **–führer** m. raftsman

flössen v. to float, to raft

Flöte f. flute

flöten v. to play the flute; to whistle; to warble; **— gehen** (sl.) to be lost (*oder* broken)

Flotille f. flotilla

flott adj. floating, afloat; (fig.) nimble, dashing; fast, gay; smart; **— machen** to set afloat; **— leben** to lead a gay, easy life

Flotte f. fleet; navy; **–nschau** f. naval review; **–nstützpunkt** m. naval base

Fluch m. oath; malediction; anathema; curse

fluchen v. to curse; to swear

Flucht f. flight; escape; suite, row, sequence (arch.) alignment; (mech.) play

flüchten v. to flee; to escape

flüchtig adj. runaway, fugitive; volatile; superficial; hasty; fleet(ing), transitory

Flüchtling m. fugitive; refugee; deserter

Flug m. flying, flight; flock (of birds); **im –e** on the wing, in haste; **–abwehr** f. anti-aircraft defense; **–bahn** f. trajectory; **–ball** m. (tennis) volley; **–blatt** neu. handbill, flyer; **–hafen** m. airport; **–lehre** f. aerodynamics; **–post** f. airmail; **–sand** m. quicksand; **–schema** neu.; **–schneise** f. flight pattern; **–schrift** f. pamphlet; **–stützpunkt** m. airbase; **–wesen** neu. aeronautics; **–sport** m. aviation

Flügel m. wing; leaf, casement; (army) flank; grand piano; **–adjutant** m. aide-de-camp; **–fenster** neu. French window;

–haube *f.* cap with lappets; (motor) hood; **–mann** *m.* (mil.) file leader, flank man; **–schlag** *m.* beat of wings

flügge *adj.* (orn.) fledged; ready to start; self-supporting

Flugzeug *neu.* airplane; **–führer** *m.* pilot; **–halle** *f.* hangar; **–modell** *neu.* mock-up; **–mutterschiff** *neu.* aircraft carrier; **–rumpf** *m.* nacelle; **–schwanzflosse** *f.* empennage; **–träger** *m.* aircraft carrier

Fluor *neu.* fluorine; **–eszenz** *f.* fluorescence

Flur *f.* field, meadow; commons; — *m.* lobby; corridor, passage; floor

Fluss *m.* river; flow(ing); flux; fusion, melting; (med.) catarrh; menstruation; fluency; **–arm** *m.* tributary stream; **–krebs** *m.* crawfish; **–mündung** *f.* mouth of a river, estuary; **–pferd** *neu.* hippopotamus

flüssig *adj.* fluid, liquid; flowing, fluent

flüstern *v.* to whisper

Flut *f.* flood; high tide (*oder* water); flow; deluge; **–welle** *f.* tidal wave; **–wende** *f.* **–wechsel** *m.* turning of the tide; **–zeichen** *neu.* high-water mark

föderativ *adj.* confederate; federal

Fohlen *neu.* colt, foal

fohlen *v.* to foal

Föhn *m.* warm, humid Alpine wind in spring; hair dryer

Föhre *f.* Scotch pine (*oder* fir)

folg: **–en** *v.* to follow, to succeed; to obey; **–endermassen** *adv.*, **–enderweise** *adv.* as follows, in the following manner; **–enschwer** *adj.* of great consequence; **–lich** *adv.* consequently; therefore; **–sam** *adj.* obedient, docile, tractable; **–ern** *v.* to conclude, to infer

Folge *f.* sequence, succession; consequence; order, series; set, suite; continuation; sequel; — **leisten** to comply with, to obey; **in der** — in the future; **–leistung** *f.* compliance, obedience; **–nde** *m.* follower; **–rung** *f.* conclusion; deduction; **–satz** *m.* corollary; **–zeit** *f.* time to come

Foliant *m.* folio, volume

Folie *f.* foil; mounting; (mirror) silvering

Folter *f.* torture, rack; **auf die** — **legen** (*or* **spannen**) to put to the rack; to keep in suspense; **–er** *m.*, **–knecht** *m.* torturer; **–kammer** *f.* torture chamber; **–qual** *f.* torture, torment

foltern *v.* to torture, to put to the rack

Fond *m.* stock; foundation; background; (auto.) back seat; **–s** *pl.* (public) funds, capital

foppen *v.* to tease; to trick, to fool

Förder: –band *neu.* conveyor belt; **–er** *m.* promoter, patron; **–korb** *m.* elevator; **–ung** *f.* promotion; **–wagen** *m.* mine railway

förderlich *adj.* useful; helpful; promoting

fordern *v.* to ask, to demand; to claim; to exact, to require; to challenge, to summon

fördern *v.* to further, to advance, to promote

Forelle *f.* trout

Forke *f.* pitchfork; manure fork

Form *f.* form, shape; figure; cut; model, pattern; good behavior, formality; (gram.) voice; (mech.) mold, block, last; **–alitäten** *f. pl.*, **–alien** *f. pl.* formalities; **–at** *neu.* size; importance; **–el** *f.* formula; **–fehler** *m.* breach of etiquette; flaw

form: –al *adj.* formal; **–ell** *adj.* according to form; **–en** *v.* to form, to mold, to shape, to block; **–ieren** *v.* to form, to arrange; (mil.) to fall in line; **–ulieren** *v.* to formulate

förmlich *adj.* formal; ceremonious; real, regular; — *adv.* really, so to speak; downright

forsch *adj.* dashing; vigorous

Forsch: –er *m.* investigator, research worker; **–ung** *f.* investigation, research; **–ungsreisender** *m.* explorer

forschen *v.* to investigate, to inquire, to search

Forst *m.* forest, wood; **–hüter** *m.* forest ranger; **–mann** *m.* forester; **–wirtschaft** *f.* forestry

Förster *m.* forester; gamekeeper; ranger; **–ei** *f.* forester's district (*oder* house)

fort *adv.* forth, forward; on(ward); away, gone, off; **in einem** — continually, without interruption; **und so** — **and so forth** (*oder* **on**); **–an** *adv.* henceforth, hereafter; **–arbeiten** *v.* to continue working; **–besteh(e)n** *v.* to continue to exist; **–bewegen** *v.* to move on (*oder* forward); to keep moving; **–dauern** *v.* to continue, to last; **–fahren** *v.* to drive away, to remove; to depart; to continue; **–führen** *v.* to lead away; to carry on; **–geh(e)n** *v.* to go away (*oder* forward, on); **sich –helfen** *v.* to make a living; **–kommen** *v.* to get away (*oder* on, along); **–lassen** *v.* to allow to go; to omit; **–laufen** *v.* to escape, to run away; **–laufend** *adj.* continuous, uninterrupted; **–machen** *v.* to make off (*oder* haste); **–müssen** *v.* to be obliged to leave; **–pflanzen** *v.* to propagate; to transmit; **–schaffen** *v.* to clear away, to remove, to eliminate; **–schreiten** *v.* to advance, to proceed; to make progress; **–schrittlich** *adj.* progressive; **–schwemmen** *v.* to wash away; **–setzen** *v.* to put away, to carry on; to pursue; **–stehlen** *v.* to steal (*oder* slip) away; **stürmen**, **–stürzen** *v.* to rush away; **–während** *adj.* continuous, incessant, perpetual; **–weisen** *v.* to send away; **–ziehen** *v.* to move away, to leave; to march off; to migrate

Fort: –bestand *m.* continuation, duration, permanence; **–bewegung** *f.* locomotion; **–bildungsanstalt** *f.*, **–bildungsschule** *f.* continuation school; institution for higher education; **–fall** *m.* cessation; abolition; discontinuance; **–führung** *f.* continuation; pursuit; **–gang** *m.* departure, leaving; continuation; progress; **–kommen** *neu.* progress; living; **–leben** *neu.* survival; life after death; **–pflanzungsorgane** *neu. pl.* sexual (*oder* reproductive) organs; **–schritt** *m.* prog-gress, advancement; improvement; **–schrittspartei** f. progressive party; **–setzung** f. continuation, prosecution; pursuit; (lit.) sequel

Foto m. (see Photo)

Fötus m. foetus, fetus

Fracht f. freight, cargo, load; freight charges; **–brief** m. bill of lading; **–er** m. freighter; shipper; **–gut** neu. freight, load, cargo; **–satz** m. freight rate

frachten v. to freight, to load; to ship

Frack m. full dress coat

frag: **–en** v. to ask, to question; to inquire; nicht lange (or viel) — to be quick about it; um Rat — to seek advice; **–lich** adj. questionable

Frage f. question; inquiry, query; interrogation; in — stellen to make uncertain; nicht in — kommen to be out of question; ohne — undoubtedly, unquestionably; **–bogen** m. questionnaire; **–rei** f. continuous (oder importunate) questioning; **–stellung** f. formulation of questions; **–wort** neu. interrogative; **–zeichen** neu. question mark

Fraktion f. fraction

Fraktur f. fracture; Gothic (oder Old English) type

frank adj. frank, open; — und frei quite frankly; **–ieren** v. (mail) to stamp, to send postpaid; **–o** adv. prepaid; all charges paid

Franken neu. Franconia

Frankreich neu. France

Franse f. fringe

fransen v. to fray (oder ravel) out

Franz m. Frank

Frass m. fodder, feed; (med.) caries; (sl.) grub

Fratze f. grimace, caricature; mask; (sl.) mug; **–n schneiden** to make faces

fratzenhaft adj. distorted, grotesque

Frau f. woman; wife; Mrs.; gnädige — madam; Unsere liebe — Our Lady; **–enarzt** m. gynecologist; **–enkloster** neu. nunnery; **–enrechtlerin** f. suffragette; **–ensleute** pl. womanfolk; **–enzimmer** neu. (lit.) female, woman

frauenhaft adj. womanly; feminine

Fräulein neu. single lady; Miss; saleslady

frech adj. impudent, insolent; cheeky, saucy

Frechdachs m. young rascal; saucy fellow

Frechheit f. impudence, insolence; cheek

Fregatte f. frigate

frei adj. free; independent; unrestrained, bold; candid, frank, open, unprotected; vacant; exempt from; gratis, prepaid; liberal; (law) acquitted, exonerated; aus **–en Stücken** of one's own free will; aus **–er Hand** freehand, offhand; ich bin so **–!** allow me! in **–er Luft**, under **–em Himmel** in the open air; **–en** v. to court, to woo; **–geben** v. to release, to set free; to give a holiday; **–gebig** adj. liberal; generous; **–geistig** adj. open-minded, unbiased; **–halten** v. to pay for all expenses, to treat; **–händig** adj. off-hand, freehand; **–heitlich** adj. liberal; **–heraus** adv. frankly, candidly; **–herr-**

–lich adj. baronial; **–lich** adv. certainly, to be sure, of course; **–mütig** adj. candid, frank; **–sinnig** adj. enlightened, liberal minded; **–sprechen** v. to acquit, to absolve; **–stehen** v. to be isolated, to be free, to be vacant; **–willig** adj. voluntary, spontaneous

Frei: **–beuter** m. freebooter, pirate; plagiarist; **–billet** neu. free pass, complimentary ticket; **–brief** m. license, permit; **–er** m. suitor, wooer; **–denker** m. free-thinker; **–exemplar** neu. presentation copy; **–fall** (avi. ohne Fallschirm) m. free fall; — **frau** f. baroness; **–hafen** m. free port; **–heit** f. freedom, liberty; **–heitskrieg** m. war of independence; **–heitsstrafe** f. imprisonment; **–herr** m. baron; **–kauf** m. redemption; **–korps** neu. volunteer corps; **–kuvert** neu. stamped envelope; **–lauf** m. free wheeling; **–lichtbühne** f. open-air theater; **–lichtkino** neu. drive-in theater; **–marke** f. postage stamp; **–maurer** m. freemason; **–maurerei** f. freemasonry; **–mut** m. frankness, candor, openness; **–schar** f. volunteers; insurgents; **–spruch** m. acquittal; **–stelle** f. scholarship; **–stoss** m. (sports) free kick; **–tod** m. suicide; **–treppe** f. grand staircase; **–werber** m. matchmaker

Freitag m. Friday

fremd adj. strange; foreign; **–es Gut** other people's property; unter **–em Namen** incognito; **–artig** adj. odd, strange; heterogeneous; **–ländisch** adj. alien, foreign; **–stämmig** adj. alien, of foreign birth (oder race)

Fremd: **–e** f. foreign country; **–e** m. stranger; foreigner; alien; guest; **–enbuch** neu. hotel register; **–enführer** m. tourist guide; **–enlegion** f. Foreign Legion; **–enstube** f. spare room; **–herrschaft** f. foreign rule; **–körper** m. foreign substance; **–ling** m. stranger; **–sprache** f. foreign language; **–wort** neu. foreign word

Frequenz f. attendance; traffic; number of persons; frequency, wave length

Fress: **–en** neu. food (for animals); ein gefundenes **–en** (coll.) windfall; **–er** m. glutton; **–erei** f. gluttony; (sl.) feast

fressen v. to eat, to feed (used only of beasts); to corrode; (fire) to spread; to devour, to gobble up

freu: **–de(n)voll** adj. cheerful, joyful **–destrahlend** adj. beaming with joy **–detrunken** adj. enraptured, overjoyed **–dig** adj. cheerful, joyous, gratifying; sich **–en** v. to rejoice, to be glad; si **–en auf** to look forward to

Freude f. gladness, joy; delight, pleasur **–nbotschaft** f. glad tidings; good news **–nfeier** f. festival; **–nfeuer** neu. bon fire; **–nhaus** neu. disorderly house **–nmädchen** neu. prostitute; **–nrausch** m. exultation, rapture; **–nstörer** m. kill joy; **–ntag** m. red-letter day; **–ntaumel** m. mad delight

Freund m. friend; **–schaft** f. friendship

freundlich adj. friendly, bright, agreeabl

freundschaftlich adj. amicable, friendly

Frevel m. crime, trespass, infringement

frevel: -haft adj., -lerisch adj. malicious, wanton; criminal; outrageous, sacrilegious; —n v. to infringe, to trespass, to blaspheme

Frevler m. malefactor; transgressor, blasphemer

Friderika f. Frederica

Fried: -e(n) m. peace; tranquillity; —ens-bruch m. breach of peace; —ensrichter m. Justice of the Peace; —ensschluss m. conclusion of peace; —ensstifter m. pacifier, mediator; —ensvertrag m. peace treaty; —hof m. churchyard, cemetery

fried: -fertig adj. peaceable, pacific; -lich adj. peaceful; -liebend adj. peace-loving

Friedrich m. Frederick

frieren v. to freeze; to feel cold; to chill

Fries m. (arch.) frieze; (fabric) baize

Fris: -ur f. hairdo, coiffure; trimming; —eur f. hairdresser; —euse f. lady hairdresser; —iersalon m. beauty (oder barber) shop

frisch adj. fresh; brisk; new; hale, vigorous; auf —er Tat in the very act; — aufl cheer up! -e Eier newlaid eggs; -e Spur hot scent; -e Wäsche clean linen; — gestrichen! wet paint! — zu! onward! let's go! —weg adv. straightway

frisieren v. (hair) to dress, to curl

Frist f. set term (oder time); respite, grace

froh adj. joyful, cheerful, joyous, happy; —gelaunt adj in a happy mood; —locken v. to exult, to triumph; —sinnig adj. cheerful, joyful

Froh: -locken neu. exult, triumph; —mut m., —sinn m. cheerfulness, happiness; —natur f. cheerful disposition

fröhlich adj. cheerful, joyful, merry, happy

fromm adj. pious, devout; patient; artless; —en v. to benefit, to avail, to profit

Frömm: —elei f. bigotry; hypocrisy; sanctimoniousness; —igkeit f. godliness, piety; devoutness; —ler m. hypocrite

Fron f. -arbeit f., -dienst m. compulsory (oder enforced) labor; drudgery; -herr m. feudal lord; -leichnam m. Corpus Christi; -vogt m. taskmaster

fronen v. to do forced labor

Front f. front; face; zone of battle

Frosch m. frog; firecracker; (mech.) bracket; -mensch m. frogman; -schenkel m. frogleg

Frost m. frost; chill, cold; -beule f. chillblain; -schutzmittel neu. anti-freeze

frösteln v. to shiver; to feel chilly

Frucht f. fruit; grain; crop; result, product; eingemachte Früchte preserves; -boden m. (bot.) receptacle; -folge f., -wechsel m. rotation of crops; -garten m. orchard; -keim m. germ; -knoten m. seed bud; ovary; -lese f. fruit harvest

früh adj. early, in the morning; premature; -er adj. earlier, prior, sooner; former, late; -estens adv. at the earliest; -lingshaft adj. vernal, springlike;

-reif adj. precocious; early (-ripe); -stücken v. to breakfast; -zeitig adj. early; untimely; premature

Früh: -aufsteher m. early riser; -e f. (early) morning; dawn; in aller -e before daybreak; -geburt f. premature birth; -konzert neu. matinée; -ling m., -jahr neu. spring; -reife f. earliness, precociousness; -saat f. spring sowing; -stück neu. breakfast; zweites -stück lunch(eon)

Fuchs m. fox; chestnut horse; freshman, cunning (oder sly) fellow; -bau m. foxhole; -eisen neu. fox trap; -schwanz m. foxtail; handsaw

füg: -en v. to join, to fit, to regulate; to add; to ordain, to dispose; sich — to accomodate, to reconcile oneself; to acquiesce in; to submit; to happen, to coincide; -lich adj. convenient, just; -sam adj. obedient, docile, pliant, yielding, submissive

Fühl: -er m., -horn neu. feeler, antenna; -ung f. touch

fühlbar adj. tangible, perceptible, marked

fühlen v. to feel, to touch, to sense; to notice, to surmise; jemand auf den Zahn — to sound someone out; Reue — to repent; sich gut — to feel well

Fuhr: -e f. conveyance; wagon load; -mann m. drayman, driver; -werk neu. vehicle, wagon

führen v. to lead; to conduct, to guide; to convey, to carry; to handle, to manage; to keep (books); to stock (goods); to bear (name, title); to show (proof); to wage (war); das grosse Wort — to brag, to boast; das Wort— to be spokesman; einen Prozess — to carry on a lawsuit; im Schilde — to intend, to plan; zum Mund — to raise to one's lips

Führer m. leader, guide; conductor; driver, operator; pilot; manual; guidebook; -schaft f. leadership, guidance; the leaders; -schein m. driver's license

Führung f. conduct, command, guidance; management, (sports) lead; behavior; -srille f. groove; -szeugnis neu. police certificate of behavior

Füll: -e f. fullness, abundance; plumpness; in Hülle und -e plenty and to spare; -federhalter m. fountain pen; -horn neu. cornucopia; -sel neu. stopgap; stuffing; -ung f. filling; stuffing; packing; (door) panel; -werk neu. padding; (arch.) rubble work; -wort neu. expletive

Füllen neu. foal, colt, filly

füllen v. to fill, to stuff; auf Flaschen — to bottle; in Fässer — to barrel

fummeln v. to fumble; to potter, to dabble

Fund m. find(ing); discovery; -büro neu. lost and found department; -grube f. rich mine (oder source); -stück neu. found article

Fundament neu. foundation, basis; -ierung f. laying of a foundation

fünf adj. five; -eckig adj. pentagonal; -erlei adj. of five kinds; -fach adj.,

–fältig *adj.* five-fold; **–mal** *adv.* five times; **–stöckig** *adj.* five-storied; **–zehn** *adj.* fifteen; **–zig** *adj.* fifty

Fünf *f.*, **Fünfer** *m.* five; **–eck** *neu.* pentagon; **–ling** *m.* quintuplet; **–tel** *neu.* fifth part

fungieren *v.* to act, to officiate; to discharge

Funk *m.* wireless; radio; **–e(n)** *m.* spark; bit; **–enfänger** *m.* spark catcher; **–er** *m.* radio operator, wireless telegrapher; **–meldung** *f.* radio message; **–sendung** *f.* radio broadcasting; **–spruch** *m.* radiogram; **–turm** *m.* radio tower; **–wagen** *m.* squad car

funk: –eln *v.* to twinkle, to sparkle; **–elnagelneu** *adj.* brand-new; **–en** *v.* to radio, to broadcast; **–ensprühend** *adj.*, **–enwerfend** *adj.* sparkling, scintillating

funktionieren *v.* to function

für *prep.* for; in favor of; for the sake (*oder* on behalf) of; in return for; instead of; **an und — sich** in (*oder* of) itself; **ein — allemal** once and for all; **–s Erste for the present; — sich** for oneself alone; (theat.) aside; **— und —** forever and ever; **— und wider** pro and con; **ich habe es — mein Leben gern** I am exceedingly fond of it; **Schritt — Schritt** step by step; **Tag — Tag** day after day; **–liebnehmen** to put up with, to content onself with

Für: –bitte *f.* intercession; **–sorge** *f.* precaution, care; relief; **–sorgeerziehung** *f.* child welfare work; education of juvenile delinquents; **–sprache** *f.* recommendation; intercession; **–sprecher** *m.* interceder; advocate; **–wort** *neu.* pronoun

Furage *f.* forage, fodder

Furche *f.* furrow; wrinkle

Furcht *f.* fear, fright; dread; anxiety; **in — setzen** to frighten

furcht: –bar *adj.* frightful, dreadful; awful; (coll.) great, tremendous; **–los** *adj.* intrepid; fearless; **–sam** *adj.* timid, faint-hearted

fürchten *v.* to fear; to be afraid of; to dread

fürchterlich *adj.* frightful, awful, terrible

Furie *f.* fury, termagant

Furier *m.* forager

Fürst *m.* prince; sovereign; **— dieser Welt** (poet.) the devil, Satan; **–entum** *neu.* principality

fürstlich *adj.* princely

Furt *f.* ford

Fuss *m.* foot; footing; base, pedestal; bottom; **auf dem –e folgen** to follow close on one's heels; **auf eigenen Füssen stehen** to be independent; **auf freien — setzen** to set free; **auf grossem –e leben** to live in grand style; **auf gutem –e steh(e)n** to be on good terms; **— fassen** to gain a footing; **stehenden –es** immediately; **zu — on** foot; **–abtreter** *m.* foot scraper; **–bank** *f.* footstool; hassock; **–boden** *m.* floor(ing); **–fall** *m.* prostration; **–gänger** *m.* pedestrian; **–gelenk** *neu.* ankle; **–gitter** *n.* grille;

–note *f.* footnote; **–spitze** *f.* point of the foot; **–spur** *f.*, **–stapfe** *f.* footprint, footstep; track; **–steig** *m.* sidewalk, **–weg** *m.* path; **–tritt** *m.* treadle, footboard; kick; **–truppen** *f. pl.*, infantry

fuss: –en *v.* to stand (*oder* depend) on; **–fällig** *adj.* on one's knees; **–frei** *adj.* foot-free

futsch *adj.* (coll.) lost, gone; ruined

Futter *neu.* feed, fodder, forage; lining, casing; **–beutel** *m.* nosebag; **–kasten** *m.* corn bin; **–neid** *m.* (coll.) professional jealousy

Futteral *neu.* case, covering, sheath

füttern *v.* to feed; to breed; to line, to cover, to case; to stuff. to fur

Fütterung *f.* feeding; forage; lining, casing

G

Gabe *f.* gift, present; donation; talent; dose

Gabel *f.* fork; **–frühstück** *neu.* lunch(eon)

gabel: –förmig *adj.*, **–ig** *adj.* forked; **sich –n** *v.* to fork, to branch off; to bifurcate

gackeln, gackern *v.* to cackle

gaffen *v.* to gape, to gaze, to stare

Gaffer *m.* gaper; idle onlooker; **–ei** *f.* gaping

Gage *f.* salary; fee (of artist)

gähnen *v.* to yawn; **–d** *adj.* yawning

Gala *f.* gala; festive dress

Galan *m.* lover (of woman)

galant *adj.* gallant, courteous, courtly; **–es Abenteuer** romantic adventure

Galanterie *f.* gallantry, courtesy; **–waren** *f. pl.* costume jewelry; finery

Galeere *f.* (naut.) galley

Galgen *m.* gallows; **–frist** *f.* reprieve; **–humor** *m.* grim humor; **–schelm** *m.*, **–strick** *m.*, **–vogel** *m.* rogue, scoundrel, good-for-nothing

Gall: –apfel *m.* gallnut; **–e** *f.* gall, bile; anger, bad humor; **–enblase** *f.* gallbladder

Gallert *neu.*, **Gallerte** *f.* gelatine, jelly, glue

galoppieren *v.* to gallop

galvanisieren *v.* to galvanize, to electrolyze

Gamasche *f.* gaiter, legging

Gambe *f.* bass viol

Gamsbart *m.* beard of the chamois; goatee

Gang *m.* walk; errand; corridor, passage; course (of meal); action, motion; (anat.) canal, duct; (mech.) gear, worm; (min.) lode, vein; (naut.) gangway; (sports) round; **aus dem — bringen** (*or* setzen) to throw out of gear; to disarrange; **im — bleiben** to stay in motion; **im — sein** to be in operation (*oder* going on, in progress); **in — bringen** to set in motion; to bring into fashion; **in — kommen** to come into action; **–art** *f.* gait, pace; **–werk** *neu.* driving gear

Gängelband *neu.* leading strings; **jemand am — führen** to lead someone by the nose

Gans f. goose; **dumme —** (coll.) silly girl

Gänse f. pl. geese; **-blümchen** neu. daisy; **-füsschen** neu. quotation marks; **-haut** f. goose skin; (fig.) goose flesh, pimples; **-küken** neu. gosling; **-leber** f. goose liver; **-marsch** m. single file; **-rich** m. gander; **-wein** m. (coll.) water

ganz adj. all, entire, whole; complete, total; intact; **ein -er Mann** every inch a man; **eine -e Zahl** an integer; many; **etwas — anderes** quite a different thing; **— besonders** particularly; **— gewiss** most certainly; **— und gar nicht** not at all; **von -em Herzen** with all my heart

Ganze neu., **Ganzheit** f. whole; totality; **im -n** on the whole, generally

gänzlich adj. entire, full, total

gar adj. done, ready, finished; well cooked; prepared; **—** adv. fully, quite, very; perhaps; even; **— mancher** many a man; **— nicht** not at all; **— nichts** nothing at all

Garant m. guarantor; **-ie** f. guarantee

garantieren v. to guarantee

Garaus m. ruin; end; death

Garbe f. sheaf; yarrow

Garderobe f. wardrobe; clothes; cloakroom; **-nmarke** f. coat check

Gardine f. curtain; **hinter schwedischen -n** (sl.) in jail; **-npredigt** f. curtain lecture

Gärbottich m. fermenting vat

gären v. to ferment; to germinate

Garn neu. yarn; twine; net, snare; **ein — spinnen** to spin a story; **jemandem ins — gehen** to be tricked into something

Garnele f. shrimp; prawn

garnieren v. to trim; to garnish

Garnison f. (mil.) garrison

Garnitur f. trimming; fittings, mountings; equipment, outfit, set, series

garstig adj. nasty; filthy, indecent; ugly

Garten m. garden; **-bau** m. gardening, horticulture; **-haus** neu. summer house; **-laube** f. arbor, bower; **-säge** f. pruning saw

Gärtner m. gardener; **-ei** f. gardening, nursery

Gärung f. fermentation; commotion, ferment

Gas neu. gas; **-anstalt** f. gasworks; **-anzünder** m. gas lighter; **-hahn** m. gas cock; **-hebel** m. (mech.) throttle; **-leitung** f. gas pipes; **-olin** neu. gasoline

Gasse f. narrow street; lane; **eine — machen** to make a path; **Hans in allen -n** Jack-of-all-trades; **-nbube** m., **-njunge** m. street Arab, gamin; **-nhauer** m. street (oder vulgar) song

Gast m. guest; visitor; customer; **-bett** neu. spare bed; **-erei** f., **-mahl** neu. banquet, feast; **-freundschaft** f. hospitality; **-geber** m. host; **-haus** neu., **-wirtschaft** f. inn, restaurant; **-hof** m. hotel; **-spielreise** f. (theat.) tour; **-stube** f. inn; guest room; **-wirt** m. innkeeper

gast: **-frei** adj., **-freundlich** adj., **-lich** adj. hospitable; **-ieren** v. to feast, to ca-

rouse; (theat.) to star

Gatt: **-e** m. husband, consort; **-in** f. wife; **-ung** f. kind, breed, sort; genus, species

gatten v. to pair; to join; to couple, to match, **sich —** to copulate; to unite

Gatter neu. grating, railing

Gauk: **-elbild** neu. phantasm, illusion, mirage; **-elei** f., **-elwerk** neu. hocuspocus, trickery, magic; **-ler** m. juggler, magician; buffoon

gaukeln v. to flutter about; to juggle

Gaul m. horse; (coll.) nag

Gaumen m. palate

Gauner m. swindler, gangster; **-ei** f. swindling, trickery; **-sprache** f. thieve's cant; **-streich** m., **-stück** neu. swindle, trick

Gaze f. gauze; gossamer

Geächtete m. ostracized person; outlaw

geädert adj. veined; grained, marbled

Gebäck neu. baked goods; pastry, confectionery

Gebärde f. bearing, air; mien; gesture; **-nspiel** neu. gesticulation; pantomime

gebären v. to bring forth, to give birth (to)

Gebäude neu. building, structure, system

Gebein neu. bony structure; skeleton; **-e** pl. corpse

geben v. to give, to present; to grant, to bestow, to yield, (cards) to deal; **einen Verweis —** to reprimand; **es gibt** there is (oder are); **etwas — auf** to value, to regard; **Fersengeld —** to run away; **in Druck —** to have printed; **in Verwahrung —** to deposit with; **Recht —** to agree with; **sich Mühe —** to take pains; **sich zu erkennen —** to make oneself known; **sich zufrieden —** to content oneself; **verloren —** to give up for lost; **von sich —** to express, to utter; to vomit; **Zeugnis —** to bear witness

Gebet neu. prayer; **jemand ins — nehmen** to question closely

Gebettel neu. begging

Gebiet neu. area, district, territory; sphere, field; **-er** m. ruler

gebieten v. to order, to command, to govern

gebieterisch adj. imperious; categorical

Gebilde neu. form(ation), structure; image

gebildet adj. educated, well-bred

Gebirg: **-e** neu. mountain chain; highland; **-sabhang** m. mountain side; **-sbewohner** m. mountaineer, highlander; **-sgrat** m., **-skamm** m. mountain ridge

gebirgig adj. mountainous

Gebiss neu. teeth, denture; bridle bit

Gebläse neu. blower

geblümt adj. flowered, flowery; figured

Geblüt neu. blood; lineage, family; race; **es steckt im —** it runs in the family

Gebot neu. order, command; bid(ding); **-e** pl. the Ten Commandments; **zu — stehen** to be at one's disposal

Gebräu neu. brew; (coll.) mixture, poor drink

Gebrauch m. use, application; custom,

usage; rite; **—sanweisung** *f.*, **—svor-
schrift** *f.* directions for use; **—sgraphik**
f. commercial art; **—smusterschutz** *m.*
registered trade mark

gebrauchen *v.* to (make) use (of), to
utilize

gebräuchlich *adj.* customary; **nicht mehr
—** obsolete

gebraucht *adj.* used, worn; secondhand

Gebrechen *neu.* want, need; (bodily) defect

gebrechlich *adj.* weak, decrepit; infirm,
frail

Gebrüder *m. pl.* brothers

Gebrüll *neu.* roaring, lowing

Gebühr *f.* duty; fees, tax; due; **nach —**
deservedly; **über —** excessively; **wider
—** quite improper, contrary to custom;
—enlass *m.*, **—ennachlass** *m.* remission
of fees (*oder* taxes)

gebühr: —en *v.* to be due, to belong to;
sich —en to be becoming (*oder* fit,
proper); **—end** *adj.* fitting, suitable;
proper, becoming, decent; **—endermassen** *adv.*, **—enderweise** *adv.* deservedly;
—enfrei *adj.* exempt from duty (*oder*
taxes); prepaid

Geburt *f.* birth; origin; product; **—enre-
gelung** *f.*, **—sbeschränkung** *f.* birth control; **—enziffer** *f.* birth rate; **—shilfe** *f.* obstetrics; **—sland** *neu.* native country;
—sliste *f.* register of births; **—stag** *m.*
birthday; **—swehen** *f.* labor pains;
—sschein *m.*, **—surkunde** *f.* birth certificate; **—szange** *f.* forceps

gebürtig *adj.* born in, native of

Gebüsch *neu.* bush(es); thicket; copse

Gedächtnis *neu.* recollection, memory;
remembrance; **aus dem —** from memory, by heart; **im — bewahren** to keep
in mind; **zum —** in remembrance of;
-feier *f.*, **-fest** *neu.* commemoration;
memorial service

Gedanke *m.* thought; conception, idea;
plan, design; **in —n sein** to be engrossed
(*oder* preoccupied); **sich —n machen** to
worry; **-nfolge** *f.*, **-ngang** *m.*, **-nreihe**
f. train of thought; **-nlesen** *neu.* mind
reading; **-nspäne** *m. pl.* aphorisms;
-nstrich *m.* (gram.) dash; **-nübertra-
gung** *f.* telepathy; mental suggestion

Gedärm *neu.* intestines, entrails

gedeihen *v.* to prosper, to thrive, to
flourish

Gedenk: -feier *f.* commemoration;
-spruch *m.* motto; **-stein** *m.* monument, memorial stone

gedenken *v.* to mention, to remember; to
intend

Gedicht *neu.* poem

gediegen *adj.* genuine, true, solid; (min.)
pure

Gedränge *neu.* crowd, throng; scrimmage;
ins — geraten (*or* **kommen**) to get into
difficulties, to get into a fix

gedrängt *adj.* crowded; pressed, urged;
concise

gedrückt *adj.* oppressed, held down; depressed

Gedruckte *neu.* printed matter

gedrungen *adj.* stocky, compact, concise

Geduld *f.* patience; forbearance; endurance

gedulden *v.* **sich —** to wait patiently

geduldig *adj.* patient; forbearing

gedunsen *adj.* bloated, turgid

geeignet *adj.* appropriate, suitable, fit,
meet

Gefahr *f.* danger, peril, risk

gefährden *v.* to endanger, to jeopardize

gefährlich *adj.* dangerous, perilous; critical

Gefährt *neu.* vehicle

Gefährte *m.* associate, companion, mate

Gefallen *m.* pleasure; favor

gefallen *v.* to please, to suit; **sich etwas —
lassen** (coll.) to swallow something

Gefallene *m.* fallen person; slain (soldier)

gefällig *adj.* accommodating, pleasant,
kind

Gefangen: -e *m.* captive, prisoner;
-nahme *f.*, **-nehmung** *f.* arrest, imprisonment; capture; **-schaft** *f.* captivity, imprisonment

Gefängnis *neu.* jail, prison; **-direktor** *m.*
warden; **-strafe** *f.* imprisonment; **-wär-
ter** *m.* jailer

Gefäss *neu.* vessel, receptacle

gefasst *adj.* calm, composed; ready; set
(jewel)

Gefecht *neu.* (mil.) action, combat; **ausser — setzen** to put out of action;
-slehre *f.* tactics; **-sübung** *f.* maneuver,
sham fight

Gefieder *neu.* feathers, plumage

gefleckt *adj.* speckled, spotted, freckled

geflissentlich *adj.* premeditated, intentional, willful; **—** *adv.* with malice
aforethought

Geflügel *neu.* poultry; birds

geflügelt *adj.* winged; **-e Worte** familiar
quotations, proverbial sayings

Geflunker *neu.* fibbing; bragging; glitter-
(ing)

Gefolge *neu.* retinue, suite, train; escort

Gefolgschaft *f.* followers, staff (of a firm);
— leisten to follow, to obey

gefrässig *adj.* gluttonous, greedy, voracious

Gefreiter *m.* (mil.) private first class

gefrieren *v.* to freeze, to congeal

Gefrierpunkt *m.* freezing point

Gefüge *neu.* structure; joints; (anat.)
articulation; (geol.) stratification

gefügig *adj.* pliant; submissive, obedient

Gefühl *neu.* emotion; feeling, sentiment;
touch; **-sart** *f.* disposition; **-sduselei** *f.*
sentimentalism; **-smensch** *m* man of
keen sensibility

gefühllos *adj.* insensitive, callous

gegebenenfalls *adj.* if suitable; eventually

gegen *prep.* against; contrary to; towards;
counter; in return for, in comparison
with; about; **— bar** for cash; **— Empfang** on receipt; **hundert — eins** a hundred to one; **-sätzlich** *adj.* contrary,
opposite; adverse; **-seitig** *adj.* mutual,
reciprocal; **-ständlich** *adj.* objective;
-standslos *adj.* without object, to no
purpose; **-teilig** *adj.* contrary; **-über**

prep. and *adv.* opposite to, facing; in relation to; **–überstellen** *v.* to oppose; to confront; to contrast; **–wärtig** *adj.* and *adv.* present; actual, current; now– (adays)

Gegen: **–angriff** *m.* counterattack; **–besuch** *m.* return visit; **–bewegung** *f.* countermove, reaction; **–forderung** *f.* counterclaim; **–gewicht** *neu.* counterweight; **–gift** *neu.* antidote; **–klage** *f.* recrimination; **–liebe** *f.* mutual affection; **–massregel** *f.* preventive measure; retaliation; **–part** *m.* opponent; **–rede** *f.* reply, objection; **–satz** *m.* contrast, opposition; antithesis; **–schrift** *f.* refutation; **–seite** *f.* opposite side; (coin) reverse; **–spieler** *m.* opponent; antagonist; **–stand** *m.* subject; theme; **–stoss** *m.* counterattack, counterthrust; **–stück** *neu.* counterpart; **–teil** *neu.* contrary, reverse; **–wart** *f.* presence; present time; (gram.) present tense; **–wehr** *f.* defense; resistance; **–wert** *m.* equivalent; **–wind** *m.* head wind; **–wirkung** *f.* reaction; **–zug** *m.* countermove

Gegend *f.* region; district; surroundings; neighborhood; direction

Gegner *m.* adversary, opponent; foe; **–schaft** *f.* opponents; opposition; antagonism

gehaben *v.* **sich** — to be slow (*oder* fussy)

Gehalt *m.* contents; capacity; proportion; intrinsic value; — *neu.* salary, pay, wages

gehalt: **–los** *adj.* empty, worthless, superficial, shallow; **–reich** *adj.*, **–voll** *adj.* of intrinsic value; substantial; solid

Gehänge *neu.* sword-belt; ears (of hunting dogs); pendants; (eccl.) drapery; (min.) slope

gehässig *adj.* malicious, spiteful

Gehäuse *neu.* (lit.) housing; case; (fruit) core; (naut.) binnacle

Gehege *neu.* game preserve; enclosure, pen; **einem ins** — **kommen** to interfere in a person's affairs

geheim *adj.* secret; concealed, hidden; private; **–nisvoll** *adj.* mysterious

Geheim: **–nis** *neu.* mystery, secret; **–polizei** *f.* secret police; **–polizist** *m.* plain-clothes man; **–schrift** *f.* cipher, code

Geheiss *neu.* command, order

gehen *v.* to go, to walk; to extend (to); to leave; to proceed (com.) to sell; (mech.) to run, to work; **an die Arbeit** — to begin to work; **das Fenster geht nach Norden** the window faces north; **das geht nicht!** that won't do! **die Geschäfte** — **schlecht** business is slack; **es wird schon** — it is feasible; **in sich** — to repent; **sich** — **lassen** to take it easy; **Wie geht es Ihnen?** How do you do?

Gehilfe *m.* helper, assistant, journeyman

Gehirn *neu.* brain; sense; brainpower; **–lähmung** *f.* cerebral palsy; **–schlag** *m.* apoplexy; **–wäsche** *f.* brain washing

Gehöft *neu.* farm, homestead

Gehölz *neu.* thicket, woods

Gehör *neu.* hearing; musical ear; — **finden** to obtain a hearing; **jemandem** — **schenken** to give someone a hearing; **nach dem** — **spielen** to play by ear

gehorchen *v.* to obey

gehör: **–en** *v.* to belong to, to be owned by; to be fitting (*oder* proper); **–ig** *adj.* owned by; appertaining to; appropriate, becoming, fit, proper, **–ig** *adv.* thoroughly, duly, properly

gehörnt *adj.* horned, horny; antlered

gehorsam *adj.* obedient, dutiful

Gehorsam *m.* obedience, dutifulness

Gehrock *m.* frock coat

Gehwerk *neu.* (mech.) movements, works; **–zeuge** *neu. pl.* (coll.) feet

Geier *m.* vulture; **–falke** *m.* gerfalcon

Geifer *m.* drivel, slaver, slobber; venom; **–er** *m.* venomous person

Geige *f.* violin; **–r** *m.* violinist

geigen *v.* to play the violin; **ich werde dir etwas** — I'll give you a piece of my mind

Geigerzähler *m.* geiger counter

geil *adj.* rank, lecherous, lewd; voluptuous

Geisel *m.*, *f.* hostage

Geiser, Geisir, Geysir *m.* geyser

Geiss *f.* goat; doe; **–blatt** *neu.* woodbine, honeysuckle; **–bock** *m.* billy goat; **–hirt** *m.* goatherd; **–lein** *neu.* kid

Geissel *f.* whip, lash; scourge, plague

geisseln *v.* to scourge, to castigate

Geist *m.* spirit; intellect, mind; ghost, sprite; **–erglaube** *m.* spirit(ual)ism; **–erseher** *m.* ghost seer, visionary; **–erstunde** *f.* witching hour; **–esarbeit** *f.* brainwork; **–esblitz** *m.* stroke of genius, brain wave; **–esfunke** *m.* flash of wit; **–esgabe** *f.* talent; **–esgegenwart** *f.* presence of mind; **–eskraft** *f.* intellectual power; **–eskrankheit** *f.* mental disease, insanity; **–esschwäche** *f.* feeblemindedness, imbecility; **–esstörung** *f.* mental derangement, psychopathy; **–esverfassung** *f.* frame of mind; **–eszustand** *m.* mental condition; **–liche** *m.* clergyman; minister, priest; **–lichkeit** *f.* clergy

geist: **–erhaft** *adj.* ghostly, spectral; **–esabwesend** *adj.* absent-minded; **–eskrank** *adj.* mentally deranged, insane; **–esschwach** *adj.* feeble-minded; **–ig** *adj.* spiritual; intellectual, mental; alcoholic, spirituous; **–lich** *adj.* spiritual, sacred; ecclesiastical; **–los** *adj.* spiritless, dull; **–reich** *adj.*, **–voll** *adj.* spirited, witty; gifted; **–tötend** *adj.* stupefying; monotonous

Geiz *m.* avarice; miserliness; stinginess; **–hals** *m.*, **–kragen** *m.* miser

geizen *v.* to be avaricious, to be thrifty

geizig *adj.* avaricious, miserly, stingy

Gejammer *neu.* lamentation, wailing

Gejauchze *neu.*, **Gejubel** *neu.* jubilation

Gejohle *neu.* howling, yelling

gekachelt *adj.* tiled

Gekeife *neu.* nagging, squabbling, wrangling

Gekicher *neu.* tittering, snickering, giggling

Geklatsche *neu.* clapping; gossip

Geklingel *neu.* tinkling; sounding (of bell)

Geknister *neu.* crackling; rustling

Geknurr(e) *neu.* growling, snarling

Gekose *neu.* caressing; billing and cooing

Gekritzel *neu.* scribbling; scrawl

gekünstelt *adj.* artificial; affected

Gelächter *neu.* laughter; (coll.) laughing-stock

Gelage *neu.* revel, feast, drinking bout

gelähmt *adj.* paralyzed, lame

Gelände *neu.* tract of ground; terrain

Geländer *neu.* railing; balustrade, bannister

gelangen *v.* to arrive at, to reach; to attain

gelassen *adj.* calm, composed, collected

geläufig *adj.* fluent, ready; familiar

gelaunt *adj.* disposed; **gut —** in good humor; **schlecht —** cross, peevish

gelb *adj.* yellow; **-e Rübe** carrot; **-lich** *adj.* yellowish, sallow; **-süchtig** *adj.* jaundiced

Geld *neu.* money; **bares —** cash; **falsches — counterfeit** money; **kleines —** small change; **öffentliche -er** public funds; **-anlage** *f.* investment of capital; **-anweisung** *f.* money order; **-gier** *f.* avarice; **-heirat** *f.* marriage for money; **-kasten** *m.* strong box; **-leute** *pl.* financiers; **-schneider** *m.* extortioner, usurer; **-schrank** *m.* safe; **-strafe** *f.* fine; **-stück** *neu.* coin; **-tasche** *f.* purse; **-umlauf** *m.,* **-umsatz** *m.* circulation of money; **-verlegenheit** *f.* financial difficulty; **-währung** *f.* currency; **-wechselgeschäft** *neu.* currency exchange; **-wesen** *neu.* finance

Gelee *neu.* jelly

gelegen *adj.* located, situated; opportune, convenient; **-tlich** *adj.* incidental, occasional; **-tlich** *adv.* as opportunity arises; at one's convenience

Gelegenheit *f.* occasion; opportunity; **-sarbeiter** *m.* casual laborer; **-skauf** *m.* bargain; **-smacher** *m.* go-between; procurer

gelehrig *adj.* docile, tractable

Gelehrsamkeit *f.* scholarship, erudition

gelehrt *adj.* learned, scholarly, bookish

Gelehrte *m.* scholar, savant, pundit

Geleier *neu.* grind organ music; monotonous playing (singing *oder* talking)

Geleis(e) *neu.* rut; track; rails

Geleit(e) *neu.* accompaniment; safe conduct; escort; convoy; **-wort** *neu.* preface

Gelenk *neu.* joint, articulation; link; **-entzündung** *f.* arthritis; **-puppe** *f.* marionette; **-ring** *m.* swivel

gelenkig *adj.* flexible, supple; nimble

Gelichter *neu.* riffraff, gang

Geliebte *m.* or *f.* beloved, lover, sweetheart

gelind(e) *adj.* gentle, soft; lenient; slight

gelingen *v.* to succeed; to be successful

Gelispel *neu.* lisping, whispering

gellen *v.* to shrill, to yell; **-d** *adj.* shrill; piercing

geloben *v.* to promise, to vow; to pledge

Gelöbnis *neu.* pledge, promise, vow

gelockt *adj.* curly

gelt? *interr.* (dial.) right? isn't it so?

gelten *v.* to have influence (*oder* value); to be valid; to be held in esteem; to be considered; **es galt unser Leben** our lives were at stake; **es gilt!** agreed! — **für** to pass for; **sich -d machen** to assert oneself (*oder* itself)

Geltung *f.* value; recognition, validity

Gelübde *neu.* vow

gelungen *adj.* successful; (coll.) funny; good

Gelüst(e) *neu.* desire, longing; lust

gelüsten *v.* **sich — lassen** to long for, to hanker (*oder* lust) after; to covet

Gemach *neu.* room; chamber; leisure

gemach, gemächlich *adj.* leisurely, easy-going

Gemahl *m.* husband; **-in** *f.* wife

Gemälde *neu.* painting

gemäss *adj.* commensurate; agreeable, conformable; suitable; **—** *prep.* in accordance with

Gemäuer *neu.* masonry; **altes —** ruins

gemein *adj.* common, ordinary; vulgar; coarse, base, low, mean; **-fasslich** *adj.* **-verständlich** *adj.* easy to understand, popular; **-gefährlich** *adj.* dangerous to the public; **-gültig** *adj.* generally admitted; **-hin** *adv.* commonly, generally, customarily; **-nützig** *adj.* beneficial to the public; **-sam** *adj.* common; **-schaftlich** *adj.* in common; mutual

Gemein: -besitz *m.* public property; **-e** *m.* (mil.) private first class; **-geist** *m.* public spirit; **-gut** *neu.* common property; **-heit** *f.* baseness; meanness; vulgarity; **-platz** *m.* platitude; **-schaft** *f.* community; congeniality; fellowship; **-wesen** *neu.* commonwealth; **-wohl** *neu.* common welfare

Gemeinde *f.* community, municipality; congregation, parish; **-acker** *m.,* **-anger** *m.* village common; **-haus** *neu.* town hall; **-rat** *m.* municipal (*oder* town) council; **-schule** *f.* primary school; **-verwaltung** *f.* local government; **-vorstand** *m.* local board; **-vorsteher** *m.* mayor

Gemenge *neu.* mixture; affray; melee

gemessen *adj.* measured; formal, grave, sedate

Gemetzel *neu.* slaughter, massacre; carnage

Gemisch *neu.* mixture

Gemme *f.* gem

Gemse *f.* chamois

Gemunkel *neu.* mutterings, gossip, rumors

Gemurmel *neu.* murmur(ing); mumbling

Gemüse *neu.* vegetables, greens; **junges —** (coll.) young people

Gemüt *neu.* soul; heart; sentiment; **-sart** *f.,* **-sbeschaffenheit** *f.* disposition; temper; **-sbewegung** *f.* emotion; **-slage** *f.,* **-sverfassung** *f.* mood, frame of mind; **-sleben** *neu.* inner life; **-smensch** *m.* sentimental person; (coll.) rude fellow; **-sruhe** *f.* peace of mind, composure

gemüt: -**lich** *adj.* cozy; homelike, informal; snug, comfortable; good-natured; -**skrank** *adj.* melancholy; -**voll** *adj.* emotional

gen *prep.* towards, to

genau *adj.* accurate, exact; precise; particular, scrupulous; sparing; close-fisted

genehm *adj.* agreeable; welcome; -**igen** *v.* to agree (to); to approve; to grant; to sanction; **einen** -**igen** (coll.) to take one (drink)

geneigt *adj.* inclined; favorable, disposed to

General *m.* general; -**direktor** *m.* general manager; -**feldmarschall** *m.* Field Marshall General; (coll.) five-star general; -**ität** *f.* (body of) generals; generality; -**nenner** *m.* (math.) lowest common denominator; -**probe** *f.* final rehearsal; -**stab** *m.* General Staff; -**vollmacht** *f.* general power of attorney

genesen *v.* to recover; to regain health; **eines Kindes** — to give birth to a child

Genever *m.* gin

Genf *neu.* Geneva

Genialität *f.* powers (*oder* gifts) of genius; creative ability, originality; geniality

Genick *neu.* nape, neck

Genie *neu.* genius; creative ability

genieren *v.* to inconvenience; to embarrass; **sich** — to be embarrassed, to be shy

geniessen *v.* to enjoy, to relish; to have the benefit of; **nicht zu** — unpalatable, unsavory; (fig.) intolerable

Genitalien *f. pl.* genitals

Genius *m.* genius; guardian angel

Genosse *m.* companion, comrade; colleague; confederate, partisan; fellow member; (law) abettor, accomplice; -**nschaft** *f.* association; c-ooperative

Genua *neu.* Genoa

genug *adj.* enough, sufficient; —! *interj.* enough! stop it!

Genüge *f.* sufficiency; satisfaction

genügen *v.* to suffice, to satisfy

Genugtuung *f.* satisfaction; compensation

Genuss *m.* enjoyment; indulgence; use; -**mensch** *m.* voluptuary, sensualist; -**mittel** *neu.* luxuries; -**sucht** *f.* craving for pleasure

Geographie *f.* geography

Geologie *f.* geology

Geometrie *f.* geometry

Georg *m.* George

Georgine *f.* dahlia

Gepäck *neu.* baggage, luggage; -**abfertigung** *f.*, -**aufgabe** *f.*, -**ausgabe** *f.* baggage room; -**marsch** *m.* (mil.) march with full equipment; -**träger** *m.* porter

Gepflogenheit *f.* custom, usage

Geplänkel *neu.* skirmish

Geplapper *neu.* babbling, chattering

Geplätscher *neu.* splashing, purling

Geplauder *neu.* chatting, prattle

Gepolter *neu.* rumble; loud scolding

Gepräge *neu.* coinage; impression, stamp

Geprahle *neu.* brag, boast

Gepränge *neu.* pageantry, pomp

Geprassel *neu.* crackling, clatter

Gequake *neu.* croaking, quacking

Gequieke *neu.* squeaking, squealing

gerad: -**e** *adj.* direct; erect; even; straight(forward); constant, upright; -**e das Gegenteil** the very opposite; -**e und ungerade** even and odd; **ich bin** -**e gekommen** I have just come; **ich war** -**e dort** I happened to be there; **nun** -**e** now more than ever; -**eaus** *adv.* straight ahead; -**eheraus** *adv.* frankly, bluntly; -**ehin** *adv.* straight on; point-blank; -**eüber** *adv.* just opposite; -**e(s)wegs** *adv.* directly, at once; -**ezu** *adv.* straight ahead; downright, plainly, flatly; -**linig** *adj.* in a straight line, rectilinear; -**sinnig** *adj.* straightforward, upright

Gerade *f.* straight line

Geranie *f.*, **Geranium** *neu.* geranium

Gerassel *neu.* clanking, clatter, rattling

Gerät *neu.* implement, tool, apparatus; -**ekammer** *f.* storeroom; -**ekasten** *m.* tool box (*oder* chest); -**schaften** *f. pl.* utensils; household effects; equipment, fittings

Geratewohl *neu.* **aufs** — haphazardly, at random

geraum *adj.* ample; considerable; **seit** -**er Zeit** for a long time

geräumig *adj.* roomy, capacious, spacious

Geräusch *neu.* noise, bustle, stir

geräuschlos *adj.* noiseless, quiet

geräuschvoll *adj.* noisy, tumultuous

Geräusper *neu.* clearing of the throat; coughing

gerben *v.* to tan; **den Buckel** (*or* **das Fell, die Haut**) — (coll.) to flog severely

gerecht *adj.* just, righteous; fair; **in allen Sätteln** — **sein** to be a Jack-of-all-trades

Gerechtigkeit *f.* justice, impartiality

Gerechtsame *f.* prerogative, privilege

Gerede *neu.* empty talk; gossip, rumor

gereichen *v.* to conduce (*oder* redound) to

Gereiztheit *f.* irritation

gereuen *v.* **es gereut mich** I regret it

Gerhard *m.* Gerard

Gericht *neu.* court of justice, tribunal; judgment; dish; **Jüngstes** — (bibl.) Last Judgement; -**sbarkeit** *f.* jurisdiction; -**sbeamter** *m.* magistrate; -**sbefehl** *m.* warrant, writ; -**spräsident** *m.* presiding judge; -**sschranke** *f.* bar of justice; -**sverhandlung** *f.* trial; -**svollzieher** *m.* bailiff; sheriff

gerichtlich *adj.* judicial; forensic; legal

gerieben *adj.* grated; (coll.) cunning; sly

gering *adj.* small, slight; trifling, unimportant; inferior, low; — **achten** to think little of; to disdain; **nicht im** -**sten** not in the least; **ohne den** -**sten Zweifel** without the shadow of a doubt; -**fügig** *adj.* insignificant, trifling; -**schätzen** *v.* to attach little value to, to despise; -**schätzig** *adj.* derogatory, disdainful

gerinnen *v.* to curdle; to clot; to coagulate

Gerippe *neu.* skeleton; framework

gerippt *adj.* corded; ribbed; fluted

gerissen *adj.* torn; cunning, sly, wily

gern *adv.* gladly, with pleasure; readily,

willingly; — geschehen! don't mention it! — gesehen welcome everywhere; –e haben to be fond of

Gernegross *m.* would-be great; four-flusher

Geröll(e) *neu.* rubble; boulders

Gerste *f.* barley; –nkorn *neu.* grain of barley; sty (in eye); –nsaft *m.* (poet.) beer

Gerte *f.* twig; switch

Geruch *m.* (sense of) smell; odor, scent

Gerücht *neu.* rumor

geruhen *v.* to condescend

Gerümpel *neu.* old equipment; lumber, rubbish

Gerüst *neu.* scaffold(ing); platform, stage; kran *m.* gantry

Gerüttel *neu.* shaking, jolting

gesamt *adj.* entire, whole; total; joint, all

Gesamt: –absatz *m.* total sale; –ausgabe *f.* complete edition; –begriff *m.* general concept; –eindruck *m.* general impression; –ertrag *m.* entire proceeds; total output, –gut *neu.* joint property; –haftung *f.* joint liability; –heit *f.* total(ity), the whole; –wohl *neu.* common (*oder* public) weal

Gesandte *m.* envoy; ambassador, minister; (rel.) nuncio

Gesandtschaft *f.* embassy, legation

Gesang *m.* singing; song; –buch *neu.* song-book; hymn book; –lehrer *m.* voice teacher; –verein *m.* choral society

Gesäufe *neu.* carousing; drinking; boozing

Gesäusel *neu.* murmurs; rustling

Geschäft *neu.* business; transaction; affair; occupation; office, shop, store; ein (natürliches) — verrichten to relieve oneself; –sbetrieb *m.* business management; –sführer *m.* business manager; –sgegend *f.* business district; –smann *m.* businessman; –sordnung *f.* order of business; agenda; –personal *neu.* staff; –sreisende *m.* salesman; –sschluss *m.* closing time; –sträger *m.* representative; charge d'affaires; –sviertel *neu.* shopping center; –szimmer *neu.* office

geschäft: –ig *adj.* active, busy; –lich *adj.* relating to business; commercial; –slos *adj.* dull

geschehen *v.* to happen, to occur; to take place; to be done, es geschieht ihm recht! it serves him right! es ist um mich —! I am done for! — lassen to tolerate

Geschehnis *neu.* event, happening, occurrence

gescheit *adj.* intelligent, smart; clear-headed, judicious; nicht recht — a bit cracked

Geschenk *neu.* gift, present

Geschicht: –e *f.* story, tale; narrative; history; affair, incident, occurrence; –enbuch *neu.* storybook; –sbuch *neu.* history; historical work; –sforscher *m.* historian

geschichtlich *adj.* historic(al)

Geschick *neu.* destiny, fate; aptitude; –lichkeit *f.*, –theit *f.* dexterity, ingenuity, skill

geschickt *adj.* dexterous, ingenious, skilled

Geschirr *neu.* vessels; crockery, dishes; harness, trappings (of horses)

Geschlecht *neu.* sex; kind; genus, species; gender; family, stock; generation; –erkunde *f.* genealogy; –sfall *m.* genitive case; –sfolge *f.* lineage; –sglieder *neu. pl.*, –steile *m.* and *neu. pl.* genitals; –skrankheit *f.* venereal disease; –sname *m.* family name, surname; generic name; –sregister *neu.* pedigree; –sreife *f.* puberty; –strieb *m.* sexual desire; –sverkehr *m.* sexual intercourse; –swort *neu.* (gram.) article

Geschmack *m.* (sense of) taste; liking; –sache *f.* matter of taste; –slehre *f.* esthetics

Geschmeide *neu.* jewelry, trinkets

geschmeidig *adj.* malleable, supple, pliant

Geschmeiss *neu.* excrement; droppings; vermin; dregs, scum

Geschmetter *neu.* (trumpets) flourish; blare

Geschnatter *neu.* cackling, gabbling; jabbering

Geschnörkel *neu.* flourishes

Geschöpf *neu.* creature; production; minion

Geschoss *neu.* missile, projectile, shell; floor, story; –bahn *f.* trajectory

geschraubt *adj.* screwed; affected, stilted

Geschrei *neu.* screaming, shouting; clamor; ado

Geschütz *neu.* cannon, gun; –bedienung *f.* gun crew; –feuer *neu.* barrage, cannonade; –kunst *f.* gunnery; –rohr *neu.* gun barrel; –stand *m.* gun emplacement

Geschwader *neu.* squadron; –chef *m.* commodore; –flug *m.* flight in formation

Geschwätz *neu.* idle talk; tittle-tattle

geschwätzig *adj.* talkative, verbose

geschwind *adj.* quick, fast, swift; nimble

Geschwind: –igkeit *f.* quickness, speed; fleetness, nimbleness; –igkeitsmesser *m.* speedometer; –schritt *m.* double-quick step

Geschwirr *neu.* whirring, whizzing, buzzing

Geschwister *pl.* brother(s) and sister(s)

Geschworene *m.* juryman; –n *pl.* jury; –nliste *f.* panel (jury)

Geschwulst *f.* swelling; tumor

Geschwür *neu.* abscess, sore, ulcer

Gesell: –e *m.* companion; pal; journeyman; fellow, chap; –schaft *f.* society, association; high society; company; party; –schafter *m.* companion; business partner; –schaftsanzug *m.* evening (*oder* full) dress

gesell: –en *v.* to associate with, to join; –ig *adj.* sociable; entertaining; –schaftlich *adj.* social

Gesetz *neu.* law; statute; rule; –buch *neu.* code; statute book; –(es)antrag *m.* (pol.) bill; –geber *m.* legislator; –gebung *f.* legislation; –(es)tafeln *f. pl.* (bibl.) decalogue; –übertretung *f.* transgression of the law gesetz: –gebend *adj.* legislative; –kräftig *adj.* legal, legally valid; –lich *adj.*, –mässig *adj.* lawful, legal, statutory; –lich geschützt patented; –t *adj.* quiet, sedate; composed; –t den Fall supposing that; von –tem Alter of mature age; –widrig *adj.* illegal, unlawful

Gesicht *neu.* sight; face; appearance; vision, hallucination; –er schneiden to make faces; zu — bekommen to catch sight (of); zweites — second sight; –ausdruck *m.* features, physiognomy; –sfarbe *f.* complexion; –skreis *m.* horizon; –spunkt *m.* point of view; aspect; –ssinn *m.* (sense of) sight; visual faculty; –stäuschung *f.* optical illusion; –sweite *f.* range of sight; –szug *m.* feature, lineament, mien

Gesims *neu.* moulding, cornice; ledge

Gesinde *neu.* domestics, servants; –l *neu.* rabble; scamps, rascals

gesinn: –t *adj.* disposed, minded; gleich –t of the same mind; –ungslos *adj.* unprincipled; –ungstreu *adj.* loyal

Gesinnung *f.* moral attitude; conviction; edle — noblemindedness; seine — ändern to change one's mind (*oder* sides); –sgenosse *m.* political friend; partisan

gesittet *adj.* well-bred, civilized

Gesittung *f.* good manners, civilization

Gespann *neu.* vehicle; draft animals; team

gespannt *adj.* stretched, taut; eager, intense, anxious; strained. tense

Gespenst *neu.* ghost, spectre; apparition

gespenst: –erhaft *adj.*, –ig *adj.*, –isch *adj.* ghostlike, spectral

Gespiele *m.* playmate; childhood companion; — *neu.* playing

Gespinst *neu.* spun yarn

Gespött *neu.* mockery, derision; laughingstock

Gespräch *neu.* dialog; conversation; (tel.) call; –sgegenstand *m.*, –sstoff *m.* topic of conversation

gesprächig *adj.* talkative; communicative

gespreizt *adj.* spread; affected, stilted

gesprenkelt *adj.* flecked, speckled

Gestade *neu.* (lit.) coast, shore, beach

Gestalt *f.* form, build, stature; manner

gestalten *v.* to fashion, to shape; to create

Gestaltung *f.* formation

Gestammel *neu.* stammering, stuttering

Geständnis *neu.* confession; acknowledgment

Gestank *m.* stench, bad smell; stink

gestatten *v.* to allow, to permit

Geste *f.* gesture

gestehen *v.* to admit, to confess; to acknowledge

Gestehungskosten *f. pl.* prime cost; cost of production

Gestein *neu.* rock; stone; –sgang *m.* (min.) lode, streak

Gestell *neu.* rack, stand; frame; trestle; –ung *f.* appearance; presentation

gestern *adv.* yesterday; ich bin nicht von — I wasn't born yesterday, don't try to kid me

gestiefelt *adj.* booted; der –e Kater Puss-in Boots

gestikulieren *v.* to gesticulate

Gestirn *neu.* star; constellation

Gestöber *neu.* snow flurries; storm

Gestotter *neu.* stuttering, stammering

Gesträuch *neu.* bushes, shrubbery; copse

gestreift *adj.* striped, streaky

gestrichelt *adj.* broken (line); hatched

gestrig *adj.* yesterday's, of yesterday

Gestrüpp *neu.* shrubbery; underbrush; thicket

Gestümper *neu.* botching, bungling

Gesuch *neu.* request; application, petition

gesucht *adj.* in demand, desired, sought after; affected, unnatural, artificial

gesund *adj.* healthy, sane; sound; durch und durch — in the pink; frisch und — hale and hearty; –er Menschenverstand common sense; –en *v.* to convalesce; to become healthy; –heitlich *adj.* sanitary, hygienic; –machen *v.* to restore to health, to cure

Gesund: –e *m.* person in good health; –heit *f.* health; (drinking) toast; exclamation (when sneezing); –heitsamt *neu.* board of health; –heitslehre *f.* hygiene, hygienics; –heitsschein *m.* clean bill of health

Getäfel *neu.* paneling; wainscoting

Getändel *neu.* dallying, toying, trifling

Getier *neu.* (bibl.) animals; animal kingdom

Getobe *neu.* raging, raving; roaring

Getose, Getös(e) *neu.* noise; uproar; din

Getrampel *neu.* trampling, stamping

Getränk *neu.* beverage, drink; potion

Getrappel *neu.* pattering (of feet)

getrauen *v.* sich — to dare, to venture

Getreide *neu.* grain; cereals; –brand *m.* (bot.) smut; –mangel *m.* shortage of grain; –schwinge *f.* winnow; –speicher *m.* granary

getreu *adj.* exact, true

Getriebe *neu.* machinery; driving gear; bustle

getrost *adj.* confident, hopeful; — *adv.* cheerfully

Getue *neu.* affected attitude; (coll.) fuss

Getümmel *neu.* tumult, tussle

Gevatter *m.* godfather, sponsor; relative, (lit.) neighbor; talkative company

Geviert *neu.* square

Gewächs *neu.* plant; vintage; excrescence, growth; –haus *neu.* greenhouse; conservatory

gewachsen *adj.* grown; jemand — sein to be a person's equal

gewagt *adj.* risky

gewahr *adj.* aware of; –en *v.* to notice, to perceive

Gewähr *f.* guarantee; bail, surety; –smann *m.* guarantor; authority

gewähren *v.* to grant; to permit; to concede

Gewahrsam *m.*, *neu.* custody; detention

Gewalt *f.* might, power; authority; force, violence; höhere — superior force; –herrschaft *f.* despotism, tyranny;

-herrscher m. despot, tyrant; **-marsch** m. (mil.) forced march; **-massregel** f. drastic (oder violent) measure; **-streich** m. bold stroke, arbitrary act

gewalt: -haberisch adj. despotic; **-ig** adj. powerful; gigantic; **-sam** adj. forcible, highhanded; **-tätig** adj. brutal, violent

Gewand neu. garment, gown; robe, vestment

gewandt adj. agile; skillful

gewärtig adj. expecting, prepared for

Gewässer neu. lake, pond; — pl. waters

Gewebe neu. web; fabric, textile; (biol.) tissue; **-lehre** f. histology

geweckt adj. alert, bright, wide-awake

Gewehr neu. gun, rifle

Geweih neu. antlers, horns

gewerb: -etreibend adj. industrial; manufacturing; **-lich** adj. industrial; **-smässig** adj. professional

Gewerbe neu. craft, trade; vocation; **-ausstellung** f. industrial exhibition; **-freiheit** f. free enterprise; **-kammer** f. Board of Trade; **-schule** f. polytechnic (oder trade) school

Gewerk neu. craft, guild; **-schaft** f. labor (oder trade) union

Gewicht neu. weight; importance, significance; — **legen auf** to lay stress on; **ins — fallen** to weigh heavily (in decision)

gewichtig adj. significant, weighty; serious

Gewieher neu. neighing; horselaugh

gewillt adj. willing; disposed, inclined

Gewimmel neu. throng, crowd, swarm, crush

Gewinde neu. (screw) worm; garland, festoon

Gewinn m. profit, yield; prize, advantage, benefit; **-anteil** m. dividend, royalty; **-beteiligung** f. profit-sharing; **-er** m. winner; **-liste** f. list of prizes; **-los** neu., **-nummer** f. winning number

gewinn: -en v. to earn, to gain, to get, to win; to extract, to produce; **die Oberhand — en** to prevail upon, to conquer; **es über sich — en** to bring oneself to; **-end** adj. attractive, engaging; **-süchtig** adj. greedy, covetous

Gewinsel neu. whimpering, lamentation, wailing

gewiss adj. sure; fixed; certain; — adv. certainly, indeed; probably, apparently; **-enhaft(ig)** adj. conscientious; scrupulous; dependable; **-enlos** adj. unscrupulous; unprincipled; **-ermassen** adv. so to speak, to a certain degree

Gewiss: -en neu. conscience; **-ensbiss** m. twinge of conscience; remorse; **-ensfreiheit** f. freedom of conscience, religious liberty; **-enszwang** m. coercion of conscience; religious intolerance; **-heit** f. certainty, surety

Gewitter neu. thunderstorm; (coll.) outburst

gewitter: -n v. **es -t** it is thundering and lightning; **-schwer** adj., **-schwül** adj. (air) sultry

gewitz(ig)t adj. taught by experience;

shrewd

gewogen adj. well disposed, favorably inclined

gewöhnen v. to accustom, to habituate; **sich an etwas —** to become accustomed to (oder familiar with)

Gewohnheit f. habit, custom

gewohnheitsmässig adj. habitual; — adv. in the usual way; mechanically, routine

gewöhnlich adj. customary, usual; everyday, ordinary; low, vulgar

gewohnt adj. habitual, customary, usual

Gewölbe neu. (lit.) arched roof (oder ceiling), vault; impressive construction

Gewühl neu. turmoil; bustle, throng, agitation

gewunden adj. twisted; winding; tortuous

gewürfelt adj. checkered; variegated

Gewürz neu. spice; condiment, seasoning; **-nelke** f. clove; **-pflanze** f. aromatic herb

gezahnt, gezähnt adj. notched

Gezänk, Gezanke neu. quarreling, wrangling

Gezeter neu. screaming, outcry, clamor

geziem: -en v. to be fit, to become; **-end** adj., **-lich** adj. decorous; becoming; proper; due

geziert adj. affected; dandyish, foppish

Gezirpe neu. chirping

Gezücht neu. breed, brood; (coll.) rabble

Gezwitscher neu. chirping, twitter, warbling

gezwungen adj. compulsory, forced; affected

Gicht f. gout, arthritis

Giebel m. gable; **-balken** m. rooftree, ridgepole; **-feld** neu. pediment; **-stube** f. attic, garret

Gier f. greed(iness); avidity

gieren v. to yaw

gierig adj. greedy, avaricious, covetous

Giess: -bach m. torrent; **-er** m. caster, founder, molder; **-kanne** f. sprinkling can

giessen v. to pour; to spill; to cast, to found, to mold; to water

Gift neu. poison, venom; virus; toxin; virulence; malice; anger; **darauf kannst du — nehmen!** (coll.) that is certain; **-hauch** m. blight; **-nudel** f. (coll.) cigar; **-schwamm** m. poisonous mushroom, toadstool; **-zahn** m. poison fang

giftig adj. poisonous, venomous; toxic; malicious, virulent

Gilde f. guild

Gimpel m. bullfinch; simpleton

Gipfel m. peak, summit; pinnacle; limit; **-leistung** f. record performance; **-punkt** m. culminating (oder highest) point; limit

Gipfelkonferenz f. summit conference

gipfeln v. to culminate

Gips m. gypsum, plaster of Paris; **-abdruck** m., **-abguss** m. plaster cast; **-bewurf** m. plastering; **-form** f. plaster mold

girieren v. (com.) to clear; to endorse

Girlande f. garland, festoon, wreath

Giro neu. endorsement; **-bank** f. clearing

house

Gischt *m.* spray, foam; yeast

Gitter *neu.* lattice, trellis; fence, grating, railing, grid; **-fenster** *neu.* grille window; **-tor** *neu.* trellised gate

Glanz *m.* luster; gloss, polish; splendor; glory; **-leder** *neu.* patent leather; **-leistung** *f.* splendid achievement; (sports) record; **-punkt** *m.* culminating point, climax

glänzen *v.* to be bright (*oder* brilliant); to shine; to stand out, to be striking; **-d** *adj.* bright, brilliant; lustrous, excellent, splendid

Glas *neu.* glass; tumbler; **-bläser** *m.* glass blower; **-er** *m.* glazier; **-karaffe** *f.* decanter; **-kitt** *m.* putty; **-kuppel (Pilotenkanzel)** *f.* canopy; **-platte** *f.*, **-scheibe** *f.* glass pane (*oder* plate); **-schleifer** *m.* glass cutter (*oder* grinder); **-ur** *f.* glaze; icing; enamel

gläsern *adj.* of glass; glassy, vitreous

glasieren *v.* to glaze; to ice, to frost; to varnish; to enamel

glasig *adj.* glassy; **-e Augen** glazed eyes

glatt *adj.* smooth, even; slippery; slick; — *adv.* smoothly; offhand, directly, quite; entirely; plainly; **-machen** *v.* to level; **eine Sache -machen** to settle a matter; **-weg** *adj.* flatly, plainly; **-züngig** *adj.* honey-tongued

Glätte *f.* evenness, smoothness; slipperiness

Glatteis *neu.* slippery ice; **jemand aufs — führen** to get someone into a scrape

glätten *v.* to sleek, to smooth; to calender; to iron; to settle

Glatze *f.* bald spot (on head); bald head

glaub: **-en** *v.* to believe, to trust, to have faith in; to suppose; **-haft** *adj.*, **-lich** *adj.*, **-würdig** *adj.* reliable; credible; authentic

Glaube(n) *m.* belief, faith; credence; trust; creed; **-nsheld** *m.*, **-nszeuge** *m.* martyr; **-nslehre** *f.*, **-nssatz** *m.* dogma; **-nszwang** *m.* religious intolerance

gläubig *adj.* believing, faithful

Gläubige *m.* believer; **-r** *m.* creditor

leich *adj.* like, identical; same; even, level, similar; uniform; equal; — *adv.* at once, immediately; alike, equally; **an Kräften —** be a match for; **es ist ganz —** it makes no difference; — **zur Hand** ready at hand; **von -em Werte** equivalent; **-altrig** *adj.* of the same age, coeval; **-artig** *adj.* of the same kind, homogeneous; **-bedeutend** *adj.* synonymous; **-empfindend** *adj.* sympathetic; **-en** *v.* to equal; to resemble, to correspond to; **-ermassen** *adv.*, **-erweise** *adv.*, **-falls** *adv.* and *conj.* likewise, also; **-förmig** *adj.* uniform; monotonous; **-gestellt** *adj.* equal in rank; co-ordinate; **-gestimmt** *adj.* in accord; tuned to the same pitch; **-gültig** *adj.* indifferent, unconcerned; **-kommend** *adj.* equivalent to; **-laufend** *adj.* parallel; **-mässig** *adj.* equable; uniform; unvaried; regular; **-mütig** *adj.* eventempered; imperturbable; **-namig** *adj.* of the same name, homonymous; **-sam** *adv.* so to speak, to a certain degree; **-setzen, -stellen** to put on a par with; **-temperiert** *adj.* isothermal; **-tun** to compete with; to equal, to match; **-viel** *adv.* all the same; no matter; **-wertig** *adj.* equivalent; **-wohl** *adv.* and *conj.* nevertheless, notwithstanding; **-zeitig** *adj.* simultaneous

Gleich: **-e** *f.* equinox; **-e** *neu.* (the) same; **-es mit -em vergelten** to give tit for tat; **-gewicht** *neu.* balance, equilibrium, equipoise; **-heit** *f.* equality, likeness; **-heitszeichen** *neu.* (math.) sign of equation; **-klang** *m.* accord, unison, consonance; **-mut** *m.* equanimity; **-nis** *neu.* image; comparison; parable; **-stand** *m.* (tennis) deuce; **-strom** *m.* direct (*oder* continuous) current; **-strom/Wechselstrom Transformator** *m.* inverter; **-ung** *f.* equation

Gleit: **-bahn** *f.* slideway; **-boot** *neu.* hydroplane; **-schutzreifen, m.** nonskid tire

gleiten *v.* to glide, to slide, to slip

Gletscher *m.* glacier; **-spalte** *f.* crevasse

Glied *neu.* limb, member; link; file, rank; (bibl.) generation; (math.) term; **-erbau** *m.* structure; articulation; build; **-erlähmung** *f.* paralysis; **-erpuppe** *f.* marionette; **-ermassen** *pl.* limbs

glimmen *v.* to glimmer, to glow, to smolder

glimpflich *adj.* indulgent; mild

glitsch(r)ig *adj.* slippery

glitzern *v.* to glisten, to glitter, to twinkle

Globus *m.* globe

Glocke *f.* bell; (glass) shade; clock; **etwas an die grosse — hängen** to make a big fuss about something; **-nhaus** *neu.*, **-nstube** *f.*, **-nstuhl** *m.* belfry; **-nklöppel** *m.* bell clapper; **-nschlag** *m.* stroke of the bell (*oder* hour); **-nspiel** *neu.* chimes; **-nturm** *m.* bell tower, steeple

Glöckner *m.* bell ringer, sexton

Glorie *f.* glory; **-nschein** *m.* halo; aureole

glorreich *adj.* glorious, illustrious

Gloss: **-ar** *neu.* glossary; **-e** *f.* marginal note, gloss; **-enmacher** *m.* commentator

glotzen *v.* to gape, to stare

Glück *neu.* fortune, luck; happiness; **auf gut —** hopeful for the best; **Freunde im — fairweather friends**; **— ab!** (avi.) happy landing! **— auf!** good luck! **— wünschen** to congratulate; **im — schwimmen** to be in clover; **sein — machen** to make one's fortune; **viel —!** good luck! many happy returns! **zum — fortunately**; **-sbringer** *m.* mascot; **-sfall** *m.* lucky incident, stroke of good fortune; **-sgüter** *neu. pl.* worldly possessions; **-skind** *neu.*, **-spilz** *m.* lucky fellow; **-srad** *neu.* wheel of fortune; **-sritter** *m.* fortune hunter; adventurer; **-sspiel** *neu.* game of chance (*oder* hazard); **-ssträhne** *f.* stroke of luck; **-stag** *m.* red-letter day; **-wunsch** *m.* congratulation

glück: **-en** *v.* to succeed; **-lich** *adj.* lucky, successful; happy; glad; advantageous;

–licherweise *adv.* fortunately; **–selig** *adj.* blissful; **–strahlend** *adj.* beaming with happiness

Glucke, Gluckhenne *f.* mother hen

glucksen *v.* to gurgle; to sob; to burp

Glüh: –birne *f.* electric light bulb; **–hitze** *f.* intense heat; **–lampe** *f.* incandescent lamp; **–wein** *m.* mulled wine; **–wurm** *m.* glowworm

glühen *v.* to glow, to be ardent (*oder* fervent)

Glut *f.* heat; glowing embers; ardor, fervor

Gnade *f.* mercy, pardon; favor; grace; clemency; — **für Recht ergehen lassen** to temper justice with mercy; **–nbund** *m.* (rel.) convenant of grace; **–nfrist** *f.* reprieve, respite; **–ngeschenk** *neu.* gratification

gnädig *adj.* lenient, merciful; affable, favorable; **–e Frau** (salutation) dear madam

Gockel *m.* (coll.) rooster

Gold *neu.* gold; **–arbeiter** *m.*, **–schmied** *m.* goldsmith; **–blech** *neu.* gold foil; **–finger** *m.* ring finger; **–fink** *m.* goldfinch; **–fuchs** *m.* (horse) palomino; (coll.) gold coin; **–gewicht** *neu.* troy weight; **–gräber** *m.* gold digger; **–käfer** *m.* rose beetle (*oder* chafer); **–kind** *neu.* darling; **–klumpen** *m.* gold nugget; **–legierung** *f.* gold alloy; **–macherkunst** *f.* alchemy; **–regen** *m.*, **–rute** *f.* laburnum; goldenrod; **–schaum** *m.* tinsel; **–schnitt** *m.* (book) gilt edge; **–waage** *f.* gold balance; **–währung** *f.* gold standard

Golf *m.* gulf

Golfstrom *m.* Gulf Stream

Gondel *f.* gondola; (coll.) small boat

gönnen *v.* not to begrudge, to wish well

Gönner *m.* patron, protector; benefactor

Gosse *f.* gutter, drain

Gott *m.* God; deity; **gerechter** (*or* grosser) **–I** good Heavens! — **behüte** God (*oder* Heaven) forbid! **grüss –I** good day (*oder* morning)! — **befohlen!** good-by! **um –es willen!** for goodness sake! **–esacker** *m.* churchyard; **–esdienst** *m.* divine service; **–esgelehrtheit** *f.* theology; **–eshaus** *neu.* church, chapel; **–eslästerung** *f.* blasphemy; **–esleugner** *m.* atheist; **–essohn** *m.* Son of God; **–esurteil** *neu.* ordeal; **–heit** *f.* divinity, deity

gott: –ähnlich *adj.* godlike; **–begnadet** *adj.* endowed with divine grace; highly gifted; **–ergeben** *adj.* resigned to the will of God; **–esfürchtig** *adj.* God-fearing; pious; **–eslästerlich** *adj.* blasphemous; **–los** *adj.*, **–vergessen** *adj.* wicked; **–selig** *adj.* godly; devout; **–verlassen** *adj.* Godforsaken

Gött: –er *m. pl.* gods, deities; **–erbrot** *neu.*, **–erspeise** *f.* ambrosia; **–erdämmerung** *f.* twilight of the gods; **–erlehre** *f.* mythology; **–erspruch** *m.* oracle; **–ertrank** *m.* nectar; **–in** *f.* goddess

Gottfried *m.* Godfrey, Geoffrey

göttlich *adj.* divine, godlike; (coll.) droll, funny; magnificent

Götze *m.* idol, false god; **–nbild** *neu.* idol; **–ndienst** *m.* idolatry

Gouvernante *f.* governess

Gouverneur *m.* governor

Grab *neu.* grave, tomb; sepulchre; **–en** *m.* ditch; (mil.) trench; **–geläute** *n.* knell; **–legung** *f.* burial, interment; **–mal** *neu.*, **–stein** *m.* tombstone; **–schrift** *f.* epitaph; **–stätte** *f.* place of burial

graben *v.* to dig; to trench; to engrave

Grad *m.* degree; rate; grade, rank, title, stage; (math.) power; **im gewissen –e** to a certain degree; **im hohen –e** extraordinarily

grad: –ieren *v.* to graduate; to alloy, to refine; **–uell** *adv.*, **–weise** *adv.* gradually; by degrees

Graf *m.* count; (England) earl

Gräfin *f.* countess

Gram *m.* grief, sorrow; **jemanden — sein** to bear a grudge against someone

grämen *v. sich* — to fret, to grieve, to worry

grämlich *adj.* morose, sullen, peevish

Gramm *neu.* gram

Grammatik *f.* grammar

grammat(ikal)isch *adj.* grammatical

Gran *neu.* (weight) grain

Granat *m.* garnet; **–apfel** *m.* pomegranate

Granate *f.* grenade, shell

grandios *adj.* grand, magnificent

Granit *m.* granite

Graphik *f.* graphic arts

graphisch *adj.* graphic

Graphit *m.* graphite, plumbago, black lead

grps(ch)en *v.* (coll.) to grab, to snatch

Gras *neu.* grass; **das — wachsen hören** to know everything better; **ins — beissen** to die; **–halm** *m.* blade of grass; **–hüpfer** *m.* grasshopper; (lit.) frog; **–land** *neu.* pasture

grasen *v.* to graze

grassieren *v.* (med.) to rage, to spread

grässlich *adj.* horrible, ghastly, hideous

Grat *m.* sharp edge; crest; ridge (pole)

Gratifikation *f.* gratuity; extra pay

Gratulant *m.* congratulator, well wisher

Gratulation *f.* congratulation

gratulieren *v.* to congratulate

grau *adj.* gray; ancient; **–braun** *adj.* dun; **–en** *v.* to turn gray, to dawn

grau: –en *v.* to have a horror of; **–enhaft** *adj.*, **–envoll** *adj.* horrible, gruesome; **–lich** *adj.* fearful, uncanny; **–sam** *adj.* cruel, inhuman; **–sen** *v.* to shudder; to dread; **–sig** *adj.*, **–slich** *adj.* dreadful frightful, horrid

Graupe *f.* hulled barley (*oder* wheat)

Grautier *neu.* (lit.) donkey

Graveur *m.* engraver

gravieren *v.* to engrave

Gravierung *f.* rotogravure

gravitätisch *adj.* grave, solemn

Gravitationskraft (der Erde) *f.* G-force

Grazie *f.* charm, grace

graziös *adj.* graceful

Greif *m.* griffin

greifbar *adj.* seizable; on hand; palpable
greifen *v.* to catch hold of; to grasp; to seize, to affect; to strike (chord); **aus der Luft gegriffen** pure invention; **ineinander — to interlock; nach jedem Mittel — to snatch at every straw; um sich — to gain ground, to spread; unter die Arme — to aid, to give a lift; zu den Waffen — to take up arms**
greinen *v.* (coll.) to whine, to blubber, to cry
Greis *m.* old man; **−enalter** *neu.* old age; senility; **−in** *f.* old woman
grell *adj.* shrill; glaring; crude
Grenz−bezeichnung *f.* demarcation; **−e** *f.* border, boundary, frontier; limit(ation); **−er** *m.* frontiersman; boundary guard; customs officer; **−linie** *f.*, **−scheide** *f.* borderline; **−mal** *neu.*, **−stein** *m.* landmark; **−stadt** *f.* frontier town; **−verkehr** *m.* traffic across the border
grenzen *v.* to border (on); to adjoin; **−los** *adj.* boundless, infinite, unlimited, immense
Greuel *m.* abomination, atrocity, outrage
greulich *adj.* atrocious, frightful, horrible
gries: −grämig, −grämisch, −grämlich *adj.* morose, surly
Griesgram *m.* surly (*oder* morose) person
Griff *m.* grasp, grip; hold; handle, haft, hilt; (mil.) manipulation (of gun); (mus.) touch; **−brett** *neu.* (mus.) keyboard, finger board
Griffel *m.* slate pencil; (bot.) pistil, style
Grille *f.* cricket; caprice, whim; **−nfänger** *m.* whimsical person; pessimist, crank
grillenhaft *adj.* capricious, moody, surly
Grimasse *f.* grimace
Grimm *m.* grimness; fury, anger
Grimmen *neu.* gripes; **— pl.** colic
grimmig *adj.* enraged, furious; grim
Grind *m.* scab, scurf, mange
grinsen *v.* to grin; to smirk
grob *adj.* rude, rough, coarse, gross
Groll *m.* rancor, resentment; grudge
Grönland *neu.* Greenland
Groschen *m.* penny; Austrian coin; trifle
gross *adj.* great; tall, high; big, large; grown-up; spacious, vast; eminent; grand; **— auftreten** to assume airs; **— denken** to think nobly; **— und klein** grownups and children; high and low; **— ziehen** to raise, to bring up; **der Buchstabe** capital letter; **−es Los** first prize; **sich — tun** to boast, to swagger; **−artig** *adj.* grand(iose), imposing; **−en-teils** *adv.* to a large extent, mostly; **−herzig** *adj.* generous, noble-minded, magnanimous; **−jährig** *adj.* of age, mature; **−mächtig** *adj.* high and mighty; giant-sized; **−mäulig** *adj.* boastful; **−mütig** *adj.* generous, broadminded; **−spurig** *adj.* arrogant; **−städtisch** *adj.* metropolitan; fashionable; **−tuerisch** *adj.* swaggering; **−zügig** *adj.* on a large scale; broadminded
Gross−aufnahme *f.* (film) close-up; **−betrieb** *m.* big business; **−e** *neu.* im **−en wholesale, on a large scale; −eltern**

pl. grandparents; **−fürst** *m.* grand duke; **−handel** *m.* wholesale trade; **−herzog** *m.* grand duke; **−ist** *m.* wholesale dealer; **−macht** *f.* first-rate power; **−mast** *m.* mainmast; **−maul** *neu.* boaster; **−mut** *f.* magnanimity; **−mutter** *f.* grandmother; **−sprecher** *m.* braggart; **−sprecherei** *f.* boasting, bragging; **−stadt** *f.* metropolis; **−städter** *m.* urbanite; **−tuer** *m.* swaggerer; **−vater** *m.* grandfather; **−wild** *neu.* big game
Grösse *f.* dimension, size; amplitude; height; volume; celebrity; (ast.) magnitude; (math.) quantity, value; **−nwahn** *m.* megalomania
grösstenteils *adv.* chiefly, mostly
grotesk *adj.* grotesque
Grotte *f.* grotto
Grübchen *neu.* dimple
Grube *f.* excavation; cavity; hole, den, mine, pit; (bibl.) grave; **− narbeiter** *m.* miner; **−nlampe** *f.*, **−nlicht** *neu.* miner's (safety) lamp; **−nwetter** *neu.* firedamp
Grübelei *f.* meditation; rumination; brooding
grübeln *v.* to brood, to ponder, to ruminate
Gruft *f.* vault; mausoleum; (poet.) grave, tomb
Grum(m)et *neu.* aftermath
grün *adj.* green; verdant; immature; **auf einen −en Zweig kommen** to prosper; **vom −en Tisch aus** only in theory; **−en** *v.* to become green; to flourish; **−lich** *adj.* greenish
Grün *neu.* green; (cards) spades; **im −en** out-of-doors; **−futter** *neu.* green fodder; **−kohl** *m.* kale; **−kramladen** *m.* greengrocery; **−schnabel** *m.* inexperienced person
Grund *m.* ground; foundation; valley; bottom; estate; soil; cause, motive, reason; (art) priming; **auf den — gehen** to investigate thoroughly; **auf — von** on the basis of; **aus welchem −e?** for what reason? **im −e** fundamentally; after all; **von − aus** from the very bottom, thoroughly; **−akkord** *m.* fundamental chord; **−anstrich** *m.* first coat (paint); **−begriff** *m.* fundamental idea, basic principle; **−besitz** *m.* real estate; **−buch** *neu.* legal register of real estate; **−farbe** *f.* (art) priming; **−fehler** *m.* radical fault; **−feste** *f.* (poet.) foundation; **−fläche** *f.* base; **−gedanke** *m.* fundamental idea; **−gesetz** *neu.* fundamental law; organic statute; **−kapital** *neu.* original stock; **−lage** *f.* groundwork, foundation; assumption; **−linie** *f.* base line; **−mauer** *f.* foundation wall; substructure; **−peilung** *f.* (naut.) sounding; **−rente** *f.* ground rent; **−riss** *m.* ground plan; outline; sketch; syllabus; compendium; **−satz** *m.* axiom, principle; **−schuld** *f.* mortage; **−stein** *m.* cornerstone; **−steuer** *f.* land tax; **−stoff** *m.* element; raw material; **−strich** *m.* down stroke; **−stück** *neu.* real estate; **−ton** *m.* (mus.) keynote; **−zahl** *f.* cardinal number, radix

grund: **–ehrlich** adj. thoroughly honest; **–falsch** adj. fundamentally wrong; **–legend** adj. fundamental; **–los** adj. bottomless; groundless, unfounded; **–verkehrt** adj. altogether wrong; **–verschieden** adj. entirely different

Gründ: **–er** m. founder; promoter; **–ling** m. (ichth.) groundling, gudgeon; **–ung** f. foundation, establishment

gründlich adj. thorough; scrupulous; profound

grunzen v. to grunt

Gruppe f. group, section; smallest battle unit

gruppieren v. to group

Grus m. coal slack

gruselig adj. uncanny, creepy

gruseln v. **es gruselt mich** my flesh creeps; **— machen** to cause to shudder

Gruss m. greeting, salutation; regards; salute

grüssen v. to greet, to welcome; to give regards to; to salute

Grütze f. grits, groats; (coll.) brains

gucken v. to look, to peer

Gulasch neu. goulash; **–kanone** f. (mil.) field kitchen; (coll.) beanery

Gulden m. florin, guilder

gültig adj. valid; legal; binding; authentic

Gummi neu. gum; **— m.** rubber, eraser; **–absatz** m. rubber heel; **–band** neu. elastic band; **–mantel** m. rubberized raincoat; **–reifen** m. rubber tire; **–schlauch** m. rubber hose; **–schuhe** m. pl. galoshes; **–stempel** m. rubber stamp

Gunst f. favor; partiality; advantage

günstig adj. favorable, advantageous

Günstling m. favorite; minion

Gurgel f. throat; **die — spülen** (coll.) to drink, to spray the tonsils; **–wasser** neu. gargle

gurgeln v. to gargle; to gurgle

Gurke f. cucumber; gherkin; (coll.) nose; **saure –n** pickled cucumbers, pickles

Gurt m. belt; girdle; girth; strap

Gürtel m. belt, girdle; zone; **–flechte** f., **–rose** f. (med.) shingles

gürten v. to gird(le)

Guss m. (act of) pouring; downpour; cast(ing), founding; (cooking) icing; (typ.) font; **–eisen** neu. cast iron; **–stahl** m. cast steel; **–waren** f. pl. foundry goods

gut adj. good; beneficial; kind; considerable, useful; **— adv.** well; **ein –es Wort einlegen** to put in a good word; **es — haben** to be well off; **im –en** amicably; **jemand — sein** to like someone; **kurz und —** in short; **man muss –e Miene zum bösen Spiel machen** one must grin and bear it; **nicht für Geld und –e Worte** not for love or money; **schon —!** all right! **Sie haben — lachen** it is very easy for you to laugh; **–artig** adj. good-natured; (med.) benign; **–geartet** adj. well-mannered; **–gelaunt** adj. in good spirits; **–gemeint** adj. well-meant; **–gesinnt** adj. well-disposed; **–gläubig** in good faith; credulous; **–heissen** to approve, to sanction; **–herzig** adj. good-

hearted, charitable; **–machen** to make amends for; **nicht wieder –zumachen** irreparable; **–mütig** adj. good-natured; **–sagen** to be security (oder surety) for; **–schreiben** to credit; **–willig** adj. readily, voluntarily

Gut neu. farm, estate; property; merchandise; goods; **–sbesitzer** m. owner of an estate (oder farm)

Gut: **–achten** neu. expert (oder professional) opinion; **–dünken** neu. judgment, opinion; **–haben** neu. credit, balance due; **–schein** m. credit note

Güte f. kindness; purity; goodness, value, quality; nature

Güter pl. goods; **–gemeinschaft** f. joint property, common ownership; **–transport** m. freight traffic; **–wagen** m. truck; **–zug** m. freight train

gütig adj. affable, good, kind; charitable

gütlich adv. and adj. amicable, friendly; **sich — tun** to enjoy

Gymnasialbildung f. high-school (oder junior-college) education

Gymnasiast m. high-school student; college undergraduate

Gymnasium neu. high school; university preparatory school

Gymnastik f. gymnastics

gymnastisch adj. gymnastic

Gynäkologe m. gynecologist

H

Haar neu. hair; nap; pile; **aufs — precisely**; **das hat an einem — gehangen** it was a close shave; **ein — in etwas finden** to find a flaw in a thing; **–e lassen müssen** to suffer damages; **mit Haut und –en** entirely; **sich in die –e geraten** to come to blows; **um ein — nearly**, narrowly; **um kein — besser** not a bit better; **–ausfall** m. loss of hair; **–esbreite** f. hair's breadth; **–flechte** f. braid of hair; **–frisur** f. hairdress, hairdo; **–gefäss** neu. capillary; **–künstler** m. hairdresser; **–nadel** f. hairpin; **–spalterei** f. hairsplitting; **–tracht** f. hairdress, style; **–wasser** neu. hair tonic

haar: **–en** v. to shed one's hair; **–ig** adj. hairy; haired; stunning; **–klein** adv. minutely, with all details; **–scharf** adj. very sharp; hypercritical; **–sträubend** adj. shocking

Hab: **–e** f. belongings; property; **–enichts** m. penniless person; **–en** neu. credit; asset; **–gier** f., **–sucht** f. greediness, avarice

haben v. to have, to own, to possess; to be obliged (to); **am Schnürchen — to** have at one's finger tips; **auf sich — to** signify, to mean; **da hast du's!** there you are! **etwas — wollen** to ask for, to desire; **gern — to** like; **nichts auf sich — to** be of no consequence; **recht (oder unrecht) — to** be right (oder wrong); **sich — to** put on airs; **unter sich — to** be in charge of; **was hast du?** what's the matter with you?

habgierig, habsüchtig adj. greedy, ava-

ricious
Habicht m. hawk; **-nase** f. hooked nose
Habilitation f. prerequisite for teaching at a German university
Hack: -beil neu., **-messer** neu. chopper; hatchet; **-block** m. chopping block; **-brett** neu. chopping board; (mus.) dulcimer; **-e** f. mattock, hoe; **-en** m. heel; **-epeter** m. chopped raw pork; **-fleisch** neu. minced meat
hacken v. to hack; to hoe; to chop, to split; to mince; (birds) to pick
Hader m. dispute, quarrel; feud; (dial.) rag; **-er** m. quarreler; **-lump** m. (dial.) ragamuffin
hadern v. to quarrel; to argue, to dispute
Hafen m. harbor, port; haven, refuge; (dial.) earthenware vessel; **-arbeiter** m. longshoreman; **-damm** m. jetty, mole; **-räumer** m. dredge; embargo; **-platz** m., **-stadt** f. seaport
Hafer m. oats; **ihn sticht der —** good luck has spoilt him; **-brei** m. porridge; **-flocken** f. pl. rolled oats; **-grütze** f. oatmeal; **-schleim** m. gruel
Haft f. arrest; custody; **-el** f. clasp, pin, hook; **-befehl** m. warrant (of arrest); **-pflicht** f. liability; responsibility; **-ung** f. security, bail; **mit beschränkter -ung** with limited liability; **-vollzug** m. imprisonment
haftbar adj. liable, responsible
haften v. to adhere (oder stick) to; **— für** to be liable, to vouch for
Häftling m. prisoner
der Haag m. the Hague
hageln v. to hail
hager adj. haggard, gaunt
Hahn m. cock, rooster; male bird; (gun) hammer; faucet, valve, tap; **danach kräht kein —** nobody pays any attention to that; **der rote —** fire; **— im Korb** cock of the walk; **-enbart** m. wattles; **-enkamm** m. cock's comb; **-enschrei** neu. cock's crowing; **-rei** m. cuckold
Hai(fisch) m. shark
Hain m. (poet.) grove, wood
Häkchen neu. small (oder crochet) hook
Häkelei f. crocheting; (coll.) teasing
Haken m. hook; check mark; **einen — schlagen** to dodge around a corner; to trip up; **— und Öse** hook and eye; **-kreuz** neu. swastika
halb adj. half; partial; incomplete; **— adv.** by halves; **auf -em Wege** halfway, midway; **-e Note** (mus.) semitone; **— soviel** half as much; **um — zwei** at one thirty; **-amtlich** adj. semiofficial; **-blütig** adj. half-breed, half-caste; **-entschlummert** adj. dozing; **-er** prep. for the sake (oder on account, by reason) of; **-fertig** adj. semi-manufactured; **-ieren** v. to halve; to bisect; **-jährlich** adj. semiannual; **-militarisch** adj. paramilitary; **-rund** adj. semicircular; **-wegs** adv. halfway; reasonably well; **-wüchsig** adj. adolescent
Halb: -bildung f. superficial education; **-bruder** m. stepbrother; **-dunkel** neu.

dusk, twilight; **-e** neu. half; **-geschwister** pl. stepbrothers (oder sisters); **-gott** m. demigod; **-heit** f. incompleteness; **-insel** f. peninsula; **-kreis** m. semicircle; **-kugel** f. hemisphere; **-messer** m. radius; **-part machen** to go halves; **-schlummer** m. drowsiness; **-schuh** m. low shoe; slipper; **-schwester** f. stepsister; **-schwergewicht** neu. light heavyweight; **-welt** f. demimonde; **-wissen** neu. smattering
Hälfte f. half; **auf der — des Weges** halfway
Halfter m. halter; saddlebag (for pistols)
Hall m. sound, noise, reverberation
Halle f. hall; vestibule; lounge
hallen v. to sound, to resound
Halm m. blade, stalk; **-früchte** pl. cereals
Hals m. neck, throat, gullet; **aus vollem -e lachen** to split with laughter; **einer Flasche den — brechen** to drink up a bottle; **es geht ihm an den —** he is doomed; **es hängt mir zum -e heraus** I'm fed up with it; **— über Kopf** head over heels; **um den — fallen** to embrace; **vom -e schaffen** to get rid of; **-abschneider** m. profiteer; cutthroat; **-ader** f. jugular vein; **-binde** f. necktie; **-bräune** f. quinsy; **-kette** f. necklace; **-kragen** m. collar; cape; **-schmerzen** m. pl., **-weh** neu. sore throat; **-tuch** neu. scarf
hals: -brecherisch adj. dangerous, foolhardy, rash; **-en** v. to embrace; (naut.) to veer round; **-starrig** adj. headstrong; stubborn; obstinate
Halt m. halt, stop; hold; support; footing; **-eplatz** m. stopping place; **-er** m. holder; **-estelle** f. stop, station; **-ezeichen** neu. stop signal; **-ung** f. bearing, carriage; behavior, conduct
haltbar adj. defensible; tenable; durable
halten v. to hold; to check; to halt, to stop; to observe; to keep; to support; to deliver (speech); to contain; to subscribe to: **es — mit** to side with; **grosse Stücke — auf** to think highly of; **— für** to consider, to take for; **sich bereit — to be ready; **sich — to hold out; to endure; **was — Sie von?** what do you think of? **zu jemand — to adhere (oder stick) to someone
Halunke m. scoundrel; rascal; rogue; swindler
Hammel m. wether; **-braten** m. roast mutton; **-sprung** m. (pol.) pairing off
Hammer m. hammer; forge; **-schlag** m. stroke of the hammer; hammer scales; **-werk** neu. forge
Hampelmann m. puppet; jumping jack
Hand f. hand; **auf der — liegen** to be obvious; **an die — geben** to supply: **an die — gehen** to assist, to help; **auf Händen tragen** to coddle; **aus bester — from the best source; **bei der — sein** to be ready; **die öffentliche — the government; **eine — wäscht die andere** one good turn deserves another; **einem die — geben** to shake hands; **— an sich legen** to commit suicide; **— ans**

Werk legen to put the shoulder to the wheel; — im Spiel haben to have a finger in the pie: unter der — secretly; von der — weisen to deny, to reject; vor der — for the present, just now; **-arbeit** f. handicraft, manual labor; needlework; **-arbeiter** m. manual laborer; **-aufheben** neu. (voting) show of hands; **-beil** neu. hatchet; **-buch** neu. manual, handbook; **-feger** m. hand brush; **-fertigkeit** f. manual skill, dexterity; **-schellen** f. pl. handcuffs, manacles; **-feuerwaffen** f. pl. (mil.) small arms; **-geld** neu. earnest money; advance; **-gelenk** neu., **-wurzel** f. wrist; **-gemenge** m. hand-to-hand fight; **-gepäck** neu. hand baggage; **-griff** m. grasp; **-habe** f. handle; manipulation, pretext; **-harmonika** f. accordion, concertina; **-karren** m. handcart; **-koffer** m. handbag, suitcase; **-langer** m. handy man; **-reichung** f. aid, assistance; **-schlag** m. handshake (as pledge); **-schrift** f. handwriting; manuscript; **-schuh** m. glove; **-seife** f. toilet soap; **-tasche** f. handbag; **-tuch** neu. towel; **-tuchhalter** m. towel rack; **-werk** neu. handicraft; trade; **-werker** m. craftsman; artisan

hand: **-fest** adj. robust, stalwart, sturdy; **-gemacht** adj. handmade; **-gemein** adv. at blows (oder close quarters); **-gerecht** adj. handy; **-greiflich** adj. palpable; obvious; **-haben** v. to handle, to manipulate; to manage; **-lich** adj. easy to use, manageable; **-schriftlich** adj. written, in writing (oder manuscript)

Händ: **-edruck** m. handshake, **-elmacher** m. brawler, quarreler; **-ler** m. trader, dealer

Handel m. commerce; business, transaction; trade; bargain; lawsuit; affair; **-sakademie** f. commercial college; **-samt** neu. Board of Trade; **-sbilanz** f. balance of trade; **-sblatt** neu. trade journal; **-sbuch** neu. ledger; **-sfirma** f. commercial firm; **-sflotte** f. merchant marine; **-sgenossenschaft** f. business partnership; **-sgericht** neu. commercial court; **-sgeschäft** neu., **-sgesellschaft** f. commercial concern, business corporation; **-skammer** f. Chamber of Commerce; **-sminister** m. secretary of commerce; **-ssperre** f. embargo; **-svertrag** m. commercial treaty; **-szeichen** neu. trademark

handel: **-n** v. to act, to proceed; to trade; to traffic; **-n mit** to deal with (oder in); **-n um** to bargain for; **es -t sich um** the question is; **-n von** to treat of; **-seinig** adj., **-seins** adj. agreed on terms; **-treibend** adj. trading; commercial; **-süblich** adj. usual in trade

händelsüchtig adj. quarrelsome

Handlung f. deed, act; undertaking; business house; (lit.) plot; **-sdiener** m., **-gehilfe** m. clerk; **-sweise** f. proceeding

Hanf m. hemp

Hänfling m. linnet

Hang m. slope; inclination, disposition

Häng: **-ebacke** f. jowl; **-ebahn** f. suspended railroad; **-ebauch** m. paunch; potbelly; **-eboden** m. loft; **-ebrücke** f. suspension bridge; **-edach** neu. penthouse; **-ematte** f. hammock

hängen v. to hang, to suspend, to hook; **— an** to adhere (oder cling) to, to be fond of

Hannover neu. Hanover

Hans m. Jack

hänseln v. to tease, to ridicule; to hoax

Hansnarr, Hanswurst m. buffoon, clown

Hantel f. dumbbell

hantieren v. to handle, to manipulate

Happen m. mouthful; morsel, piece

häretisch adj. heretical

Harfe f. harp; **-nist** m., **-nspieler** m. harpist

Harke f. rake; jemand zeigen, was eine **— ist** (coll.) to give somebody a piece of one's mind

Harm m. grief, sorrow; insult, wrong, injury

Harmon: **-ie** f. harmony, **-ika** f. accordion; **-ikazug** m. corridor train; **-ielehre** f. theory of harmony

harmlos adj. harmless, innocent, guileless

Harn m. urine; **-blase** f. (urinary) bladder

Harnisch m. armor; in — geraten to fly into a rage; in — jagen to infuriate

harpunieren v. to harpoon

harren v. (poet.) to wait, to hope

harsch adj. harsh; hard, rough

hart adj. hard; tough, severe; burdensome; cruel; (phy.) penetrating; **-e Eier** hardboiled eggs; **-e Züge** stern features; **-er Verlust** heavy loss; **-gesotten** adj. hardboiled; hardened; **-herzig** adj. hardhearted, callous; **-hörig** adj. hard of hearing; **-köpfig** adj. headstrong; **-leibig** adj. constipated; **-näckig** adj. obstinate, stubborn; (med.) chronic

Härte f. hardness; harshness, sternness

Hartgeld neu. coined money

Hartgummi m. vulcanized rubber

Harz neu. resin; rosin

Hasardspiel neu. game of chance, gambling

Haschee neu. hash

haschen v. to catch, to seize; **— nach** to snatch at; to strive for

Hase m. hare; rabbit; da liegt der — im Pfeffer (or begraben) there's the hitch; falscher — meat loaf; **-nfuss** m. hare's foot; coward; **-nklein** neu., **-npfeffer** m. rabbit stew

Haspe f. hasp, hinge; **-l** f. reel, windlass

Hass m. hate, hatred; **-er** m. hater

hässlich adj. ugly; odious; repulsive; nasty

Hast f. haste, hurry, precipitation

hasten v. to hasten, to hurry, to precipitate

hastig adj. hasty, precipitate

hätscheln v. to caress, to fondle; to pamper

Haube f. cap, hood; helmet; bonnet; (rail.) dome; (biol.) crest; **unter die — kommen** to get married; **-nlerche** f.

crested lark

Hauch m. breath; breeze, puff (of wind); touch, trace; aspiration

hauchen v. to breathe, to exhale; to aspirate

hauen v. to hew; to chop; to strike; to lash, to whip; to cut (stone); — und **stechen** to cut and thrust; **übers Ohr — to cheat

häuf: -eln v. to heap up (around plant); **-en** v. to heap (up); to accumulate, to amass; **-ig** adj. frequent, repeated

Haufe(n) m. heap; pile; number, crowd; **etwas über den -n werfen** to upset; **-nwolke** f. cumulus cloud

Haupt neu. head; chief, leader; **aufs — schlagen** to vanquish; **-altar** m. high altar; **-anstifter** m. ringleader; **-bahnhof** m. central station; **-bestandteil** m. and neu. chief constituent (oder ingredient); **-buch** neu. ledger; **-büro** neu. central office; **-eingang** m. main entrance; **-fach** neu. main subject; **-gewinn** m. first prize; **-kerl** m. head man; **-leitung** f. (elec.) main wire; **-mann** m. captain; **-nenner** m. (math.) common denominator; **-post** f., **-postamt** neu. central post office; **-probe** f. (theat.) dress rehearsal; **-quartier** neu. headquarters; **-redakteur** m. editor-in-chief; **-rolle** f. (theat.) leading part; **-sache** f. main (oder most important) thing; **-satz** m. (gram.) principal sentence; **-schiff** neu. central aisle; (naut.) flagship; **-schlagader** f. aorta; **-segel** neu. mainsail; **-spass** m. capital joke; **-stadt** f. capital, metropolis; **-strasse** f. main road; **-streich** m. master stroke; **-ton** m. principal accent; **-treffer** m. first prize; **-verkehrsstunden** f. pl. rush hours; **-versammlung** f. general meeting; **-wort** neu. noun; **-zug** m. main feature; principal train

Häuptling m. chief(tain); (coll.) leader

häuptlings adv. head over heels

hauptsächlich adj. chief, foremost, main

Haus neu. house; home; household; dynasty; parliamentary body; firm; **das — bestellen** to make a will; **das — hüten** to be confined to the house; **ein fideles — a jolly fellow; — und Hof** house and home; **von — e aus** originally, by birth; **zu — e** at home; **-andacht** f. family devotions; **-angestellte** f. domestic, servant; **-arbeit** f. indoor work; domestic work; **-arzt** m. family doctor; **-besitzer** m. landlord; **-bewohner** m. tenant; **-dame** f. housekeeper; **-flur** m. hall, vestibule; **-frau** f. housewife, homemaker; **-freund** m. family friend; **-genosse** m. fellow lodger; **-gesetz** neu. family law; **-gesinde** neu. domestics; **-halt** m. household; **-hälterin** f. housekeeper; **-haltsplan** m. budget; **-haltung** f. housekeeping; **-haltungskosten** f. pl. household expenses; **-herr** m. host; **-ierer** m. peddler; **-knecht** m. porter, handyman; **-kreuz** neu. (coll.) domestic affliction, bad wife; **-lehrer** m. family tutor; **-mädchen** neu. woman servant.

maid of all work; **-meister** m. janitor; caretaker; **-mittel** neu. home remedy; **-ordnung** f. house regulations; **-rat** m. household furniture; **-schuhe** m. pl. slippers; **-stand** m. household; **-suchung** f. (police) house search; **-tier** neu. domestic animal; **-tor** neu. gate; **-tür** f. front door; **-verwalter** m. steward; **-wirt** m. landlord; **-wirtschaft** f. home management; **-zins** m. house rent

haus: -backen adj. home-baked; plain, prosaic; **-en** v. to dwell, to reside; to economize; **übel -en** to devastate, to ravage; **-halten** v. to manage a household; **-hälterisch** adj. economical; thrifty; **-ieren** v. to peddle

Häuschen neu. small house; cottage; **aus dem — sein** to be excited (oder beside oneself)

Häusler m. cottager

häuslich adj. domestic; housekeeping; economical; home-loving; **-e Aufgaben** homework

Hausse f. rise (of prices); boom

Haut f. skin; hide; coat; film; membrane; **auf blosser — tragen** to wear next to one's skin; **aufgesprungene — chapped** (oder cracked) skin; **aus der — fahren** (coll.) to hit the ceiling; **eine ehrliche — an honest fellow; jemandem die — über die Ohren ziehen** to fleece someone; **mit — und Haar** completely; **mit heiler — davonkommen** to have a close shave; **-bläschen** neu. pimple; **-farbe** f. complexion

häuten v. to skin; to flay; **sich — to cast off skin, to slough

Heb: -amme f. midwife; **-earm** m. leverarm; **-el** m. lever; **-ebühne** f. platform elevator; **-ekran** m. hoisting crane; **-er** m. siphon; **-ung** f. elevation, removal; accented syllable; improvement, advancement

heben v. to lift, to raise; to heave, to elevate; to bring up; to cancel; to improve, to favor; **sich — to rise

hech: -eln v. to hackle, to carp, to gossip; **-blau** adj. grayish blue; **-grau** adj. bluish gray

hecken v. to breed, to hatch

Heer neu. army; crowd, multitude, swarm; **-(es)bann** m. levies, military force; **-esabteilung** f. (mil.) division; **-esleitung** f. army command; **-esmacht** f. (mil.) forces; **-esverpflegung** f. (mil.) commissariat; **-esverwaltung** f. military administration; **-folge** f. military duty; **-führer** m. army commander; **-lager** neu. army camp; **-schar** f. (poet.) army; **-schau** f. army parade (oder review); **-strasse** f. broad highway; **-zug** m. (mil.) expedition

Hefe f. barm, leaven, yeast; dregs, sediment

Heft neu. haft, hilt; copy book; (magazine) issue; **das — in der Hand haben** to be master of a situation; **-faden** m. basting thread; **-klammer** f. paper fastener; **-pflaster** neu. adhesive plaster; –stich *m.* tack, basting

heften *v.* to stitch, to pin; to baste; to fix, to rivet; **sich an jemandes Sohlen —** to stick close to someone's heels

heftig *adj.* violent, vehement, irascible

hegen *v.* to preserve, to protect, to tend; to entertain (suspicion, hope, etc.)

Hehl *neu.* concealment; secret; –er *m.* receiver of stolen goods; fence; –erei *f.* (act of) receiving stolen goods

hehlen *v.* to conceal, to keep secret

hehr *adj.* sublime; venerable; **hoch und —** high and mighty

Heid: –e *f.* heath; –e *m.* heathen, pagan; –ekraut *neu.* heather; –elbeere *f.* bilberry; –elerche *f.* wood lark; –engeld *neu.* immense sum; fortune; –enmission *f.* foreign mission; –eröschen *neu.* brier rose

heidnisch *adj.* heathenish, pagan

heikel *adj.* delicate, difficult, ticklish

heil *adj.* healthy; healed; whole; –! *interj.* hail! good luck! –bar *adj.* curable; –bringend *adj.* salutary; –en *v.* to heal, to cure; –kräftig *adj.* curative, healing; –kundig *adj.* skilled in medical arts; –los *adj.* (coll.) wicked; awful; tremendous; –sam *adj.* wholesome

Heil *neu.* welfare; luck; salvation; –and *m.* Saviour, Redeemer; –anstalt *f.* sanatorium; –bad *neu.* medicinal bath; spa; –brunnen *m.* mineral spring; –butt *m.* halibut; –kraft *f.* healing power; –kunde *f.* medical science, therapeutics; –mittel *neu.* drug, remedy; –mittellehre *f.* pharmacology; –quelle *f.* mineral spring; –sarmee *f.* Salvation Army; –serum *neu.* antitoxin; –stätte *f.* sanatorium; –ung *f.* cure, healing; –verfahren *neu.* medical treatment

heilig *adj.* holy; sacred; –en *v.* to hallow, to sanctify; **der Zweck –t die Mittel** the end justifies the means

Heilig: –e *m.* saint; **das –e Abendmahl** the Lord's Supper; **der –e Abend** Christmas Eve; **die –e Schrift** Holy Writ, the (Holy) Scriptures; –enschein *m.* halo; –keit *f.* sanctity; **Seine –keit** His Holiness (the Pope); –tum *neu.* sanctuary, relic; –tumsentweihung *f.*, –tumsschändung *f.* sacrilege

Heim *neu.* home; –arbeiter *m.* homeworker; –at *f.* native country; homeland; habitat; (law) domicile; –atkrieger *m.* stay-at-home soldier; –atschein *m.* certificate of domicile (*oder* naturalization); –atvertriebene *m.* displaced person; –chen *neu.* house cricket; tiny person; –fahrt, –reise *f.* homeward journey; –gang *m.* going home; death; –gegangene *m.* deceased; –stätte *f.* homestead; –weh *neu.* homesickness; nostalgia

heim *adv.* home(ward); –atlich *adj.* native; –elig *adj.* comfortable, snug; homey; –fallen *v.* to revert; –isch *adj.* native, indigenous; domestic; homey, accustomed; **sich –isch fühlen** to feel at home; –kehren *v.* to return home; –leuchten *v.* (coll.) to send (one) about

his own business; –suchen *v.* to visit; to afflict; –zahlen *v.* to retaliate; to repay

heimlich *adj.* clandestine, secret; snug

heimtückisch *adj.* malicious, deceitful; underhanded

Heinrich *m.* Henry

Heinzelmännchen *neu.* brownie, goblin

Heirat *f.* marriage; –santrag *m.* marriage proposal; –sbüro *neu.* matrimonial agency; –sgut *neu.* dowry; –skandidat *m.* suitor, wooer; –sschein *m.* marriage license; –sstifter *m.* matchmaker; marriage broker

heirat: –en *v.* to marry, to wed; –sfähig *adj.* marriageable; –slustig *adj.* desirous of marrying

heiser *adj.* hoarse, husky; raucous

heiss *adj.* hot; ardent, vehement; –hungrig *adj.* ravenously hungry; –laufen *v.* (mech.) to overheat

heissen *v.* to call, to name; to be called (*oder* named); to command; to designate, to signify; **es heisst** it is said; **jemand willkommen —** to bid someone welcome

heiter *adj.* bright, serene; cheerful, gay

Heiz: –anlage *f.* heating installation; –er *m.* stoker; fireman; –kissen *neu.* heating pad; –körper *m.* radiator; –material *neu.* fuel; –rohr *neu.* flue; fire tube; –sonne *f.* electric heater; –ung *f.* heating (installation)

heizen *v.* to heat; to fire; to give off heat

Hektar *neu.* hectare (2.41 acres)

Held *m.* hero; –endichtung *f.* epic poem; –enrolle *f.* (theat.) part of the hero; –entum *neu.* heroism; –in *f.* heroine

heldenhaft, heldenmütig *adj.* heroic

helfen *v.* to help; to aid, to assist; to be useful, to serve; **es hilft nichts** it is of no use; **sicht nicht zu — wissen** to be at wit's end

Helfer *m.* helper, rescuer, assistant; –shelfer *m.* (law) aider and abettor, accomplice

hell *adj.* bright, shining; fair, light; pale; smart; **am –en Tage** in broad daylight; **–es Gelächter** hearty laughter; **in –en Haufen** in great numbers; –hörig *adj.* keen-eared

Hell: –e *neu.* (coll.) pale beer; –e *f.*, –igkeit *f.* brightness, brilliancy; distinctiveness; –ebarde *f.* halberd; –er *m.* farthing; Austrian coin

Hellas *neu.* Greece

Helm *m.* helmet; (arch.) dome, cupola; –busch *m.* crest (*oder* plume) of a helmet

Helvetien *neu.* Switzerland

Hemd *neu.* shirt; chemise; **jemand bis aufs — ausziehen** (coll.) to strip someone to the skin; –brust *f.* dicky; –cher *neu.* chemisette; –einsatz *m.* shirt front; –särmel *m.* shirt sleeve

Hemm: –nis *neu.* hindrance, impediment, obstruction; –schuh *m.* brake shoe; –ung *f.* restraint, retardation; (watch) escapement; (gun) safety catch

hemmen *v.* to check, to stop; to retar

to curb, to restrain
Hengst *m.* stallion; male (of ass, camel, zebra); –**fohlen** *neu.*, –**füllen** *neu.* colt
Henk: –**el** *m.* handle (of basket, pot, etc.); –**er** *m.* hangman, executioner; –**ersknecht** *m.* hangman's assistant; torturer
henken *v.* to hang
Henne *f.* hen
her *adv.* here, hither, this way, near; ago, since; from; **hin und —** to and fro; **hinter etwas — sein** to be after something; **nicht weit — sein** to live near by; **to be of little importance; um mich —** around me; **von alters —** of old, for a long time; **–bestellen** *v.* to send for; **–fallen** *v.* to fall towards; **über jemand –fallen** to pounce upon; to attack; **–geben** *v.* to hand over; to give away; **sich dazu –geben** to be a party to; **–gehen** *v.* to go on; to set about; to happen; **–halten** *v.* to hold forth; to bear the brunt; **–kommen** *v.* to come hither, to approach; to arise from; **–kömmlich** *adj.* traditional, customary; **–leiten** *v.* to lead hither; to derive; **–machen** *v.* to set about; to fall upon; **–nehmen** *v.* to obtain; (coll.) to take to task; **–richten** *v.* to prepare; to make ready; **–sagen** *v.* to recite; to repeat; **–schaffen** *v.* to bring hither; to provide, to procure; **–stellen** *v.* to set up; to produce, to manufacture; **–ziehen** *v.* to draw (*oder* march) hither; **–ziehen über jemand** (coll.) to run a person down
herab *adv.* down(ward); **von oben — from above**; **–drücken** *v.* to depress; **–lassend** *adj.* condescending; **–sehen** *v.* to look down; **–setzen** *v.* to lower; to disparage; to reduce; **–würdigen** *v.* to debase, to degrade
Heraldik *f.* heraldry
heran *adv.* along, near, on; hither; **–bilden** *v.* to train; to educate; **–kommen** *v.* to come on, to approach; **–nahen** *v.* to approach; **–nehmen** *v.* to discipline; **–rücken** *v.* to draw near; to advance; **–treten** *v.* to approach, to step up to; **–wachsen** *v.* to grow up; **–ziehen** *v.* to draw near; to educate
heraus *adv.* out; from within; forth; **frei (*oder* offen) —** frankly, bluntly; **— damit! out with it!** **–bekommen** *v.* to get back (change); to elicit; to puzzle out; to make out; **–bringen** *v.* to bring (*oder* find) out; **–fordern** *v.* to challenge; to provoke; **–geben** *v.* to deliver, to hand out; to give change; to publish; to issue; **–geh(e)n** *v.* to go out; **aus sich –geh(e)n** to become communicative; **–kommen** *v.* to come out; to appear; to be published (*oder* issued); **auf eins –kommen** to be all the same; **–nehmen** *v.* to take out; **sich etwas –nehmen** to venture, to presume; **–reden** *v.* to speak out; **–reissen** *v.* to tear out; **sich –reissen** to extricate oneself; **–rücken** *v.* to come out with; to hand over; **–rufen** *v.* to call forth (*oder* out); **–schlagen** *v.* to knock out; **–stellen** *v.* to place outside; **sich –stellen** to turn out to be; **–streichen** *v.* to

strike out; to single out; to praise; **–treten** *v.* to step out, to emerge, to protrude; **–ziehen** *v.* to extract
herbei *adj.* hereto, hither; near to; **—! come here!** **–führen** *v.* to bring near (*oder* about); to cause; to give rise to; **–schaffen** *v.* to provide
Herberge *f.* lodging, shelter; inn
Herbst *m.* fall, autumn; harvest time; **–zeitlose** *f.* meadow-saffron
Herd *m.* hearth, fireplace, kitchen range; home; focus; central (*oder* starting) point
Herde *f.* herd, flock; drove; crowd, multitude; **–nmensch** *m.* one of the mass of humanity; **–ntier** *neu.* gregarious animal
herein *adv.* in (here), into this place; **—! come in!** **–brechen** *v.* to beset; to befall; **–dringen** *v.* to enter forcibly; **–fallen** *v.* to fall into; (coll.) to be taken in; **–gehen** *v.* to enter; **–legen** *v.* to put in; (coll.) to cheat; **–schneien** *v.* to snow in; (coll.) to appear suddenly
Hergang *m.* course of events
hergebracht *adj.* traditional, customary
Hering *m.* herring
Herkunft *f.* derivation; descent, origin
Hermelin *neu.* ermine
hernach *adv.* afterwards, thereafter; subsequently
hernieder *adv.* downward
Hero: –**ismus** *m.* heroism; –**ld** *m.* herald; –**s** *m.* hero
heroisch *adj.* heroic(al)
Herr *m.* master; owner, principal; gentleman; Sir, Mr., Lord; **als grosser — leben** to live in grand style; **— werden** to master, to overcome; **sein eig(e)ner — sein** to be independent; **–enabend** *m.* stag party; **–enartikel** *m.* gentlemen's apparel; **–enhaus** *neu.* manor, mansion; **–enzimmer** *neu.* study; **–gott** *m.* Lord God; **–in** *f.* mistress, lady; **–schaft** *f.* mastery, dominion; power; authority; master and mistress; **–scher** *m.* ruler, sovereign; **–schsucht** *f.* ambition
herüber *adv.* over, across; to this side
herum *adv.* (round) about, near; around; (coll.) finished, over; **hier — hereabouts; rings (*oder* rund) — all around; überall — everywhere; –bringen** *v.* to bring around; to persuade, to induce; **–drücken** *v.* to squeeze around; **sich –drücken** (coll.) to hang around; **–irren** *v.* to wander aimlessly; **–irrend** *adj.* stray, vagrant; **–kommen** *v.* to come around; to travel about; to become known; **–kriegen** *v.* to talk over; **–reichen** *v.* to pass around; **–schnüffeln** *v.* to poke one's nose into everything; **–stöbern** *v.* to rummage about; **–streichen** *v.* to roam about; **–treiben** *v.* to drive around; **sich –treiben** to gad about; to rove around
herunter *adv.* down(ward); off; **–giessen** *v.* to pour down; **–holen** *v.* to bring down; (avi.) to shoot down; **–klappen** *v.* to turn down (collar, etc.); **–kommen**

r. to come down; to decline; (coll.) to go to the dogs; **-lassen** v. to let down; to lower; **-reissen** v. to pull down; (oder to pieces); **-setzen** v. to reduce, to lower; to downgrade; to disparage

hervor adv. forth, forward; out; **-brechen** v. to break through; to emerge; **-bringen** v. to bring forth; to produce; to utter; to engender, to generate; **-drängen** v. to press forward; **-geh(e)n** v. to go forth; to result from; **-heben** v. to make conspicuous (oder prominent), (typ.) to display; to emphasize, to stress; **-ragen** v. to stand out, to project; **-ragend** adj. excellent, outstanding, prominent; **-rufen** v. to call forth; to cause; **-stechen** v. to stand out; to be conspicuous; **-steh(e)n** v. to stand out; to project; **-treten** v. to step forward; to be prominent; **sich -tun** to distinguish oneself; to excel; **-ziehen** v. to draw forth, to produce

Herz neu. heart; center, core; (cards) hearts; courage; **ans — legen** to enjoin, to urge; **das — auf der Zunge haben** to wear one's heart on one's sleeve; **ein Kind unterm -en tragen** to be pregnant; **ein Mann nach meinem -en** a man to my liking; **etwas auf dem -en haben** to have something on one's mind; **ins — schliessen** to become fond of; **sein — an etwas hängen** to set one's heart on something; **sich das — aus dem Leibe ärgern** to eat one's heart out with vexation; **sich ein — fassen** to take courage; **von -en gern** with the greatest of pleasure; **-ader** f. aorta; **-blut** neu. heart's blood; the very life; **-dame** f. queen of hearts; **-ensangelegenheit** f. love affair; **-ensbrecher** m. lady-killer, **-enseinfalt** f. simplicity; simple-mindedness; **-ensgüte** f. kindheartedness; **-enslust** f. heart's content; **-geräusch** neu. heart murmurs; **-kammer** f. heart ventricle; **-klopfen** neu. palpitation of the heart; **-liebchen** neu., **-liebste** f. true love; **-muskel** m. miocardium; **-schlag** m. heart beat; apoplexy; **-weh** neu. heartache; grief

herz: -allerliebst adj. sweet, lovely; **-bewegend** adj. heart-stirring, touching; **-brechend** adj. heart-breaking; **-en** v. to hug, to embrace, to caress; **-ensfroh** adj. very glad; **-ensgut** adj. very kind; **-ergreifend** adj. moving; **-erhebend** adj. heart-stirring; **-förmig** adj. heart-shaped; **-haft** adj. stouthearted, valiant, vigorous; **-ig** adj. charming, lovely; **innig** adj. heart-felt; **-lich** adj. hearty, cordial, affectionate; **-los** adj. heartless, cruel; **-zerreissend** adj. heart-rending

Herzog m. duke; **-in** f. duchess; **-tum** neu. duchy

herzu adv. up (to) towards

Hetz: -blatt neu. (coll.) hate-sheet; yellow journal; **-er** m., **-redner** m. agitator, instigator; **-presse** f. yellow press; **-rede** f. inflammatory speech

Hetze f. hunt, hunting with hounds; agitation; hurry, mad race

Heu neu. hay; **-boden** m. hayloft; **-er** m. haymaker; **-fieber** neu. hay fever; **-gabel** f. pitchfork; **-schober** m. haystack; **-schrecke** f. grasshopper

heuch: -eln v. to play the hypocrite; to feign; to pretend, to simulate; **-lerisch** adj. hypocritical

Heuch: -elei f. hypocrisy; **-ler** m. hypocrite

heuen v. to make hay

heulen v. to howl, to hoot, to yelp; to cry

heute adv. today; nowadays; **— vor acht Tagen** a week ago today! **-abend** adv. tonight; **-früh** adv. this morning

heutig adj. of today; modern

heutzutage adv. nowadays

Hexe f. witch, sorceress; hag; **-nkessel** m. hurly-burly, hubbub; **-nkreis** m. magic circle; **-nkunst** f. witchcraft, sorcery, magic art; **-nmeister** m. magician, sorcerer; **-nschuss** m. lumbago; **-rei** f. sorcery; black magic

Hieb m. blow, cut, stroke; gash, slash; hit

hier adv. here; **— sein** to be present; **— und da** now and then; in various places; **-an** adv. hereon; **-auf** adv. hereupon, on (oder after, at, by) this; **-aus** adv. from this; hence; **-bei** adv. hereby, herewith; enclosed; **-durch** adv. through here, this way; by this means; hereby; **-gegen** adv. against this; **-her** adv. this way, hither; **bis -her** so far; hitherto, up to now; **-herum** adv. hereabouts; **-hin** adv. in this direction; **-mit** adv. herewith; **-nach** adv. hereafter; according to this; **-orts** adv. here; **-über** adv. over here; concerning this; **-um** adv. around here; **-unter** adv. beneath this; among these **-von** adv. hereof, herefrom; **-zu** adv. in addition to this; moreover; **-zulande** adv. in this country

hiesig adj. of this country (oder place), local

Hilf: -e f. help; aid, assistance; relief; **-sarbeiter** m. temporary worker; **-sgelder** neu. pl. subsidies; **-skasse** f. charitable fund; **-slehrer** m. substitute teacher; **-smittel** neu. remedy, resource; expedient; **-smotor** m. servomotor; booster; **-sprediger** m. curate; **-squelle** f. resource; **-struppen** f. pl. auxiliary troops; **-s(zeit)wort** neu. auxiliary verb; **-szug** m. relief train

Himbeere f. raspberry

Himmel m. heaven; sky, firmament; canopy; **aus allen -n fallen** to be bitterly disappointed; **-bett** neu. fourposter (bed); **-blau** neu. sky-blue, azure; **-fahrt** f. (rel.) Ascension; Assumption; **-reich** neu. kingdom of heaven; **-sgegend** f., **-srichtung** f. quarter of the heaven, direction; point of the compass; **-skörper** m. celestical body; **-skunde** f. astronomy; **-sschlüssel** m. primrose, primula; **-sstrich** m. climate, region, zone; latitude; **-szeichen** neu. sign of the zodiac; **-szelt** neu. (lit.) celestial dome, firmament

himmlisch adj. heavenly, celestial; divine

hin *adv.* there, thither, toward(s); along, till; forth; (coll.) gone, lost, dead; ruined; exhausted; **aufs Ungewisse —** at random; **es zieht sich —** it drags on; **Fahrkarte — und zurück** round-trip ticket; **— ist —** there's no use crying over spilt milk; **— und her** to and fro; **— und her überlegen** to rack one's brain; **— und wieder** now and then; **— und zurück** coming and going; **überall —** in all directions; **-bringen** *v.* to bring (*oder* carry) to; to pass, to spend; **-deuten** *v.* to point at; **-fallen** *v.* to fall down; **-fällig** *adj.* decaying, frail, weak; **-geben** *v.* to give away, to surrender, to sacrifice; **sich -geben** to devote oneself; **-geh(e)n** *v.* to go there; to pass away; to elapse; **-halten** *v.* to hold out; to keep in suspense; **-länglich** *adj.* sufficient; **-legen** *v.* to lay (*oder* put) down, **sich -legen** to lie down; **-nehmen** *v.* to take; to accept; to suffer; **-raffen** *v.* to cut off (by death); **-reichen** *v.* to stretch out; to hand over; to suffice; **-reichend** *adj.* sufficient; **-reissen** *v.* to overpower; to enchant, to charm; **-reissend** *adj.* charming, enchanting; **-scheiden** *v.* to die, to pass away; **-schleppen** *v.* to drag on; **-schwinden** *v.* to dwindle, to vanish; **-setzen** *v.* to set down; **sich -setzen** to sit down; **-sichtlich** *adj.* with reference to; in view of; **-stellen** *v.* to put down; to represent; **-strecken** *v.* to stretch out; to kill; **sich -strecken** to lie down, to lay low; to last; **-weisen** *v.* to refer (*oder* point) to; **-weisend** *adj.* demonstrative; **-werfen** *v.* to throw down; to sketch; **-ziehen** *v.* to draw to; to attract; to move there; **sich -ziehen** to draw out, to drag on

Hin: -blick *m.* glance; regard; **im -blick auf** in view of; **-fahrt** *f.* journey (*oder* voyage, trip) there; **Hin- und Rückfahrt** round trip; **-gabe** *f.* abandonment; devotion; indulgence; **-gang** *m.* decease; **-reise** *f.* journey (*oder* voyage) to; **-richtung** *f.* execution; **-sicht** *f.* respect, regard; **-weg** *m.* (the) way toward; **-weis** *m.* hint, indication; reference, allusion

hinab *adv.* down, downward(s); **den Fluss —** downstream

hinauf *adv.* up to; upward(s); **den Fluss — upstream; die Treppe — upstairs; -setzen** *v.* to raise; **-steigen** *v.* to ascend, to mount

hinaus *adv.* out(side); **—! ** *interj.* get out! **hoch — wollen** to aim high; **über etwas — sein** to be beyond something; **-gehen** *v.* to go out; to exceed; **auf etwas -gehen** to end in, to aim at; **-schieben** *v.* to defer, to postpone, to put off; **-werfen** *v.* to throw out; to expel; **-ziehen** *v.* to draw out; to march (*oder* move) out(side); to protract

hindern *v.* to hinder, to impede; to obstruct

Hindernis *neu.* hindrance; impediment; obstacle; deterrence; **-rennen** *neu.*

steeplechase; hurdle-race

hinein *adv.* in (thither), into; **mitten— right into the middle; -arbeiten** *v.*, **sich -arbeiten in** to work one's way into; to familiarize oneself with; **-fallen** *v.* to fall into; (coll.) to be taken in; **sich -finden** *v.* to accomodate (*oder* reconcile) oneself to; **-geh(e)n** *v.* to go in(to); to enter; **-geraten** *v.* to get into

hinfort *adv.* henceforth; in the future

hingegen *adv.* and *conj.* on the contrary; on the other hand; but, whereas

hinken *v.* to limp; to hobble; to drag along

hinten *adv.* behind; in the rear; (naut.) aft; **-über** *adv.* upside down, backwards

hinter *adj.* back; hind(er); posterior; — *adv.* back(wards), behind; — *prep.* behind, after; back of, in the rear of; — **die Sache (or Schliche) kommen** to find out something; **— die Schule gehen** to play truant; **— einer Sache her sein** to be persistent about; **— Schloss und Riegel bringen** to jail; **sich lassen** to outdistance, to outstrip; **jemand — das Licht führen** (coll.) to cheat someone; **-bringen** *v.* to inform (*oder* report) secretly; **-drein** *adv.* afterwards, subsequently; following; **-einander** *adv.* successively; one after the other; **-geh(e)n** *v.* to deceive, to hoodwink; **-hältig** *adj.* deceitful; **-her** *adv.* behind; subsequently; eagerly; **-lassen** *v.* to leave behind; to bequeath; **-legen** *v.* to deposit; **-listig** *adj.* cunning; treacherous; **-rücks** *adv.* from behind; deceitfully; **-st** *adj.* hindmost, last; **-treiben** *v.* to frustrate; to thwart; **-wärts** *adv.* backwards, behind; **-ziehen** *v.* to drag back; to embezzle; to defraud

Hinter: -backe *f.* buttock; **-bein** *neu.* sich auf die -beine setzen to strain oneself; **-bliebene** *m.* survivor, mourner; **-deck** *neu.*, **-schiff** *neu.* sterndeck; **-gedanke** *m.* mental reservation; **-grund** *m.* background; **-halt** *m.* ambush; **-hof** *m.* back yard; **-lader** *m.* breechloader; **-lassenschaft** *f.* inheritance; estate; **-list** *f.* deceit, treachery; **-n** *m.* (coll.) buttock; **-pforte** *f.* back gate; **-reihe** *f.* (mil.) rear file; **-steven** *m.* sternpost; (sl.) buttocks; **-teil** *neu.* back part; hindquarter; buttock; (naut.) stern; **-treffen** *neu.* rearguard; **ins -treffen geraten** to be at a disadvantage; **-treppenroman** *m.* cheap novel; **-viertel** *neu.* hindquarter; loin; **-wand** *f.* back wall; (theat.) backdrop

hinunter *adv.* down(ward); **-giessen** *v.* (coll.) to toss off (drink); **-schlucken** *v.* to swallow; **-spülen** *v.* to wash down; **-würgen** *v.* to gulp down

hinweg *adv.* away; off; **—!** *interj.* get away! out you go! **-gerafft** *adj.* dead; **-gehen (über)** to overlook; **-kommen (über)** to overcome; **-sehen (über)** to shut one's eyes to; **-setzen, sich -setzen (über)** to reconcile oneself to, to ignore

hinwieder(um) *adv.* again, once more; on

the other hand

hinzu *adv.* toward; near; in addition to, supplementing; **-fügen** *v.* to add, to annex; **-kommen** *v.* to come up; to be added; **-ziehen** *v.* to add; to include; to consult

Hiob *m.* Job

Hiobsbote *m.* bearer of ill tidings

Hippe *f.* scythe; billhook

Hirn *neu.* brain; **-gespinst** *neu.* fancy, notion, whim; vision, chimera; **-hautentzündung** *f.* meningitis; **-schädel** *m.*, **-schale** *f.* skull, cranium

Hirsch *m.* stag; hart; **-fänger** *m.* hanger, bowie knife; **-geweih** *neu.* antlers, hart's horns; **-kalb** *neu.* fawn; **-kuh** *f.* hind, female deer; **-leder** *neu.* buckskin

Hirse *f.* millet; **-brei** *m.* millet gruel

Hirt(e) *m.* herdsman; shepherd; pastor; **-enamt** *neu.* shepherd's duties; pastorate; **-enbrief** *m.* pastoral letter; **-engedicht** *neu.* pastoral (*oder* bucolic) poem, eclogue; **-enleben** *neu.* pastoral life; **-enstab** *m.* shepherd's staff; (eccl.) crosier; **-envolk** *neu.* pastoral people; nomadic tribe; **-in** *f.* shepherdess

hissen *v.* to hoist, to pull up

Historiker *m.* historian

historisch *adj.* historic(al)

Hitz: **-e** *f.* heat; ardor, passion; **-egradmesser** *m.* pyrometer; **-eschild** (bemannte Rakete) *neu.* heat shield; **-kopf** *m.* hothead; **-schlag** *m.* heat stroke, sunstroke

hitzig *adj.* hot; heated; inflamed; angered, hotheaded; vehement; irascible

Hobel *m.* plane; **-bank** *f.* carpenter's (*oder* joiner's) bench; **-späne** *m. pl.* shavings

hoch *adj.* high; tall; noble, sublime; — *adv.* highly; greatly, very; **das ist mir zu** — that is beyond my reach; **die See ging** — the sea was rough; **es geht** — **her** there is much merrymaking; **Hände** —**!** hands up! — **angeschrieben sein to be in great favor;** — **anrechnen** to value greatly; — **leben lassen** to toast, to give three cheers for; — **spielen** to play for high stakes; — **und heilig** (*or* **teuer**) **versprechen** to promise solemnly; **-achtungsvoll** *adj.* respectfully yours; **-bejahrt** *adj.*, **-betagt** *adj.* very old; **-fahrend** *adj.* haughty, overbearing; **-fein** *adj.* superfine, exquisite; **-fliegend** *adj.* flying high; ambitious; **-gehend** *adj.* running high; rough (sea); **-gemut** *adj.* in good spirits; **-gesinnt** *adj.* noble-minded; **-gespannt** *adj.* high-tensioned; exaggerated; **-gestimmt** *adj.* high-pitched; high-minded; **-gradig** *adj.* to a high degree; intense; **-halten** *v.* to cherish, to esteem highly; **-herzig** *adj.* noble, high-minded, magnanimous; **-klingend** *adj.* high-sounding; bombastic; **-mütig** *adj.* haughty, arrogant; **-näsig** *adj.* supercilious, (coll.) stuck-up; **-rot** *adj.* bright red; highly inflamed; **-selig** *adj.* of blessed memory, late; **-stimmig** *adj.* tall, standard; **-trabend** *adj.* pompous, bombastic; **-wertig** *adj.* of high value, valuable

Hoch *neu.* cheer; (meteorology) high pressure area; **-achtung** *f.* high esteem, deep respect; **-amt** *neu.* (eccl.) high mass; **-antenne** *f.* overhead aerial; **-bahn** *f.* elevated railroad; **-bau** *m.* tall construction, skyscraper; **-betrieb** *m.* intensive activity, hustle; **-burg** *f.* stronghold; **-druck** *m.* high pressure; great hurry; relief printing; **-ebene** *f.* plateau; **-(ehr)würden** *m.* Right Reverend; **-genuss** *m.* great enjoyment; real treat; **-gericht** *neu.* place of execution; gallows; **-gesang** *m.* anthem, ode; **-haus** *neu.* skyscraper; **-mut** *m.* haughtiness; arrogance; **-ofen** *m.* blast furnace; **-schule** *f.* college; university; **-sommer** *m.* midsummer; **-spannung** *f.* (elec.) high voltage; **-sprung** *m.* high jump; **-stapelei** *f.* swindling; criminal imposture; **-stapler** *m.* swindler; confidence man; **-verrat** *m.* high treason; **-wasser** *neu.* high water (*oder* tide); flood; **-wild** *neu.* big game

höchst *adj.* highest; extreme; utmost; maximum; — *adv.* extremely, most, very; **aufs -e** to the last extremity; — **schädlich** highly injurious; **-ens** *adv.* at most; **-wahrscheinlich** *adj.* very probably, in all likelihood

Höchst: **-geschwindigkeit** *f.* top speed; **-leistung** *f.* maximum output; record performance; **-preis** *m.* maximum price; **-mass** *neu.* maximum

Hochzeit *f.* wedding, nuptials; marriage; **-er** *m.* bridegroom; **-erin** *f.* bride; **-sreise** *f.* honeymoon trip; **-sschmauss** *m.* wedding dinner; **-szug** *m.* bridal procession

hocken *v.* to crouch, to squat; (coll.) to stick

Höcker *m.* knoll; protuberance; hunchback; hump

Hof *m.* yard; courtyard; farm; estate; court; (ast.) corona, halo; **den** — **machen** to court; **-besitzer** *m.* owner of an estate; **-brauch** *m.*, **-sitte** *f.* court etiquette; **-burg** *f.* royal residence; **-dame** *f.* lady in waiting; lady of the court; **-dichter** *m.* poet laureate; **-haltung** *f.* royal household; **-hund** *m.* watchdog; **-meister** *m.* private tutor; manager of an estate; **-rat** *m.* privy councilor; **-staat** *m.* princely household; court dress; **-schranze** *f.* courtier

Höf: **-lichkeit** *f.* politeness; **-lichkeitsbezeigungen** *f. pl.* marks of attention, compliments; **-ling** *m.* courtier

hoff: **-en** *v.* to hope, to expect; **-entlich** *adv.* it is to be hoped; **-nungsvoll** *adj.* hopeful, promising; **-nungslos** *adj.* hopeless

Hoff: **-art** *f.* haughtiness, arrogance, conceit; **-nung** *f.* hope; expectation; **in guter -nung** pregnant; expectation; **-nungsschimmer** *m.* gleam of hope; **-nungsstrahl** *m.* ray of hope, silver lining

hoffärtig *adj.* haughty, arrogant; conceited

höflich *adj.* courteous, polite

Höhe *f.* height; altitude; elevation; **auf der** — up to par; up to date; in the latitude (of); **auf gleicher —** on a level with; **das ist die —!** that's the limit!; **Ehre sei Gott in der —!** Glory to God in the Highest; **–nkrankheit** f. aeroembolism; **–nmesser** m. altimeter; **–nzug** m. mountain range; **–npunkt** m. peak; zenith; climax

Hoheit f. sovereignty; Highness; **–sgewässer** n. pl. territorial waters

höher adj. higher; superior

hohl adj. hollow; concave; empty; flimsy; **–äugig** adj. hollow-eyed; **–bäckig** adj. hollow-cheeked; **–geschliffen** adj. hollow-ground; concave; **–köpfig** adj. empty-headed, shallow-witted, vacuous

Hohl: **–bohrer** m. post-hole digger; **–heit** f. hollowness; **–kehle** f., **–rinne** f. (arch.) groove, channel; **–kopf** m. empty-headed fellow; **–naht** f., **–saum** m. hemstitch; **–raum** m. hollow; cavity; **–weg** m. ravine; narrow pass; defile

Höhle f. cave(rn); hollow, cavity; den; **–nbewohner** m. cave dweller; troglodyte

Höhlung f. hollow; cavity; excavation

Hohn m. disdain; scorn; derision; **–gelächter** neu. mocking laughter

höhnen v. to jeer; to scorn, to deride

höhnisch adj. disdainful, scornful; derisive

Höker m. street vendor

hold adj. charming, graceful, lovely; **jemandem — sein** to favor someone; **–selig** adj. most charming, enchanting

holen v. to fetch; (naut.) to lower; to haul up; **— lassen** to send for; **sich —** to catch (cold, etc.) **sich Rat —** to consult

Hölle f. hell; **Himmel und — aufbieten** to move heaven and earth; **jemand die —heiss machen** to make it hot for someone; **–nangst** f. mortal fright; **–nbrand** m. hell-fire; tremendous conflagration; **–nmaschine** f. infernal machine

höllisch adj. diabolical; (coll.) tremendous

holp(e)rig adj. rugged, rough, uneven

holpern v. to jolt; to stumble

Holunder m. elder (shrub oder tree)

Holz neu. wood; timber; forest; **— sägen** (coll.) to snore; **–apfel** m. crab apple; **–bekleidung** f. wooden lining, wainscoting; **–bildhauer** m. woodcarver; **–birne** f. wild pear; **–bock** m. sawhorse; (ent.) tick; **–bohrer** m. auger, gimlet; wood beetle; **–essig** m. wood vinegar; **–fäller** m., **–hacker** m., **–hauer** m. woodcutter; lumberman; **–fäule** f. dry rot; **–frevel** m. forest damage; **–geist** m. wood alcohol; **–häher** m. jay; **–hof** m. lumberyard; **–kohle** f. charcoal; **–nagel** m. wooden peg; **–schlag** m. forest clearing; felling of timber; **–schneider** m. wood engraver (oder carver); **–schnitt** m. woodcut; **–schuh** m. clog; **–späne** m. pl. shavings; **auf dem —weg sein** to be on the wrong track; **–wolle** f. excelsior

holz: **–en** v. to fell timber; to gather wood; (coll.) to cudgel; **–ig** adj. containing wood fibers; **–reich** adj. woody

hölzern adj. wooden; stiff; tedious; dull

homogen adj. homogeneous

honett adj. honorable; decent

Honig m. honey; **— um den Mund schmieren** to coax, to wheedle; to fawn; **–kuchen** m. gingerbread; **–monat** m., **–mond** m. honeymoon; **–saft** m. nectar; **–scheibe** f., **–wabe** f. honeycomb; **–seim** m. liquid honey

Honorar neu. honorarium; fee; **–professor** m. honorary professor

Honoratioren pl. notables; City Fathers

honorieren v. to honor; to pay an honorarium

Hör: **–bild** neu. sound picture; **–ensagen** neu. hearsay; **–er** m. hearer, auditor, noncredit student; (tel.) receiver; **–erschaft** f. audience; **–folge** f. (rad.) program; **–saal** m. auditorium; lecture room; **–spiel** neu. radio play; **–weite** f. earshot

hör: **–bar** adj. audible; **–en** v. to hear; to listen; to obey; to attend (lectures); **auf einen Namen –en** to answer to a name; **das lässt sich –en** that sounds all right; **Flöhe husten** (or **Gras wachsen**) **–en** to have sharp hearing, to be keenly alert; **schwer –en** to be hard of hearing; **von sich –en lassen** to send news of oneself; to write; **Berlin –en** (rad.) to get Berlin; **–ig** adj. dependent; living in bondage

horchen v. to hearken; to eavesdrop

Horizont m. horizon

horizontale Luftströmung f. advection

Horn neu. horn; bugle; peak; (ent.) feeler; **die Hörner zeigen** to oppose vigorously; **sich die Hörner abstossen** to learn by experience; **–bläser** m. hornblower, bugler; **–haut** f. horny skin; callous; cornea; **–hecht** m. garfish; **–isse** f. hornet; **–rabe** m. hornbill; **–signal** neu. bugle call; **–ung** m. (poet.) February; **–vieh** neu. horned cattle; (coll.) blockhead

horn(art)ig adj. like horn; horny; hardened

Hörnchen neu. small horn, cornicle; crescent

hörnern adj. of horn; like horn

horrend adj. horrible; gruesome

Horst m. eyrie; bush, thicket; den, dwelling

Hort m. (lit.) hoard, treasure; day nursery; refuge, protection

Hortensie f. hydrangea

Hose f. trousers; shorts; panties; **–nband** neu. kneeband; (Order of the) Garter **–nboden** m. seat of trousers; **sich auf den –nboden setzen** to work hard; **–nbund** m. waistband; **–nklappe** f., **–nlatz** m. fly (of trousers); **–nmatz** m. little fellow; **–nträger** m. pl. suspenders

Hospital neu. hospital

Hospiz neu. hospice

Hostie f. (rel.) the Host

Hotel neu. hotel; **–ier** m. hotel owner

Hub m. lift(ing); raising; (piston) stroke; **–schrauber** m. helicopter; **–schrauber-Nahverkehr** m. helibus

hübsch adj. pretty; handsome

Huckepack m. piggyback

Huf m. hoof; **-beschlag** m. horseshoeing; **-eisen** neu. horseshoe; **-nagel** m. horseshoe nail; **-schlag** m. hoof beat; **-schmied** m. blacksmith

Hüft: -bein neu., **-knochen** m. hipbone; **-e** f. hip, haunch; **-gelenk** neu. hip joint; **-nerv** m. sciatic nerve; **-schmerz** m., **-weh** neu. sciatica

Hügel m. hill; knoll; **-land** neu. hill country

hügelig adj. hill-shaped; hilly

Huhn neu. hen, chicken, pullet; **ein verrücktes —** a crazy fellow; a silly woman

Hühner pl. poultry; **-auge** neu. (toe) corn; **-augenoperateur** m. chiropodist; **-frikassee** f. stewed chicken; **-haus** neu., **-stall** m. hen coop; **-hof** m. poultry yard; **-hund** m. pointer, setter; **-pastete** f. chicken pie; **-stange** f. perch, roost

Huld f. grace, favor, clemency; **-igung** f. homage; **-igungseid** m. oath of allegiance

huld: -igen v. to render homage; to indulge in; **-reich** adj., **-voll** adj. gracious; clement

Hülle f. cover(ing), envelope; **in — und Fülle** in abundance; **sterbliche —** mortal frame

hüllen v. to cover, to wrap; to veil, to hide; **sich in Schweigen —** to remain silent

Hülse f. shell; pod; capsule; hull; **-nfrüchte** f. pl. legumes

human adj. humane; **-istisch** adj. humanistic; classical; **-itär** adj. humanitarian

Hummel f. bumble bee

Hummer m. lobster; **-schere** f. lobster claw

Humor m. humor; **-eske** f. humorous sketch (oder play, story); **-ist** m. humorist

humoristisch adj. humorous

Humpen m. bumper, goblet

Humus m. humus, mould

Hund m. dog, hound; (min.) truck; **auf dem — sein** to be down and out; **auf den — kommen, vor die -e gehen** to go to the dogs; **da liegt der —** there's the rub! **ein toter — beisst nicht** dead men tell no tales; **-earbeit** f. drudgery; **-efutter** neu. dog food; miserable meal; **-ehütte** f. kennel; **-ekuchen** m. dog biscuit; **-emarke** f. dog tag; **-ewache** f. (naut.) midnight watch; **-ewärter** m. kennel man; **-ewetter** neu. bad weather; **-ezucht** f. breeding of dogs; **-sfott** m. scoundrel; cur; **-sstern** m. Dog Star, Sirius; **-stage** m. pl. dog-days; **-swut** f. hydrophobia, rabies

hundert adj. hundred; **-erlei** adj. of a hundred different kinds; **-fach** adj., **-fältig** adj. hundredfold, centuple; **-jährig** adj. of a hundred years, centenary; **-tägig** adj. lasting a hundred days; **-weise** adv. by (oder in) hundreds

Hundert neu., **-er** m. hundred; **-stel** neu. hundredth part

Hündin f. bitch

hündisch adj. bootlicking, servile, fawning

Hüne m. giant; **-ngestalt** f. mighty figure; **-ngrab** neu. prehistoric barrow, cairn

Hunger m. hunger; famine; predilection, eagerness; **am -tuch nagen** to suffer hunger; **-gestalt** f. mere skeleton; **-kur** f. reducing diet; **-leider** m. needy wretch; **-lohn** m. starvation wage; **-snot** f. famine; **-tod** m. death from starvation

hungern v. to be hungry, to suffer hunger; **— lassen** to starve; **— nach** to yearn for

hungrig adj. hungry

Hupe f. (auto.) horn, siren

hüpfen v. to hop, to skip, to jump

Hürde f. hurdle, pen; stand (for drying fruit); **-nrennen** neu. hurdle race

Hure f. prostitute; whore; **-rei** f. fornication

hurtig adj. brisk, nimble, agile

huschen v. to scurry, to whisk

husten v. to cough

Husten m. cough

Hut m. hat, round cover; **unter einen — bringen** (coll.) to reconcile; **— f.** guard, protection; **auf der — sein** to be on one's guard; **in Gottes —** in God's keeping; **-krempe** f. hat brim; **-schachtel** f. hatbox

hüten v. to guard, to protect; to take care of; **das Bett —** to be confined to one's bed; **ich werde mich — !** I certainly won't do that! **sich —** to be on guard, to avoid

Hütte f. hut, cabin; chalet, shelter; foundry, smeltery; **-nkunde** f., **-wesen** neu. metallurgy

Hyäne f. hyena

Hymne f., **Hymnus** m. hymn; anthem

hypnotisieren v. to hypnotize

Hypo- -chonder m. hypochondriac; **-thek** f. mortgage; **-these** f. hypothesis; supposition, assumption

Hysterie f. hysteria

I

ich pron. I; **— selbst** I myself; **— Armer! — Elender!** poor me!

Ich neu. self; ego; **-sucht** f. egotism

ideal adj. ideal; **-isieren** v. to idealize; **-istisch** adj idealistic(al)

Idee f. idea; notion, concept; (coll.) a little (bit); **-nverbindung** f. association of ideas

ideell adj. ideal; imaginary, fanciful

identifizieren v. to identify

identisch adj. identical

Identitätsnachweis m. certificate of identity

idiotisch adj. idiotic(al)

Idyll neu., **Idylle** f. idyl

idyllisch adj. idyllic

Igel m. hedgehog; (agr.) drill-harrow; urchin

Ignorant m. ignoramus

gnorieren v. to ignore

hm pron. to him, to it

hn pron. him, it; **-en** pron. to them

hr pron. and adj. to her; hers, its; **— pl.** you; theirs; **-er** pron. (of) her (oder them, their); **-erseits** adv. in her (oder their) turn; **-esgleichen** adj. of her (oder their) kind; like her (oder them); **-ethalben** adv., **-etwegen** adv., **-etwillen** adv. on her (oder their) account; for her (oder their) sake; as far as she (oder they) is (oder are) concerned

llegitim adj. illegitimate

llegitimität f. illegitimacy

lloyal adj. disloyal

llustrieren v. to illustrate

lse f. Alice, Elsie

ltis m. polecat, ferret

maginär adj. imaginary

mbiss m. snack; **-halle** f. snack bar

mker m. beekeeper; **-ei** f. beekeeping

mmatrikulieren v. to matriculate

mme f. (poet.) bee

mmer adv. always, continually; constantly; auf **—** forever; **— mehr** more and more; **— und — wieder** over and over again; **— wieder** continuing: noch **—** still, yet, even now; nur **— zu!** keep it up! wann auch **—** whenever; was auch **—** what(so)ever; wen auch **—** whom(so)ever; wenn auch **—** (al)though; wer auch **—** who(so)ever; wie auch (or nur) **—** in whatever manner; how(so)ever; wie **—** as usual; wo auch **—** where(so)ever; wohin auch **—** wherever; whithersoever; **-dar** adv. forever; **-fort** adv. constantly, on and on; **-hin** adv. for all that, nevertheless; **-während** adj. constant, permanent; **-zu** adv. and interj. continuously; go ahead!

mmobilien pl. real estate; immovables

mmunisieren v. to render immune; to immunize

mmunität f. immunity

npfen v. to inoculate, to vaccinate; to graft

mponieren v. to impress; **-d** adj. impressive

mport m. importation, imports; **-e** f. imports (especially cigars); **-eur** m. importer

mposant adj. imposing

mpotenz f. impotence

mprägnieren v. to impregnate

mprovisieren v. to improvise; to extemporize

mpuls m. impulse

mpulsiv adj. impulsive

mstande adv. capable (of); **— sein** (coll.) to be foolish enough (to do something)

n prep. in, at; to, into; within

nangriffnahme f. start, setting about

nbegriff m. totality; embodiment; essence

nbegriffen adv. included

nbrunst f. fervor, ardor

nbrünstig adj. ardent, fervent

ndem adv. (mean)while; because, as, since; by

ndes(sen) adv. meanwhile; but; nevertheless

Indien neu. India

indigniert adj. indignant

Indiskretion f. indiscretion; tactlessness

indisponiert adj. indisposed

Individu: **-alismus** m. individualism; **-alität** f. individuality; **-um** neu. individual; personality

individuell adj. individual

Indiz neu. (law) indication of guilt; **-ienbeweis** m. circumstantial evidence

Indossament neu. endorsement

Industri: **-alisierung** f. industrialization; **-e** f. industry; **-eller** m. manufacturer; industrialist; **-estaat** m. manufacturing country

industriell adj. industrial

ineinander adv. into each other

infam adj. infamous

Infamie f. infamy

Infant m. infante; **-erie** f. infantry; **-in** f. infanta; **-rist** m. infantryman, foot soldier

Infektionskrankheit f. infectious disease

infizieren v. to infect

infolge prep. because (oder as a result) of; **-dessen** adv. consequently; therefore

Ingenieur m. engineer (degree of a technical university); **-skunst** f. engineering

Ingredienz f. ingredient

Ingwer m. ginger

Inhaber m. owner, proprietor; holder

Inhalt m. content(s), capacity; area, volume; subject, matter; **-sangabe** f., **-sverzeichnis** neu. table of contents, index, summary

inhalt: **-lich** adj. as regards the contents; **-los** adj. empty, unmeaning; **-reich** adj., **-schwer** adj., **-voll** adj. rich; significant; full of meaning

Injurie f. insult

Inkarnat neu. flesh color

Inkasso neu. cashing; collection

inklusive adj. included, including

Inkonsequenz f. inconsistency; illogicalness

Inkrafttreten neu. coming into force

Inländer m. native

inländisch adj. indigenous, domestic

Inlett neu. bedtick

inn: **-ehaben** v. to possess; **-ehalten** v. to pause, to interrupt; to comply with; **-en** adv. inside, within; **-er** adj. inner, internal; **-erhalb** adv. and prep. inside, within; **-erlich** adj. inward; internal; heartfelt; **-erst** adj. inmost; **-ewerden** v. to perceive; **-ig** adj. heartfelt, intimate

Inn: **-ere** neu. interior; heart, soul; Minister des **-eren** Secretary of the Interior; **-erste** neu. innermost, core; **-ung** f. guild, association of craftsmen

inoffiziell adj. unofficial

insbesondere adv. above all; in particular

Inschrift f. inscription, legend, epigraph

Insekt neu. insect; **-enkunde** f. entomology

Insel f. island; **-bewohner** m. islander; **-chen** neu. islet; **-staat** m. insular state

Inserat neu. advertisement

insge: -heim *adv.* secretly; -mein *adv.* in general; usually; -samt *adv.* collectively

insofern, insoweit *adv.* so far; to that extent; — *conj.* if, in this respect; as far as

insonderheit, insonders *adv.* particularly

inspirieren *v.* to inspire

inspizieren *v.* to inspect

installieren *v.* to install

instandhalten *v.* to keep up, to maintain

inständig *adj.* imploring; urgent

instandsetzen *v.* to repair; to enable

Instanz *f.* instance; legal step (*oder* division); letzte — last resort

instruieren *v.* to direct, to instruct

instrumentieren *v.* (mus.) to score

Insulaner *m.* islander; inhabitant of an island

inszenieren *v.* to stage, to arrange

Integralrechnung *f.* integral calculus

integrierend *adj.* integral

intellektuell *adj.* intellectual

intelligent *adj.* intelligent

Intelligenz *f.* intelligence, intelligentsia

Intendant *m.* manager; superintendent; intendant

Intensität *f.* intensity, intensiveness

inter: -essant *adj.* interesting; -essieren *v.* to interest; sich -essieren für to take interest in; -mittierend *adj.* intermittent; -n *adj.* internal; -nieren *v.* to intern; -pretieren *v.* to elucidate, to interpret; -venieren *v.* to intervene; -viewen *v.* to interview

Inter: -esse *neu.* interest, advantage: -essengemeinschaft *f.* community of interest; pool, trust; -essent *m.* interested party; -imsregierung *f.* provisional government; -nat *neu.* boarding school; -nierung *f.* internment; -nist *m.* internist; -punktion *f.* punctuation; -rogativ *m.* interrogative pronoun; -vall *neu.* interval

interkontinentales Fernlenkgeschoss *neu.* intercontinental ballistic missile (ICBM)

intim *adj.* intimate; private

Intimität *f.* intimacy, privacy

Intimus *m.* intimate friend

intonieren *v.* (mus.) to intone

Intrige *f.* intrigue

intrigieren *v.* to intrigue, to plot

invalid *adj.* invalid, weak; disabled

Invalide *m.* invalid; disabled person; -nversicherung *f.* old-age insurance

Invent: -ar *neu.* stock; inventory; -ur (aufnahme) *f.* taking of an inventory

Investitur *f.* investiture

inwendig *adj.* inside, interior, inward

inwiefern, inwieweit *adv.* how far, to what extent

inwohnend *adj.* inherent

inzwischen *adv.* meanwhile

irden *adj.* earthen, made of earth

irdisch *adj.* earthly; mortal; wordly

irgend *adv.* any, some; at any time, in any way; perhaps; ever; wenn — möglich if at all possible; -einer *pron.*, -jemand *pron.*, -wer *pron.* anybody, somebody, anyone, someone; -einmal *adv.* any time, sometime; -wie *adv.* anyhow somehow; -wo *adv.* anywhere, some where; -woher *adv.* from any (*ode* some) place; -wohin *adv.* to any (*ode* some) place

irisierend *adj.* iridescent

Irland *neu.* Ireland

Ironie *f.* irony

ironisch *adj.* ironic(al)

irr: -e *adj.* astray; wrong; confused, insane; -e werden to become confuse (*oder* insane); -eführen *v.* to lea astray; to mislead; -ereden *v.* to rave -ig *adj.* erroneous; false, incorrect -itieren *v.* to irritate; to disturb; -nig *adj.* insane; -tümlich *adj.* erroneous mistaken

Irr: -e *m.* insane person; -e *f.* mistake course; in die -e gehen to go astray -enanstalt *f.* mental hospital; -gan *m.*, -garten *m.* maze, labyrinth -glaube *m.*, -lehre *f.* heresy; -licht *neu* will-o'-the-wisp; -sinn *m.* insanity -tum *m.* error, oversight, mistake; -we *m.* wrong way; -wisch *m.* will-o'-the wisp; boisterous child; fickle person

Ischias *neu.* sciatica

Island *neu.* Iceland

isolieren *v.* to isolate; to insulate

Isotope *f.* isotope

Italien *neu.* Italy

J

ja *adv.* yes; aye; -wohl *adv.* indeed

Jacke *f.* jacket; jerkin; jersey; -tt *neu* short (morning) coat; jacket; das i (mir) — wie Hose (coll.) that's all th same (to me); die — voll kriegen (coll. to get a thrashing

Jagd *f.* hunt(ing); hunting ground; - machen to chase, to pursue; -aufsehe *m.* gamekeeper; -flieger *m.* (avi. fighter pilot; -flugzeug *neu.* fighte plane; -frevel *m.* poaching; -geheg *neu.* game preserve; -geschwader *ne* (avi.) fighter squadron; -gesetze *net* *pl.* game laws; -horn *neu.* bugle; -hun *m.* hound; setter; -rennen *neu.* steeple chase; -revier *neu.* hunting groun -schein *m.* hunting license; (sl.) pro of insanity; -verband *m.* (avi.) fighte unit

jagen *v.* to hunt; to chase, to pursue; dash; to race, to gallop; jemand a etwas — to turn somebody out, force somebody to leave

Jäger *m.* hunter, huntsman; range gamekeeper; (avi.) fighter; riflema -ei *f.* profession of hunting; -haus *ne* -hof *m.* ranger's (*oder* gamekeeper house

jäh *adj.* abrupt, sudden; steep, preci tous; -lings *adv.* suddenly, abrupt precipitously; -zornig *adj.* h tempered; quick to anger

Jahr *neu.* year; das ganze — hindur all the year round; in den besten sein to be in the prime of life; in -e kommen to grow old; schon bei sein to be advanced in years; **übers —** a year hence; **vor — und Tag** a full year ago; **-buch** neu. almanac, year-book; **-esabschluss** m. annual balance sheet; **-esbericht** m. annual report; **-esrente** f. annuity; **-estag** m. anniversary; **-eszahl** f. year (oder date); **-eszeit** f. season; **-hundert** neu. century; **-markt** m. annual fair; **-tausend** neu. millenium; **-zehnt** neu. decade

ähr: -en v. sich — to have occurred a year ago; **-ig** adj. one year old; lasting a year; occurring a year ago; **-lich** adj. annual

Jähzorn m. irascibility, violent temper
Jakob m. James, Jacob
Jalousie f. Venetian blind
Jamaikapfeffer m. allspice
Jammer m. distress, misery; lamentation, wailing; **was für ein —l** what a pity! **-bild** neu., **-gestalt** f. pitiable figure; **-holz** neu. (coll.) guitar; out-of-tune piano; **-lappen** m. (coll.) weakling; crybaby; **-tal** neu. (bibl.) vale of tears
ammer: -n v. to lament, to moan, to wail; **er -t mich** I pity him; **-schade** adv. too bad! **-voll** adj. deplorable, lamentable, piteous
ämmerlich adj. miserable; pitiable, deplorable
Janhagel m. mob, rabble, riffraff
Januar m. January
Jaspis m. jasper
äten v. to weed
auchzen v. to exult, to jubilate
Jazzkapelle f. jazz band
e adv. each (time); at any time, ever; **— drei und drei** three at a time, three by three; **— eher — lieber** the sooner the better; **— nachdem** depending on circumstances; **— und —** always; from time to time; **-denfalls** adv. at any rate, by all means; **-der** pron. each, every, any; **-dermann** pron. everybody, everyone; **-derorts** pron. everywhere; **-derzeit** adv. at all times, always; **-desmal** adv. each (oder every) time; **-doch** adv. however, still, yet; **-her** adv. **von -her** at all times; **-mals** adv. at any time, ever; **-mand** pron. somebody; someone; **irgend -mand** anyone; **-ner** pron. that (one); the former; **-nseitig** adj. on the other side, opposite; **-nseits** prep. and adj. beyond, on the other side, across, yonder; **-weilig** adj. actual, respective; **-weils** adv. at times, at any given time
längerjelieber m. and neu. honeysuckle
enseits neu. the world beyond; the life to come; **jemand ins — befördern** to kill someone
saias m. Isaiah
— neu. and m. jet, black amber
ig adj. present; existing, actual, current
—t adv. now, at present; **gleich —** at once; **von — ab** (or **an**) henceforth; **rom** this time forward
tzeit f. modern times; these days
—h m. yoke; (mountain)ridge; cross**—m**; land measure; **-bein** neu. cheek

bone
Jockei m. jockey
Jod neu. iodine
jodeln v. to yodel
Johann m. John
Johannis: -beere f. currant; **-brot** neu. (bot.) carob; **-käfer** m. June bug; glowworm; **-tag** m. St. John's day; midsummer solstice; **-trieb** m. second bloom; late love; **-würmchen** neu. glowworm
Jongleur m. juggler
jonglieren v. to juggle
Joppe f. jacket, jerkin
Jot neu. letter j; **-a** neu. iota, jot, whit
Journal neu. journal, magazine; (comm.) daybook; **-ismus** m. journalism; **-ist** m. journalist
Jub: -el m. jubilation, exultation; **-eljahr** neu. year of jubilee; **alle -eljahre einmal** (coll.) once in a blue moon; **-ilar** m. person who celebrates a jubilee; **-iläum** neu. jubilee, anniversary
jubeln v. to jubilate, to exult, to rejoice
jubilieren v. to rejoice, to jubilate
Juchzer m. shout of joy
jucken v. to itch; to feel itchy; **ihm juckt das Fell** (coll.) he is itching for a fight; **sich —** to scratch oneself
Jude m. Jew; **-nhetze** f., **-nverfolgung** f. Jew-baiting
Jugend f. youth; **-freund** m. friend of one's youth; school chum; **-gericht** neu. juvenile court; **-herberge** f. youth hostel; **-liebe** f. first love; **-schriften** f. pl. juvenile books; **-werk** neu. early work (of an artist)
jugendlich adj. youthful; juvenile
Juli m. July
jung adj. young, youthful; juvenile; immature; early, fresh; **-en** v. (zool.) to bring forth young; **-enhaft** adj. boyish; **-fer(n)haft** adj. maidenly; **-fräulich** adj. immaculate, virginal
Jung: -brunnen m. fountain of youth; **-e** m. boy, lad; apprentice; (cards) knave; **-e** neu. (zool.) young; **-fer** f. girl, virgin; maid; **alte -fer** spinster; **-fernfahrt** f. (naut.) maiden voyage; **-fernkranz** m. bridal wreath; **-fernrede** f. first public speech; **-fernschaft** f. maidenhood; virginity; **-frau** f. virgin; **-geselle** m. bachelor
Jüng: -er m. disciple, adherent; **-erschaft** f. discipleship; **-ling** m. youth, young man; **-lingsalter** neu. adolescence; **-st(geboren)e** m. youngest, last born; **der -ste Tag** doomsday; **das -ste Gericht** the last judgment
Juni m. June
Junker m. titled (oder Prussian) landowner
Jurist m. jurist; lawyer
juristisch adj. juridical, legal
Jus neu., **Jura** pl. jurisprudence
Justiz f. administration of the law; **-beamte** m. officer of the law; **-behörde** f. legal authority; **-minister** m. minister of justice; Attorney General; **-mord** m. condemnation of an innocent person;

judicial murder
Juwel *neu.* jewel; gem, precious stone; **-en(arbeit)** *f.* jewelry; **-ier** *m.* jeweler
Jux *m.* frolic; practical joke, lark

K

Kabale *f.* cabal, intrigue
Kabarett *neu.* cabaret; compartmented dish, Lazy Susan
Kabel *neu.* cable(gram); **-jau** *m.* codfish
kabeln *v.* to cable
Kabine *f.* cabin; (bathhouse) cubicle; **-tt** *neu.* cabinet; council (of governor); closet; **-ttsfrage** *f.* vital question
Kachel *f.* tile; **-ofen** *m.* Dutch tile stove
Kadenz *f.* cadence
Kadett *m.* cadet; **-enanstalt** *f.* military academy
Käfer *m.* beetle, chafer; (coll.) pretty girl
Kaff *neu.* chaff; rubbish; (sl.) poor village
Kaffee *m.* coffee; — *neu.* coffee shop; **-brenner** *m.* coffee roaster; **-(e)rsatz** *m.* coffee substitute; **-grund** *m.*, **-satz** *m.* coffee grounds; **-klatsch** *m.*, **-kränzchen** *neu.* ladies' gossip party; **-maschine** *f.* percolator; **-mühle** *f.* coffee grinder; **-pause** *f.* coffee break; **-pflanzung** *f.* coffee plantation; **-schwester** *f.* coffee lover, gossiper
Käfig *m.* cage
kahl *adj.* bare, bald; barren, bleak; — **geschoren** close-cropped; **-köpfig** *adj.* bald-headed
Kahm *m.* mould, scum
Kahn *m.* boat, skiff; barge; (sl.) slipper; bed
Kai *m.* quay, wharf
Kaiser *m.* emperor; **-in** *f.* empress; **-reich** *neu.* empire; **-schnitt** *m.* Caesarian operation
kaiserlich *adj.* imperial
Kajak *m.* kayak, Eskimo canoe
Kajüte *f.* (naut.) cabin; — **erster Klasse** stateroom; **-njunge** *m.* cabin-boy
Kakadu *m.* cockatoo
Kakao *m.* cocoa bean; cocoa
Kaktee *f.*, **Kaktus** *m.* cactus
Kalb *neu.* calf; fawn; **-fleisch** *neu.* veal; **-sbraten** *m.* roast veal; **-skeule** *f.* leg of veal; **-skotelett** *neu.* veal cutlet; **-sschnitzel** *neu.* veal steak
kalb: **-en** *v.* to calve; **-ern** *v.* (coll.) to frolic, to dally; **-erig** *adj.* silly
Kaldaunen *f. pl.* intestines, tripe
Kalender *m.* calendar, almanac
Kalfakter, Kalfaktor *m.* (prison) trusty; toady
Kali(um) *neu.* (caustic) potash; potassium
Kaliber *neu.* caliber; capacity, level; kind
Kalif *m.* caliph
Kalk *m.* lime (chem.) calcium; **mit — bewerfen** to roughcast, to plaster; **mit — tünchen** to whitewash; **ungelöschter —** quicklime; **-bewurf** *m.* roughcast, plaster; **-brennerei** *f.* limekiln
kalk: **-en** *v.* to fertilize with lime; to plaster; to whitewash; **-ig** *adj.* chalky
Kalkulator *m.* computer
kalt *adj.* cold; frigid; unemotional; —

machen (coll.) to kill; — **stellen** to keep cold; (coll.) to shelve; **-er Schlag** harmless lightning flash; **-blütig** *adj.* cold-blooded; composed
Kälte *f.* cold(ness); indifference; frigidity
Kalzium *neu.* calcium
Kambüse *f.* caboose
Kamee *f.* cameo
Kamel *neu.* camel; (coll.) stupid person; **-garn** *neu.* mohair; **-ie** *f.* camellia
Kamera *f.* camera
Kamerad *m.* comrade; companion, chum; **-schaft** *f.* comradeship, camaraderie, fellowship
kameradschaftlich *adj.* companionable; — *adv.* friendly as comrades
Kamille *f.* camomile
Kamin *m.* chimney; fireplace, fireside; cleft; crevice; **-sims** *m.* mantlepiece
Kamm *m.* comb; crest, ridge; (meats) neck, shoulder; **alles über einen — scheren** (coll.) to treat everyone (ode everything) alike
Kammer *f.* chamber; small room; board; (heart) ventricle; **-diener** *m.* valet; **-gericht** *neu.* (provincial) court of appeal; **-herr** *m.* chamberlain; **-jäger** *m.* exterminator; gamekeeper of a sovereign; **-jungfer** *f.* woman-in-waiting, lady's maid; **-musik** *f.* chamber music; **-ton** *m.* (mus.) concert-pitch
Kampf *m.* combat; fight, battle; conflict struggle; — **auf Leben und Tod** fight to the death; — **ums Dasein** struggle for existence; **-bahn** *f.* stadium; **-flugzeu** *neu.* fighter plane, bomber; **-hahn** *m.* game cock; squabbler, sorehead; **-plat** *m.* battlefield; **-preis** *m.* winnin prize; **-richter** *m.* umpire; **-spiel** *neu.* tourna ment
kämpfen *v.* to fight; to battle; to struggl
Kampfer *m.* camphor
Kämpfer *m.* fighter; warrior; (arch.) abut ment
kampieren *v.* to camp
Kanal *m.* canal; channel; conduit; sewer drain; duct; **ich habe den — voll** (coll. I am fed up; **-isation** *f.* canalization sewer system
Kanapee *neu.* sofa; settee
Kanarienvogel *m.* canary
Kandelaber *m.* candelabrum; street lam
Kandidat *m.* candidate; applicant; **-en rede** *f.* electioneering speech; **-tur** candidacy
kandidieren *v.* to run (*oder* stand) fo office
Kandis(zucker) *m.* sugar candy
Känguruh *neu.* kangaroo
Kaninchen *neu.* rabbit; **-bau** *m.* rabbi burrow; **-fell** *neu.* rabbit skin
Kanker *m.* canker; venereal disease
Kanne *f.* can; pot; jug; tankard; **-giesse** *m.* pewterer; tavern polician; politic babbler
Kannibale *m.* cannibal
Kanon *m.* canon; regulation, criterion curriculum; (Holy Scriptures) autho ized version; **-e** *f.* cannon; gun; piece ordnance; (coll.) expert; **-ier** *m.* arti

leryman, gunner

Kant: -e *f.* edge; margin, brim; border; selvage; **auf die hohe -e legen** (coll.) to save (money); **-ine** *f.* canteen, mess; **-or** *m.* choirmaster; cantor; church music director, organist; **-schu** *m.* short, thick leather whip; knout

Kanu *neu.* canoe

Kanz: -el *f.* pulpit; (avi.) cockpit, turret; (educ.) chair; elevated hunting blind; **-elrede** *f.* sermon; **-lei** *f.* (government) office; office staff; **-ler** *m.* chancellor; **-list** *m.* (government) clerk

Kap *neu.* (geog.) cape

Kapaun *m.* capon

Kap der guten Hoffnung *neu.* Cape of Good Hope

Kapelle *f.* small church; chapel; band

Kapellmeister *m.* bandmaster; conductor

Kaper *m.* pirate's ship; — *f.* caper

Kapillar *neu.* capillary

Kapital *neu.* capital; principal; **festgelegtes** — invested capital; **flüssiges** — available funds, fluid capital; — **schlagen aus** to profit by; **-anlage** *f.* investment; **-besitz** *m.* cash property; **-ismus** *m.* capitalism; **-ist** *m.* capitalist; **-verbrechen** *neu.* capital crime

Kapitän *m.* captain; skipper

kapitulieren *v* to capitulate

Kaplan *m.* chaplain

Kappe *f.* cap; hood; cowl(ing); (shoe) tip; **etwas auf seine eigene — nehmen** (coll.) to make oneself responsible for something

kappen *v.* to shorten; to trim, to top

Kapsel *f.* housing, case, capsule; (gun) cap

kaputt *adj.* broken, destroyed, unstrung

Kapuz: -e *f.* hood, cowl; **-iner** *m.* Capuchin monk; **-inerkresse** *f.* nasturtium

Karabiner *m.* carbine

Karaffe *f.* carafe, decanter

Karambolage *f.* collision; (billiards) carom

Karat *m.* carat; **-gewicht** *neu.* troy weight

Karawane *f.* caravan

Karbid *neu.* carbide

Karbonade *f.* chop, cutlet

Karbunkel *m.* carbuncle, anthrax

Kardätsche *f.* carding (*oder* curry) comb

Kardinal *m.* cardinal; drink (of white wine)

Karfreitag *m.* Good Friday

Karfunkel *m.* carbuncle (gem)

karg *adj.* paltry; stingy; (soil) sterile; **-en** *v.* to be niggardly (*oder* stingy)

kärglich *adj.* paltry; scanty; poor

kariert *adj.* checkered

Karikatur *f.* caricature; cartoon

karikieren *v.* to caricature

Karl *m.* Charles, Carl

karmesin *adj.* crimson

Karmin *m.* and *neu.* carmine

Karnickel *neu.* rabbit; bunny; (sl.) scapegoat

Kärnten *neu.* Carinthia

Karo *neu.* square; check; (cards) diamonds

Karosse *f.* state coach; **-rie** *f.* (auto.) chassis, body

Karpfen *m.* carp

Karre *f.*, **Karren** *m.* cart; (wheel)barrow; **an dem selben — ziehen** (coll.) to be in the same boat; **den —n gründlich festfahren** (coll.) to mess things up

Karree *neu.* square

karren *v.* to cart

Karriere *f.* career; full gallop

Kartätsche *f.* case (*oder* canister, grape) shot; currycomb; (plastering) trowel

Kartäuser *m.* Carthusian monk; **-likör** *m.* chartreuse

Karte *f.* card; chart, map; ticket; bill of fare, menu; **die -n abheben** to cut the cards; **die -n geben** to deal the cards; **die -n legen** (*or* **schlagen**) (cards) to tell a (person's) fortune; **ein Spiel -n** a pack of cards; **jemand in die -n sehen** (cards) to look into somebody's hand; to discover someone's designs; **-nbrief** *m.* letter card; **-ngeber** *m.* (cards) dealer; **-nkunststück** *neu.* card trick; **-nschläger** *m.* (cards) fortune teller; **-nzeichnen** *neu.* cartography; **-i** *f.* card index

Kartell *neu.* cartel; trust; pool

Karthago *neu.* Carthage

Kartoffel *f.* potato; (sl.) watch; **-brei** *m.* mashed potatoes; **-puffer** *m.* potato pancake

Karton *m.* cardboard; carton; (art) cartoon; **-age** *f.* secure packing

Kartothek *f.* card index

Kartusche *f.* cartridge; (arch.) cartouche

Karussel *neu.* carousel, merry-go-round

Karwoche *f.* Holy Week (before Easter)

Karzer *m.* lockup; (coll.) prison

käs: -en *v.* to curd(le); **-eweiss** *adj.* chalk-white; **-ig** *adj.* cheesy; caseous; pale

Käse *m.* cheese; **-blatt** *neu.* (coll.) small newspaper, rag; **-rei** *f.* cheese factory

Kasematte *f.* casemate

Kaserne *f.* (mil.) barracks; **-narrest** *m.* confinement to barracks

Kasper(le) *m.* Punch; **-theater** *neu.* Punch-and-Judy show

das Kaspische Meer *neu.* Caspian Sea

Kass: -e *f.* cashbox; cash money; pay office; health insurance association; ticket (*oder* box) office; **-enabschluss** *m.* balancing (*oder* closing) of (cash) accounts; **-enbestand** *m.* cash balance; **-enbote** *m.* bank messenger; **-enführer** *m.* cashier; **-enprüfer** *m.*, **-enrevisor** *m.* auditor; **-enschrank** *m.* safe; **-enübersicht** *f.* balance sheet; **-ette** *f.* (money) casket; cashbox; (arch.) coffer; caisson; (phot.) plateholder; **-ierer** *m.* cashier; teller

kassieren *v.* to take in money; (law) to annul, to invalidate; (mil.) to discharge

Kastagnette *f.* castanet

Kastanie *f.* chestnut

Kaste *f.* caste; class

kasteien *v.* to castigate, to mortify

Kastell *neu.* citadel; fortress

Kastrat *m.* eunuch

kastrieren *v.* to castrate

Katakombe *f.* catacomb

Katalog m. catalog, list

katalogisieren v. to catalog

Katapultflugzeug n. catafighter

katastrophal adj. catastrophic

Kate f. cottage, hut

Kate: –chismus m. catechism; –gorie f. category

Kater m. tomcat; (coll.) hangover; –idee f. (coll.) crazy idea

Kathed: –er neu. (educ.) desk; –erblüte f. (educ.) malapropism, boner; –erweisheit f. academic wisdom; –rale f. cathedral

Kathol: –ik m. Catholic; –izismus m. Catholicism

katholisch adj. Catholic

Kattun m. calico; cotton print

Katz: –balgerei f. (act of) scuffling, brawling; –e f. cat; feline: cat-o-nine-tails; money bag; **das ist für die –e** (coll.) that's futile; **die –e im Sack kaufen** to buy a pig in a poke; –enauge neu. cat's eye; (traffic) reflector light; –enjammer m. hangover; –enkopf m. box on the ear; round paving stone; –enmusik f. caterwauling; mock serenade; –ensprung m. (coll.) a stone's throw

Kätzchen neu. kitten; catkin

Kauderwelsch neu. gibberish; jargon

kauen v. to chew

kauern v. to cower, to crouch

Kauf m. purchase; **er ist leichten –s davon gekommen** he got off cheaply; **mit in — nehmen** to take into the bargain (oder the bad with the good); –brief m. bill-of-sale; –haus neu. commercial firm; department store; –laden m. shop, store; –leute pl. merchants, dealers; –mann m. shopkeeper, merchant

kauf: –en v. to buy, to purchase; to bribe; –lustig adj. keen to buy; –männisch adj. commercial, mercantile

Käufer m. buyer, purchaser; customer

käuflich adj. marketable; corruptible, venal; — adv. by purchase

Kaulquappe f. tadpole

kaum adv. barely, hardly, scarcely; just now

Kaution f. security; (law) bail

Kautschuk m. and neu. caoutchouc; rubber

Kauz m. small owl; (coll.) queer fellow

keck adj. bold, forward, direct; pert, saucy

Keg: –el m. cone; bowling pin, tenpin; **mit Kind und –el** with the whole family; with bag and baggage; –elbahn f. bowling alley; –elkugel f. bowling ball; –ler m. bowler

Kehle f. throat; gullet; fluting; gorge; (bastion) rear entrance; **aus voller —** loudly, heartily

Kehr: –aus m. last dance; **den –aus machen** to bring to a close; –besen m. broom; –bürste f. whisk broom; –e f. turn(ing), bend; –er m. sweeper; –frau f. charwoman; –icht m. sweepings; rubbish; –reim m. refrain; –seite f. reverse;

(fig.) drawback; –t neu. (mil.) about-face. –wisch m. duster

kehr: –en v. to sweep; to turn around (oder over, back); **den Rücken –en** to cold-shoulder; **sich –en an** to mind; –tmachen v. to face about

keifen v. to scold; to bark; to yelp

Keil m. wedge; (arch.) keystone; (dress) gore, gusset; (mech.) key; (typ.) quoin; –e f. (coll.) thrashing; drubbing; –er m. mature wild boar; –erei f. scuffle, drubbing fight; –schrift f. cuneiform writing

Keim m. sprout, bud; germ; **im — ersticken** to nip in the bud; –träger m. (med.) carrier

keimen v. to germinate; to sprout, to bud

kein adj. no (one), none; –er adj. nobody; –er von beiden neither of the two; –erlei adj. not of any kind; not any; –erseits adv. on neither side; –esfalls adv. in no case, on no account; certainly not; –eswegs adv. by no means, not at all; –mal adv. not once

Keks m. cookie

Kelch m. goblet; calyx; chalice; cup

Kell: –e f. ladle; trowel; –er m. cellar –erei f. wine cellar; –ergeschoss neu. basement; –erladen m. basement shop –ner m. waiter; –nerin f. waitress

Kelter f. wine (oder fruit) press

keltern v. to press (grapes, fruits)

kenn: –bar adj. recognizable; –en v. to know, to be acquainted (with); –en lernen to become acquainted (with) to get to know; –tlich adj. distinguishable; conspicuous, marked; –zeichnen v. to characterize; to (ear)mark

Kenn: –buchstabe m. key letter; –er m connoisseur, expert; adept; –erblick m sure eye; –ermiene f. mien (oder attitude) of an expert; –karte f. identity card; –tnis f. knowledge, experience acquirements; **etwas zur –tnis nehmen** to take note of something; –ung f characteristic; (naut.) landmark; –wort neu. device, motto, password; –zeichen neu. characteristic mark; identity badge, token; symptom

kentern v. (naut.) to capsize

Keramik f. ceramics; potter's art

Kerb: –e f. notch; **in die gleiche –e hauen** (coll.) to pursue the same goal; –tier neu. insect

kerben v. to notch; (coin) to mill

Kerker m. (lit.) jail

Kerl m. fellow; chap

Kern m. core, nucleus; kernel; essence heart; –frucht f. stone fruit; –gehäus neu. core; –fleisch neu. prime cut, soli meat; –holz neu. heartwood; –spaltung f. nuclear fission; –schuss m. bull's-ey shot; –spruch m. pithy saying; –waffen krieg m. nuclear war

kern: –en v. to granulate; to churn, t curdle; –gesund adj. thoroughly healthy; –ig adj. full of kernels (ode stones, pips); granular; substantial strong; vigorous, pithy

Kerze f. candle; taper; –ngiesser

candlemaker; **–nhalter** m. candleholder, candlestick; **–nstärke** f. (elec.) candle power

kerzengerade adj. as straight as an arrow

Kessel m. kettle; tank; boiler; caldron; valley; basin; **–flicker** m. tinker; **–pauke** f. kettledrum; **–schmied** m. coppersmith; boilermaker; **–wagen** m. tank truck

Kette f. chain; bracelet, necklace; row, series; (orn.) flock; **–nbrücke** f. suspension bridge; **–nfaden** m. warp thread; **–nglied** neu. chain link; **–nhandel** m. wholesaling; chain store; **–nhund** m. watchdog; **–npanzer** m. coat of mail; **–nraucher** m. chain smoker; **–nstich** m. chain stitch

ketten v. to (tie to a) chain

Ketzer m. heretic; **–ei** f. heresy; heterodoxy

ketzerisch adj. heretical; heterodox

keuchen v. to pant, to puff; to gasp

Keuchhusten m. whooping cough

Keule f. club; Indian club; pestle; (zool.) hind leg

keusch adj. chaste, pure; virginal, maidenly

kichern v. to snicker; to chuckle, to giggle

Kiebitz m. lapwing, peewit; (coll.) kibitzer

Kiefer m. jawbone; mandible; **—** f. pine

Kiel m. quill; keel; **–holen** neu. keelhauling; **–raum** m. ship's hold; **–wasser** neu. (naut.) wake

Kieme f. gill

Kies m. gravel; pyrite; **–el** m. pebble; flint; silica, silex; **–grube** f. gravel pit; **–weg** m. gravel path (oder walk)

Kimme f. notch; (gun) sight

Kind neu. child; offspring; **an –es Statt annehmen** to adopt; **das — beim rechten Namen nennen** to call a spade a spade: **totgeborenes —** stillborn child; **von — auf** from childhood on; **–bett** neu. childbed; **–heit** f. childhood, infancy; **–taufe** f. christening (of child)

kind: –erleicht adj. extremely easy; **–erlieb** adj. fond of children; **–isch** adj. childish; silly, immature; **–lich** adj. childlike, naïve

Kinder pl. children, **die –schuhe ausziehen** to grow up, to mature; **–art** f. children's way; **–ei** f. childish idea; trifle; **–frau** f., **–mädchen** neu. nurse; governess; **–gärtnerin** f. kindergarten teacher; **–jahre** neu. pl. infancy; **–lieder** neu. pl. nursery songs; **–literatur** f. juvenile literature; **–märchen** neu. fairy tale; **–mord** m. infanticide; **–spiel** neu. child's play; trifling matter; **–sprache** f. prattle; **–stube** f. nursery; **–wagen** m. baby carriage; **–zeit** f. babyhood, childhood, infancy

Kindes: –alter neu. tender age; **–kind** neu. grandchild; **–liebe** f. filial affection; **–not** f., **–nöte** pl. childbed labor; **–räuber** m. kidnapper

Kinkerlitzchen neu. pl. superfluous efforts; pointless overspending

Kinn neu. chin; **–backen** m., **–backe** f.,

–lade f. jaw

Kino neu. motion-picture theater

kippen v. to seesaw; to tip, to tilt; **ein Glas —** (coll.) to hoist one (drink)

Kirch: –dorf neu. village around a church; **–e** f. church; **–gang** m. churchgoing; **–gänger** m. churchgoer; **–hof** m. churchyard; cemetery; **–sprengel** m. diocese; **–turm** m. steeple, spire

Kirchen: –älteste m. church elder; **–amt** neu. church office; ecclesiastical function; **–bann** m. excommunication; **–buch** neu. parish register; **–busse** f. church penance; **–chor** m. church choir; **–diener** m. sexton, sacristan; **–gesang** m. congregational song (oder singing); **–geschichte** f. ecclesiastical history; **–gesetz** neu. canonical law; **–jahr** neu. ecclesiastical year; **–lehre** f. church doctrine; **–musik** f. sacred music; **–patron** m. patron saint of a church; **–politik** f. ecclesiastical politics; **–raub** m., **–schändung** f. sacrilege; **–sänger** m. chorister; **–steuer** f. church tax; **–streit** m. ecclesiastical dissension; religious controversy; **–stuhl** m. pew; **–vater** m. Church Father; early Christian writer

kirchlich adj. ecclesiastic(al)

Kirmes f. annual parish fair

Kirsch: –branntwein m., **–geist** m. cherry brandy; **–e** f. cherry; **–rot** neu. cerise; **–wasser** neu. cherry cordial

Kissen neu. cushion; pillow; **–bezug** m, **–überzug** m. cushion cover; pillow case

Kiste f. box, chest, case; (sl.) auto; airplane

Kitsch m. trash; trumpery; gingerbread

Kitt m. cement; putty; lute; **der ganze —** the whole kit and caboodle

Kittel m. smock; frock

kitten v. to cement; to glue (together)

Kitz: **–e** f. fawn; kid; kitten; **–el** m. tickling, titillation; pruriency; **–ler** m. tickler

kitzeln v. to tickle, to titillate

klaffen v. to gape, to yawn; to be ajar

kläffen v. to yap, to yelp; to scold, to carp

Klafter m. fathom; (wood) cord

klag: –bar adj. (law) actionable; **–elustig** adj., **–süchtig** adj. litigious; **–en** v. to complain; to lament, to mourn, to wail; (law) to bring an action; to sue; **–los** adj. without complaint; **–los stellen** (law) to satisfy

Klage f. complaint; lamentation, moaning; lawsuit; **–lied** neu. dirge, elegy; **–punkt** m. (law) count of an indictment; **–schrift** f. (law) bill of complaints

Kläger m. plaintiff

kläglich adj. lamentable, pitiable, plaintive

Klamm f. ravine; gorge; **–er** f. clasp; clamp; paper clip; bracket, parenthesis

Klang m. sound, tone; **von gutem —** of good repute; **–boden** m. sounding board; **–farbe** f. timbre; **–lehre** f. acoustics

klangvoll, klangreich adj. sonorous

Klapp m. slap, blow; **–bett** neu. folding bed; **–e** f. flap; lid; valve; (mus.) key, stop, damper; (sl.) mouth; **in die -e gehen** (*or* **steigen**) (coll.) to go to bed; **zwei Fliegen mit einer -e schlagen** to kill two birds with one stone; **-fenster** *neu.* trap (*oder* skylight) window; **-hornvers** *m.* limerick; **-messer** *neu.* jackknife; **-stuhl** *m.* folding chair; **-sitz** *m.* jump seat; **-tür** *f.* trapdoor

klappen *v.* to clap, to clack; **es klappt** this comes at the right moment; **zum -en kommen** to come to a head

Klaps *m.* slap, smack; **-smühle** *f.* (sl.) mental hospital

klar *adj.* clear; bright; pure; (naut.) ready; shipshape; distinct; plain; obvious; **das ist — wie Klossbrühe** (coll.) that's obvious; **-legen, -machen, -stellen** *v.* to clear up, to explain

klären *v.* to purify; to clarify; to clear

Klarinette *f.* clarinet

Klasse *f.* class; rank; **das ist —** (coll.) that's tops; **-narbeit** *f.* (educ.) written exercise; **-neinteilung** *f.* classification; **-nzimmer** *neu.* classroom, schoolroom

klassifizieren *v.* to classify

Klassik *f.* classical period; **-er** *m.* (art.) old master; classic

klassisch *adj.* classic(al); first-class

Klatsch *m.* slap, clap; (whip) crack; gossip; **-base** *f.*, **-maul** *neu.* gossiper, scandalmonger; chatterbox; **-e** *f.* fly swatter; gossiper; **-en** *neu.* applause; gossiping; **-erei** *f.* gossip; **-mohn** *m.*, **-rose** *f.* (European) red field poppy

klatsch! *interj.* pop! smack! **-en** *v.* to clap, to slap; to gossip; **Beifall -en, in die Hände -en** to applaud; **-süchtig** *adj.* fond of gossip; **-nass** *adj.* soaked to the skin

Worte — to split hairs

Klaue *f.* claw; fang, talon; hoof; (sl.) bad handwriting; **in den -n haben** (coll.) to have in one's grip

Klaus: **-e** *f.* hermitage; cell; **-ner** *m.* hermit, recluse; **-ur** *f.* secluded cloister room; written examination under supervision

Klausel *f.* clause, proviso, stipulation

Klavi: **-atur** *f.* (mus.) keyboard; **-er** *neu.* piano; **-erauszug** *m.* piano arrangement; **-erstimmer** *m.* piano tuner

Klebe: **-mittel** *neu.*, **-stoff** *m.* adhesive; agglutinant; **-pflaster** *neu.* adhesive tape; sticking plaster; **-r** *m.* billposter; gluten

kleben *v.* to glue, to gum, to paste; **jemandem eine —** (sl.) to box someone's ears; **-bleiben** to adhere to; to cling

kleckern, klecksen *v.* to blot(ch); to daub

Klee *m.* clover, trefoil; **über den grünen — loben** (coll.) to praise to the skies; **-blatt** *neu.* cloverleaf; inseparable trio; **-blattkreuzung** *f.* (auto.) cloverleaf

Kleid *neu.* garment, dress, frock, gown, covering; **-er** *pl.* clothing; raiment; **-erablage** *f.* cloak room; **-erbügel** *m.* coat hanger; **-erbürste** *f.* clothes brush; **-erpuppe** *f.* clothes dummy; **-erschrank** *m.* closet, wardrobe; **-erstoff** *m.* dress material; **-ung** *f.* clothing, raiment;

-ungsstück *neu.* garment; **-verleiher** *m.* costumer

kleiden *v.* to clothe, to dress; to become to suit; **in Worte —** to express in words

Kleie *f.* bran

klein *adj.* little, small; young; minor, petty; humble; **ein — bisschen** (*or* wenig) a little bit; **gross und —** great and small; old and young; **im -en verkaufen** to retail; **-er Geist** narrow mind; **-es Geld** change; small coins; **-es Schläfchen** short nap; **kurz und — schlagen** to break into small pieces; **sich — machen** to humble oneself; **um ein -es** almost; **von — auf** from childhood; **-denkend** *adj.*, **-geistig** *adj.* narrow-minded; **-laut** *adj.* subdued, deflated; **-lich** *adj.* pedantic, fussy; **-mütig** *adj.* faint-hearted; **-städtisch** *adj.* provincial; small townlike

Klein *neu.* giblets; fragments; **-asien** *neu.* Asia Minor; **-bahn** *f.* narrow-gauge railroad; **-bauer** *m.* small farmer; **-betrieb** *m.* small business; **-bildkamera** *f.* miniature camera; **-bürger** *m.* prosaic person; philistine; **-funkgerät** *neu.* walkie-talkie; **-geld** *neu.* small coins, change; **-handel** *m.* retail business; **-holz** *neu.* wood kindling; **-igkeit** *f.* trifle; small matter; **-kind** *neu.* small child; **-kinderbewahranstalt** *f.* day nursery; **-kram** *m.* trifles; **-krieg** *m.* guerilla warfare; **-kunst** *f.* industrial arts; cabaret programs; **-mut** *m.* faint-heartedness; **-stadt** *f.* small town; **-wagen** *m.* compact car; **-vieh** *neu.* rabbits, poultry

Kleinasien *neu.* Asia Minor

Kleinod *neu.* gem, jewel

Kleister *m.* paste

Klemme *f.* clamp; cramp; pinch; trouble; **in einer — sein** (*or* **sitzen, stecken**) to be in a fix; **-r** *m.* pince-nez

Klempner *m.* tinsmith; **-ei** *f.* tinsmith shop

Klepper *m.* old nag, hack, jaded horse

Kleriker *m.* clergyman

Klerus *m.* clergy

Klette *f.* bur; burdock; **haften wie eine — to stick like a bur; **-rpflanze** *f.* climber, creeper

klettern *v.* to climb; to ascend

Klient *m.* client; customer; **-el** *f.* clientele

Klima *neu.* climate; **-anlage** *f.* air conditioning

klimatisch *adj.* climatic

Klimbim *m.* (coll.) painting the town red; fanfare; (medals) fruit salad; fuss and feathers

klimmen *v.* to climb

klimpern *v.* to jingle, to tinkle; (mus.) strum

kling(e)ling! *interj.* ding-dong!

Klinge *f.* blade; (poet.) sword; **-nspender** *m.* blade dispenser

Klingel *f.* small bell; **-beutel** *m.* (church) collection bag

klingeln *v.* to pull the bell, to ring, tinkle

klingen *v.* to sound; to clink, to tinkle

-de Münze hard cash
Klinik f. clinical hospital; clinical instructions
klinisch adj. clinical
Klinke f. latch; door handle; ratchet; switchboard plug
klinken v. to operate (latch); to shut (door)
Klinker m. clinker
klipp! interj. click! — und klar definitely and clearly; obvious; -ig adj. craggy, rocky
Klipp: -e f. cliff, crag; reef; -er m. (naut.) clipper; -fisch m. dried cod; -klapp neu. click-clack; flip-flap
klirren v. to clink, to clash, to clatter
Klischee neu. cliché, stereotype plate
Kloake f. cesspool, sewer; (zool.) cloaca
kloben v. to split cordwood; log; block, pulley
klobig adj. weighty, massive; rude, clumsy
klopfen v. to knock, to rap; to beat; auf den Busch — (coll.) to sound out; jemandem auf die Finger — (coll.) to reprimand someone
Klopfer m. beater, knocker
Klöppel m. club, cudgel; bobbin; drumstick; (bell) clapper
klöppeln v. to make (bobbin) lace
Klops m. meat ball
Klosett neu. toilet; -papier neu. toilet paper
Kloss m. clod, lump; dumpling
Kloster neu. cloister; monastery, convent; -bruder m. monk, friar; -frau f., -fräulein neu. nun; -wesen neu. monasticism
klösterlich adj. conventual; monastic
Klotz m. block; clog; (coll.) lout
klotzig adj. coarse, clumsy; (sl.) enormous
Klub m. club; -kamerad m. clubmate, fellow member; -sessel m. lounge (oder club) chair
Kluft f. abyss, chasm; gorge, defile, ravine; (sl.) clothes; uniform
klug adj. intelligent; judicious; prudent; shrewd, clever; durch Schaden — werden to learn by experience; ich kann nicht — daraus werden I can't make head or tail of it
Klügelei f. sophistry; subtilization
klügeln v. to affect wisdom; to criticize
klüglich adv. judiciously, prudently, wisely
Klumpen m. clump, lump; clod; clot; nugget
klumpen v. to conglomerate; to clot, to lump
Klumpfuss m. clubfoot
klumpig adj. lumpy, clotted, agglomerated
Klüngel m. clique; der ganze — the whole crew
knabbern v. to gnaw, to nibble
Knabe m. boy, lad; -nalter neu. boyhood
knack: -s! interj. crack! snap! -en, -sen v. to crack, to snap, to break, to click; eine harte Nuss zu -en haben to have a tough job

Knäckebrot neu. rye wafer
Knall m. bang; (coll.) insanity; — und Fall suddenly; unexpectedly; -bonbon m. cracker bonbon; -büchse f. popgun; -erbse f. pea-shaped firecracker
knallen v. to detonate, to crack; to bang
knallig adj. glaring (colors); crazy; goofy
knapp adj. tight, narrow; scarce; concise; scanty; limited; -e Mehrheit bare majority; — halten to keep a tight rein; — werden to run short; mit -er Not with great difficulty; by the skin of one's teeth
knarr! interj. creak! -en to creak, to groan
Knaster m. (coll.) inferior tobacco; grumbler
knattern v. to rattle; to crackle
Knäuel m. and neu. (yarn) ball; entanglement, mixup; cluster; crowd
Knauf m. knob; (arch.) capital; pommel
Knauser m. niggard, miser; -ei f. stinginess
knaus(e)rig adj. niggardly, stingy; miserly
knausern v. to be stingy (oder a miser)
knautschen v. to crumple
knautschig adj. creased, crumpled
Knebel m. gag; toggle; short stick; -bart m. twisted moustache; imperial
knebeln v. to gag; to muzzle, to suppress
Knecht m. farmhand; servant; (lit.) slave; jack; — Ruprecht Santa Claus; -schaft f. slavery; bondage, servitude; -ssinn m. servile spirit
knechten v. to keep in servitude; to enslave
kneifen v. to pinch; to flinch; to shirk
Kneifer m. pince-nez; coward, flincher
Kneifzange f. tweezers; flat-nosed pliers
Kneipe f. (coll.) tavern, inn; -rei f. drinking bout, carousal
kneipen v. to pinch, to tipple, to carouse
kneten v. to knead
Knick m. flaw, crack; bend; hedge; -er m. miser, niggard; folding knife; -beine neu. pl. knock-kneed legs; -s m. curtsy
knick: -en v. to break, to crack, to bend; to dispirit; -(e)rig adj. stingy; -ern v. to be stingy; to crackle; -sen v. to curtsy
Knie neu. knee; bend; (mech.) elbow, joint; -band neu. garter; knee ligament; -fall m. going down on one's knees; -geige f. bass viol; -gelenk neu. knee joint; -riemen m. shoemaker's strap; Meister -riem m. (coll.) shoemaker; -rohr neu. elbow pipe; -scheibe f. knee cap; -schützer m. kneepad
Kniff m. pinch; crease, fold; dodge, knack, trick
knipsen v. to punch; to clip; to snip; to snap
Knirps m. little fellow; dwarf; (coll.) shrimp
knirschen v. to crunch, to gnash, to grate
knistern v. to crackle, to rustle; to crepitate
knittern v. to crackle; to ruffle; to crumple
Knoblauch m. garlic; -zehe f. garlic clove
Knöchel m. knuckle; ankle; (sl.) dice

Knochen m. bone; (sl.) house key; **bis auf die —** right to the core; **–bau** m. bony frame (oder structure); **–bruch** m. bone fracture; **–frass** m. caries; **–gerüst** neu. skeleton; **–gewebe** neu. bone tissue; **–haus** neu. charnel house; **–lehre** f. osteology; **–mann** m. (poet.) Death; **–mehl** neu. bone meal; **–splitter** m. bone splinter

knöchern adj. of bone, bony, osseous
Knödel m. dumpling
Knolle f., **Knollen** m. bulb, tuber; clod; lump
Knopf m. button; stud; knob; boss; pommel; head; **der — geht ihm auf** (coll.) he finally gets the idea
knöpfen v. to button; to finger buttons
Knorpel m. cartilage; gristle
knorpelig adj. gristly; cartilaginous
knorrig adj. gnarled, knobby, knotty
Knospe f. bud; tender young person
knospen v. to bud, to sprout; to blossom
Knötchen neu. small knot; nodule, tubercle
Knoten m. knot; difficulty; plot; **hier hat es einen —** there's a hitch in it; **–punkt** m. junction; **–stock** m. knotty stick
knoten v. to knot
knotig adj. knobby; lumpy; crude, vulgar
Knuff m. cuff, thump, push
knüllen v. to crumple, to crush
knüpfen v. to tie, to knot; **ein Bündnis —** to form an alliance
Knüppel m. club, cudgel; log; (bakery) small roll; mallet; (avi.) stick; **der — liegt beim Hunde** there is no choice; **–damm** m. corduroy road
knüppeldick adj. very thick (oder much); **er hat es — hinter den Ohren** he's a very sly fellow
knurren v. to growl, to snarl; to grumble; (stomach) to rumble
knusp(e)rig adj. crisp
knuspern v. to crunch; to nibble
Knute f. knout
knutschen v. to crush; to cuddle
Knüttel m. club, cudgel; **–vers** m. doggerel
koalisieren v. to form a coalition
Kobold m. sprite, (hob)goblin, imp
Koch m. cook; **–er** m. cooker; cooking apparatus; **–erei** f. inferior cooking; **–geschirr** neu. pots and pans; soldiers' (oder campers') mess kit; **–herd** m. kitchen range; **–kiste** f. insulated box (for keeping foods hot); **–kunst** f. culinary art; **–löffel** m. ladle
kochen v. to cook; to boil; to stew; to scald; to seethe, to be exited; **überall wird mit Wasser gekocht** people are the same everywhere
Köcher m. quiver
Köchin f. cook
Kode m. code, cipher; **–x** m. (law) code
ködern v. to bait, to decoy, to lure
Koffer m. bag, box, suitcase, trunk; **–träger** m. porter, redcap; **–grammofon** neu. portable phonograph
Kognak m. cognac, brandy
Kohl m. cabbage; cole, kale; **aufgewärmter —** an old story; **–kopf** m. head of

cabbage; **–rabi** m. kohlrabi; **–rübe** f. rutabaga; **–weissling** m. cabbage butterfly
Kohle f. coal; charcoal; (elec.) carbon; **auf glühenden —** nsitzen to sit on pins and needles; **–narbeiter** m. coal miner; collier; **–nbecken** neu. coal field; brazier; **–nbergwerk** neu. coal mine; **–nblende** f. anthracite; **–neimer** m. coal scuttle; **–nflöz** neu. coal seam; **–ngrube** f. coal mine; **–nkasten** m. coal box; **–nkeller** m. coal cellar; **–nlager** neu. coal deposit (oder seam); **–nschiff** neu. collier; **–nstoff** m. carbon; **–nzeichnung** f. charcoal drawing
Köhler m. charcoal burner; coalfish; **–glaube** (n) m. blind faith, superstition
Koje f. (naut.) cabin, berth
Koka f. coca; **–in** neu. cocaine
kokett adj. coquettish; **–ieren** v. to flirt
Kokon m. cocoon
Kokos: –baum m., **–palme** f. coconut tree; **–nuss** f. coconut; **–öl** neu. coconut oil
Koks m. coke; (sl.) cocaine; money
Kolben m. club, mace; (rifle) butt; flask; (chem.) still; soldering iron; piston, plunger; (bot.) spike, spadix
Kolibri m. hummingbird
Kolik f. colic, gripes
kollaborieren v. to collaborate
Kolleg neu. (university) lecture course; **–e** m. colleague; **–ialität** f. fellowship; **–iengelder** neu. pl. students' fees; **–ium** neu. faculty, staff, board
kollegial adj. harmonious; collegiate
Kollekt: –e f. collect(ion); **–eur** m. collector; **–ion** f. collection; **–iv** neu. group association
kollektiv adj. collective; united
Koller m. choler, frenzy, rage; (horses) blind staggers; leather jerkin
kollern v. to roll; to rumble; to gobble
kollidieren v. to collide
Kollisionskurs (Rakete) m. collision course
Kolloquium neu. scientific conference
Köln neu. Cologne
Koloni: –alwaren f. pl. groceries; colonial produce; **–e** f. colony; **–st** m. settler
kolonisieren v. to colonize
Kolonne f. (mil.) column; formation
Kolor: –atur f. coloratura; **–ierung** f. coloring; **–it** neu. coloring
kolorieren v. to color
Koloss m. colossus
Kolportage f. colportage; cheap, sensational publication
kolportieren v. to hawk; to circulate rumors
Kolumne f. pillar; column
kombinieren v. to combine
Kombüse f. caboose, ship's galley
Komik f. funniness, comic deportment, drollery; **–er** m. comedian; comic actor
komisch adj. comical, funny, strange
Komma neu. comma; (math.) decimal point
Kommand: –ant m., **–eur** m. commandant, commander; **–antur** f. commander's office; garrison headquarters; **–itgesellschaft** f. company with limited

liability (*oder* membership); **-o** *neu.*
command; detachment; **-obrücke** *f.*
(pilot) bridge; **-ostab** *m.* commanders'
baton; **-oturm** *m.* control tower

kommandieren *v.* to command

kommen *v.* to come; to approach, to arise.
to result (from); to arrive; to occur;
to cost; **an die Reihe** — to have one's
turn; **aneinander** — to come to blows;
auf etwas — to hit upon; to remember;
hinter etwas — to detect something;
in Verlegenheit — to get into trouble;
— **lassen** to send for; — **seh(e)n** to
foresee; **nach Hause** — to get home;
nicht dazu — to have no time; **um
etwas** — to lose (*oder* come for) something; **wie** — **Sie dazu?** How do you get
it? How dare you? **zu etwas** — to
acquire something; **zu kurz** — to lose
out; **zu sich** — to recover

Komment *m.* students' club code; **-ar** *m.*
commentary; annotation; **-ator** *m.* an-
notator

kommentieren *v.* to annotate

kommissarisch *adj.* provisional

Kommode *f.* chest (of drawers)

Kommun: **-albeamte** *m.* municipal official; **-alschule** *f.* council school; **-als-
teuer** *f.* local tax; **-e** *f.* community;
(coll.) Communist Party; **-ikant** *m.*
(rel.) communicant; **-ion** *f.* (rel.) Holy
Communion; **-ismus** *m.* communism

kommun: **-al** *adj.* communal; municipal;
-istisch *adj.* communistic; **-izieren** *v.*
to communicate

Komödi: **-ant** *m.* comedian, actor; **-an-
tentum** *neu.* bohemianism; **-e** *f.* comedy; pretense; **-enhaus** *neu.* playhouse;
theater (for comedies)

Kompa(g)nie *f.* company; firm

Kompagnon *m.* (com.) partner; collaborator

Kompass *m.* compass; **-häuschen** *neu.*
binnacle; **-peilung** *f.* compass bearing

Komplementärfarbe *f.* complementary
color

komplett *adj.* complete; **-ieren** *v.* to complete

Kompliment *neu.* compliment; bow

Komplize *m.* accomplice

komplizieren *v.* to complicate

kompliziert *adj.* complicated; **-er Bruch**
compound fracture

Komplott *neu.* plot, conspiracy

komponieren *v.* to compose; to set to
music

Komponist *m.* (mus.) composer; arranger

Kompott *neu.* compote; stewed fruit

Kompresse *f.* (med.) compress

komprimieren *v.* to compress; to condense

Kompromiss *m.* compromise

kompromittieren *v.* to compromise; to expose

Komtesse *f.* countess

Kondensator *m.* condenser

kondensieren *v.* to condense

Kondensstreifen *m.* (avi.) contrail

Konditor *m.* confectioner; **-ei** *f.* confectionery; **-ware** *f.* confectionery; pastries. sweets

kondolieren *v.* to condole (with)

Kondukt *m.* (funeral) procession; **-eur** *m.*
(traffic) conductor; **-or** *m.* (phys.) conductor

Konfekt *neu.* confectionery, sweets; **-ion**
f. ready-made clothing; **-ionär** *m.* out-
fitter

Konferenz *f.* conference; meeting; convention

konferieren *v.* to confer; to act as announcer

Konfession *f.* confession; creed; **-sschule**
f. denominational school

konfessionell *adj.* denominational

konfessionslos *adj.* nondenominational

Konfirmand *m.* (rel.) person being con-
firmed; **-enunterricht** *m.* confirmation
classes

konfirmieren *v.* to confirm

konfiszieren *v.* to confiscate

Konfitüre *f.* confectionery; candied fruit;
preserves; marmalade

Konflikt *m.* conflict

konform *adj.* conformable; exact; **-gehen**
to agree

konfrontieren *v.* to face; to confront

konfus *adj.* confused, muddled

König *m.* king; **-in** *f.* queen; **-reich** *neu.*
kingdom; realm; **-smord** *m.* regicide;
-stiger *m.* Bengal tiger; **-streue** *m.*
royalist; **-tum** *neu.* kingship, royalty

königlich *adj.* royal; wonderful, grand,
regal

konisch *adj.* conic(al)

Konjunktiv *m.* subjunctive (mood)

Konjunktur *f.* high level of business; bear
market; **-politiker** *m.* (pol.) coattail
rider

konkav *adj.* concave

konkret *adj.* concrete; real; palpable

Konkubinat *neu.* concubinage

Konkurrent *m.* competitor

Konkurrenz *f.* competition

konkurrieren *v.* to compete

Konkurs *m.* bankruptcy; failure; **-erklä-
rung** *f.* declaration of insolvency;
-masse *f.* bankrupt's estate; **-verfahren**
neu. proceedings in bankruptcy; **-ver-
walter** *m.* trustee in bankruptcy

können *v.* to be able; to know; to be
possible; to be permitted to; **es kann
sein** it may be; **nicht mehr** — to be
exhausted; **sie** — **nichts dafür** it wasn't
their fault

Könner *m.* expert, adept

Konrad *m.* Conrad

Konsens *m.* consent, agreement

konsequent *adj.* consistent; persistent

Konsequenz *f.* consistency; consequence

Konserv: **-atorium** *neu.* academy of music, conservatory; **-e** *f.* preserve; canned
food; **-enbüchse** *f.* tin can; **-enfabrik**
f. cannery

konservieren *v.* to conserve; to preserve,
to can

Konsistorium *neu.* (rel.) consistory

konsolidieren *v.* to consolidate; to make
safe

Konsorte *m.* accomplice; associate member

Konsortium *neu.* syndicate
Konspiration *f.* conspiracy
konstatieren *v.* to give evidence
konstituieren *v.* to constitute; **sich — als** to resolve itself into
konstitutionell *adj.* constitutional; consistent with the constitution
konstruieren *v.* to construct, to design, to plan; to construe; (phil.) to establish
Konsul *m.* consul; **-at** *neu.* consulate; **-tation** *f.* consultation; counseling
konsularisch *adj.* consular
konsultieren *v.* to counsel; to consult
Konsum *m.* consumption; **-ent** *m.* consumer; **-verein** *m.* co-operative society
konsumieren *v.* to consume
Konter: **-admiral** *m.* Rear Admiral; **-bande** *f.* contraband; smuggling, smuggled goods; **-fei** *neu.* portrait, likeness; **-tanz** *m.* square dance
kontinuierlich *adj.* continuous, connected
Kontinuität *f.* continuity, connection
Konto *neu.* account; **-korrent** *neu.* current account; **-r** *neu.* office; **-rist** *m.* office clerk
Kontra *neu.* (cards) double; **-alt** *m.* contralto; **-altistin** *f.* contralto singer; **-bass** *m.* contrabass; **-hent** *m.* contracting party, contractor; opponent; **-punkt** *m.* counterpoint
kontrakt: **-brüchig** *adj.* contract-breaking; **-lich** *adj.* fixed, stipulated; **-pflichtig** *adj.* bound by contract
Kontrakt *m.* contract, agreement; **-bruch** *m.* breach of contract
kontrollieren *v.* to control; to check; to audit; to keep time
Kontroll-(*oder* **Warn-**)**station** *f.* (radio *oder* Radar) beacon; **-stelle** (avi. & mil.) check point
Kontur *f.* contour (line)
Konvent *m.* assembly (of clergy, student bodies, French Revolution); (eccl.) conventicle; **-ion** *f.* custom, tradition; convention, agreement; **-ionalstrafe** *f.* penalty for breach of contract
konventionell *adj.* conventional
Konversation *f.* conversation; **-slexikon** *neu.* encyclopedia; **-sstück** *neu.* society comedy
Konvertit *m.* convert
konzentrieren *v.* to concentrate, to saturate
konzentrisch *adj.* concentric
Konzert *neu.* (mus.) concert(o)
konzertieren *v.* to give a concert
Konzession *f.* concession, license, patent
Konzil *neu.* (eccl.) council
Köper *m.* twill
Kopf *m.* head; knob, button; top; brains; **alles auf den —** stellen to turn everything upside down; **auf seinen — bestehen, seinen — aufsetzen** to be stubborn; **aus dem -e wissen** to know by heart; **durch den — gehen (lassen)** to (let) revolve in one's mind; **er handelt nur nach seinem —** he follows no one's advice but his own; **es ist ganz nach meinem —** it's quite to my liking; **im — behalten** to remember; **im**

— rechnen to compute mentally, **— an —** closely packed; **mit einem dicken — dasitzen** to be overwhelmed with worries; **nicht auf den — gefallen sein** to be no fool; **nicht von seinem — abgehen, seinen — durchsetzen** to stick to one's guns; **sich den — zerbrechen** to rack one's brains; **sich etwas in den — gesetzt haben** to be obstinate; **über den — wachsen** to outgrow; **vor den — stossen** to offend; **-arbeit** *f.* brain (*oder* mental) work; **-bahnhof** *m.* terminal railroad station; **-ende** *neu.* head; **-hängerei** *f.* dejection; **-haut** *f.* scalp; **-hörer** *m.* headphone; **-kissen** *neu.* pillow; **-kissenbezug** *m.* pillow case; **-nicken** *neu.* nod; **-nuss** *f.* head blow; box on the ear; **-putz** *m.* coiffure; **-rechnen** *neu.* mental arithmetic; **-salat** *m.* head lettuce; **-schmerz** *m.*, **-weh** *neu.* headache; **-sprung** *m.* (swimming) header; **-steuer** *f.* poll tax; **-stimme** *f.* falsetto; **-stück** *neu.* headpiece; (coll.) box on the ear; **-tuch** *neu.* head-cloth, kerchief; **-waschen** *neu.* shampoo; **-zerbrechen** *neu.* brain cudgeling
kopf: **-hängerisch** *adj.* moping; **-los** *adj.* headless; disconcerted; **-über** *adv.* head foremost, head over heels; **-unter** *adv.* headlong
köpfen *v.* to behead; to lop, to top
Kopie *f.* copy, facsimile; duplicate; proof sheet; reproduction; imitation; (contact) print
kopieren *v.* to copy; to make a contact print
Koppel *f.* coupling; group of dogs, train of horses; paddock, enclosure; **—** *neu.* sword (*oder* shoulder) belt
koppeln *v.* to couple, to link
kopulieren *v.* to copulate; to marry
Koralle *f.* coral; amber bead
Korb *m.* basket, hamper; creel, pannier, hive; gondola (of balloon); (coll.) refusal; **Hahn im —** sein to be cock of the walk; **-geflecht** *neu.* wickerwork
Kord *m.* corduroy; **-el** *f.* cord, string, twine
Korinthe *f.* currant
Kork *m.* cork; stopper; **-enzieher** *m.* corkscrew
korken *adj.* of cork; **—** *v.* to cork
Korn *neu.* grain; cereal, (Germany) rye; small particle; (coins) fine weight; (gun) sight; **auf's — nehmen** to aim at, to keep a sharp eye upon; **von altem** (*oder* **echtem**) **Schrot und —** of the good old sort; **-ähre** *f.* spike of grain; **-boden** *m.*, **-speicher** *m.* granary; silo; **-börse** *f.* grain exchange; **-branntwein** *m.* whisky; **-kammer** *f.* granary; breadbasket
Kornett *neu.* (mus.) cornet; **—** *m.* (mil.) cornet, mounted standard bearer
Korona *f.* corona; (sl.) circle of listeners participants
Körper *m.* body; bulk; substance; **-bau** *m.* body structure, build; **-bemalung** *f.* tattooing; **-beschaffenheit** *f.* constitu

tion, physique; **-fehler** m. bodily defect, deformity; **-fülle** f. corpulence; **grösse** f., **-wuchs** m. stature; **-haltung** f. bearing, attitude; carriage; **-inhalt** m. solid contents; **-kraft** f. physical strength; **-mass** neu. cubic measure; **-pflege** f. physical culture; **-schaft** m. corporation; group, association; **-übung** f. gymnastics; **-welt** f. material world

körperlich adj. bodily; material

körperschaftlich, korporativ adj. corporate, collective

Korps neu. corps; (coll.) group

korpulent adj. corpulent, obese

Korpulenz f. corpulence, obesity

Korrekt: -or m. proofreader; **-ur** f. correction; proofreading; **-urabzug** m., **-urbogen** m., **-urfahne** f. printer's proof; galley proof

Korrespondenz f. correspondence; **-büro** neu. press association

korrigieren v. to correct; to proofread

korrumpiert adj. corrupt; venal; immoral

Korsar m. corsair, freebooter; pirate's ship

Korsett neu. corset; **-stange** f. corset stay

kosen v. to caress, to fondle; to hug

Kosename m. pet name

Kosmetik f. cosmetics; cosmetic care

kosmisch adj. cosmic

Kosmonaut m. cosmonaut

Kost f. food; board, diet; **-gänger** m. boarder; **-geld** neu. board allowance; (law) alimony; **-probe** f. sample, relish; **-verächter** m. dainty (oder fastidious) person; scorner

kost: -bar adj. precious; costly; **-en** v. to cost; to take; to require; to taste; to experience the effect (of); **-enfrei** adj., with free board; **-spielig** adj. expensive, costly

Kosten pl. costs, expenses; charges; **auf seine — kommen** not to regret expenditures; **-anschlag** m. estimate of costs; **-aufwand** m. expenditure; **-punkt** m. problem of expense

köstlich adj. fine, precious; delicious

Kostüm neu. costume; dress, clothes; jacket and skirt; **-fest** neu. fancy dress ball; **-probe** f. dress rehearsal

Kot m. dirt, filth; mud; excrement; **-au** m. kowtow; **-blech** neu., **-flügel** m. mudguard; fender

Kotelett neu. cutlet, chop

Köter m. cur; watchdog

Krabbe f. crab, shrimp; (coll.) lively girl

krabbeln v. to grovel, to crawl

krach! interj. crash! **-en** v. to crack; to crash

Krach m. crash; collapse; quarrel, scene

krächzen v. to caw, to croak

Kraft f. strength, power, force; vigor; validity; hand, laborer, worker; **ausser — setzen** to annul, to abrogate; **-anstrengung** f., **-aufwand** m. effort; **-ausdruck** m. strong expression; **-äusserung** f. manifestation of force; **-brühe** f. strong broth; **-droschke** f. taxi; **-fahrer** m. motorist; **-fahrzeug** neu. motor vehicle; **-probe** f. trial of strength; **-rad**

neu. motorcycle; **-stoff** m. fuel, gasoline; **-verstärker** m. servomotor; **-wagen** m. automobile; **-werk** neu. power plant (oder station)

kraft prep. by virtue of, on the basis of

kräftig adj. strong, vigorous; robust; nourishing; **-en** v. to strengthen, to invigorate

Kragen m. collar; neck; (zool.) ruff; **beim — nehmen** to collar; **es geht ihm an den —** it will cost him his neck; **-knopf** m. collar stud

Krähe f. crow, rook; **-nfüsse** m. pl. crow's feet, wrinkles (around eye); bad handwriting, hen tracks

krähen v. to crow

Krakeel m. brawl, aquabble, row, wrangle

Kralle f. claw, talon, clutch

krallen v. to claw, to scratch

Kram m. odds and ends; rubbish; (coll.) business; **-laden** m. hole-in-the-wall shop

kramen v. to rummage; to stir, to move

Krämer m. small shopkeeper; petty person

Krampf m. cramp, spasm; convulsion; fit; **-ader** f. varicose vein

krampf: -artig adj., **-haft** adj. convulsive, spasmodic; **-en** v. to contract, to convulse, to clench; **-stillend** adj. antispasmodic

Kran m. (mech.) crane; hoist

Krangerüstturm m. gantry tower

Kranich m. (orn.) crane

krank adj. ill; sick; suffering; (hunting) wounded; **— am Beutel sein** to be short of money; **sich — stellen** to feign illness; **-en** v. to be ailing; to suffer from; **-haft** adj. morbid; pathological; **-heitshalber** adv. owing to illness

Krank: -e m. sick person, patient; **-heit** f. illness, disease; (zool.) distemper; **-heitserreger** m. disease germ; **-heitserscheinung** f. symptom; **-heitslehre** f. pathology; **-heitsübertragung** f. infection; **-heitsurlaub** m. sick-leave

kränk: -eln v. to be in poor health; **-en** v. to offend; to anger; to grieve; **-lich** adj. sickly, susceptible to illness

Kranken: -anstalt f., **-haus** neu. hospital; **-bericht** m. doctor's report; bulletin; **-bett** neu., **-lager** neu. sick-bed; **-dienst** m. care of the sick; **-kasse** f. hospitalization insurance, sick benefit fund; **-kost** f. diet; **-pflege** f. nursing; **-saal** m. hospital ward; (naut.) sick bay; **-schwester** f., **-wärterin** f. nurse; **-stube** f. sickroom; **-tragbahre** f. stretcher; **-träger** m. stretcher bearer; **-wagen** m. ambulance; **-wärter** m. male nurse; **-zimmer** neu. sickroom

Kränkung f. offense; vexation, insult; grievance

Kranz m. garland, wreath; (arch.) cornice; **-jungfer** f. bridesmaid

Kränzchen neu. small garland; ladies' circle

kränzen v. to wreath, to crown

Krapfen m. doughnut, fritter

Krater m. crater

Kratz: -e f. scraper; carding comb; -bürste f. wire (oder hard) brush; intractable person; -eisen neu. scraping iron; -er m. scraper; scratch; -fuss m. scraping bow

kratzbürstig adj. cross, quick-tempered

Krätze f. itch; -r m. sour wine

kratzen v. to scratch; to scrape; to grate

krätzig adj. itchy, mangy, full of scabs

kraus adj. curly, frizzled; dishevelled; queer; die Stirne — ziehen to knit one's brow; -haarig adj. curly-haired

Krause f. frill, ruff

kräuseln v. to curl, to frizzle, to ripple; (smoke) to wreathe

Kraut neu. herb, plant; herbage; cabbage; weed; ins — schiessen to grow rankly

Kräuter neu. pl. herbs; -käse m. green cheese; -kunde f. botany

Krawall m. uproar, row, free-for-all fight

Krawatte f. cravat, necktie

Kreatur f. creature; favorite, minion

Krebs m. crayfish; crab; (ast.) Cancer; (med.) cancer; -gang m. crab's walk; retrogression

Kredenz f. sideboard, buffet

Kredit m. credit; -iv neu. power of attorney; credentials; -or m. creditor

kreditfähig adj. (com.) solvent, sound

Kreide f. chalk, crayon; in die — geraten to go into debt; tief in der — stehen to be deeply (oder heavily) in debt

Kreis m. circle; orbit; district; province; sphere, ring; (biol.) phylum; -bahn f. orbit; -bogen m. arc; -elachse m. gyroscope; -lauf m. circulation, rotation; -säge f. circular saw; -umfang m., -linie f. circumference, periphery

kreischen v. to scream, to shriek, to screech; -de Stimme shrill voice

kreisen v. to circulate, to circle; to revolve

Krempe f. (hat) brim

Krempel m. rubbish; — f. carding machine

Kremserweiss neu. white lead

krepieren v. (coll.) to die; to burst, to explode

Krepp m. crêpe, crape

Kresse f. cress; nasturtium

Krethi und Plethi m. riffraff; rag, tag, and bobtail

Kreuz neu. cross; crucifix; loins; backbone; (cards) clubs; (horse) croup; (mus.) sharp; (typ.) dagger; affliction; ans — heften (oder schlagen) to crucify; das — auf sich nehmen to take up the cross, to be willing to bear consequences; das — schlagen to make the sign of the cross; drei -e hinter jemand machen to be glad to be rid of someone; über — legen to lay crosswise; zu — kriechen to submit humbly; -band neu. crossbeam; mailing wrapper (for printed matter); -er m. copper coin; cruiser; -fahrer m., -ritter m. crusader; -gang m. cloisters; -otter f. adder, viper; -schmerz m. lumbago; -schnabel m. crossbill; -ung f. intersection; crossbreeding; -verhör neu. crossexamination; -weg m. crossroad; Way of

the Cross; -worträtsel neu. crossword puzzle; -zug m. crusade

kreuz: — und quer crisscross; in all directions; -brav adj. honest to the core; -en v. to cross, to intersect; to crossbreed; to cruise; -igen v. to crucify; -lahm adj., -steif adj. lame (oder stiff) in the back

kribbeln v. to crawl, to itch, to tickle

kriechen v. to crawl, to creep, to sneak; to fawn; to cringe

Krieg m. war, feud; in den — ziehen to go to war; — führen to wage war; -er m. soldier, old fighter; -erverein m. association of war veterans; -sausrüstung f. armaments; -sbaukunst f. military engineering; -sbereitschaft f. preparedness for war; -sdienstverweigerer m. conscientious objector; -sentschädigung f. war indemnity; -serklärung f. declaration of war; -sgebiet neu. warzone; -sgefährte m.. -skamerad m. fellow-soldier; -sgefangene m. prisoner of war; -sgericht neu. court-martial; -sgeschrei neu. war cry; -sgewinnler m. war profiteer; -shandwerk neu. military profession; -shetzer m. warmonger; -smacht f. military forces; -srat m. council of war; -srecht neu. martial law; -sschauplatz m. theater of war; -sschiff neu. battleship, warship; -sschuld f. war guilt; war debt; -ssteuer f. war tax; -streiber m. warmonger; -szucht f. military discipline; -szug m. military campaign (oder expedition)

krieg: -en v. to wage war; to catch, to seize; to obtain, to receive; -erisch adj. bellicose; martial; -führend adj. belligerent; -spflichtig adj. liable for military service

die Krim f. Crimea

Kriminal: -beamte m. detective; -gericht neu. criminal court; -roman m. detective story; -gesetzbuch neu. criminal (oder penal) code

kriminell adj. criminal

Krimskrams m. rubbish, trash

Krippe f. crib, manger; crèche; day nursery; -nspiel neu. nativity play; -nbeisser m., -nsetzer m. (coll.) old horse (oder man)

Krise, Krisis f. crisis

Kristall m. crystal; — neu. crystal glass

Kriterium neu. criterion

Kritik f. criticism; evaluation; review; -er m. critic; reviewer; -losigkeit f. lack of judgment

kritisch adj. critical, judicious; precarious

kritisieren v. to criticize; to review

Krittelei f. carping criticism; fault-finding

kritzeln v. to scrawl; to scribble

Krokodil neu. crocodile

Kron: -e f. crown; coronet, corona; diadem; crest; (bot.) corolla; (coll.) head; das setzt dem Fass die -e auf that tops everything; -enblatt neu. petal; -engold neu. 18 carat gold; -leuchter m. chandelier; -zeuge m. state's evidence; chief witness

krönen v. to crown

Kropf m. (orn.) crop, craw; goiter; **–taube** f. pouter pigeon

Kröte f. toad; (coll.) coin; **kleine —** impertinent girl

Krücke f. crutch; T-shaped tool

Krug m. jug, pitcher; inn, tavern

Krume f. crumb; topsoil

krümeln v. to crumble; to crumb; to pulverize

krumm adj. crooked, bent; hooked; arched, curved; sinuous; **die Hand — machen** (coll.) to beg; **— ansehen** v. to look askance; **— liegen** (coll.) to have no money; **— nehmen** (coll.) to take amiss; **–e Wege gehen** to pursue dishonest ways; **–beinig** adj. bowlegged; knock-kneed

Krumm: –holz neu. dwarf shrub; underbrush; **–stab** m. crozier

krümmen v. to bend, to curve, to crook; to wind, to meander; **sich —** to cringe; to stoop; to wriggle, to writhe

Krupp m. croup, diphtheria

Kruppe f. crupper

Krüppel m. cripple

krüppelhaft, krüpp(e)lig adj. crippled

Kruste f. crust; scab; **–ntier** neu. crustacean

Kruzifix neu. crucifix

Krypta f. crypt

Kübel m. bucket; tub; vat

kubisch adj. cubic(al)

Küch: –e f. kitchen; **in des Teufels –e kommen** (coll.) to be in danger of losing one's neck; **kalte –e** cold dinner; **–enherd** m. kitchen range; **–enmeister** m. chef; **–enzettel** m. bill of fare; **–lein** neu. small cake; chicken

Kuchen m. cake; clot; **–bäcker** m. pastry cook

Kuckuck m. cuckoo; **–sei** neu. cuckoo's egg; dubious gift

Kufe f. vat; (cradle) rocker; (sledge) runner

Kugel f. ball, sphere; bullet; (gym.) shot; **–lager** neu. ball bearing; **–mass** neu. caliber; **–schreiber** m. ball-point pen; **–stossen** neu. shot-put

kugel: –fest adj. bulletproof; **–förmig** adj. spherical; globular; **–ig** adj. round, globular; **–n** v. to bowl, to roll; to ballot

Kuh f. cow; **blinde —** blindman's buff; **das geht auf keine –haut** that's beyond all measure; **–euter** neu. cow's udder; **–fladen** m. cow-dung; **–handel** m. shady deal; **–hirt** m. cowboy, cowherd

kühl adj. cool, chilly; fresh; unfriendly, stiff; **–en** v. to cool; **sein Mütchen an jemandem –en** to take one's temper out on someone

Kühl: –anlage f., **–haus** n. cold-storage plant; **–apparat** m. refrigerator; **–e** f. coolness, freshness; unfriendliness; stiffness; **–er** m. cooler; radiator; **–mittel** neu. refrigerant; **–raum** m. cold storage room; **–ung** f. cooling; refrigeration

kühn adj. bold, daring; intrepid; audacious

Küken neu. small chicken

Kulisse f. (theat.) wing; scene; **–nschieber** m. scene shifter

Kult m. cult; **–ivierung** f. cultivation; **–ur** f. culture, civilization; forestation; (agr.) cultivation; **–urfilm** m. educational film; **–urpflanzen** f. pl. cultivated plants; **–usminister** m. Minister of Culture

Kümmel m. caraway (seed); cumin brandy

Kummer m. grief; worry; sorrow

kümmer: –lich adj. miserable; pitiful; stunted; **–lich** adv. barely, scarcely; **–n** v. to trouble, to take pains; **sich –n um** to care for; to be concerned about; to mind

Kümmernis f. grief; affliction; anxiety

Kum(me)t neu. horse collar

Kumpan m. companion, fellow

kund adj. known; **–geben** v. to demonstrate; to manifest; **–machen, — tun** v. to make known, to publish; to proclaim; **–ig** adj. experienced, familiar with; **–schaften** v. to reconnoiter, to scout

Kund: –e m. customer; (sl.) tramp; **—** f. information, news; **–ige** m. wellinformed person; expert; **–schaft** f. customers; (mil.) reconnoitering, scouting; **–schafter** m. scout, spy; emissary

künd: –bar adj. recallable, redeemable; **–en** v (bibl.) to announce, to make known; **–igen** v. to give notice; to call off; to denounce

künftig adj. future; later; **seine –e Frau** (coll.) his wife-to-be; **–hin** adv. henceforth, from now on

Kunkel f. distaff

Kunst f. art; ingenuity, skill; **das ist keine —** it's easy; **schwarze —** black magic; **–akademie** f. academy of arts; **–dünger** m. chemical fertilizer; **–flug** m. (avi.) stunt flight; **–gärtner** m. nursery gardener; horticulturist; **–gewerbe** neu. applied art; arts and crafts; **–händler** m. art dealer; **–handwerker** m. artisan, craftsman; **–kenner** m. art connoisseur; **–kniff** m. ruse; **–lauf** m. figure skating; **–leder** neu. imitation leather; **–liebhaber** m. amateur; **–reiter** m. circus rider; **–richter** m. art critic; **–seide** f. artificial silk; **–springen** neu. fancy diving; **–stoff** m. plastics; **–stück** neu. feat, trick; **–tischler** m. cabinetmaker

kunst: –fertig adj. possessing artistic skill; **–gemäss** adj., **–gerecht** adj. artistically correct; **–los** adj. inartistic; artless; simple; **–reich** adj. artistic; ingenious; **–sinnig** adj. appreciative of art; **–verständig** adj. expert in art; **–voll** adj. highly artistic

Künst: –elei f. artificiality; affectation; **–ler** m. artist; virtuoso; **–lerwerkstatt** f. artist's studio

künst: –eln v. to elaborate, to overrefine; to attitudinize; **–lerisch** adj. artistic; **–lich** adj. artificial; arty

Kupfer neu. copper; **–druck** m. copperplate print(ing); **–stich** m. copperplate engraving (oder print); **–tiefdruck** m.

photogravure

kupfern, kupfrig *adj.* of copper, coppery

Kuppe *f.* (nail) head; top, summit; **-l** *f.* cupola, dome; firmament

Kupp(e)lung *f.* coupling, clutch

kuppeln *v.* to couple; to make a match; to clutch

Kur *f.* cure; course of treatment; **einer Dame die — schneiden** to pay court to a woman; **-arzt** *m.* physician (at health resort); **-atel** *f.* guardianship, trusteeship; curatorship; **-ator** *m.* guardian; trustee; supervisor (at German university); **-atorium** *neu.* board of trustees; governing body; **-fürst** *m.* (German) elector; **-fürstentum** *neu.* electorate; **-gast** *m.* health resort patient; **-haus** *neu.* health resort hotel; casino; pump room; **-ort** *m.* health resort, spa; **-pfalz** *f.* Palatinate; **-pfuscher** *m.* quack

Kür *f.* choice; **-assier** *m.* cuirassier; **-bis** *m.* pumpkin; gourd; (sl.) head; **-bisflasche** *f.* calabash; **-schner** *m.* furrier

Kurbel *f.* crank; **-kasten** *m.* (coll.) movie camera; **-welle** *f.* crankshaft

kurbeln *v.* to crank

Kurie *f.* curia; (eccl.) court of justice; magistracy

Kurier *m.* courier, express

kurieren *v.* to cure

kurios *adj.* odd, strange, rare

Kuriosität *f.* oddity, rarity, curiosity

Kurrentschrift *f.* cursive writing, italics

Kurs *m.* course; currency; rate of exchange; **-abweichung (Rakete)** *f.* yaw; **ausser — setzen** to withdraw from circulation; **in — setzen** to circulate; **-bericht** *m.* stock exchange quotations; stock market report; **-buch** *neu.* train schedules, railway guide, time tables; **-schwankungen** *f. pl.* stock exchange fluctuations

kursieren *v.* to circulate

Kursivschrift *f.* italics

Kursus *m.* course (of lectures)

kurz *adj.* short; brief; **in -em soon,** shortly; **— angebunden** brusque; **— entschlossen** quickly resolved; **— fassen** to be brief; **— treten** (mil.) to mark time; **— und bündig** concise; **— und gut** in a word; **— und klein schlagen** to smash into bits; **über — oder lang** sooner or later; **vor -em** recently; **zu — kommen** to come off the loser; **-atmig** *adj.* short-winded, asthmatic; **-erhand** *adv.* without hesitation, abruptly; **-fristig** *adj.* short-termed; short-dated; **-gefasst** *adj.* briefly worded, concise; **-lebig** *adj.* short-lived; **-schliessen** *v.* to handcuff; (elec.) to short circuit; **-sichtig** *adj.* nearsighted, shortsighted; **-um** *adv.* in short, in a word; **-weilig** *adj.* amusing, funny

Kurz: -geschichte *f.* short short story; feature article; **-schluss** *m.* (elec.) short circuit; **-schrift** *f.* shorthand, stenography; **-streckenläufer** *m.* sprinter; **-waren** *f. pl.* notions; haberdashery; **-weil** *f.* amusement, pastime; **-wellensender** *m.* short-wave transmitter

kürzen *v.* to shorten, to diminish, to reduce; to curtail; (math.) to simplify

kürzlich *adv.* lately, recently

Kusine *f.* cousin

Kuss *m.* kiss; **-hand** *f.* blown kiss

küssen *v.* to kiss

Küssen *neu.* kissing

kussfest *adj.* kissproof

Küste *f.* coast, shore; **-nfahrer** *m.* coaster; **-nstrich** *m.*, **-nland** *neu.* maritime country

Küster *m.* sexton, verger

Kustos *m.* custodian, curator; canon

kutschieren *v.* to drive (coach)

Kutte *f.* monk's robe, cowl

Kuvert *neu.* envelope; table setting

L

Lab: -e *f.*, **-sal** *neu.*, **-ung** *f.* refreshment; restorative; comfort; **-etrank** *m.*, **-etrunk** *m.* refreshing drink

labbern *v.* to lap; (sl.) to babble

laben *v.* to refresh; **sich —** to enjoy; to restore oneself

Laborant *m.* laboratory assistant

laborieren *v.* to work in a laboratory; **mit seiner Krankheit —** to labor with one's sickness, to show off one's affliction

Lach: -anfall *m.*, **-krampf** *m.* laughing fit; **-e** *f.* laughter; puddle, slough; **-en** *neu.* laughter, laugh(ing); **-er** *m.* laugher; **-gas** *neu.* laughing gas, nitrous oxide; **-taube** *f.* ring dove; (coll.) gay girl

lächeln *v.* to smile, to simper, to smirk

lächerlich *adj.* laughable; ridiculous; foolish; absurd; **— machen** to ridicule

Lachs *m.* salmon; cordial made in Danzig; **-schinken** *m.* fillet of smoked ham

Lack *m.* lac; **-firnis** *m.* lacquer, varnish; **-ierarbeit** *f.* lacquered ware; **-ierer** *m.* lacquerer; **-leder** *neu.* patent leather; **-muspapier** *neu.* litmus paper; **-schuh** *m.* patent-leather shoe

lackieren *v.* to lacquer; **da war ich lackiert** I was cheated on that

Lade *f.* box, chest, shrine; drawer; (organ) wind chest

Lade: -baum *m.* boom, derrick; **-fähigkeit** *f.* tonnage; **-platz** *m.* wharf; freight platform; **-r** *m.* loader; longshoreman; **-raum** *m.* loading space, ship's hold; (gun) chamber; **-schein** *m.* bill of lading; **-stock** *m.* ramrod

Laden *m.* shop, store; shutter; **-besitzer** *m.* shopkeeper; **-dieb** *m.* shoplifter; **-hüter** *m.* dead stock, white elephant; **-kasse** *f.* till; **-preis** *m.* retail price; **-tisch** *m.* counter

laden *v.* to load; to freight; to invite; (elec.) to charge; (law) to cite, to summon

Ladung *f.* invitation; load, freight; (law) citation, summons; (elec.) charge; (mil.) volley; (naut.) cargo

Lage *f.* position, situation; condition; state; layer; round (of beer); (fencing) guard; (mus.) pitch; (naut.) broadside; (paper) quire; **bedrängte —** distress;

in der — sein to be able; **in die rechte — bringen** to put into proper order; **missliche** — predicament

Lager *neu.* bed; lodging; camp; lair; stock; supply; store; (geol.) deposit, layer, stratum; (mech.) bearing; support; party, side; **auf** — in stock; **aufs — bringen** to store, to warehouse; **nach langem** — after a long illness; **–aufnahme** *f.* stock inventory; **–aufseher** *m.*, **–ist** *m.* storekeeper; **–feuer** *neu.* campfire; **–gebühr** *f.*, **–geld** *neu.*, **–miete** *f.* storage charges; demurrage; **–haus** *neu.* storehouse, warehouse; **–patz** *m.*, **–statt** *f.*, **–stätte** *f.* resting place; bed; (geol.) deposit; **–schein** *m.* warrant; **–ung** *f.* storage, warehousing; stratification; **–vorrat** *m.* stock; **–wache** *f.* camp watch

lagern *v.* to lie down; to rest, to camp; to store, to warehouse; to be in stock; to stratify

Lagune *f.* lagoon; **–nriff** *neu.* atoll

lahm *adj.* lame, limpid; paralyzed; (coll.) tired, tedious; **–en** *v.* to limp; to be lame; **–legen** *v.* to render ineffective

lähmen *v.* to lame; to paralyze, to enervate

Lähmung *f.* paralysis; palsy

Laib *m.* (bread) loaf; rounded mass

Laich *m.* spawn; **–zeit** *f.* spawning time

Laie *m.* layman; amateur; **–nbruder** *m.* lay brother

Lake *f.* brine, pickle

Laken *neu.* (bed) sheet, shroud; (coll.) sail

lakonisch *adj.* laconic

Lakritze *f.* licorice

lallen *v.* to mumble, to stammer, to babble

lamentieren *v.* to lament

Lamm *neu.* lamb; **–zeit** *f.* lambing time

Lämm: –chen *neu.* lambkin; **–erhüpfen** *neu.* (sl.) teen-age dancing; hop

lammfromm *adj.* gentle as a lamb

Lamp: –e *f.* lamp; **–e** *m.*, **eins auf die –e giessen** to hoist one (drink); **–endocht** *m.* wick; **–enfieber** *neu.* stage fright; **–enschirm** *m.* lamp shade

Land *neu.* land; country; state; continent; territory; ground. soil; **ans — bringen** (or setzen) to bring ashore; **ausser –es sein** to be abroad; **das Gelobte —** the Promised Land; **des –es verweisen** to banish, to exile; **über — geh(e)n** to go overland; **Unschuld vom –e** country cousin; **vom –e eingeschlossen** landlocked; **vom –e stossen** to put to sea; **–arbeiter** *m.* farm hand; **–arzt** *m.* country doctor; **–bau** *m.* agriculture; **–bewohner** *m.* countryman; **–briefträger** *m.*, **–bote** *m.* rural mailman; **–brot** *neu.* farmer's bread; **–dienst** *m.* (naut.) duty on shore; **–enge** *f.* isthmus; **–flucht** *f.* migration from the country (to cities); **–friede** *m.* public peace; **–gericht** *neu.* country court; **–gut** *neu.* country estate; **–karte** *f.* map; **–kreis** *m.* rural district; **–macht** *f.* continental power; (mil.) land forces; **–mann** *m.* farmer; countryman; **–mark** *f.* national boundary; territory; **–marke** *f.* landmark; **–messer** *m.* sur-

veyor; **–partie** *f.* outing, picnic; **–plage** *f.* public calamity; **–pomeranze** *f.* country bumpkin; **–post** *f.* rural mail delivery; stagecoach; **–rat** *m.* district magistrate; **–ratte** *f.* (naut.) landlubber; **–recht** *neu.* common law; **–regen** *m.* steady rain; **–richter** *m.* country judge; **–rücken** *m.* ridge (of land); **–schaft** *f.* district, province; landscape, scenery; **–see** *m.* inland lake; **–sitz** *m.* country seat; **–smann** *m.* compatriot, fellow countryman; **was für ein –smann sind Sie?** What's your native country? **–spitze** *f.* cape, headland; **–steuer** *f.* land tax; **–strasse** *f.* highway; **–streicher** *m.* tramp, vagabond; **–strich** *m.* region, zone; **–ung** *f.* landing, disembarkation; **–ungsbrücke** *f.* landing stage; pier; **–vermessung** *f.* land surveying; **–wehr** *f.* militia; **–wirtschaft** *f.* agriculture, farming

land: –en *r.* to land. to disembark; **–flüchtig** *adj.* fugitive; **–flüchtig werden** to flee one's country; **–fremd** *adj.* strange; foreign; **–läufig** *adj.* customary, universally known; **–schaftlich** *adj.* scenic

Länd: –erkunde *f.* geography; **–ler** *m.* slow waltz

Landes: –beschreibung *f.* topography; **–farben** *f. pl.* national colors; **–kirche** *f.* national church; **–obrigkeit** *f.* public authority; **–sitte** *f.* national custom; **–sprache** *f.* language of a country, vernacular, idiom; **–tracht** *f.* national costume; **–trauer** *f.* public mourning; **–vater** *m.* sovereign; **–verfassung** *f.* constitution of a country; **–verrat** *m.* high treason; **–verweisung** *f.* banishment, exile

landes: –kundig *adj.* familiar with a country; well-known; **–kundlich** *adj.* geographical; **–üblich** *adj.* customary in a country; **–verräterich** *adj.* treasonable

ländlich *adj.* rural, rustic; provincial

lang *adj.* long; tall; lengthy; **auf die –e Bank schieben** to put off; **auf –e hinaus** for a long time to come; **die Zeit wird mir —** time hangs heavy on my hands; **einen –en Hals machen** to crane one's neck; **ein –es Gesicht machen** to make a long face; **eine –e Nase machen** to thumb one's nose; **entsetzlich — endless**; **es ist noch — nicht fertig** it is far from done; **in nicht zu –er Zeit** before long; **— und breit** at full length; **–e Finger machen** to pilfer; **— hin a long time yet; **über kurz oder — sooner or later; **— adv.** for a long time; **–e nicht** not by far; not nearly; **–atmig** *adj.* long-winded. prolix; **–en** *v.* (coll.) to suffice; to reach for; **–gespitzt** *adj.* sharp pointed; **–her** *adv.* long ago; **–hin** *adv.* far and away; **–mütig** *adj.* forbearing, patient; **–sam** *adj.* slow, lingering; **–stielig** *adj.* long-stemmed; long-handled; **–weilen** *v.* to bore, to weary; **–weilig** *adj.* tedious, boring; **–wierig** *adj.* lengthy, protracted, chronic

Lang: **-bein** m. long-legged person; **-eweile** f. boredom, tedium, ennui; **-finger** m. pickpocket, pilferer; **-mut** f. forbearance; patience; **-schiff** neu. (church) nave; **-schläfer** m. late riser

läng: **-lich** adj. longish, elongated; **-s** adv. along; **-st** adv. for a long time; by far; **-stens** adv. at most, at the latest

Läng: **-e** f. length; duration; lengthiness; longitude; **-engrad** m., **-enkreis** m. meridian; **-enmass** neu. linear measure; **-srichtung** f. longitudinal direction; **-sschwelle** f. (rail.) stringer; **-ststreifen** m. crossline

Lanze f. lance, spear; **eine — für jemand brechen** to go to bat for someone; **-tte** f. lancet

lapidar adj. lapidary, pithy; forceful, concise

Lappalie f. trifle, bagatelle

lappen v. to lap, to sip

Lappen m. rag, tatter; duster; (bot., zool.) lobe; wattle; flap; (dog) ear; inhabitants of Lapland; **durch die — gehen** (coll.) to escape

Läpperei f. trifle, bauble; silliness

läppern v. (coll.) to lap, to sip; **sich zusammen —** (coll.) to mount up, to accumulate

läppisch adj. silly, childish, foolish

Lärm m. noise; din, clamor; **viel — um nichts** much ado about nothing

lärmen v. to clamor, to bluster, to row

Larve f. mask; larva, grub; specter

lasch adj. loose, flabby; lax; limp

Laser abbr. (Lichtverstärkung durch Strahlungsanregung unter Verwendung einer fremden Strahlungsquelle) laser

lasieren v. to glaze, to coat

lassen v. to let, to allow, to permit; to tolerate; to make possible; to cause, to effect; to leave undone (oder off, open, shut); to abandon; to deposit; to give up, to renounce; **ausser Acht —** to disregard; **das Licht brennen —** to keep the light burning; **das muss man ihm — one** must give him credit for that; **es beim alten —** to leave things as they were; **etwas sein —** to abstain from something; **holen —** to send for; **ich habe mir sagen —** I have been told; **lass das!** stop it! **lass nur!** never mind! **mit sich reden —** to be reasonable; **sagen —** to send word; **sein Leben —** to lose one's life; **sich Zeit —** to take time; **vermuten —** to give ground to believe; **zufrieden —** to let alone

lässig adj. negligent, remiss; careless; dilatory; idle, lazy; indolent

Last f. load; burden; freight, cargo, tonnage; trouble; **-en** pl. tax, impost; **einem etwas zur — legen** to make someone responsible for something; **einem zur — fallen** to be a burden (oder inconvenience) to someone; **zu -en des Käufers** paid for by the purchaser; **-enaufzug** m. freight elevator; **-igkeit** f. ship's tonnage (oder capacity); **-kahn** m. barge, lighter; **-(kraft)wagen** m. motor truck; **-schrift** f. debit; **-tier** neu.

beast of burden; **-träger** m. porter

last: **-en** v. to weigh (on); to encumber; to press upon; to load; **-enfrei** adj. unburdened, exempt from encumbrances; **-ig** adj. freighted; heavy, weighty; (naut.) listing, careening

läst: **-erlich** adj. blasphemous; abusive, slanderous; **-ern** v. to slander, to revile, to malign; **-ig** adj. troublesome; unpleasant

Laster neu. vice; bad habit; **langes — (coll.)** very tall person, stringbean; **-höhle** f. den of iniquity

Läster: **-er** m. blasphemer; reviler; maligner; slanderer; **-maul** neu. scandalmonger; **-ung** f. blasphemy; abuse; slander

lasterhaft adj. vicious, wicked, dissolute

Latein neu. Latin; **mit seinem — zu Ende sein** to be at the end of one's rope (oder wits)

Laterne f. lantern; street lamp; **-nanzünder** m. lamplighter; **-npfahl** m. lamp post

Latsch m. (coll.) untidy fellow; sloven; **-e** f. slipper; dwarf pine

Latt: **-e** f. lath; batten; (coll.) lanky person; **-enkiste** f. crate; **-enverschlag** m. latticework partition; **-enzaun** m. picket fence

Lattich m. lettuce

lau adj. lukewarm, tepid; indifferent

Laub neu. foliage, leaves; **-e** f. arbor, summerhouse; **fertig ist die -e!** ready we are! **-engang** m. arbored walk; arcade; **-baum** m. deciduous tree; **-fall** m. defoliation; **-frosch** m. tree frog; **-säge** f. fret saw; **-wald** m. deciduous forest; **-werk** neu. foliage; leafwork

Lauer f. lurking; ambush; **auf der — liegen** to lie in ambush for

Lauf m. run, race; career; (ast.) movement, speed; current; way, course; (gun) barrel; (mus.) quick run; (zool.) leg; **das ist der — der Welt** that's how it goes; that's life; **einer Sache freien — lassen** to let something take its course; **in vollem -e** at top speed; **-bahn** f. course; career; **-brett** neu. running board; **-brücke** f. plank bridge; pontoon; gangway; **-bursche** m., **-junge** m. errand boy; **-erei** f. running about; **-käfer** m. ground beetle; **-katze** f., **-kran** m. traveling (oder overhead) crane; **-pass** m. dismissal, sack; **-rädchen** neu. caster; **-riemen** m. endless belt; **-schiene** f. guide rail; **-schritt** m. (mil.) double pace; **im -schritt!** on the double! **-werk** neu. movement, wheelwork; **-zeit** f. running time; rutting season; **-zettel** m. bill of lading; handbill; circular

Laufstall m. play-pen

laufen v. to run; to rush; to flow, to pass, to leak; to continue, to go on; to strand; **in den Hafen —** to put into port; **in den Weg —** to come across; **— lassen** to let go; **Rollschuh —** to rollerskate; **Schlittschuh —** to skate; **Spiessruten — to** run the gauntlet; **Sturm — to**

assault. to storm; **vom Stapel — lassen** to launch; **-d** *adj.* running, current, recurring; **auf dem -den sein** to be up to date; **-de Nummern** consecutive numbers; **-de Rechnung** open account

Läufer *m.* runner; messenger; (mech.) slider; upper millstone; hall (*oder* stair) carpet

Lauge *f.* lye. leach; (coll.) sarcasm

laun: **-enhaft** *adj.* capricious, changeable; **-ig** *adj.* humorous; entertaining; **-isch** *adj.* moody; cross; ill-humored

Laune *f.* mood; caprice; fancy, whim; temper; **bei guter — sein** to be in good humor

Laus *f.* louse; **-bub(e)** *m.*, **-ejunge** *m.* young rascal; rogue

lauschen *v.* to hearken, to listen, to eavesdrop

lausen *v.* to delouse; **mich laust der Affe!** (coll.) that beat's all!

lausig *adj.* lousy; (sl.) shabby, pitiful; mean

laut *adj.* loud; noisy; audible, distinct, sonorous; (mus.) forte; **— werden** to become known (*oder* public); **—** *adv.* aloud; **—** *prep.* in accordance with; **-bar** *adj.* notorious known; **-en** *v.* to sound, to run; to read, to say; **-los** *adj.* silent, inaudible

Laut *m.* sound, tone; audible noise; utterance; **-bildung** *f.* formation of sounds; **-e** *f.* lute; **-lehre** *f.* science of sound; **-schrift** *f.* phonetic writing; **-sprecher** *m.* loud-speaker

läuten *v.* to ring; to toll, to peal; **etwas — hören** to learn via the grapevine

lauter *adj.* pure, unalloyed, unsullied; flawless; genuine, true, sincere; nothing but, mere; **aus — Neid** out of sheer envy

läutern *v.* to purify; to refine; to clarify

Läutewerk *neu.* alarm bell

Lawine *f.* avalanche

lax *adj.* lax, loose; licentious

Lazarett *neu.* (mil.) hospital

Leb: **-emann** *m.* playboy; man about town; **-ewesen** *neu.* living being; **-kuchen** *m.* gingerbread; spice cake; **-tage** *m. pl.* days of one's life; **-(e)wohl** *neu.* farewell, goodbye

Leben *neu.* life; existence; ȧctivity, animation; reality; **am — bleiben** to survive; **am — sein** to be alive; **bei Leib und — under** penalty of death; **das — schenken** to give birth (to); to spare life; **ins — rufen** (mil.) to activate; **Kampf auf — und Tod** life and death struggle; **mit dem — davonkommen** to escape with one's life; **mit Leib und — with** body and soul; **ums — bringen** to kill; **ums — kommen** to perish; **-de** *m.* living person; **-salter** *neu.* age, period of life; **-sart** *f.* manners, good breeding; **-saufgabe** *f.* lifework; **-sbild** *neu.* biography; **-sfähigkeit** *f.* vitality; **-sfrage** *f.* vital question; **-sfreude** *f.* enjoyment of life; **-sführung** *f.* conduct of life; **-sgefahr** *f.* mortal danger; **-sgefährte** *m.* life companion;

spouse; **-sgeister** *m. pl.* animal spirits; **-sgrösse** *f.* life size; **-shaltung** *f.* standard of living; **-skraft** *f.* vital energy; **-slauf** *m.* course of life; biographical sketch; **-slicht** *neu.* lamp of life; **-sraum** *m.* essential space to subsist on; **-srente** *f.* life annuity; **-sstrafe** *f.* capital punishment; **-sunterhalt** *m.* livelihood, subsistence; **-sversicherung** *f.* life insurance; **-swandel** *m.* moral conduct; **-swasser** *neu.* water of life; (sl.) brandy; **-sweisheit** *f.* practical philosophy; wisdom of experience; **-szeit** *f.* lifetime; **-szweck** *m.* goal in life

leben *v.* to live; to be alive; to dwell, to reside; to stay; **einen (hoch) — lassen** to drink to someone's health; to starve; **in den Tag hinein —** to lead a careless life; **nichts zu — haben** to be destitute; **-d** *adj.* living, alive; **-des Bild** tableau; **-dig** *adj.* alive, living; vivid, active; **-sfroh** *adj.* joyful; **-sgefährlich** *adj.* perilous; **-sgross** *adj.* life-sized; **-skräftig** *adj.* vigorous; **-slang**, **-slänglich** *adj.* lifelong; **-slustig** *adj.* jovial, merry, cheerful; **-smüde** *adj.* weary (*oder* sick) of life; **-swichtig** *adj.* vital

Leber *f.* liver; **frei von der — weg reden** to speak freely; **-fleck** *m.* freckle, mole; **-tran** *m.* cod-liver oil; **-wurst** *f.* liver sausage

lebhaft *adj.* lively, vivacious, impulsive; sprightly, brisk, vivid; acute; animated

leblos *adj.* lifeless; dull, rigid

lechzen *v.* to languish (*oder* thirst, long) for

Leck *neu.* leak, leakage; **ein — bekommen** to spring a leak

leck: **-en** *v.* to leak; to lick; to trickle; **-er** *adj.* tasty, delicious, appetizing, fastidious, attractive; **-ern** *v.* to nibble

Lecker *m.* licker; **-bissen** *m.* dainty morsel, tidbit; **-ei** *f.* delicacy, sweetmeat; **-maul** *neu.* sweet tooth; dainty feeder

Leder *neu.* leather; (coll.) football; leather apron; **in — gebunden** calf-bound; **vom — ziehen** to unsheathe a weapon; **zäh wie — as** tough as leather; **-haut** *f.* thick skin; **-hosen** *f. pl.* leather breeches

ledern *adj.* leathery; tough

ledig *adj.* unmarried; vacant, empty; except (*oder* free) from; **—** *adv.* exclusively; purely, simply; **los und —** absolutely free; **-lich** *adv.* only, solely, quite, merely

leer *adj.* empty; void; vacant; unoccupied; vain; **— ausgehen** to be left empty-handed; **-e Ausrede** lame excuse; **— laufen** (mech.) to idle; **-er Schein** empty show; **-er Vorwand** idle pretext; **-en** *v.* to empty, to clear, to void; to vacate; to drain

Legalität *f.* legality

Legat *m.* legate; **— neu.** legacy; **-ion** *f.* legation

legen *v.* to lay; to put, to place; **sich — to** abate, to slacken; to cease; to lie (*oder* calm) down; **an den Tag — to** evince, to show; **etwas nahe — to** suggest; to urge; **Hand an etwas** — to turn one's hand to something; **Hand an sich** — to commit suicide; **Karten** — (cards) to tell a fortune; **letzte Hand an etwas** — to put the finishing touches to; **sich ins Mittel** — to intervene; **Wert auf etwas** — (*oder* importance) to attach value (*oder* importance) to something; **zurecht** (*oder* **bereit**) — to arrange, to keep in readiness

Legende *f.* legend

legitim *adj.* legitimate; **-ieren** *v.* to legalize; to legitimize; **sich** — to identify oneself

Legitim: -ation *f.* legitimation; proof of identity; **-ierung** *f.* legitimization; **-ität** *f.* legitimacy

Leh(e)n *neu.* fief; **-sbesitz** *m.* feudal tenure; **-sherr** *m.* feudal lord; **-smann** *m.* vassal; **-swesen** *neu.* feudalism

Lehm *m.* clay, loam; **-mauer** *f.* **-wand** *f.* mud wall

Lehn: -e *f.* chair back; rest, support; slope; **-sessel** *m.*, **-stuhl** *m.* armchair, easy chair

lehnen *v.* to lean (against), to rest (upon) to bend (over)

Lehr: -amt *neu.* teacher's position; professorship; **-anstalt** *f.* educational establishment; school; academy; **-auftrag** *m.* professorship; **-buch** *neu.* textbook; **-bursch(e)** *m.*, **-junge** *m.*, **-ling** *m.* apprentice; **-e** *f.* precept; moral; doctrine; apprenticeship; (mech.) gauge; **-er** *m.* teacher; instructor; **-erbildungsanstalt** *f.* teacher's college; **-erin** *f.* teacher, instructress; **-erkollegium** *neu.*, **-schaft** *f.* staff of teachers; **-fach** *neu.* teaching profession; branch of instruction; **-film** *m.* educational film; **-gang** *m.* course of studies; **-gebäude** *neu.* system (of science); **-geld** *neu.* fee for apprenticeship; tuition; **-geld bezahlen** *m.* to pay for one's wisdom; **-herr** *m.* master of apprentices; **-jahre** *neu. pl.* (years of) apprenticeship; **-körper** *m.* teaching body (*oder* staff); **-kunst** *f.* pedagogy; **-plan** *m.* curriculum; **-saal** *m.* classroom; **-satz** *m.* proposition; theorem; dogma; doctrine; **-schriften** *f. pl.* didactic writings; **-spruch** *m.* maxim, aphorism; **-stand** *m.* educational profession; **-stoff** *m.* subject matter of instruction; **-stuhl** *m.* academic chair; **-zeit** *f.* (term of) apprenticeship

lehren *v.* to teach, to inform, to instruct

lehrreich *adj.* instructive

Leib *m.* body; abdomen, belly; **am ganzen -e** all over; **auf den — rücken** to attack; **bei lebendigem -e** while still alive; **bei -e nicht** on no account; **es ging ihm an — und Leben** his life was at stake; **gesegneten -es** (poet.) pregnant; **vom -e bleiben** to stay away (from someone); **-arzt** *m.* court physician; **-binde** *f.* waistband, abdominal belt; sash; **-chen** *neu.* bodice; **-eigene** *m.* serf; **-eigenschaft** *f.* serfdom; **-esbeschaffenheit** *f.* constitution; physique;

-eserbe *m.* heir; **-eskraft** *f.* **aus -eskräften** with all one's might; **-esstrafe** *f.* corporal punishment; **-esübungen** *f. pl.* gymnastics, calisthenics, physical training; **-garde** *f.*, **-wache** *f.* bodyguard; **-gericht** *neu.*, **-speise** *f.* favorite dish; **-haftige** *m.* the devil; **-rente** *f.* life annuity; **-schmerz** *m.* stomach ache, colic; **-wäsche** *f.* underwear

leib: -eigen *adj.* in serfdom (*oder* bondage); **-haftig** *adj.* embodied, incarnate; personified; real; **-lich** *adj.* corporeal, bodily, material; **sein -licher Sohn** his own son

Leich: -dorn *m.* (dial.) corn (on toe); **-e** *f.* corpse; cadaver; (coll.) funeral; (typ.) omission; **-enausgrabung** *f.* exhumation; **-enbahre** *f.* bier; **-enbegängnis** *neu.* funeral; **-enbeschauer** *m.* coroner; **-enbestatter** *m.* undertaker; **-enhalle** *f.* mortuary; **-enhemd** *neu.* shroud; **-enschändung** *f.* desecration of the dead; **-enschau** *f.* inquest; **-enstarre** *f.* rigor mortis; **-enstein** *m.* tombstone; **-enträger** *m.* pallbearer; **-entuch** *neu.* pall; shroud; **-enverbrennung** *f.* cremation; **-enwagen** *m.* hearse; **-enzug** *m.* funeral procession; **-nam** *m.* corpse; dead body

leicht *adj.* light; easy; mild, slight; insignificant; frivolous; — *adv.* easily, lightly, gently; — **entzündlich** highly inflammable; **-en Herzens** lightheartedly; **-er Absatz** ready sale; **-blütig** *adj.* sanguine; playful; **-faßlich** easy to understand; **-fertig** *adj.* careless; frivolous; thoughtless; **-flüssig** *adj.* mobile, easily fusible; **-füssig** *adj.* lightfooted; **-gläubig** *adj.* credulous, gullible; **-herzig** *adj.* light-hearted; **-hin** *adv.* lightly, carelessly; **-lebig** *adj.* happy-go-lucky; **-sinnig** *adj.* careless, frivolous; **-ern** *v.* (naut.) to unload

Leicht: -er *m.* (naut.) lighter; **-fuss** *m.* happy-go-lucky fellow; **-igkeit** *f.* lightness, ease, facility; **-matrose** *m.* ordinary seaman; **-sinn** *m.* carelessness, levity, frivolity

Leid *neu.* grief, sorrow; harm, hurt, injury; pain; **in Lieb' und — in** good and evil days; **sich ein — antun** to commit suicide; **-eform** *f.* passive voice; **-en** *neu.* pain, torture; disease; **-enschaft** *f.* passion, emotion; **-tragende** *m.* mourner; **-wesen** *neu.* affliction; grief; **zu unserem -wesen** to our regret

leid *adj.* sorrowful; painful; **es tut mir —** I am sorry; **-en** *v.* to suffer; to bear, to endure; to permit; to tolerate; **Ich kann ihn nicht -en** I can't stand him; **ich mag ihn wohl -en** I rather like him; **-enschaftlich** *adj.* passionate; **-enschaftslos** *adj.* dispassionate; **-er** *adv.* unfortunately; regrettably; **-er!** *interj.* alas! **-ig** *adj.* disagreeable, troublesome; sore; **-lich** *adj.* tolerable; mediocre

Leier *f.* lyre; (ast.) Lyra; (mech.) crank; **die alte — the** same old story; **-mann** *m.* organ grinder; **-kasten** *m.* grind organ, hurdy gurdy; **-schwanz** *m.*

lyrebird

leiern v. to grind; to turn (a winch); to harp on one string; (coll.) to reel off

Leih: –bibliothek f., –bücherei f. rental library; –er m. lender, borrower; –haus neu. pawnshop, loan firm

leihen v. to lend; to loan; to borrow

leihweise adv. as a loan

Leim m. glue, size; birdlime; **auf den — geh(e)n** to be taken in; **aus dem — geh(e)n** to fall to pieces

leimen v. to glue; (coll.) to cheat, to entrap

Lein m. flax(plant); –e f. line, cord, rope; leash, rein; **an der –e haben** to have in one's power; –en neu. linen; –kuchen m. linseed cake; –öl neu. linseed oil; –samen m. flaxseed, linseed; –wand f. linen (cloth); canvas; movie screen

leinen adj. linen

leise adj. low, soft, faint, light; gentle

Leist: –e f. border, ledge, margin; selvage; (anat.) groin; (book) edge; –en m. shoemaker's last; **alles über einen — schlagen** to treat everything alike; –ung f. performance, execution; output, effect; result; (com.) payment; –ungsfähigkeit f. productivity, efficiency; (mech.) power

leisten v. to do, to perform; to offer, to extend, to provide; **einen Eid —** to take an oath; **es sich — können** to be able to afford; **Genugtuung —** to give satisfaction; **sich etwas —** to treat oneself to; **Vorzügliches —** to achieve excellent results

leistungsfähig adj. productive; efficient; (com.) solvent

Leit: –artikel m. leading article; –er m. leader; guide, conductor; manager; principal; –er f. ladder; (mus.) scale; –ersprosse f. ladder rung; –erwagen m. rack wagon; –faden m. clue; guide, key, manual; –fähigkeit f. conductivity; –gedanke m. main thought; keynote; –motiv neu. theme melody; –regel f. guiding principle; –schiene f. switch; –stern m. guiding star; polar star; –strahl m. (avi.) vector; –ung f. leading, leadership, guidance, direction, management; pipe line; (phy. and elec.) conduction, circuit; **eine lange –ung haben** (coll.) to be slow to comprehend

leiten v. to lead, to steer, to guide; to direct, to control, to manage; to conduct

Lek: –tion f. lesson; lecture; reprimand; –tor m. lecturer; (publisher's) reader; –türe f. reading matter

Lende f. loin, hip; –nbraten m. roast loin; –nschurz m. loin cloth

lenk: –bar adj. guidable; dirigible; –en v. to drive, to steer; to govern; to guide; to direct, to lead; to manage; to rule; **die Aufmerksamkeit –en auf** to call attention to; –sam adj. docile; manageable, flexible

Lenker m. driver; guide; ruler; pilot

Lenkstange f. handle bar; connecting rod

Lenz m. (poet.) spring; prime (of life)

Lerche f. lark; –ngesang m. song of a lark

lernen v. to learn; to study

Les: –art f. reading, version; –ebuch. neu. reader; –ehalle f. public reading room; –epult neu. reading desk; –er m. reader; –eratte f. bookworm; –erkreis m., –erschaft f. circulation; –esaal m. lecture (oder reading) room; –estoff m. reading material; –estücke neu. pl. selections for reading; –ezeichen neu. bookmark; –ezirkel m. reading club (oder circle); –ung f. recitation; (pol.) reading

les: –bar adj. legible; readable; worth reading; –en v. to read; to lecture; to gather, to glean; –erlich adj. legible

Lese f. gleaning; gathering, harvesting; vintage; culling; –r m. gleaner

Lettland neu. Latvia

letzt adj. last, final; ultimate; **der –ere** the latter; **in den –en Zügen liegen** to breathe one's last; **in –er Zeit** lately, of late; **–e Ölung** (rel.) extreme unction; **–er Wille** last will and testament; **zu guter —** last but not least; **zum –en, am –en** finally, ultimately; **–hin** adv., **–lich** adv. lately; recently; lastly, finally

Letzte neu. (the) last; **das ist das —** that's the limit

Leucht: –e f. (coll.) light; lantern; sage; luminary; –en neu. radiation, shining, glow; sparkling; –er m. candlestick, candelabra; chandelier; –feuer neu. flare; beacon light; –gas neu. illuminating gas; –käfer m. firefly; –turm m. lighthouse; –uhr f. luminous clock; –zifferblatt neu. luminous dial

leuchten v. to light, to illuminate; to shine; to beam, to radiate

leugnen v. to deny; to disavow; to gainsay

Leugnen neu. denial, disavowal, retraction

Leukoplast neu. adhesive tape

Leumund m. reputation

Leute pl. people, persons; folk(s); (mil.) men, subordinates; servants; public, world; –schinder m. oppressor; slavedriver, extortioner

Leutnant m. (second) lieutenant; (avi.) pilot officer; (naut.) lieutenant junior grade

leutselig adj. affable, friendly

Lexikograph m. lexicographer

Lexikon neu. dictionary; encyclopedia

Libell neu. libel; –e f. dragonfly; (mech.) water level

Librettist m. librettist, textbook writer

Licht neu. light; brightness, luster; clarity; candle; eye (of game); highlight; (diamond) fire; **ans — bringen** to bring to light; **bei — besehen** to examine closely; **das — der Welt erblicken** to be born; **einem ein — aufstecken** to set someone straight, to open someone's eyes; **in gutem –e erscheinen** to make a good impression; **ins falsche — setzen** to misrepresent; **— in etwas bringen** to clear up a matter; **mir geht ein — auf** I see the point; **–bad** neu. solar bath; **–bild** neu. photograph; **-blick** m. ray of hope; **-bogen** m. (elec.) arc; **-druck** m. phototype, photogravure; **-kegel** m. cone of light; searchlight beam; **-körper** m. luminary; **-mess(e)** f. Candlemas; **-leitung** f. lighting circuit; **-pause** f. blueprint; **-pausverfahren** neu. photographic printing; **-reklame** f. illuminated advertising; **-seite** f. bright (oder sunny) side; **-spielhaus** neu. motion-picture theater; **-stärke** f. candle power; **-strahl** m. ray (oder beam) of light; **-ung** f. clearing; **-zieher** m. candlemaker

licht adj. bright, light; shining; **am -en Tage** in broad daylight; **-echt** adj. light-fast, fadeless; **-empfindlich** adj. sensitive to light; (phot.) sensitized; **-en** v. to light (up); to clear; to thin; to lighten; to lift; to weigh (anchor); **-erloh** adj. blazing; flaring; **-erloh** adv. ablaze

Lid neu. eyelid

lieb adj. dear, beloved, cherished; agreeable, amiable; sweet, charming; **den -en langen Tag** the livelong day; **mir zu -e** for my sake; **sich — Kind machen** to ingratiate oneself; **-äugeln** v. to ogle; **-eln** v. (coll.) to dally, to flirt; **-en** v. to love, to like, to be fond of; **-end** adj. affectionate, loving; **-enswert** adj. worthy of love, attractive, charming; **enswürdig** adj. pleasing, amiable; **-evoll** adj. loving, affectionate, kindhearted; **-gewinnen** v. to take a fancy (oder liking) to; **-haben** v. to be fond of; to like, to love; **-kosen** v. to caress, to fondle; **-lich** adj. lovely, charming; pleasing; sweet; **-los** adj. loveless, unkind; **-reich** adj. loving, benevolent; kind; **-reizend** adj. winning, charming, lovable

Lieb: **-chen** neu., **-ste** m. and f. beloved, darling, sweetheart; **-e** f. love, affection; passion; charity; kindness; (coll.) sweetheart; **aus -e** for love; **-elei** f. flirtation; **-esdienst** m. act of charity; **-esgabe** f. charitable gift; **-esgeschichte** f. love story (oder affair); **-eshandel** m. love affair; **-esheirat** f. love match; **-espfand** neu., **-eszeichen** neu. love token; **-estrank** m. love potion; **-eswerke** neu. pl. charitable deeds; **-haber** m. lover, admirer; amateur, fancier, collector, dilettante; **-haberei** f. hobby; **-habervorstellungen** f. pl. amateur theatricals; **-kosung** f. caress(ing), fondling, petting; **-ling** m. darling, pet; favorite; **-lingsbeschäftigung** f. favorite occupation, hobby; **-lingssünde** f. besetting sin; **-reiz** m. charm; fascination; **-schaft** f. love affair

Lied neu. song; air, melody, tune; ballad; **das ist das Ende vom —** that's how it all came out; **immer das alte —** the same old complaint; **-chen** neu. short song, ditty; **-erabend** m. song (oder ballad) concert; **-erbuch** neu. songbook; hymnbook; **-erdichter** m. songwriter, lyrical

poet; **-erkranz** m., **-ertafel** f. choral society; glee club; song collection

Liederjahn m. wastrel; scoundrel, rake **liederlich** adj. careless, negligent, slovenly; disorderly; dissolute; profligate; loose

Liefer: **-ant** m. seller, supplier; contractor; **-bedingungen** f. pl. terms of delivery; **-frist** f., **-zeit** f. term of delivery; **-schein** m. delivery ticket; **-ung** f. delivery, supplying

lieferbar adj. deliverable

liefern f. to deliver; to furnish; to provide, to supply; to yield; to issue (in series); to fight (battle); **ans Messer —** to ruin, to kill; **er ist geliefert** he is lost

liegen v. to lie, to be situated; to camp; to be quartered; **es ist mir nichts daran gelegen** it is of no importance (oder consequence) to me; **es liegt an ihm** it is up to him; **es liegt in ihm** it's characteristic of him; **im Anschlag —** (gun) to aim; to lie in ambush; **in den Ohren — to** pester; **jemand links — lassen** to disregard someone; **— bleiben** to keep to (one's bed); (car) to break down; to be discontinued; (goods) to remain on hand; **mir ist daran gelegen** I value (oder esteem) it; **nach Osten —** to face east; **wem liegt daran?** who cares about it? **zutage —** to be obvious

Lift m. elevator; **-boy** m. elevator operator **Liga** f. league; association, club

Likör m. liqueur, cordial

Lila neu. lilac

Lilie f. lily

lind adj. gentle, mild, soft; **-ern** v. to soften; to assuage; to mitigate; to appease

Lind: **-e** f. linden, basswood, lime tree; **-wurm** m. (poet.) dragon

Lineal neu. ruler, straightedge; (typ.) guide

Linie f. line, stroke; boundary; route; descent, lineage; (mil.) position; **in erster —** first of all, above all; **-npapier** neu. ruled paper; **-nschiff** neu. liner; battleship; **-nzieher** m. ruler

linieren v. to rule, to draw lines

link adj. left; left-handed; **-e Seite** wrong side; (coin) reverse; (com.) debit side; (naut.) port; **mit dem -en Bein zuerst aufstehen** to get up out of the wrong side of bed; **-erhand** adv. on the left hand (oder side); **-isch** adj. awkward, clumsy; **-s** adv. on (oder to) the left; **-s liegen lassen** to ignore; **-s stehen** to belong to the party of the left; **-s um!** turn left! **-shändig** adj. left-handed, counterclockwise

Linke f. (the) left; party of the left

Linnen neu. linen (see under Lein)

Linse f. lentil; lens; **-ngericht** neu. dish of lentils; (bibl.) mess of pottage

Lippe f. lip; **-nblütler** m. labiate (flower); **-nlaut** m. labial; **-nstift** m. lipstick

liquidieren v. to liquidate, to wind up; to clear accounts

lispeln v. to lisp; to whisper

List f. cunning, craft; ruse, trick, strata-

. gem; **–e** f. list, register, roll

listig adj. cunning, crafty, sly, wily, tricky

Litanei f. litany; (coll.) endless talk

Liter m. and neu. liter; 1.0567 liquid quarts, 0.9081 dry quart

literarisch adj. literary; **–er Diebstahl** plagiarism

Literat m. man of letters; writer; **–entum** neu. literary vocation; **–ur** f. literature

lithographieren v. to lithograph

Liturgie f. liturgy

liturgisch adj. liturgic(al)

Livland neu. Livonia

Livree f. livery

Lizentiat m. licentiate

Lizenz f. license, permit

Lob neu. praise, commendation; **–eserhebung** f. high praise, encomium; **–gesang** m. song of praise; **–hudelei** f. exaggerated praise; **–hudler** m. adulator, toady, flatterer; **–rede** f. eulogy; panegyric; **–spruch** m. eulogy

lob: –en v. to praise, to commend, to extol; **–esam** adj. (poet.) praiseworthy, upright; **–hudeln** v. to overpraise, to laud extravagantly; **–preisen, –singen** v. to extol, to glorify

löblich adj. laudable, praiseworthy, commendable

Loch neu. hole; aperture, cave, hollow; gap; (billiard) pocket; (sl.) jail; **auf dem letzten — pfeifen** (coll.) to be on one's last legs; **er säuft wie ein —** (sl.) he drinks like a fish; **jemand ein — in den Bauch reden** (coll.) to talk someone's ear off; **–er** m., **–eisen** neu. punch, perforator

löch(e)rig adj. porous, perforated

Lock: –e f. lock, curl; **–enkopf** m. curly head; **–enwickel** m., **–enwickler** m. curler, curl paper

lock: –en v. to curl, to wave; to allure, to entice; to decoy; **–ig** adj. curly, crimped

Locker m. tempter, seducer; decoyer; **–mittel** neu. bait, lure; **–ruf** m. bird call; siren call; **–speise** f. bait; **–spitzel** m. agent provocateur; **–vogel** m. decoy bird

locker adj. loose, not solid; slack; lax, dissolute; **nicht –er lassen** (coll.) not to give in; **–n** v. to loosen, to slacken; to break up (soil); to relax; **Sitten –ern** to demoralize; **–ig** adj. curly, crimped

lodern v. to blaze, to flare

Löffel m. spoon, ladle; (rabbit, hare) ear; **jemand eins hinter die — geben** (coll.) to box someone's ear; **–ente** f., **–gans** f. shoveller

löffeln v. to ladle (out); to spoon

Log: –e f. lodge; (theat.) box; secret society; **–engang** m. (theat.) lobby

Logarithmus m. logarithm

logieren v. to lodge, to stay

logisch adj. logical

Lohe f. blaze, flare; tanner's bark

lohen v. to blaze, to flare, to tan

Lohn m. wages; compensation; payment; **–arbeiter** m. laborer, workman; hireling; **–diener** m. temporary servant; **–druckerei** f. exploitation of workers;

–empfänger m. wage earner; **–satz** m. wage scale; **–tüte** f. pay envelope

lohnen v. to compensate, to remunerate; to be profitable; **sich der Mühe —** to be worth while; **–d** adj. advantageous, remunerative

lokal adj. local; **–isieren** v. to locate

Lokal neu. locale, locality; place; office; inn; **–behörde** f. local authority; **–ität** f. locality; **–kenntnisse** f. pl. knowledge of (oder familiarity with) a place; **–nachrichten** f. pl. local news; **–patriotismus** m. parochialism; narrow patriotism; **–verkehr** m. local traffic; **–zug** m. local (oder suburban) train

Lokomo: –bile f. traction engine; **–tive** f. locomotive; engine; **–tivführer** m. locomotive engineer; **–tivschuppen** m. engine shed

Lorbeer m. laurel, bay; **–kranz** m. crown of laurel; honor, fame

Los neu. lot; chance, destiny, fate; (lottery) ticket; (ground) parcel, allotment; **das grosse —** to win first prize; to have a windfall; **–trennung** f. separation

los adj. loose; free; slack, released; **dort ist der Teufel —** hell broke loose there; **— werden to get rid of; mit ihm ist nicht viel —** he is no bargain; **was ist —?** what's the matter? **–arbeiten** v. to extricate; to work off; **–binden** v. to unbind, to untie; (naut.) to unfurl; **–brechen** v. to break loose; **–bröckeln** v. to crumble away; **–drehen** v. to twist off; **–drücken** to squeeze off; (coll.) to fire, to shoot; **–e** adj. loose, slack; incoherent; free; frivolous; **–en** v. to raffle, to draw lots; **–fahren** v. to drive away; to become loose; to fly off; (coll.) to blow up; **–feuern** v. to fire off; **–geben** v. to release; **–geh(e)n** v. to go off, to become loose; **–kaufen** v. to ransom, to redeem; **–lassen** v. to release, to unleash; **–legen** v. to loosen; (coll.) to set about; to inveigh (against); **–lösen** v. to detach; **–machen** v. to undo; to set free; **–reissen** v. to tear off; to separate; **–sagen** v. to break with; **sich –sagen** to renounce; **–schiessen** v. to fire off (oder away); **–schlagen** v. to knock off; to sell (cheaply); to attack; **–schnallen** v. to unbuckle; **–schrauben** v. to unscrew; **–sprechen** v. to absolve; to acquit; **–stürmen** v. to rush forth; **–trennen** v. to rip off; **–ziehen** v. to pull off; to start; to inveigh

lös: –bar adj., **–lich** adj. soluble; **–en** v. to loosen; to relax; to free; to undo; to cancel; to unravel, to clear up; to (dis)solve; to buy (tickets)

Lösch: –blatt neu., **–papier** neu. blotting paper; **–eimer** m. fire bucket; **–er** m. extinguisher; blotter; **–gerät** neu. fire-fighting apparatus; **–kalk** m. quicklime; **–mannschaft** f. fire brigade

löschbar adj. extinguishable, quenchable

löschen v. to extinguish, to quench, to slake; to blot (out), to cancel; (naut.) to unload

Lösegeld *neu.* ransom
Losung *f.* password; watchword; dung (of game)
Lot *neu.* lead, plummet; plumb line; one-half ounce; (geom.) perpendicular line; **er ist nicht ganz im —** (coll.) he does not feel quite well; **-se** *m.* pilot
Löt: -er *m.* solderer; **-kolben** *m.* soldering iron; **-lampe** *f.* blowtorch; **-rohr** *neu.* blowpipe
löten *v.* to solder
Lothringen *neu.* Lorraine
Lotterie *f.* lottery; **-los** *neu.* lottery ticket
lotterig *adj.* disorderly, slovenly, dissipated
Löw: -e *m.* lion; (ast.) Leo; **-enmaul** *neu.* lion's mouth; snapdragon; **-enzahn** *m.* lion's tooth; dandelion; **-in** *f.* lioness
Loyalität *f.* loyalty
Luchs *m.* lynx; **schlau wie ein —** very cunning
Lücke *f.* gap, hole, void; breach; omission; deficiency; **-nbüsser** *m.* stopgap
lückenhaft *adj.* gapped; defective, incomplete
Luder *neu.* carrion, bait, decoy; hussy; (sl.) sly fox; **armes —** poor wretch; **-leben** *neu.* dissolute life
Luft *f.* air, atmosphere; breeze, draft; **aus der — gegriffen** unfounded, fictitious; **das hängt in der —** it is uncertain (*oder* undecided); **dicke —** (coll.) great danger; tense atmosphere; **er ist — für mich** he means nothing to me; **in die — fliegen** to blow up, to explode; **in freier —** in the open air; outdoors; **jemand an die — setzen** to throw a person out; **sich — machen** to give vent to (one's feelings); **-akrobat** *m.* aerialist; **-angriff** *m.* air raid; **-aufklärung** *f.* air reconnaisance; **-bild** *neu.* phantom, vision; aerial photograph; **-blase** *f.* bubble; **-brücke** *f.* airlift; **-druck** *m.* atmospheric pressure; **-druckbremse** *f.* air brake; **-druckmesser** *m.* barometer; **-fahrt** *f.* aviation; **-fahrtmedizin** *f.* aeromedicine; **-fahrzeug** *neu.* aircraft; **-geschwader** *neu.* air wing; **-gespinst** *neu.* chimera; **-gewehr** *neu.* air rifle; **-heizung** *f.* air heating; **-ikus** *m.* scatterbrain; **-kanal** *m.* air passage; **-klappe** *f.* air valve; **-landetruppen** *f. pl.* airborne troops; **-linie** *f.* air line; beeline; **-loch** *neu.* air pocket; **-post** *f.* airmail; **-raum** *m.* air space, atmosphere; **-reifen** *m.* pneumatic tire; **-reiniger** *m.* air filter; **-reklame** *f.* sky writing; **-röhre** *f.* windpipe; trachea; **-röhrenentzündung** *f.* bronchitis; **-schacht** *m.* air shaft; **-schaukel** *f.* flipflap; **-schiff** *neu.* airship; **-schiffahrt** *f.* aeronautics; **-schlange** *f.* streamer; **-schlauch** *m.* inner tube; **-schraube** *f.* propeller; **-schutz** *m.* air defense; **-schutzkeller** *m.* air raid shelter; **-spiegelung** *f.* mirage; **-sprung** *m.* caper, leap; **-streitkräfte** *f. pl.* air forces; **-strömungsmesser** *m.* anemometer; **-strom** *m.* air current; **-stützpunkt** *m.* air base; **— und Raumfahrt** *f.* aero-

space; **-waffe** *f.* air force; **-widerstand** *m.* gust load; air resistance; **-zug** *m.* current (*oder* draft) of air
luft: -dicht *adj.* airtight; hermetical; **-gekühlt** *adj.* air-cooled; **-ig** *adj.* airy, light; breezy, aerial; **-krank** *adj.* airsick; **-leer** *adj.* airless; **-leerer Raum** vacuum; **-tüchtig** *adj.* airworthy
Lüftchen *neu.* breeze
lüften *v.* to lift; to air, to ventilate; to reveal, to unveil; **den Hut —en** to tip the hat
Lüg: -e *f.* lie, falsehood; **harmlose -e** white lie; **-en haben kurze Beine** one doesn't get far with lies; **-enmaul** *neu.* **-ner** *m.* liar
lüg: -en *v.* to lie, to tell stories; **-enhaft** *adj.*, **-nerisch** *adj.* mendacious; lying, false
Luke *f.* dormer window; (naut.) hatch
lullen *v.* to lull, **in den Schlaf —** to sing to sleep
Lümmel *m.* hooligan, hoodlum, lout; **-ei** *f.* hooliganism, rudeness
Lump *m.* bum, scamp, ragamuffin; **-en** *m.* rag; **-engeld** *neu.* paltry sum; **-engesindel** *neu.*, **-enpack** *neu.*, **-envolk** *neu.* riffraff, rabble; **-ensammler** *m.* ragpicker; **-erei** *f.* shabby trick; meanness
lumpen *v.* to lead a dissolute life; **sich nicht — lassen** (coll.) not to act shabbily
lumpig *adj.* ragged, tattered; shabby, stingy
Lunge *f.* lung; **-n** *pl.* (zool.) lights; **-nblutung** *f.* hemorrhage of the lungs; **-nkrankheit** *f.*, **-nschwindsucht** *f.* pulmonary tuberculosis; **-rer** *m.* idler, loafer
lungern *v.* to loaf, to loiter, to idle
Lupe *f.* magnifying glass; pocket lens; **unter die — nehmen** to examine closely
Lust *f.* delight, pleasure; inclination, desire; lust; **— haben zu** to like to do; **mit — und Liebe** with heart and soul; **-barkeit** *f.* merriment, gaiety; entertainment; **-barkeitssteuer** *f.* entertainment tax; **-fahrt** *f.* pleasure trip; **-haus** *neu.* summerhouse, pavilion; **-mord** *m.* rape and murder; **-spiel** *neu.* comedy
lust: -erweckend *adj.* appetizing, savory; **-ig** *adj.* joyous, merry, gay; amusing, funny; **sich -ig machen über** to mock at; **-los** *adj.* listless; dull; **-wandeln** *v.* to stroll, to promenade
Lüst: -er *m.* chandelier; luster; gloss; (cloth) alpaca; **-ernheit** *f.* lustfulness; concupiscence; **-ling** *m.* sensualist, voluptuary, debauchee
lüstern *adj.* lustful, covetous; lascivious
lutschen *v.* (coll.) to suck
Lüttich *neu.* Liège
luxuriös *adj.* luxurious
Luxus *m.* luxury; **-ausgabe** *f.* de luxe edition; **-waren** *f. pl.*, **-artikel** *m. pl.* fancy goods, luxuries
lynchen *v.* to lynch
Lynchgesetz *neu.*, **Lynchjustiz** *f.* lynch (*oder* mob) law
Lyrik *f.* lyric(al) poetry; **-er** *m.* lyric poet

lyrisch *adj.* lyric(al)

Lyzeum *neu.* lyceum; (Germany) high school and junior college for girls

M

Maat *m.* (naut.) mate

Mach (Geschwindigkeitsmasseinheit nach dem Physiker Ernst Mach) einmalize Schallgeschwindigkeit *f.* Mach

Mach: -enschaft *f.* machination, intrigue

machen *v.* to make, to do; to create, to manufacture; to cause; to arrange, to progress; **da ist nichts zu —** nothing can be done about it; **das macht nichts** that doesn't matter; **er macht sich jetzt** he is getting on now; **Freude —** to give pleasure; **Holz —** to split wood; **möglich —** to render possible; **Mut —** to encourage; **niemand kann es ihm recht —** nobody can satisfy him; **sich auf den Weg** (*or* **die Beine**) **—** to get on one's way; **sich aus dem Staube —** to make off; **jemand schlecht —** to defame a person; **sich viel Mühe —** to go to a lot of trouble; **Vorwürfe —** to reproach; **zu etwas —** to convert to

Macht *f.* might, force, strength, power; sovereign state, authority; army; **-befugnis** *f.* full authority (*oder* power); competence; **-bereich** *m.* sphere of influence; **-haber** *m.* ruler, dictator; **-vollkommenheit** *f.* absolute power

machthaberisch *adj.* despotic, dictatorial

mächtig *adj.* mighty, powerful; (min.) thick, rich; **seiner —** in control of himself; **—** *adv.* much; in great degree

machtlos *adj.* impotent, powerless

Mädchen *neu.* girl; maiden; maidservant; **-fürälles** *neu.* maid-of-all-work; **-handel** *m.* white slave traffic; **-name** *m.* maiden name

mädchenhaft *adj.* girlish, maidenly

Made *f.* maggot; grub

madig *adj.* maggoty; worm-eaten; **— machen** (coll.) to run down (*oder* defame)

Magazin *neu.* storehouse; depot; magazine

Magd *f.* maid servant, housemaid; (poet.) maiden

Magen *m.* stomach; maw; **er liegt mir im —** (coll.) I am fed up with him; **seine Augen waren grösser als der —** he took more than he could eat; **-beschwerden** *f. pl.* indigestion; **-brennen** *neu.* heartburn; **-entzündung** *f.* gastritis; **-säure** *f.* gastric acid; **-schwäche** *f.* dyspepsia

mager *adj.* lean, meager; (milk) skimmed; (soil) devitalized; (wine) lacking body

Magi: **-e** *f.* magic; **-er** *m.* magician; magi; **-ster** *m.* (school)master; **-strat** *m.* magistracy; city (*oder* town) council

Magnat *m.* magnate; grandee; **-en** *pl.* body of nobles

Magnet *m.* magnet; loadstone; **-ismus** *m.* magnetism; mesmerism; **-nadel** *f.* magnetic needle; **-ofongerät** *neu.* magnetic tape recorder

magnet: **-isch** *adj.* magnetic; hypnotic;

-isierbar *adj.* magnetizable; **-isieren** *v.* to magnetize; to mesmerize

mähen *v.* to mow, to reap; to bleat

Mäher *m.* mower, reaper

Mahl *neu.* meal; **-zeit** *f.* repast; meal; **—** *interj.* (coll.) what a mess! **gesegnete -zeit** may your meal be blessed!

mahlen *v.* to mill, to grind; to crush

Mahn: **-brief** *m.* request to pay; dunning (*oder* monitory) letter; **-er** *m.* admonisher; dun; **-ung** *f.* warning; admonition

Mähne *f.* mane; (coll.) long hair

mahnen *v.* to remind; to admonish, to dun

Mähre *f.* mare; plug, hack

Mähren *neu.* Moravia

Mai *m.* May; **-baum** *m.* maypole; **-feier** *f.* May Day (labor) demonstration; **-fest** *neu.* May Day; **-glöckchen** *neu.* lily of the valley; **-käfer** *m.* cockchafer; **-kätzchen** *neu.* (birch) catkin

Mailand *neu.* Milan

Mainz *neu.* Mayence

Mais *m.* maize; Indian corn; **-hülse** *f.* corn husk; **-kolben** *m.* corncob, ear of corn

majestätisch *adj.* majestic(al)

Major *m.* (mil.) major; (avi.) squadron leader; **-at** *neu.* primogeniture; entail; **-ität** *f.* majority

majorenn *adj.* of age; major

Majuskel *f.* capital letter; (typ.) small capital

Makel *m.* blemish, defect, stain, spot

mäkeln *v.* to find fault; to be fastidious

Makler *m.* broker, middleman; **-gebühr** *f.* brokerage; **-geschäft** *neu.* broker's business

Mäkler *m.* faultfinder; fastidious person

Makrele *f.* mackerel

Makrone *f.* macaroon

Makulatur *f.* wastepaper; **— reden** (coll.) to talk nonsense

Mal *neu.* mole, spot; sign; monument; (boundary) mark; (sports) base, goal; time; **das wievielte —** how many times; **manches —** often, many a time; **mit einem —** suddenly; **nicht ein einziges —** not once; **zum ersten —** for the first time; **zu wiederholten -en** repeatedly; again and again

mal *adv.* multiplied by; (coll.) once

male: **-n** *v.* to paint; to portray; to draw, to delineate; (lit.) to describe; **-erisch** *adj.* picturesque; graphic

Maler *m.* painter; artist; **-ei** *f.* (art of) painting

Malheur *neu.* misfortune, accident

Malstrom *m.* maelstrom

malträtieren *v.* to maltreat

Malz *neu.* malt; **da ist Hopfen und — verloren** (coll.) this case is hopeless

Mammut *neu.* and *m.* mammoth

Mamsell *f.* girl, miss, housekeeper

man *pron.* one, somebody; we, you; they, people

manch *pron.* and *adj.* many a (one); **-e** *pron.* some, several; **-erlei** *adj.* of several kinds, various; **-mal** *adv.* sometimes; many a time; often; now and again

Mand: **-ant** *m.* client; (pol.) constituent; **-at** *neu.* mandate, authorization, power of attorney

Mandarine *f.* tangerine

Mandel *f.* almond; tonsil; **-entzündung** *f.* tonsillitis

Mandoline *f.* mandolin

Mangan *neu.* manganese

Mangel *f.* mangle; — *m.* defect, want; lack; deficiency, scarcity; **aus — an** for want of; **— leiden** to be destitute

mangel: **-haft** *adj.* imperfect, incomplete; defective; **-n** *v.* to be deficient, to want, to lack; to mangle, to calender; **-s** *adv.* for want of

Mani: **-e** *f.* mania, craze

mani: **-eriert** *adj.* affected, stilted, mannered; **-erlich** *adj.* well-mannered, mannerly, civil

Manier *f.* manner, deportment; way, fashion; **-iertheit** *f.* mannerism

manifestieren *v.* to manifest, to declare

maniküren *v.* to manicure

Manko *neu.* deficiency, deficit; shortage

Mann *m.* man; male; husband; soldier, sailor, worker; **alle — an Deck** all hand on deck; **an den — bringen** (coll.) to sell; **an den unrechten — kommen** to come up against a better man; **ein — ein Wort** a man's word is his bond; **er wird seinen — schon finden** he'll find his match; **seine Tochter an den — bringen** to marry off one's daughter; **seinen — stellen** to hold one's own, to be brave; **-e** *m.* vassal; **-esalter** *neu.* years of manhood; **-eskraft** *f.* virility; **-sbild** *neu.* male; **-schaft** *f.* body of men, personnel; (mil.) ranks; squad; (naut.) crew; (sports) team; **-sleute** *pl.* menfolk; **-(e)szucht** *f.* (mil.) discipline; **-weib** *neu.* manlike woman, amazon

mann: **-bar** *adj.* marriageable; **-haft** *adj.* manly; resolute; virile; **-shoch** *adj.* of a man's height; **-stoll** *adj.* man-crazy, nymphomaniac

mannigfach, mannigfaltig *adj.* various, manifold, diverse

Manöver *neu.* maneuver

manövrieren *v.* to maneuver

Manövrierfähigkeit *f.* maneuverability

Mansarde *f.* attic room; garret

Manschette *f.* cuff; **-n haben** (coll.) to be afraid; **-nknopf** *m.* shirt stud, cuff button

Mantel *m.* mantle; cloak, overcoat; (mech.) jacket, casing; (naut.) case; (tire) cover; **-kragen** *m.* (cloak) cape; **-sack** *m.* (poet.) valise

Manu: **-al** *neu.* manual; notebook; (mus.) keyboard; **-faktur** *f.* manufacture; factory; **-skript** *neu.* manuscript; (typ.) copy

Mappe *f.* portfolio; briefcase; file folder

Mär, Märe *f.* tale; tidings; **-chen** *neu.* fairy (*oder* folk) tale; (coll.) story, fib

märchenhaft *adj.* fabulous, wonderful, legendary

Marder *m.* marten

Marien: **-fäden** *m. pl.* Indian summer;

gossamer; **-glas** *neu.* isinglass; **-käfer** *m.* ladybug

Marine *f.* marine, navy; **-flieger** *m.* naval airman; **-flugzeug** *neu.* seaplane; **-station** *f.* naval base; **-wesen** *neu.* naval affairs

marinieren *v.* to pickle, to marinate

Mark *neu.* marrow, pulp; core, essence; vigor — *f.* boundary, border country (money unit) mark; **-stein** *m.* boundary stone; landmark

mark: **-ant** *adj.* striking; characteristic; **-ieren** *v.* to mark; (coll.) to simulate, to pretend; **-ig** *adj.* pithy, vigorous

Marke *f.* mark, sign; (identification) check; stamp, trademark; token; sort; quality, vintage

Marketender *m.* sutler, canteen clerk

Markise *f.* awning, blind

Markt *m.* market; trade; fair; **-flecken** *m.* small country town; **-kurs** *m.* market quotation; **-schreier** *m.* high-pressure salesman

Marmelade *f.* jam; marmalade

Marmor *m.* marble; **-bruch** *m.* marble quarry; **-platte** *f.* marble slab

Marodeur *m.* marauder

marodieren *v.* to maraud, to pillage

Marotte *f.* caprice, whim; fad, hobby

marschieren *v.* to march

Marter *f.* torment, torture; **-bank** *f.* torture rack; **-er** *m.* tormentor, torturer; **-holz** *neu.* cross of torture; **-pfahl** *m.* torture stake; **-tod** *m.* martyr's death

martern *v.* to torment, to torture

martialisch *adj.* martial; warlike

Märtyrer *m.* martyr; **-geschichte** *f.* martyrology

Martyrium *neu.*, **Märtyrertum** *neu.* martyrdom

März *m.* March

Marzipan *m.* and *neu.* marzipan; marchpane

Masche *f.* mesh; stitch (in knitting)

Maschine *f.* machine, engine; typewriter; motorcycle, bicycle; **-narbeiter** *m.* machinist; **-nbauer** *m.* mechanical engineer; **-nführer** *m.* engineer; **-nschreiberin** *f.* typist; **-nschrift** *f.* typewriting, typescript; **-nwesen** *neu.* engineering; **-rie** *f.* machinery

maschinemässig *adj.* machine-like; mechanical

Maser *f.* (wood) streak, vein; spot, speckle; **-n** *pl.* measles

Maske *f.* mask; disguise; **-nball** *m.* masked (*oder* fancy dress) ball; **-nscherz** *m.* mummery; **-rade** *f.* masquerade

maskieren *v.* to mask; to disguise

Mass *neu.* measure; proportion; degree; limit; measurement; criterion; moderation; **nach — angefertigt** tailor-made; **made to measure**; **über alle -en** beyond measure, exceedingly; **-arbeit** *f.* custom work; **-einheit** *f.* unit of measurement; **-gabe** *f.* proportion; **nach -gabe** in accordance with; **-nahme** *f.* measure; **-regeln** *f. pl.* measures; remedies gesetzliche **-regeln ergreifen** to take legal steps; **-reg(e)lung** f. reprimand, disciplinary punishment; **-stab** m. scale; rule, standard; yardstick; **-verhältnis** neu. dimension; **-werk** neu. (arch.) carved work, tracery

mass: -enhaft adj. in masses; abundant; numerous; **-enweise** adv. in masses, in bulk; **-gebend** adj. authoritative, decisive; standard; **-halten** v. to keep within bounds; to observe moderation; **-ig** adj. massive, bulky, large; **-iv** adj. massive, solid; **-los** adj. boundless; exorbitant; limitless; **-regeln** v. to take to task, to reprimand; to inflict disciplinary punishment; **-voll** adj. moderate, measured

Masse f. mass, bulk; substance; multitude; (law) assets, estate; **-nabsatz** m. wholesale trade; **-narmut** f. pauperism; **-naufgebot** neu. general levy; **-nmord** m. general massacre; **-nversammlung** f. mass meeting

massieren v. to massage

mässig adj. moderate, temperate; reasonable; **-en** v. to moderate; to check, to mitigate

Mässigung f. moderation, restraint, control

Mast f. (food) mast; **-(baum)** m. mast; pole; **-darm** m. rectum; **-ix** m. mastic; putty; **-kalb** neu. fatted calf; **-korb** m. (naut.) masthead, top; **-kur** f. fattening diet

mästen v. to fatten

Material neu. (raw) material; equipment; **rollendes —** (rail.) rolling stock; **-ismus** m. materialism

Materie f. matter; substance; subject

materiell adj. material; real

Mathematik f. mathematics; **-er** m. mathematician

mathematisch adj. mathematic(al)

Matratze f. mattress; (gym.) mat

Mätresse f. (kept) mistress

Matrikel f. register, roll; matriculation

Matrize f. matrix; mold

Matrone f. matron

Matrose m. sailor

Matsch m. pulp, mash; slush, mud

matschen v. to mash; to splash. to (s)quash

matt adj. exhausted, feeble; faint, dim; insipid; **-setzen** (chess) to mate

Matt neu. (chess) checkmate

Matte f. (mountain) meadow, pasture

Maturität f. maturity

Matz m. little fellow; (dicky)bird

Mauer f. wall; **-blümchen** neu. wallflower; **-brecher** m. battering ram; **-kelle** f. trowel; **-stein** m. brick; **-werk** neu. stonework, masonry

mauern v. to build masonry, to immure; (cards) to risk nothing

Maul neu. (zool.) mouth; **halt's —!** shut up! **— und Klauenseuche** foot-and-mouth disease; **-esel** m., **-tier** neu. mule; **-held** m. braggart, blowhard; **-korb** m. muzzle; **-schelle** f. slap in the face; **-sperre** f. lockjaw; **-trommel**

f. mouth organ; **-werk** neu. gift of gab

maul: -en v. to sulk, to mope; **-voll** adj. mouthful

Maulbeere f. mulberry

Maulwurf m. mole

Maure m. Moor

Maurer m. mason, bricklayer; **-handwerk** neu. building trade

Maus f. mouse; (thumb) base; **-efalle** f. mouse trap

maus: -en v. to catch mice; (coll.) to filch, to pilfer; **-etot** adj. dead as a doornail; stone-dead; **-farben** adj. mousecolored, dun; **-ig** adj. mousy

Maut f. duty, excise, toll

Maxime f. maxim

Mechan: -ik f. mechanics; **-iker** m. mechanic(ian); **-isierung** f. mechanization; **-ismus** m. mechanism; works

mechanisch adj. mechanical

meckern v. to bleat; (coll.) to criticize, to laugh foolishly

Medaille f. medal

Medaillon neu. medallion, locket

meditieren v. to meditate

Medizin f. medicine; art of healing; **-albeamte** m. medical officer; **-albehörde** f. Board of Health; **-algewicht** neu. troy weight; **-er** m. medical student; medical man; (coll.) medic

medizinisch adj. medical, medicinal

Meduse f. jellyfish; sea jelly

Meer neu. ocean, sea; **-busen** m. bay, gulf; **-enge** f., **-esstrasse** f. channel, straits; **-esbrandung** f. surf, breakers; **-esspiegel** m. sea level; **-frau** f. mermaid; **-katze** f. long-tailed monkey; **-rettich** m. horseradish; **-schaum** m. sea foam; meerschaum; **-schweinchen** neu. guinea pig; **-spinne** f. king crab

Mehl neu. flour, meal; dust; **-kloss** m. dumpling; **-speise** f. pastry; pudding; **-suppe** f. gruel

mehr adv. more; **es dauert nicht — lange** it won't last much longer; **es ist nichts — da** there is nothing left; **immer — more and more; — als** more than; **noch — even more; umso —** all the more; **-en** v. to augment, to increase; **-ere** adj. pl. several; **-erlei** adj. various, sundry; **-fach** adj. manifold; multiple; repeated, frequent; **-jährig** adj. for several years; **-malig** adj. repeated, frequent; **-mals** adv. more than once, several times; **-silbig** adj. polysyllabic; **-stellig** adj. (math.) of several places; **-stimmig** adj. (mus.) for several voices, concerted

Mehr: -aufwand m., **-ausgabe** f. increased (oder additional) expenditure; **-bedarf** m. surplus demand; **-betrag** m. surplus amount; **-gebot** neu. overbid; **-heit** f. majority; **-kosten** pl. additional expenses; **-ung** f. increase, augment; **-wert** m. surplus value; **-zahl** f. plural(ity)

meiden v. to avoid, to shun

Meier m. manager (of an estate); farm tenant; **-ei** f. farm(house); dairy farm; dairy

Meile *f.* mile; **-nstein** *m.* milestone
meilenweit *adj.* extending for miles, many miles away
mein *pron.* and *adj.* my, mine; **gedenke — remember me**; **-erseits** *adv.*, **-esteils** *adv.* for my part; **-ethalben** *adv.*, **-etwegen** *adv.*, **-etwillen** *adv.* so far as I am concerned; **um -etwillen** on my account; **-ig** *adj.* mine, my; **-tag** *adv.* as long as I live; for a long time
Meineid *m.* perjury; **-ige** *m.* perjurer
meinen *v.* to mean; to think, to suppose, to believe; to intend
Meinung *f.* opinion, meaning; intention; view, belief; **jemand die — sagen** to give someone a piece of one's mind; **-sverschiedenheit** *f.* difference of opinion, disagreement
Meise *f.* titmouse
Meissel *m.* chisel
meist *adj.* most; **—** *adv.* generally, mostly; **die —en Menschen** most of the people; **-enorts** *adv.* almost everywhere; **-ens** *adv.*, **-enteils** *adv.* mostly, in most cases; generally, usually
Meist: -begünstigung *f.* preference; **-begünstigungsklausel** *f.* most-favored-nation clause; **-betrag** *m.* maximum amount; **-bietende** *m.* highest bidder
Meister *m.* master; champion; **-schaft** *f.* mastery; championship; **-stück** *neu.*, **-werk** *neu.* masterpiece (*oder* work)
meister: -haft *adj.*, **-lich** *adj.* excellent, masterful; **-n** *v.* to master; to subdue; to excel, to outdo; (coll.) to find fault with
melancholisch *adj.* melancholy
Melasse *f.* molasses
Meld: -eamt *neu.* registration office; **-edienst** *m.* intelligence service; **-er** *m.* orderly; messenger; **-ereiter** *m.* (mil.) dispatch rider; **-estelle** *f.* local reporting station; **-ezettel** *m.* registration form; **-ung** *f.* report; announcement; information; notification; (sports) entry
melden *v.* to inform, to report; to notify; **sich — lassen** to send in one's name
melken *v.* to milk
Melod: -ie *f.* melody; **-ik** *f.* melodics; **-rama** *neu.* melodrama
Melone *f.* melon; derby hat
Meltau *m.* mildew, blight
Membrane *f.* membrane; (tel.) diaphragm
Memme *f.* coward; poltroon
memorieren *v.* to memorize
Menage *f.* menage; household; housekeeping; set of dishes (*oder* cruets)
Menge *f.* quantity, multitude; heap, swarm, crowd; **eine — Geld** plenty of money
mengen *v.* to mix, to mingle, to blend; **sich in etwas —** to meddle (*oder* interfere) with something
Mensch *m.* human being; person; (bibl.) man; **kein —** nobody; **-enaffe** *m.* anthropoid ape; **-enalter** *neu.* generation; average age of man; **-enfeind** *m.* misanthrope; **-enfresser** *m.* cannibal; ogre; **-enfreund** *m.* philanthropist; **-enge-**

denken *neu.* (from) time immemorial; **-engeschlecht** *neu.* human race; mankind; **-enhandel** *m.* slave trade; **-enliebe** *f.* philanthropy; charity; **-enraub** *m.* kidnapping; **-enrechte** *neu. pl.* human rights; **-enscheu** *f.* unsociableness; **-enschinder** *m.* exploiter, extortioner; **-enschlag** *m.* race of men; **-ensohn** *m.* Christ; **-heit** *f.* mankind; **-werdung** *f.* incarnation
mensch: -enfeindlich *adj.* misanthropic; **-enfreundlich** *adj.* philanthropic; **-enleer** *adj.* deserted; **-enmöglich** *adj.* humanly possible; **-enscheu** *adj.* unsociable; **-lich** *adj.* human, humane
menstruieren *v.* to menstruate
Mensur *f.* mensuration; (fencing) distance; standard (for organ pipes); diapason
Mentalität *f.* mentality
Menü *neu.* menu
Menuett *neu.* minuet
Merk: -blatt *neu.* instructional pamphlet; **-buch** *neu.* notebook; **-er** *m.* marker (poet.) critic; **-mal** *neu.* distinguishing mark; characteristic feature; **-wort** *neu* catchword; (theat.) cue; **-zeichen** *neu* distinctive mark
merk: -bar, **-lich** *adj.* noticeable, perceptible; **-en** *v.* to mark; to remember; to notice; **das werde ich mir —en** I wil bear that in mind; **-en lassen** to show; **lass dir nichts -en** do not let it be seen; **-enswert** *adj.* remarkable; **-würdig** *adj* noteworthy; strange; memorable; **-würdigerweise** *adv.* strange to say
Merkur *m.* Mercury; **—** *neu.* (chem. mercury
Merle *f.* blackbird
Mesner *m.* (Roman Catholic) sacristan sexton
Mess: -amt *neu.* celebration of the Mass; **-buch** *neu.* missal; **-e** *f.* trade fair Mass; (mil.) mess; **-ebude** *f.* booth (at a fair)
Mess: -band *neu.* measuring tape; **-kunde** *f.* surveying; **-ung** *f.* measurement; mensuration
mess: -bar *adj.* measurable; **-en** *v.* to measure; to compare (with); to survey **sich -en mit** to be a match for; to compete with
Messer *neu.* knife; **—** *m.* measurer; measuring apparatus; **-scheide** *f.* scabbard; **-schneide** *f.* knife-edge; **auf -sschneide** on the razor's edge; **-schmied** *m.* cutler; **-stecher** *m.* cutthroat
Messing *neu.* brass; **-beschlag** *m.* brass mounting
Met *m.* mead
Meta: -morphose *f.* metamorphosis; **-pher** *f.* metaphor; **-physik** *f.* meta physics
Metall *neu.* metal; **edle -e** preciou metals; **unedle -e** base metals; **-geld** *neu.* hard cash; **-urgie** *f.* metallurgy; **-probe** *f.* assay; **-waren** *f. pl.* hardware
metaphysisch *adj.* metaphysical
Meteor *neu.* meteor; **-it** *m.* meteorite; **-ologie** *f.* meteorology

Meter *m.* and *neu.* meter (1.0936 yards); **-mass** *neu.* metric measure

Methode *f.* method

Methodik *f.* theory of method

Metier *neu.* profession, trade

Metr: -ik *f.* metrics; **-onom** *neu.* metronome; **-opole** *f.* metropolis; **-um** *neu.* meter

metrisch *adj.* metrical

Mette *f.* matins

Mettwurst *f.* German Bologna sausage

Metz: -elei *f.* massacre; **-ger** *m.* (dial.) butcher; **-gerei** *f.* butcher's shop

metzeln, metzgen *v.* to slaughter, to massacre

Meuchelmord *m.* assassination; **-er** *m.* assassin

meuchl: -n *v.* to assassinate; **-erisch** *adj.* murderous, treacherous; **-ings** *adv.* insidiously, treacherously

Meute *f.* pack of hounds; (coll.) gang, crowd

Meuter: -ei *f.* mutiny; **-er** *m.* mutineer

meuter: -isch *adj.* mutinous; **-n** *v.* to mutiny

miau! *interj.* miaow! **-en** *v.* to mew

mich *pron.* me

Mieder *neu.* bodice, corselette

Miene *f.* air, expression; mien; countenance; **gute — zum bösen Spiel machen** to make a virtue of necessity; **-nspiel** *neu.*, **-nsprache** *f.* play of the features; pantomime

Miet: -e *f.* rent, hire; lease, tenancy; (theat.) season ticket; (agr.) rick, shock, pit; **-er** *m.* renter, tenant; **-erschaft** *f.* tenancy; **-geld** *neu.* rent; **-kontrakt** *m.* rental agreement; **-ling** *m.* hireling; **-shaus** *neu.* apartment house; **-skaserne** *f.* tenement house; **-sleute** *pl.* lodgers, tenants, roomers; **-svertrag** *m.* lease; **-swohnung** *f.* rented dwelling, apartment; **-zins** *m.* rental

nieten *v.* to rent; to hire; to charter

Miez(e) *f.* pussycat; pussy; girl's pet name

Migräne *f.* migraine; sick headache

Mikro: -be *f.* microbe; **-fon** *neu.* microphone; **-millimeter** *m.* micron; **-skop** *neu.* microscope

Mikrorillen *adj.* (Schallplatten) microgroove

Milch *f.* milk; **-bart** *m.* (coll.) milksop; greenhorn; **-brei** *m.* porridge; **-brot** *neu.* French (*oder* Vienna) bread; **-bruder** *m.* foster brother; **-gesicht** *neu.* baby face; immature youth; **-glas** *neu.* milk tumbler; opalescent glass; **-händler** *m.* dairyman, milkman; **-kuh** *f.* milk cow; **-kur** *f.* milk diet; **-schwester** *f.* foster sister; **-strasse** *f.* Milky Way; **-suppe** (avi. Nebel) *f.* soup; **-wirtschaft** *f.* dairy farm(ing); **-zahn** *m.* milk tooth

milch: -en *v.* to give milk; **-ig** *adj.* milky; translucent; **-weiss** *adj.* milk-white

Mild: -e *f.* gentleness; indulgence; benevolence; clemency; **-erungsgrund** *m.* mitigating circumstance

mild(e) *adj.* mild; gentle, mellow, soft; bland; indulgent; charitable; **-ern** *v.* to mitigate, to moderate; to soften, to soothe; to reduce; **-ernde Umstände** (law) extenuating circumstances; **-gesinnt** *adj.* of gentle disposition; **-herzig** *adj.*, **-tätig** *adj.* charitable, openhanded, kindhearted

Milieu *neu.* environment; setting; local color; background; sphere

Militär *neu.* (the) military; army; **— m.** professional soldier; **-arzt** *m.* army surgeon; **-behörden** *f. pl.* military authorities; **-dienst** *m.* military (*oder* active) service; **-herrschaft** *f.*, **-ismus** *m.* militarism; **-kapelle** *f.* military band; **-polizei** *f.* military police; **-wesen** *neu.* army affairs; war department

militärisch *adj.* military, soldierlike, martial

Miliz *f.* militia

Mill: -iarde *f.* milliard; billion (in U.S.); **-ion** *f.* million; **-ionär** *m.* millionaire

Milz *f.* milt, spleen

Mim: — e *m.* mimic; **-ik** *f.* mimicking; mimicry; **-ikry** *f.* mimesis; mimicry

mimen *v.* to act; to mimic; to imitate

mimisch *adj.* mimic, acting

minder *adj.* less(er); inferior, minor; **nicht mehr, nicht —** neither more or less; **-jährig** *adj.* under age; **-n** *v.* to diminish, to slacken; to lessen; **-wertig** *adj.* of inferior quality

Minder: -betrag *m.* deficiency, deficit; **-einnahme** *f.*, **-ertrag** *m.* decrease of receipts; **-heit** *f.* minority; **-jährigkeit** *f.* minority (of age); **-wertigkeitsgefühl** *neu.* inferiority complex; **-zahl** *f.* minority

mindest *adj.* least, slightest, smallest; **nicht das -e** not a bit; **nicht die -e Aussicht** not the ghost of a chance; **nicht im -en** not at all, by no means; **zum -en** at least; **-ens** *adv.* at least

Mindest: -betrag *m.* minimum amount; **-gebot** *neu.* lowest bid; **-gehalt** *m.* lowest percentage; minimum wages; **-mass** *neu.* minimum

Mine *f.* mine; (pencil) refill; **-nräumer** *m.*, **-nsucher** *m.* mine sweeper; **-nsperre** *f.* mine blockade; **-ntrichter** *m.* mine crater

Mineral *neu.* mineral; **-ogie** *f.* mineralogy; **-reich** *neu.* mineral kingdom

Miniatur *f.*, **Miniaturgemälde** *neu.* miniature

minimal *adj.* minimum

Minister *m.* minister; **-ium** *neu.* ministry; **-präsident** *m.* Prime Minister; **-rat** *m.* Cabinet, Council

Minne *f.* (poet.) love; **-sang** *m.* old chivalric love song; **-sänger** *m.* minnesinger, troubadour

minorenn *adj.* under age, minor

Minorität *f.* minority

minus *adv.* minus

Minus *neu.* deficit; loss; **-kel** *f.* miniscule; **-zeichen** *neu.* subtraction sign

minut: -enlang *adv.* lasting a (*oder* for) minute(s); **-iös** *adj.* minute

Minute *f.* minute; **-nzeiger** *m.* minute

hand

Minze *f.* (bot.) mint

mir *pron.* (to) me, (to) myself

Mirakel *neu.* miracle

Misch: -**dünger** *m.* compost; -**ehe** *f.* mixed marriage; -**ling** *m.* half-breed, mongrel, hybrid; -**masch** *m.* hodge-podge; medley; -**rasse** *f.*, -**volk** *neu.* mixed race; -**ung** *f.* mixing, mixture; combination, composition; alloy

mischen *v.* to mix; to mingle; to blend; to alloy; (cards) to shuffle; **sich in etwas —** to interfere in something

Misere *f.* misery

miss: -**achten** *v.* to disregard, to despise; to undervalue; -**behagen** *v.* to displease; -**behaglich** *adj.* displeasing; uncomfortable; -**billigen** to disapprove, to disavow; -**brauchen** *v.* to abuse, to misuse; -**bräuchlich** *adj.* improper; -**deuten** *v.* to misinterpret, to misconstrue; -**en** *v.* to miss; to lack; -**fallen** *v.* to displease; -**fällig** *adj.* unpleasant, disparaging; -**gebildet** *adj.* malformed; -**gestaltet** *adj.*, -**gestaltig** *adj.* misshapen, deformed; -**gestimmt** *adj.* peevish, discordant, depressed; -**glücken** *v.* to fail; -**gönnen** *v.* to grudge, to envy; -**günstig** *adj.* envious, jealous; -**handeln** *v.* to maltreat; -**hellig** *adj.* dissonant, incongruous; -**leiten** *v.* to mislead; -**lich** *adj.* unpleasant, precarious; difficult; -**liebig** *adj.* unpopular; obnoxious; -**lingen** *v.* to fail; -**mutig** *adj.* ill-humored, discontented; -**raten** *v.* to turn out badly; -**stimmen** *v.* to depress, to upset; -**tönend** *adj.*, -**tönig** *adj.* discordant; -**trauen** *v.* to mistrust; -**trauisch** *adj.* distrustful, suspicious; -**vergnügt** *adj.* dissatisfied, malcontent; -**verständlich** *adj.* misleading, erroneous; -**versteh(e)n** *v.* to misunderstand, to misconstrue

Miss: -**achtung** *f.* disdain, disregard; -**behagen** *neu.* uneasiness; -**belieben** *neu.* displeasure; -**bildung** *f.* malformation, deformity; -**brauch** *m.* abuse; -**erfolg** *m.* failure; -**ernte** *f.* crop failure; -**etat** *f.* misdeed, crime; -**etäter** *m.* evildoer, criminal; -**fallen** *neu.* dislike; displeasure; disapproval; -**geburt** *f.* abortion; monster; -**geschick** *neu.* misfortune; mishap; -**gestalt** *f.* deformity; monster; -**griff** *m.* mistake; -**gunst** *f.* envy, jealousy; grudge; -**handlung** *f.* maltreatment; (law) assault and battery; -**helligkeit** *f.* difference, discord; -**klang** *m.* disharmony, dissonance; -**laut** *m.* discordant sound; -**stand** *m.* inconvenience; grievance; -**stimmung** *f.* discordance; depression; -**ton** *m.* dissonance; -**trauen** *neu.* mistrust, suspicion; -**verständnis** *neu.* misunderstanding, dissension; -**wirtschaft** *f.* maladministration, mismanagement

Mission *f.* mission; -**är** *m.* missionary

Mist *m.* dung, manure; (coll.) junk; (naut.) mist, fog; **er hat Geld wie —** (coll.) he has a lot of money; -**beet** *neu.* hotbed; -**haufen** *m.* dunghill; -**käfer** *m.*

dung beetle

Mistel *f.* mistletoe

misten *v.* to manure; to clean (out); (naut.) to fog

mit *prep.* and *adv.* with; also, likewise; at, by; too; **Böses — Gutem vergelten** to return good for evil; — **Absicht** intentionally; — **dabei sein** to be one of the party; — **der Zeit** in time, gradually; — **einem Wort** in a word; — **fünfzig Jahren** at the age of fifty; — **Namen nennen** to call by name; -**arbeiten** *v.* to collaborate; to contribute; -**beteiligt** *adj.* participating; interested (in); -**bewerben** *v.* to compete for (*oder* with); -**einander** *adv.* together, jointly; -**eingebriffen** *adj.*, -**eingeschlossen** *adj.* included, inclusive; -**empfinden**, -**fühlen** *v.* to sympathize; -**halten** *v.* to share; -**helfen** *v.* to assist; -**hin** *adv.* and *conj.* consequently, therefore; -**hören** *v.* to overhear; -**laufen** *v.* to run along with; to do as (others do); -**leidig** *adj.* compassionate; -**machen** *v.* to take part in; to follow; to go through with; -**nehmen** to take along with; to exhaust; to treat harshly; to profit by; -**nichten** *adv.* by no means; -**reden** *v.* to join in conversation; -**samt** *prep.* together with; -**schuldig** accessory (to crime); übel -**spielen** to play a trick on; -**teilen** *v.* to impart; to communicate; to announce; -**unter** *adv.* sometimes, now and then; -**wirken** *v.* to assist; to collaborate; to take part in; -**wissen** *v.* to know of, to share (secret); -**zählen** *v.* to count in; to take into account

Mit: -**arbeiter** *m.* co-worker, contributor; -**besitzer** *m.* joint owner; -**bewerber** *m.* competitor, rival; -**bringsel** *neu.* present, souvenir; -**bürger** *m.* fellow citizen; -**erbe** *m.* coheir; -**esser** *m.* (med.) blackhead; parasite; -**fahrerzentrale** *f.* carpool; -**gefühl** *neu.* compassion; sympathy; -**gift** *f.* dowry; -**giftjäger** *m.* fortune hunter; -**glied** *neu.* member; -**gliedschaft** *f.* membership; -**helfer** *m.* assistant; accessory, accomplice; -**hilfe** *f.* assistance; -**inhaber** *m.* copartner; -**laut** *m.* consonant; -**leid** *neu.* pity; -**leidsbezeugung** *f.* condolence; -**mensch** *m.* fellow man; -**schuld** *f.* complicity; -**schuldner** *m.* codebtor; -**schüler** *m.* schoolmate, classmate; -**welt** *f.* our contemporaries; -**wirkung** *f.* assistance, participation

Mittag *m.* midday, noon; south; **zu — essen** to dine; -**brot** *neu.*, -**essen** *neu.* dinner; -**slinie** *f.* meridian; -**stunde** *f.* noon, lunch time

mittägig, **mittäglich** *adj.* midday, meridional; southern

mittags *adv.* at midday, at noon

Mitte *f.* middle, center, midst; mean, medium; **das Reich der —** the Middle Kingdom, China; **die goldene —** the golden mean; **in die — nehmen** to attack from both sides; to take between; **— Vierzig** in the middle forties

Mittel *neu.* means; expedient; remedy; average, mean; medium; — *pl.* money; **kein —** unversucht lassen to leave no stone unturned; **sich ins —** legen to mediate; **-alter** *neu.* Middle Ages; **-arrest** *m.* (mil.) solitary confinement; neutral zone; **-mächte** *f. pl.* Central Powers; **-punkt** *m.* center; **-schiff** *neu.* middle aisle; **-schule** *f.* secondary school; **-smann** *m.* go-between; broker; mediator; **-stand** *m.* middle classes; **-strasse** *f.*, **-weg** *m.* middle course, compromise, mean; **-stufe** *f.* middle step; intermediate degree (*oder* grade); **-treffen** *neu.* center (of army); **-wort** *neu.* participle

mittel-: -alterlich *adj.* medieval; (coll.) middle-aged; **-bar** *adj.* indirect; mediate; **-bar** *prep.* with the aid of; **-gross** *adj.* medium-sized; **-ländisch** *adj.* Mediterranean; **-los** *adj.* without means; destitute; **-mässig** *adj.* mediocre, average; indifferent; **-s** *prep.* by means of

ittelmeer *neu.* Mediterranean Sea

tten *adv.* midway, amidst; **— auf der Strasse** in the open street; **— in der Luft** in midair; **— ins Herz** right into the heart; **-drin** *adv.* in the center; **-durch** *adv.* right across; **-entzwei** *adv.* broken in the middle

Mitternacht *f.* midnight, north

mitternächtig, mitternächtlich *adj.* taking place at midnight; nocturnal, northern

mitternachts *adv.* at midnight

Mittler *m.* mediator; intercessor

mittler *adj.* middle, central; middling; average; medium; mediocre; **-weile** *adv.* in the meantime, meanwhile

ittwoch *m.* Wednesday

ixtur *f.* mixture

öbel *neu.* piece of furniture; **-schoner** *m.* slipcover; **-spediteur** *m.* furniture mover; **-tischler** *m.* cabinetmaker; **-wagen** *m.* furniture van

nobil *adj.* mobile; active, nimble; **-isieren, -machen** *v.* to mobilize

Mobil: -iar *neu.* furniture; **-ien** *pl.* movables; personal property; **-isierung** *f.*, **-machung** *f.* mobilization

möblieren *v.* to furnish; **möbliertes Zimmer** furnished apartment

Mode *f.* mode, fashion, vogue; **-artikel** *m. pl.*, **-waren** *f. pl.* fancy goods; novelties; **-dame** *f.* lady of fashion; **-journal** *neu.* ladies' (*oder* fashion) magazine; **-schau** *f.* fashion show; **-schriftsteller** *m.* popular (*oder* fashionable) author; **-welt** *f.* world of fashion; **-wort** *neu.* slogan in vogue

Modell *neu.* model, pattern, mold; sample, draft; **-ierer** *m.* patternmaker, molder, modeller

modellieren, modeln *v.* to model; to mold, to shape, to fashion

Moder *m.* mold, mud, decay; **-geruch** *m.* musty smell

moder: -ig *adj.* moldy, musty; decaying, putrid; **-n** to decay, to putrefy, to rot; **-n** *adj.* modern, fashionable; **-nisieren**

v. to modernize

modifizieren *v.* to modify

modulieren *v.* to modulate

Modus *m.* mode, manner; (gram.) mood

Mogelei *f.* cheating, trickery

mögen *v.* to like, to want, to desire; to be willing, to let; **das mag sein** that may be so; **lieber —** to like better; to prefer; **mag kommen was will** no matter what happens; **wie dem auch sein mag** that as it may

möglich *adj.* possible, feasible, practicable; eventual; **alles -e** all kinds of things; everything possible; **nicht —!** you don't say so! **sein -stes tun** to do one's utmost; **so bald wie —** as soon as possible; **-enfalls** *adv.*, **-erweise** *adv.* possibly, perhaps

Möglichkeit *f.* possibility; potentiality

Mohär *m.* mohair

Mohn *m.* poppy; **-same(n)** *m.* poppyseed

Mohr *m.* Moor; Negro; **-enwäsche** *f.* vindication

Möhre, Mohrrübe *f.* carrot

mokieren *v.* **sich — über** to ridicule, to mock

Molch *m.* salamander

Mole *f.* mole, jetty, pier; **-kül** *neu.* molecule

Molke *f.* whey; **-rei** *f.* dairy; creamery

Moll *neu.* (mus.) minor; **alles in —** doleful, sad

mollig *adj.* cozy, snug; soft; rounded

Moment *m.* moment; instant; **— ** *neu.* momentum; impulse; **-aufnahme** *f.* snapshot

momentan *adj.* momentary, instantaneous; **— ** *adv.* for the moment (*oder* present); just now

Monarch *m.* monarch; **-ie** *f.* monarchy

Monat *m.* month; **-abschluss** *m.*, **-bericht** *m.* monthly balance (*oder* report); **-sfluss** *m.* menstruation; **-sfrist** *f.* one month's grace (*oder* time); **-sgeld** *neu.* monthly allowance; **-sgehalt** *neu.* monthly pay (*oder* salary); **-skarte** *f.* monthly ticket; **-sschrift** *f.* monthly magazine

monatelang *adj.* for months

monatlich *adj.* monthly

Mönch *m.* monk, friar; **-skappe** *f.* monk's hood; **-skloster** *neu.* monastery; **-skutte** *f.* cowl; **-sorden** *m.* monastic order; **-swesen** *neu.*, **-tum** *neu.* monasticism; **-szelle** *f.* friar's cell; **-szucht** *f.* monastic discipline

Mond *m.* moon; (ast.) satellite; (poet.) month; **den — betreffend** lunar; **-bahn** *f.* orbit; **-finsternis** *f.* lunar eclipse; **-hof** *m.* halo around the moon; **-rakete** *f.* circumlunar rocket; **-sichel** *f.* moon crescent; **-stein** *m.* moonstone; **-sucht** *f.* somnambulism

Mono: -gamie *f.* monogamy; **-gramm** *neu.* monogram; **-kel** *neu.* monocle; **-log** *m.* monolog; **-pol** *neu.* monopoly; **-polisierung** *f.* monopolization

monoton *adj.* monotonous

Monstranz *f.* monstrance

monströs *adj.* monstrous

Monstrum neu. monster

Monsun m. monsoon

Montag m. Monday

Montage f. mounting, fitting

Mont: –eur m. fitter, mounter; mechanic; –ierung f. erection, assemblage; adjusting; (mil.) equipment; –ur f. uniform

montieren v. to fit, to erect, to assemble

Monument neu. monument

Moor neu. bog, fen, marsh, swamp; –bad neu. mud bath; –land neu. marshy country

Moos neu. moss; (coll.) money

moosig adj. mossy

Mop m. (dust) mop; –s m. pug

mopsen v. (sl.) to pilfer; **sich** — (coll.) to be bored

Moral f. moral(s); morality; morale; **den –ischen haben** to feel the prick of conscience; –pauke f., –predigt f. severe reprimand, moral lecture

moralisch adj. moral

moralisieren v. to moralize

Morast m. morass, marsh, swamp, slough

Mord m. murder; –(io)! interj. murder! –anschlag m. murderous attack (oder plot); –brenner m. incendiary; –gier f., –lust f. bloodthirstiness, murderous lust; –kommission f. homicide squad; –skerl m. devil of a fellow; –spektakel m. dreadful din, hullabaloo

mord: –en v. to murder, to kill; –gierig adj. bloodthirsty, sanguinary; –smässig adj. (coll.) enormous

Mörder m. murderer; **gedung(e)ner** — hired assassin; **aus seinem Herzen keine –grube machen** (coll.) to wear one's heart on one's sleeve; to be very outspoken

mörderisch, mörderlich adj. murderous; awful; terrible, cruel, enormous; deadly, fatal

morg: –endlich adj. matutinal; –enfrüh adv. tomorrow morning; –ens adv. in the morning; –ig adj. of tomorrow; –enländisch adj. oriental

Morgen m. morning daybreak; (the) morrow; acre; east; –andacht f. morning devotions; –dämmerung f., –grauen neu. dawn, morning twilight; –gabe f. bridegroom's gift; –land neu. Orient; –luft wittern to scent an advantage; –rock m. negligée

Morphium neu. morphine

morsch adj. rotten; decayed; rickety; carious

Mörser m. mortar; –keule f. pestle

Mörtel m. mortar; –trog m. hod

Mosaik neu. mosaic

mosaisch adj. Mosaic

Moschee f. mosque

Moschus m. musk; –bock m. musk beetle; musk deer

Moskito m. mosquito

Most m. must; fruit wine

Motiv neu. motive;

motivieren v. to motivate

Motor m. motor; –hotel neu. tourist court; –rad neu. motorcycle; –schaden m. engine trouble

motorisieren v. to motorize

Motte f. moth; **Ach, Du kriegst die –n!** (coll.) holy cow! –nfrass m. damage by moths; –npulver neu. insecticide

Möwe f. gull, sea mew

Mucke f. whim, caprice; (dial.) gnat; –r m. bigot, hypocrite

Mücke f. gnat, midge; –nstich m. gnat bite

mucken v. to grumble; to mutter; to be glum

mucksen v. (fig.) to stir; **er darf sich nicht** — he dare not say a word

müde adj. tired, weary; exhausted

Muff m., –e f. muff; (mech.) socket; sleeve; moldy smell; –el f. muffle

muffig adj. fusty, moldy; sulky, cross

muhl interj. moo; –en to moo, to low

Müh: –e f. trouble; toil; effort; pains; **es ist der –e wert** it's worth while; **mit –e und Not** with difficulty; **sich –e geben** to take pains; –ewaltung f. care, exertion; –sal f. hardship; distress

müh: –elos adj. effortless, easy; –en v. to labor, to toil; –evoll adj. difficult, hard, laborious; –sam adj. wearisome, intricate, tiring; –selig adj. toilsome, wretched, unpleasant

Mühl: –bach m. millstream; –e f. mill, game (played on a board); **das ist Wasser auf seine –e** that's grist for his mill; –wehr neu. milldam

Muhme f. (dial.) aunt; older woman

Mulatte m. mulatto

Mulde f. tray; trough; hollow, valley

Mull m. mull, muslin

Müll neu. garbage, dust, rubbish, sweepings; –abfuhr f. garbage collection; –eimer m., –kasten m. dustbin; –schippe f. dustpan; –wagen m. garbage van

Müller m. miller

multiplizieren v. to multiply

Mum: –ie f. mummy

Mumme: –rei f., –nschanz m. mummery, masquerade

mumifizieren v. to mummify

mummeln v. to mumble

Mumpitz m. nonsense, bosh

München neu. Munich

Mund m. mouth; **den — halten** to hold one's tongue; **den — vollnehmen** to brag; **die Bissen im –e zählen** to be grudge every morsel; **im –e führen** to talk constantly about; **kein Blatt vo den — nehmen** to speak freely; **nac dem — reden** to flatter; **nicht auf de — gefallen sein** to have a ready tongue; **reinen — halten** to keep a secret; **sic den — verbrennen** to give onese away; **sich vom –e absparen** to scrimp; **über den — fahren** to cut short; –a f. dialect; –höhle f. oral cavity; –sperr f. lockjaw; –stück neu. mouthpiece (cigarette) tip; –vorrat m. victual provisions; –wasser neu. mouthwas gargle; –werk neu. (coll.) glib tongue gift of gab; –winkel m. corner of th mouth

Münd: –el neu. ward, minor; –elgeld neu

money held in trust; **–igkeit** *f.* coming of age, majority

münd:–en *v.* to flow (*oder* run) into; **–lich** *adj.* oral; **–lich** *adv.* by word of mouth

mündig *adj.* of age

Mündung *f.* mouth, estuary, orifice; (gun) muzzle; outlet, terminus

Munition *f.* ammunition; **–slager** *neu.* ammunition dump; **–snachschub** *m.* ammunition supply

munkeln *v.* to mutter, to whisper; (coll.) to plot; **im Dunkeln ist gut —** night covers all

Münster *neu.* minster, cathedral

munter *adj.* brisk, lively, sprightly, gay, merry; **— werden** to awake

Münz:–anstalt *f.* mint; **–e** *f.* coin, money, change, medal; **für bare –e nehmen** to take words at face value; **klingende –e** hard cash; **mit gleicher –e bezahlen** to give tit for tat; **–einheit** *f.* monetary unit; **–fernsprecher** *m.* telephone booth; **–fuss** *m.* standard of coinage; **–kunde** *f.* numismatics; **–prägung** *f.* coinage; **–recht** *neu.* right of coinage; **–system** *neu.,* **–wesen** *neu.* monetary system; **–zusatz** *m.* alloy

mürbe *adj.* tender, mellow; well-boiled; brittle, crisp; unnerved, worn-down; **— machen** to break (one's) spirit; (mil.) to soften up; **— werden** to give in

Mürbekuchen *m.* shortcake

murmeln *v.* to murmur; to mutter; to play marbles

Murmeltier *neu.* marmot; **wie ein — schlafen** to sleep like a log

murren *v.* to growl; to grumble

mürrisch *adj.* sullen, morose; surly, sulky

Mus *neu.* jam, stewed fruit; purée; pap

Muschel *f.* mussel; shell (fish); conch; earpiece

Muse *f.* muse; **–nross** *neu.* Pegasus; **–nsohn** *m.* poet; university student; **–um** *neu.* museum

Muselman *m.* moslem

musi:–kalisch *adj.* musical; **–zieren** *v.* to perform music

Musik *f.* music, band; **in — setzen** to set to music; **–alienhandlung** *f.* music shop; **–ant** *m.,* **–er** *m.,* **–us** *m.* musician; **–antenknochen** *m.* funny bone; **–direktor** *m.* bandmaster; conductor; **–dose** *f.* music box; **–korps** *neu.* military band; **–schule** *f.* conservatory; **–werk** *neu.* music mechanism, musical work

Musk:–at *m.* nutmeg; **–ateller** *m.* muscatel wine (*oder* grape)

Muskel *m.* muscle; **–kater** *m.* stiffness, soreness; **–schwund** *m.* muscular dystrophy; **–zerrung** *f.* sprain

Musket:–e *f.* musket; **–ier** *m.* musketeer

muskelig, muskulös *adj.* muscular; sinewy

Musse *f.* leisure; **mit –e** at one's leisure

Musselin *m.* muslin

müssen *v.* to have to, to be obliged (*oder* compelled) to; **alle Menschen — sterben** all men must die; **sie — bald kommen** they are bound to come soon; **Sie — wissen** you should know

müssig *adj.* idle, unemployed; superfluous; useless; **— gehen** to idle, to loaf

Müssiggänger *m.* idler, loafer; lazybones

Muster *neu.* design, model, pattern; sample, example, standard; specimen; **–bild** *neu.* ideal, paragon; **–knabe** *m.* model boy; prig; **–schutz** *m.* trademark; **–werk** *neu.* classical (*oder* standard) work; **–wirtschaft** *f.* model farm; **–zeichner** *m.* designer; **–zimmer** *neu.* sample (*oder* show) room

muster:–gültig *adj.* ideal, model, exemplary; standard, classical; **–haft** *adj.* and *adv.* perfectly; **–reisende(r)** *m.* traveling salesman

mustern *v.* to examine, to inspect, to review

Mut *m.* courage, boldness; valor, spirit, mood; **den — nehmen** to discourage; **den — verlieren** (*oder* **sinken lassen**) to become discouraged; **guten –es sein** to be full of hope (*oder* good cheer); **— fassen** to summon up courage; **— machen** to encourage; **–massung** *f.* surmise; suspicion; presumption

mut:–ig *adj.* fearless, brave; **–los** *adj.* discouraged; **–massen** *v.* to presume, to guess, to suppose; **–masslich** *adj.* probable, presumptive, presumable; **–willig** *adj.* playful, wanton

Mütchen *neu.* mood; **sein — kühlen** to vent one's anger (on)

Mutter *f.* mother; (mech.) nut; (zool.) dam; **–boden** *m.* native (*oder* fertile) soil; humus; **–gottesbild** *neu.* image of the Holy Virgin; **–land** *neu.* native (*oder* mother) country; **–leib** *m.* womb; **vom –leibe an** from birth on; **–mal** *neu.* birthmark, mole; **–mord** *m.* matricide; **–pferd** *neu.* mare; **–schaf** *neu.* ewe; **–schaft** *f.* maternity; **–schoss** *m.* mother's lap; **–schwein** *neu.* sow; **–söhnchen** *neu.* mother's darling; mama's boy; spoiled child; **–sprache** *f.* mother tongue

mütterlich *adj.* maternal; motherly; **–erseits** *adv.* from (*oder* on) the mother's side

mutterseelenallein *adv.* all (*oder* quite) alone

Mütze *f.* cap; **–nschirm** *m.* visor (of cap)

Myrrhe *f.* myrrh

Myrte *f.* myrtle

myst:–eriös *adj.* mysterious; **–ifizieren** *v.* to mystify, to dupe; **–isch** *adj.* mystical

Myst:–erium *neu.* mystery; **–ik** *f.,* **–izismus** *m.* mysticism

Myth:–e *f.* myth; **–ologie** *f.* mythology; **–os** *m.,* **–us** *m.* myth

myth:–enhaft *adj.,* **–isch** *adj.* mythical; **–ologisch** *adj.* mythological

N

na *interj.* now! well! **— nu?** what next?: **— und?** well, and afterward?

Nabe *f.* (mech.) nave, hub; boss

Nabel *m.* navel; **–schnur** *f.,* **–strang** *m.* umbilical cord

nach *prep.* after(wards); behind; past; according to; to(wards); along, by, from; **einer — dem anderen** one by one; **— der Reihe** in turn; **— deutchem Gelde** in German money; **— jemand ausschauen** to look out for someone; **— adv.** after, behind; **mir —I** follow me! **— und —** little by little; gradually; **— wie vor** now as before, as usual

nachäffen v. to ape, to mimic

nachahmen v. to imitate, to copy, to counterfeit; **-swert** *adj.* worthy of imitation

Nacharbeit *f.* additional (*oder* finishing) work

nacharten v. to resemble, to take after

Nachbar *m.* neighbor; **-dorf** *neu.* neighboring village; **-schaft** *f.* neighborhood; **-sleute** *pl.* neighbors; **-volk** *neu.* neighboring nation

nachbauen v. to build after (a model); to build subsequently

nachbestellen v. to repeat

nachbeten v. to pray after; (coll.) to parrot; to echo

Nachbeter *m.* blind adherent; satellite

nachbilden v. to copy, to imitate; to mold from, to counterfeit

nachbleiben v. to remain behind; to be left over; to survive; **— müssen** (school) to be kept in

Nachbleibsel *neu.* remains; rest; aftereffect

nachblicken v. to look (*oder* gaze) after

nachdatieren v. to postdate

nachdem *adv.* afterward(s); **— conj.** after, when; **je —** according to

nachdenken v. to meditate (on), to reflect

nachdenklich *adj.* thoughtful, meditative

Nachdichtung *f.* free version (*oder* limitation) of a literary work

nachdrängen v. to press (*oder* drive) after

nachdringen v. to pursue; to press after

Nachdruck *m.* stress, emphasis; reprint(ing), reproduction; pirated edition; **— verboten** copyright reserved

nachdrucken v. to reprint; **unerlaubt —** to pirate

nachdrücklich *adj.* energetic, emphatic

Nacheiferer *m.* emulator, rival

nacheilen v. to hurry after; to pursue

nacheinander *adv.* one after another; by turns; successively; **-folgend** *adj.* subsequent

nachempfinden v. to feel (for); **-d** *adj.* sympathetic, receptive

Nachen *m.* (poet.) skiff, fishing boat

nacherzählen v. to repeat; **dem Deutschen nacherzählt** adapted from the German

Nachfahr(e) *m.* descendant, successor

nachfahren v. to drive (*oder* follow) after

nachfliegen v. to fly after

Nachfolge *f.* succession; disciples; **— Christi** Imitation of Christ; **-r** *m.* successor

nachfolgen v. to follow, to succeed; **-d** *adj.* subsequent, following

nachforschen v. to investigate, to inquire (*oder* search) after

Nachfrage *f.* inquiry, request; demand

nachfragen v. to inquire after; **er fragt nicht danach** he does not care about it

nachfühlen v. to feel with, to empathize; **-d** *adj.* sympathetic

nachfüllen v. to fill up (*oder* in); to add

nachgeben v. to give way (*oder* up); to yield; **jemand nicht —** to be a match for someone

nachgeboren *adj.* younger; posthumous

Nachgebühr *f.* excess postage (*oder* fee)

Nachgeburt *f.* afterbirth

nachgeh(e)n v. to follow, to pursue; to trace; (clock) to be slow; (com.) to attend to

nachgemacht *adj.* counterfeit, imitated, sham, artificial; **-e Waren** imitation goods

nachgerade *adv.* by now, by this time; after all; gradually, by degrees

Nachgeschmack *m.* aftertaste

nachgiebig *adj.* compliant; flexible; tractable, yielding; obliging; indulgent, easygoing

nachgraben v. to dig after (*oder* for)

nachgrübeln v. to ruminate; to ponder

Nachhall *m.* echo, resonance, reverberation

nachhaltig *adj.* enduring, lasting; persistent

nachhause *adv.* homewards; **— gehen** to go home

nachhelfen v. to help; to lend a hand; to retouch; to prompt; to push forward

nachher *adv.* after that; afterwards; later; **-ig** *adj.* later, subsequent, posterior

Nachhilfe *f.* help, aid, assistance

nachholen v. to recover; to finish later

Nachhut *f.* (mil.) rear(guard)

nachjagen v. to hunt (*oder* chase) after, to pursue; **jemand eine Kugel —** to fire a shot after someone

Nachklang *m.* reverberation; resonance; reminiscence

Nachkomme *m.* descendant; **ohne -n** without issue; **-nschaft** *f.* posterity, descendants

nachkommen v. to come after, to follow; to overtake; to execute, to fulfill; **Ihrem Wunsche —** in accordance with your wishes; **seinem Versprechen —** to keep one's promise

Nachkriegszeit *f.* postwar period

Nachlass *m.* legacy, heritage; estate; (com.) reduction, discount; allowance; **-en** *neu.* remission; reduction; relaxation; diminution; ceasing; **-enschaft** *f.* estate, inheritance; **-gericht** *neu.* probate court; **-steuer** *f.* inheritance tax; **-versteigerung** *f.* auction of an estate; **-verwalter** *m.* executor

nachlassen v. to leave behind; to transmit; (com.) to reduce; to grant; to relax, to give over (*oder* up); to yield; to diminish; to cease, to slacken, to temper

nachlässig *adj.* negligent, careless; remiss

nachlaufen v. to run after

Nachlese *f.* gleaning(s); (lit.) supplement; **-n** *neu.* rereading

nachlesen v. to look up again, to reread

nachmachen v. to copy, to imitate; to mimic; to counterfeit

nachmal: **-en** v. to paint after, to copy; **-ig** adj. subsequent; **-s** adv. afterward(s)

Nachmittag m. afternoon; **-svorstellung** f. afternoon performance

nachmittägig, nachmittäglich adj. taking place (oder occurring) in the afternoon

nachmittags adv. in the afternoon

Nachnahme (per) f. cash on delivery; c.o.d.; **unter —** paid on delivery; **-gebühr** f. collection fee

nachordnen v. to rearrange

nachplappern v. to repeat by rote; to parrot

Nachporto neu. excess postage; surcharge

nachprüfen v. to verify; to check, to test

nachrechnen v. to count again; to verify figures (oder a calculation); to audit

Nachrede f. epilogue; slander, rumor: in üble — bringen to slander; **-r** m. slanderer

Nachredner m. later speaker

Nachricht f. news; information; **ausführliche —** detailed account; **-enamt** neu., **-enbüro** neu. press agency; **-endienst** m. news service; (mil.) signals; **-entechnik** f. means of communication; **-entruppen** f. pl. signal corps; **-enwesen** neu. intelligence service; **-er** m. hangman

Nachruf m. posthumous reputation; obituary notice, memorial poem (oder speech)

nachrufen v. to call after

Nachruhm m. posthumous fame

Nachsatz m. concluding sentence; postscript

nachschicken v. to forward; to send after

Nachschlag m. afterstroke; (mus.) complementary (oder grace) note; **-ebuch** neu., **-ewerk** neu. reference book, encyclopedia

nachschlagen v. to strike afterwards; to resemble; (mus.) to syncopate; to consult (book); to look up (word); to counterfeit (coins)

nachschleppen v. to drag after; (naut.) to tow

Nachschlüssel m. picklock; master key

nachschmieren v. to copy poorly; to relubricate

nachschreiben v. to copy; to plagiarize

Nachschrift f. copy; transcript; postscript; lecture notes

Nachschub m. supply; reinforcement

Nachschuss m. new (oder additional) payment

nachsehen v. to look after (oder for); to examine, to revise; to check, to look up; to see (whether); jemand etwas — to overlook (oder excuse) someone's faults

Nachsehen neu. revising, rereading; das — haben to have one's trouble for nothing; to come too late

nachsenden v. to send after, to forward; to redirect (mail); Bitte — please forward

nachsetzen v. to set behind (oder after); to pursue; to consider inferior

Nachsicht f. indulgence; forbearance; clemency; **— haben mit** to make allowances for

nachsicht: **-ig** adj. forbearing, indulgent; **-slos** adj. unrelenting, stern; **-svoll** adj. considerate; lenient, indulgent

Nachsilbe f. suffix

nachsinnen v. to muse, to meditate, to reflect

nachsitzen v. to be kept in

Nachsommer m. Indian summer

Nachspeise f. sweets, desert

Nachspiel neu. (theat.) afterpiece; epilogue; (mus.) postlude; (fig.) sequel

nachsprechen v. to repeat (someone's) words

nachspüren v. to track, to trace out; to investigate; to spy upon

nächst adj. next, nearest; shortest; closest; bei der **-en** Gelegenheit at the first opportunity; mit **-er** Post by return mail; **—** adv. next; soon; **—** prep. next to, after; **-beste** adj. second best; **-dem** adv. thereupon, soon; **-ens** adv. shortly, very soon; **-folgend** adj. next (in order); **-liegend** adj. nearest

Nächste m. (the) next; fellow man, neighbor; jeder ist sich selbst der **-e** everybody thinks first of himself; **-nliebe** f. charity

nachstehen v. to stand after; to be inferior to; wie **-d** bemerkt as mentioned below

nachstellen v. to place behind; (clock) to put back; (mech.) to adjust; to pursue

Nachstellung f. pursuit, persecution

nachstreben v. to strive after; to aspire to emulate

nachsuchen v. to search for

nachsynchronisieren v. to dub

Nacht f. night; bei **— und Nebel davongehen** to escape under cover of darkness; **mit einbrechender —** at nightfall; **über — bleiben** to stay overnight; **über — kommen** to come unexpectedly; **-essen** neu. supper; **-eule** f. screech owl; **-geschirr** neu., **-topf** m. chamber pot; **-gleiche** f. equinox; **-hemd** neu., **-kleid** neu., **-rock** m. nightshirt, nightdress; **-lager** neu. night's lodging; **-igall** f. nightingale; **-lokal** neu. night club; **-mahr** m. nightmare; **-musik** f. serenade; **-schicht** f. night shift; **-schwalbe** f. night hawk; **-schwärmer** m. moth; night reveller; **-wächter** m. watchman; **-wandler** m. sleepwalker; **-zeug** neu. nightwear

nacht: **-s** adv. at (oder by) night; **-schlafend** adj. zu **-schlafender Zeit** when everyone sleeps; **-wandlerisch** adj. somnambulistic; **mit -wandlerischer Sicherheit** with absolute certainty

nächt: **-elang** adv. for nights; **-igen** v. to pass the night; **-lich** adj. nightly, nocturnal; **-licherweise** adv. at night time

Nachteil m. disadvantage, prejudice, detriment; im **— sein** to be at a disadvantage

nachteilig *adj.* detrimental, disadvantageous; prejudicial; disparaging; derogatory

Nachtisch *m.* dessert

Nachtrag *m.* supplement; codicil; postscript

nachtragen *v.* to carry after; to add; to bear a grudge; **-d** *adj.* resentful, vindictive

nachträglich *adj.* additional, supplementary; subsequent, further, later

nachtun *v.* to imitate; to emulate; **es jemandem — wollen** to try to compete

nachwachsen to grow again (*oder* up)

nachweinen *v.* to mourn; to bewail, to lament

Nachweis *m.* proof, evidence; agency

nachweisbar, nachweislich *adj.* traceable, demonstrable; evident, authentic

Nachwelt *f.* posterity; future generations

Nachwirkung *f.* after-effect, consequence

Nachwort *neu.* epilogue; concluding remarks

Nachwuchs *m.* aftergrowth; (fig.) new blood

nachzahlen *v.* to pay extra (*oder* additionally)

nachzählen *v.* to recount; to count one's change

nachzeichnen *v.* to draw from, to copy

nachziehen *v.* to drag along, to pencil (eyebrow); to follow

Nachzügler *m.* straggler

Nacken *m.* (nape of) neck; **jemand auf dem — sitzen** to harass someone; **jemand den — beugen** to curb someone's wilfulness; **-schlag** *m.* blow from behind; mischief

nackend, nackt *adj.* naked, nude; bare; plain

Nadel *f.* needle; pin; **wie auf -n sitzen** to be on pins and needles; **-arbeit** *f.* needlework; **-baum** *m.*, **-holz** *neu.* conifer; **-geld** *neu.* pin money; **-kissen** *neu.* pincushion; **-kopf** *m.* pinhead; **-öhr** *neu.* eye of a needle; **-stich** *m.* stitch, prick; pinprick

Nagel *m.* nail; peg; stud; spike; tack; **an den — hängen** to give up; **auf den Nägeln brennen** to be urgent; **-bürste** *f.* nailbrush; **-kuppe** *f.* nailhead; **-pflege** *f.* manicure; **-schmied** *m.* nail maker

nageln *v.* to nail, to spike

nagelneu *adj.* brand-new

nagen *v.* to gnaw, to nibble; to corrode

Nager *m.*, **Nagetier** *neu.* gnawer, rodent

nah *adj.*, **-e** *adj.* near, close; imminent; approaching; **-e** *adv.* nearby; **-egehen** *v.* to affect, to grieve; **-ekommen** *v.* to come near; to get at; **-elegen** to suggest, to urge; **-eliegen** *v.* to be obvious; **-en** *v.* to approach, to draw near; **-estehen** *v.* to be closely connected; **-etreten** *v.* to come near; **jemandem -etreten** to hurt someone's feelings; **-ezu** *adv.* almost

Nah: -aufnahme *f.* close-up; **-kampf** *m.* close fight; **-verkehr** *m.* local traffic

Näh: -e *f.* nearness, proximity, vicinity; **in der -e** at hand, close by; **-ere** *neu.* particulars, details

Näh: -erei *f.* needlewor·, sewing; **-garn** *neu.* sewing cotton; **-korb** *m.* sewing basket; **-maschine** *f.* sewing machine; **-nadel** *f.* sewing needle; **-zeug** *neu.* sewing implements

nähen *v.* to sew, to stitch; to suture

näher *adj.* nearer, closer; intimate, detailed; **-n** *v.* to bring (*oder* place) near; to approach

Nähr: -boden *m.* nurturing soil; culture medium; **-kraft** *f.* nutritive power; **-präparat** *neu.* patent food; **-wert** *m.* nutritive value; **-stand** *m.* (the) farmers

nähren *v.* to feed, to nurse; to suckle; to nourish, to entertain; **sich — von** to live (*oder* maintain oneself) on

nahrhaft *adj.* nourishing, nutritious, nutritive, substantial; lucrative

Nahrung *f.* food, nourishment; **-smangel** *m.* want of nourishment; **-smittel** *neu. pl.* provisions, food(stuff); victuals; **-s(mittel)sorgen** *f. pl.* cares of subsistence, struggle for livelihood

Naht *f.* seam; (med.) suture

naiv *adj.* naïve, harmless, ingenuous, artless

Name *m.* name; reputation; **auf meinen -n** on my account; **jemand dem -n nach kennen** to know someone by name; **wie war doch Ihr —?** may I ask your name? **-saufruf** *m.* roll call; **-ngebung** *f.* naming; christening; **-nliste** *f.*, **-nverzeichnis** *neu.* list of names, nomenclature; **-nsvetter** *m.* namesake; **-nszug** *m.* signature

namhaft *adj.* renowned, notable; considerable; **— machen** to name; to specify

nämlich *adj.* same, very; **— ** *adv.* namely

Napf *m.* bowl, basin; **-kuchen** *m.* pound-cake

Narbe *f.* scar, cicatrice; grain; (bot.) stigma

narbig *adj.* scarred, grained

Narkose *f.* narcosis, anaesthesia

narkotisieren *v.* to narcotize, to anaesthetize

Narr *m.* fool, buffoon; **einen -en fressen an** to take a great fancy to; **zum -en machen** (*oder* **halten**) to dupe; **-enfreiheit** *f.* liberty at carnival; riotous merrymaking; **-enhaus** *neu.* madhouse; **-enkappe** *f.* fool's cap; **-enpossen** *f. pl.*, **-enstreich** *m.* tomfoolery; foolish trick; **-etei** *f.* folly; **-heit** *f.* craziness

närrisch *adj.* foolish; mad, odd, strange

Narzisse *f.* narcissus; **gelbe —** daffodil

Nasch: -erei *f.*, **-werk** *neu.* dainties, sweets; **-katze** *f.* sweet tooth

naschen *v.* to eat sweets on the sly; to have a sweet tooth

Nase *f.* nose; snout; (dog) scent; (coll.) rebuke; **auf der — liegen** (coll.) to be ill (*oder* in trouble); **das sticht ihm in die —** he covets that; **die — rümpfen** to sneer; to fool; **etwas an der — ansehen** to see at a glance; **immer der — nach** follow your nose; straight on; **jemand auf der — herumtanzen** to

make a fool of someone; **unter die —
reiben** (coll.) to rub it in; **–nbein** *neu.*
nasal bone; **–nbluten** *neu.* nosebleed;
–loch *neu.* nostril; **–rücken** *m.* bridge
(of nose)

naseweis *adj.* saucy, pert, cheeky

nasführen *v.* to fool, to trick, to dupe

Nashorn *neu.* rhinoceros

nass *adj.* wet, damp, moisty, rainy;
–auern *v.* (coll.) to sponge; to cadge

Nass *neu.* liquid; (coll.) water; rain; drink

Nässe *f.* wetness, humidity, dampness

nässen *v.* to moisten, to wet

Nation *f.* nation; **–alfarben** *f. pl.*, **–al-
flagge** *f.* national colors (*oder* flag);
–alhymne *f.* national anthem; **–alöko-
nomie** *f.* political economy; **–ialität** *f.*
nationality

national *adj.* national; **–isieren** *v.* to
nationalize

Natter *f.* viper, adder

Natur *f.* nature; constitution; temper-
(ament); **in —** in kind; **von — aus** by
nature; **wider die —** against the grain;
–anlage *f.* disposition; **–bursche** *m.*
child of nature, unceremonious fellow;
–dichter *m.* self-taught poet; **–ell** *neu.*
temper, nature; **–erscheinung** *f.* phenomenon; **–forscher** *m.* investigator of
nature; **–gabe** *f.* gift of nature, talent;
–geschichte *f.* natural history; **–kraft**
f. power of nature; **–kunde** *f.* natural
science; **–recht** *neu.* natural right;
–reich *neu.* kingdom of nature; **–trieb**
m. instinct; **–volk** *neu.* primitive race;
–wissenschaften *f. pl.* natural sciences

Natural: –ien *f. pl.* products of nature;
natural history specimen; victuals;
–ienkabinett *neu.*, **–iensammlung** *f.*
natural history collection; **–ist** *m.*
naturalist; **–leistung** *f.* payment in kind

natürlich *adj.* natural; innate, genuine;
simple; **–es Kind** illegitimate child; **—**
adv., **–erweise** *adv.* of course, certainly,
naturally

Navigationsraum *m.* chartroom

n. Chr. *abbr.* **nach Christus** A.D., after
Christ

Nebel *m.* fog, haze, mist; **künstlicher —**
smoke screen; **–fleck** *m.* (ast.) nebula;
–horn *neu.* foghorn; **–mond** *m.*, **–monat**
m., **–ung** *m.* (lit.) November; **–schwaden** *m. pl.* damp fog

nebel: –haft *adj.* hazy; nebulous, **–ig**,
neblig *adj.* foggy, hazy, misty; damp;
–n *v.* to be foggy

neben *adv.* and *prep.* beside, near, close
to; alongside; besides, in addition to;
–an *adv.* close by, next door; **–bei** *adv.*,
–her *adv.*, **–hin** *adv.* adjoining, alongside; by the way, incidentally; moreover; **–einander** *adv.* side by side;
–sächlich *adj.* subordinate, unimportant, incidental

Neben: –absicht *f.* secondary objective;
–anschluss *m.* (elec.) shunt; (tel.) extension; **–arbeit** *f.* extra work; **–ausgang**
m. side exit; **–bedeutung** *f.* secondary
meaning; **–beruf** *m.* additional occupation, sideline; **–beschäftigung** *f.* avoca-

tion; **–buhler** *m.* competitor, rival;
–eingang *m.* side entrance; **–einkünfte**
pl., **–einnahmen** *f. pl.* additional income, perquisites; **–fluss** *m.* tributary;
–gebäude *neu.* lean-to, annex; **–geleis**
neu. sidetrack; **–handlung** *f.* episode;
byplay; **–kosten** *pl.* incidental costs,
extras; **–mann** *m.* next man; **–mensch**
m. fellow creature; **–person** *f.* (theat.)
subordinate character; **–produkt** *neu.*
by-product; **–rolle** *f.* subordinate part;
–sache *f.* side issue; **–satz** *m.* (gram.)
subordinate clause; **–strasse** *f.* by-
street; **–tisch** *m.* sidetable

nebst *prep.* together (*oder* along) with;
besides; in addition, including

necken *v.* to tease, to banter, to fool

Neckerei *f.* teasing, banter, raillery

Neffe *m.* nephew

Neger *m.* Negro; **–in** *f.* Negress

nehmen *v.* to take; to accept, to receive;
to appropriate; to remove; to seize;
aufs Korn — to take aim at; **die Folgen
auf sich —** to bear the consequences;
ein Ende — to come to an end; **es
genau —** to be pedantic; **es sich nicht
— lassen** to insist on; **etwas zu sich
—** to eat something; **jemand beim
Wort —** to take someone at his word;
jemand gefangen — to capture someone; **— wir den Fall** let us suppose;
Partei — to side with; **streng genommen** strictly speaking; **Urlaub —** to
take a vacation; to go on furlough; **wie
man's nimmt** according to the way you
take it; **zur Ehe —** to marry

Neid *m.* envy; jealousy; grudge; **–er** *m.*,
–hammel *m.* envious person; grudger

neidisch *adj.* envious, jealous

Neig: –e *f.* slope; remainder; dregs, heel-
tap; **auf die** (*or* **zur**) **–egeh(e)n** to
decline, to run short; to come to an
end; **–ung** *f.* declivity, inclination,
tendency; taste; **–ungsehe** *f.* love match

neigen *v.* to bend, to bow; to incline, to
slope; to lower, to dip

nein *adv.* no

Nekro: –log *m.* necrology; **–manie** *f.*
necromancy

Nelke *f.* carnation, pink; clove

nenn: –bar *adj.* mentionable; **–en** *v.* to
name, to call, to enter; to term; to
mention; **–enswert** *adj.* worth mentioning

Nenn: –er *m.* denominator; **–ung** *f.* naming; nomination; entry; **–wert** *m.* nominal value; **zum –wert** (com.) at par;
–wort *neu.* noun

Nerv *m.* nerve; **auf die –en fallen** (*or*
gehen) to drive one mad; **–enentzün-
dung** *f.* neuritis; **–enheilanstalt** *f.*
mental hospital; **–enkrankheit** *f.* neurosis; **–enkunde** *f.*, **–enlehre** *f.* neurol-
ogy; **–enschmerz** *m.* neuralgia; **–ensystem** *neu.* nervous system; **–enzelle** *f.*
neuron; **–osität** *f.* nervousness

nerv: –enkrank *adj.* neurotic ; **–ig** *adj.*
nervy; pithy; sinewy; **–ös** *adv.* nervous

Nerz *m.* mink

Nessel *f.* nettle; **–tuch** *neu.* unbleached

muslin (*oder* calico)

Nest *neu.* nest; aerie, eyrie; (coll.) small town; **–häkchen** *neu.* nestling

nett *adj.* nice, pretty, kind

netto *adj.* net

Nettogehalt *neu.* take-home pay

Netz *neu.* net(work), trap; **in seine –e ziehen** to ensnare, to fascinate; **seine –e auswerfen** to allure, to entice; **–hemd** *neu.* mesh shirt; **–werk** *neu.* network

neu *adj.* new, fresh; recent, modern; **aufs –e, von –em** anew, again; **die –e Mode** latest fashion; **–ere Sprachen** modern languages; **–ste Nachrichten** late news; **–(ge)backen** *adj.* just baked; **–erdings** *adv.* recently, lately; **–erlich** *adj.* anew, late; **–gemacht** *adj.* renovated; **–gestalten** to reorganize; **–gierig** *adj.* curious, inquisitive; **–lich** *adv.* recently; **–modisch** *adj.* fashionable; **–vermählt** just married; **–zeitlich** *adj.* modern

Neu: **–angeworbene** *m.* fresh recruit; **–anschaffung** *f.* new purchase; **–auflage** *f.* new edition; **–bau** *m.* new construction; rebuilding; **–bearbeitung** *f.* revised version; **–druck** *m.* reprint; **–(e)rer** *m.* innovator; **–(e)rung** *f.* innovation, reform; **–gestaltung** *f.* reorganization; modification; **–gier(de)** *f.* curiosity, inquisitiveness; **–heit** *f.* newness, novelty; **–igkeit** *f.* news; **–igkeitskrämer** *m.* newsmonger; **–jahrsabend** *m.* New Year's Eve; **–land** *neu.* unknown territory; new field of research; **–ling** *m.* beginner, novice; **–regelung** *f.* rearrangement; **–reiche** *m.* parvenu; newly rich; **–stadt** *f.* newest part of a city; **–vermählten** *pl.* bridal couple; **–zeit** *f.* modern times

neun *adj.* nine; **–erlei** *adj.* of nine kinds; **–fach** *adj.*, **–fältig** *adj.* ninefold; **–te** *adj.* ninth; **–zehn** *adj.* nineteen; **–zig** *adj.* ninety

Neur- **–algie** *f.* neuralgia; **–asthenie** *f.* neurasthenia; **–ose** *f.* neurosis

neutral *adj.* neutral; **–isieren** *v.* to neutralize

Neuyork *neu.* New York

nicht *adv.* not; **auch —** not even; nor; **das — no** such thing; **durchaus —** by no means; **gar —** not at all; **ganz und gar — not** in the least; **ich auch —** nor I, either; **mit –en** not at all; **— doch** certainly not; don't; **— einmal** not even; **— verantwortlich** irresponsible; **— wahr?** isn't it? **— wenig** not a little; **nur das —** anything but that; **zu –e machen** to nullify; **zu –e werden** to become spoiled; **–ig** *adj.* null, vain, void; transitory; **für –ig erklären** to annul

Nicht: **–achtung** *f.* disrespect; disregard; **–befolgung** *f.* nonobservance; **–erscheinen** *neu.* nonappearance; nonpublication; **–igkeitserklärung** *f.* annulment; **–wissen** *neu.* ignorance; **–zulassung** *f.* nonadmission

Nichte *f.* niece

nichts *pron.* nothing; **es ist — damit** there

is nothing to it; **fast gar —** hardly anything; **gar —** nothing at all; **mir —, dir —** without ado or ceremony; **so viel wie —** next to nothing; **–destominder** *adv.*, **–destoweniger** *adv.* nevertheless, notwithstanding; **–nutzig** *adj.* useless, naughty; **–sagend** *adj.* meaningless; insignificant; **–würdig** *adj.* worthless; base, contemptible

Nickel *m.* (coin) nickel; **—** *neu.* (min.) nickel

nicken *v.* to nod; (coll.) to doze, to nap

nie *adv.* never, at no time; **fast —** hardly ever

nieder *adj.* low, base, mean; inferior; **—** *adv.* down, low; **–beugen** *v.* to bend down; to discourage; **–brechen** *v.* to fall (*oder* break) down; **–deutsch** *adj.* low (*oder* North) German; **–drücken** to press down; to depress; **–fahren** to drive down; to descend; **–gedrückt** *adj.* depressed, dejected; **–geh(e)n** to go down; **–halten** *v.* to keep down; to curb, to suppress; **–holen** *v.* to haul down, to lower; **–kämpfen** *v.* to subdue, to master; **–knüppeln** *v.* to club, to bludgeon; **–kommen** *v.* to descend; to be confined; **–lassen** *v.* to let down, to lower; **sich –lassen** to settle down; to establish; (avi.) to land; to light; **–machen** *v.* to cut down, to massacre; **–metzeln** *v.* to slaughter; **–schlagen** to knock down, to fell; to calm down; to quash, to stop; (chem.) to precipitate; to discourage; **–schmettern** *v.* to dash to the ground, to crush; **–schreiben** *v.* to write down; **–trächtig** *adj.* base, vile, infamous; **–wärts** *adv.* downwards; **–werfen** to throw down, to overcome; **sich –werfen** to prostrate oneself

Nieder: **–fahrt** *f.* descent; **–fall** *m.* downfall; **–gang** *m.* decline; (ast.) setting; (mech.) downstroke; **–kunft** *f.* confinement, childbed; **–lage** *f.* (com.) branch establishment; depot; (act of) depositing; defeat; **–schlag** *m.* sediment; (chem.) knockout blow; rain; result; (radioaktiv) fallout; **–schrift** *f.* writing; copy; **–tracht** *f.* baseness, infamy; **–ung** *f.* lowland, plain; **–werfung** *f.* overthrow, suppression

Niederlande *pl.* Netherlands

niedlich *adj.* pretty, neat, nice

Niednagel *m.* hangnail

niedrig *adj.* low, humble, inferior; base, mean

niemals *adv.* never, at no time

niemand *pron.* no one, nobody

Niere *f.* kidney

nieseln *v.* to drizzle

niesen *v.* to sneeze

Niet *m.* and *neu.* rivet

nieten *v.* to rivet

Nihilismus *m.* nihilism

Nikotin *neu.* nicotine

Nilpferd *neu.* hippopotamus

Nimbus *m.* nimbus; prestige

nimmer *adv.* never; **–mehr** *adv.* nevermore; **–satt** *adj.* insatiable

Nimmersatt m. glutton
Nippel m. nipple
nippen v. to sip
Nippesachen f. pl. knickknacks, gimcracks, gewgaws
nirgend(s) adv. nowhere
Nische f. niche
nisten v. to (build a) nest
Nitrat neu. nitrate
Niveau neu. level, standard
nivellieren v. to level, to equalize
Nivellierwaage f. spirit level
Nix m. nix, water elf; **-e** f. nymph, mermaid
nobel adj. noble, generous, distinguished
noch adv. still, yet; besides, in addition; **er hat weder Geld — Freunde** he has neither money nor friends; **— am gleichen Tag** the very same day; **— dazu** in addition, into the bargain; **— einmal** once more; **— etwas** something more, anything else; **— immer still; — lange nicht** far from it; **— nichts** nothing yet; **— obendrein** over and above that; **sei es — so klein** be it ever so small; **-malig** adj. repeated; **-mal(s)** adv. again, once more
Nocke f., **Nockerl** neu. dumpling; **-n** m. cam
Nomade m. nomad
Nominalbetrag m., **Nominalwert** m. nominal value
Nonne f. nun; **-nkloster** neu. nunnery, convent
Nord m. north; (poet.) north wind; **-en** m. (the) North, northern region; **-licht** neu. northern lights, aurora borealis; **-pol** m. North Pole; **-polfahrt** f. Arctic expedition
nordisch adj. northern
nordwärts adv. northward(s)
nörgeln v. to nag, to grumble, to carp
Norm f. norm, standard; rule; criterion; **-alarbeitstag** m. ordinary workday; **-algeschwindigkeit** f. average (oder normal) speed; **-algewicht** neu. standard weight; **-alspur** f. (rail.) standard gauge; **-alzeit** f. mean time
norm: -al adj. normal, standard; **-alisieren** v. to normalize; **-en** v. to regulate, to standardize
Norwegen neu. Norway
Not f. want, need, necessity; distress; danger, emergency; misery; **aus —** from necessity; **in — geraten** to become destitute; **mit knapper — entrinnen** to have a narrow escape; **von Nöten sein** to be hard pressed; **seine liebe — haben** to have enough trouble; **zur — at** the worst; **-anker** m. sheet (oder spare) anchor; **-ausgang** m. emergency exit; **-ausstieg** m. (bemannte Rakete) escape hatch; **-behelf** m. makeshift; stopgap; expedient; last resource; **-bremse** f. emergency brake; **-fall** m. emergency; **-kapsel** f. (aerospace) escape capsule; **-lage** f. calamity; **-landung** f. (avi.) forced landing; **-leine** f. (rail.) communication cord; **-lüge** f. white lie; **-pfennig** m. savings; **-ruf** m., **-schrei**

m. cry of distress; **-signal** neu. signal of distress; danger signal; **-stand** m. critical state, urgent case; **-standsarbeiten** f. pl. relief work; **-tür** f. fire escape; **-verband** m. temporary dressing; **-wehr** f. self-defense; **-zucht** f. rape
not: -dürftig adj. needy, makeshift; **-gedrungen** adj. compulsory, forced; **-landen** (avi.) to make a forced landing; **-leidend** adj. poor, distressed; **-wendig** adj. necessary, urgent, indispensable; **-züchtigen** v. to rape
Nota f. memorandum, bill; **-blen** m. pl. notabilities; **-r** m. notary; **-riat** neu. notary's office
Note f. note; annotation; bank note; memorandum; (pol.) communique; **nach -n** thoroughly; **nach -n singen** to sing at sight; **-nausgabe** f. issue of bank notes; **-nbank** f. issuing bank; **-nblatt** neu. sheet of music; **-nbuch** neu. music book; **-nhalter** m., **-nständer** m. music stand; **-nschlüssel** m. clef; **-nsystem** neu. staff
notieren v. to note, to book, to score
Notierung f. quotation, notation, entry
nötig adj. necessary, required, indispensable; **— haben** to need; **-en** v. to compel, to force, to urge; to invite; **sich -en lassen** to need pressing; **-enfalls** adv. if need be
Notiz f. notice, note, memorandum; **-block** m. scratch pad; **-buch** neu. notebook
Notturno, Nokturno neu. nocturne
Novelle f. short story; supplementary law
November m. November
Novität f. novelty
Novize m. and f. novice
Nu m. and neu. moment; **im — in** an instant, in no time
nüchtern adj. sober, dry; prosy; insipid
Nudel f. noodle; **komische — (sl.) funny** fellow; **-holz** neu. rolling pin
Null f. zero, nought; **-punkt** m. zero
numerieren v. to number; **numerierter Platz** reserved seat
Nummer f. number; copy, issue; size; ticket; **auf — Sicher bringen** (coll.) to save; to put in jail; **eine grosse — sein** (coll.) to be influential; **-nfolge** f. numerical order; **-nscheibe** (tel.) dial; **-nschild** neu. license plate
nun adv. now, then; henceforth; **-! interj.** well! **— und nimmermehr** never; **-mehr** adv. now, by this time, since then; **-mehrig** adj. actual, present
nur adv. only, solely, merely; but, except; just; **Du weisst — zu gut** you know well enough; **— etwa** only about; **— mehr, — noch** only just; **— weiter!** to go on! **wenn — provided that; wer — immer** whoever
Nürnberg neu. Nuremberg
Nuss f. nut; (mech.) tumbler; **-kern** m. kernel (of nut); **-knacker** m. nutcracker; **-schale** f. nutshell
Nüstern f. pl. nostrils
nutz, nütze adj. useful; **zu nichts — quite useless; good for nothing; zu -e machen**

to utilize; **-bar** *adj.* useful; **-bringend**
adj. profitable; **-en** *r.* to serve, to be
of use; to make use of; **-los** *adj.* unprofitable, useless; **-niessen** *v.* to enjoy
the profits

Nutz: -anwendung *f.* practical application; **-barmachung** *f.* utilization; **-en**
m. use, profit, advantage; utility;
-garten *m.* kitchen garden; **-holz** *neu.*
timber; **-last** *f.* payload; **-ung** *f.* produce, yield, revenue

nützen *v.* to be of use; to utilize, to serve

nützlich *adj.* useful; of use, advantageous

Nymphe *f.* nymph

O

o! *interj.* oh! ah! — **weh!** oh dear!

Oase *f.* oasis

ob *conj.* whether, if; **na —!** rather! I
should say so! — *prep.* on account of;
above; **-gleich** *conj.*, **-schon** *conj.*,
-zwar *conj.* although

Ob: -acht *f.* care, attention; **-acht geben**
to pay attention; **-dach** *neu.* shelter;
-dachlose *m.* homeless person; **-dach-
losenheim** *neu.* house of refuge; **-hut**
f. guardianship, protection, care; **-lie-
genheit** *f.* incumbency, duty; **-mann**
m. chairman; foreman

Obduktion *f.* autopsy

oben *adv.* above, aloft, on high, on top,
overhead, upstairs; on the surface; **da**
(*or* **dort**) — up there; nach — upwards;
von — bis unten from top to bottom;
weiter — further (*oder* higher) up; **wie
—erwähnt** as mentioned above; **-an**
adv. at the top, in the first place; **-auf**
adv. on top of; uppermost; on the surface; **-auf sein** to be in great form;
-drein *adv.* over and above, into the
bargain; **-erwähnt** *adj.*, **-genannt** *adj.*
above-mentioned; **-hin** *adv.* superfi-
cially, perfunctorily; **-hinaus** *adv.*
ambitiously

ober *adj.* upper, higher, superior; leading;
-faul *adj.* very lazy; bad (excuse);
-flächlich *adj.* superficial, shallow;
-halb *adv.* and *prep.* above; **-irdisch**
adj. above ground, overhead; **-lastig**
adj. topheavy; **-st** *adj.* topmost, highest, supreme; first; head

Ober *m.* waiter; (cards) knave; **-appella-
tionsgericht** *neu.* High Court of Appeal;
-arm *m.* upper arm; **-arzt** *m.* head
physician; **-aufsicht** *f.* superintendence;
-bau *m.* superstructure; **-befehl** *m.*
supreme command; **-befehlshaber** *m.*
commander-in-chief; **-bett** *neu.* coverlet; **-bürgermeister** *m.* Lord Mayor;
-deck *neu.* (naut.) upperdeck; **-e** *m.*
(eccl.) Father Superior; **-fläche** *f.* surface, area; **-gericht** *neu.* superior court;
-geschoss *neu.* upper story; **-gewalt** *f.*
supreme authority; **-hand** *f.* upper
hand; predominance; **-haupt** *neu.* chief,
head, sovereign; leader; **-haus** *neu.*
upper house, Senate; House of Lords;
-haut *f.* epidermis; **-hemd** *neu.* shirt;
-herrschaft *f.* supremacy; **-in** *f.* (eccl.)

Mother Superior; **-kiefer** *m.* upper jaw;
-kellner *m.* headwaiter; **-kommando**
neu. supreme command; **-körper** *m.*
upper part of the body, torso; **-land**
neu. upland, upper country; **-landes-
gericht** *neu.* Supreme Court of the
country; **-leder** *neu.* uppers; **-lehrer** *m.*
headmaster; **-leitung** *f.* top management; (elec.) overhead conveyor system; **-leutnant** *m.* first lieutenant;
-licht *neu.* skylight; **-priester** *m.* high
priest; **-quartiermeister** *m.* quartermaster general; **-rock** *m.* overcoat; **-s**
neu. (dial.) whipped cream; **-schicht** *f.*
upper classes; **-st** *m.* colonel; **-schwes-
ter** *f.* head nurse; **-staatsanwalt** *m.*
attorney general; **-steiger** *m.* (min.)
foreman; **-stimme** *f.* treble, soprano;
-stube *f.* attic, garret; **-stleutnant** *m.*
lieutenant colonel; **-stufe** *f.* upper
grade; **-wasser haben** to have the upper
hand

obig *adj.* above(-mentioned), foregoing

Objekt *neu.* object; **-iv** *neu.* lens; **-ivität**
f. objectivity

Oblate *f.* wafer; (eccl.) host

obligat *adj.* indispensable, necessary;
-orisch *adj.* obligatory, compulsory

Obrigkeit *f.* authorities, government

obrigkeitlich *adj.* official, governmental,
magisterial; — *adv.* by authority

Observatorium *neu.* observatory

Obst *neu.* fruit(s); **-garten** *m.* orchard;
-kelter *f.* fruit press

obszön *adj.* obscene

Ochse *m.* ox, bullock; (sl.) blockhead;
-nbraten *m.* roast beef; **-ngespann** *neu.*
ox team; **-nschwanzsuppe** *f.* oxtail
soup; **-nziemer** *m.* horsewhip

öde *adj.* bare, bleak, deserted, desolate;
dreary, dull

Öde *f.* desert, desolation; solitude

Odem *m.* (poet.) breath

oder *conj.* or; or else; — **aber** or instead

Ofen *m.* furnace, stove, oven; **-hocke**
m. stay-at-home; **-klappe** *f.* damper
-loch *neu.* oven mouth; **-rohr** *neu.*
-röhre *f.* stovepipe; **-schirm** *m.* fir
screen; **-setzer** *m.* stovemaker; **-vor**
setzer *m.* fender

offen *adj.* open, frank, vacant; public
candid, severe; **auf -er Strecke** on th
open road; **frei und** — **handeln** to act
straightforwardly; **-e Rechnung** (com.
current account; **-e See** high sea; **-e**
Kredit unlimited credit; — **gesagt**, —
gestanden frankly speaking; — **lasse**
to leave blank; **-bar** *adj.* obvious, mani
fest, evident; **-baren** *v.* to disclose, t
reveal, to manifest; **-halten** *v.* to re
serve; **-herzig** *adj.* openhearted; frank
-kundig *adj.* notorious; public; —
Handlung overt act; **-sichtlich** *adj*
apparent; **-stehen** *v.* to stand open; t
remain unpaid; to be at liberty to

öffentlich *adj.* public

Öffentlichkeit *f.* publicity, (the) publi

Offerte *f.* offer, proposal, tender

Offizier *m.* officer; **-smesse** *f.* (naut.
wardroom; **-spatent** *neu.* officer's com

mission

öffnen r. to open, to uncork; (med.) to dissect

Öffnung f. opening, aperture, hole; mouth; gap, slit, slot; dissection

öfter adj. repeated, more frequent; —s adr., des —en adr. frequently, now and then

oft(mals) adv. frequently, often

Oheim, Ohm m. uncle

ohne prep. without, but for, except; nicht — not so bad; — weiteres without much ado; —dem adv., —dies adv.. —hin adr. anyhow; besides; —gleichen adj. unequalled, unparalled

Ohnmacht f. powerlessness, weakness; faint, unconsciousness; —sanfall m. fainting spell

ohnmächtig adj. helpless, powerless. unconscious; — werden to faint

Ohr neu. ear; bis über beide —en (coll.) up to the eyes; die —en spitzen (coll.) to listen attentively; die —en steif halten (coll.) to keep a stiff upper lip; ein geneigtes — finden to get a favorable hearing; eins übers — bekommen to get one's ears boxed; er hat es dick hinter den —en he is a sly fellow; jemand das Fell über die —en ziehen to fleece someone; jemand übers —hauen (coll.) to cheat someone; mir klingen die —en my ears are ringing; someone is talking about me; sich aufs — legen to take a nap; sich etwas hinter die —en schreiben (coll.) to note well; —enarzt m. ear specialist, otologist; —enbläser m. flatterer, slanderer; —enklingen neu., —sausen neu. ringing in the ear; —enschmalz neu. ear wax; —enschmaus m. musical treat; —schützer m., —enwärmer m., —klappe f. earflap; —feige f. box on the ear; —gehänge neu., —ring m. earring

Öhr neu. (needle) eye

ohrenzerreissend adj. earsplitting

Ökonom m. farmer, steward. housekeeper; —ie f. economy, economics, housekeeping; agriculture

ökonomisch adj. economic(al)

oktroyieren v. to impose, to dictate

Okular neu. eyepiece

okulieren v. to inoculate; to graft

Okzident m. occident

Öl neu. oil; — auf die Wogen giessen (coll.) to pacify; — ins Feuer giessen (coll.) to add fuel to the fire; —baum m. olive tree; —berg m. (bibl.) Mount of Olives; —bild neu. oil painting; —kanne f. oilcan, oiler; —kuchen m. oilcake; —ung f. oiling, lubrication; anointment; letzte —ung extreme unction; —zweig m. olive branch

ölen r. to oil, to lubricate, to anoint; wie geölt as if oiled; very fast, very easily

ölig adj. oily; unctuous

Olive f. olive

Olympiade f., olympischen Spiele neu. pl. Olympiad; Olympic games

ominös adj. ominous

ondulieren v. to wave (hair)

Onkel m. uncle

Oper f. opera; opera house; —ette f. operetta; —nglas neu., —gucker m. opera glasses; —ntext m. libretto

oper: —ativ adj. operatic; —ieren v. to operate (on); —nhaft adj. in operatic style

Opera: —teur m. operator; operating surgeon; —tion f. operation; —tionsgebiet neu. (mil.) theater of operations

Opfer neu. sacrifice, oblation; victim; casualty; —gabe f. offering; —kasten m.. —stock m. poor box; —lamm neu. sacrificial lamb; victim; —tod m. sacrifice of one's life; —trank m. libation; —ung f. sacrifice, sacrificing

opfer: —n r. to sacrifice, to immolate; —willig adj. —freudig adj. self-sacrificing

opponieren r. to oppose

Opt: —ik f. optics; —iker m. optician

optieren r. to choose

Optimismus m. optimism

optisch adj. optic(al)

Orakel neu. oracle

Orange f. orange; —nschale f. orange peel

oratorisch adj. oratoric(al)

Oratorium neu. oratory

orchestrieren v. to orchestrate

Orchidee f. orchid

Orden m. order, decoration, medal; —sbruder m. member of an order; friar, monk; —sgeistlichkeit f. regular clergy; —skleid neu. monastic garb; —sschwester f. nun; —szeichen neu. badge, order

ordentlich adj. orderly, regular; tidy, decent; respectable; good, sound; — adv. fairly, downright

ordin: —är adj. common, ordinary; low, vulgar; —ieren v. to ordain

Ordinarius m. professor in ordinary, headmaster

ordnen v. to put in order, to arrange, to classify; to regulate

Ordnung f. arrangement, regulation; order; tidiness; class; classification; der — nach in due order; —sruf m. (pol.) call to order; —sstrafe f. fine; —szahl f. ordinal number

ordnungs: —gemäss adj., —mässig adj. orderly, regular, lawful; —liebend adj. order-loving; —swidrig adj. contrary to order; illegal

Ordonnanz f. (mil.) orderly; order

Organ neu. organ; official voice (oder publication); —isation f. organization; —isator m. organizer; —ismus m. organism; —ist m. organist

organisch adj. organic

organisieren v. to organize

Orgel f. organ; —pfeife f. organ pipe

Orgie f. orgy

Orient m. orient; —ierung f. orientation; information; —ierungssinn m. sense of direction

orientalisch adj. oriental

orientieren v. to orient(ate), to locate, to inform

Original neu. original; —handschrift f. autograph; —ität f. originality, peculiarity originell *adj.* original, peculiar

Orkan *m.* hurricane, typhoon

Ornat *m.* official robes

Ornithologe *m.* ornithologist

Ort *m.* place, spot, locality; (mil.) termination; **am unrechten — ** out of place; **an — und Stelle gelangen** to arrive at one's destination; **–sbehörde** *f.* local authorities; **–sbeschreibung** *f.* topography; **–sbestimmungswort** *neu.* local option; **–schaft** *f.* village, place; **–sgespräch** *neu.* (tel.) local call; **–skenntnisse** *f. pl.* local knowledge, familiarity with a place; **–ssinn** *m.* sense of location; **–sveränderung** *f.* change of location; **–svorsteher** *m.* village magistrate; **–szeit** *f.* local time

Ortho: **–doxie** *f.* orthodoxy; **–graphie** *f.* orthography; **–pädie** *f.* orthopedics, orthopedy

ortho: **–dox** *adj.* orthodox; **–graphisch** *adj.* orthographic; **–pädisch** *adj.* orthopedic

örtlich *adj.* local

Öse *f.* loop, ring; (hook) eye; (shoe) eyelet

Ost *m.* east; (poet.) east wind; **–en** *m.* east; Orient

ostentativ *adj.* ostentatious

Oster: **–fest** *neu.*, **–n** *neu.* Easter; Passover; **–hase** *m.* Easter bunny; **–lamm** *neu.* Paschal lamb; **–mond** *m.* (poet.) April

Österreich *neu.* Austria

östlich *adj.* eastern, easterly, Oriental

Ostsee *f.* Baltic Sea

Otter *m.* otter; **— ** *f.* adder

Ouvertüre *f.* overture

oval *adj.* oval

oxidieren *v.* to oxidize

Oxyd *neu.* oxide; **–dation** *f.*, **–ierung** *f.* oxidation; rusting

Ozean *m.* ocean; **–flieger** *m.* transocean airman

Ozon *neu.* ozone

P

p.A. *abbr.* per Adresse c/o, care of

Paar *neu.* pair, couple; brace

paar *adj.* some, few; even, like, matching; in pairs; **— oder unpaar** even or odd; **–en** *v.* to pair; to mate, to couple, to copulate; **–ig** *adj.* in pairs; **–mal** *adv.* **ein –mal** several times; **–weise** *adr.* in pairs, two by two

Pacht *f.* tenure, lease, rent; **–ertrag** *m.* rental; **–kontrakt** *m.*, **–vertrag** *m.* lease; **–zeit** *f.* term of lease; **–zins** *m.* rent

pachten *v.* to lease, to rent, to farm; (coll.) to monopolize

Pächter *m.* leaseholder, tenant, tenant farmer

pachtweise *adv.* on lease

Pack *m.* package, bundle, pile; **mit Sack und — ** with bag and baggage; **— ** *neu.* rabble; **–eis** *neu.* pack ice; **–en** *m.* bale; **–er** *m.* packer; **–erei** *f.* packing; **–esel** *m.* pack mule; **–hof** *m.* bonded warehouse; **–papier** *neu.* packing paper; **–raum** *m.* packing (*oder* stowage) room;

–ung *f.* pack(ing); wrappings; **–wagen** *m.* baggage car

Päckchen *neu.* small parcel

packen *v.* to pack; to grasp, to seize; to grip; to fascinate, to thrill; **sich — ** (coll.) to be gone, to clear out

Pädagoge *m.* pedagogue

Pädagogik *f.* pedagogy

paddeln *v.* to paddle, to canoe

Page *m.* page; **–nkopf** *m.* bobbed hair

paginieren *v.* to page, to paginate

Pagode *f.* pagoda

Pair *m.* peer; **–swürde** *f.* peerage

Paket *neu.* parcel, package; **–ausgabe** *f.* parcel delivery; **–boot** *neu.* (naut.) packet; **–karte** *f.* dispatch note; **–post** *f.* parcel post

Pakt *m.* pact, agreement

Palast *m.* palace

palastartig *adj.* palatial

Paletot *m.* (man's) overcoat

Palm: **–e** *f.* (bot.) palm; **–in** *neu.* coconut butter; **–wedel** *m.* palm branch

Pampelmuse *f.* grapefruit

Pamphlet *neu.* pamphlet; lampoon

Paneel *neu.* panel; wainscot

Panier *neu.* banner, standard

panieren *v.* to dress with breadcrumbs, to bread

panisch *adj.* panic

Panne *f.* breakdown; puncture; mishap

Panoptikum *neu.* waxwork exhibition

Pantine *f.* clog, patten

Pantoffel *m.* slipper; **unter dem — steh(e)n** to be henpecked; **–blume** *f.* slipperwort; **–held** *m.* henpecked husband

Panzer *m.* armor; coat of mail; (mil.) tank; **–abwehr** *f.* antitank defense; **–auto** *neu.* armored car; **–faust** *f.* mailed fist; an' tank hand grenade; **–granate** *f.* ant. tank grenade; **–handschuh** *m.* gauntlet; **–hemd** *neu.* shirt of mail; **–jäger** *m. pl.* antitank troops; **–kreuzer** *m.* battle cruiser; **–platte** *f.* armor plate; **–regiment** *neu.* tank regiment; **–schiff** *neu.* ironclad; **–tür** (luftdrucksichere, army) *f.* bulkhead; **–wagen** *m.* tank; **–zug** *m.* armored train

Papagei *m.* parrot; **–enkrankheit** *f.* psittacosis

Papier *neu.* paper; (com.) securities, bonds; **–e** *pl.* identification papers; **das steht nur auf dem — ** it means nothing; **zu — bringen** to put on paper, to write down; **–abfälle** *m. pl.* wastepaper; **–bogen** *m.* sheet of paper; **–brei** *m.* paper pulp; **–fabrik** *f.* paper mill; **–format** *neu.* size of paper; **–geld** *neu.* paper money; **–handlung** *f.* stationery store; **–korb** *m.* wastebasket; **–waren** *f. pl.* stationery

Papp *m.* pap; (coll.) paste; **–band** *m.* pasteboard binding; **–e** *f.* cardboard, pasteboard; **nicht von –e** (coll.) thorough, sound, remarkable; **–enstiel** *m.* trifle; **um einen –enstiel** dirt cheap

Pappel *f.* poplar

Papst *m.* pope; **–tum** *neu.* papacy; pontificate

päpstlich *adj.* papal
Parabel *f.* parable; parabola
Parade *f.* parade; (mil.) review; parry;
 -bett *neu.* bed of state; **-platz** *m.* parade
 ground; **-schritt** *m.* goose step
paradieren *v.* to parade
Paradies *neu.* paradise
paradiesisch *adj.* paradisiac(al); heavenly
paradox *adj.* paradoxical
paralisieren *v.* to paralyze
parallel *adj.* parallel
Paralyse *f.* paralysis, palsy
paralytisch *adj.* paralytic(al), paralized
Parasit *m.* parasite
parat *adj.* ready
Parenthese *f.* parenthesis
Parforceritt *m.* steeplechase
Parfüm *neu.* perfume; **-erie** *f.* perfumery
parfümieren *v.* to perfume
pari *adv.* at par
Paria *m.* pariah
Park *m.* park, grounds; **-platz** *m.* parking
 place
Parkett *neu.* parquet; inlaid floor; (theat.)
 orchestra seats
Parlament *neu.* parliament; (U.S.A.)
 Congress; **-är** *m.* bearer of a flag of
 truce; **-arier** *m.* parliamentarian; (pol.)
 representative
parlamentarisch *adj.* parliamentary
Parodie *f.* parody
Parole *f.* parole; password; watchword
Partei *f.* party, faction; side; tenant; **—
 nehmen für** to side with; **sich zwischen
 den -en halten** to sit on the fence;
 -gänger *m.* partisan; **-gruppe** *f.* faction;
 -programm *neu.* party platform
partei: **-isch** *adj.,* **-lich** *adj.* partial,
 biased; **-los** *adj.* impartial, independent, neutral
Parterre *neu.* parterre, ground floor
Partie *f.* excursion, outing; game; (sport)
 match, set; (theat.) part; lot
Partikel *f.* particle
Partitur *f.* (mus.) score
Partner *m.* partner; **-schaft** *f.* partnership
Parzelle *f.* allotment, lot, parcel (of land)
parzellieren *v.* to divide into lots; to parcel
Pass *m.* pass(age), defile; amble, pace;
 passport; **-age** *f.* passage; (mus.) run;
 -agier *m.* passenger; **blinder -agier**
 stowaway; **-agierflugzeug** *neu.* air liner;
 -agiergut *neu.* passenger's baggage;
 -ant *m.* passer-by; **-gänger** *m.* ambling
 horse; **-ierschein** *m.* pass, permit
pass: **-abel** *adj.* tolerable; bearable; **-en**
 v. to fit, to suit; (game) to pass; to be
 becoming (*oder* convenient); **-en auf**
 to fit on; to lie in wait for; **zueinander
 -en** to match; to be harmonious; **-end**
 adj. convenient, appropriate; becoming; **für -end halten** to think proper;
 -ieren *v.* to pass, to cross; to happen
passlich *adj.* convenient, suitable, fit
Past: **-e** *f.,* **-a** *f.* paste
Pastell *neu.* pastel; **-farben** *f. pl.* pastel
 crayons (*oder* colors)
Pastete *f.* pie; pastry; **da haben wir die
 —** we are in a nice mess
pasteurisieren *v.* to pasteurize

Pastille *f.* lozenge
Pastor, *m.* pastor, minister. clergyman; **-at**
 neu. pastorate; parsonage
Pate *m.* godfather, sponsor; **-nkind** *neu.*
 godchild; **-nstelle** *f.* sponsorship
Patent *neu.* patent; **-amt** *neu.* patent
 office
Pater *m.* (eccl.) Father; priest; **-noster** *m.*
 and *neu.* Lord's Prayer; escalator
pathetisch *adj.* pathetic
Pathologe *m.* pathologist
Patient *m.* patient
Patin *f.* godmother
Patri: **-arch** *m.* patriarch; **-ot** *m.* patriot;
 -otismus *m.* patriotism; **-zier** *m.* pa-
 trician
patriarchalisch *adj.* patriarchal
patriotisch *adj.* patriotic
Patron *m.* patron; protector; fellow; **-at**
 neu. patronage
Patrone *f.* cartridge; **-ngurt** *m.* cartridge
 belt; **-ntasche** *f.* cartridge pouch
Patrouille *f.* patrol
patrouillieren *v.* to patrol, to go the
 rounds
Patsch *m.* smack, slap; **-e** *f.* dilemma,
 mess; **in der -e sitzen** (coll.) to be in a
 fix
patschen *v.* to splash; to slap, to smack
patschnass *adj.* soaked to the skin
patt *adj.* (chess) stalemate
patzig *adj.* (coll.) impudent, pert, saucy
Pauke *f.* kettledrum; **-nwirbel** *m.* roll of
 the kettledrum; **-rei** *f.* (coll.) duel;
 cramming
pauken *v.* to beat (kettledrum); (coll.) to
 cram
Paus: **-e** *f.* pause, intermission, break;
 rest; tracing, traced design; **-enzeichen**
 neu. pause signal; **-papier** *neu.* tracing
 paper
pausbäckig *adj.* chubby-faced
Pauschal: **-gebühr** *f.* flat rate; **-kauf** *m.*
 wholesale purchase; **-summe** *f.* lump
 (*oder* round) sum
Pavillon *m.* pavilion
Pech *neu.* pitch; (cobbler's) wax; bad
 luck; **-draht** *m.* (cobbler's) thread;
 -fackel *f.* pine torch; **-strähne** *f.* run of
 bad luck; **-vogel** *m.* unlucky fellow
Pedal *neu.* pedal
pedantisch *adj.* pedantic
Pedell *m.* beadle; janitor; proctor
Peil: **-(funk)gerät** *neu.* radio locator; direction finder; **-kompass** *m.* azimuth
 compass; **-ung** *f.* direction finding,
 radiolocation
Pein *f.* pain, agony, torment; **-iger** *m.*
 tormentor, torturer; **-igung** *f.* torture
peinigen *v.* to torment, to torture, to
 harass
peinlich *adj.* distressing; painful, tormenting; (law) penal, criminal; pedantic,
 punctilious
Peitsche *f.* whip, lash, scourge; **mit der
 — knallen** to crack the whip; **-nhieb**
 m. lash, whip cut; **-nschnur** *f.* whip
 thong, lash
peitschen *v.* to whip, to flog, to lash, to
 scourge; **das peitschte mich auf** this

stirred (*oder* stimulated) me
Pelikan *m.* pelican
Pelle *f.* peel, skin
pellen *v.* to peel, to skin, to pare
Pellkartoffeln *f. pl.* potatoes in their jackets
Pelotonfeuer *neu.* platoon firing
Pelz *m.* pelt, skin, hide; fur; auf den — rücken (coll.) to importune; den — ausklopfen (coll.) to thrash soundly; jemandem Läuse in den — setzen (coll.) to play a dirty trick on someone; -futter *neu.* fur lining; -händler *m.* furrier; -jäger *m.* fur trapper; -verbrämung *f.* fur trimming; -ware *f.*, -werk *neu.* furs
Pendel *m.* and *neu.* pendulum; -schwingung *f.* oscillation; -verkehr *m.* shuttle service
pendeln *v.* to oscillate, to swing
penibel *adj.* pedantic; particular; fastidious
Pension *f.* pension; boardinghouse; -är *m.* pensioner; boarder; -at *neu.* boarding school
pensionieren *v.* to pension off
Pensum *ncu.* task, lesson, curriculum
per *prep.* by; — Adresse care of; — Jahr per annum, a ,(*oder* each) year; — sofort from now on
perfekt *adj.* perfect
perfid *adj.* perfidious
Pergament *neu.* parchment; -haut *f.* membrane
Periode *f.* period; menstruation
periodisch *adj.* periodic
Peripherie *f.* periphery; circumference
Perl: -e *f.* pearl, bead; bubble; seine -en vor die Säue werfen to waste one's talents; -enkette *f.* pearl necklace: -huhn *neu.* guinea fowl; -muschel *f.* pearl oyster; -mutter *f.* mother-of-pearl; -schrift *f.* (typ.) pearl
perlen *v.* to effervesce, to sparkle; to pearl
Perpendikel *m.* and *neu.* pendulum, perpendicular
perplex *adj.* perplexed
Perron *m.* (rail.) platform
Person *f.* person(age); (theat.) character, part; in — personally, personified; -al *neu.* employees; staff, personnel; servants; (theat.) performers; -alien *f. pl.* personal data; -alverzeichnis *neu.* list of employees; -enaufzug *m.* passenger elevator; -enstand *m.* state of population; -enverzeichnis *neu.* (theat.) cast; -enwagen *m.* passenger car
personifizieren *v.* to personify
persönlich *adj.* personal; — *adv.* in person
Persönlichkeit *f.* person(ality)
Perspektiv *neu.* small telescope; -e *f.* perspective: prospect, outlook
Perücke *f.* wig
pessimistisch *adj.* pessimistic
Pest *f.*, Pestilenz *f.* pestilence, plague
Petersilie *f.* parsley
Petschaft *neu.* seal, signet
Petunie *f.* petunia
petzen *v.* to bear tales, to tattle, to inform
Pfad *m.* path; -finder *m.* pioneer; boy

scout
Pfaffe *m.* (coll.) cleric; -ntum *neu.* clericalism
Pfahl *m.* stake, pole, post, pile, prop; -bau *m.* pilework; lake dwelling; -werk *neu.* palisade, stockade
Pfalz *f.* Palatinate; imperial palace
Pfand *neu.* pledge, security; -brief *m.* mortgage bond; -gläubiger *m.* mortgagee; -haus *neu.*, -leihe *f.* pawnshop: -leiher *m.* pawnbroker; -recht *neu.* lien: -schein *m.* pawn ticket; -schuldner *m.* mortgagor; -verschreibung *f.* mortgage deed
Pfänd: -erspiel *neu.* game of forfeits; -ung *f.* distraint, distress, seizure: -ungsbefehl *m.* warrant of distress
Pfanne *f.* pan; (anat.) socket
Pfannkuchen *m.* pancake; doughnut: omelet
Pfarr: -amt *neu.*, -bezirk *m.*, -gemeinde *f.* parish; -e(i) *f.* parsonage, pastorate: -er *m.* parson, pastor, minister; -haus *neu.* parsonage; -kind *neu.* parishioner
Pfau *m.* peacock; -enrad *neu.* peacock's fan; -henne *f.* peahen
Pfeffer *m.* pepper; -streuer *m.* peppershaker; -gurke *f.* gherkin; -kuchen *m.* gingerbread; -ling *m.* mushroom; -minze *f.* peppermint; -nuss *f.* ginger-(bread) nut
pfeffern *v.* to (season with) pepper; to make spicy: (coll.) to throw
Pfeife *f.* whistle, pipe; fife; -n *neu.* whistling; (theat.) hissing; -nkopf *m.* pipe bowl
pfeifen *v.* to whistle, to pipe; (mice) to squeak; (wind) to howl; (theat.) to hiss; er pfeift auf dem letzten Loch he is on his last legs; ich pfeife darauf I don't give a hoot for it
Pfeil *m.* arrow, dart; -hagel *m.* shower of arrows; -spitze *f.* arrowhead
Pfeiler *m.* pillar, post
Pfennig *m.* pfennig, penny; -fuchser *m.* pinchpenny, miser; -kraut *neu.* moneywort
Pferd *neu.* horse; (chess) knight; (gym.) vaulting horse; das — beim Schwanze aufzäumen to put the cart before the horse; zu -e on horseback; -ebremse *f.* horsefly; -edecke *f.* saddlecloth; -ehändler *m.* horse dealer; -eknecht *m.* groom; hostler; -ekoppel *f.* paddock; -ekraft *f.* horsepower; -erennen *neu.* horse race; -eschwemme *f.* horse pond; -ezucht *f.* breeding of horses
Pfiff *m.* whistle; -ikus *m.* smart fellow
pfiffig *adj.* smart; artful, crafty, sly, sharp
Pfingst: -en *neu.* Pentecost, Whitsuntide; -rose *f.* peony; -sonntag *m.* Whitsunday
Pfirsich *m.* peach
Pflanz: -e *f.* plant; -enbutter *f.* vegetable butter; -enfaser *f.* vegetable fiber; -enkost *f.* vegetable diet; -enkunde *f.* botany; -enreich *neu.*, -enwelt *f.* vegetable kingdom; -ensaft *m.* (bot.) sap; -er *m.* planter, colonist, settler; -schule *f.* nursery; -stätte *f.* (fig.) seminary;

source; hotbed; **-ung** *f.* plantation; colony

pflanz: -en *v.* to plant; **-enfressend** *adj.* herbivorous, graminivorous; **-lich** *adj.* vegeta(b)l(e)

Pflaster *neu.* plaster; pavement; **Paris ist ein teures — Paris is very expensive; -er** *m.* paver; **-stein** *m.* paving stone; **-treter** *m.* loafer; **-ung** *f.* paving

Pflaume *f.* plum; **getrocknete** (*or* **gedörrte**) **-e** prune; **-nmus** *neu.* plum jam

Pfleg: -e *f.* care, nursing; rearing; cultivation; **-ebefohlene** *m.* ward; **-eeltern** *f.* foster parents; **-ekind** *neu.* foster child; **-emutter** *f.* foster mother; **-er** *m.*, **-erin** *f.* nurse, guardian, curator; **-esohn** *m.* foster son; **-ling** *m.* foster child; **-schaft** *f.* guardianship

pflegen *v.* to care for, to nurse, to foster; to cultivate; to be accustomed, to be in the habit; **der Ruhe — to take one's ease; Umgang — to associate with**

Pflicht *f.* duty, obligation; **-anteil** *m.*, **-beitrag** *m.* quota; **-eifer** *m.* zeal; **-gefühl** *neu.* sense of duty; **-leistung** *f.* performance of duty; **-teil** *m.* legitimate portion

Pflock *m.* peg, pin, plug, picket; **einen — zurückstecken** (coll.) to moderate one's demands

pflücken *v.* to gather, to pick, to pluck; **sie hat ein Hühnchen mit ihm zu —** she has a bone to pick with him

Pflug *m.* plow; **-schar** *f.* plowshare

pflügen *v.* to plow, to till

Pforte *f.* gate, door; Porte

Pförtner *m.* doorkeeper, janitor, porter; (anat.) pylorus

Pfosten *m.* post; pale, stake, jamb

Pfote *f.* paw

Pfriem(en) *m.*, **Pfrieme** *f.* awl; punch, bodkin

Pfropf(en) *m.* stopper, plug, cork, wad; **-enzieher** *m.* corkscrew; **-messer** *neu.* grafting knife; **-reis** *neu.* scion, graft

pfropfen *v.* to cork; to plug; to cram, to stuff; (hort.) to graft

Pfründe *f.* benefice; sinecure; prebend

Pfründner *m.* beneficiary; prebendary

Pfuhl *m.* pool, puddle; (fig.) slough, pit

pfui *interj.* phooey! phew! shame on you!

Pfund *neu.* pound; **mit seinem -e wuchern** to make the most of one's talent; **sein — vergraben** to hide (*oder* bury) one's talent

Pfusch: -arbeit *f.*, **-erei** *f.* bungling; botching; **-er** *m.* botcher, bungler; quack

pfuschen *v.* to botch, to bungle; to scamp

Pfütze *f.* puddle, bog, quagmire

phänomenal *adj.* phenomenal, extraordinary

Phant: -asie *f.* imagination, fancy; fantasy; **-asiegebilde** *neu.* fantastic vision; chimera; **-ast** *m.* dreamer, visionary; **-om** *neu.* phantom

phant: -asieren *v.* to daydream; to improvise; to rave, to ramble; **-asievoll** *adj.* imaginative, fanciful; **-astisch** *adj.* fantastic, fanciful

Pharmaz: -eut *m.* pharmacist; druggist; **-ie** *f.* pharmacy

Phil: -anthrop *m.* philanthropist; **-anthropie** *f.* philanthropy; **-ologe** *m.* philologist; **-ologie** *f.* philology; **-osoph** *m.* philosopher; **-osophie** *f.* philosophy

phil: -anthropisch *adj.* philanthropic(al); **-ologisch** *adj.* philologic(al); **-osophieren** *v.* to philosophize; **-osophisch** *adj.* philosophic(al)

Phiole *f.* phial, vial

Phlegma *neu.* phlegm; equanimity; **-tiker** *m.* phlegmatic person

Phon (Lautstärkemasseinheit) *n.* decibel

phonetisch *adj.* phonetic(al)

Photo *m.*, **-apparat** *m.* camera; **-grametrie** *f.* space control; **-graph** *m.* photographer; **-graphie** *f.* photograph(y); **-montage** *f.* photographic layout

photographieren *v.* to photograph

Physik *f.* physics; **-er** *m.* physicist

physikalisch *adj.* physical, of physics

Physio: -gnomie *f.* physiognomy; **-loge** *m.* physiologist; **-logie** *f.* physiology

physisch *adj.* physical

picken *v.* to pick, to peck

Picknick *neu.* picnic

Piedestal *neu.* (arch.) pedestal

piepen *v.* to chirp, to cheep, to squeak; **bei dir piept's wohl?** (sl.) Are you crazy?

Piet: -ät *f.* piety, reverence; **-ätlosigkeit** *f.* irreverence; **-ismus** *m.* pietism, bigotry

Pik *m.* pique, grudge; **— neu.** (cards) spade; **-anterie** *f.* piquancy, pungency

Pikkolo *m.* boy waiter; **-flöte** *f.* piccolo

Pil: -ger *m.* pilgrim; **-gerfahrt** *f.*, **-gerschaft** *f.* pilgrimage

pilgern *v.* to go on a pilgrimage

Pilz *m.* mushroom, fungus, agaric; **giftiger — toadstool**

Pinguin *m.* penguin

Pinie *f.* stone pine

pinkeln *v.* (sl.) to make water; to piddle

Pinne *f.* peg, tack; pivot; (naut.) tiller

Pinsel *m.* (paint)brush; (coll.) simpleton; **-ei** *f.* daubing; **-strich** *m.* stroke of the brush

pinseln *v.* to paint; to daub

Pinzette *f.* tweezers

Pionier *m.* pioneer; (mil.) engineer, sapper

Pirat *m.* pirate

Pirol *m.* (orn.) oriole

pirschen *v.* to hunt, to stalk game

Pistazie *f.* pistachio

Pistole *f.* pistol; **-ntasche** *f.* holster

Piston *m.* piston; **— neu.** (mus.) cornet

pitschnass *adj.* wet to the skin, wet through

pittoresk *adj.* picturesque

r'acken *v.* to torment, to drudge

Plackerei *f.* drudgery, vexation, trouble

plädieren *v.* to plead

Plage *f.* plague, affliction, torment, nuisance; **-geist** *m.* bore, tormentor

plagen *v.* to plague, to annoy, to pester; **sich — to drudge, to toil**

Plagiat *neu.* plagiarism; **-or** *m.* plagiarist

plagiieren *v.* to plagiarize

Plak: -at *neu.* placard, bill, poster; -atsäule *f.* advertisement pillar; -ette *f.* plaque

Plan *m.* plan, design, project, plot

plan *adj.* plain, level, flat; -ieren *v.* to plane, to level

plan: -en *v.* to plan, to project, to plot; -los *adj.* without a plan, desultory; -mässig *adj.* planned; systematic, methodical

Plane *f.* tarpaulin, awning

Planet *m.* planet; -arium *neu.* planetarium

planetarisch *adj.* planetary

Planierungsraupenfahrzeug *n.* bulldozer

Plänkelei *f.* skirmish

Plantage *f.* plantation

Planung *f.* planning

Planwirtschaft *f.* economic planning

Plapper: -ei *f.* babble, chatter; -maul *neu.*, -tasche *f.* chatterbox

plappern *v.* to babble, to chatter

plärren *v.* to bawl; to blubber, to wail

Plastik *f.* plastic art; sculpture

plastisch *adj.* plastic

Platane *f.* plane tree

Platin *neu.* Platinum

platonisch *adj.* Platonic

plätschern *v.* to splash; to murmur, to plash

platt *adj.* flat, even; insipid, dull, commonplace; die -e Wahrheit the plain truth; — heraus sagen to speak frankly; — sein (coll.) to be dumbfounded; -deutsch *adj.* Low German; -erdings *adv.* absolutely, decidedly, flatly; -füssig *adj.* flat-footed; -weg *adj.* flatly

Platt: -e *f.* plate; plateau; slab; (mus.) disk, record; (coll.) baldness; -enteller *m.* turntable; -form *f.* platform; -fuss *m.* flat foot; -fusseinlage *f.* arch support

Plätt: -brett *neu.* ironing board; -eisen *neu.* flat iron; -wäsche *f.* laundry (to be ironed)

plätten *v.* to iron, to press

Platz *m.* place; locality, site; square; seat; (sport) ground, court; am -e sein to be opportune; nicht am -e out of place; — greifen to gain ground, to spread; — machen to clear the way; — nehmen to sit down; seinen — behaupten to stand one's ground; -karte *f.* ticket (for reserved seat); -kommandant *m.* military commandant; -patrone *f.* blank cartridge; -regen *m.* torrential rain; downpour; -wärter *m.* groundman; -wechsel *m.* change of place; (com.) local draft; (sports) change in lineup

Plätzchen *neu.* small place; fancy cookie

platzen *v.* to burst, to crack; to explode

platzraubend *adj.* space-stealing

Plauder: -er *m.* chatterer; talker; -stündchen *neu.* cozy chat; -tasche *f.* chatterbox; gossiper; -ton *m.* conversational tone

plaudern *v.* to chat, to chatter, to blab, to talk; aus der Schule — to act as talebearer

Plebejer *m.* plebeian

plebejisch *adj.* plebeian

Pleite *f.* (coll.) bankruptcy

Plejaden *f. pl.* (ast.) Pleiades

Plenarsitzung *f.*, **Plenum** *neu.* plenary meeting

Pleuelstange *f.* connecting rod

Plombe *f.* lead seal; dental filling

plombieren *v.* to seal with lead; to fill (tooth)

plötzlich *adj.* sudden, unexpected; — *adv.* suddenly, abruptly, offhandedly

Pluderhosen *f. pl.* wide breeches

plump *adj.* blunt; heavy, clumsy; awkward, shapeless; -s! thump! -sen *v.* to plump, to plop

Plunder *m.* lumber, rubbish, trash

plündern *v.* to plunder, to pillage, to sack

Plüsch *m.* plush

Pneu(matik) *m.* pneumatic tire

Pöbel *m.* mob, rabble; -herrschaft *m.* mob rule

pöbelhaft *adj.* vulgar, low, plebeian

pochen *v.* to knock, to rap; to beat. to throb; — auf to insist on, to boast about

Pochspiel *neu.* poker

Pochwerk *neu.* stamping mill; pounding machine

Pocke *f.* pock; -n *pl.* smallpox; -nimpfung *f.* vaccination; -nnarbe *f.* pockmark

pockennarbig *adj.* pockmarked

Podex *m.* (coll.) buttocks

Podium *neu.* platform, rostrum

Poesie *f.* poetry

poetisch *adj.* adj. poetic(al)

Pointe *f.* point (of joke *oder* story)

Pokal *m.* goblet; cup

Pökel: -fleisch *neu.* salted meat; -hering *m.* pickled herring; -rindfleisch *neu.* corned beef

pökeln *v.* to pickle, to salt

Pol *m.* pole; (elec.) terminal; -arforscher *m.* polar explorer; -arfuchs *m.* arctic fox; -arkran *m.* gantry; -arlicht *neu.* northern lights; -arzone *f.* frigid zone

polarisieren *v.* to polarize

polemisch *adj.* polemic(al)

poli: -tisch *adj.* political; -tisieren to dabble in politics; -zeilich *adj.* (of the) police; -zeiwidrig *adj.* contrary to police regulations

Police *f.* (insurance) policy

polieren *v.* to polish, to burnish

Politik *f.* politics; policy; -er *m.* politician

Politur *f.* polish; gloss; varnish

Poliz: -ei *f.* police; -eibüro *neu.*, -eiwache *f.* police station; -eiaufsicht *f.* police supervision; unter -eiaufsicht on parole; -eibeamte *m.* police officer; -eibehörde *f.* police authorities; -eikommissar *m.* police inspector; -eipräsident *m.* police commissioner; -eisspitzel *m.* police informer; -eistreife *f.* police raid; -eistunde *f.* closing hour; curfew; -ist *m.* policeman

Polster *neu.* cushion; bolster; -er *m.* upholsterer; -möbel *neu. pl.* upholstered furniture; -sessel *m.*, -stuhl *m.* easy

chair; **-ung** f. stuffing, upholstery
polstern v. to stuff, to upholster, to pad
Polter: -abend m. eve before a wedding;
-er ml blusterer; **-geist** m. hobgoblin
poltern v. to be noisy, to rumble; to
bluster
Polytechnikum neu. technical college
pomadig adj. (coll.) phlegmatic
Pommern neu. Pomerania
Pomp m. pomp, ostentation
pomphaft, pompös adj. pompous, mag-
nificent
Popanz m. bugbear; dummy
Popo m. (coll.) behind, buttocks
populär adj. popular; — **machen** to popu-
larize
Popularität f. popularity
Pore f. pore
porös adj. porous
Portal neu. portal
Porte: -feuille neu. portfolio; **-monnaie**
neu. purse; **-pee** neu. sword knot
Portier m. doorkeeper; porter; **-e** f. door
curtain
Portion f. portion, helping, ration
Porto neu. postage; **-kasse** f. petty cash
portofrei adj. postpaid, prepaid
Porträt neu. portrait, likeness
Porzellan neu. porcelain, china; **-bren-
nerei** f. porcelain manufactory; **-erde**
f. kaolin; **-service** neu. set of china
Posamentier m. lacemaker; haberdasher;
-waren f. pl. lacework; trimmings;
haberdashery
Posaune f. trombone; (bibl.) trumpet;
-nengel m. angel with chubby cheeks
Pose f. pose, attitude; quill
posieren v. to pose, to strike an attitude
Positiv m. (gram.) positive degree; —
neu. (phot.) positive; small organ
Positur f. posture
Posse f. drollery; farce, burlesque; **-n** m.
prank, trick; **-nreisser** m. buffoon,
jester
possenhaft adj. clownish, farcical
possierlich adj. droll, funny, quaint
Post f. mail; post (office); news, message;
-amt neu. post office; **-anweisung** f.
money order; **-beamte** m. post office
clerk; **-beutel** m. mailbag; **-bote** m.
mailman; **-kasten** m. mail box;
-schliessfach neu. post office box;
-stempel m. postmark; **-wertzeichen**
neu. postage stamp
Postament neu. pedestal, base
Posten m. post, (com.) sum, item, entry;
(mil.) outpost, sentry; **auf dem — sein**
(coll.) to feel well; **-jäger** m. position
hunter; **-kette** f., **-linie** f. (mil.) outpost
line
Postille f. postil, book of family sermons
post: -alisch adj. postal; **-lagernd** adj.
general delivery; **-wendend** adj. by
return mail
Potenz f. power; potency
Pott: -asche f. potash; **-fisch** m., **-wal** m.
sperm whale
Prä: -dikat neu. predicate; title; (school)
mark; **-gestock** m. die, matrix; **-lat** m.
prelate; **-mie** f. premium, prize; bonus;

-parat neu. preparation; **-position** f.
preposition; **-sens** neu. present (tense);
-sent neu. present, gift; **-sident** m.
president; chairman; **-sidium** neu.
presidency; chair; **-tendent** m. pre-
tender; **-teritum** neu. preterite, past
tense; **-zedenzfall** m. precedent; **-zision**
f. precision
prä: -destinieren v. to predestinate;
-historisch adj. prehistoric(al); **-mie-
ren** to award (prize to); **-numerando**
adv. in advance, beforehand; **-parieren**
v. to prepare; **-sentieren** to present, to
offer; **-sidieren** to preside; **-zis** adj.
precise; concise; punctual
Pracht f. magnificence, splendor, luxury;
-exemplar neu. splendid specimen
prächtig, prachtvoll adj. magnificent,
gorgeous
prachtliebend adj. ostentatious, fond of
show
Prag neu. Prague
prägen v. to coin, to shape
prägnant adj. significant
Prägnanz f. terseness, significance
Prahl: -er m., **-hans** m. boaster, braggart;
-erei f. vainglory
prahlen v. to boast, to brag; to show off
prahlerisch adj. boastful; vainglorious,
showy
prakt: -ikabel adj. practicable; **-isch** adj.
practical, useful; **-ischer Arzt** general
practitioner; **-izieren** v. to practice
Praktik f. practice; **-ant** m. probationer;
-er m. practical person, expert
Prall m. collision; bounce, rebound, impact
prallen v. to bounce, to dash, to rebound
prangen v. to make a show; to shine
Pranger m. pillory
Prärie f. prairie
prasseln v. to crackle, to patter
prassen v. to carouse, to revel, to feast
Praxis f. practice; exercise; usage; (law)
clients; (med.) patients
predigen v. to preach; to sermonize
Prediger m. preacher, clergyman
Predigt f. sermon; lecture
Preis m. price; prize; praise; **um jeden —**
at any price; **um keinen —** not for all
the world; **-angabe** f. quotation of
prices; **-aufgabe** f. prize question; **-aus-
schreiben** neu. competition, award;
-drückerei f. close bargain; **-gabe** f.,
abandonment, surrender; exposure;
-richter m. arbiter, judge; **-schiessen**
neu. shooting match; **-schwankungen**
f. pl. fluctuation of prices; **-sturz** m.
fall of prices; **-träger** m. prize winner;
-treiberei f. forcing up of prices;
-zuschlag m. markup
preis: -en v. to praise, to extol, to glorify;
-geben to abandon, to surrender, to
expose; **-krönen** to award a prize to;
-wert adj. cheap; **-würdig** adj. praiseworthy
Preis(s)elbeere f. cranberry
Prell: -bock m. bulkhead, buffer; **-er** m.
cheat; tosser; ricochet shot; **-erei** f.
cheating, fraud; **-schuss** m. ricochet

-stein *m.* curbstone; –stoss *m.* drop kick

prellen *v.* to toss; to cheat, to swindle
Premiere *f.* (theat.) first night
Presbyterium *neu.* presbytery
Press: –e *f.* press; journalism; (coll.) crammer, tutorial college; –estimme *f.* press comment; –etribüne *f.* press gallery; –glas *neu.* moulded glass; –kohle *f.* briquette; –luft *f.* compressed air
pressen *v.* to press; to squeeze; to urge
pressieren *v.* to be urgent; to dun
Preussen *neu.* Prussia
Priester *m.* priest; –amt *neu.*, –schaft *f.*, –tum *neu.* priesthood; –hemd *neu.* alb; surplice; –herrschaft *f.* hierarchy; –rock *m.* cassock; –weihe *f.* ordination of a priest
priesterlich *adj.* priestly, sacerdotal
Prima *f.* highest class (of a junior college); –ner *m.* student of the highest class (of a junior college); –s *m.* primate; –t *neu.* primacy
prima *adj.* prime; first-class; — vista (mus.) at first sight; (com.) payable on sight
primär *adj.* primary
Primel *f.* primrose, primula
primitiv *adj.* primitive
Prinz *m.* prince; –essin *f.* princess; –gemahl *m.* prince consort
Prinzip *neu.* principle; –al *m.* principal, head, boss; –ienreiter *m.* stickler for principles
prinzipiell *adj.* on principle
prinzlich *adj.* princely
Prior *m.* prior; –ität *f.* priority; –itätsaktie *f.* preferred stock
Prise *f.* (naut.) prize; pinch (of snuff)
Pritsche *f.* wooden sword; plank bed
privat *adj.* private; –im *adv.* privately; –isieren *v.* to free-lance, to live on one's means (oder resources)
Privat: –dozent *m.* university lecturer; –mann *m.* private person; –recht *neu.* civil law
Privileg(ium) *neu.* privilege
probat *adj.* proved, tried, tested
Probe *f.* trial, test, proof; sample; probation; rehearsal; auf die — stellen to put to the test; auf — on trial; –abzug *m.* (typ.) proof sheet; –zeit *f.* probation
Probier: –er *m.* assayer, tester; –glas *neu.* test tube; –mamsell *f.* (coll.) mannequin; –stein *m.* touchstone
prob(ier)en *v.* to test, to try; to taste; to sample; to assay; to rehearse
Problem *neu.* problem
problematisch *adj.* problematic(al)
produktiv *adj.* productive
Produzent *m.* producer
produzieren *v.* to produce; sich — to show off, to perform
profan *adj.* profane; –ieren *v.* to profane
Profess: –ion *f.* profession; trade; –or *m.* professor; –ur *f.* professorship, professoriate
Profil *neu.* profile
profitieren *v.* to profit (oder gain by)

Prognose *f.* prognosis; forecast
Programm *neu.* program; (pol.) platform
Projekt *neu.* project; –il *neu.* projectile; –ion *f.* projection; –ionsapparat *m.* projector
proklamieren *v.* to proclaim
Prokur: –a *f.* procuration; –ator *m.* procurator; –ist *m.* (com.) authorized manager
Proletarier *m.* proletarian
Prolog *m.* prologue
Promotion *f.* promotion; graduation
promovieren *v.* to graduate, to take a degree
propagieren *v.* to propagandize
Propeller-Turbinenmotor *m.* turboprop
Prophet *m.* prophet
prophetisch *adj.* prophetic(al)
proportioniert *adj.* proportionate; proportioned
Propst *m.* provost; prior
Prosa *f.* prose; –iker *m.*, –ist *m.* prose writer; prosaic person
prosaisch *adj.* prosaic
prosit! prost! *interj.* cheers! here's to your health! — Neujahr! happy New Year!
Prospekt *m.* prospect; prospectus; view
Prostituierte *f.* prostitute
Proszeniumsloge *f.* stage box
Protekt: –ion *f.* protection; –ionswirtschaft *f.* protectionism; –or *m.* protector; sponsor; –orat *neu.* protectorate; sponsorship
Protest *m.* protest; mit — zurückkommen (com.) to be dishonored; –ant *m.* Protestant; –antismus *m.* Protestantism
protestantisch *adj.* Protestant
protestieren *v.* to protest
Protokoll *neu.* protocol; record; minutes; –buch *neu.* minute book; –führer *m.* recording clerk
protokollarisch *adj.* in the minutes; on record
protokollieren *v.* to protocol; to record
protzen *v.* to show off; to put on airs
Proviant *m.* provisions, supplies; –amt *neu.* supply depot; –kolonne *f.* supply column
Provinz *f.* province; –ler *m.* provincial
Provis: –ion *f.* commission, percentage; –ionsreisende *m.* salesman on commission; –or *m.* druggist's assistant; –orium *neu.* temporary arrangement (oder state)
provisionsweise *adv.* on commission
provisorisch *adj.* provisional, temporary
provozieren *v.* to provoke
Prozent *neu.* per cent, percentage; –satz *m.* percentage; rate of interest
Prozess *m.* process; lawsuit, action; einen — anstrengen to sue (at law); kurzen — machen mit to make short work of; –akten *f. pl.* minutes of a law case; pleadings; –führer *m.* litigant; –führung *f.* conduct of a case; –ion *f.* procession; –ordnung *f.* rules of court
prozesssüchtig *adj.* litigious
prüde *adj.* prudish
Prüf: –er *m.* examiner, assayer; –ling *m.* examinee; –stein *m.* touchstone; crite-

rion; **-ung** f. examination; inspection; testing; (bibl.) affliction; **-ungsausschuss** m., **-ungskommission** f. board of examiners

Prüfzählen neu. countdown

prüfen v. to examine; to inspect; to test; to investigate; (com.) to audit, to check

Prügel m. cudgel, stick; — pl. thrashing; **-ei** f. fight; free-for-all; **-knabe** m. scapegoat; **-strafe** f. corporal punishment

prügeln v. to thrash; **sich** — to fight

Prunk m. splendor, pomp, ostentation

prunk: -en v. to show off, to boast; **-süchtig** adj. ostentatious; **-voll** adj. gorgeous, splendid, sumptuous

prusten v. to sneeze, to snort; to burst out

Psalm m. psalm; **-ist** m. psalmist

Pseudonym neu. pseudonym, fictitious

Psych: -iater m. psychiatrist; **-iatrie** f. psychiatry; **-oanalyse** f. psychoanalysis; **-ologe** m. psychologist; **-ologie** f. psychology; **-ose** f. psychosis

psych: -isch adj. psychic(al); **-ologisch** adj. psychological; **-opathisch** adj. psychopathic

Pubertät f. puberty

Publi: -kum neu. public; audience; **-zist** m. journalist; **-zität** f. publicity

publizieren v. to publish

Pudel m. poodle; **wie ein begossener** — crestfallen; **-mütze** f. fur cap

Puder m. powder; **-quaste** f. powder puff

pudern v. to powder

Puff m. push; bang, pop; crush; puff; (coll.) bordello; **-ärmel** m. puffed sleeve; **-bohne** f. horsebean; **-er** m. potato pancake; buffer; **-spiel** neu. backgammon

puffen v. to puff, to jolt, to nudge; to pop

Puls m. pulse; **-ader** f. artery; **-schlag** m. pulse beat, pulsation; **-wärmer** m. wristlet

puls(ier)en v. to pulsate

Pult neu. desk, lectern

Pulver neu. powder, gunpowder; **er hat das — nicht erfunden** (coll.) he isn't very bright; **sein — unnötig verschiessen** (coll.) to try in vain; **-fass** neu. powder barrel; **-ladung** f. powder charge

pulverisieren v. to pulverize; to demolish

Pump m. (coll.) borrowing, credit; **-e** f. pump; **-enschwengel** m. pump handle; **-hosen** f. pl. baggy trousers

pumpen v. to pump; (coll.) to borrow, to loan

Punkt m. point; dot; period; place; moment; item; matter; subject; **bis zu einem gewissen — to** some extent; **— ein Uhr** at one o'clock sharp; **springender — main** point; **-um** neu. period, end; **-zahl** f. score

punktieren v. to dot; to puncture, to punctuate

pünktlich adj. punctual, prompt, exact

Punsch m. (beverage) punch

Pupille f. (eye) pupil

Puppe f. doll, puppet; chrysalis, pupa; shock (of grain); **-nmacher** m. doll-maker; **-nspiel** neu., **-ntheater** neu. puppet show; **-nstube** f. doll's house; **-nwagen** m. doll buggy

pur adj. pure, sheer

Pur: -itaner m. Puritan; **-itanertum** neu. Puritanism

Püree neu. puree, mash

purgieren to purge

puritanisch adj. Puritan

Purpur m. purple

Purzelbaum m. somersault

purzeln v. to tumble

Puste f. (coll.) breath; **-rohr** neu. blowpipe

Pustel f. pustule

pusten v. to puff; to blow; to pant

Pute f. turkey hen; **-r** m. turkey cock

Putsch m. putsch, revolutionary outbreak, riot

Putz m. trimmings; ornaments; attire, finery; (arch.) plaster, roughcast; **-er** m. clean(s)er; **-frau** f. charwoman; **-geschäft** neu. milliner's shop; **-händlerin** f. milliner; **-waren** f. pl. millinery; **-wolle** f. cotton waste; **-zeug** neu. cleaning utensils

putzen v. to clean; to polish; to adorn; to shine; (horse) to groom; (nose) to blow; (arch.) to plaster, to roughcast; (candle) to snuff; **sich** — to dress up

Pygmäe m. pygmy

Pyjama m. and neu. pajama

Pyramide f. pyramid

Q

Quabbe f. fatty growth; jellyfish

quabb(e)lig adj. flabby, jellylike

Quack: -elei f. silly talk; gabble; **-salber** m. quack; **-salberei** f. quackery

quacksalbern v. (med.) to quack

Quader m. and f. square stone; ashlar

Quadrat neu. square; **ins — erheben** to square; **-wurzel** f. (math.) square root

quadratisch adj. square; quadratic

quadrieren v. to square

quaken v. to quack, to croak

Quäker m. Quaker

Qual f. pain; torment; agony; **-ität** f. quality; **-itätsware** f. high-class article

qual: -ifizieren v. to qualify; **-itativ** adj. qualitative

Quäl: -er m., **-geist** m. tormentor; torturer; bore; **-erei** f. tormenting, pestering; drudgery

quälen v. to torment, to torture, to harass, to worry; to anoy; **sich** — to drudge, to toil

Qualm m. dense smoke; fumes

qualm: -en v. to smoke; **-ig** adj. smoky

qualvoll adj. painful; tormenting; distressing

Quant: -entheorie f. quantum theory; **-ität** f. quantity; **-um** neu. quantum

Quappe f. tadpole, eelpout

Quarantäne f. quarantine

Quark m. curd; cottage cheese; nonsense, trifle

Quart neu. quart; (typ.) quarto; **-e** f. (mus.) fourth; (fencing) quarte; **-a** f.

(secondary school) third grade; **-al** *neu.* quarter (of year); **-aner** *m.* (secondary school) pupil of the third grade; **-ett** *neu.* quartet

Quartier *neu.* quarters; lodging; (mil.) billet; **-macher** *m.*, **-meister** *m.* quartermaster

Quarz *m.* quartz

quasseln *v.* to talk nonsense, to jabber

Quast *m.* knot, tuft; **-e** *f.* tassel; brush

Quatemberfasten *neu.* Ember days

Quatsch *m.* nonsense, twaddle; rubbish

Quecke *f.* quick grass, couch grass

Quecksilber *neu.* quicksilver, mercury; **-kur** *f.* mercurial treatment; **-säule** *f.* column of mercury

quecksilberig, quecksilbern *adj.* of quicksilver, mercurial; restless, lively

Quell *m.* (poet.) spring, well; **-e** *f.* source, spring, fountain; origin

quellen *v.* to gush, to swell; to spring (from)

quer *adj.* cross, transverse, oblique; queer — *adv.* across, diagonally; athwart; **-en** *v.* to traverse; **-feldein** *adv.* cross-country; **-köpfig** *adj.* stubborn, cranky; **-über** *adv.* across

Quer: -balken *m.* crossbeam; **-e** *f.* diagonal direction; **jemand in die -e kommen** to thwart someone's designs; **-feldeinlauf** *m.* cross-country race; **-kopf** *m.* queer fellow; crank; **-pfeife** *f.* fife; **-strasse** *f.* cross street; **-strich** *m.* crossline; **-treiberei** *f.* intriguing, plotting

Quetsch: -e *f.* crush; **-kartoffeln** *f. pl.* mashed potatoes; **-kommode** *f.* (dial.) accordion; **-ung** *f.*, **-wunde** *f.* contusion; bruise

quetschen *v.* to crush, to squeeze; to contuse

quick *adj.* quick, alert; brisk, lively

quietschen *v.* to squeak, to creak

Quint: -a *f.* (secondary school) second grade; **-aner** *m.* (secondary school) second grade student; **-e** *f.* quinte; (mus.) fifth; **-essenz** *f.* quintessence; **-ett** *neu.* quintet

quirlen *v.* to twirl, to beat, to whisk

quitt *adj.* even, free, rid; quits; **-ieren** *v.* to acknowledge receipt; to quit, to abandon

Quitte *f.* quince

Quittung *f.* receipt

Quote *f.* quota, share

R

Rabatt *m.* discount; rebate

Rabbi(ner) *m.* rabbi

Rabe *m.* raven; **weisser —** rare bird; **-naas** *neu.* carrion; **-neltern** *pl.* cruel parents; **-nstein** *m.* place of execution

rabenschwarz *adj.* raven-black; pitch-dark

Rach: -e *f.* revenge, vengeance; **-egefühl** *neu.* resentment, vengefulness; **-gier** *f.*, **-sucht** *f.* vindictiveness

rach: -edurstig *adj.*, **-gierig** *adj.*, **-süchtig** *adj.* vindictive, vengeful

Rachen *m.* throat; jaws; (coll.) mouth; (poet.) abyss; **-putzer** *m.* (coll.) sour wine; strong brandy

rächen *v.* to avenge, to revenge; **das wird sich an ihr —** it will come home to her

Rächer *m.* avenger; vindicator

Rachitis *f.* rickets

Racker *m.* rogue, rascal

Rad *neu.* wheel; bicycle; **unter die Räder kommen** (coll.) to perish; **-achse** *f.* axletree; **-bremse** *f.* wheel lock; hub brake; **-dampfer** *m.* paddle steamer; **-fahrer** *m.* cyclist; **-kranz** *m.* rim; **-ler** *m.* cyclist; **-macher** *m.* wheelwright; **-reifen** *m.* tire; **-rennen** *neu.* bicycle race; **-schaufel** *f.* paddle wheel; **-speiche** *f.* spoke; **-spur** *f.* rut; wheel track; **-zahn** *m.* cog

Radar *neu.* radar; **-gerät** *neu.* radar indicator; radio direction finder; **-auffanggerät** *neu.* lobe

radeln, radfahren *v.* to bike, to cycle

Radau *m.* noise, row

radebrechen *v.* to speak badly

Rädelsführer *m.* ringleader

Radier: -gummi *m.* rubber eraser; **-messer** *neu.* penknife; **-nadel** *f.* etching needle; **-ung** *f.* etching erasure

radieren *v.* to etch

Radieschen *neu.* radish

radikal *adj.* radical

Radio *neu.* radio; **-apparat** *m.* radio set; **-peilung** *f.* radio homing; **-röhre** *f.* radio tube

radioaktiv *adj.* radioactive

Radium *neu.* radium; **-heilverfahren** *neu.* radiotherapy

raffen *v.* to snatch, to gather

raffinier: -en *v.* to refine; **-t** *adj.* crafty, cunning; refined

Ragout *neu.* ragout, hash; hodge-podge

Rah: -e *f.* (naut.) yard; **-segel** *neu.* (naut.) square sail; **-tau** *neu.* (naut.) headrope

Rahmen *m.* frame; (shoe) welt; background; surroundings; **-enantenne** *f.* loop aerial; **-sucher** *m.* view finder

Rain *m.* (agr.) balk, ridge, edge

Rakete *f.* rocket; **-abschuss** *m.* blast-off; **-abschussbasis** *f.* launching pad; **-nabschussführungsschiene** *f.* launching rail; **-nabwehrgeschoss** *neu.* anti-missile missile; **-nbasis** *f.* rocket base; **-nbunker** *m.* silo; **-nfähre** *f.* ferry rocket; **-ngeschoss (ferngelenkt)** *neu.* ballistic missile; **-nstart** *m.* jet-assisted take-off, jato; **Rückfeuerungs- f.** retro-rocket; **Träger-** carrier rocket

Ramm: -bär *m.*, **-block, -e** *f.* rammer, pile driver; **-ler** *m.* ram, buck rabbit

rammen *v.* to ram; to drive in; to butt

Rampe *f.* ramp; platform; **-nlicht** *neu.* footlights

Rand *m.* rim; brim; edge, margin; (wound) lip; verge; **ausser — und Band sein** to be out of hand; **halt deinen —!** (coll.) shut up! **-bemerkung** *f.* marginal note

ländern *v.* to border, to rim; (coins) to mill

Rang m. rank; order; position; quality; (theat.) balcony; **den — ablaufen** to outrun; **ersten –es** first class; **–abzeichen** neu. badge of rank; **–älteste** m. senior in rank; **–ordnung** f. order of precedence

Range f. scamp, tomboy

Rangier: –bahnhof m. (rail.) switchyard; **–er** m. switcher; **–gleis** neu. (rail.) siding

rangieren v. (rail.) to switch; to rank

Ranke f. tendril; shoot; branch

Ränke m. pl. intrigues, machinations, tricks; **–schmied** m. intriguer, plotter, schemer

Ranzen m., **Ränzel** neu. knapsack; schoolbag

ranzig adj. rancid

Rappe m. black horse; **auf Schusters –n reiten** (coll.) to travel on foot

rappel: –n v. to rattle; **bei ihm –ts** he is crazy; **er –te sich auf** (coll.) he recuperated

rapportieren v. (mil.) to report

Raps m. (bot.) rape; **–saat** f., **–samen** m. rapeseed

rar adj. rare, scarce; exquisite; **er macht sich —** (coll.) one hardly sees him

Rarität f. rarity, scarcity; curiosity

rasch adj. quick, swift, hasty

rascheln v. to rustle

Rasen m. grass, lawn; turf; **–mähmaschine** f. lawn mower; **–sprenger** m. lawn sprinkler

rasen v. to rage, to rave; to speed; **–d** adj. raging, raving; rapid; **jemand –d machen** to drive someone mad; **–d** adv. (coll.) very much

Raserei f. rage, raving; frenzy; speeding

Rasier: –apparat m., **–messer** neu. razor; **–klinge** f. razor blade; **–pinsel** m. shaving brush; **–seife** f. shaving soap; **–zeug** neu. shaving utensils

rasieren v. to shave; (mil.) to raze

räsonieren v. to reason, to argue, to grumble

Raspel f. rasp; grating iron

raspeln v. to rasp; to grate; **Süssholz —** to spoon, to flirt, to coax, to fawn

Rasse f. race; breed; **–nhygiene** f. eugenics; **–nkreuzung** f. crossbreeding; **–nvermischung** f. miscegenation; **–nwahn** m. racism

rasseln v. to rattle, to clank

rassig adj. racy, thoroughbred

Rast f. rest; repose; (mil.) halt; **–losigkeit** f. restlessness; **–tag** m. day of rest

rasten v. to rest; to repose; to relax; to halt

rastlos adj. restless, indefatigable

Rasur f. erasure, shave

Rat m. advice, counsel; counsellor; council board; deliberation; means, expedient; **keinen — mehr wissen** to be at wit's end; **mit — und Tat** by word and deed; **— schaffen** to devise a remedy; **zu –e ziehen** to consult; **–geber** m. adviser; **–haus** neu. city hall; **–losigkeit** f. helplessness; **–schlag** m. advice, counsel; **–schluss** m. resolution; decree;

–sherr m. councilman; **–skeller** m. tavern in the basement of a city hall; **–sschreiber** m. clerk to the council

rat: –en v. to advise; to counsel; to guess, to solve; **–los** adj. helpless, embarrassed; **–sam** adj. advisable, expedient; **–schlagen** v. to deliberate

Rate f. rate; instalment; **in –n** by instalments

Ratifizierung f. ratification

Ratio: –n f. ration; **–nalisierung** f. rationalization; **–nalismus** m. rationalism

ratio: –nal adj. rational; **–nalistisch** adj. rationalistic; **–nalisieren** v. to ration; **–nell** adj. reasonable; rational; economical

rätlich adj. advisable; expedient

Rätsel neu. riddle, puzzle, enigma

rätselhaft adj. puzzling, enigmatical

Ratte f. rat; **–nfänger** m. ratcatcher

rattern v. to rattle, to clatter

Raub m. robbery; piracy; rape; prey; **–bau** m. wasting (of natural resources); **–gier** f. rapacity; **–krieg** m. predatory war; **–mord** m. murder with robbery; **–ritter** m. robber knight; **–tier** neu. beast of prey; **–überfall** m. predatory attack; **–zug** m. raid

rauben v. to rob; to plunder; to deprive

Räuber m. robber; brigand; **–ei** f. robbery; **–höhle** f. den of thieves; **–geschichte** f. cock-and-bull story; **–hauptmann** m. gang leader

Rauch m. smoke; **–er** m. smoker; **–erabteil** neu. smoking compartment; **–fang** m. chimney, flue; **–fass** neu. censer; **–fleisch** neu. smoked meat; **–zimmer** neu. smoking room

rauch: –en v. to smoke; **–geschwärzt** adj. smokestained; **–ig** adj. smoky

Räucher: –fass neu. censer; **–hering** m. kipper; **–waren** f. pl. smoked meat, smoked fish

räuchern v. to smoke, to fumigate

Rauchwerk neu. furs

Räude f. mange, scab

räudig adj. mangy, scabby

Rauf: –bold m., **–degen** m. bully; rowdy; **–erei** f. scuffle, row; **–lust** f., **–sucht** f. pugnacity, combativeness

Raufe f. rack

raufen v. to pluck, to pull; **sich —** (coll.) to scuffle, to fight

rauh adj. rough; hoarse; raw; uneven; coarse, rude; **–beinig** adj. caddish; **–en** v. to roughen

Rauhreif m. hoarfrost

Raum m. room; space; place; district; (naut.) hold; **freier —** open space; **luftleerer —** vacuum; **— geben** to give way to; to indulge in; to grant; **–ersparnis** f. saving of space; **–inhalt** m. volume; capacity; **–kunst** f. (art of) interior decoration; **–meter** m. cubic meter; **–schiff** neu. spaceship

Räum: –lichkeit f. locality, premises; space; **–ung** f. removal, clearance, evacuation; **–ungsausverkauf** m. clearance sale

räumen v. to clear away, to remove; to

make room, to evacuate; to leave, to quit

räumlich *adj.* spatial

raunen *v.* to whisper; **man raunt sich zu** there is a rumor

Raupe *f.* caterpillar; **–nantrieb** *m.* caterpillar drive; **–nfrass** *m.* damage done by caterpillars; **–nschlepper** *m.* caterpillar tractor

Rausch *m.* drunkenness, intoxication; ecstasy; **–gift** *neu.* narcotic, dope; **–gold** *neu.* brass foil, tinsel

rauschen *v.* to rush, to rustle; to roar

räuspern *v.* **sich —** to clear one's throat, to hem, to hawk

Rayon *m.* rayon; district; department; circuit

Reagens *neu.* reagent; **–glas** *neu.* test tube; **–papier** *neu.* test (*oder* litmus) paper

reagieren *v.* to react

Reaktion *f.* reaction; **–är** *m.* reactionary

reaktionär *adj.* reactionary

real *adj.* real; material, substantial; **–isieren** *v.* to realize; **–istisch** *adj.* realistic

Real: **–gymnasium** *neu.*, **–schule** *f.* secondary school (for modern subjects); **–injurie** *f.* (law) assault and battery; **–ismus** *m.* realism; **–ist** *m.* realist; **–ität** *f.* reality; **–wert** *m.* actual value

Reb: **–e** *f.* grape, vine; tendril; **–enblut** *neu.*, **–ensaft** *m.* grape juice; wine; **–enhügel** *m.* vineclad hill; **–laus** *f.* vine louse; **–stock** *m.* vine

Rebell *m.* rebel; **–ion** *f.* rebellion, mutiny

rebellieren *v.* to rebel, to revolt, to mutiny

Rebhuhn *neu.* partridge

Rebus *m.* and *neu.* rebus; picture puzzle

rechen *v.* to rake

Rechen *m.* rake; rack

Rechen: **–aufgabe** *f.*, **–exempel** *neu.* arithmetic problem; **–buch** *neu.* arithmetic book; **–fehler** *m.* miscalculation; **–kunst** *f.* arithmetic; **–lehrer** *m.* teacher of arithmetic; **–maschine** *f.* calculating machine; **–schaft** *f.* account; **–schieber** *m.* slide rule; **–tafel** *f.* slate

rechnen *v.* to count, to calculate, to reckon; **alles in allem gerechnet** taking all in all; **— auf** to count upon; **— zu** to include; to rank amongst; to class with

Rechnung *f.* calculation; account; bill; **auf eigene —** at one's own risk; **auf — setzen** to charge, to put to one's account; **auf seine — kommen** to benefit (by); **den Umständen — tragen** to act according to circumstances; **in — ziehen** to take into account; **–sabschluss** *m.* closing of accounts; **–sführer** *m.* accountant, bookkeeper; **–sjahr** *neu.* fiscal year; **–sprüfer** *m.* auditor

recht *adj.* right, correct; just; due, lawful, legitimate; real; genuine; **— ** *adv.* right, well; very; quite; **es geht nicht mit –en Dingen zu** there is something wrong about it; **es geschieht ihm —** it serves him right; **es ist mir —** I don't mind; **ich weiss nicht — wie** I don't quite know how; **jetzt erst —** now more than

ever; **— behalten** to be right in the end; **— haben** to be right; **— und schlecht** fairly good; **wenn ich es — bedenke** when I consider it properly; **–eckig** *adj.* rectangular; **–en** *v.* to litigate; **–ens** *adv.* legally; **–erhand** *adv.* on the right hand; **–fertigen** *v.* to justify; to vindicate; **–gläubig** *adj.* orthodox; **–haberisch** *adj.* disputatious, dogmatic; **–lich** *adj.* lawful, legal; **–los** *adj.* illegal, outlawed; **–mässig** *adj.* legitimate; **–s** *adv.* at (*oder* on) the right; **–schaffen** *adj.* honest, righteous; **–sgültig** *adj.*, **–skräftig** *adj.* legal, valid; **–sum!** (mil.) right about! **–swidrig** *adj.* illegal; **–winklig** *adj.* rectangular; **–zeitig** *adj.* in time

Recht *neu.* right; privilege; claim; justice, law; **allgemeines —** common law; **an den –en kommen** to meet one's match; **mit vollem —** for good reasons; **nach dem –en sehen** to see to things; **— sprechen** to administer justice; **sich selbst — verschaffen** to take law into one's own hands; **von –s wegen** by rights; **zu — bestehen** to be legally valid; **–e** *f.* right hand; (pol.) Right; **–e** *m.* (boxing) right; **–eck** *neu.* rectangle; **–gläubige** *m.* orthodox person; **–haberei** *f.* dogmatism; **–sanwalt** *m.* lawyer, attorney; **–sausdruck** *m.* legal term; **–sbeistand** *m.* legal adviser; **–schreibung** *f.* orthography; **–sgang** *m.* legal procedure; **–sgelehrsamkeit** *f.* jurisprudence; **–sgelehrte** *m.* jurist; **–sgrund** *m.* legal argument; **–sgültigkeit** *f.* legality; **–shandel** *m.* lawsuit, legal action; **–skraft** *f.* legal force; validity; **–smittel** *neu.* legal measure; **–snachfolger** *m.* assignee; **–sperson** *f.* (law) body corporate; **–sprechung** *f.* administration of justice; **–sspruch** *m.* sentence; verdict; **–sstaat** *m.* constitutional state; **–streit** *m.* lawsuit; **–sverfahren** *neu.* legal procedure; **–swissenschaft** *f.* jurisprudence

Reck *neu.* (gym.) horizontal bar

Recke *m.* hero, warrior, swordsman

recken *v.* to stretch, to extend; to crane (neck); **–haft** *adj.* heroic, valiant

Red: **–e** *f.* speech; talk, conversation; address; oration; rumor; **davon kann keine –e sein** that is out of the question; **es geht die –e davon** it is being rumored that; **es ist nicht der –e wert** it is not worth mentioning; **–in die –e fallen** to interrupt; **jemand zur –e stellen** to call someone to account; **–e stehen** to answer (for); **–egabe** *f.*, **–ekunst** *f.* rhetoric; oratory; **–ensart** *f.* phrase, saying; expression; empty talk; **–erei** *f.* prattle; **–eschwall** *m.* verbosity; **–eschwulst** *m.* bombast; **–eweise** *f.* manner of speech, style; **–ewendung** *f.* phrase, idiom; **–ner** *m.* orator, speaker; **–nerbühne** *f.* platform

red: **–ebegabt** *adj.*, **–egewandt** *adj.* fluent in speech, eloquent; **–en** *v.* to speak, to talk; to converse; **mit sich –en lassen** to listen to reason; **das Wort –en** to put in a good word for; **–nerisch** *adj.* oratorical, rhetorical; **-selig** adj. talkative; loquacious; garrulous

Redak: -teur m. editor; **-tion** f. editing; editorial staff; editorial office; **-tionsschluss** m. deadline

redlich adj. honest, upright, just, sincere

Redlichkeit f. honesty, integrity

reduzieren v. to reduce; to diminish

Reede f. (naut.) roadstead; **-r** m. shipowner; **-rei** f. shipping line; shipping trade

reell adj. fair, honest, good; solid

Refektorium neu. refectory

Refer: -at neu. report, lecture; **-endar** m. junior lawyer; **-ent** m. reporter, lecturer; **-enz** f. reference, information

referieren v. to report, to lecture

reflektieren v. to reflect; **auf etwas —** to have something in view

Reflex m. reflex; **-bewegung** f. reflex action; **-ion** f. reflection

Reform f. reform; **-ation** f. reformation; **-ator** m. reformer; **-ierte** m. member of the Reformed Church

reformieren v. to reform

Refrain m. refrain; **-sänger** m. crooner

Refraktor m. refractor; refracting telescope

Regal neu. (book)shelf; stand

rege adj. active, animated; brisk, lively

Regel f. rule, regulation; norm; precept; (med.) menses; **in der —** as a rule; **-detrie** f. (math.) rule of three

regel: -mässig adj. regular; **-mässig** adv. regularly, usually; **-n** v. to regulate; to adjust; to arrange; to settle; **-recht** adj. regular; correct; **-widrig** adj. irregular

Regen m. rain; **aus dem — in die Traufe kommen** to jump from the frying pan into the fire; **-bogen** m. rainbow; **-guss** m. downpour; **-mantel** m. raincoat; **-schirm** m. umbrella; **-wurm** m. earthworm; **-zeit** f. rainy season

regen v. to stir, to move

regendicht adj. rainproof, waterproof

regenerieren v. to regenerate

Regensburg neu. Ratisbon

Regent m. regent; **-schaft** f. regency

Regie f. administration, state monopoly; stage management

regieren v. to govern, to rule; to reign

Regierung f. government; reign, rule; **-santritt** m. accession (to presidency oder throne); **-sbeamte** m. government official; **-sbezirk** m. administrative district; **-sgewalt** f. supreme power

Regiment neu. government; regiment

Regionalprogramm neu. (rad. & TV) closed-circuit

Regist: -er neu. register; index; table of contents; (organ) stop; **-rator** m. registrar, recorder; **-ratur** f. registry; **-rierkasse** f. cash register; **-rierung** f. registration

registrieren v. to register, to record; to file

Reglement neu. regulations; bylaw

Regler m. regulator

regnen v. to rain; **es regnet Bindfaden** it's raining cats and dogs

regnerisch adj. rainy

regsam adj. active, agile. mobile

regulieren v. to regulate; to adjust; to settle

Regung f. motion, movement; emotion, impulse

regungslos adj. motionless, immovable

Reh neu. roe, deer; **-geiss** f. doe; **-kitz** neu. fawn; **-posten** m. buckshot

Reib: -e f., **-eisen** neu. grater; **-erei** f. friction; **-fläche** f. rough (oder striking) surface; **-ung** f. friction; collision; conflict; **-ungsfläche** f. (fig.) source of irritation

reiben v. to rub, to grate; to grind; **jemand etwas unter die Nase —** to tell a person something to his face

reich adj. rich, wealthy; substantial, copious; **-haltig** adj., **-lich** adj. abundant, full, copious

Reich neu. empire, realm, kingdom; **-sautobahn** f. German express highway; **-sapfel** m. imperial globe; **-sfarben** f. pl. national flag (oder colors); **-skleinodien** neu. pl. imperial crown jewels

Reich: -e m. rich person; **-tum** m. riches, wealth

reichen v. to reach, to extend; to hand, to present, to pass; to suffice

Reichweite f. range, reach

reif adj. ripe; mature; mellow; **-en** to ripen, to mature; **-lich** adj. mature; thorough

Reif m. ring; circle; **-eisen** neu. hoop iron; **-en** m. ring; hoop, tire; **-enpanne** f., **-enschaden** m. tire puncture; **-rock** m. hoop skirt, crinoline

Reif m. hoarfrost

Reife f. ripeness; maturity; **-prüfung** f. final examination

reifen v. to form hoarfrost, to rime

Reigen m., **Reihen** m. round dance

reih: -en v. to range, to rank, to string; **-enweise** adv. by (oder in) rows; **-um** adv. by (oder in) turns, alternately

Reihe f. row, range, series; line, sequence; rank, file; **ausser der —** out of turn; **der — nach** successively; **er ist an der —** it is his turn; **-nfolge** f. succession, sequence

Reiher m. heron

Reim m. rhyme; **-erei** f. inferior poetry; **-schmied** m. poetaster; rhymester

reimen v. to rhyme; (coll.) to make sense

rein adj. pure, unalloyed, unadulterated; clean, genuine; net; mere, sheer; **-adr.** entirely, quite; **-en Mund halten** to keep a secret; **-en Wein einschenken** to tell the plain truth; **-es Deutsch** correct German; **-es Gewissen** clear conscience; **— unmöglich** quite impossible; **-igen** v. to clean, to cleanse, to purify; to refine; **-lich** adj. clean, neat, tidy; **-rassig** adj. purebred

Rein: -emachefrau f. cleaning woman; **-ertrag** m. net proceeds; **-fall** m. failure; **-gewinn** m. net gain

Reis m. rice; **-brei** m. rice boiled in milk

Reis neu. twig, scion, sprig; **-ig** neu.

brushwood; **-igbündel** neu. fagot

Reise f. journey; trip; travel; **-büro** neu. tourist agency; **-führer** m. guide book; guide; **-gefährte** m. fellow traveler; **-gepäck** neu. baggage; **-nde** m. traveler; salesman; **-scheck** m. traveler's check; **-zeit** f. tourist season; **-ziel** neu. destination

reisen v. to travel, to journey; to go (to)

Reiss: -aus nehmen to take to one's heels; **-brett** neu. drawing board; **-er** m. bestseller; thriller; box-office success; **-feder** f. drawing pen; **-kohle** f. charcoal crayon; **-nagel** m., **-zwecke** f. thumbtack; **-verschluss** m. zipper; **-zahn** m. canine tooth; **-zeug** neu. drawing instruments

reissen v. to tear, to drag, to pull; to burst, to split; **an sich —** to snatch; to seize; to usurp; to monopolize; **ihm riss die Geduld** he lost his patience; **in Stücke —** to tear to pieces; **Possen —** to clown; **wenn alle Stränge —** if worst comes to worst; **Witze —** to crack jokes; **-d** adj. rapid, rapacious; acute; violent; **die Ware geht -d** the goods sell like hot cakes

Reit: -bahn f. riding academy; **-er** m. horseman; rider; **-erei** f. cavalry; **-erstandbild** neu. equestrian statue; **-gerte** f. whip, switch; **-hose** f. riding breeches; **-knecht** m. groom; **-kunst** f. horsemanship; **-pferd** m. saddle horse; **-stiefel** m. pl. riding boots; **-weg** m. bridle path; **-zeug** neu. riding equipment

reiten v. to ride, to go on horseback; **Galopp —** to gallop; **Schritt —** to amble, to pace; **Trab —** to trot: **über den Haufen —** to ride down; **vor Anker —** (naut.) to ride at anchor; **-d** adj. on horseback, mounted

Reiz m. attraction, charm; stimulus; irritation; **-mittel** neu. incentive; stimulant; **-stoff** m. irritant

reiz: -bar adj. irritable; sensitive; **-en** v. to excite, to stir up; to irritate, to provoke; to entice; to charm; (cards) to bid; **-end** adj., **-voll** adj. attractive, charming; **-los** adj. insipid; unattractive

rekapitulieren v. to recapitulate

rekeln, räkeln v. to loll about

Reklamation f. reclamation, protest; complaint

Reklame f. advertisement; publicity; **-film** m. advertising film; **-schild** neu. billboard; **-zeichner** m. advertising designer

rekognoszieren v. to reconnoiter

rekonstruieren v. to reconstruct

Rekonvaleszent m. convalescent

Rekord m. record performance (oder event)

Rekrut m. recruit; **-enunteroffizier** m. drill sergeant; **-ierung** f. recruiting

rekrutieren v. to recruit; to be recruited

Rektor m. rector; headmaster; **-at** neu. rectorship; headmastership

Relais neu. relay

relativ adj. relative; relating to

Relegation f. expulsion; rustication

Relief neu. relief; **-karte** f. relief map; **-stickerei** f. raised embroidery

Religion f. religion; **-sgebräuche** m. pl. rites

religiös adj. religious; pious

Religiosität f. religiousness; religiosity

Reling f. and neu. (naut.) main rail

Reliquie f. relic; **-nschrein** m. reliquary

Reminiszens f. reminiscence, recollection

Remise f. coach house; shed

remittieren v. to remit, to return

Remonte f. remount

Rempelei f. jostling; rumpus

rempeln v. to jostle, to push; to look for a fight; to barge (into)

Renegat m. renegade

renitent adj. obstinate, refractory

Renn: -bahn f. race track; **-boot** neu. hydroplane; **-en** neu. race; **totes -en** undecided race; **-er** m. race horse; **-fahrer** m. race cyclist; car racer; **-mannschaft** f. race crew; **-sport** m. racing, turf; **-tier** neu. reindeer; **-tierflechte** f. reindeer moss; **-wagen** m. racing car; **-ziel** neu. goal line

rennen v. to run, to rush; to race

Renommee neu. reputation

renovieren v. to renovate, to redecorate

Rent: -abilität f. lucrativeness, profitableness; **-amt** neu., **-kammer** f. revenue office; **-e** f. revenue, income; annuity; pension; **-ier** m., **-ner** m. pensioner; man of private means

rentabel adj. lucrative, profitable

rentieren v. sich — to be profitable; to pay

reorganisieren v. to reorganize

Reparat: -ion f. reparation; **-ur** f. repair(ing); **-urwerkstätte** f. repair shop

reparieren v. to repair

repatriieren v. to repatriate

repetieren v. to repeat

Repetiergewehr neu. repeating rifle; repeater

Replik f. rejoinder, reply; replica

Report m. (com.) extra charge; **-age** f. (rad.) report; **-er** m. reporter

Repräsentant m. representative

repräsentieren v. to represent

Reproduktion f. reproduction; rendering

reproduzieren v. to reproduce

Reptil neu. reptile

Republik f. republic; **-aner** m. republican

republikanisch adj. republican

requirieren v. to requisition

Requisiten neu. pl. requisites; (theat.) properties, props

Reserv: -ation f. reservation; **-e** f. reserve; **-oir** neu. reservoir; tank; **-rad** neu. spare wheel; **-truppen** f. pl. reserves

reservieren v. to reserve

Residenz f. seat (of government), residence

resignieren v. to resign

resolut adj. resolute, determined

Resolution f. resolution

Resonanz f. resonance; **-boden** m. sounding board

Respekt *m.* respect, esteem; **–sperson** *f.* person held in respect; notability; notable

respekt: –abel *adj.* respectable; **–ieren** *v.* to respect, to esteem; **–ive** *adv.* respectively; **–los** *adj.* irreverent; **–voll** *adj.* respectful; **–widrig** *adj.* disrespectful

Rest *m.* rest; remainder; remnant; balance; dregs; **den — geben** to finish off; to kill; **irdische –e** mortal remains; **–auflage** *f.* remainders; **–bestand** *m.* reminant, residue; **–betrag** *m.* remainder

Restaurant *neu.* restaurant

Restauration *f.* restoration; repair; (pol.) reinstatement; restaurant

restaurieren *v.* to restore, to renew, to repair

Resultat *neu.* result; outcome

Retirade *f.* retreat; rest room

retirieren *v.* to retreat

Retorte *f.* (chem.) retort

retour *adv.* back

Rett: –er *m.* rescuer, deliverer; Redeemer; **–ungsboot** *neu.* lifeboat; **–ungsgürtel** *m.,* **–ungsring** *m.* life belt; **–ungsmittel** *neu.* remedy; expedient; last straw; **–ungsstation** *f.* first-aid post

retten *v.* to save, to rescue, to deliver; **sich —** to escape

Rettich *m.* radish

rettungslos *adj.* past help; irretrievable

retuschieren *v.* to retouch

reu: –en *v.* **es –t mich** I am sorry for it; **–ig** *adj.,* **–mütig** *adj.,* **–evoll** *adj.* repentant, remorseful; **–los** *adj.* impenitent

Reue *f.* repentance; regret; remorse; **–egeld** *neu.* forfeit, penalty

Revanche *f.* revenge; **–partie** *f.* return match

revanchieren *v.* **sich —** to revenge oneself; to return a favor

revidieren *v.* to revise; to audit, to check

Revier *neu.* hunting ground; preserve; district; quarter; (mil.) sick bay

Revis: –ion *f.* revision, revisal, auditing; (law) appeal; rehearing; **–ionsbogen** *m.* (typ.) revise; **–or** *m.* reviser; auditor, controller

Revol: –te *f.* insurrection; **–ution** *f.* revolution; **–utionär** *m.* revolutionist

Revue *f.* review; (theat.) revue

Rezens: –ent *m.* reviewer, critic; **–ion** *f.* review; critique

Rezept *neu.* prescription; recipe

rezitieren *v.* to recite

Rhapsodie *f.* rhapsody

Rhabarber *m.* rhubarb

Rhein *m.* Rhine River

Rhesusfaktor *m.* (med.) RH-factor

Rhetorik *f.* rhetoric; **–er** *m.* rhetorician

rhetorisch *adj.* rhetorical

Rheuma *neu.,* **Rheumatismus** *m.* rheumatism

Rhinozeros *neu.* rhinoceros

rhythmisch *adj.* rhythmic(al)

Rhythmus *m.* rhythm

Richt: –balken *m.* traverse beam; **–blei** *neu.* plummet; **–er** *m.* judge; adjuster; **–eramt** *neu.* judgeship, judicature; **–erspruch** *m.* sentence; judgment; **–erstand** *m.* judiciary; **–erstuhl** *m.* tribunal; judge's chair; **–kanonier** *m.* gunner; **–linie** *f.* direction; guiding principle; **–mass** *neu.* standard; guage; **–platz** *m.,* **–statt** *f.* place of execution; **–scheit** *m.* and *neu.* level, ruler; **–schnur** *f.* plumb line; guiding principle; guide; **–ung** *f.* direction; course; bearing; tendency; adjustment

richt: –en *v.* to set straight; to adjust; (mil.) to dress; (min.) to straighten; to prepare; (watch) to set; to direct, to turn; to judge, to sentence; to execute; **sich –en nach** to conform with; to be guided by; **zugrunde –en** to ruin; **–erlich** *adj.* judicial; **–ig** *adj.* right, correct; accurate; suitable, fair; genuine, real; **–ig!** *interj.* quite right! **–ig gehen** to go right; (watch) to keep good time; **–igstellen** *v.* to rectify

Riech: –er *m.* (coll.) smeller; nose; **–fläschchen** *neu.* scent bottle; **–salz** *neu.* smelling salts; **–stoffe** *m. pl.* scents; perfumes; **–werkzeuge** *neu. pl.* olfactory organs

riechen *v.* to smell, to scent; **den Braten** (or **Lunte**) **—** to smell a rat; **ich kann ihn nicht —** I can't stand him

Riege *f.* section; (gym.) squad; team

Riegel *m.* bolt, bar; (clothes) rack; (mil.) switch line; **einen — vorschieben** to bar; to hinder; **hinter Schloss und —** under lock and key

Riemen *m.* strap, thong; oar; sling; **–antrieb** *m.* belt drive; **–scheibe** *f.* pulley; **–werk** *neu.* straps, harness

Ries *neu.* ream (1000 sheets of paper)

Riese *m.* giant; ogre; **–narbeit** *f.* tremendous work; **–nerfolg** *m.* smash hit; **–nschlange** *f.* python; boa constrictor

Rieselfeld *neu.* irrigated field

rieseln *v.* to drizzle, to ripple, to trickle

riesengross, riesig *adj.* gigantic, enormous

Riff *neu.* reef

Rigorosum *neu.* (doctor's degree) examination

Rille *f.* small groove

Rind *neu.* ox, cow; horned cattle; **–erbraten** *m.* roast beef; **–erbremse** *f.* gadfly; **–erbrust** *f.* brisket of beef; **–erhirt** *m.* cowboy; **–fleisch** *neu.* beef; **–sleder** *neu.* cowhide; **–vieh** *neu.* bovine; (coll.) blockhead

Rinde *f.* bark; crust; rind

Ring *m.* ring; circle; (com.) pool, trust; (mech.) link; **–bahn** *f.* circular railroad; **–finger** *m.* ring finger; **–mauer** *f.* circular wall

Ring: –er *m.,* **–kämpfer** *m.* wrestler; **–kampf** *m.* wrestling match; **–richter** *m.* umpire

Ringel *m.* ringlet, curl; **–blume** *f.* marigold; **–locke** *f.* curl; **–reigen** *m.,* **–reihen** *m.* ring-around-a-rosy; **–söckchen** *neu. pl.* bobby socks

ringen *v.* to struggle; to wrest(le); to wring

rings *adv.* (a)round; **–herum** *adv.* **–um(her)** *adv.* all around; round about

Rinn: -e *f.* groove. gutter, channel; furrow; -sal *neu.* watercourse, rill; -stein *m.* gutter

Ripp: -chen *neu.* small rib; chop; -e *f.* rib; (arch.) groin; -enfellentzündung *f.* pleurisy; -enstoss *m.* nudge in the ribs; -enspeer *m.* sparerib

Risiko *neu.* risk

riskant *adj.* risky

riskieren *v.* to risk

Riss *m.* tear, cleft, split, scratch; fracture; sketch, plan; (fig.) schism; breach

Ritt *m.* ride; -meister *m.* cavalry captain

Ritter *m.* knight, cavalier; **arme — fritters; fahrender — knight-errant; -gut** *neu.* estate, manor; -orden *m.* order of knighthood; -schaft *f.* knights; knighthood; -schlag *m.* knighting, dubbing; -sporn *m.* larkspur; -tum *neu.*, -wesen *neu.* chivalry

ritterlich *adj.* knightly; chivalrous; gallant

rittlings *adv.* astride, astraddle

rituell *adj.* ritual

Ritus *m.* rite

Ritz *m.*, **Ritze** *f.* cleft, fissure; rift; crack; chink; scratch

ritzen *v.* to cut, to scratch, to graze, to slit

Rivale *m.* rival

rivalisieren *v.* to rival, to compete

Rivalität *f.* rivalry

Rizinusöl *neu.* castor oil

Robbe *f.* (zool.) seal; -fang *m.* sealing; -fänger *m.* sealer; seal hunter

Robber *m.* (cards) rubber

Roboter *m.* robot

robust *adj.* robust, sturdy

röcheln *v.* (throat) to rattle, to rasp

rochieren *v.* (chess) to castle

Rock *m.* coat; skirt; -schoss *m.* coattail; front of a skirt

Rocken *m.* distaff

Rodel *f.* toboggan; -bahn *f.* toboggan run; -schlitten *m.* toboggan; bobsled

rodeln *v.* to toboggan

roden *v.* to clear land, to root out, to stub

Roggen *m.* rye

roh *adj.* raw; crude; brutal; rough, rude; vulgar uncultured

Roh: -bau *m.* bare brickwork; -einnahmen *f. pl.* gross receipts; -eisen *neu.* pig iron; -kost *f.* vegetarian food; -köstler *m.* vegetarian; -ling *m.* cruel person; brute; -material *neu.*, -stoff *m.* raw material; -metall *neu.* crude metal

Rohr *neu.* cane; reed; pipe, tube; (gun) barrel; -dach *neu.* reed thatch; -dommel *f.* bittern; -geflecht *neu.* wickerwork; -kolben *m.* (bot.) cattail; -leger *m.* pipe fitter; plumber; -leitung *f.* pipeline; -mündung *f.* (gun) muzzle; -netz *neu.* pipes, conduit; -spatz *m.* reed sparrow; wie ein -spatz schimpfen to swear like a fishwife; -stock *m.* bamboo; -stuhl *m.* basket chair; -zucker *m.* cane sugar

Röhr: -e *f.* tube, pipe; conduit; -icht *neu.* reeds; canebrake

Roll: -e *f.* roll; roller; pulley; reel, spool; calender, mangle; caster; list, register;

(theat.) part; **aus der -e fallen** to misbehave; -enbesetzung *f.*, -enverteilung *f.* (theat.) cast; -er *m.* roller; canary; (toy) scooter; -feld *neu.* (avi.) runway; -film *m.* roll film; -kommando *neu.* raiding (*oder* murder) squad; -kutscher *m.* carrier, carter; -mops *m.* rolled pickled herring; -schiene *f.* rail; -schuhe *m. pl.* roller skates; -schuhbahn *f.* skating rink; -stuhl *m.* wheel chair; -treppe *f.* escalator; -wäsche *f.* laundry for mangling

rollen *v.* to roll; to mangle; to rumble; (avi.) to taxi; -des **Material** rolling stock

Roman *m.* novel; romance; -literatur *f.* fiction; -schriftsteller *m.* novelist; -tik *f.* romantic period; romanticism; -ze *f.* romance; ballad

romantisch *adj.* romantic

Römer *m.* Roman; rummer; large wine-glass

römischkatholisch *adj.* Roman Catholic

Romme *neu.* rummy (game)

Ronde *f.* (mil.) round; -ll *neu.* round (flower) bed; round tower

röntgen *v.* to X ray

Röntgen: -aufnahme *f.*, -bild *neu.* X-ray photograph; -strahlen *m. pl.* X rays

Ros: -e *f.* rose; (med.) erysipelas; -enkohl *m.* Brussel sprouts; -enkranz *m.* wreath of roses; rosary; -enkreuzer *m.* Rosicrucian; -enmontag *m.* last Monday before Lent; -enöl *neu.* attar of roses; -enstock *m.*, -enstrauch *m.* rose bush; -ette *f.* rosette

rosa *adj.* pink, rose-colored

rosig *adj.* rose, rosy, roseate

Rosine *f.* raisin; currant

Ross *neu.* horse, steed; **auf dem hohen — sitzen** to sit on one's high horse; -händler *m.* horse dealer; -kamm *m.* currycomb; -kastanie *f.* horse chestnut

Rösselsprung *m.* (chess) knight's move; riddle

Rost *m.* rust; gridiron; grate, grill; -braten *m.* (meat) roast; -fleck(en) *m.* ironmold; -schutz *m.* antirust

rost: -en *v.* to rust; -frei *adj.* (steel) stainless; -ig *adj.* rusty

Röstbrot *neu.* toast

rösten *v.* to roast, to grill, to toast

rot *adj.* red, ruddy; **der -e Hahn** (the) fire; **— werden** to blush; -bäckig *adj.* red-cheeked; -blond *adj.* auburn; -glühend *adj.* red-hot; -haarig *adj.* red-haired; -ieren to rotate, to revolve; -ten, sich zusammen -ten to form gangs

Rot *neu.* red; -auge *neu.*, -feder *f.* (ichth.) roach; -dorn *m.* pink hawthorn; -drossel *f.* redwing; -fuchs *m.* bay horse; -haut *f.* redskin; Indian; -käppchen *neu.* Red Riding Hood; -kehlchen *neu.* robin; -kohl *m.* red cabbage; -lauf *m.* (med.) erysipelas; -schwänzchen *neu.* (orn.) redstart; -spon *m.*, -wein *m.* red wine; claret; port; -stift *m.* red pencil; -tanne *f.* spruce; -welsch *neu.* thieves' argot; -wild *neu.* red deer

röt: -en *v.* to redden; -lich *adj.* reddish;

-lichbraun *adj.* russet
Röte *f.* redness; blush; **-l** *m.* red chalk (*oder* ochre); **-ln** *f. pl.* German measles
Rotte *f.* band, gang; troop
Rotz *m.* mucus; nasal discharge
Rou- **-lade** *f.* rolled meat; roulade; **-leau** *neu.* Venetian (*oder* roller) blind
Rüb- **-e** *f.* turnip; beet; **gelbe -e carrot;** **-enzucker** *m.* beet sugar; **-saat** *f.*, **-samen** *m.* rapeseed
Rubin *m.* ruby
Rubrik *f.* heading; rubric; column
rubrizieren *v.* to head; to arrange in columns
ruchbar *adj.* notorious, public; **— werden** to become known; to get about
ruchlos *adj.* infamous, impious, wicked
Ruck *m.* jerk, jolt; start; **auf einen — at one pull; sich einen — geben to pull oneself together; -sack** *m.* rucksack, shoulder bag
Rück- **-anspruch** *m.* (law) counterclaim; **-antwort** *f.*, **-äusserung** *f.* reply; **-berufung** *f.* recall; **-bleibsel** *neu.* remainder, residue; **-blick** *m.* retrospect; backward glance; **-erinnerung** *f.* reminiscence; **-fahrkarte** *f.* round-trip ticket; **-fahrt** *f.* return journey; **-fall** *m.* relapse; (law) reversion; **-gabe** *f.* restitution, return; **-gang** *m.* decrease; retrogression; recession; decline; **-grat** *neu.* backbone; **-halt** *m.* support; reserve; **-hand** *f.* (tennis) backhand; **-kauf** *m.* redemption, repurchase; **-kehr** *f.* return; **-lage** *f.* reserve fund; **-porto** *neu.* return postage; **-prall** *m.* rebound, recoil; **-ruf** *m.* recall; **-schlag** *m.* recoil; backstroke; reverse; **-schritt** *m.* regression, relapse; **-seite** *f.* back, wrong side; reverse; **-sicht** *f.* consideration, regard; **-sitz** *m.* back seat; **-sprache** *f.* consultation, discussion; **-stand** *m.* arrears, residue; **-stoss** *m.* rebuff; recoil; **-stossmotor** *m.* jet propulsion; **-tritt** *m.* retirement; resignation; **-trittbremse** *f.* coaster brake; **-vergütung** *f.* reimbursement; **-wärtsgang** *m.* reverse gear; **-weg** *m.* way back, return; **-wirkung** *f.* retroaction; reaction; **-zahlung** *f.* repayment; **-zug** *m.* retreat, withdrawal
Rückkoppelung *f.* feedback
rück- **-bezüglich** *adj.* reflexive; **-erstatten** to refund; **-fällig** *adj.* relapsing; (law) revertible; **-gängig** *adj.* going backward; **-gängig machen** to cancel, to recall, to break off; **-haltlos** *adj.* unreserved; open; **-läufig** *adj.* retrograde; **-lings** *adv.* backwards, from behind; **-schrittlich** *adj.* reactionary; **-sichtsvoll** *adj.* considerate, thoughtful; **-ständig** *adj.* in arrears; old-fashioned; **-wärtig** *adj.* retrograde; rearward; behind the lines; **-wärts** *adv.* back(wards); **-wirkend** *adj.* retroactive; retrospective; **-zahlen** *v.* to repay
Rücken *m.* back; rear; ridge; (nose) bridge; **es läuft mir eiskalt über den —** my spine tingles; **in den — fallen** to attack in the rear; **jemand den — kehren** to turn one's back to (*oder* on)

someone; **-flug** *m.* upside-down flying; **-lehne** *f.* (chair) back; **-mark** *neu.* spinal cord
rücken *v.* to move; to push; to draw; **an jemandes Stelle —** to take a person's place; **ins Feld —** to take the field; **jemand zu Leibe —** to press someone hard; **sich nicht von der Stelle —** not to budge an inch
Rüde *m.* male dog (*oder* fox, wolf)
Rudel *neu.* herd, troop, crowd, pack
Ruder *neu.* rudder, helm, oar; **ans — kommen** to come into power; **-bank** *f.* rower's seat; (naut.) thwart; **-boot** *neu.* rowboat; **-er** *m.* rower, oarsman; **-pinne** *f.* tiller
rudern *v.* to row; to pull an oar
Rüdiger *m.* Roger
Ruf *m.* cry, shout; call; summons; reputation; fame, name; credit; **im -e stehen** to be reputed (to be); to be generally considered (as); **er hat einen — als Professor erhalten** he has been offered a professorship; **in üblen — bringen** to defame; **Mann von — celebrity; -name** *m.* Christian name; **-nummer** *f.* (tel.) number; **-weite** *f.* earshot; **in -weite** within call; **-zeichen** *neu.* (tel.) call signal
rufen *v.* to cry, to shout; to call; to summon; **etwas ins Leben —** to call something into being; **ins Gedächtnis —** to recall to mind, to remind; **— lassen** to send for; **wieder ins Leben —** to restore to life; **wie gerufen kommen** to appear at the right moment
Rüffel *m.* reprimand, dressing down; rebuke
Rüge *f.* rebuke, reproach, reprimand, censure
rügen *v.* to blame, to censure, to reprimand
ruh- **-elos** *adj.* restless, disquieted; **-en** *v.* to rest, to repose; to sleep; to be buried; **eine Sache -en lassen** to drop a matter; **es -t auf ihm** it is his duty; **-en auf** to rest on, to be based on; **-endes Kapital** dead capital; **-ig** *adj.* quiet, still, silent; composed, calm; **-ig** *adv.* with pleasure, safely
Ruhe *f.* rest, repose; quiet, silence, calm; **in aller — very calmly; in — lassen** to let alone; **sich zur — setzen** to retire; **zur — bringen** to calm; to pacify; **zur — gehen** to go to bed; **-bett** *neu.* couch; **-gehalt** *neu.* pension; **-punkt** *m.* point of rest; pause; **-stand** *m.* retirement; **-stätte** *f.* resting place; **letzte -stätte** grave; **-störung** *f.* disturbance; **-tag** *m.* day off
Ruhm *m.* glory; renown; fame; **-eshalle** *f.* Hall of Fame, pantheon
ruhm- **-los** *adj.* inglorious; **-redig** *adj.* vainglorious; **-süchtig** *adj.* ambitious
rühmen *v.* to praise, to extol; to glorify; **sich —** to be proud (of); to brag
rühmlich *adj.* glorious, honorable
Ruhr *f.* dysentery
Rühr- **-ei** *neu.* scrambled eggs; **-löffel** *m.* ladle; **-stück** *neu.* melodrama, sob stuff;

-ung *f.* feeling, emotion; compassion
rühr: **-en** *v.* to move, to stir; to touch; to beat (drum); to affect; **-t euch!** (mil.) at ease! **-end** *adj.* affecting, touching; **-ig** *adj.* active, busy; agile, alert, nimble; **-selig** *adj.* sentimental, emotional
Ruin *m.* ruin; destruction; decay; **-e** *f.* ruins, debris; (coll.) wreck
ruinieren *v.* to ruin, to destroy
Rummel *m.* bustle; hubbub; amusement park; **den — kennen** (coll.) to know what's what; **den — verstehen** (coll.) to know a trick or two
rumoren *v.* to slam-bang; to rummage; to rumor
Rumpelkammer *f.* junk closet
Rumpf *m.* trunk; body; torso; (naut.) hull; fuselage; **-versteifung** (avi.) bulkhead
rümpfen *v.* **die Nase —** to turn up one's nose
rund *adj.* round, circular, plump; **-en** *v.* to round; to go around; (baseball) to make a run; **-heraus sagen** to speak frankly; **-herum** *adv.* all around; **-lich** *adj.* rounded, plump; **-weg** *adv.* bluntly, flatly
Rund: **-bau** *m.* circular building; **-blick** *m.* view all around; panorama; **-bogen** *m.* Roman arch; **-e** *f.* circle; (sports) lap; round; (coll.) party; **-erlass** *m.* circular (notice); **-fahrt** *f.* circular tour; **-frage** *f.* questionnaire; **-funk** *m.* radio, broadcasting; **-funkansager** *m.* radio announcer; **-funkempfänger** *m.* radio receiver; **-funkgerät** *neu.* radio set; **-funkhörer** *m.* radio listener; **-funksender** *m.* radio transmitter; **-funksendung** *f.* broadcasting; **-funkstation** *f.* radio station; **-funkzeitung** *f.* radio magazine; **-gang** *m.* round; stroll; **-gemälde** *neu.* panorama; **-reise** *f.* round trip; **-reisebillet** *neu.* round-trip ticket; **-schau** *f.* panorama; review; **-schreiben** *neu.* circular; **-ung** *f.* rounding; curve; roundness
Rune *f.* rune; **-nschrift** *f.* runic writing
Runkelrübe *f.* beet root
Runzel *f.* wrinkle; pucker
runzeln *v.* to wrinkle; **die Stirn —** to frown
runzlig *adj.* wrinkled, puckered
rupfen *v.* to pluck, to pull up; (coll.) to fleece
ruppig *adj.* unkempt; unmannered; shabby
Rüsche *f.* frill(ing), ruche
Russ *m.* soot
Russe *m.* Russian
Rüssel *m.* (zool.) trunk, snout, proboscis; **-käfer** *m.* weevil
russ(art)ig *adj.* sooty
Russland *neu.* Russia
Rüst: **-kammer** *f.* armory, arsenal; **-ungsanlage** *f.*, **-ungsbetrieb** *m.* munition works, armament plant; **-zeug** *neu.* tools, equipment; implements
rüsten *v.* to prepare; to equip; to arm
rüstig *adj.* robust, vigorous; active

Rute *f.* rod, switch, twig; tail; **-nbündel** *neu.* fasces; **-ngänger** *m.* dowser
Rutsch *m.* glide, slide; landslip; (coll.) short visit; **-bahn** *f.* slide, chute
rutschen *v.* to glide, to slide, to slip, to skid
rütteln *v.* to shake, to jog; to jolt; **gerüttelt voll** heaped, crammed

S

Saal *m.* hall, large room
Saat *f.* seed, sowing; young crop; **-feld** *neu.* grain field; **-gut** *neu.*, **-korn** *neu.* seed grain; **-krähe** *f.* rook
Sabbat *m.* Sabbath
Säbel *m.* sabre, sword; **-beine** *neu. pl.* bow legs; **-hieb** *m.* sword cut
sabotieren *v.* to sabotage
Sach: **-bearbeiter** *m.* administrator; **-e** *f.* thing; matter, subject; (law) case; **-en** *pl.* goods, clothes; **bei der -e sein** to pay attention to; **nicht bei der -e sein** to be absent minded; **nicht zur -e gehören** to be irrelevant; **seine sieben -en** (coll.) all his personal effects; **seiner -e gewiss sein** to be sure of one's facts; **zur -e!** come to the point! (pol.) question! **-kenner** *m.*, **-kundige** *m.* expert; **-kenntnis** *f.*, **-kunde** *f.* expert knowledge; **-lage** *f.* state of affairs; **-leistung** *f.* payment in kind; **-register** *neu.* index, list of contents; **-verhalt** *m.* facts of a case, **-verständige** *m.* specialist, authority; **-verwalter** *m.* attorney; counsel; **-wert** *m.* real value
sach: **-dienlich** *adj.* pertinent, relevant; useful; **-gemäss** *adj.* appropriate; proper; **-gemäss** *adv.* in a suitable manner; **-kundig** *adj.*, **-verständig** *adj.* competent, expert; **-lich** *adj.* real; objective; **-lich** *adv.* to the point
Sachsen *neu.* Saxony
sacht(e) *adj.* soft, gentle; easy-going, slow
Sack *m.* sack, bag; (dial.) pocket, purse; **mit — und Pack** with bag and baggage; **-erlot! -erment!** *interj.* Darn it! **-garn** *neu.* twine; **-gasse** *f.* blind alley (fig.) deadlock; **-hüpfen** *neu.*, **-laufen** *neu.* sack race; **-leinen** *neu.*, **-leinewand** *f.* sackcloth; **-pfeife** *f.* bagpipe; **-tuch** *neu.* (dial.) handkerchief
sacken *v.* to sack; to pocket; to sink
säen *v.* to sow
Säer, Sämann *m.* sower
Saft *m.* sap, juice; fluid, liquid; **voll —** succulent; **weder — noch Kraft haben** to have no energy, to be insipid
saftig *adj.* juicy; spicy, coarse
Sage *f.* legend; myth; saga; **es geht die —** the story goes
Säge *f.* saw; **-blatt** *neu.* saw blade; **-bock** *m.* sawhorse; **-mehl** *neu.*, **-späne** *m. pl.* sawdust; **-mühle** *f.*, **-werk** *neu.* sawmill
sagen *v.* to say, to tell; to signify; **das hat nichts zu —** that does not matter; **er lässt sich nichts —** he will not listen to reason; **gesagt, getan** no sooner said than done, **ich habe mir — lassen** I was told; **ich muss —** I must admit;

lassen Sie es sich gesagt sein believe me; let it be a warning to you; **— lassen** to send word; **— wollen mit** to mean by; **-haft** adj. legendary, mythical

sägen v. to saw; (coll.) to snore

Sahne f. cream

Saison f. season; **-arbeiter** m. seasonal worker; **-ausverkauf** m. clearance sale

Saite f. (mus.) string, cord; **andere -n aufziehen** to change one's attitude; **-ninstrument** neu. stringed instrument; **-nspiel** neu. lyre; string music

Sakrament neu. sacrament

Sakristei f. vestry

Säkularfeier f. centennial; centenary

säkularisieren v. to secularize

Salat m. salad; **da haben wir den —!** (coll.) that's a fine mess; **grüner —** lettuce

Salb: **-e** f. salve, ointment; **-ung** f. anointment, unction

salbadern v. to wheedle, to prattle

Salbei m. and f. (bot.) sage

salben v. to anoint, to salve

salbungsvoll adj. unctuous; smug, pathetic

saldieren v. to balance, to settle

Saldo m. (com.) balance; **— ziehen** to strike a balance; **-vortrag** m. balance forward

Salm m. salmon

Salmiak m. sal ammoniac; **-geist** m. liquid ammonia

Salon m. drawing room; (naut.) saloon; **-held** m., **-löwe** m. playboy; **-wagen** m. Pullman car

Salpeter m. saltpeter, sodium nitrate

Salto m. somersault; **-mortale** m. breakneck leap

Salut m. (mil.) salute; **-schuss** m. gun salute

salutieren v. to salute

Salve f. volley; salvo; (naut.) broadside

Salz neu. salt; (coll.) wit; **-bergwerk** neu. salt mine; **-fass** neu. salt shaker; **-gurke** f. pickled cucumber; **-hering** m. pickled herring; **-lake** f., **-lauge** f. brine, pickle; **-lecke** f. salt lick; **-sole** f. salt water; brine

salz: **-artig** adj. saline; **-bildend** adj. saltforming; **-en** v. to salt, to season; **gesalzene Preise** exorbitant prices; **-ig** adj. salty

Säm: **-aschine** f. seeding machine; **-ereien** f. pl. seeds; **-ling** m. seedling

Samariter m. Samaritan

Same(n) m. seed; sperm; **-nkapsel** f. seedcase; **-nkorn** neu. grain of seed; **-nstaub** m. pollen

Samm: **-elband** m. (lit.) omnibus; volume; **-elbecken** neu., **-elbehälter** m. reservoir; **-elbüchse** f. collecting box; **-elplatz** m. meeting place; **-elruf** m. (mil.) assembly; **-elstelle** f. central depot; collecting station; **-elsurium** neu. medley; **-elwort** neu. collective noun; **-ler** m. collector; compiler; **-lung** f. collection; composure, concentration

sammeln v. to gather, to collect; to accumulate; to assemble, to rally; to con-

centrate; **sich —** to compose oneself

Samstag m. (dial.) Saturday

samt prep. and adv. together with; **— und sonders** each and all, jointly and severally

Sam(me)t m. velvet; **jemanden mit -handschuhen anfassen** to handle someone very delicately

sämtlich adj. all (together); **—** adv. collectively, as a whole

Sand m. sand, grit; **auf — bauen** to build on an uncertain foundation; **im -e verlaufen** to come to naught; **wie — am Meer** (bibl.) innumerable; **-bahn** f. dirt track; **-boden** m. sandy soil; **-korn** neu. grain of sand; **-läufer** m. sandpiper; **-mann** m. sandman; **-papier** neu. sandpaper; **-stein** m. sandstone

Sandale f. sandal

sandig adj. sandy, gritty

sanft adj. soft, smooth; gentle, mild; slight; **-mütig** adj. gentle, mild, goodnatured; meek

Sänfte f. sedan chair; litter

Sanftmut m. gentleness, mildness

Sang m. song, singing; **ohne — und Klang** silently, unceremoniously

Sänger m. singer; songster; poet

sanieren v. to cure; to restore

Sanierung f. restoration, reorganization

sanitär adj. sanitary

Sanität: **-er** m. ambulance man; **-sbehörde** f. Board of Health; **-shund** m. first-aid dog; **-skolonne** f. ambulance corps; **-soffizier** m. medical officer; **-swache** f. first-aid station; **-swagen** m. motor ambulance

Sankt adj. saint; **-ion** f. sanction; **-ionierung** f. confirmation, recognition; ratification

sanktionieren v. to sanction

Saphir m. sapphire

Sarg m. coffin; **-deckel** m. coffin lid; **-tuch** neu. pall

sarkastisch adj. sarcastic

satanisch adj. satanic

Satellit m. satellite

Satin m. satin, sateen

Satire f. satire

satirisch adj. satiric(al)

satt adj. satisfied; satiated; deep, intense; rich; saturated; **etwas — haben** to be fed up with something; **nicht — werden** never to tire of; **nicht — zu bekommen** insatiable; **sich — essen** to eat one's fill; **-sam** adv. sufficiently, enough

Sattel m. saddle; bridge (of nose); ridge; **aus dem — heben** to unhorse; to supersede; **fest im — sitzen** to be firmly established; **in allen Sätteln gerecht sein** to have all-around experience, to be Jack-of-all-trades; **-dach** neu. ridged roof; **-knopf** m. (saddlebow) pommel; **-pferd** neu. saddle horse; left horse; **-zeug** neu. saddle and harness

sattelfest adj. firm in the saddle; proficient; knowing one's business (oder trade), mastering one's trade

satteln v. to saddle

sättigen v. to satiate, to satisfy; to saturate; **sich —** to appease one's hunger

Sattler *m.* saddler; **-ei** *f.* saddlery

Satyr *m.* satyr

Satz *m.* sentence; proposition, thesis, theorem; composition; phrase; bound, leap; set; sediment; (com.) rate, charge; (typ.) matter; **in — geben** to give to the typesetter; **-bau** *m.* (gram.) construction; **-bild** *neu.* (typ.) setting; **-fehler** *m.* misprint; **-gefüge** *neu.* complex sentence; **-lehre** *f.* syntax; **-spiegel** *m.* (typ.) face; page proof; **-ung** *f.* statute; ordinance; regulations; **-zeichen** *neu.* punctuation mark

satzungsgemäss, satzungsmässig *adj.* statutory

Sau *f.* sow; **unter aller —** (sl.) beneath contempt; **-bohne** *f.* broad bean; **-kerl** *m.* dirty fellow; **-stall** *m.* pigsty; dirty place; **-wetter** *neu.* bad weather

sauber *adj.* clean, neat, tidy; (coll.) fine

säubern *v.* to clean, to clear, to purge

Sauce *f.* sauce; gravy

sauer *adj.* sour, acid, pickled; hard; morose; cross; **-töpfisch** *adj.* peevish, sour, sullen

Sauer:-ampfer *m.* (bot.) sorrel; **-braten** *m.* marinated beef roast; **-kohl** *m.*, **-kraut** *neu.* sauerkraut; **-milch** *f.* curdled milk; **-stoff** *m.* oxygen; (flüssig) lox; **-teig** *m.* sourdough; **-stoffmangel** *m.* anoxia

säuern *v.* to make sour; to leaven

Sauf:-bold *m.* drunkard; **-en** *neu.* drinking; **-erei** *f.*, **-gelage** *neu.* drinking bout; booze

saufen *v.* to drink; to booze; to carouse

Säufer *m.* drunkard; **-wahnsinn** *m.* delirium tremens

Saug:-er *m.* sucker; (bottle) nipple; **-flasche** *f.* feeding bottle; **-heber** *m.* siphon; **-rüssel** *m.* proboscis; **-scheibe** *f.* suction disk

Säug:-en *neu.* suckling, nursing; lactation; **-etier** *neu.* mammal; **-ling** *m.* suckling; baby; infant; **-lingsfürsorge** *f.* infant welfare; **-lingsheim** *neu.* nursery; home for infants

saugen *v.* to suck(le); to absorb; **sich etwas aus den Fingern —** to invent tales

säugen *v.* to suckle, to nurse

Säule *f.* column, pillar; (phys.) pile; **-nfuss** *m.* pedestal; **-gang** *m.*, **-halle** *f.* colonnade, arcade; portico; **-knauf** *m.* (arch.) capital

Saum *m.* seam, hem; border, edge; **-pfad** *m.* mule track; **-pferd** *neu.* pack horse; **-tier** *neu.* pack mule (*oder* horse)

säumen *v.* to hem; to border; to tarry; to hesitate; to lag behind; to delay

saumselig *adj.* tardy; lazy; negligent

Säure *f.* sourness, tartness; acidity; acid; **-messer** *m.* acidimeter

Saus *m.* **in — und Braus leben** to live riotously

säuseln *v.* to rustle, to whisper, to buzz

sausen *v.* to rush, to dash; to sough

Saxophon *neu.* saxophone

Schabe *f.* cockroach

Schabe:-fleisch *neu.* scraped meat; **-r** *m.* scraper; **-rnack** *m.* trick, hoax

schaben *v.* to scrape, to grate; to rasp; to graze; (art) to rub

schäbig *adj.* shabby; stingy; mean

Schablon: -enhaft *adj.*, **-enmässig** *adj.* mechanical; stereotyped; **-isieren** *v.* to stencil

Schablone *f.* model, pattern; stencil

Schach *neu.* chess; **in — halten** to keep in check; **— bieten** to (give) check; **-brett** *neu.* chessboard; **-feld** *neu.* (chess) square; **-figur** *f.* chessman; **-meister** *m.* chess champion; **-partie** *f.* game of chess; **-zug** *m.* (chess) move; clever move

Schach: -er *m.* bargaining, jobbery; **-erer** *m.* haggler

Schächer *m.* (bibl.) thief; poor wretch

schachern *v.* to bargain, to haggle, to job

schachmatt *adj.* checkmated; knocked out

Schacht *m.* shaft, pit

Schachtel *f.* box; **alte —** old frump; **-deckel** *m.* box lid

Schächter *m.* (kosher) butcher

schad: -e *adj.* regrettable; **dafür ist es zu -e** it's too good for that; **es ist -e** it's a pity; **wie -e!** what a pity! too bad! **-en** to damage, to harm, to hurt; **das -et dir nichts** that serves you right; **das -et nichts** that does not matter, never mind; **-enfroh** *adj.* rejoicing over another's misfortune, malicious; **-haft** *adj.* damaged, defective, faulty; **-los** *adj.* undamaged; **sich -los halten** to indemnify; to recoup oneself

Schad: -en *m.* damage, harm, injury; defect; loss; disadvantage, detriment; mischief; **durch -en wird man klug** a burnt child fears the fire; **jemand -en zufügen** to harm someone; **mit -en verkaufen** to sell at a loss; **-en leiden** to come to grief; **-enersatz** *m.* compensation, indemnification; **-enersatzklage** *f.* action for damages; **-enfeuer** *neu.* destructive fire; **-loshaltung** *f.* indemnification

Schäd: -igung *f.* damage; prejudice; **-ling** *m.* noxious person (*oder* animal); vermin; parasite

Schädel *m.* skull; (fig.) head; **-bohrer** *m.* (med.) trepan; **-bruch** *m.* skull fracture

schädigen *v.* to damage, to injure, to harm

schädlich *adj.* injurious, hurtful; noxious

Schaf *neu.* sheep; **weibliches —** ewe; (coll.) simpleton; **-bremse** *f.* botfly; **-bock** *m.* ram; **-fell** *neu.* sheepskin, fleece; **-fleisch** *neu.* mutton; **-garbe** *f.* yarrow; **-herde** *f.* flock of sheep; **-hirt(e)** *m.* shepherd; **-hürde** *f.* sheepfold; **-schur** *f.* sheep shearing; **-skopf** *m.* sheepshead; **-stand** *m.* stock of sheep; **-zucht** *f.* sheep breeding

Schäf: -chen *neu.* lamb(kin); **seine -chen ins Trockene bringen** to feather one's nest; **-chenwolke** *f.* cirrus (cloud); **-er** *m.* shepherd; **-erei** *f.* sheep farm; **-ergedicht** *neu.* pastoral, idyll, eclogue; **-erin** *f.* shepherdess; **-erspiel** *neu.* pastoral play; **-erstunde** *f.* lover's hour

schaffen *v.* to create, to produce; to work;

to accomplish; to provide; to convey; to remove; **an Ort und Stelle** — to bring to the agreed place; **er weiss immer Rat zu** — he is never at a loss; **ich habe nichts damit zu** — it doesn't concern me; **jemanden aus dem Wege (or beiseite)** — to kill (*oder* remove) someone; **jemandem viel zu** — **machen** to give someone a lot of trouble; **sich zu** — **machen** to putter about

Schaffner *m.* conductor; **-in** *f.* housekeeper; female conductor

Schafott *neu.* scaffold; execution place

schäkern *v.* to joke, to dally, to flirt

schal *adj.* insipid; stale; flat, dull

Schal *m.* shawl, scarf, comforter; **-e** *f.* shell; peel, skin; hull, husk; pod; cup, dish, bowl, basin; scale; **-entier** *neu.* crustacean

Schäl: -hengst *m.* stallion; **-maschine** *f.* peeling machine; **-pflug** *m.* breastplow

schälen *v.* to peel, to pare; to husk, to shell; to bark; **sich** — to peel (off), to cast one's shell; to shed (bark); to scale

Schalk *m.* rogue, wag; jester; **-haftigkeit** *f.*, **-heit** *f.* waggishness; archness; roguery; **-snarr** *m.* court jester

schalkhaft *adj.* roguish, waggish; jocular

Schall *m.* sound, reverberation; **-becken** *neu.* cymbal; **-boden** *m.* soundboard; **-dämpfer** *m.* silencer, muffler; **-explosion** *f.* sonic boom; **-grenze** *f.* sound barrier; **-lehre** *f.* acoustics; **-platte** *f.* record; **-plattenrille** *f.* microgroove; **-rille** *f.* groove; **-trichter** *m.* bell; horn; megaphone; **-welle** *f.* sound wave

schall: -dicht *adj.* soundproof; **-en** *v.* to ring; to (re)sound; **-end** *adj.* resonant; sonorous

Schalt: -anlage *f.* switch gear; **-brett** *neu.* switchboard; dashboard; instrument panel; **-er** *m.* switch; ticket window, counter; **-getriebe** *neu.* main gearshift; **-jahr** *neu.* leap year; **-schlüssel** *m.* ignition key; **-tafel** *f.* switchboard; **-ung** *f.* gearshift; (elec.) connection

schalten *v.* to rule, to direct; (elec.) to switch, to connect; to put into gear; to deal with; **jemand** — **und walten lassen** to give someone full control

Scham *f.* shame; bashfulness, modesty; (anat.) genitals; **-bug** *m.* (anat.) groin; **-gefühl** *neu.* sense of shame; **-röte** *f.* blush; **-teile** *m. pl.* genitals

scham: -haft *adj.* bashful, chaste; **-los** *adj.* shameless, impudent; **-rot** *adj.* blushing

schämen *v.* **sich** — to be ashamed (of)

Schand: -bube *m.* scoundrel; **-e** *f.* shame; disgrace; **-fleck** *m.* blemish, stain; **-gedicht** *neu.*, **-schrift** *f.* libelous writing; **-geld** *neu.*, **-preis** *m.* scandalous price; **-mal** *neu.* brand; mark of infamy; **-maul** *neu.* evil tongue, slanderer; **-pfahl** *m.* pillory; whipping post; **-tat** *f.* crime, misdeed, infamous action

Schän: -er *m.* violator; ravisher; **-lichkeit** *f.* infamy, baseness; **-ung** *f.* defamation; desecration; disfigurement; violation, rape

schandbar *adj.* shameful; infamous

schänden *v.* to dishonor, to defame; to sully, to brand; to desecrate, to profane; to rape

schändlich *adj.* infamous, atrocious

Schank *m.* sale (of liquors); **-berechtigung** *f.* liquor license; **-bier** *neu.* tap beer; **-tisch** *m.* bar; **-wirtschaft** *f.* tavern, bar

Schanz: -arbeiten *f. pl.* entrenchments; **-e** *f.* redoubt; entrenchment; **sein Leben in die -e schlagen** to risk one's life

Schar *f.* troop; flock; crowd; plowshare; **-führer** *m.* platoon leader; **-mützel** *neu.* skirmish; **-wache** *f.* watch; patrol

Scharade *f.* charade

scharen *v.* **sich** — to assemble; to flock

scharf *adj.* sharp, cutting; pointed; harsh, caustic; acute; shrill; keen; rigorous; — **bewachen** to watch closely; **-e Patrone** live cartridge; **-e Zucht** rigid discipline; — **reiten** to ride hard; **-sichtig** *adj.* sharp-sighted; penetrating; **-sinnig** *adj.* sagacious, ingenious

Scharf: -blick *m.* penetrating glance; keen eye; acuteness; **-macher** *m.* agitator; firebrand; **-richter** *m.* executioner; **-schütze** *m.* sharpshooter; **-sicht** *f.* perspicacity; **-sinn** *m.* sagacity, acumen, ingeniousness

Schärfe *f.* sharpness, acuteness; severity; pungency; precision; edge

schärfen *v.* to sharpen, to point; to whet; to intensify, to increase, to strengthen

Scharlach *m.* scarlet; **-fieber** *neu.* scarlet fever

scharlachfarben, scharlachrot *adj.* scarlet, vermilion

scharmant *adj.* charming, fascinating

Scharnier *neu.* hinge, joint

Schärpe *f.* sash

scharren *v.* to scrape, to scratch; (horse) to paw; to shuffle (feet)

schartig *adj.* dented, jagged, notchy

scharwenzeln *v.* to fawn, to toady

schatt: -enhaft *adj.* shadowy; unreal, ghostly; **-ieren** *v.* to shade, to tint; to hatch (drawing); **-ig** *adj.* shady, shaded

Schatten *m.* shade, shadow; phantom, spirit; **in den** — **stellen** to place (*oder* throw) in the shade; to eclipse; (elec.) **-bild** *neu.* silhouette; phantom; **-könig** *m.* mock king, kinglet; **-reich** *neu.* underworld, Hades; **-riss** *m.* silhouette; **-spiel** *neu.* shadow play; phantasmagoria

Schatulle *f.* cash box; private fund

Schatz *m.* treasure, riches; hoard; darling, sweetheart; **-amt** *neu.* treasury; exchequer; **-anweisung** *f.* treasury note; **-gräber** *m.* treasure hunter; **-kammer** *f.* treasury; **-meister** *m.* treasurer

schätz: -bar *adj.*, **-enswert** *adj.* estimable; valuable; **-en** *v.* to estimate; to value, to judge; to esteem; to appreciate; to respect; **-ungsweise** *adv.* approximately, probably

Schätzung *f.* estimate; appraisal, esteem; appreciation; **-swert** *m.* estimated value

Schau f. show, view; display, exhibition; review; **zur — stellen** to exhibit, to display; **-brot** neu. (bibl.) shewbread; **-bude** f. booth (at a fair); **-budenbesitzer** m. showman; **-bühne** f. stage, theater; **-fenster** neu. show window; **-fensterreklame** f. window display; **-gefecht** neu. sham battle; **-gerüst** neu. platform, grandstand; **-haus** neu. mortuary, morgue; **-kasten** m. showcase; **-münze** f. medal; **-packung** f. dummy; **-platz** m. scene, theater; **-spiel** neu. play; drama; spectacle, scene, sight; **-spieldichter** m. dramatist, playwright; **-spieldirektor** m. theatrical manager; **-spieler** m. actor, player; **-spielerin** f. actress; **-spielkunst** f. dramatic art; **-spieltruppe** f. touring company; **-stellung** f. exhibition, show; **-stück** neu. show piece; specimen; **-turnen** neu. gymnastic display

schau! interj. look! **-en** v. to see, to observe, to look, to gaze; **-lustig** adj. curious; **-spielern** v. to act; to sham; to play-act

Schauder m. shudder(ing), shivering; fright

schauder: -erregend adj., **-haft** adj. horrible; shocking, awful, terrible, atrocious; **-n** v. to shudder, to shiver, to feel creepy

Schauer m. shuddering; fit; awe; thrill; shower; **-drama** neu. thriller; **-leute** pl. stevedores; **-roman** m. dime novel, ghastly novel

schauer: -lich adj., **-rig** adj. awful, horrible; ghastly; **-n** v. to feel awe (for); to shudder

Schaufel f. shovel, scoop; paddle; **-rad** neu. paddle wheel

schaufeln v. to shovel

Schaukel f. swing; **-pferd** neu. rocking horse; **-stuhl** m. rocking chair

schaukeln v. to swing, to rock; **wir werden das Kind schon —** (coll.) we'll take care of the matter

Schaum m. foam, spume, froth; (soap) lather; **-gold** neu. tinsel; **-kelle** f., **-löffel** m. skimmer, skimming ladle; **-schläger** m. empty talker, windbag; **-wein** m. sparkling wine; champagne

schäumen v. to foam, to froth, to effervesce, to sparkle; (soap) to lather; **vor Wut —** to boil with rage

Scheck m. (bank) check; **-buch** neu. checkbook; **-formular** neu. blank check; **-inhaber** m. bearer

scheckig adj. piebald, dappled, speckled

scheel adj. envious; squint-eyed; askew; **-süchtig** adj. envious, jealous

Scheffel m. bushel

Scheibe f. disk; slice; (ast.) orb; honeycomb; (mech.) dial; (mil.) practice target; (potter's) wheel; (window) pane; **-ngardine** f. cafe curtain; **-nhonig** m. honey in the comb; **-nschiessen** neu. target shooting; **-nstand** m. target range; **-nwischer** m. windshield wiper

Scheich m. sheik

Scheide f. sheath, scabbard; boundary, limit; (anat.) vagina; **-blick** m. parting glance; **-brief** m. farewell letter; **-gruss** m. farewell; **-kunst** f. analytical chemistry; **-mauer** f., **-wand** f. partition; **-münze** f. small coin, change; **-weg** m. parting of ways; crossroad

scheiden v. to separate, to divide; to analyze, to divorce; **sich —** to part; to separate, to depart; **sich — lassen** to get divorced

Scheidung f. separation; divorce

Schein m. shine, light; appearance; certificate; receipt; banknote; **es ist alles nur —** it's nothing but make-believe; **sich den — geben** to feign, to pretend; **zum —** as a matter of form; **-angriff** m. sham attack; **-grund** m. pretense; sophism; **-heilige** m. hypocrite; **-könig** m. mock king; **-werfer** m. searchlight, headlight, spotlight

schein: -bar adj. seeming, apparent, pretended; **-en** v. to shine; to appear, to seem; **-heilig** adj. hypocritical; **-tot** adj. seemingly dead

Scheit m. and neu. log

Scheitel m. (hair) parting; vertex, summit; **-punkt** m. vertex, zenith

scheiteln v. to part (hair)

scheitern v. to run aground, to wreck, to fail

Schelle f. (small) bell; manacle; (dial.) box on the ear; **-n** pl. (cards) diamonds; **-ngeläut** neu. tinkling of bells; **-nkappe** f. fool's cap and bells

schellen v. to ring (oder pull) a bell

Schelm m. rogue; knave; **-enstreich** neu., **-enstück** neu., **-erei** f. roguery, prank

schelmisch adj. roguish; arch

schelten v. to scold, to reprimand, to abuse

Schema neu. scheme; model, patter; schedule; diagram; order, arrangement

Schenk m. (lit.) cupbearer; **-e** f. bar, inn, tavern

Schenkel m. thigh; shank; leg; (geom.) side; **-bruch** m. fracture of the thighbone

schenken v. to pour out; to retail liquor; to donate, to present, to grant; **das Leben —** to give birth; to grant life

Schenker m. donor

Schenkungsurkunde f. deed of gift

Scherbe f. fragment; potsherd; (sl.) monocle

Schere f. scissors; shears; clippers; claw (of crabs); **-nfernrohr** neu. periscope; **-nschleifer** m. scissors grinder; **-nschnitt** m. silhouette

scheren v. to shear, to clip; to shave; to warp; (naut.) to sheer; to bother, to disturb; **sich fort —** to be off, to go away

Schererei f. vexation; bother, trouble

Scherflein neu. mite; **sein — beitragen** to do one's bit

Scherge m. executioner; beadle; bailiff

Scherz m. jest, joke, pleasantry; **— treiben mit** to make fun of; **-wort** neu. joke

scherz: -en v. to make merry, to jest, to joke; **-haft** adj. jocular, playful; **-liebend** adj. frolicsome, waggish; **-weise** adv. for fun

Scheu f. shyness; timidity; awe; **ohne —** bold; **-sal** neu. monster

scheu adj. shy; timid; skittish; **— machen** to intimidate; **-chen** v. to scare, to frighten

Scheuche f. scarecrow; bugbear

scheuen v. to shy (at), to avoid, to shun; **sich —** to be afraid (of), to hesitate; **keine Mühe —** to spare no trouble

Scheuer f. barn, shed

Scheuer: -bürste f. scrubbing brush; **-frau** f. cleaning woman; **-lappen** m. scouring cloth; **-leiste** f. baseboard

scheuern v. to scour, to scrub; to rub, to chafe

Scheune f. barn, shed

scheusslich adj. atrocious, hideous, horrible

Schicht f. layer, bed, stratum; shift; coating; class, rank; (wood) pile; **-enbildildung** f. stratification; **-meister** m. (min.) overseer; **-wechsel** m. change of shift

schichten v. to arrange in layers; to pile up; to stratify; to classify

Schick m. skill, fitness; elegance, chic; **-lichkeitsgefühl** neu. sense of propriety, tact; **-sal** neu. destiny, fate; lot; **-salsglaube** m. fatalism; **-salsschlag** m. misfortune; **-ung** f. affliction; dispensation; Providence

schick adj. chic, stylish; smart; **-en** v. to send, to dispatch; to transmit; **es -t sich** to be becoming (oder proper); **sich für** (or zu) **etwas -en** to be adapted for something; **-lich** adj. proper, decent; becoming

Schieb: -efenster neu. sash window; **-er** m. slide (rule); profiteer; **-etür** f. sliding door; **-karren** m. wheelbarrow; **-ung** f. profiteering

schieben v. to push, to shove; to slide; to shift; to profiteer; **die Schuld auf jemand —, jemandem etwas in die Schuhe —** to put the blame on someone; **Kegel —** to bowl

Schieds: -gericht neu. court of arbitration; **-smann** m., **-srichter** m. arbitrator; referee; **-spruch** m. arbitration, decision

schief adj. slanting, inclined; crooked; bent; wry; **-er Winkel** oblique angle; **— adv.** awry; **das geht —** that fails; **jemand — ansehen** to look askance at someone; **— gewickelt** (coll.) in error

Schiefer m. slate; **-bruch** m. slate quarry; **-dach** neu. slate roof; **-decker** m. slater; **-tafel** f. (school) slate

schielen v. to squint; to be cross-eyed; **— nach** to leer at

Schien: -bein neu. shinbone; **-e** f. rail; (med.) splint; **aus den — kommen** to derail; **-ennetz** neu. railway system; **-enstrang** m. railroad track; **-enweite** f. gauge

schier adj. pure, sheer; **— adv.** almost

Schiess: -ausbildung f. gunnery drill; **-baumwolle** f. guncotton; **-bedarf** m. ammunition; **-bude** f. shooting gallery; **-gewehr** neu. gun, rifle; **-lehre** f. ballistics; **-platz** m. firing range; **-prügel** m. (coll.) firearm; **-pulver** neu. gunpowder; **-scharte** f. loophole, embrasure; **-scheibe** f. target; **-stand** m. rifle range

schiessen v. to shoot, to fire; (sports) to score; to dart, to rush; (plants) to spring up; **die Zügel — lassen** to give rein to; **einen Bock —** to pull a boner; **einen Purzelbaum —** to somersault; **es ist zum —** it's just too funny; **hinterrücks —** to snipe; **in Samen —** to run to seed

Schiff neu. ship, boat; (arch.) nave; (mech.) shuttle; **-(f)ahrt** f. navigation; **-bau** m. shipbuilding; **-bruch** m. shipwreck; **-brüchige** m. castaway; **-er** m. skipper, sailor, navigator; **-erklavier** neu. (coll.) accordion; **-sbesatzung** f. ship's crew; **-sbrücke** f. pontoon bridge; **-sjournal** neu. logbook; **-sjunge** m. cabin boy; **-skörper** m., **-srumpf** m. hull; **-sladung** f. ship's cargo; **-smakler** m. ship broker; **-sraum** m. hold, tonnage

schiff: -bar adj. navigable; **-brüchig** adj. shipwrecked; **-en** v. to navigate, to ship

Schikane f. chicanery, vexation, annoyance

schikanieren v. to annoy, to vex, to irritate

schikanös adj. vexatious

Schild m. shield, buckler; escutcheon; **etwas im -e führen** to have something up one's sleeves; **—** neu. signboard; nameplate; label; peak (of cap); **-bürger** m. duffer; **-drüse** f. thyroid gland; **-erhaus** neu. sentry box; **-knappe** m. shield bearer, squire; **-kröte** f. tortoise, turtle; **-wache** f. sentry, sentinel

schildern v. to describe, to depict, to paint

Schilderung f. description, depiction

Schilf neu. reed, sedge; **-rohr** neu. reed(s)

schillern v. to change colors; **-d** adj. iridescent, opalescent

Schimäre f. chimera, phantom

Schimmel m. mildew; mold; white horse

schimmelig adj. mildewy, moldy, musty

Schimmer m. glimmer, gleam, shimmer; **er hat keinen —** he hasn't the faintest idea

schimmern v. to glimmer, to glitter, to glisten

Schimpanse m. chimpanzee

Schimpf m. affront, insult; disgrace; **-name** m. abusive name; **-wort** neu. invective

schimpfen v. to abuse, to revile, to scold

schimpflich adj. disgraceful, scandalous

Schindel f. shingle

schinden v. to flay, to skin; to exploit, to sweat; **sich —** to drudge, to slave

Schinken m. ham; (sl.) old book, bad painting

Schippe f. spade, shovel, scoop

schippen v. to shovel

Schirm m. umbrella; screen; peak (of

cap); shelter, protection; **–dach** *neu.* penthouse; lean-to; **–er** *m.*, **–herr** *m.* patron, protector; **–herrschaft** *f.* protectorate; **–mütze** *f.* peaked cap; **–ständer** *m.* umbrella stand

schirmen *v.* to protect, to shield, to screen

schirren *v.* to harness

Schisma *neu.* schism; **–tiker** *m.* schismatic

schlabbern *v.* to slobber, to slaver; to babble

Schlacht *f.* battle, fight; **–bank** *f.* shambles; **–enbummler** *m.* camp follower; **–feld** *neu.* battlefield; **–getümmel** *neu.*, **–gewühl** *neu.* affray; melee; **–haus** *neu.*, **–hof** *m.* slaughterhouse, abattoir; **–messer** *neu.* butcher's knife; **–opfer** *neu.* victim; sacrifice; **–ordnung** *f.* order of battle; **–ruf** *m.* battle cry; **–schiff** *neu.* battleship; **–vieh** *neu.* fattened stock

schlachten *v.* to slaughter, to massacre

Schlächter *m.* butcher; **–ei** *f.* butcher shop; butchery, massacre, slaughter

Schlacke *f.* slag; cinder, dross, scum

schlacken *v.* to form slag

Schlaf *m.* sleep; fester — sound (*oder* deep) sleep; **im — liegen** to be asleep; **–anzug** *m.* pajamas; **–bursche** *m.* night lodger; **–enszeit** *f.* bedtime; **–gefährte** *m.*, **–genosse** *m.* bedfellow; **–gewand** *neu.* nightgown; **–lied** *neu.* lullaby; **–losigkeit** *f.* sleeplessness, insomnia; **–mittel** *neu.* soporific, sleeping pill; **–mütze** *f.* nightcap; sleepyhead; **–rock** *m.* dressing gown; **–saal** *m.* dormitory; **–sack** *m.* sleeping bag; **–stelle** *f.* night's lodging; **–stube** *f.*, **–zimmer** *neu.* bedroom; **–wagen** *m.* Pullman, sleeping car; **–wandler** *m.* sleepwalker, somnambulist

schlaf: **–en** to sleep; **–en gehen** to go to bed; **–mützig** *adj.* sluggish, sleepy; **–trunken** *adj.* drowsy; **–wandeln** to sleepwalk

Schläf: **–chen** *neu.* doze, nap, forty winks; **–er** *m.* sleeper

schläfern *v.* to feel sleepy

Schläfe *f.* (anat.) temple

schläf(e)rig *adj.* sleepy, drowsy, somnolent

schlaff *adj.* slack; flabby; loose; limp; lax

Schlag *m.* blow, stroke, slap; punch; coach door; (bird's) song; (clock) striking; (heart) beat; apoplexy; (pigeon) loft; (thunder) clap; (wood) cut; (fig.) race, kind; **ein Mann von meinem –e** a man after my own heart; **elektrischer — electric shock; — drei Uhr** three o'clock sharp; **–ader** *f.* artery; **–anfall** *m.*, **–fluss** *m.* apoplectic stroke; **–ball** *m.* bat and ball; **–baum** *m.* turnpike; **–bolzen** *m.* firing pin; **–er** *m.* song hit; **–fertigkeit** *f.* quickness at repartee; **–holz** *neu.*, **–instrument** *neu.* percussion instrument; **–kraft** *f.* striking power; **–obers** *neu.*, **–rahm** *m.*, **–sahne** *f.* whipped cream; **–wort** *neu.* catchword; slogan; **–zeile** *f.* headline; **–zeug** *neu.* percussion instruments

schlag: **–artig** *adv.* all of a sudden; **–en** *v.* to strike, to beat, to hit; to knock, to

kick; (birds) to sing; to coin (money); to cut (wood); **Alarm –en** to sound alarm; **ans Kreuz –en** to crucify; **ans schwarze Brett –en** to announce on the blackboard; **aus der Art –en** to vary from type; **das schlägt nicht in mein Fach** that's not in my line; **die Beine übereinander –en** to cross one's legs; **die Zinsen zum Kapital –en** to add the interest to the capital; **eine Brücke –en** to build a bridge; **ein Figur –en** (chess) to take a piece; **eine geschlagene Stunde** a whole hour; **einen Knoten –en** to tie a knot; **einen Kreis –en** to describe a circle; **ein Kreuz –en** to make the sign of the cross; **in Falten –en** to fold; **in Papier –en** to wrap up in paper; **klein –en** to break into pieces; **mit den Flügeln –en** to flap one's wings; **sich –en** to fight a duel; **sich –en zu** to side with; **Takt –en** (mus.) to beat time; **Wunden –en** to inflict wounds; **Wurzeln –en** to take root

Schläger *m.* beater, kicker; rapier, sword; bat, racket, golf club; (bird) warbler; **–ei** *f.* brawl, scuffle, free-for-all fight

Schlamm *m.* mud, ooze, slime; **–bad** *neu.* mud bath; **–beisser** *m.* mudfish

Schlämmkreide *f.* whiting, whitener

Schlampe *f.* slut, slattern, sloven; **–erei** *f.* disorder, untidiness; slovenliness; mess

Schlange *f.* snake, serpent; **— stehen** to stand in line; **–nbeschwörer** *m.* snake charmer; **–nbiss** *m.* snakebite; **–nbrut** *f.* (fig.) generation of vipers; **–nlinie** *f.* wavy line; **–nmensch** *m.* contortionist

schlängeln *v.* **sich —** to wind, to meander

schlank *adj.* slender, slim; lean, lanky; **–weg** *adv.* right away; downright, flatly

schlapp *adj.* flabby, limp, slack; tired; **— machen** (coll.) to collapse, to faint

Schlapp: **–e** *f.* defeat, failure, reverse; **–hut** *m.* slouch hat; **–schwanz** *m.* coward, weakling

Schlaraffe *m.* lazybones, sluggard; **–nland** *neu.* land of milk and honey; **–nleben** *neu.* life of idleness and luxury

schlau *adj.* sly; artful, crafty, cunning

Schlauch *m.* hose; tube; (leather) bag; (bot.) utricle; **–boot** *neu.* rubber dinghy

Schlauf *m.*, **Schlaufe** *f.* loop, sling, ring

schlecht *adj.* bad, wicked; inferior, poor, ill; wretched; **–e Luft** foul air; **–e Zeiten** hard times; **mir ist — I** feel ill; **— machen** to run down; **— und recht** plain and honest, somehow; **— werden** to go bad, to turn sour; **— *adv.* badly, ill; **–erdings** *adv*, absolutely; by all means; **–gelaunt** *adj.* in bad humor; **–hin** *adv.*, **–weg** *adv.* plainly, simply, absolutely, quite

schlecken *v.* to lick; to eat dainties

Schleckermaul *neu.* sweet tooth; epicure

Schlegel *m.* drumstick; (baseball) bat; (bell) clapper; (mech.) mallet; (veal) leg

Schlehdorn *m.* blackthorn

Schleich: **–er** *m.* sneak; **–ware** *f.* smuggled goods, contraband; **–handel** *m.* smuggling; black market; **–händler** *m.* smuggler; black marketer; **–weg** m. secret path (*oder* means)

schleichen v. to slink, to sneak, to creep; **–d** adj. creeping; furtive, stealthy; **–des Gift** slow poison

Schleier m. veil, haze; (smoke) screen; **–eule** f. barn owl; **–flor** m. crape

schleierhaft adj. hazy, mysterious

Schleif: **–bahn** f. slide; **–e** f. bow, tie; loop, curve, bend; sledge; slide; **–er** m. grinder; cutter; glide (waltz); **–lack** m. grinding paste; enamel; **–lackmöbel** neu. pl. enameled furniture; **–stein** m. grindstone

schleifen v. to grind, to whet; to polish; to cut; to drag, to slide; to slur; to demolish

Schleim m. slime; mucus, phlegm; **–absonderung** f., **–fluss** m. expectoration, mucous secretion; **–haut** f. mucous membrane; **–suppe** f. gruel

schlemmen v. to feast, to gormandize

Schlemmer m. glutton; gourmand, gourmet; **–ei** f. gluttony, revelry; gormandizing

schlendern v. to saunter, to stroll, to loiter

Schlendrian m. beaten track; old humdrum way

schlenkern v. to dangle, to swing, to fling

Schlepp: **–dampfer** m. tugboat; **–e** f. train (of dress); trail; **–enträger** m. trainbearer; **–er** m. dragger; tug; **–kleid** neu. dress with a train; **–lohn** m. towage; **–netz** neu. dragnet; **–tau** neu. towrope; **ins –tau nehmen** to take in tow

schleppen v. to drag, to trail, to tug

Schlesien neu. Silesia

Schleswig-Holstein neu. Schleswig-Holstein

Schleuder f. sling, catapult; centrifuge; **–er** m. slinger; price cutter; **–honig** m. strained honey; **–preis** m. cut price; **zum – preis** dirt cheap; **–sitz** m. (avi.) ejection seat

schleudern v. to hurl, to sling, to fling; to swing; to undersell

schleunig adj. prompt, speedy, quick; **–st** adv. in all haste, immediately

Schleuse f. lock, sluice; **–ngeld** neu. lock charges; **–nmeister** m., **–nwärter** m. lock keeper; **–ntor** neu. lock gate

Schlich m. dodge, trick; **jemand auf die –e kommen** to see through someone's tricks

schlicht adj. plain, simple; unpretentious; sleek; **–en** v. to smooth, to plane; to settle

Schlichter m. mediator; arbitrator; peacemaker; (mech.) dresser, sizer

Schlichtungsausschuss m. arbitration committee

schliessen v. to close, to shut; to lock; to conclude; to finish; to break up; to infer (from); to judge (by); to contract; **an die Brust** (*or* in die Arme) **—** to embrace; **ein Bündnis —** to form an alliance; **einen Vergleich —** to come to an agreement; **Frieden —** to make peace; **geschlossen dafür sein** (*or* dafür

stimmen) to vote unanimously for; **in's Herz —** to take a great liking to; **in sich —** to include, to comprise

schliesslich adj. final, conclusive, last; — adv. finally, after all, at last

Schliff m. polish; (glass, diamonds) cut

schlimm adj. bad, evil; ill, sick; serious; **–stenfalls** adv. if worst comes to worst

Schling: **–e** f. sling, loop, snare, noose; **sich aus der –e ziehen** to get out of a difficulty; **–pflanze** f. climbing plant, creeper

Schlingel m. rascal, naughty boy, imp

schlingen v. to wind; to tie (a knot); to sling, to twist; to devour; to gulp

Schlips m. (neck)tie; cravat; **–nadel** f. tie pin

Schlitt: **–en** m. sled, sleigh; toboggan; sliding platform; (ship's) cradle; **mit jemand –en fahren** (coll.) to abuse somebody; **unter den –en kommen** to come off badly; **–erbahn** f. slide, shoot; **–schuh** m. skate; **–schuh laufen** to skate; **–schuhläufer** m. skater

Schlitz m. slit, slash, slot

schlitzen v. to slit, to slash

Schloss neu. (pad)lock; clasp, snap; castle, palace; **ins — fallen** (door) to snap to; **unter — und Riegel** under lock and key; **–er** m. locksmith; (mech.) fitter; **–erei** f. locksmith's workshop; **–hof** m. castle yard

Schlosse f. hailstone

schlott(e)rig adj. flabby, loose, shaky; tottery, wobbly; rickety; trembling

schlottern v. to hang loosely, to fit badly; to shake, to tremble, to wobble, to totter

Schlucht f. gorge, gully, ravine, glen

schluchzen v. to sob

Schluck m. gulp, draught, sip; **–auf** m., **–en** m. hiccups; **–er** m. hiccups; **armer –er** poor wretch

schlucken v. to gulp, to swallow

Schlummer m. slumber; **–lied** neu. lullaby; **–rolle** f. round pillow, bolster

schlummern v. to slumber

Schlund m. gullet, throat; abyss

Schlupf: **–loch** neu. hiding place; loophole; **–winkel** m. hiding place, hidden corner; refuge

schlüpfen v. to slip, to glide, to slide

schlüpfrig adj. slippery; indecent, obscene

schlürfen v. to sip, to lap; to shuffle

Schluss m. closing; end, termination; closure; conclusion; **–akt** m. last act; **–antrag** m. motion for closure; **–ergebnis** m. final result; **–folgerung** f. conclusion; inference; **–formel** f. closing phrase; **–licht** neu. taillight; **–rechnung** f. final account; **–rede** f. final speech, epilogue; **–runde** f. (sports) final; **–satz** m. closing sentence; finale; **–stein** m. keystone; **–verkauf** m. clearance sale; **–wort** neu. last word, summary

Schlüssel m. key; spanner; cipher, code; solution; (mus.) clef; **–bart** m. key bit; **–bein** neu. collarbone; **–blume** f. (bot.) cowslip; **–bund** neu. bunch of keys; **–loch** neu. keyhole; **–wort** neu. keyword; codeword

Schmach f. disgrace, humiliation; shame

schmachten v. to languish, to pine; — **nach** to long for; **-d** adj. languishing, languid

schmachvoll adj. disgraceful, humiliating

schmackhaft adj. appetizing, palatable, tasty, savory

Schmäh: -er m. defamer, slanderer; **-rede** f. abuse, diatribe, philippic; **-schrift** f. libelous writing; **-sucht** f. abusiveness

schmäh: -en to abuse, to revile, to defame, to slander; **-end** adj. abusive, slanderous; **-lich** adj. disgraceful, humiliating

schmal adj. narrow, slender; slim; scanty, poor; **-brüstig** adj narrow-chested; **-spurig** adj. (rail.) narrow-gauged

Schmal: -film m. 8-millimeter film; **-hans** m. lanky fellow; **da ist -hans Küchenmeister** they are on short rations; **-spur** f. narrow gauge

schmälen v. to abuse, to scold, to chide

schmälern v. to diminish; to curtail; to impair, to belittle, to disparage

Schmalz neu. lard; drippings

schmalzen v. to lard, to add fat to, to grease

schmalzig adj. fatty, greasy; sentimental

schmarotz: -en v. to be a parasite, to sponge; **-erhaft** adj., **-erisch** adj. parasitic(al)

Schmarotzer m. parasite; sponger; **-tum** neu. parasitism

Schmarre f. scar, gash, slash

schmatzen v. to smack, to buss

schmauchen v. (dial.) to smoke, to puff (at a pipe)

Schmaus m. feast, banquet; **-erei** f. feasting, banquet; carousal

schmausen v. to feast, to carous, to banquet

schmecken v. to taste; **— nach** to taste of

schmeich: -elhaft adj., **-lerisch** adj. fawning, wheedling; flattering; **-eln** v. to flatter; to wheedle, to coax; to fawn; to fondle

Schmeich: -elei f. flattery, coaxing; **-elkatze** f. caressing girl; **-ler** m. toady, wheedler

schmeissen v. to fling, to throw, to hurl

Schmelz m. enamel; glaze; bloom; sweetness; **-arbeit** f. enamel(ing); **-e** f. melt(ing); **-er** m. smelter; **-erei** f , **-hütte** f. foundry, smeltery; **-ofen** m. smelting furnace; **-punkt** m. melting point; **-tiegel** m. crucible; **-wasser** neu. melting (oder melted) snow

schmelz: -bar adj. fusible, meltable; **-en** v. to melt, to fuse; to diminish; **-end** adj. melting; languishing; mellow

Schmerz m. ache, pain; grief, suffering; **-ensgeld** neu. damage compensation; **-enskind** neu. child of sorrow; **-enslager** neu. bed of suffering

schmerz: -beladen adj., **-erfüllt** adj. greatly afflicted; **-en** v. to pain, to hurt, to ache; to grieve; to distress; **-haft** adj., **-lich** adj., **-voll** adj. painful, grievous; **-lindernd** adj., **-stillend** adj.

soothing; (med.) analgesic

Schmetter: -ling m. butterfly

schmettern v. to smash, to dash; to shat ter; to throw (down); to blare; to bray to peal, to yell; to warble; **einen —** (coll.) to drink

Schmied m. smith; **-e** f. smithy, forge **-eeisen** neu. wrought iron; **-ehamme** m. sledge hammer

schmied: -bar adj. malleable; **-eeisen** adj. of wrought iron; **-en** v. to forge; t plan, to fabricate; to hatch, to plot, t concoct

schmiegen v. to bend; **sich —** to nestl (against); to twine around, to clin (to)

schmiegsam adj. flexible, pliant; suppl

Schmier: -e f. grease; troop of strollin, actors; (sl.) gaff; **-er** m. greaser scribbler; dauber; **-fink** m. dirty fellow **-geld** neu. (coll.) bribe; palm oil; **-käs** m. soft cheese; **-mittel** neu. lubricant **-öl** neu. lubricating oil; **-plan** m. lubri cation chart; **-seife** f. soft soap

schmieren v. to smear, to grease, to lu ricate; (butter) to spread; to scrawl to scribble; (art) to daub; to bribe **jemand Honig um den Mund — t** flatter someone

schmierig adj. greasy; dirty, filthy; sordi

Schminkdose f. rouge pot; make-up s

Schminke f. rouge, paint; make-up

schminken v. to paint the face, to roug

Schmirgel m. emery; **-papier** neu. emer (oder sand) paper; **-scheibe** f. emer wheel

schmirgeln v. to polish with emery

Schmöker m. old (oder trashy, trivial book

schmökern v. to pore over (a book)

schmollen v. to pout, to be sulky

Schmorbraten v. stewed meat

schmoren v. to stew, to swelter

Schmu m. (sl.) unfair gain; **— mache** to swindle

Schmuck m. decoration, ornament; fin ery; jewelry; **-kasten** m. jewel bo **-sachen** f. pl. jewels; **-stück** neu. piec of jewelry

schmuck adj. neat, trim, smart, spru

schmücken v. to adorn, to decorate; t trim

Schmugg: -el m., **-elei** f. smuggling; **-l** m. smuggler; **-waren** f. pl. smuggle goods

schmuggeln v. to smuggle

schmunzeln v. to smirk, to grin

schmusen v. to prattle; (coll.) to fli

Schmutz m. dirt, filth, mud; **-blech** ne mudguard; **-fink** m. dirty fellow; **-fle** m. stain, spot; **-titel** m. (typ.) half tit

schmutzen v. to soil, to get dirty

schmutzig adj. dirty, filthy, soiled; shabb

Schnabel m. beak, bill, prow; spou (coll.) mouth; **-schuhe** m. pl. pointe shoes

Schnack m. chit-chat; twaddle; chatte gossip

schnacken v. (dial.) to talk; to chatt

Schnadahüpfel neu. Alpine folk song

Schnalle f. buckle, clasp

schnallen v. to buckle, to fasten, to strap up

schnalzen v. to snap (fingers); to click (tongue)

schnappen v. to snap, to snatch; to clutch; **nach Luft —** to gasp for breath

Schnäpper m. catch, snap; (med.) lancet; (orn.) flycatcher

Schnaps m. schnapps, strong liquor

schnarchen v. to snore

Schnarre f. rattle

schnattern v. to cackle, to quack; to jabber

schnauben v. to snort; to puff, to blow; **nach Rache —** to breathe vengeance; **sich die Nase —** to blow one's nose; **vor Wut —** to fret and fume. to foam with rage

schnaufen v. to breathe heavily, to pant

Schnauzbart m. mustache

Schnauze f. snout, muzzle, spout, nozzle; **die — voll haben** (sl.) to be fed up (with)

Schnecke f. snail, slug; gastropod; **–nbohrer** m. screw auger; **–ngang** m. winding alley; **im –ngang at a snail's pace; –nhaus** neu. snail shell; **–npost** f. slow coach; **–ntempo** neu. snail's pace

Schnee m. snow; beaten egg whites; **–ball** m. snowball; **–brille** f. snow goggles; **–fall** m. snowfall; **–flocke** f. snowflake; **–gestöber** neu., **–treiben** neu., **–wehe** f. snowdrift; **–glöckchen** neu. snowdrop; **–grenze** f. snow line; **–huhn** neu. white grouse; **–kette** f. skid chain; **–könig** m. **sich wie ein –könig freuen** to be merry as a lark; **–pflug** m. snowplow; **–schläger** m quick sweep; **–schuh** m. ski; **–sturm** m. snow storm; blizzard; **–wasser** neu. slush; **–wittchen** neu. Snow White

schneeig adj. snowy, snow-white

Schneid m. dash, energy

Schneide f. edge, blade, bit; **–bank** f. chopping bench; **–bohnen** f. pl. French beans; **–mühle** f., **–werk** neu. sawmill; **–zahn** m. incisor

schneiden v. to cut, to carve; to mow; to trim; to intersect; **Gesichter —** to make faces; **in Streifen —** to shred; **–d** adj. cutting, sharp; biting, piercing; glaring; sarcastic

Schneider m. tailor; cutter; **–erei** f. tailor's business; **–in** f. dressmaker; **–puppe** f. dummy

schneidern v. to do tailoring (oder dressmaking); (coll.) to make

schneidig adj. sharp, cutting, dashing, smart

schneien v. to snow

Schneise f. forest aisle; (avi.) flying lane

schnell adj. fast, quick, rapid, speedy, swift; prompt; **–en** v. to jerk, to toss

Schnell: –hefter m. letterfile; **–igkeit** f. rapidity; speed; velocity; quickness; **–kraft** f. elasticity; **–presse** f. steam press; **–schritt** m. quickstep; **–waage** f. steelyard; **–zug** m. express train

Schnepfe f. snipe, woodcock

schneuzen v. (coll.) to trim (a wick); **sich — to blow one's nose**

Schnickschnack m. tittle-tattle, prank, chat

schniegeln v. to dress up

schnipp: –ern v., **–(s)eln** v. to cut up; **–ig** adj. snappish, pert; **–(s)en** v. to snap, to punch

Schnippchen neu. snap (of fingers); **ein — schlagen to play a trick (on)**

Schnitt m. cut(ting), section; incision; shape, pattern; harvest, reaping; (book) edge; **einen guten — machen** (coll.) to make a good profit; **–blumen** f. pl. cut flowers; **–bohnen** f. pl. string beans; **–e** f. slice, cut; **–er** m. mower, reaper; **–lauch** m. chive; **–linie** f. intersecting line; **–muster** neu. dress pattern; **–punkt** m. point of intersection; **–waren** f. pl. dry goods; **–wunde** f. cut gash

Schnitz m. cut, snip; (dial.) slice; **–arbeit** f., **–erei** f., **–werk** neu. wood carving; **–er** m. cutter, carver; blunder, slip

Schnitzel m. chip; parings, shavings; **Wiener –el** breaded veal cutlet; **–jagd** f. paper chase

schnitze(l)n v. to cut, to carve, to chip

schnöd(e) adj. vile, base, disdainful

Schnorchel m. snorkel

Schnörkel m. scroll; flourish

schnörkelhaft adj. full of flourishes

schnorren v. (coll.) to sponge, to peddle

schnüffeln v. to sniff, to snuffle; to spy out, to snoop (around)

Schnupf: –en m. cold, catarrh; **den — bekommen** to catch a cold; **–tabak** m. snuff; **–tuch** neu. (coll.) handkerchief

schnupfen v. to (take) snuff

Schnuppe f. (candle) snuff; shooting star; **das ist mir —** (coll.) that's all the same to me

schnuppern v. to snuffle, to smell out

Schnur f. cord, string, line, lace; **über die — hauen** to kick over the traces

Schnür: –band neu. lace; **–boden** m. (theat.) loft, gridiron; **–chen** neu. thin string; **am –chen haben** to have at one's fingertips; **wie am –chen** like clockwork; **–leib** m., **–leibchen** neu. corset; **–loch** neu. eyelet; **–riemen** m. lace, strap; **–senkel** m. shoelace

schnüren v. to lace; to tie up; to cord, to rope; **sein Bündel —** to depart; **sich — to wear a corset**

schnurgerade adj. as straight as an arrow

schnurr! interj. buzz! whirl! purr! **–en** v. to buzz; to whir; to purr; **–ig** adj. droll; funny, odd, queer

schnurstracks adv. directly, straight away; immediately, at once

Schnurrbart m. mustache

Schober m. barn, shed, rick, stack

Schock neu. threescore; heap, shock; **— m.** shock; **–schwerenot!** confound it!

Schöffe m. juror, juryman; **–ngericht** neu. trial by jury

Schokolade f. chocolate; **–ntafel** f. chocolate bar

Scholastik f. scholasticism; **–er** m. scholastic

Scholle f. clod, lump; (fig.) land, soil; floe

schon adv. already, so far, as yet; even, indeed; das ist — wahr that's true enough; das kennen wir — it's an old story; es wird sich — machen lassen it will come out all right; — am nächsten Tage the very next day; — gut! that's all right! wenn — although; wenn — denn — in any event

schön adj. beautiful; lovely; fine; handsome, great, considerable; das —e Geschlecht the fair sex; das ist alles — und gut that's all very fine; das wäre noch —er! certainly not! das werde ich — bleiben lassen I'll take good care to avoid it; die —en Künste the fine arts; die —e Literatur belles-lettres; eine —e Summe a good round sum; sich — machen to spruce up; —en Dank many thanks; — machen (dog) to beg; — tun to flirt; —geistig adj. aesthetic

Schon: —ung f. careful treatment; forebearance; mercy; nursery for trees; —zeit f. closed season

Schön: —färberei f. heightening, coloring; optimism; —geist m. aesthete, bel esprit; —heit f. beauty; —heitsmittel neu. cosmetic; —heitspflege f. beauty culture; —heitssalon m. beauty shop; —heitswasser neu. beauty lotion; —redner m. spouter; fine talker; —schreibekunst f., —schrift f. caligraphy; —tuerei f. coquetting, flirting

Schoner m. schooner; antimacassar

Schopf m. top (of head); forelock, tuft; crest, crown

Schöpf: —brunnen m. draw well; —eimer m. bucket; —er m. creator; —kelle f., —löffel m. bailer, skimmer; —rad neu. bucket wheel; —ung f. creation; —werk neu. hydraulic engine

schöpfen v. to scoop, to ladle, to draw; to conceive; Hoffnung — to gather fresh hope; wieder Atem — to recover one's breath

schöpferisch adj. creative, productive

Schoppen m. half a pint; mug

Schöps m. wether; simpleton; —enfleisch neu. mutton; —enbraten m. roast mutton

Schorf m. scurf, scab

Schornstein m. chimney, smokestack; funnel; —feger m. chimney sweep

Schoss m. shoot, sprig, sprout; scion; lap; womb; coattail; flap; die Hände in den — legen to idle; es ist ihm in den — gefallen it just fell into his lap; im —e seiner Familie in the bosom of his family; —hund m. lap dog; —kind neu. darling, pet

Schössling m. offshoot, shoot

Schote f. husk, pod; —n pl. green peas; —nfrüchte f. pl. legumes

schräg(e) adj. oblique, slanting; diagonal; transversal; —über adv. across, aslant

Schräge f. obliquity, slope, slant, bevel

Schramme f. scratch, scar; crack

Schrank m. cupboard, wardrobe; —koffer m. trunk

Schranke f. barrier turnpike; (law) bar (rail.) gate; limit, bound(s); in die —n fordern to challenge; in —n halten to restrain; —n setzen to put a stop to; —nwärter m. (rail.) gatekeeper, signalman

schränken v. to cross (arms), to set (a saw)

schrankenlos adj. boundless; unbridled

Schranze m. and f. cringing courtier, flunkey

Schrapnell neu. shrapnel

schrappen r. to scrape

Schrat m. faun, satyr

Schraube f. screw; propeller; bei ihm ist eine — locker he has a screw loose; —nschlüssel m. wrench, spanner; —zieher m. screwdriver

schrauben v. to screw, to turn, to twist, to spiral; seine Forderungen höher — to increase one's demands; seine Hoffnungen niedriger — to come down a peg

Schraubstock m. vise

Schreck, Schrecken m. fright, horror; in —en setzen to terrify; —bild neu. horrible sight, bugbear; —ensbotschaft f. alarming news; —ensherrschaft f. reign of terror; —nis neu. horror; —schuss m. warning shot; false alarm; idle threat

schreck: —en v. to frighten, to alarm, to terrify; to startle; —haft adj. fearful, timid; —lich adj. dreadful, frightful, horrible; awful; tremendous

Schrei m. cry, shout, scream, shriek; letzter — latest fashion; —er m. crier; —hals m. crybaby; —vögel m. pl. (orn.) screechers

Schreib: —art f. style; spelling; —bedarf m. writing material, stationery; —block m. writing pad; —en neu. writing; letter; communication, note; —er m. writer, clerk, secretary; —erei f. writing, scribbling; —feder f. pen, nib; —fehler m. slip of the pen, error in writing; —heft neu. exercise book; —mappe f. writing case; portfolio; —maschine f. typewriter; —papier neu. writing paper; —stube f. office; (mil.) orderly room; —tisch m. desk; —unterlage f. blotting pad; —waren f. pl. stationery; —warenhändler m. stationer; —zeug neu. pen and ink set

schreib: —en v. to write, to spell; mit der Maschine —en to type; —faul adj. lazy about writing; —fertig adj. ready to write

schreien v. to shout, to scream, to howl; —d adj. shrill, glaring, loud; flagrant

Schrein m. shrine; —er m. carpenter, joiner, cabinetmaker; —erei f. carpenter's workshop

schreiten v. to stride, to stalk; zum Äussersten — to take extreme measures; zur Entscheidung — to proceed towards a decision

Schrift f. (hand)writing; work; publication; (law) writ; (rel.) Scriptures; (typ.) font, typeface; —art f. type; —auslegung f. exposition of the Scriptures, exegetics; **–bild** *neu.* (typ.) setting, face; **–deutsch** *neu.* literary German; **–führer** *m.* secretary; **–gelehrte** *m.* scribe; **–leiter** *m.* editor; **–leitung** *f.* editors, editorship; **–probe** *f.* specimen of writing (*oder* type); **–satz** *m.* composition; **–setzer** *m.* typesetter; **–steller** *m.* author, writer; **–stück** *neu.* document; **–tum** *neu.* literature; **–wechsel** *m.* correspondence; **–zeichen** *neu.* letter, type, character; **–zug** *m.* character, flourish

schrift: **–lich** *adj.* by letter, written; **–stellerisch** *adj.* literary; **–stellern** *v.* to do literary work

schrill *adj.* shrill; **–en** *v.* to sound shrilly

Schritt *m.* step, pace, stride, gait; **auf – und Tritt** everywhere; **den ersten – machen** to move first; **– für –** step by step; **– halten** to keep pace; **–macher** *m.* pacemaker

schrittweise *adv.* by steps, step by step

schroff *adj.* steep; harsh; abrupt, blunt

Schröpf: **–eisen** *neu.* cupping instrument; **–er** *m.* cupper, fleecer; **–kopf** *m.* cupping glass

Schrot *m.* and *neu.* small shot; crushed grain; (coin) weight; **–brot** *neu.* wholemeal bread; **–flinte** *f.* shotgun; **–mehl** *neu.* coarse flour; **–mühle** *f.* rough-grinding mill; **–säge** *f.* pitsaw

schroten *v.* to rough-grind, to crush; (casks) to lower

schrubben *v.* to scrub

Schrubber *m.* scrubber

Schrulle *f.* whim, fad, crochet, caprice

schrumpfen, schrumpeln *v.* to shrink, to shrivel; to contract; to wrinkle

Schub *m.* shoving; push, thrust; batch, heap; **–fach** *neu.*, **–kasten** *m.*, **–lade** *f.* drawer; **–karren** *m.* wheelbarrow

schüchtern *adj.* bashful, timid, shy

Schuft *m.* scoundrel, rascal; **–erei** *f.* drudgery

schuften *v.* (coll.) to drudge, to plod

schuftig *adj.* rascally, base, mean, shabby

Schuh *m.* shoe; boot; (measure) foot; **jemand etwas in die – schieben** to pass the buck; **–anzieher** *m.* shoehorn; **–band** *neu.* (boot) lace; **–flicker** *m.* cobbler; **–knöpfer** *m.* button hook; **–krem** *m.*, **–wichse** *f.* shoe polish; **–macher** *m.* shoemaker; **–putzer** *m.* shoeblack; **–waren** *f. pl.*, **–werk** *neu.*, **–zeug** *neu.* footwear

Schul: **–amt** *neu.* school administration; **–arbeit** *f.* homework; **–ausgabe** *f.* school edition; **–bank** *f.* form, bench; **–behörde** *f.* Board of Education; **–bildung** *f.* educational background; **–diener** *m.* porter, janitor; **–e** *f.* school; **hinter die –e gehen, die –e schwänzen** to play truant; **höhere –e** secondary school; **–e machen** to establish a precedent; **–ferien** *pl.* school vacations; **–freund** *m.*, **–kamerad** *m.* schoolfellow, chum; **–fuchs** *m.* pedant; **–geld** *neu.* tuition; **–heft** *neu.* exercise book; **–jugend** *f.* schoolchildren; **–klasse** *f.*, **–zimmer** *neu.* classroom; **–kollegium** *neu.* teaching staff; **–lehrer** *m.* schoolteacher; **–mappe**

f. schoolbag; **–meister** *m.* schoolmaster, pedant; **–ordnung** *f.* school regulations; **–pferd** *neu.* trick horse; **–rat** *m.* school board; school inspector; **–reiter** *m.* trick rider; **–schiff** *neu.* training ship; **–stunde** *f.* lesson; **–tafel** *f.* blackboard; **–ung** *f.* instruction, training; **–wesen** *neu.* educational system, school affairs; **–zeugnis** *neu.* school report(card)

schul: **–en** *v.* to school, to instruct; to train; **–meistern** *v.* to teach, to censure; **–pflichtig** *adj.* obliged to attend school

Schuld *f.* guilt, fault; debt, obligation; blame, sin; **es ist seine –** it's his fault; **jemand die – geben** to lay the blame at someone's door; **–beweis** *m.* proof of guilt; **–brief** *m.* promissory note; **–buch** *neu.* ledger; account book; **–entilgung** *f.* discharge of debts; **–forderung** *f.* claim, demand, debt; **–haft** *f.* imprisonment for debts; **–ige** *m.* guilty person; trespasser; culprit; **–igkeit** *f.* obligation; duty; **–ner** *m.* debtor; **–schein** *m.*, **–verschreibung** *f.* promissory note

schuld: **–bewusst** *adj.* conscious of guilt; **–en** *v.* to owe; **–enfrei** *adj.* free from debt, unencumbered; **–ig** *adj.* guilty, culpable; owing, due; **–los** *adj.* guiltless, innocent

Schüler *m.* pupil, student; disciple, follower; **–in** *f.* schoolgirl; **–schaft** *f.* discipleship

schülerhaft *adj.* schoolboylike, immature

Schulter *f.* shoulder; **–bein** *neu.* humerus; **–blatt** *neu.* shoulder blade; **–klappe** *f.*, **–stück** *neu.* shoulder strap

schultern *v.* to shoulder

Schultheiss, Schulze *m.* (lit.) village mayor

Schund *m.* rubbish, trash, junk; **–roman** *m.* cheap novel; literary trash

Schuppe *f.* scale, scurf, dandruff

schuppen *v.* to scale, to scrape, to peel off; **sich –** to form scales

Schuppen *m.* shed, garage, hangar

schüren *v.* to poke, to rake, to add fuel (to); to stir (up), to incite

schürfen *v.* (min.) to dig; to prospect; to graze, to scratch; **–d** *adj.* (fig.) thorough

Schurke *m.* scoundrel, rascal; **–nstreich** *m.*, **–erei** *f.* rascality, villainous trick

schurkisch *adj.* knavish, rascally, villainous

Schurz *m.* apron, loincloth, kilt; **–fell** *neu.* leather apron

Schürze *f.* apron; **–nband** *neu.* apron string; **–nherrschaft** *f.* petticoat government; **–njäger** *m.* woman chaser

schürzen *v.* to tie (*oder* tuck) up; **den Knoten eines Dramas –** to weave a plot

Schuss *m.* shot; rush; (bullet) wound; (bot.) shooting; **einen – abgeben** to fire a round; **einen – Kognak** a dash of brandy; **in – kommen** to get into working order; **jemand in den – kommen** to come across someone; **weit vom – out** of danger; **–feld** *neu.* firing zone; **–waffe** *f.* firearm; **–weite** *f.* firing range; **ausser –weite** out of reach; **–wunde** *f.*

gunshot wound

schuss: –bereit *adj.* ready to fire; –fest *adj.*, –sicher *adj.* bulletproof; invulnerable

Schüssel *f.* dish, tureen, basin, bowl

Schuster *m.* shoemaker; **auf –s Rappen on foot**; –ahle *f.* awl; –pech *neu.* cobbler's wax

schustern *v.* to cobble, to mend shoes

Schutt *m.* garbage, rubble; debris; –abladeplatz *m.* garbage dump

Schütte *f.* heap; granary

Schüttelfrost *m.* shaking chills, shivers

schütteln *v.* to shake; **sich —** to shiver, to tremble

schütten *v.* to pour; **es schüttet the rain pours down**

Schutz *m.* protection; shelter, cover, screen; safeguard; custody; **in — nehmen to defend; to protect; — suchen to take shelter**; –befohlene *m.* charge, ward, protégé; –blech *neu.* mudguard; –brief *m.* letter of safe conduct; –brille *f.* protective goggles; –bündnis *neu.* defensive alliance; –engel *m.* guardian angel; –färbung *f.* protective coloring; –frist *f.* term of copyright; –gebiet *neu.*, –herrschaft *f.* protectorate; –geleit *neu.* safe conduct, escort; convoy; –haft *f.* protective custody; –heilige *m.* patron saint; –herr *m.* protector, patron; –insel *f.* safety island; –mann *m.* policeman; –männer *m. pl.*, –leute *pl.* policemen; –marke *f.* trademark; –umschlag *m.* jacket, wrapper; –wall *m.* (Sandsäcke) revetment; bulwark

Schütz: –er *m.* protector; guardian; –ling *m.* protégé

Schütze *m.* rifleman; (ast.) Sagitarius; –nfest *neu.* shooting match; –ngraben *m.* (mil.) trench; –nkönig *m.* champion shot; –nloch *neu.* rifle pit

schützen *v.* to protect, to defend, to guard

Schwabe *m.* Swabian; –nstreich *m.* tomfoolery

Schwabe *f.* cockroach

Schwaben *neu.* Swabia

schwach *adj.* weak, feeble; frail; faint; infirm; scanty; **–e Seite weak point; –er Verstand feeble intellect; –es Gedächtnis bad memory; –es Licht dim light**; –sichtig *adj.* dim-sighted; –sinnig *adj.* feeble-minded; imbecile

Schwach: –heit *f.* weakness; frailty; –kopf *m.* imbecile, simpleton; –sinn *m.* imbecility; –strom *m.* low tension

Schwäch: –*e f.* weakness; debility; faintness; –lichkeit *f.* feebleness, delicacy; –ling *m.* weakling; pushover; –ung *f.* enervation. diminution; defloration

Schwadron *f.* and *neu.* squadron; –eur *m.* braggart, gasbag, swaggerer

Schwager *m.* brother-in-law

Schwägerin *f.* sister-in-law

Schwägerschaft *f.* relations by marriage

Schwalbe *f.* swallow; –schwanz *m.* swallowtail; dovetail

Schwall *m.* swell, flood; torrent (of words)

Schwamm *m.* sponge; fungus; dry rot

Schwan *m.* swan; –engesang *m.*, –enlied *neu.* swan song; (lit.) last song

Schwang *m.* vogue; **im –e sein to be in fashion**

schwanger *adj.* pregnant

Schwangerschaft *f.* pregnancy

schwank *adj.* flexible, pliable; slender; –en *v.* to waver, to vacillate; to sway, to totter; to fluctuate; –end *adj.* wavering, unsteady; irresolute

Schwank *m.* funny story; prank; (theat.) farce; –ung *f.* oscillation, fluctuation

Schwanz *m.* tail, end; –riemen *m.* crupper

schwänzen *v.* to play truant; to idle about

Schwäre *f.* abscess, ulcer, boil

schwären *v.* to suppurate, to ulcerate

Schwarm *m.* swarm, flock, herd; crowd, throng; (coll.) idol; –geist *m.* fanatic, reveller

schwärmen *v.* to swarm, to rove, to revel; **— für to be enthusiastic (about)**

Schwärmer *m.* reveller; dreamer; enthusiast; (ent.) hawk moth; (fireworks) cracker; (rel.) fanatic; –erei *f.* reverie; fanaticism

Schwarte *f.* rind, skin; old book: **dass die — kracht** (sl.) vigorously; –enmagen *m.* headcheese

schwarz *adj.* black; dark; dirty; **das –e Brett the bulletin board; –e Kunst black magic; — sehen to take a gloomy view (of)**

Schwarz: –amsel *f.*, –drossel *f.* blackbird; –arbeit *f.* scab labor; –brot *neu.* rye bread; –e *m.* Negro; devil; –e *neu.* black (color); blackness, darkness; ins –e treffen to hit the bull's eye; –fahrer *m.* joy rider; –handel *m.* black market; –künstler *m.* magician, necromancer; –schlachten *neu.* illegal slaughtering; –rock *m.* black coat; (coll.) cleric; –seher *m.* pessimist; –wild *neu.* wild boars

Schwärze *f.* blackness; printer's ink; baseness

schwärzen *v.* to blacken, to ink; to defame

Schwarzwald *m.* Black Forest

schwatzen, schwätzen *v.* to chatter, to gossip

Schwätzer *m.* babbler, prattler, gossip

Schwebe *f.* suspense, balance; **in der — sein to be undecided; –bahn *f.* suspension railway**

schweben *v.* to be suspended, to hover; to dangle; to soar; to be undecided (*oder* pending); **es schwebt mir auf der Zunge I have it on the tip of my tongue; in Gefahr — to be in jeopardy; –de Schulden floating debts**

Schweden *neu.* Sweden

Schwefel *m.* sulphur; –bad *neu.* sulphur bath; sulphurous springs; –hölzchen *neu.* match

schwefel: –farbig *adj.*, –gelb *adj.* sulphuryellow; –(halt)ig *adj.* sulphurous; –sauer *adj.* sulphuric

Schweif *m.* tail; train; –stern *m.* comet

schweifen *v.* to rove, to roam; to curve

schweigen *v.* to be (*oder* keep) silent; to hold one's tongue; to keep mum

schweigsam *adj.* taciturn, reticent

Schwein *neu.* hog, pig, swine; — **haben** to be lucky; **-ebraten** *m.* roast pork; **-efett** *neu.* lard; **-efleisch** *neu.* pork; **-ehirt** *m.* swineherd; **-ehund** *m.* filthy dog; **-ekoben** *m.*, **-estall** *m.* pigsty; **-epökelfleisch** *neu.* salt pork; **-erei** *f.* filthiness; obscenity; **-igel** *m.* smutty fellow, obscene talker; (dial.) hedgehog; **-igelei** *f.* obscenity; **-sleder** *neu.* pigskin; **-sschwarte** *f.* rind of bacon, crackling

die Schweiz *f.* Switzerland

schweinisch *adj.* swinish, filthy; obscene

Schweiss *m.* sweat, perspiration; (hunting) blood; toil; **-arbeit** *f.* welding; **-blätter** *neu. pl.* perspiration guards; **-er** *m.* welder

schweiss: **-(be)fördernd** *adj.* sudorific; **-en** *v.* to weld; (hunting) to bleed; **-ig** *adj.* sweaty; perspiring; (hunting) bloody

schwelen *v.* to smoulder

schwelgen *v.* to feast, to revel, to indulge in

Schwelger *m.* epicure, glutton, reveller; **-ei** *f.* revelry; gluttony; debauchery

schwelgerisch *adj.* luxurious, debauched

Schwelle *f.* sill; threshold; doorstep; architrave; beam, joist; (rail.) sleeper

schwellen *v.* to swell, to rise; to bloat, to inflate; to increase, to distend

Schwemme *f.* watering place; horse pond

Schwengel *m.* swingle; clapper; (pump) handle

schwenken *u.* to swing; to wave; to brandish; to rinse; to turn; to change (one's mind)

schwer *adj.* heavy; weighty; ponderous; hard, difficult; serious, severe; grave; etwas — **nehmen** to take something to heart; **mit -em Herzen** reluctantly; — **daniederliegen** to be seriously ill; — **fallen** to be difficult; **-e** See rough sea; **-e** Zeiten hard times; **-e** Zunge slow tongue; **-er** Atem short breath; **-er** Fehler great blunder; **-er** Junge gangster, mobsman; **-er** Wein full-bodied wine; **-es** Essen indigestible food; **-es** Geld round sum; **-es** Verbrechen atrocious crime; — **verwundet** mortally wounded; **-betrübt** *adj.* deeply grieved; **-blütig** *adj.* melancholy; **-fällig** *adj.* clumsy, sluggish, slow; **-hörig** *adj.* hard of hearing; **-lich** *adv.* hardly, scarcely; **-mütig** *adj.* melancholy, sad, mournful; **-verständlich** *adj.* abstruse; **-wiegend** *adj.* grave, serious

Schwer: **-e** *f.* heaviness; weight; gravity; **-elosigkeit** *f.* weightlessness; **-enöter** *m.* gay rascal; playboy; **-gewicht** *neu.* heavyweight; chief stress; emphasis; **-industrie** *f.* heavy industry; **-kraft** *f.* force of gravity; **-kriegsbeschädigte** *m.* disabled soldier; **-mut** *f.* melancholy, sadness; **-punkt** *m.* center of gravity; main point

Schwert *neu.* sword; **-feger** *m.* furbisher; **-lilie** *f.* iris

Schwester *f.* sister; registered nurse; nun; **-nschaft** *f.* sisterhood; sorority

Schwibbogen *m.* archway; flying buttress

Schwieger: **-eltern** *pl.* parents-in-law; **-mutter** *f.* mother-in-law; **-sohn** *m.* son-in-law; **-tochter** *f.* daughter-in-law; **-vater** *m.* father-in-law

Schwiele *f.* wale; callus

schwierig *adj.* difficult; hard; complicated; delicate, particular; fastidious; trying

Schwimm: **-anstalt** *f.* swimming establishment; **-blase** *f.* air bladder; water wings; **-dock** *neu.* floating dock; **-er** *m.* swimmer; (mech.) float; **-flosse** *f.* fin; **-fuss** *m.* webfoot; **-gürtel** *m.* life belt; **-hose** *f.* bathing trunks; **-kraft** *f.* buoyancy; **-weste** *f.* life jacket

schwimmen *v.* to swim, to float; to welter

Schwind: **-el** *m.* dizziness; swindle; fraud, cheat; **-elei** *f.* swindle; **-elfirma** *f.*, **-elgesellschaft** *f.*, **-elunternehmen** *neu.* bogus (oder fraudulent) company; **-elgefühl** *neu.* giddy sensation; **-ler** *m.* swindler, cheat, imposter; **-sucht** *f.* tuberculosis of the lungs

schwind: **-en** *v.* to dwindle, to shrink; to vanish; **-süchtig** *adj.* consumptive

schwindel: **-haft** *adj.* causing dizziness; very high; fraudulent, swindling; **-ig** *adj.* dizzy, giddy; **-n** *v.* to swindle, to cheat; mir **-t** I feel dizzy

schwingen *v.* to swing, to oscillate, to vibrate

Schwips *m.* tipsiness; **einen** — **haben** to be tipsy

schwirren *v.* to whir, to whiz, to buzz; **umher** — to flit to and fro

Schwitzbad *neu.* Turkish bath

schwitzen *v.* to sweat, to perspire; to toil

schwören *v.* to swear, to take an oath; **Rache** — to vow vengeance; — **auf** to swear by; to have confidence in

schwül *adj.* sultry, oppressive, close

Schwulst *m.* bombast, turgidity

schwülstig *adj.* bombastic, turgid

Schwund *m.* dwindling; falling off; disappearance, shrinkage; atrophy; (rad.) fading

Schwung *m.* swing(ing); vault(ing); ardor; verve; flight; **edler** — noble strain; **in** — **bringen** to set going; **-feder** *f.* (orn.) pinion; **-kraft** *f.* centrifugal force; energy; buoyancy; **-rad** *neu.* flywheel; **-seil** *neu.* slack rope

schwunghaft *adj.* lively, flourishing, brisk

Schwur *m.* oath; **-gericht** *neu.* (law) jury

Sechs *f.* six; **-eck** *neu.* hexagon; **-pfünder** *m.* six pounder; **-tel** *neu.* sixth part

Sechs *adj.* six; **-eckig** *adj.* hexagonal; **-fach** *adj.*, **-fältig** *adj.* sixfold, sextuple; **-jährig** *adj.* six-year-old; **-monatlich** *adj.* six monthly; every six months; **-te** *adj.* sixth; **-teilig** *adj.* in six parts; **-tens** *adv.* sixthly

sechzehn *adj.* sixteen; **-te** *adj.* sixteenth

Sechzehn *f.* sixteen; **-tel** *neu.* sixteenth part

sechzig *adj.* sixty; **-jährig** *adj.* sixty year old; **-ste** *adj.* sixtieth

Sechzig *f.* sixty; **-er** *m.* sexagenarian; **-stel** *neu.* sixtieth part

See m. lake; — f. sea; **an der —** at the seashore; **an der — gelegen** maritime; **auf hoher —** at sea; **in — stechen** to put to sea; **zur — gehen** to go to sea; **-bad** neu. seaside resort; **-bär** m. fur seal; (coll.) old salt; **-beben** neu. seaquake; **-dienst** m. naval service; **-fahrer** m. seafarer, sailor; navigator; **-fahrt** f. cruise, navigation; **-flugzeug** neu. seaplane; **-gefecht** neu. naval action; **-gesetz** neu. maritime law; **-gras** neu. seaweed; **-herrschaft** f. naval supremacy; **-hund** m. (zool.) seal; **-igel** m. sea urchin; **-jungfer** f. mermaid; dragonfly; **-kadett** m. midshipman, naval cadet; **-karte** f. sea chart; hydrographic map; **-leute** pl. seamen; **-löwe** m. sea lion; **-mann** m. seaman, sailor; **-meile** f. nautical mile; **-möwe** f. seamew, gull; **-not** f. distress; **-räuber** m. pirate; **-rose** f. water lily; **-schlacht** f. sea battle; **-schlange** f. sea serpent; **-schwalbe** f. tern; **-stern** m. starfish; **-streitkräfte** f. pl. naval forces; **-tang** m. seaweed; **-teufel** m. devilfish; **-volk** neu. maritime nation; **-warte** f. naval observatory; **-weg** m. sea route; **auf dem -wege** by sea; **-zunge** f. sole

Seele f. soul; mind, heart; (gun) bore; **eine — von Mensch** a love of a man; **jemand aus der — sprechen** to guess someone's thoughts; **von ganzer —** with all one's heart; **-namt** neu., **-nmesse** f. service for the dead, requiem; **-ngrösse** f. magnanimity; **-nheil** neu. spiritual welfare; salvation; **-nhirt** m. pastor; **-nleiden** neu. mental trouble; **-nnot** f., **-npein** f., **-nqual** f. mental distress; **-nwanderung** f. transmigration of souls; **-nwärmer** m. (coll.) comforter

seelen: -froh adj., **-vergnügt** adj. very glad; **-voll** adj. soulful; sentimental

Seelsorge f. ministerial work; **-r** m. pastor; clergyman, minister

Segel neu. sail, canvas; **die — einziehen** (oder **streichen**) to shorten sail; to give in; **unter — gehen** to set sail; **-boot** neu. sailboat; **-flug** m. (avi.) gliding; **-flugzeug** neu. (avi.) glider; **-klasse** f. (avi. and naut.) rating; **-macher** m. sailmaker; **-schiff** neu. sailing ship; **-schlitten** m. iceboat; **-sport** m. yachting; **-stange** f. (naut.) yard; **-tuch** neu. sailcloth, canvas

Segen m. benediction, blessing; grace; luck; **-swunsch** m. benediction; good wishes

segensreich adj. blessed; lucky, prosperous

segnen v. to bless, to give benediction; to consecrate; **das Zeitliche — to die; gesegneten Leibes** pregnant

Seh: -en neu. sight; **ihm verging Hören und -en** he lost consciousness; **-enswürdigkeiten** f. pl. sights, objects of interest, curiosities; **-er** m. seer, prophet; **-feld** neu. field of vision; **-kraft** f. visual power; **-nerv** m. optic nerve; **-rohr** neu. periscope; **-schärfe** f. sight, focus; **ausser -weite** out of

sight; **-werkzeug** neu. organ of sight, eye

sehen r. to see. to look; to notice, to perceive, to experience, to realize, **darauf — to see to, to watch; durch die Finger — to connive; schlecht — to have poor eyesight; — lassen** to display, to show; **-swert** adj., **-swürdig** adj. worth seeing; remarkable

Sehn: -e f. sinew, tendon; (bow) string; (geom.) secant; chord; **-enverzerrung** f. sprain of a tendon

sehn: -en v. **sich -en** to long (oder yearn) for; **sich nach Hause -en** to be homesick

Sehnsucht f. longing, yearning, ardor, desire

sehr adv. very, much, greatly, most; **wie — auch immer** however much

seicht adj. shallow, flat; superficial, insipid; **-e Redensarten** platitudes

seid: -en adj. silk(en); **-enartig** adj., **-ig** adj. silky

Seide f. silk; **-nbau** m. silkworm culture; **-nernte** f. yield of cocoons; **-nflor** m. silk gauze (oder crepe); **-nglanz** m. silky luster; **-npapier** neu. tissue paper; **-nraupe** f. silkworm

Seidel neu. beer glass; pint, mug

Seife f. soap; **-nblase** f. soap bubble; **-nflokken** f. pl. soap flakes; **-nlauge** f. soapsuds; **-nschaum** m. lather

seihen v. to filter, to strain

Seil neu. rope; line, cable; **— springen** to skip; **-bahn** f. cable railway, funicular; **-er** m. ropemaker; **-erei** f. rope-making; ropery; **-tänzer** m. ropewalker; **-werk** neu. cordage; (naut.) rigging; **-winde** f. rope winch; windlass; **-ziehen** neu. tug of war; **-zug** m. tackle

sein v. to be, to exist; **etwas — lassen** to leave something alone, to stop something; **— pron.** and adj. his, its, one's; of him; **-erseits** adv. on his part; with regard to him; **-erzeit** adv. in his (oder its) time; formerly; **-esgleichen** pron. his equals; people like him; **-ethalben** adv., **-etwegen** adv., **-etwillen** adv. for his sake; on his account; **-ig** pron. his, its

Sein neu. being, existence; essence; **-en** pl. his people; **-ige** neu. his (oder one's) property; his (oder one's) duty

seit prep. and conj. since; **— damals** since then; **— einigen Tagen** these last few days; **— kurzem** lately, of late; **-dem** adv. and conj. since then, ever since; **-ens** prep. on the part (oder side) of; **-her** adv. up to now, since then; **-lich** adj. (col)lateral, side; **-lich** adv. at the side; **-wärts** adv. toward the side, sideways, aside; laterally

Seite f. side; flank, wing; age; party; (geom.) face; (math.) member; **auf die — geh(e)n** to step aside; **auf jemandes — sein** (oder **treten**) to side with someone; **nach allen -n** in all directions; **schwache —** weakness; **von allen -n** from every quarter; **von -n** on the part of; **zur — steh(e)n** to stand by, to help;

-nansicht *f.* side view; profile; **-nbewegung** *f.* (avi.) yawing; **-nblick** *m.* side glance; **-nflügel** *m.*, **-ngebäude** *neu.* (arch.) wing; **-ngewehr** *neu.* side arms; bayonet; **-nhieb** *m.* side blow; sarcastic remark; **-nkulisse** *f.* (theat.) side wing; **-nlehne** *f.* arm rest; **-nschiff** *neu.* aisle; **-nsprung** *m.* side leap; evasion, escapade; **-nstück** *neu.* counterpart; **-nzahl** *f.* number of pages; page number

Sekret: **-är** *m.* secretary; desk; secretary bird; **-ariat** *neu.* secretary's office, secretariat

Sekt *m.* dry wine, champagne

Sekt: **-e** *f.* sect; **-ierer** *m.* sectary; **-ion** *f.* section; post-mortem examination; **-ionsbefund** *m.* findings of a post-mortem examination; **-or** *m.* sector

Sekund: **-a** *f.* second highest class of college; **-aner** *m.* student of the second highest class of college; **-ant** *m.* (sports) second; **-e** *f.* second; **-enzeiger** *m.* (watch) second hand

sekundär *adj.* secondary, subordinate

selbst *pron.* self, in person, myself, himself; herself, itself, themselves; **das versteht sich von —** that's a matter of course; **von —** of one's own accord, voluntarily, automatically; **— adv.** even; **-bewusst** *adj.* self-confident; **-gefällig** *adj.* self-satisfied; complacent; **-genügsam** *adj.* self-sufficient; **-gerecht** *adj.* self-righteous; **-herrlich** *adj.* autocratic; **-isch** *adj.* selfish, egotistic; **-los** *adj.* unselfish, disinterested; **-mörderisch** *adj.* suicidal; **-redend** *adj.* self-evident; obvious; **-sicher** *adj.* self-assured; **-süchtig** *adj.* selfish; **-tätig** *adj.* automatic; self-acting; **-vergessen** *adj.* forgetful of oneself; **-verständlich** *adj.* self-evident, natural, obvious; **-verständlich** *adv.* of course; **das ist -verständlich** that stands to reason; **-willig** *adj.* wilful

Selbst *neu.* (the) self, individuality, personality; ego; **-achtung** *f.* self-respect; **-anlasser** *m.* self-starter; **-anschluss** *m.* dial telephone; **-aufopferung** *f.* self-sacrifice; **-befleckung** *f.* masturbation; **-beherrschung** *f.* self-control; **-bekenntnis** *neu.* voluntary confession; **-bestimmung** *f.* self-determination; **-bewusstsein** *neu.* self-confidence; **-bildnis** *neu.* self-portrait; **-binder** *m.* necktie; (agr.) binder; **-biographie** *f.* autobiography; **-erhaltung** *f.* self-preservation; **-erkenntnis** *f.* knowledge of oneself; **-erniedrigung** *f.* self-abasement; **-fahrer** *m.* owner-driver; **-gefälligkeit** *f.* complacency; **-gefühl** *neu.* self-reliance; **-gespräch** *neu.* monologue, soliloquy; **-herrlichkeit** *f.* sovereignty; vanity; **-hilfe** *f.* self-help; self-defense; **-kostenpreis** *m.* cost price; **-kritik** *f.* self-criticism; **-ladepistole** *f.*, **-lader** *m.* automatic pistol; **-laut** *m.* vowel; **-losigkeit** *f.* unselfishness; **-mord** *m.* suicide; **-sucht** *f.* selfishness; egotism; **-täuschung** *f.* self-deception; **-überhebung** *f.*, **-überschätzung** *f.*

presumptuousness; **-überwindung** *f.* self-conquest; **-unterricht** *m.* self-instruction; **-verblendung** *f.* infatuation; **-verleugnung** *f.* self-denial; **-ständlichkeit** *f.* matter of course; foregone conclusion; **-vertrauen** *neu.* self-confidence; **-zucht** *f.* self-discipline; **-zünder** *m.* automatic lighter; **-zündung** *f.* hypergolic ignition

selig *adj.* blessed, blissful, happy; deceased, late; (coll.) tipsy; **-sprechen** *v.* to beatify

Selig: **-e** *m.* the departed; **-preisung** *f.* (bibl.) beatitude, **-sprechung** *f.* beatification

Sellerie *m.* and *f.* celery

selten *adj.* rare, scarce, extraordinary, unusual; **— adv.** seldom, rarely

Selterswasser *neu.* Seltzer water; soda water

seltsam *adj.* strange, odd, queer, curious

Semester *neu.* semester, term, session

Seminar *neu.* seminar, seminary; training college; **-ist** *m.* theological student

Semmel *f.* bun, roll; **-knödel** *m.* *pl.*, **-klösse** *m.* *pl.* dumplings

semmelblond *adj.* flaxen-haired

Senat *m.* senate; **-or** *m.* senator

Send: **-bote** *m.* messenger, delegate, emissary; **-brief** *m.*, **-schreiben** *neu.* open letter; **-efolge** *f.* radio program; **-er** *m.* transmitter; **-eraum** *m.* (rad.) studio; **-espiel** *neu.* radio play; **-estation** *f.*, radio station; **-estörung** *f.* (rad.) dead air; **-ling** *m.* emissary; **-ung** *f.* sending; mission; consignment; shipment; transmission; broadcast

senden *v.* to send, to forward, to transmit, to broadcast

Senf *m.* mustard; **seinen — dazugeben** (coll.) to put in one's two cents' worth; **-korn** *neu.* mustard seed

sengen *v.* to singe, to scorch, to burn

Senk: **-blei** *neu.*, **-lot** *neu.* plummet, sounding lead; **-e** *f.* low ground; **-er** *m.* (hort.) layer; **-fuss** *m.* flat foot; **-fusseinlage** *f.* arch support; **-grube** *f.* cesspool; **-kasten** *m.* caisson; **-leine** *f.* fathom line; **-rechte** *f.* perpendicular; **-schnur** *f.* plumb line; **-ung** *f.* lowering; reduction; declivity; unaccented syllable

Senkel *m.* shoelace

senken *v.* to sink, to lower; (hort.) to lay; to bow (one's head), to cast down; **sich —** to sink, to settle; to incline

senkrecht *adj.* vertical, perpendicular

Senn *m.* Alpine cowherd; **-erei** *f.* Alpine dairy; **-erin** *f.* Alpine dairymaid; **-hütte** *f.* chalet

Sense *f.* scythe; **-nmann** *m.* mower; (lit.) Death

sensibel *adj.* sensitive, touchy

Sentenz *f.* aphorism, maxim

Separatvertrag *m.* special agreement

Sept: **-ember** *m.* September; **-ett** *neu.* septet; **-ime** *f.* (mus.) seventh

Sequenz *f.* sequence

sequestrieren *v.* to sequestrate, to sequester

Serail *neu.* seraglio

Serbien *neu.* Serbia

Serie *f.* series; issue, set; (billiard) break

Sermon *m.* sermon; tedious lecture

Serpentine *f.* serpentine road

Serum *neu.* serum

Service *neu.* set of china

Servierbrett *neu.* tray, salver

servieren *v.* to serve, to wait (at table)

Serviette *f.* table napkin

Sesam *m.* sesame

Sessel *m.* armchair

sesshaft *adj.* established, resident; sedentary

Setz: **-er** *m.* (typ.) compositor; **-fehler** *m.* typographical error; **-kasten** *m.* letter case; **-ling** *m.* seedling; **-maschine** *f.* typesetting machine

setzen *v.* to set, to place, to put; to plant; (typ.) to set, to compose; to erect (monument); to stake, to wager; **alles daran** — to move heaven and earth; **ans Land** — to disembark; **aufs Spiel** — hazard, to risk, to stake; **ausser Kraft** — to annul, to invalidate; **den Fall** — to suppose; **in Angst und Schrecken** — to frighten, to terrify; **in Rechnung** — to charge (to); **in Szene** — (theat.) to stage; **in Verlegenheit** — to embarrass; **jemand auf die Strasse** — to turn someone out of doors; **Kinder in die Welt** — to beget children; — **über** to leap over; to cross (river); **sich aufs Pferd** — to mount a horse; **sich** — to sit down; (birds) to perch; **sich zur Wehr** — to defend oneself; **unter Wasser** — to submerge, to flood

Seuche *f.* epidemic; pestilence; **-nherd** *m.* center of infection; **-nlazarett** *neu.* hospital for contagious diseases

seufzen *v.* to sigh, to groan, to moan

Seufzer *m.* sigh, groan

Sext: **-a** *f.* sixth (*oder* lowest) class of an undergraduate college; **-aner** *m.* student of the lowest class of an undergraduate college; **-ant** *m.* sextant; **-e** *f.* (mus.) sixth; **-ett** *neu.* sextet

sexuell *adj.* sexual

Sezier: **-besteck** *neu.* dissecting case; **-messer** *neu.* scalpel; **-ung** *f.* dissection

sich *pron.* himself, herself, itself, themselves; oneself; one another; each other; **an** — in itself

Sichel *f.* sickle; crescent

sicher *adj.* safe, secure; steady; sure, certain; reliable; **aus -er Hand** from good authority; **seiner Sache** — **sein** to be certain of something; **seines Lebens nicht** — **sein** to be in danger; — **gehe(e)n** to make quite sure; — **stellen** to put in safe keeping; **-heitshalber** *adv.* for safety's sake; **-lich** *adv.* surely, certainly; **-n** *v.* to secure; to guarantee

Sicher: **-heit** *f.* safety, security; assurance; **-heitskette** *f.* door chain; **-heitslausel** *f.* safeguard; **-heitsleistung** *f.* security, bail; **-heitsnadel** *f.* safety pin; **-heitsschloss** *neu.* safety lock; **-heitsventil** *neu.* safety valve; **-stellung** *f.* safeguarding, guarantee; **-ung** *f.* protection, safety device; (elec.) fuse; safety bolt

Sicht *f.* sight, view; visibility; **auf** —, **bei** — at sight; **auf lange** — long-term; **-bereich** *m.*, **-weite** *f.* visual range; **-tage** *m. pl.* days of grace; **-vermerk** *m.* visa; **-wechsel** *m.* sight draft

sicht: **-bar** *adj.* visible, apparent, evident; **-en** *v.* to sight; to sort, to sift; **-lich** *adv.* evidently, obviously; visibly

sickern *v.* to trickle, to ooze, to leak

sie *pron.* she; her; they; them

Sie *pron.* you

Sieb *neu.* sieve; colander, strainer; sifter

Sieb: **-en** *f.* seven; **böse -en** shrew, termagant; **-engestirn** *neu.* Pleiades; **-enmeilenstiefel** *m. pl.* seven-league boots; **-ensachen** *f. pl.* goods and chattels; **-enschläfer** *m.* lazybones; dormouse; **-entel** *neu.* seventh part; **-zehn** *f.* seventeen; **-zig** *f.* seventy; **-ziger** *m.* septuagenarian

sieb: **-en** *adj.* seven; **-enerlei** *adr.* of seven different kinds; **-enfach** *adj.*, **-enfältig** *adj.* sevenfold; **-enjährig** *adj.* septennial; **-enmal** *adv.* seven times; **-ente** *adj.* seventh; **-tens** *adr.* in the seventh place; **-zehn** *adj.* seventeen; **-zig** *adj.* seventy

sieben *v.* to sift, to strain; to eliminate

siech *adj.* sickly, infirm; **-en** *r.* to pine away

Siechtum *neu.* sickliness, long illness

Sied: **-ler** *m.* settler; **-lung** *f.* settlement, colony; **-lungsgesellschaft** *f.* building and loan association

Siede: **-grad** *m.*, **-punkt** *m.* boiling point

siedeln *v.* to settle, to colonize

sieden *r.* to boil, to seethe; **-dheiss** *adj.* boiling hot

Sieg *m.* victory; **den** — **davontragen** to win the day; — **durch Zielfotografie** photo finish; **-er** *m.* victor, winner; **-esbeute** *f.* victor's spoils; **-esbogen** *m.* triumphal arch; **-eszeichen** *neu.* trophy; **-eszug** *m.* triumphal procession

sieg: **-en** *r.* to be victorious; to win; **-esgewiss** *adj.* confident of victory; **-estrunken** *adj.* elated with victory; **-haft** *adj.*, **-reich** *adj.* victorious, triumphant

Siegel *neu.* seal; **unter dem** — **der Verschwiegenheit** in strict confidence; **-bewahrer** *m.* keeper of the seal; **-lack** *m.* sealing wax; **-ring** *m.* signet ring

siegeln *v.* to (affix a) seal

Signal *neu.* signal; bugle call; **-buch** *neu.* code of signals; **-ement** *neu.* personal description; **-leine** *f.* bell rope; communication cord; **-mast** *m.* signal mast; semaphore; **-pfeife** *f.* warning whistle; **-wärter** *m.* signalman

signalisieren *r.* to signal

Signet *neu.* collophon; printer's trade mark

Silbe *f.* syllable; **-nfall** *m.* (lit.) rhythm; **-nmass** *neu.* syllabic quantity; meter; **-nmessung** *f.* prosody; **-nrätsel** *neu.* charade; **-nstecher** *m.* quibbler, hair-

splitter; **-ntrennung** f. syllabication
Silber neu. silver; silverware; **-arbeiter** f. silversmith; **-geschirr** neu. silver plate; **-legierung** f. silver alloy; **-ling** m. (bibl.) silver coin; **-pappel** f. white poplar; **-plattierung** f. silver plating; **-reiher** m. egret, white heron; **-währung** f. silver standard; **-zeug** neu. silverware

silber: -(art)ig adj., -n adj. silvery, argentine; **-hell** adj. silvery
Silvesterabend m. New Year's Eve
Simili(stein) m. artificial gem
simpel adj. simple, naïve, plain
Sims neu. ledge; sill; cornice, molding
simulieren v. to simulate, to feign
simultan adj. simultaneous
Sinfonie f. symphony
Sing: -**akademie** f. singing school; **-drossel** f. (orn.) thrush; **-erei** f., **-sang** m. singsong; **-spiel** neu. musical comedy; **-stimme** f. singing voice; vocal part; **-vogel** m. songster, warbler; **-weise** f. tune, melody
singen v. to sing; to carol, to warble; **nach dem Gehör** — to sing by ear; **nach Noten** —, **vom Blatt weg** — to sing at sight
sinken v. to sink; to fall, to decline, to decrease; **den Mut** — **lassen** to lose heart; **die Stimme** — **lassen** to lower one's voice; **in Ohnmacht** — to faint away
Sinn m. sense; intellect, mind; opinion; meaning; taste, wish; tendency; **and(e)ren -es werden** to change one's mind; **bei** — **sein, seine fünf** — **beisammen haben** to have one's wits about one; **seinen** — **auf etwas richten** to turn one's attention to something; **sich etwas aus dem** — **schlagen** to dismiss something from one's mind; **von** -**en sein** to be out of one's mind; **-bild** neu. symbol, emblem; allegory; **-enlust** f. sensual enjoyment; voluptuousness; **-enmensch** m. sensualist; **-enwelt** f. material world; **-esänderung** f. change of mind; **-esart** f. character, disposition; **-esorgan** neu., **-eswerkzeug** neu. organ of sense; **-estäuschung** f. illusion, hallucination; **-gedicht** neu. epigram; **-spruch** m. epigram; motto
sinn: -**bildlich** adj. symbolic, allegoric(al); **-en** v. to think; to speculate (upon), to reflect; to meditate, to ponder, to muse; **auf etwas** — to plan, to plot; **auf Mittel und Wege** — to devise means and ways; **-fällig** adj. obvious; **-getreu** adj. faithful; **-ig** adj. thoughtful; ingenious; sensible; **-lich** adj. sensual; material; **-los** adj. senseless; foolish; **-reich** adj. sensible, clever; ingenious; witty; **-verwandt** adj. synonymous; **-voll** adj. significant, pregnant
sintemal conj. whereas, since
Sintflut f. deluge; (bibl.) the Flood
Sippe f., **Sippschaft** f. kindred, kith and kin
sistieren v. to inhibit, to stop, to arrest
sitt: -**enlos** adj. immoral, dissolute, profli-

gate; **-enrein** adj. morally pure, chaste; **-enstreng** adj. puritanical; **-ig** adj. well-bred, modest; **-lich** adj. moral; **-sam** adj. modest, decent; reserved, respectable
Sitt: -**e** f. custom, habit, usage; **-en** pl. morals, manners; **das ist nicht mehr -e** that's out of date; **feine -en** good manners; **lockere -en** loose morals; **-engesetz** neu. moral code; **-enprediger** m. moralizer; **-enrichter** m. censor; moralist; **-enverfall** m. demoralization; moral corruption
Sittich m. parakeet
situiert adj. **gut** (or **wohl**) — well-off; well-to-do
Sitz m. seat, place; domicile, residence; fit (of clothes); **-arbeit** f. sedentary work; **-fläche** f. seat (of chair); **-fleisch** neu. perseverance; **er hat kein -fleisch** he can't sit still; he does not persevere; **-gelegenheit** f. seating accomodation; **-platz** m. seat; **-stange** f. perch; **-streik** m. sit-down strike; **-ung** f. sitting; session; meeting; **-ungsbericht** m. minutes of a meeting; **-ungsperiode** f. (law) term
sitzen v. to sit; (birds) to perch; to fit; to hold a meeting; to adhere, to stick fast; (coll.) to be imprisoned; **hinter Schloss und Riegel** — to sit in jail; **jemand auf dem Halse** — to be a burden to someone; — **bleiben** to remain seated; to be a wallflower; to remain a spinster; (educ.) not to pass; — **lassen** to abandon, to leave in the lurch
Skala f. scale; **bewegliche** — sliding scale
Skalp m. scalp
Skalpell neu. scalpel
Skandal m. scandal, noise, row
skandal: -**ieren** v. to abuse, to slander; **-isieren** v. to scandalize; **-ös** adj. scandalous
Skelett neu. skeleton
Skepsis f. skepticism
Skeptiker m. skeptic
skeptisch adj. skeptic(al)
Ski m. ski; **-lauf** m. skiing; **-läufer** m. skier; **-springen** neu. ski jumping
skilaufen v. to ski
Skizze f. sketch, **-nbuch** neu. sketchbook
skizzenhaft adj. sketchy
Sklave m. slave; **-ndienst** m., **-rei** f. slavery
sklavisch adj. slavish, servile
Skonto m. and neu. discount
Skorbut m. scurvy
Skrofeln f. pl. scrofula
Skrupel m. scruple
skrupellos adj. unscrupulous
Smaragd m. emerald
so adv. so, thus; such; approximately; anyhow; as, —? interj. indeed? really? — conj. if, therefore, then; — **auch** however; — **doch** nevertheless, yet; — **ein Mensch** such a person; — **gross wie** as big as; — **oft** whenever; **um** — **besser** so much the better; **-bald** adv. as soon as; **-dann** adv. then, after (oder upon) that; **-eben** adv. just now; **-fern** conj.,

–weit *conj.* so far as; **–fern nur** as long as, if only; **–fort** *adv.* at once, immediately; **–fortig** *adj.* immediate; instantaneous, prompt; **–gar** *adv.* even; **–genannt** *adj.* so-called; **–gleich** *adv.* directly, promptly; **–lange** *adv.* as (*oder* so) long (as); whilst; **–mit** *adv.*, **–nach** *adv.* consequently, therefore; **–viel** *conj.* as far (*oder* much) as; the same as; **–wie** *conj.* as soon as; just as; also; **–wieso** *adv.* in any case, anyhow; **–wohl** *conj.* as well (as); not only; **–zusagen** *adv.* so to speak, as it were

Socke *f.* sock; **–nhalter** *m.* garter, suspender

Sockel *m.* base, pedestal

Soda *neu.* soda; **–wasser** *neu.* soda water

Sodbrennen *neu.* heartburn, pyrosis

Sofa *neu.* sofa; **–schoner** *m.* antimacassar

Sohle *f.* sole; bottom; (min.) floor

Sohn *m.* son; **der verlorene —** (bibl.) the Prodigal Son

Sojabohne *f.* soybean

Solawechsel *m.* promissory note

Solbad *neu.* saltwater (*oder* brine) bath

solch *pron.* and *adj.* such, the same, **–enfalls** *adv.* in such a case; **–ergestalt** *adv.* in such a form (*oder* manner, way); **–erlei** *adj.* of such a kind; **–ermassen** *adv.*, **–erweise** *adv.* to such a degree, in such a way

Sold *m.* pay, wages; **–buch** *neu.* (mil.) pay book

Soldat *m.* soldier; **–eska** *f.* gang of soldiers

soldatisch *adj.* soldierlike, military; of soldierly bearing

Söldling, Soldner *m.* hireling, mercenary

solid *adj.* solid, substantial; respectable; thorough; reliable; solvent; **–arisch** *adj.* joint; unanimous

Solid: –arität *f.* solidarity, unanimity; **–arschuldner** *m.* joint debtor; **–ität** *f.* solidity; soundness; reliability, respectability

Solist *m.*, **Solistin** *f.* soloist

Soll *neu.* debit; **–bestand** *m.* calculated assets

sollen *v.* to be obliged, to be bound to, to have to; to be supposed to; **das hat nicht sein —** that was not to be; **er hätte schreiben —** he ought to have written; **sollte er krank sein?** can he be ill? **Was soll das?** what is the use of that?

Solo *neu.* solo; **–stimme** *f.* solo part; **–tänzer** *m.* principal dancer

Sommer *m.* summer; **–aufenthalt** *m.*, **–frische** *f.* summer resort; **–fäden** *m. pl.* gossamer; **–frischler** *m.* summer vacationer; **–getreide** *neu.* spring grain; **–sonnenwende** *f.* summer solstice; **–sprosse** *f.* freckle; **–wohnung** *f.* summer residence

sommersprossig *adj.* freckled

somnambul *adj.* somnambulistic

Sonate *f.* sonata

sonder *prep.* without; **–bar** *adj.* strange, odd; peculiar; **–barerweise** *adv.* strange to say; **–gleichen** *adj.* unique, unequalled; **–lich** *adj.* particular, special, remarkable; **–n** *conj.* but; **–s** *adv.* **samt und –s** all together

Sonder: –(ab)druck *m.* special reprint, extract; **–berichterstatter** *m.* special correspondent; **–fall** *m.* exceptional case; **–ling** *m.* eccentric person, original; **–meldung** *f.* special announcement; **–recht** *neu.* special privilege; **–zug** *m.* special train

sondern *v.* to separate, to sever

sondieren *v.* to probe; to sound, to fathom

sonn: –en *v.* to (expose to the) sun; to bask; **–enklar** *adj.* clear as daylight; evident; **–(en)verbrannt** *adj.* sunburnt, tanned; **–ig** *adj.* sunny; **–täglich** *adj.* taking place on Sunday(s); **–täglich** *adv.* every Sunday

Sonn: –abend *m.* Saturday; **–e** *f.* sun; **–enaufgang** *m.* sunrise; **–enbad** *neu.* sunbath; **–enbahn** *f.* orbit of the sun, ecliptic; **–enblume** *f.* sunflower; **–enbrand** *m.* sunburn; **–endach** *neu.*, **–ensegel** *neu.* awning; **–enfinsternis** *f.* solar eclipse; **–enfleck** *m.* sunspot; **–enjahr** *neu.* solar year; **–ennähe** *f.* perihelion; **–enscheibe** *f.* solar disk; **–enschirm** *m.* sunshade; **–enseite** *f.* sunny side; **–enstäubchen** *neu.* mote; **–enstich** *m.* sunstroke; **–ensystem** *neu.* solar system; **–enuhr** *f.* sundial; **–enuntergang** *m.* sunset; **–enwende** *f.* solstice; **–tag** *m.* Sunday; **–tagsanzug** *m.* (clothes) Sunday best; **–tagsausflügler** *m.* week-ender; **–tagsfahrkarte** *f.* weekend ticket; **–tagskind** *neu.* person born on Sunday (*oder* under a lucky star); **–tagsstaat** *m.* Sunday finery

sonst *adv.* otherwise; else, besides, moreover; usually; before, formerly; **— nichts als** nothing but; **— nirgends** nowhere else; **wenn es — nichts ist** if that's all; **–ig** *adj.* other, former, remaining; **–wie** *adv.* in some other way; **–wo** *adv.* elsewhere, somewhere else; **–woher** *adv.* from somewhere else; **–wohin** *adv.* to another place, somewhere else

Sopran *m.* soprano; **–ist** *m.*, **–istin** *f.* soprano

Sorg: –e *f.* sorrow, anxiety; concern, care; worry, trouble; **lass das meine –e sein** leave that to me; **sich –en machen** to trouble oneself (about); **–e tragen** to take care of; to see to; **–enkind** *neu.* problem child; **–enstuhl** *m.* easy chair; **–falt** *f.* carefulness, precision; care

sorg: –en *v.* **sich –en** to be anxious, to worry; to trouble oneself (about); **–en für** to care for, to provide for; to see to; **dafür lass mich –en** I'll take care of that; **–enfrei** *adj.* free from trouble; lighthearted; **–envoll** *adj.* careworn; worried; **–fältig** *adj.* careful; precise, scrupulous; **–lich** *adj.* careful, anxious; **–los** *adj.* careless; thoughtless; carefree; lighthearted; **–sam** *adj.* cautious, circumspect

Sort: –e *f.* sort, kind, species; quality, brand; **–ierer** *m.* sorter; **–iment** *neu.* assortment; retail book trade; **–imenter**

m. bookseller

sortieren *v.* to (as)sort; to arrange, to sift

Sosse *f.* sauce, gravy

Souffleur *m.*, **Souffleuse** *f.* prompter; **-kasten** *m.* prompter's box

souffleuren *v.* to prompt

Souper *neu.* supper

Souverän *m.* sovereign; **-ität** *f.* sovereignty

sozial *adj.* social; **-isieren** *v.* to socialize; **-istisch** *adj.* socialistic

Sozial: -demokratie *f.* social democracy; **-ismus** *m.* socialism; **-ist** *m.* socialist; **-versicherung** *f.* social security; **-wissenschaft** *f.* sociology

Spachtel *m.* and *f.* spatula

Späh: -er *m.* spy, scout, secret observer; **-erblick** *m.* prying glance; **-trupp** *m.* patrol

spähen *v.* to spy, to scout, to reconnoiter

Spalier *neu.* espalier; trellis; — **stehen** to form a lane; **-obst** *neu.* wall fruit

Spalt *m.*, **Spalte** *f.* crack, gap; slit, slot; fissure; crevasse; **-e** *f.* (typ.) column; **-holz** *neu.* firewood; **-ung** *f.* splitting, fission; dissension, schism

spalt: -bar *adj.* cleavable, fissile; **-en** *v.* to cleave, to split; to divide; to decompose, to ferment; **-enweise** *adv.* (typ.) in columns

Span *m.* chip, splinter; **-ferkel** *neu.* sucking pig

Spange *f.* buckle; clasp; brooch; **-nschuh** *m.* buckled shoe

Spanien *neu.* Spain

Spann: -e *f.* span; interval; **-er** *m.* boot tree, last; (ent.) looper; **-feder** *f.* spring; **-kraft** *f.* elasticity; tension; energy; **-ung** *f.* stretching; tension; strain; (arch.) span; (elec.) voltage; potential; **-ungsmesser** *m.* voltmeter; **-weite** *f.* spread; (arch.) span

spannen *v.* to stretch; to strain; to tighten; (bow) to bend; (gun) to cock; to excite; **gespannt sein** to be anxious (*oder* curious); **vor den Wagen** — to hitch to the wagon; **-d** *adj.* exciting, fascinating, thrilling

Spar: -büchse *f.* money box; **-einlage** *f.* savings deposit; **-er** *m.* saver, economizer; **-flamme** *f.* pilot light; **-kasse** *f.* savings bank; **-pfennig** *m.* savings, nest egg

sparen *v.* to spare, to save, to economize

Spargel *m.* asparagus

spärlich *adj.* scanty, frugal; thin, sparse

Sparren *m.* spar, rafter

sparsam *adj.* economical, thrifty; parsimonious

Spass *m.* joke, jest; fun; — **machen** to amuse; **zum** — for fun; **-macher** *m.*, **-vogel** *m.* wag, clown, buffoon; jester; **-verderber** *m.* spoil-sport

spass: -en *v.* to jest, to joke, to make fun; **-eshalber** *adv.* for fun; **-ig** *adj.*, **-haft** *adj.* joking, amusing, funny, droll

spät *adj.* late: wie — **ist es?** what time is it? **zu — kommen** to be late; **-er** *adj.* later; **-er** *adv.* afterwards; **-erhin** *adv.* later on; **-estens** *adv.* at the latest

Spät: -herbst *m.* late autumn; **-ling** *m.* latecomer; late fruit; **-obst** *neu.* late fruit

Spatel *m.* spatula

Spaten *m.* spade; **-stich** *m.* spade cut

Spatz *m.* sparrow; **das pfeifen die -en schon von den Dächern** that's the talk of the town

spazieren *v.* to walk, to stroll; **-fahren** *v.* to go for a drive; **-führen** *v.* to take out for a walk; **-geh(e)n** *v.* to go for a walk

Spazier: -fahrt *f.* drive; boating; **-gang** *m.* walk, stroll; **-gänger** *m.* stroller, walker, promenader; **-stock** *m.* walking stick

Specht *m.* woodpecker

Speck *m.* bacon; fat; lard; — **ansetzen** to become fat; **wie die Made im — sitzen** to be in clover; **-schwarte** *f.* bacon rind; **-seite** *f.* flitch of bacon; **-stein** *m.* soapstone

spedieren *v.* to dispatch, to forward

Spedit: -eur *m.* forwarding agent; **-ion** *f.* forwarding; shipping department; **-ionsgeschäft** *neu.* forwarding agency; furniture removal business

Speer *m.* spear, lance; javelin

Speiche *f.* spoke

Speichel *m.* spittle; slaver; **-drüse** *f.* salivary gland; **-fluss** *m.* salivation; **-lecker** *m.* lickspittle, toady

Speicher *m.* warehouse; storeroom; reservoir; loft; granary, accumulator; silo

speichern *v.* to store, to warehouse

speien *v.* to spit, to expectorate, to vomit

Speise *f.* food, nourishment; meal, dish; dessert; **-eis** *neu.* ice cream; **-fett** *neu.* cooking fat; **-kammer** *f.* pantry, larder; **-karte** *f.*, **-zettel** *m.* bill of fare; **-nauftzug** *m.* dumb-waiter; **-nfolge** *f.* menu; **-öl** *neu.* salad oil; **-rohr** *neu.* supply pipe; **-röhre** *f.* esophagus, gullet; **-saal** *m.*, **-zimmer** *neu.* dining room; **-wagen** *m.* (rail.) diner

speisen *v.* to eat, to dine; to feed, to nourish, to supply

Spektakel *m.* and *neu.* noise, row, fracas

Spektrum *neu.* spectrum

Spekulant *m.* speculator

spekulieren *v.* to speculate

Spelunke *f.* den; low tavern

Spend: -e *f.* gift, contribution, donation; **-er** *m.* donor, benefactor; **-ung** *f.* contribution, donation

spenden *v.* to give, to contribute; to deal out; **Almosen** — to bestow alms; **das Abendmahl** — to administer the sacrament

spendieren *v.* to spend, to pay for; to treat

Spengler *m.* plumber; tinsmith

Sper: -ber *m.* sparrow hawk; **-ling** *m.* sparrow

Sperr: -e *f.* shutting, bar(ring); blockade; embargo; **-feuer** *neu.* curtain fire; **-frist** *f.* period of grace; **-gebiet** *neu.* prohibited area; blockade zone; **-gut** *neu.* bulky goods; **-haken** *m.* catch; ratchet; **-holz** *neu.* plywood; **-sitz** *m.*

(theat.) orchestra seat; **–ung** f. stoppage; blockade; embargo; **–vorrichtung** f. locking device; lock
sperrangelweit adv. ajar; **— offen** wide open
sperren v. to close, to lock; to block(ade), to stop; (legs) to straddle; (typ.) to space; **sich —** to oppose
Spesen f. pl. charges, expenses, costs
Spezerei f. spice
spezial, speziell adj. special, particular; **–isieren** v. to specialize
Spezial–arzt m. (med.) specialist; **–fach** neu., **–ität** f. specialty, special branch
spezifisch adj. specific; **–es Gewicht** specific gravity
Sphäre f. sphere, range, province
Spick–aal f. smoked eel; **–gans** f. smoked goose breast; **–nadel** f. larding pin
Spiegel m. mirror; (med.) speculum; tab, facing; (fig.) model, paragon; **–bild** neu. reflected image; **–ei** neu. fried egg; **–fechterei** f. jugglery, humbug; **–fernrohr** neu. reflecting telescope; **–pfeiler** m. (arch.) pier; **–schrift** f. mirror writing; **–ung** f. reflection, mirage
spiegel–blank adj. shining; **–glatt** adj. as smooth (oder slippery) as a mirror; **–n** r. to shine; to reflect; **sich –n** to be reflected, to look at oneself in the mirror
Spiel neu. play(ing), game, sport; gamble; (mus.) touch; (theat.) performance; acting; set, suit, pack (of cards); **auf dem –e stehen** to be at stake; **aufs — setzen** to hazard, to risk; **aus dem –e lassen** to leave out of question; **die Hand mit im –e haben** to have a finger in the pie; **ehrliches — fair** play; **leichtes — haben** to have no difficulty; **sein — treiben mit** to make game of; **–art** f. manner of playing; special type; (bot.) variety; **–ball** m. ball; (fig.) plaything; puppet; **–bank** f. gambling table (oder house); **–dose** f. musical box; **–er** m. player, gambler; actor, performer; **–erei** f. play, sport; trifle; **–ergebnis** neu. score; **–feld** neu. field, ground, court; **–film** m. feature movie; **–gefährte** m., **–genosse** m. playmate; **–hölle** f. gambling den; **–karte** f. playing card; **–leiter** m. stage manager, producer; **–mann** m. musician, fiddler, minstrel; **–marke** f. chip, counter; **–plan** m. repertory; program; **–platz** m. playground; **–raum** m. elbowroom, free scope; **–sachen** f. pl., **–waren** f. pl., **–zeug** neu. toys; **–schar** f. (mus. and theat.) amateur company; **–schuld** f. gambling debt; **–schule** f. kindergarten; **–uhr** f. musical clock; **–verderber** m. killjoy; spoilsport; **–werk** neu. chime
spiel–bar adj. (theat.) stageable; **–en** r. to play, to gamble; to act, to perform; to simulate; to flash; **–end** adr. playing; with the utmost ease
Spiess m. spear, pike, lance; spit; **den — umdrehen** to turn the tables on; **–bürger** m., **–er** m. narrow-minded fellow;

Philistine; **–er** m. stag, young buck; **–geselle** m. accomplice; crony; **–rute** f. gauntlet; **–ruten laufen** to run the gauntlet
spiess–bürgerlich adj., **–ig** adj. narrowminded; **–en** v. to spear, to spit
Spinat m. spinach
Spind neu. wardrobe, locker, cupboard
Spindel f. spindle, distaff; mandrel; axis
Spinett neu. spinet
Spinn–e f. spider; **–er** m. spinner; silkworm; **–erei** f. spinning (mill); **–faser** f. synthetic fiber; **–gewebe** neu., **–webe** f. cobweb; **–maschine** f. spinning jenny; **–rad** neu. spinning wheel; **–rocken** m. distaff; **–stoffindustrie** f. textile industry
spinnen v. to spin; (cat) to purr; to be crazy
Spion m. spy, scout; **–age** f. espionage; **–ageabwehr** f. counterespionage
spionieren r. to spy, to scout; to pry
Spiralsturzflug m. spiral dive
Spirit–ismus m. spiritualism; **–uosen** f. pl. alcoholic liquors; **–us** m. spirit, alcohol; **–usbrennerei** f. distillery
Spital neu. hospital
Spitz m. Pomeranian dog; **einen — haben** (coll.) to be tipsy; **–bart** m. pointed beard; **–bogen** m. pointed arch; **–bube** m. thief, rascal; **–e** f. point; peak, top; head; (pen) nib; (tongue) tip; lace; sarcastic remark; **an der –e stehen** to act as leader; **die –e abbrechen** to take the edge off; **etwas auf die –e treiben** to carry something to extremes; **jemand die –e bieten** to defy someone; **–enbesatz** m. lace trimming; **–enklöppelei** f. bobbin lacemaking; **–enleistung** f. peak performance (oder power output); **–enlohn** m. maximum pay; **–entanz** m. toe dance; **–hacke** f. pickaxe; **–maus** f. shrewmouse; **–name** m. nickname
spitz adj. pointed, acute; sharp; sarcastic; **–bübisch** adj. roguish, rascally; **–en** to point; to sharpen; **den Mund –en** to purse one's lips; **die Ohren –en** to prick up one's ears; **sich –en auf** to be eager about; **–findig** adj. subtle; hairsplitting, captious; sophistical; **–winklig** adj. acute-angled
Spitzel m. informer, spy; police agent
spleissen v. to split, to splice
Splitter m. splinter, chip; fragment; mote
splitter–(faser)nackt adj. stark naked; **–ig** adj. splintered, splintery; **–n** v. to splinter
spontan adj. spontaneous
Sporen m. spur; incentive, stimulus; **die — geben** to put spurs to
spornen v. to spur; to stimulate
spornstreichs adr. at full speed, directly
Sport m. sport; **–abzeichen** neu. sports badge; **–eln** f. pl. perquisites; fees; **–funk** m. (rad.) sports news; **–ler** m. sportsman; **–wagen** m. gocart; sport car
sportlich adj. sportsmanlike; athletic
Spott m. mockery, derision, ridicule; butt; **Gegenstand des –es** laughingstock; **seinen — treiben** to make sport of; **–drossel** f. mockingbird; **–geburt** f.

monstrosity; **–gedicht** *neu.* satirical poem; **–geld** *neu.*, **–preis** *m.* low price; trifling sum; **–name** *m.* nickname

spott: **–billig** *adj.* dirt-cheap; **–en** *v.* to mock, to ridicule; **–lustig** *adj.* satirical

Spötte: **–lei** *f.*, **–rei** *f.* banter, chaff; raillery; mockery, derision, sneer; **–r** *m.* jeerer; mocker, scoffer; (bibl.) blasphemer

spöttisch *adj.* mocking, ironical, sarcastic

Sprach: **–armut** *f.* lack of words; **–e** *f.* speech; language, tongue; diction; articulation; **jemand die –e benehmen** to strike one dumb; **mit der –e herausrücken** to speak freely; **mit der –e nicht herauswollen** to beat about the bush; **zur –e bringen** to broach a subject; **–eigenheit** *f.*, **–eigentümlichkeit** *f.* idiomatic peculiarity; **–fehler** *m.* speech defect; **–forscher** *m.* linguist, philologist; **–forschung** *f.* linguistics, philology; **–führer** *m.* colloquial guide, phrase book; **–gebrauch** *m.* usage (of a language); **–grenze** *f.* linguistic frontier; **–lehrer** *m.* language teacher; **–regel** *f.* grammatical rule; **–rohr** *neu.* speaking tube; (coll.) mouthpiece, spokesman; **–schatz** *m.* vocabulary; **–schnitzer** *m.* solecism; **–talent** *neu.* talent for acquiring languages; **–unterricht** *m.* teaching of languages; **–verwirrung** *f.* confusion of tongues; **–wissenschaft** *f.* linguistics, philology

sprach: **–kundig** *adj.* proficient in languages; **–lich** *adj.* linguistic, grammatical; **–los** *adj.* speechless, dumb; **–widrig** *adj.* ungrammatical; **–wissenschaftlich** *adj.* philological

Sprech: **–er** *m.* speaker, spokesman; lecturer; (rad.) announcer; **–film** *m.* talking motion picture; **–gesang** *m.* recitative; **–stunde** *f.* consulting hour; **–stundenhilfe** *f.* doctor's receptionist; **–übung** *f.* exercise in speaking; **–weise** *f.* diction; **–zimmer** *neu.* consultation room

sprechen *v.* to speak, to talk; to say, to discuss; **ausführlich** (*or* **weitläufig**) **—** to enlarge on; **dafür —** to speak in favor of; **er ist nicht zu —** he is engaged; **er lässt nicht mit sich —** he won't listen to reason; **frei —** to extemporize; **to find innocent; schuldig —** to find guilty; **sich herum —** to be the talk of the town; **— wir nicht davon** don't mention it; **–de Ähnlichkeit** striking resemblance; **–der Beweis** conclusive evidence; **Urteil — to pronounce judgment; vor Gericht —** to plead

spreiten *v.* to spread, to extend

spreizen *v.* to spread, to stretch out, to straddle; **sich —** to be affected; to resist

Spreng: **–bombe** *f.* bomb; **–er** *m.* sprinkler, spray; **–körper** *m.* explosive shell; **–ladung** *f.* explosive charge; **–stoff** *m.* explosive; **–wagen** *m.* street sprinkler

Sprengel *m.* parish, diocese

sprengen *v.* to blow up, to burst open; to force; to break up (*oder* open); to sprinkle, to water; to ride at full speed

sprenkeln *v.* to speckle, to spot; to marble

Sprey *f.* chaff

Sprichwort *neu.* proverb; adage, saying

Spring: **–brunnen** *m.* fountain; jet (of water); **–er** *m.* jumper, vaulter; (chess) knight; **–flut** *f.* spring tide; **–insfeld** *m.* harum-scarum fellow; romp; **–seil** *neu.* skipping rope

springen *v.* to jump, to leap; to spring; to dive; (fountain) to spout, to play; to crack, to burst; **in die Augen —** to strike the eye; **in die Bresche — to fill the breach; Seil — to skip rope; über die Klinge — lassen** to put to the sword; to kill

Sprit *m.* spirit, alcohol

Spritz: **–arbeit** *f.* firemen's work; marbled work; **–bewurf** *m.* roughcast; **–e** *f.* fire engine, sprayer; squirt; injection, syringe; **–enhaus** *neu.* fire engine shed; **–er** *m.* splash, squirt; spot; **–fahrt** *f.* outing; **–kuchen** *m.* fritter

spritzen *v.* to squirt; to sprinkle, to spray; to spout; to inject; to gush forth

spröde *adj.* brittle; fragile, inflexible; chapped; shy, coy; prudish

Spross *m.* shoot, sprout, sprig; (stag) antler; offspring

Sprosse *f.* rung, round, step; sprout; freckle

sprossen *v.* to sprout, to shoot, to germinate

Sprössling *m.* shoot, sprout; offspring, scion

Spruch *m.* aphorism, maxim, saying; verse (of Scriptures); motto; sentence, verdict

Sprudel *m.* bubbling water, mineral spring; overflow (of humor *oder* words)

sprudeln *v.* to bubble, to gush forth, to effervesce, to sparkle; to brim (over)

sprühen *v.* to drizzle; to sparkle, to flash

Sprung *m.* leap, bound, jump; crack; split; **auf dem –e sein** zu to be on the point of; **jemand auf die** (*or* **hinter jemandes**) **Sprünge kommen** to find someone out; **nur ein — bis dahin** only a stone's throw away; **–brett** *neu.* springboard; **–federmatratze** *f.* spring mattress; **–gelenk** *neu.* hock; **–hügel** *m.*, **–schanze** *f.* ski jump platform; **–tuch** *neu.* (life-saving) jumping net

Spucke *f.* (coll.) spittle, saliva

spucken *v.* to spit, to expectorate

Spucknapf *m.* spittoon

Spuk *m.* spook, apparition, ghost, specter; noise; **–geschichte** *f.* ghost story

spukhaft *adj.* ghostly, haunted

Spul: **–e** *f.* spool, bobbin; coil; quill; **–maschine** *f.* spooling machine, bobbin frame; **–rad** *neu.* spooling wheel; **–wurm** *m.* bellyworm

Spül: **–eimer** *m.* slop pail; **–fass** *neu.* wash tub; **–frau** *f.* scullery maid; dishwasher; **–icht** *neu.*, **–wasser** *neu.* dish water, rinsings; slops; **–kasten** *m.* flush tank; **–stein** *m.* sink

spülen *v.* to rinse, to flush, to cleanse

Spund *m.* bung, plug, stopper; faucet, tap; **–bohrer** *m.* tap borer; **–loch** *neu.* bunghole

Spur f. trace, scent, track, rut; footprint; (fig.) mark, sign, vestige; **jemand auf die — kommen** to be on someone's tracks; **keine — nicht a bit; —weite** f. (rail.) gauge

Spür: —hund m. bloodhound, pointer; (coll.) spy; **—nase** f. good nose; keen sense of smell; **—sinn** m. sagacity, shrewdness

spüren v. to feel, to notice, to perceive; **— nach** to track, to scent out; to search for

spurlos adj. trackless; — adv. without a trace

sputen r. **sich —** to hurry, to make haste

Staat m. state; government; pomp, finery; **in vollem — in** full dress; **— mit etwas machen** to parade; to show off; to boast; **—enbund** m. confederation; **—enlose** m. person without nationality; **—sakt** m. state ceremony; **—saktion** f. political event; **—sangehörige** m. citizen; **—sangehörigkeit** f. nationality; citizenship; **—sanwalt** m. public prosecutor; **—sanzeiger** m. official gazette; **—sarchiv** neu. government record office; **—sbeamte** m. government official; **—sbürger** m. citizen; **—sdienst** m. civil service; **—seinkünfte** pl. public revenues; **—sgefangene** m. prisoner of state; **—sgeheimnis** neu. state secret; **—sgelder** neu. pl. public money; **—sgewalt** f. supreme power; **—shaushalt** m. budget, finances; **—skerl** m. fine fellow; **—skleid** neu. gala dress; **—skunst** f. statecraft, politics; **—smann** m. statesman, politician; **—sordnung** f. political system; **—spapiere** neu. pl. government bonds; **—srecht** neu. constitutional law; **—sschuld** f. national debt; **—sstreich** m. coup d'état; **—swesen** neu. state affairs; **—swissenschaft** f. political science; **—swohl** neu. general welfare; **—szuschuss** m. government subsidy

Stab m. staff, stick; rod, bar; baton; personnel; headquarters; **den — über jemand brechen** to condemn someone; **—(hoch)sprung** m. pole jump; **—ilität** f. stability; **—reim** m. alliteration; **—sarzt** m. surgeon major; **—squartier** neu. headquarters; **—träger** m. sergeant at arms

Stäbchen neu. small rod; (coll.) cigarette

stabil adj. stable; **—isieren** v. to stabilize

Stachel m. sting, goad, tongue, spike, thorn; prick(le), stimulus, spur; **—beere** f. gooseberry; **—draht** m. barbed wire; **—schwein** neu. porcupine

stach(e)lig adj. prickly, thorny; sarcastic

Stadion neu. stadium, arena

Stadium neu. phase, stage

Stadt f. city, town; **—bahn** f. metropolitan railroad; **—bezirk** m., **—teil** m., **—viertel** neu. city district, ward; **—bild** neu. panorama; city plan; **—gemeinde** f. municipality; **—kern** m. center of a city; **—koffer** m. suitcase; **—randsiedlung** f. suburban settlement; **—rat** m. alderman, city council; **—väter** m. pl. city fathers; **—verordnete** m. city councilor; **—verord-**

netenversammlung f. city council; **—waage** f. public scales

Städt: —ebau m. city planning; **—eordnung** f. municipal ordinance; **—er** m. townsman

städtisch adj. municipal, urban

Stafette f. courier; dispatch rider; **—nlauf** m. relay race

Staffage f. accessories

Staffel f. rung, step; (avi.) squadron; (mil.) echelon, detachment; (sport) relay; **—ei** f. easel; **—lauf** m. relay race; **—tarif** m. sliding tariff; graduated wage scale

Stahl m. steel; **—feder** f. steel spring; steel pen; **—helm** m. steel helmet; **—kammer** f. strong-room; **—panzer** m. steel armor; **—stich** m. steel engraving; **—waren** f. pl. hardware, cutlery; **—werk** neu. steelworks

stählen v. to (convert into) steel; to harden

stählern adj. made of steel; steely, hard

Staken m. stake, pile, pole

Staket neu. palisade, fence, stockade

Stall m. stable, stall; (pig)sty; kennel, shed; **—dienst** m. stable work; **—geld** neu. stable fee; **—knecht** m. groom, hostler; **—magd** f. dairy maid; **—meister** m. riding master, equerry; **—ung** f. stables; stabling

Stamm m. stem, trunk, stalk; family, race, tribe, clan; breed; main part; stock; **—aktie** f. original share; **—baum** m. pedigree; **—buch** neu. genealogical register; album; **—eltern** pl. ancestors; first parents; **—folge** f. lineage; **—gast** m. regular guest; **—halter** m. eldest son; son and heir; **—holz** neu. standing timber; **—kapital** neu. original capital; **—kneipe** f., **—lokal** neu. favorite pub; **—rolle** f. muster roll; **—sitz** m. ancestral estate; **—tafel** f. genealogical table; **—vater** m. ancestor; **—wort** neu. root word, stem

stammeln v. to stammer, to stutter

stammen v. to descend, to originate, to derive; to come (oder spring) from

stämmig adj. sturdy, strong, robust, vigorous

Stammler m. stammerer, stutterer

stammverwandt adj. cognate, kindred, akin

stampfen v. to stamp, to pound, to ram, to crush; to trudge, to paw; (naut.) to pitch

Stampfkartoffeln f. pl. mashed potatoes

Stand m. stand(ing); position; stall, booth; condition, situation; state; profession; rank, class; **einen schweren — haben** to have a hard fight; **—bild** neu. statue; **—er** m. (mil.) pennant; **—esamt** neu. registrar's office; **—esbeamte** m. registrar; **—esehre** f. professional honor; **—esgenosse** m. equal in rank; **—esregister** neu. vital statistics; **—esvorurteil** neu. class prejudice; **—esperson** f. person of rank; **—geld** neu. booth fee; **—gericht** neu. court martial; **—licht** neu. parking lights; **—ort** m., **—platz** m. site, station, position; garrison; **–punkt** m. point of view; stand; **–quartier** neu. permanent quarters; **–recht** neu. martial law; **–rede** f. harangue; **–uhr** f. pendulum clock

stand: **–esgemäss** adv., **–esmässig** adv. in accordance with one's rank; **–haft** adj. steady, constant, firm; steadfast; **–halten** v. to hold out, to resist, to withstand; **–rechtlich** adj. according to martial law

Standarte f. standard, ensign

Ständchen neu. serenade

Ständer m. stand, post, pillar

ständig adj. permanent, constant; **— adv.** continuously

Stange f. pole, rod, perch, bar, stake; **bei der — bleiben** to persevere; **eine — Geld** a lot of money; **jemand die — halten** to back someone; **von der —** ready-made; **–nbohne** f. pole bean; **–spargel** m. asparagus served whole

Stänker m. stinker, quarrelsome fellow; **–erei** f. brawl, quarrel, squabble, slander

Staniol neu. tinfoil; **–streifen** (Radarstörung) m. (avi.) window; chaff

Stanze f. punch, stamp, die; (lit.) stanza

Stapel m. pile, heap; (naut.) slips, stocks; depot, dump; **vom — lassen** to launch; **vom — laufen** to be launched; **–lauf** m. launch(ing); **–platz** m. depot, dump

stapeln v. to pile up, to stack up

Star m. starling; (med) cataract; (movie) star; **den — stechen** to remove a cataract; (fig.) to open someone's eyes

stark adj. strong, sturdy, intense; corpulent, stout; violent; considerable, numerous; voluminous; **— auftragen** to exaggerate; **–e Erkältung** severe cold; **–er Esser** hearty eater; **–e Seite** (fig.) strong point; **— adv.** very, much, hard

Stärke f. strength, force, power; intensity; largeness; violence; thickness; number, quantity; forte, strong point; starch; **–grad** m. degree of strength, intensity; **–mehl** neu. cornstarch; **–zucker** m. glucose

stärke: **–haltig** adj containing starch, starchy; **–en** v. to strengthen, to invigorate; to starch; **sich –en** to take refreshments; **–end** adj. restorative, strengthening; tonic

Starkstrom m. (elec.) high tension; **–leitung** f. power line, power circuit

Stärkungsmittel neu. restorative

starr adj. stiff, rigid; staring; unbending; **— vor Entsetzen terror-stricken; — vor Erstaunen** (or **Überraschung**) flabbergasted, thunderstruck; **–en** r. to stare; to gape; **–köpfig** adj. headstrong, obstinate

Starr: **–heit** f. stiffness, rigidity; inflexibility; **–krampf** m. tetanus

Start m. start; take-off; **–bahn** f. (avi.) runway; **–er** m. starter; **–ordnung** f. starting order; **–rakete** f. booster rocket; **–zählung** f. countdown

starten v. to start; (avi.) to take off

startklar adj. (avi.) ready for the take off

Statik f. statics

Station f. station; stop; (hospital) ward; **freie — free** board and lodging; **–svorsteher** m. stationmaster

stationieren v. to station

Statist m. (film, theat.) extra, supernumerary; **–ik** f. statistics; **–iker** m. statistician

statistisch adj. statistic(al)

Stativ neu. stand, support; tripod

Statt f. place, stead; **an Eides — in lieu of an oath; an Kindes — annehmen** to adopt a child; **–halter** m. governor

statt prep. and conj. instead of, in lieu of; **— meiner** in my place; **–finden, –haben** r. to take place, to happen; **–geben** v. to permit, to grant; **–haft** adj. admissible, allowable; legal; **–lich** adj. stately; imposing; considerable; grand

Stätte f. place, room

Statue f. statue

statuieren v. to establish; **ein Exempel — to make an example of; to set up as a warning

Statur f. stature; figure, height; size

Status m. state of affairs

Statut neu. statute, regulations

Staub m. dust; powder; pollen; **in den — ziehen** to drag through the mire; **sich aus dem –e machen** to escape, to abscond; **viel — aufwirbeln** to cause a stir; **–beutel** m. (bot.) anther; **–blatt** neu., **–gefäss** neu. (bot.) stamen; **–faden** m. (bot.) stamen, filament; **–fleck** m. dust speck; **–geborene** m. (bibl.) mortal man; **–kamm** m. fine-tooth comb; **–korn** neu. dust particle; **–lappen** m., **–tuch** neu. dustcloth; **–mantel** m. dust coat; **–sauger** m. vacuum cleaner; **–wedel** m. feather duster; **–zucker** m. powdered sugar

stäuben v. to dust; to raise dust; to spray

staubig adj. dusty, powdery

Staude f. shrub, bush, tall plant

stauen f. to stow (goods); to dam (water); **sich —** to block; to bank up; to rise

staunen v. to be astonished; to be amazed; to marvel; **–enswert** adj. astonishing, amazing

Stearinkerze f. tallow (oder paraffin) candle

Stech: **–apfel** m. thorn, apple; **–becken** neu. bedpan; **–eisen** neu. punch; piercer; **–er** m. engraver; (gun) hair trigger; **–fliege** f. gadfly; **–ginster** m. juniper; **–mücke** f. gnat; **–palme** f. holly, ilex; **–schritt** m. goose step

stechen v. to prick; to sting; to pierce; to stab; (flea) to bite; to engrave; to cut; (cards) to trump; to tap (smelting furnace); (sun) to burn; to stick (pig); **durch und durch — to transfix; ihn sticht der Hafer** he is in high spirits; **in die Augen — to take one's fancy; in See —** to put to sea

Steck: **–brief** m. warrant of arrest; **–dose** f. (elec.) wall plug; **–en** m. stick, staff; **–enpferd** neu. fad, hobby; **–er** m. (elec.) plug; **–kissen** neu. cushion for carrying a baby; **–kontakt** m. (elec.) plug; **–ling**

m. (bot.) cutting; seedling; **-nadel** *f.* pin; **-rübe** *f.* turnip; **-schlüssel** *m.* box wrench

stecken *v.* to stick; to put, to set, to plant; to fix; to pin up; to be attached, to be stuck; to be hidden; to be involved; **Geld in ein Geschäft —** to invest money in a business; **im Elend —** to be in great misery; **in Brand —** to set on fire; **jemand in den Sack —** to outdo someone; **unter einer Decke —** to have a secret understanding; **to be an accomplice; — bleiben** *v.* to be stuck; to break down; **— lassen** to leave (key in door, etc.)

Stefan *m.* Stephen

Steg *m.* path; footbridge; (mus.) bridge; (trouser) strap; (typ.) stick; **-reif** *m.* extempore; **aus dem -reif sprechen to** extemporize

Steh: -bierhalle *f.* tavern; **-kragen** *m.* stand-up collar; **-lampe** *f.* floor lamp, **-leiter** *f.* stepladder; **-platz** *m.* standing place

stehen *v.* to stand; to stop; to be erect; to be; to suit, to become; (dog) to point; **an der Spitze —** to be at the head; **es steht bei Dir** its up to you; **für jemand gut —** to vouch for someone; **geschrieben —** to be written; **mir steht der Verstand still** I am at my wit's end; **Modell —** to serve as a model; **unter Waffen —** to be under arms; **wie steht's mit dir?** what about you? **zu Diensten —** to be at one's service; **— bleiben** to stop; **-d** *adj.* standing; **allein —d** isolated; lonely; **-den Fusses** on the spot; **-des Kapital** fixed capital; **-des Wasser** stagnant water; **— lassen** to let alone, to leave

stehlen *v.* to steal, to rob, to pilfer; **dem lieben Gott die Zeit —** to idle away one's time; **sich davon —** to sneak away

steif *adj.* stiff, rigid; benumbed; formal; **halt die Ohren —!** be brave! **— und fest behaupten** to assert obstinately; **-en** *v.* to stiffen

steigen *v.* to climb, to ascend; to mount; to increase; **herunter —** to descend; **ins Bett —** to go to bed; **— lassen** to fly (a kite)

steigern *v.* to raise, to increase; to heighten; to intensify; (auction) to bid; (gram.) to compare

steil *adj.* steep, precipitous

Stein *m.* stone, rock; monument; gravestone; kernel; gem; (checkers) piece; **einen — im Brett haben** to be in favor with someone; **es fiel mir ein — vom Herzen** that's a load off my mind; **-des Anstosses** stumbling block; **— und Bein frieren** to freeze hard; **— und Bein schwören** to swear on a stack of bibles; **über Stock und — laufen** to run at full speed; **-adler** *m.* golden eagle; **-block** *m.* boulder; **-brecher** *m.* quarryman; stone crusher; **-bruch** *m.* quarry; **-damm** *m.* pier, mole; paved road; **-druck** *m.* lithography; **-eiche** *f.* holm oak; **-garten** *m.* rock garden; **-geröll(e)**

neu. rubble, shingle; **-gut** *neu.* earthenware, crockery; **-hauer** *m.*, **-metz** *m.* stone mason; **-kohle** *f.* (pit)coal; **-pflaster** *neu.* stone pavement; **-pilz** *m.* edible mushroom; **-salz** *neu.* rock salt; **-schleifer** *m.* stone polisher; **-schneider** *m.* lapidary; **-setzer** *m.* paver; **-wand** *f.* stone wall; **-wurf** *m.* stone's throw; **-zeit** *f.* Stone Age

stein: -alt *adj.* as old as the hills; **-ern** *adj.*, **-ig** *adj.* rocky, stony; **-igen** *v.* to stone; **-reich** *adj.* full of stones; immensely rich

Steiss *m.* buttocks; rump; **-bein** *neu.* coccyx

Stell: -age *f.* stand; shelf; **-dichein** *neu.* rendezvous; tryst; **-e** *f.* place, spot, stand; position, situation; (book) passage; **an jemandes -e treten** to replace someone; **an Ort und -e sein** to be in place; **an -e von** instead of; **auf der -e** immediately; **offene -e** vacancy; **von der -e kommen** to make progress; **zur -e schaffen** to deliver; **zur -e sein** to be present; **-enjäger** *m.* job hunter; **-ennachweis** *m.*, **-envermittlung** *f.* employment agency; **-macher** *m.* cartwright, wheelwright; **-motor** *m.* servomotor; **-ung** *f.* position; posture; attitude; situation; (mil.) line; **seine -ung nehmen** to express one's opinion; **-ungnahme** *f.* comment; **-ungsgesuch** *neu.* application; **-vertreter** *m.* representative; deputy; substitute; proxy; **-wagen** *m.* omnibus for outings; **-werk** *neu.* signal box

stell: -bar *adj.* adjustable, movable; **-en** *v.* to put, to place; to set; to regulate; to furnish; to provide; to corner, to arrest; **auf sich selbst gestellt sein** to be independent; **einen Antrag -en** to propose; (pol.) to move; **einen Bürgen -en** to find bail; **gut gestellt sein** to be well off; **in Frage -en** to question; **in Zweifel -en** to doubt; **nach dem Leben -en** to make an attempt on (someone's) life; **sich feindlich -en** to oppose; **sich -en** to (take a) stand; to feign, to pretend; to give oneself up; **sich -en auf** to cost; **sich -en zu** to behave towards; **vor Augen -en** to expose to view; **zur Diskussion -en** to invite a discussion upon; **zur Rede -en** to call to account; **zur Schau -en** to exhibit; **Zeugen -en** to produce witnesses; **-vertretend** *adj.* vicarious, supplementary; delegated

Stelz: -bein *neu.*, **-fuss** *m.* wooden leg; **-e** *f.* stilt; **-vogel** *m.* (orn.) wader

Stemmeisen *neu.* chisel

stemmen *v.* to prop, to support; to stem; to lift (weight); **sich —** to resist; to oppose

Stempel *m.* stamp; die, puncheon; postmark; brand; (bot.) pistil; (mech.) piston; **-gebühr** *f.* stamping fee; **-kissen** *neu.* ink pad; **-schneider** *m.* stamp cutter; die sinker

stempeln *v.* to stamp, to mark; **— gehen** to be on the dole

Stengel *m.* stalk, stem

Steno: **-gramm** *neu.* shorthand notes; **-graph** *m.* stenographer; **-graphie** *f.* stenography, shorthand; **-typist** *m.*, **-typistin** *f.* stenographer and typist

stenographieren *v.* to write (*oder* take down) shorthand

stenographisch *adj.* stenographic; shorthand

Stepp: **-decke** *f.* quilt; **-stich** *m.* back-stitch

steppen *v.* to quilt

Sterbe: **-bett** *neu.*, **-lager** *neu.* deathbed; **-fall** *m.* death; **-hemd** *neu.* shroud; **-kasse** *f.* burial fund; **-liste** *f.* register of deaths; **-sakramente** *neu. pl.* last sacraments

sterben *v.* to die; **im — liegen** to be dying; **vor Langeweile —** to be bored to death; **-skrank** *adj.* fatally ill; **-smüde** *adj.* dead-tired

sterblich *adj.* mortal

Sterblichkeitsziffer *f.* death rate

Stereo: **-metrie** *f.* stereometry; **-skop** *neu.* stereoscope; **-typ** *m.* stereotype

stereotyp *adj.* stereotype(d)

steril *adj.* sterile; **-ilisieren** *v.* to sterilize

Stern *m.* star; (typ.) asterisk; **-bild** *neu.* constellation; **-deuter** *m.* astrologer; **-enbanner** *neu.* Star-Spangled Banner; **-kunde** *f.* astronomy; **-schnuppe** *f.* shooting star; **-warte** *f.* astronomical observatory

stet(ig) *adj.* steady, constant, continual

stets *adv.* always; constantly, continually

Steuer *neu.* helm, rudder; **-bord** *neu.* starboard; **-knüppel** *m.* (avi.) control stick; **-mann** *m.* helmsman; deck officer; **-mannskunst** *f.* art of navigation; **-rad** *neu.* steering wheel; **-ruder** *neu.* rudder, helm; **-ung** *f.* steering (gear); **-vorrichtung** *f.* steering apparatus (*oder* gear)

Steuer *f.* tax; **-amt** *neu.* revenue office; **-anschlag** *m.* assessment; **-beamte** *m.* revenue officer; **-einnehmer** *m.* tax collector; **-erklärung** *f.* income tax return; **-hinterziehung** *f.* tax fraud; **-politik** *f.* fiscal policy; **-satz** *m.* tax rate; **-zahler** *m.* taxpayer; **-zuschlag** *m.* surtax

steuerfrei *adj.* tax-exempt

steuern *v.* to steer, to navigate, to drive; to pilot; **einer Sache —** to repress something; **— zu** to contribute to

steuerpflichtig *adj.* subject to taxation

Stich *m.* sting, bite, prick; stitch, puncture; stab; engraving; (cards) trick; (fencing) thrust; (mil.) hitch, knot; (spade) cut; (fig.) gibe, taunt; **einen — haben** to turn sour; (coll.) to have a screw loose; **im — lassen** to forsake, to desert; **— halten** to stand the test; **-blatt** *neu.* (sword) guard; trump card; **-el** *m.* engraving tool; graver; **-elei** *f.* (coll.) needlework; gibe, sneer, taunt; **-ler** *m.* taunter; giber, sneerer; **-ling** *m.* stickleback; **-probe** *f.* sample taken at random; **-tag** *m.* fixed day; **-waffe** *f.* pointed weapon; **-wahl** *f.* final ballot; **-wort** *neu.* catchword; cue; **-wortverzeichnis** *neu.* list of subjects; index; **-wunde** *f.* stab

stich: **-elhaarig** *adj.* wire-haired; **-eln** *v.* to stitch; to taunt, to gibe, to sneer; **-fest** *adj.*, **-haltig** *adj.* standing the test; valid; sound, plausible

Stick: **-erei** *f.* embroidery; **-garn** *neu.* embroidery cotton; **-gaze** *f.* needlepoint canvas; **-husten** *m.* hooping cough; **-luft** *f.* stuffy air; **-muster** *neu.* embroidery pattern; **-rahmen** *m.* embroidery hoop; **-stoff** *m.* nitrogen; **-zeug** *neu.* embroidery materials

stick: **-ig** *adj.* stuffy, close; suffocating; **-stoffhaltig** *adj.* nitrogenous

sticken *v.* to embroider

stieben *v.* to disperse, to scatter; to fly about; to spray; to give off (dust, etc.)

Stief: **-bruder** *m.* stepbrother; **-eltern** *pl.* stepparents; **-kind** *neu.* stepchild; **-mutter** *f.* stepmother; **-mütterchen** *neu.* pansy; **-sohn** *m.* stepson; **-vater** *m.* stepfather

Stiefel *m.* boot; **-anzieher** *m.* shoehorn; **-knecht** *m.* bootjack; **-putzer** *m.* bootblack; **-schaft** *m.* (boot) leg; **-wichse** *f.* shoe polish

Stiege *f.* staircase, stairs; score (20)

Stieglitz *m.* goldfinch, thistle finch

Stiel *m.* handle, stick; stem, stalk; **mit Stumpf und —** with root and branch; **-stich** *m.* hemstitch

Stier *m.* bull; Taurus; **-kampf** *m.* bullfight; **-kämpfer** *m.* bullfighter, matador

Stift *m.* peg, pin; pencil, crayon; (coll.) apprentice; **—** *neu.* charitable foundation; convent, chapter; **-er** *m.* founder; donor; **-sherr** *m.* canon, prebendary; **-shütte** *f.* (bibl.) Tabernacle; **-skirche** *f.* collegiate church; **-ungsfest** *neu.* founder's (*oder* commemoration) day

stiften *v.* to found, to establish; to donate

stigmatisieren *v.* to stigmatize

Stil *m.* style; manner, usage, kind; **-blüte** *f.* pun; **-istik** *f.* style of composition

still *adj.* still; silent, quiet; calm; motionless; taciturn, peaceful; **-e Messe** Low Mass; **-e Neigung** unexpressed love; **-e Woche** Holy Week; **-e Zeit** (com.) dull season; **-er Gesellschafter** (com.) silent partner; **-er Vorbehalt** mental reservation; **-bleiben** *v.* to keep quiet; **-(l)egen** *v.* to shut down; **-en** *v.* to calm; to stanch; to quench; to appease; to nurse, to suckle; **-halten** *v.* to keep still, to stop; **-(l)iegen** *v.* to lie quietly; to stand still; **-schweigen** *v.* to be silent; **-schweigen** *v.* to take no notice (of); **-schweigend** *adj.* silent; tacit, implied; **-sitzen** *v.* to sit quietly; **nicht -sitzen können** to be fidgety; **-stehen** *v.* to stand still, to stop; **stillgestanden!** (mil.) attention! **-stehend** *adj.* stationary, stagnant; **-vergnügt** *adj.* quietly enjoying, inwardly serene

Still: **-e** *f.* silence; calmness; peace; **in aller -e** in secret, privately; silently; **-eben** *neu.* (art.) still life; **-(l)egung** *f.* shutdown; **-schweigen** *neu.* silence; **-stand** *m.* standstill, stoppage; deadlock; (wirtschaftlich) *m.* recession

der Stille Ozean *m.* the Pacific Ocean

Stimm: −**abgabe** f. voting, vote; −**band** neu. vocal cord; −**bruch** m. breaking of the voice; −**e** f. voice; vote; comment; (mus.) part; **gut bei** −**e sein to be in good voice;** −**enfang** m. canvassing; −**engleichheit** f. voting parity; −**enmehrheit** f. majority of votes; −**enminderheit** f. minority of votes; −**er** m. tuner; −**gabel** f. tuning fork; −**lage** f. register, pitch; −**recht** neu. suffrage; −**umfang** m. range of a voice; −**ung** f. tuning; pitch, key; frame of mind; mood; atmosphere; impression; −**ung machen to canvass, to cheer up;** −**ungsmensch** m. moody person; −**vieh** neu. (coll.) mass of voters; henchmen; −**wechsel** m. breaking of the voice; −**zettel** m. ballot

stimm: −**berechtigt** adj. entitled to vote; −**en** v. to tune; to vote; to prejudice; to put in a good (oder bad) humor; to suit; to be correct, to correspond (to); −**haft** adj. voiced; −**los** adj. voiceless

stink: −**en** v. to stink; −**end** adj., −**ig** adj. stinking; rancid; −**faul** adj. very lazy

Stinkbombe f. stinkpot, stink bomb

Stinktier neu. skunk

Stipendiat m. holder of a scholarship

Stipendium neu. scholarship

stippen v. to dip, to steep

Stirn f. forehead; (fig.) impudence; face; **die** − **bieten to defy; to face;** −**binde** f. headband; −**locke** f. forelock; −**riemen** m. (horse) frontlet; −**runzeln** neu. frowning; −**seite** f. front

stöbern v. to hunt; to rummage; to drift

stochern v. to poke, to stir; **in den Zähnen** − **to pick one's teeth**

Stock m. stick, staff, cane; rod; stem; trunk; floor, story; (bee) hive; (mus.) baton; (printing) block; **über** − **und Stein up hill and down dale;** −**engländer** m. typical Englishman; −**fisch** m. dried cod; (fig.) blockhead; −**fleck** m. mildew: −**haus** neu. (dial.) jail; −**makler** m. stockbroker; −**rose** f. hollyhock; −**werk** neu. floor, story

stock: −**blind** adj. stone-blind; −**dumm** adj. utterly stupid; −**en** v. to stop, to stagnate; to pause, to hesitate; to falter, to flag; to coagulate; to curdle; to turn mouldy; −**finster** adj. pitch-dark; −**ig** adj. decayed; −**steif** adj. stiff as a poker; −**taub** adj. stone-deaf

Stoff m. stuff, material; matter, substance; subject; fabric; −**wechsel** m. metabolism

stöhnen v. to groan, to moan

Stoiker m. stoic

stoisch adj. stoic(al)

Stola f. stole

Stolle f., −**n** m. loaf-shaped Christmas cake; −**n** m. post; deep dugout; (min.) gallery

stolpern v. to stumble, to trip; to blunder

stolz adj. proud; haughty; arrogant; majestic; −**ieren** v. to strut, to stalk, to flaunt

Stolz m. pride, haughtiness, arrogance

Stopf: −**en** m. (dial.) cork, stopper; −**er** m.

stuffer; darner; −**garn** neu. darning cotton; −**mittel** neu. astringent; −**nadel** f. darning needle

stopfen v. to stuff, to cram; to plug, to stop up: to darn; **jemand den Mund** − **to silence someone;** −**d** adj. constipating; astringent

Stopp: −**licht** neu. stop light; −**uhr** f. stop watch

Stoppel f. stubble

stoppeln v. to glean; to patch

stoppen v. to stop, to interrupt

Stör m. sturgeon

Stör: −**enfried** m. intruder; mischief-maker; marplot; −**ung** f. disturbance; (rad.) jamming, statics; **geistige** −**ung mental disorder**

Storch m. stork; −**schnabel** m. stork's bill; cranesbill; pantograph

stören v. to disturb; to trouble; to intrude; (rad.) to jam, to interfere

störr: −**ig** adj., −**isch** adj. intractable; headstrong; restive

Stoss m. push, thrust; blow, knock; punch; kick; jolt; recoil, shock; stroke; impact; heap, pile; −**dämpfer** m. shock absorber, bumper; −**degen** m. foil, rapier; −**kraft** f. impetus; impact; −**kurs (Rakete)** m. collision course; −**seufzer** m. deep sigh; −**stange** f. bumper, push rod; −**truppen** f. pl. shock troops; −**verkehr** m. rush-hour traffic; −**welle** f. shock wave; −**zahn** m. tusk

stossen v. to push, to shove, to bump; to thrust; to kick; to nudge; to pound, to crush; to punch, to knock, to strike; **auf Hindernisse** − **to encounter obstacles, in die Trompete** − **to sound the trumpet; sich an etwas** − **to be shocked by something;** − **an to knock against; to border on;** − **aus to expel; über den Haufen** − **to overthrow; von Land** − **to put to sea; von sich** − **to cast off, to repudiate; vor den Kopf** − **to affront; to offend; zu jemand** − **to join someone**

stottern v. to stutter, to stammer

stracks adv. directly, straight ahead

Straf: −**anstalt** f. penitentiary; −**e** f. punishment; fine; penalty; **bei** −**e von on penalty of; eine** −**e absitzen to serve time (in prison);** −**erlass** m. (law) pardon; amnesty; −**fälligkeit** f. culpability; −**gefangene** m. convict; −**gericht** neu. criminal court; (bibl.) judgment; −**gesetz** neu. penal law; −**losigkeit** f. impunity; −**mandat** neu. penalty; −**porto** neu. postage fine; −**prozess** m.; −**sache** f. criminal case; −**recht** neu. criminal law; −**richter** m. criminal judge; −**verfahren** neu. criminal procedure; −**vollzug** m. execution of a sentence

straf: −**bar** adj. criminal; punishable, culpable; −**en** v. to punish, to chastise; to fine; −**ender Blick reproachful look;** −**fällig** adj. punishable; −**frei** adj., −**los** adj. exempt from punishment; unpunished; −**mündig** adj. of responsible age; −**rechtlich** adj. criminal, penal; −**würdig**

adj. deserving punishment

straff *adj.* tight, stretched; taut; rigid, strict; **–en** *v.* to tighten, to stretch

sträflich *adj.* punishable; unpardonable

Sträfling *m.* convict, prisoner

Strahl *m.* beam, ray; jet; flash; (geom.) radius; **–enbrechung** *f.* refraction; **–enkranz** *m.*, **–enkrone** *f.* halo; aureole; nimbus; **–ung** *f.* radiation

strahl: –en *v.* to beam, to radiate; **–enbrechend** *adj.* refractive; **–end** *adj.* radiant; **–ig** *adj.* radial, radiating

Strähne *f.* strand (of hair); skein (of yarn)

stramm *adj.* stretched, tight, taut; robust; strapping; **— stehen** (mil.) to stand at attention

strampeln *v.* to fidget, to struggle; **sich bloss — to** kick the bedclothes off

Strand *m.* beach, strand; seashore; **auf — laufen** to strand; **–bad** *neu.* seaside resort; **–gut** *neu.* flotsam, jetsam; **–hafer** *m.* (bot.) bent grass; **–hütte** *f.* cabana; **–korb** *m.* beach chair; **–läufer** *m.* sandpiper; **–räuber** *m.* wrecker; **–recht** *neu.* right of salvage; **–schuhe** *m. pl.* beach slippers; **–wächter** *m.* coast guardsman

stranden *v.* to strand, to run ashore

Strang *m.* rope, cord, trace; strand (of hair); skein (of yarn); (rail.) track; **am gleichen — ziehen** to act in unison; **über die Stränge schlagen** to kick over the traces; **wenn alle Stränge reissen** if worst comes to worst; **zum — verurteilen** to condemn to the gallows

strangulieren *v.* to strangle

Strapaze *f.* exertion, strain, hardship

strapazieren *v.* to overexert, to strain; to wear out

Strasse *f.* street; highway, road; strait(s); **an der — by** the wayside; **jemand auf die — setzen** to turn someone out; **–narbeiter** *m.* roadman; **–nbahn** *f.* streetcar; **–nbau** *m.* road construction; **–ndamm** *m.* roadway; **–ndirne** *f.* streetwalker; **–nfeger** *m.*, **–nkehrer** *m.* street cleaner; **–nhändler** *m.* street vendor; **–njunge** *m.* street arab; **–nlaterne** *f.* street lamp; **–nräuber** *m.* highwayman; **–nrennen** *neu.* road race; **–nschild** *neu.* street sign; **–nüberführung** *f.* overpass; **–nzug** *m.* row of streets

Stratosphäre *f.* stratosphere; **–nflugzeug** *neu.* stratocruiser

sträuben *v.* to ruffle, to bristle; **das Haar sträubt sich** the hair stands on end; **sich — gegen** to struggle against; to resist

Strauch *m.* shrub, brush; **–dieb** *m.* footpad; **–werk** *neu.* shrubbery, brushwood

straucheln *v.* to stumble; (fig.) to sin, to err

Strauss *m.* ostrich; struggle, combat, fight; bouquet, bunch (of flowers)

streb: –en *v.* to strive, to aspire; to struggle (for); to endeavor; **zum Mittelpunkt –ende Kraft** centripetal force; **–erhaft** *adj.*, **–erisch** *adj.* ambitious; **–sam** *adj.* industrious, zealous

Strecke *f.* stretch; extent; tract; distance; (geom.) straight line; (hunt.) bag;

(min.) gallery; (rail.) line; **zur — bringen** to shoot down, to bag; **–narbeiter** *m.* track worker; platelayer; **–nwärter** *m.* trackwalker

streck: –bar *adj.* extensible, ductile, malleable; **–en** *v.* to stretch; to extend; to eke; **die Waffen –en** to lay down arms, to surrender; **in gestrecktem Lauf** at full speed; **zu Boden –en** to knock down; **–enweise** *adv.* in some parts; here and there

Streich *m.* stroke, blow; prank. trick; **auf einen —** at one blow; **jemand einen — spielen** to play a trick on somebody; **–holz** *neu.*, **–hölzchen** *neu.* match; **–instrument** *neu.* (mus.) stringed instrument; **–quartett** *neu.* string quartet; **–riemen** *m.* razor strop

streicheln *v.* to caress, to stroke gently

streichen *v.* to stroke; to paint; to rush (past); to sweep (over); to stroll; to mitigate; to spread (butter); to strop; to strike (match); to lower (sails, flag); to play (violin); to cancel, to obliterate; **frisch gestrichen!** wet paint! **gestrichen voll** full to the brim; **vor jemand die Segel —** to submit to someone

Streif: –e *f.* patrol; raid; **–en** *m.* stripe, band; streak, strip; **–jagd** *f.* shooting expedition; **–kolonne** *f.*, **–kommando** *neu.* raiding party; **–licht** *neu.* side light; **–zug** *m.* expedition; scouting raid

streifen *v.* to stripe, to streak; to strip; to touch slightly; to graze, to scrape; to ramble, to roam; (mil.) *v.* to buzz; to strafe; **die Ärmel in die Höhe —** to turn up the sleeves

Streik *m.* strike; **in den — treten** to go on strike; **–brecher** *m.* strikebreaker; scab; **–kasse** *f.* strike fund; **–posten** *m.* picket

streiken *v.* to (be on) strike

Streit *m.* quarrel, fight; dispute, competition; **–axt** *f.* battle-ax; **–er** *m.* combatant, fighter; disputant; **–fall** *m.* controversy, quarrel; **–frage** *f.* matter in dispute; question at issue; **–hammel** *m.* (coll.) brawler, squabbler; **–igkeit** *f.* difference; quarrel; **–kräfte** *f. pl.* (mil.) forces; **–punkt** *m.* point of controversy; **–sache** *f.* controversial matter; **–schrift** *f.* polemical pamphlet

streit: –bar *adj.* pugnacious, warlike; valiant; **–en** *v.* to quarrel, to fight, to dispute; **–ig** *adj.* debatable; doubtful; **–ig machen** to contest; **–lustig** *adj.* pugnacious; **–süchtig** *adj.* contentious; quarrelsome

streng *adj.* severe, rigorous, stern, harsh; strict; austere; stringent; sharp; **–er Arrest** close confinement; **–er Kritiker** carping critic; **–genommen** *adv.* strictly speaking; **–gläubig** *adj.* orthodox

Strenge *f.* rigor, sternness, harshness; severity, austerity; strictness, sharpness

Streu *f.* litter; bed of straw; **–büchse** *f.*, **–er** *m.* shaker; dredger; **–zucker** *m.* powdered sugar

streuen *v.* to strew, to scatter; to spread; to litter

Strich *m.* dash, stroke, line; (compass) point; district, region, zone; (birds) flight; migration; (fabric) grain; **auf den — gehen** (coll.) to walk the streets; **es geht mir gegen den —** it goes against the grain; **jemand auf den — haben** (coll.) to bear a grudge against someone; **nach — und Faden** thoroughly; **-einteilung** *f.* graduation; **-regen** *m.* local shower

strichweise *adv.* locally; by zones; in flights

Strick *m.* cord, rope; (coll.) rascal; **wenn alle —e reissen** if worst comes to worst; **-arbeit** *f.*, **-erei** *f.* knitting; **-leiter** *f.* rope ladder; **-nadel** *f.* knitting needle

stricken *v.* to knit

Striegel *m.* currycomb

striegeln *v.* to currycomb; to handle roughly

Strieme *f.*, **Striemen** *m.* stripe, streak, weal

striemig *adj.* covered with wales; streaked

strittig *adj.* debatable, disputed; doubtful

Stroh *neu.* straw, thatch; **leeres — dreschen** to waste one's words; **-dach** *neu.* thatched roof; **-halm** *m.* blade of straw; **-köpf** *m.* simpleton; **-mann** *m.* scarecrow; dummy; **-sack** *m.* straw mattress; **-witwe** *f.* grass widow; **-witwer** *m.* grass widower

stroh- **-farben** *adj.*, **-gelb** *adj.* straw-colored; **-ig** *adj.* strawy

Strolch *m.* loafer, tramp, vagabond, bum

Strom *m.* stream; torrent; flow; current; **-erzeuger** *m.* dynamo; **-kreis** *m.* (elec.) circuit; **-schnelle** *f. pl.* rapids; **-spannung** *f.* voltage; **-unterbrecher** *m.* (elec.) circuit breaker, cutout; **-zähler** *m.* electricity meter

strom- **-ab(wärts)** *adv.* downstream; **-auf(wärts)** *adv.* upstream; **-linienförmig** *adj.* streamlined; **-weise** *adv.* in floods

strömen *v.* to stream, to flow, to gush, to pour; to flock, to crowd

Stromer *m.* tramp, loafer

Strömung *f.* current, flow, drift; tendency

Strontium *neu.* strontium

Strophe *f.* stanza, verse

strotzen *v.* to be puffed up; to exuberate; **-d** *adj.* crammed full; robust, vigorous; **vor Gesundheit -d** in the pink of health

Strudel *m.* whirlpool, eddy; rush; strudel

Strumpf *m.* stocking, hose; (gas) mantle; **sich auf die Strümpfe machen** to make off; **-band** *neu.* garter; **-halter** *m.* suspender; **-waren** *f. pl.* hosiery

struppig *adj.* bristle, shaggy; unkempt, rough

Stube *f.* room, apartment, chamber; **gute — living room, parlor; -narrest** *m.* confinement to one's room; **-nfliege** *f.* common fly; **-ngelehrte** *m.* (fig.) bookworm; **-ngenosse** *m.* roommate; **-nhocker** *m.* stay-at-home; **-nluft** *f.* close air; **-nmädchen** *neu.* housemaid, chambermaid; **-nmaler** *m.* house painter

stubenrein *adj.* housebroken (pets)

Stuck *m.* stucco; **-decke** *f.* stuccoed ceiling

Stück *neu.* piece, bit; fragment; lump; (cattle) head; passage; play; **aus freien -en** of one's own accord; **ein starkes —** a bit thick; **grosse -e halten auf** to think much of; **in vielen -en** in many respects; **sich grosse -e einbilden** to be very conceited; **-arbeiter** *m.* pieceworker; **-enzucker** *m.* lump sugar; **-giesserei** *f.* cannon foundry; **-güter** *neu. pl.* piece goods; **-lohn** *m.* piece-work rates; **-werk** *neu.* imperfect work, patchwork

stück- **-eln** *v.* to cut into pieces; to piece; **-en** to piece, to patch; **-weise** *adv.* in pieces, piece by piece

Student *m.* student, undergraduate; **-enblume** *f.* marigold; **-enjahre** *neu. pl.* college days; **-enschaft** *f.* student body

Studi- **-e** *f.* study, sketch, essay; **-endirektor** *m.* headmaster (high school); **-engang** *m.* course of study; **-erstube** *f.*, **-o** *neu.* study; **-osus** *m.* (coll.) student; **-um** *neu.* study, education

studieren *v.* to study, to go to college; to investigate, to do research on

Stufe *f.* step, stair, rung; shade, stage; degree; **auf gleicher — mit** on a level with; **-nfolge** *f.* gradation, succession; **-nleiter** *f.* scale, gradation

stufen *v.* to graduate, to scale; **-artig** *adj.* steplike; graduated; **-weise** *adv.* by degrees, gradually

Stuhl *m.* chair; seat; stool; pew; **der Heilige —** the Holy See; **jemand den — vor die Tür setzen** to turn someone out; **-bein** *neu.* leg of a chair; **-gang** *m.* evacuation of the bowels; **-lehne** *f.* chair back

Stulle *f.* (coll.) slice of bread and butter

stülpen *v.* to turn up; to clap (*oder* put) on

stumm *adj.* dumb, mute; mum, silent, speechless

Stummel *m.* stump, end; butt

Stumpen *m.* stump; (hat) rough body; Swiss cigar

Stümper *m.* blunderer, bungler; **-ei** *f.* bungling

stumpf *adj.* blunt; obtuse; dull; **-sinnig** *adj.* dull-witted, stupid

Stunde *f.* hour; lesson, period; **zur — at the present moment, immediately; **-nbuch** *neu.* prayer book; **-ngeld** *neu.* fee for lessons; **-nglas** *neu.* hourglass; **-nlohn** *m.* hourly wage rate; **-nplan** *m.* schedule

stunden *v.* to grant a respite, to allow time; **-lang** *adj.* for hours; **-weise** *adv.* by the hour

stündlich *adj.* hourly; every hour

Stundung *f.* respite, short grace; delay in payment; **-sfrist** *f.* grace (for payment due)

Stupsnase *f.* snub nose; turned-up nose

Sturm *m.* storm; tempest; assault; fury, turmoil; **ein — im Wasserglas** a tempest in a teapot; **im — nehmen** to take by storm; **— laufen** to assault, to storm; **— läuten** to ring the alarm; **-bataillon** *neu.* shock battalion; **-glocke**

f. alarm bell, tocsin; **–leiter** *f.* scaling ladder; **–riemen** *m.* chin strap; **–schritt** *m.* double quickstep; **–wind** *m.* hurricane, heavy gale; **–zentrum** *neu.* cell

stürmen *v.* to (take by) storm; to dash, to rush along; to rage; to be stormy

Stürmer *m.* stormer, assaulter; (sport) forward

stürmisch *adj.* stormy, tempestuous; (fig.) impetuous, turbulent; passionate

Sturz *m.* fall, tumble; plunge, crash; overthrow; ruin; **zum — bringen** to overthrow; **–acker** *m.* newly plowed field; **–bach** *m.* torrent; **–flug** *m.* nose dive; **–helm** *m.* crash helmet; **–kampfflieger** *m.* dive bomber

stürzen *v.* to fall, to tumble, to plunge; to (over)throw; to rush, to dash; to stream; (avi.) to dive, to crash; **ins Verderben — to ruin; sich in Kosten —** to incur heavy expenses; **vom Thron —** to dethrone

Stuss *m.* (coll.) nonsense, foolish talk

Stute *f.* mare; **–nfüllen** *neu.* filly; foal

Stütz: –balken *m.* supporting beam, joist; **–e** *f.* prop, stay, support; help; **–mauer** *f.* buttress, retaining wall; **–pfeiler** *m.* pillar, support; (fig.) base; strong point; fulcrum

Stutz: –bart *m.* trimmed beard; **–en** *m.* short rifle, carbine; nozzle; **–er** *m.* dandy, fop; **–flügel** *m.* baby grand piano; **–ohr** *neu.* cropped ear; **–uhr** *f.* mantelpiece clock

stutz: –en *v.* to curtail, to crop, to dock, to trim, to lop; to clip; to be startled, to hesitate; to become suspicious; **–erhaft** *adj.* dandified, foppish; **–ig** *adj.* startled, taken aback; flabbergasted, perplexed

Sub: –jekt *neu.* subject; fellow; **–jektivität** *f.* subjectivity; **–limat** *neu.* sublimity; **–skribent** *m.* subscriber; **–stantiv** *neu.* substantive, noun; **–stanz** *f.* substance, matter; **–strat** *neu.* substratum; **–vention** *f.* subsidy

subtil *adj.* subtle, fine, delicate

Suche *f.* search, quest, tracking; **auf der — nach** in search for; **–er** *m.* seeker; spotlight; searchlight; (phot.) viewfinder

suchen *v.* to search, to look for; to seek; to try (to do); to be at a loss (for); **das Weite — to run away; hier haben Sie nichts zu —** I you have no business here!

Sucht *f.* mania, passion, rage; disease

süchtig *adj.* having a mania for; addicted to

Sud *m.* boiling, decoction; **–elei** *f.* dirty (*oder* slovenly) work; daubing; scribbling; **–ler** *m.* bungler; dauber; scribbler; quack

Süd, Süden *m.* south; **–früchte** *f. pl.* tropical fruits; **–länder** *m.* southerner

sudeln *v.* to bungle, to botch; to daub

südlich *adj.* southern; **— adv.** southerly **das Südliche Eismeer** *neu.* Antarctic Ocean

Südpol *m.* South Pole

süffig *adj.* tasty; delicious; pleasant to drink

suggerieren *v.* to suggest; to influence

Sühn: –e *f.*, **–ung** *f.* atonement; reconciliation; **–opfer** *neu.* expiatory sacrifice

sühnen *v.* to expiate, to atone for

Sulz *m.*, **Sülze** *f.* jelly; meat jelly; brawn

summarisch *adj.* summary

Summe *f.* sum, total; amount; **die — ziehen** to sum up; **höchste —** maximum

summen *v.* to buzz, to hum; to tingle

Summer *m.* buzzer

summieren *v.* to add up; **sich — to run up**

Sumpf *m.* swamp, bog, marsh, fen; morass; (min.) sump; **einen — austrocknen** to drain a marsh; **–fieber** *neu.* swamp fever; malaria; **–huhn** *neu.* coot; (coll.) boozer; **–lache** *f.* slough; **–vögel** *m. pl.* wading birds

sumpfig *adj.* boggy, swampy, marshy

Sund *m.* sound, strait(s)

Sünd: –e *f.* sin, trespass, misdeed; **–enbock** *m.* scapegoat; **–enfall** *m.* (bibl.) fall of man; **–engeld** *neu.* ill-gotten money; enormous sum; **–entlgung** *f.* propitiation; **–envergebung** *f.* absolution; **–er** *m.* sinner, transgressor; **armer –er** culprit; poor wretch; **–flut** *f.* the Deluge

sünd: –ig *adj.*, **–haft** *adj.* sinful, culpable; **–igen** *v.* to sin, to transgress

superklug *adj.* overwise; too clever, pert

superlativisch *adj.* superlative

Suppe *f.* soup, broth; **die — auslöffeln müssen** to have to take the rap; **jemand die — versalzen** (coll.) to spoil someone's pleasure; **–nkräuter** *neu. pl.* potherbs; **–nlöffel** *m.* tablespoon; **–nschüssel** *f.* soup tureen; **–nwürfel** *m.* soup cube; **–nwürze** *f.* seasoning

suppig *adj.* soupy; souplike, liquid

Supremat *neu.* supremacy

surren *v.* to hum, to whir, to whiz, to buzz

Surrogat *neu.* substitute

suspendieren *v.* to suspend

süss *adj.* sweet; lovely; **–en** *v.* to sweeten; **–lich** *adj.* sweetish; saccharine

Süss: –e *f.* sweetness; **–holz** *neu.* licorice; **–holz raspeln** to spoon; to flirt; **–igkeit** *f.* sweetness; suavity; **–igkeiten** *pl.* sweets; **–(s)peise** *f.* dessert; **–(s)toff** *m.* saccharine; **–wasser** *neu.* fresh water

Symbol *neu.* symbol; **–ik** *f.* symbolism

symbolisch *adj.* symbolic(al)

Symmetrie *f.* symmetry

symmetrisch *adj.* symmetric(al)

Sympathie *f.* sympathy; **–streik** *m.* sympathetic strike

sympathisch *adj.* sympathetic; congenial, pleasant

Symphonie *f.* symphony

symptomatisch *adj.* symptomatic(al)

Synagoge *f.* synagogue

Syndik: –at *neu.* syndicate, cartel; **–us** *m.* magistrate

Synode *f.* synod

synonym *adj.* synonymous

Synthese *f.* synthesis

synthetisch *adj.* synthetic(al)

Syphilis *f.* syphilis

syphilitisch *adj.* syphilitic
Syrien *neu.* Syria
Syringe *f.* lilac
systematisch *adj.* systematic
Szen: -arium *neu.* scenario; **-e** *f.* stage, scene; **in -e setzen** (theat.) to rehearse, to stage; **sich in -e setzen** to show off; **-erie** *f.* scenery; landscape
Szepter *neu.* scepter

T

Tabak *m.* tobacco; **-bau** *m.* cultivation of tobacco; **-sbeutel** *m.* tobacco pouch; **-sdose** *f.* snuff box
tabellarisch *adj.* tabular, tabulated
Tabelle *f.* table; index; schedule
Tabernakel *neu.* tabernacle
Tablett *neu.* tray, salver; **-e** *f.* lozenge
tabu *adj.* taboo
Taburett *neu.* taboret, stool
Tachometer *m.* speedometer
Tadel *m.* reprimand, blame; fault; **ohne — blameless, faultless; über allen — erhaben** beyond reproach
tadel: -los *adj.* faultless, irreproachable; **-n** *v.* to blame, to find fault with; to reprimand; **-nswert** *adj.* blamable, objectionable; **-süchtig** *adj.* censorious, faultfinding
Tafel *f.* table, tablet; blackboard; slate; plate, slab; (chocolate) bar; dinner; chart, index, diagram; **die — aufheben** to rise from the table; **-aufsatz** *m.* centerpiece; **-berg** *m.* plateau; **-besteck** *neu.* knife, fork and spoon; **-butter** *f.* best butter; **-geschirr** *neu.* dinner service; **-glas** *neu.* plate glass; **-musik** *f.* dinner music; **-obst** *neu.* dessert (fruit); **-runde** *f.* guests; round table; **-tuch** *neu.* tablecloth; **-zeug** *neu.* table linen and plateware
tafeln *v.* to dine, to banquet, to feast
täfeln *v.* to inlay, to wainscot, to panel
Taf(fe)t *m.* taffeta
Tag *m.* day; daylight; lifetime; **an den — bringen** to bring to light; **auf seine alten — e** in his old age; **dieser — e** one of these days; **einen — um den anderen** every other day; **er hat seinen guten —** he is in a good mood; **es ist heller —** it is broad daylight; **es wird — day is breaking; in den — hineinleben** to live from day to day; **-s darauf** the next day; **unter — e arbeiten** (min.) to work underground; **vor Jahr und — a** long time ago; **-ebau** *m.* strip mining; **-eblatt** *neu.* daily newspaper; **-ebuch** *neu.* diary; daybook; **-edieb** *m.* idler; **-egeld** *neu.* daily allowance; **-elöhner** *m.* day laborer; **-esanbruch** *m.* daybreak; **-esangabe** *f.* date; **-esbefehl** *m.* (mil.) order of the day; **-eskasse** *f.* (theat.) daytime box office; **-eskurs** *m.* (com.) daily quotation; **-esordnung** *f.* agenda; **-espresse** *f.* daily press; **-esstempel** *m.* date stamp; **-eszeitung** *f.* daily newspaper; **-ewerk** *neu.* day's work; **-schicht** *f.* day shift; **-undnachtgleiche** *f.* equinox; **-ung** *f.* meeting,

session
tag: -elang *adj.* for days; **-en** *v.* to dawn; to meet, to sit, to confer; **-süber** *adv.* during the day; **-täglich** *adj.* daily, every day
täglich *adj.* daily; every day
Taifun *m.* typhoon
Taille *f.* waist, bodice; (cards) round
Takel *neu.* (naut.) tackle; **-age** *f.*, **-ung** *f.*, **-werk** *neu.* rigging
Takt *m.* tact; (mus.) measure, time; **den — angeben** (*or* **schlagen**) to beat time; **den — halten** to keep time; **-gefühl** *neu.* tactfulness; **-stock** *m.* (mus.) baton; **-strich** *m.* (mus.) bar
takt: -fest *adj.* keeping good time; sound; firm; **-ieren** *v.* (mus.) to beat time, to conduct; **-los** *adj.* tactless, indiscreet; **-mässig** *adj.* well-timed, rhythmical
Taktik *f.* tactics
taktisch *adj.* tactical
Tal *neu.* valley; dale, glen; **-fahrt** *f.* descent; trip downstream; **-kessel** *m.* basin; **-mulde** *f.*, **-senke** *f.* depression of a valley; **-sohle** *f.* bed of a valley; **-sperre** *f.* dam
Talar *m.* judge's gown, robe
Talent *neu.* talent, ability
Talg *m.* tallow; suet; **-licht** *neu.*, **-kerze** *f.* tallow candle
Talk *m.* talc(um); **-erde** *f.* magnesia
Tam: -bour *m.* drummer; **-bourmajor** *m.* drum major; **-burin** *neu.* tambourine; **-tam** *neu.* tom-tom; **-tam schlagen** to make a great fuss
Tand *m.* bauble, gew-gaw; trifle; toy
tändeln *v.* to dally, to trifle; to flirt
Tank *m.* tank; **-anlage** *f.* fuel tank; **-stelle** *f.* filling station; **-wagen** *m.* tank car; **-wart** *m.*, **-wärter** *m.* gas station attendant
tanken *v.* to tank; (auto.) to fill up
Tann *m.* (poet.) pine forest; **-e** *f.* fir; **-enzapfen** *m.* fir cone
Tante *f.* aunt
Tanz *m.* dance; **das -bein schwingen** (coll.) to dance; **-bär** *m.* dancing bear; **-boden** *m.*, **-saal** *m.* dance hall; ballroom; **-erei** *f.* dance, hop
tänzeln *v.* to trip, to mince; to amble
Tänzer *m.*, **Tänzerin** *f.* dancer
Tapet *neu.* carpet; **etwas aufs — bringen** to broach a subject; **-e** *f.* wallpaper
tapezieren *v.* to (hang) wallpaper
Tapezierer *m.* paper hanger; upholsterer
tapfer *adj.* brave, fearless, valiant
Tapisseriewaren *f. pl.* tapestry goods
tappen *v.* to walk heavily; to grope; to fumble
täppisch, tapsig *adj.* awkward, clumsy
Tarantel *f.* tarantula
Tarif *m.* tariff; (rail.) rates; list of charges; wage scale; **-lohn** *m.* standard wages; **-vertrag** *m.* wage agreement
tarnen *v.* to camouflage, to disguise, to screen
Tarnkappe *f.* magic hood
Tasche *f.* pocket; bag, pouch; purse; **jemand in die — stecken** (coll.) to be superior to someone; **-nausgabe** *f.*

pocket edition; **–ndieb** m. pickpocket; **–nfeuerzeug** neu. pocket lighter; **–ngeld** neu. allowance; **–nkrebs** m. common crab; **–nlampe** f. flashlight; **–nspieler** m. juggler; **–ntuch** neu. handkerchief

Tasse f. cup (and saucer); **–nkopf** m. cup

Tast: –atur f. keyboard; **–e** f. (piano, typewriter) key; **–sinn** m. sense of touch, feeling; **–werkzeug** neu. organ of touch, feeler

tasten v. to touch, to feel; to grope; to fumble

Tat f. deed, act, action; **auf frischer — ertappen** to catch red-handed; **in der — indeed**; as a matter of fact; **–bestand** m. facts (of a case); **–einheit** f. (law) coincidence; **–kraft** f. energy; **–sache** f. fact

tat: –enlos adj. inactive, idle; **–kräftig** adj. energetic; **–sächlich** adj. factual, real; **–sächlich** adv. in fact

Tät: –er m. perpetrator, culprit; **–erschaft** f. guilt, perpetration; **–igkeit** f. activity, action; occupation; **–igkeitswort** neu. verb; **–lichkeit** f. (law) assault and battery

tät: –ig adj. active, busy, employed; **–igen** v. to do, to settle; **–lich** adj. violent; **–lich werden** to assault

Tatze f. paw; claw

Tau neu. cable, rope; **— m.** dew; **–werk** neu. cordage, rigging; **–wetter** neu. thaw; **–ziehen** neu. tug of war

taub adj. deaf; dead; empty, hollow; numb; **- stumm** adj. deaf-mute

Taub: –e f. pigeon, dove; **–enschlag** m. dovecot; **–enzüchter** m. pigeon fancier; **–er** m., **Täuberich** m. male pigeon; **–stumme** m. deaf-mute

Tauch: –batterie f. plunge battery; **–er** m. diver; **–erglocke** f. diving bell; **–erkolben** m. (mech.) plunger

tauchen v. to plunge; to dive, to submerge

tauen v. to thaw; to melt; (naut.) to tow

Tauf: –becken neu., **–stein** m. baptismal font; **–buch** neu. parish register; **–e** f. baptism, christening; **aus der –e heben** to be godfather (oder godmother); to initiate, to originate; **–kapelle** f. baptistry; **–name** m. Christian (oder given) name; **–pate** m. godfather; **–schein** m. certificate of baptism

taufen v. to baptize, to christen; **Wein — to water** (oder adulterate) wine

Täufling m. child (oder person) to be baptized

taugen v. to be fit (oder good for); to be of use (oder value); **nichts — to be worthless**

Taugenichts m. good-for-nothing

tauglich adj. fit, good; adapted; useful, able

Taumel m. giddiness, ecstasy, frenzy

taumeln v. to reel, to stagger; to be giddy

Tausch m. exchange, barter; **–geschäft** neu., **–handel** m. barter

tauschen v. to exchange, to barter

täuschen v. to deceive, to delude, to cheat; to trick; **sich — to be mistaken; –d** adj. delusive; illusory; **–de Ähnlichkeit**

striking resemblance; **–d nachgemacht** copied perfectly

tausend adj. thousand; **–fach** adj., **–fältig** adj. thousandfold; **–jährig** adj. millenial; **–mal** adv. a thousand times

Tausend neu. thousand; **vom — per thousand; –er** m. thousand; 1,000 banknote; **–künstler** m. jack-of-all-trades; conjurer; **–schön(chen)** neu. daisy; **–stel** neu. a thousandth

Tax: –ameter m. taximeter; **–ator** m. appraiser

Taxe f. valuation; tax, fee, charge, rate; taxicab

taxieren v. to evaluate, to assess; to tax

Technik f. technics; industry; technology; technique, skill; **–er** m. technician, engineer; **–um** neu. technical school

technisch adj. technical

Teckel m. dachshund

Tee m. tea; **–brett** neu. tea tray; **–kanne** f. teapot; **–kessel** m. teakettle; **–löffel** m. teaspoon; **–rose** f. tea rose; **–sieb** neu. tea strainer; **–strauch** m. tea plant

Teer m. tar; **–farben** f. pl. aniline dyes; **–jacke** f. (coll.) sailor

teeren v. to tar

Teich m. pond; **–binse** f. bulrush; **–kolben** m. cattail; **–rose** f. water lily; **–wirtschaft** f. fish culture (in ponds)

Teig m. dough, paste; **–waren** f. pl. noodle products

teigig adj. doughy

Teil m. part; portion; share; party, side; **edle –e** vital parts; **ein grosser — a great deal; ich für mein — so far as I am concerned; sich seinen — denken** to have one's own ideas; **zum — partly,** to some extent; **–chen** neu. particle; **–er** m. divider; divisor; **–haber** m. partner, joint proprietor; participant; **–nahme** f. participation; interest, sympathy; **–nehmer** m. participant; subscriber; **–strecke** f. section; **–ung** f. division, partition; **–zahlung** f. part-payment, instalment

teil: –bar adj. divisible; **–en** v. to divide; to distribute; to share; **sich –en** to share in; to branch off; **geteilte Gefühle** mixed feelings; **geteilter Meinung sein** to be of different opinions; **–haben** v. to participate (oder share) in; **–nahms-los** adj. unconcerned; indifferent, apathetic; **–nehmen** v. to participate; to sympathize; **–s** adv. partly; **–weise** adj. partial; **–weise** adv. partly, to some extent

Teint m. complexion

Tele: –fon neu. telephone; **–fonanruf** m. telephone call; **–fonanschluss** m. telephone connection (oder extension); **–fonist** m., **–fonistin** f. telephone operator; **–fonzelle** f. telephone booth; **–fonzentrale** f. telephone exchange; **–gramm** neu. telegram; **–graf** m. telegraph; **–grafie** f. telegraphy; **–grafist** m. telegrapher; **–skop** neu. telescope

tele: –fonieren v. to telephone; **–fonisch** adj. telephonic; **–grafieren** v. to telegraph; **–grafisch** adj. telegraphic(al);

-skopisch *adj.* telescopic(al)

Teller *m.* plate; **-eisen** *neu.* double-jawed trap; **-mütze** *f.* flat cap; **-tuch** *neu.* dish towel

Temp: **-el** *m.* temple; **-elherr** *m.*, **-ler** *m.* Knight Templar; **-elraub** *m.*, **-elschändung** *f.* sacrilege

temper: **-amentslos** *adj.* spiritless; **-amentsvoll** *adj.* high-spirited, passionate; **-erieren** *v.* to temper; to moderate, to assuage

Tempera *f.* (art.) tempera, distemper

Temperatur *f.* temperature

Temperenzler *m.* teetotaler

Tempo *neu.* tempo; measure, time; pace; rate

Tendenz *f.* tendency; **-stück** *neu.* play with a purpose

tendenziös *adj.* tendentious, biased

Tenne *f.* threshing floor

Tennis *neu.* tennis; **-platz** *m.* tennis court; **-schläger** *m.* tennis racket

Tenor *m.* tenor; substance, topic

Teppich *m.* carpet, rug; **-kehrmaschine** *f.* carpet sweeper; **-nagel** *m.* tack

Termin *m.* term, time; fixed day; (law) summons; deadline; **-geschäft** *neu.* (com.) futures; **-grenze** *f.* deadline; **-ologie** *f.* terminology; **-us technicus** *m.* technical term

Terpentin *m.* and *neu.* turpentine

Terr: **-ain** *neu.* ground, terrain; **-asse** *f.* terrace; **-itorium** *neu.* territory

terrorisieren *v.* to terrorize

Tertia *f.* fourth class of an undergraduate college; **-ner** *m.* student of a Tertia

Testament *neu.* testament, will; **ohne — sterben** to die intestate; **-svollstrecker** *m.* executor

testamentarisch *adj.* testamentary; **— adr.** by will

teuer *adj.* costly, expensive; dear; beloved; cherished; **wie — ist es?** what does it cost?

Teu(e)rung *f.* dearth; scarcity; high cost of living; **-szuschlag** *m.* cost-of-living increase

Teufel *m.* devil; demon; fiend; **das weiss der — nobody** knows that; **den — an die Wand malen** talk of the devil and he will appear; **in -s Küche geraten** (*or* **kommen**) to get into an awful mess; **jemand zum — jagen** to send someone packing; **pfui —!** how disgusting! **zum — gehen** to go to rack and ruin; **zum — noch einmal!** the deuce! **-ei** *f.* deviltry; **-sbraten** *m.* (coll.) rake, scamp; **-sbrut** *f.* hellish crew

teuflisch *adj.* devilish, diabolical; inhuman

Text *m.* text; libretto; **aus dem — kommen** (fig.) to lose the thread; **jemand den — lesen** to reprimand someone; **-buch** *neu.* textbook, libretto; **-ilien** *f. pl.* textiles

Theater *neu.* theater; stage; **-besuch** *m.* playgoing; **-besucher** *m.* playgoer; **-direktor** *m.* theater manager; **-kasse** *f.* box office; **-stück** *neu.* drama, play; **-vorstellung** *f.* theatrical performance;

-zettel *m.* playbill; program

theatralisch *adj.* theatrical

Theke *f.* (restaurant) counter, bar

Thema *neu.* topic, subject, theme

Theo: **-loge** *m.* theologian; **-logie** *f.* theology; **-rie** *f.* theory; **-soph** *m.* theosophist; **-sophie** *f.* theosophy

theoretisch *adj.* theoretical

Theorie *f.* theory

These *f.* thesis

Thron *m.* throne; **-besteigung** *f.* accession to the throne; **-folge** *f.* succession to the throne; **-himmel** *m.* canopy; **-rede** *f.* (sovereign's) address to the people

thronen *v.* to be enthroned; to reign

Thun(fisch) *m.* tunny, tuna

Thymian *m.* thyme

ticken *v.* to tick

tief *adj.* deep; low; far; dark; profound; innermost; utmost; **das lässt — blicken** that tells a tale; **-er stimmen** to lower the pitch; **zu — singen** to sing flat; **-gehend** *adj.* profound; (naut.) deep-drawing; **-greifend** *adj.* far-reaching, radical; **-gründig** *adj.* deep, profound; **-liegend** *adj.* low-lying, deep-seated; (eyes) sunken; **-schürfend** *adj.* thorough, profound; **-sinnig** *adj.* pensive; melancholy

Tief *neu.* depression; **-angriff** *m.* low-flying attack; **-bau** *m.* underground building (*oder* engineering); **-blick** *m.* penetration; **-druck** *m.* low pressure; copperplate printing; **-e** *f.* depth, profundity; lowness; (bibl.) the deep; **-ebene** *f.*, **-land** *neu.* lowland(s), plain; **-gang** *m.* (naut.) draft; **-schlag** *m.* hit below the belt; **-stand** *m.* low level; lowness; low water mark

Tiegel *m.* saucepan, crucible

Tier *neu.* animal; beast; **ein grosses — (coll.)** a big shot; **-art** *f.* species of animal; **-arzneikunde** *f.* veterinary science; **-arzt** *m.* veterinarian; **-bändiger** *m.* tamer of wild animals; **-garten** *m.* zoological garden; **-kreis** *m.* zodiac; **-kunde** *f.* zoology; **-quälerei** *f.* cruelty to animals; **-reich** *neu.* animal kingdom; **-schutzverein** *m.* society for the prevention of cruelty to animals

tierärztlich *adj.* veterinary

tierisch *adj.* animal; bestial, brutal

Tiger *m.* tiger; **-in** *f.* tigress

tilgen *v.* to extinguish; to blot out; to annul; to amortize; (typ.) to delete; to redeem

Tilgung *f.* cancellation; amortization; (typ.) deletion; redemption; **-sfond(s)** *m.* sinking fund

Tingeltangel *neu.* low-class revue theater

Tinktur *f.* tincture

Tinte *f.* ink; **in der — sitzen** (coll.) to be in the soup; **-nfass** *neu.* inkwell; **-nfisch** *m.* cuttlefish; **-nklecks** *m.* ink blot; **-nstift** *m.* indelible pencil; **-nwischer** *m.* pen wiper

tippeln *v.* to tiptoe; to tramp, to hike

tippen *v.* to tap; to touch lightly; to type (write); **— auf** to suspect; to set *or* place

Tippfräulein *neu.*, **Tipse** *f.* (coll.) female

typist

Tirol *neu.* Tyrol

Tisch *m.* table; board; meal; **am grünen — at the conference table; reinen — machen** to make a clean sweep; **unter den — fallen** not to come under consideration; **vor — before a meal; zu — bitten** (*or* **laden**) to invite to dinner; **–dame** *f.*, **–herr** *m.* dinner partner; **–decke** *f.*, **–tuch** *neu.* tablecloth; **–gebet** *neu.* grace at meals; **–gesellschaft** *f.* dinner party; **–karte** *f.* place card; **–lade** *f.* table drawer; **–leindeckdich** *neu.* magic table; **–ler** *m.* carpenter; **–lerei** *f.* carpentry, carpenter's shop; **–platte** *f.* table top; **–rede** *f.* after-dinner speech; toast; **–rücken** *neu.* table turning; **–tennis** *neu.* ping-pong; **–zeit** *f.* dinner time

Titan(e) *m.* Titan; **—** *neu.* titanium

Titel *m.* title; head(ing); claim; **–bild** *neu.* frontispiece; **–blatt** *neu.* title page; **–halter** *m.*, **–verteidiger** *m.* title holder

Titulatur *f.* titles

titulieren *v.* to title, to style, to call

Toast *m.* toast, health; toasted bread

toben *v.* to rage, to rave; to roar; to romp

Tobsucht *f.* frenzy, raving madness

Tochter *f.* daughter; **–haus** *neu.* (com.) branch; **–kirche** *f.* branch church; **–land** *neu.*, **–staat** *m.* colony; **–sprache** *f.* derivative language

Töchterschule *f.* girls' school; **Höhere — girl's college**

Tod *m.* death; decease; **auf den — liegen** to be mortally ill; **der weisse — avalanche;** death by freezing; **des –es sein** to be doomed; **Kampf auf Leben und —** mortal combat; **–esangst** *f.* agony; mortal fear; **–esanzeige** *f.* death notice; **–esart** *f.* manner of death; **–esfall** *m.* (case of) death; casualty; **–esgefahr** *f.* deadly peril; **–eskampf** *m.* death struggle, last agony; **–eskandidat** *m.* dying (*oder* doomed) person; **–esstoss** *m.* death blow; **–esstrafe** *f.* capital punishment; **–estag** *m.* anniversary of someone's death; **–esurteil** *neu.* death sentence; **–feind** *m.* mortal enemy; **–sünde** *f.* deadly sin

tod: **–bringend** *adj.* deadly, fatal; **–krank** *adj.* deathly sick, mortally ill; **–müde** *adj.* dead tired; **–wund** *adj.* mortally wounded

tödlich *adj.* deadly; fatal; mortal, murderous

Toilette *f.* dress; dressing table; toilet; **— machen** to dress; to spruce up; **–ngarnitur** *f.* toilet set; **–npapier** *neu.* toilet paper

Toleranz *f.* tolerance, toleration

toll *adj.* mad, raving; frantic; excessive; extravagant; **—** *en v.* to fool about; to frolic; to romp

Toll: **–e** *f.* (coll.) tuft; topknot; **–haus** *neu.* lunatic asylum; **–häusler** *m.* madman; **–kirsche** *f.* deadly nightshade, belladonna; **–kopf** *m.* madcap; **–wut** *f.* hydrophobia, rabies

Tolpatsch, Tölpel *m.* awkward (*oder* clumsy) person

Tomate *f.* tomato

Ton *m.* clay; tone, note; accent, stress; tint; fashion; **–art** *f.* (mus.) key; **–bandgerät** *neu.* tape recorder; **–dichtung** *f.* musical composition; **–fall** *m.* cadence; intonation, modulation; **–fanatiker** *m.* audiophile; **–farbe** *f.* timbre; **–film** *m.* sound film; **–folge** *f.* (mus.) scale; melody; **–führung** *f.* melody; **–gefäss** *neu.* earthen vessel; **–höhe** *f.* pitch; **–ika** *f.* (mus.) tonic; **–kunst** *f.* musical art; **–künstler** *m.* musician; **–lage** *f.* (mus.) range, pitch; **–leiter** *f.* (mus.) scale; gamut; **–mass** *neu.* metrical quantity; **–papier** *neu.* tinted paper; **–setzer** *m.* composer; **–silbe** *f.* accented syllable; **–stufe** *f.* pitch; **–taube** *f.* clay pigeon; **–waren** *f. pl.* pottery

tönen *v.* to (re)sound; to ring; to shade; to tint, to tone

tönern *adj.* of clay, earthen

Tonne *f.* tun, butt; barrel, cask; (naut.) ton (1,000 kilograms, 2,205 pounds); **–ngehalt** *m.* tannage; **–ngewölbe** *neu.* barrel vault

Tonsur *f.* tonsure

Topas *m.* topaz

Topf *m.* pot, crock, jar; **alles in einen — werfen** to treat all alike; **–gucker** *m.* meddlesome person; **–lappen** *m.* potholder

Töpfer *m.* potter; **–ei** *f.* potter's workshop (*oder* trade); **–scheibe** *f.* potter's wheel; **–waren** *f. pl.* crockery, pottery, earthenware

topp! *interj.* agreed! all right!

Tor *neu.* gate(way); (sports) goal; **–hüter** *m.* gatekeeper; porter; goalkeeper; **–latte** *f.*, **–pfosten** *m.* goal post; **–schluss** *m.* closing of the gates; **kurz vor –esschluss** just before the end; **–schütze** *m.* (sports) scorer; **–stoss** *m.* goal kick; **–wart** *m.* goalkeeper

Tor *m.* fool, simpleton; **–heit** *f.* folly, silliness

Torf *m.* peat; **–moor** *neu.* peat bog

töricht *adj.* foolish, stupid, silly

Tornister *m.* knapsack, schoolbag; (mil.) pack

torpedieren *v.* to torpedo

Torpedo *m.* torpedo; **–bootzerstörer** *m.* (torpedo boat) destroyer

Torte *f.* fancy (*oder* layer) cake; tart; **–nbäcker** *m.* pastry cook; **–nheber** *m.* cake server

Tortur *f.* torture

tosen *v.* to rage, to roar

tot *adj.* dead; lifeless; desolate; dull; stagnant; (sports) out of play; **–e Hand** (law) mortmain; **–er Punkt** dead center; deadlock; **–es Fleisch** (med.) proud flesh; **–es Rennen** dead heat; **–enblass** *adj.*, **–enbleich** *adj.* deathly pale; **–geboren** *adj.* stillborn; **–lachen** *v.*, **sich –lachen** to split one's sides with laughter; **–schlagen** *v.* to kill; to waste (time); **–schweigen** *v.* to hush up; **–sicher** *adj.* cocksure; **–stellen** *v.*, **sich –stellen** to feign death

Tot: **-e** *m.* dead person; corpse; **-enacker** *m.* cemetery; **-enamt** *neu.* burial service; **-enbahre** *f.* bier; **-enbett** *neu.* deathbed; **-enfeier** *f.* obsequies; **-engeläut(e)** *neu.* knell; **-engeleit** *neu.* funeral procession; **-engerippe** *neu.* skeleton; **-engräber** *m.* gravedigger; **-engruft** *f.* vault; **-enhemd** *neu.* shroud; **-enkopf** *m.* skull; **-enliste** *f.* death roll; casualty list; **-enmarsch** *m.* funeral .march; **-enmaske** *f.* death mask; **-enmesse** *f.* mass for the dead, requiem; **-enschau** *f.* coroner's inquest; **-enschein** *m.* certificate of death; **-enstarre** *f.* rigor mortis; **-enstille** *f.* dead silence; **-entanz** *m.* dance macabre; **-enwagen** *m.* hearse; **-geburt** *f.* stillborn child; **-schlag** *m.* manslaughter; **-schläger** *m.* murderer; loaded cane

totalitär *adj.* totalitarian

das Tote Meer *neu.* the Dead Sea

töten *v.* to kill, to slay; to deaden; to mortify; **sich —** to commit suicide

Tour *f.* journey, trip; round; (dance) figure; (mech.) revolution, turn; in einer **—** without stopping; **-enrad** *neu.* roadster; **-enwagen** *m.* station wagon; **-enzahl** *f.* number of revolutions; **-enzähler** *m.* speed indicator; **-ist** *m.* tourist; **-nee** *f.* (theat.) tour(ing)

Trab *m.* trot; im **—** at a trot; on the run; **jemand auf den —** **bringen** (coll.) to make someone speed up; **-er** *m.* trotter; **-rennbahn** *f.* trotting course

Trabant *m.* satellite

traben *v.* to trot; (coll.) to hurry

Tracht *f.* dress, costume; fashion; load; **eine — Prügel** a sound thrashing

trachten *v.* **— nach** to desire, to strive for; to seek after; to aspire to; **jemand nach dem Leben —** to make an attempt on someone's life

traditionell *adj.* traditional

Trag: **-bahre** *f.*, **-e** *f.* litter, stretcher; **-balken** *m.* beam, girder; **-band** *neu.* brace, strap, suspender; **-fähigkeit** *f.* carrying capacity; (naut.) tonnage; (soil) productiveness; **-fläche** *f.* (avi.) wing; **-himmel** *m.* canopy; **-riemen** *m.* strap; **-sessel** *m.* sedan chair; **-weite** *f.* range; import(ance); consequence; **-zeit** *f.* (zool.) period of gestation

trag: **-bar** *adj.* portable; endurable; **-en** *v.* to carry, to bear; to wear; to support; to yield; to produce; to endure; to be pregnant; **bei sich —en** to have about one; **sich gut —en** to wear well; **sich —en mit** to plan, to work on; **Sorge —en um** to be anxious about; **-fähig** *adj.* capable of bearing

Träg: **-er** *m.* carrier, porter; holder; bearer, wearer; prop, support, girder; **-heit** *f.* slowness; **-heitsgesetz** *neu.* law of inertia; **-heitssteuerung** (Rakete) *f.* inertial guidance

träge *adj.* lazy, indolent; sluggish; inert

Tragik *f.* tragic art; calamity

tragisch *adj.* tragic(al); calamitous, sad

Tragöd: **-e** *m.* tragic actor; **-ie** *f.* tragedy; **-in** *f.* tragic actress

Train *m.* (mil.) train; army service corps; **-er** *m.* trainer; **-ing** *neu.* training; coaching; **-ingsanzug** *m.* training suit; **-kolonne** *f.* transport column

trainieren *v.* to train, to coach

Traktat *m.* and *neu.* treatise; tract; treaty

traktieren *v.* to treat, to entertain

Tramp: **-el** *m.* and *neu.* awkward (*oder* clumsy) person; **-tier** *neu.* dromedary; **-olin** *m.* and *neu.* trampoline; springboard

Tran *m.* train oil; (whale) blubber; **im — sein** (coll.) to be drunk (*oder* sleepy); **-chierbesteck** *neu.* carving set

tranchieren *v.* to carve, to cut up

Träne *f.* tear; **-ngas** *neu.* tear gas

tränen *v.* to run with tears; (eyes) to water

Trank *m.* drink, draught, beverage; potion

Tränke *f.* watering place; horse pond

tränken *v.* to give to drink; to water; to drench; to soak, to saturate, to impregnate

Trans: **-formator** *m.* (elec.) transformer; **-mission** *f.* transmission; **-missionsapparat** *m.* transmitter; **-missionswelle** *f.* connecting shaft; **-parent** *neu.* transparency; **-piration** *f.* perspiration; **-port** *m.* transportation, carriage, shipment; **-porteur** *m.* transporter, carrier; (geom.) protractor; **-portschiff** *neu.* troop ship, transport

trans: **-ferieren** *v.* to transfer; **-pirieren** *v.* to perspire; **-ponieren** *v.* transpose; **-portabel** *adj.* transportable, movable; **-portieren** *v.* to transport, to convey, to ship; **-zendent(al)** *adj.* transcendent(al), beyond conception

trappe(l)n *v.* to patter, to trot, to trip

trassieren *v.* to draw (a draft on)

Tratsch *m.* (coll.) gossip; tittle-tattle

Tratte *f.* (com.) draft

Trau: **-altar** *m.* marriage altar; **-handlung** *f.* marriage ceremony; **-rede** *f.* clergyman's address to the bridal pair; **-ring** *m.* wedding ring; **-schein** *m.* marriage certificate; **-ung** *f.* marriage ceremony; wedding; **-zeuge** *m.* witness to a wedding

Traube *f.* grape; bunch of grapes; cluster, raceme; **-nblut** *neu.* (poet.) wine; **-ngeländer** *neu.* vine trellis; **-nlese** *f.* vintage; **-nmost** *m.* grape juice, new wine, must; **-npresse** *f.* wine press; **-nzucker** *m.* grape sugar

trauen *v.* to trust, to confide; to marry

Trauer *f.* grief, sorrow; affliction; mourning; **-anzeige** *f.* announcement of a death; **-botschaft** *f.* sad news; **-fall** *m.* death; **-flor** *m.* crape; **-gefolge** *neu.* **-zug** *m.* funeral procession; **-gottesdienst** *m.* funeral service; **-haus** *neu.* house of mourning; **-marsch** *m.* funeral march; **-rand** *m.* black edge; **-schleier** *m.* mourning veil; **-spiel** *neu.* tragedy **-weide** *f.* weeping willow; **-zeit** *f.* time of mourning

trauern *v.* to grieve; to be in mourning

Traufe *f.* gutter, eaves; **vom Regen in die — ** from the frying pan into the fire

traulich *adj.* intimate, familiar; cozy. snug

Traum *m.* dream, fancy, illusion; **quällen-der** — nightmare; **-bild** *neu.*, **-gesicht** *neu.* vision; **-deuter** *m.* interpreter of dreams; **-spiel** *neu.* phantasmagoria; **-welt** *f.* realm of dreams

träumen *v.* to dream, to daydream; to imagine

Träumer *m.* dreamer; **-erei** *f.* dreaming; daydream; fancy, reverie, musing

traumhaft *adj.* dreamlike, fairylike, unreal

traurig *adj.* sad, sorrowful, mournful; dreary

traut *adj.* beloved, dear; cozy, snug, homey

travestieren *v.* to travesty

Treber *pl.* husks of grapes; brewer's grains

Trecker *m.* tractor

Treff *neu.* (cards) club(s); (coll.) meeting place; **-en** *neu.* meeting, encounter; battle; **-er** *m.* hit; prize, winning ticket; luck; **-punkt** *m.* rendezvous; (mil.) point of impact

treff: **-en** *v.* to hit, to strike; to affect; to find, to meet, to encounter; to join; to befall, to concern; to take (measures); to make (preparations); (art and phot.) to achieve likeness; **das Los traf ihn** the lot fell on him; **das trifft sich gut** that's lucky; **empfindlich** — (fig.) to cut to the quick; **sich getroffen fühlen** to feel hurt; **-end** *adj.* well-aimed, striking; appropriate; **-lich** *adj.* excellent, exquisite; **-sicher** *adj.* accurate, sure of one's aim

Treib: **-eis** *neu.* drift ice; **-er** *m.* driver, drover, beater; **-haus** *neu.* hothouse, conservatory; **-holz** *neu.* driftwood; **-jagd** *f.* battue; **-riemen** *m.* drivebelt; **-sand** *m.* quicksand; **-stoff** *m.* fuel, propellant

treiben *v.* to drive, to propel; to float, to drift; (bot.) to germinate; to chase (metal); to impel, to urge; to expel; to pursue; to practice; to study, to cultivate; **etwas auf die Spitze** — to push something to extremes; **in die Ecke** — to corner; **jemand aus dem Haus** — to eject somebody; **vor sich her** — (sports) to dribble; **Wild** — to beat up game

trennbar *adj.* separable, divisible

trennen *v.* to separate, to sever; to interrupt, to disconnect; to divide; to undo, to rip (seam); **sich** — to part, to separate; to branch off

Trennung *f.* separation, severance; dissolution; division; **-slinie** *f.* demarcation line; (mil.) formation boundary; **-sstrich** *m.* hyphen

trepp: **-ab** *adv.* downstairs; **-auf** *adv.* upstairs; **-enförmig** *adj.* rising like steps

Treppe *f.* staircase, stairs; **eine** — **hoch wohnen** to live on the second floor; **-nabsatz** *m.* landing; **-ngeländer** *neu.* banisters; railing; **-nhaus** *neu.* well of a staircase; **-nläufer** *m.* stair carpet; **-witz** *m.* afterwit; bad joke

Tresse *f.* lace; (mil.) stripe

treten *v.* to tread, to step, to walk; to pedal, to treadle; **auf der Stelle** —

(mil.) to mark time; **ins Haus** — to enter the house; **in Verbindung** — to make connections; **jemand unter die Augen** — to face someone; **jemand zu nahe** — to offend (*oder* hurt) someone; **über die Ufer** — to overflow the banks; **zutage** — to come to light

treu *adj.* faithful, true; loyal; accurate; retentive (memory); **-brüchig** *adj.* faithless, perfidious; **-herzig** *adj.* candid, guileless; simple-minded; **-lich** *adj.* faithfully, truly; **-los** *adj.* faithless, perfidious

Treu *f.* **auf** — **und Glauben** in good faith; **-bruch** *m.* breach of faith, perfidy; **-e** *f.* faithfulness, fidelity, loyalty, accuracy; **-händer** *m.* trustee; **-handgesellschaft** *f.* trust company

Triangel *m.* triangle

Tribun *m.* tribune; **-al** *neu.* tribunal

Tribüne *f.* platform, grandstand; gallery

Tribut *m.* tribute

tributpflichtig *adj.* tributary

Trichine *f.* trichina

Trichter *m.* funnel; crater

Trick *m.* trick, dodge; **-film** *m.* stunt (*oder* animated) film

Trieb *m.* shoot, sprout; driving; impetus; instinct; inclination; **-feder** *f.* mainspring; motive; **-kraft** *f.* motive power **-rad** *neu.* driving wheel; **-sand** *m.* quicksand; **-stange** *f.* connecting rod; **-wagen** *m.* rail car; **-werk** *neu.* gear; mechanism; driving unit

Trift *f.* drift, floating; pastur(ag)e

triftig *adj.* cogent, plausible, good, weighty

Trigonometrie *f.* trigonometry

Trikot *m.* and *neu.* tricot; tights; **-agen** *f. pl.* knitted goods; hosiery

Triller *m.* (mus.) trill, quaver; warble

Trink: **-er** *m.* drinker; drunkard; **-gelage** *neu.* drinking bout, carousal; **-geld** *neu.* tip, gratuity; **-glas** *neu.* drinking glass; **-halle** *f.* pump room; **-spruch** *m.* toast; **-wasser** *neu.* drinking water

trinken *v.* to drink; to imbibe, to absorb; — **auf** to drink to, to toast

Trio *neu.* trio; **-le** *f.* (mus.) triplet

trippeln *v.* to trip

Tritt *m.* pace, step; tread(ing), kick; footfall, footprint; treadle; footboard; footstool; — **halten** to keep in step; **-brett** *neu.* running board; **-leiter** *f.* stepladder

Triumph *m.* triumph; **-ator** *m.* victor; conquering hero; **-bogen** *m.* triumphal arch

triumphieren *v.* to triumph

trocken *adj.* dry, arid; boring, dull, tedious; **noch nicht** — **hinter den Ohren** to be green; **-legen** *v.* to drain, to dry up

Trocken: **-apparat** *m.* dehydrator; **-batterie** *f.* dry cell battery; **-boden** *m.* drying loft; **-dock** *neu.* dry dock; **auf dem** **-en sitzen** to be high and dry (*oder* without money); **sein Schäfchen im** **-en haben** to have one's share secure; **-eis** *neu.* dry ice; **-milch** *f.* powdered milk

Trockenrasierer *m.* electric razor

trocknen v. to dry, to drain, to dehydrate

Tröd: -el m. secondhand goods; rubbish, junk; -elei f. dawdling, loafing; -elgeschäft neu., -elladen m. secondhand store; -elmarkt m. old clothes market; -ler m. secondhand dealer; dawdler

trödeln v. to dawdle, to loiter, to hesitate, to be slow

Trog m. trough

Troja neu. Troy

Trommel f. drum; (anat.) tympanum; (mech.) tumbler, cylinder; -fell neu. drumhead; tympanic membrane; -feuer neu. drumfire: -schlag m. drumbeat; -schlegel m. drumstick; -wirbel m. roll of drums

trommeln v. to (beat the) drum; mit den Fingern — to beat the devil's tattoo

Trommler m. drummer

Trompete f. trumpet; -ngeschmetter neu. blare of trumpets; -nschall m. sound of trumpets; -nstoss m. flourish of trumpets

Tropen pl. tropics; -helm m. sun (oder pith) helmet; -koller m. tropical frenzy

Tropf m. simpleton; armer — poor wretch; -en m. drop; (perspiration) bead; -enfänger m. drip catcher; -stein m. stalactite

tropf: -en v. to drop, to drip, to trickle; -nass adj. dripping wet; -enweise adv. by drops, drop by drop

tröpfeln v. to drop, to drip, to trickle

Trophäe f. trophy

tropisch adj. tropic(al)

Tross m. (mil.) supply train; baggage; followers, crowd

Trost m. consolation, comfort, solace; nicht (recht) bei -e sein not to be in one's right mind; -preis m. consolation prize

trost: -bringend adj., -reich adj. comforting, consolatory; cheering; -los adj. disconsolate, hopeless; cheerless, desolate

trösten v. to console, to comfort, to solace

Tröster m. comforter, consoler

Trott m. trot; -el m. dunce, idiot, fool; -oir neu. sidewalk, pavement

trotten v. to trot

Trotz m. obstinacy, defiance, insolence; — bieten to defy; zum — in defiance (oder in spite) of; -kopf m. stubborn (oder bullheaded) person

trotz prep. in spite of, notwithstanding; -dem adv. and conj. nevertheless, in spite of that; (al)though; -en v. to defy; to be obstinate (oder stubborn); to sulk; -ig adj., -köpfig adj. defiant, obstinate, refractory, sulky, sullen

trüb adj. muddy, turbid; dim, dull, gloomy, cloudy; sad; dreary; -en v. to make muddy; to dull, to darken; to spoil, to sadden; der Himmel trübt sich the sky is overcast; er sieht aus, als ob er kein Wässerchen -en könnte he is the picture of innocence; -selig adj. sad, wretched; -sinnig adj. melancholy

Trüb: im -en fischen to fish in troubled waters; -sal f. affliction, distress, misery; -sal blasen (coll.) to be in the dumps; -sinn m. melancholy, gloom

Trubel m. turmoil, confusion; commotion bustle

trudeln v. to trundle; (avi.) to spin

Trug m. deception, fraud; delusion, illusion; -bild neu. phantom, optical illusion; -schluss m. false conclusion fallacy

trügen v. to deceive, to delude, to mislead

trügerisch adj. deceitful, deceptive, delusive

Truhe f. chest, trunk

Trümmer pl. ruins, debris, remains; fragments

Trumpf m. trump, trump card; seine Trümpfe ausspielen to use every advantage

trumpfen v. to trump

Trunk m. draught, drink(ing); dem — ergeben addicted to drink; sich dem — ergeben to take to the bottle; -enbold m. drunkard; -sucht f. dipsomania -süchtige m. dipsomaniac

trunken adj. drunk, tipsy; elated; exuberant

trunksüchtig adj. dipsomaniacal, drink craving

Trupp m. troop, band, gang, squad; -e f troupe, company; (mil.) troop, body unit; -en pl. forces; -enaushebung f levy of troops; -engattung f. branch of the service; -enschau f. military review; -enteil m. military unit; -enübungsplatz m. maneuver grounds -enverband f. (mil.) formation, unit -enverbandplatz m. regimental first-aid post

Truthahn m. tom turkey

Truthenne f. turkey hen

Trutz m. defiance, resistance, offensive

die Tschechoslowakei f. Czechoslovakia

Tube f. tube

Tuberk: -el f. tubercle; -elbildung f tuberculation; -ulose f. tuberculosis

tuberkulös adj. tuberculous

Tuch neu. cloth, fabric; scarf, shawl -fabrik f. textile mill; -fühlung f. close touch; -händler m. clothier, draper -waren f. pl. clothing, drapery

tüchtig adj. qualified, capable, efficient thorough; good; — adv. very much thoroughly

Tücke f. malice, trick, spite; whim

tückisch adj. malicious, deceitful, spiteful; (med.) malignant; (animals) vicious

tüfteln v. to puzzle (over), to split hairs

Tugend f. virtue; -bold m. self-righteous person; paragon of virtue; shan moralist; -richter m. moralist, censor

tugend: -haft adj., -sam adj. -reich adj virtuous

Tüll m. tulle; -spitze f. net lace

Tulpe f. tulip; -nzwiebel f. tulip bulb

tummeln v. to put in motion; to exercise, sich — to bustle about, to hurry

Tummelplatz m. playground; scene of activity

Tümpel m. pool, puddle

Tumult m. tumult, riot; -uant m. rioter

tun r. to do, to execute; to perform, to act; to work, to be busy; to put; to affect. to pretend; **das tut nichts** that doesn't matter. **des Guten zuviel —** to overdo something; **es ist ihm nur um das Geld zu —** he cares only about the money; **es ist mir sehr darum zu —** I am anxious about it; **es mit jemand zu — bekommen** to get into trouble with someone; **es tut mir leid** I am sorry; **nichts mit jemand zu —** haben to have no business with someone; **schön —** to flirt; **so — als ob** to pretend to; **weh —** to grieve, to hurt; **-lich** adj. feasible, practicable, advisable; **-lichst** adj. utmost; **-lichst** adv. if possible

Tun neu. doing(s), action, conduct; **-ichtgut** m. ne'er-do-well

Tünche f. whitewash; (fig.) varnish, veneer

tünchen v. to whitewash; (fig.) to varnish

Tunke f. sauce, gravy

tunken v. to dip, to soak, to steep, to dunk

Tunnel m. tunnel

Tüpfel m. and neu. dot, spot, tittle, jot; **etwas bis aufs -chen wissen** to know something in minute detail

tüpfeln v. to dot, to spot, to stipple

tupfen r. to touch lightly, to dab; to dot

Tür f. door; **jemand die — weisen, jemand den Stuhl vor die —** setzen to turn somebody out; **mit der — ins Haus fallen** to blurt out; **offene —** einrennen to belabor the obvious; **vor der — stehen** to be imminent; **zwischen — und Angel** on the point of leaving; **in a dilemma; -angel** f. door hinge; **-flügel** m. door wing; **-füllung** f. door panel; **-griff** m. door handle; **-hüter** m., **-steher** m. doorkeeper, porter, janitor; **-klinke** f. door latch; **-schild** neu. doorplate; **-schwelle** f. threshold

Turbine f. turbine; **-nanlage** f. turbine plant; **-nluftstrahlmotor** m. turbojet

die Türkei f. Turkey

Türkis m. turquoise

Turm m. tower, steeple; turret; (chess) castle, rook; **-fahne** f. vane; **-falke** m. kestrel; sparrow hawk; **-lukendeckel** m. (mil.) turret door (oder hatch); **-schwalbe** f. (orn.) swift; **-spitze** f. spire; **-uhr** f. church clock; tower clock

türmen v. to pile up; (coll.) to scamper off; **sich —** to tower, to rise high

Türmer m. watchman (oder warder) of a tower

Turn: -en neu., **-erei** f. gymnastics; **-er** m. gymnast; **-erschaft** f., **-verein** m. gymnastic club; **-gerät** neu. gymnastic apparatus; **-halle** f. gym(nasium); **-hosen** f. pl. gym bloomers

turnen v. to practice gymnastics

Turnier neu. tournament; tilting; **-platz** m. tiltyard; **-schranken** f. pl. lists

Turteltaube f. turtledove

Tusch m. (mus.) flourish; **-e** f. India ink; **-farbe** f. water color; **-kasten** m. paint box

tuscheln v. to whisper

tuschen v. to draw with India ink

Tüt: -e f. paper bag; cone (for ice cream); **-tel** m., **-telchen** neu. dot; jot

Typ m., **-us** m., **-e** f. type; **-hus** m. typhoid fever; **-ograf** m. typographer; **-opografie** f. typography

Tyrann m. tyrant; **-ei** f. tyranny; **-enmord** m., **-enmörder** m. tyrannicide

tyrannisch adj. tyrannic(al)

U

übel adj. bad, evil; ill, sick; **dabei kann einem — werden** it is enough to make one sick; **es sieht — mit ihm aus** he is in a bad way; **mir ist —** I feel sick; **nicht —** not bad; **— (auf)nehmen** to take amiss; **wohl oder —** willing or not; **-gelaunt** adj. ill-humored; cross, sulky; **-nehmerisch** adj. easily offended; touchy; **-wollend** adj. malevolent

Übel neu. evil; ailment, illness; **-befinden** neu. indisposition; **-keit** f. nausea, sickness; **-stand** m. inconvenience; drawback, abuse; **-tat** f. misdeed; **-täter** m. evil-doer

üben v. to exercise, to practice, to drill, to train; **Geduld —** to have patience; **geübt sein** to be skilled; **Gewalt —** to use violence; **Rache —** to take revenge

über prep. above, over; exceeding, higher than; beyond, across; (up)on; more than; during; about, concerning; — adv. over, in excess; completely; thoroughly; **die ganze Zeit —** all the while; **etwas — haben** to be tired of something; **heute — acht Tage** a week from today; **jemand — sein** to surpass someone; **— alle Massen** exceedingly, indescribably; **— kurz oder lang** sooner or later; **— Liverpool nach Hamburg** to Hamburg via Liverpool; **-s Jahr** next year; **wir sind noch nicht — den Berg** we are not yet out of the woods

überall adv. everywhere; all over; throughout

überaltert adj. overaged

überanstrengen v. to overexert, to overstrain

überantworten v. to deliver up; to surrender; (law) to extradite

überarbeiten v. to revise, to retouch; **sich — to overwork oneself

überaus adv. exceedingly, extremely

Überbau m. superstructure

überbelichten v. (phot.) to overexpose

überbieten v. to outbid; to excel, to surpass

Überbleibsel neu. remainder, residue, leftover

Überblick m. survey, view; summary, synopsis

Überbrettl neu. special kind of cabaret

überbringen v. to deliver, to bring to

Überbringer m. bearer, carrier

überbrücken v. to bridge (over); to span

überdachen v. to roof, to shelter

überdenken v. to think over, to reconsider

überdies adv. moreover

Überdruck m. excess pressure; overprint; compression; **- kombination** f. space suit

Uberdruss m. disgust; repletion, satiety

überdrüssig adj. tired of; satiated

übereignen v. to assign, to convey

übereilen v. to precipitate; to scamp (work)

überein adv. conformably; in accordance; **-ander** adv. one above the other; **die Beine -ander schlagen** to cross one's legs; **-kommen** v. to come to an agreement; **-stimmen** v. to agree; to correspond; **-stimmend** adj. corresponding

Uberein: -kommen neu., **-kunft** f. agreement, arrangement; **-stimmung** f. harmony, conformity

überessen v. sich — to overeat

überfahren v. to pass (oder run) over; to drive across, to cross

Überfahrt v. passage, crossing

Überfall m. sudden attack, raid; surprise; **-kommando** neu. (police) flying squad

überfallen v. to attack suddenly; to raid; to overtake; to surprise

überfällig adj. overdue

überflügeln v. (mil.) to outflank; to surpass

Überfluss m. abundance, plenty; redundancy; **im — abundantly; zum —** needlessly

überflüssig adj. superfluous; redundant

überfluten v. to overflow, to inundate

überfordern v. to overcharge; overweight

überführen v. to convey; to convict; to convince; (chem.) to convert, to transform

Überführung f. conveying, transfer; conviction; (chem.) conversion, transformation; overpass

überfüllen v. to overfill, to overload; to overcrowd; to overstock

Übergabe f. delivery; surrender; handing over

Übergang m. crossing; transition; change; **-smantel** m. light topcoat; **-szeit** f. transition period; **-szustand** m. transitional state

übergeben v. to deliver, to hand over, to surrender; **sich —** to vomit

übergeh(e)n v. to go (oder pass) over; to change into (oder over); to ignore, to omit

Übergewicht neu. overweight; preponderance, superiority; **das — bekommen** to become top-heavy; to get the upper hand

Übergriff m. encroachment, infringement

Überhandnahme f. increase, spread, prevalence

überhandnehmen v. to increase, to spread; to become prevalent (oder too numerous)

überhäufen v. to overburden; to overwhelm

überhaupt adv. in general, on the whole; altogether; **— nicht** not at all

überheben v. to spare, to exempt from; **sich —** to injure oneself (by overlifting); to be overbearing (oder presumptuous)

überheblich adj. arrogant, overbearing

überhitzen v. to overheat; to superheat

überholen v. to haul over; to outdistance to outstrip, to surpass; to overhaul, t check

überholt adj. out of date, antiquated

überhören v. to fail to hear; to ignore; t hear someone's homework (or lessons

überirdisch adj. supernatural, unearthly

überkippen v. to tip over, to keel

Überkleid neu. upper garment

überkochen v. to boil over; to fret an fume

überladen v. to overload; to overdo; de **Magen —** to overeat; **—** adj. overdone too profuse

Überlandflug m. (avi.) cross-country flight

überlassen v. to leave, to give up; to cede to transfer; to abandon; to give way

überlaufen v. to run over, to overflow (mil.) to desert; to pester, to impor tune; **es überläuft mich** I am overcome (by a feeling)

Überläufer m. deserter; renegade

überleb: -en v. to outlive, to survive **-engross** adj. bigger than life-size; - adj. out of date, antiquated, old fashioned

Überlebende m. survivor

überlegen v. to lay over, to cover; (coll. to whip; to consider, to reflect upon; — adj. superior; **er ist ihm —** he excel him

Überlegenheit f. superiority, preponder ance

Überlegung f. reflection, consideration deliberation; **mit — verübtes Verbre chen** premeditated crime; **ohne —** thoughtlessly

überleiten v. to lead over (oder across) to form a transition

überlesen v. to reread; to skim; to peruse to overlook

überliefern v. to deliver, to hand over; t transmit, to pass (on); to surrender

Überlieferung f. delivery; tradition; sur render

überlisten v. to outwit, to dupe, to deceive

übermachen v. to transmit; to bequeath

Übermacht f. superior power; predomi nance

übermächtig adj. too powerful; over whelming

übermangansauer adj. permanganic

übermannen v. to overcome, to overpower

Übermass neu. excess; **im — excessively**

übermässig adj. excessive, exorbitant

Übermensch m. superman

übermenschlich adj. superhuman

übermitteln v. to send, to convey; t transmit

übermorgen adj. the day after tomorrow

übermüdet adj. overtired, overfatigued

Übermut m. high spirits, wantonness insolence

übermütig adj. high-spirited, frolicsome presumptuous, insolent

übernachten v. to stay over night

Übernahme f. taking over; undertaking **-bedingungen** f. pl. conditions of ac ceptance

übernatürlich adj. supernatural

übernehmen v. to take over (oder in hand); to undertake; to assume responsibility; **sich —** to overwork oneself; to overeat

überquer adv. crossways, across; **-en** to cross

überragen v. to overtop; to excel, to surpass

überraschen v. to surprise

überreden v. to persuade

überreich adj. too rich; abounding in, **-en** to hand over, to present; **-lich** adj. superabundant

überreif adj. overripe

Überrest m. remainder, rest; remains; residue

Überrock m. overcoat, topcoat

überrumpeln v. to take (by) surprise

Überrumpelung f. surprisal; sudden attack

übersatt adj. satiated; glutted, surfeited

überschallgeschwindigkeit f. supersonic speed; ultrasonic speed

überschätzen v. to overestimate, to overrate

überschauen v. to overview; to survey

überschäumen v. to foam over; to exuberate

Überschicht f. extra shift; overtime

überschiessen v. to overshoot; to fall forward; to overflow; to exceed; **-de Summe** surplus

Überschlag m. estimate; rough calculation; somersault; (dress) facing

überschlagen v. to estimate; to skip; **sich —** to tumble over, to turn a somersault; (avi.) to loop the loop; **die Stimme überschlägt sich** the voice breaks

überschnappen v. to go crazy; **mit der Stimme —** to squeak, to shrill

überschneiden v. to intersect, to overlap

überschreiben v. to transfer; to superscribe; to head, to title; to carry over

überschreien v. to cry down; **sich —** to overstrain one's voice

überschreiten v. to cross over; to exceed; to transgress; to infringe; (com.) to overdraw

Überschrift f. superscription; heading, title

Überschuh m. overshoe, galosh

überschuldet adj. involved in debts

Überschuss m. surplus, excess, profit

überschüssig adj. surplus, excess, leftover

überschütten v. to cover; to overwhelm

Überschwang m. exuberance, rapture

überschwemmen v. to flood, to inundate

überschwenglich adj. exuberant, rapturous

überseeisch adj. oversea(s), transoceanic

übersehen v. to survey; to overlook

übersenden v. to send, to transmit, to consign

Übersender m. sender, consignor; remitter

übersetzen v. to pass (oder carry) over, to cross; to translate

Übersetzung f. translation; (mech.) gear

Übersicht f. survey; view; summary,

synopsis, abstract; **-skarte** f. general plan

übersichtlich adj. clear, lucid; easily seen

übersiedeln v. to move; to emigrate

übersinnlich adj. transcendental; metaphysical

überspannen v. to stretch over; to carpet, to cover with; to overstrain; to exaggerate

überspannt adj. overstrained; eccentric

überspringen v. to overleap; to skip, to omit

überstechen v. (cards) to overtrump

überstehen v. to stand over; to project; to endure; to get over; to survive

übersteigen v. to step (oder climb) over; to surmount, to exceed

übersteigern v. to overbid, to outbid

überstimmen v. to tune too high; to outvote

Überstunde f., **-n** pl. overtime

überstürzen v. to topple; to hurry; to precipitate; **sich —** to act rashly

übertönen v. to drown out; to deafen

übertragbar adj. transferable; contagious

übertragen v. to carry over; to transfer; to give up to, to entrust with; to transmit; to transcribe; to infect with; **-e Bedeutung** figurative sense

übertreffen v. to excel, to surpass; to beat

übertreiben v. to exaggerate, to overdo

übertreten v. to go (oder step) over; to change sides; to violate, to transgress, to trespass; to sprain (ankle)

übertrieben adj. exaggerated, excessive; extravagant; extreme; exorbitant

Übertritt m. going over; (rel.) conversion

übertrumpfen v. to overtrump; to outwit

übertünchen v. to whitewash; to gloss over

übervölkert adj. overpopulated

übervorteilen v. to overreach; to defraud

überwachen v. to supervise; to control; to shadow

überwältigen v. to overcome, to overpower; to overwhelm; to subdue; **-d** adj. imposing

überweisen v. to assign, to transfer; to remit

Überweisungsscheck m. transfer check

überwiegen v. to outweigh; to predominate; **-d** adj. predominant; **-d** adv. mainly, chiefly

überwinden v. to overcome; to conquer; to get over, to surmount; **ein überwundener Standpunkt** an outmoded viewpoint

überwintern v. to winter; to hibernate

überwuchern v. to overgrow; to overrun

Überwurf m. loose gown, cloak; wrap, shawl

Überzahl f. surplus; odds; majority

überzählig adj. supernumerary, superfluous

überzeugen v. to convince, to persuade

Überzeugung f. conviction, belief

überziehen v. to put on; to pull over; (com.) to overdraw; **Bett —** to change bed linen; **einen Sessel —** to upholster a chair; **sich —** to become overcast

Überzieher m. overcoat, topcoat

überzuckern v. to sugar coat; to candy, to frost, to ice

Überzug m. cover, coat(ing); crust; slip, case

üblich adj. usual, customary, prevailing

übrig adj. left over, remaining; **die –en** the others, the rest; **ein –es tun** to do more than is necessary; **etwas für jemand — haben** to care for someone; **im –en** for the rest, in other respects; **nichts zu wünschen — lassen** to leave nothing to be desired; **–ens** adv. by the way, after all; besides, moreover

Ufer neu. bank, beach, shore; coast; **–damm** m. embankment; **–seite** f. riverside

uferlos adj. boundless; extravagant

Uhr f. clock, watch; hour, time; **es ist ein** — it's one o'clock; **wieviel — ist's?** what's the time? **–werk** neu. clockwork; **–zeiger** m. hand of a clock (oder watch)

Uhu m. great horned owl

Ulan m. (mil.) uhlan, lancer

Ulk m. fun, joke, merry prank

ulken v. to have fun, to crack jokes, to tease

ulkig adj. funny, amusing, comical

Ulme f. elm

Ultimo m. (com.) last day of the month

um prep. about, round; at; because of, for; by; **einen Tag — den anderen** day after day; every other day; **rechts —!** right face! **— die Hälfte mehr** half as much again; **— drei Uhr** at three o'clock; **— ein Jahr älter** a year older; **–s Leben kommen** to die; **— so besser!** so much the better! **— sein** to be over; to expire; **—** adv. about; **— und —** from (oder on) all sides; **—** conj. **— zu** in order to

umadressieren v. to redirect (mail)

umändern v. to alter, to change; to transform

umarbeiten v. to recast, to remodel; to rework

umarmen v. to embrace, to hug

Umbau m. reconstruction, alterations

umbauen v. to rebuild, to reconstruct

umbehalten v. to keep on (wrap, etc.)

umbiegen v. to bend, to turn back (oder down)

umbilden v. to recast, to remodel, to transform; to reconstruct; to reform

umbinden v. to tie round; to put on; to rebind

umblasen v. to blow down (oder over)

umblättern v. to turn over (leaf of book)

umblicken v. to look around; to glance back

umbrechen v. to break down (oder up); (typ.) to make up, to page

umbringen v. to kill, to murder; to make away with; **sich —** to commit suicide

Umbruch m. radical change, revolution; (typ.) paging; page proof

umdrehen v. to turn over (oder around); **den Hals —** to wring somebody's neck; **den Spiess —** to turn the tables on someone; **sich —** to rotate, to revolve, to turn round

umdüstert adj. dark, gloomy

umeinander adv. round (oder for) ea other

umfahren v. to run over; to drive (od sail) around); to circumnavigate

umfallen v. to fall down; to upset

Umfang m. circumference, periphery; e tent, size; compass, range; bulk, v ume

umfangen v. to embrace; to surround

umfangreich adj. extensive, voluminou wide

umfassen v. to embrace, to encircle; include; (mil.) to outflank; **mit eine Blick —** to take in at a glance; **–d a** comprehensive, extensive

umflort adj. veiled; muffled; (eyes) di

umformen v. to transform; to remodel; reform, to convert

Umformer m. transformer, converter; r former

Umfrage f. inquiry, poll, canvass

Umfriedung f. enclosure, fence

Umgang m. (going) round, circuit; proce sion; social intercourse, associatio (arch.) circular gallery; **–sformen** f. manners; **–ssprache** f. colloquial la guage

umgänglich adj. sociable, companionab

umgarnen v. to ensnare, to trap; to e mesh

umgaukeln v. to flit (oder hover) aroun to wrap in (illusions)

umgeben v. to surround; to enclose; fence in

Umgebung f. surroundings, neighbo hood; associates, company; bac ground, environment

Umgegend f. neighborhood, vicinity, e virons

umgeh(e)n v. to go around; to circulat (mil.) to outflank; to avoid, to evad (ghost) to haunt; **mit etwas —** to occupied with something, to plan to something; **mit jemand — to** associa with someone; **–d** adj. **mit –der Po** by return mail; **–d** adv. immediate

umgekehrt adj. contrary, opposite, verse; **—** adv. on the contrary, vi versa

umgestalten v. to alter, to transform, reorganize; to metamorphose

umgraben v. (soil) to dig (oder break)

umgrenzen v. to encircle; to circumscrib to limit; to fence

umhaben v. to have around one (oder o

umhalsen v. to embrace, to hug

Umhang m. cape, shawl, wrap

Umhängetasche f. shoulder bag

umhauen v. to cut down, to fell

umher adv. around; about; here and the

umhin adv. **ich kann nicht — I** can't he it

umhüllen v. to wrap, to encase, to protec to veil, to cover

Umkehr f. turning back; return; conve sion; **–ung** f. reversal, subversion, version

umkehren v. to turn back (oder abou

round, over); to return; to reverse; to invert; to convert; to overthrow, to subvert

umkippen v. to overturn; to tip over

umklammern v. to clasp; to clutch; to encircle

umklappen v. to turn down (collar)

umkleiden v. to clothe; to cover; **sich —** to change one's dress

Umkleideraum m. dressing room

umkommen v. to die, to perish; to be wasted

Umkreis m. circumference, circuit; radius

umkreisen v. to turn (oder circle, revolve) round; to encircle; to rotate; (**die Erde**) v. to orbit

umlagern v. to surround; to besiege

Umlauf m. circulation; rotation; revolving, revolution, turn; circular; **in — setzen** to circulate; to spread (rumors)

umlaufen v. to run down; to revolve, to circulate

umlegen v. to lay down; to put on; to shift, to relay; to lay around (someone or something); (sl.) to kill

umleiten v. to conduct in another direction; to divert

umlenken v. to turn round (oder back)

umlernen v. to readjust one's views

umliegend adj. surrounding, neighboring

ummauern v. to wall in, to fortify

umnachtet adj. wrapped in darkness; deranged

umnebeln v. to wrap in fog; to becloud

umpacken v. to repack

umpflanzen v. to transplant; to plant around

umpflügen v. to plow up

umquartieren v. to remove to other quarters

umranken v. to twine around

umrechnen v. (com.) to change, to convert

Umrechnungskurs m. rate of exchange

umreissen v. to pull down; to outline

umringen v. to encircle, to encompass

Umriss m. outline, contour, sketch

umrühren v. to stir up (oder around)

umsatteln v. to resaddle; to change one's occupation; (pol.) to change sides

Umsatz m. sales, turnover, returns

umsäumen v. to hem; to surround

umschalten v. to switch (oder change) over

Umschalter m. switch, commutator; (typewriter) shift key

Umschau f. look(ing) round; **— halten** to look around; to reconnoiter, to scout

umschauen v. **sich —** to look around

umschichtig adv. by turns, alternately

umschiffen v. to circumnavigate; to double (a cape)

Umschlag m. cover, wrapper; envelope; (book) jacket; hem, cuff; (com.) transfer, reshipment; (med.) compress; change, turn; **-papier** neu. wrapping paper; **-shafen** m. port of reshipment; **-tuch** neu. wrap, shawl

umschlagen v. to topple; to overturn, to knock down; to shift; (naut.) to capsize; (voice) to break; to turn (a hem) up (oder down); to turn over (a page);

to change, to degenerate

umschliessen v. to enclose, to surround

umschlingen v. to embrace; to clasp around

umschmelzen v. to recast, to remelt

umschreiben v. to rewrite; to transcribe; to circumscribe; to reindorse, to transfer

Umschreibung f. transcription; paraphrase

umschütten v. to spill; to decant; to transfuse

umschwärmen v. to swarm round; to adore

Umschweif m. digression; circumlocution; **-e machen** to digress; **ohne -e** bluntly, plainly

umschwenken v. to wheel around; to change one's mind

Umschwung m. change; revulsion; revolution; (gym.) swing round the bar

umsehen v. **sich —** to look back (oder around); to go sightseeing

Umsehen neu. **im —** in a twinkling

umsetzen v. to transpose; to transplant; to sell, to turn over; to convert

Umsichgreifen neu. spread(ing)

Umsicht f. circumspection, prudence, caution

umsichtig adj. circumspect, prudent, cautious

umsonst adv. for nothing, gratis; in vain

umspannen v. to change (horses); to enclose, to encompass; (elec.) to transform

umspringen v. to jump around; to change, to veer; **— mit** to treat, to manage

Umstand m. circumstance, fact; **-skleid** neu. maternity dress; **-swort** neu. adverb

Umstände m. pl. particulars; ceremonies, formalities; fuss, trouble, ado; **grosse — machen** to raise great difficulties; **in anderen -n sein** to be pregnant; **mildernde —** (law) extenuating circumstances; **ohne —** without ceremony; **unter allen -n** in any case, at all events; **unter keinen -n** on no account; **unter solchen -n** as matters stand; **unter -n** circumstances permitting

umständlich adj. circumstantial, involved; ceremonious, formal; fussy

umstehen v. to stand round (oder about); to surround; **-d** adj. on the next page

Umsteige: -billet neu., **-(fahr)karte** f., **-fahrschein** m., **-r** m. transfer ticket

umsteigen v. to change (trains), to transfer

umstellen v. to arrange differently; to shift, to transpose; to invert; to convert; to surround, to beset; **sich —** to adapt oneself

umstimmen v. to tune to another pitch; **jemand —** to change someone's mind

umstossen v. to knock down; to upset, to overturn; to annul, to invalidate

umstricken v. to ensnare, to entangle

umstritten adj. controversial, disputed

umstülpen v. to tip over; to turn upside

down

Umsturz *m.* overthrow; subversion; revolution

Umstürzler *m.* anarchist, revolutionist

umtaufen *v.* to rebaptize; to give a new name

Umtausch *m.* exchange

umtauschen *v.* to exchange

Umtriebe *m. pl.* intrigues, machinations

umtun *v.* to put on; **sich —** to look for

umwälzen *v.* to roll round; to revolutionize

Umwälzung *f.* radical change; revolution

umwandeln *v.* to change, to transform, to convert

Umwandlungsprozess *m.* metamorphosis

umwechseln *v.* to exchange; to change (money)

Umweg *m.* roundabout way, detour; bypass; **auf -en** indirectly; **-e machen** to bypass

Umwelt *f.* environment, milieu

umwenden *v.* to turn over; **sich —** to turn around, to look back

umwerben *v.* to court, to woo

umwerfen *v.* to overturn, to upset; to throw round (*oder* over); to put on (coat)

umwerten *v.* to revaluate

umwühlen *v.* to uproot, to rummage all around

umzäunen *v.* to fence in, to enclose

umziehen *v.* to change (clothes); to move (to); to surround; to cover all around; to become overcast; to walk round

umzingeln *v.* to encircle, to surround

Umzug *m.* moving; procession, demonstration

unab: -änderlich *adj.* unalterable, irrevocable; **-hängig** *adj.* independent; **-kömmlich** *adj.* indispensable, reserved; **-lässig** *adj.* incessant; **-sehbar** *adj.* unbounded, immeasurable, immense; **-sichtlich** *adj.* unintentional; accidental; **-weisbar** *adj.*, **-weislich** *adj.* imperative; unavoidable; **-wendbar** *adj.* inevitable

Unabhängigkeit *f.* independence; **-serklärung** *f.* Declaration of Independence

unähnlich *adj.* unlike, dissimilar

unan: -fechtbar *adj.* incontestable, indisputable; **-gebracht** *adj.* out of place, unsuitable; **-gefochten** *adj.* undisputed; unhindered; **-gemessen** *adj.* inadequate, unsuitable; improper; **-greifbar** *adj.* unassailable; incontestable; **-nehmbar** *adj.* unacceptable; **-sehnlich** *adj.* poor-looking, plain; insignificant; **-tastbar** *adj.* inviolable, unassailable; unimpeachable

Unannehmlichkeit *f.* inconvenience, annoyance

Unart *f.* bad habit (*oder* behavior)

unartig *adj.* badly behaved, naughty, rude

unauf: -findbar *adj.* undiscoverable; **-geschlossen** *adj.* unexploited, undeveloped; **-haltbar** *adj.*, **-haltsam** *adj.* irresistible; incessant; **-hörlich** *adj.* incessant, constant; **-lösbar** *adj.*, **-löslich** *adj.* indissoluble, inexplicable; **-schieb**

bar *adj.*, **-schieblich** *adj.* pressing, urgent

unaus: -bleiblich *adj.* inevitable, certain; **-führbar** *adj.* impracticable, unfeasible; **-gesetzt** *adj.* uninterrupted, incessant; **-löschbar** *adj.*, **-löschlich** *adj.* inextinguishable, indelible; **-sprechlich** *adj.* inexpressible, indescribable; immense; **-stehlich** *adj.* unbearable, intolerable; **-weichbar** *adj.*, **-weichlich** *adj.* unavoidable; inevitable

unbändig *adj.* unruly, intractable; tremendous

unbarmherzig *adj.* unmerciful, pitiless, cruel

unbeabsichtigt *adj.* unintentional

unbeachtet *adj.* unnoticed, disregarded

unbeanstandet *adj.* unopposed; unobjectionable

unbebaut *adj.* uncultivated

unbedacht(sam) *adj.* inconsiderate, thoughtless

unbedenklich *adj.* unobjectionable, harmless; **—** *adv.* unhesitatingly, without scruples

unbedeutend *adj.* insignificant, trifling

unbedingt *adj.* unconditional, absolute, implicit

unbeeinflusst *adj.* unprejudiced, unbiased

unbeeinträchtigt *adj.* uninjured, unhindered

unbefahrbar *adj.* impassable, impracticable

unbefangen *adj.* impartial, unprejudiced, natural

unbefleckt *adj.* unsullied, spotless; immaculate

unbefriedigt *adj.* unsatisfied; disappointed

unbefugt *adj.* unauthorized, incompetent

unbegreiflich *adj.* incomprehensible, inconceivable; mysterious

unbegrenzt *adj.* unlimited, unbounded

unbegründet *adj.* unfounded; baseless

Unbehagen *neu.* uneasiness, discomfort

unbehaglich *adj.* uncomfortable, uneasy

unbehelligt *adj.* undisturbed, unmolested

unbeholfen *adj.* awkward, clumsy; ungainly

unbeirrbar, unbeirrt *adj.* imperturbable

unbekannt *adj.* unknown; unacquainted (with); ignorant (of)

unbekümmert *adj.* unconcerned; carefree

unbelästigt *adj.* unmolested

unbelebt *adj.* inanimate, lifeless; dull, empty

unbemerkt *adj.* unnoticed, unperceived

unbemittelt *adj.* impecunious, poor

unbenutzt *adj.* unused, unemployed; uninvested

unberechenbar *adj.* incalculable; unreliable

unberechtigt *adj.* unauthorized; unfounded; unjustified; unlawful

unberücksichtigt *adj.* unconsidered; disregarded

unberufen *adj.* unbidden, unauthorized; **—!** knock on wood! — *adv.* intrusively

unberührt *adj.* untouched; intact; virgin

unbeschädigt *adj.* uninjured, undamaged

unbescheiden *adj.* immodest; arrogant; insolent

unbescholten *adj.* blameless, irreproachable; (law) without previous conviction

unbeschränkt *adj.* unrestricted; absolute

unbeschreiblich *adj.* indescribable; — *adv.* exceedingly, extremely

unbeschwert *adj.* unburdened, light

unbeseelt *adj.* soulless, inanimate

unbesehen *adv.* without examination (*oder* inspection); without hesitation

unbesetzt *adj.* unoccupied; vacant; plain

unbesiegbar, unbesieglich *adj.* invincible

unbesonnen *adj.* thoughtless, heedless; rash

unbesorgt *adj.* unconcerned, carefree; sei —! don't worry!

Unbestand *m.*, Unbeständigkeit *f.* inconstancy; changeableness; unsteadiness

unbeständig *adj.* unstable; inconstant

unbestechbar, unbestechlich *adj.* incorruptible

unbestellbar *adj.* not deliverable

unbestimmbar *adj.* indeterminable, nondescript

unbestimmt *adj.* undetermined, undecided; uncertain; indistinct; indefinite

unbestreitbar *adj.* incontestable, indisputable

unbestritten *adj.* uncontested, undisputed

unbeteiligt *adj.* not concerned; indifferent

unbetont *adj.* unaccented, unstressed

unbeträchtlich *adj.* inconsiderable, trifling

unbeugsam *adj.* inflexible; stubborn, obstinate

unbewacht *adj.* unwatched, unguarded

unbewaffnet *adj.* unarmed; naked (eye)

unbewandert *adj.* inexperienced; unskilled

unbeweglich *adj.* immovable; -es Gut real estate

unbewohnbar *adj.* uninhabitable

unbewohnt *adj.* uninhabited; vacant; desolated

unbewusst *adj.* unconscious; involuntary

unbezahlbar *adj.* invaluable; priceless

unbezahlt *adj.* unpaid; outstanding

unbezähmbar *adj.* untamable, indomitable

unbezwingbar, unbezwinglich *adj.* invincible; unconquerable; unsurmountable; indomitable

unbiegsam *adj.* unbending, inflexible; rigid

Unbill *f.* injury, injustice; wrong; inclemency

unbillig *adj.* unfair, unjust, unreasonable

unbotmässig *adj.* insubordinate, rebellious

unbrauchbar *adj.* useless; unserviceable; unfit

und *conj.* and; na —? well? nothing more?

Undank *m.*, Undankbarkeit *f.* ingratitude

undenkbar *adj.* unthinkable, inconceivable

undenklich *adj.* immemorial

Unding *neu.* absurdity, impossibility; nonsense

undurchführbar *adj.* impracticable, un-

feasible

undurchlässig *adj.* impermeable, impervious (to)

undurchsichtig *adj.* not transparent, opaque

uneben *adj.* uneven; rough; hilly; unsuitable; nicht — not bad, rather good; -bürtig *adj.* of inferior rank; inferior

unecht *adj.* not genuine, false; artificial; (colors) not fast; (math.) improper

unehelich *adj.* illegitimate

unehr: -enhaft *adj.* dishonorable; -erbietig *adj.* disrespectful; -lich *adj.* dishonest, insincere; underhanded; false

uneigennützig *adj.* disinterested, unselfish

uneigentlich *adj.* not literal, figurative

unein: -bringlich *adj.* irretrievable; -gedenk *adj.* regardless of; -geschränkt *adj.* unrestricted; -ig *adj.* disagreeing, discordant; -s *adv.* -s sein to disagree

unempfänglich *adj.* unsusceptible, unreceptive

unempfindlich *adj.* insensible (to), insensitive; indifferent, callous

unendlich *adj.* infinite, endless; vast

unent: -behrlich *adj.* indispensable; -geltlich *adj.* gratuitous, free; -schieden *adj.* undecided; (game) drawn; irresolute; -schiedene Frage open question: -schlossen *adj.* irresolute, hesitating; -schuldbar *adj.* inexcusable; -wegt *adj.* undeviating, steadfast, persistent; -wirrbar *adj.* inextricable; -zifferbar *adj.* undecipherable

uner: -achtet *prep.* notwithstanding, in spite of; -bittlich *adj.* inexorable, pitiless; -fahren *adj.* inexperienced; -findlich *adj.* undiscoverable, incomprehensible; -forschlich *adj.* inscrutable; -forscht *adj.* unexplored; -freulich *adj.* unpleasant, annoying; -füllbar *adj.* unrealizable; -giebig *adj.* unproductive; -gründlich *adj.* unfathomable; impenetrable; -heblich *adj.* insignificant, irrelevant; -hört *adj.* unheard (of); shocking; exorbitant; -kannt *adj.* unrecognized; -klärlich *adj.* inexplicable. perplexing; -lässlich *adj.* indispensable; -laubt *adj.* unlawful, prohibited; -ledigt *adj.* unfinished, unsettled; -messlich *adj.* immeasurable, immense; -müdlich *adj.* untiring; indefatigable; -quicklich *adj.* unpleasant; uncomfortable; -reichbar *adj.* unattainable; -reicht *adj.* unequalled; (sports) record; -sättlich *adj.* insatiable; -schlossen *adj.* undeveloped; -schöpflich *adj.* inexhaustible; -schrocken *adj.* intrepid, fearless; -schütterlich *adj.* imperturbable, firm; -schwinglich *adj.* beyond one's means; unattainable; -setzlich *adj.* irreplaceable; irreparable; -spriesslich *adj.* unprofitable; unpleasant; -träglich *adj.* intolerable; -wartet *adj.* unexpected; -weislich *adj.* undemonstrable; -widert *adj.* unanswered; unrequited; -wünscht *adj.* undesirable; unwelcome; -zogen *adj.* uneducated; ill-bred

unfähig *adj.* incapable; unable; disabled

Unfall *m.* accident; **–station** *f.* first-aid station; **–versicherung** *f.* accident insurance

unfassbar, unfasslich *adj.* inconceivable, incomprehensible. unintelligible

unfehlbar *adj.* infallible; — *adv.* certainly

unfein *adj.* coarse, indelicate, unmannerly

unfern *adv.* not far off, near(by); — *prep.* not far from, near

unfertig *adj.* unfinished, unready; immature

Unflat *m.* dirt, filth, nasty mess

unflätig *adj.* dirty, filthy; obscene

unförmig *adj.* deformed, misshapen; monstrous

unfrankiert *adj.* (mail) not prepaid; unfranked

unfreiwillig *adj.* involuntary, compulsory

Unfriede *m.* discord, dissension

unfruchtbar *adj.* unfruitful; barren, sterile

Unfug *m.* mischief, nuisance; misbehavior; **grober —** (law) disturbance of the peace

ungeachtet *adj.* not esteemed; — *prep.* notwithstanding, despite; — *conj.* although

ungeahndet *adj.* unpunished

ungeahnt *adj.* not anticipated, unexpected

ungebärdig *adj.* unruly, wild; unmannerly

ungebeten *adj.* unbidden, uninvited

ungebräuchlich *adj.* unusual; obsolete

Ungebühr *f.* indecency, impropriety; injustice

ungebührlich *adj.* indecent, improper; undue

ungebunden *adj.* unbound; unrestrained, free, loose; dissolute; **–e Rede** prose

ungedeckt *adj.* uncovered, unsheltered; (com.) dishonored; (table) not yet set

Ungeduld *f.* impatience

ungefähr *adj.* approximate; — *adv.* about, nearly; **von —** by chance, accidentally; **–det** *adj.* safe; not endangered; **–lich** *adj.* harmless

ungegliedert *adj.* unjointed, inarticulate

ungehalten *adj.* unkept; indignant; impatient

ungeheissen *adj.* unbidden; — *adv.* voluntarily

ungeheuchelt *adj.* unfeigned, sincere

Ungeheuer *neu.* monster; **–lichkeit** *f.* atrocity

ungeheuer *adj.* monstrous; colossal, enormous; — *adv.* exceedingly; **–lich** *adj.* monstrous

ungehobelt *adj.* unplaned; unmannered, rude

ungehörig *adj.* undue, unbecoming, improper

Ungehorsam *m.* disobedience; insubordination

ungekünstelt *adj.* artless; unaffected, natural

ungeladen *adj.* (gun) unloaded; uninvited

ungeläufig *adj.* unfamiliar; not fluent

ungelegen *adj.* inconvenient, inopportune

Ungelegenheit *f.* inconvenience, annoyance

ungelenk(ig) *adj.* awkward, clumsy, stiff

ungelernt *adj.* unskilled, untaught

ungelöscht *adj.* unquenched; unslaked (lime)

Ungemach *neu.* misfortune, hardship, adversity

ungemein *adj.* uncommon, extraordinary

ungemütlich *adj.* uncomfortable; unpleasant

ungenannt *adj.* unnamed; anonymous

ungenau *adj.* inaccurate, inexact

ungeniert *adj.* unceremonious; free and easy

ungeniessbar *adj.* uneatable, unpalatable

ungenügend *adj.* insufficient; unsatisfactory

ungenügsam *adj.* insatiable

ungeordnet *adj.* unarranged, unsettled

ungepflegt *adj.* untended; untidy, neglected

ungerade *adj.* not straight; uneven; odd

ungeraten *adj.* spoilt; undutiful; abortive

ungerecht *adj.* unjust, unfair; **–fertigt** *adj.* unjustified, unwarranted

ungereimt *adj.* rhymeless; absurd

ungern *adv.* unwillingly, reluctantly

ungesäuert *adj.* unleavened

ungesäumt *adj.* seamless, unhemmed; immediate, prompt; — *adv.* without delay, at once

ungeschehen *adj.* undone

Ungeschick *neu.* misfortune

ungeschickt *adj.* inept, unskillful; awkward

ungeschlacht *adj.* uncouth; coarse; clumsy

ungeschliffen *adj.* unpolished; rude, uncouth

ungeschoren *adj.* unshorn, unshaven; unmolested; **— lassen** to leave alone; not to bother

ungesehen *adj.* unseen, unnoticed

ungesetzlich *adj.* illegal, unlawful

ungestalt(et) *adj.* deformed, misshapen

ungestört *adj.* undisturbed, uninterrupted

ungestraft *adj.* unpunished; — *adv.* with impunity

ungestüm *adj.* impetuous, violent, raging

Ungestüm *m.* and *neu.* impetuosity, violence

ungeteilt *adj.* undivided; unanimous; entire

Ungetüm *neu.* monster

ungewiss *adj.* uncertain, doubtful

Ungewissheit *f.* uncertainty; **in — lassen** to keep in suspense

Ungewitter *neu.* thunderstorm; violent storm

ungewöhnlich *adj.* uncommon, unusual; strange

ungewohnt *adj.* unaccustomed, unfamiliar

ungezählt *adj.* uncounted; innumerable

Ungeziefer *neu.* vermin

ungeziemend *adj.* unseemly; improper

ungezogen *adj.* naughty; ill-bred; uncivil

ungezwungen *adj.* unforced; unaffected, easy

Unglaube *m.* disbelief, unbelief

ungläubig *adj.* incredulous, unbelieving

unglaublich *adj.* incredible

ungleich *adj.* unequal; uneven; odd; unlike, dissimilar; different; — *adv.* incomparably, much; **–artig** *adj.* dissimilar, heterogeneous; **–förmig** *adj.* unequal, irregular; **–mässig** *adj.* disproportionate, unsymmetrical

Unglimpf *m.* harshness; affront; insult; wrong

Unglück *neu.* misfortune; bad luck; accident; calamity, disaster; **–sbotschaft** *f.* evil tidings; **–sfall** *m.* accident, mishap; casualty; **–srabe** *m.* hoodoo; **–sstunde** *f.* fatal hour; **–svogel** *m.* bird of ill omen; unlucky person

unglück: –lich *adj.* unhappy; fatal, unrequited; **–licherweise** *adv.* unfortunately, by mischance; **–selig** *adj.* unfortunate, disastrous

Ungnade *f.* disgrace, disfavor; **in — fallen** to be disgraced; to incur displeasure

ungnädig *adj.* ungracious, unkind, illhumored

ungültig *adj.* invalid; not available; non current; **für — erklären**, **— machen** to invalidate, to void; to annul, to cancel

Ungunst *f.* disfavor; inclemency; unkindness

ungünstig *adj.* unfavorable, disadvantageous

ungut *adj.* unkind; **nichts für —!** no harm meant! don't be offended!

unhaltbar *adj.* not durable; untenable

unharmonisch *adj.* inharmonious, discordant

Unheil *neu.* evil, harm; disaster, calamity; **–stifter** *m.* mischief-maker

unheil: –bar *adj.* incurable; **–bringend** *adj.* disastrous, ruinous; **–schwanger** *adj.* fraught with disaster; **–voll** *adj.* calamitous

unheimlich *adj.* gruesome, sinister; **ihm wurde — zumute** he began to feel alarmed (*oder* uneasy); **— adv.** tremendously

unhöflich *adj.* impolite, uncivil, disrespectful

Unhold *m.* fiend, demon, monster

unhörbar *adj.* inaudible

unhygienisch *adj.* unsanitary

Uni: –form *f.* uniform; **–kum** *neu.* unique example (*oder* person); **–versalerbe** *m.* sole heir; **–versalmittel** *neu.* universal remedy, panacea; **–versität** *f.* university; **–versum** *neu.* universe

uni: –formiert *adj.* uniformed, uniform; **–versal** *adj.*, **–versell** *adj.* universal

Unke *f.* toad; (coll.) croaker

unkenntlich *adj.* unrecognizable

Unkenntnis *f.* ignorance

unkeusch *adj.* unchaste; impure, lewd

unklar *adj.* indistinct; unintelligible, obscure

unklug *adj.* imprudent, unwise

unkörperlich *adj.* incorporeal, immaterial

Unkosten *pl.* costs, charges, expenses

Unkraut *neu.* weed(s); **— vergeht nicht** evil doesn't perish

unkündbar *adj.* unredeemable; consolidated; permanent (position)

unkundig *adj.* unacquainted (with); ignorant

unlängst *adv.* not long ago, recently, lately

unlauter *adj.* impure; insincere, unfair

unleugbar *adj.* undeniable; incontestable

unlieb *adj.* disagreeable; **–enswürdig** *adj.* unfriendly; **–sam** *adj.* disagreeable, unpleasant

unliniert *adj.* unruled, without lines

unlogisch *adj.* illogical

unlösbar, unlöslich *adj.* insoluble

Unlust *f.* dislike, disinclination; aversion

unlustig *adj.* listless; disinclined, reluctant

unmännlich *adj.* unmanly

Unmass *neu.*, **Unmasse** *f.* vast quantity, inmense number

unmassgeblich *adj.* unauthoritative; **nach meiner –en Meinung** in my humble opinion

unmässig *adj.* immoderate; excessive

Unmenge *f.* vast quantity (*oder* number)

Unmensch *m.* monster, brute

unmenschlich *adj.* inhuman, brutal; monstrous; barbarous; **–e Kraft** enormous strength

unmerklich *adj.* imperceptible

unmittelbar *adj.* immediate, direct

unmöbliert *adj.* unfurnished

unmodern *adj.* unfashionable; out-of-date

unmöglich *adj.* impossible; out of the question; **sich — machen** to compromise oneself

unmoralisch *adj.* immoral

unmündig *adj.* minor; under age

Unmut *m.* displeasure, ill humor, peevishness

unnachahmlich *adj.* inimitable

unnachgiebig *adj.* unyielding, relentless

unnahbar *adj.* unapproachable, inaccessible

unnatürlich *adj.* unnatural, affected

unnötig *adj.* unnecessary, superfluous; **–erweise** *adv.* unnecessarily, needlessly

unnütz *adj.* useless, unprofitable; idle, vain; (coll.) fresh, naughty

Unordnung *f.* disorder, untidiness; confusion; **in — bringen** to throw into confusion; to disarrange; **in — sein** to be in a mess

unparteiisch *adj.* impartial, unbiased

Unparteiische *m.* referee, umpire

unpassend *adj.* unfit, unsuitable; improper; unbecoming; inopportune; **sie benahm sich sehr —** she behaved in an unladylike way

unpässlich *adj.* indisposed; ailing

unpolitisch *adj.* unpolitic; undiplomatic

unpraktisch *adj.* impracticable; unskilful

unqualifiziert *adj.* unqualified

Unrat *m.* dirt, garbage, refuse; excrements; **— wittern** to smell a rat

unrätlich, unratsam *adj.* inadvisable

Unrecht *neu.* injustice; wrong; error; **an den –en kommen** to meet one's match; **im — sein, — haben** to be mistaken (*oder* wrong); **jemand — geben** to decide against someone; **jemand — tun** to wrong someone

unrecht *adj.* wrong; unfair, unjust; improper, inopportune; **am –en Ort sein** to be out of place; **–mässig** *adj.* unlawful, illegal

unregelmässig *adj.* irregular; abnormal
unrein *adj.* unclean, impure; **-er Diamant** clouded (*oder* flawed) diamond; **-er Ton** (mus.) discord; **ins -e schreiben** to make a rough copy; **-lich** *adj.* dirty, filthy
unrentabel *adj.* unremunerative
unrettbar *adj.* past help, irrecoverable; **— verloren** irretrievably lost
unrichtig *adj.* incorrect, wrong; erroneous
Unruh *f.* (watch) balance; **-e** *f.* uneasiness; commotion, disturbance; riot; **-estifter** *m.* agitator, disturber of the peace
unruhig *adj.* restless, unquiet; uneasy; agitated; turbulent; **-e See** rough sea; **-es Pferd** restive horse; **-e Zeiten** troubled times
uns *pron.* (to) us; ourselves; **ein Freund von —** a friend of ours; **unter —** between ourselves; **wir sehen — nie** we never see each other; **-er** *pron.* our, ours; of us; **erbarme dich -er** have mercy upon us; **-(e)rige** *adj.* ours; our people; **-ereiner** *pron.*, **-ereins** *pron.* one of us, such as we; **-esgleichen** *adj.* people like us; **-erthalben** *adv.*, **-ertwegen** *adv.*, **-ertwillen** *adv.* on our account; for our sakes
unsachlich *adj.* not to the point; subjective
unsagbar, unsäglich *adj.* inexpressible; unutterable; immense
unsanft *adj.* ungentle, harsh
unsauber *adj.* unclean, dirty; filthy; unfair
unschädlich *adj.* harmless, innocuous; **— machen** to render harmless; to disarm; to neutralize
unschätzbar *adj.* invaluable; priceless
unscheinbar *adj.* unpretentious; plain
unschicklich *adj.* improper, unseemly; indecent
unschlüssig *adj.* irresolute; undecided
unschön *adj.* unlovely, unsightly; unfair
Unschuld *f.* innocence
unschuldig *adj.* innocent, guiltless; harmless
unschwer *adj.* not difficult, easy
unselbständig *adj.* dependent (on others)
unselig *adj.* unfortunate; fatal, accursed
unsicher *adj.* insecure, unsafe; unsteady; uncertain; irresolute; precarious
unsichtbar *adj.* invisible
Unsinn *m.* nonsense, absurdity
unsinnig *adj.* nonsensical, unreasonable; absurd
Unsitte *f.* bad habit; abuse
unsittlich *adj.* immoral; indecent
unstatthaft *adj.* inadmissible, illicit; illegal
unsterblich *adj.* immortal; **— machen to** immortalize
Unstern *m.* unlucky star; disaster, misfortune
unstet *adj.* unsteady; inconstant; restless
unstillbar *adj.* unappeasable, unquenchable
unsträflich *adj.* irreproachable; blameless

unstreitig *adj.* incontestable, indisputable; **— adv.** undoubtedly
unsympathisch *adj.* unpleasant, disagreeable; **er ist mir —** I don't like him
untadelhaft, untadelig *adj.* blameless; irreprochable
Untat *f.* crime, outrage
untätig *adj.* inactive, idle
untauglich *adj.* unfit; useless; disabled
unteilbar *adj.* indivisible
unten *adv.* below; downstairs; at the bottom; **nach —** downward; **— durch sein** (coll.) to be despised; **von oben bis —** from top to bottom; **von — auf dienen** to rise from the ranks; **-an** *adv.* at the lower end
unter *prep.* under; below, beneath, underneath; among(st); by; during; **nicht — drei Pfund** not less than three pounds; **— der Hand** privately; **— dieser Bedingung** on this condition; **— freiem Himmel** in the open air; **— seiner Regierung** in his reign; **— Tage** (min.) underground; **— uns** among ourselves; between us; **— adj.** under, lower, inferior
Unter *m.* (cards) jack, knave
Unterabteilung *f.* subdivision; subunit
Unterarm *m.* forearm
Unterbau *m.* substructure, foundation
unterbauen *v.* to build a substructure; to lay a foundation; to undergird
Unterbeamte *m.* subordinate official
unterbelichten *v.* (phot.) to underexpose
Unterbett *neu.* underbedding, feather bed
Unterbewusstsein *neu.* (the) subconscious
unterbieten *v.* to underbid, to undercut, to undersell; (sports) to lower (record)
Unterbilanz *f.* (com.) deficit
unterbleiben *v.* to be left undone; **not to** take place; to cease, to be discontinued
unterbrechen *v.* to interrupt; to cut short; to stop; to intercept; to break (circuit)
Unterbrechung *f.* interruption; intermission; break, stop; disturbance
unterbreiten *v.* to spread underneath; **jemand —** to lay (*oder* submit to) someone
unterbringen *v.* to place; to accomodate; to shelter; to sell; to billet (troops)
unter der Hand *adv.* secretly
underdes(sen) *adv.* meanwhile, in the meantime
Unterdruckkammer *f.* altitude chamber
unterdrücken *v.* to oppress; to repress; to suppress; to crush, to quell
untereinander *adv.* each other; among themselves; mutually, reciprocally
unterernährt *adj.* undernourished, underfed
unterfangen *v.* to dare; to undertake
Unterfangen *neu.* undertaking, venture
Unterfertigte *m.* (the) undersigned
Unterführung *f.* subway; underpass
Untergang *m.* setting; sinking; decline; destruction, ruin, fall
Untergebene *m.* subordinate, menial; inferior
unterge(h)en *v.* to sink, to founder; (ast.) to set; to decline, to perish

untergeordnet *adj.* subordinate; **-e Rolle** minor part; **von -er Bedeutung** of secondary importance

Untergeschoss *neu.* basement

Untergestell *neu.* undercarriage, chassis

Untergewicht *neu.* underweight

untergraben *v.* to undermine, to sap

Untergrund *m.* subsoil; substructure; background; underground; **-bahn** *f.* (rail.) subway

unterhalb *prep.* below, under, at the lower end

Unterhalt *m.* maintenance, support, livelihood; **-ung** *f.* conversation; amusement, entertainment; maintenance; **-ungslektüre** *f.*, **-ungsliteratur** *f.* light reading

unterhalt: **-en** *v.* to support, to maintain, to keep up; to entertain, to amuse; **sich -en** to converse (with); to enjoy oneself; **-end** *adj.*, **-sam** *adj.* amusing, entertaining

unterhandeln *v.* to negotiate, to parley

Unterhändler *m.* negotiator, mediator; agent; (coll.) go-between

Unterhandlung *f.* negotiation; **in -en stehen** to carry on negotiations

Unterhaus *neu.* Lower House, House of Commons; House of Representatives

Unterhemd *neu.* undershirt

unterhöhlen *v.* to undermine; to tunnel

Unterholz *neu.* underwood, underbrush

Unterhosen *f. pl.* underpants, drawers

unterirdisch *adj.* underground; subterranean

unterjochen *v.* to subdue, to subjugate

Unterkiefer *m.* lower jaw

Unterkleid *neu.* slip; **-ung** *f.* underwear

unterkommen *v.* to find accommodations (*oder* lodging); to get employment

Unterkommen *neu.* accommodation, lodging, shelter; employment

Unterkörper *m.* underbody

unterkriegen *v.* to get the better of; **sich nicht — lassen** to hold one's own (ground)

Unterkunft *f.* accommodation, lodging, shelter

Unterlage *f.* foundation, basis; support; document, evidence, record; blotting pad; (geol.) substratum

Unterlass *m.* **ohne —** without intermission; incessantly

unterlassen *v.* to neglect, to omit; to fail to do; to abstain (from)

unterlaufen *v.* to slip in; to occur; **es können leicht Fehler —** mistakes can easily be made; **mit Blut —** suffused with blood, bloodshot

unterlegen *v.* to lay (*oder* put) underneath; to attach (meaning to); to set (words to music)

Unterleib *m.* abdomen; bowels

unterliegen *v.* to succumb; to be defeated (*oder* overcome); **es unterliegt keinem Zweifel** there is not doubt about it

Unterlippe *f.* underlip; lower lip

untermengen, untermischen *v.* to intermix; to mix up; to intermingle

unterminieren *v.* to undermine; **-d** *adj.*

(mil.) subversive

unternehmen *v.* to undertake; to attempt; **-d** *adj.* enterprising, lively; bold, daring

Unternehmer *m.* contractor; entrepreneur; employer; **-verband** *m.* syndicate, pool

Unternehmung *f.* enterprise; operation

Unteroffizier *m.* (mil.) noncommissioned officer; corporal; (naut.) petty officer

unterordnen *v.* to subordinate; **von untergeordneter Bedeutung** of secondary importance

Unterpfand *neu.* pledge, security

Unterprima *f.* lower division of the highest grade of a German Junior college

unterreden *v.* **sich —** to converse, to confer

Unterricht *m.* teaching, training; instruction, lesson; **-sbriefe** *m. pl.* instruction by correspondence; **-sfach** *neu.* branch of instruction, educational subject; **-swesen** *neu.* public instruction, educational matters

unterrichten *v.* to instruct, to teach; to educate, to train; to inform; **sich von etwas —** to inform oneself

Unterrock *m.* petticoat

untersagen *v.* to forbid, to prohibit; to interdict

Untersatz *m.* basis; stand; pedestal; saucer; (phil.) minor proposition

unterschätzen *v.* to underestimate, to underrate

unterscheiden *v.* to distinguish; to differentiate; to discern; **sich — von** to differ from

Unterscheidungsmerkmal *neu.* distinctive mark

Unterschenkel *m.* (anat.) shank

unterschieben *v.* to push (*oder* shove) under; to substitute; to foist upon; to insinuate

Unterschied *m.* difference, distinction; **ohne —** indiscriminately

unterschied: **-en** *adj.*, **-lich** *adj.* different, distinct; **-slos** *adv.* indiscriminately, without distinction (*oder* exception)

unterschlagen *v.* to embezzle; to intercept; to suppress; to defraud

Unterschleif *m.* embezzlement, fraud

Unterschlupf *m.* refuge, shelter

unterschreiben *v.* to sign; to subscribe to

Unterschrift *f.* signature; caption

Unterseeboot *neu.* submarine

unterseeisch *adj.* submarine

Untersekunda *f.* lower division of the second grade of a German secondary school

untersetzt *adj.* thick-set, stocky, dumpy

Unterstaatssekretär *m.* Undersecretary of State

Unterstand *m.* cover, shelter; (mil.) dugout

unterstehen *v.* to stand under; to take shelter; to be subordinate to; **sich —** to dare, to venture

unterstreichen *v.* to underline; to emphasize

Unterstufe *f.* (school) lower grade

unterstützen *v.* to aid, to assist, to support; to second; to patronize, to subsidize

Unterstützungsfonds m. relief fund

untersuchen v. to inquire (*oder* search) into; to examine; to scrutinize; to explore; to analyze; to investigate; to probe

Untersuchung f. investigation; **–sgefangene** m. prisoner under trial; **–shaft** f. detention before trial; **–srichter** m. examining judge

Untertan m. subject; serf, vassal

untertänig adj. humble, submissive, subject

Untertasse f. saucer

untertauchen v. to dive, to dip; to submerge

Unterteil m. lower part; base, bottom

Untertitel m. subtitle, subheading

Unterton m. undertone; (phys.) accessory sound

unterwärts adj. downwards; underneath

Unterwäsche f. underwear

Unterwasserbombe f. depth charge

unterwegs adv. on the way; immer — always on the move

unterweisen v. to instruct, to teach

Unterwelt f. underworld, lower regions; Hades

unterwerfen v. to subjugate, to subdue; to subject; **sich —** to submit, to be resigned

unterwinden v. sich — to venture upon; to undertake; to attempt

unterwühlen v. to undermine

unterwürfig adj. submissive; servile

Unterzeichn: –er m. signatory; **–ete** m. undersigned; **–ung** f. signing; ratification

Unterzeug neu. underwear

unterziehen v. to draw under; to put on underneath; **sich einer Operation —** to submit (*oder* undergo) an operation; **sich einer Sache —** to undertake something

Untiefe f. shallow place, sandbank; (fig.) bottomless depth, abyss

Untier neu. monster; savage animal

untilgbar adj. indelible; irredeemable

untrennbar adj. inseparable

untreu adj. unfaithful, disloyal; **einer Sache — werden** to desert a cause

Untreue f. unfaithfulness, disloyalty; **im Amt** breach of trust

untröstlich adj. disconsolate, inconsolable

untrüglich adj. infallible, unmistakable

untüchtig adj. incapable, unfit; incompetent

Untugend f. bad habit, vice

unüber: –legt adj. inconsiderate, rash; **–sehbar** adj. incalculable; immense, vast; **–setzbar** adj. untranslatable; **–steigbar** adj. insurmountable; **–tragbar** adj. not transferable; unassignable; **–treffbar** adj., **–trefflich** adj. unsurpassable, unequalled; **–troffen** adj. unexcelled, unsurpassed; **–windlich** adj. invincible, unconquerable; insurmountable

unum: –gänglich adj. indispensable; inevitable; **–schränkt** adj. unlimited; absolute; **–stösslich** adj. irrefutable, irrevocable; **–wunden** adj. unreserved; candid, frank, plain

ununterbrochen adj. uninterrupted; incessant

unveränderlich adj. unchangeable; invariable

unverantwortlich adj. irresponsible; inexcusable

unverbesserlich adj. incorrigible

unverbindlich adj. disobliging, unkind

unverblümt adj. blunt, plain; unadorned

unverbrennbar adj. incombustible

unverbürgt adj. unwarranted; unconfirmed

unverdaulich adj. indigestible

unverderbt, unverdorben adj. uncorrupted, unspoiled; unblemished; pure, spotless

unverdient adj. undeserved, unmerited; unjust; **–ermassen** adv. undeservingly, unjustly

unverdrossen adj. indefatigable, untiring

unverdünnt adj. undiluted

unverehelicht adj. unmarried; single

unvereinbar adj. incompatible, irreconcilable

unverfälscht adj. unadulterated; genuine, pure

unverfänglich adj. not captious, harmless

unverfroren adj. unabashed, audacious; impudent

unvergänglich adj. imperishable; immortal

unvergesslich adj. unforgettable

unvergleichlich adj. incomparable; unique

unverhältnismässig adj. disproportionate; excessive

unverheiratet adj. unmarried

unverhofft adj. unexpected; unforeseen; **–es Glück** windfall

unverhohlen adj. unconcealed; frank, open

unverkäuflich adj. unsaleable, unmarketable; **–e Ware** dead stock

unverkennbar adj. unmistakable; evident

unverkürzt adj. uncurtailed; unabridged

unverletzbar adj. invulnerable; inviolable

unverletzt adj. unhurt, uninjured; undamaged

unvermählt adj. unmarried

unvermeidbar, unvermeidlich adj. unavoidable; inevitable; fatal

unvermerkt adj. unperceived; unnoticed

unvermischt adj. unmixed; unadulterated; unalloyed; pure

unvermittelt adj. abrupt, sudden

Unvermögen neu. incapacity; impotence

unvermögend adj. incapable; impotent; powerless; penniless, poor

unvermutet adj. unexpected, unforeseen

unvernehmlich adj. inaudible; unintelligible

Unvernunft f. unreasonableness; folly

unvernünftig adj. unreasonable; irrational

unverrichtet adj. unperformed, not carried out

unverrückt adv. immovably; fixedly; **–ansehen** to gaze steadily at

unverschämt adj. shameless, impudent; **-e Preise** exhorbitant prices

unverschuldet adj. undeserved, unmerited; not in debt; unencumbered; **-erweise** adv. undeservedly; innocently

unversehens adv. unawares, unexpectedly

unversehrt adj. uninjured; intact, safe

unversichert adj. uninsured

unversiegbar, unversieglich adj. inexhaustible

unversöhnlich adj. irreconcilable; implacable

unversorgt adj. unprovided for, destitute

Unverstand m. want of judgment (oder sense); lack of intelligence; folly, stupidity

unverständig adj. imprudent; foolish, unwise

unverständlich adj. unintelligible; incomprehensible; **die Sache ist mir ganz —** I cannot make head or tail of the affair

unversteuerbar adj. untaxable

unversucht adj. unattempted, untried; **nichts — lassen** to leave no stone unturned

unvertilgbar adj. indelible, indestructible

unverträglich adj. unsociable, incompatible; intolerant, quarrelsome

unverwandt adj. unmoved, steadfast, fixed

unverweilt adv. without delay, immediately

unverweslich adj. incorruptible, undecaying

unverwundbar adj. invulnerable

unverwüstlich adj. indestructible; inexhaustible; everlasting; irrepressible (humor)

unverzagt adj. undismayed, undaunted, bold

unverzeihlich adj. unpardonable, inexcusable

unverzinsbar, unverzinslich adj. paying no interest

unverzüglich adj. immediate, instant, prompt

unvoll: -endet adj. uncompleted, unfinished; **-kommen** adj. imperfect, defective; **-ständig** adj. incomplete

unvor: -bereitet adj. unprepared; extempore; **-denklich** adj. immemorial; **-hergesehen** adj. unforeseen, unexpected; **-sätzlich** adj. unpremeditated, unintentional; **-sichtig** adj. incautious; imprudent; **-teilhaft** adj. unprofitable, disadvantageous; unbecoming; **-teilhaft aussehen** not to look one's best

unwahr adj. untrue, false; **-haftig** adj. untruthful, insincere; **-scheinlich** adj. improbable, unlikely

unwandelbar adj. immutable, unchangeable

unwegsam adj. impassable, impracticable

unweit adj. not far off, near(by); — prep. not far from, close to, near

unwert adj. unworthy

Unwesen neu. disorder; annoyance, nuisance; **sein — treiben** to be up to one's tricks; to haunt (a place)

unwesentlich adj. unessential, immaterial; unimportant; **das ist —** that doesn't matter

Unwetter neu. bad weather; thunderstorm

unwichtig adj. unimportant, insignificant

unwider: -legbar adj., **-leglich** adj. irrefutable; **-ruflich** adj. irrevocable; **-stehlich** adj. irresistible

unwill: -ig adj. unwilling; reluctant; indignant; **-kommen** adj. unwelcome; unpleasant; **-kürlich** adj. involuntary, instinctive

Unwille m. indignation; wrath, reluctance

unwirklich adj. unreal

unwirksam adj. ineffectual, inoperative; void

unwirsch adj. cross, rude, uncouth

unwirtschaftlich adj. uneconomic

unwissen: -d adj. ignorant; **-schaftlich** adj. unscientific; **-tlich** adv. unknowingly

unwohl adj. unwell, indisposed

Unwohlsein neu. indisposition; menstruation

unwohnlich adj. uninhabitable; uncomfortable

unwürdig adj. unworthy

Unzahl f. immense number

unzählbar, unzählig adj. innumerable, countless

Unze f. ounce

Unzeit f. wrong time; **zur —** inopportunely

unzeitgemäss adj. behind the times, inopportune

unzeitig adj. untimely, ill-timed; premature

unzerbrechlich adj. unbreakable, infrangible

unzerreissbar adj. untearable, solid

unzerstörbar adj. indestructible, imperishable

unzertrennlich adj. inseparable; inherent

unziemend, unziemlich adj. unbecoming, improper

unzivilisiert adj. uncivilized; barbarous

Unzucht f. unchastity; prostitution

unzüchtig adj. unchaste; lewd; obscene

unzufrieden adj. dissatisfied, discontented

unzu: -gänglich adj. inaccessible; reserved; **-länglich** adj. inadequate, insufficient; **-lässig** adj. inadmissible; **-rechnungsfähig** adj. irresponsible; imbecile; **-reichend** adj. insufficient; **-sammenhängend** adj. disconnected; incoherent; **-ständig** adj. incompetent; **-träglich** adj. disadvantageous; unwholesome; **-treffend** adj. incorrect; **-verlässig** adj. unreliable, uncertain

unzweckmässig adj. inexpedient, unsuitable

unzweideutig adj. unequivocal, unambiguous

unzweifelhaft adj. undoubted, indubitable

üppig adj. luxuriant; exuberant; voluptuous; abundant; well-developed (shape)

Urahn m. great-grandfather; ancestor; **-e** f. great-grandmother; ancestress

uralt adj. old as the hills; ancient, primeval

Uran *neu.* uranium
Uraufführung *f.* first performance
urbar *adj.* arable; cultivated; **— machen** to bring under cultivation, to cultivate
Urbewohner *m. pl.* aborigines
Urbild *neu.* original, prototype, archetype
Urchristentum *neu.* primitive Christianity; the early Church
Ureinwohner *m. pl.* native inhabitants
Ureltern *pl.* first parents; ancestors
Urenkel *m.* great-grandchild; greatgrandson; **-in** *f.* great-granddaughter
Urgross: -eltern *pl.* great-grandparents; **-mutter** *f.* great-grandmother; **-vater** *m.* great-grandfather
Urheber *m.* author, originator, creator; **-recht** *neu.* copyright; **-schaft** *f.* authorship
Urin *m.* urine
urinieren *v.* to urinate
Urkunde *f.* document; record; charter; evidence
Urlaub *m.* leave; furlough; vacation; **-er** *m.* soldier on furlough
Urmensch *m.* primitive man
Urne *f.* urn; ballot box; **zur — gehen** to vote
urplötzlich *adj.* very sudden
Urquell *m.* primary source; origin
Ursache *f.* cause, reason, motive; **keine —** don't mention it
ursächlich *adj.* causal; causative
Urschrift *f.* original text; first draft
Ursprache *f.* primitive (*oder* original) language
Ursprung *m.* source; origin; beginning, cause
ursprünglich *adj.* original, primitive, primary
Urstoff *m.* primary matter; element
Urteil *neu.* judgment, opinion; sentence, verdict; **-seröffnung** *f.* publication of a judgment; **-skraft** *f.*, **-svermögen** *neu.* power of judgment; **-sspruch** *m.* sentence, verdict
urteil: -en *v.* to express one's opinion; to judge; to pass sentence; **-sfähig** *adj.* competent to judge, judicious; **-slos** *adj.* without judgment, injudicious
Urtext *m.* original text
Urtier *neu.* protozoan, primitive animal
Ururelltern *pl.* progenitors, early ancestors
Urvater *m.* first progenitor
Urvolk *neu.* primitive people; aborigines
Urwahl *f.* primary election
Urwald *m.* primeval forest
urwüchsig *adj.* native, original; rough, blunt
Urzeit *f.* primeval period
Usurpator *m.* usurper
usurpieren *v.* to usurp
Utensilien *f. pl.* utensils, tools, implements
Utopie *f.* Utopian scheme, chimera
utopisch *adj.* utopian
uzen *v.* (coll.) to tease, to fool

V

vag *adj.* vague; **-abundieren** *v.* to tramp, to roam, to stroll about

Vagabund *m.* vagabond, tramp, bum; **-entum** *neu.* vagrancy
Vakanz *f.* vacancy
Valuta *f.* rate (of exchange); currency
Vampir *m.* vampire
Van Allens Radiationsgürtel *m.* Van Allen Radiation Belt
Vanille *f.* vanilla; **-nschote** *f.* vanilla bean
Var: -iante *f.* variant; **-iation** *f.* variation; **-ieté** *neu.* variety theater
variieren *v.* to vary; to compose variations
Vas: -all *m.* vassal; **-allenstaat** *m.* satellite
Vase *f.* vase
Vaselin *neu.*, **Vaseline** *f.* Vaseline
Vater *m.* father; **-haus** *neu.* parental house; **-land** *neu.* native country; **-landsliebe** *f.* patriotism; **-mörder** *m.* parricide; (coll.) high stiff collar; **-schaft** *f.* paternity, fatherhood; **-sname** *m.* surname; **-stadt** *f.* native city; **-stelle** *f.*, **-stelle vertreten** to be a father to; to father; **-teil** *neu.* patrimony; **-unser** *neu.* Lord's Prayer
vater: -ländisch *adj.* national, patriotic; **-landsliebend** *adj.* patriotic; **-los** *adj.* fatherless
väterlich *adj.* fatherly, paternal; **-erseits** *adv.* on the father's side
vege: -tarisch *adj.* vegetarian; **-tativ** *adj.* vegetative; vegetable; **-tieren** *v.* to vegetate
Vegetarier *m.* vegetarian
Vehemenz *f.* vehemence
Veilchen *neu.* violet; **-wurzel** *f.* orris root
Veitstanz *m.* St. Vitus' dance
Vene *f.* vein; **-nentzündung** *f.* phlebitis
venerisch *adj.* venereal
Ventil *neu.* valve; **-ator** *m.* ventilator; fan
verab: -folgen *v.* to deliver, to hand over; to remit; **-reden** *v.* to agree upon; **sich -reden** to make an appointment (*oder* a date); **-redetermassen** *adv.* as agreed upon; **-reichen** *v.* to give, to hand over; **-säumen** to neglect, to omit; **-scheuen** *v.* to abhor, to detest; **-scheuenswert** *adj.*, **-scheuenswürdig** *adj.* abominable, detestable; **-schieden** *v.* to discharge, to dismiss; to disband; **ein Gesetz -schieden** to pass a bill; **sich -schieden** to take leave of, to bid farewell
verachten *v.* to despise, to disdain
verächtlich *adj.* contemptuous; contemptible
verallgemeinern *v.* to generalize
veraltet *adj.* antiquated, obsolete
veran: -kern *v.* to anchor, to moor; to establish firmly; **-lagen** *v.* to assess; **-lagt** *adj.* gifted, talented; **-lassen** *v.* to cause, to occasion; to induce; **-schaulichen** *v.* to illustrate; to make clear; **-schlagen** *v.* to estimate, to rate; **-stalten** *v.* to arrange, to organize
Veran: -lagung *f.* assessment; talent, disposition; **-staltung** *f.* arrangement; (sport) event; performance
Veranda *f.* veranda, porch
veränderlich *adj.* changeable, variable; unstable; unsettled; fluctuating
verändern *v.* to alter, to change; to vary;

to transform; **sich —** to become changed; (coll.) to take another position

verantwort: -en v. to answer (*oder* account) for; **sich -en** to justify oneself; **-lich** adj. responsible; **-ungslos** adj. irresponsible; **-ungsvoll** adj. imposing responsibility

Verantwortung f. responsibility; justification; **auf seine —** at his own risk; **zur — ziehen** to call to account

verar: -beiten v. to work up; to manufacture; to assimilate; to digest; to wear out; **-gen** v. to take amiss, to misconstrue; **-men** v. to become impoverished; **-zten** r. (coll.) to doctor

verauktionieren v. to (sell at) auction

verausgaben v. to spend; **sich —** to run short of money

veräusserlich adj. alienable; saleable

veräussern v. to alienate; to dispose of

verballhornen v. to edit ridiculously

Verband m. union; formation, unit; (med.) bandage, dressing; **-flug** m. formation; **-päckchen** neu. (mil.) field dressing; **-platz** m. first-aid station; **-smitglied** neu. member of a society; **-stoff** m., **-zeug** neu. bandaging material

verbannen v. to banish, to exile; to outlaw

verbarrikadieren v. to barricade, to block

verbauen v. to build (*oder* block) up; to obstruct; to spend in building, to build badly

verbergen v. to conceal, to hide

verbessern v. to correct; to improve

verbeugen v. **sich —** to (make a) bow

verbiegen v. to bend, to twist, to warp

verbieten v. to forbid, to prohibit

verbilligen v. to reduce in price, to cheapen

verbinden v. to bind (up); to bandage, to dress (wound); to join, to unite; to combine; (tel.) to connect; **ich bin Ihnen sehr verbunden** I am very much obliged to you

verbindlich adj. binding, obligatory; obliging

Verbindlichkeit f. obligation; liability; obligingness, courtesy

Verbindung f. combination, union; association, society, contact; communication, connection; blending (of colors); amalgamation; compound; **sich in — setzen** to get into touch, to contact; **-sbahn** f. (rail.) branch line; **-sgang** m. connecting passage; **-smann** m. mediator; **-soffizier** m. liaison officer; **-sstück** neu. joint; coupling, tie

verbissen adj. obstinate; crabbed, dogged

verbitten v. not to permit; **das verbitte ich mir** I won't stand that

verbittern v. to embitter

verblassen v. to fade, to (turn) pale

verblättern v. to lose one's place (in book)

Verbleib m. whereabouts

verbleichen v. to (turn) pale; to fade

verblenden v. to blind; to screen; to mask; to face (wall); to delude, to infatuate

verblichen adj. faded; deceased

Verblichene m. deceased

verblüffen v. to bewilder, to dumbfound

verblühen v. to fade, to wither

verblümt adj. veiled; figurative, allusive

verbluten v. **sich —** to bleed to death

verbohrt adj. obstinate, stubborn; mad

verborgen v. to lend; **—** adj. concealed, hidden, secret; **-erweise** adv. stealthily

Verbot neu. prohibition, veto

verboten adj. forbidden, prohibited; illicit; **-er Eingang!** no admission!

Verbrauch m. consumption; expenditure; **-er** m. consumer; **-steuer** f. excise tax

verbrauchen v. to consume, to use; to wear out

Verbrech: -en neu. crime; **-er** m. criminal, felon; **-erkolonie** f. penal colony; **-tum** neu. outlawry

verbrechen v. to commit (a crime)

verbrecherisch adj. criminal

verbreiten v. to spread, to diffuse; to disseminate; to circulate; **sich — über** to enlarge upon (a theme); to expatiate on

verbrennbar adj. combustible

verbrennen v. to burn; to scorch; to cremate

Verbrennung f. burn(ing); combustion; cremation; **-smotor** m. combustion engine; **-sofen** m. crematory, incinerator

verbriefen v. to guarantee by documents

verbringen v. to pass (time); to spend

verbrüdern v. **sich —** to fraternize

verbrühen v. to scald

verbuchen v. to book

Verb(um) neu. verb; **-alinjurie** f. (law) libel

verbummeln v. to trifle (*oder* idle) away; (coll.) to forget, to neglect

verbunden adj. united, connected; obliged

verbünden o. **sich — mit** to ally (*oder* unite) oneself with

Verbündete m. ally, confederate

verbürgen v. to guarantee; **sich — für** to vouch (*oder* answer) for

verbüssen v. to suffer the consequences; to serve time; to complete a sentence

Verdacht m. suspicion; distrust

verdächtig adj. suspicious; doubtful

verdächtigen v. to cast suspicion on; to distrust; to accuse, to incriminate

Verdächtigung f. insinuation; false charge

verdamm: -en v. to condemn; to damn; **-enswert** adj. damnable; **-t!** interj. damn it!

Verdammnis f. damnation, perdition

Verdammung f. condemnation; damnation

verdampfen v. to evaporate; to vaporize

verdanken v. to owe to; to be obliged to

Verdau: -lichkeit f. digestibleness; **-ung** f. digestion; **-ungsbeschwerden** f. pl., **-ungsstörung** f. indigestion

verdauen v. to digest

Verdeck neu. (mech.) top, hood; (naut.) deck

verdecken v. to cover; to conceal; to veil

verdenken v. to take amiss; to blame

Verderb m. ruin; decay; waste; **-en** neu. corruption; destruction; ruin; **-er** m. corrupter; destroyer

verderb: -en v. to spoil; to destroy, to,

ruin; to corrupt; to perish; es mit jemand **–en** to lose someone's favor; sich den **Magen –en** to upset one's stomach; **–lich** *adj.* perishable, pernicious; fatal; **–t** *adj.* corrupted; depraved

verdeutlichen *v.* to elucidate; to make plain

verdeutschen *v.* to translate into German

verdichten *v.* to condense, to compress; to solidify; to consolidate

verdicken *v.* to thicken, to condense

verdien: –en *v.* to earn; to deserve; to merit; **er hat sich um sein Land –t gemacht** he has served his country well; **habe ich das um Sie –t?** have I deserved that from you? **–stlich** *adj.*, **–stvoll** *adj.*, **–t** *adj.* deserving; meritorious; **–termassen** *adv.*, **–terweise** *adv.* deservedly; according to one's merit

Verdienst *m.* earnings; gain, profit; — *neu.* merit; **–spanne** *f.* margin of profit

verdingen *v.* to hire out; **sich** — to take a position

verdolmetschen *v.* to interpret

verdonnern *v.* (coll.) to condemn, to punish

verdoppeln *v.* to double; to redouble

verdorben *adj.* spoiled, tainted; depraved

verdorren *v.* to dry up, to wither

verdrängen *v.* to push aside; to displace; to repress, to supplant; to inhibit

verdrehen *v.* to twist; to sprain; (eyes) to roll; to distort, to misrepresent; **jemand den Kopf** — to turn someone's head **verdreht** *adj.* distorted, twisted; cracked, crazy, mad; misrepresented

verdreifachen *v.* to treble, to triple

verdriessen *v.* to annoy, to grieve; **es sich nicht** — **lassen** not to be discouraged by; **sich keine Mühe** — **lassen** to spare no pains

verdriesslich *adj.* annoyed, cross, peevish; ill-humored; annoying, irksome, unpleasant

verdrossen *adj.* sulky, listless, cross

verdrucken *v.* to misprint

Verdruss *m.* annoyance, vexation, trouble

verduften *v.* to evaporate; (coll.) to slip away, to vanish

verdummen *v.* to make (*oder* become) stupid

verdunkeln *v.* to darken, to cloud; to black out; to eclipse; to obscure

Verdunk(e)lung *f.* darkening; black-out; eclipse; dimming; **–sgefahr** *f.* (law) danger of prejudicing the course of justice

verdünnen *v.* to thin; to dilute; to rarefy

verdunsten *v.* to evaporate

verdursten *v.* to die of thirst

verdüstern *v.* to darken, to cloud; to obscure

verdutzen *v.* to bewilder, to disconcert

verdutzt *adj.* dumbfounded, startled

veredeln *v.* to ennoble; to improve, to refine; (bot.) to graft

vereh(e)lichen *v.* to marry

verehr: –en *v.* to respect; to revere; to adore, to worship; **jemand etwas –en** to give someone a present; **–lich** *adj.*,

–t *adj.* esteemed, honored; **–ungswert** *adj.*, **–ungswürdig** *adj.* estimable, admirable, respected

Verehrer *m.* admirer, worshiper, lover

vereid(ig)en *v.* to swear in, to put under oath

Verein *m.* association, club, society; **im** — **mit** in conjunction with; **–igung** *f.* union; combination; junction; unification; alliance, coalition; fusion; **–zelung** *f.* isolation; detachment

verein: –bar *adj.* combinable, compatible; consistent; **–baren** *v.* to agree upon; to arrange; **–(ig)en** *v.* to unite, to combine, to join; **sich –(ig)en** to associate, to ally, to reconcile; **–fachen** *v.* to simplify; **–heitlichen** *v.* to unify; to standardize; **–nahmen** *v.* to take in (money); **–samen** *v.* to become isolated (*oder* lonely); **–zelt** *adj.* isolated; sporadic; solitary

die Vereinigten Staaten *pl.* the United States

vereisen *v.* to turn to ice; to freeze; to glaciate

vereiteln *v.* to frustrate, to baffle

verelenden *v.* to become wretched, to pauperize

verenden *v.* to die, to perish

verenge(r)n *v.* to narrow; to contract; to tighten, to constrict

vererben *v.* to bequeath, to leave; to transmit; **sich** — to be hereditary; **sich** — **auf** to devolve on

Vererbung *f.* (act of) bequeathing; hereditary transmission; **–sforschung** *f.* genetics

verewigen *v.* to perpetuate; to immortalize

verewigt *adj.* deceased; late; immortalized

verfahren *v.* to deal with, to treat; to proceed; to spend money (*oder* time) in driving; to muddle; **sich** — to miss one's way; to be on the wrong track; — *adj.* bungled; muddled; hopeless

Verfahren *neu.* proceeding(s); procedure; process; method, dealing

Verfall *m.* decay, decline; deterioration; degeneracy; (com.) maturity; foreclosure

verfälschen *v.* to falsify, to forge; to adulterate; to counterfeit

verfänglich *adj.* insidious; embarrassing; risky

verfärben *v.* to use (*oder* spoil) in dyeing; **sich** — to change color; to turn pale, to fade

verfass: –en *v.* to compose, to write; **eine Urkunde –en** to draft (*oder* draw up) a document; **–ungsmässig** *adj.* constitutional; **–ungswidrig** *adj.* unconstitutional

Verfass: –er *m.* author; **–erin** *f.* authoress

Verfassung *f.* condition, state; \disposition, mood; constitution

verfaulen *v.* to rot, to putrefy; to decay

verfechten *v.* to fight for, to defend; to advocate, to champion

verfehlen *v.* to miss; to fail to do

verfehlt *adj.* unsuccessful; spoiled; bungled

Verfehlung f. mistake, failure; lapse: offense

verfeinden v. sich — mit to fall out with; to make an enemy of

verfeinern v. to refine; to improve, to polish

verfemen v. to outlaw

verfertigen v. to make, to manufacture

Verfettung f. fatty degeneration

verfeuern v. to burn, to blaze away; to waste

verfilmen v. to film, to picture, to screen

verfinstern v. to darken; to eclipse

verfitzen v. to entangle

verflachen v. to become flat (oder shallow); to decline (intellectually)

verflechten v. to interlace; to implicate

verfliegen v. to fly away; to evaporate; to vanish; to pass quickly; sich — (avi.) to lose one's way

verfliessen v. to flow away; to elapse

verflixt! interj. (coll.) confound it!

verflossen adj. past; late

verfluchen v. to curse, to damn

verflucht adj. accursed, damned; —! interj. darn it! — adv. (coll.) very

verflüchtigen v. to volatilize; sich — to evaporate

Verfolg m. course, progress; -er m. pursuer; prosecutor; -ung f. pursuit; prosecution; -ungswahn m. persecution complex

verfolgen v. to pursue; to persecute

verfrachten v. to load, to ship; to charter

verfressen adj. (coll.) voracious

verfrüht adj. premature

verfügbar adj. available

verfügen v. to decree, to order, to ordain; sich — to betake oneself; — über to dispose of; to have control of, to be master of

Verfügung f. decree; order; disposal

verführen v. to entice, to tempt; to seduce

verführerisch adj. enticing; seductive

vergaloppieren v. sich — (coll.) to blunder

vergangen adj. past, bygone, last

Vergangenheit f. past; (gram.) past tense

vergänglich adj. transitory, transient; perishable

Vergaser m. carburetor

vergeb: -en v. to give away, to dispose of; to bestow, to confer; (cards) to misdeal; to forgive, to pardon; sich etwas -en to degrade oneself; -en sein to be engaged; to be filled (position); -ens adv. in vain; -lich adj. futile, unavailing; idle

vergegenwärtigen v. to represent; sich — to realize, to imagine

vergeh: -en v. to pass; to fade; to perish; to elapse; sich — to offend (against), to injure; to assault, to violate; — vor to die of; vor jemand — to feel inferior

vergeistigen v. to spiritualize; to alcoholize

vergelten v. to repay; to retaliate; to return

vergessen v. to forget; to neglect

Vergessenheit f. oblivion

vergesslich adj. forgetful

vergeuden v. to squander, to waste; to lavish, to dissipate

vergewaltigen v. to violate; to rape

vergewissern v. sich — to make sure of; to ascertain

vergiessen v. to shed, to spill

vergiften v. to poison; to contaminate

vergilbt adj. yellowed

Vergissmeinnicht neu. forget-me-not

vergittern v. to enclose with latticework

Vergleich m. comparison; agreement; compromise

vergleich: -bar adj. comparable; -en v. to compare; to collate; to settle; sich -en mit to come to terms with; to compromise; -sweise adv. by way of agreement

verglimmen v. to cease glimmering; to burn out; to die away

Vergnüg: -en neu. amusement; pleasure; fun; -ung f. entertainment, pleasure; -ungsreise f. pleasure trip

vergnügen v. to amuse; to divert; sich — to enjoy (oder amuse) oneself

vergnügt adj. gay, cheerful; delighted, glad

vergolden v. to gild

vergönnen v. to permit; to grant; not to begrudge

vergöttern v. to deify; to idolize, to adore

vergraben v. to hide in the ground; to bury

vergrämt adj. grief-stricken, woebegone

vergreifen v. sich — to seize by mistake; (mus.) to touch the wrong key; sich — an to lay hands on; to violate; to steal

vergrössern v. to enlarge; to extend; to increase; to magnify; to exaggerate

Vergrösserung f. enlargement; -sapparat m. enlarging camera; -sglas neu. magnifying glass

Vergünstigung f. favor; privilege, concession; (com.) rebate

vergüten v. to reimburse, to compensate; to indemnify; to refund, to restore

verhaften v. to arrest; to take into custody

Verhaftung f. arrest; -sbefehl m. arrest warrant

verhallen v. (sounds) to die (oder fade) away

verhalten v. to suppress, to restrain; sich — to behave, to conduct (oneself); sich — zu to be in proportion to (oder the ratio of)

Verhalten neu. behavior, conduct, attitude

Verhältnis neu. relation; proportion, ratio; love affair; -se pl. circumstances, situation; -wort neu. preposition

verhältnismässig adj. proportional, relative

verhältniswidrig adj. disproportionate

Verhaltungsmassregeln f. pl. rules of conduct; instructions

verhandeln v. to negotiate, to parley; (law) to plead; to debate; to sell; to barter away

Verhandlung f. negotiation, parley; trial

verhängen v. to hang over, to veil; eine Strafe — to inflict a punishment

Verhängnis *neu.* destiny, fate; disaster
verhängnisvoll *adj.* fatal, fateful; unfortunate, disastrous
verharren *v.* to remain, to persevere
verhärten *v.* to harden, to grow hard
verhaspeln *v.* to tangle up; **sich —** to become confused; to break down (in speech)
verhasst *adj.* hated, odious
verhätscheln *v.* to coddle, to pamper, to spoil
verhauen *v.* (coll.) to thrash; **sich —** (coll.) to blunder
verheeren *v.* to devastate, to ravage; **-d** *adj.* devastating; catastrophic; (coll.) awful
verhehlen *v.* to conceal, to hide
verheimlichen *v.* to keep secret; to disguise
verheiraten *v.* to marry; to get married
verheissen *v.* to promise
verheissungsvoll *adj.* promising
verhelfen *v.* **jemand zu etwas —** to help a person obtain something
verherrlichen *v.* to glorify, to extol
verhetzen *v.* to instigate, to stir up
verhexen *v.* to bewitch, to enchant
verhindern *v.* to hinder, to prevent
verhöhnen *v.* to deride; to sneer
Verhör *neu.* trial; examination, interrogation
verhören *v.* to interrogate, to examine, to hear; **sich —** to misunderstand
verhüllen *v.* to cover, to veil; to disguise
verhundertfachen *v.* to multiply a hundredfold
verhungern *v.* to die of hunger; to starve
verhunzen *v.* to bungle, to spoil
verhüten *v.* to prevent, to avert; **-d** *adj.* preventive, preservative; prophylactic
verirren *v.* **sich —** to go astray, to err
Verirrung *f.* straying, aberration; mistake
verjagen *v.* to drive away, to expel
verjähren *v.* to become superannuated, to grow obsolete
verjährt *adj.* superannuated; **-es Recht** prescriptive right
verjüngen *v.* to rejuvenate; (art and geom.) to reduce; **es verjüngt sich** it tapers off
verkalken *v.* to calcify, to calcine
verkalkulieren *v.* **sich —** to miscalculate
verkappt *adj.* disgusted; secret
verkatert *adj.* (coll.) suffering from a hangover
Verkauf *m.* sale; **-spreis** *m.* selling price
verkaufen *v.* to sell; to dispose of
Verkäufer *m.* seller; retailer; salesman
verkäuflich *adj.* saleable; for sale; venal
Verkehr *m.* traffic; commerce, trade; intercourse; communication; **aus dem — ziehen** to withdraw from service (*oder* circulation); **-sader** *f.* traffic artery; **-sampel** *f.* traffic light; **-sandrang** *m.* traffic rush; **-sordnung** *f.* traffic regulations; **-sstockung** *f.*, **-störung** *f.* traffic block; bottleneck; breakdown; **-swesen** *neu.* traffic; train service
verkehren *v.* to turn (the wrong way); to invert; to convert; to transform; to

pervert; to frequent, to visit, to have intercourse (with); **sich — in** to change into
verkehrt *adj.* inverted, reversed; upside down; incorrect, wrong; absurd
verkennen *v.* to misjudge; to underrate
verketten *v.* to chain (*oder* link) together
Verkettung *f.* concatenation; coincidence
verketzern *v.* to charge with heresy; to calumniate; to slander
verkitten *v.* to cement; to putty up
verklagen *v.* to accuse; to sue
Verklagte *m.* accused; defendant
verklären *v.* to glorify; to transfigure
verklausulieren *v.* to stipulate; to limit by provisos; to guard by clauses
verkleben *v.* to paste (*oder* glue, gum) up
verkleiden *v.* to disguise, to mask; to line, to face, to wainscot
verkleinern *v.* to diminish; to reduce; to belittle; to disparage
Verkleinerung *f.* miniaturization; **-swort** *neu.* (gram.) diminutive
verklingen *v.* (mus.) to die (*oder* fade) away
Verknappung *f.* scarcity, shortage
verknittern *v.* to crumple, to crease
verknöchern *v.* to ossify; to grow pedantic
verknoten *v.* to knot; to entangle
verknüpfen *v.* to knot (*oder* tie) together; to link; to combine; to entail, to involve
verkochen *v.* to boil away, to use in cooking
verkohlen *v.* to carbonize; (coll.) to hoax
verkommen *v.* to deteriorate, to decay; to degenerate; **—** *adj.* ruined; degenerate; depraved
verkorken *v.* to cork (up)
verkörpern *v.* to embody; to personify
verkrachen *v.* (coll.) to become bankrupt; **sich — mit** (coll.) to fall out with
verkramen *v.* (coll.) to disarrange, to mislay
verkriechen *v.* **sich —** to hide; to creep away
verkrümmt *adj.* bent, crooked; misshapen
verkrüppelt *adj.* crippled; deformed; maimed
verkrustet *adj.* incrusted
verkühlen *v.* **sich —** to catch cold
verkümmern *v.* to become stunted; to atrophy; to pine away; to embitter, to curtail
verkünd(ig)en *v.* to announce, to make known; to proclaim; **das Evangelium —** to preach the gospel; **ein Urteil —** to pronounce sentence
verkuppeln *v.* to couple; to procure, to pander
verkürzen *v.* to shorten; to abridge; to curtail; to diminish; to contract; **sich die Zeit —** to pass away the time
verlachen *v.* to deride, to ridicule
verladen *v.* to load, to ship, to entrain
Verlag *m.* publishing house; **-sartikel** *m.* publication; **-sbuchhändler** *m.* publisher; **-srecht** *neu.* copyright; **-szeichen** *neu.* colophon
verlangen *v.* to demand; to require; to

desire; — **nach** to long for, to crave for

Verlangen *neu.* demand; request; desire; longing; **auf —** by request, on demand

verlängern *v.* to lengthen; to extend, to prolong

verlangsamen *v.* to slow down, to retard

Verlass *m.* **auf ihn ist kein —** he cannot be relied on

verlassen *v.* to leave, to quit; to abandon, to forsake, to desert; **sich — auf** to rely on; — *adj.* forsaken, abandoned; lonely

verlässlich *adj.* reliable, trustworthy

Verlaub *m.* **mit —** with your permission

Verlauf *m.* course; expiration; progress; **einen schlimmen — nehmen** to take a bad turn; **nach — von** after the lapse of

verlaufen *v.* to pass, to expire; to take its course; to proceed; to turn out; **sich —** to lose one's way; to disperse, to scatter; — *adj.* stray, lost; forlorn

verlautbaren *v.* to make known; to divulge

verlauten *v.* to become known; **— lassen** to give 🐝 understand; to hint; **wie verlautet** as reported

verleben *v.* to spend, to pass

verlebt *adj.* past, spent; worn out, decrepit

verlegen *v.* to shift, to transfer, to remove; to misplace; to block, to obstruct; to defer, to postpone; to publish; **sich auf etwas —** to take up (*oder* go in for) something; — *adj.* confused, embarrassed; **um etwas — sein** to be at a loss for something

Verlegenheit *f.* dilemma, embarrassment

Verleger *m.* publisher

Verlegung *f.* shifting, transfer; postponement, misplacement; publishing

verleiden *v.* to disgust (with); to spoil

verleihen *v.* to lend out, to loan; to bestow, to confer (on); to grant; **seinen Gefühlen Ausdruck —** to express one's feelings

verleiten *v.* to mislead; to induce; to seduce

verlernen *v.* to unlearn; to forget (how to do)

verlesen *v.* to read aloud; to call (the roll); to pick (vegetables); **sich — to** misread

verletz: -bar *adj.*, **-lich** *adj.* damageable; vulnerable; susceptible, touchy; **-en** *v.* to damage; to hurt, to injure, to wound; to violate; **-end** *adj.* offensive, insulting

verleugnen *v.* to deny; to disavow; to renounce; **sich — lassen** to pretend not to be at home

verleumden *v.* to slander, to defame

verlieben *v.* **sich — to** fall in love

verlieren *v.* to lose; to shed; to waste; **sich — to** get lost; to disperse; to disappear

Verlies *neu.* dungeon

Verlob: -te *m.* fiancé; **-te** *f.* fiancée; **-ung** *f.*, **Verlöbnis** *neu.* betrothal, engagement

verloben *v.* **sich — to** become engaged (to)

verlocken *v.* to allure, to entice; to seduce; **-d** *adj.* enticing, tempting

verlogen *adj.* mendacious, lying, untruthful

verlohnen *v.* **es verlohnt sich nicht der Mühe** it is not worth while, it doesn't pay

verloren *adj.* lost, forlorn, stray; lonely; fruitless; **der -e Sohn** the Prodigal Son; **-e Eier** poached eggs; **— geben** to give up for lost; **-geh(e)n** to be lost

verlöschen *v.* to extinguish; to efface, to obliterate; to go (*oder* burn) out

verlosen *v.* to dispose of by lot; to raffle

verlöten *v.* to solder up

verlottern, verludern, verlumpen *v.* to waste, to squander, to ruin; to go to tho dogs

Verlust *m.* loss, privation; bereavement; leak, waste; **bei — von** under pain of, with forfeiture of; **-e** *pl.* (mil.) casualties

verlustig *adj.* **einer Sache — gehen** to lose (*oder* forfeit) something

vermachen *v.* to bequeath

Vermächtnis *neu.* bequest, legacy

vermählen *v.* to marry; to give in marriage

vermaledeien *v.* to curse, to execrate

vermauern *v.* to wall in (*oder* up)

vermehren *v.* to increase, to augment; to multiply; to enlarge; to propagate

vermeid: -bar *adj.*, **-lich** *adj.* avoidable; **-en** *v.* to avoid; to evade; to shun; to elude

vermeinen *v.* to believe, to think, to suppose

vermeintlich *adj.* alleged, supposed, pretended

vermelden *v.* to announce, to notify

vermengen *v.* to blend, to mingle, to confound

Vermerk *m.* note, comment, entry

vermerken *v.* to note down, to record; to observe; to remark; **übel — to** take amiss

vermessen *v.* to measure; to survey; **sich — to** measure incorrectly; to dare (*oder* presume) to; — *adj.* bold, audacious

Vermessenheit *f.* boldness; presumption

vermieten *v.* to rent, to lease, to hire out

Vermieter *m.* landlord; lessor

vermindern *v.* to decrease, to diminish; to abate, to impair; to reduce

vermischen *v.* to mix; to mingle; to blend

vermissen *v.* to miss; to deplore, to regret

vermitteln *v.* to mediate, to negotiate, to bring about; to intercede, to interpose

vermittels(t) *prep.* by means of, through

Vermittler *m.* mediator, arbitrator; agent, go-between; matchmaker

Vermittlung *f.* mediation, negotiation; agency; (tel.) exchange, operator

vermodern *v.* to mould; to decay, to rot

vermöge *prep.* by virtue of, through; **-n** *v.* to be able (*oder* in a position) to do; to have influence (over); to prevail upon; **-nd** *adj.* wealthy, rich

Vermögen *neu.* ability, power; capacity, faculty; means, property, wealth; **-sabgabe** *f.* capital levy; **-sverhältnisse** *neu. pl.* pecuniary circumstances

vermummen *v.* to muffle up, to mask

vermuten v. to presume, to surmise, to suspect

vermutlich adj. presumable, likely, probable

vernachlässigen r. to neglect, to slight

vernageln v. to nail up

vernähen v. to sew up

vernarben v. to cicatrize, to heal up

vernarren r. sich — in to become infatuated with, to dote on

Vernehm: -en neu. dem -en nach from what we hear, according to report; -ung f. examination; hearing; interrogation; trial

vernehmen v. to perceive; to hear, to understand; (law) to interrogate, to examine; sich — lassen to speak, to intimate

vernehmlich adj. distinct, intelligible

verneigen v. sich — to curtsy, to bow

verneinen v. to answer in the negative; to deny, to disavow; -d adj. negative

vernichten v. to annihilate, to destroy

vernickeln v. to (plate with) nickel

vernieten v. to rivet

Vernunft f. reason; intelligence; judgment; sense; die gesunde — common sense; jemand zur — bringen to bring someone to his senses; — annehmen to listen to reason

vernünftig adj. sensible; logical, reasonable; rational; wise, judicious

veröden v. to become desolate; to devastate

Verödung f. desolation, devastation; depopulation, stagnation; (med.) obliteration

veröffentlichen v. to make public, to publish; ein Gesetz — to promulgate a law

verordnen v. to order; to decree; to prescribe

verpachten v. to lease; to farm out

verpacken v. to pack (oder wrap) up

Verpackungsgewicht neu. tare (weight)

verpassen v. to let slip; to miss, to lose

verpesten v. to infect; to poison

verpfänden v. to pawn, to pledge, to mortgage

verpflanzen v. to transplant

verpflegen v. to board, to feed, to cater for

Verpflegung f. feeding, board; food, diet; maintenance; provision(ing)

verpflichten v. to oblige, to engage; sich zu etwas — to pledge oneself to do something; zu Dank — to put under obligation

Verpflichtung f. obligation; duty; commitment, engagement; gemeinsame -en joint liabilities

verpfuschen v. to bungle, to botch, to scamp

verplappern, verplaudern v. to waste in gossip; sich — to blab, to give oneself away

verplempern v. to spend foolishly; to fritter

verpönt adj. prohibited, taboo

verprassen v. to dissipate, to waste

verproviantieren v. to provision, to supply

verprügeln v. to thrash soundly

verpulvern v. to pulverize; (coll.) to squander

verpuppen v. sich — to change into a pupa

verpusten v. sich — (coll.) to recover one's breath; to rest

verputzen v. to roughcast, to plaster; (coll.) to eat, to polish off

verqualmt adj. filled with smoke

verquicken v. to amalgamate; to combine, to mix

verquollen adj. bloated, swollen, warped (wood)

verrammeln v. to bar, to block, to barricade

Verrat m. treason, treachery; betrayal

verraten v. to betray; to disclose, to show

Verräter m. betrayer, traitor; informer; -ei f. treachery; treasonable conduct

verräterisch adj. treacherous; perfidious

verräuchern v. to blacken (oder fill) with smoke; to burn up incense

verrauschen v. to die (oder rush, pass) away

verrechnen v. to reckon up, to charge; sich — to miscalculate, to be mistaken

Verrechnung f. reckoning; balancing (of account); -sscheck m. (com.) counter check; -sstelle f. (com.) clearinghouse

verregnen v. to be spoiled by rain

verreiben v. to grind well, to rub away

verreisen v. to go on a trip, to travel

verreissen v. to tear to pieces; to criticize sharply

verrenken v. to dislocate, to sprain

verrennen v. sich — to adhere stubbornly (to); to run the wrong way; to get stuck

verrichten v. to accomplish, to perform, to do

verriegeln v. to bolt; to bar, to barricade

verringern v. to diminish, to lessen, to reduce

verrinnen v. to run off (oder away); to elapse

verrohen v. to become brutal

verrosten v. to rust

verrucht adj. infamous, vile; wicked

verrücken v. to remove, to shift; to displace

verrückt adj. crazy, mad, cracked; er macht mich — he drives me mad

Verrückte m. lunatic, madman, insane person

Verruf m. in — kommen to fall into discredit

verrufen v. to condemn, to decry; — adj. infamous, disreputable, notorious

Vers m. verse; stanza, strophe; ich kann mir keinen — daraus (or darauf) machen I can't make head or tail of it

versagen v. to deny, to refuse; to fail, to break down; (gun) to misfire; versagt sein to be engaged; to have a prior appointment

Versager m. failure; misfire

versalzen v. to oversalt; to spoil

versammeln v. to assemble, to bring together; to convene; sich — to meet, to assemble

Versammlung *f.* assembly, meeting, convention

Versand *m.* dispatch; shipment; export(ation); **-geschäft** *neu.* export business; mail-order house

versanden *v.* to become choked up with sand; (fig.) to stick

Versatz *m.* pawn(ing), pledge; **-amt** *neu.* pawnshop; **-stück** *neu.* (theat.) movable scenery

versauern *v.* to turn sour; to become morose

versaufen *v.* (coll.) to waste in drinking

versäumen *v.* to miss, to neglect, to omit

Versäumnis *neu.* neglect, omission; delay; loss of time

verschachern *v.* to barter away

verschaffen *v.* to procure, to provide; **jemand Recht —** to obtain justice for someone; **sich Recht —** to take the law into one's own hands

verschämt *adj.* ashamed, bashful

verschanzen *v.* to entrench, to fortify; **sich — hinter** to take shelter behind

verschärfen *v.* to sharpen; to aggravate; to intensify; to make worse; **die Gegensätze — sich** the contrasts become more pronounced

verscharren *v.* to bury (without ceremony)

verscheiden *v.* to die, to expire, to pass away

verschenken *v.* to give away, to make a present; to donate; to pour out (beverages)

verscherzen *v.* to trifle away, to lose (by folly)

verscheuchen *v.* to scare away; to banish

verschicken *v.* to send away; to dispatch, to forward; to deport (criminals)

Verschiebebahnhof *m.* (rail.) switchyard

verschieben *v.* to shift, to displace; (rail.) to shunt; to postpone; to black-market

verschieden *adj.* different; dissimilar; diverse; **-e Artikel** sundries; **zu —en Malen** on various occasions; **-artig** *adj.* various, heterogeneous; **-erlei** *adj.* of various kinds, divers; **-farbig** *adj.* variegated; **-lich** *adv.* repeatedly, differently

verschiessen *v.* to use up (ammunition); to fade, to lose color

verschiffen *v.* to ship, to export

verschimmeln *v.* to become moldy

verschlafen *v.* to miss by sleeping; to spend sleeping; to sleep off; to oversleep; — *adj.* sleepy, drowsy

Verschlag *m.* wooden partition; box, shed

verschlagen *v.* to board up; to nail up; to partition off; to spoil by beating; to lose one's place (in books); **das verschlägt einem dem Atem** that takes away one's breath; **— werden** to be driven out of one's course; — *adj.* lukewarm; cunning, sly

verschlammen *v.* to silt up, to get muddied

verschlechtern *v.* to make worse, to impair; **sich —** to become worse, to deteriorate

verschleiern *v.* to veil, to screen; to conceal

verschleiert *adj.* veiled; clouded, hazy; **mit —er Stimme** with a husky voice

verschleifen *v.* to ruin in grinding; to slur

verschleimen *v.* to choke up with mucus

verschleissen *v.* to wear out, to be used up

verschleppen *v.* to carry off; to misplace; to delay, to protract; to spread (disease)

verschleudern *v.* to hurl away; to dissipate; to squander; to sell at a loss, to dump

verschliessen *v.* to close, to shut, to lock up; **sein Herz —** to harden one's heart; **sich einer Sache —** to shut one's eyes to something

verschlimmern *v.* to make worse; to aggravate; **sich —** to grow worse

verschlingen *v.* to devour, to swallow; to intertwine; to twist, to entangle

verschlossen *adj.* closed, locked; reserved

verschlucken *v.* to swallow; **sich —** to swallow the wrong way

Verschluss *m.* lock(ing), fastener, zipper; clasp, plug, zeal; (phot.) shutter; **unter — under** lock and key; **-laut** *m.* (gram.) explosive consonant; **-stück** *neu.* plug, stopper

verschmachten *v.* to languish, to pine away

verschmähen *v.* to disdain, to despise, to scorn

verschmelzen *v.* to melt (together); to fuse; to blend; to coalesce, to amalgamate

verschmerzen *v.* to get over (the loss of)

verschmieren *v.* to smear; to daub; to use up in greasing; to waste (paper) in scribbling

verschmitzt *adj.* cunning, sly, crafty

verschmutzt *adj.* dirty, filthy, soiled

verschnappen *v.* **sich —** to let the cat out of the bag; to give oneself away

verschnaufen *v.* **sich —** to recover one's breath; to rest

verschneiden *v.* to cut away (*oder* badly); to trim, to prune, to clip; to blend, to adulterate (wine); to castrate

verschneit *adj.* snowed in, covered with snow

verschnörkelt *adj.* adorned with flourishes

verschnupft *adj.* stuffed up with a cold; annoyed, piqued, vexed, miffed

verschnüren *v.* to tie up, to cord, to lace

verschollen *adj.* lost, missing; long past

verschonen *v.* to spare; to exempt

verschönern *v.* to beautify, to embellish, to adorn; to improve

verschossen *adj.* discolored, faded; **er ist mächtig in sie —** (coll.) he is madly in love with her

verschrauben *v.* to screw on; to overscrew

verschreiben *v.* to use up in writing; to order, to write for; to prescribe; to assign; (law) to make over; to write incorrectly; **sich —** to make a slip (in writing); to sell oneself (to); to set one's heart upon

verschrien *adj.* in bad repute, decried

verschroben *adj.* eccentric, odd, queer

verschrumpelt *adj.* shrivelled, wrinkled

verschüchtern *v.* to intimidate

verschulden *v.* to be guilty (*oder* the cause) of; to become involved in debts

verschuldet *adj.* indebted; encumbered

verschütten *v.* to spill; to fill up, to bury

verschwägert *adj.* related by marriage

verschwatzen, verschwätzen *v.* to spend in chatting (*oder* gossiping)

verschweigen *v.* to keep secret; to conceal

verschwenden *v.* to lavish, to squander

Verschwender *m.* spendthrift, squanderer, prodigal

verschwenderisch *adj.* wasteful, prodigal

verschwiegen *adj.* discreet; reticent

verschwinden *v.* to disappear, to vanish

verschwistert *adj.* brother and sister; closely united

verschwitzen *v.* to soil (*oder* exhale, get rid of) by perspiration; (coll.) to forget

verschwommen *adj.* indistinct, hazy, vague

verschwören *v.* to forswear, to abjure; **sich — mit** to conspire (*oder* plot) with

versehen *v.* to equip with, to provide; to perform, to administer; to keep; **ehe man sich versieht** unexpectedly; suddenly: **sich —** to overlook; to make a mistake; **-tlich** *adv.* inadvertently, by mistake

Versehen *neu.* oversight, mistake, slip

versehren *v.* to hurt, to injure, to damage

versenden *v.* to send, to dispatch, to forward

versengen *v.* to singe, to scorch, to parch

versenken *v.* to sink; to submerge; to lower; **sich —** to become absorbed in

Versenkung *f.* sinking; (theat.) trap door

versessen *v.* **— auf** to be eager for; to bent on; to be mad about, to be obsessed by

versetzen *v.* to displace, to transfer, to shift; to promote; to transpose; to transplant; to pawn, to pledge; to mix; to alloy; to give, to deal; to put into; to reply

versichern *v.* to assure, to affirm; to insure; **sich —** to make sure of, to ascertain

Versicherung *f.* assurance, affirmation; insurance; **-sschein** *m.* insurance policy

versiegeln *v.* to seal (up)

versilbern *v.* to silver, to plate; (coll.) to turn into money

versinken *v.* to sink, to become submerged; to be absorbed (in)

versinnbildlichen *v.* to symbolize, to allegorize

versinnlichen *v.* to make perceptible; to grow (*oder* make) sensual; to materialize

versoffen *adj.* (coll.) drunk(en)

versohlen *v.* (coll.) to thrash

versöhnen *v.* to appease; **sich — mit** to reconcile oneself with (*oder* to)

versöhnlich *adj.* conciliatory, forgiving

versorgen *v.* to furnish (with), to provide, to supply; to maintain; to care for

Versorger *m.* breadwinner, supporter

versorgt *adj.* worried; provided for

verspäten *v.* to delay, to retard; **sich —** to be (*oder* come) too late

Verspätung *f.* delay, lateness; **der Zug hat eine Stunde —** the train is an hour overdue

verspeisen *v.* to eat up; to consume

versperren *v.* to bar, to block; to obstruct, to close, to lock up

verspielen *v.* to lose (in gambling); **es bei jemand —** to lose a person's favor

verspotten *v.* to deride, to ridicule

versprechen *v.* to promise; **sich etwas — von** to expect much of; **sich —** to make a slip of the tongue

versprengen *v.* to disperse, to scatter

verspritzen *v.* to squirt, to shed, to spill

verspüren *v.* to feel, to perceive; to be aware

verstaatlichen *v.* to nationalize

Verstand *m.* intelligence, intellect; comprehension; judgment; **da steht mir der — still** I'm at my wit's end; **das geht über meinen —** that's past my comprehension; **den — verlieren** to go out of one's mind; **gesunder —** common sense; **-esmensch** *m.* matter-of-fact person; **-esschärfe** *f.* mental acumen, sagacity

verständ- **-ig** *adj.* intelligent; reasonable; sensible; judicious; **-igen** *v.* to inform; **sich -igen mit** to come to terms with; **-lich** *adj.* comprehensible, intelligible; clear; **sich -lich machen** to make oneself understood; **-nislos** *adj.* devoid of understanding; unappreciative; imbecile; **-nisvoll** *adj.* understanding; appreciative; intelligent

Verständ- **-igkeit** *f.* prudence; good sense; **-igung** *f.* understanding; agreement; (tel.) reception; **-nis** *neu.* comprehension; sympathy

verstärken *v.* to strengthen, to reinforce; to amplify; to intensify; to increase

Verstärker *m.* amplifier; intensifier

verstatten *v.* to allow, to permit, to grant

verstauben *v.* to become dusty

verstäuben *v.* to spray

verstauchen *v.* to sprain

Versteck *neu.* hiding place, retreat; ambush; **-spiel** *neu.* hide-and-seek (game)

verstecken *v.* to conceal, to hide

versteckt *adj.* concealed, hidden; underhanded, veiled, secret; **-e Absicht** ulterior motive

verstehen *v.* to understand, to comprehend; to know; **es versteht sich von selbst** it goes without saying; **etwas zu — geben** to hint, to intimate; **falsch — to misunderstand, to misconstrue; sich — auf** to be skilled at; **sich zu etwas — to agree to; was — Sie darunter?** what do you mean by it?

versteifen *v.* to stiffen, to prop; **sich — auf** to insist upon, to make a point of

versteigern *v.* to (sell by) auction

versteinern *v.* to turn to stone, to petrify

verstellbar *adj.* adjustable

verstellen *v.* to shift; to misplace; to

block, to obstruct; to disguise; **sich —** to feign

versteuern v. to pay tax on

verstimmen v. to put out of tune; to annoy, to upset

verstimmt adj. out of tune; cross, upset

verstockt adj. obdurate; impenitent; stubborn

verstohlen adj. stealthy, furtive, secret

verstopfen v. to stop up; to block; to constipate

verstorben adj. deceased, late

verstört adj. disconcerted, bewildered; upset, troubled; disordered (mind); haggard

Verstoss m. offense, fault; infraction, violation; **–ene** m. outcast, outlaw

verstossen v. to transgress; to violate; to cast out, to repudiate; to banish; to expel

verstreichen v. to pass, to slip by, to elapse; to use up in smearing (oder painting)

verstreuen v. to disperse, to scatter; to litter

verstricken v. to use up in knitting; to ensnare; **sich —** to become involved

verstümmeln v. to maim, to mutilate, to cripple

verstummen v. to become silent (oder speechless); to be struck dumb

Versuch m. experiment; trial; test; attempt; **–er** m. tempter, seducer; **–sanstalt** f. research institute; **–sballon** m. research balloon; (fig.) kite; **–skaninchen** neu. guinea pig; victim (of experiments)

versuchen v. to try, to attempt; to test; to taste; to sample; to tempt, to entice

versuchsweise adv. by way of experiment; tentatively; **— annehmen** to accept on approval

versumpfen v. to become marshy; to become corrupt; to grow dissolute

versündigen v. **sich —** to sin (against); to offend, to trespass

versunken adj. sunk; (fig.) lost, absorbed

versüssen v. to sweeten

vertagen v. to adjourn; to put off

vertändeln v. to idle (oder trifle) away

vertauschen v. to exchange; to mistake; to permute, to substitute

verteidigen v. to defend; to advocate

Verteidiger m. defender; defense counsel; (sports) back

verteilen v. to distribute; to apportion; to allot; to dispense; to assign

verteuern v. to raise the price of

verteufelt adj. devilish, infernal; **—** adv. awfully

vertiefen v. to deepen, to make deeper; **sich —** in to become absorbed in; to plunge into

Vertieftsein neu. preoccupation

Vertiefung f. deepening; cavity, hollow; absorption, engrossment

vertiert adj. bestial, brutal, brutish

vertilgen v. to exterminate, to eradicate; to destroy; to consume

vertonen v. to set to music, to compose

Vertrag m. agreement, contract; treaty; **–sbruch** m. breach of contract

vertrag: –en v. to carry away; to bear, to endure; to wear out; **es verträgt sich nicht** it is incompatible; **ich kann diese Speise nicht –en** this food doesn't agree with me; **sich –en mit** to agree (oder get on well) with; **sich wieder –en** to settle differences, to make it up; **–lich** adj. contractual; **–lich** adv. as stipulated, as agreed upon; **–smässig** adv. in accordance with an agreement; **–sschliessend** adj. contracting; **–swidrig** adj. contrary to an agreement

verträglich adj. compatible, sociable

vertrau: –en v. to rely upon, to trust; **–enselig** adj. too trusting; **–ensvoll** adj. full of confidence; **–enswürdig** adj. trustworthy, reliable; **–lich** adj. confidential, private, intimate; **–t** adj. intimate, familiar; **–t mit** conversant with; versed in

Vertrauen neu. confidence, reliance, trust; **im — between** ourselves; **jemand sein — schenken** to place confidence in someone; **–smann** n. trustworthy person, confidant; **–sseligkeit** f. blind confidence; **–sstellung** f. position of trust; **–svotum** neu. vote of confidence

vertrauern v. to mourn (oder grieve) away

verträumen v. to dream away

vertreiben v. to drive away; to expel; to turn out; to banish; to sell, to distribute; **sich die Zeit —** to pass away the time

vertreten v. to substitute for; to represent; to answer for, to plead for; **jemand den Weg —** to block (oder stand in) someone's way; **sich den Fuss — to** sprain one's foot; **sich die Beine — to** stretch one's legs

Vertreter m. proxy, substitute; representative, deputy; advocate; (com.) agent

Vertretung f. representation; replacement; **in — acting** (oder signed) for

Vertrieb m. sale, distribution

vertrinken v. to spend on drink

vertrocknen v. to dry up, to wither

vertrödeln v. to fritter (oder idle) away

vertrösten v. to give hope to, to console; to put off

vertrusten v. (com.) to pool, to monopolize

vertun v. to squander, to waste

vertuschen v. to hush up; to hide, to conceal

verübeln v. to blame for; to take amiss

verüben v. to commit, to perpetrate

verulken v. to make fun of, to tease

verun: –ehren v. to disgrace, to dishonor; **–einigen** v. to disunite; **sich –einigen** to fall out, to quarrel; **–glimpfen** v. to slander, to revile; **–glücken** v. to meet with an accident; to fail; to die, to perish; **–reinigen** v. to soil; to defile, to pollute; **–stalten** v. to disfigure, to deface; **–treuen** v. to embezzle, to misappropriate; **–zieren** v. to disfigure, to mar

verursachen v. to cause, to give rise to;

to bring about; to originate; to provoke

verurteilen *v.* to condemn, to sentence

vervielfachen, vervielfältigen *v.* to multiply; to duplicate, to copy; to reproduce

Vervielfältigungsmaschine *f.* duplicator; mimeograph

vervollkommnen *v.* to perfect, to improve

vervollständigen *v.* to complete, to replenish

verwachsen *v.* to grow together; to heal up; to be engrossed in; — *adj.* grown together; deformed

verwahr: **-en** *v.* to guard, to keep; **jemand zu -en geben** to entrust to someone's care; **sich -en** to protest (against), to resist; **-losen** *v.* to neglect; to be neglected; **-lost** *adj.* neglected; abandoned, uncared for

Verwahrung *f.* custody, guard(ing); keeping, care; — **einlegen** to enter a protest (against)

verwaist *adj.* orphaned; deserted

verwalten *v.* to administer, to manage; to supervise; to govern, to hold (office)

Verwaltung *f.* administration; management, supervision; **-sdienst** *m.* civil service; **-srat** *m.* board of management

verwandeln *v.* to convert; to transform, to metamorphose; to turn into

Verwandlung *f.* conversion; transformation; metamorphosis; (theat.) shifting of scenes; **-skünstler** *m.* quick-change artist

verwandt *adj.* kindred, related; similar, cognate; **-schaftlich** *adj.* kindred, as (among) relatives

Verwandt: **-e** *m.* and *f.* relative, kinsman; **-schaft** *f.* kinship, relationship; relatives; congeniality, affinity

verwarnen *v.* to warn, to caution; to admonish

verwaschen *v.* to wash out, to use up in washing; — *adj.* hazy, vague, indistinct; faded

verweben *v.* to interweave

verwechseln *v.* to (mis)take for; to exchange; to confuse, to confound

verwegen *adj.* bold, daring, audacious

verwehen *v.* to blow away; to be scattered; to cover (by drifting)

verweichlichen *v.* to coddle, to become effeminate (*oder* weak, delicate); to enervate

verweigern *v.* to deny, to refuse

verweilen *v.* to stay, to linger, to stop; — **bei** to dwell on

verweint *adj.* tear-stained, tearful

Verweis *m.* rebuke, reprimand, reproof; reference; **-ung** *f.* banishment, exile; **unter -ung auf** with reference to

verweisen *v.* to rebuke, to reprimand, to reprove; **des Landes** — to banish, to exile; **— auf** to refer to

verwelken *v.* to fade, to wither

verweltlichen *v.* to make (*oder* become) worldly; to secularize

verwenden *v.* to use, to utilize; to employ; to apply; to spend; **sich — für** to intercede for

Verwendung *f.* use; utilization; **-sfähig-**

keit *f.* usability; (mil.) accessibility

verwerfen *v.* to reject; to disapprove; (cards) to play the wrong card; (law) to dismiss (case); to quash (verdict); (zool.) to miscarry

verwerflich *adj.* objectionable; blamable

verwerten *v.* to utilize, to turn to account

verwesen *v.* to rot, to decompose, to putrefy; (poet.) to administer, to supervise

verwichen *adj.* bygone, former, last, past

verwickeln *v.* to entangle, to embroil, to involve; to complicate

verwildern *v.* to grow wild; to become unmanageable (*oder* depraved); to be neglected

verwinden *v.* to get over, to overcome; to distort; (avi.) to twist, to warp

verwirken *v.* to forfeit, to incure, to lose

verwirklichen *v.* to realize, to materialize

verwirren *v.* to entangle, to confuse, to perplex; to bewilder, to embarrass

verwischen *v.* to wipe out, to efface

verwittert *adj.* weather-beaten; dilapidated

verwitwet *adj.* widowed

verwöhnen *v.* to coddle, to pamper, to spoil

verworfen *adj.* depraved; infamous, abandoned

verworren *adj.* confused, intricate

verwund: **-bar** *adj.* vulnerable; touchy; **-en** *v.* to wound; to hurt, to injure; **-erlich** *adj.* astonishing; **-ern** *v.* to astonish; **sich -ern** to be amazed (*oder* surprised); to wonder

verwunschen *adj.* enchanted, bewitched

verwünschen *v.* to bewitch; to curse; to cast a spell (on); to execrate

verwünscht *adj.* cursed, confounded; — *interj.* damn it! hang it!

verwurzeln *v.* to become firmly rooted

verwüsten *v.* to lay waste, to devastate

verzagen *v.* to lose heart, to grow despondent

verzählen *v.* **sich —** to miscount, to miscalculate

verzapfen *v.* to draw from a tap; to join by mortise

verzärteln *v.* to coddle, to pet, to pamper

verzaubern *v.* to bewitch, to charm, to enchant

verzehren *v.* to eat (up); to consume

verzeichnen *v.* to misdraw; to record, to list, to register

Verzeichnis *neu.* list, register, roll; inventory; catalogue; index; specification

verzeihen *v.* to pardon, to forgive; — **Sie!** excuse me! I beg your pardon

verzerren *v.* to distort; to twist; to grimace

verzetteln *v.* to scatter; to fritter away

Verzicht *m.* renunciation; resignation; — **leisten** to renounce

verzichten *v.* to renounce, to forgo, to waive

verziehen *v.* to remove; to stay; to distort; to be slow, to delay; to spoil (child); **keine Miene** — not to move a muscle; **sich —** to warp; to disappear, to disperse, to vanish

verzieren v. to adorn, to trim, to embellish

Verzierung f. adornment, ornament, flourish

verzögern v. to delay, to retard; **sich —** to be late (*oder* deferred)

verzollen v. to pay duty on; **Haben Sie etwas zu —?** Do you have anything to declare?

verzücken v. to enrapture, to entrance

verzuckern v. to sweeten, to ice, to sugar-coat

Verzug m. delay; **Gefahr im —!** danger ahead! **ohne —** immediately; **–stage** m. pl. days of grace; **–szinsen** m. pl. interest on back payments

Verzweiflung f. despair; despondency; **aus reiner —** out of sheer desperation; **zur — bringen** to drive mad

verzweigen v. to branch out, to ramify

verzwickt adj. complicated, intricate; queer

Vesper f. vespers; **–zeit** f. afternoon snack

Veteran m. veteran (soldier)

Veterinär m. veterinarian

Veto neu. veto; **ein — einlegen** to veto something

Vettel f. hag, slut, witch

Vetter m. male cousin; **–nwirtschaft** f. nepotism

Vexier: –bild neu. picture puzzle; **–schloss** neu. puzzle lock; **–spiegel** m. distorting mirror

vibrieren v. to vibrate

Vieh neu. cattle; beast; **–bestand** m. livestock; **–hof** m. stockyard; farmyard; **–seuche** f. cattle plague; foot-and-mouth disease; **–zucht** f. cattle breeding

viehisch adj. bestial, brutish, brutal

viel adj. and adv. much; numerous; often; **das –e Geld** all that money; **das will — sagen** that says a great deal; **ein bisschen —** a little too much; **in –em** in many respects; **mehr als zu —** more than enough; **noch einmal so —** as much again; **recht —, sehr —** plenty of, a great deal; **um –es besser** better by far; **–e** many; **–artig** adj. manifold, various; **–bändig** adj. many-volumed; **–beschäftigt** adj. very busy; **–deutig** adj. ambiguous, equivocal; **–erlei** adj. of many kinds, divers; **–fach** adj. multifarious, repeated; **–fach** adv. in many cases, frequently; **–fältig** adj. various; manifold; **–gestaltig** adj. multiform; **–jährig** adj. of many years, of long standing; **–köpfig** adj. many-headed, numerous; **–leicht** adv. perhaps; **–malig** adj. often repeated; frequent; **–mals** adv. many times, often, frequently; **–mehr** adv. rather, much more; **–mehr** conj. rather; on the contrary; **–sagend** adj. expressive, significant; **–seitig** adj. many-sided; versatile; **–silbig** adj. polysyllabic; **–sprachig** adj. polyglot; **–stimmig** adj. polyphonic; **–verheissend** adj., **–versprechend** adj. most promising; **–zellig** adj. multicellular

Viel: –eck neu. polygon; **–frass** m. glut-

ton; wolverine; **–götterei** f. polytheism; **–heit** f. multiplicity, multitude; **–liebchen** neu. darling; **–stufenrakete** f. multistage rocket; **–weiberei** f. polygamy

vier adj. four; **auf allen –en** on all fours; **unter — Augen** privately; **zu –en** by fours; **–blätt(e)rig** adj. four-leafed; **–eckig** adj. quadrangular, square; **–erlei** adj. of four kinds; **–fach** adj., **–fältig** adj. fourfold, quadruple; **–füssig** adj. four-footed, quadruped; **–gestrichen** adj. (mus.) four-times accented; **–händig** adj. four-handed; **–händig spielen** to play a duet; **–jährig** adj. of (*oder* lasting) four years; **–mal** adv. four times; **–malig** adj. occurring four times; **–schrötig** adj. square-built, clumsy; **–seitig** adj. four-sided, quadrilateral; **–spännig** adj. drawn by four horses; **–stellig** adj. of four digits; **–stimmig** adj. for four voices; **–stöckig** adj. four storied; **–tägig** adj. of four days; **–te** adj. fourth; **–teilen** to quarter; **–teilig** adj. in (*oder* of) four parts; **–teljährlich** adj. quarterly; **–telstündig** adj. lasting a quarter of an hour; **–telstündlich** adj. every quarter of an hour; **–tens** adv. fourthly; **–zehn** adj. fourteen; fourteenth; **–zehnte** adj. fourteenth; **–zeilig** adj. four-lined; **–zig** adj. forty; **–zigste** adj. fortieth

Vier f. four; **–eck** neu. square, quadrangle; **–er** m. four; four-oared boat; **–füss(l)er** m. quadruped; **–gespann** neu. team of four horses; quadriga; **–ling** m. quadruplet; **–radbremse** f. four-wheel brake; **–spänner** m. four-in-hand (coach); **–taktmotor** m. four-stroke engine; **–tel** neu. fourth part, quarter; district; **–telnote** f. quarter note; **–ung** f. (arch.) crossing; **–vierteltakt** m. (mus.) common measure; **–ziger** m. person forty (*oder* more) years old; **–zigstel** neu. fortieth part

Vierwaldstättersee m. Lake Lucerne

Vikar m. vicar, curate

Viktor-Viktor! (avi. **Verstanden!**) Roger!

Viktualien pl. victuals, provisions

Villenkolonie f. garden city

Viol: –a f. (mus.) viola; **–e** f. (bot.) viola, violet; **–ine** f. violin; **–in(en)schlüssel** m. treble clef; **–oncell(o)** neu. (violin) cello

violett adj. violet

virtuos adj. artistic, masterly, brilliant

Virtuos: –e m., **–in** f. virtuoso, artist; **–ität** f. virtuosity, mastery

visieren v. to adjust, to gauge; to aim at; to visa, to endorse, to examine (passport)

Vision f. vision, phantom; **–är** m. visionary

Visitation f. search; inspection

Visite f. visit, call; **–nkarte** f. calling card

visitieren v. to search, to inspect

Visum neu. visa

vivat! interj. long live! hurrah!

Vize: –admiral m. vice-admiral; **–kanzler** m. vice-chancellor; **–könig** m. viceroy

Vlies neu. fleece

Vogel m. bird; **den — abschiessen** to

carry off the prize; **einen — haben to** be cracked; **komischer —** queer fellow; **–bauer** *m.* bird cage; **–beerbaum** *m.* mountain ash, rowan; **–fänger** *m.*, **–steller** *m.* bird catcher, fowler; **–futter** *neu.* birdseed; **–haus** *neu.* aviary; **–hecke** *f.* breeding cage; **–herd** *m.* fowling place, decoy; **–kenner** *m.* ornithologist; **–kunde** *f.* ornithology; **–leim** *m.* birdlime; **–perspektive** *f.* bird's eye view; **–scheuche** *f.* scarecrow; **–stange** *f.* perch, roost; **–strich** *m.*, **–zug** *m.* migration of birds; **–warte** *f.* ornithological station

vogelfrei *adj.* free as a bird; outlawed

Vogesen *pl.* Vosges Mountains

Vogt *m.* overseer, steward; bailiff; governor

Vokabel *f.* word

Vokabular(ium) *neu.* vocabulary, stock of words

Vokal *m.* vowel; **–musik** *f.* vocal music

Volk *neu.* people; nation; tribe; crowd; lower classes; (bees) swarm; (partridges) covey; **der Mann aus dem —** the man in the street; **–sabstimmung** *f.*, **–sentscheid** *m.* plebiscite; **–saufruhr** *m.*, **–saufstand** *m.* general uprising; **–sausgabe** *f.* popular edition; **–sbewegung** *f.* national movement; **–sbibliothek** *f.* public library; **–sbildung** *f.* national education; **–sdichte** *f.* density of population; **–sdichter** *m.* popular (*oder* national) poet; **–sfest** *neu.* national festival; **–sgenosse** *m.* fellow countryman; **–sgunst** *f.* popularity; **–shaufe(n)** *m.* crowd; mob; **–sjustiz** *f.* lynch law; **–sküche** *f.* soup kitchen; **–slied** *neu.* folk song; **–smärchen** *neu.* popular fairy tale; **–sredner** *m.* popular speaker; stump orator; **–sschlag** *m.* race; **–sschule** *f.* primary school; **–ssitte** *f.* national custom; **–ssprache** *f.* national speech; popular language; **–sstamm** *m.* tribe; race; **–stracht** *f.* national costume; **–stum** *neu.* nationality; national characteristics; **–sversammlung** *f.* public meeting; **–svertreter** *m.* representative of the people; **–swirt** *m.* political economist; **–switschaft** *f.* political economics; **–swirtschaftslehre** *f.* political economy; **–swohlfahrt** *f.* national welfare; **–szählung** *f.* census

Völker–bund *m.* League of Nations; **–kunde** *f.* ethnology; **–recht** *neu.* international law; **–schlacht** *f.* battle of nations; armageddon; **–wanderung** *f.* migration of nations

völkisch *adj.* national, racial

volkreich *adj.* populous

volkstümlich *adj.* national, popular

voll *adj.* full, filled; replete; complete, entire; whole; rounded; (coll.) drunk; **aus dem –en schöpfen** to draw freely from one's store (of ideas, information, wealth); **aus –em Herzen** from the bottom of one's heart; **aus –er Brust** heartily; **aus –er Kehle** at the top of one's voice; **den Mund — nehmen** to brag, to boast; **die Uhr hat — geschla**-

gen the clock has struck the full hour; **in –er Arbeit** in the midst of work; **in –er Fahrt** at full speed; **mit –em Recht** with perfect right; **nicht für — nehmen** (coll.) not to take seriously; **sich –essen** to eat one's fill; **–auf** *adv.* abundantly, plentifully; **–blütig** *adj.* full-blooded, plethoric; **–bringen** *v.* to accomplish; **–enden** *v.* to finish, to complete; **–ends** *adv.* completely; finally; altogether; quite; **–er** *adj.* full of; **–führen** *v.* to carry out, to execute; **–gepfropft** *adj.*, **–gestopft** *adj.* crammed (full); **–gültig** *adj.* of full value, valid; **–jährig** *adj.* of (full) age; **–kommen** *adj.* perfect; complete; **–(l)eibig** *adj.* corpulent; **–machen** *v.* (coll.) to fill up, to complete; to dirty; **–spurig** *adj.* (rail.) standard-gauged; **–ständig** *adj.* complete, entire; **–ständig** *adv.* quite perfectly; **–strecken** *v.* to execute; **–tönend** *adj.* sonorous; stereophonic; **–wertig** *adj.* of high quality, of full value; **–zählig** *adj.* complete; **–ziehen** *v.* to accomplish, to execute; to take place

Voll–bad *neu.* complete bath; **–bart** *m.* full beard; **–besitz** *m.* full possession; **–blut** *neu.* thoroughbred (horse); **–blütigkeit** *f.* plethora; **–dampf** *m.* full steam; **–gefühl** *neu.* full consciousness; **–gummi** *m.* solid rubber; **–jährigkeit** *f.* full age; majority; **–kraft** *f.* full vigor; prime; **–macht** *f.* full power; power of attorney; warrant, authority; **–matrose** *m.* able-bodied seaman; **–milch** *f.* whole milk; **–schiff** *neu.* full-rigged ship; **–spurbahn** *f.* standard gauge railroad; **–strecker** *m.* executor; **–streckungsbeamte** *m.* executive officer; **–streckungsbefehl** *m.* writ of execution; **–treffer** *m.* direct hit; **–versammlung** *f.* General Assembly; **–ziehung** *f.*, **–zug** *m.* accomplishment, execution

Völlerei *f.* debauchery, gluttony

völlig *adj.* full, entire, complete, thorough; **–er Ablass** plenary indulgence; **—** *adv.* quite, entirely, completely; **–wach** wide awake

Volontär *m.* volunteer; unsalaried clerk

Volt *neu.* (elec.) volt; **–e** *f.* (sports) vault; volt; (cards) sleight of hand; **eine –e schlagen** (cards) to make a pass; **–messer** *m.* voltmeter

Volumen *neu.* volume; capacity; content

von *prep.* from; about; by; of; in; on; **einer — vielen** one out of many; **— mir aus** as far as I am concerned; if you like it; **— Rechts wegen** by right(s); **— Sinnen kommen** to lose one's head; **–einander** *adv.* apart, separate; from (*oder* of) each other; **–nöten** *adv.* necessary; **–statten** *adv.* **–statten gehen** to proceed; to progress

vor *prep.* before, previous; in front of; ahead of; in the presence of; with, for, of; from, against; **fünf Minuten — drei Uhr** five minutes to three; **nach wie —** now as before; as usual; **— acht Tagen** a week ago; **— allem** above all; **— der Tür sein** to be at the door; **— der Zeit**

prematurely; — **sich gehen** to take place, to occur; **–sich hin** to oneself

Vorabend *m.* eve

vorahnen *v.* to have a foreboding

Vorahnung *f.* propensity

voran *adv.* before, at the head; in front; on(wards); first; **–!** go ahead (*oder* on)! **–geh(e)n** *v.* to take the lead; to precede; **mit gutem Beispiel –geh(e)n** to set a good example; **–kommen** *v.* to advance, to progress; **–stellen** *v.* to place in front of; to prefer

Voranschlag *m.* rough calculation, estimate

Voranzeige *f.* preliminary announcement

Vorarbeit *f.* preliminary (*oder* preparatory) work; **–er** *m.* foreman; **–erin** *f.* forewoman

vorarbeiten *v.* to prepare one's work (*oder* the ground) to show how to work

voraus *adv.* ahead of, in front; **etwas — haben** to have an advantage over; **im —** in advance, beforehand, in anticipation; **–bedingen** *v.* to stipulate in advance; **–bezahlen** *v.* to prepay; **–gehen** *v.* to lead the way, to precede; **–nehmen** *v.* to anticipate, to forestall; **–sagen** *v.* to forecast, to predict; **–sehen** *v.* to foresee; **–setzen** *v.* to assume, to presume; to (pre)suppose; **als bekannt –setzen** to take for granted; **–sichtlich** *adj.* probable, presumable, prospective

Voraus: –setzung *f.* assumption; supposition; hypothesis; **–sicht** *f.* foresight, prudence; **–truppe** *f.* vanguard; advance guard

Vorbau *m.* front building; projecting structure

vorbauen *v.* to build out (*oder* in front of); to take precautions against; to prevent

Vorbedacht *m.* forethought, premeditation; **mit —** deliberately, on purpose

Vorbedeutung *f.* foreboding, omen, portent

vorbedingen *v.* to stipulate beforehand

Vorbehalt *m.* reservation, proviso; ohne **—** unconditionally; **unter —** aller Rechte all rights reserved

vorbehalt: –en *v.* **sich –en** to reserve to oneself; **–lich** *prep.* with reservations; on condition that; **–slos** *adj.* unconditional

vorbei *adv.* along, by; over, past; done, gone; **–geh(e)n** *v.* to go (*oder* pass) by; to miss the mark; **–lassen** *v.* to let pass; **–reden** *v.* to be at cross purposes; **–schiessen** *v.* to miss (target)

Vorbeimarsch *m.* march(ing) past, review

Vorbemerkung *f.* preliminary remark; preamble

vorbereiten *v.* to prepare; **–d** *adj.* preparatory

Vorbesprechung *f.* preliminary discussion

vorbeugen *v.* to obviate, to prevent; sich **—** to bend forward; **–d** *adj.* precautionary, preventive, prophylactic

Vorbild *neu.* model; prototype, original; **–ung** *f.* preparatory training

vorbildlich *adj.* exemplary, ideal; typical

vorbinden *v.* to put (*oder* tie) on

Vorbote *m.* forerunner; harbinger, precursor

vorbringen *v.* to bring forward; to produce; to state, to advance, to propose; to utter

Vorbühne *f.* proscenium

vorchristlich *adj.* pre-Christian

vordatieren *v.* to antedate

vordem *adv.* formerly, of old

Vorder: –achse *f.* front axle; **–ansicht** *f.* front view; **–fuss** *m.* forefoot; **–grund** *m.* foreground; **–hand** *f.* forehand; (cards) lead; **–lader** *m.* muzzle loader; **–lauf** *m.* (zool.) foreleg; **–mann** *m.* previous endorser; front rank man; **–radantrieb** *m.* front-wheel drive; **–reihe** *f.* front rank; **–seite** *f.* front (side); face (of coin); **–steven** *m.* (naut.) stem; **–teil** *m.* and *neu.* front; forepart; (naut.) prow; **–treffen** *neu.* (mil.) front line

vordrängen *v.* to push (*oder* press) forward

vordringen *v.* to advance; to gain ground

vordringlich *adj.* urgent; intrusive

Vordruck *m.* (printed) form

vorehelich *adj.* prenuptial

voreilig *adj.* overhasty, precipitate, rash

voreingenommen *adj.* biased, prejudiced

Voreltern *pl.* forefathers, ancestors

vorenthalten *v.* to keep back, to withhold

Vorfahr *m.* ancestor, progenitor

vorfahren *v.* to drive up (to); to stop at; to drive in advance of; to pass in driving

Vorfahrtsrecht *neu.* right-of-way (in traffic)

Vorfall *m.* incident, occurrence; event; case; (med.) prolapse

vorfallen *v.* to happen, to occur

Vorfeier *f.* preliminary celebration

vorfinden *v.* to find, to meet, to come upon

vorflunkern *v.* jemand etwas **—** to tell someone a fib

Vorfreude *f.* joy of anticipation

Vorfrühling *m.* early (*oder* premature) spring

vorführen *v.* to bring forward; to demonstrate, to present, to produce; (horse) to trot out

Vorgabe *f.* (sports) points given, handicap

Vorgang *m.* event, incident; precedent

Vorgänger *m.* predecessor

Vorgarten *m.* front garden

vorgeben *v.* to pretend, to allege; (sports) to give (*oder* allow) points

Vorgebirge *neu.* promontory, cape; foothills

vorgeblich *adj.* pretended, so-called

vorgefasst *adj.* preconceived (opinion)

vorgeh(e)n *r.* to advance; to go first, to proceed; to occur; to take (*oder* have) precedence; (watch) to be fast

Vorgeh(e)n *neu.* advance, proceedings; precedence; **gemeinschaftliches —** concerted action

Vorgeschichte *f.* prehistory; antecedents

vorgeschichtlich *adj.* prehistoric(al)

Vorgeschmack *m.* foretaste

Vorgesetzte *m.* superior, chief, principal

vorgestern *adv.* the day before yesterday

vorhaben v. to have on, to wear; to be busy with; to intend, to have in mind

Vorhalle f. entrance hall, vestibule, lobby

Vorhand f. (cards) lead; (com.) precedence; (tennis) forehand

vorhanden adj. on hand, in stock; existent; existing; present, available

Vorhang m. curtain

Vorhängeschloss neu. padlock

Vorhaut f. foreskin. prepuce

Vorhemd neu. dicky; shirt front

vorher adv. before(hand); in advance, previously; **–bestimmen** v. to predetermine, to predestine; **–geh(e)n** v. to precede; **–gehend** adj. preceding, foregoing; **–ig** adj. previous, preceding, former; **–sagen** v. to foretell, to predict; **–sehen** v. to foresee, to anticipate

vorherrschen v. to predominate, to prevail; **–d** adj. predominant, prevailing, prevalent

vorheucheln v. to feign, to pretend

vorhin adv. a little while ago; **erst —** only just now

Vorhof m. forecourt; front yard; vestibule; (heart) auricle

Vorhut f. (mil.) vanguard

vorig adj. former, preceding; last, past

Vorinstanz f. (law) lower court

vorjährig adj. of last year, last year's

Vorkammer f. anteroom; (heart) auricle

Vorkämpfer m. champion, pioneer

Vorkaufsrecht neu. right of pre-emption, option

Vorkehrung f. precaution; arrangement; **–en treffen** v. to take precautions; **–smassregeln** f. pl. preventive measures

Vorkenntnisse f. pl. preliminary (oder basic) knowledge; rudiments (of a subject)

vorkommen v. to come forward; to occur, to take place; to be found; to appear, to seem

Vorkommnis neu. event, occurrence

Vorkriegszeit f. prewar days (oder period)

vorladen v. (law) to cite, to summon

Vorlage f. model, pattern; (pol.) bill

vorlängst adv. long ago

vorlassen v. to give precedence; to admit

Vorlauf m. start; elimination race

Vorläufer m. forerunner, precursor; pioneer

vorläufig adj. provisional, temporary; — adv. for the present, in the meantime

vorlaut adj. forward, immodest; pert

Vorleg **–ebesteck** neu. carvers; **–er** m. mat, rug; **–eschloss** neu. padlock

vorlegen v. to put before (oder on); (meal) to help (to); to produce, to submit; to display, to show; **sich —** to lean forward

vorlesen v. to read aloud to; to gather the first ripe grapes

Vorlesung f. lecture, recital

vorletzt adj. last but one, penultimate

Vorliebe f. predilection; preference

vorliebnehmen v. to be satisfied (with)

vorliegen v. to lie before; to be under consideration; to exist, to be; **–d** adj. present, in question, in hand

vorlügen v. to tell lies (to)

vormachen v. to put on (oder before), to show how to do; to impose upon, to deceive

Vormacht f. leading power; supremacy

vormalig adj. former

vormals adv. formerly, once upon a time

Vormann m. foreman; front rank man; previous endorser

Vormarsch m. advance, march onward

Vormittag m. forenoon; morning

vormittags adv. in the forenoon

Vormund m. guardian, trustee; **–schaft** f. guardianship, tutelage

vorn adv. in (oder on the) front; before; **nach —** forward; **nach — heraus wohnen** to have front rooms; **von –(e)** opposite, facing; **von — anfangen** to begin anew (oder at the beginning); **von –herein** from the first, to begin with; **–an** adv. in front; **–ehin** adv. to the front; **–(e)weg** adv. from the start; to begin with; **–über** adv. (bent) forward

Vorname m. first (oder Christian) name

vornehm adj. of high rank; distinguished; noble; **— tun** to put on airs; **–en** v. to put on (apron); **jemand –en** to take someone to task, to reprimand someone; **sich –en** to take up; to intend, to resolve; **–lich** adv. especially, chiefly; **–st** adj. foremost; **die –ste Pflicht** the first (oder principal) duty

Vorort m. suburb; **–sbewohner** m. suburbanite; **–sverkehr** m. suburban traffic

Vorposten m. outpost

Vorrang m. precedence, priority; pre-eminence

Vorrat m. stock, store(s); provisions, supply; **–shaus** neu. storehouse, warehouse; **–skammer** f. storeroom, pantry; **–sverzeichnis** neu. inventory; **–swagen** m. (rail.) tender

vorrätig adj. in stock, on hand, available; **nicht mehr —** out of stock

vorrechnen v. to reckon up (for someone); to give an account of

Vorrecht neu. privilege, prerogative; **älteres —** priority, seniority

Vorrede f. introduction; preamble, preface; prologue

vorreden v. to tell a plausible tale; to talk (someone) into

Vorredner m. previous speaker

vorreiten v. to ride in front of; to put (a horse) through (its) paces; **jemand etwas —** (fig.) to parade something before someone

vorrichten v. to prepare, to make ready

Vorrichtung f. preparation, arrangement; apparatus, appliance; device, mechanism

vorrücken v. to move forward; to advance, to progress; (watch) to set ahead

Vorsaal m. entrance hall; lobby

vorsagen v. to tell, to recite; to prompt

Vorsänger m. leader of a choir, precentor

Vorsatz m. intention, plan, purpose; resolution; **mit —** intentionally, on purpose; deliberately

vorsätzlich adj. intentional, deliberate; (law) with malice aforethought

Vorschein m. **zum — bringen** to bring forward; to produce; **zum — kommen** to come to light

vorschieben v. to push (oder shove) forward; to use as pretext; to pretend; **einen Riegel —** to slip a bolt

vorschiessen v. to shoot (oder rush) forth; to show how to shoot; to advance (money)

Vorschlag m. proposal, proposition; offer; (mus.) grace (note); (pol.) motion; **ein — zur Güte** conciliatory suggestion

vorschlagen v. to propose, to suggest, to offer; (mus.) to beat time; (pol.) to move

Vorschlussrunde f. (sports) semifinal

Vorschneidebrett neu. carving board

vorschneiden v. to carve (at table)

vorschreiben v. to write beforehand (oder in front of); to direct, to order; **ich lasse mir nichts —** I won't be dictated to

Vorschrift f. instruction, regulation, order, prescription

vorschriftsmässig adj. according to direction

Vorschub m. aid, support; (mech.) feed, advance; **— leisten** to further, to favor

Vorschule f. preparatory school

Vorschuss m. payment in advance

vorschützen v. to plead, to pretend

vorschwindeln v. **jemand etwas —** to humbug (oder bamboozle) someone, to tell someone lies

vorsehen v. to provide for; **sich —** to take care of, to be cautious; to beware of

Vorsehung f. providence

vorsetzen v. to place (oder put) before; to offer, to serve (food); to set over (someone); **sich —** to intend, to purpose

Vorsicht f. foresight, caution, prudence; providence; **—! beware! look out! take care! –smassregel** f. precaution(ary measure)

vorsichtig adj. cautious, prudent, careful

Vorsilbe f. prefix

vorsingen v. to sing to; to lead (a choir)

vorsintflutlich adj. antediluvian

Vorsitz m. chairmanship, presidency; **den — führen** to be in the chair, to preside; **den — übernehmen** to take the chair; **–er** m., **–ende** m. chairman, presiding officer

Vorsommer m. early summer

Vorsorge f. precaution, foresight

vorsorglich adj. provident, cautious; **—** adv. as a precaution

vorspannen v. to put (horses) to; to span before, to stretch in front of

Vorspeise f. hors d'oeuvre, appetizer, relish

vorspiegeln v. to deceive, to delude

Vorspiegelung f. pretense; delusion; **— falscher Tatsachen** misrepresentation of facts

Vorspiel neu. prelude, overture; curtain raiser

vorspielen v. to play to (oder before)

vorsprechen v. to pronounce to; to teach how to pronounce; to recite; to call on, to visit

vorspringen v. to leap forward; to project, to jut out; **–d** adj. projecting; prominent

Vorsprung m. projection; advantage, lead

Vorstadt f. suburb

Vorstädter m., **–in** f. suburbanite

vorstädtisch adj. suburban

Vorstand m. board of directors; governing committee; chairman, president

vorstechen v. to be conspicuous (oder prominent); to predominate; to prepare holes by pricking

Vorstecknadel f. scarf pin

Vorsteh: –er m. chief, head; director, manager, superintendent; (church) elder; **–erdrüse** f. prostate gland; **–hund** m. pointer, setter

vorsteh(e)n v. to jut out, to project; to administer, to direct, to manage

vorstellen v. to put forward; to set ahead (watch); to introduce, to present; to represent; to mean, to signify; to point out; to remonstrate, to protest; **sich etwas —** to conceive, to imagine, to fancy; **das kann man sich nicht —** that's inconceivable

Vorstellung f. introduction, presentation; performance; remonstrance; notion, idea; **–svermögen** neu. imagination, imaginative faculty

Vorstoss m. advance, thrust; forward push

vorstrecken v. to stretch forward; to stick out; **Geld —** to advance money

Vorstufe f. first step(s); preliminary stage; introduction, first elements

Vortänzer m. leader of a dance

vortäuschen v. to feign, to pretend

Vorteil m. advantage; benefit, profit

vorteilhaft adj. advantageous, favorable, profitable; **— aussehen** to look one's best

Vortrag m. lecture; delivery, elocution; performance, recitation; discourse, report; (com.) balance carried forward; recital; **–ende** m. lecturer, speaker, performer; **–skünstler** m. elocutionist, recitalist; performer

vortragen v. to lecture; to recite; to report; to perform; to carry forward; to express

vortrefflich adj. excellent; splendid

vortreten v. to come (oder step) forward; to project, to protrude

Vortritt m. precedence; **unter — preceded** by

Vortrupp m. outpost, vanguard

vorüber adv. over, past, by, along; gone; **–gehen** v. to pass by (oder over, away); **–gehend** adj. transitory; passing; temporary

Vorübergehende m. passer-by

Vorübung f. preparatory exercise, previous practice

Voruntersuchung f. preliminary examination

Vorurteil neu. prejudice; bias, prepossession

Vorverkauf *m.* advance sale (*oder* booking)

vorvor: -**gestern** *adv.* three days ago; -**ig** *adj.* penultimate; -**letzt** *adj.* third last

Vorwand *m.* pretext, pretense; excuse

vorwärts *adv.* forward(s); onward; —**!** *interj.* go ahead! move on! start! -**geh(e)n** *v.* to advance; to progress, to improve; -**kommen** *v.* to make headway, to get on, to prosper; -**treiben** *v.* to drive forward; to propel

vorweg *adv.* beforehand; -**nehmen** *v.* to anticipate

vorweisen *v.* to exhibit, to show, to produce

Vorwelt *f.* former ages; prehistoric world

vorwerfen *v.* to throw before (*oder* forward); **jemand etwas —** to reproach someone with something

vorwiegen *v.* to outweigh; to predominate; to prevail; -**d** *adj.* predominant, prevalent; -**d** *adv.* mostly, chiefly, principally

Vorwissen *neu.* previous knowledge; **ohne mein —** without my knowledge, unknown to me

Vorwitz *m.* curiosity; inquisitiveness; forwardness; impertinence; pertness

Vorwort *neu.* foreword, preface

Vorwurf *m.* reproach, blame; subject, motif

vorwurfs: -**frei** *adj.*, -**los** *adj.* irreproachable, unimpeachable; -**voll** *adj.* reproachful

vorzählen *v.* to count before (*oder* over); to enumerate

Vorzeichen *neu.* omen; sign; (mus.) signature

vorzeichnen *v.* to sketch, to trace out, to mark, to indicate

vorzeigen *v.* to produce, to show, to display; **einen Wechsel —** to present a draft

Vorzeit *f.* antiquity; prehistoric times; **die graue —** the dawn of history

vorziehen *v.* to draw (forth); to prefer

Vorzimmer *neu.* antechamber; waiting room

Vorzug *m.* preference; priority, superiority; advantage; merit; excellence; -**spreis** *m.* special (*oder* exceptional) price

vorzüglich *adj.* excellent, choice; first-class; — *adv.* especially

vorzugsweise *adv.* by preference, chiefly

Vulkan *m.* volcano; -**fiber** *f.* vulcanized fiber

vulkanisch *adj.* volcanic

vulkanisieren *v.* to vulcanize, to retread

Vulkanisierung *f.* retread

W

Waage *f.* balance, scales; weighing machine; (ast.) Scales, Libra; (gym.) horizontal position; **jemand die — halten** to be a match for someone; **sich die — halten** to counterbalance; -**schale** *f.* scale(s), balance

waagerecht *adj.* horizontal, level

wab: -**b(e)lig** *adj.* wobbly; -**beln** *v.* to wobble; -**bern** *v.* to flicker

Wabe *f.* honeycomb

wach *adj.* awake, brisk, alert; **ganz —** wide awake; **— werden** to awake; -**ehabend** *adj.* on duty; -**en** *v.* to be (*oder* keep) awake; to watch, to guard; -**sam** *adj.* watchful, vigilant

Wach: -**e** *f.* guard, sentry; watch(man); guard room; police station; **auf -e ziehen** to mount guard; **die -e ablösen** to relieve the guard; **-e stehen** to be on guard; -**traum** *m.* daydream

Wacholder *m.* juniper; gin

Wachs *neu.* wax; -**abdruck** *m.* wax impression; -**figurenkabinett** *neu.* waxworks; -**leinwand** *f.*, -**tuch** *neu.* oilcloth; -**stock** *m.* wax taper; -**zieher** *m.* wax goods manufacturer

wachsen *v.* to grow, to increase; to thrive; to wax; **er ist ihm ans Herz gewachsen** he has become very fond of him; **jemand gewachsen sein** to be a match for someone

wächsern *adj.* waxen; of wax; pale (as wax)

Wachstum *neu.* growth; increase

Wacht *f.* guard, watch; -**dienst** *m.* guard duty; -**meister** *m.* sergeant-major (of cavalry); -**posten** *m.* sentry; -**stube** *f.* guard-room; -**turm** *m.* watchtower

Wachtel *f.* quail; -**hund** *m.* spaniel; -**schlag** *m.* call of the quail

Wächter *m.* watchman, warden; lookout man

wack: -**(e)lig** *adj.* shaky, tottering, rickety; (tooth) loose; -**eln** *v.* to shake, to rock; to totter; to be loose

wacker *adj.* brave, upright; — *adv.* bravely; heartily; soundly

Wade *f.* calf (of leg); -**nbein** *neu.* fibula

Waffe *f.* weapon, arm(s); **die -n ergreifen** to take up arms; **unter -n stehen** to be under arms; -**ndienst** *m.* military service; -**ngang** *m.* armed conflict; -**ngattung** *f.* (mil.) branch of service; -**nrock** *m.* (mil.) uniform coat; -**nruhe** *f.* ceasefire; truce; -**nschein** *m.* gun license; -**nschmied** *m.* armorer; -**nstillstand** *m.* armistice, truce

Waffel *f.* waffle

waffnen *v.* to arm

Wag: -**ehals** *m.* daredevil; -**emut** *m.* daring; -**estück** *neu.* daring enterprise; -**halsigkeit** *f.* foolhardiness; -**nis** *neu.* risk, hazard

wagen *v.* to venture, to dare; to hazard, to risk; to attempt

Wagen *m.* carriage, coach; vehicle; car, van, wagon; **der grosse —** (ast.) the Big Dipper; -**burg** *f.* barricade of wagons; -**decke** *f.* tarpaulin cover; -**heber** *m.* jack; -**lenker** *m.* driver; -**macher** *m.* cartwright; -**schlag** *m.* carriage door; -**schmiere** *f.* lubricant

wägen *v.* to weigh; to consider

Waggon *m.* (rail.) car; truck

Wahl *f.* choice, selection; option; election, poll(ing); **seine — treffen** to make one's choice; **vor die — stellen** to let one choose; **zur — vorschlagen** to nominate; **–bericht** *m.* election return; **–bezirk** *m.* electoral district; constituency; ward; **–fach** *neu.* optional subject; **–fähigkeit** *f.* eligibility; franchise; **–handlung** *f.* election; **–heimat** *f.* country of one's choice; **–kreis** *m.* ward, constituency; **–kugel** *f.* ballot; **–liste** *f.* register of electors; **–lokal** *neu.* polling place; **–programm** *neu.* (pol.) platform; **–recht** *neu.* right to vote, franchise; **allgemeines –recht** *neu.* universal suffrage; **–spruch** *m.* motto, device; maxim; **–stimme** *f.* vote; **–urne** *f.* ballot box; **–versammlung** *f.* election meeting; caucus; **–verwandtschaft** *f.* elective affinity; congeniality; **–zelle** *f.* polling booth; **–zettel** *m.* ballot

wähl: **–bar** *adj.* eligible; **–en** *v.* to choose, to pick out, to select; to elect, to vote; (tel.) to dial; **–erisch** *adj.* choosy; fastidious

Wähler *m.* voter; **–schaft** *f.* body of voters; constituency; **–scheibe** *f.* (tel.) dial

Wahn *m.* delusion, illusion; hallucination; fancy, folly; **–bild** *neu.* phantom, chimera; **–sinn** *m.* insanity, madness; **–sinnige** *m.* lunatic, madman; **–witz** *m.* frenzy, absurdity

wähnen *v.* to imagine, to presume, to fancy

wahnsinnig *adj.* insane, mad; frantic; (coll.) terrific

wahnwitzig *adj.* absurd, senseless, foolish

wahr *adj.* true; genuine; real, proper, veritable; **er will es nicht — haben** he won't admit it; **nicht —!** isn't it! isn't it! **Wort — machen** to keep one's promise; **so — mir Gott helfe!** so help me God! **— werden** to come true; **–en** *v.* to keep (up); to watch over; to preserve; **–haft(ig)** *adj.* sincere, truthful; genuine; real, actual, **–heitsgemäss** *adj.*, **–heitsgetreu** *adj.*, **–heitsliebend** *adj.* true, truthful; **–lich** *adv.* truly, certainly; (bibl.) verily; **–nehmbar** *adj.* perceivable, noticeable; **–nehmen** *v.* to notice, to perceive; to make use of; to look after; **–sagen** to tell fortunes; to prophesy; **–scheinlich** *adj.* probable, likely

Wahr: **–heit** *f.* truth; **jemand die –heit sagen** to speak bluntly; **–nehmung** *f.* perception; observation; care (of); **–nehmungsvermögen** *neu.* perceptive faculty; **–sager** *m.* fortuneteller, soothsayer; **–sagung** *f.* fortunetelling, prophecy; **–scheinlichkeitsrechnung** *f.* theory of probabilities; **–spruch** *m.* (law) verdict, **–zeichen** *neu.* landmark; token, sign, omen

währen *v.* to continue, to last; to endure; **–d** *prep.* during; **–d** *conj.* while, whilst; **–ddem** *adv.*, **–ddessen** *adv.* in the meantime, meanwhile

Währung *f.* currency, monetary standard

Waise *f.* orphan; **–nhaus** *neu.* orphanage; **–nknabe** *m.* orphan boy; **er ist der reinste –nknabe** he doesn't know a thing

Wal, Walfisch *m.* whale; **–fischfahrer** *m.* whaler; **–fischfang** *m.* whaling; **–fischtran** *m.* train oil; **–ross** *neu.* walrus

Wald *m.* wood, forest; **–brand** *m.* forest fire; **–einsamkeit** *f.* woodland retreat; **–erdbeere** *m.* wild strawberry; **–esdunkel** *neu.* forest gloom; **–essaum** *m.* forest edge; **–esel** *m.* wild ass; **–eule** *f.* brown owl; **–gegend** *f.* woodland; **–gehege** *neu.* forest preserve; **–geist** *m.* faun, satyr; **–horn** *neu.* French horn; **–hüter** *m.* forest ranger; **–läufer** *m.* forester; **–meister** *m.* (bot.) woodruff; **–nymphe** *f.* dryad; **–schnepfe** *f.* woodcock; **–schrat** *m.* forest sprite; **–ung** *f.* wood(land); **–wiese** *f.* glade; **–wirtschaft** *f.* forestry

Wäldchen *neu.* bush, grove; shrubbery; thicket

waldig *adj.* wooded, woody; forested

walken *v.* to full (cloth)

Walküre *f.* Valkyrie

Wall *m.* rampart; embankment; **–graben** *m.* moat

wallen *v.* to bubble, to simmer, to boil; to undulate; to float, to flutter; to become agitated; (poet.) to wander, to roam

wallfahren *v.* to go on a pilgrimage

Wallfahrer *m.* pilgrim

Wallfahrt *f.* pilgrimage

Walnuss *f.* walnut; **weisser –baum** hickory

Walpurgisnacht *f.* Witches' Sabbath

walten *v.* to govern, to rule; to carry out, to execute; **das walte Gott!** God grant it! **Gnade — lassen** to show mercy

walzen *v.* to roll (out); to waltz

wälzen *v.* to roll; **Bücher — to consult** many weighty books; **die Schuld auf jemand anderen —** to lay the blame on somebody else; **Gedanken — to ponder**; **sich —** to roll; to wallow, to welter

Wams *neu.* jacket; doublet; jerkin

Wand *f.* wall; partition; side; (med.) coat; **jemand an die — drücken** to shove someone aside; **spanische — folding** screen; **–bekleidung** *f.* wainscot(ing); **–gemälde** *neu.*, **–malerei** *f.* fresco; mural painting; **–karte** *f.* wall map; **–leuchter** *m.* bracket (for lighting); **–schirm** *m.* screen; **–spiegel** *m.* pier glass; **–tafel** *f.* blackboard; **–teppich** *m.* tapestry; **–ung** *f.* wall, partition

Wandel *m.* change, alteration; behavior, conduct; **Handel und — trade and traffic; **–gang** *m.*, **–halle** *f.* foyer, lobby; **–stern** *m.* planet

wandelbar *adj.* changeable, variable; fickle

Wander: **–bühne** *f.* traveling theater; **–bursche** *m.* traveling journeyman; **–er** *m.* wanderer, hiker; **–heuschrecke** *f.* migratory locust; **–niere** *f.* floating kidney; **–prediger** *m.* itinerant preacher; **–preis** *m.* challenge cup (*oder* trophy); **–ratte** *f.* brown (*oder* sewer) rat; **–raupe** *f.* larvae of processionary moth; **–schaft** *f.* travels, hiking; migration; **–smann**

m. wanderer, wayfarer; traveler; **–stab** m. walking stick; **zum –stab greifen to** set out on travels; **–trieb** m. roving spirit; migratory instinct; **–truppe** f. (theat.) strolling players; **–ung** f. walking tour; hike; excursion; migration; **–vögel** m. pl. birds of passage; members of a German hiking movement; **–volk** neu. nomadic people

wandern v. to wander, to travel; to hike

Wandlung f. change; transformation; (rel.) transsubstantiation

Wange f. cheek

wankelmütig adj. inconstant, fickle

wanken v. to stagger, to totter; to waver

wann adv. when; **dann und — now and** then; sometimes; **seit — ist er hier?** how long has he been here?

Wanne f. tub; bath; (agr.) winnowing fan

Wappen neu. coat of arms; escutcheon; **–kunde** f. heraldry; **–schild** neu. escutcheon; **–schmuck** m. emblazonry; **–spruch** m. heraldic motto; **–tier** neu. heraldic animal

wappnen v. to arm

Ware f. ware, article; **–n** pl. goods, merchandise; **–nbestand** m. stock on hand; **–nhaus** neu. department store; **–nlager** neu. stock in trade; warehouse; **–nniederlage** f. magazine, warehouse; **–nprobe** f. sample; **–nzeichen** neu. trade-mark

warm adj. warm, hot; **jemand den Kopf — machen to excite someone; sich** jemand **— halten to keep someone in** good humor; **Speisen — stellen to keep** food hot; **–blütig** adj. warm blooded

Warm: –bier neu. hot ale; **–wasserheizung** f. hot water (or central) heating; **–wasserversorgung** f. hot-water supply

Wärm: –e f. warmth; heat; ardor; **–eabgabe** f. loss of heat; **–eeinheit** f. thermal unit; **–egrad** m. degree of heat, temperature; **–ehre** f. science of heat; **–eleiter** m. conductor of heat; **–emesser** m. calorimeter, thermometer; **–flasche** f. hot-water bottle

wärmen v. to warm, to heat; **sich — to** warm oneself; to bask

Warn: –er m. warner; **–ungssignal** neu. danger signal; **–nungstafel** f. warning signboard

warnen v. to warn, to admonish, to caution

warten v. to wait, to stay; to attend to, to nurse, to look after; **da können sie lange — they may wait till doomsday;** **er lässt immer auf sich — he is never** on time; **— auf to wait for; — lassen** to keep waiting

Wärter m. attendant, keeper; care-taker; warder; (male) nurse; **–in** f. nurse

warum adv. why, for what reason

Warze f. wart; nipple, teat

was pron. what; that which, that, which; something; **— auch immer, — nur** what(so)ever; no matter what; **— für (ein)?** what kind (or sort) of?

Wasch: –anstalt f. laundry; **–automat** (öffentlich) m. laundromat; **–bär** m.

raccoon; **–becken** neu. wash basin; **–frau** f. laundress, washerwoman; **–geschirr** neu. washstand set; **–kessel** m. wash boiler; **–küche** f. laundry; **–lappen** m. wash cloth; (coll.) weakling; **–leder** neu. chamois; **–mittel** neu. lotion; **–raum** m. washroom; lavatory; **–tisch** m., **–toilette** f. washstand; **–zettel** m. laundry list; publisher's blurb

Wäsche f. wash(ing); linen; **heute ist grosse — today is wash day; in die —** geben to send to the laundry; **–beutel** m. laundry bag; **–geschäft** neu. lingerie, underclothing business; **–klammer** f. clothespin; **–leine** f. clothesline; **–mangel** f., **–rolle** f. mangle; **–rei** f. laundry; **–rin** f. laundress; **–schrank** m. linen cupboard

waschecht adj. (color-)fast; (coll.) genuine

waschen v. to wash; **jemand den Kopf —** (coll.) to scold someone; **mit allen Wassern gewaschen sein to be sly** (oder crafty)

Wasser neu. water; luster (of stones); (poet.) watercourse, sea; **ins — fallen** (coll.) to come to naught; **jemand nicht das — reichen können to be inferior to** someone; **Kölnisches — eau de Cologne; mit allen –n gewaschen sein** (coll.) to be cunning; **sich über — halten** (coll.) to keep one's head above water; **unter — setzen to inundate, to** flood; **— abschlagen** (or lassen) **to** urinate; **— ziehen to leak; zu — werden** to melt away; **zu — und zu Lande by** land and sea; **–armut** f. drouth; **–ball** m. water polo; **–baukunst** f. hydraulics; **–behälter** m. cistern, reservoir, water tank; **–blase** f. bubble; vesicle; **–bombe** f. depth charge; **–druck** m. hydrostatic pressure; **–fall** m. waterfall; **–farbe** f. water color, distemper; **–fläche** f. water level (oder surface); **–flugzeug** neu. seaplane; **–graben** m. ditch, drain; moat; **–hahn** m. faucet, tap; **–heilanstalt** f. water cure establishment; **–hose** f. waterspout; **–huhn** neu. coot; **–jungfer** f. naiad, nymph; mermaid; dragonfly; **–karte** f. hydrographic chart; **–kopf** m. hydrocephalus; **–kraft** f. water power; **–krug** m. pitcher; **–kunst** f. artificial fountain; hydraulics; **–lache** f. pool; **–lauf** m. water-course; **–leitung** f. water pipes; aqueduct; **–linse** f. duckweed; **–mann** m. water sprite; (ast.) Aquarius; **–messer** m. hydrometer; **–pest** f. pondweed; **–pflanze** f. aquatic plant; **–ratte** f. water rat; old sailor; sea dog; good swimmer; **–rinne** f gutter; **–scheide** f. watershed; **–rutschbahn** f. water chute; **–scheu** f. hydrophobia; **–schlange** f. water snake; (ast.) Hydra; **–schlauch** m. water hose; **–schraube** f. hydraulic screw; **–snot** f. flood; **–speier** m. gargoyle; **–spiegel** m. surface of the water; water level (oder table); **–sport** m. aquatics; **–stand** m. water level; tide level; **–standsmesser** m. water gauge; **–stiefel** m. pl. rubber boots; **-stoff** m. hydrogen; **-stoffsupe-roxyd** neu. hydrogen peroxide; **-strahl** m. jet of water; **-strasse** f. waterway, navigable river; **-sucht** f. dropsy; **-suppe** f. thin gruel; **-tier** neu. aquatic animal; **-verdrängung** f. (naut.) water displacement; **-vögel** m. pl. waterfowl; **-waage** f. water level; **-werk** neu. waterworks; **-zeichen** neu. watermark

wasser: **-arm** adj. arid; **-dicht** adj. waterproof; watertight; **-frei** adj. anhydrous; **-haltig** adj. containing water, hydrated; **-reich** adj. abounding in water resources; **-scheu** adj. hydrophobic; **-süchtig** adj. dropsical

wässerig adj. watery; insipid; **jemand den Mund — machen** to make someone's mouth water

wässern v. to water, to irrigate; to soak, to steep; (phot.) to wash

waten v. to wade

Watt neu. (elec.) watt; sand banks (covered at high tide), muddy shallows

Watte f. wadding; (med.) cotton; **-bausch** m. cotton ball

wattieren v. to pad, to wad, to quilt

Wauwau m. (child's) doggie; (coll.) bugbear

Web: **-e(r)baum** m. weaver's beam; warp beam; **-ekante** f. selvage; **-er** m. weaver; **-erei** f. weaving (mill); texture; **-erknecht** m. (ent.) daddy longlegs; **-erschiffchen** neu. shuttle; **-stuhl** m. loom; **-waren** f. pl. textiles

weben v. to weave; (poet.) to float

Wechsel m. change, alteration; turn, rotation; fluctuation; exchange; relay; bill of exchange; (hunting) runway; **eigener** — note of hand; **gezogener** — draft; **offener** — credit letter; **-balg** m. changeling; **-bewegung** f. reciprocal movement; **-beziehung** f. correlation; **-fälle** m. pl. ups and downs, vicissitudes; **-fieber** neu. intermittent fever; **-folge** f. alternation; **-geld** neu. change, small coin(s); **-gesang** m. antiphony; **-gespräch** neu. dialogue; **-getriebe** neu. change gear; **-jahre** neu. pl. (med.) climacteric; **-kurs** m. rate of exchange; **-reiter** m. speculator in drafts; **-schaltung** f. change-over switch; **-seitigkeit** f. reciprocity; **-strom** m. (elec.) alternating current; **-stube** f. exchange office; **-winkel** m. adjacent angle; **-wirkung** f. reciprocal action; **-wirtschaft** f. rotation of crops

wechseln v. to change, to alternate; to exchange; (hunting) to pass; to shift (scene); **die Zähne** — to cut new teeth; **den Aufenthaltsort** — to move elsewhere

Wechselseitiger Verkehr m. intercom

Wechsler m. money changer, banker

wecken v. to wake, to awaken; to rouse, to call

Wecker m. alarm clock; awakener

Wedel m. fan; duster; frond, palm leaf; (zool.) brush, tail

weder conj. neither

Weg m. way, course, path; road, passage,

route; trip, errand, walk; method, means; **am —e** by the roadside; **auf halbem —e** halfway; **auf gütlichem —e** amicably; **aus dem —(e) geh(e)n** to get out of the way; to evade; **aus dem —(e) räumen** to remove; **ein tüchtiges Stück —es** a good distance; **in die —e leiten** to prepare; **kürzester —** short cut; **nicht über den — trauen** not to trust; **verbotener —!** no trespassing! **-bereiter** m. forerunner, pioneer; **-ebau** m. road making; **-edorn** m. buckthorn; **-elag(e)rer** m. highwayman; **-enge** f. defile; **-erich** m. plantain; **-(e)geld** neu. (turnpike) toll; **-scheide** f. crossroads, road fork; **-strecke** f. length of the way; distance; **-stunde** f. distance per hour; **-warte** f. chicory; **-weiser** m. guide-(book); signpost; **-zehrung** f. provisions (for a trip); **-zug** m. departure; removal

weg adv. away; off; gone, lost, disappeared; **er hat einen —** (coll.) he is tipsy; **ganz — sein** (coll.) to be enraptured (about); **— da!** be off there! **-bar** adj., **-sam** adj. passable, accessible; **-begeben** v., **sich -begeben** to go away; to withdraw; **-bekommen** v. to get off; (fig.) to grasp; **-bleiben** v. to stay away; to be omitted; **-bringen** v. to carry away, to remove; (spot) to take out; **-dürfen** v. to be allowed to go away; **-en** prep. on account of, because of; in consideration of; for the sake of; in consequence of; owing to; **von Rechts -en** by right; **-fahren** v. to cart away; to drive off; **-fallen** v. not to take place; to be omitted; **-haben** v. to have received; to be well up in; **-helfen** v. to help to get away; **-holen** v. to fetch away; to catch (cold); **-jagen** v. to drive away; to gallop off; **-kommen** v. to get away (oder lost); **-können** v. to be able to get away; **-lassen** v. to let go; to omit; **sich -machen** to make off; **-müssen** v. to be obliged to go away; **-nehmen** v. to take away; to confiscate; to occupy (space); **-räumen** v. to clear away, to remove; **-reisen** v. to depart; **-rücken** v. to move away; to withdraw; **-schaffen** v. to clear away, to remove; **-scheren** v. to shear off; **sich -scheren** to be off; **-sehen** v. to look away; to shut one's eyes to; **-setzen** v. to put aside; to jump (over); **-treten** v. to step aside; (mil.) to break ranks; **-wenden** v. to turn away; **-werfen** v. to throw away; **sich -werfen** to degrade oneself; **-werfend** adj. contemptuous, disdainful; **-ziehen** v. to draw away; to move; to migrate

Weh neu. pain; woe; grief; **-e** f. drift; **-en** pl. labor pains; **-mutter** f. midwife

Wehr f. defense, resistance; weapon, arm; bulwark; **— neu.** weir, spillway; **-bezirk** m. military district; **-dienst** m. (mil.) service; **-gang** m. battlement, parapet; **-gehänge** neu., **-gehenk** neu. sword belt; **-gesetz** neu. military service law; **-kraft** f. armed forces; **-macht**

f. Armed Forces; **–pflicht** *f.* compulsory military service; **–stand** *m.* military profession; **–vorlage** *f.* military service bill

wehr: –en *v.* to restrain, to hinder, to forbid; **sich (seiner Haut) –en** to defend oneself, to resist; **–fähig** *adj.*, **–haft** *adj.* able to bear arms; strong; **–los** *adj.* defenseless; unarmed; **–los machen** to disarm; **–pflichtig** *adj.* subject to military service

Weib *neu.* female; woman; wife; **–chen** *neu.* little woman; (zool.) female; **–erart** *f.* woman's way(s); **–erfeind** *m.* woman hater; misogynist; **–erheld** *m.* ladies' man; **–erherrschaft** *f.* petticoat government; **–sbild** *neu.* female; (coll.) hussy, wench; **–svolk** *neu.* womankind, womanfolk

weiblich *adj.* feminine; female

weich *adj.* soft, tender; weak; mellow; smooth; **–es Ei** soft-boiled egg; **— werden** to soften; to be moved; **–en** *v.* to give way (*oder* in); to withdraw; to yield; to soften, to soak; (prices) to decline; **nicht von der Stelle –en** not to budge an inch; **von jemand –en** to abandon someone; **zum –en bringen** to push back, to repel; **–gestimmt** *adj.* in a gentle mood; **–herzig** *adj.* tenderhearted; **–lich** *adj.* soft; flabby; sloppy; effeminate; weak, indolent

Weich: –bild *neu.* precincts (of city); **–e** *f.* softness; (anat.) flank, groin; (rail.) switch; **–ensteller** *m.* switchman

Weichsel *f.* Vistula

weid: –en *v.* to graze, to pasture; **sich –en an** to feast on, to delight in; **–en** *adj.* willow; **–gerecht** *adj.*, **–männisch** *adj.* huntsmanlike; sportsmanlike; **–lich** *adv.* thoroughly, very much; **–wund** *adj.* shot in the intestines; death wound

Weid: –e *f.* pasture; willow, osier; **–engeflecht** *neu.* wickerwork; **–enkätzchen** *neu.* willow catkin; **–mann** *m.* hunter, sportsman; **–mannsheil** *neu.* hunter's greeting; **–messer** *neu.* hunting knife; **–werk** *neu.* chase, hunting

weigern *v.* to decline, to refuse; **sich —** to refuse (to do)

Weih *m.*, **–e** *f.* (orn.) kite; **–bischof** *m.* suffragan bishop; **–e** *f.* consecration; ordination; inauguration; solemnity; **–gabe** *f.* votive offering; **–nacht** *f.*, **–nachten** *pl.* Christmas; **–nachtsabend** *m.* Christmas Eve; **–nachtsbescherung** *f.* distribution of Christmas gifts; **–slied** *neu.* Christmas carol; **–smann** *m.* Santa Claus; **–rauch** *m.* incense; **–rauchfass** *neu.* censer; **–wasser** *neu.* holy water; **–wasserbecken** *neu.* font; holy-water vessel; **–(wasser)wedel** *m.* holy-water sprinkler

weihen *v.* to consecrate; to dedicate, to ordain

Weiher *m.* pond

weihevoll *adj.* solemn, hallowed

weil *conj.* because, since; (poet.) as long as; **–and** *adv.* (poet.) formerly, of old; deceased; **–en** *v.* to stay; to linger; to

delay

Weile *f.* while; (space of) time; leisure; **damit hat es gute —** there's no hurry about that; **Eile mit —** make haste slowly

Weiler *m.* hamlet

Wein *m.* wine; vine; grapes; **jemand reinen — einschenken** to tell someone the whole truth; **wilder —** Virginia creeper; **–bau** *m.* wine growing, viticulture; **–beere** *f.* grape; **–berg** *m.* vineyard; **–bergschnecke** *f.* edible snail; **–brand** *m.* cognac, brandy; **–ernte** *f.* vintage; **–fass** *neu.* wine cask; **–gegend** *f.* wine district; **–geist** *m.* ethyl alcohol; **–händler** *m.* wine merchant; **–hefe** *f.* dregs of wine; **–karte** *f.* wine list; **–kelter** *f.* winepress; **–kenner** *m.* connoisseur of wine; **–küfer** *m.* wine cooper; **–laub** *neu.* vine leaves; **–laube** *f.* vine arbor; **–lese** *f.* vintage; **–probe** *f.* sample (*oder* tasting) of wine; **–rebe** *f.*, **–stock** *m.* grapevine; **–säure** *f.* acidity of wine; tartaric acid; **–schank** *m.* retail(ing) of wine; **–schenk** *m.* cupbearer; **–schenke** *f.* wine tavern; **–stein** *m.* tartar; **–traube** *f.* (bunch of) grape(s); **–trester** *pl.* husks of pressed grapes; **–zwang** *m.* obligation to order wine (with meal)

weinen *v.* to weep, to cry, to shed tears

weis: –e *adj.* wise; prudent; **–en** *v.* to point out (*oder* at); to show; to direct; to refer (to); **von sich (***or*** der Hand) –en** to reject, to decline; **–en aus** to expel; **–lich** *adv.* wisely; prudently; **–machen** *v.* to make (one) believe a thing; to hoax; **–sagen** *v.* to predict, to prophesy

Weis: –e *m.* wise man, sage; **–e** *f.* way, manner; custom, habit; melody, tune; **auf diese –e** in this way; **auf keine –e** by no means; **–el** *m.* queen bee; **–er** *m.* indicator, pointer; **–ung** *f.* order, instruction

Weisheit *f.* wisdom; prudence; **mit seiner –heit am Ende sein** to be at one's wits' end; **–sager** *m.* prophet, fortuneteller; **–sagung** *f.* prophecy

weiss *adj.* white; clean, blank; hoary; **eine –e Weste haben** to be innocent; **jemand — waschen** to whitewash someone; **–er Sonntag** Sunday after Easter; **–en** to whiten; to whitewash; **–glühend** *adj.* white-hot, incandescent; **–lich** *adj.* whitish

weit *adj.* wide, extensive, spacious; capacious; distant, far, remote; immense, vast; loose; **bei –em** by far; **be –em nicht** not at all; **das geht zu —** that's going too far; **es — bringen** (coll.) to get on in the world; **im –este. Sinne des Wortes** in the broadest sense of the word; **nicht — her sein** (coll. to be of little value; **so — ist es als gekommen!** things have come to such a point! **Treib es nicht zu —!** Don' overdo it! **— gefehlt!** quite wrong **wenn alles so — ist** when everything 's ready; **–ab** *adv.* far away; **–aus** *adv.* b

far; much; **–blickend** *adj.* farsighted;
–en *v.* to widen, to expand; to stretch;
–gehend *adj.* extensive, vast; **–greifend**
adj. far-reaching; **–her** *adv.* from afar;
–hergeholt *adj.* far-fetched; **–herzig**
adj. broad-minded; magnanimous; tolerant; **–hin** *adv.* far away (*oder* off);
–läufig *adj.* distant; spacious; detailed,
circumstantial; **–maschig** *adj.* wide-
meshed; **–reichend** *adj.* far-reaching;
–schweifig *adj.* long-winded; prolix;
tedious; **–sichtig** *adj.* farsighted; long-
sighted; **–spurig** *adj.* (rail.) broad-
gauge; **–tragend** *adj.* far-reaching; of
long range; **–verbreitet** *adj.* widespread,
prevalent, general

Weit: **–blick** *m.* farsightedness; **–e** *f.*
width; extensiveness; distance; size;
capacity; range; **das –e suchen** to take
to one's heels; **–sprung** *m.* broad jump

weiter *adj.* wider; farther, further; **— —** *adv.*
farther, further; more, else; on, for-
ward; **bis auf –es** until further notice;
for the present; **nur —!** go on! **ohne –es**
without more ado, immediately; **und so
— and so on; — niemand** no one else;
–befördern *v.* to forward; **–bestehen** *v.*
to continue to exist; **–bringen** *v.* to help
on; **es –bringen** to make progress;
–führen *v.* to carry on; **–geben** *v.* to
pass on (to); **–geh(e)n** *v.* to walk on;
to continue; **–hin** *adv.* in future, after
that; **–kommen** *v.* to get on; **–können**
v. to be able to go on; **–leiten** *v.* to
transmit, to forward; **–lesen** *v.* to go on
reading; **–sagen** *v.* to tell (others)

Weizen *m.* wheat; **sein — blüht** he seems
to be in clover (*oder* doing well)

welch *pron.* and *adj.* what, which, who,
that; some, any; **–er auch immer** who-
soever; **–erart** *adv.*, **–ergestalt** *adv.* in
what way, by what means, how; **–erlei**
adv. of what kind

welk *adj.* withered, faded, flabby, limp;
–en *v.* to wither, to fade; to droop

Well: **–blech** *neu.* corrugated sheet iron;
–e *f.* wave; billow; breaker; (mech.)
shaft, spindle; axle; (brushwood) bundle; **–enbad** *neu.* swimming pool with
artificial waves; **–enbereich** *m.* (rad.)
wave range; **–enberg** *m.* mountainous
wave; **–enbewegung** *f.* undulation;
–enbrecher *m.* breakwater; **–enkamm**
m. crest of wave; **–enlänge** *f.* wave
length; **–enlinie** *f.* wavy line; **–enreiter**
m. surf rider; **–enschlag** *m.* dashing of
waves; **–ensittich** *m.* parakeet; **–ental**
neu. wave trough; **–entheorie** *f.* theory;
–fleisch *neu.* freshly slaughtered boiled
pork; **–pappe** *f.* corrugated cardboard

wellen *v.* to wave to corrugate; to simmer

welsch *adj.* Italian, French; outlandish

Welt *f.* world; universe; people; **auf der
— on earth; aus der — schaffen** to put
out of the way; **in die — setzen, zur —
bringen** to give birth to; **zur — kommen, das Licht der — erblicken** to be
born; **–all** *neu.* universe; **–alter** *neu.*
age; period of history; **–anschauung** *f.*
philosophical conception of the world

(*oder* history); **–ausstellung** *f.* world
fair; **–beschreibung** *f.* cosmography;
–bildung *f.* good breeding; **–bürger** *m.*
cosmopolite; **–entstehungslehre** *f.* cos-
mogony; **–enbummler** *m.* globe-trotter;
–ereignis *neu.* event of world-wide importance; **–erfahrung** *f.* experience in
worldly affairs; **–friede(n)** *m.* universal
peace; **–gebäude** *neu.* cosmic system;
–geistliche *m.* secular priest; **–gericht**
neu. Last Judgment; **–handel** *m.* international trade; **–kind** *neu.* worldling;
–körper *m.* celestial body, sphere;
–kugel *f.* globe; **–lage** *f.* general political
situation; **–lauf** *m.* course of the world;
–macht *f.* world power; **–meer** *neu.*
ocean; **–meister** *m.* world champion;
–ordnung *f.* cosmic system; natural
laws; **–postverein** *m.* International
Postal Union; **–raum** *m.* space; **–raum-
fahrer** *m.* astronaut; **–raummedizin** *f.*
space medicine; **–raumnavigation** *f.* astronavigation; **–raumschiff** *neu.* space
capsule; **–sprache** *f.* universal language;
–stadt *f.* metropolis; **–untergang** *m.* end
of the world; **–wende** *f.* turning point in
world history

welt: **–bekannt** *adj.*, **–berühmt** *adj.* world-
famous; **–entrückt** *adj.* isolated; **–erfahren** *adj.*, **–klug** *adj.* worldly-wise;
–erschütternd *adj.* world-shaking;
–fremd *adj.* ignorant of the world;
solitary; **–lich** *adj.* worldly; secular;
profane; temporal; **–männisch** *adj.* well-
bred, gentlemanly; **–umspannend** *adj.*
world-embracing; universal

Wemfall *m.* dative case

Wend: **–e** *f.* turn(ing); change, new
epoch; **–ehals** *m.* (orn.) wryneck;
–ekreis *m.* tropic; **–eltreppe** *f.* spiral
staircase; **–epunkt** *m.* turning point;
crisis; solstice; **–ung** *f.* turn(ing);
change; crisis; (mil.) wheeling; phrase,
saying

wenden *v.* to turn (round); (avi.) to yaw;
bitte —! please turn to (page)! **Geld —
an** to spend money on; **sich — an** to
turn (*oder* apply) to

wenig *adj.* little; few; **das –ste** the least;
die –sten only a few; **ein — a** little;
somewhat; **fünf –er drei** five minus
three; **nichts –er als** anything but;
nicht –er als no less than; **nicht zum
–sten** last but not least; **so — auch**
however few; **–er** less; fewer; **–er werden** to decrease, to diminish; **zwei
Dollar zu — two dollars** short; **–stens**
adv. at least

Wenigkeit *f.* small quantity; trifle; **meine
— my humble self**

wenn *conj.* when; if, in case; **— auch**
however, even if; **— auch noch** howsoever; **— doch** if only; **— etwa** if by
chance; **— nur** provided that; **–gleich**
conj., **–schon** *conj.* (al)though, even if

wer *pron.* (he) who; which; (coll.) someone; **— auch immer** whoever; **— da?**
who goes there?

Werb: **–eabteilung** *f.* advertising department; **–enummer** *f.* complimentary

copy; **-eoffizier** m. recruiting officer; **-er** m. suitor, wooer; recruiting officer; **-etrommel** f., **die -etrommel rühren** to make propaganda; to publicize clamorously; **-ung** f. courting, courtship; recruiting; canvassing; advertising, publicity, propaganda; **-ungskosten** pl. advertising expenses

werben v. to recruit, to enlist; to court, to woo; to sue (for); to propagandize, to publicize; to advertise; to canvass

Werdegang m. development; process; evolution; career

werden v. to become, to grow; to turn out; **aus ihm wird nichts** — he will never amount to anything; **es muss anders** — there must be a change; **geliebt** — to be loved; — **zu** to turn into; **-de Mutter** mother-to-be

werfen v. to throw; to fling, to hurl, to pitch; to cast; to project; to bring forth (young); **aufs Papier** — to jot down on paper; **durcheinander** — to muddle up; **sich** — to warp; **sich** — **auf** to apply oneself to; **über den Haufen** — to overthrow; to upset

Werft f. shipyard, wharf; (avi.) workshops

Werk neu. work; labor; act(ion), deed; creation; works; production; factory, workshops; mechanism; **ans geh(e)n, Hand ans** — **legen** to set to work; **ins** — **setzen** to set going; **zu -e gehen** to proceed; **-meister** m. foreman; **-leute** pl. workmen, hands; **-spionage** f. industrial spying; **-statt** f., **-stätte** f. workshop; **-stoff** m. material; **-student** m. working student; **-tag** m working day; weekday; **-zeug** neu. tool, implement; (fig.) organ

Wermut m. wormwood; vermouth; bitterness

wert adj. worth(y); valuable; dear, esteemed; **-beständig** adj. stable, of fixed value; **-en** v. to evaluate, to estimate, to appraise; **-geschätzt** adj. esteemed; **-los** adj. worthless; **-schätzen** v. to esteem highly; to appreciate; to value; **-voll** adj. precious, valuable

Wert m. worth, value; price, rate; importance, use; stress; merit; **fester** — (math.) fixed quantity; **gleicher** — equivalent; **im -e von** at a price of; — **legen auf** to attach great importance to; **-angabe** f. declaration of value; **-bestimmung** f. evaluation; **-brief** m. registered letter; **-gegenstände** m. pl., **-sachen** f. pl. valuables; **-igkeit** f. (chem.) valence; **-messer** m. standard of value; **-paket** neu. registered parcel; **-papiere** neu. pl. securities; **-sendung** f. shipment of declared valuables; **-urteil** neu. value judgment; **-zeichen** neu. paper money; stamp

wes pron., **-sen** pron. whose; **-halb** adv. and conj., **-wegen** adj. and conj. why, wherefore, on account of which, therefore, so

Wesen neu. being, creature; essence; nature, character; manners, way, con-

duct; system, organization; fuss, ado; **sein** — **treiben** to go about; to haunt; **viel -s machen** to make a fuss about; **-seinheit** f. consubstantiality; **-szug** m characteristic feature

wesen: -los adj. unsubstantial, unreal shadowy; **-seigen** adj. characteristic **-sgleich** adj. homogeneous; **-tlich** adj essential, substantial; basic material intrinsic

Wespe f. wasp; **-nstich** m. wasp's sting

West m. west; (poet.) west wind; **-en** m (the) West, Occident; **-mächte** f. pl Western Powers

Weste f. vest; **eine reine** (or **weisse**) —t **haben** to be unimpeachable

Westfalen neu. Westphalia

Westpreussen neu. West Prussia

westwärts adv. westward

wett adj. equal, even; **-eifern** to rival, t emulate, to compete; **-en** v. to bet, t wager; **-machen** v. to make up for **-rüsten** v. to compete in armament

Wett: -bewerb m. competition; (sports event; **-bewerber** m. competitor, rival **-e** f. bet, wager; **eine -e eingehen t** lay a bet; **um die -e laufen** to race **Was gilt die -e?** What do you bet **-eifer** m. emulation, rivalry; **-fahrt** f (boat, car, etc.) race; **-flug** m. air race **-kampf** m. contest, match; prize fight **-lauf** m. footrace; **-rennen** neu. race **-rudern** neu. rowing match; **-spiel** neu match, tournament; **-streit** m. com petition, contest, match

Wetter neu. weather; storm, tempest **alle** —! good gracious! **schlagendes** — firedamp; **-bericht** m. meteorologica report; **-dienst** m. weather bureau meteorological service; **-fahne** f weather vane; **-häuschen** neu. weathe box (barometer); **-karte** f. weathe map; **-kunde** f. meteorology; **-lage** f atmospheric conditions; **-leuchten** neu sheet lightning; **-sturz** m. sudden fall i temperature; **-umschlag** m. change o weather; **-voraussage** f. weather fore cast; **-warte** f. meteorological station **-zeichen** neu. storm signal

wetter: -fest adj. weatherproof; **-leuchte** v. to lighten (without thunder); **-n** to lighten and thunder; to be stormy to curse and swear; **-wendisch** adj changeable, fickle

wetzen v. to whet, to sharpen, to hon **Wetzstein** m. whetstone, hone

Wichs m. (coll.) full dress; **-bürste** f polishing brush; **-e** f. polish; (coll. thrashing

wichsen v. to polish; (coll.) to thras

Wicht m. creature; chit; imp; **-elmann** m brownie, goblin; **-igtuer** m. pompou person

wichtig adj. important, momentous; sic — **machen**, — **tun** to assume an air o importance

Wickel m. wrapping; curler; **beim** – **kriegen** (oder **nehmen**) to collar; **-ban** neu. swaddling band; **-kind** neu. bab **wickeln** v. to wind (round); to roll (up to wrap; to swaddle; (hair) to curl

Widder *m.* ram; (ast.) Aries

wider *prep.* against, contrary (*oder* in opposition) to; versus; **–borstig** *adj.* obstinate; **–fahren** *v.* to happen to, to befall; to meet with; **–hallen** *v.* to echo, to resound; **–legen** *v.* to refute; **–lich** *adj.* repugnant, repulsive, disgusting; **–n** *v.* to disgust; **–natürlich** *adj.* unnatural; **–raten** *v.* to dissuade (from); **–rechtlich** *adj.* illegal, unlawful; **–rufen** *v.* to recant, to retract, to revoke; to withdraw; **–ruflich** *adj.* revocable; **–scheinen** *v.* to reflect; **–setzen** *v.*, **sich –setzen** to oppose, to resist; **–setzlich** *adj.* insubordinate, refractory; **–sinnig** *adj.* nonsensical, absurd; contradictory; **–spenstig** *adj.* obstinate, refractory; unruly; intractable; **–spiegeln** *v.* to reflect, to mirror; **–sprechen** *v.* to contradict; to oppose; **–sprechend** *adj.* contradictory; **–steh(e)n** *v.* to resist, to withstand; **–streben** *v.* to struggle against, to resist; **–strebend** *adj.* reluctant; **–streiten** *v.* to conflict; to be contrary to; **–wärtig** *adj.* disgusting, annoying; **–willig** *adj.* reluctant, unwilling

Wider: **–haken** *m.* barbed hook; **–hall** *m.* echo, reverberation; response; **–part** *m.* opponent, adversary; opposition; **–rede** *f.* contradiction; **–rist** *m.* withers; **–ruf** *m.* recantation; disavowal; (law) disclaimer; **bis auf –ruf** until recalled; **–sacher** *m.* adversary; **–schein** *m.* reflection; **–sinn** *m.* absurdity; nonsense; **–spruch** *m.* contradiction; **–stand** *m.* resistance; (elec.) rheostat; **–streit** *m.* conflict; opposition; contest; **–wille** *m.* aversion; dislike, disgust; reluctance; antipathy

widmen *v.* to dedicate; **sich einer Sache — widmen** to devote oneself to something

Widmung *f.* dedication; **–sexemplar** *neu.* presentation copy

widrig *adj.* contrary, adverse; disgusting; repugnant; **–enfalls** *adv.* failing which

wie *adv.* how; — *conj.* as, like, such; — **auch immer** however; — **bitte?** beg your pardon? — **dem auch sei** be that as it may be; — **du mir so ich dir** tit for tat; **–so** *adv.* why; **–viel** *adv.* how much (*oder* many); **der –vielte ist heute?** what day of the month is it? **–wohl** *conj.* although

wieder *adv.* again; anew; back, in return; **hin und — now and then; immer —** again and again; — **zu sich kommen** to recover; **–anknüpfen** *v.* to renew (acquaintance); **–anstellen** *v.* to reinstall; **–aufbauen** *v.* to reconstruct; **–aufkommen** *v.* to come into fashion again; to recover; **–aufleben** *v.* to revive; **–aufnehmen** *v.* to resume; **–bekommen** *v.* to get back; to recover; **–beleben** *v.* to reanimate; to revive; **–bringen** *v.* to return, to restore; **–einsetzen** *v.* to replace; to reinstate; **–erkennen** *v.* to recognize; **–ersetzen** *v.*, **–erstatten** *v.* to restore, to refund; **–finden** *v.* to find; to recover; **–geben** *v.* to return; to repro-

duce; **–gutmachen** *v.* to compensate; **–herstellen** *v.* to re-establish, to repair; to restore; **–holen** *v.* to fetch back; to repeat, to reiterate; **–holt** *adv.* repeatedly, often; **–käuen** *v.* to ruminate; **–kehren** *v.* to return, to come back; to recur; **–um** *adv.* again, anew

Wiederbelebung (durch künstliche Atmung) *f.* resuscitation

Wiege *f.* cradle; **–messer** *neu.* mincing knife; **–nlied** *neu.* lullaby

wiegen *v.* to weigh; to rock; to mince; **sich in Hoffnungen —** to soothe oneself with hopes

wiehern *v.* to neigh; **–des Gelächter** horselaugh

Wien *neu.* Vienna

Wiese *f.* meadow; **–l** *neu.* weasel; **–ngrund** *m.* grassy valley; meadow land; **–nschaumkraut** *neu.* (bot.) lady's smock, cuckooflower

Wiking *m.* Viking

wild *adj.* wild, savage; fierce, ferocious, unruly; enraged, turbulent; untidy; **–e Ehe** common-law marriage; **–e Flucht** headlong flight; rout; **–er Wein** Virginia creeper; **–er Streik** wildcat strike; **–es Fleisch** (med.) proud flesh; **–es Haar** dishevelled hair; **— machen** to exasperate; **— werden** to become furious; (horse) to shy; **–ern** *v.* to poach; **–fremd** *adj.* quite strange; **–ledern** *adj.* buckskin

Wild *neu.* game, deer, venison; **–bach** *m.* torrent; **–bad** *neu.* thermal springs (*oder* baths); **–bahn** *f.* hunting ground; **–bret** *neu.* game, venison; **–dieb** *m.*, **–erer** *m.* poacher; **–e** *m.* savage; **–fang** *m.* unruly child; tomboy; **–gehege** *neu.*, **–park** *m.* game preserve; **–hüter** *m.* gamekeeper; **–leder** *neu.* suede; **–ling** *m.* wild tree (*oder* animal, etc.); **–nis** *f.* wilderness; **–schaden** *m.* damage caused by game; **–schütz(e)** *m.* poacher; **–schwein** *neu.* wild boar; **–stand** *m.* stock of game; **–wasser** *neu.* torrent

Wilhelm *m.* William

Will: –e *m.* will; volition; determination; intention; **aus freiem –en** of one's own accord; voluntarily; **böser –e** malice; **jemand zu –en sein** to comply with someone's wishes; **mit –en** on purpose, intentionally; **–ens sein** to be ready (to do something); **wider –en** unwillingly; unintentionally; **–enskraft** *f.* will power; **–komm** *m.*, **–kommen** *neu.* welcome; **–kür** *f.* arbitrary action; despotism; **er ist ihrer –kür preisgegeben** he is at their mercy

will: –enlos *adj.* lacking will power; irresolute; **–entlich** *adj.* intentional; **–fahren** *v.* to comply with; to grant; **–fährig** *adj.* compliant, accomodating; **–ig** *adj.* willing, ready; **–kommen** *adj.* welcome; opportune; acceptable; **–kürlich** *adj.* arbitrary, despotic, unlimited

wimmeln *v.* to swarm (*oder* be crowded) with

wimmern *v.* to whimper, to moan

Wimpel *m.* pennant, pennon

Wimper f. eyelash; **ohne mit der — zu zucken** without turning a hair

Wind m. wind, breeze; (med.) flatulence; **bei — und Wetter** in storm and rain; **den Mantel nach dem — hängen** to trim one's sails to the wind; **in den — reden** to speak in vain; **in den — schlagen** to disregard; **vor dem — segeln** to run before the wind; **— bekommen von** to get scent of; **— machen** to boast, to brag; **—beutel** m. cream puff; (coll.) windbag; **—beutelei** f. bragging, humbug; **—bruch** m. windfall; **—e** f. winch; windlass; reel; (bot.) bindweed; **—ei** neu. addled egg; **—el** f. diaper; **—eln** pl. swaddling clothes; **—eseile** f. (fig.) lightning speed; **—fahne** f. weather vane; **—fang** m. windbreak; **—harfe** f. Aeolian harp; **—hose** f. whirlwind; **—hund** m. greyhound; (coll.) windbag; **—jacke** f. weatherproof jacket; **—licht** neu. hurricane lamp; **—messer** m. anemometer; **—mühle** f. windmill; **—mühlenflugzeug** neu. helicopter; **—pocken** f. chicken pox; **—röschen** neu. anemone; **—rose** f. compass card; **—sack** m. wind cone; **—sbraut** f. gale, hurricane; **—(schutz)scheibe** f. windshield; **—stille** f. calm; **—stoss** m. gust of wind; **—ung** f. winding, turn; sinuosity; coil, whorl; worm (of screw); **—zug** m. draft, current of air

wind: —elweich adj. compliant; **—elweich schlagen** to beat to a pulp; **—en** to wind, to reel; to hoist; to bind (wreath); **sich —en** to wind, to twine (round); to meander; to writhe; **—ig** adj. windy; (coll.) unreliable; **—schief** adj. warped; **—still** adj. calm; **—wärts** adv. windward

Windel f. diaper; **—n** pl. swaddling clothes

Windung f. winding, turn; sinuosity; coil, whorl; worm (of screw)

Wink m. wink; hint, tip; insinuation; **—er** m. signaler; **—zeichen** neu. semaphore

Winkel m. angle; corner, nook; (mil.) chevron; **—advokat** m. shyster lawyer; **—blatt** neu. obscure local newspaper; **—eisen** neu. steel square (oder rule); **—haken** m. try square, rule; (typ.) composing stick; **—mass** neu. square; **—messer** m. protractor; goniometer; **—poet** m. obscure poet; **—zug** m. trick, dodge; subterfuge

winkelrecht adj. at right angles

winken v. to wink, to wave, to make a sign; to semaphore; **mit dem Laternpfahl** (or **Zaunpfahl, Scheunentor**) **— to give a broad hint

winseln v. to whimper, to whine, to wail

Winter m. winter; **—aufenthalt** m. winter resort; **—frucht** f., **—getreide** neu., **—korn** neu. winter grain; **—garten** m. conservatory; **—schlaf** m. hibernation; **—schlussverkauf** m. winter clearance sale; **—überzieher** m. winter overcoat

Winzer m. vinegrower; vintager

winzig adj. diminutive, minute; tiny

Wipfel m. treetop

Wippe f. seesaw

wir pron. we; **— alle** all of us

Wirbel m. whirl(pool); eddy; vertebra; (drum) roll; (hair) whorl; (violin) peg; **—kasten** m. (violin) neck for pegs; **—knochen** m. vertebra; **—säule** f. spine; **—sturm** m. cyclone, tornado, hurricane; **—tier** neu. vertebrate; **—wind** m. whirlwind

wirk: —en v. to work, to effect, to produce; to knit (hosiery); to knead (dough); **—en auf** to affect, to influence, to impress; **—lich** adj. real, actual; true, genuine; **—sam** adj. effective, efficacious, efficient

Wirk: —ung f. effect, result; **—ungskreis** m. sphere of activity (oder influence); province; **—waren** f. pl. knitwear

wirr adj. confused, dishevelled; chaotic

Wirr: —en f. pl. disorders, troubles; **—kopf** m. muddlehead; **—nis** f., **—sal** neu. confusion, disorder; **—warr** m. medley: jumble, muddle; chaos

Wirsingkohl m. savoy (cabbage)

Wirt m. host; innkeeper; landlord; **—in** f. hostess; innkeeper; landlady; **—schaft** f. housekeeping; household; inn; economics, economy; doings; (coll.) mess; **—schafter** m., **—schafterin** f. housekeeper; manager; steward(ess); **—schaftler** m. teacher of economics; industrial leader; **—schaftsgebäude** neu. pl. farm buildings; **—schaftsgeld** neu. housekeeping money; **—schaftsgruppe** f. trust, corporation; **—schaftsjahr** neu. fiscal year; **—schaftspolitik** f. economics; **—schaftsprüfer** m. auditor; **—shaus** neu. tavern; inn; **—sleute** pl. host and hostess

wirt: —lich adj. hospitable, habitable; **—schaften** to keep house; to manage; to economize; (coll.) to rummage; **—schaftlich** adj. economic(al); profitable; thrifty

Wisch m. (paper) scrap (straw) wisp; **—er** m. wiper; (drawing) stump; (coll.) rebuke; **—lappen** m. dust cloth, wiping rag

wischen v. to wipe; (drawing) to stump

Wismut m. and neu. bismuth

wispern v. to whisper

Wissbegierde f. thirst for learning, curiosity

wissen v. to know, to be acquainted with; **er will alles besser —** he's a know-it-all; **jemand Dank —** to be grateful; **sie will ihn glücklich —** she wishes him to be happy; **sie will nichts von ihm —** she wants to have nothing to do with him; **weder aus noch ein —** not to know which way to turn; **—schaftlich** adj. scientific, scholarly; **—tlich** adj. knowing; deliberate; **—tlich** adv. on purpose

Wissen neu. knowledge; learning; **meines —s** as far as I know; **nach bestem — und Gewissen** most conscientiously; **wider besseres —** against one's better judgment; **—schaft** f. science, knowledge; **—schaftler** m. scientist, scholar; **—sdrang** m., **—sdurst** m. thirst for knowledge

wittern v. to scent, to perceive, to suspect

Witterung f. weather; scent; **-sumschlag** m. change of weather; **-sverhältnisse** neu. pl. atmospheric conditions

Witwe f. widow; dowager; **-nschaft** f., **-nstand** m. widowhood; **-ntracht** f. widow's weeds; **-r** m. widower

Witz m. wit(tiness); joke; witticism; **-e machen** to crack jokes; **-blatt** neu. comic paper; **-bold** m. joker; **-elei** f. joking, banter

witzeln v. to ridicule; to joke

wo adv. where, when; in which; **— auch immer** wherever; **— nicht** if not, unless; **-anders** adv. somewhere else, elsewhere; **-bei** adv. where(at); whereby; in (oder through) which; **-durch** adv. by what (oder which) means; **-fern** adv. so far as; provided that; if; **-fern nicht** unless; **-für** adv. for which; what for; **-gegen** adv. against what (oder which); in return for what (oder which); **-gegen** conj. whilst, whereas, on the other hand; **-her** adv. wherefrom; from what place; **-her weiss er das?** how does he know that? **-hin** adv. whither; where to, to what (oder which) place; **-hinaus** adv. which way, to what place; **-mit** adv. by what (means), wherewith; **-möglich** adv. perhaps, possibly; **-nach** adv. after what (oder which); whereafter, whereupon; **-ran** adv. whereon; at (oder by, of) what; **-rauf** adv. whereupon; **-raus** adv. out of what; from which; **-rein** adv. into what (oder which); **-rin** adv. in what (oder which); wherein; **-rüber** adv. over which; of (oder about) what; whereat; **-rum** adv. about what (oder which); **-runter** adv. beneath what; among which; **-selbst** adv. where; **-von** adv. whereof; about what; of which; **-vor** adv. before what, of which; **-zu** adv. for which; what for; why

Woche f. week; **-n** f. pl., **-nbett** neu. childbed; **-nblatt** neu. weekly paper; **-nende** neu. weekend; **-nlohn** m. weekly wages; **-nschau** f. weekly review; newsreel; **-ntag** m. weekday

wochen- **-lang** adj. for weeks; **-tags** adv. on weekdays; **-weise** adj. by the week

wöchentlich adj. weekly; every (oder a, by the) week

Wöchnerin f. woman in childbed

Woge f. wave, billow

wogen v. to surge, to wave, to heave; **hin und her —** to fluctuate, to undulate

wohl adv. well; probably, presumably, very likely; **— prep.** about; **er wird — reich** sein he is rich, I suppose; **leben Sie —!** good-bye! **sich's — sein lassen** to enjoy oneself; **— bekomm's!** your health! here's to you! **— dem, der** happy he who; **— oder übel** whether one likes it or not; **-an!** interj. now then! come on! **-auf** adv. well, in good health; **-bedacht** adj. well-considered; **-behalten** adj. safe and sound; **-bekannt** adj. well-known, familiar; **-beleibt** adj. corpulent; **-erzogen** adj.

well-bred; **-feil** adj. cheap; **-geartet** adj. well-disposed; well-bred; **-gefällig** adj. pleasant; complacent; **-gelitten** adj. well liked, popular; **-gemeint** adj. well-meant; **-gemut** adj. cheerful, gay; **-genährt** adj. well-fed; **-geneigt** adj. well-affected; **-gestaltet** adj. well-shaped; **-habend** adj. wealthy; **-ig** adj. comfortable, happy; **-klingend** adj. harmonious, melodious; **-meinend** adj. well-meaning, benevolent; **-riechend** adj. fragrant, sweet-scented; **-schmeckend** adj. tasty, savory; **-tätig** adj. beneficent, charitable; **-tuend** adj. comforting, pleasant; **-tun** v. to do good; to be pleasant; **-überlegt** adj. well-considered; **-unterrichtet** adj. well-informed; **-verdient** adj. well-deserved; **-versorgt** adj. well-provided; **-verstanden** adj. well-understood; **-weislich** adv. prudently, wisely; **-wollend** adj. kindly, benevolent

Wohl neu. well-being, welfare, prosperity; **auf Ihr —!** your health! good luck! **-befinden** neu. good health, well-being; **-behagen** neu. (feeling of) comfort, ease; **-ergeh(e)n** neu. welfare, prosperity; **-fahrt** f. welfare; **-fahrtspflege** f. welfare work; **-gefallen** neu. pleasure, satisfaction; **sich in -gefallen auflösen** (coll.) to end peacefully; to come to naught; **-geruch** m. fragrance, perfume; **-geschmack** m. pleasant flavor; **-habenheit** f. opulence, wealth; **-klang** m., **-laut** m. melodious sound; harmony; **-leben** neu. luxurious living; life of pleasure; **-sein** neu. well-being; good health; **-stand** m. prosperity; **-tat** f. comfort, blessing; charity; **-täter** m. benefactor; **-wollen** neu. good will, benevolence

wohn: **-en** v. to live, to dwell, to reside, to stay; **-haft** adj. living, resident; **-lich** adj. cosy, snug, comfortable

Wohn: **-gebäude** neu., **-haus** neu. dwelling (oder apartment) house; **-küche** f. room with kitchenette; **-ort** m., **-sitz** m. domicile, legal residence; **-stube** f., **-zimmer** neu. living room; **-ung** f. dwelling, habitation; rooms, apartment; flat; **-ungsnachweis** m. housing agency; **-ungsnot** f. housing shortage; **-ungswechsel** m. change of residence; **-viertel** neu. residential section; **-wagen** m. trailer

Wölbung f. vault(ing); arch, dome; curvature

Wolf m. wolf; (med.) abrasion; **-seisen** neu. wolf trap; **-shunger** m. ravenous hunger; **-smilch** f. (bot.) spurge; **-ram** neu. tungsten

Wolke f. cloud; **aus allen -n fallen** to be thunderstruck; **-nbruch** m. cloudburst; **-nhöhe** f. ceiling; **-nkratzer** m. skyscraper; **-nkuckucksheim** neu. dreamland, Utopia; **-nschicht** f. stratum (of clouds); **-nwand** f. cloudbank; overcast

wolkig adj. clouded, cloudy

Woll: **-decke** f. woolen blanket; **-e** f. wool; fleece; **in die -e geraten** (coll.) to start a fight; **-stoff** m. woolen material

Woll: **-en** neu. will(ingness), volition; **-ust** f. voluptuousness, lust; **-üstling** m. voluptuary

woll: **-en** v. to want, to wish; to be willing; to intend; to be about to; **das will etwas heissen!** that's something! **das will ich meinen** I should say so; **dem mag sein wie es -e** be that as it may be; **er mag -en oder nicht** whether he likes it or not; **er will dagewesen sein** he claims to have been there; **hoch hinaus -en** to have lofty ideas; **ich -te lieber** I would rather; I prefer; **wir -en gehen** let us go

wollen adj. woolen, worsted

Wonne f. delight, bliss; **-monat** m., **-mond** m. month of May

wonne: **-sam** adj. delightful; **-trunken** adj. enraptured

worfeln v. to winnow

Wort neu. word; expression, term; saying; promise; **aufs — gehorchen** to obey implicitly; **das grosse — führen** to brag; **das — ergreifen** to begin to speak; **das — erteilen** to give permission to speak; **einer Sache das — reden** to speak for something; **ein — gibt das andere** one word leads to another; **es ist kein wahres — daran** there isn't a grain of truth in it; **ins — fallen** to interrupt; **jemand zu -e kommen lassen** to let a person have his say; **kein — mehr!** not another word! **um nicht viele -e zu machen** to cut a long story short; **— halten** to keep (one's) word; **-e verschwenden** to waste (one's) breath; **-ableitung** f. derivation of words; etymology; **-aufwand** m. verbosity; **-bildung** f. word formation; **-bruch** m. breach of promise; **-emacher** m. verbose speaker; **-fechter** m. stickler for words; **-folge** f. word order; **-fügungslehre** f. syntax; **-führer** m. speaker; spokesman; **-gefecht** neu. dispute; **-klauber** m. hairsplitter, quibbler; **-laut** m. text, wording; **-schatz** m. vocabulary; **-schwall** m. bombast, verbosity; **-spiel** neu. pun; **-wechsel** m. dispute, altercation

Wörterbuch neu. dictionary

wörtlich adj. verbal, verbatim; literal

Wrack neu. wreck

wringen v. to wring

Wucher m. usury; profiteering; **-er** m. usurer, profiteer; **-gewinn** m. inordinate profit; **-ung** f. exuberance; growth, tumor; **-zins** m. usurious interest

wuchern v. to grow luxuriantly; to practice usury, to profiteer; to make the most of; **mit seinem Pfunde — to** utilize one's talent

Wuchs m. growth; stature, development; figure

Wucht f. burden, weight; force, impetus

wuchtig adj. heavy, weighty

Wühl: **-arbeit** f. subversive activity; **-er** m. agitator; **-erei** f. agitation; **-maus** f. vole

wühlen v. to dig; to root; to burrow; to rummage; to stir up, to agitate; im

Gelde — to be rolling in money

Wulst m. and f. swelling; roll, pad; protuberance; **-lippen** f. pl. blubber lips

Wund: **-arzt** m. surgeon; **-e** f. wound; **-mal** neu. scar; **-male** pl. stigmata; **-schorf** m. scab

Wunder neu. miracle; marvel, wonder; **es grenzt an ein — it** borders on the supernatural; **sein blaues — erleben** (coll.) to be amazed; **-bild** neu. miracleworking image; **-ding** neu. marvellous thing; marvel; **-doktor** m. quack; **-glaube** m. belief in miracles; **-horn** neu. magic horn; **-kind** neu. infant prodigy; **-land** neu. fairyland; **-täter** m. miracle worker; **-tier** neu. monster; prodigy; **-welt** f. enchanted world; **-zeichen** neu. miraculous sign

wunder das nimmt mich — I am surprised; **sich — was einbilden** (coll.) to be very cocky; **-bar** adj. wonderful, marvelous; amazing; **-barerweise** adv. strange to say; **-hübsch** adj. exceedingly pretty; **-lich** adj. strange, odd; moody; **sich -n v. über** to wonder at, to be surprised at; **-sam** adj. wonderful, strange; **-schön** adj. very beautiful, exquisite; **-tätig** adj. wonder-working; miraculous; **-voll** adj. wonderful, marvelous; admirable

Wunsch m. wish, desire; **auf — by** request; **mit den besten Wünschen zum Fest** with the compliments of the season; **nach — as** desired; **-bild** neu. ideal; **-form** f. (gram.) optative form; **-zettel** m. list of things desired; letter to Santa Claus

Wünschelrute f. divining rod

wünschen v. to wish, to desire; **Glück — to** congratulate; **-swert** adj. desirable

Würd: **-e** f. dignity; honor; rank, title; **akademische -e** academic degree; **unter aller -e** beneath contempt; **-enträger** m. dignitary

würd: **-elos** adj. undignified; **-evoll** adj. dignified; **-ig** adj. worthy; deserving of; dignified, respectable; **-igen** v. to appreciate; to evaluate; to honor; **nicht eines Wortes -igen** not to grant a word (to)

Wurf m. cast, throw(ing); brood, litter; **alles auf einen — setzen** to stake all on one throw; **zum — ausholen** to get ready to throw; **-bahn** f. trajectory; **-geschoss** neu. projectile; **-scheibe** f. discus; **-sendung** f. direct mail advertising; **-speer** m., **-spiess** m. javelin; **-weite** f. range of throw

Würfel m. die; cube; **der — ist gefallen** the die is cast; **-becher** m. dice box; **-bude** f. booth for dice throwing; **-muster** neu. checkered pattern; **-spiel** neu. dice game; **-zucker** m. lump sugar

würfel: **-förmig** adj. cubic form; **-ig** adj. cubical; checkered; **-n** v. to play at dice; to checker

würgen v. to choke; to retch, to strangle; to throttle

Würger m. strangler; murderer; butcherbird

Wurm *m.* worm; grub, maggot; (poet.) dragon; — *neu.* (coll.) poor little thing; **-fortsatz** *m.* vermiform appendix; **-frass** *m.* damage done by worms; **-mehl** *neu.* worm cast; **-stich** *m.*, **-loch** *neu.* wormhole

Wurst *f.* sausage; **das ist mir** — (coll.) I don't care; **— wider** — (coll.) tit for tat; **-blatt** *neu.* (coll.) small obscure newspaper; **-waren** *f. pl.* sausages

Württemberg *neu.* Wurtemberg

Würze *f.* seasoning, flavor, spice; zest, piquancy; **in der Kürze liegt die** — brevity is the soul of wit

Wurzel *f.* root; **— fassen (or schlagen)** to take root; **-behandlung** *f.* (dent.) root treatment; **-faser** *f.* root fiber, rootlet; **-gemüse** *neu.* edible roots; **-keim** *m.* radicle; **-knolle** *f.*, **-knollen** *m.* bulb, tuber; **-schössling** *m.* layer, runner, sucker; **-werk** *neu.* root system; **-zeichen** *neu.* radical sign; **-ziehen** *neu.* extraction of roots

würzen *v.* to season, to spice, to flavor

Wust *m.* confusion; chaos; mess

wüst *adj.* waste, desolate; desert(ed); confused; unruly, disorderly; vulgar, rude; dissolute; **-en** *v.* to spoil; to live profligately

Wüst: **-e** *f.* desert, wilderness; **-enei** *f.* desolate region; **-enschiff** *neu.* (poet.) camel; **-ling** *m.* debauchee, dissolute person

Wut *f.* fury, rage; frenzy; in **— geraten** to fly into a rage; **-anfall** *m.* fit of rage; paroxysm

wut: **-entbrannt** *adj.* infuriated, enraged; **-schnaubend** *adj.*, **-schäumend** *adj.* foaming with rage; frenzied, rabid

wüt: **-en** *v.* to rage, to be furious; **-end** *adj.*, **-ig** *adj.* furious, enraged; mad

Wüterich *m.* ruthless (*oder* frantic) fellow

X

X *neu.*, **man kann ihm kein — für ein U machen** he is not easily taken in

X-Beine *neu. pl.* knock-knees

x-beinig *adj.* knock-kneed

x-beliebig *adj.* any, whatever; whoever

Xenie *f.* (satirical) epigram

x-mal *adv.* many times; ever so often

X-Strahlen *m. pl.* X-rays

xte *adj.* nth; **zum —n Male** for the umpteenth time

Xylophon *neu.* xylophone

Y

yankeehaft *adj.* Yankee-like

Ypsilon *neu.* the letter Y

Ysop *m.* hyssop

Z

Zacke *f.*, **Zacken** *m.* peak, point; (fork) prong; (mountain) crag; (saw) dent, tooth; (wall) crenel, spike; (wheel) cog; scallop

zackig *adj.* indented, notched; pointed; scalloped; serrated, crenate; pinked

zaghaft *adj.* faint-hearted, timid; hesitant

zäh(e) *adj.* tough, tenacious; viscous

Zähegrad *m.* viscosity

Zahl *f.* number; figure, cipher; **gerade —** even number; **ungerade —** odd number; **-er** *m.* payer; **-karte** *f.* money order blank; **-kellner** *m.* headwaiter; **-meister** *m.* paymaster; **-stelle** *f.* cashier's office; **-tag** *m.* payday; due date; **-ung** *f.* payment; **-ungsfähigkeit** *f.* solvency; **-ungsfrist** *f.*, **-ungsbedingung** *f.* term of payment; **-ungsmittel** *neu.* (legal) tender; **-ungsschwierigkeiten** *f. pl.* pecuniary difficulties; **-wort** *neu.* numeral

zahl: **-bar** *adj.* payable; **-en** *v.* to pay; **-enmässig** *adj.* numerical; **-los** *adj.* innumerable, countless; **-reich** *adj.* numerous; **-ungsfähig** *adj.* solvent; **-ungsunfähig** *adj.* insolvent

Zähl: **-er** *m.* counter, meter, numerator; **-ung** *f.* counting; census; computation; **-werk** *neu.* meter, counter, register

zählen *v.* to count, to enumerate; to reckon, to score; **— auf** to rely upon; **— zu** to belong to, to count with

zahm *adj.* tame, domestic, tractable

zähmen *v.* to tame, to domesticate; to break in; to subdue, to restrain, to curb

Zahn *m.* tooth; fang, tusk; cog; **jemand auf den — fühlen** (coll.) to sound out someone; **-arzt** *m.* dentist; **-bein** *neu.* dentine; **-bürste** *f.* toothbrush; **-ersatz** *m.* artificial teeth; **-fäule** *f.* caries, tooth decay; **-fleisch** *neu. pl.* gums; **-entzündung** *f.* gingivitis; **-geschwür** *neu.* gumboil; **-heilkunde** *f.* dentistry; **-höhle** *f.* (tooth) socket; **-lücke** *f.* gap between teeth; **-pasta** *f.* tooth paste; **-rad** *neu.* cogwheel; **-radbahn** *f.* rack railroad; **-reissen** *neu.*, **-schmerz** *m.* toothache; **-schmelz** *m.* (tooth) enamel; **-stein** *m.* tartar, scale; **-stocher** *m.* toothpick; **-wasser** *neu.* mouthwash; **-wechsel** *m.* second dentition

zahn: **-en** *v.* to teethe; **-förmig** *adj.* dentiform; **-los** *adj.* toothless

Zähne: **-fletschen** *neu.* showing one's teeth; **-klappern** *neu.* chattering of teeth; **-knirschen** *neu.* gnashing of teeth

Zange *f.* pliers; pincers; tongs; tweezers; forceps; forcipated claw

Zank *m.* quarrel; altercation, wrangle; **-apfel** *m.* bone of contention; **-teufel** *m.* shrew

zank: **-en** *v.* to quarrel, to wrangle; **-haft** *adj.*, **-süchtig** *adj.* quarrelsome, contentious

Zänker *m.* quarrelsome person; wrangler

Zapf: **-en** *m.* plug, peg, pin; bung, tap; tenon, pivot, trunnion; (bot.) cone; **-enloch** *neu.* mortise; **-enstreich** *m.* (mil.) tattoo; **-er** *m.* tapster, barman

Zäpfchen *neu.* small plug; uvula

zapfen *v.* to tap

zappeln *v.* to fidget, to struggle; **jemand — lassen** to keep someone in suspense

zart *adj.* tender; delicate, frail, fragile;

young; **-besaitet** *adj.* sensitive; **-füh-**
lend *adj.* tactful, sensitive; tenderhearted

zärtlich *adj.* affectionate, fond; tender

Zauber *m.* magic, spell, charm, enchant-
ment; **-buch** *neu.* conjuring book; **-ei**
f. magic, sorcery; **-er** *m.* magician,
conjurer; charmer; **-formel** *f.* magic
formula, incantation; **-in** *f.* sorceress,
witch; **-kunst** *f.* black magic; **-künstler**
m. illusionist; conjurer; **-kunststück**
neu. conjuring trick; **-posse** *f.* fairy
play; **-spruch** *m.* incantation; **-trank**
m. magic potion

zauber: -haft *adj.*, **-isch** *adj.* magical,
fascinating; **-kräftig** *adj.* magical; **-n** *v.*
to practice magic; to conjure; to pro-
duce by magic

zaudern *v.* to delay, to hesitate; to tarry

Zaum *m.* bridle; **im — halten** to keep a
tight rein on, to restrain; to check, to
curb

zäumen *v.* to bridle; to restrain, to check

Zaun *m.* fence; **einen Streit vom -e**
brechen to pick a quarrel; **-gast** *m.*
nonpaying spectator; **-könig** *m.* wren;
-pfahl *m.* fence post; **mit dem -pfahl**
winken to give a broad hint

zausen *v.* to tug (*oder* pull) about; to
tousle

Zech: -bruder *m.* tippler, boozer; **-e** *f.*
bill, reckoning; **die -e bezahlen** to pay
the bill; **-er** *m.* tippler, carouser;
-gelage *neu.* carousal, drinking bout;
-prellerei *f.* evading payment of bill

zechen *v.* to carouse, to tipple; to drink

Zeder *f.* cedar

Zehe *f.* toe; **-nspitze** *f.* tiptoe

zehn *adj.* ten; **-erlei** *adj.* of ten kinds;
-fach *adj.*, **-fältig** *adj.* tenfold; **-te** *adj.*
tenth; **-tens** *adv.* tenthly, in the tenth
place

Zehn *f.*, **-er** *m.* ten; **-eck** *neu.* decagon;
-ender *m.* stag with ten antlers;
-erreihe *f.* column of tens; **-te** *m.* tithe;
tenth; **-tel** *neu.* tenth part

Zehrung *f.* consumption; waste; expenses;
provisions; **letzte — extreme unction**

Zeichen *neu.* sign, signal; mark, token;
brand. stamp; badge; indication, symptom; omen; **seines -s ein Tischler sein**
to be a carpenter by trade; **-brett** *neu.*
drawing board; **-buch** *neu.* sketch book;
-kunst *f.* (art of) drawing; **-lehrer** *m.*
drawing instructor; **-setzung** *f.* punctuation; **-sprache** *f.* sign language;
-stift *m.* crayon, drawing pencil; **-vor-**
lage *f.* drawing copy

zeichnen *v.* to draw, to sketch, to design;
to mark; to sign; to subscribe

Zeichner *m.* draftsman; designer; subscriber

Zeige: -finger *m.* forefinger, index; **-r** *m.*
(clock) hand; **-stab** *m.*, **-stock** *m.*
pointer

zeigen *v.* to show, to point; to display, to
manifest; to exhibit; to prove, to
demonstrate; **sich — to appear; to**
turn out

Zeile *f.* line; row; **-ngussmaschine** *f.*

linotype

Zeisig *m.* siskin; **lockerer —** (sl.) fast
fellow

Zeit *f.* time, term; epoch, period, age;
season; tense; **auf — on credit; damit**
hat es — there is no hurry; die ganze
— über ever since; du liebe —! Good
heavens! **mit der — fortschreiten to**
keep pace with the times; **nach gerau-**
mer — after a considerable period; vor
der — prematurely; während der —
in the meantime; **— seines Lebens**
during his lifetime; **zu gleicher —**
simultaneously; **zur — at present; in**
time; in the time of; **zu -en** now and
then; **-abschnitt** *m.* epoch, period;
-alter *neu.* age, generation; **-angabe** *f.*
time, date; **-aufnahme** *f.* time exposure;
-aufwand *m.* time spent; **-einheit** *f.*
unit(y) of time; **-einteilung** *f.* timing,
timetable; **-folge** *f.* chronological order;
-form *f.* tense; **-funk** *m.* (rad.) topical
talk; **-genosse** *m.* contemporary; **-ge-**
schäft *neu.* installment business; **-ge-**
schichte *f.* contemporary history;
-karte *f.* season ticket; **-karteninhaber**
m. commuter; **-lage** *f.* juncture, state
of affairs; **-lauf** *m.* course of events,
period; **-lupe** *f.* slow motion; **-mass**
neu. (mus.) time; (poet.) quantity;
-messer *m.* chronometer, metronome;
-nehmer *m.* timekeeper; **-ordnung** *f.*
chronological order; **-punkt** *m.* moment; **-raffer** *m.* (film) quick motion;
-raum *m.* period, interval; **-rechnung**
f. chronology; **christliche -rechnung**
Christian era; **-schrift** *f.* journal,
periodical, magazine; **-tafel** *f.* chronological table; **-umstände** *m. pl.* circumstances; junctures; **-vertreib** *m.*
pastime, amusement; **-wort** *neu.* verb;
-zeichen *neu.* time signal; **-zünder** *m.*
time fuse

zeit: -gemäss *adj.* timely, opportune;
up-to-date; seasonable; **-genössisch**
adj. contemporary; **-ig** *adj.* early,
timely; mature; **-igen** *v.* to mature; to
effect; **-lebens** *adv.* for (*oder* during)
life; **-lich** *adj.* temporal; **-weilig** *adj.*
temporary, provisional; **-weise** *adv.* for
a time, from time to time

Zeitung *f.* newspaper; **-sausschnitt** *m.*
press clipping; **-sbeilage** *f.* supplement;
-sente *f.* canard, newspaper hoax;
-sexpedition *f.* newspaper office;
-sjunge *m.* paper boy; **-skiosk** *m.*
newsstand; **-snotiz** *f.* press item; **-swe-**
sen *neu.* journalism, the (daily) press

zelebrieren *v.* to celebrate; to read (Mass)

Zell: -e *f.* cell; **-gewebe** *neu.* cellular
tissue; **-stoff** *m.*, **-ulose** *f.* cellulose

Zelot *m.* zealot

Zelt *neu.* tent; **-bahn** *f.* tarpaulin; **-lager**
neu. camp; **-platz** *m.* tourist court

Zement *m.* cement; **-stahl** *m.* reinforced
concrete

zementieren *v.* to cement

Zenit *m.* zenith

zensieren *v.* to censor, to give grades

Zensor *m.* censor

Zensur f. censoring, censorship; school marks

Zent: −enarfeier f. centenary; −imeter m. and neu. centimeter; −ner m. hundredweight; fifty kilograms; −nerlast f. (fig.) heavy burden

zentnerschwer adj. very heavy

Zentral: −e f. central office; telephone exchange; −heizung f. central heating

zentralisieren v. to centralize

zentrisch adj. centric(al)

Zentrum neu. center (party); bull's eye

Zepter neu. scepter

zerbeissen v. to bite into pieces; to crunch

zerbersten v. to burst, to split in pieces

zerbrechen v. to break up, to smash, to shatter; **sich den Kopf** − to rack one's brains

zerbrechlich adj. breakable, fragile, brittle

zerdrücken v. to crush, to squash; to crumple

Zeremonie f. ceremony

Zeremonienmeister m. master-of-ceremonies (M.C.)

zeremoniell adj. ceremonial

zerfahren v. to crush (oder ruin) by driving over; − adj. absent-minded, scatter-brained

zerfallen v. to fall to pieces; to decay; to disintegrate; to be divided (into); − sein mit to be on bad terms with

zerfetzen v. to shred; to mutilate, to slash

zerfleischen v. to lacerate, to mangle

zerfliessen v. to flow (oder melt) away; to dissolve; to disperse

zerfressen v. to gnaw away; to corrode

zergeh(e)n v. to dissolve, to melt; to dwindle

zergliedern v. to dismember; to dissect; to analyze; to decompose

zerhacken v. to chop to pieces; to mince

zerhauen v. to cut up

zerkauen v. to chew well

zerkleinern v. to reduce to bits; to chop up

zerklopfen v. to pound to pieces

zerknautschen, zerknittern, zerknüllen v. to crush, to crumble

zerknirscht adj. contrite

zerkratzen v. to mar with scratches, to scratch

zerlegbar adj. separable, divisible, collapsible

zerlegen v. to divide, to part; to cut up; to carve (roast); to dissect; to analyze

zerlumpt adj. ragged, tattered

zermahlen v. to grind up, to pulverize

zermalmen v. to crush, to crunch, to pulverize

zernagen v. to gnaw through; to corrode

zerplatzen v. to burst apart

zerquetschen v. to crush, to squash; to bruise

Zerrbild neu. caricature

zerreiben v. to rub away, to grind down

zerreissen v. to tear up; to lacerate; to wear out; **die Ohren** − to grate on the ears

zerren v. to drag; to pull; to strain (muscle)

zerrinnen v. to melt away; to vanish

Zerrissenheit f. tattered (oder torn) condition; raggedness; disunion; mental conflict

zerrütten v. to disorganize; to ruin; to undermine (health); to derange

zerschiessen v. to shoot to pieces

zerschlagen v. to batter, to shatter; to destroy; **ganz** − **sein** to be completely exhausted; **sich** − to come to naught; − adj. battered, broken

zerschmettern v. to shatter, to smash

zerschneiden v. to cut into pieces; to sever

zersetzen v. to decompose; to undermine, to demoralize; to dissolve

zerspalten v. to cleave, to split

zersprengen v. to blast, to burst open

zerspringen v. to burst, to break; to crack

zerstampfen v. to crush; to trample down

zerstäuben v. to pulverize; to spray

Zerstäuber m. atomizer; sprayer

zerstören v. to destroy, to demolish, to ruin; to disorganize; to devastate

zerstreuen v. to disperse; to dissipate, to dispel; to divert

zerstreut adj. scattered, dispersed; diffused; absent-minded, preoccupied

Zerstreutheit f. absent-mindedness

Zerstreuung f. dispersion; diversion

zerteilen v. to divide; to cut up; to disperse

zertreten v. to crush (oder trample) down

zertrümmern v. to lay in ruins; to demolish, to wreck, to smash; to split (atoms)

Zerwürfnis neu. dissension, discord, quarrel

zerzausen v. to pull to pieces; to dishevel

Zetergeschrei neu. cry of murder; outcry

Zettel m. scrap (oder slip) of paper; label; bill; poster; −kasten m. filing cabinet

Zeug neu. stuff, material; fabric, cloth; matter; implements, tools; trash; **arbeiten, was das** − **hält** to work with might and main; **das** − **haben zu** to have the ability to do; **dummes** − nonsense; **jemand am** −e **flicken** to slander someone; **sich ins** − **legen** to put one's shoulder to the wheel; −haus neu. armory, arsenal

Zeuge m. witness; −naussage f. testimony; deposition

Zeugnis neu. evidence, testimony; attestation; testimonial; school report

zeugen v. to testify, to give evidence (of); to beget, to procreate, to generate; to produce

Zibetkatze f. civet cat

Zichorie f. chicory

Zicke f., **Zicklein** neu. kid

Zickzack m. zigzag

Ziege f. (she-)goat; doe; −nbart m. goatee; −nbock m. he-goat; buck; −nleder neu. kid leather; −npeter m. mumps

Ziegel m. brick; tile; −brenner m. brickmaker; −(brenner)ei f. brickyard; −dach neu. tiled roof; −ofen m. brick kiln; −stein m. brick

Zieh: −brunnen m. draw well; −harmonika

f. accordion; **-kind** *neu.* foster child; **-tag** *m.* moving day; **-ung** *f.* (lottery) drawing; **-ungsliste** *f.* (lottery) list of prize-winners

ziehen *v.* to pull, to draw; to haul, to tow; to extract; to cultivate, to breed; to move; to march along; to be drafty, to ache; to attract; to weigh; to make (comparison); to take off (hat); to build (wall); to dig (trench); **auf Fäden —** to string; **auf Flaschen —** to bottle; **den kürzeren —** to get the short end of it; **die Bilanz —** (com.) to strike balance; **ein Geschützrohr —** to rifle a gun; **in die Fremde —** to go abroad; **in die Länge —** to draw out, to protract; **in Erwägung —** to take into consideration; **nach sich —** to have consequences; **sich —** to warp, to extend; **Wasser —** to leak, to absorb water

Ziel *neu.* aim, object; destination; goal, target, winning post; term, limit; **sich ein — setzen** to aim at; **-band** *neu.* (sport) tape; **-fernrohr** *neu.* telescopic sight; **-findung** *f.* (avi.) homing; **-gerät** *neu.* gunsight; **-scheibe** *f.* target

ziel: -bewusst *adj.* steadily pursuing one's aim; resolute; **-en** *v.* to aim; to allude; **-los** *adj.* aimless; **-sicher** *adj.* sure of one's aim

ziemen *v.* to be seemly (*oder* suitable)

ziemlich *adj.* suitable, fit; becoming; — *adv.* fairly, very; tolerably, rather; — **dasselbe** almost alike; — **oft** pretty often

Zier *f.*, **-at** *m.*, **-de** *f.* decoration, ornament; embellishment; **-affe** *m.* (coll.) dandy, fop; **-erei** *f.* affectation; **-garten** *m.* flower (*oder* ornamental) garden; **-leiste** *f.* ornamental border; **-puppe** *f.* (coll.) clotheshorse

zieren *v.* to adorn; to decorate; to embellish; to honor; **sich —** to be affected (*oder* coy)

zierlich *adj.* graceful; delicate; pretty

Ziffer *f.* figure, number, numeral; digit, cipher; **-blatt** *neu.* (watch) dial, face

ziffernmässig *adj.* numerical; — *adv.* by figures

Zigarette *f.* cigarette; **-netui** *neu.* cigarette case; **-nspitze** *f.* cigarette holder

Zigarre *f.* cigar; **-ndeckblatt** *neu.* wrapper; **-nkiste** *f.* cigar box; **-nspitze** *f.* cigar tip; cigar holder

Zigeuner *m.* gipsy

Zimbel *f.* cymbal

Zimmer *neu.* room; apartment; **-antenne** *f.* indoor aerial; **-arbeit** *f.* carpentry; **-decke** *f.* ceiling; **-einrichtung** *f.* furniture; (act of) furnishing; **-flucht** *f.* suite of rooms; **-geselle** *m.* journeyman carpenter; **-herr** *m.* lodger; **-mädchen** *neu.* housemaid; **-mann** *m.* carpenter; **-pflanze** *f.* indoor plant; **-vermieterin** *f.* landlady

zimmern *v.* to carpenter; to timber; to make

zimperlich *adj.* prim, prudish; supersensitive

Zimt *m.* cinnamon

Zink *neu.* and *m.* zinc

Zinke *f.* prong; tooth; tennon; cornet; secret mark (on cards)

Zinn *neu.* tin; pewter; **-kraut** horsetail

Zinne *f.* battlement; pinnacle

zinnenförmig *adj.* crenelated

zinnern *adj.* (of) tin, pewter

zinnoberrot *adj.* vermillion

Zins *m.* rent, tax; (bibl.) tribute; **-en** *pl.* interest; **mit — und -eszins** in full measure; **-fuss** *m.*, **-satz** *m.* rate of interest; **-schein** *m.* coupon; dividend warrant

zins: -bar *adj.*, **-pflichtig** *adj.* tributary; **-(en)bringend** *adj.* interest-bearing; **-(en)bringend anlegen** to put out at interest

Zipfel *m.* point, tip, corner; lappet; **-mütze** *f.* tasseled cap; nightcap

zipf(e)lig *adj.* peaked, pointed

Zipperlein *neu.* (coll.) gout

Zirk: -el *m.* circle; compasses; **-ular** *neu.* circular, pamphlet; **-us** *m.* circus

zirkulieren *v.* to circulate

zirpen *v.* to chirp, to stridulate

zischeln *v.* to whisper

zischen *v.* to hiss; to whiz; to fizzle

Zischlaut *m.* hissing sound; (gram.) sibilant

Zisterne *f.* cistern

Zisterzienser *m.* Cistercian monk

Zitadelle *f.* citadel

Zitat *neu.* citation, quotation

zitieren *v.* to cite, to quote; to summon, to call up; **falsch —** to misquote

Zitron: -at *neu.* candied lemon peel; citron; **-e** *f.* lemon; **-enfalter** *m.* brimstone butterfly; **-ensäure** *f.* citric acid

zitterig *adj.* trembling, tremulous; shaky

zittern *v.* to shake, to tremble; to shiver

Zitze *f.* nipple, teat, dug

zivil *adj.* civil; moderate, reasonable; **-isatorisch** *adj.* civilizing; **-isieren** *v.* to civilize; **-rechtlich** *adj.* according to civil law

Zivil *neu.* civilians; **in —** in civilian dress; **-bevölkerung** *f.* civilian population; **-isation** *f.* civilization; **-ist** *m.* civilian; **-prozess** *m.* (law) civil suit; **-prozessordnung** *f.* civil procedure code

Zofe *f.* lady's maid

zögern *v.* to delay; to hesitate; to linger

Zögling *m.* pupil; boarder

Zölibat *neu.* celibacy

Zoll *m.* inch; duty, tariff; customs; tribute; **-abfertigung** *f.* customs clearance; **-amt** *neu.* customhouse; **-angabe** *f.* customs declaration; **-revision** *f.* customs examination: **-schein** *m.* clearance paper; **-speicher** *m.* bonded warehouse; **-stock** *m.* yardstick; **-verband** *m.*, **-verein** *m.* customs union; **-vergünstigungen** *f. pl.* preferential tariff; **-verschluss** *m.* customs seal, bond

zoll: -en *v.* to pay duty (*oder* respect); **-frei** *adj.* duty-free; **-pflichtig** *adj.* dutiable

Zöllner *m.* customs collector; (bibl.) publican

Zoo *m.* zoo; **-loge** *m.* zoologist; **-logie** *f.* zoology

zoologisch *adj.* zoologic(al)

Zopf *m.* pigtail; plait, tress; (coll.) pedantry, red tape; **falscher —** (hair) switch

Zorn *m.* anger, rage, wrath

zornig *adj.* angry, enraged, wrathful

Zote *f.* obscenity, smutty joke; **-nreisser** *m.* obscene talker

zottig *adj.* matted, shaggy

zu *prep.* in, at; by, on; (up) to; as; for; with; **—** *adv.* too; towards; closed; **ab und —** now and then; **mach —!** close it! (coll.) hurry up! **nur —!** go on! **— Fuss** on foot; **-m Beispiel** for instance; **-m Glück** fortunately; **-m Teil** partially; **-r See** at sea; **— zweien** by (*oder* in) twos

zuallererst *adv.* first of all

zuallerletzt *adv.* last of all

Zubehör *neu.* and *m.* accessories, appurtenances; conveniences; trimmings

zubeissen *v.* to bite, to snap at; to eat away

zubekommen *v.* to get in addition, to get closed

Zuber *m.* tub

zubereiten *v.* to prepare; to cook, to mix

zubilligen *v.* to grant, to concede

zubinden *v.* to bind (*oder* tie) up; **die Augen —** to blindfold

zubleiben *v.* to remain closed (*oder* locked)

zublinzeln *v.* to wink at

zubringen *v.* to bring to; to prompt; **die Zeit —** to pass (*oder* spend) time

Zucht *f.* breed(ing); rearing; cultivation; growing; training, drill; discipline; decency; **in — halten** to keep strict discipline; **-buch** *neu.* studbook; **-haus** *neu.* penitentiary; **-häusler** *m.* convict; **-hausstrafe** *f.* penal servitude; **-hengst** *m.* stallion; **-meister** *m.* disciplinarian, taskmaster; **-mittel** *neu.* means of correction; **-rute** *f.* rod, scourge; **-sau** *f.* brood sow; **-schaf** *neu.* breeding ewe; **-stute** *f.* brood mare; **-vieh** *neu.* breeding cattle; **-wahl** *f.* natural selection

zücht|-en *v.* to breed, to grow, to cultivate; to propagate; **-ig** *adj.* chaste, decent; **-igen** *v.* to chastise, to scourge, to flog; to punish

zuchtlos *adj.* insubordinate, undisciplined; dissolute, loose

zucken *v.* to twitch, to jerk, to wince; (lightning) to flash; **mit den Schultern** (*or* Achseln) **—** to shrug one's shoulders

zücken *v.* to draw

Zucker *m.* sugar; **-bäcker** *m.* confectioner; **-dose** *f.* sugar bowl; **-erbse** *f.* sweet pea; **-guss** *m.* icing; **-hut** *m.* sugar loaf; **-krankheit** *f.* diabetes; **-mäulchen** *neu.* (coll.) sweet tooth; **-melone** *f.* honeydew melon; **-rohr** *neu.* sugar cane; **-rübe** *f.* sugar beet; **-syrup** *m.* molasses; **-werk** *neu.* confectionery, sweets

Zuckung *f.* convulsion, twitch

zudecken *v.* to cover up; to conceal

zudem *adv.* besides, moreover, in addition

zudenken *v.* to intend (as a present) for

zudiktieren *v.* to decree; to inflict

Zudrang *m.* rush (to), run (on)

zudrehen *v.* to turn off; **jemand den Rücken —** to turn one's back on someone

zudringlich *adj.* obtrusive, importunate

zudrücken *v.* to close, to shut; **ein Auge —** to overlook, to connive at

zueignen *v.* to dedicate; **sich widerrechtlich —** to usurp; **sich —** to appropriate

zueilen *v.* to hasten (*oder* run, rush) towards

zueinander *adv.* to each other

zuerkennen *v.* to award, to adjudge, to sentence to

zuerst *adv.* firstly, first of all; first

zuerteilen *v.* to allow, to apportion; to bestow

zufahren *v.* to drive (*oder* go) on; to rush upon

Zufahrt *f.* driveway; **-sstrasse** *f.* approach road

Zufall *m.* chance, accident; occurrence; **durch —** accidentally; **-streffer** *m.* chance hit

zufallen *v.* to fall to, to close; to devolve on

zufällig *adj.* accidental, casual, fortuitous

Zufälligkeit *f.* chance; contingency

zufassen *v.* to lend a hand; to catch hold of

zufliessen *v.* to flow towards (*oder* into); (words) to come readily

Zuflucht *f.* refuge, shelter; recourse

zuflüstern *v.* to whisper to; to prompt

zufolge *prep.* according to, in consequence of

zufrieden *adj.* content, satisfied; **lass ihn —!** let him alone! **sich — geben** to acquiesce in; **-stellen** *v.* to content, to satisfy; **-stellend** *adj.* satisfactory

zufrieren *v.* to freeze up (*oder* over)

zufügen *v.* to add; to do, to cause; **Schaden —** to inflict harm

Zufuhr *f.* supply(ing); provisions

zuführen *v.* to bring (*oder* lead) to; (mech.) to feed; to supply; to convey

Zug *m.* drawing, pull(ing); draft; current; procession; expedition; train; (birds) flight, migration; (chess) move; (cloud) drift; (mil.) platoon, squad, troop; (mountain) range; (pen) stroke, dash; (fig.) characteristic, feature; inclination; **dem — des Herzens folgen** to obey the inner voice; **den — erreichen** to catch the train; **er ist am -e** it's his move; **im rechten — sein** to be in full swing; **in den letzten Zügen liegen** to breathe one's last; **in einem — uninterruptedly; in vollen Zügen** deeply, very thoroughly; **— um —** without delay, move for move; **durchgehender — through train; -abteil** *neu.* (rail.) compartment; **-brücke** *f.* drawbridge; **-führer** *m.* (rail.) conductor; platoon (*oder* squad) leader; **-kraft** *f.* tractive power; attraction; **-leine** *f.* towrope; **-luft** *f.* draft, current of air; **-mittel** *neu.* attraction; **-netz** *neu.* dragnet; **-pflaster** *neu.* blister, vesicatory; **-stück** *neu.*

popular play, attraction; **–tier** *neu.* draft animal; **–verkehr** *m.* railroad traffic; **–vogel** *m.* bird of passage

Zugabe *f.* addition, extra; (theat.) encore

Zugang *m.* access, admittance; entrance; increase; approach, way to

zugänglich *adj.* accessible; approachable

zugeben *v.* to add, to give into the bargain; to allow; to confess, to admit

zugegen *adj.* present

zugeh(e)n *v.* to close, to shut; to move on; to walk faster; to happen; jemandem — to come to one's hand; — lassen to forward

zugehören *v.* to belong to, to be part of

Zugehörigkeit *f.* membership; relationship

zugeknöpft *adj.* (fig.) uncommunicative, reserved

Zügel *m.* bridle, rein; (fig.) check, curb; die — schiessen lassen to give full rein to; to let loose (one's passions, etc.)

zügellos *adj.* unbridled; unrestrained, unruly

zugeritten *adj.* broken in (for riding)

zugesellen *v.* to associate with, to join

zugestandenermassen *adv.* admittedly

Zugeständnis *neu.* concession, admission

zugestehen *v.* to concede, to grant; to admit

zugetan *adj.* attached (*oder* devoted) to

zugiessen *v.* to add (by pouring); to fill up

zugig *adj.* drafty

zugleich *adv.* simultaneously; also; together

zugreifen *v.* to grasp at; to help oneself (at table); to lend a hand; to take (opportunity)

zugrunde *adv.*, — gehen to perish; to become ruined; –legen *v.* to base upon; — liegen to be based upon; — richten to destroy; to ruin

zugunsten *adv.* in favor of; for the benefit of

zugute *adv.*, — halten to allow for; to pardon; — kommen to be for the benefit of; jemand etwas –kommen lassen to give a person the benefit of something; –tun, sich etwas –tun to indulge in something; to be proud (of)

zuguterletzt *adv.* finally, last of all

zuhalten *v.* to keep closed

Zuhälter *m.* pimp, procurer

zuhängen *v.* to hang (*oder* cover) with

Zuhause *neu.* home

zuheilen *v.* to heal up

Zuhilfenahme *f.* unter — von with the aid of

zuhinterst *adv.* at the very end, last of all

Zuhörer *m.* listener; –schaft *f.* audience

zujauchzen, zujubeln *v.* to cheer, to hail

zukehren *v.* to turn to(wards); das Gesicht — to face; den Rücken — to turn one's back to

zuklappen *v.* to slam, to bang; to close

zukleben *v.* to paste (*oder* glue) up; to gum

zuklinken *v.* to latch

zuknöpfen *v.* to button up

zukommen *v.* to be due to; to fall to the share of; to befit; das kommt ihr nicht

zu she has no right to that; — auf to approach

zukorken *v.* to cork up

Zukunft *f.* future; time to come; future tense

zukünftig *adj.* future; — *adv.* in future

zulächeln *v.* to smile at

Zulage *f.* increase, addition; extra pay, bonus

zulande *adv.*, bei uns — in my country

zulangen *v.* to hand (to); to help oneself (at table)

zulänglich *adv.* sufficient, adequate

zulassen *v.* to leave closed; to admit; to allow

zulässig *adj.* admissible; permissible; das ist nicht — that is not allowed

Zulauf *m.* crowd, rush; grossen — haben to draw crowds; to be much run after

zulaufen *v.* to run to (*oder* towards, on, faster); spitz — to taper off

zuleide *adv.* — tun to hurt, to (do) harm

Zuleitung *f.* conducting; lead, supply

zuletzt *adv.* finally, ultimately; last

zuliebe *adv.* for the sake of

zumachen *v.* to close, to shut; to stop up; to button

zumal *adv.* chiefly, especially, particularly

zumauern *v.* to wall (*oder* brick) up

zumeist *adv.* mostly, for the most part

zumessen *v.* to mete out; to allot, to apportion

zumindest *adv.* at least

zumute *adv.* in the mood of; mir ist nicht wohl — I feel out of sorts; –n *v.* to expect of; sich zuviel –n to attempt too much

Zumutung *f.* unreasonable demand; eine starke — an impudent demand, imputation

zunächst *prep.* next (*oder* close) to; — *adv.* first; above all; to begin with

zunageln *v.* to nail down (*oder* up)

zunähen *v.* to sew up (*oder* together)

Zunahme *f.* increase, growth

Zuname *m.* surname; family name

Zünd: -er *m.* fuse, igniter; -holz *neu.*, -hölzchen *neu.* match; -hütchen *neu.* percussion cap; -kabel *neu.* ignition cord; -kapsel *f.* detonator; -kerze *f.* spark plug; -loch *neu.* (gun) vent; touchhole; -nadelgewehr *neu.* needle gun; -schnur *f.* fuse; -stoff *m.* combustible (*oder* inflammable) material; fuel; -ung *f.* ignition, priming

zünden *v.* to catch fire; to kindle, to ignite; to inflame; -d *adj.* inflammatory; inciting

Zunder *m.* tinder, punk

zunehmen *v.* to increase; -de Jahre advancing years; -der Mond waxing moon

zuneigen *v.*, sich — to bend toward; to incline to; sich dem Ende — to draw to a close

Zuneigung *f.* affection; sympathy; inclination; — fassen zu to take a liking to

Zunft *f.* corporation, guild; -genosse *m.* guild member; fellow craftsman

zünftig *adj.* according to the rules of a

guild; skilled, expert; (coll.) proper, thorough

Zunge f. tongue; language; (ichth.) sole; (mus.) reed; **belegte —** furred tongue; **eine feine — haben** to be a gourmet; **eine schwere — haben** to speak thickly; **er trägt das Herz auf der —** he wears his heart on his sleeve; **es schwebt mir auf der —** I have it on the tip of my tongue; **–ndrescher** m. babbler; **–nlaut** m. lingual sound

zunichte adv. ruined; **–machen** v. to annihilate; to destroy, to frustrate; **–werden** v. to come to nothing

zunicken v. to nod to

zunutze adv. **sich — machen** to profit by, to utilize; to turn to account

zuoberst adv. at the top; uppermost

zupacken v. to grasp at; to set to work

zupfen v. to pick, to pluck; to pull, to tug

Zupfgeige f. (coll.) guitar

zuraten v. to advise, to recommend

zurechnen v. to add; to attribute to, to impute

zurechnungsfähig adj. accountable; responsible, of sound mind

zurecht adv. right(ly); in (good) time; with reason; **–bringen** v. to accomplish; **–finden** v. **sich –finden** to find one's way; to begin to know; **–kommen** v. to arrive in time; to get on well; **–legen** v. to lay out; **sich etwas –legen** to figure out something; **–machen** v. to prepare; **sich –machen** to make up, to dress; **–rücken** v. to put right; **–setzen** v. **jemand den Kopf –setzen** to set someone straight; **–weisen** v. to show the way; to reprimand

Zurechtweisung f. instruction; reprimand

zureden v. to urge on, to encourage

zureichen v. to hand to, to suffice; **–d** adj. sufficient, adequate

zurichten v. to prepare, to make ready; to dress; to cook; **übel —** to maltreat

zuriegeln v. to bolt (up)

zürnen v. to be angry (with)

Zurschaustellung f. display, exhibition

zurück adv. back(wards); behind; in arrears; late; **—!** interj. stand back! **–beben** v. to shrink back; to recoil; **–begeben** v. to return; **–behalten** v. to keep back; to detain; **–bekommen** v. to get back; to retrieve; **–berufen** v. to recall; **–bleiben** v. to stay behind; **–bringen** v. to bring back; to retard; to recall; **–datieren** v. to antedate; **–drängen** v. to push back; **–eilen** v. to hurry back; **–erinnern** v. to recollect; to remind; **–erobern** v. to reconquer; **–fahren** v. to drive back; to start back; **–fallen** v. to fall back; to relapse; **–fordern** v. to reclaim; **–führen** v. to lead (oder trace) back; to attribute (oder reduce) back; **–geben** v. to give back; **–geh(e)n** v. to go back, to retreat; to decrease, to decline; to fall off; **–gehen auf** to originate in; **–greifen** v. to go back (to), to refer (to); **–gezogen** adj. retired, secluded; **–halten** v. to hold back; to restrain; to curb, to repress;

to delay; to conceal; to refrain from; to reserve; **–haltend** adj. reserved; **–kehren** v., **–kommen** v. to go back, to return; **–legen** v. to lay back (oder aside); to spare; to clear (distance); to attain (age); to go through (course); to lie back; **–liegen** v. to belong to the past; **–nehmen** v. to take back, to withdraw; to revoke; **–prallen** v. to rebound, to recoil; **–rufen** v. to recall; **ins Leben –rufen** to revive; **–schlagen** v. to strike back; to repel, to repulse; to throw off (quilt); to throw open (coat); to return (ball); **–schrecken** v. to frighten away; to shrink (from); **–sehnen** v. to long to return; **–sein** to be back(ward); to be behind the times; **–setzen** v. to put back; to reduce; to neglect, to slight; **–springen** v. to jump back; to rebound; (arch.) to recede; **–stehen** v. to stand back; to be inferior to; **–stellen** v. to put back (oder aside); (mil.) to defer; **–stossen** v. to push back; to repel; **–stossend** adj. repulsive; **–strahlen** v. to reflect; **–treten** v. to step back; to recede; to retire, to resign; **–versetzen** v. to put back; to restore; **–verweisen** v. to refer back; **–weichen** v. to fall back; to retreat; to yield; to recede; to shrink back (from); **–weisen** v. to send back; to reject; to repel; to refer back; **–werfen** v. to throw (oder drive) back; to reflect; to repulse; **–wirken** v. to react (upon); **–zahlen** v. to repay, to refund; **–ziehen** v. to draw back; to withdraw, to retract; **sich –ziehen** to retreat, to move (oder march) back; to retire

Zurück: –gabe f. giving back, restitution; **–kunft** f. return; **–nahme** f. taking back; withdrawal; retraction; revocation; recantation; **–setzung** f. disregard, slight, snub

Zuruf m. acclamation; call, shout

zurufen v. to call (oder shout) to

zurüsten v. to prepare; to fit out, to equip

Zusage f. promise, assent

zusagen v. to promise; to agree, to please, to suit; **jemand auf den Kopf —** to tell to someone's face; **–d** adj. suitable

zusammen adv. (all) together; in all; **–ballen** v. to clench (fist); to concentrate; to conglomerate; (clouds) to gather, to draw near; **–beissen** v. to grit one's teeth; **–berufen** v. to convoke; **–brechen** v. to break down, to collapse; **–bringen** v. to amass; to assemble, to collect; **–drängen** v. to compress; to concentrate, to condense; **–drehen** v. to twist together; **–drücken** v. to compress; **–fahren** v. to collide; to start, to wince; **–fallen** v. to collapse; to coincide; **–falten** v. to fold up; **–fassen** v. to summarize; to combine, to concentrate; **–flicken** v. to patch together; **–fliessen** v. to flow together, to meet; **–fügen** v. to join together; to unite; **–führen** v. to bring together; **–geben** v. to marry; **–geh(e)n** v. to go together; to match, to agree well; to shrink; **–gehörig** adj.

homogeneous; correlated; **–geraten** v. to collide; to quarrel; **–gesetzt** adj. composite; compound; complex; **–gewürfelt** adj. motley; **–halten** v. to keep (oder stick) together; to compare; **–hängen** v. to be connected (with); to cohere; **–hanglos** adj. disconnected, incoherent; **–hauen** v. to cut to pieces; to thrash soundly; **–häufen** v. to accumulate, to amass; **–klappbar** adj. collapsible, folding; **–klappen** v. to fold up; (coll.) to collapse; **–klingen** v. to harmonize; **–kommen** v. to come together, to meet; **–laufen** v. to run together; to shrink; to curdle; **–legen** v. to lay (oder club) together; to fold up; to fuse; **–nehmen** v. to gather (up); sich **–nehmen** v. to collect oneself; to be on one's good behavior; **–passen** v. to adjust, to fit, to match; **–pferchen** v. to squeeze together, to crowd; to pen up (cattle); **–raffen** v. to snatch up; sich **–raffen** to pull oneself together; **–rechnen** v. to add up; **–reimen** v. to understand; sich **–reimen** to fit in, to make sense; **–rotten** v. to assemble a gang; sich **–rotten** to flock together, to conspire; **–rücken** v. to draw nearer; **–rufen** v. to convoke, **–schiessen** v. to shoot down; to contribute; **–schlagen** v. to strike together; to smash; to clap (hands); to click (heels); (water) to close over; **–schliessen** v. to join, to amalgamate; to close (ranks); **–schmelzen** v. to melt away (oder together); **–schnüren** v. to tie together (oder up); to wring (heart); **–schrecken** v. to startle; **–schrumpfen** v. to shrivel up, to shrink; **–schweissen** v. to weld together; **–setzen** v. to combine, to compound, to compose; sich **–setzen** to sit down together; to consist of; **–sinken** to sink down; **–stecken** v. to pin (oder put) together; to conspire; **–stellen** v. to put together; to collate; to compile; **–stoppeln** v. (coll.) to bungle; **–stossen** v. to collide, to clash; to clink (glasses); to conflict; to adjoin; **–stückeln** v. to patch up, to piece together; **–stürzen** v. to collapse; **–tragen** v. to carry together; to compile; **–treffen** v. to encounter; to coincide; **–treten** v. to meet; to convene, **–wirken** v. to co-operate; **–zählen** v. to add up; **–ziehen** v. to draw together; to concentrate, to contract

Zusammen: **–arbeit** f. co-operation; **–bruch** m. breakdown, collapse; **–fluss** m. confluence; junction; **–halt** m. coherence, cohesion; **–hang** m. connection; cohesion; **–klang** m. consonance; harmony, accord; **–kunft** f. assembly, meeting; conference, convention; interview; **–schluss** m. federation, union; amalgamation; **–setzung** f. combination, synthesis; structure; compound; **–spiel** neu. teamwork; **–stoss** m. collision; conflict; encounter; **–treffen** neu. meeting, simultaneity

Zusatz m. addition; appendix; supplement; postscript; codicil; alloy; (pol.)

rider
zuschanden adv. frustrated; **— machen** to destroy, to foil, to thwart, to frustrate; **— werden** to be ruined; to come to naught

zuscharren v. to fill up (hole)

zuschauen v. to look on, to watch

Zuschauer m. spectator, onlooker; **— pl.** audience; **–raum** m. seats, auditorium

zuschicken v. to forward to; to remit

zuschieben v. to push towards; to close by pushing; **die Schuld —** to put the blame on

Zuschlag m. addition, increase; **extra** charge; surtax; bonus; (auction) knocking down; (min.) flux; **–karte** f. additional ticket

zuschlagen v. to strike; to bang, to slam; (auction) to knock down; to add as a flux

zuschliessen v. to lock up; to close

zuschmeissen v. to slam; to throw to

zuschnallen v. to buckle; to strap up

zuschnappen v. to snap at

zuschneiden v. to cut up (oder out)

Zuschnitt m. cut; style; structure

zuschreiben v. to attribute (oder ascribe, owe) to; to credit with; to accept an invitation (by letter)

zuschreiten v. to step up to; to walk briskly

Zuschrift f. communication, letter

zuschütten v. to add to; to fill up

zusehen v. to look on, to watch; to take care of, to see to

zusetzen v. to add to; to lose (time, money, health); to put on (fire)

zusichern v. to assure of, to promise

Zuspeise f. side dish

zusperren v. to bar, to close, to lock

zuspitzen v. to point, to sharpen; **sich —** to taper; to become critical

Zusprache f. kindly encouragement; consolation

zusprechen v. **dem Essen —** to eat heartily; **jemand etwas —** to adjudge something to a person; **Mut —** to encourage; **Trost —** to comfort

Zuspruch m. encouragement, consolation; customers; approval, praise

Zustand m. condition, state; **in gutem —** in good order (oder repair); **Zustände** pl. nervous attack, hysterical fit

zustande adv. **–bringen** to bring about, to accomplish; **–kommen** to take place, to come about; **nicht –kommen** not to come off

zuständig adj. pertaining (oder belonging) to; authorized, competent, responsible

zustatten adv. **— kommen** to be useful to

zustecken v. to pin up; **jemand etwas —** to slip something to a person

zusteh(e)n v. to belong (oder be due) to; **es steht ihr nicht zu** she has no right to it

zustellen v. to deliver (oder forward, ship) to; to block up, to obstruct

Zustellungsurkunde f. writ of summons

zustimmen v. to agree to; **–d** adj. affirmative

zustopfen v. to stop up; to mend, to darn

zustossen v. to push to; to shut; to thrust forward; to befall, to happen to

zustreben v. to stream to; to flow into

Zustrom m. influx; crowd, multitude; flow

zustürzen v. to rush upon

zustutzen v. to trim, to fit, to adapt

zutage adv. — bringen, — fördern to bring to light; to uncover; — liegen to be evident; — treten to come to light; to crop out

Zutat f. ingredient, seasoning; trimming

zuteil adv. — werden to fall to one's share; jemand etwas — werden lassen to allot (oder grant) something to a person; -en v. to allot, to assign; to apportion; to adjudge; to bestow

Zuteilung f. allotment

zutragen v. to carry to; to report; sich — to happen, to take place

Zuträger m. gossip, scandalmonger; informer; -ei f. talebearing, slandering

zuträglich adj. advantageous; useful, beneficial; wholesome; schwere Speisen sind ihm nicht — rich food does not agree with him

zutrauen v. jemand etwas — to give one credit for something; jemand nicht viel — to have no high opinion of someone

Zutrauen neu. confidence, trust

zutraulich adj. confiding, trusting; sociable

zutreffen v. to come true, to prove correct; -d adj. correct, right, true; to the point

zutrinken v. to drink to

Zutritt m. access, admission; entrance; überall — haben to be welcome everywhere

Zutun neu. help, assistance; interference

zuunterst adv. at the very bottom

zuverlässig adj. dependable, reliable, certain; von -er Seite on good authority

Zuversicht f. confidence, trust

zuviel adv. too much; des Guten — tun to go too far; mehr als — more than enough

zuvor adv. before, previously; first (of all); -kommen v. to anticipate; to forestall; -kommend adj. obliging, complaisant; -tun, es jemand –tun to surpass someone

Zuwachs m. increase, growth, enlargement; auf — berechnet allowing for growth

zuwachsen v. to grow together; to become overgrown; to heal up; to fall to one's share

zuwege adv. — bringen to bring about; to accomplish, to effect

zuweilen adv. sometimes, at times, occasionally

zuweisen v. to allot (oder assign) to

zuwenden v. to turn to(wards); to bestow on, to devote to

zuwerfen v. to throw to(wards); to slam (door); to cast (glances); to fill (with earth)

zuwider adj. repugnant, distasteful; — prep. against, contrary to; -handeln v. to contravene; -laufen to run counter to,

to be contrary to; -sein to be repugnant to; to displease

zuwinken v. to wave (oder nod) to

zuzahlen v. to pay extra

zuzeiten adv. at times, sometimes

zuziehen v. to draw together; to tighten; to call in, to consult; to move in; to immigrate; sich — to incur; to catch (disease)

Zuzug m. immigration; reinforcements

zwacken v. (dial.) to pinch; to torment

Zwang m. compulsion; constraint, restraint; force; sich keinen — antun (or auferlegen) to be free and easy; sich — antun to restrain oneself; -sanleihe f. forced loan; -sarbeit f. compulsory labor; -sbeitreibung f. forced collection; -sgestellung f. arrest; -sjacke f. strait jacket; -slage f. embarrassing position; -smassregel f. coercive measure; -sversteigerung f. forced sale; -svollstreckung f. (law) distress; -svorstellung f. hallucination; -swirtschaft f. government control

zwanzig adj. twenty; -erlei adj. of twenty kinds; -fach adj., -fältig adj. twentyfold; -ste adj. twentieth

Zwanzig f. twenty; -er m. twenty; man of twenty; -stel neu. twentieth part

zwar adv. indeed; no doubt; although; und — namely, that is

Zweck m. purpose, aim, design, goal; das hat wenig — that's of no use; der — heiligt die Mittel the end justifies the means

zweck: -dienlich adj., -entsprechend adj., -mässig adj. serviceable, expedient, appropriate; -en to peg, to tack; -los adj. aimless, useless; -s prep. for the purpose of; -widrig adj. unsuitable; inexpedient; inappropriate

zwei adj. two; zu -en in pairs; two by two; -beinig adj. two-legged; -bettig adj. with two beds; -deutig adj. ambiguous, doubtful; obscene; -erlei adj. of two kinds; different; -fach adj., -fältig adj. double, twofold; in -facher Ausführung in duplicate; -geschlechtig adj. hermaphrodite; bisexual; -gestrichen adj. (mus.) twice accented; -gleisig adj. double-tracked; -gliedrig adj. in two ranks; (math.) binomial; -händig adj. two-handed; for two hands; -jährig adj. two years old; biennial; -jährlich adj. occurring every two years; -mal adv. twice; -malig adj. (done) twice; -motorig adj. twin-engined; -reihig adj. having two rows; (coat) double-breasted; -schläfrig adj. for two sleepers; -schneidig adj. double-edged; ambiguous; -silbig adj. disyllabic; -spännig adj. drawn by two horses; -sprachig adj. bilingual; -stimmig adj. for two voices; -stündig adj. of (oder lasting) two hours; -stündlich adj. occurring every two hours; -te adj. second; another; aus -ter Hand secondhand; -teilig adj. two-piece; bipartite; -tens adv. secondly, in the second place; -tletzte adj. penultimate; -wertig adj.

bivalent; **–zackig** *adj.* two-pronged; **–zeilig** *adj.* of (*oder* in) two lines; **–züngig** *adj.* double-tongued; double-dealing, hypocritical

Zwei *f.* two; deuce; **–decker** *m.* biplane; **–er** *m.* two; **–gespann** *neu.* two-horse team; **–händer** *m.* two-handed sword; **–heit** *f.* duality; **–hufer** *m.* cloven-footed animal; **–kampf** *m.* duel; **–röhrenapparat** *m.* two-tube (radio) set; **–sitzer** *m.* two-seater; **–taktmotor** *m.* two-stroke engine; **–unddreissigstelnote** *f.* (mus.) demisemiquaver; **–vierteltakt** *m.* (mus.) two-four time; **–zeiler** *m.* couplet, distich

Zweifel *m.* doubt, suspicion; **ohne –** undoubtedly; certainly; **–sfall** *m.* doubtful case; **–sucht** *f.* skepticism

zweifel: –haft *adj.* doubtful, dubious; suspicious; **–los** *adj.* doubtless, certain; **–n** to doubt; to question; to suspect

Zweifler *m.* doubter, skeptic

Zweig *m.* branch; bough, twig; line, section; **er wird nie auf einen grünen –kommen** (coll.) he will never prosper; **–bahn** *f.* (rail.) branch line; **–geschäft** *neu.*, **–niederlassung** *f.* subsidiary firm; **–stelle** *f.* branch office

Zwerchfell *neu.* (anat.) diaphragm

Zwerg *m.* dwarf, midget; pygmy; brownie

Zwick: –el *m.* gusset; gore; (arch.) spandrel; clock (of stocking); **–er** *m.* eye glasses; pince-nez

zwicken *v.* to pinch, to nip; to twitch

Zwie: –gespräch *neu.* dialogue, conversation, colloquy; **–licht** *neu.* twilight; **–spalt** *m.*, **–tracht** *f.* dissension, discord; schism; **–sprache** *f.* conversation, dialogue

zwie: –fach *adj.*, **–fältig** *adj.* double, twofold; **–spältig** *adj.*, **–trächtig** *adj.* discordant, disunited, conflicting

Zwieback *m.* zwieback, biscuit, rusk

Zwiebel *f.* onion; bulb; (coll.) pocket watch; **–fische** *m. pl.* jumbled type

Zwil(li)ch *m.* ticking (fabric)

Zwilling *m.* twin; **–e** *pl.* (ast.) Gemini

Zwing: –burg *f.* stronghold; **–e** *f.* vise, clamp; ferrule; **–er** *m.* cage; dungeon; kennel; arena; **–herr** *m.* despot, tyrant

zwingen *v.* to compel, to force; to subdue; to accomplish; **–d** *adj.* urgent; forcible, cogent

zwinkern *v.* to blink, to wink, to twinkle

Zwirn *m.* thread, twine, twisted yarn

zwischen *prep.* between, among(st); **–durch** *adv.* in between, at times;

through, in the midst; **–her** *adv.* meanwhile; **–planetarisch** *adj.* interplanetary; **–staatlich** *adj.* international

Zwischen: –akt *m.* interlude, entr'acte; **–bemerkung** *f.* interpolated remark; **–deck** *neu.* lower deck, steerage; **–ergebnis** *neu.* preliminary result; **–fall** *m.* incident; episode; **–flügel** *m.* (avi.) flap; **–frage** *f.* question; **–gericht** *neu.* intermediate dish; **–glied** *neu.* connecting link; **–handel** *m.* transportation business; jobbing; **–händler** *m.* wholesaler; agent; jobber; **–handlung** *f.* episode; **–lage** *f.* interposition; **–landung** *f.* intermediate landing; **Flug ohne –landung** non-stop flight; **–mauer** *f.* partition wall; **–pause** *f.* interval, interlude; break; **–raum** *m.* intervening space, interstice; interval; **–rede** *f.* interruption; interjection; **–regierung** *f.* interregnum; **–ruf** *m.* loud interruption; exclamation; **–satz** *m.* insertion; parenthesis; **–spiel** *neu.* intermezzo, interlude; **–stecker** *m.* adapter (plug); **–stock** *m.* intermediate story; mezzanine; **–stück** *neu.* inset; **–stufe** *f.* intermediate grade (*oder* stage); **–träger** *m.* scandalmonger, talebearer; **–vorhang** *m.* drop curtain; **–zeit** *f.* intervening time, interval; **in der –zeit** in the meantime; **–zünder** *m.* booster

Zwist *m.* dissension, discord, quarrel

zwitschern *v.* to chirp, to twitter

zwitterhaft *adj.* mongrel, hybrid

zwölf *adj.* twelve; **–eckig** *adj.* dodecagonal; **–erlei** *adj.* of twelve kinds; **–fach** *adj.*, **–fältig** *adj.* twelvefold; **–flächig** *adj.* dodecahedral; **–jährig** *adj.* twelve-year-old; **–malig** *adj.* occurring twelve times; **–stündig** *adj.* of twelve hours; **–te** *adj.* twelfth; **–tens** *adv.* twelfthly

Zwölf *f.* twelve; **–eck** *neu.* dodecagon; **–fingerdarmgeschwür** *neu.* (med.) duodenal ulcer; **–te** *m.* twelfth; **–tel** *neu.* twelfth part

Zyklon *m.* cyclone; **–e** *f.* (weather) low pressure area

Zyklop *m.* Cyclops; **–en** *pl.* Cyclopes

Zyklotron *neu.* cyclotron, Elektronenbeschleuniger

Zylinder *m.* cylinder; lamp chimney; silk (*oder* top) hat; **–presse** *f.* roller press

Zyniker *m.* Cynic; cynic

Zynismus (not present)

Zypern *neu.* Cyprus

Zypresse *f.* cypress

Zyste *f.* cyst

ENGLISH — GERMAN

A

a *art.* ein

abandon *v.* aufgeben, verlassen; überlassen; **-ed** *adj.* verworfen; aufgegeben, verlassen

abase *v.* erniedrigen, demütigen

abate *v.* ermässigen, verringern, nachlassen; (law) aufheben

abbey *n.* Abtei

abbot *n.* Abt

abbreviate *v.* abkürzen, reduzieren

abbreviation *n.* Abkürzung

abdicate *v.* abdanken; aufgeben, entsagen

abdication *n.* Abdankung; Verzicht

abdomen *n.* Unterleib; Bauch

abduct *v.* entführen, wegführen; (med.) abziehen; **-ion** *n.* Entführung

aberration *n.* Abweichung; Abirrung

abet *v.* aufhetzen, anstiften; Vorschub leisten

abeyance *n.* Unentschiedenheit; **in —** herrenlos; unentschieden, in der Schwebe

abhor *v.* verabscheuen; **-rence** *n.* Abscheu

abide *v.* bleiben, warten; wohnen; **— by** verharren bei; standhalten; **I cannot — him** ich kann ihn nicht ausstehen

ability *n.* Fähigkeit; *pl.* geistige Anlagen; **to the best of one's —** nach besten Kräften

able *adj.* fähig, tüchtig, geschickt; **be — to** imstande sein zu, können

able-bodied *adj.* dienstfähig, tauglich; kräftig

abnormal *adj.* abnorm, regelwidrig

aboard *adv.* an Bord; **all —!** an Bord! (rail.) einsteigen!

abolish *v.* abschaffen

abolition *n.* Abschaffung

abominable *adj.* abscheulich, widerwärtig

aborigine *n.* Ureinwohner

abort *n.* (mech.) Fehler; (avi.) unvollständiger Fliegereinsatz

abortion *n.* Fehlgeburt; Abtreibung

about *prep.* um, herum; über; etwa; **send someone — his business** jemandem heimleuchten; **what —?** was soll das heissen? — *adv.* etwa, ungefähr; herum, umher; **all —** überall; **be — to do something** im Begriff sein etwas zu tun; **set — in** Angriff nehmen

about-face *n.* Kehrtwendung

above *prep.* über, mehr als; — *adv.* oben, darüber; — **all** vor allem; **be — erhaben** sein über; — *adj.* obig

aboveboard *adj.* offen, ehrlich

above-mentioned *adj.* oben erwähnt

abrasion *n.* Abschürfung, Abnutzung

abrasive *adj.* abschabend, abschleifend; — *n.* Schmirgelpapier, Politur

abreast *adv.* nebeneinander; **be — of the times** mit der Zeit Schritt halten

abridge *v.* verkürzen; beschränken

abroad *adv.* im (ins) Ausland; im Freien; **get — bekannt** werden

abrupt *adj.* plötzlich; schroff

abscess *n.* Geschwür

absence *n.* Abwesenheit; Mangel; **leave of — Urlaub**

absent *adj.* abwesend, fehlend; **-ee** *n.* Abwesende

absent-minded *adj.* geistesabwesend, zerstreut

absolute *adj.* unbedingt; absolut; unabhängig; unbeschränkt; vollkommen; **-ly** *adv.* durchaus; unbeschränkt

absolution *n.* Lossprechung, Absolution

absolve *v.* freisprechen, entbinden

absorb *v.* aufsaugen, absorbieren; ganz in Anspruch nehmen

absorption *n.* Aufsaugung; Vertieftsein

abstain *v.* sich enthalten

abstinence *n.* Enthaltsamkeit

abstract *n.* Abriss, Auszug; Inbegriff; — *v.* abstrahieren; abziehen; ablenken; — *adj.* abstrakt; schwer verständlich; **-ion** *n.* Abstraktion; Absonderung; Zerstreutheit

abstruse *adj.* schwer verständlich, dunkel

absurd *adj.* absurd; albern, sinnwidrig; **-ity** *n.* Sinnwidrigkeit, Ungereimtheit

abundance *n.* Überfluss, Fülle; Überschwang; **in — in** Hülle und Fülle

abundant *adj.* reich an; überschüssig

abuse *n.* Missbrauch; Beschimpfung; — *v.* missbrauchen; misshandeln

abusive *adj.* missbräuchlich; schimpfend

academy *n.* Akademie, Hochschule

accede *v.* zustimmen; beitreten; antreten

accelerate *v.* beschleunigen

acceleration *n.* Beschleunigung

accelerator *n.* Gashebel, Gaspedal

accelerometer *n.* Beschleunigungsmesser

accent n. Akzent; Betonung; Aussprache; — v., **-uate** v. akzentuieren; betonen

accept v. annehmen; akzeptieren; gelten lassen; **-able** adj. annehmbar; akzeptabel; angenehm; **-ance** n. Annahme, Aufnahme

access n. Zutritt, Zugang; Anfall; **-ible** adj. erreichbar, zugänglich; **-ibility** n. (mil. avi.) Verwendungsfähigkeit

accessory n. (law) Mitschuldige; — pl. Zubehör; — adj. zugehörig; hinzukommend

accident n. Zufall; Unfall; **-al** adj. zufällig; unwesentlich

acclamation n. Beifall, Zuruf; Jubel

accommodate v. anpassen; unterbringen; versehen, versorgen; schlichten

accommodating adj. gefällig, entgegenkommend

accommodation n. Anpassung; Aushilfe; Beilegung; Bequemlichkeit; Unterkunft

accompaniment n. Begleitung

accompany v. begleiten

accomplice n. Mitschuldige, Komplice

accomplish v. ausführen, vollenden; **-ed** adj. ausgebildet; **-ment** n. Vollendung, Ausführung; Bildung, Talent; — pl. Fertigkeiten, Kenntnisse

accord n. Übereinstimmung; Einklang; **of one's own** — freiwillig, aus eigenem Antrieb; **with one** — einstimmig, einmütig; — v. übereinstimmen; gewähren, gestatten; **-ance** n. Übereinstimmung; **in -ance with** gemäss, übereinstimmend mit; **-ing** prep. **-ing to** entsprechend, nach; **-ingly** adv. demgemäss

account n. Rechnung, Konto; Bericht, Darstellung; **be of no** — unbedeutend sein; nichts taugen; **call (someone) to** — von (jemandem) Rechenschaft verlangen; **give an** — Rechenschaft ablegen; berichten; **keep an** — ein Konto (or Guthaben) halten (or haben); **on** — of wegen; **on no** — auf keinen Fall, um keinen Preis; **take into** — berücksichtigen; — v. — **for** erklären, Rechenschaft ablegen; **-able** adj. erklärlich, rechenschaftspflichtig; verantwortlich; **-ant** n. Rechnungsführer, Buchhalter; Bücherrevisor; **-ing** n. Buchhaltung; Erklärung

accumulate v. anhäufen, aufhäufen; ansammeln; (coll.) zusammenscharren

accuracy n. Richtigkeit; Genauigkeit; Sorgfalt; Pünktlichkeit

accurate adj. richtig; genau; sorgfältig; pünktlich

accusation n. Anklage, Beschuldigung

accuse v. anklagen, beschuldigen; vorwerfen; **-d** n. Angeklagte, Beschuldigte

accustom v. gewöhnen; — oneself to, **become** **-ed** to sich gewöhnen an; **-ed** adj. gewöhnt

ace n. (cards) As; (sports) Meister, Kanone

acetate n. Azetat; essigsaures Salz

acetic adj. essigsauer

acetone n. Azeton

acetylene n. Azetylen

ache n. Schmerz, Weh; — v. weh tun, schmerzen

achieve v. vollbringen; zustandebringen; erlangen, gewinnen; **-ment** n. Ausführung; Gewinn, Werk; — pl. Errungenschaften

aching adj. schmerzhaft, schmerzend

acid n. Säure; — **test** Säureprobe; (fig.) Feuerprobe; — adj. sauer; herb; **-ity** n. Säure; Herbheit, Schärfe

acknowledge v. anerkennen; zugestehen; (com.) bestätigen, erkenntlich sein für

acknowledgment n. Anerkennung; Eingeständnis; Bestätigung

acme n. Gipfel, Höhe; Höhepunkt

acne n. Akne, Hautfinne, Pickel

acorn n. Eichel

acoustics n. Akustik, Schallehre

acquaint v. bekanntmachen, vertraut machen; mitteilen, berichten; **be -ed with** bekannt sein mit, kennen; **become** **-ed** with kennenlernen, bekanntwerden mit; **-ance** n. Bekanntschaft, Kenntnis; Bekannte

acquire v. erwerben, erlangen; erreichen, gewinnen; erlernen

acquisition n. Erwerb; Errungenschaft

acre n. Acker, pl. Ländereien; **-age** n. Flächeninhalt, Umfang

acrobat n. Akrobat; **-ics** n. Akrobatik

across adv. hinüber, herüber; — prep. über, quer (über); (mitten) durch; — **the street** auf der anderen Strassenseite

act n. Tat, Handlung; Werk; Schritt; Akte; Beschluss, Gesetz; Akt, Aufzug; **in the** — im Begriff, auf frischer Tat; **put on an** — sich aufspielen; **Acts** (rel.) Apostelgeschichte; — v. wirken, tätig (or aktiv) sein, handeln; funktionieren; (theat.) darstellen, spielen; — **on** handeln; **-ing** n. Tat, Handeln; Spiel(en), Schauspielkunst; **-ing** adj. handelnd, tätig; **-or** n. Schauspieler, Darsteller; **-ress** n. Schauspielerin, Darstellerin

action n. Handlung, Wirkung, Tätigkeit; Tat; (law) Klage, Prozess; (mech.) Gang, Werk; (mil.) Gefecht, Schlacht; **be killed in** — fallen; **bring an** — **against** verklagen; **in full** — auf Hochtouren, in vollem Gange; **take** — vorgehen

activate v. ins Leben rufen; aktivieren; (mil.) aufstellen

activation n. Aktivierung

active adj. tätig, aktiv; geschäftig, lebhaft; wirksam

activity n. Tätigkeit, Betriebsamkeit, Aktivität

actual adj. tatsächlich, wirklich, eigentlich; gegenwärtig, aktuell; **-ity** n. Wirklichkeit

acute adj. scharf, brennend; akut; spitz betont; schrill; (med.) hitzig; (fig.) scharfsinnig; — **angle** spitzer Winkel

ad n. Annonce, Anzeige

A.D. abbr. Anno Domini, im Jahre des Herrn

adapt v. anpassen, zurechtmachen; bear

beiten; –able *adj.* anpassungsfähig; **–ability** *n.* Anpassungsfähigkeit

add *v.* hinzufügen; beifügen; addieren; vermehren; **— up** zusammenzählen, summieren; **–ing** *adj.* addierend; **–ing machine** Additionsmaschine; **–ition** *n.* Zusatz, Beifügung; Addition; Vermehrung; **in –ition** ausserdem, übrigens, noch dazu; **in –ition to** ausser, neben; **–itional** *adj.* zusätzlich, hinzukommend, Zusatz-

adder *n.* Natter, Otter

addict *n.* Rauschgiftsüchtige; **–ed** *adj.* zugetan, ergeben; verfallen

address *n.* Adresse, Anschrift; (fig.) Anrede, Ansprache; **—** *v.* adressieren; (fig.) anreden, sich wenden (or richten); **–ee** *n.* Empfänger, Adressat

adenoid *n.* Adenoide, Drüsenschwellung

adept *adj.* eingeweiht, erfahren, geschickt

adequate *adj.* angemessen, entsprechend; hinreichend, genügend, zulänglich

adhere *v.* ankleben; anhaften, festhalten, zugetan sein

adhesive *adj.* anhaftend, anklebend; (fig.) anhänglich; **— plaster** Leukoplast, Heftpflaster; **— tape** Klebestreifen

adjacent *adj.* anliegend, anstossend, benachbart

adjective *n.* Adjektiv, Eigenschaftswort; **—** *adj.* adjektivisch

adjoin *v.* angrenzen an; **–ing** *adj.* benachbart, angrenzend

adjourn *v.* vertagen, aufschieben; **–ment** *n.* Vertagung, Aufschub

adjust *v.* anpassen, berichtigen, einstellen; (ad)justieren, eichen; (fig.) schlichten; **–able** *adj.* anpassbar, verstellbar; **–ment** *n.* Anordnung; Berichtigung, Ausgleichung; Justierung; Schlichtung

adjutant *n.* Adjutant; **— general** *n.* Generaladjutant

ad-lib *n.* dem Interpreten überlassen, nach Belieben; Extempore; **—** *v.* improvisieren, extemporieren

administer *v.* verwalten, handhaben; darreichen, spenden, austeilen

administration *n.* Verwaltung; Ausgabe, Verteilung; Darreichung; (law) Handhabung

administrative *adj.* verwaltend, Verwaltungs-

admirable *adj.* vortrefflich, bewundernswert

admiral *n.* Admiral; **rear —** Konteradmiral

admiration *n.* Bewunderung, Verehrung

admire *v.* bewundern, verehren; **–r** *n.* Bewunderer, Verehrer, Anbeter

admiringly *adv.* bewunderungsvoll, verehrungsvoll

admission *n.* Eintritt, Zutritt; Zulassung, Aufnahme; (fig.) Bekenntnis, Zugeständnis; **— charge** Eintrittsgeld

admit *v.* zulassen, Zutritt gewähren; (her)einlassen; gestatten; (fig.) zugeben, gestehen; **–tance** *n.* Zulassung, Zutritt; Einlass

admonish *v.* ermahnen; warnen, verwarnen

ado *n.* Wesen, Getue, Aufheben, Lärm; Mühe

adolescence *n.* Jugendzeit; Jünglingsalter

adolescent *adj.* jugendlich; (fig.) unreif

adopt *v.* annehmen, adoptieren; (fig.) sich aneignen; **–ed** *adj.* angenommen; **–ion** *n.* Annahme; Adoption

adorable *adj.* anbetungswürdig

adoration *n.* Anbetung, Verehrung

adore *v.* anbeten, verehren; leidenschaftlich lieben

adorn *v.* schmücken, zieren, verschönern

adrenalin *n.* Adrenalin

adrift *adj.* treibend; (fig.) ratlos

adult *n.* Erwachsene; **—** *adj.* erwachsen, reif

adulterate *v.* verfälschen, verderben

adultery *n.* Ehebruch; **commit —** ehebrechen

advance *n.* Vorwärtsgehen, Vorrücken, Vormarsch; Beförderung; Fortschritt; Antrag; Vorschuss, Auslage; Aufschlag, Preiserhöhung; (mil.) Angriff; **in —** im voraus, als Vorschuss; **—** *v.* hervortreten, vorwärtsgehen, vordringen, vorrücken, vorschreiten; befördern; vorausbezahlen, vorschiessen, auslegen; steigen; (mil.) angreifen; **–ment** *n.* Beförderung, Förderung, Fortschritt

advantage *n.* Vorteil, Vorzug; Überlegenheit; (com.) Nutzen, Gewinn; **have the — übertreffen; take — of** einen Vorteil (or Gewinn) ziehen aus, benutzen, ausnutzen; **–ous** *adj.* vorteilhaft, günstig

advent *n.* Ankunft, Herannahen; **Advent** Advent (szeit)

adventure *n.* Abenteuer, Wagestück; **—** *v.* wagen, riskieren; **–r** *n.* Abenteurer

adverb *n.* Adverb, Umstandswort; **–ial** *adj.* adverbial

adversary *n.* Gegner, Widersacher, Feind

advertise *v.* anzeigen, annoncieren, inserieren; **–ment** *n.* Anzeige, Annonce, Inserat; Reklame, Ankündigung; **–r** *n.* Anzeiger; Inserent; Anzeigeblatt

advertising *n.* Reklame; Werbung

advice *n.* Rat(schlag); Gutachten; (com.) Bericht; **ask — of** sich Rat holen bei

advisable *adj.* ratsam, rätlich

advise *v.* belehren, (be)raten; melden, benachrichtigen; **— against** abraten von; **–r** (oder **advisor**) *n.* Ratgeber, Berater

advisory *adj.* ratgebend, beratend

advocate *n.* Fürsprecher, Anwalt

aerial *n.* (rad.) Antenne; **—** *adj.* luftig

aerodynamics *n.* Fluglehre, Aerodynamik

aeroembolism *n.* Höhenkrankheit

aeromedicine *n.* Luftfahrtmedizin

aerospace *n.* Luftund Raumfahrt

aesthetic *adj.* ästhetisch; **–n.** *pl.* Ästhetik

affair *n.* Sache, Angelegenheit, Affäre; (com.) Geschäft, Handel; **foreign –s** auswärtige Angelegenheiten

affect *v.* (be)rühren, betreffen, einwirken; angreifen; (er)heucheln; **–ation** *n.* Affektiertheit, Ziererei; Verstellung; **–ed** *adj.* affektiert, erkünstelt; **–ing** *adj.* rührend, ergreifend

affection n. Anhänglichkeit, Zuneigung, Liebe; -ate adj. liebevoll, zärtlich; herzlich, gütig; your -ate dein dich liebender

affidavit n. schriftliche Eideserklärung

affiliation n. Angliederung, Aufnahme

affinity n. Verwandtschaft

affirm v. behaupten, bejahen; bekräftigen; beteuern; (law) bestätigen; -ation n. Behauptung, Bejahung, Versicherung; Bekräftigung; (law) Bestätigung; -ative adj. bejahend; -ative n. Jawort; Bejahung

affix n. Anhang, Beilage; — v. anheften, befestigen; anhängen; beifügen; aufdrücken

afflict v. betrüben, kränken; peinigen, quälen, heimsuchen; -ed with heimgesucht von; -ion n. Betrübnis, Schmerz, Elend, Not, Pein

affluence n. Überfluss, Reichtum

afford v. sich leisten, erschwingen; gewähren, bieten

affront n. Beleidigung, Schimpf; — v. beschimpfen, beleidigen

afghan n. gestrickte (or gehäkelte) Decke

afield adv. vom rechten Wege ab; (von Hause) weg; ins Feld; im Felde

afire adj. brennend; in Flammen

aflame adj. in Flammen; brennend, lodernd

afloat adj. flott, schwimmend; umlaufend, im Gange

afoot adv. zu Fuss; in Bewegung, im Gange

aforesaid adj. vorher erwähnt, vorerwähnt

afraid adj. ängstlich, erschrocken; besorgt, bange; be — of sich fürchten (or Angst haben) vor

after prep. nach; hinter; gemäss; — all nach alledem; schliesslich; eben doch; — that nachher, danach, daraufhin; — this in Zukunft; day — day Tag für Tag; day — tomorrow übermorgen; look — sich kümmern um; one — the other hintereinander; take — ähneln; — conj. nachdem; — adv. darauf, nachher; -ward(s) adv. nachher, später

afterburner n. (avi.) Nachverbrenner

aftereffect n. Nachwirkung

afterglow n. Nachglanz, Abglanz; Abendrot

afterlife n. späteres (or zukünftiges) Leben

aftermath n. Folge, Nachwirkung Nachernte

afternoon n. Nachmittag; this — heute nachmittag

afterthought n. nachträglicher Einfall

again adv. wieder(um), von neuem, nochmals; zurück; ausserdem, dagegen;— and — immer wieder

against prep. gegen, wider; vor, an, bei

age n. Alter, Lebenszeit; Zeit(alter), Epoche; Geschlecht; in -s seit einer Ewigkeit; of — mündig, volljährig; old — hohes Alter, Greisenalter; under — unmündig; — v. altern, alt werden; -ed adj. alt, bejahrt

agency n. Agentur, Vermittlung

agenda n. Agenda, Tagesordnung

agent n. Vertreter, Agent; Geschäftsträger; (chem.) wirkende Kraft, Agens

aggravate v. erschweren, verstärken, verschlimmern; (fig.) reizen, ärgern

aggravating adj. erschwerend, verschärfend; (fig.) ärgerlich, unangenehm; verdriesslich

aggravation n. Erschwerung, Verschlimmerung; Verärgerung

aggregate n. Aggregat, Anhäufung; Masse, Summe; in the — insgesamt, im ganzen

aggression n. Angriff, Anfall

aggressive adj. angreifend, streitlustig

aggressor n. Angreifer, Aggressor

aggrieve v. betrüben, kränken; bedrücken

aghast adj. bestürzt, entsetzt

agile adj. flink, behend, gewandt, agil

agility n. Behendigkeit, Beweglichkeit

agitate v. bewegen, schütteln; agitieren, werben; aufregen, beunruhigen

agitation n. Unruhe, Aufregung; Agitation

agitator n. Agitator, Aufwiegler, Hetzer

aglow adv. and adj. (er)glühend; gerötet

agnostic n. Agnostiker; — adj. agnostisch

ago adv. vergangen, vorüber; vor; long — vor langer Zeit, lang her; not long — vor kurzem

agonize v. (mit dem Tode) ringen; quälen

agonizing adj. qualvoll, peinlich

agony n. Qual, Seelenangst

agrarian adj. agrarisch, landwirtschaftlich

agree v. einverstanden sein; übereinstimmen; — on sich einigen über; — with übereinstimmen mit; zuträglich sein, zusagen; -able adj. angenehm, gefällig; -ment n. Übereinkommen, Vereinbarung; Abkommen, Vertrag, Abmachung; be in -ment (sich) einig sein; by -ment laut Übereinkommen, im Einverständnis

agricultural adj. landwirtschaftlich

agriculture n. Landwirtschaft, Ackerbau

aground adv. gestrandet, aufgelaufen

ague n. Schüttelfrost, Wechselfieber

ahead adv. nach vorn, voraus, vorwärts; get — vorwärtskommen; go — weitermachen; vorwärts streben; vorangehen; straight — geradeaus

aid n. Hilfe, Beistand; Hilfsmittel; — v. helfen, beistehen

aide(-de-camp) n. Adjutant

ail v. unpässlich sein; what -s you? was fehlt dir? -ing adj. leidend, kränklich, unpässlich; -ment n. Krankheit, Leiden

aileron n. Quersteuer

aim n. Ziel, Zweck, Absicht; — v. zielen; trachten, beabsichtigen; (mil.) visieren; -less adj. ziellos, zwecklos

air n. Luft; Miene, Gebärde; Melodie, Lied; (fig.) Öffentlichkeit; give oneself -s, put on -s sich grosstun (or aufspielen); in the open — im Freien, unter freiem Himmel; — base Luftstützpunkt; Flughafen; — blast Windstoss; — brake Luftdruckbremse; — chamber Luftkammer; Windkammer; — corps Luftwaffe; — cushion Luftkissen;

force Luftwaffe; — gun Luftgewehr; — hole Luftloch; — lift Luftbrücke; — mail Luftpost, Flugpost; — passage Luftkanal; — power Luftmacht; — pump Luftpumpe; — raid Luftangriff, Fliegerangriff; — shaft Luftschacht, Wetterschacht; — valve Luftventil; — v. (aus)lüften; abkühlen, trocknen; (fig.) veröffentlichen; -ing n. Lüftung; (fig.) Spaziergang; -y adj. luftig; leicht, dünn; (fig.) munter, leichtsinnig

airborne adj. auf dem Luftwege transportiert

airbrush n. pneumatischer Zerstäuber

air-condition v. mit einer Klimaanlage versehen; -ing n. Klimaanlage

air-cool v. luftkühlen

aircraft n. Flugzeug; — carrier Flugzeugträger, Flugzeugmutterschiff

airfield n. Flugplatz, Flugfeld

air-launch n. Raketenabschuss vom Flugzeug

airline n. Luftverkehrslinie; -r n. Verkehrsflugzeug

air lock n. Eintrittsschleuse

air meet n. Luftkampf; Luftschau

airplane n. Flugzeug

air pocket n. Luftloch

airport n. Flughafen

airship n. Luftschiff

airtight adj. hermetisch, luftdicht

airway n. Wetterschacht; Luftweg, Fluglinie; (rad.) Welle

aisle n. Gang; Seitenschiff

ajar adj. angelehnt, halb offen

alacrity n. Bereitwilligkeit, Lebhaftigkeit

alarm n. Alarm; Lärm; (mil.) Warnruf; (fig.) Furcht, Besorgnis; **fire** — Feueralarm; **sound the** — (mil.) Alarm schlagen (or blasen); — adj. — clock Wecker; — v. alarmieren, lärmen; beunruhigen, erschrecken; -ing adj. beunruhigend, erschreckend; -ist n. Miesmacher, Bangemacher

alas! interj. ach! o weh! leider!

album n. Stammbuch; Gästebuch; Album

albumen n. Albumin, Eiweissstoff, Eiweiss

alcohol n. Alkohol; **rubbing** — Alkohol zum Einreiben; -ic n. Alkoholiker; -ic adj. alkoholisch

alderman n. Stadtverordnete, Ratsherr; Aldermann

alert adj. wachsam, aufgeweckt; flink; munter; **be on the** — sich bereithalten, auf der Hut sein; -ness n. Wachsamkeit, Flinkheit; Munterkeit

alga n. Alge

algebra n. Algebra

alias n. angenommener Name, Pseudonym, Künstlername; — adj. sogenannt, alias

alibi n. Alibi

alien n. Fremde, Ausländer; — adj. fremd, ausländisch; andersartig; -ate v. entfremden, abspenstig machen

alight v. absteigen, aussteigen, absitzen; sich niederlassen, landen

align v. ausrichten; in Linie bringen; -ment n. Ausrichten; Richtung

alike adj. ähnlich, gleich; — adv. ebenso,

in gleicher Weise; gleichmässig

alimentary adj. nährend, nahrhaft; — canal Verdauungskanal

alimony n. Unterhaltsbeitrag; pl. Alimente

alive adj. lebendig; lebhaft, munter; (fig.) empfänglich; **be** — leben, am Leben sein; **be** — with belebt sein von; wimmeln von; **keep** — am Leben bleiben; über Wasser halten

alkali n. Alkali, Laugensalz; -ne adj. alkalisch, laugenhaft

all adj. ganz; alle; — kinds (oder sorts) of allerlei; — the world die ganze Welt, jedermann; — year (round) das ganze Jahr (hindurch); by — means gewiss; auf jeden Fall; for — that trotzdem; for — the world durchaus, gerade; on — fours auf allen Vieren; one and — alle insgesamt; that is — punktum, genug; with — my heart aus vollem Herzen; — adv. ganz, gänzlich, völlig; above — vor allem, vor allen Dingen; after — schliesslich, letzten Endes; along (schon) immer, die ganze Zeit über; — around ringsumher; — at once auf einmal, plötzlich; — clear die Luft ist rein; Entwarnung; — gone fort, hin, alle; — in ganz kaputt, hin; (—) in — im ganzen, alles in allem; — of a sudden mit einem Mal, ganz plötzlich; — out ganz dafür, unbedingt; — over überall; — right schön, gut; in Ordnung; — the better um so besser; — the same trotzdem; ganz gleich; — told alles in allem, im ganzen genommen; at — überhaupt, durchaus; for — I know soviel ich weiss; not at — überhaupt nicht, keineswegs, gar nicht; nothing at — gar nichts; once and for — ein für allemal

allege v. behaupten, anführen; -ed adj. angeblich

allegiance n. Treue, Gehorsam

allegory n. Allegorie, Sinnbild

allergic adj. allergisch, überempfindlich

allergy n. Allergie

alleviate v. erleichtern, mildern, lindern

alley n. Gasse, Durchgang, Gang; Allee

alliance n. Allianz, Bündnis; (fig.) Verwandtschaft

allied adj. verbündet, alliiert; (fig.) verwandt, verbunden

alligator n. Alligator, Krokodil

alliteration n. Alliteration, Stabreim

allocate v. zuteilen, anweisen

allocation n. Zuteilung, Anweisung

allot v. zuteilen; austeilen

all-out adj. vollkommen, mit voller Kraft; erschöpft

allow v. erlauben, gestatten; anrechnen, ansetzen; — oneself sich gönnen; -able adj. zulässig, erlaubt; -ance n. Taschengeld; (com.) Abzug, Rabatt; (fig.) Rücksicht, Nachsicht; **make** -ance for zugute halten

alloy n. Legierung, Mischung; — v. legieren, (ver)mischen

all-round adj. vieseitig, in allen Sätteln gerecht

allspice n. Piment
all-time adj. allzeitig
allude v. hinweisen, anspielen
alluring adj. verlockend, reizend
allusion n. Hinweis, Anspielung
ally n. Verbündete, Alliierte, Bundesgenosse; — v. verbünden, vereinigen; verbinden
almanac n. Almanach, Kalender
almighty adj. allmächtig
almond n. Mandel; — **brittle** Mandelnougatstücke; — **tree** Mandelbaum
almost adv. fast, beinahe
alms n. Almosen
alone adj. allein, einzeln, einzig; — adv. einfach, nur; **let** (oder **leave**) — **in Ruhe** (or **Frieden**) **lassen**
along adv. entlang, dahin, weiter; längs; **all** — schon immer; **get** — **with** auskommen mit; **take** — mitnehmen; — prep. entlang, längs
alongside adv. längsseits, Seite an Seite
aloof adv. fern, von ferne; weitab
aloud adv. laut, hörbar
alphabet n. Alphabet; **-ic(al)** adj. alphabetisch
already adv. bereits, schon
also adv. auch, ebenfalls; ausserdem
altar n. Altar
alternate n. Stellvertreter; — v. abwechseln; — adj. abwechselnd, wechselseitig; **on** — **days** einen Tag um den anderen
alternating adj. wechselnd; — **current** Wechselstrom
alternative n. Alternative, Auswahl; — adj. alternativ, abwechselnd
altimeter n. Höhenmesser
although conj. obgleich, wenn auch, obwohl
altitude n. Höhe; — **chamber** n. Unterdruckkammer
alto n. Alt(stimme)
altogether adv. insgesamt; durchaus
altruism n. Altruismus; Nächstenliebe, Uneigennützigkeit
alum n. Alaun
aluminum n. Aluminium
always adv. immer, stets, jederzeit
a.m., A.M. abbr. am Vormittag, vormittags
amalgamate v. (sich) verschmelzen
amass v. anhäufen, ansammeln
amateur n. Amateur, Liebhaber; Dilettant; **-ish** adj. amateurhaft, dilettantisch
amaze v. in Erstaunen setzen, verblüffen; **-ment** n. Erstaunen, Verwunderung
amazing adj. erstaunlich, wunderbar, verblüffend
ambassador n. Gesandte, Botschafter
amber n. Bernstein; Bernsteingelb; — adj. bernsteinfarben, bernsteinen; Bernstein-
ambiguity n. Zweideutigkeit, Doppelsinn
ambiguous adj. zweideutig; zweifelhaft; dunkel
ambition n. Ehrgeiz, Streben
ambitious adj. ehrgeizig, begierig
amble v. im Passgang gehen (or reiten)

ambulance n. Ambulanz, Krankenwagen
ambush n. Hinterhalt, Versteck, Lauer; — v. im Hinterhalt liegen, auflauern; überfallen
amen n. Amen; — adv. amen, so soll es sein: so ist es
amenable adj. zugänglich, willfährig
amend v. berichtigen, abändern; verbessern; **-ment** n. Ergänzung, Änderung; (pol.) Verbesserungsantrag
amends n. Ersatz, Genugtuung; (law) Vergütung, Erstattung; **make** — ersetzen, wiedergutmachen
amenity n. Annehmlichkeit
americanize v. amerikanisieren
amethyst n. Amethyst
amiable adj. freundlich, liebenswürdig
amicable adj. freundschaftlich, friedlich
amid(st) prep. inmitten, mitten unter
ammonia n. Ammoniak; **liquid** — Salmiakgeist
ammunition n. Munition, Schiessbedarf
amnesia n. Amnesie, Gedächtnisverlust
amnesty n. Amnestie, Straferlass, Begnadigung
amoeba n. Amöbe
among(st) prep. unter, zwischen; — **other things** unter anderem; **from** — aus . . . hervor
amorous adj. amorös; verliebt; Liebes-
amount n. Summe, Anzahl, Betrag; — v. sich belaufen, betragen, ausmachen; — **to** sich belaufen auf; **he** — **ed to very little** er war nicht viel wert
ampere n. Ampere
amphibious adj. amphibisch
amphitheater n. Amphitheater
ample adj. weit; geräumig; genügend, reichlich
amplification n. Erweiterung, Vergrösserung; Verstärkung
amplifier n. Verstärker
amplify v. erweitern, vergrössern, ausdehnen; ausführlich darstellen; (rad.) verstärken
amplitude n. Weite, Umfang; Stärke, Fülle; — (oder **frequency**) **modulation** (rad.) Wellenschwingungsweite
amply adv. reichlich, hinlänglich; geräumig
amputate v. amputieren, abnehmen
amputation n. Amputation
amputee n. Amputierte
amuse v. unterhalten, amüsieren; — oneself sich die Zeit vertreiben; **-ment** n. Unterhaltung, Amüsement; Zeitvertreib; Vergnügen; **-ment park** Vergnügungspark
amusing adj. amüsant, unterhaltend, ergötzlich
analysis n. Analyse, Zergliederung, Zerlegung
analytical adj. analytisch
analyze v. analysieren, zergliedern, zerlegen
anarchy n. Anarchie, Gesetzlosigkeit
anatomical adj. anatomisch
anatomy n. Anatomie
ancestor n. Vorfahr, Ahnherr, Stammvater; pl. Ahnen

ancestral *adj.* angestammt, vererbt

ancestry *n.* Geschlecht, Geburt; Abstammung, Vorfahren

anchor *n.* Anker; (fig.) Zuflucht; **lie** (*oder* **ride**) **at** — vor Anker liegen; **weigh** — den Anker lichten; — *v.* (ver)ankern, vor Anker gehen; **-age** *n.* Ankerplatz, Ankergrund

ancient *adj.* (ur)alt, ehrwürdig; ehemalig

and *conj.* und; — **so on** und so weiter

andiron *n.* Kaminbock

anecdote *n.* Anekdote

anemometer *n.* Luftströmungsmesser, Anemometer

anemic *adj.* blutarm, anämisch

anesthesia *n.* Anästhesie; Unempfindlichkeit

anesthetic *n.* Betäubungsmittel

anew *adv.* wieder(um); noch einmal, von neuem

angel *n.* Engel; — **food cake** Mürbeteigkuchen; **-ic(al)** *adj.* engelhaft, engelgleich

anger *n.* Zorn, Wut, Unwille; — *v.* ärgern, erzürnen, verdriessen

angina *n.* Angina; — **pectoris** Angina Pektoris, Brustbräune

angle *n.* Winkel, Ecke; — **iron** Angelhaken; **from all -s** von allen Seiten; — *v.* angeln; zu fangen suchen; **-r** *n.* Angler

angry *adj.* wütend, zornig, ärgerlich, böse; **become** — wütend werden, sich ärgern

anguish *n.* Angst, Pein, Qual; Seelenschmerz

angular *adj.* winkelig, eckig; spitzig; steif, ungelenk

animal *n.* Tier; — *adj.* tierisch, animalisch; Tier-; (fig.) sinnlich

animate *v.* beleben, beseelen; anregen, aufmuntern; **-d** *adj.* belebt, lebendig, lebhaft; beseelt

animation *n.* Belebung, Beseelung; (film) Trickzeichnung; (fig.) Lebhaftigkeit, Munterkeit

anise *n.* Anis

ankle *n.* Fussknöchel, Fussgelenk, Enkel

annex *n.* Anhang, Zusatz; Nachtrag; (arch.) Anbau, Nebengebäude; — *v.* sich aneignen, annektieren, anhängen, beifügen; **-ation** *n.* Aneignung, Einverleibung, Annektierung; Anfügung, Beifügung

annihilate *v.* vernichten, zerstören; abschaffen

annihilation *n.* Vernichtung

anniversary *n.* Jahrestag, Jahresfeier

annotation *n.* Anmerkung, Note, Glosse

announce *v.* melden, anzeigen, ankündigen; **-ment** *n.* Anzeige, Ankündigung; **-r** *n.* Ansager

annoy *v.* belästigen, plagen, verdriessen; **-ance** *n.* Belästigung, Plage, Störung; **-ing** *adj.* lästig, ärgerlich

annual *adj.* jährlich, alljährlich; einjährig; — *n.* Jahrbuch; (bot.) einjährige Pflanze

annuity *n.* Jahresrente; Jahreszahlung; **life** — Lebensrente

annul *v.* aufheben, abschaffen; annullieren, für ungültig erklären; **-ment** *n.* Aufhebung, Abschaffung

anode *n.* Anode

anoint *v.* salben

anomaly *n.* Anomalie, Abweichung

anon *adv.* sogleich, sofort; bald

anonymous *adj.* anonym, ungenannt

another *adj.* ein anderer (*or* zweiter); noch ein; **one** — einander, sich gegenseitig

anoxia *n.* Sauerstoffmangel

answer *n.* Antwort, Beantwortung; Resultat, Lösung; — *v.* (be)antworten, erwidern, entgegnen; **-able** *adj.* verantwortlich

ant *n.* Ameise

antagonism *n.* Antagonismus, Widerstand, Feindschaft

antagonist *n.* Antagonist, Widersacher, Gegner; **-ic** *adj.* antagonistisch, widerstreitend

antagonize *v.* vor den Kopf stossen, entgegenwirken

antartic *adj.* antarktisch

antecedent *n.* Vorausgehende; *pl.* frühere Ereignisse (*or* Umstände); Vorleben; — *adj.* früher; vorausgehend, vorhergehend

antedate *v.* zurückdatieren; vorwegnehmen

antelope *n.* Antilope

antenna *n.* (rad.) Antenne; (zool.) Fühler

anteroom *n.* Vorzimmer

anthem *n.* Hymne

anthology *n.* Anthologie, Gedichtsammlung

anthracite *n.* Anthrazit

anthropology *n.* Anthropologie, Menschenkunde

antiaircraft *adj.* Flugabwehr-, Fliegerabwehr-, Flak-

antibiotic *adj.* antibiotisch; — *n.* Antibiotikum, keimtötende Bakterie

antibody *n.* Antikörper, Schutzstoff

anticipate *v.* vorwegnehmen, zuvorkommen; voraussehen

anticipation *n.* Erwartung, Vorgefühl

anticlimax *n.* Antiklimax, Niedergang

antidote *n.* Gegengift

antifreeze *n.* Frostschutzmittel

antihistamine *n.* Antihistamin

antimissile *n.* Abwehrgeschoss

antimissile missile *n.* Raketenabwehrgeschoss

antipathy *n.* Antipathie, Widerwille, Abneigung

antiquated *adj.* altmodisch, veraltet

antique *n.* Antike; — **dealer** Antiquitätenhändler; — *adj.* antik

antiquity *n.* Altertum, Antiquität

anti-Semitic *adj.* antisemitisch

antiseptic *adj.* antiseptisch

antisocial *adj.* ungesellig, unsozial

antisubmarine *adj.* U-bootabwehr-

antitank *adj.* Panzerabwehr-

antithesis *n.* Gegensatz

antitoxin *n.* Gegengift

antitrust *adj.* gegen Kartelle gerichtet

antler *n.* Geweihsprosse; *pl.* Geweih

antonym *n.* Antonym, Gegenbegriff

anvil *n.* Amboss

anxiety n. Angst, Besorgnis; Beklemmung

anxious adj. ängstlich, bang; besorgt; gespannt; **be — to do** begierig sein zu tun

any adj. irgendein, irgendwelcher; jeder; **— more** mehr; **not — kein; not — more** nicht(s) mehr

anybody pron. irgendeiner; (irgend)jemand; jeder(mann)

anyhow adv. jedenfalls, trotzdem; irgendwie

anyone pron. irgendeiner, (irgend)jemand; jeder(mann)

anything pron. (irgend)etwas; alles; **— but** nichts weniger als; **— else** sonst etwas; **not for —** um keinen Preis

anyway adv. jedenfalls, trotzdem; irgendwie

anywhere adv. irgendwo(hin)

apart adv. getrennt; auseinander; für sich, beiseite; **— from** abgesehen von; **take — auseinandernehmen; tell —** unterscheiden

apartment n. Wohnung; **—ment house** Wohnhaus, Mietshaus

apathetic adj. apathisch

apathy n. Apathie, Gleichgültigkeit

ape n. Affe; **— v.** nachahmen, nachäffen

apex n. Spitze, Gipfel

apiary n. Bienenhaus, Bienenstand

apiece adv. je, für das Stück

apogee n. Erdferne; höchster Punkt der Flugbahn (Rakete)

apologize v. sich entschuldigen, um Entschuldigung bitten, Abbitte tun

apology n. Entschuldigung, Abbitte

apoplexy n. Schlag(anfall), Schlagfluss

apostle n. Apostel, Jünger

apothecary n. Apotheker

apparatus n. Apparat, Gerät, Vorrichtung

apparent adj. augenscheinlich, scheinbar, offenbar; **-ly** adv. scheinbar, anscheinend

apparition n. Gespenst, Erscheinung

appeal n. dringende Bitte; Reiz, Anziehungskraft; (law) Berufung, Aufruf; **— v.** ersuchen, dringend bitten, wirken, gefallen; (law) Berufung einlegen, appellieren; **-ing** adj. flehend; reizend

appear v. erscheinen, sich zeigen, scheinen; (law) sich stellen; (theat.) auftreten; **it —s that** es stellt sich heraus, dass; **-ance** n. Erscheinen, Auftreten; Erscheinung, Aussehen; Schein; **to all -ances** allem Anschein nach

appease v. befriedigen, beruhigen, stillen, mildern; beilegen; **-ment** n. Befriedigung, Beruhigung

append v. beifügen, anhängen; hinzufügen; **-age** n. Anhang, Anhängsel

appendectomy n. (med.) Blinddarmoperation

appendicitis n. Blinddarmentzündung

appendix n. Blinddarm; (lit.) Anhang, Zusatz

appetite n. Appetit

appetizer n. Vorspeise, Appetitanreger

appetizing adj. appetitlich

applaud v. Beifall spenden; loben, beklatschen

applause n. Beifall, Applaus

apple n. Apfel; **— adj. — pie** Apfelkuchen

applesauce n. Apfelmus

appliance n. Gerät, Vorrichtung

applicable adj. anwendbar, passend

applicant n. Antragsteller, Bewerber

application n. Bewerbung, Gesuch; Anwendung, Anlegung; Gebrauch; Fleiss; (med.) Verband, Umschlag; **— blank** Bewerbungsformular

applied arts n. pl. angewandte Künste; Kunstgewerbe

apply v. anwenden, gebrauchen; sich wenden; auflegen; **— for** sich bewerben um; **— to** gelten für, sich beziehen auf

appoint v. ernennen; festsetzen, bestimmen; **-ment** n. Ernennung, Festsetzung, Bestimmung; Verabredung; **make an -ment** sich berabreden; sich anmelden

apposition n. in — beigefügt

appraisal n. Abschätzung, Taxierung

appraise v. abschätzen, taxieren; **-r** n. Taxator

appreciable adj. merklich, schätzbar

appreciate v. würdigen; schätzen; wahrnehmen; aufwerten; **— it für** etwas dankbar sein

appreciation n. Dank, Anerkennung; Verständnis; Preissteigerung, Wertzunahme

appreciative adj. dankbar, anerkennend

apprehend v. ergreifen, verhaften; (fig.) erfassen, verstehen, befürchten

apprehension n. Besorgnis, Angst; Verhaftung, Fassungskraft

apprehensive adj. furchtsam, besorgt; **become —** argwöhnisch werden

apprentice n. Lehrling; **— v.** in die Lehre geben; **-ship** n. Lehre

approach n. Annäherung, Herannahen; Zugang, Auffahrt; (mil.) Laufgraben; **use the right —** richtig an die Sache herangehen; **— v.** näher kommen, sich nähern; sich wenden an; herantreten an

approbation n. Billigung, Genehmigung; Beifall

appropriate adj. angebracht, passend; **— v.** sich aneignen; bewilligen, aussetzen

appropriation n. Geldbewilligung; Aneignung; Verwendung

approval n. Billigung, Beifall; **on — auf** Probe, zur Ansicht

approve v. billigen, gutheissen

approximate v. (sich) nähern, nahe (or näher) bringen; **— adj., -ly** adv. annähernd

approximation n. Annäherung

apricot n. Aprikose, Marille

April n. April; **— shower** Aprilwetter

apron n. Schürze, Schurz; **— string** Schürzenband; **.be tied to one's mother's — strings** ein Muttersöhnchen (or Mutterkind) sein

apropos adv. apropos; **— of** bezüglich; **— adj.** passend; **—! interj.** ja so! was ich noch sagen wollte! apropos!

apt adj. tüchtig, fähig; passend; geneigt

aptitude n. Fähigkeit, Tauglichkeit, Eignung; Geneigtheit

aquamarine n. Aquamarine; Meergrün

aquaplane *n.* Gleitbrett, Wellenreiter

aquarium *n.* Aquarium

aquatic *adj.* im Wasser lebend, Wasser-

aqueduct *n.* Aquädukt, Wasserleitung

aquiline *adj.* adlerartig, Adler-

arable *adj.* pflügbar, bestellbar, urbar

arbiter *n.* Schiedsrichter, Unparteiische; Gebieter

arbitrary *adj.* willkürlich, eigenwillig

arbitrate *v.* entscheiden, schlichten

arbitration *n.* Schiedsspruch, Entscheidung

arbor *n.* Laube

arc *n.* Bogen; (elec.) Lichtbogen

arcade *n.* Arkade, Bogengang

arch *n.* Bogen, Gewölbe; **fallen –es** Senkfüsse; — *v.* (sich) wölben; bogenförmig machen; — *adj.* schlau; schelmisch; **–ed** *adj.* gewölbt, bogenförmig; **–er** *n.* Bogenschütze; **–ery** *n.* Bogenschiessen, Kunst des Bogenschiessens

archaeology *n.* Archäologie, Altertumskunde

archaic *adj.* archaisch, altertümlich

archbishop *n.* Erzbischof

archduke *n.* Grossherzog; (Austrian) Erzherzog; (Russian) Grossfürst

architect *n.* Architekt, Baumeister; **–ural** *adj.* architektonisch, baulich; **–ure** *n.* Baukunst, Baustil; Architektur

archway *n.* Bogengang, überwölbter Torweg

arctic *adj.* arktisch

ardent *adj.* glühend, feurig; leidenschaftlich

ardor *n.* Eifer, Inbrunst; Glut

area *n.* Fläche; Flächeninhalt; Ausdehnung; Gebiet, Gegend, Areal

arena *n.* Kampfplatz, Arena

Argentine *n.* Argentinien

argue *v.* (sich) streiten, erörtern; behaupten; bestreiten

argument *n.* Argument; Auseinandersetzung, Erörterung, Wortwechsel; **–ation** *n.* Beweisführung

aria *n.* Arie

arise *v.* aufstehen, sich erheben; entstehen, aufkommen, auftauchen

aristocracy *n.* Aristokratie, Adel

aristocrat *n.* Aristokrat; **–ic** *adj.* aristokratisch, vornehm

arithmetic *n.* Arithmetik, Rechenkunst; **–al** *adj.* arithmetisch

ark *n.* Arche

arm *n.* Arm; Armstütze, Seitenlehne; (bot.) Ast, Zweig; (geog.) Abzweigung; *pl.* Waffen; Wappen; **be under —** unter Waffen stehen; **bear —** als Soldat dienen; **by force of —** mit bewaffneter Hand; **small —** Handfeuerwaffen; **up in —** in vollem Aufruhr, empört; — *v.* bewaffnen, rüsten

armament *n.* Aufrüstung; Kriegsausrüstung; Kriegsmacht; Bewaffnung

armature *n.* Rüstung, Waffen; Armature

armchair *n.* Lehnstuhl, Armsessel

armhole *n.* Armloch

armistice *n.* Waffenstillstand

armor *n.* Rüstung; Panzer; Panzerung; **— plate** Panzerplatte; — *v.* panzern

armory *n.* Arsenal, Zeughaus

armpit *n.* Achselhöhle

army *n.* Armee, Heer

aroma *n.* Aroma; **–tic** *adj.* aromatisch, würzig, wohlriechend

around *prep.* um . . . herum; — *adv.* (rund)herum; ringsherum; umher; im Kreise; von Ort zu Ort; nahebei, dabei, in der Nähe; ungefähr

arouse *v.* aufwecken; erwecken, erregen

arrange *v.* einrichten, ordnen; ausmachen, beilegen; (mus.) bearbeiten; **–ment** *n.* Einrichtung, Ordnung, Anordnung; (mus.) Bearbeitung; **make –ments** Vorbereitungen treffen

arrears *n.* **in —** rückständig

arrest *n.* Arrest, Verhaftung; **under — in** Arrest, verhaftet; — *v.* verhaften, festnehmen

arrival *n.* Ankunft, Auftreten; Ankömmling

arrive *v.* (an)kommen, erscheinen; **— at** erreichen, erlangen; ankommen in

arrogance *n.* Arroganz, Anmassung

arrogant *adj.* arrogant, anmassend, hochmütig

arrow *n.* Pfeil

arrowhead *n.* Pfeilspitze

arsenal *n.* Arsenal, Zeughaus; (naut.) Kriegswerft

arsenic *n.* Arsen

arson *n.* Brandstiftung

art *n.* Kunst; Geschicklichkeit; List, Verschlagenheit; Kniff; *pl.* **the fine —** die schönen Künste; **–ful** *adj.* listig, schlau, verschlagen; **–isan** *n.* Handwerker, Kunsthandwerker; **–ist** *n.* Künstler; **–istic** *adj.* künstlerisch; **–less** *adj.* einfach, schlicht, kunstlos

arteriosclerosis *n.* Arterienverkalkung

artery *n.* Arterie, Pulsader

arthritis *n.* Gelenkentzündung, Gicht

artichoke *n.* Artischoke

article *n.* Gegenstand, Sache; Artikel, Ware, Posten; (lit.) Aufsatz

articulate *adj.* artikuliert, deutlich, vernehmbar; — *v.* artikulieren, deutlich aussprechen

artifice *n.* Kunstgriff; Schlauheit, List

artificial *adj.* künstlich

artillery *n.* Artillerie

as *conj.* and *adv.* wie, (eben)so wie; so, als; da, denn, weil; wenn, während; was; **— far —** bis (zu); soweit; soviel; **— far — I am concerned** was mich betrifft, von mir aus; **— good —** so gut wie; **— if** als ob (or wenn); **— soon —** sobald, sowie; **— yet** bis jetzt, bisher

asbestos *n.* Asbest

ascend *v.* (hin)aufsteigen, besteigen; hinauffahren; (time) hinaufreichen; **–ancy** *n.* Überlegenheit, Übergewicht, Einfluss

ascension *n.* Auffahrt, Aufsteigen; (rel.) Himmelfahrt

ascent *n.* Aufstieg, Hinaufsteigen

ascertain *v.* ermitteln, feststellen; sich vergewissern

ascetic *n.* Asket; — *adj.* asketisch

ascribe *v.* zuschreiben, beilegen, beimessen

ash n. Esche; pl. Asche, sterbliche Überreste; — **tray** Aschbecher; **Ash Wednesday** Aschermittwoch; **-en** adj. eschen; aschgrau, aschfarben

ashamed adj. beschämt, verschämt, **be — sich** schämen

ashore adv. gelandet, gestrandet; am (or ans) Ufer

Asia n. Asien

Asia Minor n. Kleinasien

aside adv. beiseite, abseits; getrennt; seitwärts; — **from** abgesehen von; **put** (oder **set**) — beiseitelegen; zurücklegen; **stand** — zur Seite gehen (or treten)

asinine adj. eselhaft, dumm; Esels-

ask v. fragen, sich erkundigen; verlangen, fordern; bitten, ersuchen; einladen, auffordern; — **a question** eine Frage stellen; — **for** fragen (or verlangen) nach

askance adv. schief, quer; (coll.) scheel

askew adv. schief, von der Seite

asleep adj. and adv. schlafend; **be — schlafen**, eingeschlafen sein; **fall — einschlafen**

asparagus n. Spargel

aspect n. Anblick; Aussehen; Aussicht, Lage; Gesichtspunkt, Vorzeichen

aspen n. Espe, Zitterpappel

aspersion n. Verleumdung, Schmähung

asphalt n. Asphalt

asphyxia n. Pulsstockung, Scheintod, Erstickungstod; **-te** v. ersticken

asphyxiation n. Erstickung

aspiration n. Streben, Trachten, Sehnen

aspire v. streben, trachten

ass n. Esel; (fig.) Dummkopf

assail v. angreifen, überfallen, bestürmen; **-ant** n. Angreifer

assassin n. Attentäter, Meuchelmörder; **-ate** v. (meuchlerisch) ermorden; **-ation** n. Ermordung, Attentat, Meuchelmord

assault n. Angriff, Anfall; Sturm, Bestürmung; (law) tätliche Beleidigung; — **and battery** tätlicher Angriff; — v. angreifen, bestürmen; (law) tätlich beleidigen

assay v. proben, probieren, prüfen

assemblage n. Versammlung; Verbindung

assemble v. (sich) versammeln, zusammenrufen; zusammensetzen; (mech.) montieren

assembly n. Versammlung, Gesellschaft; (mech.) Montage, Montierung; (mil.) Sammelsignal; (pol.) Repräsentantenhaus, Unterhaus; — **line** laufendes Band; Fliessband

assert v. behaupten, erklären; verteidigen; **-ion** n. Behauptung, Erklärung; Verteidigung

assess v. beteuern; (ab)schätzen, taxieren; **-ment** n. Einschätzung; Steuer, Abgabe; **-or** n. Assessor; **-or of taxes** Steuereinschätzer, Taxator

asset n. Guthaben, Aktiva, Aktivbestand

assign v. erteilen, zuteilen, zuweisen; auferlegen; ernennen, bestimmen; (law) übertragen; (fig.) angeben; **-ment** n. Aufgabe, Hausarbeit; Auftrag: Zuteilung, Zuweisung

assimilate v. (sich) assimilieren, einverleiben, anpassen

assimilation n. Assimilierung, Einverleibung, Anpassung

assist v. helfen, mitwirken, beistehen; **-ance** n. Hilfe, Mitwirkung, Beistand; **-ant** n. Gehilfe, Beistand, Assistent

associate n. Teilhaber, Kompagnon, Gesellschafter, Partner; Kollege, Genosse; — v. verkehren, (sich) verbinden; — adj. verbunden, assoziiert, verbündet; begleitend

association n. Vereinigung, Verein, Verband, Gesellschaft; Verbindung

assort v. sortieren, ordnen; **-ed** adj. gemischt; **-ment** n. Auswahl, Sortiment

assume v. annehmen, voraussetzen; übernehmen; sich anmassen; **-d** adj. angenommen

assumption n. Annahme, Voraussetzung; Übernehmen

assurance n. Versicherung, Zusicherung, Gewähr; Selbstvertrauen

assure v. sichern; versichern; **-d** adj. selbstbewusst; **-dly** adv. sicherlich, gewiss

asterisk n. (typ.) Sternchen

asthma n. Asthma, Atemnot

astigmatism n. Sehstörungen

astonish v. in Erstaunen setzen, staunen; **-ing** adj. erstaunlich, wunderbar; **-ment** n. Erstaunen, Überraschung, Verwunderung

astound v. in Staunen (or Schrecken) versetzen, verblüffen

astray adv. irre, vom rechten Wege ab; **go — irregehen**, fehlgehen; **lead — irreführen**; verführen

astrobiology n. Astrobiologie

astrology n. Astrologie, Sterndeuterei

astronaut n. Weltraumfahrer, Astronaut

astronavigation n. Weltraumnavigation

astronomer n. Astronom, Sternenforscher

astronomy n. Astronomie, Sternenkunde

astrophysics n. Astrophysik

asunder adj. getrennt, auseinander

asylum n. Asyl; (fig.) Zufluchtsort; **insane** (oder **lunatic**) — Irrenhaus

at prep. an, aus, bei, durch, für, in, mit, nach, über, um; von, vor, zu; — **all** überhaupt; — **all costs** um jeden Preis; — **all events** auf jeden Fall, jedenfalls; — **best** bestenfalls; — **first** zuerst; — **home** daheim, zuhause; — **large** in Freiheit, frei; — **last** endlich; — **least** wenigstens, mindestens; — **length** schliesslich; — **most** höchstens; — **noon** mittags; — **once** sofort; auf einmal; — **peace** im Frieden; — **pleasure** nach Belieben; — **your** (oder **our**) **house** bei dir (or uns); — **sea** auf See; (fig.) ratlos, ungewiss; — **stake** auf dem Spiel(e); — **that** dabei; — **times** zuweilen; — **war** im Krieg(e); — **will** nach Belieben; — **work** bei der Arbeit; — **your service** zu Ihren (or deinen) Diensten

atheism n. Atheismus, Gottesleugnung

atheist n. Atheist, Gottesleugner

athlete *n.* Athlet; —'s foot ringförmige Fussflechte

athletic *adj.* athletisch; kräftig, stark; — *n.* (*pl.*) Athletik

atlas *n.* Atlas, Kartenwerk

atmosphere *n.* Atmosphäre

atoll *n.* Atoll, Koralleninsel

atom *n.* Atom; — bomb (A-bomb) Atombombe; -ic *adj.* atomisch; -ic energy Atomenergie, Atomkraft; -ic pile Atomsäule

atomizer *n.* Zerstäuber

atone *v.* büssen, sühnen; -ment *n.* Busse, Sühne; Genugtuung; (rel.) Versöhnung, Sühneopfer; Day of Atonement Versöhnungstag

atrocious *adj.* abscheulich, grässlich, grausam

atrocity *n.* Greueltat, Abscheulichkeit, Barbarei

attach *v.* befestigen, verknüpfen, anhängen, anheften; zuteilen; pfänden lassen; — importance Bedeutung beilegen; -ed *adj.* be -ed to hängen an, gehören zu; -ment *n.* Zuneigung, Anhänglichkeit

attaché *n.* Attaché, Gesandtschaftsrat

attack *n.* Angriff; (med.) Anfall; — *v.* angreifen, anpacken; (med.) befallen

attain *v.* erreichen, erlangen, gewinnen; -able *adj.* erreichbar; -ment *n.* Erreichung, Erlangung; Gewinn; -ment *pl.* Kenntnisse, Fertigkeiten

attempt *n.* Versuch, Anschlag; Attentat; — *v.* versuchen, wagen

attend *v.* beiwohnen, anwesend sein, besuchen; (med.) behandeln, pflegen; aufwarten; — to erledigen; -ance *n.* Bedienung; Anwesenheit, Besuch, Zuhörerschaft; -ant *n.* Wärter, Diener; -ant *adj.* begleitend, anwesend; diensttuend

attention *n.* Aufmerksamkeit, Achtung; call — to hinweisen (*or* Aufmerksamkeit lenken) auf; give — to aufmerksam sein; pay — aufpassen; pay — to beachten, achtgeben auf; (fig.) den Hof machen; pay no — ignorieren; stand at — strammstehen

attentive *adj.* aufmerksam, achtsam; be — aufmerksam sein; (fig.) den Hof machen

attest *v.* bezeugen, beglaubigen, bescheinigen

attic *n.* Dachstube, Boden; *pl.* Dachgeschoss

attire *n.* Kleidung, Tracht; — *v.* (an)kleiden, schmücken

attitude *n.* Haltung, Stellung, Lage

attorney *n.* Anwalt; — at law Rechtsanwalt; Attorney General Justizminister; power of — schriftliche Vollmacht

attract *v.* anziehen, reizen, fesseln; — attention Aufmerksamkeit erregen; without -ing attention unauffällig; -ion *n.* Anziehung(skraft), Reiz; (theat.) Glanznummer, Attraktion; -ive *adj.* anziehend, vorteilhaft, verlockend; attraktiv

attribute *n.* Eigenschaft; Merkmal, Attribut; Eigenschaftswort; — *v.* zuschrei-

ben, beimessen, beilegen

auburn *n.* Rotbraun, Kastanienbraun; — *adj.* rotbraun, kastanienbraun

auction *n.* Auktion, Versteigerung; — *v.* (ver)auktionieren, versteigern; -eer *n.* Auktionator, Versteigerer

audacity *n.* Kühnheit, Unverschämtheit, Frechheit

audible *adj.* hörbar, vernehmbar, vernehmlich

audience *n.* Publikum; Zuhörer(schaft); Zuschauer; Audienz, Empfang

audiophile *n.* Tonfanatiker, Audiophile

audit *n.* Rechnungsprüfung; — *v.* Rechnungen (*or* Bücher) prüfen; (educ.) als Gasthörer studieren; -or Bücherrevisor, Rechnungsprüfer; Zuhörer

audition *n.* Vorsprechen, Vorsingen

auditorium *n.* Auditorium, Hörsaal

auditory *adj.* Gehör; — nerve Gehörnerv

auger *n.* Bohrer; (avi.) abtrudeln

aught *n.* Etwas; (math.) Null; — *adv.* etwas, irgendetwas, irgendwie

augment *v.* zunehmen, vermehren, vergrössern

august *adj.* erhaben, herrlich, hehr

August *n.* August

aunt *n.* Tante

aura *n.* Hauch, Duft

aureomycin *n.* Aureomyzin

auspices *n. pl.* Auspizien, Vorbedeutungen; under the — of unter dem Schutz(e) von

auspicious *adj.* günstig, glücklich

austere *adj.* streng, ernst, hart; herb; mässig, enthaltsam

austerity *n.* Strenge, Ernst, Härte; Mässigkeit, Enthaltsamkeit

Austria *n.* Österreich

authentic *adj.* zuverlässig, glaubwürdig, verbürgt; echt; -ate *v.* verbürgen, als echt erweisen; -ity *n.* Glaubwürdigkeit, Echtheit

author *n.* Autor, Verfasser; Schriftsteller

authoritative *adj.* autorisiert, bevollmächtigt

authorities *n. pl.* Behörde

authority *n.* Autorität; Befugnis, Gewalt; Ansehen; Glaubwürdigkeit; Quelle; on one's own — auf eigene Verantwortung; without — unberechtigt

authorization *n.* Ermächtigung, Bevollmächtigung

authorize *v.* berechtigen, ermächtigen, autorisieren

autobiography *n.* Autobiographie

autocracy *n.* Autokratie

autocrat *n.* Autokrat; -ic *adj.* autokratisch

autogiro *n.* Hubschrauber, Windmühlenflugzeug

autograph *n.* Autogramm; Originalhandschrift; Urschrift; — *v.* eigenhändig unterschreiben

automatic *n.* Selbstladepistole; — *adj.* automatisch; -ally *adv.* mechanisch

automation *n.* Automation, Automatisierung

automaton *n.* Automat; Robot(er)

automobile *n.* Automobil, Wagen

automotive *adj.* mit Selbstantrieb; Automobil-
autonomy *n.* Selbstverwaltung, Autonomie
autopsy *n.* Autopsie, Leichenschau
autumn *n.* Herbst; **-al** *adj.* herbstlich
auxiliary *n.* Helfer, Beistand; Verbündete; — *adj.* helfend, Hilfs-; — **forces** Hilfstruppen; — **verb** Hilfszeitwort
avail *n.* Nutzen, Vorteil; — *v.* nützen, helfen; — oneself of Gebrauch machen von, benutzen; **-able** *adj.* verfügbar, erhältlich, zugänglich
avalanche *n.* Lawine
avenge *v.* rächen, ahnden; **-r** *n.* Rächer
avenue *n.* Strasse, Chaussee, Allee, Promenade
average *n.* Durchschnitt; **on the** — durchschnittlich; — *adj.* durchschnittlich; — *v.* im Durchschnitt rechnen; durchschnittlich betragen (*or* arbeiten, zahlen)
averse *adj.* abgeneigt, widerwillig
aversion *n.* Abneigung, Widerwille(n), Aversion, Abscheu
avert *v.* ablenken, abwenden, verhüten
aviary *n.* Vogelhaus
aviation *n.* Flugwesen, Fliegerei; Aviatik
aviator *n.* Flieger; Aviatiker
avocado *n.* Avokado (Birne)
avocation *n.* Steckenpferd, Zeitvertreib; Nebenbeschäftigung
avoid *v.* (ver)meiden, scheuen, entgehen; **-able** *adj.* vermeidlich, vermeidbar; **-ance** *n.* Vermeidung, Meiden
await *v.* erwarten, entgegensehen
awake *v.* (er)wecken; erwachen; — *adj.* wach, munter; aufgeweckt; **-n** *v.* (er)wecken
award *n.* Preis; Urteil, Entscheidung; — *v.* zuerkennen, zusprechen; gewähren
aware *adj.* bewusst; **be — of** Kenntnis haben von, sich bewusst sein
away *adv.* (hin)weg, ab, fort; abwesend; auswärts, entfernt; — **from** entfernt (*or* abwesend) von; — **from home** von Hause fort; **far** — weit entfernt
awe *n.* Ehrfurcht, Furcht, Scheu
awe-struck *adj.* von Ehrfurcht (*or* Scheu) ergriffen
awful *adj.* furchtbar, schrecklich, entsetzlich
awhile *adv.* eine Weile (*or* Zeitlang)
awkward *adj.* ungeschickt, linkisch; plump; (fig.) peinlich, unangenehm
awl *n.* Ahle, Pfriem
awning *n.* Markise, Sonnensegel
ax(e) *n.* Axt, Beil
axiom *n.* Axiom, Grundsatz; **-atic** *adj.* grundsätzlich, unumstösslich
axis *n.* Achse, Mittellinie; Staatenbund
axle *n.* Achse
aye *adv.* ja

B

babble *n.* Geschwätz, Gewäsch; Murmeln; — *v.* schwatzen, plappern; stammeln; murmeln
babe *n.* Säugling, kleines Kind

babushka *n.* farbiges (*or* gemustertes) Kopftuch
baby *n.* Baby; Nesthäkchen; — **boy** Bübchen; — **buggy** Kinderwagen; — **carriage** Kinderwagen; — **girl** kleines Mädchen; — *v.* verhätscheln, wie ein Baby behandeln; — oneself sich verpimpeln; **-hood** *n.* erste (*or* frühe) Kindheit, Säuglingsalter; **-ish** *adj.* kindisch, kindlich; einfältig
bachelor *n.* Junggeselle; (educ.) Bakkalaureus
bacillus *n.* Bazillus, Bazille, Mikrobe
back *n.* Rücken, Kreuz; Rückseite; Kehrseite; Lehne; (sports) Verteidiger; — **to** — Rücken an Rücken; **behind one's** — hinter jemandes Rücken; heimlich; **flat on one's** — bettlägrig; **his — is up** er ist aufgebracht; **turn one's** — den Rücken kehren; im Stich lassen; — *adj.* letzt, hinter; entlegen; rückständig; — **door** Hintertür; — **number** alte Nummer, frühere Ausgabe; — **payment** rückständige Zahlung; — **seat** Rücksitz; (fig.) untergeordnete Stellung; — **stairs** Hintertreppe; — **street** Hintergasse; — **talk** Widerspruch; — *adv.* zurück; wieder; vorher, früher; — **and forth** auf und ab, hin und her; (**in**) — **of** hinter; **come** — zurückkommen; **go** — zurückgehen, sich zurückziehen; **stand** —! *interj.* zurück! **step** — zurücktreten; — *v.* beistehen, unterstützen; favorisieren; hinter (jemandem) stehen; rückwärtsfahren; zurückgehen, zurücktreten; — **up** zurückgehen, zurückfahren, rückwärtsfahren; **-er** *n.* Unterstützende, Beistand; (theat.) Geldgeber; **-ing** *n.* Unterstützung; (theat.) Finanzierung
backbone *n.* Rückgrat; (fig.) Willenskraft
backdrop *n.* Prospekt
backfire *n.* Frühzündung, Rückzündung
backgammon *n.* Puffspiel
background *n.* Hintergrund; (fig.) Vorbildung
backlog *n.* nicht ausgeführte Bestellungen (*or* Arbeiten)
backslide *v.* abfallen; rückfällig werden
backspin *n.* (sports) Rückwärtsdrehung; **put a** — **on a ball** dem Ball eine Rückwärtsdrehung geben
backstage *adv.* (theat.) hinter den Kulissen
backstop *n.* Ballfänger
backstroke *n.* Rückenschwimmen
backward *adj.* rückwärts gerichtet; langsam, träge; rückständig; zurückgeblieben; schüchtern; **-s** *adv.* rückwärts, zurück; nach hinten; verkehrt; — **and forward** hin und her
backwoodsman *n.* Hinterwäldler
bacon *n.* Speck
bacteria *n. pl.* Bakterien; **-l** *adj.* bakteriell
bacteriology *n.* Bakteriologie
bad *adj.* schlecht, schlimm; arg, böse; übel, lasterhaft; ungesund; minderwertig; — **debt** uneinbringliche Schuld; **from** — **to worse** aus dem Regen in die Traufe, immer schlimmer; **have a** —

cold stark erkältet sein; **too — zu schade; -ly** *adv.* schlecht; ernstlich, dringend, sehr; **he is -ly off** es geht ihm sehr schlecht; **I want this -ly** ich brauche dies sehr

badge *n.* Abzeichen, Dienstzeichen, Amtszeichen; (fig.) Kennzeichen, Merkmal

badger *n.* Dachs; **— v.** hetzen, plagen

badminton *n.* ein Federballspiel

baffle *v.* verspotten, vereiteln, verwirren; durchkreuzen

bag *n.* Sack, Tüte, Beutel, Tasche; Koffer; **— and baggage** Sack und Pack; **sleeping —** Schlafsack; **to be left holding the —** die Suppe auslöffeln müssen; **— v.** fangen, schiessen; (coll.) einstecken; **-gy** *adj.* bauschig, beutelig

baggage *n.* Gepäck; **excess —** Zusatzgepäck, Übergewicht; **— car** Gepäckwagen; **— check** Gepäckschein; **— master** Gepäckmeister; **— office** Gepäckaufgabe, Gepäckausgabe

bagpipe *n.* Dudelsack(pfeife)

bail *n.* Bürgschaft, Kaution; **be out on —** durch Kautionsstellung freikommen; **put up —** Kaution stellen; **— v.** ausschöpfen; **— out** Bürgschaft leisten für (avi.) mit dem Fallschirm abspringen

bailiff *n.* Gerichtsdiener

bait *n.* Köder, Lockspeise; (fig.) Lockung; **— v.** ködern, anlocken; (fig.) quälen, hetzen; **— one's hook with** an die Angel stecken

bake *v.* backen; braten; brennen; **-r** *n.* Bäcker; **-r's dozen** Bäcker Dutzend (13); **-ry** *n.* Bäckerei

baking *n.* Backen; Braten; Brennen; **— adj. — powder** Backpulver; **— soda** Speisesoda, Natron

balance *n.* Waage; Gleichgewicht; (com.) Bilanz, Rechnungsabschluss, Saldo, Bestand, Rest; **amount of —** Saldobetrag; **— of power** politisches Gleichgewicht, Kräfteausgleich; **— of trade** Handelsbilanz; **— sheet** Bilanzbogen; **his life hung in the —** er schwebte zwischen Tod und Leben; **strike a —** Bilanz ziehen; **— v.** (aus)balancieren; (com.) ausgleichen, Bilanz ziehen, saldieren

balcony *n.* Balkon; (theat.) Rang

bald *adj.* kahl, kahlköpfig; (fig.) nackt, unverhüllt; **— spot** kahle Stelle, Glatze; **-ness** *n.* Kahlheit; (fig.) Nacktheit

bale *n.* Ballen, Bündel; **— v.** in Ballen (*or* Bündel) packen; ballen, bündeln

balk *v.* aufhalten, durchkreuzen, verhindern

ball *n.* Kugel, Ball; Knäuel; **keep the — rolling** im Gang erhalten; **—bearing** Kugellager

ballad *n.* Ballade

ballast *n.* Ballast; (rail.) Schotter

ballerina *n.* Ballerina, Ballettänzerin

ballet *n.* Ballett; **— dancer** Ballettänzer

ballistic missile *n.* ferngelenktes Raketengeschoss

ballistics *n.* Schiesslehre; Wurflehre

balloon *n.* Ballon, Luftballon

ballot *n.* Stimmzettel; Wahlkugel; Wahl (durch Abgabe von Kugeln), Abstimmung; **— box** Wahlurne; **secret —** geheime Wahl; **— v.** abstimmen, wählen

ballplayer *n.* Ballspieler

ball-point pen *n.* Kugelschreiber

ballroom *n.* Tanzsaal, Ballsaal

ballyhoo *n.* Marktschreierei

balm *n.* Balsam, Linderung, Trost; **-y** *adj.* balsamisch, duftend, lindernd; (coll.) verrückt

balsam *n.* Balsam

Baltic Sea *n.* Ostsee

balustrade *n.* Balustrade, Geländer

bamboo *n.* Bambus, Bambusrohr

bamboozle *v.* betrügen, beschwindeln

ban *n.* Bann, Verbannung; **— v.** bannen, ächten; verbieten

banana *n.* Banane

band *n.* Band, Schnur; Gürtel; Borte, Streifen; (mus.) Kapelle; (fig.) Schar, Bande; **— leader** Kapellmeister; **— wagon** (pol. coll.) Triumphwagen; **— v. — together** sich vereinigen

bandage *n.* Verband, Binde, Bandage; **— v.** verbinden, bandagieren

bandbox *n.* Hutschachtel, Putzschachtel

bandit *n.* Bandit

bandstand *n.* Musikpavillon

bang *n.* Schlag, Hieb, Knall; Ponyfrisur; **— v.** (zu)schlagen; knallen, krachen; **— around (up)** misshandeln; **—! interj.** bums! krach!

banish *v.* verbannen; **-ment** *n.* Verbannung

banister *n.* Geländer

bank *n.* Bank; Spielbank; Ufer, Strand; Erhöhung; Damm, Böschung; **— account** Bankkonto; **— bill** Bankwechsel; **— note** Banknote; **savings —** Sparkasse; **— v.** auf die Bank bringen, hinterlegen; eindämmen; (fire) unterhalten; **— an airplane** mit dem Flugzeug zur Kurve ansetzen; **— on** bauen auf; **-er** *n.* Bankier; Bankhalter; **-ing** *n.* Bankgeschäft; **— house** Bankhaus

bankbook *n.* Bankbuch

bankrupt *adj.* bankrott; zahlungsunfähig; **— n.** Bankrotteur, Gemeinschuldner; **-cy** *n.* Konkurs, Bankrott

banner *n.* Fahne, Flagge, Banner

banns *n. pl.* Aufgebot; **publish the —** aufbieten

banquet *n.* Bankett, Festmahl, Festessen; **— v.** bankettieren, festlich bewirten, schmausen

Bantam *n.* Bantamhuhn, Zwerghuhn

baptism *n.* Taufe; **— of fire** Feuertaufe

baptize *v.* taufen

bar *n.* Bar; Stange, Barre, Stab; Tafel; Büfett, Theke; (gymn.) Barren, Reck; (law) Schranke, Advokatur; (mus.) Takt, Taktstrich; (fig.) Hindernis, Querstrich; **be admitted to the —** als Rechtsanwalt zugelassen sein; **prisoner at the —** Gefangener vor Gericht; **— v.** verriegeln; versperren; ausschliessen; **-(ring) prep.** ausser, ausgenommen; **-red** *adj.* gestreift

barb n. Widerhaken, Stachel; **-ed** adj. mit Widerhaken versehen; **-ed wire** Stacheldraht

barbarian n. Barbar, Unmensch, Rohling; — adj. barbarisch, roh

barbarity n. Grausamkeit, Roheit; Barbarei

barbarous adj. barbarisch, roh

barbecue n. grosser Bratrost; im Ganzen gebratenes Tier; — v. im Ganzen braten

barber n. Friseur, Barbier; — **shop** Friseurladen

bare adj. bar, nackt, unbekleidet; offen; leer; rein; kahl, entlaubt; — v. entblössen, enthüllen; **-ly** adv. kaum, knapp

barefaced adj. unverschämt, schamlos, frech

barefoot(ed) adj. barfuss, barfüssig

bareheaded adj. barhäuptig, mit blossem Kopf

barelegged adj. nacktbeinig, mit blossen Beinen

bargain n. Vertrag; Handel, Kauf, Geschäft; Gelegenheitskauf; — **counter** Ladentisch für herabgesetzte waren; **into the** — in den Kauf, obendrein; **it's a** —! topp! abgemacht! — v. handeln, feilschen; — **for** erwarten

barge n. Barke, Schute; Hausboot; Lastkahn, Leichter

baritone n. Bariton

bark n. (bot.) Rinde, Borke; (dog) Bellen, Kläffen Gebell; (naut.) Barke; **his** — **is worse than his bite** Hunde, die bellen, beissen nicht; — v. bellen, kläffen; abstossen, abschürfen; — **at** anbellen; — **up the wrong tree** auf falscher Fährte sein

barley n. Gerste

barmaid n. Kellnerin, Bardame

barn n. Scheune, Scheuer

barnacle n. Entenmuschel; (fig.) Klette

barnyard n. Scheunenhof, Scheunenplatz

barometer n. Barometer

baron n. Baron, Freiherr; (fig.) Industriemagnat; **-ess** n. Baronin, Baronesse, Freifrau; **-et** n. Baronet

baroque adj. barock; (fig.) seltsam

barrack n. Baracke, Hütte. (agr.) Schober; pl. Kaserne; (coll.) Mietskaserne

barracuda n. Pfeilhecht

barrage n. Sperrfeuer; — **balloon** Sperrballon

barrel n. Tonne, Fass

barren adj. unfruchtbar; steril; kahl; trokken, unproduktiv; **-ness** n. Unfruchtbarkeit, Dürre, Dürftigkeit; Leere, Geistesarmut

barricade n. Barrikade, Sperre, Hindernis; — v. verbarrikadieren, versperren, verhindern

barrier n. Schranke; Barriere; (mil.) Verschanzung; (rail.) Schlagbaum; (fig.) Hindernis

barroom n. Barraum, Schenkstube

bartender n. Barkellner

barter n. Tausch, Tauschhandel; — v. eintauschen, vertauschen; (coll.) verschachern

basal metabolism n. Stoffwechselbasis

base n. (arch.) Sockel; Fundament, Grundfläche; (avi., mil., naut.) Stützpunkt; (chem.) Base, Lauge; (geom.) Grundlinie; (sports) Mal; (fig.) Grundlage; — **hit** Treffer; — v. basieren, stützen, gründen, begründen; **be -d on** beruhen auf; — adj. klein, niedrig; gemein; geringwertig; (fig.) verächtlich; **-less** adj. grundlos; **-ment** n. Keller; **-ness** n. Niedrigkeit, Niederträchtigkeit; Gemeinheit; Unechtheit

baseball n. Baseball (amerikanisches Schlagballspiel)

baseboard n. untere Wandtäfelung, Wandsockel

bashful adj. scheu, schüchtern; **-ness** n. Scheu, Schüchternheit

basic adj. fundamental, grundlegend; (chem.) basisch

basin n. Becken, Bassin; (geol.) Flussbecken, Stromgebiet

basis n. Grundlage, Basis; Grund

bask v. sich wärmen (or sonnen)

basket n. Korb; **-ful** n. Korbvoll

basketball n. Korbball(spiel)

bas-relief n. Flachrelief

bass n. (ichth.) Barsch; (mus.) Bass, Bassist; — **clef** F-Schlüssel, Bassschlüssel; — **drum** Riesentrommel; — **horn** Tuba; — **viol** Violincello; — adj. niedrig, tief

bassoon n. Fagott

bastard n. Bastard, uneheliches Kind; — adj. unehelich; (fig.) falsch, unecht

baste v. (cooking) mit Fett übergiessen; (sewing) heften

bat n. (baseball) Schläger, Schlagholz; (zool.) Fledermaus; **be at** — am Schlagen (or an der Reihe) sein; **go to** — **for** unterstützen; — v. schlagen, treffen; **without -ting an eye** ohne mit der Wimper zu zucken; **-ter** n. (baseball) Schläger; (cooking) Teig; **-ter** v. zerschlagen, zertrümmern; klopfen, schlagen, stossen; **-ter down** einschlagen, **-ting** n. Schlagen (des Balles)

batch n. Schub; Menge; Trupp, Schicht, Partie

bath n. Bad; — **towel** Badetuch; **-e** r. baden; **be -ed in** umgeben sein von; **be -ed in tears** in Tränen schwimmen; **-ing** n. Bad, Baden; **-ing beach** Badestrand; **-ing cap** Badekappe; **-ing suit** Badeanzug, Schwimmanzug; **-ing trunks** Badehosen, Schwimmhosen

bathhouse n. Badeanstalt, Schwimmanstalt

bathrobe n. Bademantel

bathroom n. Badezimmer

bathtub n. Wanne, Badewanne

baton n. Taktstock, Stab

battery n. Batterie; (law) tätlicher Angriff; — **cell** Batterieelement; **dry** — Trockenelement; **the** — **is dead die** Batterie ist ausgebrannt (or tot)

battle n. Kampf, Schlacht, Gefecht; — **cry** Schlachtruf, Feldruf; — **front** Schlachtfront; — **royal** allgemeine Rauferei; **that's half the** — das heisst halb gewonnen; — v. kämpfen, streiten, fechten; — **it out** es austragen

battlefield *n.* Schlachtfeld

battleground *n.* Kriegsschauplatz

battleship *n.* Schlachtschiff

Bavaria *n.* Bayern

bawl *c.* schreien, brüllen, plärren; ausrufen, — **out** ausschimpfen

bay *n.* (arch.) Nische, Erker; (bot.) Lorbeer; (geog.) Bucht, Bai, Meerbusen; (horse) Fuchs; — **rum** Bairum, Pimentrum; — **window** Erkerfenster, Fensternische; **hold** (*oder* **keep**) **at** — in Schach halten, stellen; **stand at** — sich widersetzen sich zur Wehr setzen; — *v.* bellen

bayonet *n.* Seitengewehr, Bajonett; — *v.* mit dem Bajonett niederstossen (*or* treiben)

bayou *n.* Nebenarm, Nebenfluss

bazaar *n.* Basar, Verkaufshalle

bazooka *n.* Panzerabwehrgeschütz, Pak

be *v.* sein, werden; existieren; — **ill** krank sein; — **in a hurry** es eilig haben; — **off** sich fortmachen; — **right** recht haben; — **well** sich wohl befinden (*or* fühlen), gesund sein; **that is to** — zukünftig; **-ing** *n.* Sein, Dasein, Existenz; (poet.) Wesen; **for the time -ing** einstweilen, augenblicklich

beach *n.* Strand, Ufer; — *v.* auf den Strand ziehen (*or* setzen, laufen lassen)

beachcomber *n.* Vagabund

beachhead *n.* Landungskopf

beacon *n.* Leuchtfeuer, Signalfeuer; Leuchtturm; (avi.) Kontroll- (*or* Warn)station (Funk *or* Radar)

bead *n.* Glasperle, Perle; Kügelchen; Tropfen; *pl.* Halsband; Rosenkranz; **-work** *n.* Perlstickerei

beagle *n.* Vorstehhund, Spürhund

beak *n.* Schnabel; Tülle; **-er** *n.* Becher

beam *n.* (arch.) Baum; Balken; Schwelle; (naut.) Breite; (opt.) Strahl, Lichtstrahl; (rad.) Signal; (fig.) Glanz; — *v.* strahlen, glänzen; **-ing** *adj.* glänzend, strahlend, leuchtend

bean *n.* Bohne; **kidney** — Feuerbohne; **string** — grüne Bohne; **wax** — Wachsbohne

bear *n.* (zool.) Bär; (com.) Baissier; **grizzly** — Grizzlybär, Graubär; — *v.* tragen, ertragen, gebären; aushalten, leiden; überbringen; — **a grudge** nachtragen, — **down** überwinden; niederdrücken; — **in mind** nicht vergessen; — **oneself** sich benehmen; — **witness** Zeugnis ablegen; **-able** *adj.* ertragbar, erträglich; **-er** *n.* Träger, Überbringer; (com.) Wechselinhaber; **-ing** *n.* Haltung; (mech.) Lager; Beziehung, Verhältnis; **get one's -ings** sich orientieren, **have -ing** on zu tun haben mit; **lose one's -ings** seinen Halt verlieren

beard *n.* Bart; — *v.* Trotz bieten, entgegentreten; **-ed** *adj.* bärtig; **-less** *adj.* bartlos; (fig.) jugendlich

beast *n.* Tier, Vieh; Bestie; (fig.) roher (*or* brutaler) Mensch; — **of burden** Lasttier; **-liness** *n.* Bestialität; Roheit, Ekelhaftigkeit; **-ly** *adj.* bestialisch,

viehisch; brutal, ekelhaft

beat *n.* Schlag; (mus.) Takt, Taktschlag; Runde, Rundgang, Revier; (coll.) Sphäre, Bereich; **dead** — Schmarotzer; — *v.* schlagen, prügeln; klopfen; rühren; besiegen; gewinnen; — **a path** einen Weg bahnen; — **around the bush** Umschweife machen; — **into shape** in richtige Form bringen; — **someone's brain out** jemandem den Schädel einschlagen; — **time** Takt schlagen; — **to it** zuvorkommen; — **up** verhauen, verprügeln; **that —s everything** das übertrifft alles; **that —s me** das geht über meinen Horizont; **-en** *adj.* geschlagen, besiegt; gebahnt, ausgetreten; **-en track** herkömmliche Art und Weise; **-er** *n.* Schläger, Schlegel, Stössel; (hunting) Treiber; **egg -er** Schneeschläger; **-ing** *n.* Schlagen, Prügeln; **give a good -ing** eine tüchtige Tracht Prügel verabreichen

Beatitudes *n. pl.* Seligpreisungen

beatify *v.* seligsprechen, seligmachen

beau *n.* Liebhaber, Anbeter

beautiful *adj.* schön, prächtig; (fig.) ausgezeichnet

beautify *v.* verschönern

beauty *n.* Schönheit; schöne Frau, Schöne; Pracht; — **parlor**, — **shop** Schönheitssalon; — **sleep** Schönheitsschlaf; — **spot** Schönheitspflästerchen

beaver *n.* Biber

because *conj.* weil, denn da; — **of** wegen

beck *n.* **be at one's** — **and call** jemandem vollständig zur Verfügung stehen

beckon *v.* (zu)winken, zunicken, auffordern

become *v.* werden; wohl anstehen, sich schicken, sich eignen; gut kleiden; **what has** — **of him?** was ist aus ihm geworden? wo ist er hingekommen?

becoming *adj.* passend, kleidsam, schicklich

bed *n.* Bett, Lager; (agr.) Beet; (geol.) Lagerung; — **and bedding** Bett und Bettzeug; — **of thorns** Schmerzenslager; — **sheet** Leintuch, Betttuch; **get out of** — aufstehen; **go to** — zu Bett gehen, schlafengehen; **make the** — das Bett machen; **put to** — zu Bett bringen; **river** — Flussbett; **stay in** — im Bett bleiben; **take to** — bettlägerig werden; **-ding** *n.* Bettzeug

bedbug *n.* Bettwanze

bedclothes *n. pl.* Bettbezüge

bedcover *n.* Bettüberzug, Bettbezug

bedeck *v.* zieren, schmücken

bedfellow *n.* Bettgenosse

bedpan *n.* Stechbecken

bedquilt *n.* Steppdecke

bedridden *adj.* bettlägerig

bedrock *n.* festes Gebirge; Grundlage

bedroom *n.* Schlafzimmer

bedside *n.* Bettseite; — **manner** Krankenzimmermanieren

bedspread *n.* Bettdecke

bedspring *n.* Sprungfeder (im Bett)

bedstead *n.* Bettstelle

bedtime *n.* Schlafenszeit

bee n. Biene; **spelling —** Buchstabierwettbewerb

beech n. Buche

beechnut n. Buchecker

beef n. Rindfleisch; (coll.) Rindvieh; **— tea** Kraftbrühe; **chipped —** getrocknete Rindfleischstreifen; **corned —** geräuchertes (or gesalzenes) Rindfleisch; Pökelfleisch; Büchsenfleisch; **roast —** Roastbeef, Rostbraten; **-y** adj. fleischig

beefsteak n. Beefsteak

beehive n. Bienenkorb, Bienenstock

beeline n. Luftlinie

beer n. Bier; **— barrel** Bierfass, Biertonne

beeswax n. Bienenwachs

beet n. (rote) Rübe, Runkelrübe; **— greens** Runkelrübenkraut; **— sugar** Rübenzucker

beetle n. Käfer; Schabe

before adv. vorn, voran; vorher, zuvor, vormals, eher, ehemals; früher, bereits, schon; **an hour —** eine Stunde früher; **the day —** am vorigen Tag; **never —** noch nie; **— prep.** vor; **— long** bald; es dauert nicht mehr lang; **the day — yesterday** vorgestern; **— conj.** ehe, bevor, eher als; lieber als

beforehand adv. zuvor, im voraus; vorher

befriend v. sich anfreunden; begünstigen, beistehen

beg v. bitten, ersuchen; flehen; betteln; erbetteln; **— leave** um Erlaubnis bitten; **I — your pardon** ich bitte um Verzeihung, entschuldigen Sie; wie bitte? **I — to be excused** ich bitte um Entschuldigung; ich bitte, gehen zu dürfen; **-ging** n. Betteln, Bettelei; **-ging** adj. bettelnd, bittend

beget v. erzeugen, hervorbringen

beggar n. Bettler; Arme, Elende; **-ly** adj. bettelhaft; armselig, verächtlich

begin v. beginnen, anfangen; entstehen; **to —** with anfänglich, erstens; **-ner** n. Anfänger, Neuling; **-ning** n. Anfang, Beginn; Ursprung; **-nings** n. Anfangsgründe, Grundelemente; **at the -ning** im Anfang; **from the -ning** von Anfang an; **from -ning to end** von Anfang bis zu Ende, von A bis Zet

begrudge v. misgönnen, nicht gönnen; beneiden

behalf n. **in** (oder **on**) **— of** zugunsten von; im Namen von

behave v. sich betragen (or benehmen); **— yourself** benimm dich anständig

behavior n. Betragen, Benehmen; Verhalten, Aufführung; **be on one's good —** sich gut benehmen; sich zusammennehmen; **-ism** n. Psychologie des guten Betragens

behead v. enthaupten, köpfen

behind prep. hinter; **be — the eight ball** in der Patsche sitzen; **— adv.** hinten, dahinter, hinterher, nach hinten; zurück; rückständig; **be — nachgehen**; stecken hinter; rückständig sein; **fall — zurückbleiben**

behold v. anblicken, erblicken, betrachten; **-l** interj. siehe da!

beige n. Beige, Gelbgrau

belated adj. verspätet

belch n. Aufstossen, Rülpsen; **— v.** aufstossen, rülpsen; **— forth** ausspeien

belfry n. Kirchturm, Glockenturm

Belgium n. Belgien

belie v. verleumden; Lügen strafen; widersprechen, täuschen

belief n. Glaube; Vertrauen; Meinung, Überzeugung; (rel.) Glaubensbekenntnis; **to the best of my —** meiner innersten Überzeugung nach

believable adj. glaublich, glaubhaft

believe v. glauben, meinen, vertrauen; **— in** glauben an; **-r** n. Gläubige, Glaubende

belittle v. verkleinern, herabsetzen

bell n. Glocke, Klingel, Schelle; (naut.) Stunde

bellboy n. Hotelpage

belle n. Schönheit; **— of the ball** Ballkönigin

bellhop n. Hotelpage

belligerence n. Kampflust

belligerent n. kriegführende Partei; **— adj.** kriegführend; kriegsliebend

bellows n. Blasebalg, Gebläse

bell-shaped adj. glockenförmig, glockenartig

belly n. Bauch, Wanst; **— v.** (an)schwellen

belong v. gehören, angehören; betreffen; **-ings** n. pl. Eigentum, Besitztum, Habe

beloved adj. geliebt, teuer

below adv. unten, nach unten; hinunter, herunter; unter, niedriger, tiefer; **— prep.** unter(halb)

belt n. Gürtel, Gurt, Koppel; (geog.) Region, Meerenge; (mech.) Treibriemen; **transmission —** Transmissionsriemen; **hit below the —** gemein sein; **tighten one's —** den Gürtel enger schnallen, hungern

bemoan v. beklagen, betrauern

bench n. Bank; (law) Gerichtshof, Richterbank; (mech.) Werkbank, Arbeitstisch; (pol.) Sitz, Reihe

bend n. Biegung, Krümmung; **— v.** beugen, biegen, krümmen; neigen; (fig.) bezwingen, unterwerfen; **— down, — over** sich neigen, sich bücken

beneath adv. unten; **— prep.** unter, unterhalb

benediction n. Segen

benefactor n. Wohltäter

beneficent adj. wohltätig

beneficial adj. nützlich, vorteilhaft, zuträglich; (law) nutzniessend

beneficiary n. Almosenempfänger, Erbe

benefit n. Nutzen, Vorteil, Wohltat; (theat.) Benefiz; **for the — of** zum Nutzen (or Vorteil) von; **he always gives me the — of the doubt** im Zweifelsfalle entscheidet er immer zu meinen Gunsten; **— v.** nützen, begünstigen, fördern; **— by** Vorteil ziehen aus

benevolence n. Wohlwollen, Güte; Wohltat

benevolent adj. wohlwollend, gütig; wohltätig; **— society** Wohltätigkeitsverein

benighted adj. umnachtet

benign adj. gütig, liebreich; günstig, wohltuend; mild; (med.) gutartig

bent n. Richtung, Neigung; — adj. gebogen, krumm; geneigt; — **on** erpicht auf, entschlossen zu

Benzedrine n. Benzedrin

benzine n. Benzin

bequeath v. vermachen, hinterlassen

bequest n. Vermächtnis, Legat

bereave v. berauben; -ed adj. leidtragend, hinterblieben; -ment n. Beraubung; schmerzlicher Verlust

beret n. Barett

Bering Strait n. Beringstrasse

berry n. Beere

berserk adj. wütend

berth n. Bett, Koje; Ankergrund; **give a wide** — to weit aus dem Wege gehen

beseech v. bitten, beschwören, flehen

besetting adj. — **sin** Gewohnheitssünde

beside prep. neben, bei; ausser; — **one-self**, ausser sich; **that is** — **the question** (oder point) das hat nichts damit zu tun; — adv. ausserdem; -s adv. ausserdem; übrigens; -s prep. ausser, neben

besiege v. belagern, bestürmen

bespeak v. (vorher) bestellen

best adj. beste; — **girl** Schatz, Geliebte; — **man** Brautführer; — **seller** Erfolgswerk; **put one's** — **foot forward** sein Bestes tun; — adv. am besten, aufs beste; — n. Beste; **at** — bestenfalls; **do one's** — sein Möglichstes tun; **for the** — zum Besten; **get the** — of übervorteilen; **make the** — of sich abfinden mit; gute Miene zum bösen Spiel machen; **to the** — **of my knowledge** soviel ich weiss; **to the** — **of one's ability** nach besten Kräften; — v. übertreffen

bestow v. erteilen, schenken; gebrauchen; — (up)on verleihen

bet n. Wette, Einsatz; — v. wetten, setzen; -ter (oder -tor) n. Wettende

betray v. verraten; missbrauchen; verführen; -al n. Verrat

better adj. besser; — **half** bessere Hälfte, Ehehälfte; **for the** — zum Vorteil; **get the** — of übertreffen; — adv. besser; mehr; **all the** — umso besser; **be** — **off** besser dran sein; — **and** — immer mehr (or besser); **so much the** — umso (or desto) besser; **think** — **of it** sich eines Besseren besinnen; **we'd** — go es ist besser, wir gehen, wir sollten lieber gehen; -s n. pl. Vorgesetzten; — v. (ver)bessern; übertreffen; befördern

between prep. zwischen, unter; **few and far** — selten; — **you and me** unter uns, unter vier Augen; — adv. dazwischen

betweentimes adv. dann und wann, bisweilen

bevel n. Schrägung, Schrägmass; — v. abschrägen

beverage n. Getränk, Trank; **cold** — Erfrischung

bevy n. Trupp, Rudel, Schar, Schwarm

beware v. sich in acht nehmen, sich hüten; achtgeben; —! interj. gib acht! hüte dich!

bewilder v. verwirren, bestürzen; irreführen; -ed adj. verwirrt; -ment n. Verwirrung, Bestürzung

bewitch v. behexen, bezaubern; -ing adj. bezaubernd, reizend

beyond prep. jenseits, über, ausser, auf der anderen Seite, nach; — **belief** unglaublich; — **hope** hoffnungslos; — **one's reach** unerreichbar; — **recovery** unheilbar; **it is** — **me** es übersteigt meine Kräfte, das verstehe ich nicht; — adv. darüber hinaus, ausserhalb, jenseits; — n. Jenseits

biannual adj. zweimal jährlich

bias n. Vorurteil, Neigung; **free from** — vorurteilsfrei; **on the** — schräg; — v. beeinflussen; -ed adj. beeinflusst, voreingenommen

bib n. Schürzenlatz, Kinderlätzchen

Bible n. Bibel, Heilige Schrift

Biblical adj. biblisch

bibliography n. Bibliographie

bicarbonate of soda n. doppelkohlensaures Natron

biceps n. Bizeps

bicker v. zanken, streiten

bicycle n. Fahrrad; **ride a** — radfahren, radeln

bicyclist n. Radfahrer

bid n. Gebot, Angebot; (cards) Ansage; — v. bieten, gebieten, befehlen; (cards) melden, ansagen; — **adieu** Lebewohl sagen; -der n. Bieter, Bietende; -ding n. Bieten; Gebot, Befehl

bide v. erwarten, abwarten

biennial adj. zweijährig, zweijährlich

bier n. Bahre, Totenbahre

bifocals n. pl. Bifokalgläser

big adj. gross, dick; (fig.) hoch, vornehm; **Big Dipper** Grosser Wagen (or Bär); — **game** Grosswildjagd; — **talk** Prahlerei; — **words** starke Worte; -ness n. Grösse, Dicke; Umfang

bigamist n. Bigamist

bigamy n. Bigamie, Doppelehe

bighearted adj. grossherzig, grosszügig

bigot n. Frömmler; -ed adj. bigott; -ry n. Bigotterie, Frömmelei

bike n. Fahrrad

bilateral adj. zweiseitig, bilateral

bile n. Galle; (fig.) Bitterkeit

bilingual adj. zweisprachig

bill n. Schnabel; Schein, Note; Zettel; (com.) Rechnung; (pol.) Gesetz, Gesetzesentwurf, Gesetzesvorlage; — **of exchange** Wechsel, Kurszettel; — **of fare** Speisekarte; — **of health** Gesundheitsattest; — **of lading** Frachtbrief; **Bill of Rights** Freiheitsurkunde; — **of sale** Kaufvertrag, Schuldverschreibung; **hand** — Reklamezettel; **true** — berechtigte Anklage; — v. berechnen; — **for** in Rechnung stellen; n. pl. — **payable** fällige Rechnungen; — **receivable** noch nicht fällige Rechnungen; **post no** — Ankleben (von Plakaten) verboten

billboard n. Anschlagebrett

billet n. Billett, Zettel; (mil.) Quartier;

— v. einquartieren
billfold n. Brieftasche
billiard ball n. Billardkugel
billiards n. Billard(spiel)
billion n. (USA) Milliarde (1.000.000.000);
  Billion (1.000.000.000.000); **-aire** n.
  (USA) Milliardär; Billionär
billow n. Woge, Sturzwelle; **-y** adj. wogend, schwellend, wogig
bimonthly adj. zweimonatig, zweimonatlich
bin n. Kasten, Kiste; Behälter
bind v. binden, zwingen, verpflichten;
  (med.) verbinden; — **off** abketten; **-er**
  n. Binder; Buchbinder; **-ery** n. Buchbinderei; **-ing** n. Einband; **cloth -ing**
  Leineneinband; **paper -ing** Pappeinband; **-ing** adj. verbindlich
bingo n. Bingo, Lotteriespiel
binoculars n. pl. Ferngläser; Operngläser
binomial adj. binomisch, zweigliedrig; —
  theorem binomischer Lehrsatz
biochemistry n. Biochemie
biographer n. Biograph
biographical adj. biographisch
biography n. Biographie
biological adj. biologisch; — **warfare**
  biologischer Krieg
biology n. Biologie
bipartisan adj. beide Parteien vertretend
biplane n. Doppeldecker
birch n. Birke
bird n. Vogel; — **cage** Vogelkäfig; — **dog**
  Hühnerhund; — **watcher** Vogelbeobachter; — **of prey** Raubvogel
birdie n. ein Schlag zu wenig (or unter
  par)
bird's-eye view n. Vogelperspektive
birth n. Geburt; Abstammung, Herkunft;
  Entstehung, Veranlassung; — **certificate** Geburtsschein; — **control** Geburtenbeschränkung; — **rate** Geburtenziffer; **by** — von Geburt; **give** — gebären;
  ins Lebenrufen
birthday n. Geburtstag
birthmark n. Muttermal
birthplace n. Geburtsort
biscuit n. Keks, Biskuit
bisect v. in zwei Teile zerschneiden, halbieren
bishop n. Bischof; (chess) Läufer
bison n. Bison, Büffel, Auerochs, Wisent
bit n. Kleinigkeit; Gebiss; (mech.)
  Bohrspitze; pl. Trümmer; **a** — ein
  wenig, etwas; — **by** — allmählich;
  every — ganz und gar; **not a** — nicht
  im geringsten
bitch n. (zool.) Hündin; (sl.) Weibsbild
bite n. Biss, Stich; (ichth.) Anbeissen; —
  v. beissen, anbeissen; schneiden, stechen; — **the dust** ins Gras beissen,
  sterben
biting adj. beissend, schneidend, scharf
bitter adj. bitter, herb, schmerzhaft;
  -ness n. Bitterkeit, Verbitterung
bittern n. Rohrdommel
bituminous adj. bituminös, erdpecharts;
  — **coal** bituminöse Kohle
biweekly adj. zweiwöchentlich; — adv.
  alle vierzehn Tage

bizarre adj. bizarr, seltsam
blab v. schwatzen, ausplaudern
black adj. schwarz; dunkel; (fig.) finster,
  düster; — **list** schwarze Liste; — **magic**
  schwarze Magie (or Kunst); — **market**
  Schwarzmarkt, Schleichhandel; —
  sheep schwarzes Schaf, Taugenichts;
  — **widow** amerikanische Riesenspinne;
  — n. Schwarz, Schwärze; Neger; — v.
  wichsen; **-en** v. schwarz (or dunkel)
  werden; schwärzen; (fig.) anschwärzen,
  verleumden; **-ness** n. Schwärze, Dunkelheit
blackberry n. Brombeere
blackbird n. Amsel
blackboard n. Wandtafel, Tafel,
  schwarzes Brett
Black Forest n. Schwarzwald
blackhead n. Mitesser, Talkdrüsenverstopfung
black-list v. auf die schwarze Liste setzen
blackmail n. Erpressung; — v. erpressen
blackout n. Verdunkelung; (med.) Ohnmacht
blacksmith n. Schmied
bladder n. Blase, Harnblase
blade n. (bot.) Blatt, Halm; (mech.)
  Klinge; — **of a propeller** Propellerflügel
blade dispenser n. Klingenspender
blame n. Tadel; Schuld; Verantwortung;
  — v. tadeln, schelten, rügen; **-less** adj.
  untadelhaft, unschuldig
blanch v. bleichen, weissen; (cooking)
  abrühen
bland adj. sanft, mild
blank n. Formular; Weisse; leerer Raum,
  Lücke; unbeschriebenes Blatt, Blanko;
  (fig.) Nichts, Niete; — adj. weiss,
  blanko, leer; — **cartridge** Platzpatrone;
  — **check** Blankoscheck; — **verse**
  Blankvers
blanket n. Decke; — **instructions** Blankovollmacht; Blankobefehl; (mil.) künstliche Vernebelung; — v. bedecken
blare v. schmettern; brüllen
blaspheme v. lästern, fluchen
blasphemous adj. lästernd
blasphemy n. Gotteslästerung, Blasphemie
blast n. Sturm, Windstoss; Blasen; Explosion; Gebläse; Luftdruck; — **furnace**
  Hochofen; — v. sprengen, vernichten;
  (fig.) verderben, vereiteln; **-ing** n.
  Sprengung
blast-off n. Raketenabschuss
blaze n. Flamme, Glut; Lichtschein,
  Strahl; Brand; — v. flammen; lodern;
  leuchten
blazing adj. prall
bleach v. bleichen, weiss machen; **-ing** n.
  Bleiche; Bleichen
bleachers n. pl. offene Tribüne
bleak adj. kahl, öde; kalt, frostig; (fig.)
  freudlos
bleed v. bluten; (med.) zur Ader lassen;
  -ing n. Blutung; Aderlass; **-ing** adj.
  blutend; **-ing heart** Goldlack
blemish n. Makel, Fehler; Gebrechen;
  (fig.) Schandfleck; — v. beflecken
blend n. Mischung, Zusammenstellung;
  — v. (ver)mischen, verschmelzen; zu-

sammenpassen

bless v. segnen; beglücken; **–ed** adj. selig, gesegnet, glücklich; **–ing** n. Segen, Wohltat; Tischgebet

blight n. Mehltau, Brand; Rost; Frostschaden; Gifthauch

blimp n. Luftschiff

blind adj. blind; **— alley** Sackgasse; **fly —** blind (or nur mit Hilfe der Instrumente) fliegen; **— man** Blinde; **— spot** Punkt des mangelnden Verständnisses; **—** v. blenden; (fig.) verblenden; **—** n. Blende; (sports) Versteck; (fig.) Vorwand; **Venetian –s** Jalousien, Rouleaus, Rolläden; **-ly** adv. blind, unbesonnen, **-ness** n. Blindheit

blindfold n. Augenbinde; **—** v. die Augen verbinden; **—** adj. mit verbundenen Augen; (fig.) verwegen

blindman's buff n. Blindekuh(spiel)

blink n. Blinken, blinzeln; schimmern; (fig.) nicht sehen wollen; **—** n. Blinken, Schimmer; **-er** n. Blinkfeuer; **-ers** n. pl. Scheuklappen

bliss n. Wonne; Freude; Entzücken; **-ful** adj. wonnevoll, selig

blister n. Blase, Pustel; (mech.) Luftblase; **—** v. Blasen bilden (or ziehen)

blizzard n. Blizzard, Schneesturm

bloat v. aufblasen, aufblähen

bloc n. Zweckverband, Zweckvereinigung

block n. Block, Klotz; Häuserblock; (mech.) Kloben, Rolle, Hutform; (fig.) Sperrung, Stockung; **— and tackle** Flaschenzug; **— system** Blocksystem, Absperrsystem; **—** v. hindern, hemmen, blockieren; (ver)sperren; (art) skizzieren; (hats) pressen

blockade n. Blockade; **run a —** Blockade brechen; **-ade** v. blockieren

blockhouse n. Blockhaus

blond(e) n. Blonde, Blondine; **peroxide —** Wasserstoffblondine; **—** adj. blond, hell

blood n. Blut; Abstammung, Menschenschlag; **— bank** Blutbank; **— count** Zählung der Blutkörper; **— donor** Blutspender; **— group** Blutgruppe; **— plasma** Blutplasma; **— poisoning** Blutvergiftung; **— pressure** Blutdruck; **— test** Blutprobe; **— transfusion** Blutübertragung; **— vessel** Blutgefäss, Ader; **in cold —** kaltblütig; **-y** adj. blutig, blutbefleckt

bloodhound n. Bluthund, Schweisshund; (fig.) Verfolger

bloodshed n. Blutvergiessen, Mord

bloodshot adj. blutunterlaufen

bloodstain n. Blutfleck; **-ed** adj. blutbefleckt

bloodsucker n. Blutsauger; (fig.) Erpresser

bloodthirsty adj. blutdürstig, blutrünstig

bloom n. Blüte; Blume; Flaum; (fig.) Blütezeit, Jugendfrische; **—** v. blühen, erblühen; florieren

bloomers n. pl. Reformhosen für Frauen

blossom n. Blüte; **—** v. blühen, Blüten treiben

blot v. Klecks, Fleck; **—** v. löschen;

beklecksen, beflecken; **— out** versperren, ausstreichen; **-ter** n. Löscher, Löschpapier

blotch n. Pustel; Klecks

blouse n. Bluse

blow n. Schlag, Streich, Hieb; (fig.) Unglücksfall; **—** v. blasen, wehen; **— away** wegwehen; **— one's brains out** sich eine Kugel durch den Kopf jagen; **— one's nose** sich die Nase putzen; **— out** ausblasen; platzen; **— over** vorübergehen; **— the horn** hupen; **— up** sprengen, explodieren; aufblasen

blower n. Gebläse

blowout n. Reifenpanne, Platzen

blowpipe n. Blasrohr; Lötrohr

blowtorch n. Lötlampe

blubber n. Tran; **—** v. flennen, plärren, weinen

blue n. Blau; (fig.) Himmel, Meer; **— jay** Blauhäher; **—** adj. blau, bläulich; (fig.) schwermütig, traurig; **—** v. blau färben, blauen; n. pl. Schwermut, Melancholie

blueberry n. Blaubeere

bluebird n. Blaukehlchen

blue-blooded adj. blaublütig, aristokratisch

blue-eyed adj. blauäugig

blueprint n. Blaupause, Blaudruck; Heliographie

bluff n. Abhang; Bluff, Irreführung; **—** adj. schroff, steil; rauh, barsch; **—** v. bluffen, verblüffen

bluing, **blueing** n. Waschblau

bluish adj. bläulich

blunder n. Fehler, Missgriff, Schnitzer; **—** v. Fehler (or Schnitzer) machen; (sports) stolpern

blunt adj. stumpf, grob, plump; **—** v. abstumpfen; (fig.) unterdrücken

blur n. Flecken, Klecks; (fig.) Makel; Undeutlichkeit; **—** v. beflecken, verwischen, auslöschen

blurt v. **— out** herausplatzen

blush n. Erröten, Schamröte; **—** v. erröten; (fig.) verwirrt sein, sich schämen

boa n. Boa, Riesenschlange; **— constrictor** Abgottschlange; Boa Constrictor

boar n. Eber, Keiler; **wild —** Wildschwein

board n. Brett; Tafel, Tisch; (naut.) Board; (fig.) Kost, Pension; **— and lodging** Kost und Logis; **— of education** Unterrichtsamt; **— of examination** Prüfungskommission; **— of health** Gesundheitsamt; **— of trade** Handelsamt, Börsenkommission; **— of trustees** Direktorium, Verwaltungsrat; **free on —** (f.o.b.) frei Schiff; **on —** an Bord; **school —** Schulbehörde; **—** v. an Bord gehen, einsteigen, beköstigen; in Pension; entern; **— up** belegen; **-er** n. Kostgänger, Pensionär

boarding house n. Pension

boarding school n. Internat, Pensionat

boast n. Prahlerei, Rühmen; **—** v. prahlen, grosstun; **— about** (oder of) sich rühmen, herausstreichen, stolz sein auf; **-ful** adj. prahlerisch

boat n. Boot, Kahn, Barke; Schiff, Fahrzeug; **be in the same —** in der gleichen

Lage sein; **–ing** n. Bootfahren, Rudersport; Wasserfahrt
boathouse n. Bootshaus
boatman n. Bootsgast, Bootsführer
bob n. Stoss, Ruck; Bubikopf; (mech.) Pendelgewicht; Flott; — v. rücken; baumeln; stutzen; kurz schneiden
bobbin n. Spule, Klöppel
bobby pin n. Haarspange
bobby sox (oder **socks**) n. Söckchen
bobby soxer n. Halbwüchsige, ausgelassener Backfisch
bobcat n. Luchs
bobolink n. amerikanischer Reisstar
bobsled n. Bob(sleigh)
bodily adj. leiblich, körperlich; (fig.) gewaltätig
body n. Körper, Leib; Rumpf, Stamm; Leiche, Leichnam; Körperschaft, Gesellschaft; (mil.) Abteilung
bodyguard n. Leibwache; (mil.) Leibgarde
bog n. Sumpf, Moor; — v. versinken, versenken
bogus adj. nachgemacht, unecht
Bohemia n. Böhmen
Bohemian adj. Bohemien-, aussergewöhnlich
boil n. Kochen, Sieden; (med.) Furunkel, Geschwür; — v. kochen, sieden, wallen; **–er** n. Kessel; (mech.) Dampfkessel; **–ing** adj. kochend, siedend; (fig.) aufwallend, erregt; **–ing point** Siedepunkt
boisterous adj. rauh, stürmisch, ungestüm; (fig.) lärmend, geräuschvoll
bold adj. unverschämt; kühn, mutig; unerschrocken; hervortretend; **–ness** n. Kühnheit, Verwegenheit; Unverschämtheit
boldface n. (typ.) Fettdruck
bold-faced adj. unverschämt, frech; (typ.) fett
boll n. Samenkapsel; — **weevil** Baumwollkäfer; **cotton** — Baumwollsamen
boloney n. Jagdwurst; (sl.) Wertlosigkeit, Nichtswürdigkeit
bolster n. Polster, Kissen; — v. (aus)polstern; — **up** unterstützen
bolt n. Riegel, Schraube; Bolzen; (cloth) Ballen, Rolle; — **out of the blue** Blitz aus heiterem Himmel; — v. verriegeln, zuriegeln; durchgehen; (pol.) verlassen, nicht unterstützen
bomb n. Bombe; (fig.) Überraschung; **–shelter** Luftschutzkeller; — v. bombardieren, bomben; **–er** n. Bomber, Bombenflugzeug
bombard v. bombardieren, beschiessen; **–ier** n. Offizier, der das Bombardement leitet; **–ment** n. Bombardement, Beschiessung
bombproof adj. bombenfest, bombensicher
bombshell n. Bombe; (fig.) Überraschung
bombsight n. Bombenzielgerät
bonbon n. Bonbon, Zuckerwerk
bond n. Band; (com.) Obligation, Schuldverschreibung; **government –s** Staatspapiere; — v. sicher anordnen (or einteilen, festlegen); (com.) Sicherheit anbieten; **–age** n. Gefangenschaft;

Knechtschaft, Sklaverei
bondholder n. Wertpapierbesitzer, Obligationsinhaber
bondsman n. Bürge; Leibeigene
bone n. Knochen, Bein; (ichth.) Gräte, Fischbein; — **china** Steingut; — v. Knochen (or Gräten) entfernen, entgräten; (sewing) Fischbein einsetzen; **–less** adj. knochenlos, grätenlos; (fig.) haltlos
bonfire n. Freudenfeuer
bonnet n. Damenhut; Haube
bonus n. Vergütung, Prämie, Gratifikation, Bonus; (com.) Gewinnanteil, Dividendenerhöhung
bony adj. beinern, knöchern
booby n. Tölpel; — **trap** Falle
book n. Buch; (mus.) Textbuch, Libretto; (com.) Geschäftsbuch, Kassenbuch; — **end** Buchstütze; — **review** Buchbesprechung, Buchkritik; — **value** Bilanzüberschuss, Buchwert; — v. buchen, eintragen; anschreiben, aufschreiben; bestellen; **–ie** n. Winkelbuchmacher; **–ing** n. Buchung, Eintragung; Platzbestellung; **–ing office** Billettschalter, Fahrkartenschalter; (theat.) Tageskasse; **–let** n. Broschüre; Büchlein
bookbinder n. Buchbinder
bookcase n. Bücherschrank, Bücherkiste
bookkeeper n. Buchhalter, Buchführer
bookkeeping n. Buchführung, Buchhaltung; **double entry** — doppelte Buchführung; **single entry** — einfache Buchführung
bookmaker n. Buchmacher
bookmark n. Lesezeichen, Buchzeichen
bookplate n. Exlibris, Eigentumszeichen
bookseller n. Buchhändler
bookshelf n. Bücherbrett
bookstand n. Büchergestell, Buchladen
bookstore, bookshop n. Buchhandlung
boom n. Dröhnen, Donnern; (com.) Hochkonjunktur, Aufschwung, Hausse; (naut.) Spiere; **sonic** — Schallexplosion; — **town** emporschiessende Stadt; — v. dröhnen, donnern; (fig.) florieren
boomerang n. Bumerang
boon n. Wohltat, Gnade, Gabe
boondoggle v. frivole Dinge tun
boor n. Lümmel; **–ish** adj. lümmelhaft, grob
boost n. Schub, Stoss; — v. Reklame (or Lärm) machen für; herauftreiben, ankurbeln; **–er** n. (com.) Preissteigerer; (elec.) Hilfsmotor; Puf5ersatz; Zwischenzünder; (pol.) Anhänger; **–er rocket** n. Startrakete, Antriebsrakete
boot n. Stiefel; **riding** — Reitstiefel; **to** — obendrein; **–ee** n., **–ie** n. Kinderschuh
booth n. Bude; **telephone** — Telefonzelle
bootleg v. Alkohol schmuggeln; **–ger** n. Alkoholschmuggler
booty n. Beute, Raub
booze n. Trank, Getränk; — v. trinken
border n. Grenze, Rand; Einfassung, Saum, Borte; — **line** Grenzlinie; — v. einfassen, besetzen; grenzen, begrenzen; — **on** angrenzen, anstossen
borderland n. Grenzland, Nachbarland

borderline case n. Grenzfall
bore n. Bohrung, Bohrloch; Kaliber; langweiliger Mensch; — v. bohren; langweilen, belästigen
boric adj. Bor-; — **acid** Borsäure
boring adj. langweilig
born adj. geboren, bestimmt; **be — to** bestimmt sein zu
borrow v. leihen, borgen, entlehnen; -er n. Borger, Entleiher
bosom n. Busen, Brust; (fig.) Schoss, Tiefe; — **of a shirt** Hemdbrust; — adj. — **friend** Busenfreund
boss n. Chef, Herr, Vorgesetzte; — v. treiben; (coll.) herumkommandieren; -y adj. herrisch, gebieterisch
botanical adj. botanisch
botany n. Botanik
botch n. Pfuscharbeit; — v. pfuschen, stümpern
both pron. and adj. beide, beides; — conj. sowohl
bother v. belästigen, plagen; sich bemühen; — n. Belästigung, Plage; Mühe
bottle n. Flasche, Karaffe; — v. auf Flaschen ziehen
bottleneck n. Flaschenhals; Engpass; Strassenverengung; Verkehrsstockung
bottom n. Boden, Grund; Unterteil, Grundfläche, Basis; (fig.) Ursache; Tiefe; **at —** im Grunde; **be at the —** die Triebfeder (or Seele) einer Sache sein; zugrunde liegen; **false —** Doppelboden; **from top to —** von oben bis unten; — adj. unter; unterst, niedrigst; letzt; — **drawer** unterste Schublade; — **land** reiche Flussebene; -less adj. bodenlose, grundlos; (fig.) unergründlich
bough n. Zweig, Ast
bouillon n. Bouillon, Fleischbrühe
boulder n. Geröll, Felsblock
bounce v. aufspringen (lassen); hinauswerfen; — n. Sprung; -er n. Rausschmeisser
bound n. Grenze, Schranke; Grenzstein, Markstein; Sprung; **beyond all —s** alle Grenzen überschreitend; **keep within —s** sich in Schranken halten; **out of —s** ausserhalb des Erlaubten; **within —s** mässig; innerhalb des Erlaubten; — v. beschränken; begrenzen; springen; — adj. gebunden; verpflichtet; entschlossen; (naut.) unterwegs; — **for** auf der Reise nach; **it is — to** es muss; -ary n. Grenze, Grenzlinie; -less adj. unbeschränkt, grenzenlos, unbegrenzt
bounteous, bountiful adj. gütig, freigebig; reichlich
bounty n. Güte, Freigebigkeit; Belohnung
bouquet n. Blumenstrauss, Bukett; (wine) Blume
bout n. Streit, Kampf; (med.) Anfall; (sports) Wettkampf; **drinking —** Trinkgelage
bow n. (courtesy) Verbeugung, Verneigung; (fashion) Schleife; (naut.) Bug; (sports) Bogen; — v. sich verbeugen, neigen; sich unterwerfen; den Bogen führen; einen Bogen machen

bowels n. pl. Eingeweide; — **of the earth** Erdinnere
bower n. Laube, Landsitz
bowl n. Schale, Schüssel; Bowle, Humpen; (sports) Kugel, Ball; Sportplatz; — v. rollen, schieben, kugeln; (sports) kegeln; -er n. Kegler; -ing n. Kegeln; -ing alley Kegelbahn; -ing pin Kegel
bowlegged adj. krummbeinig; (coll.) o-beinig
box n. Schachtel, Karton, Kiste; Behälter, Büchse; Stand, Bude; (bot.) Buchsbaum; (law) Geschworenenbank; (mail) Briefkasten; (theat.) Loge; — **on the ear** Ohrfeige; **hot —** (rail.) heissgelaufenes Getriebe; (prisoner's) — Anklagebank; — **elder** Eschenahorn; — **office** Theaterkasse; — **seat** Logenplatz; — v. boxen; in Schachteln (or Kartons, Kisten) packen; -er n. Boxer; -ing n. Boxen; -ing glove Boxhandschuh
boxcar n. Güterwagen
boy n. Knabe, Junge, Bube, Bursche; Bediente; — **scout** Pfadfinder; -hood n. Knabenalter; -ish adj. knabenhaft
boycott n. Boykott; — v. boykottieren
boysenberry n. Brombeere mit Himbeergeschmack
bra, brassiere n. Büha, Büstenhalter
brace n. Band, Gurt; Paar; (arch.) Winkelband, Stützbalken; (med.) Spange, Klammer; (mech.) Drillbohrer; — v. absteifen, abspreizen; stemmen; gürten, klammern; (fig.) anspannen; — **up** sich zusammennehmen
bracelet n. Armband
bracing adj. stärkend, erfrischend
bracket n. Klammer; (arch.) Konsole; (fig.) Klasse; — v. einklammern
brag v. prahlen; aufschneiden; -gart n. Prahler, Aufschneider
braid n. Zopf; Borte, Litze, Schnur; — v. flechten
braille n. Braille, Blindenschrift
brain n. Gehirn; pl. Verstand, Kopf; (coll.) Hirn; **blow one's —s out** sich eine Kugel durch den Kopf jagen; **rack one's —s** sich den Kopf zerbrechen; — **storm** Gedankenblitz; — **trust** Ratgebergruppe; — v. den Schädel einschlagen; — **wash** v. das Gehirn waschen; -y adj. geistreich, gescheit
brake n. (bot.) Breche; (mech.) Bremse, Bremsvorrichtung; — **band** Bremsband; **four-wheel —** Vierradbremse; **put on** (oder **apply) the —s** bremsen; **release the —s** die Bremse loslassen; — v. bremsen
brakeman n. Bremser
bramble n. Brombeerstrauch, Dorngebüsch
bran n. Kleie
branch n. Zweig, Ast; (com.) Filiale, Zweigniederlassung; (geol.) Flussarm; (zool.) Geweihsprosse; (fig.) Abzweigung; Abschnitt; — **of** (art, science, trade, etc.) Fach; — **of the sea** Meeresarm; — **line** Zweigbahn; — v. — **off** abstammen, abzweigen; — **out** sich

verzweigen, grösser werden

brand *n.* Marke, Sorte; Brand; (fig.) Schandfleck; — *v.* einbrennen; (fig.) brandmarken

brandish *v.* schwingen, schwenken

brand-new *adj.* (funkel)nagelneu

brandy *n.* Kognak, Weinbrand

brass *n.* Messing; (mil. sl.) hohes Tier; — **band** Blasorchester; (mil.) Trompeterkorps; — *adj.* messingartig

brassie *n.* messingbeschlagener Golfstock

bravado *n.* Drohung, Herausforderung

brave *adj.* brav, tapfer, mutig; kühn, unerschrocken; (fig.) stattlich, glänzend; — *v.* herausfordern, trotzen; mutig begegnen; — *n.* Krieger; **-ry** *n.* Mut, Tapferkeit, Unerschrockenheit

brawn *n.* Muskelkraft

brazier *n.* Kohlenpfanne

Brazil *n.* Brasilien

breach *n.* Bruch, Riss, Sprung; (law) Übertretung, Verletzung; (mil.) Bresche, Durchbruch; (fig.) Uneinigkeit, Zwist; — **of faith** Treubruch; — **of promise** Wortbruch

bread *n.* Brot; (slice of) — **and butter** Butterbrot; (fig.) Lebensunterhalt; — **-and-butter letter** Dankbrief für Gastfreundschaft

breadbasket *n.* Brotkorb; (fig.) Kornkammer; (sl.) Magen

breadth *n.* Breite, Fülle, Weite; (fig.) Hochherzigkeit

breadwinner *n.* Brotverdiener; Ernährer

break *n.* Pause; Chance; (law) Fluchtversuch; **bad** — Pech; — **of day** Tagesanbruch; — *v.* brechen; zerschlagen; einschlagen; auflösen; beibringen; ruinieren; kassieren; dressieren; — **down** zusammenbrechen; stecken bleiben; — **in** anlernen; — **into** einbrechen; — **of (a habit)** abgewöhnen; — **one's neck** sich das Genick brechen; — **open** aufbrechen, erbrechen; — **out** ausbrechen; — **the bank** die Bank sprengen; — **the ice** das Eis brechen; — **through** durchbrechen; — **to pieces** zerbrechen; — **up** (sich) auflösen; **-able** *adj.* zerbrechlich; **-age** *n.* Brechen, Zerbrechen; Bruch; **-er** *n.* Brecher, Sturzsee; **-ing** *adj.* (zer)brechend; **-ing point** Festigkeitsgrenze

breakdown *n.* Zusammenbruch; Panne; Betriebsstörung; Misslingen; **nervous** — Nervenzusammenbruch

breakfast *n.* Frühstück; — *v.* frühstücken

breast *n.* Brust; (fig.) Busen; Gewissen; (arch.) Brüstung; — **stroke** Brustschwimmen; **make a clean** — **of** alles eingestehen; — *v.* sich entgegenstemmen; trotzen, die Stirn bieten

breath *n.* Atem; Hauch; (fig.) Augenblick, Moment; — **of air** Lüftchen; **catch one's** — Atem holen (*or* schöpfen); **out of** — atemlos; **-e** *v.* atmen, einatmen, ausatmen; leise äussern, verlauten; (fig.) leben; **-ing** *n.* Atmen, Hauchen; **-ing space** Atempause; **-less** *adj.* atemlos, ausser Atem

breath-taking *adj.* atemraubend

breech *n.* Steiss; — **of a gun** Kanonenverschluss; **-es** *n. pl.* Sporthosen, Reithosen, Breeches

breed *n.* Brut, Art, Rasse, Zucht; (fig.) Herkunft, Schlag; — *v.* züchten, aufziehen; gebären, erzeugen, sich vermehren; **-er** *n.* Züchter; **-ing** *n.* Züchten; (fig.) Bildung, Herkunft, Lebensart

breeze *n.* Brise, Wind; — *v.* stürmen

brethren *n. pl.* Brüder

brew *n.* Gebräu; — *v.* brauen, mischen; (fig.) anstiften, anzetteln; **-er** *n.* Brauer; **-ery** *n.* Brauerei

briar, brier *n.* Dornstrauch, Hagebuttenstrauch; Bruyèrepfeife

bribe *n.* Bestechung, Bestechungsgeld; — *v.* bestechen; **-ry** *n.* Bestechung

bric-a-brac *n.* Antiquitäten; Nippsachen Nippes; Krimskrams

brick *n.* Ziegel, Backstein; — *adj.* ziegelartig, ziegelförmig

brickbat *n.* Ziegelstück, Ziegelbrocken

bricklayer *n.* Maurer

brickwork *n.* Rohbau (aus Ziegeln); Backsteinbau

brickyard *n.* Ziegelei, Ziegellager

bridal *adj.* bräutlich, hochzeitlich

bride *n.* Braut; (fig.) junge Frau, Neuvermählte

bridegroom *n.* Bräutigam; Neuvermählte

bridesmaid *n.* Brautjungfer

bridge *n.* Brücke; (cards) Bridge; (mus.) Steg; — *v.* eine Brücke schlagen; überbrücken

bridgehead *n.* Brückenkopf

bridgework *n.* Brückenbau; (dent.) Zahnbrücke

bridle *n.* Zügel, Zaum; — *adj.* — **path** Reitweg; — *v.* zügeln, (auf)zäumen; (fig.) den Kopf zurückwerfen

brief *n.* kurze Darstellung des Klagepunktes; Klagebeantwortung; — **case** Aktentasche; **hold a** — **for** befürworten; **in** — mit kurzen Worten, kurz gesagt; — *adj.* kurz, bündig; flüchtig, knapp; **-ing** *n.* Einsatzbesprechung; Befehlsausgabe; Lagebesprechung

brigade *n.* Brigade

brigadier general *n.* Brigadegeneral

brigand *n.* Räuber

bright *adj.* hell, glänzend, heiter; (fig.) geistreich, fröhlich; gescheit, aufgeweckt, lebhaft; — **and early** in aller Frühe; **-en** *v.* erleuchten, erhellen; polieren; wieder Mut fassen; **-ness** *n.* Glanz, Helle, Klarheit; Heiterkeit

Bright's disease *n.* Bright'sche Krankheit, Nierenkrankheit

brilliance *n.* Glanz; Scharfsinn

brilliant *adj.* glänzend, brillant, strahlend, leuchtend; (fig.) geistreich; ausgezeichnet; — *n.* Brillant

brim *n.* Rand, Krempe; — *v.* bis zum Rand füllen, übervoll sein; **-ful** *adj.* bis zum Rande voll

brimstone *n.* Schwefel

brine *n.* Salzwasser, Sole

bring *v.* bringen, mitbringen, herbringen;

(law) erheben, einbringen; — **about** bewerkstelligen, herbeiführen; — **along** mitbringen; — **down** herunterbringen; — **forth** hervorbringen; — **out** herausbringen, aufdecken; — **to** wieder zu sich bringen; — **to bear** geltend machen; — **up** erziehen; heraufbringen; vorbringen

brink n. Rand, Kante; steiles Ufer

brisk adj. lebhaft, rasch; flink; frisch; **–ness** n. Lebhaftigkeit

bristle n. Borste, Stachel; — v. sträuben, starren

Britain n. Britannien

Brittany n. Bretagne

brittle adj. spröde, brüchig; zerbrechlich; (fig.) schwach, leicht zerstörbar

broad adj. breit, weit; gross; liberal, deutlich; (coll.) dreist; — **jump** Weitsprung; **in — daylight** am hellen Tage; **–en** v. ausweiten, ausbreiten; erweitern, verbreitern

broadcast n. Sendung, Rundfunksendung; — v. senden; **–ing** n. Rundfunk; **–ing station** Sender, Rundfunkstation

broadcloth n. feines Baumwolltuch

broad-minded adj. weitherzig, duldsam; **–ness** n. Weitherzigkeit, Duldsamkeit

broadside n. Breitseite

brocade n. Brokat

brochure n. Broschüre

brogue n. (gebrochene) Mundart

broil v. unter der Flamme braten; schmoren; **–er** n. Bratrost; Brathühn

broke (sl.) adj. ruiniert; **–n** adj. gebrochen, zerbrochen; **be —** kaputt sein; **— English** gebrochenes (or geradebrechtes) Englisch

broker n. Makler, Agent; Zwischenhändler; **insurance —** Versicherungsagent; **–age** n. Maklergeschäft; Maklergebühr

bromide n. Brom; Gemeinplatz

bronchial adj. bronchial; — **tube** Bronchie, Luftröhre

bronchitis n. Bronchitis

bronco n. ungezähmtes Pferd

bronze n. Bronze, Bronzefarbe; **Bronze Age** Bronzezeit; — v. bronzieren

brooch n. Brosche, Spange

brood n. Brut; — v. (aus)brüten, ersinnen

brook n. Bach; — v. ertragen, erdulden, aushalten

broom n. Besen; (bot.) Ginster

broomstick n. Besenstiel

broth n. Suppe, Fleischbrühe

brother n. Bruder; **–hood** n. Brüderschaft; Brüderlichkeit; **–ly** adj. brüderlich

brother-in-law n. Schwager

brow n. Stirn; Augenbraue; (geol.) Abhang

brown n. Braun; — adj. braun, brünett, bräunlich; — **paper** braunes Papier, Packpapier; — **sugar** brauner Zucker, Rohzucker; **dark —** dunkelbraun; — v. (sich) bräunen, braun machen (or werden)

Bruges n. Brügge

bruise n. Quetschung; — v. zermalmen, zerquetschen; (coll.) braun und blau schlagen

brunch n. zweites Frühstück

brunet(te) n. Brünett(e); — adj. brünett

Brunswick n. Braunschweig

brunt n. Stoss, Heftigkeit; Anprall, Gewalt

brush n. Bürste; (art) Pinsel; (bot.) Gebüsch, Gestrüpp, Unterholz; (elec.) Strahlenbündel; (mil.) Scharmützel; Lunte; (zool.) Rute; — v. fegen, bürsten; kehren, wischen; — **against** anstreifen; — **aside** beiseiteschieben; — **off** abbürsten; (fig.) abweisen; — **one's teeth** sich die Zähne putzen; — **up on** auffrischen

brushwood n. Gestrüpp, Reisig

brutal adj. roh, brutal; **–ity** n. Roheit, Brutalität

brute n. Rohling; Tier; (coll.) Scheusal; — adj. tierisch, viehisch

BTU (British Thermal Unit) n. britische Wärmeeinheit (Hitzemenge erforderlich um 1 Pfd. Wasser 1° zu erwärmen)

bubble n. Blase; Tand, Bagatelle; (coll.) Schwindel; — v. sieden, sprudeln, Blasen werfen; (fig.) gurgeln, murmeln; — **over** überschäumen, übersprudeln

bubonic plague n. Beulenpest

buccaneer n. Seeräuber, Freibeuter

bucket n. Eimer, Kübel

buckle n. Schnalle; — v. schnallen, zuschnallen; sich werfen; — **down to** sich ins Zeug legen, um

buckram n. Steifleinen

buckshot n. Rehposten

buckwheat n. Buchweizen

bud n. Knospe, Auge; Keim, Sprosse; (sl.) Debütantin; **nip in the —** im Keime ersticken; — v. knospen, keimen, sprossen; sich entwickeln; okulieren, veredeln; **–ding** adj. knospend; (fig.) angehend

buddy (coll.) n. Gefährte, Genosse, Kamerad

budge v. sich regen (or rühren); von der Stelle gehen

budget n. Budget, Haushaltsplan, Etat; — v. einteilen

buff n. Lederfarbe, Braungelb; — adj. lederfarben, braungelb; — v. (ab)ledern, polieren; **–er** n. Polierinstrument, Nagelpolierer

buffalo n. Büffel

buffer n. Puffer; — **state** Pufferstaat

buffet n. Büffet, Anrichte, Kredenz; Geschirrschrank; Schenktisch; — v. puffen

bug n. Käfer; Wanze

bugbear n. Popanz, Schreckbild

buggy n. Einspänner; **baby —** Kinderwagen

bugle n. Signalhorn, Waldhorn; — **call** Hornsignal; **–r** n. Hornbläser, Hornist

build v. bauen, erbauen, aufbauen; (fig.) bilden, gründen; — **up** aufbauen; **–er** n. Erbauer; Baumeister; Konstrukteur; (fig.) Schöpfer; **–ing** n. Gebäude, Bau(werk); Erbauen, Konstruktion

bulb n. (bot.) Zwiebel, Knolle; (elec.) Birne

bulge n. Anschwellung, Wulst; (arch.) Ausbauchung; — v. hervorragen, ausbauchen

bulk n. Masse, Menge, Umfang, Volumen; **in** — in Bausch und Bogen; **-y** adj. gross, dick; unhandlich, sperrig

bulkhead n. (mil.) luftdrucksichere Panzertür; (naut.) Schott; (avi.) Rumpfversteifung

bull n. Stier, Bulle; (com.) Haussier

bulldog n. Bulldogge

bulldoze v. einschüchtern, ins Bockshorn jagen; **-r** n. Planierungsraupenfahrzeug

bullet n. Kugel, Geschoss

bulletin n. Bulletin, Tagesbericht; kurze Bekanntmachung; — **board** Anschlagebrett

bulletproof adj. kugelfest, kugelsicher

bullfight n. Stierkampf, Stiergefecht; **-er** n. Stierkämpfer, Torero

bullfrog n. Ochsenfrosch

bullion n. Goldbarren, Silberbarren

bull's-eye n. Zentrum einer Schiesscheibe; Schuss ins Zentrum

bulrush n. Teichbinse, Sumpfbinse

bulwark n. Bollwerk, Bastei; (fig.) Schutz

bum n. Taugenichts, Landstreicher

bumblebee n. Hummel

bump n. Beule; Schlag, Stoss; — v. stossen, schlagen; — **into** stossen gegen; (fig.) sehen; **-er** n. (auto.) Stosstange; **-er** adj. riesengross; höchst, best; **-y** adj. holperig

bun n. Brötchen, Semmel

bunch n. Bund; Bündel, Büschel; Menge; (coll.) Bande; — **of flowers** Blumenstrauss; — **of grapes** Weintraube; — v. zu einem Bündel zusammenstellen

bundle n. Bund, Bündel; Paket; Rolle; **small** — Päckchen; — v. bündeln, einpacken, zusammenrollen; — **up** bündeln; warm einwickeln

bungalow n. einstöckiges Sommerhaus; Bungalow

bungle v. stümpern, pfuschen

bunion n. Schwellung am Ballen (or grossen Zeh)

bunk n. Koje; Wandbett; (sl.) Geschwätz, leeres Gerede

bunker n. Bunker; Behälter; (golf) Hindernis vor dem Golfloch

bunkhouse n. Herberge

buoy n. Boje, Ankerboje; — v. — **up** flott erhalten; (fig.) aufrechterhalten; **-ant** adj. schwimmend; (fig.) heiter

burden n. Last, Bürde; — v. beladen, belasten; (fig.) beschweren

bureau n. Büro; Amtszimmer, Geschäftszimmer; Kommode; **-crat** n. Bürokrat

bureaucracy n. Bürokratie; (fig.) Amtsschimmel

burglar n. Einbrecher; — **alarm** Einbruchsalarm; **-y** n. Einbruch

burial n. Beerdigung, Begräbnis; — **ground** Begräbnisplatz; Friedhof

burlap n. grobe Leinwand

burlesque n. Burleske, Posse, Satire; — v. lächerlich machen, travestieren

burn n. Brandmal, Brandwunde; — v. brennen, verbrennen; anbrennen; bräu-

nen; — **down** niederbrennen; **-ing hot** glühend heiss; — **one's bridges behind one** alle Brücken hinter sich abbrechen; — **up** verbrennen; **money to** — Geld wie Heu; **-er** n. Brenner

burnish v. polieren, glätten

burrow n. Bau, Loch; — v. Löcher graben, sich eingraben; (fig.) sich verkriechen

burst n. Bersten, Platzen; Explosion; (fig.) Ausbruch; — v. bersten, platzen; zerspringen, aufspringen; explodieren; — **in(to)** hereinplatzen; — **into tears** in Tränen ausbrechen; — **out laughing** in lautes Gelächter ausbrechen

bury v. begraben, beerdigen; vergraben; (fig.) verbergen; — **the hatchet** die Streitaxt begraben, Frieden schliessen

bus n. Bus, Omnibus; — **boy** Pikkolo

bush n. Busch, Strauch; Dickicht, Gebüsch; **-y** adj. buschig

bushel n. Scheffel; (fig.) grosse Menge, Haufen

bushing n. (elec.) Durchführungsisolator

busily adv. fleissig, geschäftig; rastlos

business n. Geschäft, Handel; Beschäftigung, Beruf; Arbeit, Tätigkeit; (fig.) Angelegenheit, Sache; — **before pleasure** erst kommt die Arbeit, dann das Vergnügen; **do** — **with** Geschäfte machen mit; **mind your own** — kümmere dich um deine eigenen Angelegenheiten; **on** — geschäftlich; **that's none of your** — das geht dich nichts an

businesslike adj. geschäftsmässig, kaufmännisch; (fig.) praktisch

businessman n. Kaufmann, Geschäftsmann

bust n. Büste; Brust, Busen

bustle n. Lärm, Getöse; Geschäftigkeit; (clothing) Tornüre; — v. sich tummeln (or rühren)

busy adj. beschäftigt, rührig, tätig, eifrig; **the number is** — die Nummer ist besetzt; — v. beschäftigen

busybody n. Zudringliche; einer, der seine Nase in fremde Angelegenheiten steckt

but conj. aber, jedoch; sondern; ausser dass; — prep. ausser; **all** — fast; bis auf; — adv. nur

butcher n. Fleischer, Metzger, Schlächter; (fig.) Mörder; — **shop** Fleischerei; — v. (ab)schlachten; (fig.) morden; **-y** n. Metzelei

butler n. Haushofmeister; Kellermeister; **—'s pantry** Speisekammer

butt n. Kolben; Stummel; Zielscheibe; — v. stossen, anstossen; — **in** sich einmischen

butter n. Butter; — **dish** Butterdose; — **knife** Buttermesser; — v. buttern, mit Butter bestreichen; — **up** (sich) einschmeicheln

buttercup n. Butterblume

butterfingered adj. mit ungeschickten Händen

butterfly n. Schmetterling; (fig.) Unbeständige

buttermilk n. Buttermilch

butterscotch n. Butterkaramelle

button n. Knopf; — v. anknöpfen, zuknöpfen

buttonhole n. Knopfloch

buttress n. (arch.) Strebe(pfeiler); (fig.) Stütze; **flying —** Strebebogen; **—** v. stützen

buy v. kaufen; einkaufen; (fig.) erkaufen, bestechen; **— for cash** gegen Barzahlung kaufen; **— off** abfinden; **— on credit** auf Kredit kaufen; **— out** den Anteil abkaufen von; **— secondhand** gebrauchte Sachen kaufen; **— up** aufkaufen; **—er** n. Käufer, Einkäufer

buzz v. (mil.) schwirren; streifen

by prep. an, bei, neben; über; auf; bis zu; gegen, um; innerhalb, während; für, nach, durch, mit, von; vermittels, vermöge; gemäss, zufolge; **— far** weitaus; bei weitem; **— oneself** allein; **— that** damit, darunter; **— the way** apropos; **—** adv. nahe, dabei, zugegen; ab, beiseite, nebenbei, weg; vorbei; vorüber; **— and —** nach und nach

bygone adj. vergangen, veraltet; früher; **-s** n. pl. vergangene Dinge, alte Sachen

bylaw n. Satzung, Statut; Nebengesetz

bypass n. Umgehungsstrasse, Entlastungsstrasse; Nebenweg; **—** v. umgehen, einen Umweg machen; entlasten

bypath, byway n. Nebenweg

by-product n. Nebenprodukt

bystander n. Umstehende, Zuschauer

byword n. Sprichwort

C

cab n. Taxi; (rail., truck) Führerstand

cabana n. Strandhütte; Wohnlaube

cabaret n. Kabarett; (coll.) Musikkaffeehaus

cabbage n. Kohl, Kraut; (sl.) Geld

cabin n. Hütte, Häuschen; (naut.) Kabine, Kajüte, Koje; **— boy** Schiffsjunge

cabinet n. Kabinett, Ministerium; Stube; Schrank

cabinetmaker n. Kunsttischler

cable n. Kabel, Seil; Ankertau, Trosse; Kabeldepesche; **— address** Telegrammadresse; **— car** Drahtseilbahnwagen; **—** v. kabeln

cablegram n. Kabel(depesche)

caboodle n. **the whole —** (coll.) der ganze Klimbim, die ganze Gesellschaft

caboose n. Personenwagen an einem Güterzug

cabstand n. Taxistand, Taxihalteplatz

cackle n. Gegacker, Geschnatter; **—** v. gakkern, schnattern

cactus n. Kaktus

cad n. Prolet, ungebildeter Mensch

cadaver n. Kadaver; **-ous** adj. leichenhaft, leichenblass

caddie, caddy n. Golfstockträger, Golfjunge

cadence n. Kadenz; Tonfall; Takt

cadenza n. Kadenz

cadet n. Kadett

Caesarean adj. cäsarisch; **— (section)** Kaiserschnitt

café n. Kaffeehaus, Café; Kaffeerestaurant

cafeteria n. Restaurant mit Selbstbedienung

caffeine n. Koffein

cage n. Käfig; (mech.) Förderkorb; (coll.) Gefängnis; **—** v. einsperren

cake n. Kuchen, Torte; (fig.) Stuck; **— of soap** Seifenstück; **—** v. hart werden (or machen)

calamity n. Kalamität, Unglück, Elend

calcify v. verkalken

calcimine n. Kalkmilch

calcium n. Kalzium; **— carbonate** Kalziumkarbonat; (coll.) kohlensaurer Kalk

calculate v. kalkulieren, berechnen; (fig.) abwägen, vermuten; beabsichtigen

calculating adj. kalkulierend, berechnend; **— machine** Rechenmaschine

calculation n. Kalkulation, Berechnung

calculator n. Kalkulator, Berechner; Rechenmaschine

calculus n. Rechnung; **differential —** Differentialrechnung; **integral —** Integralrechnung

caldron n. Kessel

calendar n. Kalender; (law) Liste der Gerichtsfälle; **—** v. registrieren

calf n. Kalb; Kalbleder; (anat.) Wade

calfskin n. Kalbfell, Kalbleder

caliber n. Kaliber; (fig.) geistige Befähigung, Wert

calibrate v. kalibrieren, richtige Weite (or Grade, Masse) finden

calibration n. Eichung; Gradeinteilung

calico n. Kaliko

caliper n. Kaliberzirkel

calisthenics n. Freiübungen

call n. Ruf, Schrei; Anspruch, Forderung; kurzer Besuch; (com.) Nachfrage; (mil.) Appell; (orn.) Lockruf; (tel.) Anruf, Gespräch; **long distance —** Ferngespräch; **on —** bereit, verfügbar; **—** v. rufen, ausrufen; schreien; herbeirufen; wecken; Besuch machen; nennen, benennen; (cards) ansagen; (law) vorladen; **— down** ausschelten; **— for** abholen, fordern; **— off** absagen, abberufen; **— on** besuchen; **— together** berufen, zusammenrufen; **— the roll** die Namensliste verlesen; **— to order** zur Ordnung rufen; **— up** anrufen; (mil.) aufrufen; **-er** n. Besucher; Rufer; **-ing** n. Beruf, Beschäftigung; **-ing** adj. **-ing card** Visitenkarte

calm n. Ruhe, Stille; (naut.) Windstille; **—** adj. ruhig, still; gelassen; **keep —** die Ruhe bewahren; **—** v. beruhigen; **— down** sich beruhigen; sich legen, nachlassen; **-ness** n. Ruhe, Stille

caloric adj. Wärme-, Heissluft-

calorie n. Kalorie; Wärmeeinheit

calumny n. Verleumdung, falsche Anschuldigung

Calvinism n. Kalvinismus

calyx n. Kelch

cam n. Nocken

camaraderie n. Kameradschaft

cambric n. Battist

camel n. Kamel; **-'s hair** Kamelhaar

camellia n. Kamelie

cameo n. Kamee

camera n. Kamera, Fotoapparat; candid — Geheimkamera; motion picture — Filmkamera

camouflage n. Tarnung; — v. tarnen

camp n. Lager; Feldlager; army — Heerlager; — v. lagern, kampieren; -er n. Lagerbewohner, Kampierende

campaign n. Feldzug, Kampagne; — v. an einem Feldzug (or einer Kampagne) teilnehmen

campfire n. Lagerfeuer

campground n. Lagerplatz

campus n. Gebäude und Grundbesitz einer Hochschule; Sportplatz

camshaft n. Nockenwelle

can n. Büchse, Dose; — opener Büchsenöffner; — v. können; (coll.) dürfen; konservieren, einmachen, einkochen; -ned adj. konserviert, in Konservendosen eingemacht; -ned goods Konservendosen; -nery n. Konservenfabrik, Konservendosenfabrik

canal n. Kanal

canary n. Kanarienvogel

canasta n. Canasta, Kanasta

cancel v. aufheben, ungültig machen; durchstreichen; absagen; (stamps) abstempeln, entwerten; -lation n. Annulierung, Aufhebung; Ausstreichen; Abbestellung, Abstemplung

cancer n. Krebs; -ous adj. krebsartig, krebskrank

candelabrum n. Kandelaber, Armleuchter

candid adj. aufrichtig, offen

candidate n. Kandidat, Bewerber

candle n. Kerze, Licht; burn the — at both ends seine Kräfte (or Mittel) verschwenden; he can't hold a — to her er kann ihr das Wasser nicht reichen; — power Kerze, Lichtstärke

candlelight n. Kerzenlicht

candlestick n. Leuchter

candy n. Süssigkeit(en), Bonbon(s), Zuckerwerk; — v. kandieren, verzukkern

cane n. Rohr; Spazierstock; — sugar Rohrzucker

canine adj. hündisch, Hunde-

canker n. Krebs; (bot.) Brand; (fig.) Krebsschaden

cannibal n. Kannibale, Menschenfresser; — adj. kannibalisch; -ism n. Kannibalismus

cannon n. Kanone, Geschütz; (billiards) Karambolage; — ball Kanonenkugel; — v. beschiessen; (billiards) karambolieren; -ade n. Kanonade; Beschiessung (coll.) Karombolage

canny adj. schlau; vorsichtig; sparsam

canoe n. Kanu, Paddelboot; Einbaum

canon n. Regal, Richtschnur; (rel. and mus.) Kanon; — law kanonisches Recht, Kirchenrecht; -ize v. heiligsprechen; (fig.) verherrlichen

canopy n. Baldachin; (avi.) Glaskuppel des Piloten

cantaloupe n. Zuckermelone

cantata n. Kantate

canteen n. Kantine; Feldflasche

canton n. Bezirk, Kanton, Kreis; -ment n. Kantonnement; Einquartierung

canvas n. (art) Leinwand, Ölgemälde; (camping) Zeltleinwand; (naut.) Segeltuch, Segel

canvass n. Sichtung, Prüfung; Bewerbung; (pol.) Wahlprüfung; — v. sichten, prüfen; bewerben; (pol.) Wahlreden halten, Stimmen fangen

canyon n. Felsenschlucht

cap n. Mütze, Kappe; (dent.) Krone; (mech.) Deckel, Verschluss, Haube; — and gown Barett und Talar, akademische Tracht; — v. bedecken, mit einer Kappe versehen; (fig.) übertreffen; — the climax das Äusserste erreichen

capability n. Fähigkeit; Vermögen

capable adj. tüchtig, fähig, imstande, geeignet

capacious adj. geräumig, umfassend, weit

capacity n. Gehalt, Rauminhalt, Aufnahmefähigkeit; Kapazität; Befähigung, Fähigkeit; Eigenschaft, Funktion

cape n. (geog.) Kap, Vorgebirge; (clothing) Kape, Kragenmantel

Cape of Good Hope n. Kap der guten Hoffnung

caper n. Kapriole, Luftsprung; (bot.) Kaper; (fig.) toller Streich; cut -s Kapriolen machen; — v. hüpfen, springen

capillary n. Kapillargefäss, Haargefäss; — adj. Kapillar-; haarfein, haarförmig; — attraction Kapillarität

capital n. Hauptstadt; (arch.) Kapitell, Säulenkopf; (com.) Kapital, Stammvermögen; (typ.) grosser Buchstabe; make — of Nutzen ziehen aus; — adj. Kapital-, Haupt-; besonders, überragend; vortrefflich; (law) peinlich, Todes-; — crime Kapitalverbrechen; — goods Produktionsgüter; — letters grosse Buchstaben; — punishment Todesstrafe; — stock Aktienkapital; -ism n. Kapitalismus; -ist n. Kapitalist; -ize v. gross schreiben; kapitalisieren; (fig.) gewinnen

capitol n. Kapitol, Regierungsgebäude

capitulate v. kapitulieren

capitulation n. Kapitulation

capon n. Kapaun, Kapphahn

caprice n. Kaprize, Einfall, Laune

capricious adj. kapriziös, launenhaft

capsize v. kentern, umschlagen

capsule n. Kapsel, Hülle, Hülse; (chem.) Probiertiegel

captain n. (mil.) Hauptmann, Rittmeister; (naut. and sports) Kapitän; (fig.) Anführer

caption n. (film) Untertitel; (typ.) Titelzeile, Überschrift

captivate v. bestricken, bezaubern, fesseln

captivating adj. fesselnd, reizend

captive n. Gefangene; (fig.) Bezauberte; — adj. gefangen; (fig.) bestrickt, bezaubert, gefesselt

captivity n. Gefangenschaft, Knechtschaft

captor n. Erbeuter, Fänger; (naut.) Kaperer

capture *n.* Einnahme, Gefangennahme; (law) Verhaftung; (naut.) Kapern; Prise; — *v.* einnehmen, fangen; erbeuten; (law) verhaften; (naut.) kapern

car *n.* Wagen, Auto; (avi.) Gondel; (rail.) Waggon; **armored —** Panzerwagen; **— pool** Fahrbereitschaft; Interessengemeinschaft von Wagenbesitzern; **— port** Autoschuppen

caramel *n.* Karamel(le)

caravan *n.* Karawane

caraway *n.* Kümmel

carbide *n.* Karbid

carbolic *adj.* karbolsauer; **— acid** Karbolsäure, Phenol

carbon *n.* Kohlenstoff; (elec.) Kohlestift; **— copy** Durchschlag; **— dioxide** Kohlendioxyd; **— monoxide** Kohlenmonoxyd; **— paper** Kohlepapier, Blaupapier

carbonic *adj.* Kohlen-; **— acid** Kohlensäure

carborundum *n.* Siliziumkarbid, Karborundum

carbuncle *n.* Karfunkel; Karbunkel, Furunkel

carburetor *n.* Vergaser

carcass *n.* Aas, Kadaver

card *n.* Karte; Mitteilung, Geschäftsanzeige; **it's in the —s** es steht in den Karten; **— index** Kartei; **— table** Spieltisch; — *v.* krempeln, rauhen

cardboard *n.* Pappe, Pappdeckel

cardiac *adj.* (med.) Herz-; (pharm.) herzstärkend

cardinal *n.* (eccl.) Kardinal; (orn.) Rotfink; — *adj.* Kardinal-, Haupt-; vorzüglich; **— number** Grundzahl

cardiogram *n.* Kardiogramm

cardiology *n.* Kardiologie

care *n.* Sorge, Vorsicht, Pflege; Behandlung; Aufsicht, Wartung; **— of** per Adresse; **take —!** *interj.* Achtung! Vorsicht! **take — not to** sich hüten zu; **take — of** sich kümmern um, sorgen für; erledigen; aufbewahren; schonen; **take — of oneself** sich pflegen; **take — to** dafür sorgen, dass; — *v.* sorgen, sich kümmern; pflegen; beaufsichtigen; **— for** mögen, geneigt sein; sich kümmern um, pflegen; **—d for** versorgt; **for all I —** meinetwegen; **I don't —** es ist mir gleich (*or* einerlei); **I don't — much for it** ich mache mir nicht viel daraus; **what do I —!** Was geht's mich an! **who —s?** Wen interessiert das? **—ful** *adj.* vorsichtig, sorgfältig; **be —ful not to** sich hüten zu; **—fulness** *n.* Vorsicht, Sorgfalt; **—less** *adj.* sorglos, unbekümmert; unachtsam, nachlässig; leichtsinnig; **—lessness** *n.* Unachtsamkeit, Nachlässigkeit

career *n.* Laufbahn, Beruf; Karriere; — *v.* eilen, rasen, rennen

carefree *adj.* sorglos

caress *n.* Liebkosung; — *v.* liebkosen, streicheln; schmeicheln

caretaker *n.* Wärter, Wächter

careworn *adj.* abgehärmt, gramerfüllt

carfare *n.* Fahrgeld, Fahrpreis

cargo *n.* Kargo, Fracht, Schiffsladung

caribou *n.* Karibu, amerikanisches Renntier

caricature *n.* Karikatur; — *v.* karikieren

Carinthia *n.* Kärnten

carload *n.* Wagenladung

carnal *adj.* fleischlich, sinnlich

carnation *n.* Nelke

carnival *n.* Karneval, Fasching; Lustbarkeit

carnivorous *adj.* fleischfressend

carol *n.* Lobgesang, Jubellied; — *v.* singen; lobpreisen, jubilieren

carouse *v.* saufen, zechen; **-l** *n.* Karussell

carp *n.* Karpfen; — *v.* bekritteln, verspotten; **-ing** *adj.* tadelsüchtig

carpenter *n.* Zimmermann, Tischler

carpentry *n.* Zimmerhandwerk, Tischlerarbeit

carpet *n.* Teppich; **— sweeper** Teppichkehrmaschine; **— v.** mit Teppichen belegen

carpetbagger *n.* politischer Abenteurer; Nutzniesser

carpool *n.* Mitfahrerzentrale

carriage *n.* Wagen, Fuhrwerk; Haltung. Benehmen; (avi. and mech.) Gestell, Lafette

carrier *n.* Träger, Bote. Überbringer, Spediteur (med.) Bazillenträger; **— pigeon** Brieftaube

carrot *n.* Karotte, Mohrrübe. Möhre

carry *v.* tragen, fahren, führen, befördern, bringen, transportieren, übertragen; fortsetzen; (mil.) einnehmen, erobern; durchsetzen, gewinnen; **— a motion** einen Antrag durchbringen; **— away** fortreissen, fortschaffen; **— on** weiterführen; — oneself sich betragen (*or* benehmen); **— out** (*oder* **through**) erfüllen, ausführen, durchführen; **— weight** Gewicht haben; **-ing** *adj.* **-ing charge** Transportspesen

cart *n.* Karre(n); Wagen; **put the — before the horse** das Pferd am Schwanz aufzäumen; **turn — wheels** radschlagen; — *v.* karren; **— away** wegschaffen; **-age** *n.* Fuhrlohn, Transportkosten

Carthage *n.* Karthago

cartilage *n.* Knorpel

carton *n.* Karton

cartoon *n.* Karikatur(enserie); Musterzeichnung; (film) Zeichenfilm, Trickfilm; **-ist** *n.* Karikaturenzeichner

cartridge *n.* Kartusche, Patrone

carve *v.* (meat) zerlegen, tranchieren, vorschneiden; (metal) gravieren; (stone) aushauen, meisseln; (wood) schnitzen; **-r** *n.* (meat) Tranchierer, Vorschneider; (stone) Bildhauer, Steinmetz; (wood) Schnitzer

carving knife *n.* Tranchiermesser, Schnitzmesser

carving set *n.* Tranchierbesteck

cascade *n.* Kaskade, Wasserfall; (fig.) Feuerwerk

case *n.* Behälter, Etui, Futteral; Gehäuse, Kasten, Kiste; Fach; Besteck; Hülle; Fall, Lage, Sache; (gram.) Fall; (law) Prozess; (typ.) Schriftart, Setzkasten;

in any — auf jeden Fall; in — falls, im
Falle dass; in — of bei, im Falle von
casemate *n.* bombensicheres Arsenal;
Kasematte
casement *n.* Fensterflügel, Verschalung
cash *n.* Bargeld, Barschaft; — **and carry**
Barverkauf (zum Mitnehmen); — in
advance Vorauszahlung; — on delivery
Lieferung per Nachnahme; — on hand
Bargeld; in — bar; — register Registrierkasse; — *v.* einkassieren, einlösen;
— in on verdienen bei; -ier n. Kassierer; -ier's check voll gedeckter Banks-
check
cashbook *n.* Kassabuch; Kassenbuch
cashbox *n.* Geldkassette
cashew *n.* Cachou, brasilianische Akazie
cashmere *n.* Kaschmir
casing *n.* Überzug, Verkleidung; Futteral,
Gehäuse
casino *n.* Kasino; Klubhaus
cask *n.* Tonne, Fass
casket *n.* Kästchen; Sarg
Caspian Sea *n.* das Kaspische Meer
casserole *n.* Kasserole, Tiegel
cassock *n.* Soutane, Priesterrock
cast *n.* Werfen; Wurf; Wurfweite; (art)
Färbung, Schattierung; (mech.) Guss,
Gussform, Gussstück; (med.) Gipsverband; (naut.) Auswerfen; (theat.)
Besetzung; (fig.) Art, Form, Gattung;
Äussere; — *adj.* — iron Gusseisen; — *v.*
werfen; auswerfen; (mech.) formen,
giessen; (theat.) besetzen; — aside
fortwerfen; — a vote abstimmen,
wählen; — lots auslosen; — on anschlagen; the die is — der Würfel ist
gefallen; -er *n.* Laufrolle; -ing *n.*
(mech.) Giessen, Gussform; (theat.)
Rollenverteilung; -ing *adj.* ausschlag-
gebend, entscheidend
castanet *n.* Kastagnette
castaway *n.* Verworfene; (naut.)
Schiffbrüchige
castdown *adj.* gedemütigt, entmutigt
caste *n.* Kaste, Klasse; lose — seine
Stellung in der Gesellschaft verlieren
castle *n.* Schloss, Burg, Kastell; (chess)
Turm; — in the air (oder in Spain)
Luftschloss; — *v.* rochieren
castoff *adj.* weggeworfen; abgelegt; wertlos
castor oil *n.* Rizinusöl
castrate *v.* kastrieren
casual *adj.* zufällig; gelegentlich; —
acquaintance flüchtige Bekannte; -ty *n.*
Unfall, Todesfall; (mil.) Verlust
cat *n.* Katze; let the — out of the bag
die Katze aus dem Sack lassen; — nap
Nickerchen; -ty *adj.* tückisch, hinterlistig
catacombs *n. pl.* Katakomben
catafighter *n.* Katapultflugzeug
catalogue *n.* Katalog, Verzeichnis; — *v.*
katalogisieren
catapult *n.* Katapult
cataract *n.* Katarakt, Wasserfall, Wolkenbruch; (med.) grauer Star
catarrh *n.* Katarrh
catastrophe *n.* Katastrophe

catch *n.* Fang; Beute; Vorteil; Griff;
Verschluss, Haken; Klinke; Stockung;
(sports) Auffangen; a good — ein guter
Fang; eine gute Partie; — of a door
Türklinke, Schliesshaken; play — Ball
spielen; — *v.* fangen; erreichen, bekommen, erwischen; überfallen; (er)fassen;
treffen; (mech.) ineinandergreifen;
(med.) sich holen, angesteckt werden;
(sports) auffangen; — a train einen Zug
erreichen; — cold sich erkälten; — fire
Feuer fangen, in Brand geraten; —
hold of ergreifen, habhaft werden; —
on hängen bleiben; (coll.) kapieren; —
one's eye ins Auge fallen; — up nachkommen; — up with einholen; — basin
Abflussbassin, Bewässerungsbecken;
-er *n.* Fänger; -ing *adj.* ansteckend;
-ing tune einschmeichelnde Melodie;
-y *adj.* anziehend, einnehmend, pac-
kend; verfänglich
catchall *n.* Sammelkasten
catchword *n.* Schlagwort, Stichwort; Losungswort; (pol.) Parteiparole
catechism *n.* Katechismus
category *n.* Kategorie
cater *v.* mit Nahrungsmittelversorgen;
für die Tafel (or Unterhaltung, Bedürf-
nisse) sorgen; -er *n.* Lebensmittellie-
ferant, Proviantmeister; Versorger
cater-cornered *adj.* diagonal, schräglau-
fend
caterpillar *n.* Raupe; — tractor Raupen-
schlepper
caterwaul *n.* Katzenmusik; — *v.* miauen
catgut *n.* Darmsaite
cathedral *n.* Dom, Kathedrale, Münster
cathode *n.* Kathode; — rays Katho-
denstrahlen
Catholic *n.* Katholik; — *adj.* katholisch;
-ism *n.* Katholizismus
catnip *n.* Katzenminze
cat's-paw *n.* Gefoppte, (willenloses)
Werkzeug
catsup *n.* Ketchup, pikante Tomatensauce
cattle *n.* Vieh, Rinder; — breeding Vieh-
zucht; — car Viehwagen; — ranch
Viehweide, Rinderfarm; — show Vieh-
ausstellung
cattleman *n.* Viehzüchter
caucus *n.* Vorversammlung
cauliflower *n.* Blumenkohl
causal *adj.* kausal, ursächlich
cause *n.* Grund, Ursache; (fig.) Angelegenheit, Sache; show — Rechtsgründe
angeben; — *v.* veranlassen, verursachen; erregen; bewirken; -less *adj*
grundlos, unbegründet
caustic *adj.* kaustisch, ätzend; (fig.) satirisch, beissend
cauterize *v.* ausbrennen, beizen
caution *n.* Vorsicht, Behutsamkeit; Warnung, Verwarnung; — *v.* warnen, verwarnen
cautious *adj.* vorsichtig, behutsam
cavalcade *n.* Kavalkade
cavalier *n.* Kavalier; — *adj.* hochmütig
verächtlich
cavalry *n.* Kavallerie

cavalryman n. Kavallerist

cave n. Höhle, Grube; — dweller Höhlenbewohner, Troglodyt; — man Höhlenmensch, Troglodyt; — v. — in einstürzen

cavern n. Höhle, Kaverne

caviar n. Kaviar

cavil v. bekritteln, nörgeln

cavity n. Höhlung, Vertiefung; Höhle

caw v. krächzen

cease v. aufhören, ablassen; abstehen, einstellen; (fig.) ruhen; — fire das Feuer einstellen; -less adj. unaufhörlich

cedar n. Zeder; — adj. zedern, aus Zederholz

cede v. abtreten, überlassen

ceiling n. Decke; (avi.) Flughöhe, Steighöhe; — price Höchstpreis; — zero Flughöhe Null

celebrate v. feiern; preisen, verherrlichen; (rel.) lesen; -d adj. berühmt, gefeiert

celebration n. Feier, Fest; (fig.) Verherrlichung

celebrity n. Berühmtheit

celery n. Sellerie

celestial adj. himmlisch, göttlich

cell n. (biol.) Zelle; (elec.) galvanisches Element; Sturmzentrum; — of a party (pol.) Parteikern

cellar n. Keller

cello n. Cello

cellophane n. Zellophan

cellular adj. zellig, zellförmig

celluloid n. Zelluloid

cellulose n. Zellulose

cement n. Zement; Kitt, Mörtel; rubber — flüssiger Klebstoff; — v. zementieren; (fig.) fest verbinden

cemetery n. Friedhof, Kirchhof

censor n. Zensor; — v. der Zensur unterwerfen, (über)prüfen, zensieren; -ship n. Zensur, Zensoramt

censure n. Tadel, Rüge, Verweis; — v. tadeln, kritisieren

census n. Volkszählung, Zensus

cent n. Cent; Pfennig; Hundert

centenary n. Jahrhundertfeier, hundertjähriges Jubiläum; — adj. hundertjährig

centennial n. Hundertjahrfeier; — adj. hundertjährig

center n. Mitte, Mittelpunkt Zentrum; — of gravity Schwerpunkt; — v. konzentrieren; in den Mittelpunkt stellen

centerboard n. (naut.) Schwert

centerpiece n. Tafelaufsatz

centigrade adj. hundertgradig, hundertteilig

centimeter n. Zentimeter

central adj. zentral; — heating Zentralheizung; -ization n. Zentralisierung; Zentralisation; -ize v. zentralisieren

Central Alps n. Mittelalpen

centrifugal adj. zentrifugal, vom Mittelpunkt wegstrebend; — force Zentrifugalkraft

centripetal adj. zentripetal, zum Mittelpunkt strebend; — force Zentripetalkraft

century n. Jahrhundert

ceramics n. pl. Keramik; Töpferkunst

cereal n. Getreide(pflanze)

cerebral palsy n. (med.) Gehirnlähmung

ceremonial n. Zeremoniell; — adj. zeremoniell, feierlich, förmlich

ceremonious adj. zeremoniell, förmlich

ceremony n. Umstand, Zeremonie; Feier; without — ohne Umstände

certain adj. gewiss, sicher, unzweifelhaft; unfehlbar, unvermeidlich; -ly adv. bestimmt, zuverlässig, allerdings, sicherlich; -ty n. Gewissheit, Sicherheit, Bestimmtheit; with -ty mit Zuverlässigkeit (or Bestimmtheit)

certificate n. Attest, Zeugnis, Schein

certification n. Beglaubigung, Bescheinigung

certified adj. beglaubigt, bescheinigt; — check beglaubigter Scheck; — public accountant amtlicher Rechnungsführer

certify v. bezeugen, beglaubigen, bescheinigen

certitude n. Gewissheit, Sicherheit

cessation n. Aufhören, Einstellen; Schluss; — of hostilities Einstellung der Feindseligkeiten

cession n. Abtretung

cesspool n. Senkgrube

chafe v. reiben, frottieren; (med.) wundreiben, sich scheuern; (fig.) aufregen, erzürnen

chaff n. Häcksel, Spreu; (fig.) Neckerei; (auch window avi.) Staniolstreifen zur Störung von Radar; — v. aufziehen, necken

chagrin n. Ärger, Verdruss; — v. ärgern

chain n. Kette, Fessel; Reihe; pl. Sklavenketten, Gefangenschaft; — gang Abteilung zusammengeketteter Verbrecher; — reaction Kettenreaktion; — smoker Kettenraucher; — stitch Kettenstich; — store Kettenladen, Zweiggeschäft (eines Warenkonzerns); — v. fesseln, (an)ketten

chair n. Stuhl, Sessel; Sitz; Professur; (pol.) Präsidium; Vorsitzende; address the — sich an den Vorsitzenden wenden; take the — den Vorsitz übernehmen; — car Salonwagen

chairman n. Vorsitzende

chalice n. Kelch

chalk n. Kreide; — v. mit Kreide zeichnen (or schreiben, mischen); — up to auf Konto schreiben

challenge n. Aufforderung, Herausforderung; (law) Verwerfung; (mil.) Anruf; — v. auffordern, herausfordern; (law) verwerfen; (mil.) anrufen

chamber n. Kammer, Zimmer; (law) Gerichtszimmer; — of commerce Handelskammer; — music Kammermusik; -lain n. Kammerherr; Kämmerer

chambermaid n. Kammermädchen, Zimmermädchen

chamois n. Gemse; Gemsenleder, Sämischleder

champagne n. Champagner, Sekt

champion n. Meister, Champion; (fig.) Verfechter; — v. verteidigen, beschützen; -ship n. Meisterschaft; (fig.)

Verteidigung

chance n. Gelegenheit, Chance, Möglichkeit; Wahrscheinlichkeit; Los, Zufall; **by —** zufällig; **not a —** keine Spur; **on the —** mit der Hoffnung; **stand a —** Aussicht haben; **take a —** das Glück versuchen, es darauf ankommen lassen; **— v.** sich begeben, geschehen; wagen, es ankommen lassen auf; **— adj.** zufällig, gelegentlich

chancel n. Altarplatz, Hochchor

chancellor n. Kanzler

chandelier n. Kronleuchter, Lüster; Kandelaber, Armleuchter

change n. Änderung, Veränderung; Wechsel, Abwechselung, Übergang; Kleingeld; (mus.) Modulation, Variation; **— of heart** Gefühlsveränderung; **for a —** zur Abwechslung; **give — for** herausgeben auf; **make — in** Kleingeld umwechseln; **— v.** (sich) (ver)ändern; tauschen, wechseln; (baby) trockenlegen; (rail.) umsteigen; **— clothes** sich umziehen; **— for the better** sich verbessern; **— for the worse** sich verschlechtern (or verschlimmern); **— hands** den Besitzer wechseln; **— one's mind** sich anders besinnen, anderen Sinnes werden; **-able** adj. veränderlich, unbeständig; (color) schillernd; **-less** adj. unveränderlich, beständig

channel n. Kanal; Flussbett; Rinne, Gosse; (naut.) Fahrwasser; (pol.) Dienstweg, Amtsweg; (rad.) Sender; **— v.** kanalisieren, aushöhlen, furchen

chant n. Gesang, Melodie, Weise; **— v.** singen, besingen; (coll.) herunterleiern

chanticleer n. Hahn

chaos n. Chaos; Wirrwarr

chaotic adj. chaotisch; verworren

chap n. (coll.) Bursche, Kerl; pl. Lederüberkleid; **— v.** aufspringen, rissig werden; spalten; **-ped** adj. aufgesprungen, rissig

chapel n. Kapelle

chaperon n. Anstandsdame; **— v.** (als Anstandsdame) begleiten

chaplain n. Kaplan; army — Feldprediger; navy — Schiffsgeistliche

chapter n. Kapitel, Abschnitt

char v. verkohlen

character n. Charakter; Art; Rang; Person, Figur; Festigkeit; Buchstabe; (theat.) Rolle; (fig.) Original; Zeugnis; **act out of —** aus der Rolle fallen; **in — dem** Charakter gemäss; **-istic** n. Eigenschaft; Kennzeichen; **-istic** adj. eigentümlich, charakteristisch; **-ize** v. charakterisieren

charade n. Scharade

charcoal n. Holzkohle; **— burner** Köhler

charge n. Preis, Forderung; Last, Belastung; Anweisung, Auftrag; Ladung; Aufsicht, Verwahrung; Mündel, Pflegling; (law) Anklage, Beschuldigung; Rechtsbelehrung; (mil.) Angriff; **be in — of** leiten; **in** Verwahrung haben; **extra —** Nebenkosten, Aufschlag; **free of —** unentgeltlich, gratis; **in — of** die Aufsicht über; **take — of** sich anneh-

men, die Leitung übernehmen; **— account** Spesenkonto; **— v.** anrechnen, berechnen; belasten; anweisen, beauftragen; (elec.) laden; (law) anklagen, beschuldigen; (mil.) angreifen; **— for** verlangen, fordern; **— to one's account** auf die Rechnung setzen, das Konto belasten; **— with** beschuldigen; **-r** n. Dienstpferd; Schlachtross

chariot n. Triumphwagen; Staatswagen; **-eer** n. Wagenlenker

charitable adj. wohltätig, barmherzig, mildtätig; (fig.) gütig, nachsichtig

charity n. Wohltätigkeit, Barmherzigkeit, Mildtätigkeit; Güte, Nachsicht; (fig.) Liebeswerk, Stiftung; Almosen

charm n. Charme; Reiz, Zauber; Anmut; (fig.) Amulett, Zauber(mittel); **— v.** (be)zaubern; fesseln, entzücken; (fig.) behexen; **-ing** adj. charmant, reizend, entzückend

chart n. Tabelle; (naut.) Karte, Seekarte; **— v.** auf einer Karte verzeichnen; **-er** n. Stiftungsurkunde; Privilegium; (fig.) Vorrecht; **-er member** Stiftungsmitglied; **-er** v. durch Urkunde festsetzen; privilegieren; (naut.) chartern; befrachten, verfrachten; (fig.) bevorrechten

charwoman n. Scheuerfrau, Reinemachefrau

chase n. Jagd, Verfolgung; **give — nach-** jagen, nachsetzen; **— v.** jagen, hetzen; nachsetzen, verfolgen; **-r** n. (coll.) leichtes Getränk (neben alkoholischen Getränken)

chassis n. Fahrgestell, Rahmen; (mil.) Lafette

chaste adj. keusch, züchtig; (fig.) edel, rein; **-n** v. strafen; reinigen; (ver)bessern; (fig.) demütigen

chastise v. züchtigen; (rel.) kasteien; **-ment** n. Strafe, Züchtigung

chastity n. Keuschheit, Reinheit

chat n. Geplauder, Plauderei; Unterhaltung; **— v.** plaudern, schwatzen; **-ter** n. Geplauder, Geplapper, Geschwätz; Klappern; (orn.) Geschnatter, Gezwitscher; **-ter** v. plappern, schwatzen; klappern; schnattern, zwitschern; his teeth **-ter** with cold er klappert vor Kälte mit den Zähnen; **-ting** n. Klappern; (orn.) Gezwitscher; Geschnatter; (fig.) Tratsch; **-ty** adj. geschwätzig, schwatzhaft

chattel n. bewegliche Gut, Habe; **goods and -s** Hab und Gut

chatterbox n. Plaudertasche, Schwätzer(in)

chauffeur n. Chauffeur, Fahrer

cheap n. billig, wohlfeil; gering, gemein, ordinär; **feel —** sich gering (or klein) fühlen; **get off —** mit blauem Auge davonkommen; **-en** v. herabsetzen, verbilligen; **-ness** n. Billigkeit, Wohlfeilheit; (fig.) Gemeinheit

cheat n. Betrüger, Schwindler; **— v.** betrügen, (be)schwindeln, mogeln; **— out of** betrügen um; **-er** n. Betrüger, Schwindler, Gauner

check n. Scheck; Hemmnis, Hindernis,

Einhalt, Unterbrechung; Marke,
Schein; Kontrolle; (chess) Schach;
(fabrik) Karo, karierte Muster; (mil.)
Schlappe; (fig.) Dämpfer, Zügel; Unfall; **coat** (*oder* hat) — Garderoben-
marke; **hold** (*oder* keep) **in** — in Schach
halten; **traveler's** — Reisescheck; —
list Kontrollverzeichnis; — *v.* hemmen,
hindern; einhalten, unterbrechen; kontrollieren, nachsehen; abgeben, zur
Aufbewahrung geben; bezeichnen, markieren; (chess) Schach bieten; (fig.)
dämpfen, zügeln; — **in** eintragen; — **off**
abhaken, abstreichen; — **up on** kontrollieren, sich erkundigen über; — **with**
übereinstimmen mit
checker *v.* karieren; **-ed** *adj.* kariert
checkerboard *n.* Damebrett
checkers *n.* Damespiel
checking account *n.* Bankkonto
checkmate *n.* Schachmatt; — *v.* schachmatt setzen
check point *n.* Kontrollstelle
checkup *n.* gründliche Untersuchung
cheek *n.* Wange, Backe; (coll.) Dreistigkeit, Stirn; — **by jowl** dicht beieinander, in vertraulicher Gemeinschaft;
with one's tongue in one's — schalkhaft
cheekbone *n.* Backenknochen
cheer *n.* Heiterkeit; Stimmung; Ermutigung, Trost; Beifallsruf, Zujauchsen;
pl. Beifall, Applaus, Hochlebenlassen;
be of good — guter Dinge sein; — *v.*
ermutigen, trösten; aufmuntern; (zu)-
jubeln, Beifall spenden, mit Beifall
begrüssen; — **up** aufheitern; sich
trösten; **-ful** *adj.* froh, heiter, munter;
-fulness *n.* Heiterkeit, Frohsinn; **-ing**
adj. tröstend, trostreich; **-ing** *n.* Bei-
fallrufen; **-less** *adj.* freudlos, trostlos
cheese *n.* Käse
cheesecloth *n.* Wachstuch
chef *n.* Küchenchef
chemical *adj.* chemisch; — **engineering**
Chemotechnik; — **warfare** chemischer
Krieg; **-s** *n. pl.* Chemikalien
chemist *n.* Chemiker; **-ry** *n.* Chemie
chemosphere *n.* Luftschicht ca 32–80 Km.
über der Erde
cherish *v.* mit Liebe behandeln, hegen,
pflegen; festhalten an; — **the hope** die
Hoffnung aufrechterhalten (*oder* hegen)
cherry *n.* Kirsche; — *adj.* kirschrot; Kir-
schenholz-; — **brandy** Kirschbrannt-
wein; **—stone** Kirschkern
cherub *n.* Cherub
chess *n.* Schach(spiel)
chessboard *n.* Schachbrett
chessman *n.* Schachfigur
chest *n.* Kiste, Kasten, Koffer; Lade,
Truhe; Kommode; (anat.) Brust(kasten); — **of drawers** Kommode
chestnut *n.* Kastanie; — *adj.* kastanienbraun; — **tree** Kastanienbaum
chevron *n.* Wappensparren; (mil.) Winkel, Tresse
chew *v.* kauen; (coll.) grübeln; **-ing** *adj.*
-ing gum Kaugummi
chic *n.* Schick; (fig.) Geschmack; — *adj.*

schick, geschmackvoll, stilgerecht
Chicago *n.* Chicago
chicanery *n.* Schikane, Rechtsverdre-
hung; Haarspalterei
chick *n.* Küken; **-en** *n.* Huhn, Hühnchen,
Küken, Küchlein; **-en** *adj.* **-en pox**
Windpocken
chicken-hearted *adj.* furchtsam, feige
chick-pea *n.* Kichererbse
chickweed *n.* Vogelmiere, rotes Sand-
kraut
chicory *n.* Zichorie, Wegwarte
chide *v.* schmähen, tadeln; keifen, schelten
chief *n.* Chef, Haupt, Oberhaupt; Anführer, Häuptling; — **of staff** General-
stabschef; — *adj.* erst, höchst, oberst;
hauptsächlich, vorzüglichst; Ober-,
Haupt; — **clerk** Hauptbuchhalter;
Chefsekretär; — **justice** Richter am
Obersten Gerichtshof
chieftain *n.* Stammeshäuptling, Hauptmann
chiffon *n.* Chiffon; **-iere** *n.* Kommode;
Kästchen
chilblain *n.* Frostbeule
child *n.* Kind; **ever since I was a** — von
Kindheit an; **with** — in anderen
Umständen, schwanger; **-ish** *adj.* kindisch; **-like** *adj.* kindlich
childbirth *n.* Geburt, Niederkunft
childhood *n.* Kindheit; **second** — zweite
Kindheit, Kindischwerden im Alter
chili *n.* spanischer Pfeffer; — **sauce**
gepfefferte Tomatensauce
chill *adj.* eisig, frostig, kalt; (fig.) ent-
mutigend, niederdrückend; — *n.* Frost,
Kälte, Schauer; (med.) Frösteln, Schüttelfrost; (fig.) Entmutigung; — *v.*
erkälten, erstarren; abkühlen; (metal)
abschrecken; (fig.) dämpfen, entmutigen; niederschlagen; **-y** *adj.* frostig,
kühl; **I feel** — *y* mich fröstelt
chime *n.* Glockenspiel, Geläute; (fig.)
Einklang, Harmonie; — *v.* ertönen
lassen, zusammenklingen; (fig.) übereinstimmen harmonieren
chimera *n.* Chimäre, Schimäre; Hirnges-
pinst, Schreckbild
chimerical *adj.* schimärisch, phantastisch
chimney *n.* Kamin, Schornstein, Esse;
(lamp) Zylinder; — **sweep** Schornsteinfeger
chimpanzee *n.* Schimpanse
chin *n.* Kinn; — **up!** Kopf hoch!
china(ware) *n.* Porzellan
chinchilla *n.* Chinchilla
chink *n.* Riss, Ritze; Spalt, Spalte; — *v.*
— **up** ausfüllen
chintz *n.* Möbelkattun
chip *n.* Splitter, Span; Spielmarke; **a** —
off the old block aus demselben Holz
geschnitzt; — *v.* bearbeiten, behauen;
abschleifen; — *n.* beitragen zu
chipmunk *n.* gestreiftes Erdhörnchen
chiropodist *n.* Pedikürer; Fussspezialist
chiropractor *n.* Chiropraktiker, Handauf-
leger
chirp *n.* Zirpen, Zwitschern; — *v.* zirpen,
zwitschern; piepen, pfeifen

chisel n. Meissel, Stemmeisen; Stichel; — n. meisseln; (sl.) betrügen; **-er** n. Betrüger, Gauner

chitchat n. Schnickschnack, Geschwätz

chivalrous adj. chevaleresk, ritterlich, galant

chivalry n. Ritterlichkeit; Rittertum

chives n. pl. Schnittlauch

chloremia n. (med.) Bleichsucht

chlorine n. Chlor

chloroform n. Chloroform; **administer —** mit Chloroform betäuben; **— v.** chloroformieren

chloromycetin n. Chloromycetine

chlorophyll n. Chlorophyll, Blattgrün

chock-full adj. gedrängt voll, übervoll

chocolate n. Schokolade; Praliné

choice n. Wahl, Auswahl; Ausgewähltes; Sortiment, Vorrat; — adj. (aus)erlesen, ausgesucht, vorzüglich

choir n. Chor

choirmaster n. Chorleiter

choke n. Würgung; Erstickungsanfall; (auto) Drosselklappe; — v. ersticken, würgen; (mech.) verstopfen; drosseln; **— back** herunterschlucken; **-r** n. Halsbinde, Krawatte; Stehkragen

cholera n. Cholera

choleric adj. cholerisch, jähzornig; hitzig

cholesterol n. Cholesterin, Gallenfett

choose v. wählen, auswählen; belieben; mögen, vorziehen, wollen

choosy adj. wählerisch

chop n. Hieb, Schlag; Kotelett(e); Rippenstück; Scheibe, Schnitte, Stück; pl. Kinnbacken; **breaded —** paniertes Kotelett; **lick one's —s** sich das Maul lecken; **— v.** zerhauen, zerhacken; schlagen; **— down** fällen, niederhauen; **— off** abhacken; **-ped meat** Hackfleisch; **— up** zerhacken; **-per** n. Hackmesser; **-py** adj. stürmisch; abgebrochen; plötzlich umschlagend; unbeständig, unstet

choral adj. chorartig; Chor-; **-e** n. Choral

chord n. Akkord, Zusammenklang

chore n. leichte Arbeit, Auftrag; pl. Farmarbeiten, Hausarbeiten

choreography n. Choreographie

chorister n. Chorist, Chorsänger; Chorleiter

chorus n. Chor; Refrain; Kehrreim

chosen adj. erwählt, auserlesen; **— few** die wenigen Auserwählten

chowder n. dicke Suppe. Milchsuppe

Christ n. Christus; **-endom** n. Christentum, Christenheit

christen v. taufen; **-ing** n. Taufe

Christian n. Christ; — adj. christlich; **— name** Taufname, Vorname; **-ity** n. Christentum; **-ize** v. zum Christentum bekehren

Christmas n. Weihnacht(en), Christfest, Weihnachtsfest; **Merry —!** Fröhliche Weihnachten; **— adj.** — **carol** Weihnachtslied; **— Day** Weihnachtstag; **— Eve** Weihnachtsabend, Heilige Abend; **— present** Weihnachtsgeschenk; **— tree** Weihnachtsbaum, Christbaum

chromium n. Chrom

Chromosome n. Chromosom

chronic adj. chronisch

chronicle n. Chronik; **— v.** in eine Chronik aufnehmen, aufzeichnen

chronological adj. chronologisch; **in — order** in der richtigen Zeitfolge

chronology n. Chronologie, Zeitfolge; Zeitrechnung

chrysalis n. Puppe

chrysanthemum n. Chrysanthemum, Chrysanthemum

chubby adj. plump, rundlich

chuckle n. Kichern; Kakeln; — v. kichern, in sich hineinlachen; gackern, kakeln

chum n. Freund, Kamerad; **school —** Schulkamerad; **-my** adj. intim

chunk n. Klumpen; kurzes, dickes Stück

church n. Kirche; — adj. kirchlich; **Kirch-churchgoer** n. Kirchgänger

churchman n. Geistliche; Klerikale

churchyard n. Kirchhof; Friedhof

churlish adj. grob, plump, roh; (fig.) geizig; schwierig

churn n. Butterfass; — v. buttern; (fig.) erschüttern, schütteln; schäumen

chute n. Abwurfschacht; Gleitbahn; Stromschnelle

cicada n. Zikade; Baumgrille

cider n. Zider, Apfelwein

cigar n. Zigarre; **— butt** Zigarrenstummel; **— box** Zigarrenkiste; **— case** Zigarrenetui; **— holder** Zigarrenspitze

cigarette n. Zigarette; **— butt** Zigarettenstummel; **— case** Zigarettenetui; **— holder** Zigarettenhalter, Zigarettenspitze; **— lighter** Feuerzeug

cinch n. Sattelgurt; (fig.) Gewissheit; (sl.) eine sichere Sache; Kleinigkeit, Kinderspiel

cinder n. Schlacke; Kohlenstäubchen; **burnt to a —** verkohlt

Cinderella n. Aschenbrödel, Aschenputtel

cinnamon n. Zimt

cipher n. Chiffre, Geheimschrift; Null; Nummer, Zahl, Ziffer; **— v.** chiffrieren; (aus)rechnen

circle n. Kreis, Zirkel; Umfang, Umkreis, Ring; **dress —** erster Rang; **family —** Familienkreis; **vicious —** Zirkelschluss; **— v.** (um)kreisen, zirkeln

circuit n. Kreis, Umkreis; Kreislauf; (elec.) Stromkreis, Leitung, Schaltung; (law) Gerichtsbezirk; (fig.) Ausdehnung, Fläche; **short —** Kurzschluss; **— breaker** Stromunterbrecher; **— court** Bezirksgericht; **-ous** adj. weitläufig, weitschweifig

circular n. Rundschreiben; — adj. kreisförmig, Kreis-; **-ize** v. zirkulieren; Rundschreiben versenden

circulate v. zirkulieren; in Umlauf setzen; umlaufen

circulating adj. zirkulierend, umlaufend; (math.) periodisch; **— library** Leihbibliothek

circulation n. Zirkulation, Umlauf, Kreislauf; Verbreitung; Auflage; **— (of the blood)** Blutkreislauf; **put into — in** Umlauf bringen

circumcise v. beschneiden

circumcision n. Beschneidung

circumference n. Umfang, Kreisumfang

circumflex n. Zirkumflex; — adj. gebogen, gekrümmt

circumlocution n. Umschreibung

circumnavigate v. umschiffen, umsegeln, die Erde umgehen

circumscribe v. umschreiben; umgrenzen, begrenzen, beschränken

circumspect adj. umsichtig, behutsam, vorsichtig

circumstance n. Umstand; Zufall; Sachlage, Zustand; pl. Verhältnisse, Einzelheiten

circumstantial adj. umständlich, eingehend; (fig.) unwesentlich, zufällig; — evidence Indizienbeweis

circumvent v. umgehen, überlisten; umstellen; —tion n. Überlistung

circus n. Zirkus

cirrhosis n. Schrumpfung

cistern n. Zisterne, Wasserreservoir

citation n. Erwähnung; (law) Vorladung; Zitierung; (lit.) Zitat, Aufführung

cite v. erwähnen, nennen; (law) zitieren, vorladen; (lit.) anführen

cither n. Zither

citified adj. städtisch; bürgerlich; eingebürgert

citizen n. Bürger, Städter; Staatsbürger; Zivilist; fellow — Mitbürger; —ry n. Bürgerschaft; -ship n. Staatsangehörigkeit; Bürgerrecht

citric adj. zitronensauer; Zitronen-; — acid Zitronsäure

citron n. Zitrone

citrus adj. citrusartig; — fruit Citrusfrucht

city n. Stadt, — adj. städtisch; Stadt-; — hall Rathaus; — manager Stadtverwalter; — planning Stadtplanung

civet (cat) n. Zibetkatze

civic adj. bürgerlich; Bürger-; -s n. Bürgerkunde; Zivilrecht

civil adj. bürgerlich, zivil; Bürger-; höflich, gesittet; (law) zivilrechtlich, gesetzlich; — engineer Zivilingenieur; — law bürgerliches Recht; — liberty bürgerliche Freiheit; — right bürgerliches Ehrenrecht; — servant Staatsbeamt; — service Zivilverwaltung; — war Bürgerkrieg; -ian n. Zivilist; -ian adj. -ian clothes Zivilkleider, Zivil; -ian life Zivilleben; -ity n. Höflichkeit, Artigkeit; -ization n. Kultur; Gesittung, Zivilisation; -ize v. zivilisieren

clad adj. bekleidet, gekleidet

claim n. Anspruch, Anrecht; (law) Rechtsanspruch; (min.) Grubenanteil; lay — to Anspruch erheben auf; — v. beanspruchen, fordern, verlangen

clairvoyance n. Hellsehen, Vorausschauen; (fig.) Scharfsinn

clam n. Muschel

clambake n. Muschelbacken, Muschelkochen

clamber v. klimmen, klettern

clammy adj. feucht, kalt, klebrig, klamm

clamor n. Geschrei, Lärm; Getöse, Tumult; — v. schreien, verlangen; -ous adj. lärmend, schreiend

clamp n. Krampe, Klampe, Klammer; — v. klammern, klemmen

clan n. Clan, Sippe, Stamm; (pol.) Clique; (sl.) Sippschaft; -ish adj. Sippen-; zu einer Clique angehörig; anhänglich

clandestine n. Untergrundbewegung

clank n. Geklirr, Gerassel; — v. klirren rasseln

clansman n. Stammesmitglied

clap n. Klaps, Schlag; Beifallsklatschen; — of thunder Donnerschlag; — v. klappen, klatschen, klopfen; schlagen; Beifall klatschen; — hands in die Hände klatschen; — into jail ins Gefängnis werfen; -per n. Klöppel; -ping n. Applaus

claptrap n. Effekthascherei; Unsinn, Windbeutelei

clarification n. Aufklärung; Läuterung

clarify v. (auf)klären; läutern

clarinet n. Klarinette; — player Klarinettist

clarity n. Klarheit, Glanz

clash n. Geklirr, Geschmetter; Schlag, Stoss; Zusammenstoss; (fig.) Widerstreit, Widerspruch; — v. klirren, schmettern; schlagen, (zusammen)stossen; (fig.) widerstreiten

clasp n. Haken; Klammer, Spange; Schloss; (fig.) Umarmung, Umklammerung; hand — Händedruck; — adj. — knife Klappmesser, Taschenmesser; — v. einhaken, schliessen; ergreifen, festhalten; (fig.) umarmen, umklammern; — hands sich die Hände schütteln; -ed adj. (hands) gefaltet

class n. Klasse; Stunde, Vorlesung, Kurs; Stand, Gesellschaftsklasse; Kategorie; Jahrgang; — v. ordnen, klassifizieren; -ification n. Klassifizierung; -ify v. klassifizieren, einordnen

classic(al) adj. klassisch; mustergültig; -ism n. Klassizismus

classmate n. Klassenkamerad

classroom n. Klassenzimmer, Schulraum

clatter n. Gerassel, Geklapper; (fig.) Geschwätz; — v. rasseln, klappern; (fig.) schwatzen

clause n. Klausel; Redeteil; Satzteil

claustrophobia n. Platzangst

clavicle n. Schlüsselbein

claw n. Klaue, Kralle; Pfote, Tatze; — v. klauen, krallen, (zer)kratzen

clay n. Ton, Lehm; (fig.) Asche, Staub; — pigeon Tontaube; — pit Lehmgrube

clean adj. rein, sauber, blank, unbeschrieben; unvermischt; fehlerrei; glatt; geschickt; gänzlich, völlig; — v. reinigen, säubern; saubermachen, aufräumen; putzen, polieren; — house Grossreinemachen; — out ausräumen; — up sich waschen; -er n. Reiniger, Putzer; Reinigungsmittel; -ers n. Reinigungsanstalt; -ing n. Reinigung, Aufräumen, Säuberung; -ing adj. -ing rag Putztuch, Wischtusch; -ing woman Putzfrau; -liness n. Reinlichkeit, Sauberkeit; (fig.) Reinheit; -se v. reinigen, säubern, putzen, scheuern; ausfegen, auskehren; spülen, waschen; (fig.) befreien, lossprechen; **-ser** n. Putzmittel, Scheuerpulver

clean-cut adj. genau begrenzt (or bestimmt, bezeichnet)

clear adj. klar; hell, rein; deutlich, unzweifelhaft; vollständig, unbedingt; frei, offen; (com.) netto; (weather) heiter; (fig.) fleckenlos, unschuldig; — **profit** Nettogewinn; **in the** — von aller Schuld rein; — v. klären, aufklären; aufheitern; leeren, räumen; vorbeigehen, Hindernisse nehmen; entlasten; (com.) bar einnehmen; freimachen; verzollen; (law) rechtfertigen; (naut.) klar machen; lossprechen; — **away** wegräumen; — **one's throat** sich räuspern; — **out** ausräumen; ausreissen, sich aus dem Staube machen; — **the way** den Weg freimachen; — **the table** den Tisch abräumen; — **up** aufklären; sich aufhellen; **-ance** n. Freimachung, Räumung; Zwischenraum; (com.) Ausverkauf; Verzollung; (naut.) Klarmachen; **-ing** n. Abholzen; Lichtung; (com.) Abrechnung; **-ing in the forest** Waldlichtung; **-ly** adv. deutlich, genau; augenscheinlich, offenbar; **-ness** n. Klarheit, Deutlichkeit, Helligkeit; Freiheit

clear-cut adj. gedrängt, kurz; abgesondert, unterschieden

clear-headed adj. verständig, einsichtig

clearing-house n. Abrechnungsstelle

clear-sighted adj. klarsehend

cleave v. (sich) spalten; zerreissen; eindringen; haften, kleben; aufspringen, bersten; **-r** n. Hackmesser

cleft n. Kluft, Riss, Ritze; Spalt, Spalte; — adj. — **palate** Gaumenspalte

clemency n. Gnade, Milde, Nachsicht

clement adj. gnädig, mild, nachsichtig

clench v. festhalten, ergreifen; packen; — **one's fist** die Faust ballen; — **one's teeth** die Zähne zusammenbeissen

clergy n. Geistlichkeit

clergyman n. Geistliche

clerical adj. klerikal, geistlich; schriftlich, Schreib-; — **error** Schreibfehler; — **work** Büroarbeit, schriftliche Arbeit

clerk n. Büroangestellte; Schreiber; Sekretär; **town** — Stadtsekretär; — v. als Angestellter arbeiten

clever adj. geschickt, gewandt, tüchtig; klug, gescheit; — **fellow** geriebener Bursche; **-ness** n. Geschicklichkeit, Gewandtheit, Tüchtigkeit

cliché n. Klischee

click n. Ticken, Knipsen, Knistern; Einschnappen; Knacken; (mech.) Sperrhaken, Klinke; — v. ticken, knipsen, knistern, knacken; (sl.) klappen; einschlagen; — **one's heels** die Hacken zusammenschlagen

client n. Klient; Kunde; **-ele** n. Klientel; Kundschaft

cliff n. Abhang, Klippe; — **dweller** Felsenbewohner, Vorfahre der Pueblo-Indianer

climate n. Klima

climax n. Klimax, Höhepunkt

climb v. besteigen; (er)klettern; steigen; — **indicator** n. Aufstiegmessgerät

clinch n. (mech.) Klinke, Niet, Vernietung; (sports) Clinch; (fig.) Halt, Umklammerung; — v. (mech.) vernieten; festmachen; (fig.) abschliessen; endgültig erledigen; **-er** n. (mech.) Klammer Klampe; (fig.) treffende Antwort; Trumpf; **that's a -er** das trifft den Nagel auf den Kopf

cling v. anhaften; sich klammern, festhalten; (clothes) eng anliegen; **-ing** adj. **-ing vine** Ranke

clinic n. Klinik; **-al** adj. klinisch

clink n. Klingen, Geklirr; — v. klingen, klirren; — **glasses together** mit den Gläsern anstossen; **-er** n. Klinker, Backstein

clip n. Klipp, Spange; Klammer; Schlag; rascher Gang; (mil.) Patronenrahmen; **paper** — Büroklammer, Klammer; — v. (ab)schneiden, beschneiden, ausschneiden; scheren, stutzen; — **together** zusammenklammern; **-per** n. (avi.) Transozeanflugzeug; (mech.) Schere, Haarschneidemaschine; (naut.) Klipper, Schnellsegler; **-ping** n. Ausschnitt

clique n. Clique, Sippschaft

cloak n. Mantel; (fig.) Deckmantel, Vorwand; — v. einhüllen; (fig.) bemänteln, verbergen

cloakroom n. Garderobe, Kleiderablage

clock n. Uhr; Tageszeit; (hosiery) Zwickel; **punch the** — die Zeit(karte) stempeln; **round the** — **zwölf volle Stunden**; — v. abstoppen, mit der Stoppuhr messen

clockwise adv. wie die Uhrzeiger laufend

clockwork n. Uhrwerk; **like** — pünktlich wie ein Uhrwerk

clod n. Klumpen; Erdscholle; (fig.) Tölpel

clodhopper n. Bauernlümmel

clog n. Holzschuh; Beschwerde; (fig.) Fessel, Hindernis; — v. hemmen; verstopfen; stocken

cloister n. Kloster; (arch.) Kreuzgang; **-ed** adj. einsam, abgeschieden

close n. Abschluss, Ende, Schluss; — v. (zu-)schliessen, zumachen; abschliessen, beendigen; verschliessen, sperren; — **in on** hereinbrechen über, umzingeln; — **off** abschliessen, sperren; — **up** verschliessen; (mil.) die Reihen schliessen; — adj. nah(e), dicht, eng; geizig, genau; verschwiegen; (weather) drückend, schwül, dumpf; — **call** knappes Entkommen; — **fight** gleichwertiger Kampf; — **quarters** Handgemenge, Nahkampf; **pay** — **attention** gut aufpassen; — adv. nahe, dicht, eng; genau; — **by** dicht bei, nahe, in der Nähe; — **to** nahe bei; — **to the wind** dicht am Winde; **from** — **up** in (or von) der Nähe; **-ed** adj. verschlossen, versperrt; **-ed shop** Betrieb unter Gewerkschaftszwang; **-ness** n. Enge, Knappheit; Kargheit; Schwüle; Sparsamkeit; Genauigkeit; Festigkeit; **-ing** n. Schliessen, Schluss closed-circuit n. (rad. and TV) Regionalprogramm

closefisted adj. filzig

closet n. Wandschrank; Kabinett; Klosett; — adj. geheim, privat; (fig.) unpraktisch; — v. in einen Wandschrank schliessen; beiseitenehmen

close-up n. Grossaufnahme

clot n. Klümpchen; — v. gerinnen, verdichten

cloth n. Stoff, Tuch, Zeug, Gewebe; Leinwand, Lappen; make up out of whole — aus der Luft greifen; -e v. kleiden, bekleiden, einkleiden; pl. Kleider, Kleidung, Wäsche; suit of -es Anzug; -es closet Kleiderschrank; -es dryer, -es hanger Kleiderbügel; -es hook Kleiderhaken; -es rack, -es tree Kleiderständer; -ing n. Kleider, Kleidung; article of -ing Kleidungsstück

clothesbasket n. Wäschekorb

clothesbrush n. Kleiderbürste

clothesline n. Wäscheleine

clothespin n. Wäscheklammer, Klammer

cloture n. Abschluss; (pol.) Diskussionsschluss

cloud n. Wolke; Trübung; — v. umwölken, bewölken, bedecken, verdunkeln; — up sich bewölken; -iness n. Bewölkung, Umwölkung; Unklarheit; Trübe; -y adj. bewölkt, wolkig; düster, trübe; (fig.) traurig, unklar

cloudburst n. Wolkenbruch

clout n. Knuff, Schlag; — v. schlagen

clove n. Gewürznelke

cloven-footed adj. spaltfüssig, zweihufig

clover n. Klee; live in — wie die Made im Speck leben; -leaf (auto.) Kleeblattkreuzung

clown n. Clown; Hanswurst, Possenreisser

club n. Verein, Klub; Keule, Schlegel, Stock; (cards) Treff, Kreuz; (sports) Schläger, Schlagholz; — car Klubwagen; — sandwich mehrschichtiger Sandwich; — v. niederschlagen; besteuern, zusammenlegen; sich vereinigen

clubfoot n. Klumpfuss

clubhouse n. Klubhaus

clubroom n. Klubzimmer

cluck v. gluck(s)en

clue n. Anhaltspunkt, Leitfaden, Schlüssel

clump n. Klumpen, Klotz; (fig.) Gruppe; — v. trampeln; schwerfällig gehen

clumsiness n. Plumpheit, Ungeschicklichkeit

clumsy adj. plump, ungeschickt

cluster n. Büschel, Traube; Schwarm, Haufen; — v. sich sammeln; (bee) schwärmen; (fig.) sich häufen

clutch n. Griff, Festhalten; Haken; (auto.) Kuppelung; pl. Klauen; release the — die Kuppelung loslassen; step on the — auf die Kuppelung treten; throw in the — die Kuppelung einschalten; throw out the — auskuppeln; — pedal Kuppelungspedal; — v. greifen, packen, festhalten

clutter n. Unordnung, Wirrwarr; — v.

durcheinanderwerfen, in Verwirrung (or Unordnung) bringen; — up verwirren

coach n. Kutsche, Wagen; Personenwagen; Privatlehrer; Repetitor; (sports) Trainer; — v. einpauken; (sports) trainieren

coachman n. Kutscher

coagulate v. koagulieren, gerinnen (machen)

coal n. Kohle, Steinkohle; — car Tender; — field Kohlenflöz, Kohlenrevier; — gas Leuchtgas, Steinkohlengas; — mine Kohlenbergwerk; — oil Rohpetroleum; — tar Kohlenteer

coalbin n. Kohlenbehälter, Kohlenkasten

coalesce v. sich verbinden (or verschmelzen, vereinigen)

coalition n. Koalition, Verbindung, Bund

coarse adj. gemein, grob, rauh, roh; — language anstössige Sprache; -n v. grob werden (or machen); -ness n. Gemeinheit, Grobheit, Rauheit; Roheit; (grain) Grobkörnigkeit

coarse-grained adj. grobkörnig, grobfaserig

coast n. Küste, Strand, Ufer; the — is clear die Bahn ist frei, die Luft ist rein; — guard Küstenwache; Strandwächter; — line Uferlinie; — v. hinunterfahren; abwärtsgleiten; -er n. (naut.) Küstenfahrer; -er adj. -er brake Rückbremse

coaster n. Gläseruntersatz

coat n. Mantel, Rock, Überzieher; Jacke; (zool.) Fell, Pelz; — of arms Wappenschild; — of mail Panzerhemd; — of paint Anstrich; — hanger Kleiderbügel; — v. bekleiden, belegen; überstreichen; überziehen; -ing n. Bedeckung, Bekleidung; Anstrich, Überzug

coatroom n. Garderobenraum

coauthor n. Mitautor, Mitarbeiter

coax v. beschwatzen, erschmeicheln; (fig.) bereden, überreden

coaxial cable n. Achsenkabel

cob n. kleines, kräftiges Pferd; Klumpen; männlicher Schwan; Maiskolben

cobalt n. Kobalt

cobble v. flicken; -r n. Flickschuster; (fig.) Pfuscher; (cooking) Obsttörtchen

cobblestone n. Kieselstein, Feldstein, Kopfstein

cobra n. Kobra, Brillenschlange

cobweb n. Spinngewebe

cocaine n. Kokain

cock n. Hahn; — v. (gun) spannen; — the ears die Ohren spitzen; — the head den Kopf hochtragen; -er n. Kampfhahnzüchter; -y adj. eingebildet

cockade n. Kokarde

cockatoo n. Kakadu

cockcrow n. Hahnenschrei; (fig.) Tagesanbruch

cockeyed adj. schielend; (sl.) schief; besoffen

cockfight(ing) n. Hahnenkampf

cockle n. (bot.) Kornrade; (zool.) Herzmuschel

cockney n. Cockney, waschechter Londoner; Londoner Dialekt

cockpit *n.* Hahnenkampfarena; (avi.) offene Kanzel; (naut.) Raumdeck; Schiffsverbandplatz

cockroach *n.* Küchenschabe, Kakerlake

cocksure *adj.* bombensicher, ganz sicher

cocktail *n.* Cocktail; Vorspeise

cocoa *n.* Kakao; Kakaopulver, Kakaotrank; Kokospalme

coconut *n.* Kokosnuss; — **milk** Kokosmilch; — **tree** Kokospalme

cocoon *n.* Kokon

cod *n.* Dorsch, Kabeljau

c.o.d. *abr.* per Nachnahme

coddle *v.* dämpfen; verhätscheln, verwöhnen

code *n.* (law) Gesetzbuch; (naut.) Signalbuch; (fig.) Chiffre, Geheimschrift; — *v.* chiffrieren

codeine *n.* Kodein; Methylmorphin

codfish *n.* Dorsch, Kabeljau

cod-liver oil *n.* Lebertran

coed *n.* Schülerin in einer Schule für Gemeinschaftserziehung

coeducation *n.* Gemeinschaftserziehung; **-al** *adj.* gemeinschaftlich erzogen

coefficient *n.* Koeffizient

coerce *v.* einschränken; anhalten, zwingen

coercion *n.* Einschränkung; Zwang

coexist *v.* koexistieren, gleichzeitig vorhanden sein; **-ence** *n.* Koexistenz, Gleichzeitigkeit

coffee *n.* Kaffee; — **bean** Kaffeebohne; — **break** Kaffeepause; — **color** Kaffeebraun; — **cup** Kaffeetasse; — **grounds** Kaffeesatz; — **plantation** Kaffeeplantage; — **shop** Kaffeehaus, Café

coffeepot *n.* Kaffeekanne

coffer *n.* Koffer, Schmuckkasten; Geldkasten

coffin *n.* Sarg

cog *n.* Radzahn; — **railway** Zahnradbahn

cognac *n.* Kognak

cognition *n.* Kenntnis, Kunde; Erkennen

cogwheel *n.* Zahnrad

cohabit *v.* zusammenleben

cohere *v.* zusammenhängen; übereinstimmen; **-nce** *n.* Zusammenhang, Übereinstimmung; **-nt** *adj.* kohärent, zusammenhängend; übereinstimmend

cohesion *n.* Kohäsion. gegenseitige Anziehungskraft

coiffure *n.* Coiffure, Haartracht

coil *n.* (elec.) Spule; (mech.) Rolle, Winde, Windung; — **of rope** Taurolle; — *v.* aufrollen, aufwickeln; — **up** zusammenrollen

coincide *v.* zusammentreffen, übereinstimmen; **-nce** *n.* Zusammentreffen, Übereinstimmung

coke *n.* Koks

colander *n.* Durchschlag

cold *n.* Kälte, Frost; (med.) Erkältung, Schnupfen; **catch** — sich erkälten; — *adj.* kalt, frostig; (fig.) gleichgültig; keusch; leidenschaftslos; teilnahmlos; — **cream** Cold-Cream, Hautcreme; — **cuts** Aufschnitt; — **feet** Angst; — **front** Kaltluftfront; — **snap** plötzlicher Kälteumschwung; — **sore** Schnupfenausschlag; — **storage** Kühlraumlagerung; **Kühlhaus**; — **war** kalter Krieg, — **wave** Kältewelle; **I am** — mir ist kalt, mich friert; **turn a** — **shoulder to** über die Achsel ansehen; **-ness** *f.* Kälte

cold-blooded *adj.* gefühllos, kaltblütig

coleslaw *n.* Krautsalat

colic *n.* Kolik

coliseum *n.* Kolosseum

collaborate *v.* zusammenarbeiten

collaborator *n.* Mitarbeiter

collapse *n.* Kollaps, Zusammenbruch; Einsturz; Verfall; — *v.* zusammenbrechen, einfallen

collapsible *adj.* zusammenklappbar; — **boat** Faltboot

collar *n.* Kragen; Halsband, Halsring; (horse) Kummet; (mech.) Ring, Reifen; — *v.* mit einem Kragen versehen; beim Kragen packen; (coll.) kontrollieren

collarbone *n.* Schlüsselbein

collateral *adj.* gleichlaufend, gleichzeitig; seitlich; indirekt; parallel; Seiten-, Neben-; — **note** Schuldschein mit zusätzlicher Deckung; — *n.* zusätzliche Deckung

colleague *n.* Kollege

collect *v.* (sich) sammeln, einsammeln; einkassieren; (taxes) erheben, eintreiben; **send** — unter Nachnahme senden; **-ed** *adj.* gesammelt, gefasst; **-ion** *n.* Sammlung; (taxes) Erhebung, Eintreibung; (mail) Leerung; **-ive** *adj.* gesammelt, vereinigt; kollektiv, gemeinschaftlich; Sammel-; **-ive bargaining** Tarifabkommen; **-ive noun** Kollektivum, Sammelwort; **-ive security** Kollektivsicherheit; **-or** *n.* Sammler; Kassierer, Kollektor; **-or** (elec.) Stromabnehmer; (taxes) Steuereinnehmer; **ticket -or** Fahrkartenkontrolleur; **-or of customs** Zolleinnehmer

college *n.* höhere Schule; Hochule, Universität; Kollegium, Fakultät

collegiate *adj.* kollegial; akademisch

collide *v.* zusammenstossen, kollidieren; (fig.) widerstreiten

collie *n.* schottischer Schäferhund; Collie

collision *n.* Zusammenstoss; — **course** (Rakete) Kollisionskurs; Stosskurs

colloquial *adj.* Umgangs-, Gesprächs-, familiär; **-ism** *n.* Ausdruck der Umgangssprache

collusion *n.* heimliches Einverständnis, Durchstecherei

Cologne *n.* Köln

colon *n.* (anat.) Dickdarm; (gram.) Doppelpunkt

colonel *n.* Oberst; **lieutenant** — Oberstleutnant

colonial *adj.* kolonial

colonist *n.* Kolonist

colonize *v.* kolonisieren

colony *n.* Kolonie

color *n.* Farbe, Färbung; Anstrich; (mil.) Fahne, Flagge; (fig.) Anschein; Eigenart; Ausdruck; Deckmantel, Vorwand; **local** — Lokalfarbe; **lose** — abfärben, verfärben, verblassen; **show one's true -s** sein wahres Gesicht zeigen, die Maske abwerfen; **under false**

–s unter falscher Flagge; **with flying –s** mit fliegenden Fahnen; — *v.* färben; anmalen, anstreichen; erröten; beschönigen; **–ation** *n.* Färbung, Kolorit; Farbengebung; **–ed** *adj.* bunt, farbig, gefärbt; dunkelhäutig; **–ed man** Neger; **–ful** *adj.* farbenreich, farbenprächtig; **–ing** *n.* Färbung, Kolorit, Farbengebung; Gesichtsfarbe; **–less** *adj.* farblos

color-blind *adj.* farbenblind; **–ness** Farbenblindheit

colossal *adj.* kolossal

colt *n.* Füllen, Fohlen; (fig.) Wildfang, Neuling

column *n.* (arch.) Säule; (math. and typ.) Rubrik, Spalte; (mil.) Kolonne; **spinal — Rückgrat; –ist** *n.* Autor für eine bestimmte Zeitungsrubrik

coma *n.* Schlafsucht; Koma

comb *n.* Kamm; Striegel; (bee) Wabe; **pocket — Taschenkamm; —** *v.* kämmen; striegeln; (mech.) hecheln, krempeln; (fig.) durchsuchen; **— one's hair** sich kämmen; **–er** *n.* Schaumwelle

combat *n.* Kampf, Gefecht; **single — Einzelkampf, Zweikampf; —** *v.* (be)kämpfen, bestreiten; **–ant** *n.* Kämpfer, Kriegsteilnehmer; (fig.) Verfechter; **–ant** *adj.* kämpfend, streitend; (mil.) aktiv

combination *n.* Kombination, Verbindung, Vereinigung; Bündnis; Zusammenstellung; (fig.) Komplott

combine *n.* Geschäftsverband; Kartell; (agr.) Mähdrescher; — *v.* (sich) verbinden, (sich) vereinigen

combustion *n.* Verbrennung, Entzündung; **spontaneous — Selbstentzündung; — chamber** *n.* Brennkammer; **— engine** Brennkraftmotor

come *v.* kommen; fallen; **— about** sich ereignen, zustande kommen; **— across** stossen auf, zufällig treffen; **— after** (nach)folgen; abholen kommen; **— again** wiederkommen; **— along** mitkommen; gehen; **— apart** entzwei (*or* in Stücke) gehen; **— around** herumkommen, sich bekehren; **— back** zurückkommen; **— before** vortreten; vorgehen; **— between** dazwischentreten; **— by** vorbeikommen; zufällig erlangen; **— down** herunterkommen; (price) herabsetzen; **— down with** sich ins Bett legen mit; **— forward** vortreten; **— from** herkommen, herstammen; **— home (to)** heimkommen, nahegehen; **— in** hereinkommen, eintreten; **— in!** herein!; **— near** nahekommen; beinahe; **— now!** komm doch!; **— of** entstehen; **— off** abkommen, loskommen; **— on** herankommen; wachsen; **— on!** nur zu!; **— out** herauskommen; sich zeigen; sich erklären; **— over** herüberkommen; **— to** wieder zu sich kommen; kommen auf (*or* zu); **— to nothing** zu Wasser werden; **— to pass** geschehen; **— true** in Erfüllung gehen; **— under** fallen unter; **— up** (her)aufkommen; aufgehen; **— up to** einholen; entsprechen; **— upon** stossen auf; **–r** *n.* Kommende, Ankom-

mende; (fig.) Bewerber

comeback *n.* Rückkehr, Wiederkehr; Wiederherstellung; (theat.) Wiederauftreten; (coll.) Erwiderung

comedian *n.* Komiker; Komödiant

comedy *n.* Komödie, Lustspiel

comet *n.* Komet

comfort *n.* Bequemlichkeit, Behaglichkeit; Trost; — *v.* trösten, erquicken; **–able** *n.* Steppdecke; **–able** *adj.* bequem; **–er** *n.* Steppdecke; Tröster; **–ing** *adj.* tröstend, tröstlich, ermutigend

comic *adj.* komisch; **— opera** komische Oper; **—** *n.* Komiker; Karikatur(enreihe); **–al** *adj.* komisch

comma *n.* Komma, Beistrich

command *n.* Befehl, Gebot; (mil.) Kommando; (fig.) Herrschaft; **be in — befehlen, gebieten; by your — auf Ihren Befehl; have a — of** beherrschen; **—** *adj.* **– performance** Auftreten von Künstlern bei Hof; — *v.* befehlen, kommandieren; beherrschen; **–ant** *n.* Kommandant; **–eer** *v.* (mil.) zum Militärdienst zwingen; requirieren; in Beschlag nehmen; **–er** *n.* (mil.) Kommandeur, Befehlshaber; (naut.) Kapitän; **–er in chief** Oberbefehlshaber; **lieutenant –er** Kapitänleutnant, Fregattenleutnant; **–ing** *adj.* gebietend, befehlshaberisch, beherrschend; (mil.) kommandierend; **–ment** *n.* (bibl.) Gebot; (fig.) Vorschrift; **–o** *n.* Sturmtrupp, Stosstrupp; Sturmsoldat

commemorate *v.* gedenken, das Andenken feiern, erinnern an

commemoration *n.* Gedächtnisfeier; Erinnerung

commence *v.* anfangen, beginnen; **–ment** *n.* Anfang, Beginn; (educ.) Promotion

commend *v.* loben, rühmen; empfehlen; **–able** *adj.* lobenswert, empfehlenswert; **–ation** *n.* Lob, Empfehlung

comment *n.* Bemerkung, Anmerkung, Erläuterung; **—** *v.* kommentieren, erläutern, sich auslassen über; **–ary** *n.* Kommentar, Abhandlung; (fig.) Denkwürdigkeit; **–ator** *n.* Kommentator, Erklärer

commerce *n.* Handel, Verkehr

commercial *adj.* kaufmännisch, kommerziell; Handels-, Geschäfts-; **— plane** Verkehrsflugzeug; **—** *n.* Werbeprogramm; (rad.) Werbefunk; **–ize** *v.* in den Handel bringen

commiserate *v.* bedauern, bemitleiden

commissary *n.* Kommissar; Ausrüstungsgeschäft

commission *n.* Kommission, Auftrag, Vollmacht; (com.) Provision; (mil. and naut.) Offizierspatent; **in —** in Dienst gestellt; **on —** auf (*or* unter) Provision; **out of —** ausser Dienst; — *v.* beauftragen, bevollmächtigen; abordnen, ernennen; **–er** *n.* Kommissar, Beauftragte

commit *v.* übergeben, anvertrauen; (law) begehen, verüben; überweisen; **— oneself** sich binden; (coll.) sich eine Blösse geben; **— to memory** sich einprägen; **— to prison** ins Gefängnis stecken; —

to writing zu Papier bringen; –ment n. Anvertrauen; Überweisung; Verpflichtung; Begehung; (law) Verhaftungsbefehl

committee n. Ausschuss, Komitee, Kommission

commode n. Kommode

commodity n. Artikel, Ware

common adj. gemein, gemeinsam, allgemein, alltäglich, gewöhnlich; häufig, üblich; bürgerlich; niedrig; — carrier öffentliches Verkehrsunternehmen; — law Gewohnheitsrecht; — people gewöhnliches Volk; — sense gesunder Menschenverstand; — stock Stammaktie, Aktienstock; have in — gemein haben; in — gemeinsam, gemeinschaftlich; –er n. Bürger; Gemeine

commonplace adj. abgedroschen; gewöhnlich; — n. Gemeinplatz

commonwealth n. bürgerliche Gesellschaft (or Verfassung); Gemeinwesen; (pol.) Staat, Staatenverbindung

commotion n. Aufruhr, Tumult; Bewegung

communal adj. kommunal, Gemeinde-

commune n. Kommune; — v. sich besprechen (or unterhalten); (rel.) kommunizieren

communicant n. Kommunikant

communicate v. mitteilen; benachrichtigen; teilen; (rel.) das Abendmahl nehmen

communication n. Mitteilung, Nachricht, Verbindung; (fig.) Gedankenaustausch; lines of — Verbindungswege

communion n. Gemeinschaft; (rel.) Kommunion, Abendmahl; take — das Abendmahl empfangen

communism n. Kommunismus

communist n. Kommunist

community n. Gemeinde; Gemeinschaft; — adj. kommunal; — center öffentlicher Versammlungsort; — chest gemeinschaftlicher Wohltätigkeitsfonds

commutation n. Veränderung, Vertauschung; (law) Strafmilderung; — ticket Zeitkarte, Monatskarte, Wochenkarte

commutator n. Stromwender, Umschalter

commute v. verändern, ablösen; umwandeln; (rail.) regelmässig auf einer Strecke verkehren; (law) die Strafe mildern; –r n. Zeitkarteninhaber

compact n. Vertrag, Pakt; Puderdose; — adj. bündig, kompakt; dicht, fest; kurz; (auto.) n. Kleinwagen; — v. verbinden, verdichten; –ness n. Dichtigkeit, Festigkeit; (fig.) Gedrungenheit

companion n. Genosse, Gefährte, Kompagnon; Gegenstück, Seitenstück; –able adj. gesellig; –ship n. Gesellschaft; Genossenschaft

companionate marriage n. Kameradschaftsehe

company n. Gesellschaft, Firma; (mil.) Kompagnie; (ty.) Umgang, Verkehr; — union Betriebsgewerkschaft; keep — Gesellschaft leisten; keep — with vertraulich verkehren mit; part —

auseinandergehen

comparable adj. vergleichbar

comparative n. Komparativ; — adj. vergleichend; verhältnismässig; relativ; — degree Komparativform

compare v. (sich) vergleichen, gleichstellen; (gram.) steigern; beyond — unvergleichlich

comparison n. Vergleich, Vergleichung; Steigerung; Gleichnis, Verhältnis; beyond — ohne Frage; by way of — vergleichsweise; in — with im Vergleich mit

compartment n. Abteilung, Fach; (rail.) Abteil; smoking — Raucherabteil

compass n. Kompass; Umfang, Umkreis; Bereich, Bezirk; (mech.) Zirkel; (mus.) Stimmumfang; — card Windrose; — v. umgeben; umgehen; vollenden; anstiften

compassion n. Erbarmen, Mitleid

compassionate adj. mitleidig

compatibility n. Verträglichkeit, Vereinbarkeit

compatible adj. verträglich, schicklich

compel v. zwingen, nötigen

compendium n. Abriss, Auszug; Handbuch

compensate v. kompensieren; ausgleichen, ersetzen; entschädigen

compensation n. Ersatz, Vergütung; Entschädigung; (com.) Lohn

compete v. konkurrieren; mitbewerben, wetteifern; sich messen

competent adj. kompetent, fähig; fachkundig, zuständig; berechtigt

competition n. Konkurrenz; Wettbewerb

competitive adj. konkurrenzfähig, wettbewerbsfähig; Konkurrenz-

competitor n. Konkurrent, Mitbewerber

compile v. zusammentragen; sammeln

complacency n. Behagen, Wohlgefallen; Selbstzufriedenheit, Selbstgefälligkeit

complain v. klagen; sich beklagen (or beschweren); (law) Klage führen; –ant n. Kläger; –t n. Klage; (med.) Krankheit, Übel

complement n. Ergänzung, Komplement; Gesamtzahl, Vollständigkeit; (gram.) Prädikatsnomen; –ary adj. ergänzend, Ergänzungs-

complete adj. ganz, vollständig, komplett; — v. vervollständigen, vollenden, komplettieren; (fig.) erfüllen

completion n. Ergänzung; Vollendung, Erfüllung

complex n. Komplex; inferiority — Minderwertigkeitskomplex; — adj. kompliziert, verwickelt; zusammengesetzt; –ity n. Verwickelung, Schwierigkeit

complexion n. Gesichtsfarbe, Hautfarbe, Teint; (fig.) Aussehen, Gemütsart; Natur, Temperament

compliance n. Einwilligung, Willfährigkeit; in — with gemäss

complicate v. komplizieren, verwickeln, –d adj. kompliziert, verwickelt

complication n. Verwicklung, Komplikation

complicity n. Mitschuld

compliment n. Kompliment, Artigkeit, Schmeichelei; — v. komplimentieren; beglückwünschen; -ary adj. artig, höflich; -ary copy Freiexemplar

comply v. einwilligen, nachgeben, sich fügen

component n. Komponente, Bestandteil; — adj. einen Teil ausmachend, Bestand-

compose v. zusammensetzen, zusammenstellen; (art.) entwerfen; (lit.) verfassen, dichten; (mus.) komponieren; (typ.) setzen; (fig.) beruhigen, beilegen, schlichten; — oneself sich beruhigen (or fassen); -d adj. gefasst, ruhig; be -d of bestehen aus; -r n. (lit.) Dichter, Verfasser; (mus.) Komponist

composing room n. Setzersaal

composition n. Zusammensetzung, Zusammenstellung; (art) Anordnung, Entwurf, Stil; (chem.) Mischung, Verbindung; (lit.) Aufsatz; (mus.) Komposition; (typ.) Schriftsatz, Setzkunst

compositor n. Schriftsetzer

composure n. Gemütsruhe, Fassung

compound n. Gemisch, Masse, Zusammensetzung; (chem.) Verbindung; (gram.) Kompositum, zusammengesetztes Wort; (fig.) Umzäunung; — v. zusammensetzen; mengen, mischen; ausgleichen, tilgen; ablösen, beilegen; sich vertragen (or vergleichen); — adj. zusammengesetzt; — interest Zinseszins

comprehend v. einschliessen, enthalten; (fig.) verstehen, begreifen

comprehension n. Inbegriff, Umfang, Umfassung; Einbeziehung; (fig.) Begriffsvermögen, Fassungskraft

comprehensive adj. umfassend; bündig, kurz; (fig.) verständig

compress n. Kompresse, Umschlag; — v. zusammendrücken, zusammenpressen; (fig.) kondensieren; -ed adj. -ed air Druckluft, Pressluft; -ion n. Zusammendrücken; Druck; -or n. Kompressor

comprise v. einschliessen, in sich fassen, bestehen aus, enthalten

compromise n. Kompromiss; — v. einen Kompromiss schliessen; sich vergleichen; kompromittieren, blossstellen

comptometer n. Rechenmaschine, Komptometer

comptroller n. Kontrolleur

compulsion n. Nötigung, Zwang

compulsory adj. zwangsweise, zwingend; Zwangs-

computation n. Rechnen, Rechnung, Berechnung; Überschlag

compute v. berechnen, rechnen; -er n. Kalkulator

comrade n. Kamerad, Gefährte, Genosse

con adv. dagegen, wider; pro and — für und wider; — n. Kontra, Gegengründe; the pros and -s Gründe und Gegengründe; — v. prüfen

concave adj. konkav

conceal v. verbergen, verstecken, verhehlen; verheimlichen, verschweigen;

-ment n. Verborgenheit, Versteck; (fig.) Geheimhaltung, Verheimlichung

concede v. bewilligen, einräumen, zugestehen; (fig.) anerkennen, zugeben

conceit n. Einbildung; Einfall; günstige Meinung; Eitelkeit; -ed adj. eingebildet, dünkelhaft

conceivable adj. begreiflich, denkbar

conceive v. sich denken (or vorstellen); begreifen, erfassen; ausdrücken, fassen; (med.) empfangen; (zool.) trächtig werden

concentrate v. (sich) konzentrieren

concentration n. Konzentration, Konzentrierung; — adj. — camp Konzentrationslager

concept n. Konzept; Begriff; -ion n. Konzeption, Vorstellung, Begriff; Entwurf; Empfängnis; Immaculate Conception Unbefleckte Empfängnis

concern n. Firma, Geschäft; Konzern; Sache, Angelegenheit; Anteil, Interesse; Bedeutung, Beziehung; Sorge, Kummer, Teilnahme; — v. angehen, betreffen, interessieren; -ed adj. beteiligt, interessiert; betreten, betroffen; besorgt; as far as he's -ed was ihn betrifft; be -ed about besorgt sein um; be -ed with zu tun haben mit; the parties -ed die Beteiligten; -ing prep. in Bezug auf, hinsichtlich, betreffs

concert n. (mus.) Konzert; (fig.) Einvernehmen, Verabredung; -ed adj. gemeinschaftlich

concertina n. Konzertina

concertmaster n. Konzertmeister, erster Geiger

concession n. Konzession; Zugeständnis; -aire n. Konzessionierte

conciliate v. aussöhnen, versöhnen; gewinnen

conciliation n. Versöhnung, Aussöhnung

conclave n. Konklave; geheime Versammlung

conclude v. (be)schliessen, entscheiden

conclusion n. Schluss, Beschluss; Folgerung; in — schliesslich, zum Schluss

conclusive adj. entscheidend, abschliessend, endgültig; — evidence schlagender Beweis

concoct v. zubereiten; (fig.) aussinnen, planen; -ion n. Zubereitung; Gebräu; (fig.) Anstiftung, Ausbrütung

concomitant adj. begleitend, mitwirkend, mitverbunden; — n. Begleitumstand

concord n. Einigkeit, Einklang, Eintracht; Übereinstimmung, Harmonie

concrete n. Beton; Steinmörtel; reinforced — Eisenbeton; — adj. konkret; gegenständlich, greifbar; dicht, fest; wesentlich; — mixer Betonmischmaschine

concubine n. Konkubine

concussion n. Erschütterung

condemn v. missbilligen; verdammen, verwerfen; (law) verurteilen; -ation n. Missbilligung; Verdammung, Verwerfung; (law) Verurteilung

condensation n. Kondensierung, Verdichtung; (fig.) Abkürzung

condense v. kondensieren, eindicken, verdichten; (fig.) (ab)kürzen; **-d** adj. **-d milk** kondensierte Milch, Büchsenmilch; **-r** n. Kondensator

condescension n. Herablassung

condiment n. Würze

condition n. Bedingung; Beschaffenheit, Rang, Stand; Umstände, Verhältnisse; **on —** that unter der Bedingung, dass; **on no —** unter keinen Umständen; **-al** adj. bedingt; abhängig; eingeschränkt; Bedingungs-; **-al clause** Bedingungssatz; **-al** n. Konditional, Bedingungsform; **-ed** adj. bedingt, beschaffen, geartet; **-ed reflex** konditioneller Reflex

condole v. kondolieren, Beileid bezeigen; **-nce** n. Kondolenz, Beileid

condone v. verzeihen, nachsehen

conducive adj. dienlich, förderlich, beitragend

conduct n. Führung; (com.) Verwaltung; (elec.) Leitung; (fig.) Benehmen, Betragen; **safe —** freies (or sicheres) Geleit; **—** v. führen; (elec.) leiten; (mil.) bedecken, geleiten; (mus.) dirigieren; **— oneself** sich benehmen (or betragen); **-ion** n. Leitung, Leitungsfähigkeit; **-or** n. Anführer; (mus.) Dirigent, Kapellmeister; (phy.) Leiter, Konduktor; Blitzableiter; (rail.) Schaffner, Kondukteur

conduit n. Leitung; Röhre; Abzug, Kanal

cone n. Kegel; (bot.) Zapfen; **ice-cream —** Eiskremtüte

confab n. Geplauder, Gespräch

confection n. Mischung, Zubereitung; Konfekt; (fashion) Konfektionsartikel; **-ery** n. Konfekt; Konditorei

confederacy n. Bund, Bündnis; Bundesgenossenschaft; Konföderation

confederate n. Verbündete, Bundesgenosse; Mitschuldige; **—** adj. verbündet; **—** v. sich verbünden

confederation n. Bund, Bündnis; Staatenbund

confer v. sich besprechen, konferieren; erteilen, übertragen, verleihen; **-ence** n. Beratung, Besprechung, Konferenz, Tagung

confess v. bekennen, einräumen, (zu)gestehen; (eccl.) beichten; **-ion** n. Bekenntnis, Geständnis; (eccl.) Beichte; **-ional** n. Beichtstuhl; **-ional** adj. konfessionell; **-or** n. Beichtvater

confetti n. Konfetti, Papierschnitzel

confidant n. Mitwisser, Vertraute

confide v. anvertrauen; vertrauen, sich verlassen; **-nce** n. Vertrauen, Zuversicht; Eröffnung; **in strictest -nce** im vollsten Vertrauen; **-nce man** Bauernfänger; **-nt** adj. vertrauend, vertrauensvoll, zuversichtlich; **-ntial** adj. vertraulich, vertraut; geheim; **speaking -ntially** unter uns gesagt

confiding adj. vertrauensselig, vertrauend

confine n. Grenze, Schranke; **—** v. (be)grenzen, beschränken, einengen, einschliessen; **be -ed** niederkommen, in den Wochen liegen; **be -ed to bed** das Bett hüten müssen; **-ment** n.

Beschränkung; (law) Gefangenschaf Haft; (med.) Bettlägerigkeit; Entbir dung, Niederkunft

confirm v. bestätigen, bekräftigen, bestä ken; (eccl.) konfirmieren, einsegne firme(l)n; **-ation** n. Bestätigung, Be kräftigung, Bestärkung; (eccl.) Konfir mation, Einsegnung, Firm(el)ung; **-e** adj. bestimmt, fest; (med.) chronisc unheilbar; (fig.) unverbesserlich

confiscate v. beschlagnahmen, einziehe konfiszieren

conflagration n. Brand, Feuersbrunst

conflict n. Zusammenstoss; Kampf Konflikt, Streit; **—** v. sich widerspre chen, widerstreiten; **-ing** adj. **-in views** entgegengesetzte Ansichten

conform v. anpassen, sich fügen (or rich ten); **-ation** n. Bildung, Gestalt, Ge staltung; Bau, Zusammensetzung, Ar passung; **-ity** n. Übereinstimmung Ähnlichkeit; Fügsamkeit

confound v. verwirren, verwechseln; **him!** der Teufel soll ihn holen! **—** i verdammt! **-ed** adj. verflucht, ve wünscht; verwirrt; scheusslich

confront v. konfrontieren, gegenüberste len; entgegentreten

confuse v. verwirren, verwechseln; b stürzen, aus der Fassung bringen; **-** adj. verwirrt, verworren, unklar, ko fus; bestürzt

confusion n. Verwirrung, Konfusion; Ve wechslung; Durcheinander; Bestürzun

congeal n. erstarren; gefrieren; gerinne

congenial adj. geistesverwandt, kong nial; (fig.) sympathisch

congenital adj. angeboren

conger eel n. Seeaal

congested adj. angesammelt, überfüllt

congestion n. Anhäufung, Ansammlun (med.) Kongestion, Blutandrang

conglomeration n. Konglomerat, Anhä fung, Ansammlung

congratulate v. gratulieren, beglückwü schen

congratulation n. Glückwunsch, Gratul tion

congregate v. (sich) versammeln, zusa menkommen

congregation n. Gemeinde, Versammlun **-al** adj. Gemeinde-, Kirchengemeind unabhängig

congress n. Kongress; **-ional** adj. Kon ress-

congressman n. Kongressabgeordnete

congruity n. Kongruenz, Folgerichtigkei Übereinstimmung

conic(al) adj. konisch, kegelförmig; **section** Kegelschnitt

conjecture n. Vermutung, Konjektu Mutmassung; **—** v. mutmassen, ve muten

conjugal adj. ehelich, Ehe-

conjugation n. Konjugation, Abwandlu

conjunction n. Bindewort, Verbindu

conjunctive n. Konjunktiv, Möglichkei form; **—** adj. konjunktivisch; abhängi bedingt; verbindend

conjure v. beschwören, behexen, beza

bern; **–r** n. Beschwörer, Hexenmeister, Zauberer

connect v. (sich) verbinden, verknüpfen; zusammenfügen; anschliessen; (elec. and mech.) koppeln, schalten; **–ed** adj. verbunden, verknüpft; zusammengefügt, zusammenhängend; (fig.) verwandt; **–ing** adj. **–ing rod** n. Pleuelstange; **–ion** n. Beziehung; Zusammenhang, Verbindung; (elec.) Schaltung; (rail.) Anschluss

conniption (fit) n. Wahnsinnsanfall

connivance n. Duldung, Nachsicht; (law) stillschweigendes Einverständnis

connoisseur n. Kenner, Kunstliebhaber

conquer v. besiegen, bezwingen, erobern; erringen, überwinden; **–or** n. Sieger, Eroberer

conquest n. Eroberung, Sieg, Besitzergreifung

conscience n. Gewissen; (fig.) Bewusstsein, Vernunft

conscience-stricken adj. von Gewissensbissen gepeinigt

conscientious adj. gewissenhaft; **— objector** Kriegsdienstverweigerer; **–ness** n. Gewissenhaftigkeit

conscious adj. bei Bewusstsein; bewusst; (fig.) kundig, unterrichtet; **–ness** n. Bewusstsein; (fig.) Kenntnis

conscript n. ausgehobener Rekrut, Dienstpflichtige(xix); **—** v. zwangsweise ausheben

conscription n. Zwangsaushebung, allgemeine Wehrpflicht

consecrate v. einsegnen, heiligen; weihen, widmen

consecration n. Einsegnung, Heiligung; Weihe, Weihung, Widmung

consecutive adj. folgend, konsekutiv, folgerichtig; aufeinanderfolgend; **— clause** Folgesatz; **— narrative** zusammenhängende Erzählung

consensus n. Übereinstimmung, Zustimmung

consent n. Zustimmung, Einwilligung, Genehmigung; **—** v. zustimmen, einwilligen, genehmigen

consequence n. Konsequenz; Folge, Ergebnis; Wirkung, Einfluss, Bedeutung; (phil.) Schlusssatz; **as a** (oder in) **—** folglich, infolgedessen; **that's of no —** das ist ohne Bedeutung

consequential adj. konsequent, folgerichtig; (er)folgend, notwendig; (fig.) eingebildet, hochtrabend

consequently adv. folglich, infolgedessen, daher

conservation n. Erhaltung, Konservierung, Aufbewahrung

conservative n. Konservative; **—** adj. konservativ; (fig.) vorsichtig

conservatory n. Treibhaus, Gewächshaus; (mus.) Konservatorium

consider v. betrachten; bedenken, erwägen, überlegen; berücksichtigen; halten für; **–able** adj. beträchtlich, ansehnlich; **–ate** adj. aufmerksam; bedächtig, rücksichtsvoll; **–ation** n. Betrachtung, Erwägung, Überlegung; Bedeutung,

Wichtigkeit; Rücksicht; Entschädigung; Vergütung; (law) Gegenleistung; **be under –ation** erwogen werden, noch nicht entschieden sein; **take into –ation** in Erwägung ziehen, berücksichtigen; **–ing** prep. in Anbetracht

consign v. überweisen, übergeben, übersenden, übertragen; anvertrauen; richten an; hinterlegen; **–ee** n. Warenempfänger; **–ment** n. Übersendung, Versendung, Zustellung; **on –ment** in Kommission

consist v. bestehen; **–ency** n. Dichtigkeit, Festigkeit; Folgerichtigkeit, Übereinstimmung; **–ent** adj. konsequent; übereinstimmend

consolation n. Trost, Tröstung

console n. Konsole; (arch.) Kragstein; **—** v. trösten

consolidate v. konsolidieren, festigen; (fig.) vereinigen, zusammenziehen

consolidation n. Konsolidierung; Festigung, Verdichtung; Vereinigung

consoling adj. tröstend, trostreich

consommé n. Consommé, klare Fleischbrühe

consort n. Konsorte, Gemahl; **Prince —** Prinzgemahl; **—** v. sich gesellen; (fig.) übereinstimmen

conspicuous adj. auffallend, sichtbar; deutlich; hervorragend; **be —** hervorragen

conspiracy n. Verschwörung, Konspiration; (fig.) Zusammenwirken

conspirator n. Verschworene, Verschwörer

conspire v. sich verschwören, konspirieren; (fig.) zusammenwirken

constable n. Polizist, Schutzmann; Konstabel

constabulary n. Polizei, Schutzmannschaft

Constance, Lake of n. Bodensee

constancy n. Beständigkeit, Beharrlichkeit; Bestand, Dauer; Standhaftigkeit; Treue

constant adj. beständig, beharrlich; unverändert, ständig; treu; fortwährend, dauernd

constellation n. Konstellation, Sternbild

consternation n. Konsternation, Bestürzung

constipate v. verstopfen

constipation n. Verstopfung

constituency n. Wählerschaft; Wahlbezirk

constituent n. Wähler; Bestandteil; **—** adj. konstituierend, wählend; verfassunggebend; Grund-, Bestand-

constitute v. ausmachen; konstituieren, errichten; bestellen, ernennen; beauftragen, einsetzen, bevollmächtigen; festsetzen, herbeiführen

constitution n. Verfassung, Konstitution; Beschaffenheit, Bildung; Anordnung, Festsetzung; Körperbau, Körperbeschaffenehit; **–al** n. Verdauungsspaziergang; **–al** adj. konstitutionell, verfassungsgemäss; (fig.) begründet; natürlich, temperamentsgemäss; **–ality** n. Verfassungsmässigkeit

constrain v. zwingen, nötigen; (fig.) ein-

sperren, fesseln; –t n. Zwang, Nötigung;
Befangenheit; Haft, Einschränkung;
under –t unter Zwang

construct v. bauen, aufstellen, errichten,
konstruieren; zusammenfügen, zusammensetzen; entwerfen; bilden, erdenken, gestalten; **–ion** n. Konstruktion,
Bau, Aufführung, Errichtung; Zusammenfügung, Zusammensetzung; (arch.)
Bauart, Bauwerk; (gram.) Satzbau;
(fig.) Auslegung, Bildung, Gestaltung;
–ive adj. konstruktiv, bildend, ordnend;
aufbauend; **–or** n. Konstrukteur, Erbauer; Erfinder, Urheber

construe v. konstruieren; (fig.) auslegen,
deuten

consul n. Konsul; **–ar** adj. konsularisch;
–ate n. Konsulat

consult v. sich beraten, konsultieren; um
Rat fragen; (fig.) nachschlagen; **–ant** n.
Berater; **–ation** n. Konsultation; Beratung

consume v. verbrauchen, konsumieren; **–r**
n. Abnehmer Konsument, Verbraucher;
–rs' goods Verbrauchsgüter

consummation n. Vollendung, Vollziehung; (fig.) Ende

consumption n. Verbrauch; (med.) Auszehrung, Schwindsucht

consumptive adj. schwindsüchtig, verzehrend

contact n. Berührung, Kontakt, Verbindung; (elec.) Stromschluss; (mil.)
Fühlung; **– lens** Kontaktlinse; **– v.**
sich in Verbindung setzen mit, in
Verbindung treten mit

contagion n. Ansteckung; Seuche

contagious adj. ansteckend

contain v. enthalten, fassen; bestehen aus;
(fig.) (sich) zurückhalten; **–er** n. Behälter

contaminate v. verunreinigen, beflecken,
vergiften

contemplate v. beabsichtigen; beschauen,
betrachten; nachsinnen

contemplation n. Betrachtung; Nachdenken, Nachsinnen; Vorhaben

contemplative adj. nachdenklich

contemporary adj. gleichzeitig, zeitgenössisch; **– n.** Zeitgenosse

contempt n. Verachtung, Geringschätzung; **– of court** Missachtung des
Gerichtshofes; **–ible** adj. unwürdig,
verachtenswert; verächtlich; **–uous** adj.
verächtlich, geringschätzig; hochmütig

contend v. kämpfen, ringen, streiten; sich
bewerben; (fig.) behaupten, streben

content n. Zufriedenheit; Gehalt; pl.
Inhalt; **table of –s** Inhaltsverzeichnis;
to one's heart's – zur völligen Zufriedenheit; **– adj.** zufrieden; geneigt,
willens; **– v.** befriedigen, zufriedenstellen; **–ed** adj. genügsam, zufrieden;
–ment n. Genügsamkeit, Zufriedenheit

contention n. Streit, Hader; Beweisführung, Streitpunkt; **bone of –ion** Zankapfel

contentious adj. streitsüchtig, zänkisch

contest n. Kampf, Streit; Wettbewerb;
– v. bestreiten, anfechten; streben;

–ant n. Kampfteilnehmer; Wettkämpfer; Mitbewerber; (pol.) Wahlkandidat

context n. Zusammenhang

contiguous adj. anstossend, angrenzend

continence n. Enthaltsamkeit, Mässigung; (fig.) Keuschheit

continent n. Kontinent; **— adj.** enthaltsam, mässig; (fig.) keusch; **–al** adj.
kontinental

contingency n. Zufall, Zufälligkeit; (fig.)
Möglichkeit

contingent n. Zufall; Anteil, Beitrag;
(mil.) Kontingent, Truppenteil; **— adj.**
zufällig; (fig.) möglich; **— on** abhängig
von

continual adj. beständig, fortwährend;
unaufhörlich, ununterbrochen; (coll.)
ewig

continuance n. Fortdauer; (law) Aufschub

continuation n. Fortsetzung, Weiterführung, Prolongation, Übertragung

continue v. dauern, fortsetzen, weiterführen; beibehalten; behalten, erhalten;
verlängern; anhalten, beharren; fortfahren; **to be –d** Fortsetzung folgt

continuity n. Stetigkeit, Fortdauer; (film)
Drehbuch; (rad.) Manuskript

continuous adj. fortdauernd, fortlaufend;
stetig, ununterbrochen

contort v. krümmen, winden; (fig.) verdrehen, verzerren; **–ion** n. Drehung, Krümmung; **–ionist** n. Schlangenmensch

contour n. Kontur, Umriss

contraband n. Konterbande, Schmuggelware, Schmuggel(ei); **— adj.** gesetzlich
verboten

contract n. Vertrag, Kontrakt; **— v.**
einen Vertrag schliessen; sich vertraglich verpflichten; kontrahieren; (sich)
zusammenziehen; (fig.) sich aneignen;
(gram. and math.) abkürzen, verkürzen; **— a debt** Schulden machen; **— a
disease** sich eine Krankheit zuziehen;
–ion n. Zusammenziehung; (gram. and
math.) Abkürzung, Verkürzung; (med.)
Schrumpfung; **–or** n. Unternehmer,

contradict v. widersprechen; **–ion** n.
Widerspruch; **–ory** adj. widersprechend

contrail n. (avi.) Kondensstreifen

contralto n. Kontra-Alt; Kontra-Altistin

contraption n. (coll.) Maschine, Vorrichtung

contrary adj. konträr, entgegengesetzt,
verkehrt; ungünstig, widrig, widerspenstig; **— to gegen, zuwider; — n.**
Gegenteil, Gegensatz; **on the —** im
Gegenteil; **to the —** dagegen

contrast n. Gegensatz; Kontrast; **— v.**
vergleichen, gegenüberstellen; kontrastieren; **— with** sich abheben von,
abstechen von

contribute v. beitragen, beisteuern, spenden; mitwirken

contribution n. Beitrag, Spende, Kontribution; Mitwirkung

contributor n. Beisteuernde, Beitragende,
Mitwirkende; Mitarbeiter

contrite adj. reuevoll; bereuend, zerknirscht

contrition n. Reue, Zerknirschung

contrivance n. Erfindung; Vorrichtung; Entwurf; Kniff; (fig.) Erfindungsgabe, Findigkeit

contrive v. erfinden, ersinnen; entwerfen; ausdenken; veranstalten

control n. Kontrolle, Aufsicht, Prüfung, Überwachung; Herrschaft, Beherrschung; Einhalt, Hemmung; pl. Steuerung; **under —** in der Gewalt; **— tower** Kontrollturm; **— v.** kontrollieren; beaufsichtigen, prüfen, überwachen; beschränken, einschränken; (avi. and mech.) lenken, steuern; **— oneself** sich beherrschen; **-er** n. Kontrolleur, Leiter, Aufseher, Überwacher; Regulator

controversial adj. strittig, Streit-

controversy n. Streit, Kontroverse

conundrum n. Scherzrätsel; kaum lösbare Frage

convalesce v. genesen; **-nce** n. Genesung, Konvaleszenz; **-nt** adj. genesend; Genesungs-

convene v. (sich) versammeln, zusammenberufen

convenience n. Bequemlichkeit; Angemessenheit, Schicklichkeit; Komfort; **at your earliest —** baldmöglichst, umgehend; **at your own —** ganz nach Ihrem Belieben

convenient adj. bequem; passend, schicklich; gelegen, günstig

convent n. Kloster, Konvent

convention n. Versammlung, Zusammenkunft, Tagung; Übereinkunft, Vertrag; (fig.) Konvention, Brauch, Herkommen; **-al** adj. konventionell; **-ality** n. Haften am Hergebrachten, Konventionalismus

conversation n. Gespräch, Unterhaltung, Konversation; **-alist** n. gewandter Gesellschafter, guter Unterhalter

converse n. Umkehrung, Gegensatz; **— adj.** umgekehrt, entgegengesetzt; **— v.** reden, sich unterhalten

conversion n. Umtausch, Umwandlung; (pol.) Meinungswechsel, Übertritt; (rel.) Bekehrung

convert n. Bekehrte, Konvertit; **— v.** umwandeln, umkehren, umstellen; (rel.) bekehren; **-er** n. (elec.) Umformer; (rel.) Bekehrer; **-ibility** n. Umwandelbarkeit; (rel.) Bekehrbarkeit; **-ible** n. Kabriolett; **-ible** adj. umwandelbar, umsetzbar; vertauschbar

convex adj. konvex; erhaben, gewölbt

convict n. Sträfling, Zuchthäusler; **— v.** überführen; (law) schuldig erklären; **-ion** n. Überzeugung; (law) Überführung, Schuldigerklärung

convince v. überzeugen

convincing adj. überzeugend; **— proof** schlagender Beweis

convivial adj. festlich; gesellig; gastlich; (fig.) lustig; Fest-

convocation n. Einberufung; Versammlung

convoy n. (mil.) Bedeckung, Eskorte; (naut.) Geleitzug

convulse v. in Zuckungen versetzen; (fig.)

erschüttern; **be –d with laughter** sich vor Lachen ausschütten

convulsion n. Krampf, Zuckung

cook n. Koch, Köchin; **— v.** Kochen; **— a person's goose** jemand den Garaus machen; **— up** ausdenken; **-ery** n. Kochkunst; **-ing** n. Kochen; Küche; **-ing** adj. kochend; **-ing utensils** Küchengeräte

cookbook n. Kochbuch

cookie, cooky n. Kleingebäck, Keks

cool n. Frische, Kühle; **— adj.** kühl, frisch; kalt, gleichgültig, teilnahmslos; gelassen; (coll.) unverfroren; bar, rund; **keep —** ruhig bleiben; **— v.** (ab)kühlen, sich erfrischen; **— off** abkühlen; (sich) beruhigen; **— one's heels** lange warten; **-er** n. Kühler; Kühlmittel; (sl.) Gefängnis; **-ness** n. Kühle; (fig.) Kälte, Kaltblütigkeit; Gleichgültigkeit, Lauheit; (coll.) Frechheit

cool-headed adj. besonnen

coolie n. Kuli

coon n. Waschbär

coop n. Hühnerkäfig; (sl.) Gefängnis; **fly the —** ausbrechen; **— v. — up** einsperren

cooper n. Böttcher, Fassbinder; Küfer; **-age** n. Böttcherei, Fassbinderei

co-op. n. Kooperative, Genossenschaft; Konsumgeschäft; Genossenschaftsmiethaus; **-erate** v. mitwirken, zusammenwirken; **-eration** n. Mitwirkung, (genossenschaftliche) Zusammenarbeit; **-erative** n. Konsumverein, Kooperative; Konsumgeschäft; Genossenschaftsmiethaus; **-erative** adj. kooperativ, mitwirkend

co-ordinate v. koordinieren, zusammenfassen; gleichschalten; **— adj.** gleichgestellt; **— n.** Koordinate

co-ordination n. Koordination; Gleichschaltung; (physiol.) Zusammenwirkung

coot n. Wasserhuhn; **-ie** n. Laus

cop n. Polizist; **— v.** fangen; stehlen

copal n. Kopal

copartner n. Beteiligte, Teilhaber

cope v. kämpfen; **I can't — with it** ich kann damit nicht fertig werden

coping n. Mauerkappe

copious adj. reich(lich); übervoll; weitläufig, wortreich

copilot n. zweiter Pilot

copper n. Kupfer; Kupfermünze; Kupferfarbe; (sl.) Polizist; **— adj.** kupfern, kupferrot

copperhead n. Mokassinschlange

copperplate n. Kupferplatte; Kupferstich

coppersmith n. Kupferschmied

copra n. Kopra

copulate v. sich verbinden (or paaren)

copulation n. Verbindung; Paarung, Begattung

copy n. Abschrift, Kopie; Muster, Medell; Nachahmung, Nachbildung; Exemplar, Abdruck; Nummer; Manuskript; **— desk** Redaktion für Aktuelles und Schlagzeilen; **— v.** abschreiben, kopieren; nachahmen, nachbilden; nachmachen; abzeichnen

copybook n. Schreibheft; Kopierbuch

copycat n. Nachäffer

copyright n. Copyright, Urheberrecht, Verlagsrecht; — v. ein Copyright anmelden (or erwerben)

coquet v. kokettieren; **-ry** n. Koketterie, Gefallsucht; **-te** n. Kokette; **-tish** adj. kokett, gefallsüchtig

coral n. Koralle; — adj. korallen; korallenrot; — **diver** Korallenfischer; — **reef** Korallenriff

cord n. Schnur, Bindfaden, Kordel; Leine; (anat.) Strang, Band; (wood) Klafter; — v. (auf)klaftern

cordage n. Tauwerk

cordial adj. herzlich, freundlich; — n. Magenlikör; **-ity** n. Herzlichkeit, Wärme

corduroy n. Kord, gerippter Baumwollstoff; — **road** Knüppeldamm

core n. Kern, Herz, Mark; (bot.) Kerngehäuse

corespondent n. mitangeklagter Ehebrecher

cork n. Kork, Stöpsel, Pfropfen; (bot.) Korkeiche, Korkrinde; — v. verkorken, zustöpseln; **-age** n. Pfropfengeld

corkscrew n. Korkenzieher

corn n. Mais; Korn, Getreide; (med.) Hühnerauge; — **borer** Kornkäferlarve, Maisbohrer; — **popper** Maisröster; — r. einsalzen, einpökeln; **-y** adj. hornig; (med.) mit Hühneraugen übersät; (coll.) abgedroschen

corncob n. Maiskolben

corncrib n. Maisspeicher

corner n. Ecke, Winkel; (com.) Aufkaufen; **turn the** — um die Ecke gehen; (fig.) über den Berg kommen; — **shelf** Eckgestell; — v. in die Ecke (or Enge) treiben; aufkaufen; **-ed** adj. winkelig, eckig; (coll.) in der Klemme sein

corner stone n. Eckstein; Gedenkstein

cornet n. Kornett, Horn

cornfield n. Maisfeld

cornflower n. Kornblume

cornice n. Kranzleiste, Gesims

cornstalk n. Maisstengel

cornstarch n. Maisstärke

corollary n. Folgesatz

coronation n. Krönung

coroner n. Leichenbeschauer

coronet n. kleine Krone; (poet.) Kranz

corporal n. Korporal, Obergefreite; — adj. körperlich, leiblich

corporation n. Körperschaft, Korporation

corps n. Korps

corpse n. Leiche, Leichnam

corpulent adj. stark, fleischig, beleibt, korpulent

corpuscle n. Blutkörperchen, Zelle

correct v. verbessern, berichtigen, korrigieren; zurechtweisen; — adj. richtig, korrekt; **-ion** n. Verbesserung, Berichtigung, Korrektur; **house of -ion** Besserungsanstalt, Zuchthaus; **-ive** adj. bessernd, berichtigend; **-ive** n. Besserungsmittel

correlation n. Wechselbeziehung

correspond v. in Briefwechsel stehen, korrespondieren; entsprechen; **-ence** n. Korrespondenz; Übereinstimmung; **carry on a -ence** in Briefwechsel stehen; **-ence** adj. **-ence school** Schule für Fernunterricht; **-ent** n. Korrespondent, Berichterstatter; Briefschreiber; **-ing** adj. entsprechend, passend

corridor n. Gang, Flur, Korridor

corroborate v. bestärken, bestätigen

corrode v. zerfressen, zernagen, ätzen

corrosive adj. zerfressend, ätzend

corrupt v. verderben, verführen; korrumpieren; — adj. verderbt, korrupt; **-ible** adj. korrumpiert, bestechlich, verderbbar; **-ion** n. Verdorbenheit, Korruption, Fäulnis

corsage n. Ansteckblume

corset n. Korsett

cortisone n. Nebennierensubstanz, Kortison

cosmetic n. Kosmetik, Schönheitsmittel; — adj. kosmetisch, verschönernd; Schönheits-

cosmic adj. kosmisch; — **rays** Höhenstrahlen

cosmonaut n. Kosmonaut

cosmopolitan n. Weltbürger

cost n. Preis, Aufwand; Kosten; **at all -'s, at any** — um jeden Preis; **at less than** — unter Einkaufspreis; — **of living** Lebenshaltungskosten; — **accounting** Unkostenverrechnung; — v. kosten, zu stehen kommen; **-ly** adj. teuer, kostspielig

costume n. Tracht, Kostüm, Kleid

cot n. Feldbett

cottage n. Landhaus; Hütte, Häuschen; — **cheese** Quark, weisser Käse. Topfen

cotton n. Baumwolle; Kattun; (med.) Watte; — **flannel** Kattunflanell; — **gin** Entkernmaschine; — **goods** Baumwollwaren; — **mill** Baumwollspinnerei; — **thread** Baumwollgarn; — v. — to liebgewinnen

couch n. Sofa, Couch, Chaiselongue; — v. ausdrücken, erfassen

cough n. Husten; — **drop** Hustenbonbon; — v. husten

council n. Ratsversammlung; Beratung; **city** — Stadtrat; **-(l)or** n. Ratsmitglied, Stadtverordnete, Ratsherr, Stadtrat

counsel n. Rat; Beratung; (law) Rechtsanwalt; — v. raten; beraten; **-(l)or** n. Ratgeber, Berater, Sach(ver)walter

count n. Summe, Zahlung; Graf; (law) Anklagepunkt; — v. zählen, rechnen; — **on** rechnen mit, sich verlassen auf; **-er** n. Zahltisch, Theke; (cards) Spielmarke; Geiger **-er** Geigerzähler; **-less** adj. zahllos, unzählig

countdown n. Startzählung

countenance n. Gesicht, Miene; Fassung; Gunst; — v. begünstigen, zulassen

counter n. Ladentisch; — adv. entgegen, zuwider; — adj. entgegengesetzt, Gegen-; — v. einen Gegenschlag führen

counteract v. entgegenwirken, zuwiderhandeln

counterattack n. Gegenangriff

counterbalance n. Gegengewicht; — v. ausgleichen, aufwiegen

counterclockwise adv. in entgegengesetzter Richtung des Uhrzeigers laufend

counterfeit n. Unechte, Fälschung; Falschgeld; — v. fälschen, verfälschen, nachmachen; erheucheln; — adj. gefälscht, verfälscht; nachgemacht, unecht; erheuchelt; -er n. Fälscher; Falschmünzer; Heuchler

counterintelligence n. Gegenspionage, Spionageabwehrdienst

counteroffensive n. Gegenoffensive

counterpoint n. Kontrapunkt

countersign n. Gegenzeichnung; (mil.) Losungswort; — v. gegenzeichnen, mitunterschreiben

counterweight n. Gleichgewicht; Gegengewicht

countess n. Gräfin

country n. Land; Vaterland, Heimat; Gegend; out of the — im Ausland; Land-; — club Geselligkeitsverein; — house Villa, Landhaus

countryman n. Landsmann; Landmann, Bauer

countryside n. Landstrich, Land

county n. Kreis, Provinz; — seat Kreisstadt

coup n. Schlag, Streich; (sports) Meisterschaft; — d'état Staatsstreich; — de grace Gnadenstoss

coupe n. Coupé; Wagen (mit zwei Türen)

couple n. Paar; Ehepaar; a — of ein paar; — v. koppeln, (sich) paaren; sich ehelich verbinden; -t n. Reimpaar

coupling n. Kuppelung

coupon n. Coupon, Abschnitt

courage n. Mut, Tapferkeit, Courage; take. — beherzt sein; -ous adj. brav, tapfer, mutig

courier n. Kurier, Eilbote

course n. Lauf, Verlauf, Kurs; Gang; Reihe, Kursus; Wettrennen; as a matter of — ganz selbstverständlich; in due — zu seiner Zeit, zur rechten Zeit; in the — im Laufe; in the — of time mit der Zeit; of — natürlich, gewiss, selbstverständlich

court n. Hof; Kur; (law) Gericht, Gerichtshof; (sports) Platz, Spielplatz; — v. den Hof machen; sich bewerben; -eous adj. höflich, gefällig, -esy n. Höflichkeit; -ier n. Höfling; -ly adj. and adv. höflich, artig; schmeichlerisch; Hof-; -ship n. Werben

courthouse n. Gerichtsgebäude

court-martial n. Kriegsgericht; — v. vor ein Kriegsgericht stellen

courtroom n. Gerichtssaal

courtyard n. Hof

cousin n. Vetter, Cousin; Base, Kusine; first — leiblicher Vetter, Geschwisterkind

cove n. kleine Bucht; Obdach

covenant n. Vertrag, Kontrakt; (rel.) Bund; — v. einswerden, übereinkommen

cover n. Deckel, Decke; Überzug, Umschlag; Deckung; Kuvert, Gedeck;

(fig.) Deckmantel; under separate — mit derselben Post; — charge Bedienung; — v. (be)decken; überziehen, einwickeln, einschlagen; verbergen; schützen; zurücklegen; (gun) bestreichen; (newspaper sl.) berichten; -ing n. Decke, Bekleidung, Hülle; -let n. Bettdecke

cow n. Kuh; Weibchen; — v. entmutigen, einschüchtern

coward n. Feigling, Memme; Hasenfuss; -ice n. Feigheit; -ly adj. and adv. feige

cowboy n. Cowboy, Rinderhirt, Kuhhirt

cower v. kauern, hocken

cowherd n. Rinderhirt, Kuhhirt

cowhide n. Rinderhaut, Kuhhaut; Rindsleder

cowl n. Kappe, Kapuze

co-worker n. Mitarbeiter

cowpuncher n. Cowboy

coy adj. schüchtern, spröde; zimperlich

coyote n. Steppenwolf, Präriewolf, Kojote

cozy adj. gemütlich, behaglich; — n. Teewärmer, Kaffeewärmer

crab n. (ast.) Krebs; (zool.) Krabbe, Taschenkrebs; (sl.) Sauertopf; catch a — den Streich verfehlen, krebsen; — apple Holzapfel; — v. sich beklagen, nörgeln; -bed adj., -by adj. verärgert, mürrisch, sauertöpfisch

crack n. Sprung, Riss, Spalt(e); Krach, Knall; — of dawn Morgengrauen; — v. springen, platzen; reissen, spalten, knallen; knacken, aufbrechen; zerbrechen; — a joke einen Witz reissen; — down niederschlagen; -ed gesprungen; (coll.) verrückt; -er n. knuspriger Biskuit; -le v. knistern, knattern; -ling n. Geknister; (cooking) Grieben, Kruste

crackpot n. harmlos Verrückter

crack-up n. Absturz

cradle n. Wiege; — v. wiegen, einwiegen

craft n. Geschick(lichkeit), Fertigkeit; Gewerbe; List; (naut.) Schiff, Boot; — union Zunft, Gewerkschaft; -iness n. Schlauheit, Verschlagenheit; -y adj. listig, verschlagen

craftsman n. Handwerker

cram v. (ver)stopfen, anfüllen; nudeln; (sl.) ochsen, pauken

cramp n. Krampf; — v. beengen, einschränken

cranberry n. Preiselbeere

crane n. (mech. and naut.) Kran; (zool.) Kranich; — v. sich den Hals ausrecken; zaudern

cranium n. Schädel, Hirnschale

crank n. Windung; (mech.) Kurbel; (sl.) Verschrobene; — v. ankurbeln; -y adj. reizbar, launenhaft

crankcase n. Kurbelgehäuse, Kurbelkasten

crankshaft n. Kurbelwelle

crape n. Flor, Krepp; Trauerflor

craps(hooting) n. amerikanisches Würfelspiel

crash n. Krach, Lärm; Zusammenstoss; (avi.) Absturz; — v. krachen, knir-

schen; (ein)stürzen; (avi.) abstürzen
crash-landing n. Bruchlandung
crate n. Lattenkiste; Packkorb; **-r** n. Trichter
crater n. Krater
crave v. verlangen, sehen, flehen
craving n. Begierde, Sehnsucht
crawl v. kriechen; **be -ing with** wimmeln von; — n. Kraulen
crayfish n. Krebs
crayon n. Zeichenstift, Farbstift
crazy adj. toll, verrückt; **— bone** Ellbogenknochen, Musikantenknochen; **— quilt** Flickendecke
cream n. Sahne, Rahm; Creme, Krem; (fig.) Beste; **— of tartar** Weinsteinpulver; **— of the crop** Beste; **whipped —** Schlagsahne; **— cheese** Sahnenkäse; **— puff** Krapfen; **— separator** Entsahner; — v. abrahmen, entsahnen; schlagen; mit Sahne vermischen; (fig.) das Beste nehmen; **-ery** n. Molkerei; **-y** adj. sahnig, cremefarben
crease n. Falte, Kniff; — v. falten, kniffen, umbiegen, zerknittern
create v. (er)schaffen; verursachen; ernennen
creation n. Schöpfung; (fashion) Kreation
creative adj. schaffend, schöpferisch
creator n. Schöpfer
creature n. Geschöpf, Tier, Kreatur
credentials n. pl. Empfehlungsschreiben; Beglaubigungsschreiben
credible adj. glaubwürdig, glaublich
credit n. Kredit, Haben; Glaubwürdigkeit; Ansehen; **be a — to** Ehre machen; **give — for** anrechnen; zutrauen; **letter of —** Kreditbrief; **on —** auf Kredit; **— balance** Kreditbestand; **— side** Gutschein; — v. kreditieren, gutschreiben; glauben, trauen; **— with** gutschreiben; **-able** adj. kreditfähig; achtbar, ehrenvoll; **-or** n. Gläubiger
credulous adj. leichtgläubig
creed n. Kredo, Glaubensbekenntnis
creek n. Bach; Unterschlupf
creep v. kriechen, schleichen; **-er** n. Kriecher, Schleicher; (bot.) Schlingpflanze; **-y** adj. gruselig
cremate v. (Leichen) verbrennen
creole n. Kreole; — adj. kreolisch
creosote n. Kreosot
crepe n. Krepp; **— de Chine** Crepe de Chine; **— paper** Kreppapier
crescendo n. Krescendo; adj. and adv. crescendo, anschwellend
crescent n. Halbmond, Mondsichel; — adj. halbmondförmig; zunehmend
crest n. Wappen; Schopf; Kamm; Rükken, Gipfel
crestfallen adj. niedergeschlagen, mutlos
crevice n. Riss, Spalte
crew n. Mannschaft, Besatzung, Bemannung
crib n. Kinderbett, Krippe
cricket n. (ent.) Grille, Heimchen; (sports) Kricket
Crimea n. die Krim
crime n. Verbrechen, Frevel
criminal n. Verbrecher; — adj. kriminell,

verbrecherisch; Kriminal-. Strafcriminology n. Kriminalistik
crimson n. Karmesin, Karmin; — adj. karmesinrot, karminrot; — v. erröten
crinoline n. Krinoline, Reifrock
cripple n. Krüppel; — v. lähmen, verkrüppeln; entkräften
crisis n. Krise, Krisis, Höhepunkt, Wendepunkt
crisp adj. knusperig; kraus, frisch
crisscross adj. kreuz und quer laufend; — v. kreuz und quer laufen, durchkreuzen
critic n. Kritiker; **— art —** Kunstrichter; **-al** adj. kritisch, prüfend; entscheidend; bedenklich; **-ism** n. Kritik, Beurteilung, Besprechung; **-ize** v. kritisieren, prüfen; tadeln, bekritteln; rezensieren
croak v. quaken, krächzen; (sl.) sterben; — n. Quaken, Gekrächze
crochet n. Häkelei, Häkelarbeit; — v. häkeln
crock n. Steinguttopf; **-ery** n. Steingut, Töpferware
crocodile n. Krokodil; **— tears** Krokodilstränen
crone n. altes Weib
crony n. Busenfreund, alter Bekannte
crook n. Haken, Krümmung; (sl.) Schwindler; — v. krümmen, beugen; **-ed** adj. schräg, schief, krumm; unehrlich, lasterhaft
croon v. wimmern; leise singen
crop n. Ernte; Kropf; — v. abschneiden, stutzen; pflücken, ernten; abfressen; **— up** auftauchen
cross n. Kreuz; Kruzifix; Kreuzung; — adj. kreuzweise, quer; kreuzend; Kreuz-, Quer-; böse, ärgerlich; entgegengesetzt; **be at — purposes** sich unabsichtlich bekämpfen; **— reference** Hinweis von Buchabschnitt zu Buchabschnitt; **— section** Querschnitt; — v. übergehen, hinübergehen, kreuzen; entgegentreten; in den Weg kommen; **— one's fingers** die Daumen halten; **— out** durchstreichen; **it -es my mind** mir kam der Gedanke; **-ing** n. Übergang, Kreuzung; Kreuzweg; Überfahrt; Rassenkreuzung; **— street —** Strassenübergang
crossbreed n. Mischling; Mischrasse; — v. kreuzen; durch Kreuzung züchten
cross-country adj. querfeldein
crosscut adj. quer durchschneidend; **— saw** Kreuzsäge; — n. Kreuzhieb, Querschlag
cross-examination n. Kreuzverhör
cross-examine v. ins Kreuzverhör nehmen
cross-eyed adj. schielend
cross-question v. ein Kreuzverhör anstellen mit; hin und her fragen
crossroad n. Querstrasse, Kreuzweg; pl. Scheidewege
crosswise adj. kreuzweise, schief
crossword puzzle n. Kreuzworträtsel
crotch n. Gabelung, Haken
crouch v. sich schmiegen (or kauern), hocken
croup n. (horse) Kruppe; (med.) Kehl-

kopfbräune

crow n. Krähe; Krähen; — v. krähen; prahlen

crowbar n. Brecheisen

crowd n. Menge, Masse, Haufen; Gedränge; — of people Menschenmenge; — v. (sich) drängen, pressen; schwärmen, wimmeln; -ed adj. gedrängt, zusammengepresst, überfüllt

crown n. Krone, Kranz; Spitze, Gipfel; Scheitel; — prince Kronprinz; — v. krönen, ehren, auszeichnen

crucible n. Schmelztiegel; Feuerprobe; steel Schmelztiegelstahl

crucifix n. Kruzifix; -ion n. Kreuzigung

crucify v. kreuzigen

crude adj. roh, unreif, unbearbeitet, Roh-

cruel adj. grausam, unmenschlich, hart; -ty n. Grausamkeit

cruise n. Kreuzen, Seefahrt; — v. kreuzen; -r n. Kreuzer

crumb n. Krume, Brocken; — v. zerkrümeln; panieren; -le v. zerkrümeln, zerbröckeln

crumple v. zerdrücken, zerknüllen

crusade n. Kreuzzug; -r n. Kreuzfahrer

crush v. zerquetschen; unterdrücken; — n. Gedränge; (sl.) Zuneigung

crust n. Kruste, Rinde, Schale; -y adj. krustig, rindig, schalig; grämlich

crutch n. Krücke

cry n. Ruf, Geschrei, Schrei; Ausrufen; a far — from weit entfernt von; — v. rufen, schreien; ausrufen; weinen; -ing n. Weinen, Gejammer

crybaby n. Jammerlappen

crystal n. Kristall; — adj. kristallen; kristallklar; — gazing Kristallseherei; -line adj. kristallen; Kristall-; -lize v. kristallisieren

cub n. Junge, Junges; — adj. — reporter junger Reporter

cubbyhole n. Versteck; kleiner Raum

cube n. Würfel, Kubus

cubic(al) adj. kubisch, Kubik-

cubism n. Kubismus

cuckoo n. Kuckuck; — adj. verrückt

cucumber n. Gurke

cud n. chew one's — wiederkauen

cuddle v. herzen, liebkosen

cudgel n. Knüttel, Keule; — v. durchprügeln; — one's brains sich den Kopf zerbrechen

cue n. Stichwort; (billiards) Queue

cuff n. Manschette; Umschlag; Faustschlag; — links Manschettenknöpfe; — v. schlagen, puffen, knuffen

culinary adj. kulinarisch; Küchen-, Koch-

culminate v. kulminieren, gipfeln; den Gipfel erreichen

culprit n. Beklagte, Schuldige, Verbrecher

cult n. Kult, Kultus, Verehrung

cultivate v. bearbeiten, kultivieren; pflegen; ausbilden

cultivation n. Kultivierung; Ackerbau; Bildung; Gesittung; Ausbildung, Pflege, Zucht; Übung

cultivator n. Pfleger, Züchter; Bodenbearbeitungsgerät

culture n. Kultur, Pflege, Geistesbildung;

-ed adj. kultiviert, gebildet

culvert n. Abzugskanal

cunning n. Kenntnis, Wissen; List, Schlauheit; — adj. schlau, verschmitzt; reizend, entzückend

cup n. Tasse, Becher; (fig. and bot.) Kelch; (sports) Cup, Pokal; -ful n. Bechervoll

cupboard n. Küchenschrank, Silberschrank

cupcake n. Törtchen

cupola n. Kuppel, Kuppelgewölbe

cur n. Köter; Halunke

curable adj. heilbar

curate n. Hilfspfarrer

curative adj. heilsam; — n. Heilmittel

curator n. Kurator, Verwalter; Vormund

curb n. Beschränkung, Einschränkung; steinerne Einfassung; Kinnkette; — v. beschränken, einschränken; im Zaum halten, zügeln

curbstone n. Rinnstein, Bordschwelle

curd n. Quark, dicke Milch; -le v. gerinnen (lassen); erstarren (lassen)

cure n. Kur; Heilmittel; — v. heilen, kurieren; pökeln, räuchern; (skins) beizen, gerben

cure-all n. Allheilmittel, Wundermittel

curfew n. Abendglocke; abendliches Ausgehverbot, Polizeistunde

curio n. Rarität, Seltenheit, Kuriosität; -sity n. Neugier(de), Kuriosität; Rarität; -us adj. kurios, seltsam, sonderlich; neugierig

curl n. Locke; Kräuselung; Windung; — v. (sich) kräuseln, sich winden; sich locken; — up aufrollen; -ing adj. -ing iron Brennschere; -y adj. lockig, kraus

currant n. Johannisbeere; Korinthe

currency n. Währung, Zahlungsmittel; Verbreitung, Umlauf

current n. Strömung, Strom; Lauf, Gang; — adj. laufend, strömend; heutig; geläufig; allgemein (bekannt); kursierend; the — issue die letzte Ausgabe

curriculum n. Kurrikulum, Lehrplan

curse n. Fluch, Verwünschung; — v. (ver)fluchen, schwören; verdammen

curtail v. beschränken; (ab)kürzen, stutzen

curtain n. Vorhang; Gardine, Schleier; — call Hervorruf; — raiser Vorspiel; — rod Vorhangstange, Gardinenstange; — v. umhüllen, verhängen, verschleiern

curvature n. Krümmung

curve n. Kurve, Bogen; — v. (sich) biegen, (sich) krümmen

cushion n. Kissen, Polster; (billiard) Bande

custard n. Eierrahm

custodian n. Kustos, Verwahrer, Hüter; Vormund

custody n. Verwahrung, Aufsicht; Haft, Gewahrsam; Verhaftung

custom n. Sitte, Gebrauch, Gewohnheit; (law) Gewohnheitsrecht; pl. Zoll; -ary adj. gewöhnlich, üblich, gebräuchlich; -er n. Kunde, Käufer; (sl.) Kerl

custom-built, custom-made adj. nach Mass gemacht, Mass-

customhouse n. Zollamt
cut n. Schnitt, Hieb; Scheibe, Schnitte, Stück; (art) Stich; Holzschnitt; (cards) Abheben; Stechen; (price) Herabsetzung; (salary) Abzug, Kürzung; — v. schneiden, verwunden; (cards) abheben; stechen; (class) schwänzen; (cloth) scheren, abschneiden; (gem) schleifen; (grass) mähen; schneiden; (hair) stutzen; (meat) vorschneiden; (price) herabsetzen, drücken; (salary) kürzen; (teeth) durchbrechen; (tree) fällen; — **across** querüber gehen; — **down** fällen; vermindern; — **off** abschneiden; (elec.) unterbrechen; — **out** ausschneiden, zuschneiden; — **short** abkürzen; ins Wort fallen; — **up** zerschneiden; — adj. beschnitten, gespalten, zersägt; verwundet; — **and dried** fix und fertig; — **glass** geschliffenes Glas; -**lery** n. Messerschmiedware; Essbestecke; -**let** n. Kotelett; -**ter** n. Schneidende; Schneider, Zuschneider; Schnitzer; (naut.) Kutter; -**ting** n. Schneiden; (bot.) Ableger, Steckling; (paper) Abschnitt, Ausschnitt, Schnitzel; -**ing** adj. scharf, schneidend, beissend
cutback n. Herabsetzung, Verminderung; (film) Rückblende
cute adj. hübsch, lieblich
cuticle n. Oberhaut; Nagelhaut
cutoff n. Abkürzung; Absperrung, Unterbrechung
cutout n. Umschalter; (elec.) Sicherung; Ausschalter
cut-rate adj. Rabatt-
cutthroat n. Halsabschneider, Meuchelmörder; — adj. mörderisch, halsabschneiderisch
cyanide n. Zyan(id)
cycle n. Zyklus, Periode; Kreis, Zirkel; Fahrrad
cyclist n. Radfahrer
cyclone n. Zyklon, Wirbelsturm
cyclotron n. Zyklotron, Elektronenbeschleuniger
cylinder n. Zylinder, Walze, Rolle; — **head** Zylinderhut, Zylinderrolle
cylindric(al) adj. zylindrisch, walzenförmig
cypress n. Zypresse
Cyprus n. Cypern
cyst n. Zyste, Eitersack
czar n. Zar
Czechoslovakia n. die Tschechoslowakei

D

dab n. Klecks, Fleck; Klaps; Betupfen; — v. tappen, tippen; beschmieren, abklatschen
dabble v. bespritzen, plätschern; stümpern, pfuschen; — **in** hinein pfuschen in
dachshund n. Dackel
dacron n. Dakron
dad(dy) n. Papa(chen), Vati
daffodil n. gelbe Narzisse
dagger n. Dolch, Stilett
dahlia n. Dahlie
daily adj. täglich; — (**paper**) Tageszeitung

daintiness n. Feinheit, Zartheit; Niedlichkeit
dainty adj. elegant, fein; nett, zierlich; — n. Leckerbissen, Naschwerk
dairy n. Molkerei, Milchgeschäft; — **farm** Meierei, Milchwirtschaft
daisy n. Gänseblümchen, Massliebchen
dale n. Tal
dally v. tändeln, schäkern; vertändeln
dam n. Damm, Deich, Talsperre; (zool.) Muttertier; — v. dämmen, stauen
damage n. Schaden, Nachteil, Verlust; pl. Schadenersatz; — v. schaden, beschädigen
damask n. Damast; — adj. damasten, damastartig
dame n. Dame, vornehme Frau
damn v. verdammen, verfluchen, verwünschen; — interj. verflucht!; — **it!** verdammt! -**able** adj. verdammenswert; schändlich; -**ation** n. Verdammung, Verfluchung; (bibl.) Verdammnis; -**ed** adj. verdammt; abscheulich, scheusslich
damp n. Feuchtigkeit; (min.) Schwaden; — adj. feucht, dunstig; dumpf; -**en** v. anfeuchten, befeuchten; dämpfen; (fig.) niederschlagen; -**ness** n. Feuchtigkeit
damper n. Dämpfer; Klappe, Schieber
damsel n. Jungfrau, Fräulein, junges Mädchen
dance n. Tanz; Ball; — **hall** Tanzhalle; — v. tanzen; -**er** n. Tänzer
dandelion n. Löwenzahn
dandruff n. Schuppen, Schinn, Kopfschorf
dandy n. Dandy, Geck; — adj. vortrefflich
danger n. Gefahr; — **zone** Gefahrenzone; -**ous** adj. gefährlich
dangle v. baumeln, schwanken
dank adj. feucht, nasskalt, dunstig
Danube n. Donau
dapper adj. nett, niedlich, schmuck
dare n. Herausforderung; — v. wagen, herausfordern; sich unterstehen (or erkühnen)
daredevil n. Wagehals
daring n. Kühnheit, Dreistigkeit, Tollkühnheit; — adj. kühn, verwegen, dreist
dark adj. dunkel, finster, trübe; schwarz, schwärzlich; böse, verbrecherisch; geheimnisvoll; **Dark Ages** Mittelalter; **Dark Continent** schwarzer Kontinent, Afrika; — **horse** unbekannter Bewerber; — n. Dunkel(heit); Verborgenheit, Ungewissheit; Undeutlichkeit; Unwissenheit; **in the** — im Dunkeln; **leave in the** — im Ungewissen lassen; -**en** v. verdunkeln, verfinstern; schwärzen; (fig.) verdüstern, verwirren; -**ness** n. Dunkelheit, Finsternis
darkroom n. Dunkelkammer
darling n. Liebling, Herzblatt; — adj. teuer, lieb, wert
darn v. stopfen, ausbessern; — n. gestopfte Stelle; — **it!** interj. verwünscht! -**ing** n. Stopferei; -**ing needle** Stopfnadel
dash n. Schlag, Stoss, Streich; Sturz,

Sprung; Prise; (typ.) Gedankenstrich; — v. schlagen, stossen, schleudern; besprengen, bespritzen; zerstören, vernichten; stürzen; — off wegstürzen; skizzieren, flüchtig entwerfen; -ing adj. flott, schneidig, kühn

dashboard n. Armaturenbrett

data n. pl. Daten; Angaben, Tatsachen

date n. Datum, Zeitangabe; Jahreszahl, Zeitpunkt; Verabredung; (bot.) Dattel; up to — bis heute; zeitgemäss, modern; auf dem Laufenden; what is the —? welches Datum (or den wievielten) haben wir heute? — line Datumsgrenze, Nullmeridian; Zeitungsdatum; — v. datieren, ansetzen; ausgehen mit, verabredet sein mit; — from zurückgehen auf; -d adj. veraltet, altmodisch

daub n. Klecks, Schmiererei; (art) Geschmiere; — v. (be)schmieren, beschmutzen, besudeln

daughter n. Tochter

daughter-in-law n. Schwiegertochter

dauntless adj. furchtlos, verwegen, unerschrocken

davenport n. Sofa, Schlafsofa

dawn n. Morgendämmerung, Tagesanbruch; (fig.) Anfang, Erwachen; — v. tagen, dämmern; (fig.) sich entfalten

day n. Tag; Tageslicht; a — täglich, pro Tag; by the — tageweise, täglich; carry the — die Schlacht gewinnen; — after — von einem Tag zum anderen; — for Tag für Tag; — after tomorrow übermorgen; — before yesterday vorgestern; — by — von Tag zu Tag, täglich; -s of grace Verzugstage; every — jeden Tag; every other — jeden zweiten Tag; from — to — von Tag zu Tag; on the following — am nächsten Tage; one — eines Tages, einst; the other — neulich; these -s heutzutage; — laborer Tagelöhner, tageweise Beschäftigte; — letter verbilligtes Telegramm (ausserhalb der Geschäftsstunden); — nursery Spielschule; — school Externat; — shift Tagesschicht

daybreak n. Tagesanbruch

daylight n. Tageslicht

daylight-saving time n. Sommerzeit

daze n. Betäubung, Verwirrung; — v. betäuben, verwirren

dazzle v. blenden; verblenden, verwirren

deacon n. Diakon(us)

deactivate v. unwirksam machen; (Radiumaktivität) neutralisieren

dead adj. tot, gestorben, leblos; erloschen; unempfindlich; (bot.) verdorrt, verwelkt; (law) bürgerlich tot; (mus.) tonlos, verlöschend; (window) blind; — body Leichnam; — calm vollkommene Windstille; — center unbeweglicher Mittelpunkt; — end Sackgasse; — heat unentschiedener Wettkampf; — letter unbestellbarer Brief; — reckoning Berechnung des zurückgelegten Weges; — shot Scharfschütze; — silence Totenstille; — weight unnütze (or schwere, drückende) Last; — n. Tote; Tiefe, Stille; — adj. voll-

kommen, völlig, unbedingt; —en v. (er)töten; dämpfen, abschwächen, abstumpfen; -ly adj. tötlich; gefährlich; -ly sin Todsünde

deadline n. Termin; Redaktionsschluss

deadlock n. Stillstand, Stockung

Dead Sea n. das Tote Meer

deaf adj. taub, schwerhörig; — and dumb taubstumm; fall on — ears kein Gehör finden, tauben Ohren predigen; —en v. taub machen, betäuben; -ness n. Taubheit, Schwerhörigkeit

deaf-mute n. Taubstumme

deal n. Teil, Menge; (cards) Kartengeben; (com.) Handel, Geschäft; a good — ziemlich viel; a great — sehr viel; — v. teilen, austeilen, verteilen; handeln, vermitteln; (cards) geben; — with sich befassen mit, behandeln; —er n. (cards) Kartengeber; (com.) Händler; -ings n. pl. Handlungsweise; Umgang, Verkehr

dean n. (educ.) Dekan; (rel.) Dechant

dear adj. lieb, wert; teuer, kostspielig; Dear Sir Sehr geehrter Herr; — n. Liebling; Lieber

dearth n. Teuerung; Mangel

death n. Tod; Todesfall; put to — hinrichten; — penalty Todesstrafe; — rate Sterblichkeitsziffer; — warrant Todesurteil; -less adj. unsterblich; -like adj. totenähnlich; -ly adj. tödlich; verderblich

deathbed n. Sterbebett

debase v. verringern, verschlechtern; entwerten

debatable adj. streitig, bestreitbar

debate n. Erörterung, Debatte; Wortstreit; — v. erörtern, verhandeln, debattieren; — with oneself sich überlegen, erwägen

debauch v. verführen, verderben, verleiten; —ery n. Schwelgerei, Ausschweifung

debit n. Debet, Soll; Schuld; — balance Schuldabrechnung; — v. belasten, zu Lasten schreiben

debris n. Überbleibsel, Ruinen; (geol.) Trümmer

debt n. Schuld(en); bad — nicht einzutreibende Schuld; be in — verschuldet sein; floating — schwebende Schuld; public — öffentliche Schuld; run into — sich in Schulden stürzen; -or n. Schuldner, Debitor

debut n. Debüt, erstes Auftreten; make one's — zum ersten Mal auftreten; -ante n. Debütantin

decade n. Jahrzehnt, Dekade; Zehnerreihe

decadence n. Dekadenz, Verfall

decadent adj. dekadent, verfallen

decamp v. das Lager abbrechen, aufbrechen; ausreissen

decapitate v. enthaupten

decay n. Verfall, Verwesung; (bot.) Verblühen; (med.) Abnahme; — v. verfallen, abnehmen; verwelken

deceased adj. verstorben, abgestorben; — n. Verstorbene

deceit n. Betrug, Täuschung, Falschheit;

–ful *adj.* (be)trügerisch, täuschend, listig

deceive *v.* (be)trügen, täuschen, irreleiten

December *n.* Dezember

decency *n.* Anstand, Schicklichkeit

decent *adj.* anständig, schicklich; leidlich, ziemlich gut

deception *n.* Betrug; Irreführung, Täuschung

deceptive *adj.* (be)trügerisch, täuschend

decibel *n.* Lautstärkemesser

decide *v.* entscheiden, beschliessen, bestimmen; sich entschliessen; **–dly** *adv.* entschieden, bestimmt

decimal *adj.* dezimal; **— point** Komma; **— n.** Dezimalbruch

decipher *v.* entziffern, enträtseln

decision *n.* Entscheidung, Entschluss, Entschlossenheit

decisive *adj.* entschieden, entschlossen, entscheidend

deck *n.* Deck, Verdeck; (cards) Spielkartenpaket; **— chair** Liegestuhl; **— hand** Matrose; **—** *v.* (be)decken; bekleiden; schmücken

declaim *v.* deklamieren; eifern (gegen)

declaration *n.* Erklärung; (cards) Ansage; (law) Klageführung

declare *v.* erklären; angeben, deklarieren; behaupten

declination *n.* Neigung; Abweichung; (ast. and phy.) Deklination

decline *v.* ablehnen, verweigern; abnehmen, verfallen; (sich) neigen; (gram.) deklinieren, abwandeln; **— n.** Sinken. Abnahme; (med.) Verfall; **be on the —** zu Ende gehen, verfallen

decode *v.* entziffern

decompose *v.* (sich) zersetzen, verwesen; zerlegen

decontaminate *v.* entgiften, reinigen

decorate *v.* schmücken, verzieren, dekorieren

decoration *n.* Verzierung; Dekoration; Orden, Auszeichnung

decorator *n.* Dekorateur, Dekorationsmaler

decorous *adj.* schicklich, geziemend, anständig

decoy *n.* Köder; Lockvogel; **—** *v.* ködern, kirren, (ver)locken

decrease *v.* abnehmen, (sich) vermindern

decree *n.* Erlass, Verordnung, Dekret; Rechtsschluss; Bescheid; **—** *v.* verordnen, beschliessen

decrepit *adj.* abgelebt, gebrochen, altersschwach

dedicate *v.* widmen, weihen, dedizieren

dedication *n.* Widmung, Weihung, Zueignung

deduct *v.* abziehen, abrechnen; **–ion** *n.* Abzug, Abziehen; Herleitung, Schlussfolgerung

deed *n.* Tat, Handlung; Urkunde, Dokument; **—** *v.* überschreiben, übertragen

deep *n.* Tiefe Abgrund; **—** *adj.* tief; vertieft; gründlich, versteckt; scharfsinnig; (color) dunkel; **–en** *v.* (sich) vertiefen; dunkler werden (or machen); vergrössern; (sich) steigern

deep-freezer *n.* Tiefgefriermaschine

deep-rooted, deep-seated *adj.* tief eingewurzelt

deer *n.* Hirsch, Rotwild

defame *v.* verunglimpfen, defamieren

defeat *n.* Niederlage; Vernichtung; **— v.** vernichten, schlagen; vereiteln; ablehnen; **–ist** *n.* Defaitist, Flaumacher

defend *v.* (sich) verteidigen, beschützen, bewahren; **–ant** *n.* Beklagte, Verklagte; **–er** *n.* Verteidiger

defense *n.* Verteidigung, Rechtfertigung; Schutz; **–less** *adj.* wehrlos, schutzlos

defensive *n.* Defensive, Verteidigung; **—** *adj.* defensiv, verteidigend; Schutz-, Verteidigungs-

defer *v.* aufschieben, verschieben; zögern; **— to** überlassen, sich fügen; **–ence** *n.* Nachgiebigkeit, Rücksichtnahme; Ehrerbietung; **in –ence to** aus Rücksicht gegen; **–ential** *adj.* ehrerbietig, rücksichtsvoll; **–ment** *n.* Aufschub, Verschiebung

defiance *n.* Herausforderung; Trota, Hohn; **in — of** zum Hohn (or Trotz)

deficiency *n.* Fehler, Mangel(haftigkeit); Unzulänglichkeit

deficient *adj.* mangelhaft, unzulänglich

deficit *n.* Defizit, Fehlbetrag, Manko

defile *n.* Engpass, Hohlweg; Defilee; **— v.** defilieren; beschmutzen, verderben

define *v.* definieren, erklären, bestimmen; umgrenzen, festsetzen

definite *adj.* bestimmt, deutlich, genau

definition *n.* Definition, Begriffsbestimmung, Erklärung

definitive *adj.* bestimmt, definitiv, endgültig, entschieden, ausdrücklich

deflate *v.* Luft (or Gas) herauslassen, entleeren

deflect *v.* ablenken, abbiegen, abwenden, abweichen

deform *v.* entstellen, verunstalten; **–ed** *adj.* entstellt, verunstaltet; verwachsen; **–ity** *n.* Verunstaltung, Ungestaltheit; Missgestalt; Hässlichkeit

defraud *v.* betrügen, unterschlagen

defray *v.* bezahlen, bestreiten

defrost *v.* enteisen, auftauen; **–er** *n.* Enteiser; Frostschutzmittel

defunct *adj.* verstorben; nicht mehr vorhanden

defy *v.* herausfordern, trotzen

degenerate *v.* ausarten, entarten, degenerieren; **—** *adj.* entartet, degeneriert

degeneration *n.* Entartung, Degeneration

degrade *v.* erniedrigen; degradieren

degree *n.* Grad, Rang; Stufe; **by –s** allmählich, stufenweise

dehumidify *v.* die Feuchtigkeit entziehen

dehydrate *v.* dehydrieren, Wasserstoff entziehen

deify *v.* vergöttlichen, vergöttern

deity *n.* Gottheit, Gott

dejected *adj.* entmutigt, mutlos, niedergeschlagen

dejection *n.* Niedergeschlagenheit, Schwermut

delay *n.* Verschiebung, Verzögerung, Aufschub; **without —** unverzüglich; **— v.**

aufhalten; (ver)zögern; aufschieben

delectable *adj.* ergötzlich, köstlich

delegate *n.* Delegierte, Abgeordnete; — *v.* delegieren, abordnen; übertragen

delegation *n.* Abordnung, Delegation

delete *v.* auslöschen, streichen, tilgen

deliberate *v.* erwägen, überlegen; nachdenken; — *adj.* absichtlich, bewusst; bedächtig

deliberation *n.* Erwägung, Überlegung, Vorsicht

delicacy *n.* Feinheit, Zartheit, Zartgefühl; Delikatesse; Wohlgeschmack

delicate *adj.* zart, fein, empfindlich; delikat, wohlschmeckend, schmackhaft; heikel, wählerisch

delicatessen *n.* Feinkost, Delikatessen

delicious *adj.* köstlich, delikat

delight *n.* Vergnügen, Freude, Lust; **take — in** Freude haben an; — *v.* entzücken; (sich) erfreuen, (sich) ergötzen; **-ed** *adj.* entzückt, erfreut; **-ful** *adj.* entzückend, köstlich, reizend

delineate *v.* entwerfen, skizzieren; beschreiben

delineation *n.* Entwurf, Skizze; Beschreibung

delinquency *n.* Pflichtvergessenheit; Vergehen, Verbrechen, Kriminalität

delinquent *n.* Delinquent, Verbrecher, Missetäter

delirious *adj.* wahnsinnig, rasend; irre; **be —** wahnsinnig sein; irre reden, phantasieren

delirium *n.* Delirium, Wahnsinn; Verzückung; **— tremens** Delirium tremens, Säuferwahnsinn

deliver *v.* befreien, erlösen; (com.) (ab)liefern, abgeben, übergeben; einreichen; (lecture) halten, vortragen; (med.) entbinden; (message) ausrichten; (opinion) äussern; **-ance** *n.* Befreiung, Erlösung; Ausführung; **-y** *n.* Übergabe; (com.) Lieferung, Ablieferung; Zustellung; (lecture) Vortrag; (med.) Niederkunft; **general -y** *n.* Ausgabestelle für postlagernde Briefe

delta *n.* Delta

delude *v.* betrügen, täuschen, anführen

deluge *n.* Überschwemmung; (bibl.) Sintflut; — *v.* überschwemmen, überfluten

delusion *n.* Täuschung, Wahn, Trug, Blendwerk

de luxe *adj.* luxuriös, kostbar, kostspielig

delve *v.* graben; ergründen, erforschen

demagogue *n.* Demagoge, Aufwiegler

demand *n.* Verlangen; Forderung, Anspruch; Bedarf; Nachfrage; **in —** begehrt; **on —** auf Verlangen; bei Sicht; — *v.* verlangen, fordern; erfordern, beanspruchen

demeanor *n.* Betragen, Benehmen

demented *adj.* wahnsinnig, verrückt

demerit *n.* Fehler, Schuld; Unwürdigkeit; (educ.) Tadel

demilitarize *v.* entmilitarisieren

demise *n.* Ableben, Verscheiden

demitasse *n.* Mokkaschale

demobilize *v.* demobilisieren, abrüsten

democracy *n.* Demokratie

democrat *n.* Demokrat; **-ic** *adj.* demokratisch

demolish *v.* demolieren, abbrechen; abtragen, zerstören

demolition *n.* Niederreissen, Abtragung, Zerstörung; — **bomb** Sprengbombe

demon *n.* Dämon, böser Geist, Teufel

demonstrate *v.* beweisen, demonstrieren

demonstration *n.* Beweis; Demonstration, Massenkundgebung

demonstrative *adj.* beweisend, demonstrativ, darlegend; ausdrucksvoll

demonstrator *n.* Beweisführer, Demonstrator, Erklärer

demoralize *v.* demoralisieren

demote *v.* degradieren, erniedrigen

demotion *n.* Degradierung, Erniedrigung

demur *n.* Bedenken, Zweifel, Einwand; — *v.* bedenken, zweifeln, zögern; Einwendungen erheben

den *n.* Höhle, Grube; Bude; Herrenzimmer

denature *v.* vergällen, ungeniessbar machen; **-d** *adj.* **-d alcohol** verunreinigter Alkohol

denazification *n.* Entnazifizierung

deniable *adj.* verneinbar, abzuleugnen

denial *n.* Leugnen, Verleugnung; Verneinung; Absage

denim *n.* Drill(ich), grobes Kattungewebe

Denmark *n.* Dänemark

denomination *n.* Benennung; Anzeige; Klasse; Konfession

denominator *n.* Nenner; **common —** Generalnenner

denote *v.* bezeichnen, bedeuten

denounce *v.* anzeigen, angeben, denunzieren; anklagen

dense *adj.* dicht, fest; beschränkt

density *n.* Dichte, Dichtheit

dent *n.* Beule, Eindruck; — *v.* eindrücken, verbeulen

dental *adj.* die Zähne betreffend, Zahn-

dentifrice *n.* Zahnpasta, Zahnpulver

dentist *n.* Zahnarzt, Dentist

denture *n.* künstliches (or falsches) Gebiss

denunciation *n.* Anzeige, Anklage, Denunziation

deny *v.* leugnen, bestreiten, verneinen; verleugnen; abschlagen

deodorant *n.* geruchtilgendes Mittel

depart *v.* abreisen, wegfahren; sich trennen, scheiden; abweichen; sterben, verscheiden; **-ment** *n.* Abteilung, Bezirk; Fach, Branche; Ministerium; **-ment store** Warenhaus, Kaufhaus; **-ure** *n.* Abreise; Trennung; Abweichung; Tod

depend *v.* abhängen; hängen, schweben; sich verlassen (auf); **it -s** es kommt darauf an; **-able** *adj.* zuverlässig, verlässlich; **-ence** *n.* Abhängigkeit, Zusammenhang; Vertrauen, Zuversicht; **-ency** *n.* Zubehör; abhängiges Gebiet, Kolonie; **-ent** *n.* Abhängige, Anhänger; **-ent** *adj.* abhängig, angewiesen; in der Schwebe; **-ent upon** berufend auf

depict *v.* abmalen, schildern, beschreiben

depilatory *adj.* enthaarend; — *n.* Enthaarungsmittel

deplorable *adj.* bejammernswert; erbärmlich, kläglich

deplore v. beklagen, betrauern, bejammern

deport v. deportieren, fortschaffen; verbannen; **-ation** n. Verbannung, Ausweisung; **-ment** n. Haltung, Benehmen, Betragen

depose v. absetzen, entthronen; (law) bezeugen, erhärten

deposit n. Einzahlung; Anzahlung; Hinterlegung, Depositum; (geol. and phy.) Lager, Ablagerung; — v. deponieren, hinterlegen; einzahlen; **-ion** n. Aussage; Ablagerung; **-or** n. Deponent, Hinterleger; Einzahler; **-ory** n. Aufbewahrungsort

depot n. Bahnhof, Depot; Niederlage

deprave v. verführen, verderben, verschlechtern

deprecate v. missbilligen, tadeln

depreciate v. herabsetzen, geringschätzen; im Werte sinken

depreciation n. Herabsetzung; Geringschätzung; (com.) Entwertung, Fallen, Sinken

depress v. niederdrücken, niederschlagen, deprimieren; bedrücken, entmutigen; **-ion** n. Depression, Niedergang; Niedergeschlagenheit

deprive v. entziehen, berauben

depth n. Tiefe; in the — of winter mitten im Winter; — bomb, — charge Unterwasserbombe

deputation n. Deputation, Abordnung

deputy n. Deputierte, Abgeordnete, Stellvertreter

derail v. entgleisen, zum Entgleisen bringen

deranged adj. verrückt, verwirrt; (geistig) gestört, derangiert

derby n. steifer, runder Filzhut (mit schmaler Krempe)

derelict n. herrenloses Gut; Wrack; — adj. verlassen, herrenlos; **-ion** n. Vernachlässigung, Pflichtvergessenheit; Aufgeben, Verlassen

deride v. verlachen, verhöhnen, verspotten

derision n. Verspottung; Spott, Hohn

derivation n. Ableitung

derivative n. Ableitung

derive v. ableiten, herleiten

derogatory adj. beeinträchtigend, nachteilig, herabwürdigend

derrick n. Ladebaum; (oil) Vorturm

descend v. hinabsteigen; sich senken; (min.) einfahren; (fig.) sich herablassen; be —ed abstammen; **-ant** n. Nachkomme, Abkömmling

descent n. Niedergang, Abstieg; Abhang; (min.) Einfahrt; (fig.) Abstammung

describe v. beschreiben, schildern, darstellen

description n. Schilderung, Beschreibung; Art

descriptive adj. beschreibend, schildernd

desecrate v. entweihen, profanieren

desegregation n. Rassenrehabilitierung

desert n. Wüste, Einöde; pl. Verdienst; — v. desertieren, fahnenflüchtig werden;

verlassen; **-er** n. Deserteur, Fahnenflüchtige; Ausreisser; **-ion** n. Fahnenflucht; Abfall

deserve v. verdienen; sich verdient machen

deserving adj. verdient, verdienstvoll, würdig

design n. Entwurf, Plan; Muster; — v. entwerfen, ersinnen; planen, beabsichtigen; **-ate** v. bezeichnen, ernennen, bestimmen; **-ation** n. Bestimmung, Bezeichnung; Ernennung; **-er** n. Entwerfer; Zeichner; **-ing** adj. verschlagen, hinterlistig

desirability n. Erwünschtheit, Wünschenswerte

desirable adj. wünschenswert, begehrenswert

desire n. Wunsch; Begierde; Lust; — v. verlangen, wünschen, begehren; (er)bitten

desirous adj. begierig, lüstern

desk n. Schreibtisch, Pult; Katheder; Schultisch

desolate v. verheeren, verwüsten; — adj. einsam, öde; trostlos

desolation n. Verheerung, Verwüstung; Öde; Schwermut

despair n. Verzweiflung, Hoffnungslosigkeit; — v. verzweifeln; **-ing** adj. verzweifelnd, verzweifelt

despatch see dispatch

desperate adj. verzweifelt, hoffnungslos; verwegen

desperation n. Verzweiflung

despise v. verachten, verabscheuen

despite prep. trotz, ungeachtet

despondent adj. mutlos, verzweifelnd, verzagt

despot n. Despot, Gewaltherrscher; **-ic** adj. despotisch, unumschränkt; **-ism** n. Despotismus, Gewaltherrschaft

dessert n. Nachtisch, Dessert

destination n. Bestimmung(sort)

destiny n. Bestimmung, Schicksal, Geschick

destitute adj. hilflos, verlassen; mittellos

destitution n. Mangel, Entbehrung; Verlassenheit

destroy v. zerstören, vernichten; ausrotten; **-er** n. Zerstörer, Vernichter

destruction n. Zerstörung, Vernichtung, Untergang

destructive adj. zerstörend, vernichtend

detach v. ablösen, trennen; (mil.) abkommandieren; (fig.) abspenstig machen; **-ment** n. Abteilung, Sonderkommando; Gleichgültigkeit

detail v. eingehend darstellen, detaillieren; (mil.) abkommandieren; — n. Einzelheit, Detail; (mil.) Abkommandierung, Abkommandierte, Sonderkommando; go into — auf Einzelheiten eingehen; in — ausführlich, umständlich

detain v. aufhalten, hindern, zurückhalten; (law) in Haft behalten

detect v. entdecken, ermitteln, ertappen; **-ion** n. Entdeckung; **-ive** n. Detektiv, Geheimpolizist; **-ive** adj. Detektiv-; **-or** n. Detektor

detention n. Vorenthaltung; Verzug; Haft

detergent n. Reinigungsmittel

deteriorate v. (sich) verschlechtern, an Wert verlieren; entarten

deterioration n. Verschlechterung, Entartung

determination n. Entschlossenheit, Bestimmtheit; Entschluss, Beschluss

determine v. bestimmen, beschliessen

deterrence n. Hindernis; Hürde; Verzögerung; (mil.) Abschreckung

detest v. verabscheuen; **-able** adj. abscheulich

dethrone v. enthronen

detonate v. detonieren, explodieren (lassen); verpuffen

detonation n. Detonation, Explosion, Knall; Verpuffung

detour n. Umweg, Umleitung; — v. umleiten

detract v. abziehen, beeinträchtigen, schmälern

detriment n. Nachteil, Schaden, Abbruch; **-al** adj. nachteilig, schädlich

deuce n. (cards and dice) Zwei; (tennis) Gleichstand; (sl.) Teufel

devaluate v. entwerten

devaluation n. Entwertung

devastate v. verwüsten, verheeren

devastation n. Verwüstung

develop v. entwickeln, entfalten, erschliessen; **-ment** n. Entwicklung, Entfaltung; Ereignis

deviate v. abweichen; ableiten

deviation n. Abweichnung; Ableitung

device n. Vorrichtung; Entwurf, Plan; List, Kunstgriff; Devise, Wahlspruch

devil n. Teufel; **between the — and the deep blue sea** in der Klemme; — v. plagen; stark würzen; **-ed** adj. stark gewürzt; **-ed eggs** russische Eier; **-ish** adj. teuflisch; verteufelt; **-try** n. Teufelei; Verwegenheit

devious adj. abweichend, abwegig; abgelegen, irrig

devitalize v. der Lebenskraft berauben

devoid adj. ermangelnd, bar, leer; — of ohne

devote v. weihen, widmen; ergeben

devotion n. Hingabe; Ergebenheit; Weihe, Widmung

devour v. verzehren, verschlingen

devout adj. fromm, inbrünstig, andächtig; aufrichtig

dew n. Tau; **-y** adj. tauig; betaut

dewdrop n. Tautropfen

dextrose n. Dextrose, Traubenzucker

diabetes n. Diabetes, Zuckerkrankheit

diabetic adj. diabetisch, zuckerkrank

diabolic(al) adj. diabolisch, teuflisch; boshaft

diadem n. Diadem

diagnose v. diagnostizieren, eine Diagnose stellen

diagnosis n. Diagnose

diagonal n. Diagonale, Querlinie; — adj. diagonal, schräg

diagram n. Diagramm, Figur, graphische Darstellung, Schaubild

dial n. (clock) Zifferblatt; Sonnenuhr;

(mech.) Anzeigetafel; (tel.) Wählerscheibe, Nummernscheibe; — telephone Selbstanschlusstelefon, Wählerfernsprecher; — v. wählen

dialect n. Dialekt, Mundart

dialog(ue) n. Dialog, Zwiegespräch

diameter n. Durchmesser

diamond n. Diamant; (cards) Karo; (geom.) Rhombus, Raute; (sports) Baseballfeld; — **cutter** Diamantenschleifer

diaper n. Windel

diaphragm n. (med.) Zwerchfell; (opt.) Blende; (tel.) Membran(e)

diarrhea n. Diarrhöe, Durchfall

diary n. Tagebuch

diathermy n. Diathermie, Bestrahlung

dice n. pl. Würfel

dichotomy n. Dichotomie, Zweiteilung

dicker v. feilschen, handeln

dictaphone n. Diktafon

dictate n. Diktieren; Vorschrift, Regel, Gebot; — v. diktieren, vorschreiben

dictation n. Diktat; Vorschrift

dictator n. Diktator, unumschränkter Machthaber; **-ial** adj. diktatorisch, unumschränkt, gebieterisch; **-ship** n. Diktatur, Gewaltherrschaft

diction n. Diktion, Ausdruck, Redeweise, Stil; **-ary** n. Wörterbuch, Lexikon

die n. Würfel; Zufall, Los; (mech.) Stempel; Prägestock

die v. sterben, umkommen; vergehen; — **away** verhallen, ersterben; — **down** ausgehen, verlöschen; — **out** aussterben; **never say —!** verzweifle nie!

diesel engine n. Dieselmotor

diet n. Diät; Speise, Nahrung; Reichstag; — v. diät leben, Diät halten; **-etics** n. Ernährungslehre; **-ician** n. Diätfachmann

differ v. abweichen, sich unterscheiden; anderer Meinung sein; **-ence** n. Unterschied, Verschiedenheit, Differenz, Streit; **-ent** adj. anders, verschieden; **-ential** n. Differential; **-entiate** v. differenzieren, unterscheiden

difficult adj. schwer, schwierig, mühsam; eigensinnig; **-y** n. Schwierigkeit, Hindernis

dig v. (um)graben; wühlen; — **up** ausgraben; **-ger** n. Grabende, Gräber, Erdarbeiter; **-gings** n. pl. Minenbezirk, Minengebiet; (coll.) Wohnung

digest n. Übersicht, Auszug, Abriss; — v. verdauen, verarbeiten; **-ible** adj. verdaulich; **-ion** n. Verdauung; Digestion; **-ive** adj. verdauungsfördernd

digit n. Fingerbreite; (math.) Ziffer (unter zehn), Stelle

dignified adj. würdevoll, stattlich, erhaben

dignify v. ehren, auszeichnen

dignitary n. Würdenträger, Prälat

dignity n. Würde, Erhabenheit

dike n. Deich, Damm

dilapidate v. zerstören, verfallen (lassen)

dilemma n. Dilemma, Verlegenheit, Klemme

diligence n. Fleiss, Eifer

diligent adj. fleissig, eifrig

dilute v. verdünnen, (ab)schwächen, verwässern; — adj. verdünnt; kraftlos, schwach

dim adj. unklar, matt, trübe; dunkel; — v. (sich) verdunkeln, trüben; — **lights** abblenden; **-ness** n. Unklarheit; Dunkel; Trübheit, Mattheit

dime n. Zehncentstück; — **novel** Schundroman

dimension n. Dimension, Ausdehnung, Umfang

diminish v. verringern, (sich) vermindern, abnehmen; **-ing** adj. verringert, vermindert

diminutive adj. klein, winzig; verkleinernd

dimple n. Grübchen

din n. Lärm, Getöse; — v. betäuben

dine v. speisen, dinieren; **-r** n. Speisende; Speisewagen; **-tte** n. Essnische

dingy adj. schmutzig, schwärzlich

dining adj. Speise-; — **car** Speisewagen; — **room** Esszimmer, Speisezimmer, Speisesaal

dinner n. Essen, Mittagessen, Abendessen, Festessen; — **jacket** Smoking

dinosaur n. Dinosaurier

dint n. by — of durch, mittels, kraft, vermöge

diocese n. Diözese, Bischofssprengel

diorama n. Diorama, Reliefbild

dioxide n. Dioxyd

dip v. (ein)tauchen; färben; untersinken; (sich) senken; — n. Eintauchen, kurzes Bad; Abhang, Senkung; **-per** n. Kochlöffel, Schöpflöffel; Big (or Great) Dipper grosser Bär, grosser Wagen

diphtheria n. Diphterie, Halsbräune

diphthong n. Diphthong, Doppellaut

diploma n. Diplom, Urkunde; **-cy** n. Diplomatie; **-t** n. Diplomat; **-tic** adj. diplomatisch, taktvoll

direct adj. gerade, direkt; klar, deutlich; offen; — **current** Gleichstrom; — **hit** Volltreffer; — **object** direktes Objekt; — adv. geradeswegs; unmittelbar; — v. richten, lenken, leiten, führen, anweisen, anordnen; hinweisen, zeigen; adressieren; **-ion** n. Richtung; Leitung, Führung; Anweisung, Anordnung, Direktion; **-ions** pl. Gebrauchsanweisung; **-tion finder** Peilvorrichtung; **-ive** n. Direktive, Richtschnur, Weisung; **-or** n. Direktor, Leiter; **board of -ors** Direktorium; **-ory** n. Adressbuch; Einwohnerverzeichnis

dirndl n. Dirndl

dirt n. Schmutz, Dreck; Erde, Erdboden; — **road** Feldweg; **-y** adj. schmutzig, unsauber; gemein, schändlich; **-y trick** Schurkenstreich; — v. beschmutzen, besudeln

dirt-cheap adj. spottbillig

disability n. Unvermögen, Unfähigkeit; Rechtsunfähigkeit

disable v. unfähig (or unbrauchbar, kampfunfähig) machen; ausserstand setzen; **-d** adj. untauglich, dienstunfähig

disadvantage n. Nachteil, Schaden

disagree v. nicht übereinstimmen, nicht einverstanden sein; (food) nicht zuträglich sein; **-able** adj. unangenehm, verdriesslich; **-ment** n. Verschiedenheit; Meinungsverschiedenheit, Missstimmung, Streit

disappear v. verschwinden; **-ance** n. Verschwinden

disappoint v. enttäuschen, täuschen; vereiteln; **-ed** adj. enttäuscht; **-ment** n. Enttäuschung; Misslingen, Fehlschlag

disapproval n. Missbilligung

disapprove v. misbilligen, tadeln, verwerfen

disarm v. entwaffnen, unschädlich machen; abrüsten; **-ament** n. Entwaffnung, Abrüstung

disaster n. Unfall, Katastrophe, Unheil

disastrous adj. unheilvoll, verhängnisvoll

disband v. entlassen, (sich) auflösen

disburse v. auszahlen; vorschiessen; **-ment** n. Auszahlung; Vorschuss

disc n. Scheibe

discard v. verwerfen, weglegen; entlassen; (cards) ablegen; — n. Verwerfen; Ablegen; abgeworfene Karte; abgelegte Sache

discern v. unterscheiden; erkennen, wahrnehmen; beurteilen; **-ible** adj. unterscheidbar, erkennbar, sichtbar; **-ing** adj. unterscheidend, einsichtsvoll; **-ment** n. Unterscheidung, Einsicht

discharge n. Entlassung; (com.) Erfüllung, Bezahlung; (elec.) Entladung; (gun) Abschuss, Abfeuern; (med.) Eiter(ung), Ausfluss; — v. entlassen; abladen, löschen, entladen; feuern; eitern

disciple n. Jünger, Schüler

disciplinary adj. disziplinarisch

discipline n. Disziplin, Zucht; Züchtigung; — v. bestrafen, züchtigen; erziehen

disclose v. eröffnen, offenbaren, enthüllen

disclosure n. Eröffnung, Offenbarung, Enthüllung

discolor v. (sich) verfärben; (fig.) entstellen; **-ation** n. Verfärbung; (fig.) Entstellung

discomfort n. Unbehagen, Verdriesslichkeit

disconcert v. vereiteln, verwirren, ausser Fassung bringen

disconnect v. trennen; auskuppeln; (elec.) ausschalten

discontent n. Unzufriedenheit, Missvergnügen; — v. unzufrieden (or missvergnügt) machen; **-ed** adj. unzufrieden, missvergnügt

discontinue v. unterbrechen, aufgeben; aufhören

discord(ance) n. Zwietracht, Uneinigkeit; (mus.) Dissonanz, Disharmonie, Missklang

discount n. Diskonto, Abzug, Rabatt; — v. diskontieren, abrechnen, abziehen; (fig.) mit Vorsicht aufnehmen, nicht für voll nehmen

discourage v. entmutigen, abschrecken; **-ment** n. Entmutigung, Abschreckung

discourse n. Rede, Diskurs, Unterhal-

tung; — v. reden, sprechen, unterhalten
discourteous adj. unhöflich, unartig; grob
discourtesy n. Unhöflichkeit; Roheit
discover v. entdecken, aufdecken; erspähen; ausfindig machen; **-y** n. Entdeckung, Auffindung; Enthüllung; Fund
discredit n. schlechter Ruf, Diskredit; — v. nicht glauben; beschimpfen, verunglimpfen
discreet adj. diskret, verschwiegen; vorsichtig
discretion n. Diskretion, Verschwiegenheit; Umsicht, Besonnenheit; Takt
discriminate v. unterscheiden
discriminating adj. unterscheidend; scharfsinnig, einsichtsvoll
discrimination n. Unterscheidung; Scharfsinn
discus n. Diskus, Wurfscheibe
discuss v. besprechen, erörtern, verhandeln
discussion n. Verhandlung, Diskussion
disease n. Krankheit; **-d** adj. krank, leidend
disembark v. landen, ausschiffen, aussteigen
disfavor n. Ungnade, Missfallen
disfigure v. entstellen, verunstalten; **-ment** n. Entstellung, Verunstaltung
disgrace n. Schande; Ungnade; — v. entehren, schänden; in Ungnade fallen; **-ful** adj. entehrend, schimpflich
disguise n. Verkleidung, Maske, Vorwand; — v. verhehlen, verkleiden
disgust n. Widerwille, Abscheu, Ekel; Abneigung; **cause** — Widerwillen erregen; — v. anekeln; verleiden; **be -ed** sich ärgern; **-ing** adj. eklig, ekelhaft, widerwärtig
dish n. Schüssel; Gericht, Platte, Speise; **set of -es** Tafelgeschirr; — v. — **up** anrichten, auftragen, auftischen
dishcloth, **dishrag** n. Tischtuch; Geschirrtuch
dishearten v. entmutigen, verzagen
dishonest adj. unredlich, unehrlich; **-y** n. Unredlichkeit, Unehrlichkeit
dishonor n. Schande, Unehre; Nichtbezahlung; — v. entehren; nicht bezahlen; **-able** adj. entehrend, schimpflich, ehrlos, gewissenlos
dishpan n. Abwaschschüssel
dishwasher n. Tellerwäscher; Geschirrwaschmaschine
dishwater n. Abwaschwasser, Spülwasser
disillusion n. Enttäuschung; Ernüchterung; — v. enttäuschen, ernüchtern
disinclined adj. abgeneigt
disinfect v. disinfizieren; **-ant** n. Desinfektionsmittel
disinherit v. enterben
disintegrate v. zerfallen, (sich in seine Bestandteile) auflösen
disintegration n. Verwitterung; Auflösung
disinterested adj. uneigennützig; unparteiisch
disk n. Scheibe; — **jockey** Schallplattenjongleur; Tonoperateur
dislike n. Abneigung, Missfallen; Wider-

willen; — v. missbilligen, nicht mögen, nicht leiden können
dislocate v. verrenken, ausrenken; (fig.) verwirren
dislodge v. ausquartieren, verlegen; (hunting) verjagen
disloyal adj. treulos, verräterisch; **-ty** n. Treulosigkeit, Untreue
dismal adj. düster, trübselig, traurig, schrecklich; schaurig, öde
dismantle v. entkleiden, entblössen; (mil.) demontieren; schleifen; (naut.) abtakeln
dismay n. Bestürzung; Schrecken, Furcht; — v. bestürzen; erschrecken
dismember v. zergliedern, zerstückeln
dismiss v. entlassen, verabschieden; abweisen; **-al** n., **-ion** n. Entlassung; Abdankung, Abschied; Abweisung
dismount v. absteigen, absitzen; abmontieren
disobedience n. Ungehorsam, Widerspenstigkeit
disobedient adj. ungehorsam, widerspenstig
disobey v. nicht gehorchen, ungehorsam sein; missachten
disorder n. Unordnung, Verwirrung; Aufruhr; (med.) Krankheit; Störung; — v. in Unordnung bringen, verwirren; zerrütten; **-ly** adj. unordentlich, verwirrt; ordnungswidrig; liederlich
disorganization n. Auflösung, Zerrüttung
disorganize v. desorganisieren, zerrütten; in Unordnung bringen
disown v. verleugnen, verstossen, nicht anerkennen
disparage v. herabsetzen, verunglimpfen; **-ment** n. Verkleinerung, Herabsetzung
dispatch n. Absendung; Erledigung; Abfertigung; Depesche, Eilbrief; Eile; — v. absenden, expedieren; erledigen; eilen; beseitigen
dispel v. vertreiben, verjagen; verbannen
dispensary n. Apotheke; Klinik
dispensation n. Dispens(ation), Austeilung, Verteilung; Vergebung, Verzeihung
dispense v. austeilen, verteilen; verwalten; verzichten, erlassen; entbinden; (med.) bereiten
disperse v. zerstreuen, vertreiben, zerteilen
displace v. versetzen, verlegen, verrücken; **-d person** Heimatvertriebene, Zwangsverschleppte; **-ment** n. Verrückung, Versetzung, Verschiebung; (naut.) Wasserverdrängung
display n. Entfaltung, Aufwand; (com.) Ausstellung, Schau; Auslage; — v. zur Schau stellen, ausstellen; entfalten, zeigen
displease v. missfallen; beleidigen, verletzen
displeasure n. Missfallen, Missvergnügen; Unwille, Verdruss
disposal n. Einrichtung, Anordnung; **I'm at your** — ich stehe zu Ihrer Verfügung
dispose v. (an)ordnen, einrichten; unterbringen; verfügen; abschaffen, los-

werden; **-ed** *adj.* gesinnt, gestimmt, geneigt

disposition *n.* Einrichtung, Ordnung; Temperament, Gemütsart; Gesinnung

dispossess *v.* vertreiben, berauben; enteignen

disproportion *n.* Missverhältnis; **-ate** *adj.* unverhältnismässig, unproportioniert

disprove *v.* widerlegen

disputable *adj.* bestreitbar, streitig

dispute *n.* Auseinandersetzung, Wortwechsel; Disput, Debatte; — *v.* bestreiten, streitig machen, abstreiten; debattieren, erörtern

disregard *v.* missachten; ignorieren, übersehen; — *n.* Missachtung; Vernachlässigung, Nicht(be)achtung

disrepair *n.* schlechter Zustand

disreputable *adj.* verrufen; schimpflich

disrepute *n.* Verruf, Schande

disrespect *n.* Unehrerbietigkeit; Missachtung; Unhöflichkeit, Grobheit; **-ful** *adj.* unehrerbietig; unhöflich, unartig

disrobe *v.* entkleiden

disrupt *v.* zerreissen, spalten; **-ion** *n.* Zerreissen; Bruch, Spaltung

dissatisfaction *n.* Unzufriedenheit, Missvergnügen

dissatisfied *adj.* unzufrieden, missvergnügt

dissatisfy *v.* nicht befriedigen; unzufrieden machen

dissect *v.* zerschneiden, zerlegen; (anat.) sezieren; (fig.) zergliedern; **-ion** *n.* Zergliederung; (anat.) Sektion, Sezieren, Obduktion

dissemble *v.* verhehlen, verbergen; heucheln, schmeicheln

disseminate *v.* aussäen; aussprengen, verbreiten

dissension *n.* Zwietracht, Zwist, Streit

dissent *n.* Meinungsverschiedenheit; Abweichung; — *v.* anderer Meinung sein; abweichen, nicht übereinstimmen; **-er** *n.* Andersdenkende, Dissident

dissertation *n.* Dissertation, Abhandlung, Auseinandersetzung

dissimilar *adj.* ungleichartig, unähnlich

dissipate *v.* verschwenden; ausschweifen; zerstreuen

dissipation *n.* Verschwendung; Ausschweifung; Zerstreuung

dissolute *adj.* liederlich, wüst, ausschweifend

dissolution *n.* Auflösung, Zersetzung

dissolve *v.* (sich) auflösen, trennen; schmelzen; vergehen

dissonant *adj.* abweichend; (mus.) misstönend

dissuade *v.* abraten

distaff *n.* Rocken; — **side** weibliche Linie

distance *n.* Entfernung, Strecke, Ferne, Abstand; **at a —** von weitem; **in the —** in der Ferne; **keep at a —** fern halten; **keep one's —** sich fern halten

distant *adj.* fern, entfernt; zurückhaltend; **very —** weit entfernt

distaste *n.* Widerwillen, Ekel, Abneigung; **-ful** *adj.* ekelhaft, ekelerregend; widerwärtig

distemper *n.* (color) Leimfarbe, Temperafarbe; (dog) Staupe

distil(l) *v.* destillieren; herabtröpfeln (lassen); **-lation** *n.* Destillierung; **-lery** *n.* Branntweinbrennerei

distinct *adj.* klar, deutlich; unterschieden, verschieden; getrennt; **-ion** *n.* Unterscheidung, Unterschied; Vorzug, Würde; Auszeichnung; **-ive** *adj.* unterscheidend, eigentümlich; besonders; **-ness** *n.* Deutlichkeit; Bestimmtheit

distinguish *v.* unterscheiden; auszeichnen

distort *v.* verzerren, verdrehen, verziehen; **-ion** *n.* Verzerrung, Verdrehung

distract *v.* zerstreuen; abziehen, ablenken; beunruhigen; **-ed** *adj.* bestürzt, verrückt; **-ion** *n.* Zerstreuung; Ablenkung; Zerstreutheit

distress *n.* Not, Elend; Pein, Qual, Kummer; — *v.* quälen, peinigen; erschöpfen, überanstrengen

distribute *v.* verteilen, austeilen, verbreiten

distribution *n.* Verteilung, Austeilung, Verbreitung

distributor *n.* Verteiler, Austeiler

district *n.* Bezirk, Kreis; Gebiet, Zone; **— attorney** Staatsanwalt

distrust *n.* Misstrauen, Zweifel; — *v.* misstrauen, zweifeln; **-ful** *adj.* misstrauisch, argwöhnisch

disturb *v.* stören; in Unordnung bringen; aufrühren; beunruhigen; **-ance** *n.* Störung; Aufruhr

ditch *n.* Graben; **fight to the last —** bis zum letzten Blutstropfen kämpfen; — *v.* in einen Graben fahren (*or* werfen); (sl.) im Stich lassen

ditto *n.* Gleiche, Erwähnte; — *adv.* dito, desgleichen; — *adj.* — **marks** Anführungszeichen

ditty *n.* Liedchen

divan *n.* Diwan, Sofa

dive *n.* (sports) Tauchen; Kopfsprung; Sturzflug; (coll.) Spelunke; — *v.* (unter)tauchen; einen Sturzflug machen; **— bomber** Sturzkampfflugzeug; **-er** *n.* Taucher

diverge *v.* divergieren, auseinanderlaufen, abweichen; **-nce** *n.* Divergieren, Auseinanderlaufen, Abweichen; **-nt** *adj.* divergierend, abweichend

divers *adj.* diverse, etliche, verschiedene; **-e** *adj.* verschieden, mannigfaltig; **-ify** *v.* verschieden machen; Abwechslung bringen in; **-ity** *n.* Verschiedenheit, Mannigfaltigkeit

diversion *n.* Ablenkung, Zerstreuung, Zeitvertreib

divert *v.* abwenden, ablenken; zerstreuen, belustigen

divide *v.* teilen, dividieren; scheiden, trennen; sich spalten, sich entzweien; **— by two** durch zwei teilen (*or* dividieren); — *n.* Wasserscheide; **-nd** *n.* Dividende, Gewinnanteil; (math.) Dividend

divine *n.* Theologe, Geistliche, Priester; — *adj.* göttlich, heilig; — *v.* weissagen; ahnen

diving n. Tauchen; Kunstspringen; (avi.) Sturzfliegen; tauchend; — **bell** Taucherglocke; — **suit** Taucheranzug

divinity n. Gottheit, Göttlichkeit; Theologie

divisible adj. teilbar

division n. Division; Teilung; Abteilung; (pol.) Wahlkreis, Bezirk

divisor n. Divisor, Teiler

divorce n. Scheidung, Trennung; **get a** — sich scheiden lassen; — v. scheiden, trennen; wegnehmen

divorcé n. Geschiedene

divulge v. verbreiten, ausplaudern

dizziness n. Schwindel

dizzy adj. schwindlig, schwindelnd; (coll.) duselig; **I feel** — mir ist schwindelig

do v. tun, machen, ausführen, verrichten; passen, gehen; genügen; — **away with** abschaffen, beseitigen; — **without** entbehren müssen; **how** — **you** —? Wie geht es Ihnen? **-er** n. Täter, Vollbringer; **-ing** n. Werk; **-ings** Taten, Begebenheiten; Treiben; **-ne** adj. getan, geschehen; beendigt, fertig; (food) gar, gut

docile adj. gelehrig, lenksam, fügsam

dock n. (bot.) Ampfer; (law) Anklagebank; (naut.) Dock; (zool.) Schwanzstummel; **dry** — Trockendock; — v. stutzen, verkürzen; abziehen; (naut.) docken

doctor n. Doktor, Arzt; **-'s office** Sprechzimmer; — v. ärztlich behandeln, kurieren; (sl.) doktern, fälschen, zustutzen

doctrine n. Lehre, Doktrin

document n. Dokument, Urkunde; Beleg; — v. dokumentieren, beurkunden, belegen; **-ary** adj. dokumentarisch, urkundlich

dodge n. Seitensprung; Kniff, Schlich, Winkelzug; — v. ausweichen, vermeiden, Ausflüchte gebrauchen

doe n. Reh, Hindin; Häsin

doff v. ausziehen, ablegen

dog n. Hund; Rüde, Bock; (coll.) Kerl, Bursche; — **in the manger** Neidhammel; **go to the** —**s** auf den Hund kommen; — **days** Hundstage; — **fancier** Hundeliebhaber; **Dog Star** Hundsstern, Sirius; — v. hetzen, sich an jemandes Fersen heften; **-ged** adj. störrisch, starrköpfig, verbissen

dogcart n. leichter Jagdwagen

dogfight n. Luftzweikampf

doghouse n. Hundehütte; **be in the** — (ehelichen) Verdruss haben

dogma n. Dogma, Grundsatz; Glaubenslehre; **-tic** adj. dogmatisch; gebieterisch

dogsear n. Eselsohr

dogwood n. Kornelkirsche

doily n. Spitzendeckchen, Dessertserviette

dole n. Austeilung, Verteilung; Anteil; — v. verteilen; — **out** austeilen, herausrücken; **-ful** adj. kummervoll, kläglich, trübselig

doll n. Puppe; Zierpuppe

dollar n. Dollar; **silver** — Silberdollar

dolphin n. Delphin

domain n. Gebiet, Domäne; Gut, Herrschaft

dome n. Kuppel, Dom

domestic adj. häuslich; einheimisch, inländisch; gezähmt; Haus-, Privat-; — **animal** Haustier; **-ate** v. zähmen; heimisch werden

dominance n. Herrschen; Macht, Gewalt

dominate v. (be)herrschen, vorherrschen

domination n. Herrschaft

domineer v. beherrschen, dominieren; **-ing** adj. gebieterisch, herrisch; übermütig

dominion n. Herrschaft, Gebiet; Dominion

domino n. Domino; pl Domino(spiel)

don v. anziehen, anlegen

donate v. schenken, geben, widmen

donation n. Schenkung, Widmung

donkey n. Esel; — **engine** Hilfsmaschine

donor n. Geber, Spender; **blood** — Blutspender

doodle v. kritzeln, bekritzeln; — n. Kritzelei; **-r** n. Kritzler, Bekritzler

doom n. Schicksal, Los; Urteil; — v. verurteilen; bestimmen

doomsday n. Jüngster Tag; Weltuntergang

door n. Tür, Pforte, Tor; **out of** —**s** draussen; — **mat** Fussabtreter, Fussmatte

doorbell n. Klingel

doorkeeper, doorman n. Pförtner, Portier

doorknob n. Türknopf

doorpost n. Torpfosten, Türpfosten

doorstep n. Stufe vor der Haustür

doorway n. Torweg, Hauseingang, Tür

dope n. Rauschgift, Betäubungsmittel; (sl.) Dummkopf; vertrauliche Auskunft; — **fiend** Rauschgiftsüchtige; — v. betäuben; dopen

dormant adj. schlafend; ungebraucht, unbenutzt

dormer (window) n. Bodenfenster, Dachfenster

dormitory n. Schlafsaal

dose n. Dosis, Arzneimenge; Pille; — v. dosieren, Arznei verordnen

dot n. Punkt, Pünktchen; Tüpfel; **on the** — pünktlich; **auf die Minute;** — v. punktieren, tüpfeln

dote v. vernarrt sein; faseln

double n. Doppelte; Doppelgänger; (theat. and film) Double; pl. (sports) Doppel; — adj. doppelt; zweideutig; — **bass** Kontrabass; — **bed** zweischläfriges Bett; — **chin** Doppelkinn; — **cross** Doppelverrat, Hintergehen; — **entry** doppelte Buchführung; — **feature** Doppelvorstellung; — **talk** Doppelzüngigkeit; — **time** Laufschritt; — v. (sich) verdoppeln; zusammenlegen, falten; (cards) Kontra ansagen; — **up** sich krümmen; zusammenkrümmen

double-breasted adj. zweireihig

double-cross v. hintergehen

double-dealing n. Falschheit, Doppelzüngigkeit

double-feature n. (theat.) zwei Hauptfilme

double-quick *adj.* schnell, im Geschwindschritt

doubt *n.* Zweifel, Bedenken; **no —** zweifellos, sicherlich; **without —** ohne Zweifel, zweifellos; **—** *v.* (be)zweifeln; argwöhnen; **-er** *n.* Zweifler; **-ful** *adj.* bedenklich, zweifelnd; zweifelhaft, fraglich; verdächtig; **-less** *adj.* zweifellos, gewiss

dough *n.* Teig; (sl.) Geld

doughnut *n.* Pfannkuchen, Krapfen, Spritzkuchen

douse *v.* tauchen, ins Wasser stürzen; (naut.) laufen lassen; (sl.) auslöschen

dove *n.* Taube; **ring —** Ringeltaube

dovetail *v.* genau ineinanderpassen

dowager *n.* Frau (*or* Witwe) von Stand

dowel *n.* Dübel; Holzpflock

down *n.* Daune, Flaum; Düne, Hügel. Hügelland; **ups** and **-s** Wechselfälle; **— —** *prep.* and *adv.* nieder, unten; herab. hinab; herunter; hinunter; (nom.) bezahlt; **five dollars —** fünf Dollar als Anzahlung; **up and —** auf und ab; **—** *adj.* niedrig, wenig; (com.) billig; (sun) untergegangen; **be — and out** auf den Hund gekommen sein; **— payment** Anzahlung; **—** *interj.* nieder! (hin)ab! kusch dich! **—** *v.* niederwerfen; abschiessen; hinunterstürzen, (hin)abstürzen; **-y** *adj.* flaumig, sanft, weich

downcast *adj.* niedergeschlagen

downfall *n.* Sturz, Niedergang, Untergang, Fall

downhearted *adj.* verzagt, niedergeschlagen, gedrückt

downpour *n.* Platzregen, Wolkenbruch, Guss

downright *adv.* gerade heraus, völlig, durchaus; **—** *adj.* offenherzig, ausgesprochen; völlig

downstairs *n. pl.* unteres Stockwerk; **—** *adv.* (nach) unten, die Treppe hinunter

downtown *adv.* in die (*or* der) Stadt; **—** *adj.* in der Innenstadt liegend

downward *adj.* (sich) senkend, abschüssig; **-s** *adv.* abwärts, niederwärts; hinab

dowry *n.* Mitgift, Ausstattung

doze *n.* Schlummer, Schläfchen; **—** *v.* schlummern, duseln; **— off** einnicken

dozen *n.* Dutzend; **by the —** dutzendweise

drab *adj.* mausgrau; eintönig; trüb(e)

draft, draught *n.* Zug; (art and lit.) Entwurf; (com.) Tratte, Wechsel, Scheck; (drink) Trunk, Schluck; Trank; (mil.) Musterung; Sonderkommando; Ersatz, Nachschub; (naut.) Tiefgang; **honor a —** einen Wechsel einlösen; **on —** vom Fass; **rough —** Rohentwurf; **sight —** Sichtwechsel; **— board** Musterungskommission; **— horse** Zugpferd; **—** *v.* entwerfen, skizzieren; mustern, auswählen, einziehen; **-ee** *n.* Rekrut, Militärdienstfähige; **-ing** *adj.* **-ing board** Zeichenbrett; **-y** *adj.* zugig

draftsman *n.* Zeichner; Entwerfer

drag *v.* schleppen; eggen; mit einem Schleppnetz fischen; **—** *n.* (coll.) Einfluss; **— chute** Bremsfallschirm

dragnet *n.* Schleppnetz

dragon *n.* Drache

dragonfly *n.* Libelle, Wasserjungfer

drain *n.* Abfluss, Abzugsgraben, Ableitung; (fig.) Belastung; **—** *v.* (ent)leeren; ableiten; entwässern, trockenlegen; ablaufen; (fig.) berauben; **-age** *n.* Entwässerung, Trokkenlegung

drainpipe *n.* Abzugsrohr, Abflussrohr

drake *n.* Enterich

dram *n.* Drachme; Trunk, Schluck

drama *n.* Drama; **-tic** *adj.* dramatisch; **-tics** *n.* Dramatik, dramatische Kunst; **-tist** *n.* Dramatiker; **-tization** *n.* Dramatisierung; **-tize** *v.* dramatisieren

drape *v.* drapieren, behängen; umhüllen; in Falten legen; schmücken; **—** *n.* Vorhang; **-ry** *n.* Vorhang; Drapierung, Faltenwurf; Stoff, Gewebe, Tuchwaren

drastic *adj.* drastisch, kräftig

draw *n.* Ziehung; Lotterie; Los; (fishing) Zug, Fang; (sports) Unentschieden; (theat.) Zugstück; **in a —** unentschieden; **—** *v.* ziehen, in die Länge ziehen; (air) einatmen; (art) zeichnen, skizzieren; (bow) spannen; (curtain) aufziehen, zuziehen; (fluids) abziehen; (meat) ausnehmen, ausweiden; (theat.) anziehen, erregen; (teeth) (aus)ziehen; **— blood** Blut vergiessen, schröpfen; **— lines** Linien ziehen; **— lots** Nummern ziehen; **— near** (*or* nigh) sich nähern; **— off** abziehen; **— on** anlocken; **— out** herausnehmen; ausforschen; **— the line** eine Grenze ziehen; **— up** abfassen; aufstellen; **-er** *n.* Schublade; **-ers** Unterhose; **-ing** *n.* Ziehen, Ziehung; Zeichnung; **-ing** *adj.* **-ing account** offenes Konto; **-ing card** Zugstück; **-ing room** Empfangszimmer, Salon; Zeichensaal

drawback *n.* Schattenseite, Kehrseite; Nachteil, Hindernis

drawbridge *n.* Zugbrücke

drayman *n.* Rollkutscher

dread *n.* Furcht, Entsetzen; Ehrfurcht; Scheu; **—** *adj.* furchtbar; schrecklich; erhaben; **—** *v.* (sich) fürchten, ein Grauen empfinden; **-ful** *adj.* furchtbar, schrecklich; entsetzlich

dream *n.* Traum, Träumerei; **—** *v.* träumen, ahnen; **-er** *n.* Träumer; **-y** *adj.* träumerisch, traumhaft

dreariness *n.* Düsterkeit, Traurigkeit, Öde

dreary *adj.* traurig, trübselig, trostlos; düster, öde

dredge *n.* Bagger; Schleppnetz; **—** *v.* (aus)baggern, mit dem Schleppnetz fischen

dredging machine *n.* Bagger

dregs *n. pl.* Bodensatz; Abfall, Auswurf; Abschaum; Hefe

drench *v.* durchnässen

dress *n.* Kleid, Anzug; Kleidung; **in full —** in vollem Staat; **rehearsal** Kostümprobe; **— suit** Gesellschaftsanzug; **—** *v.* (sich) anziehen, kleiden; (hair) frisieren; (med.) verbinden; (mil.) sich ausrichten, in Linie aufstellen; **— up** sich zurechtmachen (*or* herausputzen);

get —ed sich anziehen; —er n. Kommode; —ing n. Ankleiden, Zurichten; Behandlung; (cooking) Zutat; (med.) Verband; **salad —ing** Salatsauce; **—ing gown** Schlafrock, Morgenrock; **—ing table** Frisiertoilette; **-y** adj. sich geschmackvoll kleidend; putzsüchtig; modisch

dressmaker n. Damenschneider(in)

dribble v. tröpfeln, träufeln; geifern, sabbern; (sports) dribbeln, treiben

drift n. Trieb(kraft), Antrieb; Treiben; (geol.) Geschiebe; (naut.) Abtrift; (phil.) Tendenz, Absicht; — v. dahintreiben; schwimmen; sich anhäufen

driftwood n. Treibholz

drill n. Bohrer, Drillbohrer; (mil.) Drill, Exerzieren; — v. bohren, drillen; (mil.) exerzieren

drink n. Getränk; Trank, Trunk, Schluck; — v. trinken, saufen, zechen; **— to trinken** auf; **-er** n. Trinker, Säufer; **-ing fountain** Trinkbrunnen

drip n. Tropfen; Tröpfeln; Traufe; — v. tröpfeln, tropfen, triefen; träufeln; **-ings** n. pl. Bratenfett

drive n. Fahrweg; Ausfahrt, Ausfahren, Fahren; Spazierfahrt; Kampagne; Schwung; Treiben; (hunting) Treiben, Hetzen; (mech.) Antrieb; **four-wheel —** Vierradantrieb; **go for a —** eine Autofahrt machen; — v. treiben; fahren, ausfahren, lenken; (com.) betreiben, leiten; (engine) fahren; (hit) schlagen; (hunting) jagen, hetzen; (nails) einschlagen; **— a bargain** ein gutes Geschäft abschliessen; **— at** hinauswollen auf; **— away** vertreiben; fortfahren; **— back** zurücktreiben; zurückfahren; **— crazy** (oder mad) verrückt machen; **— off** wegjagen, abweisen; **— on** zufahren; **— out** forttreiben, hinausfahren; **— to** desgisat zur Verzweiflung bringen; **— up** auftreiben; **-r** n. Fahrer, Chauffeur; **-r's license** Führerschein

drive-in n. Autobahngaststätte mit Bedienung am Wagen; Freilichtkino

driveway n. Fahrweg

drizzle n. Sprühregen; — v. sprühen, nieseln, fein regnen

drogue n. Bremsfallschirm

drone n. Drohne; Müssiggänger; Summen, Brummen; (avi.) ferngelenkte, unbemannte Rakete; — v. faulenzen

droop v. zusammenfallen; sinken lassen; verwelken; den Kopf hängen lassen

drop n. Tropfen; Fall, Sinken; pl. **drops,** Bonbons; **lemon —** Zitronendrops; **letter —** Briefeinwurf, Briefschlitz; **— curtain** Zwischen(akts)vorhang; **— hammer** elektrischer Schmiedehammer; **— leaf** Klappbrett, zusammenklappbare Tischplatte; — v. tröpfeln; lecken; fallen (lassen); absetzen, aufgeben; senken; sinken; (bombs) (ab) werfen; **— asleep** einschlafen; **— in** zufällig vorsprechen; **— off** abfallen; abgeben, einschlafen; **— out** ausscheiden

dropsy n. Wassersucht

drought, drouth n. Trockenheit, Dürre

drove n. Herde, Trieb, Trift; Getümmel, Auflauf

drown v. ertrinken, ertränken; übertönen; überfluten

drowsiness n. Schläfrigkeit

drudge n. Packesel, Schwerarbeitende; — v. sich abplacken (or abplagen); **-ry** n. Plakkerei

drug n. Droge, Arzneiware; Rauschgift; — v. Schlafmittel nehmen (or geben); **-gist** n. Apotheker, Drogist

drugstore n. Drogerie

drum n. Trommel; (anat.) Trommelhöhle; **— major** Tambourmajor; — v. trommeln; **— into** einpauken; **— up** (zusammen)trommeln; **-mer** n. Trommler, Tambour; Handlungsreisende

drumstick n. Trommelschlegel; (cooking) Keule

drunk adj. (be)trunken; **get —** sich betrinken; — n. Betrunkene, Besoffene; **-ard** n. Trunkenbold; **-en** adj. (be)trunken; **-en revel** Ausschweifung, Orgie; **-enness** n. Trunkenheit; Trunksucht

dry adj. trocken, dürr; geräuchert; gedörrt; nüchtern; langweilig; herb; **— battery** Trockenbatterie; **— cell** Trockenelement; **— cleaner** chemische Reinigung(sanstalt); **— cleaning** chemische Reinigung; **— dock** Trockendock; **— goods** n. pl. Kurzwaren, Schnittwaren, Baumwollwaren; **— ice** Trockeneis; **— measure** Trockenmass; **— rot** Schwamm, Trockenfäule; — v. (ab)trocknen, austrocknen; dörren, rösten; **-er** n. Trockner; **-ness** n. Trockenheit, Dürre

dry-clean v. chemisch reinigen

dual adj. zwei bezeichnend, zwiefach, doppelt; zweifach; **— control** Doppelkontrolle

dub v. nachsynchronisieren; nachträglich einsetzen

dubious adj. zweifelhaft; schwankend, unschlüssig

duchess n. Herzogin

duck n. Ente; — v. (unter)tauchen, sich ducken (or bücken); neigen

duct n. Gang; Röhre, Rohr; Kanal; **-less** adj. (anat. and bot.) röhrenlos

dud n. Blindgänger

dude n. Geck, Stutzer; **— ranch** Ranch mit Fremdenverkehr

due adj. schuldig; zustehend; gebührend; fällig, zahlbar; **become** (oder **fall**) — fällig werden; **— bill** Schuldschein; **— to** durch, wegen; **in — time** zur richtigen Zeit; — n. Gebühr, Schuld, Recht; Anspruch; Lohn; pl. Abgaben, Gebühren; **give someone his —s** jemandem das Seinige geben; — adv. gerade; genau nach

dugout n. Unterstand

duke n. Herzog; **-dom** n. Herzogtum

dull adj. dumm, albern; träge, schwerfällig; stumpf; dumpf; düster; (color) matt, dunkel; (com.) flau, still; — v. abstumpfen; (sich) trüben; **-ness** n. Dummheit, Stumpfsinn; Trägheit, Mattigkeit; Langweiligkeit; Teilnahmslosigkeit; Flaute, Stille

duly *adv.* angemessen, pflichtgemäss

dumb *adj.* dumm, töricht; stumm, sprachlos

dumbbell *n.* Hantel

dumb-waiter *n.* Speiseaufzug

dum(b)found *v.* zum Schweigen bringen, verblüffen

dummy *n.* Kleiderpuppe, Attrappe; (cards and fig.) Strohmann

dump *n.* Schuttabladeplatz, Abfallhaufen; **be (down) in the —s** schwermütig sein, vor sich hinstarren; **— truck** Kippwagen; **—** *v.* auskippen; abladen, abwerfen; auf den Markt werfen; **-ling** *n.* Kloss, Knödel

dumping ground *n.* Schuttabladeplatz

dunce *n.* Dummkopf, Einfaltspinsel

dune *n.* Düne, Sandhügel

dung *n.* Mist, Dünger; **—** *v.* düngen

dungeon *n.* Verliess, Kerker

dunghill *n.* Dunghaufen, Misthaufen

duodenal ulcer *n.* (*med.*) Zwölffingerdarmgeschwür

dupe *n.* Angeführte, Betrogene, Gimpel; **—** *v.* täuschen, anführen

duplex *n.* Zweifamilienwohnung; Zweifamilienhaus; **—** *adj.* doppelt, zweifach

duplicate *n.* Duplikat, Kopie; **—** *v.* verdoppeln; wiederholen; abschreiben; **—** *adj.* doppelt, zweifach

duplicity *n.* Zweideutigkeit, Falschheit; Doppelzüngigkeit

durability *n.* Dauerhaftigkeit

durable *adj.* dauerhaft, dauernd

duration *n.* Dauer, Fortdauer

duress *n.* Bedrückung, Zwang

during *prep.* während

dusk *n.* Dämmerung, Halbdunkel, Zwielicht; **-y** *adj.* dämmerig, dunkel; trübe, düster

dust *n.* Staub; Kehricht, Müll; Asche; **house — Wohnungsstaub**; **— bowl** Ursprung (*or* Quelle) des Sandsturms; **— storm** Sandsturm; **—** *v.* abstauben, ausstauben; abbürsten, abwischen; bestäuben; **-y** *adj.* staubig, bestäubt; staubartig

dustpan *n.* Kehrrichtschaufel, Müllschaufel

dutiable *adj.* steuerpflichtig, zollpflichtig; **— goods** zollpflichtige Waren

dutiful *adj.* pflichtgetreu, gehorsam; ehrerbietig

duty *n.* Pflicht, Verpflichtung, Schuldigkeit; Aufgabe; (*mil.* and *naut.*) Dienst; (tax, etc.) Zoll, Abgabe, Steuer; **be off — dienstfrei** sein; **be on — im Dienst** sein, Dienst haben

dwarf *n.* Zwerg; **—** *v.* verkrüppeln, verkleinern; zusammenschrumpfen; in den Schatten stellen; in der Entwicklung hindern; **—** *adj.* Zwerg-; niedrig, klein, winzig

dwell *v.* wohnen; **— (up)on** verweilen bei, sich aufhalten bei; **-er** *n.* Einwohner, Bewohner; **-ing** *n.* Wohnung, Behausung

dwindle *v.* sich vermindern, abnehmen; schwinden

dye *n.* Farbe, Färbung; Farbstoff; **—** *v.* färben; **-ing** *n.* Färben

dynamic *adj.* dynamisch; **-s** *n. pl.* Dynamik

dynamite *n.* Dynamit

dynamo *n.* Dynamo

dynasty *n.* Dynastie

dyspepsia *n.* Verdauungsstörung

E

each *adj.* jeder, jede, jedes; **— and every one** jeder einzelne; **— one** (ein)jeder; **— other** einander, sich; **—** *pron.* (ein)jeder

eager *adj.* eifrig, begierig; brennend; **-ness** *n.* Begierde, Eifer

eagle *n.* Adler

eagle-eyed *adj.* adleräugig, scharfsichtig

ear *n.* Ohr; Gehör; (*bot.*) Ähre, Kolben; **by — nach dem Gehör**; **— of corn** Maiskolben; **— muff** Ohrenschützer; **— specialist** Ohrenspezialist; **— trumpet** Hörrohr

earache *n.* Ohrenschmerzen

eardrum *n.* Trommelfell

earl *n.* Graf

early *adj.* früh, (früh)zeitig; **— bird** Frühaufsteher; **— life** Jugendzeit

earmark *n.* Kennzeichen; **—** *v.* kennzeichnen, vormerken

earn *v.* verdienen, erwerben, gewinnen; **-ings** *n. pl.* Lohn, Verdienst, Einkommen

earnest *adj.* ernst(haft); ernstlich, begierig; **— money** Handgeld; **—** *n.* Ernst; **I am in — es** ist mein voller Ernst; **-ness** *n.* Eifer, Sorgfalt; Ernst(haftigkeit)

earphone *n.* Kopfhörer

earring *n.* Ohrring

earshot *n.* Hörweite

earth *n.* Erde, Boden; Land; Welt; **-en** *adj.* irdisch; tönern, irden; **-ly** *adj.* irdisch, weltlich; körperlich, sinnlich; **no -ly reason** kein erdenklicher Grund, nicht der geringste Grund; **-y** *adj.* erdig; erdfarben, erdfahl

earthenware *n.* Steingut, Töpferware

earthquake *n.* Erdbeben

earwax *n.* Ohrenschmalz

ease *n.* Ruhe; Behaglichkeit, Ungezwungenheit; Behagen; Leichtigkeit; Linderung; **at — frei, ungezwungen**; rührt euch! **—** *v.* lindern, mildern, beruhigen; **— up** nachlassen

easel *n.* Staffelei, Gestell

easiness *n.* Leichtigkeit, Gemächlichkeit

east *n.* Osten, Ost; Orient, Morgenland; **—** *adj.* and *adv.* Ost-, östlich; **— of** östlich von; **-erly** *adj.* östlich, Ost-; **-erly wind** Ostwind; **-erly** *adv.* ostwärts, nach Osten; **-ern** *adj.* östlich, orientalisch, morgenländisch

Easter *n.* Ostern, Osterfest; Oster-; **— egg** Osterei

eastward *adj.* östlich; **—** *adv.* ostwärts, nach Osten

easy *adj.* leicht; bequem, behaglich, gemächlich; **— chair** Lehnstuhl; **live on — street** im Wohlstand leben; **take**

it —! nur ruhig! sachte!

easygoing adj. gemütlich, bequem; gutmütig; leichtsinnig

eat v. essen, verzehren; (chem.) zerfressen, eindringen; (zool.) fressen; — **up** aufessen

eaves n. pl. Dachrinne, Traufe

eavesdrop v. lauschen; **-per** n. Lauscher, Horcher

ebb n. Ebbe; Abnahme, Neige; — **and flow** Ebbe und Flut; — adj. — **tide** Ebbe; — v. ebben; ablaufen, abnehmen

E-boat n. Schnellboot

ebony n. Ebenholz

eccentric adj. exzentrisch, überspannt; **-ity** n. Überspanntheit

ecclesiastic n. Geistliche; — adj. geistlich, kirchlich

echelon n. Staffel(aufstellung)

echo n. Echo, Widerhall; — v. widerhallen, echoen; wiederholen

eclipse n. Finsternis, Verfinsterung; — v. verfinstern, verdunkeln

ecliptic n. Sonnenbahn, Ekliptik

economic adj. volkswirtschaftlich, ökonomisch; **-al** adj. sparsam, haushälterisch; wirtschaftlich; **-s** n. pl. Volkswirtschaftslehre; Haushaltungskunst

economist v. Nationalökonom, Volkswirtschaftslehrer; Volkswirt; Haushälter; Sparer

economize v. (er)sparen; sparsam anwenden

economy n. Wirtschaft; Haushalt(ung); Ersparnis, Ökonomie

ecstasy n. Ekstase, Verzückung

ecstatic adj. ekstatisch, verzückt, schwärmerisch

eczema n. Ekzem, Hautflechte, Hautausschlag

edge n. Schärfe, Schneide; Rand, Kante; **on** — gespannt, gereizt; — v. einfassen, säumen; sich seitwärts bewegen; vorrücken, vordringen; — **away** vorsichtig wegrücken

edible adj. essbar

edict n. Edikt, Verordnung, Erlass

edifice n. Gebäude, grosser Bau

edify v. belehren, überreden; erbauen

edit v. herausgeben, redigieren; — n. Ausgabe, Auflage; **-or** n. Redakteur, Herausgeber; **-or in chief** Chefredakteur; **-orial** n. Leitartikel; **-orial** adj. redaktionell; Redaktions-

educate v. erziehen, unterrichten, (aus)bilden; **-d** adj. gebildet, erzogen

education n. Erziehung, Unterricht, Ausbildung; Bildung; **-al** adj. erzieherisch, pädagogisch; Erziehungs-

educator n. Erzieher

eel n. Aal

efface v. auslöschen, ausstreichen; verwischen, tilgen; in den Schatten stellen; — **oneself** in den Hintergrund treten

effect n. Wirkung, Effekt; Eindruck; pl. Effekten, Habseligkeiten; **for** — um Eindruck zu machen; **go into** — in Kraft treten; **have an** — wirken; **in** — in der Tat; **put into** — in Kraft setzen;

take — wirken; — v. bewirken, ausführen; **-ive** adj. wirksam, kräftig; wirkend, effektiv

effeminate adj. weibisch, verzärtelt, verweichlicht

effervescent adj. aufbrausend; Brause-

efficacious adj. wirksam, kräftig

efficacy n. Wirksamkeit, wirkende Kraft

efficiency n. Wirksamkeit, Tüchtigkeit, Leistungsfähigkeit

efficient adj. wirkend, wirksam, tüchtig, ausgebildet, leistungsfähig

effort n. Anstrengung, Bestrebung, Bemühung; **make an** — sich bemühen (or anstrengen)

effusive adj. übertrieben; verschwenderisch; überschwenglich

egg n. Ei; **fried** — Spiegelei; **hard-boiled** — hart(gekocht)es Ei; **poached** — verlorenes Ei; **scrambled** — Rührei; **soft-boiled** — weich(gekocht)es Ei; — **cell** Eizelle; — **cup** Eierbecher; — **white** Eiweiss; — **yolk** Eidotter, Eigelb

eggnog n. Eierlikör

eggshell n. Eierschale

ego n. Ich, Ego; **-(t)ism** n. Egoismus, Selbstsucht; Selbstüberhebung; **-(t)istic(al)** adj. egoistisch, egozentrisch, selbstsüchtig

Egypt n. Ägypten

eider down n. Eiderdaune

eight adj. acht; — **ball** Billiardkugel No. 8; **behind the** — **ball** im Schlamassel sein; — n. Acht(er); **-een** adj. achtzehn; **-een** n. Achtzehn; Achtzehner; **-eenth** adj. achtzehnt; — n. Achtzehnte; Achtzehntel; **-fold** adj. achtfach; **-h** adj. acht; **-h** n. Achte; Achtel; **-ieth** adj. achtzigst; **-ieth** n. Achtzigste; Achtzigstel; **-y** adj. achtzig; **-y** n. Achtzig; Achtziger

either pron. and adj. einer, jeder; beide; **not** — keiner; — conj. entweder; — . . . **or** entweder — . . . oder

ejaculation n. Ausruf; Stossgebet

eject v. vertreiben, verjagen; ausstossen; **-ion** n. Vertreibung; (med.) Auswurf; **-ion seat** (avi.) Schleudersitz

El abbr. Hochbahn

elaborate v. ausarbeiten; — **upon** etwas genauer beschreiben; — adj. ausgearbeitet, ausgefeilt; detailliert

elapse v. verstreichen, vergehen, verfliessen

elastic adj. elastisch, federnd, dehnbar; — n. Gummiband; **-ity** n. Elastizität, Dehnbarkeit; Spannkraft

elate v. ermutigen, aufblähen; **-d** adj. erhaben, stolz

elbow n. Ellbogen; Krümmung, Biegung; (mech.) Knie, Winkel; — v. mit dem Ellbogen (weg-)stossen

elbowroom n. Ellbogenfreiheit, Bewegungsfreiheit, Spielraum

elder n. Ältere, Senior; Kirchenälteste; (bot.) Holunder; — adj. älter; **-ly** adj. ältlich, älter

eldest adj. ältest-

elect v. (er)wählen, auswählen; — adj. ausgewählt, (aus)erwählt; **-ion** n.

Wahl, Abstimmung; **-loneering** *n.*
Wahlpropaganda; **-ive** *adj.* wählend;
Wahl-; **-ive** *n.* Wahlfach; **-or** *n.*
Wähler; Kurfürst; **-oral** *adj.* die Wahl
betreffend, Wahl-; Wähler-; **-oral
college** Wahlausschuss; **-orate** *n.* Wähl-
ler (schaft); Kurfürstentum
electric *adj.* elektrisch; **—** **bulb** Glühbirne;
— **cable** elektrisches Kabel; **—** **chair**
elektischer Stuhl; **—** **charge** elektrische
Ladung; **—** **eye** Elektronenauge; Selen-
zelle; **—** **fixtures** elektrische Installation; **—** **meter** Stromzähler; **—** **motor**
Elektromotor; **—** **plant** Elektrizitäts-
werk; **—** **railroad** elektrischer Zug; **—**
shock elektrischer Schlag; **—** **welding**
elektrisches Schweissen; **-al** *adj.* elektrisch; **-al engineer** Elektrotechniker;
-al engineering Elektrotechnik; **-al
transcription** (rad.) Schallplattenüber-
tragung; **-ian** *n.* Elektriker; **-ity** *n.*
Elektrizität; **—** **razor** Trockenrasierer
electrify *v.* elektrisieren
electrocute *v.* elektrisch hinrichten (or
töten)
electrocution *n.* elektrisches Hinrichten
(or Töten)
electrode *n.* Elektrode
electrolysis *n.* Elektrolyse
electrolyte *n.* Elektrolyt
electromagnet *n.* Elektromagnet; **-ic** *adj.*
elektromagnetisch; **-ic field** elektro-
magnetisches Feld
electromotive *adj.* elektromotorisch; **—
force** elektromotorische Kraft
electron *n.* Elektron; **-ics** *n.* Elektronik,
Elektronenlehre
electroplate *v.* galvanisieren; galvanisch
versilbern (or vergolden, etc.)
electrotherapie *n.* elektrische Heilbe-
handlung
elegance *n.* Feinheit, Eleganz, Vornehmheit
elegant *adj.* elegant, fein; geschmackvoll;
vornehm
elegy *n.* Elegie, Klagelied
element *n.* Element, Bestandteil; Urstoff;
Grundstoff; *pl.* Elemente, Anfangsgründe; Naturgewalten; **-al** *adj.* elementar, naturgewaltig, wesentlich;
-ary *adj.* elementar, einfach; Natur-;
Anfangs-; **-ary school** Volksschule,
Grundschule
elephant *n.* Elefant
elevate *v.* hochheben, erhöhen, erheben;
-d *adj.* erhoben, hoch; erhaben; **-d
railroad** Hochbahn; **-d train** Hoch-
bahnzug
elevation *n.* Erhebung, Erhöhung; Höhe
elevator *n.* Fahrstuhl, Aufzug; (avi.)
Höhensteuer; **grain** — Getreidespeicher
eleven *adj.* elf; **—** *n.* Elf(er); **-th** *adj.* elfte;
-th *n.* Elfte; Elftel
elf *n.* Kobold, Elf; **-in** *adj.* elfisch, elfen-
gleich; Elfen-
eligible *adj.* wählbar; wünschenswert,
passend; heiratsfähig
eliminate *v.* ausmerzen, beseitigen; absondern, ausscheiden
elk *n.* Elch, Elen

ellipse *n.* Ellipse
elliptic(al) *adj.* elliptisch; unvollständig
elm *n.* Ulme, Rüster
elocution *n.* Aussprache, Vortragskunst
elope *v.* entlaufen, durchgehen; entführen;
sich entführen lassen; **-ment** *n.* Entlaufen, Entführung; Fortlaufen
eloquence *n.* Beredsamkeit
eloquent *adj.* beredt, beredsam
else *adj.* and *adv.* anders, weiter, sonst;
nothing — sonst nichts; **or** — sonst;
somewhere — irgendwo anders, anderswo; **what** —? was sonst? — *conj.*
sonst, wo nicht
elsewhere *adv.* anderswo, sonstwo, woan-
ders
elucidate *v.* aufklären, erläutern
elude *v.* ausweichen, geschickt umgehen
emaciate *v.* abzehren, abmagern, aus-
mergeln
emanate *v.* ausfliessen, ausstrahlen; her-
rühren
emancipate *v.* emanzipieren, befreien
emancipation *n.* Emanzipation, Befreiung
emancipator *n.* Befreier
embalm *v.* einbalsamieren; **-ment** *n.*
Einbalsamierung
embargo *n.* Hafensperre; Handelsverbot;
— *v.* (den Hafen, Handel) sperren;
(ship) beschlagnahmen
embark *v.* (sich) einschiffen; sich einlassen; **-ation** *n.* Einschiffung, Verladung
embarrass *v.* in Verlegenheit setzen, verwirren; **-ed** *adj.* verlegen; **-ing** *adj.*
peinlich; **-ment** *n.* Verlegenheit; Verwicklung, Verwirrung
embassy *n.* Gesandtschaft, Botschaft
embellish *v.* verschönern, ausschmücken
ember *v.* glühende Kohle (or Asche)
embezzle *v.* veruntreuen, unterschlagen;
-ment *n.* Veruntreuung, Unterschla-
gung; **-r** *n.* Veruntreuer, Unterschla-
gende
embitter *v.* verbittern, erbittern
emblem *n.* Emblem, Sinnbild, Kennzeichen
embody *v.* verkörpern; einverleiben;
umfassen, enthalten
embrace *n.* Umarmung; **—** *v.* (sich)
umarmen, umfassen; enthalten; annah-
men
embroider *v.* sticken; verschönern, ausschmücken; **-y** *n.* Stickerei; **-y frame**
Stickrahmen; **-y needle** Sticknadel
embryo *n.* Embryo, Leibesfrucht; (fig.)
Keim
emerald *n.* Smaragd; **—** *adj.* smaragdfar-
ben
emerge *v.* auftauchen, emporkommen;
entstehen; **-ncy** *n.* dringende Not,
schwierige Lage; unerwartetes Ereignis;
-ncy brake Notbremse; **-ncy exit**
Notausgang; **-ncy landing** Notlandung;
-ncy landing field provisorisches Lan-
defeld
emeritus *adj.* emeritiert, in den Ruhe-
stand versetzt
emery *n.* Schmirgel, Korund
emigrant *n.* Auswanderer, Emigrant
emigrate *v.* auswandern, emigrieren

emigration n. Auswanderung, Emigration

eminence n. Erhöhung, Anhöhe; hoher Rang, Auszeichnung; (eccl.) Eminenz; (fig.) Gipfel

eminent adj. hervorragend, eminent; vorzüglich; — **domain** staatliches Vorrecht, Staatsgebiet

emotion n. Rührung, Gefühl(sregung); Erregung; **-al** adj. gefühlsmässig; gefühlvoll; leicht erregbar

empennage n. Flugzeugschwanzflosse

emperor n. Kaiser

emphasis n. Nachdruck, Betonung

emphasize v. ausdrücklich betonen

emphatic adj. emphatisch, nachdrücklich, eindringlich

empire n. Reich; Herrschaft, Gewalt

empiric(al) adj. erfahrungsmässig

employ n. Beschäftigung, Dienst; Anstellung; — v. anwenden, (ge)brauchen; beschäftigen, anstellen; **-ee** n. Angestellte, Arbeitnehmer; **-er** n. Arbeitgeber; **-ment** n. Beschäftigung, Arbeit, Tätigkeit; **-ment agency** Arbeitsvermittlung, Arbeitsnachweis, Arbeitsamt

emporium n. Handelsplatz, Stapelplatz

empower v. ermächtigen, bevollmächtigen

empress n. Kaiserin

emptiness n. Leere, Nichtigkeit

empty adj. leer; hungrig; (fig.) hohl, eitel; — v. (ent)leeren, ausräumen; sich entleeren, (or ergiessen)

empty-handed adj. mit leeren Händen

emulate v. wetteifern mit, nacheifern

emulsion n. Emulsion

enable v. ermöglichen, befähigen; ermächtigen

enact v. erlassen, verfügen, verordnen; (theat.) darstellen

enamel n. Email(le), Schmelz, Glasur; — v. emaillieren, glasieren

enamored adj. verliebt

encampment n. Lager, Feldlager

enchant v. fesseln, entzücken, bezaubern; **-ing** adj. fesselnd, entzückend, bezaubernd; **-ment** n. Bezauberung; Zauberei, Zauber

encircle v. umringen, umfassen

enclose v. einschliessen, umgeben; (letter) beifügen, einlegen; enthalten; (field, etc.) einzäunen, einfrieden

enclosure n. Einschliessung; (letter) Beilage, Einlage; (field, etc.) Einzäunung; Gehege; Einfriedung; Zaun, Hecke

encompass v. umschliessen, einschliessen

encore n. Dacaporuf, Wiederholung; Zugabe; **-!** interj. noch einmal! da capo!; — v. noch einmal verlangen

encounter n. Zusammentreffen, Begegnung; (mil.) Gefecht, Treffen; Zusammenstoss; — v. (zusammen)treffen; sich begegnen, stossen auf

encourage v. ermutigen, ermuntern; fordern, unterstützen; **-ment** n. Ermutigung, Ermunterung; Forderung, Unterstützung

encouraging adj. ermutigend, aufmunternd

encroach v. Eingriffe tun; — **upon** eingreifen in, stören; — **upon someone's kindness** jemandes Güte missbrauchen

encumbrance n. Bürde; Belastung; Hindernis

encyclopedia n. Enzyklopädie, Konversationslexikon

end n. Ende; Absicht, Zweck; Ziel; Tod, Vernichtung; **be at an —** am Ende sein, aus sein; **bring to an —** zu Ende führen; **— to —** der Länge nach; **his hair stood on —** seine Haare standen zu Berge; **in the —** auf die Dauer, schliesslich; **make both -s meet** auskommen, sich nach der Decke strecken; **no —** unendlich, endlos; **on —** aufrecht; ununterbrochen; hintereinander; **put an — to** ein Ende machen mit; **the — justifies the means** der Zweck heiligt die Mittel; **to the bitter —** bis zum bitteren Ende; bis zum äussersten; **without —** unendlich; — v. (be)enden, vollenden; (fig.) vernichten; sterben; **all's well that -s well** Ende gut, alles gut; **-ing** n. Ende, Schluss; (gram.) Endung; **-less** adj. unendlich, endlos

endanger v. gefährden

endeavor n. Bemühung, Bestreben; — v. sich bemühen, sich bestreben

endorse v. übertragen, überschreiben, indossieren, girieren; (fig.) unterstützen, bestätigen, beipflichten; **-ment** n. Indossament; (fig.) Bestätigung, Unterstützung

endow v. ausstatten, aussteuern, (eccl.) dotieren; **-ment** n. Ausstattung, Aussteuer, Dotation; Stiftung; (fig.) Talent

endurable adj. erträglich, leidlich

endurance n. Ausdauer, Geduld; Erdulden, Ertragen; Dauer

endure v. dulden, aushalten, ertragen; dauern

endways, endwise adv. gerade, aufrecht

enema n. Klistier, Einlauf

enemy n. Feind, Gegner

energetic adj. energisch, kraftvoll, tatkräftig

energy n. Energie, Tatkraft; Nachdruck, Wirksamkeit

enervate v. entnerven, schwächen

enforce v. erzwingen, durchsetzen; durchführen; **-ment** n. Erzwingung, Durchsetzung; Durchführung

engage v. verpflichten, engagieren, anstellen, beschäftigen; (mil.) angreifen; — **in** betreiben, sich einlassen auf; **-ed** adj. verlobt; beschäftigt; verpflichtet; **-ment** n. Verlobung; Verabredung; (mil.) Angriff

engaging adj. einnehmend, gewinnend, reizend

engender v. (er)zeugen

engine n. Maschine; Motor; Lokomotive; Mittel; **— room** Maschinenraum; **-er** n. Ingenieur, Techniker, Maschinenbauer; Lokomotivführer; (mil.) Pionier; (naut.) Maschinist; **-er** v. durchsetzen, einrichten, bauen; **-ering** n. Ingenieurwesen, Maschinenbaukunst

England n. England

English Channel n. der Ärmelkanal

engraft v. veredeln, aufsetzen, pfropfen, okulieren

engrave v. gravieren, stechen, eingraben; (fig.) einprägen

engraving n. Gravierung, Gravieren; (metal) Stich; (wood) Schnitt

engross v. ganz in Anspruch nehmen; an sich ziehen; **–ed** adj. vertieft (fig.) vergrössern

enhance v. erhöhen, steigern; übertreiben; (fig.) vergrössern

enigma n. Rätsel; **–tic** adj. rätselhaft, dunkel

enjoin v. befehlen, auferlegen; einschärfen, vorschreiben; verbieten

enjoy v. geniessen; sich erfreuen; besitzen; **— oneself** sich (gut) unterhalten, sich amüsieren; **–able** adj. angenehm, erfreulich, genussreich; **–ment** n. Genuss; Vergnügen, Freude

enlarge v. zunehmen, weiten; ausdehnen; erweitern; (phot.) vergrössern; (fig.) sich verbreiten; **–ment** n. Zunahme; Erweiterung; (phot.) Vergrösserung

enlighten v. erleuchten, erhellen; aufklären, belehren; **–ment** n. Erleuchtung; Aufklärung

enlist v. sich anwerben lassen; (an)werben; gewinnen (für); **–ment** n. Anwerbung

enliven v. beleben, ermuntern

enmity n. Feindschaft, Feindseligkeit

enormity n. Ungeheuerlichkeit

enormous adj. enorm, ungeheuer

enough adj. and adv. genug, genügend: **be —** genügen; (aus)reichen, langen; **be good — to** so gut sein und; **— n.** Genüge

enquire v. see inquire

enrage v. wütend machen, aufbringen; **–d** adj. wütend, aufgebracht

enroll v. eintragen, einschreiben, anmelden; (mil.) anwerben; (naut.) anmustern; **–ment** n. Eintragung, Einschreiben, Anmeldung

enshrine v. einschliessen, als Heiligtum verwahren

ensign n. Abzeichen, Fahne, Flagge; (naut.) Fähnrich

enslave v. knechten, unterjochen

ensue v. folgen; sich ergeben; sich ereignen, nachfolgen

ensure v. sichern, versichern, verbürgen

entail n. Vererben; Erbfolge; **— v.** vererben; zur Folge haben, erfordern

entangle v. verwirren, verwickeln, verstricken

enter v. eintreten, betreten; eingehen; eintragen, einschreiben; (sports) melden, nennen

enteritis n. (med.) Darmverschluss

enterprise n. Unternehmen, Unternehmung; **free —** Gewerbefreiheit

enterprising adj. unternehmend; verwegen, kühn

entertain v. unterhalten, bewirten; hegen; **–er** n. Wirt; Unterhalter, Unterhaltende; **–ment** n. Unterhaltung, Zerstreuung; Bewirtung; Schaustellung, Aufführung

enthrone v. einsetzen; auf den Thron setzen

enthusiasm n. Begeisterung, Enthusiasmus

enthusiast n. Schwärmer, Enthusiast; **–ic** adj. schwärmend, begeistert, enthusiastisch

entice v. (ver)locken, reizen; **–ment** n. Verlockung, Reiz

entire adj. ganz, gesamt, vollkommen, unversehrt, ungeschmälert, vollständig, ungeteilt; **–ly** adv. gänzlich, durchaus, völlig; herzlich; entschieden; lediglich; **–ty** n. Ganzheit, Gesamtheit; Vollständigkeit, Unversehrtheit

entitle v. betiteln, benennen; berechtigen

entity n. Sein; Wesen(heit)

entomology n. Entomologie, Insektenkunde

entrance n. Eingang; Einfahrt; Einlass, Eintritt, Eintreten; (theat.) Auftreten; **— v.** entzücken, hinreissen

entreat v. bitten, ersuchen, erflehen; **–y** n. Bitte, Gesuch

entrée n. Entree, Eintritt, Zutritt; (cooking) Hauptgericht

entrench v. see intrench

entry n. Eingang; Eintritt; (com.) Eintragung, Buchung; (sports) Nennung, Meldung; (theat.) Auftritt

entwine v. (um)winden, verflechten

enumerate v. aufzählen, zählen

enunciate v. ausdrücken, aussprechen; aufstellen

enunciation n. Aussprache, Vortrag; Aufstellung

envelop v. einhüllen, einwickeln, umgeben; **–e** n. Umschlag, Hülle; Briefumschlag

enviable adj. beneidenswert

envious adj. neidisch, missgünstig

environment n. Umgebung

envoy n. Gesandte

envy n. Neid, Missgunst; **— v.** beneiden, missgönnen

enzyme n. Enzym, Ferment

epaulet n. Epaulette, Achselstück

epic n. Epos, Heldengedicht; **— adj.** episch

epidemic n. Epidemie, Seuche; **— adj.** epidemisch, seuchenartig

epidermis n. Epidermis, Oberhaut

epigram n. Epigramm, Sinngedicht, Spottgedicht

epilepsy n. Epilepsie, Fallsucht

epileptic adj. epileptisch, fallsüchtig; **— n.** Epileptiker, Fallsüchtige(r)

epilogue n. Epilog, Nachwort

episcopalian n. Mitglied einer Bischofskirche; **— adj.** bischöflich

episode n. Episode

epistle n. Brief, Epistel, Sendschreiben

epitaph n. Epitaph, Grabschrift

epithet n. Attribut, Beiwort; Benennung

epitome n. Auszug, Abriss

epoch n. Epoche, Zeitabschnitt, Zeitpunkt

equable adj. gleichförmig, gleichmässig, gleichmütig

equal n. Gleiche; **— adj.** gleich, gleich-

mässig; be — to gewachsen sein; — v.
gleichen, gleichkommen; -ity n. Gleichheit, Gleichmässigkeit; -ize v. gleichmachen, ausgleichen

equanimity n. Gleichmut

equation n. Gleichung

equator n. Äquator; -ial adj. äquatorial

equestrian n. Kunstreiter; — adj. reitend;
Reit-, Reiter-

equidistant adj. parallel, gleichweit entfernt

equilateral adj. gleichseitig

equilibrium n. Gleichgewicht

equinox n. Tag- und Nachtgleiche

equip v. ausstatten, ausrüsten; -age n.
Ausrüstung; Equipage, Kutsche; -ment
n. Ausstattung, Ausrüstung; standard
-ment Normalausrüstung

equitable adj. billig, gerecht; unparteiisch

equity n. Billigkeit, Gerechtigkeit, Unparteilichkeit; (law) Billigkeitsrecht

equivalent n. Gegenwert, Gleichwertigkeit, Äquivalent; — adj. gleichwertig,
gleichbedeutend

equivocal adj. zweideutig, doppelsinnig;
zweifelhaft, unbestimmt

era n. Ära, Zeit(rechnung); Periode,
Zeitalter

eradicate v. ausrotten, entwurzeln

eradication n. Ausrottung, Entwurzelung

erase v. ausradieren, auslöschen; verwischen; -r n. Radiergummi; Wischer

erasure n. Rasur, Ausradieren, Ausradie-
rung, Streichung

ere prep. vor; — adv. früh; — conj. ehe,
bevor

erect v. aufstellen, errichten, aufrichten;
— adj. aufrecht, gerade; -ion n. Errichtung, Aufrichtung

ermine n. Hermelin, Hermelinpelz

erode v. anfressen, zerfressen; benagen

erosion n. Auswaschung, Zerfressung

err v. sich irren; fehlen, sündigen; -atic
adj. wandernd; seltsam, exzentrisch;
-oneous adj. irrig, falsch; unrichtig;
-or n. Irrtum, Fehler, Schnitzer

errand n. Auftrag, Botengang; Bestellung; run an — einen Auftrag ausführen; — boy Laufbursche

erudition n. Gelehrsamkeit

erupt v. ausbrechen, hervorbrechen,
durchbrechen; -ion n. Ausbruch; Ausschlag

escalator n. Rolltreppe

escapade n. Eskapade, Seitensprung

escape n. Flucht; Entrinnen, Entweichen;
have a narrow — mit knapper Not davonkommen; make one's — sich aus dem
Staube machen; — capsule Notkapsel
(bemannte Rakete); — hatch Notaus-
stieg (bemannte Rakete); — v. entgehen, entfliehen, entweichen; (fig.)
entfallen

escort n. Gefolge, Begleitung; Geleit,
Eskorte; — v. begleiten, geleiten, es-
kortieren

escutcheon n. Wappenschild; Namens-
schild

esophagus n. Speiseröhre

especial adj. besonder, hauptsächlich,
speziell; vorzüglich

espionage n. Spionage; Spionieren

esquire n. Wohlgeboren, Hochwohlge-
boren

essay n. Essay, kurze Abhandlung,
Aufsatz; Versuch; — v. versuchen,
erproben

essence n. Essenz, Extrakt; Wesen(heit),
Geist

essential adj. wesentlich; wichtig; — n.
Hauptsache, Wesentliche, Wichtigste

establish v. feststellen, festsetzen; errichten, einrichten; (be)gründen; — oneself
eine Position erringen, sich niederlassen; -ment n. Gründung, Errichtung;
Festsetzung; Organisation, Haushalt;
Bestand

estate n. Gut, Besitz, Vermögen; Nachlass; Konkursmasse; Stand, Zustand

esteem n. Hochachtung, Würdigung;
Ansehen; — v. abschätzen; hochachten;
-ed adj. geachtet, hochgeschätzt

esthetic adj. ästhetisch, schöngeistig; -s
n. pl. Ästhetik, Schönheitslehre

Esthonia n. Estland

estimable adj. achtungswert; schätzbar

estimate n. Schätzung, Voranschlag,
Kosten(vor)anschlag; v. berechnen,
abschätzen

estimation n. Schätzung, Überschlag;
Voranschlag; Meinung, Achtung

estrange v. entfremden, fernhalten

etc. abbr. usw.

etch v. ätzen, radieren; -ing n. Ätzung,
Radierung

eternal adj. ewig, immerwährend

eternity n. Ewigkeit

ether n. Äther; -eal adj. ätherisch, himmlisch

ethical adj. ethisch, moralisch, sittlich

ethics n. Ethik, Sittenlehre, Moral

ethnology n. Völkerkunde

ethyl n. Äthyl; Kohlenwasserstoff

etiquette n. Etikette, gute Sitte

etymology n. Etymologie, Wortur-
sprungslehre

eucalyptus n. Eukalyptus, australischer
Gummibaum

Eucharist n. Abendmahl(sfeier); -ic adj.
eucharistisch; Abendmahls-

eugenics n. Rassenhygiene

eulogize v. loben

eulogy n. Lobpreisung, Lobrede

euphonious adj. wohllautend; euphonisch

Europe n. Europa; -an n. Europäer; -an
adj. europäisch

euthanasia n. Euthanasie; schmerzloses
Töten unheilbarer Kranker

evacuate v. evakuieren, räumen; entleeren, wegschaffen

evacuee n. Evakuierte; Ausgewiesene

evade v. ausweichen, umgehen, sich
drücken vor

evaluate v. (ab)schätzen, einschätzen

evaluation n. Abschätzung, Wertbestimmung

evangelical adj. evangelisch

evangelist n. Evangelist; Wanderprediger

evaporate v. verdampfen (lassen), verdunsten; (fig.) verduften; -d adj. -d

milk kondensierte Milch

evaporation n. Verdampfung, Verdunstung

evasion n. Entweichen; Ausflucht, Umgehung

eve n. Abend; Vorabend

even adj. gerade, eben, gleich; glatt; gleichförmig, gleichmässig; gelassen, ausgeglichen; rund, genau; **break —** auf seine Kosten kommen; **— number** gerade Zahl; **— sum** runde Summe; **get —** heimzahlen; **odd or —** gerade oder ungerade; **on — terms** in gutem Einvernehmen; **we are —** wir sind quitt; **— adv.** selbst, sogar; **— if** wenn auch, selbst wenn; **—more** noch mehr; **— now** selbst jetzt, auch jetzt; **— so** trotzdem; **— though** wenn auch, obwohl; **not —** nicht einmal; **— v.** ebnen; glätten, gleichstellen; **-ness** n. Gleichheit, Gleichförmigkeit; Ebenheit; Seelenruhe

evening n. Abend; **good —** guten Abend; **in the —** abends, am Abend; **this —** heute abend; **— adj.** Abend-; **— clothes** Abendkleider, Gesellschaftskleider; **— star** Abendstern, Venus

event n. Ereignis, Begebenheit, Vorfall; (sports) Veranstaltung; **at all —s, in any —** auf alle Fälle, jedenfalls; **in the —** im Falle; **-ful** adj. ereignisreich; wichtig, merkwürdig; **-ual** adj. eventuell, möglich; etwaig, schliesslich

ever adv. immer, stets, beständig; je, jemals; **— since** von der Zeit an; **— so long** eine Ewigkeit; **— so much** soviel wie irgend möglich; **for — and —** immer und ewig, immerfort; **auf ewig**; **hardly —** fast nie

evergreen n. Immergrün; **— adj.** immergrün

everlasting adj. ewig, unaufhörlich, unverwüstlich

evermore adv. immerfort, stets; je wieder

every adj. alle; jeder; jede, jedes; alle möglichen; **— now and then, — once in a while** dann und wann, ab und zu; **— one** jeder; **— time** jedesmal; **— two years** alle zwei Jahre

everybody pron. jedermann, jeder, jede, jedes; alle; **— else** alle anderen

everyday adj. alltäglich, allgemein; Alltags-

everyone pron. jedermann, jeder, jede, jedes; alle; **— else** alle anderen

everything pron. alles

everywhere adv. überall

evidence n. Beweis; (law) Beweismaterial, Beweismittel; Zeuge, Zeugnis; **give —** Zeugnis ablegen; **— v.** augenscheinlich machen, dartun; beweisen; zeugen

evident adj. offenbar, augenscheinlich, klar

evil n. Übel, Böse, Bosheit; **— adj.** übel, böse, schlecht, schlimm

evildoer n. Übeltäter

evil-minded adj. übelgesinnt

evoke v. hervorrufen, wachrufen; (herauf)beschwören

evolution n. Entwicklung, Entfaltung

evolve v. entwickeln, (sich) entfalten

exact adj. genau, exakt, sorgfältig; pünktlich; **— v.** erpressen, fordern, eintreiben; **-ing** adj. streng, anspruchsvoll; genau; **-ion** n. Erpressung; ungebührliche Forderung; Eintreibung; **-itude** n., **-ness** n. Exaktheit, Genauigkeit, Pünktlichkeit

exaggerate v. übertreiben, vergrössern

exalt v. erheben, erhöhen; **-ation** n. Erhebung, Erhöhung; Begeisterung, Verzückheit

examination n. Prüfung, Examen; Untersuchung; (law) Verhör; **medical —** ärztliche Untersuchung

examine v. prüfen, untersuchen; betrachten; (law) verhören, vernehmen; **-r** n. Prüfer, Untersuchende; (law) Verhörende, Vernehmende

example n. Beispiel, Vorbild; Exempel; Warnung, Lehre; Exemplar, Muster; **for —** zum Beispiel; **make an —** ein Beispiel statuieren, exemplarisch bestrafen; **set a good —** mit gutem Beispiel vorangehen; **set an —** ein Beispiel geben

exasperate v. reizen, erbittern, ärgern

exasperation n. Erbitterung, Reizung

excavate v. aushöhlen, ausgraben

excavation n. Ausgrabung, Aushöhlung; Höhle

exceed v. überschreiten, übersteigen; übertreffen; **-ingly** adv. ausserordentlich, äusserst, überaus

excel v. übertreffen, überragen; hervorragen, sich hervortun; **-lence** n. Vortrefflichkeit, Vollkommenheit; Feinheit; **-lency** n. Excellenz; **-lent** adj. ausgezeichnet, vorzüglich, (vor)trefflich

except conj. ausser, es sei denn, dass; **— prep.** ausser, ausgenommen; **— for** bis auf, abgesehen von; **— v.** ausschliessen, ausnehmen; **-ing** prep. mit Ausnahme von; **-ion** n. Ausnahme; Einwendung, Einwand; **-ional** adj. aussergewöhnlich, ungewöhnlich

excess n. Überschuss; Übermass, Unmässigkeit; **be in — of** überschüssig; **to — im** Übermass; **— adj.** überschüssig; **— baggage** Überfracht; **-ive** adj. übermässig, übertrieben

exchange n. Austausch, Tausch; Wechsel; **in — for** im Austausch für; **money —** Wechselstube; **rate of —** Kurs, Wechselkurs; (stock) **— Börse; telephone —** Fernsprechamt, Telefonzentrale; **— v.** (aus)tauschen, vertauschen, umtauschen, eintauschen; wechseln; **-able** adj. auswechselbar, austauschbar; Tausch-

excise n. Warensteuer, Verbrauchssteuer

excitable adj. reizbar, erregbar

excite v. aufregen, wachrufen; erregen, anregen, reizen; **get -d** sich aufregen; **-dly** adv. aufgeregt; **-ment** n. Aufregung, Anregung; Erregung, Reizung

exciting adj. aufregend; erregend

exclaim v. schreien, ausrufen

exclamation n. Geschrei, Ausruf(ung); **— mark, — point** Ausrufungszeichen

exclude v. ausschliessen

exclusion n. Ausschluss, Ausschliessung

exclusive adj. ausschliesslich, alleinig, exklusiv

excommunicate v. exkommunizieren

excretion n. Auswurf, Aussonderung

excursion n. Ausflug, Abstecher

excusable adj. entschuldbar; verzeihlich

excuse n. Entschuldigung; Ausflucht, Vorwand; — v. entschuldigen, verzeihen

execute v. ausführen, vollziehen; (law) hinrichten; (mus.) vorspielen

execution n. Ausführung, Durchführung; (law) Hinrichtung; (mus. and theat.) Vortrag, Spiel, Technik; **-er** n. Henker, Scharfrichter

executive n. Exekutive, Staatsgewalt; Direktor; — adj. exekutiv, ausübend, vollziehend

executor n. Testamentsvollstrecker

exemplary adj. musterhaft, nachahmenswert; exemplarisch; Muster-

exemplify v. erläutern, (durch Beispiele) belegen

exempt adj. befreit, verschont; — v. befreien, verschonen; **-ion** n. Befreiung, Freisein, Ausnahme

exercise n. Übung, Praxis; Ausübung, Anwendung; (gymn.) Leibesübung; (mil.) Exerzieren; — v. üben; sich Bewegung machen; ausüben; gebrauchen, anwenden; exerzieren; (horse) zureiten

exert v. anstrengen; geltend machen; — oneself sich bemühen; **-ion** n. Anstrengung, Bemühung; Äusserung, Anwendung

exhale v. ausatmen, aushauchen; verdunsten

exhaust v. erschöpfen, entleeren; — n. Auspuff; — **fan** Aussenventilator; — **gas** Abgas; — **manifold** Sammelleerung; — **pipe** Auspuffrohr; — **steam** Abdampf; — **valve** Auslassventil; **-ed** adj. (com.) vergriffen; **-ible** adj. erschöpfbar; **-ing** adj. ermüdend; **-ion** n. Erschöpfung; **-ive** adj. erschöpfend

exhibit n. Austellung, Schau; Ausstellungsstück; Schaustellung; Warenauslage; (law) Beweisschrift; **on** — zur Besichtigung, zur Schau gestellt; — v. ausstellen, zeigen; aufweisen; darlegen; **-ion** n. Austellung, Schau; Darstellung, Darlegung; **-or** n. Aussteller

exhilaration n. Erheiterung, Heiterkeit

exhort v. ermahnen, zureden; raten, warnen; **-ation** n. Ermahnung, Zureden; Mahnrede

exhume v. exhumieren, wieder ausgraben

exigency n. Dringlichkeit, Erfordernis, Bedarf; kritische Lage

exile n. Verbannte; Verbannung, Exil; — v. verbannen

exist v. vorhanden sein, existieren; leben; bestehen; **-ence** n. Existenz, Dasein; Leben; Bestehen; **-ent** adj. vorhanden, bestehend

exit n. Ausgang; (theat.) Abtreten, Abgang

exodus n. Auszug, Abwanderung; **Exodus** zweites Buch Mosis

exonerate v. freisprechen, reinigen; rechtfertigen; entlasten

exorbitant adj. übermässig, übertrieben

exotic fuel n. hochenergetischer Treibstoff

expand v. (sich) ausdehnen, (sich)ausbreiten; (sich) erweitern; (bot.) aufblühen

expansion n. Ausdehnung, Ausbreitung; Weite

expansive adj. ausdehnungsfähig; ausgedehnt; (fig.) gefühlvoll, mitfühlend; mitteilsam

expatriate v. aus dem Heimatland verbannen; — n. Vaterlandslose, Heimatlose

expect v. erwarten, warten; zumuten, vermuten, annehmen, glauben; **she is -ing** sie ist guter Hoffnung; **-ant** adj. erwartend; Anwartschaft habend; werdend; **-ation** n. Erwartung; Vermutung, Hoffnung; Aussicht

expediency n. Schicklichkeit, Ratsamkeit, Zweckmässigkeit; Nützlichkeitsprinzip

expedient adj. schicklich, passend; ratsam; zweckmässig, nützlich; — n. Ausweg, Notbehelf, Mittel

expedition n. Eile, Schnelligkeit; Ausführung; Forschungsreise; Expedition; (mil.) Feldzug, Kriegszug

expel v. vertreiben, ausstossen; (educ.) relegieren, ausschliessen

expend v. ausgeben, auslegen; verbrauchen, verzehren; **-able** adj. entbehrlich; **-iture** n. Ausgabe, Ausgeben; Aufwand, Verbrauch

expense n. Ausgabe, Auslage; pl. Unkosten, Kosten, Spesen; **at the — of** auf Kosten von

expensive adj. teuer, kostspielig

experience n. Erfahrung, Erlebnis; — v. erfahren, erleben, erleiden; **-d** adj. erfahren, erprobt; geschickt

experiment n. Versuch, Experiment; — v. versuchen, experimentieren; **-al** adj. erfahrungsgemäss, experimentell; Experimental-

expert n. Sachverständige, Fachmann; — adj. beschlagen, erfahren, geschickt

expiate v. sühnen, büssen

expiration n. Ablauf, Verlauf; Ende, Schluss; (fig.) letzter Atemzug, Tod; Ausatmen

expire v. sterben; verscheiden; verfliessen; ausatmen, aushauchen; ablaufen, verfallen, fällig werden, erlöschen

explain v. erklären, erläutern; auseinandersetzen

explanation n. Erklärung, Aufklärung, Auslegung; Auseinandersetzung

explicit adj. deutlich, klar, ausdrücklich; rückhaltlos, bestimmt

explode v. explodieren, platzen, sprengen, bersten

exploration n. Erforschung, Untersuchung

explore v. untersuchen, erforschen; **-r** n. Forscher, Erforscher; Forschungsreisende

explosion n. Explosion, Sprengung, Bersten; (fig.) Ausbruch

explosive adj. explosiv; Knall-, Spreng-; — n. Sprengstoff

exponent n. Erläuterer, Erklärer; Vertreter; (math.) Exponent, Potenzzahl

export v. exportieren, ausführen; — n. Export, Ausfuhr; Ausführware; -er n. Exporteur

expose v. aussetzen; ausstellen; aufdecken; blozstellen, enthüllen; (phot.) belichten

exposé n. Exposé, Darstellung; Aufdeckung

exposition n. Erklärung, Auslegung; Ausstellung; Darstellung

expostulate v. ernste Vorstellungen machen; — with Vorhaltungen machen, zur Rede stellen

exposure n. Enthüllung; Blozstellung; Ausgesetztsein; (arch.) Lage; (phot.) Belichtung

expound v. erklären, auslegen

express v. äussern, ausdrücken, darstellen; — adj. schnell; Express-, Eilausdrücklich, bestimmt, deutlich; (by) — per Express, per Eilgut; durch Eilboten; — company Paketpostgesellschaft; — train D-Zug; Schnellzug; — n. Express; Eilbote; Schnellzug, Expresszug; -ion n. Ausdruck, Äusserung; -ive adj. ausdrückend, ausdrucksvoll; -ly adv. eigens, absichtlich, ausdrücklich

expressman n. Paketpostangestellte

expressway n. Schnellstrasse

expropriate v. enteignen

expulsion n. Vertreibung, Austreibung, (educ.) Relegierung; (med.) Abführen

extemporaneous, extempory adj. extemporiert, unvorbereitet, improvisiert, aus dem Stegreif

extemporize v. extemporieren, unvorbereitet sprechen (or schreiben, spielen)

extend v. reichen, (sich) ausdehnen; verlängern, strecken; erweitern, vergrössern; erweisen, gewähren

extension n. Ausdehnung, Erweiterung; (arch.) Anbau; (tel.) Nebenanschluss, Apparat; — cord Verlängerungsschnur

extensive adj. ausgedehnt, umfassend

extent n. Weite, Grösse, Umfang; Grad, Ausdehnung; to a certain — gewissermassen, bis zu einem gewissen Grade; to the — of bis zum Betrage von

extenuate v. verdünnen, entkräften, schwächen, mildern

extenuating circumstances n. mildernde Umstände

exterior n. Äussere, Aussenseite; — adj. äusserlich

exterminate v. vertilgen, ausrotten, zerstören

extermination n. Vertilgung, Ausrottung

external adj. äusserlich, äusserst; pl. Äussere, äussere Form; Äusserlichkeiten; — adv. ausserhalb

extinct adj. erloschen, aufgehoben; ausgestorben, untergegangen; -ion n.

Erlöschen; Tilgung; Aussterben, Untergang, Vernichtung

extinguish v. auslöschen, ersticken; verdunkeln; vernichten; abschaffen, tilgen; -er n. Löscher; fire -er Feuerlöscher

extra n. Aussergewöhnliche; Sonderleistung, Sonderarbeit; (film) Chargenspieler, Statist; (newspaper) Extrablatt; — adj. extra, ungewöhnlich, ausserordentlich; übrig; Extra-; Neben-, Sonder-; — charges Nebenkosten; — pay Zulage; — work Mehrarbeit, Nebenarbeit; — adv. besonders, ausserdem, extra

extract v. Auszug, Extrakt, Zitat; — r. ausziehen, ausscheiden; ableiten; herauslocken; -ion n. Ausziehen, Auszug; Abkunft, Herkunft

extracurricular adj. Nebenstudien betreffend, Neben-

extradition n. Auslieferung

extraordinary adj. ausserordentlich, aussergewöhnlich, besonder, Extra-

extravagance n. Extravaganz, Übertreibung, Übermass; Verschwendung

extravagant adj. extravagant, übertrieben, übermässig; verschwenderisch

extreme n. Äusserste, Extrem; höchsten Grad; äusserste Massnahme; Übertreibung; carry (oder go) to -s auf die Spitze treiben; — adj. äusserst, übermässig, extrem

extremist n. Anhänger extremer Anschauungen; (pol.) Ultraradikale

extremity n. Äusserste, äusserste Not (or Verlegenheit); höchster Grad; pl. Extremitäten, Gliedmassen

extricate v. herausreissen, herauswinden, losmachen; (chem.) entwickeln

exuberance n. Überfluss, Fülle, Üppigkeit, Überschwenglichkeit

exuberant adj. üppig, überschwenglich, übermässig

exult r. frohlocken, jauchzen; -ant adj. frohlockend; -ation n. Frohlocken, Jubel

eye n. Auge; (fig.) Blick, Gesicht(skreis); (sewing) Öhr, Öse; an — for an — Auge um Auge; black — blaues Auge; catch someone's — jemandes Aufmerksamkeit fesseln; evil — böser Blick; have an — for Sinn haben für; hooks and -s Haken und Ösen; in the -s of the law vom Standpunkte des Gesetzes; in the twinkling of an — im Augenblick, im Nu; keep an — on ein wachsames Auge haben auf; see — to — im gleichen Lichte sehen; — v. anschauen, ansehen, betrachten; angucken, blicken auf

eyeball n. Augapfel

eyebrow n. Augenbraue

eyecup n. Augenglas

eyelash n. Augenwimper

eyelet n. Schnürloch; Guckloch; Öse

eyelid n. Augenlid

eyeshade n. Augenschirm

eyesight n. Augenlicht, Gesicht; Sehkraft

eyesore n. Gerstenkorn; be an — ein

Dorn im Auge sein

eyestrain n. Augen(über)anstrengung

eyetooth n. Augenzahn

eyewash n. Augenwasser, Augenbad; (coll.) Schwindel, Mumpitz

eyewitness n. Augenzeuge

F

fable n. Fabel, Sage, Märchen; Lüge; **-d** adj. fabelhaft, erdichtet

fabric n. Stoff, Gewebe; Gefüge; **-ate** v. fabrizieren, verfertigen, herstellen; erdichten, erfinden; bauen, errichten; fälschen; **-ation** n. Fabrikation, Herstellung; Erdichtung; Fälschung

fabulous adj. fabelhaft

face n. Gesicht, Angesicht; Ausdruck, Miene; (arch., furniture) Front, Vorderseite, Fassade, Aussenseite; Oberfläche; (clock) Zifferblatt; (coin) Bildseite; (geom.) Fläche; (typ.) Bildtype; (fig.) Dreistigkeit, Unverschämtheit; **at — value** für bare Münze; **— card** Bildkarte; **— lifting** Hebung der Wangenhaut; **— to —** von Angesicht zu Angesicht; persönlich; **— to — with** angesichts, gegenüber; **— value** Nennwert; **in the — of** in Gegenwart von (fig.) trotz; **in the — of heavy odds** trotz widriger Umstände; **lose — an** Ansehen verlieren; **make a —** Grimassen (or Gesichter) schneiden; **on the — of it** allem Anschein nach, augenscheinlich; **put the best — on things** gute Miene zum bösen Spiel machen; **save (one's) —** den Anschein wahren; **show one's —** sich sehen (or blicken) lassen; **— v.** ins Gesicht sehen, ansehen; gegenüber liegen, gegenüber stehen; entgegentreten, trotzen; (arch.) bedecken, bekleiden; hinausgehen auf; (sewing) aufschlagen, besetzen, einfassen; **— on** gehen (or gerichtet sein) auf; **— the music** die Folgen auf sich nehmen

facetious adj. witzig, drolling; scherzhaft, lustig

facial adj. das Gesicht betreffend; Gesichts-; **— n.** Gesichtskosmetik

facile adj. leicht; leutselig, ungänglich; nachgiebig, gefällig; flink, geschickt

facilitate v. erleichtern, fördern

facility n. Leichtigkeit, Gewandtheit, Geschicklichkeit; Schwäche, Nachgiebigkeit; Leutseligkeit

facing n. Besatz, Einfassung, Aufschlag; (arch.) Verkleidung

fact n. Tatsache; Wirklichkeit; Tat; pl. Tatbestand; **as a matter of —** zwar, tatsächlich; **in —** in der Tat, wirklich; pl. **— are —** Tatsachen bleibt Tatsache; **the — of the case** der Sachverhalt; **-ual** adj. faktisch, tatsächlich

faction n. Partei, Fraktion

factor n. Faktor; (fig.) Umstand

factory n. Fabrik

faculty n. Fakultät; Lehrerkollegium; Fähigkeit, Befähigung, Gabe

fad n. Grille, Liebhaberei; Steckenpferd;

Modetorheit

fade v. verblassen, verschiessen; (bot.) verwelken; (mus.) verklingen, abklingen; **-less** adj. lichtecht, farbecht

fade-out n. Abblenden, langsames Verschwinden

fag v. sich abarbeiten, ermüden, erschöpfen

Fahrenheit adj. Fahrenheit-

fail v. scheitern, fehlschlagen, misslingen; fehlen, mangeln; stocken, versagen, nachlassen; (agr.) missraten; (com.) Bankrott machen; (educ.) durchfallen; (med.) verfallen, abnehmen; **— n. without —** unfehlbar, ganz gewiss; **-ing** n. Fehler, Schwäche; **-ing** prep. mangels; **-ure** n. Misslingen, Versagen, Fehlschlag(en), Misserfolg; Versager, Zusammenbruch; (com.) Zahlungseinstellung, Bankrott; (med.) Sinken, Verfall; **be a -ure** keinen Erfolg haben; **heart -ure** Herzschlag

faint n. Ohnmacht; **— adj.** schwach, matt; ohnmächtig, kraftlos; **— v.** ohnmächtig werden, in Ohnmacht fallen; **-ness** n. Schwäche, Mattigkeit; Undeutlichkeit

fair n. Jahrmarkt, Markt; Messe; **— adj.** gerecht, unparteiisch, ehrlich; schön, hübsch; sauber, leserlich; (hair) blond; (complexion) hell; (sport) fair; (fig.) gewöhnlich, Mittel-; **— copy** Reinschrift; **— play** ehrliches Spiel; **— trade** gegenseitige Handelsbeziehung; **— weather** günstiges (or schönes) Wetter; **-ly** adv. schön, ehrlich, billig; leidlich, ziemlich; **-ly well** ziemlich gut; **-ness** n. Aufrichtigkeit, Ehrlichkeit; Unbescholtenheit, Redlichkeit; Billigkeit; Unparteilichkeit; Hellfarbigkeit Blondheit

fair-minded adj. vorurteilsfrei

fair-trade agreement n. gegenseitiges Handelsabkommen

fair-weather friend n. Freund im Glück

fairy n. Fee, Elfe; **— adj.** feenhaft, zauberisch; Feen-; **— tale** Märchen

fairyland n. Märchenland, Feenreich

faith n. Glauben(sbekenntnis), Religion; Vertrauen; Treue; **in good —** auf Treu und Glauben; **-ful** n. Gläubige; **-ful** adj. treu, getreu; gläubig; ehrlich; gewissenhaft; **-fully yours** hochachtungsvoll, Ihr sehr ergebener; **-less** adj. ungetreu, treulos

fake n. Schwindel, Fälschung, betrügerische Nachahmung; Schwindler; **— adj.** betrügerisch, gefälscht; **— v.** nachahmen, nachmachen, zurechtmachen, fälschen; **-r** n. Betrüger, Fälscher

falcon n. Falke

fall n. Fall(en), Sturz; Untergang, Zusammenbruch; Fällen; (com.) Sinken, Fallen; (season) Herbst; pl. Fälle, Gefälle; **— v.** fallen, hinfallen, umfallen; fällen; (arch.) einfallen, einstürzen; (bot.) abfallen, herunterfallen; (com.) sinken; (wind) sich legen; (zool.) krepieren; **— apart** (oder to pieces) zerfallen; **— asleep** einschlafen; **— away** abfallen, abmagern; **— back**

zurückfallen; sein Wort nicht halten; — back again wieder zurückweichen; — back on zurückgreifen auf; — behind zurückbleiben; im Rückstand bleiben; — for (person) sich verlieben in; — for (thing) hereinfallen auf; — in einfallen; (mil.) antreten; — in love sich verlieben; — off herunterfallen; zurückgehen; — on überfallen; — out ausfallen, sich überwerfen; (mil.) austreten; — short nicht hinreichen (or ausreichen); — sick krank werden; — through durchfallen, misslingen; — upon befallen, plötzlich angreifen; -en adj. gefallen; -en arches Senkfuss

fallacious adj. trügerisch, irreleitend

fallacy n. Täuschung; Irrtum

fallout n. radioaktiver Niederschlag

false adj. falsch; unrichtig; untwahr, treulos; — alarm blinder Alarm; — bottom Doppelboden; — pretenses Vorspieglung falscher Tatsachen; — step Fehltritt; — teeth falsche Zähne; -hood n. Lüge, Falschheit, Unwahrheit; Heuchelei, Unredlichkeit

falsetto n. Falsett, Fistelstimme; Kopfstimme

falsies n. pl. falscher Busen, Schaumgummibusen

falsify v. (ver)fälschen

falter v. schwanken, zögern, wanken; stolpern, straucheln; stottern, stammeln

fame n. Ruhm, Ruf; -d adj. berühmt

familiar adj. vertraut, vertraulich, intim; wohlbekannt; alltäglich; gewöhnlich; — with vertraut mit; -ity n. Vertraulichkeit, Vertrautheit; -ize v. vertraut machen

family n. Familie; Geschlecht; (bot. and zool.) Gattung; — doctor Hausarzt; — tree Stammbaum

famine n. Hungersnot; Teuerung, Mangel

famous adj. berühmt, famos, ausgezeichnet

fan n. Fächer; (mech.) Ventilator; Gebläse; (sl.) Anhänger; Liebhaber, Fex; — v. fächeln; anfachen; (fig.) entflammen; — oneself sich Luft zufächeln

fanatic n. Fanatiker, Schwärmer; -(al) adj. fanatisch, schwärmerisch; -ism n. Fanatismus

fanciful adj. phantastisch, schwärmerisch, wunderlich; launenhaft

fancy n. Phantasie, Einbildungskraft, Einbildung; Grille; Geschmack; Lust; Liebhaberei; — v. sich vorstellen, sich einbilden; wähnen; — adj. elegant, bunt, phantastisch, übertrieben; — goods Modeartikel, Luxusartikeln, Galanteriewaren

fancywork n. feine(weibliche)Handarbeit

fanfare n. Fanfare, Tusch

fang n. Fang(zahn), Giftzahn

fantastic adj. phantastisch, eingebildet, seltsam, wunderlich

fantasy n. Phantasie, Phantasie

far adj. fern, weit, entfernt; — away weit entfernt; — be it from me das sei fern

von mir; — cry weite Entfernung, grosser Gegensatz; — from keineswegs; — off entlegen; weit entfernt; on the — side auf der anderen Seite; — adv. fern, weit; sehr, ganz; as — as bis zu, bis an; soweit; soviel; by —, — and away bei weitem, um vieles; — and near, — and wide weit und breit; so — bis jetzt; so — as soviel

farce n. Posse, Schwank

fare n. Fahrgeld, Fahrpreis; Fahrgast; Speise, Kost; — v. fahren, ergehen; sich befinden; — ill schlimm daransein; — well gut wegkommen

farewell n. Lebewohl, Abschied; -! interj. lebe wohl! auf Wiedersehen!

farfetched adj. weit hergeholt, gesucht, gezwungen

farm n. Gut, Bauernhof, Meierei, Farm; Pachtgut; — hand Tagelöhner, Landarbeiter; — v. bearbeiten, bebauen; (ver)pachten; -er n. Bauer, Landwirt, Landmann; small -er Kleinbauer, Häusler; -ing n. Ackerbau, Landbau

farmhouse n. Bauernhaus, Gutshaus, Farmhaus

farmyard n. Wirtschaftshof, Gutshof, Bauernhof

far-off adj. weit entfernt

far-reaching adj. weitreichend, weittragend

farsighted adj. (med.) weitsichtig; (fig.) umsichtig, vorsichtig

farther adj. and adv. weiter, ferner, entfernter

farthermost adj. weitest, fernst

farthest adj. weitest, fernst, entferntest; — adv. am fernsten, am weitesten

fascinate v. bezaubern, versaubern, fesseln

fascinating adj. bezaubernd, reizend, spannend, fesselnd

fascination n. Bezauberung, Zauber, Reiz; Fassination

fascism n. Faschismus

fascist n. Faschist

fashion n. Mode; Form, Gestalt, Art; Schnitt; in — nach der Mode; latest — neueste Mode; out of — unmodern; -able adj. elegant, modisch, modern

fast n. Fasten; — day Fasttag; — v. fasten; — adj. fest, tief; unbeweglich; schnell, rasch; waschecht, lichtecht; leichtlebig, flott; the clock is — die Uhr geht vor; -ing n. Fasten, Enthaltsamkeit; -ness n. Festigkeit, Sicherheit, Stärke; Schnelligkeit; (mil.) Feste

fasten v. befestigen, festmachen, verschliessen; heften; sich halten an; -er n. Befestiger, Befestigungsmittel; patent -er Druckknopf; -ing n. Befestigungsmittel; Schloss, Riegel, Haken

fat n. Fett, Schmalz; — adj. dick, fett, feist, plump; become — dick werden; mästen; -ness n. Fettigkeit, Wohlleibtheit; -ten v. fett machen, fett werden; mästen; (agr.) fruchtbar machen, düngen; -ty adj. fettig; -ty n. Dickerchen

fatal adj. verhängnisvoll, tödlich, fatal; -ism n. Fatalismus; -ity n. Verhängnis;

Unglück(sfall); (mil.) Verlust

fate n. Schicksal, Verhängnis, Geschick; **-ful** adj. verhängnisvoll

father n. Vater; (eccl.) Pater; **-hood** n. Vaterschaft; **-less** adj. vaterlos; **-ly** adj. väterlich

father-in-law n. Schwiegervater

fatherland n. Vaterland

fathom n. (naut.) Faden; — v. sondieren, abmessen; (fig.) ergründen, eindringen; **-less** adj. unergründlich, bodenlos

fatigue n. Ermüdung, Müdigkeit, Ermattung; Strapaze; — v. ermüden, ermatten

faucet n. Hahn, Zapfen

fault n. Fehler; Verfehlung, Vergehen; Irrtum; Schuld; **be at** — schuld daran sein; **find** — etwas auszusetzen haben; **-less** adj. fehlerlos, tadellos; **-y** adj. fehlerhaft, mangelhaft; tadelnswert

faultfinder n. Tadler, Krittler, Nörgler, Mäkler

faultfinding adj. tadelsüchtig, nörgelnd, krittelnd, mäkelnd

faun n. Faun, Waldgott

favor n. Gunst, Gefallen; Gnade, Milde; **balance in your** — Saldo zu Ihren Gunsten; **be in** — in Gunst stehen; **be in** — of für etwas sein, dafür sein; **in** — of zu Gunsten von; — v. begünstigen; — **us with a song** erfreuen Sie uns mit einem Lied; — **us with your visit** beehren Sie uns mit Ihrem Besuch; **he -s his father** er ähnelt dem Vater; **-able** adj. günstig, geneigt, gewogen; dienlich, zustimmend; freundlich; **-ite** n. Günstling, Liebling; Favorit; **-ite** adj. begünstigt; Lieblings-; **-itism** n. Günstlingswirtschaft; Favorisieren

fear n. Furcht, Angst; Besorgnis; **for** — **of** aus Angst vor; — v. (be)fürchten; sich fürchten, besorgen; **-ful** adj. furchtsam, bange; furchtbar, schrecklich; **-less** adj. furchtlos, unerschrocken; **-some** adj. fürchterlich; furchtsam

feasible adj. ausführbar, möglich

feast n. Fest; Festtag; Festessen, Schmaus; (fig.) Leckerbissen; — v. speisen, festlich bewirten; schmausen, sich gütlich tun

feat n. Heldentat, Leistung, Tat; Kunststück

feather n. Feder; pl. Geflügel; — **bed** Federbett; **light as a** — federleicht; **that's a** — **in his cap** darauf kann er sich etwas einbilden; — v. befiedern, schmücken; **-ed** adj. federig, befiedert, gefiedert; **-y** adj. federartig, federig, federleicht

featherbedding n. durch Gewerkschaftsvertrag bedingte Anstellung unnötiger Arbeiter

featherweight n. Federgewicht

feature n. Hauptzug, Merkmal; Hauptfilm; pl. Züge, Gesichtszüge; — v. ausgestalten; in der Hauptrolle darstellen; (fig.) gross aufmachen

February n. Februar

federal adj. Bundes-; föderativ, verbündet; föderalistisch

federate adj. verbündet, föderiert; — v. (sich) verbünden, zu einem Staatenbund zusammenschliessen

federation n. Staatenbund, Verband, Föderation

fee n. Gebühr; Honorar, Lohn; Trinkgeld; Eintrittsgeld; Beitrag

feeble adj. schwach, matt

feeble-minded adj. schwachköpfig, geistesschwach

feed n. Futter, Nahrung; (mech.) Zuleitung, Vorsorgung; — v. füttern, speisen, nähren; essen; sich nähren; vorsorgen, versehen; **-er** n. (agr.) Fütterer, Viehmäster; (mech.) Futterapparat; (mech.) Zuführung, Zuleitung

feedback n. (recording machine) Rückkoppelung

feel n. Fühlen, Gefühl(ssinn); Empfindung; — v. fühlen, empfinden, spüren; sich fühlen; — **about** halten von; — **like** Lust haben auf (or zu); — **one's way** sich durchtasten; **-er** n. Fühler, Fühlhorn; **put out a -er** das Gelände sondieren, einen Fühler ausstrecken; **-ing** n. Gefühl, Fühlen; Empfindung, Mitgefühl; **-ing** adj. fühlend, gefühlvoll; tief empfunden; mitleidig

feign v. heucheln, sich verstellen; erdichten; simulieren; — **to do** vorgeben zu tun

feint n. Verstellung, Finte; (mil.) Scheinangriff

felicitation n. Gratulation, Glückwunsch

felicity n. Glück(seligkeit)

feline adj. katzenartig

fell v. fällen, umhauen

fellow n. Gefährte, Genosse; Kollege, Kamerad; Kerl, Bursche; Mitglied; — **citizen** Mitbürger; — **countryman** Landsmann; — **creature** Mitmensch, Mitgeschöpf; — **member** Vereinsmitglied; — **student** Studiengenosse; — **traveler** Reisegefährte; (pol.) Mitläufer; Anhänger (aber nicht Mitglied einer Partei); **-ship** n. Gemeinschaft, Kameradschaft; Mitgliedschaft; (educ.) Stipendium

felly n. Felge

felon n. Verbrecher; **-y** n. Kapitalverbrechen

felt n. Filz; — v. (sich) verfilzen

female n. Weib, Weibchen; — adj. weiblich

feminine adj. weiblich, weibisch; feminin

fence n. Zaun, Umzäunung, Einfriedung; (law) Hehler; — v. einzäunen; (sports) fechten, parieren; (fig.) abwehren; **-r** n. Fechter; Fechtmeister

fencing n. Fechten, Fechtkunst

ferment n. Gärung, Erregung; Ferment; — v. gären, in Gärung geraten; **-ation** n. Gärung; Fermentierung

fern n. Farn(kraut)

ferocious adj. wild, raubgierig; grimmig, grausam

ferocity n. Wildheit, Grausamkeit

ferret n. Frettchen; — v. — **out** heraus-

bringing, vertreiben; aufspüren
ferrous adj. eisenhaltig
ferry n. Fähre; — v. überführen, übersetzen
ferryboat n. Fähre, Fährboot
fertile adj. fruchtbar, ergiebig; (fig.) erfinderisch, schöpferisch
fertility n. Fruchtbarkeit
fertilization n. Fruchtbarmachung, Befruchtung
fertilize v. befruchten; fruchtbar machen, düngen; -r n. Dünger, Düngemittel
fervent adj. heiss, glühend, inbrünstig
fervid adj. brennend, siedend; hitzig
fervor n. Eifer; Hitze, Glut
fester v. eitern, schwären, faulen
festival n. Fest; — adj. festlich, Fest-
festivity n. Festlichkeit, Lustbarkeit
fetch v. (ab)holen, einholen, einbringen
fête n. Fest; — v. feiern
fetter v. fesseln; n. pl. Fesseln, Ketten
feud n. Leh(e)n; -al adj. feudal, lehnbar, Lehns-; -alism n. Lehnswesen
feud n. Fehde, Streit
fever n. Fieber; **yellow —** gelbes Fieber; -ish adj. fieberhaft; fieberkrank
few adj. wenige; einige; **a —** ein paar, einige wenige; **quite a —** ziemlich viel; -er adv. weniger
fiancé n. Verlobte, Bräutigam; -e n. Verlobte, Braut
fib n. Notlüge, Schwindelei, Finte; — v. flunkern, lügen
fiber, fibre n. Faser, Fiber
fickle adj. unbeständig, veränderlich, wankelmütig
fiction n. Dichtung, Erdichtung, Fiktion; Prosaliteratur, Romanliteratur
fictitious adj. fingiert, nachgemacht; erdichtet, eingebildet; unecht
fiddle n. Geige, Violine; Fiedel; **play second —** eine untergeordnete Rolle spielen; — v. fiedeln, geigen; tändeln; -r n. Geiger; Fiedler, Spielmann
fidelity n. Wahrhaftigkeit, Ehrlichkeit, Treue; **high —** höchste Tongenauigkeit (or Pflichttreue, Wahrhaftigkeit, Redlichkeit); Raumton
fidget v. unruhig sein, umher zappeln; nervös machen
field n. Feld; Acker, Weide; Grund; Schlachtfeld; (sports) Spielfeld, Sportplatz; (fig.) Bereich; — **artillery** Feldartillerie; — **day** Felddienstübung; (fig.) grosser Tag; — **glass** Feldglas, Feldstecher; — **hospital** Feldlazarett; — **kitchen** Feldküche, Gulaschkanone; — **marshal** Feldmarschall; — **mouse** Feldmaus; — **officer** Stabsoffizier; -er n. Spieler im Feld, Fänger
fierce adj. wild, hitzig, wütend; grimmig, ungestüm; -ness n. Wildheit, Ungestüm, Grimmigkeit
fife n. Pfeife, Querpfeife; -r n. Pfeifer
fifteen n. Fünfzehn(er); — adj. fünfzehn; -th n. Fünfzehnte, Fünfzehntel; -th adj. fünfzehnt
fifth n. Fünfte, Fünftel; — adj. fünft; — **column** fünfte Kolonne, Spionage- und Sabotageorganisation im Hinterland;

— **columnist** Mitglied der fünften Kolonne; — **wheel** fünftes Rad am Wagen
fiftieth n. Fünfzigste, Fünfzigstel; — adj. fünfzigst
fifty n. Fünfzig; — adj. fünfzig; **in his fifties** in den Fünfzigern
fifty-fifty adj. halb und halb, zu gleichen Teilen
fig n. Feige; (coll.) Kleinigkeit, Pfifferling; — **tree** Feigenbaum
fight n. Kampf, Streit; (mil.) Gefecht, Treffen; (sports) Ringkampf, Boxkampf; — v. kämpfen, streiten; bekämpfen; boxen, ringen, raufen; fechten; duellieren; -er n. Kämpfer, Streiter; Fechter, Boxer, Schläger; -er (plane) Kampfflugzeug, Jagdflugzeug; -ing n. Kampf
figment n. Erdichtung
figure n. Figur, Form, Gestalt; Abbildung; (math.) Zahl, Ziffer, Nummer; — **of speech** Redewendung; — **skater** Eiskunstläufer; — **skating** Eiskunstlauf; — v. formen, gestalten; abbilden, darstellen; sich zeigen; rechnen; (theat.) eine Rolle spielen; (coll.) sich vorstellen; — **on** rechnen auf; — **out** lösen, berechnen; -d adj. gemustert
figurehead n. Galionsbild, Bugfigur; nomineller Leiter
filament n. Fäserchen; Staubfaden; (elec.) Glühfaden
file n. Aktendeckel, Aktenordner; Aktenbündel; Kartei, Kartothek; (mech.) Feile; (mil.) Reihe; (sewing) Aufreihfaden; — **on** in den Akten; **single —** Gänsemarsch; — **clerk** Registraturangestellte; — **leader** Vordermann, Flügelmann; — v. (ein)ordnen, ablegen, registrieren; einbringen; (mech.) feilen; — **by** defilieren, vorbeiziehen
filibuster n. Freibeuter; (pol.) Dauerredner (um Gesetzesanträge oder Gesetzesannahme zu verhindern); Quertreiber
filing n. Registratur; Ordnung, Einordnung; pl. Feilspäne; — **card** Karteikarte; — **case** Karteischrank, Kartothekkasten
fill n. Fülle; Genüge; Füllung; **eat one's —** sich satt essen; — v. (an)füllen, ausfüllen; erfüllen, vollbringen; innehaben, besetzen; (voll)stopfen; — **an order** einen Auftrag erledigen (or ausführen); — **a tooth** einen Zahn plombieren (or füllen); — **in** eintragen, einsetzen, ausfüllen; — **out** ausfüllen; — **the bill** allen Anforderungen genügen; — **up** voll machen, auffüllen; sich füllen; -er n. Füller; Trichter; Einlage; (fig.) Lückenbüsser; -ing n. Füllung; (dent.) Plombe; — **station** Tankstelle
filet n. Stirnband; (cooking) Filet, Lendenstück
filly n. Stutenfüllen
film n. Schicht; Schleier; (med.) Membrane, Häutchen; (phot.) Film; — **strip** Filmstreifen, Bildstreifen, Bildband; **roll of —** Rollfilm; — v. filmen
filter n. Filter; — v. filtern, filtrieren,

durchseihen

filter-tip *adj.* mit Filter, Filter-

filth, filthiness *n.* Schmutz, Unrat; Schmutzigkeit; **-y** *adj.* schmutzig, unrein; trübe; (fig.) gemein, unflätig

fin *n.* Finne; Flosse; (sl.) Fünfdollarnote

final *adj.* letzt, endlich; definitiv, endgültig; End-, Schluss-; *n. pl.* (sports) Endrunde, Schlussrunde; (educ.) Schlussprüfungen; **-ist** *n.* Teilnehmer an der Schlussrunde; **-ity** *n.* Endgültigkeit, Endzustand; Endlichkeit

finance *n.* Finanzwesen; *pl.* Finanzen, Einkünfte; — *v.* finanzieren, finanziell unterstützen

financial *adj.* finanziell, wirtschaftlich

financier *n.* Geldmann, Finanzmann

finch *n.* Fink

find *n.* Fund; — *v.* finden, treffen; auffinden, ausfindig machen; entdecken, ermitteln; (law) erklären, erkennen, befinden; — **fault with** tadeln; — **out** ermitteln, herausbringen; **-er** *n.* Finder, Entdecker; (phot.) Sucher; **-ing** *n.* Fund, Entdeckung; Erkenntnis; (law) Resultat, Ausspruch, Urteil

fine *n.* Geldstrafe, Busse; — *v*, zu einer Geldstrafe verurteilen, mit einer Geldstrafe belegen; — *adj.* fein, zart, dünn; spitz; schön, herrlich, vortrefflich; verfeinert; feingebildet; vornehm, elegant; **the — arts** die schönen Künste; — *v.* zu einer Geldstrafe verurteilen, mit einer Geldstrafe belegen; **-ness** *n.* Feinheit, Eleganz; Vortrefflichkeit; (min.) Feingehalt, Reinheit

finery *n.* Staat, Glanz, Putz

finespun *adj.* feingesponnen

finger *n.* Finger; **finger wave** (ohne Wickler gelegte) Kaltwelle; **have a — in the pie** die Hand mit im Spiele haben; **keep one's -s crossed** den Daumen halten; — *v.* betasten, befühlen; (mus.) mit Fingersatz versehen, spielen, üben; **-ing** *n.* Fingern, Betasten; (mus.) Fingersatz

fingernail *n.* Fingernagel; — **polish** Nagellack

fingerprint *n.* Fingerabdruck

finicky *adj.* affektiert, geziert; wählerisch

finish *n.* Ende, Schluss; Vollendung, Fertigstellung; Lack, Politur; (sports) Endkampf; — *v.* (be)enden, beendigen; aufhören; vollenden, fertigmachen; (sports sl.) den Rest geben; — (drinking) austrinken; — (eating) aufessen; — (talking) ausreden, zuende reden; **-ed** *adj.* beendet, fertig; vollendet

finite *adj.* endlich, begrenzt

fir *n.* Tanne, Fichte, Föhre

fire *n.* Feuer, Flamme; Brand, Feuersbrunst; Licht, Glanz, Leidenschaft; (mil.) Geschützfeuer; — **alarm** Feuermelder; — **department** Feuerwehr; — **engine** Feuerspritze; — **escape** Rettungsleiter; Nottreppe; — **extinguisher** Feuerlöscher, Löschapparat; — **insurance** Feuerversicherung; — **screen** Ofenschirm; Kamingitter; — **ship** Feuerschiff; **be on** — brennen, in Brand

stehen; **build** (*oder* **make) a** — ein Feuer machen (*or* anzünden); **open** — das Feuer eröffnen; **set on** — anzünden; **set** — **to** in Brand setzen; — *v.* schiessen, feuern; entlassen, hinausschmeissen; anzünden, heizen

firearms *n. pl.* Feuerwaffen

firebrand *n.* Feuerbrand; Aufwiegler

firecracker *n.* Schwärmer, Knallkapsel, Knallbonbon, Knallfrosch

firefly *n.* Glühwürmchen, Leuchtkäfer

fireman *n.* Feuerwehrmann; (rail.) Heizer

fireplace *n.* Herd; Kamin

fireplug *n.* Hydrant

firepower *n.* Feuerstärke

fireproof *adj.* feuerfest, feuersicher

fireside *n.* Herd; Kamin; (fig.) Häuslichkeit; **by the** — am Kamin; im häuslichen Kreise

firetrap *n.* Feuerfalle; leicht entzündbares Gebäude

firewarden *n.* Branddirektor

fireworks *n. pl.* Feuerwerk, Feuerwerkskörper

firing *n.* Anzünden; Heizung, Feuerung; (mil.) Abfeuern; (coll.) Entlassung; — **line** Feuerzone, Frontlinie; — **pin** Zündnadel

firm *n.* Firma, Geschäftshaus; — *adj.* fest, sicher; beständig, standhaft; **-ness** *n.* Festigkeit, Entschlossenheit

first *adj.* erste, vorderste, vorzüglichste; — **aid** erste Hilfe; — **mate** Obersteuermann; — **name** Vorname; — **night** Première; — **nighter** Premièrenbesucher; **in the** — **place** an erster Stelle; — *adv.* zuerst, erstens; eher; **at** — zuerst; — **come** — **served** wer zuerst kommt, mahlt zuerst; — **of all** vor allen Dingen; **to go** — vorangehen; — *n.* Erste

first-aid *adj.* erste Hilfe leistend; — **kit** Erstehilfekasten

first-class *adj.* erstklassig; **private** — Gefreite

firsthand *adj.* aus erster Hand

first-rate *adj.* ersten Ranges, ausgezeichnet

fiscal *adj.* fiskalisch; Finanz-

fish *n.* Fisch; — **bowl** Goldfischglas; — **market** Fischmarkt; — **story** Anglerlatein; — *v.* fischen, angeln; (fig.) erhaschen; **-ery** *n.* Fischerei; **-ing** *n.* Fischen, Fischfang; **-ing boat** Fischerboot; **-ing line** Angelschnur; **-ing rod** Angelrute; **-ing smack** Fischereikutter; **-ing tackle** Angelgerät; **-y** *adj.* fisch(art)ig; fischreich; (coll.) verdächtig, faul

fisherman *n.* Fischer

fishhook *n.* Angelhaken

fishpond *n.* Fischteich

fission *n.* Spaltung; **nuclear** — Kernspaltung; **-able** *adj.* spaltbar

fist *n.* Faust

fit *n.* Anfall, Ausbruch; Einfall, Laune; — *adj.* fähig, geeignet, passend, tauglich; angemessen, schicklich; (sports) in guter Form; — *v.* passen; anpassen; (mech.) montieren, aufstellen; **be** —

for taugen zu; — in(to) hineinpassen; übereinstimmen; — out ausrüsten, einrichten; —ful adj. veränderlich, launenhaft, unstet; krampfartig; -ness n. Eignung, Tauglichkeit; Schicklichkeit; -ter n. Zubereiter, Zurichter; Einrichter; Monteur; Installateur; -ting n. Anprobe, Probe; Zurechtmachen, Anpassen; Montieren, Montierung; Ausrüstung; Installation; -tings pl. Zubehör; Ausrüstungsgegenstände; -ting adj. passend, geeignet

five n. Fünf(er); — adj. fünf

fix n. üble Lage, Klemme; — v. herrichten, instandsetzen, reparieren; festmachen, befestigen; heften, richten auf; bestimmen; sich niederlassen, sich festsetzen; — up ordnen, einrichten; —ation n. Festhalten, Festmachen; Fixierung; —ed adj. fest, feststehend; bestimmt; starr; (chem.) feuerfest; nicht flüchtig; —ture n. Feststehend; Einrichtung; Inventarstück

fizz n. Zischen, Sprühen, Sprudeln; (fig.) Sodawasser; — v. zischen, sprühen, sprudeln; -le n. misslungenes Unternehmen; Abfallen, Steckenbleiben; -le v. stecken bleiben; zischen

flabbergast v. verblüffen

flabby adj. schlaff, welk; (fig.) kraftlos, gehaltlos

flag n. Fahne, Flagge; (bot.) Kalmus, Schwertlilie; — officer Flaggoffizier; — of truce Friedensfahne, Parlamentärfahne; — v. ermatten, erschlaffen, nachlassen; Flaggensignale geben; — a train einen Zug durch Flaggensignale zum Halten bringen; -ging adj. schlaff werdend

flagpole n. Fahnenstange

flagrant adj. abscheulich, berüchtigt; offenkundig

flagship n. Flaggschiff

flagstaff n. Fahnenstange

flagstone n. Fliese, Platte

flail n. Dreschflegel; — v. dreschen

flair n. Spürsinn, Witterung; Sinn, feine Nase

flake n. Flocke; Schicht, Schuppe; — v. — off abschuppen; (sich) abblättern

flaky adj. flockig, schuppig; geschichtet

flamboyant adj. auffallend, flammend; (arch.) im flämischen Stil gehalten

flame n. Flamme; Feuer, Hitze; Heftigkeit; Leidenschaft; (coll.) Flamme; — thrower Flammenwerfer; — v. flammen, lodern; auffahren

flaming adj. flammend; rotglänzend; heftig, glühend

flammable adj. entzündbar, entflammbar

flank n. Flanke, Seite; (mil.) Flügel; — v. flankieren, umgehen

flannel n. Flanell; -ette n. Baumwollflanell

flap n. Klappe; (anat.) Lappen; (avi.) Bremsklappe am Flugzeug; Zwischenflügel; (coat) Schoss; (hat) Krempe; (wing) Schlag; — v. klappen, klapsen schlagen; lose herabhängen; flattern

flapjack n. Pfannkuchen

flare n. Leuchtsignal; Leuchtpatrone; (fig.) Prahlerei; — v. flackern, lodern; flimmern, schimmern; — up aufbrausen; plötzlicher Streit

flare-up n. Auflackern, Aufbrausen; plötzlicher Streit

flash n. Blitz; in a — im Augenblick (or Nu); — back Rückblende; — bulb Blitzlichtlampe; — of lightning Blitzstrahl; — v. blitzen; aufflammen, ausbrechen; aufleuchten; auflodern; -ing n. Blitzen; Flutung; -y adj. schimmernd; auffallend, sensationell; oberflächlich, geschmacklos

flashlight n. Taschenlampe

flask n. Flakon, Fläschchen

flat n. Ebene, Fläche, Niederung; Wohnung; (mus.) Flauheit, Tiefe; (naut.) Untiefe, Sandbank; (theat.) Hintergrund; — adj. flach, platt; abgestanden, geschmacklos, fade, schal; unbedingt, absolut; (color) matt; (com.) flau; (mus.) moll, tief; — tire geplatzter Reifen, Plattfuss; — silver Essbesteck, Tafelsilber: -ness n. Flachheit, Plattheit; Flauheit; (mus.) Erniedrigung; -ten v. (sich) abflachen, verflachen; ebnen; niederdrücken, entmutigen; (mus.) dämpfen, erniedrigen

flat-bottomed adj. flachbödig

flat-chested adj. flachbrüstig

flatfoot n. Plattfuss

flat-footed adj. plattfüssig; (sl.) entschieden, entschlossen

flatiron n. Plätteisen, Bügeleisen

flatter v. schmeicheln; entzücken; -er n. Schmeichler; -ing adj. schmeichelhaft, schmeichlerisch; -y n. Schmeichelei

flaunt v. prunket mit, sich aufblähen

flavor n. Geschmack; Wohlgeruch, Aroma; (wine) Blume, Bouquet; (fig.) Beigeschmack; — v. würzen; -ing n. Aroma; Würzen

flaw n. Sprung, Riss, Bruch; Fehler; Flecken; -less adj. fehlerlos, makellos

flax n. Flachs, Lein; -en adj. flachsen, flachsartig; Flachs-; blond

flaxseed n. Leinsamen

flea n. Floh

flea-bitten adj. vom Floh gestochen; gesprenkelt

flee v. fliehen, verlassen; meiden

fleece n. Schaffell; Vlies; — v. scheren; (fig.) rupfen, prellen

fleecy adj. wollig, wollreich; flockig

fleet n. Flotte; — adj. flink, schnell; flüchtig; -ing adj. flüchtig, vergänglich

flesh n. Fleisch; Körper; Fleischeslust; Fleisch-; — color Fleischfarbe; -y adj. fleischig, fett

flesh-colored adj. fleischfarben

flexibility n. Biegsamkeit; Lenksamkeit

flexible adj. biegsam, lenksam

flight n. Flucht, Entrinnen; (arch.) Treppe; (avi.) Flug; Fliegen; Kette; (orn.) Schwarm; — deck Abflugdeck; — mechanic Bordmechaniker; — of stairs Treppe(nstufen); — pattern Flugordnung über Flugplatz; Flugschema; — strip Flugstreifen, Einflugschneise; -y adj. leichtsinnig, zerstreut, unbeständig; lebhaft

flimsy adj. dünn, schwach; nichtig

flinch v. zurückweichen, zurückschrecken

fling n. Wurf, Schlag; Freiheit, Ausbruch; Stichelei; — v. werfen, schleudern; eilen, fliegen; sticheln

flint n. Kiesel; Feuerstein

flip n. Klaps; Ruck; (drink) Flip; — v. schnipsen, schnellen; klapsen

flippant adj. vorlaut; wegwerfend; leichtfertig, frivol

flirt n. Kokette; Hofmacher; — v. flirten, schäkern, liebäugeln, kokettieren; -ation n. Flirt, Liebelei

float n. Floss; Schwimmer; Flott; (naut.) Rettungsboje; — v. schwimmen, schweben, fluten; (naut.) flott sein; in Gang bringen; treiben, flössen; (coll.) flottmachen; überschwemmen; — a loan eine Anleihe auflegen; -ing adj. schwimmend, treibend; schwankend, unbestimmt; -ing dock Schwimmdock

flock n. Herde; (eccl.) Gemeinde; (orn.) Schwarm; (fig.) Haufen, Menge; — v. zusammenströmen; sich scharen

flog v. (aus)peitschen, züchtigen; schlagen, prügeln

flood n. Flut, Überschwemmung; — tide Flut, Gezeit; — v. überfluten, überschwemmen

floodgate n. Fluttor; Schleusentor

floodlight n. Scheinwerferlicht

floor n. Boden, Fussboden; (arch.) Stockwerk, Etage; (pol.) Sitzungssaal; Recht zum Wort; — leader Parteiführer; — plan Grundriss; — show Varietévorführung; ground — Erdgeschoss; — v. dielen, mit Dielen belegen; niederschlagen, überwinden; -ing n. Fussboden(belag)

floorwalker n. Verkaufsabteilungschef

flop n. Durchfall; — v. (hin)plumpsen; misslingen

flora n. Flora; Pflanzenwelt; -l adj. Blüten-; Blumen-

florid adj. blühend, blumenreich; frisch; (arch.) verziert, überladen

florist n. Blumenhändler

floss (silk) n. Florettseide; (bot.) Samenwolle

flounce n. Volant, Falbel; Krause, Faltenbesatz; hastige Bewegung; — v. plätschern, planschen; sich hastig bewegen; mit Volants besetzen

flour n. Mehl; — v. mit Mehl bestreuen; -ish n. Blüte, Verzierung, Schnörkel; (mus.) Fanfare, Tusch; -ish v. gedeihen, blühen, florieren; schwingen, schwenken

flow n. Fluss, Strom; Zufluss, Erguss, Schwall, Überfluss; — v. fliessen, strömen; überfliessen, sich ergiessen

flower n. Blume, Blüte; (fig.) Zierde, Beste, Feinste; — girl Blumenmädchen; Brautjungfer; — v. blühen; -ed adj. geblümt; -ing adj. blumig, blühend; -y adj. blumig, blumenreich, geblümt

flowerpot n. Blumentopf

flu n. Grippe, Influenza

fluctuate v. schwanken, unschlüssig sein;

fluktuieren

fluctuation n. Schwankung, Schwanken

flue n. Rauchfang, Kaminrohr; (mech.) Heizkanal

fluency n. Geläufigkeit; Fluss

fluent adj. fliessend, geläufig

fluff n. Staubflocke, Flaum; flaumartiger Überzug, flockige Schicht; — v. verpuffen; -y adj. flaumig, flockig

fluid n. Flüssigkeit; — adj. flüssig

flunk v. versagen, durchfallen

flunkey n. Lakai, Bediente; Speichellecker

fluorescent adj. fluoreszierend, schillernd

fluorine n. Fluorin

fluoroscope n. Durchleuchtungsapparat

flurry n. Verwirrung, Aufregung; Windstoss, Brise; snow — Schneegestöber; — v. aufregen, verwirren; beunruhigen, bestürzen

flush n. Erröten, Glut; Aufwallung; (fig.) Frische, Blüte; (cards) Flöte; royal — grosse (or volle) Flöte; — v. erröten; strömen, schiessen; — the toilet die Toilette (aus)spülen; — adj. frisch, blühend; reif; übervoll; glatt, gleich; be — gut bei Kasse sein

fluster v. verwirren, aufregen

flute n. Flöte; Kannelierung; — v. flöten, auf der Flöte spielen; -d adj. gerillt, geriefelt

flutist n. Flötist, Flötenspieler

flutter n. Geflatter; Verwirrung; Erregung, Unruhe; — v. flattern, zittern; erregt sein; in Aufregung bringen

fly n. Fliege; (baseball) Flugball; (fishing) künstliche Fliege; — v. fliegen; eilen, fliehen; — into a passion in Zorn geraten; -er n., flier n. Flieger; -ing n. Fliegen; -ing adj. fliegend, eilig, schnell; Flug-; -ing boat Flugboot; -ing field Flugfeld; -ing squirrel Flughörnchen; -ing adj. fliegend, eilig, schnell; -ing colors fliegende Fahnen; -ing fish fliegender Fisch; -ing fortress fliegende Festung; -ing saucer fliegende Untertasse

flyleaf n. Vorsatzblatt

flypaper n. Fliegenfänger

flyweight n. Fliegengewicht

flywheel n. Schwungrad

foal n. Fohlen, Füllen; — v. fohlen, werfen

foam n. Schaum; — v. schäumen, geifern; -y adj. schaumig, schaumbedeckt

fob n. Uhrenanhänger

focal adj. im Brennpunkt stehend

focus n. Brennpunkt, Fokus; — v. in einem Brennpunkt vereinigen; (phot.) einstellen

fodder n. Futter; Fütterung

foe n. Feind, Gegner

fog n. Nebel; Umnebelung; (fig.) Unsicherheit; — v. umnebeln, verdüstern; verwirren; -gy adj. neblig, dunstig; (fig.) benebelt

foghorn n. Nebelhorn

foil n. Folie; (mirror) Belag; (sports) Florett, Rapier; — v. vereiteln, täuschen; überwinden, übertreffen

fold n. Falte, Falz, Kniff; — v. falten, falzen; zusammenlegen; -er n. Um-

schlag; Heft, Broschüre; **-ing** *adj.*
zusammenlegbar; Falt-, Klapp-; **-ing
bed** Feldbett, Klappbett; **-ing boat**
Faltboot; **-ing chair** Klappstuhl

foliage *n.* Laub(werk)

folk *n.* Volk; Leute; **common — einfache**
Leute; Volks-; **— dance** Volkstanz; **—
music** Volksmusik; **— song** Volkslied;
— tale Volksmärchen

folklore *n.* Volkskunde; Volkssagen

follow *v.* folgen, nachgehen; nachfolgen;
befolgen; (com.) sich widmen; (phil.)
zur Richtschnur nehmen; **as —s** wie
folgt, folgendermassen; **— suit** Farbe
bekennen; bedienen; **— up** verfolgen;
-er *n.* Anhänger; Verehrer; **-ers** *pl.*
Gefolge, Anhang; **-ing** *n.* Gefolge;
Gefolgschaft, Anhängerschaft; **-ing**
adj. folgend, kommend

follow-up *adj.* verfolgend, nachlaufend

folly *n.* Torheit, Narrheit; Unsinn

foment *v.* erregen, anstiften

fond *adj.* zärtlich, vernarrt; **be — of** gern
haben, lieben; **-ness** *n.* Zärtlichkeit;
Liebhaberei; Vorliebe

font *n.* Taufbecken

food *n.* Speise, Nahrung, Lebensmittel;
(mil.) Proviant, Verpflegung; (zool.)
Futter; *pl.* Nahrungsmittel

foodstuff *n.* Nahrungsmittel

fool *n.* Narr, Tor; Hanswurst; **to make a
— out of someone** jemanden zum
besten haben; **—** *v.* betrügen, prellen;
Spass machen; **-ish** *adj.* töricht; närrisch, albern, eitel, läppisch; **-ishness**
n. Narrheit, Dummheit, Torheit; Unsinn

foolhardy *adj.* tollkühn; dummdreist

foolproof *adj.* kinderleicht; betriebssicher

foot *n.* Fuss; Fussende; (lit.) Versfuss;
(mil.) Fussvolk; **—** *by* **—** Schritt für
Schritt; **— soldier** Infanterie; **on —,**
by **—** zu Fuss; **square —** Quadratfuss;
— *v.* **— the bill** aufkommen für; **-ing**
n. Basis, Grund; Standpunkt, Stellung

foot-and-mouth disease *n.* Maul- und
Klauenseuche

football *n.* Fussball (spiel)

footboard *n.* Trittbrett

footbridge *n.* Laufbrücke, Steg

footgear *n.* Schuhwerk

foothill *n.* Vorgebirge

foothold *n.* fester Standpunkt; Tritt;
Halt. Stütze

footlights *n. pl.* Rampenlicht; **before the
—** auf der Bühne

footman *n.* Bediente, Lakai

footnote *n.* Fussnote, Anmerkung

footpath *n.* Fusspfad, Fussweg

footprint *n.* Fussabdruck, Fuzspur, Fuz-
stapfe

footrace *n.* Wettlauf

footrest *n.* Fussbank, Schemel

footsore *adj.* fusskrank, wundgelaufen

footstep *n.* Tritt, Schritt; Spur

footstool *n.* Fussbank, Schemel

footwork *n.* (sports) Fussbewegungen,
Fussarbeit

for *prep.* für, zu, wegen; während, seit;
als; nach; gegen; zum besten, zugun-

sten; (an)statt vor, um; **— all that**
trotzdem; **— example, — instance** zum
Beispiel; **what —?** wofür? wozu?
warum? **—** *conj.* denn

forbear *v.* sich enthalten, unterlassen, abstehen; **-ance** *n.* Geduld, Nachsicht;
Unterlassung, Enthaltung

forbid *v.* verbieten, untersagen; **God —!**
Gott behüte! **-den** *adj.* verboten, unerlaubt; **-ding** *adj.* abstossend, widerwärtig, abschreckend

force *n.* Kraft, Gewalt; Macht, Stärke;
Nachdruck; (law) Gesetzeskraft, Gültigkeit; *pl.* Streitkräfte, Truppen; **come
into — in** Kraft treten; **from — of
habit** aus alter Gewohnheit, die Macht
der Gewohnheit; **in — in** Kraft; **police
— Polizei(truppe)**; **—** *v.* zwingen,
nötigen; erzwingen, durchsetzen; **—
back** zurücktreiben; **— one's way** sich
hineindrängen (*or* einen Weg bahnen);
— open aufbrechen; **-d** *adj.* gezwungen,
erzwungen; erkünstelt; **— landing** Notlandung; **— march** Eilmarsch; **-ful** *adj.*
kräftig, stark; wirkungsvoll

forceps *n.* (med.) Zange, Geburtenzange

forcible *adj.* gewaltsam, wirksam; eindringlich; zwingend, ungestüm

ford *n.* Furt; **—** *v.* durchwaten

forearm *n.* Vorderarm; **—** *v.* im Voraus
bewaffnen

forebear *n.* Vorfahr, Ahn

forebode *v.* ahnen, voraussehen

foreboding *n.* Ahnung, Voraussage; Vorzeichen

forecast *n.* Voraussage, Vorhersage;
**weather — Wetterbericht, Wettervor-
hersage**; **—** *v.* voraussagen

foreclose *v.* ausschliessen, abweisen; **— a
mortgage** eine Hypothek für verfallen
erklären

foreclosure *n.* Abweisung; Sperre

forefather *n.* Vorfahr, Ahn

forefinger *n.* Zeigefinger

forego *v.* verzichten auf, aufgeben; **-ing**
adj. vorhergehend; vorig, früher; **-ne**
adj. vorausgegangen; **-ne conclusion**
vorgefasste Schlussfolgerung; Selbstverständlichkeit

foreground *n.* Vordergrund

forehead *n.* Stirn

foreign *adj.* ausländisch, fremd, auswärtig; **-er** *n.* Fremde, Ausländer

foreign-born *adj.* im Ausland geboren

foreleg *n.* Vorderbein, Vorderfuss

forelock *n.* Stirnhaar

foreman *n.* Vormann, Vorarbeiter; Aufseher, Werkmeister; (jury) Obmann

foremost *adj.* vorderst, erst; vornehmst;
— *adv.* zuerst, voran, voraus; **first and
—** zu allererst

forenoon *n.* Vormittag

forensic *adj.* gerichtlich, redegewandt

foreordain *v.* vorher verordnen (*or* bestimmen)

forepaw *n.* Vorderpfote

forequarter *n.* Vorderviertel

forerunner *n.* Vorläufer, Vorbote

foresail *n.* (naut.) Focksegel

foresee *v.* voraussehen, vorherwissen

foreshadow v. vorher andeuten, ahnen lassen

foresight n. Voraussicht, Vorsicht; **-ed** adj. voraussehend, vorsichtig

forest n. Wald, Waldung; Forst; **-er** n. Förster, Waldheger; **-ry** n. Forstkultur

foretaste n. Vorgeschmack; — v. vorausnehmen; im Voraus geniessen

foretell v. voraussagen, weissagen; vorbedeuten

forethought n. Vorbedacht, Vorsorge

forever adv. auf immer, zu aller Zeit

forevermore adv. auf immer und ewig

forewarn v. vorher warnen (or ankünden)

foreword n. Vorwort

forfeit n. Verwirkung; Strafe, Geldbusse; — v. verwirken, verlieren; verscherzen

forge n. Schmiede, Esse; — v. schmieden; fälschen, nachmachen; erdichten; **-r** n. Schmied; Fälscher, Falschmünzer; **-ry** n. Fälschung; Erfindung, Lüge

forget v. vergessen; vernachlässigen; **-ful** adj. vergesslich; achtlos, nachlässig; **-fulness** n. Vergesslichkeit; Vergessenheit; Vernachlässigung

forget-me-not n. Vergissmeinnicht

forgive v. verzeihen, vergeben; **-ness** n. Vergebung, Verzeihung

forgiving adj. versöhnlich, nachsichtig; mild

fork n. Gabel; (geog.) Gabelung; Wegarm; Flussarm; — v. (sich) gabeln; **-ed** adj. gegabelt; gabelförmig; zickzackförmig; Gabel-

forlorn adj. verloren, verlassen, einsam; hoffnungslos

form n. Form, Gestalt; Formalität, Brauch; Formular, Fragebogen; Bank, Klasse; — **letter** schematisierter Brief; **in good** — in guter Verfassung; **matter of** — Formalität, Formsache; — v. formen; (sich) bilden, (sich) gestalten; ausbilden; erdenken; (mil.) (sich) formieren; — **an alliance** ein Bündnis schliessen; — **an idea** (or opinion) sich eine Meinung bilden; — **a plan** einen Plan entwerfen; **-less** adj. formlos, ungestaltet

formal adj. förmlich, formell; **-ity** n. Formsache, Formalität; Förmlichkeit

format n. Entwurf; Matrize

formation n. Bildung, Gestaltung; (avi.) Verband; — **flying** n. Verbandfliegen

former adj. vorig; ehemalig, früher; vorerwähnt; **the** — der erstere; **-ly** adv. ehemals, früher, vormals; sonst

formic acid n. Ameisensäure

formula n. Formel; Regel; (med.) Rezept; **-te** v. formulieren; **-tion** n. Formulierung

forsake v. verlassen, aufgeben, entsagen

fort n. Festung(swerk); Fort; **-ification** n. Befestigung, Festungsbau; **-ify** v. befestigen; verstärken; **-ress** n. Festung

fortitude n. Geistesstärke, Standhaftigkeit, Mut

forth adv. hervor; vorwärts, weiter; heraus, hinaus; **and so** — und so weiter; **from this day** — von heute an

forthcoming adj. bevorstehend, bereit;

erscheinend, herauskommend

forthright adj. geradeaus, aufrichtig

forthwith adv. sofort, sogleich

fortieth adj. vierzigst; — n. Vierzigste; Vierzigstel

fortnight n. vierzehn Tage, zwei Wochen; **-ly** adj. and adv. vierzehntägig

fortunate adj. glücklich; **-ly** adv. glücklicherweise

fortune n. Glück; Vermögen; Schicksal, Zufall; — **hunter** Mitgiftjäger; Glücksjäger; **tell a** — wahrsagen

fortune teller n. Wahrsager

forty adj. vierzig; — n. Vierzig(er)

forward adj. vorder; zeitig vorgeschritten, frühreif; voreilig, naseweis, keck, vorlaut; bereit, eifrig; — **pass** Vorbeigang; — adv. vorwärts, voran; weiter, fort; — n. Stürmer; — v. absenden, versenden, befördern; nachsenden; beschleunigen; **—(s)** adv. vorwärts, voran

fossil n. Fossil; — adj. fossil, versteinert

foster v. ernähren, pflegen; hegen, nähren; (be)fördern, begünstigen; — adj. Pflege-; — **brother** Pflegebruder; — **child** Pflegekind; — **father** Pflegevater; — **mother** Pflegemutter

foul n. Zusammenstoss; unerlaubter Hieb (or Schlag); — adj. widerwärtig, ekelhaft; schmutzig, unrein; faul(ig), stinkend; verdorben; unehrlich, unerlaubt; Schimpf-; (law) ungesetzlich, verboten; (naut.) unklar; — **ball** Ball ins Aus; — **play** regelwidriges (or unehrliches) Spiel, Schwindel

found v. (be)gründen, stiften; **-ation** n. Gründung, Errichtung; Stiftung; (arch.) Fundament, Grund, Grundmauer; (fig.) Grundlage; **-er** n. Gründer, Stifter; Erbauer

foundry n. Giesserei, Schmelzhütte

fountain n. Quelle, Fontäne, Springbrunnen; — **pen** Füllfeder(halter)

fountainhead n. Urquell; (fig.) Ursprung

four adj. vier; — n. Vier(er) on **all -s** auf allen Vieren; **-some** n. Vierer; **-teen** adj. vierzehn; **-teen** n. Vierzehn(er); **-teenth** adj. vierzehnt; **-teenth** n. Vierzehnte, Vierzehntel; **-th** adj. viert; **-th** n. Vierte, Viertel; (mus.) Quarte

four-footed adj. vierfüssig

four-wheel brake n. Vierradbremse

fowl n. Vogel; Huhn; Geflügel, Federvieh

fox n. Fuchs; (fig.) Schlaukopf; — **terrier** Foxterrier; **-y** adj. fuchs(art)ig; schlau, verschmitzt

foxglove n. Fingerhut

foyer n. Foyer, Vorhalle, Wandelhalle

fraction n. Bruchstück; (math.) Bruch; **-al** adj. Bruch-; gebrochen; (fig.) unbedeutend

fracture n. Bruch; (med.) Knochenbruch; — v. (zer)brechen

fragile adj. zerbrechlich; gebrechlich, hinfällig, schwach

fragment n. Fragment, Bruchstück; **-ary** adj. bruchstückartig, lückenhaft; **-arily** adv. stückweise

fragrance n. Duft, Wohlgeruch; Aroma

fragrant adj. duftig, wohlriechend

frail adj. zerbrechlich; zart; schwach; **-ty** n. Schwäche, Schwachheit; Gebrechlichkeit

frame n. Rahmen, Einfassung; Gefüge, Bau, Gebälk, Zimmerwerk; (mech.) Gestell, Gerüst; (naut.) Spant; (fig.) Körper, Form; Stimmung; **— of mind** Gemütsverfassung; — v. (ein)rahmen, einfassen; bilden, bauen, zusammenfassen; (fig.) formen; (lit.) entwerfen, erfinden

framework n. Bau, System

France n. Frankreich

franchise n. Freiheit; (law) Vorrecht; (pol.) Wahlrecht

Franconia n. Franken

frank n. Portofreiheit; — adj. frei, offen, aufrichtig; franko, portofrei; — v. portofrei versenden; frankieren; **-ness** n. Offenheit, Aufrichtigkeit

frankfurter n. Frankfurter (Würstchen)

frantic adj. wild, toll, rasend; wahnsinnig; **-ally** adv. rasend, wahnsinnig

fraternal n. brüderlich

fraternity n. Brüderlichkeit; Bruderschaft, Orden, Zunft; (educ.) Verbindung

fraternize v. sich verbrüdern, fraternisieren

fraud n. Betrug, Schwindel; **-ulent** adj. betrügerisch

fraught adj. beladen, befrachtet; angefüllt

freak n. Missbildung, Sehenswürdigkeit; **-ish** adj. grillenhaft, launisch; wunderlich

freckle n. Sommersprosse; **-d** adj. sommersprossig

free adj. frei, unabhängig; kostenlos, unentgeltlich, gratis; freigebig; offen-(herzig); öffentlich; **— and easy** zwanglos, ungezwungen, leicht; **— on board** (f.o.b.) frei an Bord; **— port** Freihafen; **— sample** Gratisprobe; **— speech** Redefreiheit; **— trade** Freihandel; **— verse** Blankvers; **— will** freier Wille, Willensfreiheit; — v. befreien, freilassen; freimachen; **-dom** n. Freiheit, Unabhängigkeit; Freimütigkeit. Vertraulichkeit, Ungezwungenheit; Leichtigkeit; **-dom of speech** Redefreiheit

freeborn adj. freigeboren

freebooter n. Freibeuter

free fall n. (avi.) Freifall

free-for-all n. allgemeine Schlägerei

freehand adj. freihändig

free-lance adj. unabhängig, freischaffend

freeman n. freier Mann, Vollbürger

Freemason n. Freimaurer

free-spoken adj. freimütig, offen

freethinker n. Freidenker, Freigeist

freeway n. Autobahn

freewheel n. Freilauf

freeze v. (er)frieren, gefrieren (lassen); (fig.) erstarren; **-r** n. Gefrierapparat; **deep —** Tiefgefriermaschine

freezing adj. gefrierend, eisig; Gefrier-, Kälte; **— point** Gefrierpunkt

freight n. Fracht, Ladung; Frachtlohn, Frachtgeld; **— car** Güterwagen; —

elevator Güteraufzug; **— train** Güterzug; **by —** per Fracht, als Frachtgut; — v. befrachten, beladen; verladen; **-er** n. Frachter, Frachtdampfer

French adj. französisch; **— door** Flügeltür; **— dressing** Salatsauce; **— fried potatoes** pommes frites; **— horn** Waldhorn; **— leave** ohne Abschied verschwinden; **— windows** Flügelfenster; Balkontür, Verandatür

frenzy n. Wahnsinn, Tobsucht, Raserei

frequency n. Häufigkeit; (elec.) Frequenz; **— modulation** Frequenzmodulation; **high —** Hochfrequenz

frequent adj. häufig; — v. häufig besuchen; frequentieren

fresco n. Fresko, Wandmalerei; Wandgemälde

fresh adj. frisch; gesund; neu, unerfahren, erfrischt, munter; (butter) ungesalzen; (eggs) frischgelegt; (water) süss; (coll.) frech, angeheitert; **— water** Süsswasser; **-en** v. erfrischen, erneuern; auffrischen; zunehmen; **-ness** n. Frische, Neuheit; Gesundheit; (wind) Kühle; (fig.) Unerfahrenheit, Unverdorbenheit; (sl.) Frechheit

freshman n. Neuling, Anfänger; (coll.) Fuchs

fret v. (sich) ärgern; (sich) grämen; (sich) aufreiben; **-ful** adj. ärgerlich, mürrisch, reizbar

fret saw n. Laubsäge

friar n. Mönch

friction n. Reibung; **— tape** Isolierband

Friday n. Freitag; **Good —** Karfreitag

fried adj. gebraten; Brat-; **— chicken** Brathuhn; **— eggs** Spiegeleier, Setzeier; **— fish** Bratfisch; **— potatoes** Bratkartoffeln

friend n. Freund; Bekannte; (rel.) Quäker; **be close —s** nahe befreundet sein; **make —s** Freundschaften schliessen; **-less** adj. freundlos, verlassen; **-liness** n. freundschaftliche Gesinnung, Wohlwollen; **-ly** adj. freundlich, freundschaftlich, befreundet; wohlwollend; **-ship** n. Freundschaft

fright n. Schrecken, Furcht, Entsetzen; **-en** v. erschrecken; **be -ened** erschrecken, bange sein vor; **-en away** verscheuchen; **-ful** adj. schrecklich, entsetzlich

frigid adj. kalt, eisig; frostig; (fig.) herzlos, frigid

fringe n. Franse, Besatz; Rand, Saum; — v. mit Fransen besetzen; (um)säumen

frisk v. hüpfen, springen; (fig.) abtasten, filzen; **-y** adj. hüpfend, tanzend; fröhlich, munter, lustig

fritter n. Fetzen, Stückchen; (cooking) Krapfen; — v. **— away** vergeuden, vertändeln, vertrödeln

frivolity n. Leichtsinn, Leichtfertigkeit; Frivolität

frivolous adj. leichtsinnig, leichtfertig; frivol; wertlos, nichtig

fro adv. **to and —** auf und ab, hin und her

frock n. Kleid; Kinderkleid; Kittel

frog n. Frosch; (dress) Schnurverschluss; (rail.) Kreuzungsstück; **–man** Froschmensch

from prep. von, aus; seit; vor, gegen; wegen, nach; entfernt von; infolge von; **— first to last** von A bis Z; **— morning till night** von früh bis spät; **— now on** von jetzt an; **— top to bottom** von oben bis unten

front n. Front; Vorderseite; Stirn; **in — of** vor, gegenüber von; **shirt —** Vorhemd; Chemisett; **—** adj. vorder, erst; Vorder-; **— door** Haustür; **— line** Front(linie); **— row** erste Reihe; **— seat** Vordersitz; **—** v. **— on** gegenüberstehen; gegenübertreten; gerichtet sein nach; **-al** adj. frontal; Stirn-, Front-; **-age** n. Vorderfront

frontier n. Grenze, Grenzgebiet, Grenzland

frost n. Frost, Reif; (fig.) Frostigkeit; **—** v. mit Zuckerguss versehen, glasieren; **-ed** adj. bereift; glasiert, mit Zuckerguss versehen; **-ed glass** Milchglas; **-ing** n. Zuckerglasur; **-y** adj. frostig, eisig; eiskalt; (fig.) eisgrau, ergraut

frostbitten adj. erfroren

frown n. Stirnrunzeln; **—** v. die Stirn runzeln, finster blicken; **— on** missbilligen

frozen adj. gefroren, erstarrt

frugal adj. mässig, einfach, frugal; genügsam, sparsam

fruit n. Frucht, Obst; Folge, Erfolg, Gewinn; **— fly** Blütenstecher; **— grower** Obstzüchter; **— knife** Obstmesser; **— salad** Obstsalat; **— stand** Obststand; **— store** Obstladen; **— sugar** Fruchtzucker; **— tree** Obstbaum; **candied –s** kandierte Früchte; **-ful** adj. fruchtbar; ergiebig, gewinnbringend; **-less** adj. unfruchtbar; unnütz, vergeblich, fruchtlos

fruitcake n. Fruchttorte, Obstkuchen

frustration n. Vereitelung; (fig.) Querstrich

ry n. Laich; **—** v. braten; **-ing** adj. bratend; **-ing pan** n. Bratpfanne

dge n. Schokoladenmasse

el n. Heizmaterial; Feuerung; Treibstoff, Kraftstoff; **— gauge** Benzinmesser; **— oil** Heizöl; **— tank** Benzintank

fugitive n. Flüchtling; **—** adj. flüchtig

fulcrum n. Stützpunkt

fulfil(l) v. erfüllen, vollziehen; **-ment** n. Erfüllung, Vollziehung

full adj. voll ganz, völlig; vollständig, vollkommen; satt; weit; besetzt; reichlich; **at — length** in voller Länge; (fig.) ausführlich; **at — speed** mit höchster (or in voller) Geschwindigkeit; **— description** ausführliche Beschreibung; **— dress** Gesellschaftsanzug; **— moon** Vollmond; **— of** voll von, voller; **— power** unumschränkte Vollmacht; **— steam ahead!** Volldampf voraus! **— time** ganztägig, Voll–; **in — vollständig; in — swing** in freiem Lauf; **—** adv. völlig, ganz, genau; gerade; recht, sehr;

–ness n. Vollsein, Fülle; **in its –ness** in vollem Umfange; **the –ness of time** die festgesetzte Zeit

fullback n. Verteidiger

full-grown adj. völlig erwachsen, ausgewachsen; (bot.) hochstämmig

full-length adj. lebensgross

fumble n. Tölpelei; **—** v. umhertappen, umhergreifen

fume n. Dampf, Rauch, Dunst; **—** v. rauchen, räuchern; dampfen, dunsten; (fig.) rasen, aufgebracht sein

fumigate v. (aus)räuchern

fuming adj. rauchend; (fig.) aufgebracht

fun n. Spass, Scherz; **for —** zum Spass; **have —** Spass haben, sich unterhalten; **make —** of spotten (or sich lustig machen) über; **-ny** adj. komisch, spasshaft; seltsam; **-ny bone** Ellbogenknochen, Musikantenknochen; **strike as –ny** komisch vorkommen

function n. Funktion, Tätigkeit, Verrichtung; **—** v. funktionieren, tätig sein; **-al** adj. funktionell; amtlich; **-ary** n. Funktionär; Beamte, Amtsträger

fund n. Fonds, Kapital; Vorrat; pl. Gelder; Staatspapiere; Staatsschulden; **—** v. fundieren; (money) anlegen

fundamental adj. Grund-; wesentlich; **-s** n. pl. Grundlage; Hauptsache; Grundpfeiler

funeral n. Begräbnis, Leichenbegängnis; **— director** Begräbnisleiter; **— parlor** Begräbnishalle

fungus n. Pilz, Schwamm

funnel n. Rauchfang, Schornstein; Trichter

fur n. Pelz; Fell; (med.) Belag; **— coat** Pelzmantel; **-red** adj. pelzig, haarig; (med.) belegt; **-rier** n. Pelzhändler; Kürschner; **-ry** adj. pelzartig

furious adj. wütend, rasend; heftig, ungestüm

furlough n. Urlaub; **—** v. beurlauben

furnace n. Ofen; Schmelzofen; **blast —** Hochofen; **open-hearth —** Siemens-Martin Ofen

furnish v. versehen, versorgen; verschaffen, liefern; ausstatten, möblieren; **— a house** ein Haus einrichten; **-ed** adj. möbliert; **-ings** n. pl. Wohnungseinrichtung, Ausrüstungsgegenstände; Mobiliar

furniture n. Möbel; Hausrat, Mobiliar; **piece of —** Möbelstück; **set of —** Möbelgarnitur

furor n. Wut, Raserei

furrow n. Furche; (anat.) Runzel; **—** v. furchen, durchfurchen

further adj. weiter, ferner, entfernt; anderweitig; jenseitig; **— particulars** nähere Umstände; **until — notice** bis auf weiteres; **—** adv. weiter, ferner; überdies, noch dazu; **—** v. (be)fördern

furthermore adv. ausserdem, ferner, überdies

furthest adj. fernst, weitest; **—** adv. am fernsten, am weitesten; **at the —** spätestens

furtive adj. verstohlen, heimlich

furuncle n. Furunkel

fury n. Wut, Raserei; Heftigkeit; **blind —** blinde Wut

fuse n. Zünder, Zündschnur; (elec.) Sicherung; **— box** Sicherungsgehäuse; **— v.** schmelzen, verschmelzen; **-e** n. Windstreichhölzchen

fuselage n. Flugzeugrumpf

fusion n. Schmelzen, Schmelzung; (fig.) Fusion, Verschmelzung

fuss n. Störung, Aufruhr; (coll.) Wesen, Getue; **— v.** viel Aufhebens machen; **-y** adj. übertrieben umständlich, geschäftig; viel Aufhebens machend

futile adj. nutzlos, unnütz; wertlos, nichtig

future adj. künftig, zukünftig; **— n.** Zukunft; (gram.) Futurum; **in the —** in Zukunft, zukünftig

fuzz n. Flaum, Fäserchen; **-y** adj. flockig, faserig; flaumig; (coll.) angeduselt

G

gab n. Geschwätz, Geplauder; **gift of —** ein gutes Mundwerk; **— v.** schwatzen, schnattern

gabardine n. Gabardin

gable n. Giebel

gadfly n. Pferdebremse

gadget n. Vorrichtung, Einrichtung; Kniff, Pfiff

gag n. Knebel; (theat.) improvisierter Witz; (fig.) Knebel; **— v.** knebeln; mundtot machen

gaiety n. Munterkeit, Fröhlichkeit

gaily adv. lustig, munter; bunt

gain n. Gewinn, Vorteil, Nutzen; **— v.** gewinnen, erwerben, erlangen; (clock) vorgehen; **— weight** zunehmen; **-ful** adj. gewinnbringend, einträglich

gait n. Gang, Gangart; Haltung

gala adj. feierlich, prunkhaft; Gala-; **-xy** n. Milchstrasse; (fig.) glänzende Versammlung; **-xy of stars** Sternenmeer

gale n. steife Brise

gall n. Galle; (fig.) Bitterkeit, Unverschämtheit; **— bladder** Gallenblase; **— v.** belästigen, quälen; reizen, ärgern

gallant adj. brav, tapfer; höflich, galant; stattlich; **— n.** Galan, Liebhaber; **-ry** n. Tapferkeit; Galanterie, Artigkeit

gallery n. Galerie; Säulenhalle; Korridor; (min.) Stollen

galley n. (naut.) Galeere, Kombüse; Schiffsküche; (typ.) Setzschiff; **— proof** Korrekturabzug

gallivant v. umherziehen

gallon n. Gallone

gallop n. Galopp; **— v.** galoppieren (lassen); (fig.) schnell laufen

gallows n. Galgen

gallstone n. Gallenstein

galosh n. Galosche, Überschuh, Gummischuh

galvanize v. galvanisieren

gamble v. spielen, wetten; **— away** verspielen; **— n.** Glücksspiel; **-r** n. Spieler, Hasardeur

gambling n. Spiel, Glücksspiel; **— house** Spielkasino, Spielhölle

game n. Spiel, Belustigung; Partie; (hunting) Wild; **— license** Jagdschein; **— warden** Wildhüter; **big —** Grosswild; adj. spielbereit, mutig; (hunting) jagdbar; Wild-; **— leg** lahmes Bein

gamecock n. Kampfhahn

gamekeeper n. Wildheger, Wildhüter

gamma n. Gamma; **gamma globulin** Gammaglobulin; **gamma rays** Gammastrahlen

gang n. Abteilung, Truppe; Schar, Bande, Rotte; **-ster** n. Gangster

gangplank n. Laufplanke, Laufsteg

gangrene n. Krebs, Brand

gangway n. Durchgang, Mittelgang; (naut.) Fallreep, Laufplanke

gantry n. Polarkran; Gerüstkran; **— tower** Krangerüstturm; (rocket) Bedienungsturm

gap n. Lücke, Bresche; Kluft, Riss; **-e** v. gähnen, klaffen, sich spalten; gaffen; **-er** n. Gaffer

garage n. Garage

garb n. Tracht, Kleidung, Gewand

garbage n. Abfall, Auswurf; Schund; **— can** Abfallbehälter, Mülleimer; **— pail** Abfalleimer, Mistkübel

garble v. verstümmeln, entstellen

garden n. Garten; **— v.** Gartenbau betreiben; als Garten anlegen; **-er** n. Gärtner; **-ing** n. Gärtnerei; Gartenarbeit

gargle n. Gurgelwasser, Mundwasser; **— v.** gurgeln

garland n. Kranz, Girlande; (arch.) Laubgehänge; (fig.) Blumenlese; **— v.** bekränzen

garlic n. Knoblauch

garment n. Kleid, Kleidung; Gewand

garner v. aufspeichern

garnet n. Granat

garnish n. Garnierung, Schmuck, Zierrat; **— v.** garnieren, schmücken, verzieren

garnishee n. gerichtlich mit Beschlag belegen

garret n. Bodengeschoss, Dachstube

garrison n. Besatzung; Garnison; Fort; **— v.** mit einer Besatzung versehen, in Garnison legen

garter n. Strumpfband, Sockenhalter; **— snake** amerikanische Gürtelschlange; **Order of the —** Hosenbandorden

gas n. Gas, Leuchtgas; Benzin; **— attack** Gasangriff; **— cooker** Gaskocher; **— fitter** Gasinstallateur, Gasrohrleger; **— jet** Gasflamme; **— main** Gashauptleitung; **— mask** Gasmaske; **— meter** Gasmesser, Gasuhr; **— pipe** Gasrohr; **— station** Tankstelle; **— tank** Benzintank; **-eous** adj. gasartig, gasförmig; **-oline** n. Benzin; Gasolin; **-oline tank** Benzintank; **-oline station** Tankstelle

gash n. Schmarre, klaffende Wunde; **— v.** tief verwunden, aufschlitzen

gasket n. (mech.) Dichtung; (naut.) kurzes Tau

gasp n. Keuchen, Luftschnappen, schweres Atmen; **— v.** keuchen, schwer atmen; **— for breath** nach Luft schnappen; **— out** ausatmen, aushauchen

gastrorectomy n. operative Magenentfernung

gasworks n. pl. Gaswerke

gate n. Tor, Pforte; (rail.) Schranke

gatekeeper n. Portier; (rail.) Schrankenwärter

gateway n. Torweg, Einfahrt

gather v. sammeln, pflücken; sich (ver)sammeln; folgern, schliessen; zusammenziehen; **–ing** n. Versammlung

gaudy adj. bunt, prunkend, geputzt

gauge, gage n. Mass(stab), Eichmass; (arch.) Messlatte; (rail.) Spurweite; — v. abmessen, ausmessen; eichen; abschätzen

gauntlet n. Panzerhandschuh; Stulphandschuh; (fig.) Fehdehandschuh; **run the — ** Spiessruten laufen

gauze n. Gaze, Flor

gavel n. Hammer (des Vorsitzenden)

gawk v. gaffen; **–y** adj. tölpelhaft, linkisch

gay adj. lustig, fröhlich; bunt, glänzend; lebhaft, flott; (fig.) liederlich

gaze n. Anstarren, Anstaunen; — v. starren; anstaunen; — at anstaunen

gazette n. Zeitung; Amtsblatt, Staatsanzeiger

gear n. Stoff, Zeug; Kleidung, Tracht; (mech.) Triebrad, Zahnrad; Getriebe, Gang; **out of — ** ausgeschaltet; **put in — ** in Gang setzen; **shift into second — ** den zweiten Gang einschalten; **shift — ** umschalten; **throw out of — ** (den Mechanismus) ausschalten

gearshift n. (auto.) Schaltung

Geiger counter n. Geigerzähler

gelatin(e) n. Gelatine, Gallerte

gem n. Edelstein; Gemme; (fig.) Juwel, Glanzstück

gender n. Geschlecht

gene n. Gen

genealogy n. Genealogie, Geschlechterkunde; Stammbaum

general n. General, Feldherr; **— staff** (mil.) Generalstab; — adj. allgemein, gewöhnlich; Haupt-, General-; **— delivery** hauptpostlagernd; **— election** allgemeine Wahlen; **in — ** im allgemeinen; **–ity** n. Allgemeinheit; **–ization** n. Verallgemeinerung; **–ize** v. verallgemeinern

generate v. erzeugen, entwickeln

generation n. Erzeugung; Entwicklung; Generation, Menschenalter, Zeitalter

generator n. Generator; Erzeuger

generic adj. Gattungs-; generisch

generosity n. Freigebigkeit; Edelmut, Grossmut

generous adj. freigebig, grosszügig; reichlich; grossmütig

genesis n. Zeugung, Werden; **Genesis** Genesis, erstes Buch Mosis

genetics n. Genetik, Entstehungslehre

Geneva n. Genf

genial adj. freundlich; belebend, anregend, munter, lustig; **–ity** n. Freundlichkeit, Munterkeit, Lustigkeit

genitals n. pl. Geschlechtsteile, Genitalien

genius n. Genius, Genie; Schutzgeist; Schöpfungskraft

gentian n. Enzian

gentile n. Nichtjude; Heide; — adj. nichtjüdisch; heidnisch

gentility n. Vornehmheit, Lebensart

gentle adj. mild, sanft; lind; zahm; vornehm, edel; **–ness** n. Milde, Güte; Sanftmut

gentleman n. Herr; Ehrenmann, Gentleman; **–'s agreement** freundschaftliches Übereinkommen

gently adv. mild, sanft; leise

genuflection, genuflexion n. Knien, Kniebeuge

genuine adj. echt, rein; wahr, natürlich; unverfälscht; **–ness** n. Echtheit, Wahrheit

genus n. Geschlecht, Gattung

geographer n. Geograph

geographic(al) adj. geographisch

geography n. Geographie, Erdkunde

geological adj. geologisch, erdgeschichtlich

geologist n. Geologe

geology n. Geologie

geometric(al) adj. geometrisch; **— progression** geometrische Progression

geometry n. Geometrie, Raumlehre; **plane — ** Planimetrie; **solid — ** Stereometrie

geophysics n. Geophysik

geophysical adj. geophysikalisch

geopolitics n. Geopolitik

geranium n. Geranium, Storchschnabel

germ n. Keim; Erreger; **— cell** Keimzelle; **— plasm** Keimplasma; **–icide** n. keimtötendes Mittel; **–inate** v. keimen (lassen); spriessen; **–ination** n. Keimen, Spriessen

German adj. deutsch; **— measles** n. pl. Röteln

gestation n. Schwangerschaft; (zool.) Trächtigkeit

gesticulate v. gestikulieren, Gesten machen

gesture n. Gebärde, Geste; — v. gestikulieren

get v. werden; bekommen, erhalten, erlangen; besorgen, holen, sich verschaffen; finden; kommen; machen; bewegen; gewinnen; — about herumkommen; **— along** vorwärtskommen; auskommen; **— around** herumkommen (um); **— at** erreichen, anlangen; **— away** sich davon machen; wegbringen; **— away with** durchkommen mit; **— back** zurückerhalten; zurückkommen; **— behind** zurückbleiben; **— by** auskommen; **— done** machen lassen; fertig werden; **— down** herunterkommen; hinunterbringen, hinunterschlucken; **— even with** sich rächen an; **— in** einsteigen; hereinkommen, hineinbringen; ankommen; **— into** hinein geraten; einsteigen; **— off** aussteigen; davonkommen; (clothes) ausziehen; **— on** einsteigen; weiterkommen; (clothes) anziehen; **— out** aussteigen; herausbekommen; herausbringen; **— over** überwinden; **— rid of** loswerden; **— the better of** übertölpeln; **— through** durchkommen; durchbringen; — **to** ankommen; — **together** zusammenkommen; sich vereinigen; — **up** aufstehen, wecken; — **well** wieder gesund werden

getaway adj. Entweichen, Flucht

getup n. Ausstattung, Aufmachung

geyser n. Geiser, heisser Springbrunnen

G-force n. Gravitationskraft der Erde; Fliehkraft

ghastly adj. grausig, grässlich; geisterhaft

ghetto n. G(h)etto, Judenviertel

ghost n. Gespenst, Geist; — **writer** Berufschriftsteller, der für einen anderen schreibt; **have not the —** of a chance nicht die geringste Aussicht auf Erfolg haben; **-ly** adj. gespensterhaft, geisterhaft

giant n. Riese; Gigant; — adj. riesenhaft, riesig; gigantisch

giddy adj. schwindlich; schwindelerregend; (fig.) leichtsinnig

gift n. Gabe; Geschenk; (law) Schenkung; (fig.) Talent; **-ed** adj. begabt

gigantic adj. riesenhaft, riesig; gigantisch

giggle n. Kichern, Gekicher; — v. kichern

gild v. vergolden; **-ing** n. Vergolden, Vergoldung

gill n. (hen) Kehllappen; (ichth.) Kiemen; (measure) Viertelpinte

gilt n. Vergoldung; — adj. vergoldet

gilt-edged adj. mit Goldschnitt versehen; (coll.) hochfein, prima

gimmick n. sinnreiche Vorrichtung; Trick, Kniff

gin n. Gin; Entkörnungsmaschine; — **rummy** Ginrummy; — v. entkörnen

ginger n. Ingwer; — **ale** Ingwerbier; — adj. gelblichbraun; **-ly** adv. and adj. zimperlich; bedächtig, sorgfältig

gingerbread n. Pfefferkuchen, Lebuchen

gingersnap n. Ingwerkeks

gingivitis n. (med.) Zahnfleischentzündung

gird v. gürten, umgürten; **-le** n. Gurt, Gürtel; **-le** v. umgeben, umschliessen; umgürten

girder n. Träger, Tragbalken

girl n. Mädchen; (coll.) Dienstmädchen, Magd; — **scout** Pfadfinderin; **-hood** n. Mädchenzeit; Mädchenjahre; **-ish** adj. mädchenhaft

girth n. Umfang; Sattelgurt

gist n. Hauptpunkt, Kern; Wesen

give v. geben, schenken; übergeben, darbieten; verursachen; vortragen, mitteilen; gestatten, erlauben; aussprechen, ausstossen; angeben, nachgeben; — **a lift** unter die Arme greifen; — **account** Rechenschaft ablegen; — **away** verschenken; (sich) verraten; — **away the bride** Brautvater sein; die Braut (dem Bräutigam) geben; — **away the show** die Katze aus dem Sack lassen; — **birth** gebären, das Leben schenken, zur Welt bringen; — **credit** zutrauen, anerkennen; — **evidence** Zeugnis ablegen; — **in** nachgeben; — **off** von sich geben; — **out** ausgeben, austeilen; — **over** überlassen, abtreten; — **up** aufgeben, verzichten; **-n** adj.

gegeben, festgesetzt, bestimmt; geneigt; — **name** Taufname; — **time** bestimmte Zeit; **-r** n. Geber, Schenkende(r)

give-and-take n. Gedankenaustausch; Ausgleich

gizzard n. Kropf, Magen; (fig.) Stimmung

glacier n. Gletscher, Firn

glad adj. heiter, froh; erfreulich, angenehm; **I am —** to see you es freut mich Sie zu sehen; **-den** v. erfreuen, erheitern; **-ness** n. Freude, Frölichkeit

glade n. Lichtung

gladiolus n. Gladiole

glamor, glamour n. Reiz, Zauber; Blendwerk; **-ous** adj. zauberhaft, reizend

glance n. flüchtiger Blick; **at first —** auf den ersten Blick, sofort; — v. flüchtig blicken; streifen, berühren

gland n. Drüse; **-ular** adj. drüsenartig

glare n. Blenden; Schimmer; durchdringender Blick; — v. scheinen, strahlen, funkeln, glänzen; blenden; hervorstechen; wild starren

glass n. Glas; Trinkglas; Fenster; Spiegel; — **blower** Glasbläser; — **case** Glaskasten; — **cutter** Glasschleifer; — **eye** Glasauge; pl. Augengläser; — adj. glasartig, gläsern; Glas-; **-sy** adj. glasig, gläsern; glatt; starr

glasshouse n. Treibhaus

glassware n. Glasgeschirr, Glaswaren

glasswork n. Glasarbeit; Glashütte

glaucoma n. grüner Star; Glaukom

glaze v. verglasen; glasieren, lasieren; polieren, glätten; **-d** adj. verglast; glasiert; poliert

gleam n. Schein, Schimmer; Strahl, Lichtstrahl; Blitzstrahl; — v. scheinen, glänzen, schimmern, scheinen

glean v. (ein)sammeln; nachlesen, abernten

glee n. Lustbarkeit, Heiterkeit, Fröhlichkeit; (mus.) Rundgesang, Wechselgesang; — **club** Gesangverein, Liedertafel; **gleeful** adj. lustig, fröhlich

glen n. Bergschlucht, Talenge

glib adj. fliessend, glatt; schwatzhaft, zungenfertig

glide n. Gleiten; Schleifen; — v. gleiten, schleifen; (avi.) segelfliegen; **-r** n. (avi.) Segelflugzeug, Gleitflugzeug; Segelflieger

glimmer n. Schimmer, Glimmer; — v. schimmern, glimmern

glimpse n. flüchtiger Blick; Flimmer; — v. flüchtig sehen; **catch a —** of einen Augenblick flüchtig zu sehen bekommen

glint n. Lichtschein, Glanz; — v. glitzern, glänzen, blitzen

gloat v. — **over** sich weiden an

global adj. global, weltumfassend

globe n. Kugel; Globus, Erdkugel, Erde, Erdball

globe-trotter n. Globetrotter, Weltenbummler

gloom n. Dunkel(heit); Trübsinn, Schwermut; **-y** adj. düster, trüb; schwermütig, traurig, verdriesslich

glorification *n.* Verherrlichung; (rel.) Verklärung

glorify *v.* verherrlichen; (rel.) verklären

glorious *adj.* glorreich, ruhmreich; herrlich, köstlich, prächtig

glory *n.* Herrlichkeit, Glorie; Ruhm, Glanz, Stolz; (rel.) Heiligenschein; — *v.* frohlocken, sich freuen; sich rühmen

gloss *n.* Glosse, Randbemerkung; Glanz, Politur; — *v.* Randbemerkungen (or Glossen) machen; — **over** beschönigen; **-y** *adj.* glatt, glänzend

glossary *n.* Glossar, Wörterbuch

glove *n.* Handschuh; (sports) Boxhandschuh; — *v.* behandschuhen

glow *n.* Glut, Glühen; — *v.* glühen, erglühen; **-er** *v.* finster blicken, anstarren

glucose *n.* Glykose, Traubenzucker

glue *n.* Leim, Klebstoff, Bindemittel; — *v.* leimen, kleben; vereinigen

glum *adj.* mürrisch, verdriesslich

glutton *n.* Schlemmer, Schwelger; Fresser, Vielfrass; **-ous** *adj.* gefrässig; **-y** *n.* Gefrässigkeit; Völlerei

glycerin(e) *n.* Glyzerin

gnarled *adj.* knorrig

gnash *v.* knirschen; — **one's teeth** mit den Zähnen knirschen

gnat *n.* Mücke, Stechmücke

gnaw *v.* (zer)nagen, zerfressen; — **one's lips** sich auf die Lippen beissen

gnome *n.* Gnom, Erdgeist

go *v.* gehen, fahren; weggehen, wegfahren; reisen, laufen; werden; arbeiten; umlaufen; reichen, sich erstrecken; — **against** widerstreiten; — **ahead** vorangehen, vorwärtsgehen; — **astray** sich verirren; sündigen; — **at** losgehen auf; angreifen; — **away** weggehen, abreisen; — **back** on zurücknehmen; — **by** vorbeigehen; sich richten nach; führen; — **down** (hin)untergehen; fallen; — **far** weit gehen; viel gelten; — **for** holen; losgehen auf; — **in** for sich interessieren für; — **into** hineingehen; eingehen auf, untersuchen; — **off** losgehen; (sich) verlaufen; — **on** vorwärtskommen, vorwärtsgehen; — **out** ausgehen; — **over** übergehen; prüfen; — **through** durchgehen; durchmachen; (fig.) vergeuden; — **to it!** geh zu! drauf los! — **under** untergehen; unterliegen; führen; — **with** begleiten; passen zu; — **without** entbehren; **I am -ing to** ich werde; **it's no —** so geht's nicht; **let — of** loslassen; **let someone —** jemanden laufen lassen; **on the —** in steter Bewegung; **-ing** *n.* Gehen, Gang; Abreise; (fig.) Wandel; **-ing** *adj.* gehend, vorkommend, vorhanden; **-ing, -ing, -ne** zum ersten, zum zweiten, zum dritten (or letzten); **-ne** *adj.* weg, fort; hin; (fig.) tot, gestorben

goal *n.* Ziel, Pfahl; Mal; (sports) Tor; **— line** Torlinie; **— post** Torpfosten

goalkeeper *n.* Torhüter

goat *n.* Ziege, Geiss

gobble *v.* gierig verschlingen, an sich reissen; kollern; **-r** *n.* Truthahn

gobbledygook *n.* Kauderwelsch

go-between *n.* Vermittler, Unterhändler; Zwischenträger

goblet *n.* Becher

goblin *n.* Kobold; Elf

God *n.* Gott; Gottheit; Göttlichkeit; **act of —** Naturereignis; **— willing** so Gott will; **thank —** Gott sei Dank

god *n.* Abgott, Götze; Gott; **-ess** *n.* Göttin; **-less** *adj.* gottlos; **-like** *adj.* göttlich, gottähnlich; **-ly** *adj.* gottselig, gottesfürchtig

godchild *n.* Patenkind

godfather *n.* Pate; Taufzeuge, Gevatter

godmother *n.* Patin; Gevatterin

godsend *n.* Gottesgabe, unerwarteter Gewinn

goggle *v.* glotzen; **-s** *n. pl.* Schutzbrille

goiter, goitre *n.* Kropf

gold *n.* Gold; (fig.) Reichtum, Geld; Goldgelb; **— brick** Schwindel; wertvolle Ware, die nach Bezahlung in wertloses Gut umgetauscht wird; **— digger** Goldgräber; (fig.) Glücksjägerin; **— dust** Goldstaub; **— leaf** Blattgold; **— mine** Goldgrube; **— rush** Jagd nach Gold, Goldrausch; **— standard** Goldwährung; **-en** *adj.* golden; goldgelb; (fig.) kostbar, glücklich; **-en mean** goldener Mittelweg; **-en rule** goldene Regel, **-en wedding** goldene Hochzeit

goldenrod *n.* Goldrute, Goldregen

goldsmith *n.* Goldschmied

golf *n.* Golf(spiel); **— club** Golfstock; Golfklub; **— course** Golfplatz; **— links** Golffeld; **-er** *n.* Golfspieler

good *adj.* gut; heilsam, dienlich; recht; gütig; gerecht, echt, gültig; günstig; (child) artig, brav; **as — as gold** kreuzbrav; **for — für** (or auf) immer; **gone for —** fort auf Nimmerwiedersehen; **at —** geschickt zu; — **breeding** Wohlerzogenheit; — **for** gut gegen (or für); — **health** Wohlbefinden; gute Gesundheit; — **humor** gute Laune; **Good Neighbor Policy** gute Nachbarpolitik; — **news** frohe Botschaft; — **sense** gesunder Menschenverstand; — **turn** Gefallen; — **will** guter Wille; Wohlwollen; **have a — time** sich amüsieren; **in — time** rechtzeitig; **it's no —** es nützt nichts; es ist nicht zu gebrauchen; **make — Erfolg** haben; zurückzahlen; gutmachen; **too — zu** schade; **— gut!** fein! schön! **— n.** Gute; *pl.* Vermögen, Besitz; Waren, Güter; Effekten; **household -s** Hausgerät, bewegliche Habe; **-ly** *adj.* schön, anmutig, reizend; angenehm; ansehnlich; **-ness** *n.* Güte; Freundlichkeit; **for -ness sake** um Himmels willen, meine Güte; **my -ness** du meine Güte

good-by(e) *n.* Lebewohl; **—!** *interj.* lebe wohl! adieu! **say —** sich verabschieden

good-for-nothing *n.* Nichtsnutz, Taugenichts; — *adj.* untauglich, unbrauchbar

goodhearted *adj.* gutherzig

good-looking *adj.* schön, hübsch

good-natured *adj.* gutmütig

goon *n.* Schläger (im Dienst von Gangstern, Streikenden, Streikbrechern,

etc.)
goose n. Gans; Gänsebraten; **— flesh,
— pimples** Gänsehaut; **— step** Paradeschritt
gooseberry n. Stachelbeere
gopher n. Erdhörnchen
gorge n. Schlucht; Gurgel, Kehle, Schlund; **—** v. fressen, vollstopfen, verschlingen, verschlucken
gorgeous adj. prächtig, prachtvoll
gorilla n. Gorilla
gormandize v. schlemmen; fressen
gospel n. Evangelium
gossamer n. Sommerfaden, Altweibersommer; feine Gaze; **—** adj. leicht, dünn; (fig.) flüchtig
gossip n. Klatsch, Geschwätz; Schwätzer, Klatschbase; **—** v. klatschen, schwatzen
gouge n. Hohleisen, Hohlmeissel; **—** v. ausmeisseln, aushöhlen; (fig.) prellen
goulash n. Gulasch
gout n. Gicht, Podagra
govern v. regieren, (be)herrschen; lenken, leiten; **-ess** n. Gouvernante, Erzieherin; **-ment** n. Regierung; Leitung, Führung; Herrschaft; Regierungsform; **-ment bonds** Staatspapiere; **municipal -ment** Magistrat; **-mental** adj. Regierungs-; **-or** n. Statthalter, Gouverneur; Herrscher; (mech.) Regulator
gown n. Kleid; Gewand, Überwurf; Robe, Talar, Amtskleidung
grab n. Griff, Erschnappen; **—** v. ergreifen, packen, schnappen
grace n. Gnade, Gunst; Anmut, Grazie; Tischgebet; **say —** das Tischgebet sprechen; **—** v. schmücken, zieren; auszeichnen; **-ful** adj. anmutig; zierlich; graziös; günstig; **-less** adj. reizlos; verdorben, unverschämt
gracious adj. angenehm, reizend; gnädig, gütig; **— God!** gütiger Himmel! mein Gott! meine Güte! ach du liebe Zeit!
gradation n. Abstufung, Steigerung; (fig.) Grad, Stufe
grade n. Grad, Stufe, Rang; Qualität; (educ.) Note, Zensur; Klasse; **— crossing** Neigungskreuzung; **— school** Volksschule; **passing —** die Note "Bestanden"; **—** v. abstufen, ordnen; ebnen, planieren
gradient n. Steigung; Neigung
gradual adj. allmählich, stufenweise
graduate n. Graduierte, Absolvent, Promovierte; **—** v. abstufen, in Grade einteilen; absolvieren, promovieren; **be -d** einen Grad erreicht haben, promoviert haben
graduation n. Gradeinteilung; Promotion, Promovierung
graft n. Schiebung, Schwindel, Betrug; Erpressung, Bestechung; (agr.) Pfropfreis; (med.) Einimpfung, Verpflanzung; **—** v. erpressen, erschwindeln; pfropfen; verpflanzen, übertragen
grain n. Getreide; Korn; Gran, Faser; Faserung, Körnung; (wood) Struktur, Maserung; **— alcohol** Getreidealkohol; Äthylalkohol; **— merchant** Getreidehändler; **against the —** gegen den

Strich, widersinnig; **mixed —** Mischkorn; **-y** adj. körnig, gekörnt
gram n. Gramm
grammar n. Grammatik, Sprachlehre; **— school** Volksschule
grammatical adj. grammat(ikal)isch
gramophone n. Grammofon
granary n. Kornspeicher, Kornboden, Getreidekammer
grand adj. gross, grossartig; wichtig, bedeutend; oberst; Haupt-, Gross-; **—** n. (sl.) tausend Dollar; Tausenddollarnote; **-eur** n. Grösse, Grossartigkeit; Hoheit, Erhabenheit; **-iose** adj. grandios, grossartig; pomphaft
grandchild n. Enkel(kind)
granddaughter n. Enkelin
grandfather n. Grossvater
grandmother n. Grossmutter
grandparents n. pl. Grosseltern
grandson n. Enkel
grandstand n. Haupttribüne
granite n. Granit
grant n. Gewährung, Bewilligung, Erlaubnis; (law) Schenkungsurkunde; **—** v. bewilligen, gestatten, gewähren, erlauben; zugeben; **-ing that** zugestanden; **take for -ed** als erwiesen (or selbstverständlich) annehmen
granular adj. granuliert, körnig, gekörnt
granule n. Körnchen
grape n. Traube, Weinbeere; **bunch of -s** Weintraube
grapefruit n. Pompelmuse, Grapefruit
grapevine n. Weinstock, Weinrebe; **to learn something by the —** etwas läuten hören
graph n. Diagramm, graphische Darstellung
graphic adj. graphisch, anschaulich, beschreibend
graphite n. Graphit, Reissblei
grasp n. Griff, Greifen; Händedruck; Erfassen; **—** v. fassen, ergreifen; begreifen; **-ing** adj. habgierig, geizig
grass n. Gras, Rasen, Wiese, Weide; (agr. coll.) Grünfutter; **-y** adj. grasig, grasartig; grasreich; grasgrün
grasshopper n. Heuschrecke; Grashüpfer
grate n. Gitter, Gatter; Rost; **—** v. kratzen, knirschen; (zer)reiben, raspeln; **— on my nerves** an meinen Nerven reissen, mir auf die Nerven fallen; **-r** n. Reibeisen, Reibe
grateful adj. dankbar, erkenntlich
gratification n. Befriedigung, Annehmlichkeit; Belohnung
gratify v. befriedigen, erfreuen
grating n. Gitter, Gatter; Kratzen, Knirschen; Reiben; **—** adj. schrill; kratzend, knirschend; reibend; peinlich, unangenehm
gratitude n. Dankbarkeit, Erkenntlichkeit
grave n. Grab
grave adj. ernst, feierlich; ernsthaft; gewichtig; (mus.) tief; **-ly** adv. schwer
gravedigger n. Totengräber
gravel n. Kies, Sand
graveyard n. Friedhof, Kirchhof

gravitate *v.* zuneigen

ravitation *n.* Gravitation, Schwerkraft; Hang

gravity *n.* Gewicht, Schwere; (fig.) Ernst, Feierlichkeit, Bedeutung; **center of —** Schwerpunkt; **force of —** Schwerkraft, Anziehungskraft; **specific —** spezifisches Gewicht

gravy *n.* Tunke, Sauce, Bratensosse; **— boat** Sauciere, Sossenschüssel

gray, grey *n.* Grau; **—** *adj.* grau; (fig.) altersgrau; **—** *v.* grau machen, ergrauen; grauen, dämmern; **-ish** *adj.* gräulich

graze *v.* weiden, grasen, abgrasen; streifen, schrammen

grease *n.* Fett; Schmiere; **—** *v.* schmieren, einfetten, ölen

greasy *adj.* fettig, schmierig, ölig

great *adj.* gross; grossmütig; grossartig; beträchtlich, ansehnlich; berühmt; hervorragend; **-ly** *adv.* sehr, bedeutend; **-ness** *n.* Grösse, Bedeutung, Wichtigkeit; Macht, Stärke; Pracht, Erhabenheit, Herrlichkeit

Great Britain *n.* Grossbritannien

great-grandchild *n.* Urenkelkind

great-grandparents *n. pl.* Urgrosseltern

Greece *n.* Hellas

greed, greediness *n.* Gier, Habgier; Begier, Heisshunger; **-y** *adj.* gierig, gefrässig; begierig

green *n.* Grün; Laubgrün; (golf) Golfgrün; *pl.* Suppengrün, Gemüse; **—** *adj.* grün; frisch, neu; jung, unreif, unerfahren; kränklich; **-ish** *adj.* grünlich

greenback *n.* amerikanische Banknote

green-eyed *adj.* grünäugig

greenhorn *n.* Grünschnabel, Neuling

greenhouse *n.* Gewächshaus, Treibhaus

Greenland *n.* Grönland

greet *v.* grüssen, begrüssen; **-ing** *n.* Gruss, Begrüssung

grenade *n.* Granate

greyhound *n.* Windhund, Windspiel

grid *n.* Bratrost; Gitter; (elec.) Netzplatte; Zentralelektrode; Elektrofilter

griddle *n.* Kuchenblech

griddlecake *n.* Pfannkuchen

gridiron *n.* Bratrost; (sports) Fussballfeld, Fussballspiel

grief *n.* Kummer, Gram, Schmerz; Beschwerde

grievance *n.* Klagegrund, Übelstand; Verdriesslichkeit

grieve *v.* kränken, betrüben; ärgern; bekümmern; trauern, sich grämen

grievous *adj.* schmerzlich, verdriesslich; kränkend; schwer, drückend

grill *n.* Grill, Bratrost; **—** *v.* grillen, rösten

grille *n.* Gitter; Gitterfenster

grim *adj.* grimmig; finster; abstossend; scheusslich; **-ness** *n.* Grimmigkeit

grimace *n.* Grimasse, Fratze

grime *n.* Schmutz, Russ

grimy *adj.* schmutzig, russig

grin *n.* Grinsen; **—** *v.* grinsen

grind *v.* mahlen, zerreiben, schroten; wetzen, schleifen; (educ. sl.) einpauken, büffeln; (organ) drehen, spielen; **—**

one's teeth mit den Zähnen knirschen; **—** *n.* Mahlen; (coll.) Plackerei, Büffler; **-er** *n.* Mühle

grindstone *n.* Schleifstein, Mühlstein, Drehscheibe

grip *n.* Griff, Handdruck; Fassungskraft; (coll.) Reisetasche; **—** *v.* fassen, packen; erfassen; **-ping** *adj.* ergreifend, festhaltend

gripe *n.* Klage, Übel; **—** *v.* peinigen; sich beklagen; sich nicht wohl fühlen

grippe *n.* Grippe

grisly *adj.* grässlich, gräulich, grausig, scheusslich

gristle *n.* Knorpel

grit *n.* Griess, Kies, grober Sand; (fig.) Mut; *pl.* Schrot, Kleie, Grütze; **-ty** *adj.* sandig, kiesig

grizzly, grizzled *adj.* ergraut, gräulich; grau gesprenkelt; grauhaarig; **— bear** Grizzlybär, grauer Bär

groan *n.* Seufzen, Stöhnen, Murren, Ächzen; **—** *v.* stöhnen, seufzen, murren, ächzen

grocer *n.* Kolonialwarenhändler, Lebensmittelhändler; **-y** *n.* Grünkramladen, Kolonialwarenhandlung, Lebensmittelgeschäft; **-ies** *n. pl.* Lebensmittel, Kolonialwaren, Grünkram

groggy *adj.* unsicher gehend, schwankend; (sl.) betrunken, taumelnd, betäubt

groin *n.* Schamleiste, Leistengegend

groom *n.* Bräutigam; Stalljunge, Reitknecht; **—** *v.* pflegen, besorgen; vorbereiten

groove *n.* Grube, Rinne, Furche, Rille; Schallrille; Führungsrille; (mech.) Nut; **—** *v.* aushöhlen, furchen; (mech.) nuten, fugen, riefeln

grope *v.* tasten, betasten; (umher)tappen

gross *n.* Hauptmasse, Haupteil; Gros; **— amount** Gesamtsumme; Bruttobetrag; **— profit** Bruttogewinn; **— weight** Bruttogewicht; **—** *adj.* gross, dick, fett; grob, roh; unanständig; schwerfällig; dumm; brutto; **-ly** *adv.* höchst, sehr, in hohem Grade

grotesque *adj.* grotesk, seltsam

ground *n.* Grund, Boden, Erde; Erdboden; Land, Gegend; Grundlage; (art.) Grundierung; (mil.) Gelände; Anlagen; **— control** Boden-Radarpeilung; **— control approach (GCA)** Anflug mit Hilfe von Bodenradargeräten; **— crew** Bodenpersonal; **— floor** Erdgeschoss; **— hog** Murmeltier; **— squirrel** Erdhörnchen; **— swell** Grundsee; **— wire** Erdleitung; **above —** oberirdisch; **below —** unterirdisch; **down to the —** vollständig; **on the —** that weil, wegen; **stand one's —** sich behaupten; **—** *v.* niederlegen, (be)gründen; (avi.) Flugverbot erlassen; (elec., rad.) erden; (naut.) auf Grund laufen, auflaufen; **-less** *adj.* grundlos, unbegründet

groundbreaking *n.* Spatenstich

groundwork *n.* (arch.) Fundament, Grundmauer, Unterbau; Erdarbeit; (fig.) Grundlage

group *n.* Gruppe; (mil.) Geschwader; **—**

r. (sich) gruppieren, zusammenstellen
grouse n. Waldhuhn, Birkhuhn
grove n. Gehölz, Hain
grow r. wachsen; werden; zunehmen;
entstehen; aufziehen, anbauen, züchten; — **from** entstehen; — **old** altern;
— **together** verwachsen, zusammenwachsen; — **up** heranwachsen; **-er** n.
Pflanzer, Züchter; **-th** n. Wachstum,
Wuchs; (med.) Gewächs; (fig.) Gedeihen, Zunahme
growl n. Knurren, Brummen; — v. knurren, brummen
grownup n. Erwachsene
grown-up adj. erwachsen
grub n. Larve, Raupe, Made; (coll.)
Essen, Nahrung; Prolet; — v. graben,
wühlen; sich placken
grudge n. Widerwillen, Abneigung, Groll;
bear a — übelwollen, grollen; — v.
widerstreben; (be)neiden, missgönnen;
vorenthalten
grudgingly adv. murrend, widerwillig,
ungern
gruel n. Grütze, Haferschleim
gruesome adj. grausig, entsetzlich
gruff adj. rauh, schroff, barsch; mürrisch
grumble v. murren, brummen, knurren
grumpy adj. mürrisch, böse; knurrig,
brummig
grunt v. grunzen; — n. Grunzen
guarantee n. Garantie, Bürgschaft;
Bürge; — v. bürgen für, garantieren,
sichern; sich verbürgen
guarantor n. Bürge, Gewährsmann, Garant
guaranty n. Garantie, Bürgschaft, Gewähr(leistung)
guard n. Wache, Bewachung; Wacht,
Hut, Schutz; Wächter, Hüter; (mech.)
Schutzblech, Sicherheitskette; (mil.)
Wachtposten, Wachmannschaft,
Schildwache, Garde; (rail.) Schrankenwärter, Bahnwärter; (sports) Verteidigung, Auslage, Parade; **advance** —
Vorhut; **on** — auf Wache; auf der Hut;
under — unter Schutz; — v. (be)hüten,
schützen; bewachen; begleiten, geleiten; (cards) decken; — **against** sich
hüten vor; sich in acht nehmen vor;
-ed adj. behutsam, vorsichtig; **-ian** n.
Wächter, Hüter; (law) Vormund,
Pfleger; **-ian angel** Schutzengel; **-ianship** n. Vormundschaft, Obhut
guardhouse n. Wachthaus, Wachtlokal;
Lagergefängnis
guer(r)illa n. Guerillakämpfer, Partisan
guess n. Mutmassung, Vermutung; — v.
(er)raten; mutmassen, vermuten; **I** —
ich denke
guesswork n. Vermutung; Raterei
guest n. Gast
guidance n. Führung, Leitung; — **beam**
(avi.) Führungsstrahl; Fahrstrahl
guide n. Führer, Leiter, Lenker; Führung,
Leitung, Lenkung; Reiseführer; — v.
führen, leiten, lenken; **-d** adj. lenkbar;
-d missile ferngesteuertes (or lenkbares) Geschoss
guidebook n. Reisehandbuch, Reiseführer

guidepost n. Wegweiser
guild n. Gilde, Zunft, Innung
guile n. Arglist, Betrug; Kunstgriff; **-less**
adj. arglos, offen, aufrichtig
guillotine n. Guillotine, Fallbeil
guilt n. Schuld; Strafbarkeit; **-less** adj.
schuldlos, unschuldig; harmlos; **-y** adj.
schuldig; strafbar, verbrecherisch;
lasterhaft; **plead -y** sein Verbrechen
eingestehen; **plead not -y** sein Verbrechen ableugnen
guinea n. Guinee; — **pig** Meerschweinchen; (fig.) Versuchskaninchen
guitar n. Gitarre; **small** — Zupfgeige
gulch n. tiefe Schlucht
gulf n. Meerbusen, Golf; Abgrund,
Schlund; Strudel
Gulf Stream n. Golfstrom
gull n. Möwe
gullet n. Gurgel, Schlund, Speiseröhre
gullible adj. leichtgläubig, leicht zu
täuschen
gully n. Giessbachschlucht; Abzugsgraben
gulp n. Schluck; — v. (gierig) schlucken,
würgen
gum n. Gummi, Gummierung; Schleim;
(anat.) Gaumen; **chewing** — Kaugummi; — **tree** Gummibaum; — r.
gummieren, kleben; **-my** adj. gummiartig; gummiert; klebrig
gumdrop n. Gummibonbon
gumption n. Verstand, Mutterwitz
gumwood n. Eukalyptusbaum
gun n. Gewehr, Feuerwaffe; Kanone,
Geschütz; — **barrel** Gewehrlauf, Geschützrohr; — **metal** Kanonenmetall,
Rotguss; **-ner** n. Schütze; (mil.)
Artillerist, Kanonier, Feuerwerker;
(naut.) Stückmeister
gunboat n. Kanonenboot
gunfire n. Geschützfeuer, Kannonade
gunny n. Jute(leinewand); — **sack** Jutesack
gunpowder n. Schiesspulver
gunshot n. Schuss; Schussweite
gunsight n. Zielgerät
gunwale n. Schan(z)deck, Dollbord
gurgle n. Gurgeln; — v. gurgeln, glucksen
gush n. Guss, Erguss; (fig.) Hervorbrechen; Herzenserguss; — v. (sich)
ergiessen, stürzen, hervorströmen; (fig.)
schwärmen; **-er** n. Erdöldurchbruch
gust n. Bö, Windstoss; (fig.) Ausbruch;
— **load** (avi.) Luftwiderstand
gusto n. Gusto, Geschmack, Genuss
gut n. Darm; Magen, Bauch; pl. Eingeweide, Gedärm; **I haven't the -s** (sl.)
Ich habe nicht den Mut; — v. ausweiden, ausnehmen; **-ter** n. Gosse, Rinnstein; Dachrinne; **-tural** adj. kehlig,
guttural; Kehl-
guy n. Bursche, Kerl
gym(nasium) n. Turnhalle
gymnastic adj. gymnastisch; Turn-; **-s** n
pl. Gymnastik, Leibesübungen
gynecologist n. Gynäkologe, Frauenarzt
gyp n. Schwindel; — v. betrügen, beschwindeln
Gypsum n. Gips
gypsy, gipsy n. Zigeuner; — adj. zigeuner-

haft

gyroscope *n.* Kreiselachse; Gyroskop

H

habeas corpus *n.* Habeaskorpus; **writ of** — Freilassungsbefehl
haberdasher *n.* Kurzwarenhändler, Herrenmodegeschäftsinhaber; **-y** *n.* Kurzwaren, Herrenmodeartikel; Kurzwarenhandlung; Herrenmodegeschäft
habit *n.* Gewohnheit, Lebensweise; Amtstracht, Kleidung; **break oneself of the** — of sich abgewöhnen zu; **get into the** — of sich angewöhnen zu; **-able** *adj.* bewohnbar, wohnlich; **-at** *n.* Fundort, Heimat; **-ation** *n.* Wohnung, Wohnsitz; **-ual** *adj.* gewöhnlich, gewohnheitsmässig; gewohnt; Gewohnheits-; **-uate** *v.* (an)gewöhnen
hack *n.* Taxi; Miet(s)wagen; (coll.) Skribent; Klepper; — *v.* (zer)hacken; kurz (*or* trocken) husten
haddock *n.* Schellfisch
hag *n.* Hexe, Furie, hässliche Alte
haggard *adj.* hager, abgehärmt
the Hague *n.* der Haag
hail *n.* Hagel; Gruss, Grüssen; — *v.* (nieder) hageln; anrufen; grüssen; — **from** stammen, kommen aus; —! *interj.* Heil! Glückauf!
hailstorm *n.* Hagelsturm, Hagelwetter
hair *n.* Haar; **by a** — um ein Haar; **comb one's** — sich die Haare kämmen; **cut one's** — sich die Haare (ab)schneiden; — *adj.* — **dryer** Föhn; — **ribbon** Haarband; — **trigger** Gewehrabzug; **-less** *adj.* haarlos; kahl, glatzköpfig; **-y** *adj.* haarig, behaart
hairbrush *n.* Haarbürste
haircut *n.* Haarschnitt
hairdo *n.* Haartracht, Frisur
hairdresser *n.* Friseur; **-'s (shop)** Frisiersalon
hairpin *n.* Haarnadel
hair-raising *adj.* haarsträubend
hairsplitting *n.* Haarspalterei
hale *adj.* gesund, kräftig, rüstig, frisch
half *n.* Hälfte; — *adj.* halb; Halb-; — **blood** Halbblut; — **brother** Halbbruder; — **pay** Halblohn; — **sister** Halbschwester; — **sole** Halbsohle; — **(time)** Halbzeit; — **tone** Halbton; — **year** Halbjahr; **one and a** — anderthalb, eineinhalb
halfback *n.* Läufer; Deckungsspieler
half-blooded *adj.* halbblütig
half-breed *n.* Mischling; — *adj.* halbbürtig
half-caste *n.* Mischling, Halbblut
halfhearted *adj.* lau, gleichgültig
half-hour *n.* halbe Stunde; — *adj.* halbstündig
half-moon *n.* Halbmond
half-track *n.* Panzerwagen
half-witted *adj.* albern, töricht, einfältig
half-year *adj.* halbjährlich
halibut *n.* Heilbutt
halitosis *n.* Mundfäule
hall *n.* Saal, Halle; Gang, Korridor, Vor-

halle; Markthalle; Gerichtssaal; (educ.) Aula, Kollegium; **(entrance)** — Diele, Vorzimmer
hallmark *n.* Feingehaltszeichen, Echtheitsstempel
hallow *v.* heiligen; weihen
Halloween *n.* Abend vor Allerheiligen; (fig.) Hexensabbat
hallway *n.* Flur, Korridor
halo *n.* (art and rel.) Heiligenschein; (ast.) Hof
halt *n.* Halt; Halten; Haltestelle; — *v.* halten, haltmachen; anhalten; —! *interj.* Halt! — *adj.* lahm, hinkend
halter *n.* Halfter; Leibchen
halve *v.* halbieren
ham *n.* Schinken; (anat.) Schenkel; (sl.) pathetischer Schauspieler, Komödiant
hamburger *n.* Beefsteak, Bratklops, Rundstück
hamlet *n.* Dörfchen, Flecken
hammer *n.* Hammer; Schalghammer; (gun) Hahn; — *v.* hämmern, schmieden
hammock *n.* Hängematte
hamper *n.* Esskorb; **(clothes)** — Schmutzwäschekorb; — *v.* hemmen, belästigen
hand *n.* Hand; Handbreite; (aid) Hilfe; (cards) Karten (in der Hand); (labor) Mann, Arbeiter; Handfertigkeit; (naut.) Matrose; (side) Seite; (watch) Zeiger; (writing) Handschrift; (fig.) Kunst; **at** — zur Hand, bei der Hand; **at first** — aus erster Hand; **be on** — da sein, zur Hand sein; **by** — mit der Hand; **change -s** den Besitzer wechseln; **from** — **to** — von einer Hand in die andere; **get out of** — ausser Rand und Band geraten; **-s down** ohne Schwierigkeit; **-s off!** *interj.* Hände weg! **-s up!** *interj.* Hände hoch! **in** — im Gange; **in the -s of** in der Gewalt von; **lay one's -s on** ergreifen; **lend a (helping)** — behilflich sein; **of one's -s** aus den Händen; **on** — vorrätig, auf Lager; **on the one** — einerseits; **on the other** — andererseits; **shake -s** sich die Hände schütteln; **take the law in one's own -s** sich selbst Recht verschaffen; **upper** — Oberhand; **wash one's -s of** sich die Hände in Unschuld waschen wegen; **with one's own** — eigenhändig; — *v.* übergeben, überreichen; — **down** herunterreichen; — **in** einreichen; — **out** austeilen, ausgeben; — **over** überliefern; — **up** heraufreichen; **-iness** *n.* Handlichkeit; **-le** *n.* Heft, Griff; Henkel; (fig.) Handhabe; **-le bar** Lenkstange; **-le** *v.* handhaben, gebrauchen; anfassen, befühlen; leiten, führen; (fig.) behandeln; **-y** *adj.* geschickt, gewandt; handlich, bequem; nützlich; **-y man** Handlanger
handbag *n.* Handtasche
handbill *n.* Plakat; Reklamezettel
handbook *n.* Handbuch; (sl.) Geschäftsbuch eines Winkelbuchmachers
handclasp *n.* Händedruck
handcuff *n.* Handschelle, Handfessel; — *v.* Handschellen (*or* Handfesseln) anlegen

handful *n.* Handvoll

handicap *n.* Handikap, Vorgabe; — *r.* hemmen; (extra) belasten

handicraft *n.* Handarbeit, Handfertigkeit; Handwerk

handiwork *n.* Handarbeit

handkerchief *n.* Taschentuch

handmade *adj.* handgemacht

handout *n.* Aushilfe; Werbebroschüre; (sl.) Almosen, milde Gabe

hand-picked *adj.* persönlich ausgesucht, eigenhändig ausgewählt

handrail *n.* Geländerstange

handsaw *n.* Handsäge, Stichsäge

handshake *n.* Händedruck

handsome *adj.* schön, hübsch; ansehnlich, beträchtlich; freigebig

hand-to-hand *adj.* Hand-; — **fight** Handgemenge

handwriting *n.* Handschrift

hang *v.* (auf)hängen; einhängen, umhängen; schweben; **— on** sich anklammern; **— up** aufhängen; **—** *n.* Hang; Abhang, Neigung; **get the —** of vertraut werden mit, erfassen; **-er** *n.* Kleiderbügel; **-er-on** *n.* Anhänger; (coll.) Schmarotzer; **-ing** *n.* Hängen, Erhängen; **-ings** *pl.* Behang, Vorhänge; Tapeten

hangar *n.* Hangar, Flugzeughalle

hangman *n.* Henker

hangnail *n.* Niednagel, Neidnagel

hangout *n.* Stammplatz

hang-over *n.* Kater, Katzenjammer

hanker *v.* sich sehnen, verlangen

hankering *n.* Sehnsucht, Verlangen

Hanover *n.* Hannover

haphazard *n.* Zufall, Geratewohl; — *adj.* zufällig

hapless *adj.* unglücklich

happen *v.* geschehen, sich ereignen (*or* zutragen); passieren; **I — to be** ich bin zufällig; **-ing** *n.* Vorkommen, Vorfall, Ereignis

happily *adv.* glücklicherweise, auf geschickte Art; glücklich

happiness *n.* Glück; Glückseligkeit, Freude

happy *adj.* glücklich, glückselig; zufrieden; günstig, geschickt

happy-go-lucky *adj.* unbekümmert, sorglos; leichtsinnig

harass *v.* ermüden, erschöpfen; ärgern, quälen; belästigen, beunruhigen

harbor *n.* Hafen; Zuflucht; Unterkunft, Obdach; — *v.* beherbergen, hegen, schützen

hard *adj.* hart; schwer, schwierig, mühsam; fest; zäh; streng; heftig, scharf; tüchtig, fleissig; **drive a — bargain** bis zum Äussersten feilschen; **— and fast** bindend, unabänderlich; **— cash** klingende Münze, Bargeld; **— cider** (alkoholisierter) Apfelwein; **— coal** Anthrazit; **— labor** Zwangsarbeit; **— of hearing** schwerhörig; **— to believe** schwer zu glauben; **— to digest** schwerverdaulich; **— up** knapp; **try — sich** sehr bemühen; **—** *adv.* schwierig, mit Schwierigkeiten, mit Mühe; heftig; **-en** *v.* härten, stählen, abhärten; (sich)

verhärten; gewöhnen; unempfindlich werden; **-ly** *adv.* kaum, schwerlich; **-ly ever** fast nie; **-ness** *n.* Härte, Festigkeit; Schwierigkeit; Grausamkeit; Not; **-ship** *n.* Unglück, Ungemach, Bedrükkung, Mühsal; **-y** *adj.* kräftig, stark; kühn, mutig, tapfer; (bot.) winterhart

hard-boiled *adj.* hart(gekocht); (fig.) hartgesotten

hardhearted *adj.* hartherzig, unbarmherzig

hardtop *n.* Stahlverdeck; — *adj.* mit Stahlverdeck versehen

hardware *n.* Metallwaren; — **store** Metallwarengeschäft

hardwood *n.* Hartholz

hard-working *adj.* fleissig, arbeitsam

hare *n.* Hase

harelip *n.* Hasenscharte

harem *n.* Harem

hark *v.* horchen, lauschen; **—!** *interj.* horch! hört!

harlot *n.* Hure, Dirne

harm *n.* Schaden, Verletzung; Harm, Unrecht; — *v.* schaden, schädigen, ein Leid zufügen, verletzen; **-ful** *adj.* schädlich, nachteilig; verderblich, böse; **-less** *adj.* harmlos, unschädlich; schuldlos

harmonic *adj.* harmonisch, übereinstimmend; **-a** *n.* Harmonika

harmonious *adj.* harmonisch; zusammenstimmend, wohlklingend; symmetrisch; (fig.) einträchtig, friedlich

harmonize *v.* harmonieren, übereinstimmen; einig sein; in Einklang bringen

harmony *n.* Harmonie, Einklang; Ebenmass; (fig.) Eintracht

harness *n.* Geschirr; — *v.* anschirren

harp *n.* Harfe; — *v.* Harfe spielen; **— on** herumreiten auf; **-ist** *n.* Harfner, Harfenist; **-sichord** *n.* Spinett

harpoon *n.* Harpune; — *v.* harpunieren

harrow *n.* Egge; — *v.* eggen; (fig.) quälen, plagen; **-ing** *adj.* herzzerreissend, schrecklich

harsh *adj.* streng; rauh, barsch; herb, hart; grell; **-ness** *n.* Rauheit, Herbheit, Härte; Barschheit

hart *n.* Hirsch

harum-scarum *adj.* flüchtig, leichtsinnig, wild

harvest *n.* Ernte; Ertrag, Gewinn; — *v.* ernten, einbringen; **-er** *n.* Mähmaschine

hash *n.* Haschee, Gehacktes; **make — of** verderben, verpfuschen; — *v.* haschieren, zerhacken

hassock *n.* gepolsterte Fussbank; Kniekissen

haste *n.* Eile, Schnelligkeit; Hast; **be in — Eile** haben; **— makes waste** Eile mit Weile; **-n** *v.* (sich) eilen, beeilen, beschleunigen

hasty *adj.* eilig, schnell, hastig; hitzig, eifrig; übereilt, voreilig

hat *n.* Hut; **-s off!** *interj.* Hut ab! **-ter** *n.* Hutmacher; Hutverkäufer

hatband *n.* Hutband, Hutschnur

hatch *n.* Halbtür; (naut.) Luke; — *v.* aushekken, ausbrüten; schräffieren;

–ing n. Schraffieren, Schraffierung

hatchet n. Axt, Beil

hate n. Hass, Abscheu; — v. hassen, verabscheuen; **–ful** adj. verhasst, hasserfüllt, gehässig

hatpin n. Hutnadel

hatrack n. Hutrechen

hatred n. Hass, Groll

haughty adj. hochmütig, stolz; anmassend

haul n. Ziehen, Schleppen; Zug, Fang, Fischzug; (sl.) Diebesbeute; — v. ziehen, holen; schleppen; (min.) fördern; (naut.) den Kurs ändern

haunch n. Hüfte; Hinterhand; Keule

haunt n. Stammplatz; — v. häufig besuchen; heimsuchen; spuken; **–ed** adj. behext, verwunschen; heimgesucht, verfolgt

have v. haben, besitzen; erhalten, bekommen; verstehen; gestatten; (meal) einnehmen; — about one bei sich haben; — on anhaben; — done tun lassen; — made machen lassen; — to müssen; **I had better** go es wäre besser, wenn ich ginge; **I had my hair cut** ich liess mir das Haar schneiden; **I had rather** go ich möchte lieber gehen

haven n. Hafen, Freistatt, Freistätte

havoc n. Verwüstung, Verherrung

hawk n. Habicht, Falke; — v. hökern, hausieren; **–er** n. Höker, Hausierer

hawk-eyed adj. falkenäugig; (fig.) scharfsichtig

hawthorn n. Weissdorn, Hagedorn

hay n. Heu; — fever Heuschnupfen, Heufieber

hayfield n. Heufeld

hayloft n. Heuboden

haymaker n. Heumacher, Heuwender; (sports sl.) ziellos kreisender Boxhieb

haystack n. Heuschober

haze n. Dunst, Nebel; Höhenrauch

hazel n. Haselbusch, Haselstrauch; nussbraun, hellbraun

hazy adj. neblig, dunstig; dunkel, nebelhaft, verschwommen

he pron. er

head n. Kopf, Haupt; Führer, Leiter; Chef, Vorstand; Stück; Kopfende, Oberteil; Quelle; Spitze, Vorderseite, Vorderteil; Titel(kopf); Überschrift; Vorgebirge, Landspitze; **at the** — oben; am oberen Ende; an der Spitze; **by a** — um Kopfeslänge; **come to a** — sich zuspitzen, zur Krise kommen; **from** — **to foot** von Kopf bis Fuss, von oben bis unten; **go to one's** — zu Kopfe steigen; — **first** Kopf voran; — **of hair** Haarwuchs; — **over heels** Hals über Kopf; **–s or tails** Kopf oder Wappen (or Adler); **I can't make** — or tail of it ich kann daraus nicht klug werden; **keep one's** — die Fassung bewahren; **lose one's** — den Kopf verlieren; **out of one's** — verrückt; **put –s together** die Köpfe zusammenstecken, sich beraten; **take it into one's** — sich in den Kopf setzen; — adj. erst, vorderst, vornehmst, hauptsächlich; — **wind** Gegenwind; — v. leiten, anführen,

befehligen; an der Spitze stehen, der Erste sein; vorangehen; **be –ed** gehen; — **for** auf dem Wege sein nach; zusteuern auf; — **off** verhüten; **–ing** n. Titel, Überschrift; **–less** adj. kopflos; (fig.) ohne Oberhaupt; **–y** adj. übereilt, ungestüm; berauschend

headache n. Kopfschmerz(en)

headdress n. Kopfbedeckung; Kopfputz; Frisur

headgear n. Kopfschmuck; Kopfputz

headlight n. Scheinwerfer

headline n. Kopfzeile, Titelzeile

headlong adj. kopfüber; ungestüm, unbesonnen

headmaster n. Klassenlehrer

head-on adv. gerade entgegen

headpiece n. Kopfstück; (typ.) Kopfleiste; Zierleiste

headquarters n. Hauptquartier, Stabsquartier; **police** — Polizeidirektion

headset n. Kopfhörer

headstone n. Grabstein

headstrong adj. halsstarrig, hartnäckig; **be** — eigensinnig sein

headwaiter n. Oberkellner

headway n. Fortschritt, Erfolg; (naut.) Volldampf voraus; **make** — vorwärtskommen

heal v. heilen, wiederherstellen; genesen; versöhnen

health n. Gesundheit, Wohlbefinden; **be in good** — sich wohl befinden; **be in poor** — sich nicht wohl befinden, kränklich sein; **–ful** adj. gesund, wohl; heilsam, der Gesundheit zuträglich; **–y** adj. gesund, wohl

heap n. Haufe(n), Menge; Masse; — v. (an)häufen, aufhäufen; auftürmen, ansammeln, beladen

hear v. hören, erfahren; anhören, zuhören; hinhören, achtgeben; (law) verhören, gerichtlich untersuchen; **–er** n. Hörer; Zuhörer; **–ing** n. Gehör(sinn); Schallweite, Hörweite; (law) Verhör, Untersuchung; **out of –ing** ausser Hörweite

hearken v. horchen, lauschen, zuhören

hearsay n. Hörensagen, Gerücht, Gerede; **by** — vom Hörensagen

hearse n. Leichenwagen, Totenbahre

heart n. Herz; (fig.) Gemüt; Kern, Mitte, Mittelpunkt, Wesentliche; **at** — im Grunde (genommen); **by** — auswendig; **get to the** — of auf den Grund kommen; **have the** — es übers Herz bringen; — **and soul** mit Leib und Seele; **lose** — den Mut verlieren; **my** — **fails me** mein Mut sinkt; **sick at** — gemütskrank; **take** — Mut fassen; **take to** — beherzigen; **to one's –'s content** zur vollsten Zufriedenheit; **with all my** — von ganzem Herzen; — **trouble** Herzkrankheit, Herzbeschwerden; **–iness** n. Herzlichkeit, Aufrichtigkeit; Herzhaftigkeit; **–less** adj. herzlos, hartherzig, grausam, gefühllos; **–y** adj. herzlich, innig; aufrichtig; herzhaft; nahrhaft, kräftig

heartache n. Kummer, Herzensangst

heartbeat n. Herzschlag

heartbreak n. Herzenskummer, Herzeleid

heartbroken adj. tief bekümmert

heartburn n. Sodbrennen

heartfelt adj. innig, tief empfunden, aufrichtig

hearth n. Herd; (fig.) Heim, Familienkreis

hearthstone n. Herdstein; (fig.) Heim

heartsick adj. herzkrank; gemütskrank

heart-to-heart adj. freimütig, offen

heat n. Hitze, Glut; (sports) Einzelrennen; (zool.) Brunst, Läufigkeit; (fig.) Eifer, Erregung; **dead —** totes (or unentschiedenes) Rennen: **in —** brünstig, läufig; **prickly —** Hautausschlag; **— shield** hitzefestes Panzerschild (bemannte Rakete); **— wave** Hitzewelle; **—** v. (sich) erhitzen, erwärmen, heizen; **-er** n. Heizvorrichtung, Ofen, Wärmeapparat; **-ing** n. Heizung, Erwärmung; **central —** Zentralheizung; **-ing pad** Heizkissen

heath n. Heide

heathen n. Heide, Götzendiener

heat-resistant adj. feuerfest, hitzebeständig

heave n. Heben, Aufheben; Wogen, Schwellen; Keuchen, Seufzen; pl. Engbrüstigkeit; **—** v. (sich) heben, erheben; wogen, schwellen; ausstossen; keuchen; (mech.) aufwinden, emporheben; (naut.) hieven, winden

heaven n. Himmel, Firmament; **-s!** interj. (gerechter) Himmel! **-ly** adj. himmlisch; erhaben, heilig

heavily adv. schwer; träge, langsam; (fig.) traurig

heaviness n. Schwere, Gewicht, Druck; (fig.) Schwerfälligkeit, Langsamkeit; Kummer

heavy adj. schwer, drückend; fett; schwerfällig; heftig, stark; (fig.) drückend, lästig; **be —** fett sein; **— sea** hohe See

heavyweight n. Schwergewicht

heckle v. hecheln, frotzeln, necken; **-r** n. Hechler, Frotzler; Stichler

hectic adj. hektisch

hedge n. Hecke, Zaun; **— sparrow** Grasmücke; **—** v. einzäunen, einhegen

hedgehog n. Igel

heed n. Aufmerksamkeit, Acht(ung); **—** v. achtgeben auf, sorgfältig beachten; **-less** adj. achtlos, unbekümmert

heel n. Ferse; (shoe) Absatz; (sl.) Schuft; **rubber —** Gummiabsatz; **take to one's -s** das Hasenpanier ergreifen, ausreissen; **—** v. **— over** sich auf die Seite neigen; überholen

heifer n. Färse, junge Kuh, Sterke

height n. Höhe, Höhepunkt; Anhöhe, Gipfel; **-en** v. erhöhen, vergrössern, verstärken, steigern, vermehren

heir n. Erbe; **— apparent** rechtmässiger Erbe; **-dom** n. Erbschaft; Erbanspruch, Erbfolge; **-ess** n. Erbin; **-loom** n. Erbstück

helibus n. Hubschrauber-Nahverkehr

helicopter n. Hubschrauber

hell n. Hölle; **-ish** adj. höllisch, abscheulich

hello! interj. Hallo!

helm n. Steuerruder; Helm

helmet n. Helm

help n. Hilfe, Beistand; Hilfsmittel; Gehilfe, Arbeiter; (med.) Heilmittel, Kur; **—** v. helfen, beistehen, behilflich sein; verhelfen; reichen; bedienen; abhelfen, vermeiden; **— oneself** sich (selbst) bedienen; **— out** aushelfen, aus der Not helfen; **— to** verhelfen zu; **— yourself** langen Sie nur zu; **how can I — it?** was kann ich dafür? **I cannot —** it ich kann es nicht ändern; **-er** n. Gehilfe, Helfer; Beistand; **-ful** adj. hilfreich, behilflich; nützlich; **-ing** n. Portion; **-less** adj. hilflos, ratlos

helpmate n. Gefährte, Gehilfe; Gatte, Gattin

helter-skelter adv. holterdiepolter; Hals über Kopf

hem n. Saum, Rand, Einfassung; **—** v. säumen; räuspern, stottern; **— in** umsäumen, einschliessen

hemisphere n. Halbkugel, Hemisphäre

hemlock n. Hemlocktanne, Schierlingstanne; Schierling

hemorrhage n. Blutsturz

hemorrhoids n. pl. Hämorrhoiden

hemp n. Hanf

hemstitch v. mit Hohlsaum verzieren

hen n. Henne, Huhn

hence adv. daher, deshalb; von hier, von hinnen; fort, weg; von jetzt an, von nun an

henceforth adv. von nun an, fort an, hinfort

henchman n. feiler Anhänger

hencoop n. Hühnerstall; Hühnerkorb

henhouse n. Hühnerhaus

henpecked adj. unter dem Pantoffel stehend

her pron. sie, ihr; **-s** pron. ihrer; der (or die, das) ihrige; **a friend of -s** eine ihrer Freundinnen

herald n. Herold; Bote, Ausrufer; **-ic** adj. heraldisch; **-ry** n. Wappenkunde, Heraldik

herb n. Kraut; **-age** n. Futterkräuter

Herculean adj. herkulisch

herd n. Herde, Rudel, Trupp; **—** v. in Herden gehen, sich gesellen; zu einer Herde vereinigen; **-er** n. Hirt

herdsman n. Hirt

here adv. hier, her; hierher, hierin; **— and there** hier und dort; **— below** hienieden; **-'s to you!** auf dein Wohl! **that's neither — nor there** das gehört nicht zur Sache; **—** adj. hiesig

hereabout(s) adv. hier herum, in dieser Gegend

hereafter n. Zukunft, zukünftige Zustand; Jenseits; **—** adv. hiernach, in Zukunft, künftig

hereat adv. hierbei, hierüber

hereby adv. hierdurch

hereditary adj. erblich; vererbbar; ererbt

heredity n. Vererbung; Erblichkeit

hereinafter adv. hierin nachstehend

heresy n. Ketzerei

heretic n. Ketzer; **-al** adj. ketzerisch

heretofore *adv.* vorhin; vordem, ehemals

hereupon *adv.* darauf, darauf hin

heritage *n.* Erbschaft, Erbe

hermetically *adv.* hermetisch, luftdicht

hermit *n.* Einsiedler, Eremit, Klausner; **–age** *n.* Einsiedelei, Klause

hernia *n.* Bruch

hero *n.* Held; Halbgott, Heros; **–ic** *adj.* heroisch, heldenmütig, tapfer; **–ics** *n. pl.* Heldenhafte; Hochtrabende, Übertriebene; **–ine** *n.* Heldin; **–ism** *n.* Heldenmut, Heroismus

herring *n.* Hering; **smoked —** Bückling

herringbone *n.* Fischgrätenmuster, Grätenstich

herself *pron.* (sie, ihr) selbst; sich; **by —** von selbst, allein; **she is not —** sie fühlt sich nicht wohl

hesitant *adj.* zögernd, zaudernd; unschlüssig; stockend

hesitate *v.* zögern, zaudern; unschlüssig sein; stocken

hesitation *n.* Zögern, Zaudern; Unschlüssigkeit; Stocken

heterogeneous *adj.* heterogen, ungleich, verschieden, fremdartig

hew *v.* hauchen, hacken

hexagon *n.* Sechseck

hexameter *n.* Hexameter

hey! *interj.* hei! heda!

heyday *n.* Höhepunkt, Hochflut; Munterkeit

hiccup, hiccough *n.* Schlucken, Schluckauf; **—** *v.* schlucken, den Schlucken haben

hidden *adj.* verborgen, geheim, geheimnisvoll

hide *n.* Haut, Fell; **—** *v.* verbergen, verstecken; (fig.) verheimlichen

hide-and-seek *n.* Versteckspiel

hideous *adj.* scheusslich, schrecklich, grässlich, fürchterlich

hide-out *n.* Versteck, Schlupfwinkel

hiding *n.* Verbergen, Verborgenheit; **—** *adj.* verbergend; **— place** Versteck, Schlupfwinkel

hierarchy *n.* Hierarchie; Rangordnung

high *adj.* hoch, gross; erhaben, vornehm; stark; hochstrebend; (sl.) angetrunken; **— and dry** auf dem Trockenen; **— and low** auf und ab; weit und breit; (fig.) überall; **— frequency** Hochfrequenz; **High German** Hochdeutsch; **— light** Hochpunkt, Höhepunkt; **— school** Mittelschule, höhere Schule; **— sea(s)** offenes Meer; hochgehende See; **— spirits** gehobene Stimmung; **— tension** Hochspannung; **— tide** Flut; **— time** höchste Zeit; **— treason** Hochverrat; **— voltage** Starkstrom; **— water** Hochwasser; **— wind** starker Wind; **—** *n.* Hohe, Höhe; (auto.) Höchstgeschwindigkeit; höchster Gang; **–ly** *adv.* hoch, sehr; höchst, höchlich; **–ness** *n.* Hoheit; Höhe; Erhabenheit

highball *n.* Highball; Cocktail mit Eis

high-brow *adj.* hyperintellektuell; die geistige Überlegenheit fühlen lassend

highfalutin(g) *adj.* prahlend, schwülstig

high-flown *adj.* hochfliegend, aufgeblasen

high-grade *adj.* hochgradig

highhanded *adj.* anmassend, hochfahrend

highlight *v.* betonen, Nachdruck legen auf

high-minded *adj.* hochherzig, hochgesinnt

high-pitched *adj.* hoch; schrill, gellend

high-powered *adj.* (an Pferdekräften) stark (h.p.)

high-pressure *adj.* Hochdruck-; aufdringlich

high-priced *adj.* sehr teuer

highroad *n.* Landstrasse

high-sounding *adj.* hochtönend, hochtrabend

high-spirited *adj.* hochsinnig; trotzig, reizbar

high-strung *adj.* hochgespannt; übermütig

high-test *adj.* best erprobt

high-water mark *n.* Hochwassermarke

highway *n.* Landstrasse, Chaussee; **— robbery** Strassenraub; (fig.) Betrug

highwayman *n.* Strassenräuber

hike *n.* Fussmarsch, Wanderung; **—** *v.* wandern

hill *n.* Hügel, kleiner Berg; Haufen; **–y** *adj.* hügelig

hillside *n.* Bergabhang

hilltop *n.* Bergspitze

him *pron.* ihn, ihm

himself *pron.* (er, *or* ohn, ihm, sich) selbst

hinder *v.* (ver)hindern; aufhalten

hindmost *adj.* hinterst, letzt

hindquarter *n.* Hinterviertel, Hinterteil

hindrance *n.* Hindernis, Verhinderung; Schaden, Nachteil

hinge *n.* Angel, Scharnier; (fig.) Angelpunkt, Hauptpunkt; **—** *v.* **— on** abhängen von; sich drehen um

hint *n.* Wink, Fingerzeig; Andeutung, Anspielung; **take a —** sich gesagt sein lassen; **—** *v.* andeuten, zu verstehen geben; **— at** anspielen auf

hip *n.* Hüfte; (bot.) Hagebutte; **— roof** Walmdach, Satteldach

hipbone *n.* Hüftbein, Hüftknochen

hippopotamus *n.* Flusspferd, Nilpferd

hire *n.* Miete; Lohn, Arbeitslohn; **for —** zu vermieten; **—** *v.* mieten, pachten; dingen; (naut.) heuern; **–ling** *n.* Mietling

his *pron.* sein, seiner; der (*or* die, das) seinige

hiss *v.* zischen; pfeifen; auszischen; **–ing** *n.* Zischen, Gezische

historian *n.* Historiker, Geschichtsschreiber

historic(al) *adj.* historisch, geschichtlich

history *n.* Geschichte

hit *n.* Schlag, Stoss, Streich; Glücksfall; (mus.) Schlager; (sports) Treffer; (theat.) Erfolg(sschlager); **—** *v.* schlagen, stossen; treffen, erraten

hitch *n.* Ruck, Zuck; Haken, Schwierigkeit; **—** *v.* anbinden, festmachen; (naut.) festknoten

hitchhike *v.* trampen, als Anhalter reisen

hive *n.* Bienenstock, Bienenkorb; Bienenschwarm; *pl.* Hautausschlag, Nesselfieber

hoard *n.* Schatz, Vorrat, Hort; **—** *v.*

aufhäufen, horten, hamstern

hoarfrost *n.* Rauhreif

hoarse *adj.* heiser, rauh; misstönend; **–ness** *n.* Heiserkeit, Rauheit

hoary *adj.* eisgrau, altersgrau; weisslich; ehrwürdig

hoax *n.* Täuschung, Finte, Fopperei; (newspaper sl.) Ente; — *v.* foppen, täuschen

hobble *r.* hinken, humpeln; (an den Füssen) fesseln

hobby *n.* Steckenpferd, Liebhaberei

hobbyhorse *n.* Steckenpferd

hobnail *n.* Sohlennagel

hobnob *r.* auf vertrautem Fuss stehen; zusammen zechen

hobo *n.* Landstreicher, Vagabund

hockey *n.* Hockey

hodgepodge *n.* Mischmasch; Eintopfgericht

hoe *n.* Hacke, Haue; — *v.* hacken, behacken; anhäufeln

hog *n.* Schwein; (fig.) Schmutzfink; **–gish** *adj.* schweinisch, schmutzig; gierig, gefrässig

hogshead *n.* Oxhoft; Packfass

hoist *n.* Kran, Aufzug; — *v.* hochziehen, aufziehen, aufwinden; (naut.) hissen; — **a drink** einen kippen

hold *n.* Halt; Griff; Macht, Gewalt; Haft; (mil.) Festung; (naut.) Laderaum; **get — of** ergreifen; **take — of** anfassen; — *r.* halten, fassen, greifen; besitzen, festhalten; anhalten; einhalten; veranstalten, abhalten; gelten; (mus.) anhalten; **— forth** zu ausführlich vortragen (*or* darbieten); **— good** gelten, sich bewähren; **— no water** nicht Stich halten; **— off** abhalten; **— office** ein Amt bekleiden; **— on** anhalten, fortsetzen; **— one's own** sich behaupten, standhalten; **— one's tongue** schweigen, den Mund halten; **— out against** sich widersetzen; **— over** verbleiben; **— true** sich als wahr bestätigen; **— up** aufhalten; stützen; überfallen; **–er** *n.* Halter, Behälter; Inhaber, Besitzer; **cigar —** Zigarrenspitze; **–ing** *n.* Halten; Besitz; **–ing** *adj.* haltend; **–ing company** Dachgesellschaft (von Konzernen)

holdup *n.* Raubüberfall; Aufschub

hole *n.* Loch, Höhle, Grube; (coll.) Klemme, Patsche

holiday *n.* Feiertag, Festtag; freier Tag; **half —** Halbfeiertag; *pl.* Ferien, Urlaubszeit

holiness *n.* Heiligkeit; Frömmigkeit

hollow *n.* Höhle, Höhlung; Loch, Grube; (mech.) Nut, Rinne; — *adj.* hohl, leer; (fig.) falsch, wertlos; — *v.* aushöhlen, hohl machen

hollyhock *n.* Stockrose

holster *n.* Halfter

holy *adj.* heilig; fromm, tugendhaft; **— water** Weihwasser; **Holy Week** Karwoche

home *n.* Heim; Heimat; Haus, Wohnung; Wohnort, Geburtsort; (sports) Ziel; **at — zu Hause, daheim; charity begins at —** jeder ist sich selbst der Nächste; —

adj. heimisch, einheimisch; inländisch; häuslich; derb, tüchtig; (sports) nahe dem Ziel, das Ziel erreichend; — **economics** Hauswirtschaftslehre; — **plate** Ausgangsbasis, Zielbasis; — **rule** Selbst-regierung; — **run** Vierbasisrunde; — **town** Vaterstadt, Heimatstadt; — *adv.* nach Hause, heim; zurück; daheim; **strike — den Nagel auf den Kopf treffen; –less** *adj.* heimatlos; obdachlos; **–like** *adj.* heimisch, gemütlich; wie zu Hause; **–liness** *n.* Einfachheit, Schlichtheit; **–ly** *adj.* einfach, schlicht; hausbacken; hässlich

homeland *n.* Heimat(land)

homemade *adj.* zu Hause (*or* selbst) gemacht

homemaker *n.* Hausweib, Hausfrau

homeopathy *n.* Homöopathie

homesick *adj.* Heimweh habend; **–ness** *n.* Heimweh

homespun *n.* Homespun, rauhhaariges Wollgewebe; — *adj.* zu Hause (*or* selbst) gesponnen

homestead *n.* Heimstätte; Grundeigentum; Gehöft

homestretch *n.* Zielgerade

homeward(s) *adv.* heimwärts, nach Hause

homework *n.* Heimarbeit, Hausarbeit

homicide *n.* Mord, Totschlag

homily *n.* Kanzelrede, Lehrpredigt

homing *n.* (avi.) Zielfindung; Eigenpeilung

homing pigeon *n.* Brieftaube

hominy *n.* (grob gemahlener) Mais, Maisbrei

homogeneous *adj.* homogen, gleichartig

homogenized *adj.* homogenisiert; neutralisiert (Fettgehalt in Milchprodukten)

homosexual *adj.* homosexuell

honest *adj.* ehrlich, redlich; aufrichtig; **–y** *n.* Ehrlichkeit, Redlichkeit, Aufrichtigkeit

honey *n.* Honig; (fig.) Süssigkeit, Lieblichkeit; (coll.) Herzchen, Täubchen; **–ed** *adj.* mit Honig bedeckt; (fig.) süss, lieblich

honeybee *n.* Honigbiene

honeycomb *n.* Honigwabe, Honigzelle

honeydew melon *n.* weisse Zuckermelone

honeymoon *n.* Flitterwochen

honeysuckle *n.* Geissblatt, Jelängerjelieber

honk *n.* Hupe; — *r.* hupen, tuten; **— the horn** hupen

honor *n.* Ehre; Achtung, Hochachtung; Rechtschaffenheit; Keuschheit; Auszeichnung, Ehrenzeichen; *pl.* Honneurs, Ehrenbezeigungen; **in his —** ihm zu Ehren; **point of —** Ehrenpunkt; **word of —** Ehrenwort; **Your Honor** Euer Ehrwürden; — *r.* ehren, achten, verehren, hochachten; auszeichnen; (com.) honorieren, anerkennen; **–able** *adj.* ehrenvoll, rühmlich; ehrenhaft; rechtschaffen, redlich; ehrbar; **–ary** *adj.* ehrend; **–ary degree** akademischer Ehrengrad; **–ary doctor** Ehrendoktor, Doktor ehrenhalber (Dr. h.c.)

honorarium *n.* Honorar; Gebühren

hood *n.* Kapuze, Kappe; (mech.) Haube,

Deckel; — *v.* verkappen

hoodlum *n.* Strolch, Raufbold

hoodoo *n.* Unheilbringer; — *v.* Unheil bringen

hoodwink *v.* täuschen

hoof *n.* Huf, Klaue; — **-and-mouth disease** Maul und Klauenseuche

hook *n.* Haken; Türangel; (agr.) Sichel; **by — or by crook** es mag biegen oder brechen; **so oder so; -s and eyes** Haken und Ösen; — *v.* anhaken, festhaken, einhaken, zuhaken; angeln; stehlen, klemmen; (sports) Haken schlagen; — **on** anhaken; — **up** einstellen; anhaken; anspannen; **-ed** *adj.* krumm, hakenförmig, hakig; **-ed rug** handgeknüpfter Teppich

hookup *n.* (rad.) Ringsendung

hookworm *n.* Hakenwurm

hoop *n.* Tonnenband, Fassreifen; Ring; — **skirt** Reifrock

hoot *n.* Geschrei, Geheul; — *v.* schreien, heulen, auszischen

hop *n.* Hupf, Sprung; *pl.* Hopfen; — *v.* hopsen, hüpfen, springen; Hopfen ernten

hope *n.* Hoffnung, Vertrauen, Zuversicht; **he is past all** — es ist aus mit ihm, für ihn ist nichts mehr zu hoffen; — **against** — verzweifelt hoffen; — *v.* hoffen, vertrauen; — **for the best** das Beste hoffen; — *adj.* — **chest** Ausstattungstruhe; **-ful** *adj.* hoffnungsvoll, vielversprechend; **-ful** *n.* vielversprechender Junge; **-less** *adj.* hoffnungslos, verzweifelt

hopper *n.* Trichterkasten; Spülkasten

horde *n.* Horde, Bande

horizon *n.* Horizont, Gesichtskreis

horizontal *adj.* waagerecht, horizontal

hormone *n.* Hormon, Drüsensekret

horn *n.* Horn; Geweih; (ast.) Mondsichel; (auto.) Hupe; **-ed** *adj.* gehörnt; gekrümmt; **-ed owl** Ohreule, Uhu; **-y** *adj.* hörnern, hornig; Horn-

hornet *n.* Hornisse

hornpipe *n.* Hornpfeife; Matrosentanz

horoscope *n.* Horoskop; Gestirnstand

horrible *adj.* schrecklich, fürchterlich; entsetzlich, grässlich

horrid *adj.* scheusslich, abscheulich

horrify *v.* erschrecken, entsetzen; erschauern lassen

horror *n.* Greuel, Schrecken; Schauder, Grausen

horror-stricken *adj.* von Entsetzen ergriffen; von Schreck erfasst

hors d'oeuvre *n.* Hors d'oeuvre, Vorspeise, Nebengericht

horse *n.* Pferd, Ross, Gaul; (mech.) Gestell, Gerüst, Bock; **black —** Rappe; **bay —** Fuchs; **get on one's high —** sich aufs hohe Pferd setzen; **white —** Schimmel; — **chestnut** Rosskastanie; — **race** Pferderennen

horseback *n.* **on —** zu Pferde

horsefly *n.* Pferdebremse

horsehair *n.* Rosshaar, Pferdehaar

horsehide *n.* Pferdehaut

horselaugh *n.* wieherndes Lachen; Ge-

wieher

horseman *n.* Reiter; **-ship** *n.* Reitkunst

horseplay *n.* derber Spass, grober Witz

horsepower *n.* Pferdekraft, Pferdestärke

horse-radish *n.* Meerrettich

horseshoe *n.* Hufeisen

hose *n.* Strumpf; Schlauch; — *v.* mit einem Schlauch bespritzen

hosiery *n.* Strumpfwaren

hospitable *adj.* gastlich, fastfreundlich, gastfrei

hospital *n.* Krankenhaus; Hospital, Spital; (mil.) Lazarett; — **ward** Krankenhausabteilung; **-ity** *n.* Gastfreundschaft, Gastfreiheit; **-ization** *n.* Krankenhausunterbringung; **-ization insurance** Krankenkasse, Kranken(haus)versicherung

host *n.* Wirt, Gastgeber; Menge, Schwarm; (rel.) Messopfer, Hostie; **-age** *n.* Geisel, Bürge; **-ess** *n.* Wirtin; Gastgeberin

hostel *n.* Gasthof, Herberge; Studentenheim

hostile *adj.* feindlich, feindselig

hot *adj.* heiss; hitzig, heftig; eifrig; scharf, stark gewürzt; noch frisch; **be in — water** in der Patsche stecken; — **air** Heissluft; (coll.) blauer Dunst; — **dog** heisse Frankfurter (Würstchen); **grow —** erhitzen

hotbed *n.* Mistbeet, Pflanzstätte; (fig.) Brutstätte

hot-blooded *adj.* heissblütig

hotbox *n.* (rail.) heissgelaufener Getriebekasten

hotel *n.* Hotel, Gasthof

hothouse *n.* Treibhaus

hot-rod *n.* Amateurrennwagen

hot-tempered *adj.* heissblütig, jähzornig

hot-water bottle *n.* Wärmflasche

hound *n.* Jagdhund, Hetzhund, Spürhund; (coll.) Hund; — *v.* jagen, hetzen, verfolgen

hour *n.* Stunde; Zeit; Uhr; *pl.* Dienststunden; Horen, Stundengebete; **for -s** stundenlang; — **hand** Stundenzeiger; **-ly** *adv.* stündlich; häufig, fortwährend; **-ly** *adj.* stündlich, häufig

house *n.* Haus; Wohnhaus; Wohnung, Wohnsitz; Haushalt; Geschlecht, Familie; (com.) Handelshaus, Firma; (pol.) Kammer, Parlament; (theat.) Publikum; — **of cards** Kartenhaus; — **of correction** Besserungsanstalt; **House of Representatives** Repräsentantenhaus; Abgeordnetenhaus; — **party** Hausgesellschaft; **keep** — den Haushalt führen; — *v.* hausen, wohnen

houseboat *n.* Hausboot

housefly *n.* Stubenfliege

household *n.* Haushalt(ung); — **goods** Hauseinrichtung; Haushaltungsgegenstände; — **management** Hauswirtschaft; **-er** *n.* Haushaltungsvorstand, Familienoberhaupt, Hausvater; Hausherr

housekeeper *n.* Haushälterin, Wirtschafterin

housekeeping *n.* Haushaltung; — **money**

Wirtschaftsgeld
housemaid *n.* Hausmädchen
housemate *n.* Hausgenosse
housetop *n.* Dach
housewarming *n.* Einzugsfeier
housewife *n.* Hausfrau
housework *n.* Haushaltsarbeit
housing *n.* Obdach; Wohnung; (mech.) Gehäuse; **— shortage** Wohnungsnot
hovel *n.* Schuppen; Hütte
hover *v.* schweben; verweilen, zögern
how *adv.* and *interr.* wie, auf welche Weise, warum; **— are you?** wie geht es Ihnen? **— come?** wieso? wie kommt das? **— do you do?** guten Tag! **— goes it?** wie steht's? **— is it?** wie kommt es? **— many?** wieviele? **how much?** wieviel?
however *adv.* jedoch, dennoch; wie auch immer, jedenfalls; nichtsdestoweniger
howitzer *n.* Haubitze
howl *n.* Geheul; **—** *v.* heulen; wehklagen
howsoever *adv.* wie sehr auch immer; gleichwohl
hub *n.* Nabe; (fig.) Mittelpunkt
hubbub *n.* Lärm, Tumult
huckleberry *n.* Heidelbeerenart
huckster *n.* Höker, Hausierer
huddle *n.* Zusammenkauern; (football) Beratung (während des Zusammenkauerns); **—** *v.* sich schieben (or drängen); **— together** sich zusammendrängen
hue *n.* Färbung, Farbe; Schrei, Geschrei; **— and cry** Zetergeschrei; Verbrecherjagd
hug *n.* Umarmung; **—** *v.* umarmen, umfassen, liebkosen, hätscheln; (naut.) dicht anfahren
huge *adj.* riesig, kolossal, ungeheuer; unermesslich
hull *n.* (bot.) Hülse, Hülle, Schale; (naut.) Schiffsrumpf, Unterschiff; **—** *v.* schälen, enthülsen
hullabaloo *n.* Wirrwarr, Tumult, Tohuwabohu
hum *n.* Summen, Gesumme; Gebrumme, Gemurmel; **—** *v.* summen, brummen; (fig.) in Erregung sein
human *n.* Mensch; **—** *adj.* menschlich; **— being** Mensch; **-e** *adj.* human, menschenfreundlich; gutmütig, leutselig; humanistisch, philologisch; **-ism** *n.* Humanismus; Menschlichkeit; **-itarian** *n.* Menschenfreund; (phil. and rel.) Leugner der Gottheit Christi; **-itarian** *adj.* menschenfreundlich; **-ity** *n.* Menschheit; Humanität, Milde; Menschlichkeit, Menschenliebe; **-ize** *v.* vermenschlichen; Menschenliebe einflössen; menschlich werden (or machen), gesittet werden (or machen)
humankind *n.* Menschengeschlecht
humble *adj.* bescheiden, anspruchslos, demütig; niedrig, nieder, gering; **—** *v.* erniedrigen, demütigen; unterwerfen; **-ness** *n.* Demut, Bescheidenheit
humbug *n.* Humbug, Unsinn
humdrum *adj.* eintönig, uninteressant, langweilig
humid *adj.* nass, feucht; **-ify** *v.* (be)nässen,

anfeuchten; **-ity** *n.* Nässe, Feuchtigkeit; **-or** *n.* Einrichtung zur Aufrechterhaltung der Luftfeuchtigkeit
humiliate *v.* demütigen, erniedrigen
humiliation *n.* Demütigung, Erniedrigung
humility *n.* Demut, Bescheidenheit; Unterwürfigkeit
hummingbird *n.* Kolibri
humor *n.* Humor; Stimmung, Laune; **bad — ** schlechte Laune; **—** *v.* willfahren, sich anpassen; gefällig sein; den Willen lassen; **-ist** *n.* Humorist, Spassvogel; **-ous** *adj.* humoristisch, launig, spasshaft
hump *n.* Buckel, Höcker
humpbacked *adj.* bucklig, höckerig
humus *n.* Humus
hunch *n.* Buckel, Höcker; (coll.) Ahnung; **—** *v.* krümmen
hunchback *n.* Buckel; Bucklige; **-ed** *adj.* bucklig, höckerig
hundred *n.* Hundert(er); **—** *adj.* hundert; **-fold** *adj.* hundertfach; **-th** *n.* Hundertste; Hundertstel; **-th** *adj.* hundertst
hundredweight *n.* Zentner
hunger *n.* Hunger; heftiges Verlangen; **—** *adj.* **— strike** Hungerstreik; **—** *v.* hungern, darben; verlangen (nach)
hungry *n.* hungrig; verhungert; (fig.) begierig; **be —** Hunger haben
hunk *n.* grosses (or dickes) Stück
hunt *n.* Jagd; (fig.) Nachsetzen, Verfolgen, Suchen; **—** *v.* jagen, hetzen; abjagen, durchjagen; nachsetzen, verfolgen; **— for** suchen; **-er** *n.* Jäger; **-ing** *n.* Jagd; **-ing license** Jagdschein
hurdle *n.* Hürde; *pl.* Hürden, Hindernisse; Hindernisrennen
hurdy-gurdy *n.* Leierkasten, Drehorgel
hurl *v.* werfen, schleudern; (fig.) ausstossen, heftig äussern
hurly-burly *n.* Tumult, Tohuwabohu
hurrah! *interj.* hurra! **—** *n.* Hurra
hurricane *n.* Hurrikan, Orkan, Wirbelsturm
hurried *adj.* übereilt, schnell
hurry *n.* Eile, Hast; Übereilung; Unruhe; **be in a —** es eilig haben; **—** *v.* sich beeilen; beschleunigen, übereilen; hasten; **— away** entführen; **— back** eilig zurückkommen; **— on** antreiben; **— over** schnell hinweggehen über; **— up** eilen, sich beeilen
hurt *n.* Verwundung, Verletzung; Schaden, Nachteil; Übel; **—** *v.* verletzen, weh tun, schmerzen; schädigen, schaden; **—** *adj.* verletzt, verwundet
husband *n.* Mann, Gatte; **—** *v.* sparsam umgehen mit; **-ry** *n.* Landwirtschaft
hush *n.* Ruhe; Stille; **— money** Schweigegeld; **—!** *interj.* still! st! pst! **—** *v.* zum Schweigen bringen; (fig.) besänftigen; **— up** vertuschen
husk *n.* Schale, Hülse, Schote; **—** *v.* schälen, enthülsen
huskiness *n.* Heiserkeit, Rauheit (der Stimme)
husky *n.* Eskimohund; **—** *adj.* rauh, heiser, trocken; (coll.) kräftig
hustle *v.* stossen, drängen; sich drängen

hut n. Hütte; (mil.) Baracke

hybrid n. Bastard, Mischling; Kreuzung, Hybride; — adj. hybrid

hydraulic adj. hydraulisch; — engineering Wasserbau; —s n. Hydraulik

hydrochloric adj. salzsauer; — acid Chlorwasserstoff, Salzsäure

hydroelectric adj. hydroelektrisch

hydrogen n. Wasserstoff; — bomb Wasserstoffbombe; — peroxide Wasserstoffsuperoxyd

hydromatic adj. (system) automatisches hydraulisches System

hydronics n. Lehre vom Erhitzen and kühlen von Flüssigkeiten

hydroplane n. Wasserflugzeug; Rennboot

hyena n. Hyäne

hygiene n. Hygiene, Gesundheitslehre

hygienic adj. hygienisch

hymn n. Choral; –al n. Gesangbuch

hypergolic (self-igniting fuel) n. selbstzündender Treibstoff; — ignition n. Selbstzündung

hypersensitive adj. überempfindlich

hypersonic (5 Mach or more) adj. schneller als die 5malige Schallgeschwindidigkeit

hypertension n. Überspannung, Überanspannung

hyphen n. Bindestrich; –ate v. mit Bindestrich schreiben (or verbinden)

hypnosis n. Hypnose

hypnotism n. Hypnotismus

hypnotist n. Hypnotiseur

hypnotize v. hypnotisieren; einschläfern

hypocrisy n. Heuchelei

hypocrite n. Heuchler, Scheinheilige; Hypokrit

hypocritical adj. heuchlerisch, scheinheilig

hypodermic adj. unter der Haut liegend; — injection Einspritzung unter die Haut; — syringe hypodermische Spritze

hypothesis n. Hypothese

hypothetical adj. hypothetisch

hysteria n. Hysterie

hysteric(al) adj. hysterisch; (fig.) launisch

hysterics n. pl. hysterischer Anfall; hysterischer Lachkrampf

I

I pron. ich

iambic adj. jambisch

ICBM (intercontinental ballistic missile) n. interkontinentales Fernlenkgeschoss

ice n. Eis; Gefrorenes; — age Eiszeit; — bag Eisbeutel; — cream Speiseeis, Gefrorenes; — hockey Eishockey; — pack Packeis, Treibeis; (med.) Eisbeutel; — pick Eispickel; — skate Schlittschuh; Schlittschuhlaufen; — water Eiswasser; — v. glasieren, mit Zuckerguss versehen, überzuckern; gefrieren, mit Eis bedecken

iceberg n. Eisberg

iceboat n. Segelschlitten

icebound adj. Eis umschlossen, zugefroren

icebox n. Eisschrank, Eiskiste

icebreaker n. Eisbrecher

icehouse n. Gefrierhaus, Eiskeller

Iceland n. Island

iceman n. Eishändler; Eisarbeiter

ichthyology n. Fischkunde

icicle n. Eiszapfen

icing n. Zuckerguss, Zuckerglasur

Iconoscope n. Ikonoskop, Elektronenstrahlabtaster

icy adj. eisig; (fig.) kühl, kalt

idea n. Idee, Begriff, Vorstellung; Ahnung, Einfall; (mus.) Thema; clever — guter Einfall; he has no — er hat keine Ahnung; the — of such a thing! stell sich einer das vor!

ideal n. Ideal, Vorbild, Muster; — adj. ideal, vorbildlich, mustergültig; ideell; eingebildet; -ism n. Idealismus; -ist n. Idealist; -istic adj. idealistisch; -ize v. idealisieren

identical adj. identisch, gleichbedeutend

identification n. Identifikation, Identifizierung; — card Personalausweis; — papers Personalpapiere

identify v. identifizieren; — oneself sich ausweisen

identity n. Identität; Persönlichkeit; Eigenart

ideology n. Ideologie, Begriffslehre

idiocy n. Idiotie, Verstandesschwäche, Blödsinn

idiom n. Idiom, Mundart, Dialekt; Spracheigentümlichkeit; -atic(al) adj. idiomatisch, mundartlich

idiot n. Idiot, Schwachsinnige; -ic adj. idiotisch, schwachsinnig

idle adj. unbeschäftigt, untätig, müssig; faul, arbeitsscheu; eitel, leer; — v. faulenzen, müssig gehen; vertändeln; (mech.) leerlaufen; -ness n. Müssiggang, Musse; Trägheit, Faulheit; -r n. Müssiggänger, Faulenzer

idol n. Idol, Abgott; Götzenbild; Trugbild; -atry n. Abgötterei, Götzendienst; -ize v. vergöttern

idyl(l) n. Idyll(e); -lic adj. idyllisch

if conj. wenn, falls, wofern; ob, wiewohl, obschon; — not wo nicht, wenn nicht; — so in diesem Fall

igloo n. Iglu, Eskimohütte

ignite v. anzünden, entzünden; (chem.) erhitzen

ignition n. Zündung; Entzündung, Verbrennung; Erhitzung; — spark Zündfunke; — switch Zündhebel, Zündungsschalter

ignoble adj. gering, wertlos; unedel, unwürdig, niedrig

ignoramus n. Ignorant, Nichtswisser

ignorance n. Unwissenheit, Ignoranz, Unkenntniss; (fig.) Einfältigkeit

ignorant adj. unwissend, unkundig, ignorant

ignore v. keine Notiz nehmen, nicht beachten, ignorieren; nicht wissen (or kennen)

ill n. Übel; Laster, Bosheit; Unglück; — adj. krank; übel, schlecht; become — erkranken; — at ease unruhig, unbehaglich; — adv. schwerlich, kaum; -ness n. Krankheit, Unpässlichkeit

ill-advised *adj.* schlecht beraten
ill-bred *adj.* schlecht erzogen; ungebildet
ill-disposed *adj.* schlecht gelaunt; übelgesinnt
illegal *adj.* illegal, ungesetzlich, widerrechtlich
illegible *adj.* unleserlich
illegitimate *adj.* unehelich, illegitim; unrechtmässig
ill-gotten *adj.* unrechtmässig (*or* unehrlich) erworben
ill-health *n.* Unwohlsein, Unpässlichkeit
ill-humored *adj.* schlecht gelaunt
illicit *adj.* unerlaubt, verboten; unzulässig
illimitable *adj.* unbegrenzbar, grenzenlos
illiteracy *n.* Analphabetentum; Unwissenheit, Ungelehrtheit
illiterate *adj.* des Schreibens und Lesens unkundig; unwissend, ungebildet
ill-mannered *adj.* schlecht gesittet, taktlos
ill-natured *adj.* bosartig, boshaft; verdriesslich
illogical *adj.* unlogisch
ill-pleased *adj.* unzufrieden, missvergnügt
ill-starred *adj.* zum Unglück bestimmt, unglücklich
ill-tempered *adj.* verdriesslich, mürrisch
ill-timed *adj.* ungelegen
illuminate *v.* illuminieren, erhellen, beleuchten; (fig.) aufklären
illumination *n.* Illumination, Erhellung, Beleuchtung; (fig.) Aufklärung
illumine *v.* erleuchten; erläutern
illusion *n.* Illusion, Blendwerk, Wahnbild; (physiol.) Sinnestäuschung
illustrate *v.* illustrieren, erklären; bebildern; **-d** *adj.* illustriert; erklärt; bebildert
illustration *n.* Illustration; Illustrierung, Erklärung; Bebilderung
illustrative *adj.* erläuternd, erklärend
illustrator *n.* Illustrator, Illustrierende
illustrious *adj.* berühmt, glänzend, ausgezeichnet
image *n.* Bild(nis), Abbild, Ebenbild; **-ry** *n.* Bildwerk; bildliche Rede, lebhafte Schilderung
imaginable *adj.* denkbar, erdenklich
imaginary *adj.* eingebildet, imaginär
imagination *n.* Einbildung(skraft)
imaginative *adj.* erfinderisch; Einbildungs-
imagine *v.* sich einbilden, sich vorstellen; ersinnen, (er)denken; meinen; just —I denk nur!
imbecile *n.* Schwachsinnige; — *adj.* geistesschwach, schwachsinnig
imbibe *v.* einsaugen, einziehen; schlürfen
imbue *v.* einweichen, durchnetzen; tränken; tief färben
imitate *v.* nachahmen, nachmachen, imitieren
imitation *n.* Nachahmung, Imitation; — leather Kunstleder
imitator *n.* Nachahmer, Imitator
immaculate *adj.* unbefleckt, rein
immature *adj.* unreif; vorzeitig, verfrüht
immeasurable *adj.* unmessbar, unermesslich
immediate *adj.* unmittelbar, direkt; so-

fortig, unverzüglich; **-ly** *adv.* sogleich, augenblicklich, sofort
immense *adj.* unermesslich, ungeheuer
immensity *n.* Unermesslichkeit
immerse *v.* eintauchen, versenken; (fig.) vertiefen
immersion *n.* Eintauchen, Versenkung; (fig.) Vertiefung
immigrant *n.* Immigrant, Einwanderer
immigrate *v.* einwandern
immigration *n.* Einwanderung
immoderate *adj.* übermässig, unmässig, masslos
immodest *adj.* unbescheiden, anmassend; unanständig
immoral *adj.* unmoralisch, unsittlich; **-ity** *n.* Unmoral, Unsittlichkeit
immortal *adj.* unsterblich, unvergänglich; **-ity** *n.* Unsterblichkeit; **-ize** *v.* unsterblich machen (*or* werden); verewigen
immovable *adj.* unbeweglich; unabänderlich; (fig.) unerschütterlich; **-s** *n. pl.* Immobilien, Liegenschaften
immune *adj.* immun, unempfindlich; geschützt
immunity *n.* Befreiung, Freiheit; (med.) Unempfänglichkeit, Immunität
immunize *v.* immunisieren
imp *n.* Kobold; Schelm; **-ish** *adj.* koboldartig, teuflisch
impact *n.* Stoss, Aufschlag; — velocity Aufschlag (Anschlag) Geschwindigkeit
impair *v.* verschlechtern, verschlimmern; beinträchtigen
impale *v.* pfählen, aufspiessen, festnageln
impalpable *adj.* unfühlbar; (fig.) unfassbar
impart *v.* mitteilen; erteilen, verleihen, geben
impartial *adj.* unparteiisch; gerecht; **-ity** *n.* Unparteilichkeit, Objektivität
impassable *adj.* ungangbar, unwegsam
impassioned *adj.* erregt, leidenschaftlich
impassive *adj.* unempfindlich, gefühllos; unbeweglich
impatience *n.* Ungeduld; Unduldsamkeit
impatient *adj.* ungeduldig, unduldsam
impeach *v.* in Frage stellen, anfechten, anzweifeln; zur Verantwortung ziehen, beschuldigen, anklagen
impede *v.* verhindern, erschweren
impediment *n.* Hindernis
impel *v.* antreiben, vorwärtsstreiben, drängen
impend *v.* (über)hängen, schweben; (fig.) bevorstehen, drohen
impenetrable *adj.* undurchdringlich; (fig.) unerforschlich, unergründlich
impenitent *adj.* unbussfertig, vorstockt
imperative *adj.* befehlend, gebietend; notwendig, dringend; — *n.* Imperativ, Befehlsform
imperceptible *adj.* unmerklich; verschwindend klein
imperfect *adj.* unvollkommen, unvollständig; mangelhaft; — *n.* Imperfekt(um); **-ion** *n.* Unvollkommenheit; Mangelhaftigkeit; Gebrechen
imperial *adj.* kaiserlich; grossartig;

Reichs-; **–ism** n. Kaisertum; (fig.) Imperialismus, Weltherrschaftspolitik; **–ist** n. Kaisertreue; (fig.) Imperialist, Anhänger der Weltherrschaftspolitik

imperil v. gefährden

imperious adj. herrisch, herrschsüchtig, gebieterisch; herrschend; dringend

imperishable adj. unvergänglich, unzerstörbar

impersonal adj. unpersönlich

impersonate v. verkörpern; (theat.) darstellen

impersonation n. Personifikation, Verkörperung; (theat.) Darstellung

impertinence n. Frechheit, Unverschämtheit; Impertinenz

impertinent adj. frech, unverschämt

impervious adj. unzugänglich, undurchdringlich, undurchlässig

impetuous adj. ungestüm, heftig

impetus n. Antrieb

impious adj. ruchlos, gottlos, ehrfurchtslos

implacable adj. unerbittlich, unversöhnlich; unbarmherzig

implant v. einpflanzen, einimpfen

implement n. Werkzeug, Gerät; Hilfsmittel, Zubehör; — v. ausführen, erfüllen

implicate v. verwickeln, hineinziehen

implication n. Verwicklung; Teilnahme; Folgerung

implicit adj. verwickelt, stillschweigend; (fig.) unbedingt, blind

implied adj. miteinbegriffen, gefolgert

implore v. (an)flehen; erbitten, erflehen

imply v. umfassen, bedeuten; andeuten

impolite adj unhöflich, ungesittet

import n. Import, Einfuhr; Bedeutung, Wichtigkeit; Tragweite; — **duties** Einfuhrzoll; — v. importieren, einführen; (fig.) bedeuten, besagen; **–ance** n. Wichtigkeit; Bedeutsamkeit, Einfluss; Gewicht, Anmassung; **–ant** adj. wichtig, bedeutsam; anmassend; **–ation** n. Import, Wareneinfuhr; Einfuhr(artikel); Zufuhr; **–er** n. Importeur

impose v. auferlegen, aufbürden; — **upon** ausnutzen, missbrauchen; täuschen

imposing adj. eindrucksvoll, achtunggebietend; imposant, grossartig

imposition n. Auferlegung; Auflage, Steuer; Bürde, Zumutung; Betrug, Täuschung

impossibility n. Unmöglichkeit

impossible adj. unmöglich

impost n. Auflage, Abgabe; Steuer, Zoll

impostor n. Betrüger

imposture n. Betrug, Betrügerei

impotence n. Unvermögen, Unfähigkeit; (med.) Impotenz, Zeugungsunfähigkeit

impotent adj. unfähig, hinfällig; (med.) zeugungsunfähig, impotent

impound v. einpferchen, einschliessen; (law) in Verwahrung nehmen

impracticable adj. unausführbar; unbrauchbar; ungangbar

impractical adj. unpraktisch

impregnable adj. uneinnehmbar, unüberwindlich

impregnate v. schwängern, befruchten; (chem.) imprägnieren, durchtränken

impress n. Eindruck, Merkmal; Abdruck, Aufdruck; — v. Eindruck machen, beeindrucken; eindrücken; **–ion** n. Eindruck; Gepräge, Stempel; (typ.) Abdruck, Abzug, Auflage; **give the –ion** den Eindruck machen; **–ionable** adj. empfänglich, leicht zu beeinflussen; **–ive** adj. eindrucksvoll; nachdrucksvoll, ergreifend

imprint n. Aufdruck, Druckvermerk; **printer's** — Druckereiangabe; **publisher's** — Verlagsangabe; — v. aufdrücken, abdrucken; (ein)prägen

imprison v. ins Gefängnis setzen, einkerkern, einsperren; **–ment** n. Haft, Gefangenschaft; Einkerkerung; **false –ment** ungesetzliche Haft

improbable adj. unwahrscheinlich

improper adj. ungehörig, unpassend, ungeeignet; — **fraction** unechter Bruch

impropriety n. Ungehörigkeit; Untauglichkeit; Ungenauigkeit

improve v. verbessern; sich bessern, besser werden; **–ment** n. Verbesserung, Besserung; Fortschritt

improvident adj. unvorsichtig; sorglos, leichtsinnig

improvisation n. Improvisation, Stegreifdichtung; Improvisieren

improvise v. improvisieren

imprudence n. Unvorsichtigkeit, Unklugheit

imprudent adj. unvorsichtig, unklug

impudent adj. unverschämt, dreist, frech

impulse n. Trieb, Antrieb; Impuls

impulsive adj. impulsiv, antreibend

impure adj. unrein, unsauber; (fig.) unkeusch, unzüchtig

impurity n. Unreinheit, Unsauberkeit; (fig.) Unlauterkeit

impute v. zuschreiben; anrechnen, beimessen

in prep. in, innerhalb; an, auf; bei, zu; von, unter; nach; binnen, während; — adv. darin, herein, hinein; da, hier. **zu** Hause; — **itself** an und für sich; **there is nothing** — **it** da ist nichts Wahres daran

inability n. Unfähigkeit, Unvermögen; — **to pay** Zahlungsunfähigkeit

inaccessibility n. Unzugänglichkeit, Unerreichbarkeit

inaccessible adj. unzugänglich, unerreichbar

inaccuracy n. Ungenauigkeit, Unrichtigkeit

inaccurate adj. ungenau, unrichtig

inactive adj. untätig, müssig, träge; ausser Dienst

inactivity n. Untätigkeit, Beschäftigungslosigkeit

inadequacy n. Unzulänglichkeit, Unangemessenheit

inadequate adj. unzulänglich, unangemessen

inadvertent adj. unbeabsichtigt; unachtsam, versehentlich

inalienable adj. unveräusserlich

inane adj. leer; geistlos, nichtig; albern, fade

inanimate *adj.* unbeseelt, unbelebt; leblos
inapt *adj.* ungeeignet; ungeschickt
inarticulate *adj.* (zool.) gliederlos; (fig.) sinnlos, sprachlos; ungegliedert
inasmuch *adv.* insofern; insoweit
inaudible *adj.* unhörbar
inaugural *adj.* Antritts-, Einweihungs-
inaugurate *v.* feierlich einführen; einweihen; ins Leben rufen
inauguration *n.* Einweihung; Einsetzung, Einführung
inborn *adj.* angeboren, natürlich; eingeboren, ererbt
incalculable *adj.* unberechenbar, unmessbar
incandescent *adj.* erglühend, weissglühend; — **light** Glühlicht
incantation *n.* Beschwörung; Zauberformel; Entzücken
incapable *adj.* unfähig, ungeeignet
incapacitate *v.* unfähig machen, ausser Gefecht setzen
incarcerate *v.* einkerkern, einsperren
incarnation *n.* Fleischwerdung
incase *v.* einschliessen, umschliessen
incendiary *n.* Brandstifter; Aufwiegler, Aufhetzer; — **bomb** Brandbombe; — *adj.* brandstiftend; aufreizend
incense *n.* Weihrauch; — *v.* erregen, erzürnen, aufbringen; beweihräuchern, durchduften
incentive *n.* Ansporn, Antrieb; — *adj.* anfeuernd, antreibend
inception *n.* Beginn
incessant *adj.* unaufhörlich, unablässig; beständig
incest *n.* Inzest, Blutschande
inch *n.* Zoll; (fig.) Kleinigkeit; **every** — jeder Zoll, durch und durch; — *v.* zollweise vorrücken (*or* zurückweichen)
incident *n.* Ereignis, Vorfall; — *adj.* zufällig, beiläufig; vorkommend; abhängig; einfallend; **-al** *adj.* gelegentlich, nebensächlich; **-ally** *adv.* nebenbei; übrigens
incinerate *v.* einäschern
incinerator *n.* Verbrennungsofen
incipient *adj.* anfangend, beginnend; einleitend
incision *n.* Einschnitt, Schnitt
incisive *adj.* (ein)schneidend, scharf
incisor *n.* Schneidezahn
incite *v.* anspornen, anstacheln, anregen
inclement *adj.* unfreundlich, rauh
inclination *n.* Neigung; (fig.) Hang, Lust
incline *n.* Abhang, Abdachung; — *v.* (sich) neigen; geneigt sein; **-ed** *adj.* geneigt, aufgelegt; **-ed plane** schiefe Ebene
inclose *v.* einschliessen, umgeben; (letter) beifügen
inclosure *n.* Einzäunung; Einschliessung; (letter) Einlage, Beilage
include *v.* einschliessen, umfassen, enthalten; **-d** *adj.* eingeschlossen, einschliesslich
inclusion *n.* Einschliessung
inclusive *adj.* einschliessend, umschliessend; einschliesslich
incognito *n.* Inkognito; — *adj.* inkognito,

unbekannt, unerkannt
incoherent *adj.* zusammenhanglos; unzusammenhängend; inkonsequent; locker, lose
incombustible *adj.* unverbrennlich, nicht entflammbar
income *n.* Einkommen, Ertrag; — **tax** Einkommensteuer
incoming *adj.* neu eintretend; ankommend, eintreffend
incommensurable *adj.* unmessbar, unvergleichbar
incommutable *adj.* unvertauschbar
incomparable *adj.* unvergleichlich
incompatible *adj.* unvereinbar; unverträglich
incompetence *n.* Unfähigkeit, Untauglichkeit; Unzulänglichkeit; Unzuständigkeit
incompetent *adj.* unbefugt, unzuständig; unfähig; unzulänglich
incomplete *adj.* unvollständig, unvollendet, unvollkommen
incomprehensible *adj.* unbegreiflich, unverständlich
inconceivable *adj.* unfassbar, unbegreiflich
incongruous *adj.* unangemessen, unpassend; widersinnig
inconsequential *adj.* inkonsequent, folgewidrig
inconsiderate *adj.* unbedacht, unbedachtsam, unüberlegt; rücksichtslos
inconsistent *adj.* inkonsequent, unvereinbar, widersprechend; ungereimt, absurd
inconspicuous *adj.* unauffällig, unmerklich
inconstant *adj.* unbeständig, wechselnd
inconvenience *n.* Unbequemlichkeit, Ungelegenheit; — *v.* belästigen, lästig fallen
inconvenient *adj.* unbequem, lästig, störend; **at a most** — **time** zu sehr ungelegener Zeit
incorporate *v.* vereinigen, vermischen; verkörpern, einverleiben; — *adj.* verkörpert, einverleibt
incorporation *n.* Vereinigung, Vermischung; Einverleibung
incorrect *adj.* unrichtig, ungenau, falsch
incorrigible *adj.* unverbesserlich
incorruptible *adj.* unbestechlich
increase *n.* Zunahme, Wachstum; Vergrösserung, Vermehrung, Steigerung, Zuwachs; — *v.* wachsen, vermehren; zunehmen; vergrössern
increasing *adv.* mehr und mehr, in zunehmendem Masse
incredible *adj.* unglaublich
incredulity *n.* Ungläubigkeit, Unglaube, Skeptizismus
incredulous *adj.* ungläubig, skeptisch
incriminate *v.* beschuldigen, belasten
incubation *n.* Brüten; (med.) Inkubation
incubator *n.* Brutofen, Brutapparat
incumbent *n.* Amtsinhaber, Beamte; — *adj.* aufliegend; obliegend; **be** — **on** obliegen
incur *v.* sich zuziehen, auf sich laden; — **debts** Schulden machen

incurable *adj.* unheilbar

indebted *adj.* verschuldet, verpflichtet; I'm — to you for everything ich verdanke Ihnen alles; **-ness** *n.* Verschuldung, Verpflichtung

indecency *n.* Unziemlichkeit, Unschicklichkeit, Unanständigkeit

indecent *adj.* unziemlich, unschicklich; unanständig, obszön

indecision *n.* Unentschlossenheit, Unschlüssigkeit

indecisive *adj.* unentschlossen, schwankend; ungewiss, unentschieden

indeed *adv.* wirklich, allerdings; zwar; freilich; yes —! ja gewiss!

indefinite *adj.* unbestimmt, unentschieden; unbeschränkt, unbegrenzt

indelible *adj.* unauslöschlich, unvertilgbar

indemnity *n.* Sicherstellung; Entschädigung; (pol.) nachträgliche Genehmigung; — bond sichergestellte Schuldverschreibung

indent *v.* auszacken, einkerben; (law) einen Vertrag abschliessen; **-ation** *n.* Auszackung, Einschnitt; **-ure** *n.* Vertrag, Kontrakt

independence *n.* Unabhängigkeit; **Independence Day** Tag der Unabhängigkeitserklärung

independent *adj.* unabhängig, ungebunden, selbständig

indescribable *adj.* unbeschreiblich, unbeschreibbar

indestructible *adj.* unzerstörbar

indeterminable *adj.* unbestimmbar

index *n.* Index, Register, Verzeichnis; (math.) Exponent; — **finger** Zeigefinger; — *v.* registrieren, einordnen, mit einem Inhaltsverzeichnis versehen

India *n.* Indien

indicate *v.* anzeigen, andeuten

indication *n.* Anzeige, Angabe; Anzeichen, Merkmal

indicative *adj.* anzeigend, andeutend; — *n.* Indikativ

indicator *n.* Anzeiger; (elec.) Indikator; (mech.) Anzeigevorrichtung

indict *v.* verklagen, belangen, anklagen; **-ment** *n.* Anklage

indifference *n.* Gleichgültigkeit; Gleichmut

indifferent *adj.* gleichgültig, indifferent; mittelmässig; schlecht; unwesentlich

indigenous *adj.* eingeboren, einheimisch

indigent *adj.* bedürftig, arm

indigestible *adj.* unverdaulich

indigestion *n.* Verdauungsschwäche, Verdauungsstörung; Unverdaulichkeit

indignant *adj.* unwillig, indigniert, entrüstet

indignation *n.* Unwille, Entrüstung, Indignation

indignity *n.* Unwürdigkeit; Beleidigung, Beschimpfung

indirect *adj.* indirekt, mittelbar

indiscreet *adj.* indiskret, taktlos

indiscretion *n.* Indiskretion, Vertrauensbruch, Taktlosigkeit

indiscriminate *adj.* unterschiedslos, wahllos

indispensable *adj.* unerlässlich, unentbehrlich

indisposed *adj.* unpässlich, indisponiert; abgeneigt

indisposition *n.* Unpässlichkeit, Indisposition

indisputable *adj.* unbestreitbar

indistinct *adj.* undeutlich; verworren, unklar

indistinguishable *adj.* ununterscheidbar, ohne Rangunterschied

individual *n.* Individuum, Einzelwesen; — *adj.* individuell, persönlich, eigentümlich; **-ism** *n.* Individualismus; Selbstsucht; **-ity** *n.* Individualität, Eigentümlichkeit

indivisible *adj.* unteilbar, unzertrennlich

indoctrinate *v.* unterrichten, unterweisen

indolence *n.* Trägheit, Lässigkeit

indolent *adj.* indolent, träge, lässig; schlaff

indomitable *adj.* unbezwingbar, standhaft, unbezähmbar

indoor *adv.* drinnen; **-s** im Hause, zu Hause; Haus-, Zimmer-

indorse *v.* indossieren, giriren, begeben; bestätigen, annehmen; **-ment** *n.* Indossament, Giro, Übertragung; Genehmigung; **-r** *n.* Indossant, Girant

indubitable *adj.* unzweifelhaft, zweifellos

induce *v.* veranlassen, bestimmen; überreden; (elec. and phil.) induzieren; **-ment** *n.* Veranlassung, Anlass; Beweggrund; Reizmittel

induct *v.* einführen, einweihen, einsetzen; **-ion** *n.* Einführung, Einsetzung; (elec. and phil.) Induktion; **-ion coil** Induktionsrolle; **-ive** *adj.* bewegend, verleitend; erzeugend, veranlassend; (elec. and phil.) induktiv, Induktions-

indulge *v.* nachsichtig sein, schonend behandeln; gewähren; — in something sich einer Sache hingeben, einer Sache frönen; **-nce** *n.* Nachsicht, Schonung; Nachgiebigkeit; Sichgehenlassen, Zügellosigkeit; (rel.) Ablass; **-nt** *adj.* nachsichtig, schonend; mild

industrial *adj.* industriell, gewerbetreibend, Gewerbe-; **-ism** *n.* Gewerbetätigkeit; Industrialismus; **-ist** *n.* Industrielle

industrious *adj.* fleissig, betriebsam

industry *n.* Industrie; Fleiss, Betriebsamkeit; Gewerbe

ineffable *adj.* unaussprechlich

ineffective *adj.* unwirksam, fruchtlos; unfähig

inefficiency *n.* Unwirksamkeit, Untüchtigkeit

inefficient *adj.* untüchtig, unwirksam

ineligible *adj.* unwählbar; dienstuntauglich

inept *adj.* abgeschmackt, albern, unpassend; **-itude** *n.* Abgeschmacktheit, Albernheit

inequality *n.* Ungleichheit; Missverhältnis

inequitable *adj.* ungerecht, unbillig

inertial guidance *n.* Trägheitssteuerung

inescapable adj. unentrinnbar

inevitable adj. unvermeidlich

inexact adj. ungenau

inexcusable adj. unentschuldbar, unverzeihlich; unverantwortlich

inexhaustible adj. unerschöpflich

inexpedient adj. unzweckmässig, unpassend

inexpensive adj. billig, wohlfeil

inexperienced adj. unerfahren

inexplicable adj. unerklärlich, unverständlich

infallible adj. unfehlbar, untrüglich, sicher, zuverlässig

infamous adj. ehrlos, entehrend; verrufen, berüchtigt; infam

infamy n. Ehrlosigkeit, Schande; Infamie, Schändlichkeit, Niedertracht

infancy n. Kindheit, Kindesalter; (law) Unmündigkeit, Minderjährigkeit

infant n. Kind; Säugling; (law) Unmündige; — adj. kindlich, jugendlich, jung; unentwickelt; **-icide** n. Kindesmord, Kindermord; Kindermörder; **-ile** adj. kindlich, infantil; **-ile paralysis** Kinderlähmung

infantry n. Infanterie, Fussvolk

infatuation n. Betörung, Verblendung; Vernarrtheit

infect v. infizieren, anstecken; **-ion** n. Infektion, Infizierung, Ansteckung; **-ious** adj. ansteckend; Ansteckungs-

infer v. folgern, schliessen; **-ence** n. Folgerung, Schluss

inferior adj. untergeordnet, niedriger, minderwertig; **of — quality** von minderwertiger Beschaffenheit, von geringer Qualität; **-ity** n. geringerer Wert; Minderwertigkeit, Inferiorität; **-ity complex** Minderwertigkeitskomplex

infernal adj. höllisch, teuflisch, infernalisch; Höllen-

infest v. überschwemmen; plagen, heimsuchen

infidel n. Ungläubige, Heide; — adj. ungläubig; **-ity** n. Treulosigkeit, Treubruch, Untreue; Unglaube, Ungläubigkeit

infield n. Innenfeld; **-er** n. Innenspieler

infiltrate v. eindringen; durchsickern; durchdringen

infiltration n. Infiltration; Durchsickern; Eindringen

infinite n. Unendlichkeit; — adj. unendlich, unbegrenzt; zahllos, ungeheuer

infinitesimal adj. unendlich klein; — **calculus** Infinitesimalrechnung, Differential und Integralrechnung

infinitive n. Infinitiv, Nennform

infinity n. Endlosigkeit, Unendlichkeit, Unbegrenztheit; unendliche Grösse (or Menge)

infirm adj. schwach, unsicher; nicht gebrechlich, kraftlos; **-ary** n. Krankenstube; Krankenhaus, Hospital; **-ity** n. Schwäche, Schwachheit; Gebrechen; Gebrechlichkeit

inflame v. (sich) entflammen; (med.) (sich) entzünden

inflammable adj. entzündlich, feuergefährlich

inflammation n. Entzündung

inflammatory adj. erhitzend, aufregend; entflammend; aufrührerisch, hetzerisch; Hetz-; (med.) entzündlich

inflate v. aufblasen, aufblähen; künstlich steigern

inflation n. Aufblähung; Aufgeblasenheit; (money) Inflation

inflection n. Biegung, Krümmung; (gram.) Beugung; (voice) Modulation

inflexible adj. unbiegsam, unveränderlich, unbeugsam

inflict v. auferlegen, verhängen; zufügen; **-ion** n. Auferlegung, Verhängung; Zufügung; Strafe, Plage

influence n. Einfluss, Einwirkung; — v. einwirken auf, beeinflussen

influential adj. einflussreich

influenza n. Grippe, Influenza

influx n. Zufliessen, Einströmen; Zufluss, Zustrom; Zufuhr

infold v. einhüllen, umschliessen

inform v. benachrichtigen, informieren, unterrichten, in Kenntnis setzen; — **against** denunzieren, angeben; **-ant** n. Benachrichtiger, Berichterstatter; Gewährsmann; **-ation** n. Auskunft, Benachrichtigung; Unterweisung; **-ation bureau** Auskunftsbüro; **-ation desk** Auskunft(sstand); **-ed** adj. benachrichtigt, informiert, belehrt; **-er** n. Denunziant, Angeber

informal adj. unzeremoniell; formlos; regelwidrig; **-ality** n. Formlosigkeit; Regelwidrigkeit

infraction n. Brechen, Bruch; Verletzung, Übertretung

infrared adj. infrarot

infrequent adj. ungewöhnlich, selten

infringe v. eingreifen, übergreifen; übertreten, verletzen; **-ment** n. Bruch, Verletzung; Übertretung

infuriate v. wütend machen

infusion n. Einflössung; Aufguss

ingenious adj. genial, begabt, erfinderisch; geistreich, sinnreich

ingenuity n. Scharfsinn, Genie, Geist, Begabung

ingenuous adj. freimütig, offenherzig, aufrichtig; unbefangen

ingot n. Barren, Block, Stange

ingrained adj. eingewurzelt, eingefleischt

ingrate n. Undankbare

ingratitude n. Undank(barkeit)

ingredient n. Bestandteil

ingrown adj. einwärts (or nach innen) wachsend; — **nail** eingewachsener Nagel

inhabit v. (be)wohnen; **-able** adj. bewohnbar; **-ant** n. Bewohner, Einwohner

inhalation n. Einatmung; (med.) Inhalation

inhale v. einatmen; (med.) inhalieren

inherent adj. anhaftend, angeboren, eigen; innewohnend

inherit v. (be)erben; **-ance** n. Erbschaft, Erbe, Erbgut, Erbteil; (fig.) Vererbung; **-ance tax** Erbschaftssteuer

inhibit r. zurückhalten, hemmen, hindern.
Einhalt gebieten, verbieten; **–ion** n.
Verhinderung, Hemmung, Verbot

inhospitable adj. ungastlich, unwirtlich

inhuman adj. unmenschlich; **–ity** n. Un-
menschlichkeit

inimitable adj. unnachahmbar, unnachahmlich

iniquity n. Unbilligkeit, Ungerechtigkeit;
Schlechtigkeit; Missetat

initial n. Anfangsbuchstabe, Initiale; —
adj. anfänglich, beginnend; Anfangs-;
— r. mit den Anfangsbuchstaben (eines
Namens) versehen

initiate r. einführen, einweihen; anfangen,
beginnen

initiation n. Einführung, Einweihung;
Einleitung, Beginn

initiative n. Initiative; einleitende Handlung; **take the** — den ersten Schritt
tun; — adj. einleitend, einführend

inject r. injizieren, einspritzen; einwerfen,
eingiessen; **–ion** n. Injektion, Einspritzung; — **pump** n. Einspritzpumpe

injunction n. Einschärfung, Vorschrift;
(law) gerichtliche Aufforderung, Verbot

injure r. schaden, beschädigen, verletzen;
beleidigen

injurious adj. schädlich, nachteilig

injury n. Schaden, Beschädigung, Verletzung; Unrecht; Beleidigung

injustice n. Ungerechtigkeit, Unrecht

ink n. Tinte; — **blot** Tintenkleks; **India** —
Tusche; **printer's** — Druckerschwärze;
— v. mit Tinte beschmieren, beflecken;
–y adj. tint(enart)ig; Tinten-; (fig.)
dunkel

inkling n. Andeutung, Gemunkel; Ahnung

inkpad n. Stempelkissen

inkstand, inkwell n. Tintenfass; Schreib-
zeug

inlaid adj. eingelegt, getäfelt

inlay n. Furnierholz; Einlegearbeit; **gold**
— Goldeinlegearbeit; — r. einlegen,
furnieren, täfeln, Parkett legen

inmate n. Insasse, Mitbewohner; Hausgenosse

inmost adj. innerst; geheimst, verborgenst

inn n. Gasthof, Wirtshaus, Herberge

innate adj. angeboren, natürlich; eigen

inner adj. inner, inwendig; innerlich; —
tube Luftschlauch

innermost adj. innerst

inning n. Spielabschnitt; Dransein

innkeeper n. Gastwirt

innocence n. Unschuld, Schuldlosigkeit;
Harmlosigkeit; Einfalt

innocent adj. unschuldig, schuldlos; unschädlich, harmlos

innovation n. Neuerung

innumerable adj. unzählbar, unzählig;
zahllos

inoculate r. (hort.) okulieren, propfen;
(med.) (ein)impfen

inoculation n. (hort.) Okulieren; (med.)
Impfen, Impfung; (fig.) Einimpfung

inoffensive adj. unschädlich, arglos,harm-
los

inopportune adj. ungelegen, unzeitig

inorganic adj. unorganisch, unbelebt

inquest n. gerichtliche Untersuchung;
amtliche Leichenschau

inquire v. (nach)fragen, sich erkundigen;
erfragen, erforschen; **–r** n. Untersuchende, Nachfragende

inquiry n. Untersuchung; Anfrage, Nachfrage, Erkundigung; Forschung

inquisitive adj. neugierig, wissbegierig;
nachspürend; **–ness** n. Neugier, Wissbegierde

inquisitor n. Inquisitor; Untersuchende;
(law) Untersuchungsrichter

inroad n. Einfall, Beutezug, Streifzug;
(fig.) Übergriff, Anmassung

insane adj. wahnsinnig, irre, verrückt; —
asylum Irrenhaus, Irrenanstalt

insanity n. Wahnsinn, Geistesstörung,
Irrsinn, Verrücktheit

inscribe v. einschreiben, aufschreiben;
eintragen, aufzeichnen

inscription n. Inschrift, Aufschrift; Ein-
schreibung, Eintragung; Widmung

insect n. Insekt, Kerbtier; Ungeziefer;
— **poison** Insektengift; — **powder** In-
sektenpulver; **–icide** n. Insektenver-
tilgungsmittel

insecure adj. unsicher, ungewiss

insecurity n. Unsicherheit, Ungewissheit

insensibility n. Gefühllosigkeit, Empfin-
dungslosigkeit; Unempfindlichkeit, Be-
wusstlosigkeit; Gleichgültigkeit

insensible adj. gefühllos, empfindungslos;
unempfindlich; unmerklich; bewusstlos

inseparable adj. unzertrennlich, untrennbar

insert r. einlegen, einfügen, einsetzen; ein-
rücken; inserieren; **–ion** n. Inserat,
Anzeige; Einfügung, Einschaltung;
Eintragung

inset n. Einsatz; Einlage, Beilage

inside n. Innere; Innenseite; (fig.) In-
nerste, Wesentlichste; — **out** nach
aussen gekehrt; verkehrt; pl. Inneres,
Eingeweide; **on the** — drinnen; **toward
the** — nach innen gerichtet; — adj.
inner, inwendig; — adv. innen, drinnen;
— prep. innerhalb; **–r** n. Eingeweihte

insight n. Einblick, Einsicht; Scharfsinn

insignia n. Insignien, Abzeichen; Kennzeichen

insignificance n. Bedeutungslosigkeit; Geringfügigkeit; Verächtlichkeit

insignificant adj. unbedeutend, geringfügig, unwichtig; bedeutungslos

insincere adj. unaufrichtig, falsch;
täuschend

insincerity n. Unaufrichtigkeit; Falschheit; Täuschung

insinuate v. zu verstehen geben, andeuten
sich einschmeicheln

insinuation n. Einflüsterung, Ein-
schmeichlung; Anspielung, Andeutung;

insipid adj. geschmacklos, unschmackhaft

insist v. bestehen, beharren; hervorheben,
betonen; **–ence** n. Bestehen, Beharrlichkeit; Betonung, Hervorhebung;
–ent adj. hartnäckig, beharrend, beharrlich; eindringlich

insole n. Brandsohle, Einlegesohle

insolence n. Frechheit, Unverschämtheit,

Anmassung

insolent *adj.* frech, unverschämt, anmassend

insoluble *adj.* unauflöslich

insolvent *adj.* zahlungsunfähig

insomnia *n.* Schlaflosigkeit

insomuch *adv.* dergestalt, dermassen; so sehr

inspect *v.* inspizieren, besichtigen; beaufsichtigen; untersuchen; **-ion** *n.* Inspektion; Beaufsichtigung; Untersuchung, Prüfung; **tour of** — Inspektionsreise; **-or** *n.* Inspektor, Inspekteur, Aufseher

inspiration *n.* Inspiration, Eingebung; Begeisterung; (med.) Einatmung

inspire *v.* inspirieren, begeistern; inhalieren, einatmen; einhauchen

instability *n.* Unbeständigkeit, Wankelmütigkeit

install *v.* einrichten, einbauen, installieren; bestallen, einsetzen, einführen; **-ation** *n.* Installation,- Einrichtung; Bestallung, Einsetzung, Einführung

instal(l)ment *n.* Rate, Teilzahlung; Fortsetzung

instance *n.* Beispiel, Fall; Instanz; **for** — zum Beispiel

instant *n.* Augenblick, Moment, Nu; — *adj.* gegenwärtig, unmittelbar; augenblicklich, momentan; dringend, laufend; **on the 20th** — am 20. des laufenden Monats; **-ly** *adv.* sogleich, augenblicklich; **-aneous** *adj.* augenblicklich, unverzüglich, im Nu geschehend

instead *adv.* stattdessen, dafür; — **of** (an)statt

instep *n.* Spann, Rist

instigate *v.* aufreizen, antreiben; anstiften, hetzen

instigation *n.* Anstiftung, Aufhetzung; Antrieb

instil(l) *v.* einträpfeln, einträufeln; (fig.) einflössen, einprägen

instinct *n.* Instinkt, Naturtrieb; — *adj.* angeregt, belebt; erfüllt; **-ive** *adj.* unwillkürlich, instinktiv

institute *n.* Institute, Anstalt; — *v.* einrichten, errichten, einsetzen; verordnnen

institution *n.* Anstalt, Institut, Institution; Einrichtung; Anordnung

instruct *v.* lehren, unterrichten, erziehen, unterweisen; **-ion** *n.* Unterricht, Belehrung, Instruktion; Anweisung, Gebrauchsanweisung; **-ive** *adj.* lehrreich, belehrend, instruktiv; **-or** *n.* Lehrer, Unterweiser, Instrukteur

instrument *n.* Instrument; Werkzeug; Gerät, apparat, Vorrichtung; (law) Urkunde, Dokument; — **approach** (avi.) Anpeilung zur Landung, Blindanflug; — **board** Armaturenbrett; — **flight** Blindflug; — *v.* instrumentieren; **-al** *adj.* dienlich, förderlich, behilflich

insubordinate *adj.* unterwürfig

insubordination *n.* Ungehorsam

insufferable *adj.* unerträglich, unleidlich

insufficient *adj.* ungenügend, unzulänglich; untauglich; — **evidence** unzulänglicher Beweis

insular *adj.* insular, inselartig, Insel-; isoliert, alleinstehend; unduldsam

insulate *v.* isolieren, absondern

insulation *n.* Isolierung, Absonderung, Vereinzelung

insulator *n.* Isolator, Nichtleiter

insulin *n.* Insulin

insult *n.* Beleidigung, Beschimpfung; — *v.* beschimpfen, beleidigen

insupportable *adj.* unerträglich, unausstehlich

insurance *n.* Versicherung; — **agent** Versicherungsagent; — **broker** Versicherungsmakler; — **policy** Versicherungspolice; — **premium** Versicherungsprämie; **accident** — Unfallversicherung; **burglary** — Einbruchversicherung; **fire** — Feuerversicherung; **life** — Lebensversicherung

insure *v.* versichern, verbürgen

insurgent *n.* Aufständische, Aufrührer, Insurgent; — *adj.* aufrührerisch

insurrection *n.* Aufstand, Aufruhr; Empörung

intact *adj.* unberührt, unversehrt, unverletzt, intakt

intake *n.* Einmündung, Einlass; Einlauf; Einnahme

intangible *adj.* unberührbar; unfühlbar; unfassbar

integer *n.* Ganze; ganze Zahl

integrate *v.* vervollständigen, ergänzen; (math.) integrieren, ergänzen

integrity *n.* Ganzheit, Vollständigkeit; (fig.) Redlichkeit, Unbescholtenheit

intellect *n.* Intellekt, Verstand, Urteilskraft; **-ual** *n.* Intellektuelle; **-ual** *adj.* intellektuell, vernünftig, urteilsfähig; Verstandes-

intelligence *n.* Intelligenz, Verstand; Einsicht; (mil.) Nachricht, Auskunft; — **test** Intelligenztest, Intelligenzprüfung

intelligent *adj.* intelligent, verständig, gescheit, einsichtsvoll; **-sia** *n.* Intelligenz

intelligible *adj.* verständlich, fasslich; deutlich

intemperate *adj.* masslos, unmässig; ausschweifend

intend *v.* beabsichtigen, vorhaben; wollen; **-ant** *n.* Verwalter, Vorsteher; (theat.) Intendant

intense *adj.* intensiv, heftig, stark; angestrengt, angespannt

intensify *v.* (sich) verstärken, steigern, intensiver werden

intensity *n.* Stärke, Grad; Heftigkeit; Intensität, Spannung

intensive *adj.* intensiv, heftig, stark; verstärkend; angespannt

intent *adj.* gespannt, aufmerksam; eifrig, bedacht, erpicht; — *n.* Absicht, Vorhaben, Plan; **-ion** *n.* Absicht, Intention, Vorsatz; Zweck; **-ional** *adj.* absichtlich, vorsätzlich

inter *v.* beerdigen, begraben

intercede *v.* vermitteln, sich verwenden, Fürsprache einlegen

intercept *v.* abfangen, auffangen; hindern, aufhalten, unterbrechen; (rad.) abhören, mithören; **-or** *n.* Auffänger; **-or**

missile n. Abwehrrakete; **—or plane** Jagdflugzeug

intercession n. Dazwischentreten, Vermittlung, Fürbitte

interchange n. Austausch, Abwechslung; Tauschhandel; — v. austauschen, vertauschen; abwechseln; **-able** adj. austauschbar, auswechselbar

intercollegiate adj. zwischen den Hochschulen

intercom n. Wechselseitiger Verkehr

intercourse n. Verkehr, Umgang; Verbindung

interdenominational adj. zwischen den Religionen

interdepartmental adj. zwischen den Abteilungen

interdependence n. gegenseitige Abhängigkeit

interdict v. verbieten, untersagen

interest n. Interesse, Anteilnahme; Zins; Vorteil, Nutzen; Anrecht, Anteil; **compound — Zinseszins; rate of — Zinsfuss;** — v. interessieren; **be —ed in** sich interessieren für, Anteil nehmen an; **-ing** adj. interessant, anziehend, fesselnd

interfere v. sich einmischen; dazwischenkommen; dazwischentreten, einschreiten; **-nce** n. Einmischung, Einspruch; Dazwischentreten; (phys.) Interferenz; (rad.) Störung

interhemispheric adj. zwischen östlicher und westlicher Hemisphäre

interim n. Interimszeit, Zwischenzeit

interior n. Innere, Inwendige; Inland, Binnenland; — adj. inner, innerlich; inländisch, binnenländisch

interject v. dazwischenwerfen, einschieben, einschalten; n. (gram.) Ausruf; (fig.) Dazwischenwerfen, Einschieben

interlace v. durchflechten, durchweben; sich kreuzen

interlock v. ineinanderschliessen, ineinandergreifen; verschränken

interloper n. Eindringling

interlude n. Zwischenspiel; Unterbrechung

intermarriage n. Mischehe

intermarry v. untereinander heiraten

intermeddle v. sich einmischen

intermediary n. Vermittler, Zwischenhändler; — adj. vermittelnd

intermediate n. Vermittelnde; — adj. vermittelnd, Zwischen-, Mittel-

interment n. Beerdigung, Bestattung

interminable adj. grenzenlos, unendlich

intermingle v. (sich) vermischen

intermission n. Pause; Unterbrechung, Aussetzen

intermittent adj. zeitweilig aussetzend, ruckweise

intern v. internieren; **-ment** n. Internierung

intern(e) n. Hospitant, Assistenzarzt; **-ship** n. Hospitantenschaft, Hospitieren (in Krankenhäusern)

internal adj. inner, innerlich

international adj. international

interplanetary adj. zwischenplanetarisch; interplanetar

interpolate v. einschalten; einschieben

interpret v. deuten, interpretieren, auslegen; verdolmetschen, übersetzen; **-ation** n. Auslegung, Erklärung, Interpretation; (art) Auffassung; (theat.) Rollenwiedergabe; **-er** n. Dolmetscher

interrelated adj. gegenseitig verknüpft

interrogate v. verhören, förmlich befragen

interrogation n. Verhör, Fragen, Befragen; — **point** Fragezeichen

interrupt v. unterbrechen, stören; **-ion** n. Unterbrechung, Störung; Hemmung, Pause

interscholastic adj. zwischen den Schulen

intersect v. sich schneiden (or kreuzen); **-ion** n. Durchschneiden, Schnitt; (math.) Schnittpunkt; (rail.) Kreuzung

interspace n. Zwischenraum

intersperse v. dazwischensetzen, einstreuen, einmengen; untermengen

interstate adj. zwischenstaatlich

intertwine v. (sich) verflechten, ineinanderschlingen

interurban adj. zwischen den Städten

interval n. Zwischenraum, Abstand, Intervall; **at —s** in Abständen

intervene v. dazwischenkommen, intervenieren; einschreiten; vermitteln

intervention n. Dazwischenkunft, Einmischung; Vermittlung

interview n. Interview, Unterredung, Befragung; Zusammenkunft; **-er** n. Interviewer, Befrager

interwoven adj. durchflochten, ineinandergewebt

intestinal adj. die Eingeweide betreffend; Eingeweide-, Darm-

intestines n. pl. Eingeweide

intimacy n. Vertraulichkeit, Innigkeit

intimate n. Vertraute, Busenfreund; — adj. innig, vertraut, intim, eng; — v. andeuten, zu verstehen geben

intimation n. Andeutung, Fingerzeig

intimidate v. einschüchtern, furchtsam machen

intimidation n. Einschüchterung

into prep. in, auf, zu

intolerable adj. unerträglich, unausstehlich

intolerant adj. intolerant, unduldsam

intonation n. Intonation, Tongebung; Modulation; Ausdruck, Tonfall, Betonung

intoxicant n. Rauschmittel

intoxicate v. betrunken machen, berauschen

intoxication n. Rausch, Berauschung, Trunkenheit

intramural adj. innerhalb der Mauern befindlich; (anat.) innerorganisch

intransitive adj. intransitiv

intrench v. eingraben, verschanzen

intrepid adj. unerschrocken, beherzt

intricate adj. verwickelt, schwierig

intrigue n. Intrige, Truggewebe, Arglist, Ränke; — v. intrigieren, Ränke schmieden

introduce v. vorstellen, einführen, bekanntmachen; einleiten

introduction n. Einführung, Einleitung; Vorstellung, Bekanntmachen
introductory adj. einleitend
introvert n. Introvert, Nachinnengekehrte; — adj. introvertiert
intrude v. (sich) eindrängen, (sich) aufdrängen; stören; **-r** n. Eindringling, Zudringliche; Störenfried; ungebetener Gast
intrusion n. Eindrängen, Aufdrängen; Zudringlichkeit; (law) Besitzentziehung
intrust v. anvertrauen, betrauen
intuition n. Intuition, Anschauung, unmittelbare Erkenntnis
intuitive adj. intuitiv, unmittelbar erkennend
inundate v. überschwemmen
inundation n. Überschwemmung
invade v. einfallen, überfallen; **-r** n. Eindringling, Angreifer
invalid n. Invalide, Kranke; — adj. kränklich; invalide, dienstunfähig; ungültig; **-ate** v. ungültig machen; (ab)schwächen, entkräften
invaluable adj. unschätzbar
invariable adj. unveränderlich, beständig
invasion n. Invasion, Einfall, Angriff, Eingriff; (med.) Anfall
inveigh v. schimpfen, schmähen
inveigle v. verleiten, verlocken, verführen
invent v. erfinden, erdenken, erdichten; **-ion** n. Erfindung; Erdichtung, Lüge; **-ive** adj. erfindungsreich, erfinderisch; sinnreich; **-or** n. Erfinder, Urheber; Erdichter
inventory n. Inventar; Bestand; Verzeichnis; — v. Inventur aufnehmen
inverse adj. umgekehrt, entgegengesetzt
invert v. umkehren, umwenden; (gram. and mus.) umkehren; **-er** n. Gleichstrom-Wechselstrom Transformator
invest v. anlegen, investieren; bekleiden; **-ment** n. Anlage, Investierung
investigate v. erforschen, untersuchen, nachforschen
investigation n. Untersuchung; Forschung
investigator n. Untersuchende; Forscher
inveterate adj. eingewurzelt, hartnäckig
invigorate v. kräftigen, stärken, beleben
invincible adj. unbesiegbar, unüberwindlich
invisible adj. unsichtbar
invitation n. Einladung; Aufforderung; (fig.) Lockung
invite v. einladen, auffordern; herbeilocken; herausfordern
inviting adj. einladend, lockend, anziehend
invoice n. Rechnung; Frachtbrief; — **book** Rechnungsbuch; **pro forma** fingierte Rechnung; — v. in Rechnung stellen
invoke v. anrufen, anflehen; beschwören; (law) aufrufen
involuntary adj. unwillkürlich, unfreiwillig
involve v. verwickeln, einwickeln; in sich schliessen, enthalten; (fig.) verwirren; (math.) potenzieren
invulnerable adj. unverwundbar; unanfechtbar

inward adj. inner(lich); — adv. einwärts, nach innen
iodine n. Jod
ion n. Ion; **-ization** n. Ionisierung
iota n. Jota; Tüttelchen
irascible adj. reizbar, jähzornig
irate adj. zornig, wütend; gereizt
IRBM (intermediate range ballistic missile) n. Fernlenkgeschoss mittlerer Reichweite
ire n. Zorn
Ireland n. Irland
iris n. Regenbogen; (anat.) Iris, Regenbogenhaut; (bot.) Schwertlilie
irk v. ermüden, verdriessen; schmerzen; **-some** adj. ermüdend, lästig; beschwerlich
iron n. Eisen; Bügeleisen; pl. Fesseln; — **age** Eisenzeit; **angle** — Winkeleisen; **black** — Schwarzblech; Winkeleisen; **cast** — Gusseisen; **galvanized sheet** — verzinktes Eisenblech; — **lung** eiserne Lunge; **pig** — Roheisen; **white** — Weissblech; **wrought** — Schmiedeeisen; — adj. eisern; (fig.) unerschütterlich, hart; — **curtain** eiserne Vorhang; — **lung** eiserne Lunge; — **ration** eiserne Ration; — v. bügeln, plätten; — **out** in Ordnung bringen; **-ing** n. Plätten, Bügeln; **-ing board** Plättbrett, Bügelbrett
ironclad adj. gepanzert; (fig.) festgefügt
ironic(al) adj. ironisch, spöttisch
ironware n. Eisenware
ironworks n. pl. Eisenhütte, Eisengiesserei
irony n. Ironie, Spöttelei; Spottrede
irradiate v. bestrahlen, bescheinen, beleuchten; (fig.) erleuchten; strahlen machen
irrational adj. irrational, unberechenbar; unvernünftig, unsinnig
irreconcilable adj. unversöhnlich; unvereinbar
irrecoverable adj. unersetzlich, unwiederbringlich (verloren)
irredeemable adj. nicht tilgbar, nicht kündbar; nicht einlösbar; unverbesserlich
irregular adj. unregelmässig, regelwidrig; unrichtig; **-ity** n. Unregelmässigkeit, Regelwidrigkeit; Unrichtigkeit
irrelevant adj. unerheblich, belanglos; (law) nicht zur Sache gehörend
irremovable adj. nicht entfernbar; unabsetzbar
irreparable adj. unersetzlich; nicht wieder gutzumachen
irrepressible adj. unbezähmbar, ununterdrückbar
irreproachable adj. tadellos, unsträflich, vorwurfsfrei
irresistible adj. unwiderstehlich
irresolute adj. unentschlossen, unschlüssig, schwankend
irrespective prep. — of ohne Rücksicht auf, rücksichtslos gegen; unabhängig von
irresponsible adj. unverantwortlich
irreverent adj. unehrerbietig
irrigate v. bewässern, befeuchten; be-

rieseln

irrigation n. Bewässerung, Berieselung; — **canal** Berieselungskanal

irritable adj. reizbar, erregbar

irritant n. Reizmittel

irritate v. reizen, aufbringen; irritieren; (med.) entzünden

irritation n. Aufregung, Erregung; (med.) Reizung, Entzündung

irruption n. Einbruch, Einfall

isinglas n. Fischleim, Hausenblase

island n. Insel, Eiland; **-er** n. Insulaner, Inselbewohner

isle n. Insel, Eiland

isobar n. Linie gleichen Luftdruckes

isolate v. absondern, isolieren

isolation n. Abgesondertheit; Isolierung; **-ist** n. Isolationist

isosceles adj. gleichschenklig

isothermal adj. gleichtemperiert; gleichwarm

issuance n. Ausgabe

issue n. Nummer, Ausgabe; Folge, Resultat, Ergebnis; (law) Streitfrage; Nachkommenschaft; **avoid the —** der Frage ausweichen; **that's not the —** darum handelt es sich nicht; — v. (her)ausgeben

it pron. es

Italy n. Italien

itch n. Jucken; (med.) Krätze; (fig.) Verlangen, Begierde; — v. jucken; (fig.) darauf brennen; **-y** adj. juckend; krätzig

item n. Einzelheit, Punkt, Gegenstand, Posten; **-ize** v. einzeln aufzählen (or notieren)

itinerant adj. umherreisend, umherwandernd, umherziehend

itinerary n. Reisebeschreibung, Reisehandbuch; Reiseplan

its pron. sein(er); dessen, deren

itself pron. (es) selbst, sich; **by —** für sich allein, besonders; **in —** an sich

ivory n. Elfenbein; Elfenbeinfarbe; — adj. elfenbeinern, elfenbeinartig

ivy n. Efeu

J

jab n. Stich, Stoss, Schlag; (boxing) gerader Linke; — v. stechen, stossen, schlagen; (boxing) gerade (links) schlagen

jabber n. Geschnatter, Geplapper; — v. plappern, schnattern

jack n. (cards) Bube, Unter; (mech.) Wagenheber; Winde, Flaschenzug; (naut.) Matrose, Teerjacke; **— pot** Haupttreffer; **— rabbit** rammler; — v. **— up** aufschrauben; aufwinden

jackal n. Schakal

jackass n. Esel(shengst); (fig.) Esel

jackdaw n. Dohle

jacket n. Jacke, Jackett, Wams, Rock; Mantel; (potato) Schale; **book —** Buchumschlag

jack-in-the-box n. Schachtelmännchen

jackknife n. Klappmesser, Taschenmesser

jack-of-all-trades n. Hans Dampf in allen Gassen; **be a —** sich mit allen möglichen Dingen beschäftigen

jack-o'-lantern n. Kürbislaterne; Irrlicht

jag n. Kerbe, Zacke, Scharte; Ladung Last; Portion; — v. kerben; (aus)zacken; **-ged** adj. gekerbt, gezähnt, schartig

jaguar n. Jaguar

jail n. Gefängnis, Kerker; — v. einkerkern; **-er** n. Gefängniswärter, Kerkermeister

jailbird n. Galgenvogel, Zuchthäusler

jalopy n. alter Kasten

jam n. Marmelade; (coll.) Gedränge; Patsche, Klemme; — v. drücken, pressen; verklemmen, festsitzen; (rad.) stören

jamboree n. Pfadfindertreffen; laute Lustbarkeit

jangle n. Missklang, Gerassel; Lärm, Zänkerei; — v. zanken; misstönen, rasseln, schrillen

janitor n. Pförtner, Türsteher; Hausmeister

January n. Januar

jar n. Krug; Glas; Knarren; Misston, Misshelligkeit; — v. erzittern machen; misstönend berühren; in scharfem Gegensatz stehen

jargon n. Jargon, Kauderwelsch

jasmine n. Jasmin

jato (jet assisted take-off) n. Raketenstart

jaundice n. Gelbsucht

jaunt n. Wanderung, Ausflug

javelin n. Wurfspiess, Speer

jaw n. Kiefer, Kinnbacken

jawbone n. Kieferknochen, Kinnlade

jay n. Eichelhäher

jaywalk n. Fussgängerverkehssünde

jazz n. Jazz; **— band** Jazzorchester, Jazzkapelle

jealous adj. eifersüchtig; neidisch; misstrauisch; **be — of** eifersüchtig (or argwöhnisch) sein auf; **-y** n. Eifersucht, Neid; Misstrauen, Argwohn

jeans n. pl. Hosen aus blauem Baumwollköper

jeep n. Jeep

jeer n. Hohn, Spott; — v. (ver)höhnen, (ver)spotten

jelly n. Gelee; Gallert, Sülze

jellyfish n. Meduse, Qualle; (fig.) Schlappschwanz

jeopardize v. gefährden, aufs Spiel setzen

jerk n. Stoss, Ruck; (sl.) Kerl; — v. zucken; reissen; schnellen; **-y** adj. stossweise, sprungartig, krampfhaft

jersey n. Jersey; Wolljacke; feingekämmter Wollstoff

jest n. Witz, Scherz, Spass; — v. scherzen, spassen; **-er** n. Spassvogel, Possenreisser; (court) **-er** Hofnarr

Jesus Christ n. Jesus Christus

jet n. Wurf, Strahl; Röhre, Düse; **gas —** Gasflamme; Gashahn; **— plane** Düsenflugzeug; **-propulsion** Düsenantrieb; **— stream** Düsenstrahl

jet-propelled adj. mit Düsenantrieb

jettison v. über Bord werfen

Jew n. Jude; **Wandering —** ewige Jude;

-ish *adj.* jüdisch

jewel *n.* Edelstein, Juwel, Kleinod; *pl.* Geschmeide, Schmuck; **-er** *n.* Juwelier; **-ry** *n.* Schmuck, Juwelen, Juwelierarbeit

jibe *v.* umlegen, überholen; übergehen; (coll.) übereinstimmen

jiffy *n.* Augenblick, Nu

jig *n.* lustiger Tanz; — **saw** Wippsäge

jiggle *v.* hüpfen, wackeln; umherhüpfen

jigsaw puzzle *n.* Puzzlespiel

jilt *v.* täuschen; sitzen lassen

jingle *n.* Geklingel; — *v.* klingen, klingeln; klimpern; klirren

jingoist *n.* Chauvinist

jinx *n.* Unheilbringer; — *v.* Unheil bringen

jitterbug *n.* Jitterbug; Anhänger der Swingmusik

jitters *n.* Nervosität, Angst

jive *n.* Spelunke

job *n.* Arbeit, Stellung; Auftrag, Geschäft, Aufgabe; — **lot** Ramschware; — **work** Akkordarbeit; **-ber** *n.* Akkordarbeiter; Makler; **-less** *adj.* stellungslos, arbeitslos

jockey *n.* Jockey, Berufsreiter; — *v.* prellen, (be)gaunern; geschickt zu Werke gehen

jocular *adj.* scherzhaft

jocund *adj.* froh, heiter, lustig, munter

join *v.* verbinden, zusammenfügen; sich verbinden (*or* vereinigen, anschliessen), eintreten in; angrenzen, anstossen; **-er** *n.* Tischler, Zimmermann

joint *n.* (anat.) Gelenk; (geol.) Riss, Spalte; (meat) Lendenstück, Keule; (mech.) Scharnier, Fuge; (sl.) Spelunke; **throw out of** — sich verrenken; — *adj.* verbunden, vereinigt, gemeinsam; — **account** gemeinschaftliche Rechnung; — **heir** Miterbe; **-ly** *adv.* gemeinschaftlich

joke *n.* Witz, Scherz, Spass; **in** — scherzweise; **play a** — einen Witz reissen; **play a** — **on someone** jemandem einen Schabernack spielen; — *v.* scherzen, spassen; schäkern, necken; **-r** *n.* Spassmacher, Spassvogel; (cards) Joker

jollity *n.* Lustigkeit; Lustbarkeit

jolly *adj.* lustig, munter, fidel

jolt *n.* Stoss, Gerüttel; — *v.* stossen, schütteln, rütteln

jonquil *n.* Narzissenart, Binsennarzisse

jostle *v.* anstossen; wegstossen, fortstossen verdrängen

jot *n.* Jota; Pünktchen, Kleinigkeit; **not a** — nicht das Geringste; — *v.* — **down** schnell niederschreiben, kurz vermerken

journal *n.* Tagebuch; Journal; Tageblatt, Tageszeitung; (mech.) Zapfen; **-ism** *n.* Journalismus, Zeitungswesen; **-ist** *n.* Journalist, Zeitungsschreiber

journey *n.* Reise; — *v.* reisen, wandern

journeyman *n.* Geselle, Gehilfe

jovial *adj.* jovial, aufgeräumt; frohsinnig

joy *n.* Freude, Entzücken; **give** — Freude bereiten; **wish** — Glück wünschen; — **rider** Schwarzfahrer; **-ful** *adj.*, **-ous** *adj.* freudig, fröhlich, froh; erfreulich

jubilant *adj.* jubelnd, frohlockend

jubilee *n.* Jubiläum, Jubelfeier; Freuden-fest

Judaism *n.* Judentum

judge *n.* Richter, Schiedsrichter; Sachverständige; — *v.* richten, urteilen; beurteilen, Recht sprechen

judgment *n.* Urteil; Urteilsspruch; Beurteilung, Meinung, Ansicht; Urteilsvermögen; **pass** — Urteil fällen; — **day** jüngster Tag

judicial *adj.* richterlich, gerichtlich; Gerichts-; kritisch, unterscheidend; — **murder** Justizmord

judiciary *n.* Richterstand, Richtertum; — *adj.* richterlich, gerichtlich

jug *n.* Krug; (sl.) Gefängnis

juggle *v.* jonglieren, Taschenspielkunststücke machen; gaukeln, täuschen; betrügen; **-r** *n.* Jongleur, Taschenspieler; Gaukler; Betrüger

jugular *adj.* die Kehle betreffend; Hals-; — **vein** Halsschlagader

juice *n.* Saft; Kraft, Gehalt; (coll.) Strom

juicy *adj.* saftig, kraftvoll; (coll.) pikant

jujitsu *n.* Jiu-Jitsu

jukebox *n.* Musikautomat

July *n.* Juli

jumble *n.* Verwirrung, Wirrwarr, Durcheinander; — *v.* vermengen, verwirren; durcheinander werfen

jumbo *adj.* übergross; plump, dick; elefantenartig

jump *n.* Sprung, Absprung, Salta; — *v.* springen, abspringen; auffahren; überspringen; **-er** *n.* Jumper; Springer, Abspringende; Hüpfende; **-ing** *n.* Springen, Hüpfen; **-ing** *adj.* springend, hüpfend; **-ing jack** Hampelmann; **-y** *adj.* nervös, sprunghaft

junction *n.* Verbindung, Vereinigung; (geom.) Berührung(spunkt); (rail.) Knotenpunkt, Kreuzung

juncture *n.* Verbindungspunkt, Verbindungsstelle; Krisis, Konjunktur

June *n.* Juni; — **bug** Junikäfer

jungle *n.* Dschungel

junior *n.* Jüngere, Junior; Gehilfe; — **college** Juniorenhochschule; — **school** Vorstufe der Mittelschule; — *adj.* jüngere; Unter-

juniper *n.* Wacholder

junk *n.* Abfall, Kehricht; (naut.) Dschonke

junket *n.* Rahm; Näscherei; (fig.) Lustbarkeit; — *v.* schmausen

junkman *n.* Mistbauer

jurisdiction *n.* Rechtsprechung; Gerichtsbarkeit, Jurisdiktion; Gerichtsbezirk

jurisprudence *n.* Juristerei, Rechtswissenschaft

jurist *n.* Jurist, Rechtskundige

juror *n.* Geschworene; Preisrichter

jury *n.* Schwurgericht, Geschworenengericht; Preisgericht, Jury

juryman *n.* Geschworene

just *adj.* gerecht, ehrlich, ordentlich, rechtschaffen; — *adv.* gerade, genau; eben nur; richtig; — **as** gerade wie, eben als, — **as well** ebensogut, — **now** eben jetzt, soeben; **-ice** *n.* Gerechtigkeit, Justiz; Richter; **do -ice** Gerechtigkeit widerfahren lassen; **Justice of Peace** Friedensrichter; **-ifiable** adj. rechtfertigend, rechtmässig; **-ification** n. Rechtfertigung; Verteidigung; **-ify** v. rechtfertigen; **be -ified** recht haben

jut v. hervorragen, hervorstehen

jute n. Jute

juvenile adj. jugendlich, jung; Kinder-, Jugend; — **court** Jugendgericht; — **delinquency** Jugendkriminalität; — **delinquent** jugendlicher Verbrecher

K

kaleidoscope n. Kaleidoskop

kangaroo n. Känguruh

keel n. Kiel; — v. umschlagen, auf dem Rücken liegen

keen adj. eifrig, begierig, erpicht; scharf; energisch, lebhaft; **-ness** n. Schärfe; Heftigkeit, Eifer; Scharfsinn, Feinheit

keep n. Obhut, Unterhalt; Burgverliess; — v. behalten, bewahren, erhalten; halten, führen; bleiben, sich aufhalten; feiern, befolgen; — **a secret** ein Geheimnis bewahren; — **away** (sich) fernhalten; — **books** Buch führen; — **down** unterdrücken; — **from** hindern an, abhalten von, sich enthalten; — **in mind** im Gedächtnis behalten; — **off** abhalten; fernbleiben; — **on** fortfahren, dabei bleiben; — **one's temper** sich beherrschen; — **out** (sich) fernhalten; — **quiet** still sein (or bleiben); — **time** Takt (or Schritt) halten, die Zeit einhalten; — **track** of sich merken; — **up** fortfahren; — **up with** Schritt halten mit, nachkommen; — **your shirt on!** bewahre ruhig Blut! **-er** n. Aufseher; Bewahrer, Verwahrer; Wärter; Hüter, Kustos; **-ing** n. Aufsicht; Verwahrung, Bewahrung; Pflege, Obhut; Gewahrsam, Haft; Einklang, Übereinstimmung

keepsake n. Andenken, Erinnerungsgabe

keg n. Fässchen

kennel n. Hundezwinger; Hundehütte

kernel n. Kern; (fig.) Hauptsache

kerosene n. Kerosin, Leuchtpetroleum

kettle n. Kessel

key n. Schlüssel; (mech.) Keil, Splint; (mus.) Taste, Klappe; Ton; Musikschlüssel; (typewriter) Taste; — **ring** Schlüsselring, Schlüsselbund; — **man** Mann in Schlüsselstellung; **master** — Hauptschlüssel

keyboard n. Tastatur, Klaviatur

keyhole n. Schlüsselloch

keynote n. Grundton, Tonart; — **speech** Einleitungsrede

keystone n. Schlusstein; Grundstein; (fig.) Grundlage

kibitzer n. Kibitz

kick n. Tritt, Stoss; Fusstritt; Hufschlag; Rückschlag, Rückstoss; (coll.) Spass; — v. (mit dem Fuss) stossen, schlagen; treten, einen Fusstritt geben; — **the bucket**, — off ins Gras beissen; — out hinauswerfen; — **over the traces** über die Stränge schlagen

kickoff n. Abstoss

kid n. Zicklein, Kitze; (coll.) Kind, Junge; — v. zum besten haben, necken

kidnap v. Kinder (or Menschen) rauben, entführen; **-er** n. Kinderräuber, Menschenräuber; **-ing** n. Kinderraub, Menschenraub

kidney n. Niere

kidskin n. Ziegenfell, Ziegenleder

kill v. töten, erschlagen, umbringen; schlachten; — **time** die Zeit totschlagen (or vertreiben); **-er** n. Totschläger; Schlächter; **-ing** n. Töten; Schlachten

kill-joy n. Störenfried; Spassverderber

kiln n. Brennofen, Röstofen; Darre; **brick** — Kachelofen

kilocycle n. Kilozyklus; 1,000 Zyklen

kilogram n. Kilogramm; 1,000 Gramm

kilometer n. Kilometer; 1,000 Meter

kilowatt n. Kilowatt; — **hour** Kilowattstunde

kilt n. Kilt; kurzer, schottischer Rock

kimono n. Kimono

kin n. Verwandten; **next of** — die nächsten Verwandten

kind n. Art, Gattung, Geschlecht; Sorte; **all –s** of allerlei; **human** — Menschengeschlecht; **in** — in Waren; **nothing of the —!** mitnichten! **of that** — derartig; **of the** — dergleichen; **the same** — of gleichartig; **what** — of was für ein; — adj. freundlich, gütig, liebenswürdig; **would you be so** — **to** würden Sie so freundlich sein zu; **-liness** n. Güte, Freundlichkeit; **-ly** adj. gütig, mild; freundlich, liebenswürdig; angenehm, wohltätig; **-ness** n. Güte, Freundlichkeit, Gefälligkeit; **have the -ness to** sei so freundlich zu

kindergarten n. Kindergarten

kindhearted adj. gutherzig, gütig, wohlwollend

kindle v. anzünden, entzünden; (fig.) entflammen, sich entzünden

kindling n. — **wood** Holz zum Anzünden

kindred n. Verwandtschaft; Verwandten; — adj. verwandt, gleichartig, ähnlich

Kinescope n. Kinoskop, Kathodenröhre mit Bildschirm

kinetic adj. kinetisch, bewegend, motorisch; **-s** n. pl. Kinetik, Bewegungslehre

king n. König; (cards, chess) König; (checkers) Dame; **-dom** n. Königreich, Königtum; (zool.) Reich; **-dom of God** Reich Gottes; **-ly** adj. königlich

kingfisher n. Eisvogel

kingpin n. Kegelkönig, Hauptkegel

king size adj. (cigarette) Grossformat

kink n. Schleife; (coll.) Schrulle, Sparren; **-y** adj. mit Schleifen besetzt; kraus

kinsfolk n. Verwandten, Verwandtschaft

kinsman n. Verwandte

kipper n. Lachs, Räucherhering; — v. einsalzen und leicht räuchern

kiss n. Kuss; — v. (sich) küssen

kiss-proof adj. kussecht

kit n. Ausrüstung, Ausstattung; **first-aid** — Ersthilfe-Ausrüstung

kitchen n. Küche; — **police** Küchendienst; — **range**, — **stove** Küchenherd; — **utensils** Küchengeräte; **-ette** n.

Kleinküche

kite n. Drache; (orn.) Gabelweih; roter Milan; **fly a** — einen Drachen steigen lassen

kitten n. Kätzchen, junge Katze

kitty n. Kätzchen; Spieleinsatz, Sparbüchse

knack n. Kniff, Kunstgriff; Fertigkeit

knapsack n. Tornister, Ranzen

knave n. Schurke, Schelm; (cards) Bube. Unter; **—ry** n. Büberei, Schurkenstreich; Schelmerei

knead v. kneten; massieren; zusammenkneten

knee n. Knie

kneecap n. Kniescheibe; Kniekappe

knee-deep adj. knietief

kneel v. knien, auf den Knien liegen; — **down** auf die Knie fallen

kneepad n. Kniekissen

knell n. Geläute; (fig.) Grabgeläute; — v. tönen, klingen; durch Geläut verkünden

knickerbockers, knickers n. pl. Knickerbocker, halblange Pumphosen

knife n. Messer; — v. stechen, schneiden; (coll.) hinterlistig zu Fall bringen

knight n. Ritter; (chess) Springer, Pferd; (fig.) Kämpe; — v. zum Ritter schlagen; **-hood** n. Ritterschaft, Rittertum, Ritterwürde

knit v. stricken; (bone) verknüpfen, vereinigen; — **one's brows** die Stirne runzeln; **-ting** n. Stricken, Strickerei, Strickarbeit; **-ting needle** Stricknadel

knob n. Knopf, Knauf, Griff; Kuppe

knock n. Schlag, Stoss; Klopfen, Pochen; — v. klopfen, pochen; schlagen, stossen; prallen; — **down** niederschlagen; **-er** n. Klopfer, Schläger

knock-kneed adj. x-beinig; hinkend

knockout n. Knockout, Niederschlag

knoll n. Hügel, Bergspitze, Kuppe

knot n. Knoten; Knorren; Ast; — v. knoten, verknüpfen; (fig.) verwirren, verflechten; **-ted** adj. knotig, knorrig; (fig.) verworren, verschlungen; **-ty** adj. knotig, knorrig; (fig.) verwickelt

knothole n. Astloch

know v. wissen, kennen; verstehen; **he –s a thing or two** er ist durchtrieben; **I — positively** ich weiss es bestimmt; **I — what's what** ich weiss, was ich weiss; — **a thing perfectly** eine Sache vollkommen beherrschen; **-ing** adj. verständig; bewusst, wissentlich; geschickt, schlau; **-ingly** adv. wissentlich; **-ledge** n. Kenntnis(se), Wissen; Erkenntnis; Wissenschaft; **to my -ledge** soviel ich weiss; **-n** adj. gewusst; bekannt

know-how n. Spezialkenntnis; Könner

knuckle n. Knöchel; (meat) Kniestück; Eisbein, Dickbein, Dünnbein; — v. — **down**, — **under** sich unterwerfen

Kodak n. Kodak

kosher adj. koscher, rein

L

label n. Etikette, Zettel; Aufschrift; — v. etikettieren, mit einer Aufschrift ver-

sehen; auszeichnen

labor n. Arbeit; Mühe, Anstrengung; (med.) Geburtswehen; **Labor Day** Arbeiterfeiertag; — **union** Arbeitergewerkschaft; **be in** — in den Wehen liegen; **hard** — Zwangsarbeit; — v. arbeiten; sich abmühen (or anstrengen); ausarbeiten; — **under a mistake** sich im Irrtum befinden; **-er** n. Arbeiter; **day -er** Tagelöhner; kurzfristig Beschäftigte; **-ious** adj. mühselig, mühsam, mühevoll; arbeitsam, fleissig, emsig

laboratory n. Laboratorium

laborsaving adj. Arbeit ersparend; Handarbeit ersetzend

labyrinth n. Labyrinth, Irrgang; (fig.) Verwicklung

lace n. Spitze; Litze, Schnur, Borte, Tresse; — v. schnüren; besetzen

lacework n. Spitzenarbeit, Posamentierarbeit

lack n. Mangel, Bedürfnis; — v. fehlen, mangeln; entbehren, bedürfen; **be -ing** es fehlen lassen an; **there is something -ing in him** er hat seine Mängel (or Schwächen)

lackadaisical adj. gleichgültig, schlaff, träge

lackey n. Lakai, Bediente

lacquer n. Lack, Firnis; Lackarbeit; — v. lackieren, firnissen

lad n. Junge, Bursche; Gefährte

ladder n. Leiter, Stufenleiter; (naut.) Strickleiter, Schiffstreppe

laden adj. beladen, befrachtet

lading n. Ladung, Fracht; **bill of** — Frachtbrief

ladle n. Schöpflöffel; — v. (aus)schöpfen, auslöffeln

lady n. Dame; Edelfrau, Freifrau; (coll.) Liebste; **Ladies and Gentlemen** Meine Damen und Herren; **ladies' room** Damentoilette; **young** — Fräulein, junges Mädchen

ladybird, ladybug n. Marienkäfer

ladyfinger n. Biskuit

lady-killer n. Herzenbrecher, Frauenheld

ladylike adj. damenhaft, wohlerzogen

ladylove n. Geliebte

lag v. zaudern, zögern; zurückbleiben, zuletzt kommen

laggard adj. langsam, saumselig, lässig, träge; — n. Saumselige, Zauderer, Träge, Langsame

lagoon n. Lagune

laity n. Laien

lake n. See; — **dwelling** Pfahlbau

lamb n. Lamm; (meat) Lammfleisch; **Lamb of God** Lamm Gottes; — **chop** Lammkotelett

lambskin n. Lammfell, Lammleder

lame adj. lahm, verkrüppelt; hinkend; (fig.) unvollkommen, mangelhaft; — **excuse** faule Ausrede; — v. lähmen, zum Krüppel machen; **-ness** n. Lahmheit, Lähmung; (fig.) Schwäche

lament n. Wehklage, Jammer; — v. (be)klagen, jammern, trauern; **-able** adj. beklagenswert; jämmerlich, kläglich; **-ation** n. Jammer, Wehklage

lamp n. Lampe; Leuchte, Licht; **— shade** Lampenschirm; **electric —** elektrische Lampe

lampoon n. Schmähschrift; **—** v. schmähen

lamplight n. Lampenlicht

lamppost n. Laternenpfahl

lance n. Lanze, Speer, Wurfspiess; **—** v. durchbohren; (med.) aufschneiden; **-t** n. Lanzette

land n. Land; Grund, Boden, Erde; Grundstück; **—** v. landen; an Land bringen, ausladen, löschen; (fig.) in Sicherheit bringen; **-ing** n. Landung, Landen; (stairs) Treppenabsatz; **-ing place** Landeplatz, Flugfeld; **emergency -ing** Notlandung; **emergency -ing field** Notlandeplatz

landholder n. Landeigentümer, Grundbesitzer, Gutsbesitzer

landlady n. Hauswirtin; **— of an inn** Gastwirtin

landlord n. Hausbesitzer; **— of an inn** Gastwirt

landlubber n. Landratte

landmark n. Landmarke, Grenzstein; Markstein

landowner n. Grundbesitzer, Gutsbesitzer

landscape n. Landschaft; (art) Landschaftsbild; **— gardener** Gartenarchitekt; **— gardening** Landschaftsgärtnerei

landslide n. Erdrutsch, Bergsturz; (pol.) Wahlsieg (mit überwiegender Mehrheit)

landsman n. Landsmann, Landbewohner; (naut.) Landratte

lane n. Weg, Gasse; Doppelreihe, Spalier; **traffic —** Fahrbahn

language n. Sprache; Ausdrucksweise, Stil; **German —** deutsche Sprache

languid adj. schlaff, matt, schwach; langsam, schleichend, träge; flau

languish v. schmachten; ermatten, erschlaffen; dahinschwinden; **-ing** adj. schmachtend; ermattend, erschlaffend; matt, schlaff, flau

lank adj. dünn, schlank; schlicht; **-y** adj. schmächtig, dürr

lanolin(e) n. Lanolin

lantern n. Laterne

lap n. Schoss; Vorstoss; (sports) Runde; **—** v. bespülen; falten, legen, einhüllen, umschlagen; umschliessen; **— up** auflecken

lapel n. Aufschlag, Taschenklappe

lapse n. Fall, Gleiten; Verlauf, Verfall; Fehler, Fehltritt, Versehen; **—** v. verlaufen, verfliessen; verfallen; (ab)fallen

lard n. Schweinefett, Schmalz; **—** v. spicken, einfetten, schmieren

larder n. Speisekammer, Speiseschrank

large adj. gross, breit, dick, stark; weit; beträchtlich; **at —** frei, ungehindert

lariat n. Lasso; Bindeseil, Wurfschlinge

lark n. Lerche; (coll.) Schabernack

larva n. Larve, Puppe

laryngitis n. Kehlkopfentzündung

larynx n. Kehlkopf

laser n. (abbr.) (light amplification by stimulated emission of radiation) Laser (Lichtverstärkung durch Strahlungsanregung unter Verwendung einer fremden Strahlungsquelle)

lash n. Schnur; Schlag, Hieb; Peitsche; Wimper; **—** v. peitschen; (fig.) geisseln

lass n. Mädchen, junge Frau

lassitude n. Müdigkeit, Abgespanntheit, Mattigkeit

lasso n. Lasso, Wurfschlinge

last adj. letzt; vorig; **be on one's — legs** sich nicht mehr zu helfen wissen; **— judgment** Jüngstes Gericht; **— night** gestern abend; **— supper** letztes Abendmahl; **next to —** vorletzt; **—** n. Letzte; Ende; (shoe) Leisten; **breathe one's —** in den letzten Zügen liegen; **to the very —** bis zum Ende; **—** adv. zuletzt; **at —** endlich; **— of all** zuletzt, am Ende; **—** v. dauern, bestehen, bleiben, währen; ausreichen; **-ing** adj. dauerhaft, dauernd, beständig; **-ly** adv. zuletzt, endlich, schliesslich

latch n. Klinke, Drücker; Sicherheitsschloss; **—** v. einklinken, zuklinken

late adj. spät, verspätet; verstorben, selig; vorig, jüngst; **be (too) —** sich verspäten; **of —** kürzlich, jüngst; **—** adv. spät; **-ly** adv. kürzlich, neulich, unlängst, vor kurzem; **-ness** n. Zuspätkommen, Verspätung; Späte; Neuheit; **-r** adj. and adv. später; **-r on** späterhin; **-st** adj. spätest, neuest; **-st fashion** neu(e)ste Mode; **at the -st** spätestens

latent adj. latent, verborgen, geheim, versteckt; (phys.) gebunden

lath n. Latte; **—** v. mit Latten versehen

lathe n. Drehbank

lather n. Seifenschaum; **—** v. einseifen, schäumen

Latin n. Latein; Lateiner; **—** adj. lateinisch

Latin-American n. Südamerikaner; **—** adj. südamerikanisch

latitude n. Breite; (fig.) Spielraum

latter adj. letzter, später; **the —** dieser

lattice n. Gitter(werk); Lattenwerk

Latvia n. Lettland

laud n. Lob, Preis; Lobgesang; **—** v. loben, preisen; **-able** adj. löblich, lobenswert; **-atory** adj. lobend, preisend

laugh n. Lache(n), Gelächter; **—** v. lachen; **— at** auslachen; **— in one's sleeve** sich ins Fäustchen lachen; **— off** sich lachend hinwegsetzen über; **-able** adj. lächerlich; **-ing** adj. lachend; **-ing gas** Lachgas; **it is no -ing matter** es ist nicht zum Lachen; **-ter** n. Gelächter; **hearty -er** herzliches Lachen

laughingstock n. Gegenstand des Spottes, Zielscheibe des Gelächters

launch n. Stapellauf; **—** n. Abschuss; **-ing pad** Raketenabschussbasis; **-ing rail** Raketenabschussführungsschiene; **-ing tube** Raketenabschussführungsrohr; **—** v. vom Stapel lassen; schleudern; (fig.) in Gang setzen

launder v. waschen und rollen (or plätten)

laundromat n. öffentlicher Waschautomat

laundry n. Wäscherei, Wäsche

laundryman n. Wäschemann

laurel n. Lorbeer; (fig.) Lorbeerkranz, Ehre, Ruhm

lavatory n. Waschraum, Toilette, Abort

lavish adj. verschwenderisch, freigebig; — v. verschwenden, vergeuden

law n. Gesetz, Recht; Rechtswissenschaft; Prozess, Gerichtsverfahren; **according to** — gesetzmässig, rechtmässig; **at** — gerichtlich; **by** — gesetzlich; **take the — into one's own hands** sich selbst Recht verschaffen; **-ful** adj. gesetzlich, gerichtlich; rechtmässig; gültig; **-less** adj. gesetzlos, ungesetzlich; (fig.) zügellos; **-lessness** n. Gesetzlosigkeit, Ungesetzlichkeit; (fig.) Zügellosigkeit; **-yer** n. Rechtsanwalt, Advokat; Jurist, Rechtsgelehrte

law-abiding adj. die Gesetze einhaltend

lawbreaker n. Gesetzes Übertreter; (fig.) Verbrecher

lawgiver n. Gesetzgeber

lawmaker n. Verfasser von Gesetzen

lawn n. Rasen(platz); (cloth) Batist; **— mower** Rasenmähmaschine, Rasenmäher

lawsuit n. Prozess, Rechtshandel

lax adj. schlaff, locker, lose; lax, lässig; **-ity** n. Schlaffheit, Lockerheit; Laxheit

laxative n. Abführmittel; — adj. abführend

lay v. legen, stellen, setzen; wetten; **— away** aufheben, beiseite legen; **— claim to** Anspruch erheben auf; **— off** abbauen, entlassen; **—** n. Lage; Lied, Gesang; **—** adj. weltlich, Laien-; **— brother** Laienbruder; **-er** n. Schicht, Lage; (bot.) Ableger; (zool.) Legehenne; **-er cake** Schichttorte

layette n. Babyausstattung

layman n. Laie

layoff n. zeitweilige Entlassung

laziness n. Faulheit, Trägheit, Lässigkeit

lazy adj. faul, träge, müssig, langsam

lead n. Leitung, Führung; Vorsprung; (cards) Vorhand; (elec.) Leitung, Leiter; (theat.) Hauptrolle; **take the —** die Leitung (or den Vorsitz) übernehmen; **—** v. führen, leiten; vorangehen; anführen, befehligen; (cards) anspielen, ausspielen; (mus.) dirigieren; vorsingen; **— a dance** vortanzen; **— astray** irreführen; **— off** ableiten; eröffnen; **— the field** die Führung haben; **— the way** vorangehen; **— up to** hinauswollen auf; **-er** n. Führer, Leiter; Anführer, Rädelsführer; (mus.) Dirigent, Kapellmeister; **-ership** n. Führerschaft; Leitung, Aufsicht; **-ing** adj. leitend, lenkend, führend; hervorragend; erste, vornehmste; **-ing article** Leitartikel; Hauptartikel; **-ing axle** Vorderachse; **-ing horse** Spitzenpferd; **-ing lady** erste Liebhaberin (or Heldin); **-ing man** erster Liebhaber (or Held); **-ing note** grosse Septime; **-ing question** Suggestivfrage

lead n. (min.) Blei; (naut.) Lot, Senkblei; (typ.) Durchschuss; **— pencil** Bleistift; **—** adj. bleiern, **-en** adj. bleiern; blei-

farben; (fig.) düster; schwerfällig, glanzlos

leaf n. Blatt; (door) Flügel; (table) Klappe; **turn over a new —** ein neues Leben beginnen; **—** v. **— through** durchblättern, herumblättern in; **-less** adj. blattlos, entblättert; **-let** n. Blättchen, Zettel; Prospekt, Flugschrift; **-y** adj. belaubt, laubreich

league n. Bund, Liga; Bündnis; (naut.) Seemeile; **—** v. (sich) verbünden

leak n. Leck, Ritze; **spring a —** leck werden; **—** v. lecken, leck sein; **— out** auslaufen, austropfen; (fig.) bekannt werden, durchsickern; **-age** n. Leckwerden; Undichtheit, Auslaufen; (elec.) Ableitung; (gas) Verlust; (news) Durchsickern; **-y** adj. leck, undicht, durchlässig

leakproof adj. undurchlässig, undurchlöcherbar

lean v. (sich) lehnen, anlehnen, auflehnen sich neigen, schief stehen; sich stützen (or aufstützen); **— against** (sich) lehnen gegen; **— forward** sich vorlehnen; **— on** sich stützen auf; (fig.) sich verlassen auf; **-ing** n. Neigung

lean, leanness n. Magere, mageres Fleisch; **—** adj. mager, dürr, dünn

leap n. Sprung, Satz, Salto; **by -s** sprungweise; **— year** Schaltjahr; **—** v. springen, hüpfen

leapfrog n. Bockspringen; **—** v. bockspringen

learn v. (er)lernen; hören, erfahren; **-ed** adj. gelehrt, wissenschaftlich gebildet; **-edly** adv. erfahren, bewandert, in gelehrter Weise, als Gelehrter; **-ing** n. Lernen; Gelehrsamkeit, Wissen

lease n. Vermietung, Verpachtung; Miete, Pacht; Mietvertrag; Mietzeit; **—** v. vermieten, verpachten

leash n. Leine, Koppel; **—** v. koppeln, an der Leine führen

least adj. kleinste, geringste; mindeste, wenigste; **—** adv. am wenigsten; **at —** wenigstens, mindestens; **— of all am** allerwenigsten; **not in the —** nicht im geringsten, keineswegs; **the — possible** am wenigsten möglich; **—** n. Kleinste, Geringste

leather n. Leder; **—** adj. ledern, Leder-; **-ette** n. Ledertuch; Kunstleder; **-y** adj. ledern, lederartig

leave n. Urlaub; Abschied; Erlaubnis; **— of absence** Urlaub; **take —** Abschied nehmen; **take — of one's senses** den Verstand verlieren; **—** v. lassen; verlassen; übriglassen, dalassen, zurücklassen; aufgeben; vermachen, hinterlassen; abreisen, abfahren, fortgehen, weggehen; **— alone** in Ruhe (or Frieden) lassen; **— home** das Haus (or Zuhause) verlassen; **— open** offen (or unentschieden) lassen; **— word** Bescheid hinterlassen; **she -s it to you** sie überlässt es Ihnen

leaven n. Sauerteig, Hefe; **—** v. säuern, gären; (fig.) beeinflussen

leave-taking n. Abschiednehmen, Lebewohl

leavings *n. pl.* Überbleibsel, Reste

lectern *n.* Lesepult, Chorpult

lecture *n.* Vortrag, Vorlesung, Kolleg; Verweis, Strafpredigt; — *v.* vorlesen, vortragen; zurechtweisen, abkanzeln; **-r** *n.* Vortragende; (college) Dozent, Professor

ledge *n.* Sims, Leiste, Rand; (min.) Schicht, Lager

ledger *n.* (arch.) Querbalken, Schwelle; (com.) Hauptbuch; — **line** Hilfsnotenlinie

lee *n.* Schutz; (naut.) Lee(seite); — *adj.* lee

leech *n.* Blutegel; (fig.) Blutsauger

leer *n.* Seitenblick, lüsterner Blick; — *v.* schielen, lüstern blicken

lees *n. pl.* Bodensatz, Hefe

leeway *n.* Abtrifft; give — gewähren lassen

left *adj.* linke; — *adv.* links; — *n.* Linke; (pol.) Linkspartei(en); at the — of links von; on the — zur Linken, auf der Linken; to the — (nach) links; **-ist** *n.* Linke, Anhänger einer Linkspartei

left-handed *adj.* linkshändig; (fig.) linkisch

leftover *n.* Überbleibsel, Rest

leg *n.* Bein; Schenkel; (boot) Schaft; (meat) Keule, Schlegel; **he hasn't a — to stand on** er hat keinen Grund unter den Füssen; — **of a compass** Kompasschenkel; **pull someone's** — jemanden zum besten haben; **wooden** — Holzbein, Stelzfuss

legacy *n.* Vermächtnis, Legat

legal *adj.* gesetzlich, gesetzmässig, legal; rechtskräftig, rechtsgültig; Rechts-; **tender** gesetzlich anerkanntes Zahlungsmittel; **-ity** *n.* Gesetzlichkeit, Gesetzmässigkeit; Legalität; **-ize** *v.* rechtskräftig machen, gerichtlich bestätigen, für rechtmässig erklären

legation *n.* Legation, Gesandtschaft

legend *n.* Sage, Legende; Inschrift; Umschrift; **-ary** *adj.* sagenhaft, legendär

legging *n.* Gamasche

legibility *n.* Leserlichkeit, Lesbarkeit

legible *adj.* leserlich, lesbar; (fig.) erkennbar, deutlich

legislate *v.* Gesetze geben; durch Gesetze bewirken

legislation *n.* Gesetzgebung

legislative *adj.* gesetzgebend, gesetzlich, — **body** gesetzgebende Gewalt

legislator *n.* Gesetzgeber

legislature *n.* Gesetzgebung; gesetzgebender Körper

legitimate *adj.* ehelich, legitim; rechtmässig, gesetzlich

leisure *n.* Musse, Freizeit; Bequemlichkeit; at — in Musse; at one's — nach seiner Bequemlichkeit, bei passender Gelegenheit; — *adj.* frei, müssig, unbeschäftigt; **—hours** Mussestunden; -ly *adj.* mit Musse

lemon *n.* Zitrone, Limone; Zitronenbaum; — **drop** Zitronenbonbon; — **squeezer** Zitronenpresse; **-ade** *n.* Limonade

lend *v.* (aus)leihen, verleihen, verborgen; (fig.) geben, gewähren, leisten; **-er** *n.* Leihende, Leiher, Verleiher

length *n.* Länge; Dauer; Strecke, Ausdehnung; at full — in voller Länge; (art) in Lebensgrösse; at great — sehr ausführlich; at — vollständig, zuletzt; **-en** *v.* verlängern, (aus)dehnen; länger werden; **-y** *adj.* ziemlich lang, ausgedehnt; weitschweifig, langweilig

lengthwise *adv.* der Länge nach; — *adj.* der Länge nach gehend

leniency *n.* Milde, Sanftmut

lenient *adj.* mild, nachsichtig

lens *n.* Linse; **burning —** Brennglas

Lent *n.* Fasten(zeit)

lentil *n.* Linse

leopard *n.* Leopard

leper *n.* Leprakranke, Aussätzige

leprosy *n.* Lepra, Aussatz

less *adj. and adv.* kleiner, geringer; weniger; — *prep.* abzüglich; **-en** *v.* abnehmen, sich vermindern; verkleinern, verringern; **-er** *adj.* weniger, kleiner, geringer

lessee *n.* Mieter, Pächter

lesson *n.* Aufgabe; Lektion, Übungsstück; Lehrstunde, Lehre

lessor *n.* Vermieter, Verpächter

lest *conj.* damit nicht; aus Furcht, dass

let *v.* lassen, erlauben, gestatten; vermieten, verpachten; verdingen

letdown *n.* Herablassung; Enttäuschung

letter *n.* Brief, Schreiben; Buchstabe, Type; (fig.) buchstäblicher Sinn; *pl.* Literatur, Wissenschaft; **capital —** Grossbuchstabe; — **box** Briefkasten; — **carrier** Briefträger; — **drop** Briefeinwurf; — **opener** Brieföffner; — **of credit** Kreditbrief; — **of introduction** Enfürungsschreiben; **capital —** Grossbuchstabe; **lower-case —** kleiner Buchstabe; **registered —** eingeschriebener Brief; **unclaimed —** unbestellbarer Brief; — *v.* mit Buchstaben versehen, betiteln

letterhead *n.* Briefkopf

lettuce *n.* Salat, Lattich

levee *n.* Uferdamm

level *n.* Höhe; Niveau; Ebene, Fläche; Wasserwage; Richtscheit; — *adj.* waagerecht: eben, glatt, gleich, flach, gerade; — *v.* ebnen, planieren; einebnen, gleichmachen; richten

levelheaded *adj.* verständig, mit gesundem Urteil begabt

lever *n.* Hebel, Hebebaum; Schwengel; **-age** *n.* Hebelwirkung; Hebelkraft

levity *n.* Leichtheit, Leichtigkeit; (fig.) Leichtsinn, Leichtfertigkeit

lewd *adj.* unzüchtig, schlüpfrig, liederlich

lexicon *n.* Lexikon, Wörterbuch

liability *n.* Verbindlichkeit, Verpflichtung; Haftpflicht; Verantwortlichkeit; *pl.* Passiva, Schulden

liable *adj.* haftbar, haftpflichtig; verantwortlich; ausgesetzt, unterworfen

liar *n.* Lügner

libel *n.* Schmähschrift, Verleumdung; — *v.* schmähen, verleumden; **-(l)er** *n.*

Schmäher, Lästerer, Verleumder; **-(l)ous** adj. schmähend. lästernd; verleumdend

liberal adj. liberal, freigesinnt; grossmütig, vorurteilslos; freigebig; **—** n. Liberale, **-ism** n. Liberalismus; **-ity** n. Grossherzigkeit, Freisinnigkeit, Freigebigkeit; **-ly** adv. frei gewährt, reichlich; zügellos

liberate v. befreien; freigeben, freilassen

liberation n. Befreiung

liberator n. Befreier

liberty n. Freiheit; **be at —** frei sein; freie Hand haben; **set at —** befreien, in Freiheit setzen; **take liberties with** sich Freiheiten herausnehmen; **take the —** of sich die Freiheit nehmen zu

librarian n. Bibliothekar

library n. Bibliothek

license n. Konzession, Erlaubnis, Genehmigung, Lizenz, Gewerbeschein; **— number** Lizenznummer; **— plate** Nummernschild; **—** v. konzessionieren, behördlich bewilligen, berechtigen

licentious adj. übertrieben, unbändig; ausgelassen, ausschweifend, zügellos

lick n. Lecken; Schlag, Streich; Salzlecke; **—** v. (be)lecken; schlagen, prügeln; übertreffen, besiegen; **— up** auflecken

licorice n. Süssholz, Lakritze

lid n. Deckel, Klappe; (eye) Lid

lie n. Lüge, Erdichtung, Fabel; Lage; **give the — to** Lügen strafen; **tell -s** lügen; **white —** Notlüge; **—** v. liegen, ruhen; lügen, fabeln

Liège n. Lüttich

lien n. Pfandrecht

lieu n. **in — of** anstatt

lieutenant n. (mil.) Leutnant; (pol.) Stellvertreter; **— colonel** Oberstleutnant; **— commander** Korvettenkapitän; **— general** Generalleutnant; **first — Oberleutnant

life n. Leben; Lebensdauer; Person, Menschenleben; Lebensart; Wesen, Lebewesen; Lebhaftigkeit; Lebensbeschreibung; Lebensgrösse; **— annuity** Lebensrente; **— belt** Rettungsgürtel; **— buoy** Rettungsboje; **— insurance** Lebensversicherung; **— preserver** Schwimmgürtel; Totschläger; **— raft** Rettungsfloss; **come to —** zur Welt kommen; **early —** Jugend; **for — fürs** Leben, auf Lebenszeit; **from —** nach dem Leben, nach der Natur; **in the prime of —** in der Blüte des Lebens; **married —** Eheleben; **matter of — and death** Angelegenheit auf Leben und Tod; **way of —** Lebensweise; **-less** adj. leblos, unbelebt; tot; (fig.) kraftlos; **-like** adj. lebensgetreu, naturgetreu

lifeboat n. Rettungsboot

lifeguard n. Rettungsschwimmer, Bademeister

lifelong adj. lebenslang, lebenslänglich

lifesaver n. Lebensretter

life-size adj. lebensgross

lifetime n. Lebenszeit, Lebensdauer; **once in a —** einmal im Leben; **—** adj. lebenslänglich

lifework n. Lebenswerk

lift n. Heben, Aufheben; Erhebung, Aufschwung; (mech.) Hub; Aufzug; **give someone a —** jemandem helfen (or im Auto mitnehmen); **—** v. (er)heben, aufheben, lüften; sich heben, aufsteigen; (coll.) wegnehmen, stehlen

ligament n. Band, Fessel; (anat.) Sehne, Flechse

light n. Licht, Tageslicht; Helligkeit; **in the — of** wie, als; **—** v. leuchten, anzünden, entzünden; beleuchten, erhallen; hell sein, sich entzünden; **— up** (er)leuchten; aufleuchten; **—** adj. hell, licht; leicht; unbeladen; gering; mässig; schwach; **-en** v. lichter (or heller) werden; leuchten, blitzen; erleuchten; (fig.) erleichtern; **-ing** n. Beleuchtung; **-ly** adv. leicht(fertig), geringschätzig, verächtlich; **-ness** n. Leichtigkeit; Helligkeit; Leichtheit, Gewandtheit

lighter n. (naut.) Leichter; Leuchtschiff; (cigarette) Feuerzeug

lightning n. Blitz; **— heat —** Wetterleuchten; **— bug** Leuchtkäfer; **— rod** Blitzableiter

lighthearted adj. leichten Herzens, heiter; sorglos, lustig

lighthouse n. Leuchtturm

lightweight n. Leichtgewicht

like n. Gleiche, Ähnliche; pl. Neigungen; **—** adj. gleich, ähnlich, gleichartig; **—** adv. ebenso, gleich(sam), ähnlich; **—** prep. wie, gleich; **be — ähneln; — father — son** der Apfel fällt nicht weit vom Stamm; **—** v. gern haben, mögen; **be -d** beliebt sein; **-able** adj. angenehm, reizend, liebenswürdig; **-lihood** n. Wahrscheinlichkeit, Anschein; **-ly** adj. wahrscheinlich; geeignet; **not -ly** wohl schwerlich, kaum; **-n** v. vergleichen; **-ness** n. Ähnlichkeit, Gleichheit; Ebenbild

likewise adv. ebenso, gleichfalls

liking n. Neigung, Wohlgefallen

lilac n. Flieder; Lila; **—** adj. lila(farben)

lilt n. rhythmischer Schwung; Tanzen; **—** v. trällern, lustig singen

lily n. Lilie; **— of the valley** Maiglöckchen, Maiblume; **—** adj. lilienhaft, lilienweiss; rein, keusch

limb n. (anat.) Glied; (ast.) Rand; (bot.) Ast, Arm; Rand; (geol.) Ausläufer; (fig.) Stück, Teil

limber adj. biegsam, geschmeidig; (fig.) nachgiebig; **—** v. aufprotzen

lime n. Vogelleim; (bot.) Lindenbaum; Zitronenbaum; (min.) Kalk, Mörtel

limelight n. Scheinwerferlicht; Mittelpunkt des öffentlichen Interesses

limestone n. Kalkstein

limit n. Grenze, Schranke, Ziel; Frist; Gebiet, Bezirk; **there is a — to everything** alles hat seine Grenzen; **to the —** bis aufs Äusserste; **—** v. beschränken, einschränken, begrenzen; **-ation** n. Beschränkung, Einschränkung; Abgrenzung; (law) Verjährungsfrist; **-ed** adj. begrenzt, eingeschränkt; **-ed in time** befristet; **-less** adj. unbegrenzt,

unbeschränkt, grenzenlos
limousine n. Limousine
limp n. Lahmen, Hinken, Humpeln; — v.
lahmen, hinken, humpeln; — adj.
schlaff, schlapp
linden n. Linde
line n. Linie, Reihe; Leine, Schnur; (com.)
Zweig, Fach; (genealogy) Stamm.
Geschlecht; (lit.) Vers, Zeile; (rail.)
Linie, Bahn, Spur, Geleise; (tel.)
Leitung; (typ.) Zeile; (fig.) Richtung;
keep in — im Glied bleiben, in Zaum
halten; — **of argument** Beweisführung;
stand in — Schlange stehen; — v.
(ab)füttern, ausfüttern, polstern; Spalier bilden, umsäumen; lin(i)ieren,
Linien ziehen; — **up** (sich) in Linie
(or Reihen) aufstellen; **-age** n. Geschlecht, Familie; Stammbaum; **-al**
adj. gerade, direkt; g(e)radlinig, Län-
gen-; ererbt, angestammt; direkt
abstammend; **-ar** adj. linear; g(e)rad-
linie; (bot.) fadenförmig, linienförmig
lineman n. (football) Stürmer; (tel.)
Streckenarbeiter
linen n. Leinen, Linnen, Leinewand,
Leinenzeug; Wäsche, Bettwäsche; **dirty**
— Schmutzwäsche; — adj. leinen, aus
Leinwand
line-up n. Formation; (baseball) Spieler-
liste; (football) Aufstellung; (police)
Reihe vorgeführter Personen
linger v. sich aufhalten, zaudern, zögern;
säumen; **-ing** adj. langsam, schleichend,
zögernd
lingerie n. Damenwäsche
linguist n. Sprachforscher
liniment n. Salbe, Einreibung
lining n. Futter, Besatz, Ausfütterung;
(arch.) Wandbekleidung; **silver** —
Silberverbrämung
link n. Glied, Gelenk, Schleife, Band;
(fig.) Bindeglied; — v. (sich) verketten,
(sich) verbinden
linnet n. Hänfling
linoleum n. Linoleum
Linotype n. Linotype, Setzmaschine
linseed n. Leinsamen
lint n. Scharpie
lintel n. Oberbalken, Oberschwelle, Fen-
stersturz
lion n. Löwe; (lit.) Leu; (fig.) Held des
Tages; **-'s share** Löwenanteil; **-ess** n.
Löwin
lip n. Lippe; (edge) Rand; (coll.) Unverschämtheit
lipstick n. Lippenstift
liquefy v. schmelzen, flüssig machen (or
werden); auflösen
liqueur n. Likör
liquid n. Flüssigkeit; — adj. flüssig, fliessend; (mus.) sanft tönend, schmelzend;
— **air** flüssige Luft; — **measure** Flüs-
sigkeitsmass; **-ate** v. liquidieren; **-ation**
n. Liquidation, Abwicklung, Auflösung;
Bezahlung, Abtragung
liquor n. Alkohol, alkoholisches Getränk;
— **dealer** Spirituosenhändler
lisp n. Lispeln; — v. lispeln
list n. Liste, Verzeichnis; Leiste, Streifen;

Rand, Saum; (naut.) Schlagseite; pl.
Schranken; — **price** Katalogpreis; — v.
registrieren, katalogisieren, in eine
Liste eintragen, verzeichnen; (naut.)
Schlagseite haben
listen v. anhören, zuhören; horchen,
lauschen; **-er** n. Hörer, Zuhörer;
Horcher, Lauscher
litany n. Litanei, Bittgebet
liter n. Liter
literacy n. wissenschaftliche Bildung,
Belesenheit
literal adj. wörtlich, buchstäblich; Buchstaben
literary adj. literarisch, gelehrt, schrift-
stellerisch
literate adj. gebildet, literarisch
literature n. Literatur, Schrifttum
lithograph n. Lithographie, Steindruck;
— v. lithographieren; **-y** n. Lithographie, Steindruckkunst
litigation n. Prozess, Rechtsstreit
litter n. Tragbahre; Brut, Wurf; Streu,
Strohmatte; (fig.) Unordnung; — v.
umherwerfen, verstreuen, in Unordnung bringen
litterbug n. Schmutzfink, Strassenbe-
schmutzer
little n. Kleine, Wenige; Kleinigkeit; —
adj. klein; kurz; gering(fügig), wenig;
etwas; — **one** Kleines **very** — sehr
wenig; — adv. wenig; kaum; **a** — ein
wenig, etwas; — **by** — nach und nach
liturgy n. Liturgie
live v. leben; wohnen; sich nähren; — **on**
leben von; — **up to** erfüllen; **-er** n.
Lebende; Wohnende, Bewohner
live adj. lebend, lebendig; lebhaft, frisch;
(bullet) scharf; (coal) glühend; (elec.)
geladen; **-lihood** n. Lebensunterhalt,
Auskommen; **-liness** n. Lebhaftigkeit,
Munterkeit; **-ly** adj. lebhaft, munter,
lebendig, heiter
livelong adj. langanhaltend; **the** — **day**
den lieben, langen Tag
liver n. Leber
liverwurst n. Leberwurst
livery n. Livree, Uniform
livestock n. Vieh(stand)
living n. Leben; Lebensunterhalt; pl.
Lebendigen; **make a** — sein Auskommen haben; — adj. lebend(ig); glühend;
(fig.) tätig, belebend; — **room** Wohnzimmer; — **wage** angemessenes Gehalt
Livonia n. Livland
lizard n. Eidechse
llama n. Lama
load n. Last, Bürde; Ladung; (mech.)
Belastung; — v. laden; beladen,
befrachten; beschweren, belasten
loaf n. Laib; Brot; — v. müssig gehen,
bummeln, herumlungern; **-er** n. Müssiggänger, Bummler
loam n. Lehm
loan n. Darlehen, Anleihe; — v. (aus)-
leihen
loathe v. sich ekeln; hassen; verabscheuen
loathing n. Widerwille, Ekel, Abscheu
lobby n. Vorhalle, Vorsaal, Korridor;
(pol.) Wandelgang; Gruppe, die Ab-

geordnete zu beeinflussen sucht; (theat.) Foyer; — v. (pol.) beeinflussen; -ist n. (pol.) Beeinflusser

lobe n. Lappen; Keule (radar) Radarauffanggerät; — **of the ear** Ohrläppchen; — **of the lungs** Lungenflügel

local n. Lokal; Ortsbewohner; Lokalnachricht; (rail.) Ortszug; — adj. lokal, örtlich, räumlich; hiesig; -e n. Örtlichkeit; -ity n. Ort; -ize v. lokalisieren

locate v. abgrenzen; ausfindig machen; (die Grenzen) bestimmen; (mil.) erkunden; **be -d** gelegen sein; (fig.) liegen, wohnen

location n. Lage; Unterbringung; Vermietung; Landvermessung; (film) Ort der Aussenaufnahme

lock n. Schloss; Schleuse; Locke, Flocke; — **stitch** Steppstich; —, **stock and barrel** die ganze Geschichte; **air** — pneumatische Schleuse; **under** — **and key** hinter Schloss und Riegel; — v. schliessen, verschliessen, sich abschliessen; (mech.) verkuppeln; — **in** einschliessen, einsperren; — **out** ausschliessen, aussperren; — **up** abschliessen, absperren; -**er** n. verschliessbarer Kasten (or Schrank); Schliessfach; Kühlanlage; -**er room** Garderobe

locket n. Medaillon

lockjaw n. Kinnbackenkrampf

lockout n. Aussperrung

locksmith n. Schlosser

locomotion n. Ortsveränderung

locomotive n. Lokomotive

locust n. Heuschrecke, Zikade; (bot.) unechte Akazie

lodestar n. Leitstern, Polarstern

lodge n. Hütte, Häuschen; Loge; — v. wohnen, beherbergen; unterbringen; übernachten; hinterlegen, lagern; -**r** n. Mieter, Hausbewohner

lodging n. Wohnung, Logis; pl. Mietswohnung

loft n. Dachgeschoss, Dachkammer; Boden, Speicher

loftiness n. Höhe, Erhabenheit; (fig.) Stolz, Grösse

lofty adj. hoch; erhaben, stattlich

log n. Klotz, Block; (naut.) Log; — **cabin** Blockhaus; -**ging** n. Holzfällen, Holzflössen

logbook n. Logbuch, Schiffsjournal

logic n. Logik; -**al** adj. logisch, folgerichtig

logistics n. Einquartierung

logrolling n. Holzflössen; (pol.) gegenseitige Unterstützung (or Begünstigung)

loin n. Lende; Lendenstück. Nierenbraten

loiter v. sich aufhalten, zögern, trödeln, bummeln; -**er** n. Zauderer, Müssiggänger, Faulenzer, Bummler

lone adj. einsam, einzeln, weltabgeschieden; ledig; -**liness** n. Einsamkeit, Verlassenheit; -**ly** adj. einsam, verlassen; -**some** adj. einsam, vereinsamt

long adj. lang; langwierig, weitläufig; weitgehend; **a** — **time** lange; **as** — **as** solange; **in the** — **run** am Ende, zuletzt; — **ago** vor langer Zeit; — **odds** hoher Einsatz; — adv. lange, über, hindurch;

all day — den ganzen Tag lang; — n. Länge; — v. verlangen, sich sehnen; -**ing** n. Sehnsucht. Verlangen; -**ing** adj. sehnsüchtig, verlangend

long-distance adj. weit entfernt; — **call** Ferngespräch

long-haired adj. langhaarig; (coll.) übercultiviert

longhand n. Handschrift

longitude n. Länge

longitudinal adj. der Länge nach, Längen-

long-lived adj. langlebig, sich lange haltend

long-playing adj. langspielend; Langspiel-

long-term adj. langfristig

long-winded adj. langatmig

look n. Blick; Anblick; Ansehen, Aussehen, Miene; — v. blicken, sehen, schauen; scheinen; aussehen; — **after** aufpassen auf; — **around** umschauen; — **at** ansehen, betrachten; — **down** (verächtlich) herabsehen; — **for** suchen; — **forward to** sich freuen auf; — **into** untersuchen; — **on** betrachten; — **out** achtgeben; Achtung! — **over** (oder **through**) durchsehen; — **up** aufblicken; aufsuchen, nachschlagen; **that's how it** -**s to me** so kommt es mir vor; -**ing** adj. -**ing glass** Spiegel

lookout n. (mil.) Ausschau, Ausblick; Wache; (naut.) Ausguck, Auslug; (fig.) Aussicht

loom n. Webstuhl; — v. sichtbar werden; undeutlich erscheinen

loop n. Schleife, Schlinge; Biegung, Krümmung; Öse; (avi.) Looping; (sich) winden; (avi.) einen Looping fliegen

loophole n. Guckloch, Luke; (mil.) Schiessscharte; (coll.) Schlupfloch; (fig.) Ausflucht, Vorwand

loose adj. los(e), frei, locker; einzeln; unzusammenhängend; **be at** — **ends** nicht recht wissen, was zu tun; **get** — loskommen; **set** — in Freiheit setzen; — v. lösen, befreien; -**n** v. lose (or locker) machen; lösen, auflösen; losmachen, losbinden; ablösen, freimachen; (fig.) trennen; -**ness** n. Lockerheit; (fig.) Liederlichkeit

loose-jointed adj. gelenkig

loose-leaf adj. mit losen Blättern

loot n. Beute, Raubgut; — v. plündern, erbeuten

lop v. schlaff hängen; beschneiden, stutzen

lope n. Trott, langer Schritt; — v. trotten

lop-eared adj. mit Hängeohren

lopsided adj. schief, einseitig

loquacious adj. geschwätzig, redselig

lord n. Herr, Gebieter; Lord; **Lord** Herr, Gott, Herrgott; **Almighty Lord** Allmächtiger Gott; **good Lord!** grosser Gott! **Lord's Prayer** Vaterunser; **Lord's Supper** Heiliges Abendmahl; — v. — **it** den grossen Herrn spielen; — **it over** herrschen (or gebieten) über; -**ly** adj. herrenmässig; vornehm, stattlich; stolz, hochmütig; -**ship** n. Herrschaft; (title) Lordschaft

lore n. Kenntnis, Wissenschaft, Lehre, Kunde

Lorraine n. Lothringen

lose v. verlieren, einbüssen; verspielen; den Kürzeren ziehen; versäumen, verpassen; (watch) nachgehen; **— color** abfärben, sich verfärben; **— ground** Einfluss verlieren; **— heart** (or **courage**) den Mut verlieren; **— one's senses** den Verstand verlieren; **— one's temper** ärgerlich werden; **— one's way** sich verirren; **— out** vollständig verlieren; **— sight of** aus den Augen verlieren; **-r** n. Verlierer, Verspieler; **good -r** guter Verlierer

loss n. Verlust, Einbusse; Nachteil, Schaden; **be at a —** verlegen sein

lost adj. **be —** verloren gehen; **give up for —** verloren geben

lot n. Los, Geschick; Teil, Anteil; Posten; Partie, Bande, Gesellschaft, Menge; Parzelle; Kabel; **a —, -s** eine Menge, ein Haufen; **building —** Bauplatz; **draw -s** Lose ziehen

lotion n. Scheinheitswasser; **eye —** Augenwasser

lottery n. Lotterie

loud adj. laut, geräuschvoll; grell, auffallend; **-ness** n. Lautheit, Lautstärke; Geschrei, Lärm

loudspeaker n. Lautsprecher

lounge n. Foyer, Wandelgang; Sofa, Chaiselongue; **—** v. müssiggehen, schlendern; faulenzen

louse n. Laus; **plant —** Blattlaus

lousy adj. lausig; (fig.) gemein, filzig

Louvain n. Löwen

lovable adj. liebenswürdig

love n. Liebe; Liebchen, Liebste; Vorliebe, Liebschaft; (tennis) Null; **be in —** verliebt sein; **fall in —** sich verlieben; **make —** den Hof machen; **—** v. lieben, liebhaben; **-liness** n. Lieblichkeit, Liebenswürdigkeit; **-ly** adj. lieblich, liebenswürdig; allerliebst, wunderschön; **-r** n. Liebhaber, Liebende

lovebird n. Wellensittich, Sperlingspapagei

love-making n. Hofmachen, Courschneiden

lovesick adj. liebeskrank

loving adj. liebend

low n. Niedrige; **—** adj. niedrig, tief; gering, mässig; seicht, billig, wohlfeil; (med.) schwach; (mus.) dunkel, leise; (fig.) niedergeschlagen; **—** v. brüllen, muhen; **-er** adj. niedriger, tiefer; niedere, untere; **-er berth** untere Bett; **-er case** Kleinbuchstabe; **-er** v. herunterlassen, herablassen; senken, sinken; herabsetzen; schwächen; erniedrigen; **-liness** n. Erniedrigung; **-ly** adj. demütig, bescheiden; gering, gewöhnlich

lox (**liquid oxygen**) n. flüssiger Sauerstoff; **—** v. mit flüssigem Sauerstoff füllen

loyal adj. loyal, treu ergeben; (ge)treu, beständig, zuverlässig; **-ist** n. Loyale, Treugesinnte; **-ty** n. Treue, Loyalität

lozenge n. Rhombus; Pastille; Bonbon

lube n. ölen, Schmieren

lubricant n. Schmiermittel; **—** adj. schlüpfrig; schmierend

lubricate v. ölen, schmieren

lubrication n. Ölen, Schmieren

Lucerne, Lake of n. Vierwaldstättersee

lucid adj. licht, leuchtend; hell, glänzend; klar, durchsichtig

luck n. Glück(sfall); Zufall; **bad —** Unglück, Pech; **by —** glücklicherweise; **good —** Glück, Chance; **-ily** adv. zum Glück, glücklicherweise; **-less** adj. unglücklich, erfolglos; ungünstig; **-y** adj. glücklich, erfolgreich; günstig; **be -y** Glück haben; **-y chance** günstige Gelegenheit

lucrative adj. gewinnbringend, einträglich; lukrativ

lug v. ziehen, zerren, schleppen

luggage n. Gepäck, Reisegepäck; **— rack** Gepäcknetz, Gepäckständer

lukewarm adj. lauwarm; (fig.) gleichgültig

lull n. Einlullen; Windpause, Windstille; **—** v. einlullen; (fig.) beruhigen, stillen

lullaby n. Schlummerlied, Wiegenlied

lumber n. Bauholz; **— dealer** Bauholzhändler

lumberjack n. Holzfäller, Holzarbeiter

lumberman n. Holzhändler; Holzfäller

lumberyard n. Holzplatz

luminous adj. leuchtend, glänzend; lichtvoll; Licht-, Leucht-

lump n. Klumpen, Stück; Masse, Ganze, Menge, Haufen; Beule, Schlag; **— sugar** Würfelzucker, Stückzucker; **— sum** runde Summe, Gesamtsumme; **—** v. vereinigen, zusammenwerfen

lunacy n. (med.) Mondsucht; (fig.) Irrsinn, Wahnsinn, Verrücktheit

lunatic adj. (med.) mondsüchtig; (fig.) irrsinnig, wahnsinnig, verrückt; **— asylum** Irrenhaus; **—** n. Irrsinnige, Wahnsinnige

lunch n. Imbiss; Gabelfrühstück; **—** v. frühstücken; **-eon** n. formelles Essen, Mittagessen

lung n. Lunge, Lungenflügel; **iron —** eiserne Lunge

lunge n. Ausfall, Stoss; Bewegung, Ruck; **—** v. stossen, ausfallen; losstürzen

lurch n. Taumeln, Ruck; (naut.) Überholen; **leave in the —** im Stich lassen; **—** v. taumeln, wanken; (naut.) überholen

lure n. (fishing) Köder; (fig.) Lockmittel; **—** v. ködern, (an)locken, reizen

luscious adj. köstlich, schmackhaft; saftig, süss; lieblich; (fig.) übersüss, widerlich

lush adj. frisch, saftig, üppig

lust n. Begierde, Wollust; Lust, Gier; Hang, Sucht; **—** v. begehren, gelüsten; sich sehnen; **-y** adj. munter, lebhaft; lustig, fröhlich; kräftig, tüchtig, rüstig

luster n. Glanz, Schimmer

lute n. Laute

Lutheran n. Lutheraner; **—** adj. lutherisch

luxuriant adj. üppig, wuchernd

luxurious adj. luxuriös, verschwenderisch, schwelgerisch

luxury n. Luxus, Verschwendung; Üppigkeit, Wohlleben

lyceum n. Lyzeum
lye n. Lauge
lying n. Lüge, Unwahrheit; — adj. lügnerisch, lügend
lymph n. Lymphe; (med.) Impfstoff; **-atic** adj. lymphatisch; (fig.) schlaff
lynch n. Volksjustiz; Lynchen; — v. lynchen, Volksjustiz ausüben
lyre n. Leier
lyric(al) adj. lyrisch
lysol n. Lysol

M

macabre adj. todesdüster
macadam n. Schotter(strasse); Asphalt
Mach n. Geschwindigkeitsmasseinheit-1-mal die Schallgeschwindigkeit (nach Ernst Mach, Physiker)
machination n. Anstiftung. pl. Ränke
machine n. Maschine; Triebwerk, Getriebe; (pol.) Organisation; — **gun** Maschinengewehr; — **tool** Werkzeugmaschine; — v. mit Maschinen arbeiten, maschinell herstellen; **-ry** n. Maschinerie, Mechanismus
machinist n. Maschinist; Maschinenarbeiter, Maschinenmeister; Maschinenbauer, Maschinenbauingenieur
mackerel n. Makrele
mackintosh n. wasserdichter Mantel, Regenmantel
mad adj. toll, verrückt, wahnsinnig; böse, zornig; go — verrückt werden; it's **enough to drive one** — man könnte aus der Haut fahren; — **dog** toller Hund; **-den** v. toll (or rasend, böse, wütend) machen; rasend werden; **-ness** n. Tollheit, Verrücktheit, Wahnsinn; Tollwut; Wut, Zorn; (fig.) Begeisterung
madam n. gnädige Frau; Hausfrau
made adj. gemacht, angefertigt, hergestellt; ausgebildet
made-to-order adj. auf Bestellung gemacht
made-up adj. ausgedacht, zurechtgemacht; geschminkt
madhouse n. Tollhaus, Irrenhaus
madman n. Wahnsinnige, Verrückte
magazine n. Zeitschrift; Magazin; Lagerhaus, Speicher; (naut.) Pulverkammer
magic n. Zauber; Magie, Zauberei, Zauberkunst; — adj. magisch, zauberhaft; bezaubernd; **-ian** n. Magier, Zauberer, Zauberkünstler
magistrate n. Beamte, Gerichtsbeamte; Polizeirichter
magnanimity n. Grossherzigkeit, Grossmut
magnanimous adj. grossherzig, grossmütig
magnesium n. Magnesium; — **sulphate** Bittersalz
magnet n. Magnet; **-ic** adj. magnetisch; **-ism** n. Magnetismus, magnetische Kraft
magneto n. Zündapparat; Magnetzündung
magnificence n. Pracht, Herrlichkeit, Grossartigkeit

magnificent adj. prachtvoll, herrlich, grossartig
magnify v. vergrössern
magnifying glass n. Vergrösserungsglas, Lupe
magnitude n. Grösse, Umfang; (fig.) Wichtigkeit
magpie n. Elster
mahogany n. Mahagonibaum, Mahagoniholz; — adj. mahagonifarben
maid n. Mädchen, Jungfrau; Maid, Magd; **old** — alte Jungfer; **-en** n. Mädchen, Jungfrau; **-en** adj. mädchenhaft, jungfräulich; unverheiratet; (fig.) neu, frisch; **-en speech** Jungfernrede; **-en voyage** Jungfernfahrt
mail n. Post(sendung); Panzer, Rüstung; **by** — per Post; **by registered** — eingeschrieben; **by return** — postwendend, mit umgehender Post
mailbag n. Briefbeutel
mailbox n. Briefkasten
mailman n. Briefträger, Postbote
mail-order house n. Postversandgeschäft
maim v. verstümmeln, verkrüppeln
main n. Hauptrohr; Gewalt, Macht, Stärke; Hauptteil; in the — zum grössten Teil, überhaupt; — adj. hauptsächlich, wichtigst, Haupt-; gewaltig, mächtig; ganz, voll; by — **strength, by** — **force** mit voller Kraft; — **office** Zentralbüro; **rising** — Steigleitung
mainland n. Festland
mainspring n. Haupt(trieb)feder
mainstay n. (naut.) Grosstag; (fig.) Hauptstütze
maintain v. (aufrecht)erhalten, weiterführen, unterhalten; behaupten
maintenance n. Erhaltung; Aufrechterhaltung; Unterhalt; Behauptung
maize n. Mais
majestic adj. majestätisch
majesty n. Majestät; (fig.) Hoheit, Erhabenheit, Würde
major n. (educ.) Hauptstudienfach; (law) Mündige, Grossjährige; (mil.) Major; (phil.) Hauptsatz; — **general** Generalmajor; — adj. grossjährig, majorenn, mündig; grösser, wichtiger; weiter, breiter; — **part** grössten Teil; **-ity** n. Mehrzahl, Mehrheit; (law) Mündigkeit; (mil.) Majorsrang
make n. Fabrikat, Marke, Erzeugnis; Bau, Form, Gestalt; Stil, Schnitt; — v. machen, anfertigen, fabrizieren, schaffen, herstellen; zwingen; verdienen, gewinnen; ergeben; — **a choice** eine Wahl treffen; — **a speech** eine Rede halten; — **contact** den Stromkreis schliessen, anschliessen; in Kontakt treten, den Kontakt aufnehmen; — **fun** of sich lustig machen über; — **good** Wort halten; erfüllen; rechtfertigen; vergüten; — **money** Geld verdienen, reich werden; — **off** durchbrennen; — **out** entziffern; ausfertigen, ausfüllen; gelingen; — **over** umarbeiten; überweisen; — **peace** Frieden schliessen; — **sure** sich vergewissern; — **up** zusam-

menstellen; bilden, erfinden; sich versöhnen; sich schminken; nachholen; — up for wieder gutmachen; — up one's mind einen Entschluss fassen; — use of Nutzen ziehen aus; — war Krieg führen; –r n. Fabrikant; Verfertiger; the Maker der Schöpfer

make-believe n. Vorwand, Schein, Spiegelfechterei; — adj. vorgeblich, scheinbar

makeshift n. Notbehelf, Lückenbüsser; — adj. behelfsmässig; interimistisch

make-up n. Beschaffenheit, Natur; (theat.) Schminke(n), Maske, Ausstaffierung, Verkleidung, Ausstattung; (typ.) Umbruch

making n. Machen; he has the –s of er hat das Zeug zu; in the — im Werden

maladjustment n. schlechtes Anpassungsvermögen

malady n. Unpässlichkeit, Krankheit

malaprop(ism) n. Wortverdrehung

malaria n. Malaria, Sumpffieber, Wechselfieber

male n. Mann; (zool.) Männchen; — adj. männlich

malefactor n. Übeltäter, Missetäter

malevolent adj. böswillig, boshaft, feindselig, übelwollend

malice n. Bosheit, Arglist; (law) böse Absicht

malicious adj. boshaft, arglistig, heimtückisch; (law) böswillig

malign adj. unheilvoll, nachteilig, schädlich; — v. beschimpfen, verleumden, lästern; **–ant** adj. boshaft; (med.) bösartig

mallard n. Enterich, Erpel

malleable adj. hämmerbar; (fig.) schmiegsam, biegsam

mallet n. Hammer, Schlegel

malnutrition n. Unterernährung

malt n. Malz

maltreat v. schlecht (or unfreundlich) behandeln

ma(m)ma n. Mama

mammal n. Säugetier

mammoth n. Mammut; — adj. mammutartig, riesig

man n. Mann, Mensch; Diener, Arbeiter; Soldat, Matrose; (chess) Figur, Stein; — overboard! Mann über Bord! men's room Herrentoilette; — v. bemannen; **–ful** adj. männlich, mannhaft, tapfer; **–hood** n. Männlichkeit, Mannhaftigkeit; Mannesalter; Menschentum; **–ikin** n. Mannequin, Probiermamsell; Gliederpuppe; **–kind** n. Menschheit, Menschengeschlecht; **–like** adj. menschlich, menschenähnlich; männlich; **–liness** n. Männlichkeit, Mannhaftigkeit; **–ly** adj. männlich, mannhaft, tapfer

manage v. verwalten, leiten; handhaben, behandeln, gebrauchen; bändigen; sich behelfen, schonen; **–able** adj. handlich, lenksam, fügsam; **–ment** n. Leitung, Verwaltung, Direktion, Geschäftsführung; Handhabung, Behandlung; (rail.) Betriebsplan; **–r** n. Vorsteher, Leiter,

Direktor, Geschäftsführer; Verwalter; Haushalter

mandate n. Mandat; Befehl, Erlass; (law) Vollmacht, Auftrag

mandolin n. Mandoline

mane n. Mähne

maneuver n. Manöver; — v. manövrieren

manganese n. Mangan

mange n. Räude

manger n. Krippe, Futtertrog

mangle n. Mangel, Rolle; — v. zerhacken, zerfetzen; verstümmeln

manhole n. Einsteigloch

manicure n. Handpflege, Maniküre; — v. maniküren

manifest n. Kundgebung; Manifest; — adj. augenscheinlich, offenbar; — v. offenbaren, zeigen, kundtun; **–ation** n. Offenbarung; Kundgebung; **–o** n. Bekanntmachung, Proklamation, Manifest

manifold adj. mannigfaltig, mannigfach

manila paper n. Manilapapier

manipulate v. handhaben, behandeln, manipulieren

manipulation n. Handhabung, Verfahren; Kunstgriff, Manipulation

mannequin n. Mannequin, Probiermamsell

manner n. Art, Weise; (lit.) Manier, Stil; pl. Manieren, Benehmen, Sitte, Lebensart; in such a — so dass; in this — auf diese Weise; **–ism** n. Manieriertheit; Künstelei; **–ly** adj. manierlich, gesittet, höflich

manor n. Landgut, Gutsbesitz

manpower n. (verfügbares) Menschenmaterial

mansion n. (herrschaftliches) Wohnhaus

manslaughter n. Totschlag

mantel n. Kaminmantel, Mauermantel

mantle n. Mantel; (fig.) Deckmantel, Schleier, Überzug

manual n. Handbuch, Leitfaden; Manual; — adj. manuell; Hand-; — training handwerklicher Unterricht, Handarbeitsunterricht

manufacture n. Fabrikation, Anfertigung; — v. fabrizieren, verarbeiten, anfertigen; **–r** n. Fabrikant

manufacturing n. Fabrikation, Anfertigung

manure n. Dünger, Dung, Mist

manuscript n. Manuskript, Handschrift, Original

many adj. manch, mancherlei; viel, vielerlei, zahlreich; a great — sehr viele; in — ways vor vielerlei Art; — a mancher, manch ein; — a time sehr oft

map n. Karte, Landkarte, Himmelskarte; — maker Kartograph, Landkartenzeichner; road — Strassenkarte, Autokarte; — v. aufzeichnen, kartographieren; — out planen, darstellen

maple n. Ahorn

mar v. entstellen; beschädigen; verderben; (fig.) stören

marauder n. Marodeur, Plünderer

marble n. Marmor; (art) Marmorbildwerk, Marmorstatue; (game) Murmel;

— *adj.* marmorn, marmoriert; — *v.*
marmorieren

march *n.* Marsch; Gang, Schritt; (fig.)
Fortschritt; **March** *n.* März; — *u.*
marschieren, ziehen, gehen, schreiten

mare *n.* Mähre, Stute

margarine *n.* Margarine, Kunstbutter

margin *n.* Rand; (fig.) Grenze. Spielraum;
(com.) Gewinnspanne; **-al** *adj.* am
Rande, Rand-; (com.) äusserst

marigold *n.* Ringelblume, Dotterblume

marijuana, marihuana *n.* Marihuana

marina *n.* Bootsanlegestelle; Bootshafen

marine *n.* Seesoldat; Marine, Seewesen;
— *adj.* Marine-, See-, Schiffs-; **-r** *n.*
Seemann, Matrose

marionette *n.* Marionette, Drahtpuppe

marital *adj.* ehelich

maritime *adj.* an der See liegend (or
lebend); See-, Küsten-, Schiffahrts-

mark *n.* Zeichen, Merkmal, Marke;
Strieme, Narbe; Fleck, Mal; Stempel;
Spur; Ziel; (educ.) Note; **hit the** — **das
Ziel treffen**; **miss the** — **das Ziel verfehlen**; — *v.* (be)zeichnen, markieren,
kennzeichnen; zensieren; sich merken;
— **down** notieren; (price) herabsetzen;
— **my words!** merken Sie sich das! —
time auf der Stelle treten

market *n.* Markt, Messe, Jahrmarkt;
Absatz; Nachfrage; Marktpreis; Handelsplatz; — **place** Marktplatz; **meat**
— Fleischmarkt; **open** — öffentlicher
Markt; — *v.* einkaufen; auf den Markt
bringen, verkaufen; **-able** *adj.* verkäuflich, gangbar

marksman *n.* Scharfschütze

markup *n.* Verdienstaufschlag

marmalade *n.* Marmelade

marmot *n.* Murmeltier

marriage *n.* Ehe; Heirat, Hochzeit; (fig.)
enge Verbindung; **by** — angeheiratet;
civil — Ziviltrauung; **give away in** —
zur Frau geben, verheiraten; **-able** *adj.*
heiratsfähig, mannbar

married *adj.* verheiratet, verehelicht;
ehelich; **be** — verheiratet sein; **get** —
sich verheiraten, heiraten, verheiratet
werden; **newly** — neuvermählt

marrow *n.* Knochenmark; (fig.) Kern,
Beste

marry *v.* heiraten; verheiraten, trauen
vermählen

marsh *n.* Marsch(land), Sumpf, Morast;
-y *adj.* morastig, sumpfig

marshal *n.* Marschall; **field** — Feldmarschall, Generalfeldmarschall

marshmallow *n.* Süssigkeit (aus geschla-
genem Zucker)

mart *n.* Markt, Messe

martin *n.* Mauerschwalbe

martyr *n.* Märtyrer, Glaubenszeuge;
-dom *n.* Märtyrertum; (fig.) Marter-
qualen

marvel *n.* Wunder; Verwunderung, Bewunderung; — *v.* sich (ver)wundern;
-(l)ous *adj.* wunderbar, herrlich; erstaunlich, unglaublich

mascara *n.* Wimperntusche

mascot *n.* Talisman, Maskotte, Glücks-

bringer

masculine *adj.* männlich; mannhaft, kühn

mash *n.* Maische, Mischfutter; — *v.*
zerdrücken, zerquetschen; **-ed** *adj.*
zerstampft; **-ed potatoes** Kartoffelbrei,
Kartoffelpüree,   Quetschkartoffel,
Stampfkartoffel

mask *n.* Maske; Maskierung, Tarnung;
— *v.* maskieren, verkleiden; tarnen

mason *n.* Maurer, Steinmetz; **-ry** *n.*
Maurerhandwerk; Mauerwerk; **stone**
-ry Steinmetzarbeit

masquerade *n.* Maskerade

mass *n.* Masse, Menge, Haufe(n); (min.)
Mittel; (eccl.) Messe; — **production**
Massenproduktion; — *v.* (sich) anhäufen, (sich) ansammeln; **-ive** *adj.*
massiv, schwer, fest; gediegen; derb

massacre *n.* Blutbad, Gemetzel; — *v.*
niedermetzeln, massakrieren

massage *n.* Massage; — *v.* massieren

mast *n.* Mast; Mastbaum

master *n.* Meister, Herr, Gebieter;
(educ.) Lehrer; — **key** Hauptschlüssel;
— **mind** hervorragender Geist; bedeu-
tender Mensch; — **stroke**, — **touch**
Meisterstreich, Meisterstück; **-ful** *adj.*
herrisch, gebieterisch; meisterhaft; **-ly**
adj. meisterhaft; **-y** *n.* Meisterschaft,
Gewandtheit; Beherrschung, Herrschaft, Macht; Obhand, Vorrang

masthead *n.* Zeitungskopf; (naut.) Mast-
spitze

masticate *v.* (zer)kauen

mastoid *adj.* zitzenförmig, warzenförmig

mat *n.* Matte, Decke; — *v.* mit Matten
bedecken, belegen; verflechten; mat-
tieren; — *adj.* matt

match *n.* Streichholz, Zündholz; Gleiche,
Ähnliche, Passende; Heirat; Wette,
Übereinkunft; (sports) Wettkampf,
Spiel, Partie, Match; **be a** — **for someone** jemandem gewachsen sein; — *v.*
zusammenpassen, entsprechen; anpassen; paaren; **-less** *adj.* unvergleichlich,
ohnegleichen

matchbook *n.* Streichholzheft

matchbox *n.* Streichholzschachtel

matchmaker *n.* Heiratsvermittler

mate *n.* Gatte, Gattin; Genosse, Gefährte,
Kamerad; Gehilfe, Geselle; (chess)
Matt; (naut.) Maat; **first** — Obermaat;
(zool.) Männchen, Weibchen; — *v.*
(sich) vereinigen, verbinden; verheiraten, vermählen; paaren, gatten; (chess)
matt setzen

material *n.* Material, Stoff, Bestandteil;
— *adj.* materiell, körperlich; wesentlich, wichtig; **-ism** *n.* Materialismus,
materialistische Weltanschauung; **-istic**
adj. materialistisch; **-ize** *v.* materialisie-
ren, realisieren; (sich) verwirklichen

maternal *adj.* mütterlich; mütterlicher-
seits

maternity *n.* Mutterschaft; Mütterlich-
keit; — **hospital** Entbindungsheim

mathematical *adj.* mathematisch; (fig.)
exakt, beweisbar

mathematician *n.* Mathematiker

mathematics *n.* Mathematik

matinee n. Matinee

mating n. Paarung; — time Paarungszeit

matriarchy n. Mutterherrschaft

matriculate v. immatrikulieren, (sich) einschreiben

matriculation n. Immatrikulation

matrimonial adj. ehelich

matrimony n. Ehe, Ehestand

matrix n. (bot. and geol.) Mutterboden; (mech.) Matrize, Gussform; (fig.) Nährboden

matron n. Matrone; Hausmutter, Oberin, Vorsteherin

matter n. Sache, Angelegenheit; Stoff; Geschäft; (phy. and phil.) Materie, Substanz; (fig.) Wichtigkeit, Bedeutung; as a — of fact tatsächlich, wirklich; for that — was dies betrifft; — of course Selbstverständlichkeit, ausgemachte Tatsache; — of form eine blosse Formsache; no — es macht nichts (aus), es hat nichts zu sagen, gleichviel; the — in hand die vorliegende Angelegenheit; what is the —? um was handelt es sich? was ist los? what is the — with him? was fehlt ihm? — v. ausmachen, darauf ankommen, von Bedeutung sein

matter-of-course adj. selbstverständlich

matter-of-fact adj. tatsächlich, wirklich

mattress n. Matratze; air — Luftmatratze; spring — Sprungfedermatratze

mature adj. reif; fällig; reiflich; — v. reifen, zeitigen; fällig werden

maturity n. Reife; Fälligkeit, Verfallszeit

maul v. zerschlagen; misshandeln

mausoleum n. Mausoleum, Grabmal

maxim n. Maxime, Grundsatz; Denkspruch

maximum n. Maximum, Höchstmass; — adj. höchste, grösste

may v. mag, kann, darf; May n. Mai; May Day ersten Mai

maybe adv. vielleicht, möglicherweise

Mayence n. Mainz

mayonnaise n. Mayonnaise

mayor n. Bürgermeister

maze n. Bestürzung, Verwirrung; Labyrinth, Irrgang

M.C. (master-of-ceremonies) n. Conferencier, Zeremonienmeister

me pron. mir, mich

meadow n. Wiese, Anger

meager, meagre adj. mager, dünn, dürr; dürftig, arm; unfruchtbar

meal n. Mahl(zeit); Mehl, Maismehl; -y adj. mehlig; (fig.) blass

mean v. meinen, denken; bedeuten, heissen; wollen, beabsichtigen; bestimmen, sagen; gedenken, willens sein; I — business ich rede im Ernst; you don't — it! das meinst du doch nicht wirklich; — n. Mitte; Mittel; Mittelmässigkeit, Durchschnitt; pl. Mittel, Werkzeug; Vermögen, Einkommen; by all —s durchaus, jedenfalls; by —s of mittels; by no —s keineswegs; live within one's —s den Verhältnissen entsprechend leben; ways and —s das Mittel zum Zweck, Mittel und Wege; — adj. ge-

mein, niedrig; gering; niederträchtig; filzig; mittel(mässig); -ing n. Bedeutung, Sinn; Meinung, Absicht; -ness n. Gemeinheit, Niedrigkeit; Niederträchtigkeit; Armseligkeit

meantime adv. inzwischen, unterdessen; — n. Zwischenzeit; in the — inzwischen

meanwhile adv. inzwischen, unterdessen; — n. in the — mittlerweile

measles n. pl. Masern

measure n. Mass(einheit); Massnahme, Massregel; (lit.) Silbenmass; (mus.) Zeitmass, Takt, Rhythmus; beyond — ausserordentlich; in some — gewissermassen; — v. (ab)messen, ausmessen; ermessen; Mass nehmen; -ment n. Mass; Messung, Vermessung, Abmessung

meat n. Fleisch; broiled — unter der Flamme gebratenes Fleisch; dark — dunkles (or trockenes) Fleisch; fried — Braten, Schmorbraten; light — weisses (or zartes) Fleisch; roast — Braten; what is one man's — is another man's poison des Einen Tod ist des anderen Brot; eines schickt sich nicht für alle

mechanic n. Mechaniker, Maschinenarbeiter; -al adj. mechanisch; (fig.) unbewusst, unwillkürlich; -al engineering Maschinenbau; -al man Roboter, Maschinenmensch; -s n. Mechanik, Maschinenlehre

mechanism n. Mechanismus, Getriebe; Triebwerk; defense — Verteidigungsmaschinerie

medal n. Medaille, Denkmünze, Schaumünze; -lion n. Medaillon

meddle v. sich mischen (or vermengen); sich einmischen (or einlassen); -r n. Eindringling, Lästige, Unberufene

meddlesome adj. zudringlich, vorwitzig, lästig

mediate v. vermitteln

mediator n. Vermittler, Unterhändler

medical adj. medizinisch, ärztlich; — examination ärztliche Untersuchung

medicinal adj. medizinisch, heilkräftig, heilsam

medicine n. Medizin, Heilkunde; Arznei

medieval adj. mittelalterlich

mediocre adj. mittelmässig

mediocrity n. Mittelmässigkeit; kleiner Geist

meditate v. nachsinnen, grübeln; meditieren

meditation n. Nachdenken; Betrachtung; Meditation

Mediterranean Sea n. Mittelmeer

medium n. Mittel, Hilfsmittel; Mitte; Medium; — adj. mittel(mässig); Mittel-, Durchschnitts-

medium-sized adj. mittelgross

medley n. Gemisch, Mischmasch; (mus.) Potpourri

meek adj. demütig, bescheiden; mild, sanf(mütig); -ness n. Demut, Bescheidenheit; Milde, Mildheit, Sanftmut

meet v. treffen, begegnen, stossen auf; entgegenkommen; nachkommen, erfüllen; sich treffen (or versammeln); go to

— entgegengehen, entgegenkommen; **make both ends** — mit seinen Einkünften auskommen; **till we** — **again** bis wir uns wiedersehen; **-ing** n. Versammlung, Zusammentreffen, Zusammenkunft; Sitzung, Beratung; (sports) Renntag, Wettkampf

megaphone n. Megaphon, Sprachrohr

melancholy n. Schwermut, Melancholie; — adj. schwermütig, melancholisch

mellow adj. reif; weich, mürbe; sanft, angenehm; (mus.) voll, rund; (fig.) zart, freundlich; — v. reifen; weich (or mürbe) machen; weich (or mürbe, sanft) werden; sich mildern

melodious adj. melodisch, wohlklingend

melody n. Melodie, Singweise

melon n. Melone

melt v. schmelzen, (sich) auflösen, zergehen, zerfliessen; **-ing** adj. schmelzend; **-ing point** Schmelzpunkt; **-ing pot** Schmelztiegel

member n. Mitglied, Glied; — **of congress** Abgeordnete; **-ship** n. Mitgliedschaft; Mitgliederzahl

membrane n. Membrane, Häutchen

memento n. Erinnerungszeichen, Andenken, Memento

memo abbr. Notiz, Bemerkung

memoir n. Bericht, Denkschrift; — pl. Memoiren, Biographie

memorable adj. denkwürdig, merkwürdig

memorandum n. Memorandum, Denkschrift, Note; — **book** Merkbuch

memorial n. Denkmal; — adj. dem Andenken (or Gedächtnis) dienend; **Memorial Day** 30. Mai, Heldengedenktag

memorize v. auswendig lernen, memorieren

memory n. Gedächtnis, Erinnerung(svermögen); Andenken; **in** — **of** zum Andenken an

menace n. Drohung; — v. (be)drohen

menagerie n. Menagerie

mend n. Besserung; Ausbesserung; — v. ausbessern, flicken; (ver)bessern; besser werden

mendicant n. Bettler; — adj. bettelnd, bettelarm; Bettel-

menial adj. knechtisch, niedrig

meningitis n. Hirnhautentzündung

menstruation n. Menstruation, Monatskrankheit

mental adj. geistig, innerlich; Geistes-, Kopf-; — **hospital** Nervenheilanstalt, Irrenhaus; **-ity** n. Geisteskraft; Mentalität

mention n. Erwähnung, Meldung; — v. erwähnen, anführen, melden; **don't** — **it** es ist nicht der Rede wert; **not to** — geschweige denn, abgesehen von

menu n. Menü, Speisekarte

mercantile adj. merkantil, kaufmännisch, Handels-

mercenary n. Mietling, Söldner; — adj. gedungen, feil, käuflich; gewinnsüchtig

mercerize v. merzerisieren, Seidenglanz geben

merchandise n. Ware(n)

merchant n. Kaufmann; Händler, Krämer; — **marine** Handelsflotte

merciful adj. gnädig, barmherzig, mitleidvoll; gütig

merciless adj. unbarmherzig, mitleidlos; grausam

Mercurochrome n. Quecksilberchrom, Desinfektionsmittel

mercury n. Quecksilber; (ast.) Merkur

mercy n. Gnade, Barmherzigkeit, Mitleid; **be at someone's** — in jemandes Gewalt (or jemandem preisgegeben) sein

mere adj. bloss, allein; rein, lauter; **-ly** adv. nur, bloss

merge v. einverleiben, verschmelzen; aufgehen; **-r** n. Fusion, Verschmelzung, Einverleibung

meridian n. Meridian, Mittagslinie; (fig.) Gipfel, Höhepunkt

merit n. Verdienst; Lohn, Wert; (law) Hauptpunkt; — v. verdienen; sich verdient machen; **-orious** adj. verdienstlich

mermaid n. Seejungfer, Nixe

merriment n. Fröhlichkeit, Munterkeit

merry adj. fröhlich, munter, lustig, ergötzlich

merry-go-round n. Karussell, Ringelspiel

mesh n. Masche, Netz; — v. (sich) verstricken, ineinandergreifen

mess n. Unordnung, Verwirrung; (cooking) Gericht, Schüssel; (mil.) Messe; (naut.) Back; — v. verpfuschen, in Unordnung bringen

message n. Botschaft, Mitteilung, Auftrag

messenger n. Bote, Kurier

metabolism n. Stoffwechsel; Umwandlung

metal n. Metall; **-lic** adj. metallisch, metallen; **-lurgy** n. Metallurgie, Hüttenkunde

metaphor n. Metapher

metaphysical adj. metaphysisch

metaphysics n. Metaphysik

mete v. abmessen

meteor n. Meteor; **-ite** n. Meteorstein; **-ology** n. Meteorologie

meter, metre n. Meter; Vermass, Metrik; Messer; (elec.) Zähler; (gas) Gasuhr

method n. Methode, System, Lehrweise; **-ic(al)** adj. methodisch

Methodist n. Methodist

methylene n. Methylen

metric adj. metrisch, Vers-; messend, Mass-; — **system** Dezimalsystem

metropolis n. Hauptstadt, Metropole

metropolitan n. Grozstädter; — adj. grossstädtisch; Grozstadt-, Stadt-

mettle n. Grundstoff, Temperament

mezzanine n. Zwischenstock

mica n. Glimmer

microbe n. Mikrobe, Bakterie

microfilm n. Mikrofilm

microgroove n. Schallplattenrille

micron n. Mikromillimeter; Mikron

microphone n. Mikrofon

microscope n. Mikroskop

microwave n. Ultrakurzwelle; Mikrowelle

mid adj. mitten; **-dle** n. Mitte; Taille; **in the -dle of** mitten in (or auf); **-dle** adj.

mittel, mittler; **Middle Ages** Mittelalter; **-dle class** Mittelstand; **-st** n. Mitte; **in the -st** of mitten in (or (auf); **-st** prep. inmitten

midday n. Mittag

middle-aged adj. von mittlerem Alter

middleman n. Mittelsmann, Makler, Zwischenhändler

middleweight n. Mittelgewicht; Mittelgewichtler

middy (blouse) n. Matrosenbluse

midget n. Zwerg, Knirps

midnight n. Mitternacht

midshipman n. Seekadett

midsummer n. Hochsommer; Sommersonnenwende

midway n. Mittelweg; — adv. auf halbem Wege, unterwegs; — adj. in der Mitte befindlich

midwife n. Hebamme, Geburtshelferin

mien n. Miene, Haltung

might n. Macht, Gewalt; Kraft, Stärke; **-y** adj. mächtig, gewaltig; kräftig; gross, bedeutend, wichtig

migraine n. Migräne

migrant n. (orn.) Zugvogel; (zool.) Wandertier; — adj. wandernd

migrate v. auswandern, fortziehen

migration n. Auswanderung, Fortziehen; (orn. and zool.) Wanderung

migratory adj. wandern, nomadisch, umherziehend; Zug-

Milan n. Mailand

mild adj. mild, gelinde, sanft; leicht, schwach; nachsichtig, freundlich; **-ness** n. Milde, Sanftheit

mildew n. Mehltau; Brand; Moder, Schimmel; — v. brandig werden, mit Mehltau überziehen

mile n. Meile; **-age** n. Meilenlänge, Meilenzahl

milestone n. Meilenstein

militant adj. streitend, kriegführend; streitbar

militarism n. Militarismus

military n. Militär; Soldaten, Truppen; — adj. militärisch, Kriegs-; **compulsory — service** Wehrpflicht; — **police** Militärpolizei

militia n. Miliz, Bürgerwehr, Landwehr

milk n. Milch; — **of magnesia** Magnesiumhydroxyd; — v. melken; **-ing** adj. Melk-; **-ing machine** Melkapparat; **-y** adj. milchig; **Milky Way** Milchstrasse

milkmaid n. Kuhmagd, Melkerin

milkman n. Milchmann

milksop n. Milchbart, Grünling

milkweed n. Wolfsmilch

mill n. Mühle; Fabrik; — v. mahlen, zerreiben; (coin) prägen, rändeln; **-er** n. Müller

millet n. Hirse

millennium n. Jahrtausend; tausendjähriges Reich

milligram n. Milligramm

millimeter n. Millimeter

milliner n. Putzmacherin; Modistin; **-y** n. Modeware, Putzware; **-y shop** n. Putzwarengeschäft

million n. Million; **-aire** n. Millionär

millstone n. Mühlstein

Mimeograph n. Abzugsmaschine, Mimeograph

mimic n. Nachäffer; Mime, Schauspieler; — v. nachahmen, nachäffen; **-ry** n. Nachahmung, Nachäffung; (zool.) Angleichung, Mimikry

mince v. zerhacken, zerstückeln; beschönigen; sich zieren, stolzieren

mincemeat n. Gehacktes, Schabefleisch; Fleischpastetenfüllung; — **pie** Fleischpastete

mind n. Geist, Verstand; Gesinnung, Meinung, Ansicht, Urteil; Sinn, Gemüt; **make up one's —** einen Entschluss fassen; **of sound —** bei vollem Verstande; — **reader** Gedankenleser; — v. merken, achten; bemerken, beachten; achthaben, aufpassen, sich kümmern um; **I don't —** es ist mir gleich, ich habe nichts dagegen; **-ful** adj. achtsam, aufmerksam

mine pron. mein; der (or die, das) meinige

mine n. Grube, Bergwerk; (mil.) Mine; (fig.) Fundgrube; — **field** Minenfeld; — **sweeper** Minensuchboot; **-r** n. Bergmann, Bergarbeiter, Grubenarbeiter; Minenleger, Miniérer

mineral n. Mineral; — **oil** Mineralöl; — **water** Mineralwasser; — adj. mineralisch

mingle v. mischen, vermengen

miniature n. Miniatur(gemälde); — adj. in Miniatur

miniaturization n. Verkleinerung

minimize v. aufs kleinste Mass zurückführen; verkleinern, verringern

minimum n. Minimum, Kleinste, Geringste; Mindestmass; — adj. minimal; — **wage** Mindestlohn

mining n. Bergbau

minister n. (eccl.) Geistliche, Priester, Pastor; (pol.) Minister, Gesandte

ministry n. Geistlichkeit; geistliches Amt; Ministerium

mink n. Nerz

minor n. Minderjährige; — adj. minderjährig; kleiner, geringer; unbedeutend; (mus.) moll; **-ity** n. Minderheit; (law) Minderjährigkeit

minstrel n. Spielmann, fahrende Sänger; (coll.) Negersänger

mint n. Münzstätte; (bot.) Pfefferminz; — v. prägen, münzen

minuet n. Menuett

minus n. Minuszeichen; — adj. negativ; **—amount** Fehlbetrag; — prep. ohne, weniger

minute n. Minute; Augenblick; pl. Protokoll; — **hand** Minutenzeiger; — adj. klein, winzig; genau

miocardium n. Herzmuskel

miracle n. Wunder

miraculous adj. wunderbar, übernatürlich

mirage n. Luftspiegelung, Fata Morgana; (fig.) Täuschung

mire n. Kot, Schlamm

mirror n. Spiegel; (fig.) Vorbild

mirth n. Frohsinn, Freude; Fröhlichkeit;

-ful adj. fröhlich, lustig
misadventure n. Unfall, Unglück; Missgeschick
misapprehension n. Missverständnis
misbehave v. sich schlecht (or unpassend) benehmen
misbelief n. Irrglaube
miscalculate v. falsch berechnen (or abschätzen); sich verrechnen
miscarriage n. Fehlgeburt, Frühgeburt; (fig.) Fehlschlag, Misslingen
miscarry v. zu früh gebären; misslingen, missglücken; fehlschlagen
miscellaneous adj. gemischt; vermischt; vielseitig
mischance n. Missgeschick, Unfall
mischief n. Unheil, Unglück; Unfug, Unrecht; Schaden, Nachteil
mischievous adj. mutwillig, nachteilig, verderblich, boshaft
misconduct n. schlechtes Benehmen; schlechte Verwaltung
misconstrue v. missdeuten
misdeal v. sich vergeben, falsch austeilen
misdeed n. Missetat
misdemeanor n. Fehltritt; (law) Vergehen
misdirect v. irreleiten; falsch adressieren
miser n. Geizhals; **-ly** adj. geizig, filzig
miserable adj. elend, unglücklich, erbärmlich
misery n. Elend, Not
misfire v. Versager, Fehlzündung
misfit n. Nichtpassen, Fehlerhaftigkeit; Ungeeignete
misfortune n. Unglück(sfall), Missgeschick
misgiving n. Besorgnis, Befürchtung, böse Ahnung
mishap n. Unfall, Unglück
misinform v. falsch berichten (or belehren, unterrichten)
misinterpret v. missdeuten, falsch auslegen
misjudge v. falsch beurteilen, verkennen
mislay v. verlegen
mislead v. irreführen; (fig.) verführen, verleiten; **-ing** adj. irreführend
mismanagement n. schlechte Verwaltung (or Führung)
misnomer n. falsche Benennung; (law) Namensirrtum
misogynist n. Weiberfeind
misplace v. falsch stellen, verlegen; (fig.) übel anbringen
misprint n. Druckfehler; — v. verdrucken
mispronounce v. falsch aussprechen
misrepresent v. falsch (or ungenau) darstellen, verdrehen; **-ation** n. falsche Darstellung, Verdrehung
misrule n. schlechte Regierung; ungerechte Leitung
miss n. Fräulein
miss n. Fehlschuss, Fehlstoss, Fehlwurf; — v. verfehlen, versäumen, vermissen; auslassen, übergehen; missen, entbehren; — **one's mark** fehlschiessen; **-ing** adj. fehlend, ausbleibend; vermisst, verschollen; fort, abwesend
missal n. Messbuch
misshapen adj. verunstaltet, entstellt,

ungestalt
missile n. Wurfgeschoss; Projektil, Geschoss
mission n. Mission; Missionshaus; Sendung, Auftrag, Botschaft; Lebensziel; **-ary** n. Missionar
misspell v. falsch buchstabieren (or schreiben)
misstatement n. falsche Angabe
misstep n. Fehltritt; Missgriff
mist n. Nebel; **-y** adj. neblig, wolkig, feucht; (fig.) unklar, dunkel
mistake n. Irrtum, Versehen; Missgriff, Missverständnis; Fehler; **by —** aus Versehen; — v. verkennen, verwechseln; missverstehen; **-n** adj. falsch, irrig; **be —n** sich irren
Mister n. Herr
mistletoe n. Mistel
mistreat v. misshandeln; missbrauchen; **-ment** n. Misshandlung; Missbrauch
mistress n. Herrin, Gebieterin; Lehrerin; Geliebte
mistrial n. ergebnisloses Strafverfahren
mistrust n. Misstrauen, Argwohn; — v. misstrauen, argwöhnen
misunderstand v. missverstehen, falsch auslegen; **-ing** n. Missverständnis, Irrtum
misuse v. missbrauchen; misshandeln
mite n. Milbe; (fig.) Kleinigkeit
miter, mitre n. Mitra, Bischofsmütze
mitigate v. lindern, mildern, abschwächen, besänftigen
mitt(en) n. Fausthandschuh
mix v. mischen, mengen; (sich) vermischen, vermengen; **-ed** adj. vermischt, vermengt; gemischt, Misch-; **-ed up** verwirrt, verwickelt; **-er** n. Mixer; Mischer; **concrete -er** Betonmischmaschine; **electric -er** Elektromix; **-ture** n. Mischung, Gemisch; Vermischung; Mixtur
moan v. Stöhnen, Ächzen; — v. stöhnen, ächzen
mob n. Mob, Pöbel; Gesindel, Rotte; (coll.) Bande; — v. anfallen; anpöbeln
mobile adj. beweglich, mobil
mobility n. Beweglichkeit
mobilization n. Mobilmachung, Kriegsrüstung, Kriegsbereitschaft
mobilize v. mobil machen, rüsten, mobilisieren; (fig.) beweglich machen
mock v. (ver)spotten, verhöhnen; nachahmen, täuschen; — adj. falsch, unecht, nachgemacht; Schein-; — **orange** Pfeifenstrauch; **-ery** n. Spott, Spötterei; Blendwerk; **-ingly** adv. spotten, spöttisch nachahmend
mockingbird n. Spottdrossel
mock-up n. Attrappe; Flugzeugmodell
mode n. Mode, Sitte, Gebrauch; Art und Weise, Form, Modus; (mech.) Verfahren; (mus.) Tonart
model n. Modell; Muster, Schablone; (fig.) Vorbild; — adj. musterhaft, vorbildlich; — v. modellieren; (ab)formen, gestalten; (coll.) modeln
moderate v. mässigen, mildern, lindern, beruhigen; einschränken; — adj. mäs-

sig; gemässigt; mild; mittelmässig

moderation n. Mässigung, Mässigkeit, Gleichmut

moderator n. Mittelmann; Examinator

modern adj. modern, jetzig, neu; **-ism** n. Neuerungssucht; **-istic** adj. neuerungssüchtig; **-ize** v. modernisieren, erneuern

modest adj. bescheiden, anspruchslos, mässig; sittsam; **-y** n. Bescheidenheit, Anspruchslosigkeit; Sittsamkeit

modification n. Abänderung, Veränderung

modify v. abändern, einschränken, mildern; (gram.) näher bestimmen; umlauten

modulate v. modulieren, anpassen

modulator n. (rad.) Tonblende

mohair n. Mohär, Kamelhaar; Angorahaar

moist adj. feucht, nass; **-en** v. befeuchten, anfeuchten; benetzen, nässen; **-ure** n. Feuchtigkeit, Nässe

molar adj. zermalmend, zermahlend; **— tooth** Backenzahn

molasses n. Melasse, Sirup

mold n. Form; Gussform, Schablone; (agr.) Gartenerde, Blumenerde; (chem.) Schimmel; (fig.) Bildung, Körperbau; **—** v. formen, bilden; schimmeln; **-er** v. zerfallen, vermodern, verwittern; zerbröckeln; **-ing** n. Formen; (arch.) Ornament; Gesims, Fries; **-y** adj. schimmelig, modrig, dumpfig

mole n. Leberfleck, Mal, Muttermal; (zool.) Maulwurf

molecule n. Molekül

molest v. belästigen

mollify v. besänftigen; lindern, mildern

mollusk n. Molluske, Weichtier

molt v. (sich) mausern, haaren, häuten

molten adj. geschmolzen, gegossen

moment n. Augenblick, Moment; Wichtigkeit; **at the —** im Augenblick, gerade jetzt; **in a —** gleich, sofort; **the very —** gerade als; **-ary** adj. momentan, augenblicklich; vorübergehend, flüchtig; **-ous** adj. wichtig, bedeutend, folgenschwer

momentum n. Moment, Triebkraft

monarch n. Monarch, Alleinherrscher; **-ist** n. Monarchist; **-y** n. Monarchie

monastery n. Mönchskloster, Kloster

Monday n. Montag

money n. Geld; Münze, Zahlungsmittel; (fig.) Reichtum, Vermögen; **— order** Geldanweisung, Postanweisung; **-ed** adj. reich, vermögend

mongrel n. Mischling, Bastard; **—** adj. gemischt, Bastard-

monitor n. Klassenordner; (rad.) Monitor; **—** v. rückkoppeln

monk n. Mönch

monkey n. Affe; (fig.) Maulaffe; Range; **— wrench** Schraubenschlüssel, Engländer

monogamy n. Monogamie, Einehe

monogram n. Monogramm

monolith n. Monolith

monolog(ue) n. Monolog, Selbstgespräch

monoplane n. Eindecker

monopolize v. monopolisieren; (fig.) an sich reissen

monopoly n. Monopol, Alleinhandel

monotonous adj. eintönig, einförmig, monoton

Monotype Monotypsetzmaschine; Setzen an der Monotypmaschine

monoxide n. Monoxyd

monsoon n. Monsun, Passatwind

monster n. Ungeheuer, Scheusal; Missgeburt

monstrosity n. Ungeheuerlichkeit, Widernatürlichkeit

monstrous adj. ungeheuer, monströs; unnatürlich

month n. Monat; **-s allowance** Monatszuschuss, monatliches Taschengeld; **-'s pay** Monatsgehalt, Monatslohn; **next — nächster** Monat; **this — dieser** Monat; **-ly** adj. monatlich

Montreal n. Montreal

monument n. Denkmal, Monument; **-al** adj. monumental, riesig; Denkmal-, Gedächtnis-, Gedenk-

mood n. Stimmung, Laune; (gram.) Modus; **-y** adj. launisch; mürrisch, verdriesslich, verstimmt

moon n. Mond

moonbeam n. Mondstrahl

moonlight n. Mondlicht, Mondschein

moonshine n. Mondschein; (fig.) Faselei; (sl.) heimlich destillierter Alkohol

moor n. Moor, Morast; Moor n. Maure, Mohr; **—** v. vertäuen; **-ing** n. Vertäuung

moose n. Elch, Elen

moot adj. streitig, diskutierbar

mop n. Scheuerbesen, Mop; **—** v. (auf)wischen

mope v. schwermütig (or niedergeschlagen, träumerisch) sein

moral n. Moral, Sittlichkeit; Ethik, Sittenlehre; Nutzanwendung; **—** adj. moralisch, sittlich; **-ist** n. Moralist, Tugendrichter, Sittenlehrer; **-ity** n. Sittenlehre; Sittlichkeit; **-ize** v. moralisieren

morale n. Mut; Geisteszucht

morass n. Morast, Sumpf

Moravia n. Mähren

morbid adj. krankhaft

more n. Mehr, Grössere; **—** adj. mehr; ferner, andere; weiter, grösser; **—** adv. mehr, wieder(um), dazu; **— and —** immer mehr; **— or less** mehr oder weniger; **no — nicht(s)** mehr; **no — than** ebensowenig wie; **once — noch** einmal; **one — noch** eines; **some — noch** etwas; **the — the better** je mehr desto besser

moreover adv. ausserdem, überdies; auch, weiter, ferner

morgue n. Leichenschauhaus

morning n. Morgen; Vormittag; **good — guten** Morgen; **in the — am** Morgen (or Vormittag); morgens; **this — heute** morgen; **—** adj. früh, morgendlich, Morgen-

morning-glory n. Aurikelart

morocco (leather) n. Maroquin, Saffianleder

moron n. Schwachsinnige

morphine n. Morphium

morrow n. Morgen, folgender Tag

Morse code n. Morsealphabet

morsel n. Bissen, Bisschen, Stückchen

mortal n. Sterbliche, Mensch; — adj. sterblich, tödlich, todbringend; Todes-; menschlich; fürchterlich; -ity n. Sterblichkeit(sziffer)

mortar n. (arch.) Mörtel; (mil.) Mörser; — and pestle Mörser and Schlegel

mortgage n. Hypothek, Pfandgut; Verpfändung; — v. verpfänden, mit Hypotheken belasten

mortification n. Kasteiung, Ertötung; Beleidigung, Demütigung; (med.) Absterben, Brand

mortify v. kasteien, ertöten; beleidigen, demütigen; (med.) absterben, den Brand bekommen

mortise n. Zapfenloch; — v. verzapfen

mortuary n. Leichenhalle; Begräbniskapelle; — adj. Toten-, Leichen-

mosque n. Moschee

mosquito n. Moskito

moss n. Moos; Torf; Moor; -y adj. moosig, bemoost

most n. Meiste, Höchste, Äusserste; — adj. meiste, grösste, höchste; — adv. meist(ens), sehr; at — höchstens, im besten Falle; — of all am meisten; -ly adv. meisten(teil)s

motel n. Autohotel, Motel

moth n. Motte, Nachtfalter; — ball Mottenkugel; in — balls eingekampfert, eingemottet

mother n. Mutter; — tongue Muttersprache; — v. bemuttern; -hood n. Mutterschaft; -less adj. mutterlos; -ly adj. mütterlich

mother-in-law n. Schwiegermutter

mother-of-pearl n. Perlmutter

motif n. Leitmotiv

motion n. Bewegung, Gang; Antrieb. Regung; (pol.) Antrag, Vorschlag; make a — einen Antrag stellen; — picture Film; — v. ein Zeichen geben, zuwinken; -less adj. bewegungslos, regungslos

motivate v. motivieren, begründen

motive n. Motiv, Beweggrund; Antrieb; — adj. motiviert; bewegend; — power Triebkraft

motley adj. bunt(scheckig); buntgekleidet

motor n. Motor; — court Autoplatz; — launch Motorbarkasse; — v. im Wagen (or Auto) fahren; — adj. motorisch, bewegend; -ist n. Kraftfahrer

motorboat n. Motorboot

motorbus n. Autobus

motorcar n. Auto(mobil), Kraftwagen, Wagen

motorcycle n. Motorrad, Kraftfahrrad

motorman n. Motorführer

motto n. Motto, Sinnspruch, Devise

mound n. Erdhügel, Erdwall

mount n. Berg, Hügel; Reitpferd; Karton, Bilderrahmen; — v. (hinauf)steigen; aufsitzen, besteigen; montieren, errichten; aufziehen; (mil.) in Stellung bringen; -ed adj. beritten; -ing n.

Aufziehen; Einfassung; Garnitur, Ausrüstung

mountain n. Berg, Gebirge; range of — pl. Bergkette, Gebirgszug; — adj. gewaltig, berghoch; Berg-, Gebirgs-; -eer n. Bergsteiger; Bergbewohner; -ous adj. gebirgig, bergig

mourn v. (be)trauern; (be)klagen; -er n. Trauernde, Leidtragende; -ful adj. trauervoll, kummervoll, traurig; Trauer-; -ing n. Trauer, Trauern, Trauerkleidung

mouse n. Maus; — trap Mausefalle

mouth n. Mund; Mündung, Öffnung; Loch, Mundloch; (zool.) Maul; by word of — mündlich; make one's — water den Mund wässerig machen; — organ Mundharmonika; — v. in den Mund nehmen; laut (or affektiert) sprechen; -ful n. Mundvoll, Bissen

mouthpiece n. Mundstück; (coll.) Wortführer, Verteidiger, Sprachrohr

move v. Bewegung; Ausziehen, Umzug; Zug; (fig.) Schritt, Massregel; — v. bewegen, rühren; sich fortbewegen (or rühren); (aus)ziehen, umziehen; (pol.) beantragen; -ment n. Bewegung, Handlung, Gang; Schwung; (mus.) Satz; (watch) Werk, Gehwerk; -r n. Bewegende, Anstifter, Urheber; Spediteur

mov(e)able adj. beweglich, veränderlich, lose; — n. pl. Mobilien, Mobiliar; bewegliche Habe

movie n. Film; pl. Kino

moving adj. bewegend, beweglich; rührend; — picture Film(bild), Kinostück

mow v. (ab)mähen, schneiden; -er n. Mäher, Schnitter; Mähmaschine; -ing adj. mähend; -ing machine Mähmaschine

much adj. viel; — adv. weit, bei weitem, sehr; he is too — for me ich bin ihm nicht gewachsen; very — sehr

mucilage n. Gummilösung

muck n. Dünger, Kompost, Mist; Unrat, Schmutz

mucous adj. schleimig, schlüpfrig

mucus n. Schleim

mud n. Schlamm, Kot; Schlick; Lehm; -dle n. Wirrwarr, Verwirrung, Konfusion; -dle v. trüben, benebeln; konfus (or verwirrt, schlammig, betrunken) machen; -dy adj. schlammig, trübe; schmutzig, beschmutzt; verworren, konfus; irdisch

mudguard n. Kotflügel, Schutzblech

muff n. Muff(e); — v. verderben, verpfuschen

muffin n. Teegebäck

muffle v. einhüllen, verhüllen; dämpfen; -r n. Halstuch, Wollbinde; (auto) Schalldämpfer, Auspufftopf

mug n. Krug, Becher

muggy adj. schwül

mulberry n. Maulbeere

mulch n. Streu

mule n. Maulesel, Maultier

Multigraph n. Verfielfältigungsmaschine

multiplication n. Vervielfältigung; Mul-

tiplikation; — **table** Einmaleins
multiplier n. Multiplikator, Vermehrer
multiply v. multiplizieren; (sich) vermehren; vervielfältigen
multi-stage rocket n. Vielstufenrakete
multitude n. Vielzahl, Mehrheit; Menge
multitudinous adj. zahlreich, vielfältig; unermesslich
mum! interj. st! still! — adj. stumm, still; **keep —** den Mund halten
mumble n. Murmeln, Gemurmel; — v. murmeln, mummeln; muffeln; knabbern
mummy n. Mumie
mumps n. pl. Mumps, Ziegenpeter
munch v. bedächtig (or geräuschvoll) kauen, schmatzen
mundane adj. weltlich, irdisch
Munich n. München
municipal adj. städtisch; Stadt-, Gemeinde-; — **government** Magistrat; **-ity** n. Stadtbezirk
munition n. Munition; pl. Kriegsvorräte
mural adj. mauerähnlich, mauerartig; Mauer-, Wand-; — n. Wandgemälde
murder n. Mord; — v. (er)morden; n. Mörder; **-ous** adj. mörderisch; blutgierig, grausam
murmur n. Gemurmel; Murmeln; Gemurr; Gerücht; (med.) Geräusch; — v. murmeln, plätschern; rauschen; murren
muscle n. Muskel; (fig.) Muskelkraft
muscle-bound adj. übertrainiert
muscular adj. muskulös; — **dystrophy** n. (med.) Muskelschwund
muse v. nachdenken, nachsinnen
museum n. Museum
mush n. Maisbrei, Mehlbrei
mushroom n. Pilz; — v. plötzlich emporschiessen
music n. Musik; Tonkunst, Tonstück Noten; — **box** Spieldose; **-al** adj musikalisch; (fig.) wohlklingend, harmonisch; Musik-; **-al comedy** musikalische Komödie, Singspiel; **-ian** n. Musiker, Musikant; Tonkünstler
musing n. Nachdenken, Sinnen; — adj. nachdenklich, sinnend
musk n. Moschus, Bisam
musket n. Muskete, Flinte; **-eer** n. Musketier
muskrat n. Bisamratte
muslin n. Musselin, Nesseltuch
muss n. Unordnung; — v. verwirren
mussel n. Miesmuschel
must v. muss; I — **not** ich darf nicht; — n. Muss; Most
mustache n. Schnurrbart
mustard n. Senf, Mostrich; — **gas** Gelbkreuzgas, Senfgas
muster n. Musterung, Heerschau, Parade; — v. mustern; aufbringen, auftreiben
musty adj. dumpfig, schimmelig, moderig, muffig; abgestanden, schal
mutation n. Änderung, Veränderung, Wechsel; (med.) Mutieren, Mutation
mute n. Stumme; — adj. stumm; lautlos
mutilate v. verstümmeln
mutilation n. Verstümmelung
mutineer n. Meuterer, Aufwiegler

mutinous adj. meuterisch, rebellisch, aufrührerisch
mutiny n. Meuterei, Auflehnung; Aufruhr; — v. meutern
mutter n. Gemurmel, Gemurr; — v. murmeln, murren; munkeln
mutton n. Hammelfleisch
mutual adj. gegenseitig, beiderseitig; gemeinsam; **by — consent** in gegenseitigem Einvernehmen
muzzle n. Maulkorb; (gun) Mündung; (coll.) Maul, Schnauze; — v. mit einem Maulkorb versehen, den Mund stopfen, knebeln; schnüffeln
my pron. mein; **-self** pron. mich, mir; ich selbst (or selber)
myriad n. Myriade; — adj. zahllos, unzählig
mysterious adj. geheimnisvoll, rätselhaft, mysteriös
mystery n. Geheimnis, Rätsel; Mysterium; — **story** Kriminalgeschichte
mystic adj. mystisch, geheimnisvoll; — n. Mystiker; **-al** adj. mystisch; **-ism** n. Mystizismus
myth n. Mythus, Mythe; Sage, Fabel; **-ical** adj. mythisch, sagenhaft, fabelhaft; **-ology** n. Mythologie, Götterlehre

N

nab v. erwischen, ergreifen
nacelle n. Ballonkorb; Flugzeugrumpf
nag n. Pferd, Mähre, Klepper; — v. ärgern, nörgeln; quälen, zusetzen
nail n. Nagel; **-file** Nagelfeile; — v. (an)nageln, festnageln; beim Wort nehmen
naive adj. naiv natürlich; unbefangen
naked adj. nackt, bloss, entblösst; (bot.) kahl; (fig.) unverhüllt, einfach; **entirely — splitterfasernackt; -ness** n. Nacktheit, Blösse; (fig.) Offenheit, Unverhülltheit
name n. Name, Benennung, Titel; **by —** dem Namen nach; **in — only** nur dem Namen nach; **what is your —?** wie heissen Sie? — v. (be-)nennen; bezeichnen, erwähnen; ernennen, bestimmen; **be -d** heissen; **-less** adj. namenlos, unbenannt; (fig.) unsäglich; **-ly** adv. nämlich; **-sake** n. Namensvetter
nap n. Schläfchen, Nickerchen; — v. schlummern
nape n. Nacken, Genick
naphtha n. Naphtha
napkin n. Serviette, Mundtuch
narcissus n. Narzisse
narcotic n. Betäubungsmittel, Narkotikum; — adj. narkotisch
narration n. Erzählung, Schilderung
narrative n. Bericht, Geschichte; — adj. erzählend, schildernd
narrator n. Erzähler, Schilderer
narrow n. Engpass, Meerenge; — adj. eng, schmal, beschränkt; **have a — escape** mit knapper Not entrinnen; — v. (sich) verengen; schmälern, verkleinern, beschränken; **-ness** n. Enge, Schmalheit; Beschränktheit
narrow-gauge adj. schmalspurig

narrow-minded *adj.* kleindenkend, engherzig

nasal *adj.* Nasal; Nasen-; näselnd

nasturtium *n.* Kresse

nasty *adj.* garstig, schlimm, schlecht; übel

nation *n.* Nation; Volk; **-al** *adj.* national, Volks-, Staats-; **-alism** *n.* Nationalismus; **-alist** *n.* Nationalist; **-ality** *n.* Nationalität, Staatsangehörigkeit; **-alize** *v.* nationalisieren, verstaatlichen

nation-wide *adj.* weit verbreitet, von Grenze zu Grenze

native *n.* Eingeborene, Einheimische; **a —** of gebürtig aus, geboren in; **—** *adj.* (ein)heimisch, eingeboren, angeboren; **— land** Geburtsland

nativity *n.* Geburt; Nativität

natural *adj.* natürlich, naturgemäss; angeboren; unehelich; (art.) naturgetreu, lebenswahr; **— gas** Naturgas; **— history** Naturgeschichte; **— resources** Bodenschätze; **— science** Naturkunde; **—n.** (mus.) Auflösungszeichen; **-ly** *adv.* natürlich, von Natur aus; **-ism** *n.* Naturalismus, Naturzustand; **-ist** *n.* Naturalist, Naturforscher; **-ization** *n.* Naturalisierung, Einbürgerung; **-ize** *v.* naturalisieren, einbürgern

nature *n.* Natur; Wesen, Naturell; **good —** Gutartigkeit

naught *n.* Null, Nichts; Wertlose

naughty *adj.* unartig, ungezogen

nausea *n.* Übelkeit; **-te** *v.* verabscheuen; **be -ted** sich ekeln

nautical *adj.* nautisch; See-, Schiffs-, Marine-

naval *adj.* See-, Schiffs-, Flotten-, Marine-

navel *n.* Nabel

navigable *adj.* schiffbar, befahrbar; lenkbar, steuerbar

navigate *v.* navigieren, schiffen, befahren; lenken, steuern

navigation *n.* Navigation

navigator *n.* Schiffer, Seefahrer; Steuermann

navy *n.* Marine; Flotte, Seemacht; **— blue** Marineblau

nay *adv.* nein; **the yeas and -s** die Ja- und Nein-Stimmen, das Für und Wider

near *prep.* nahe, dicht; **—** *adj.* nahe-(liegend), in der Nähe; vertraut, nahe verwandt (*or* befreundet); **—** *adv.* nahe, dicht heran; beinahe, nahezu, fast; **—** *v.* sich nähern, näherkommen; **-ly** *adv.* fast, beinahe; **-ness** *n.* Nähe

nearby *adj.* nahe(liegend); **—** *adv.* in der Nähe

nearsighted *adj.* kurzsichtig; **— person** Kurzsichtige

neat *adj..* ordentlich, sauber, rein; nett, niedlich, zierlich

nebulous *adj.* neb(e)lig, wolkig; nebelhaft

necessary *adj.* notwendig, nötig; erforderlich

necessitate *v.* nötigen, zwingen; erfordern, notwendig machen

necessity *n.* Notwendigkeit, Bedarf; Zwang

neck *n.* Hals, Nacken; Genick; **— of land** Landenge

neckerchief *n.* Halstuch

necklace *n.* Halskette, Halsband

necktie *n.* Krawatte, Schlips; Halsbinde

neckwear *n.* Krawatten, Schlipse

need *n.* Not, Mangel; Bedarf; Bedürfnis; **—** *v.* brauchen, bedürfen, nötig haben; **-ful** *adj.* notwendig, nötig; **-less** *adj.* unnötig, vergeblich; **-y** *adj.* (hilfs)-bedürftig; arm(selig)

needle *n.* Nadel; **be on pins and —** *pl.* wie auf Nadeln sitzen; **darning —** Stopfnadel; **hypodermic —** Injektionsnadel

needlework *n.* Nadelarbeit, Handarbeit; Stickerei

negation *n.* Verneinung

negative *n.* Verneinung; (phot.) Negativ; **—** *adj.* negativ, verneint; verneinend, negierend

neglect *n.* Vernachlässigung, Nachlässigkeit; **—** *v.* vernachlässigen; versäumen

negligee *n.* Negligé

negligence *n.* Unachtsamkeit, Sorglosigkeit; (law) Fahrlässigkeit

negligent *adj.* unachtsam, sorglos; nachlässig; (law) fahrlässig

negligible *adj.* unwesentlich, nicht beachtenswert

negotiable *adj.* umsetzbar, verkäuflich

negotiate *v.* verhandeln, unterhandeln

negotiation *n.* Verhandlung, Vermittlung; Unterhandeln; Abschluss

Negress *n.* Negerin

Negro *n.* Neger

neigh *n.* Wiehern; **—** *v.* wiehern

neighbor *n.* Nachbar; Nächste; **-hood** *n.* Nachbarschaft; **-ing** *adj.* benachbart; **-ly** *adj.* nachbarlich

neither *conj.* weder; **—** *adj.* and *pron.* keiner

neomycin *n.* Neomycin

neon *n.* Neon; **— light** Neonlicht

nephew *n.* Neffe

nerve *n.* Nerv; (fig.) Mut; (coll.) Stirn; **-less** *adj.* entnervt, kraftlos

nervous *adj.* nervös, reizbar; nervenschwach; nervig, nachdrücklich, Nerven-; **-ness** *n.* Nervosität

nest *n.* Nest, Brutstätte; **— egg** Nestei; **-le** *v.* nisten; sich einnisten (*or* einschmeicheln)

net *n.* Netz; Schlinge, Falle, Fallstrick; **—** *adj.* netto, rein; **— balance** Nettobilanz; **— cost** Nettokosten; **— proceeds** Nettoertrag; **— profit** Reingewinn; **—** *v.* netto einnehmen

Netherlands *n.* Niederlande

nettle *n.* Nessel; **—** *v.* anstacheln

network *n.* Rundfunknetz

neuralgia *n.* Nervenschmerz, Neuralgie

neuritis *n.* Nervenentzündung

neuron *n.* Nervenzelle

neurosis *n.* Neurose

neurotic *adj.* neurotisch

neutral *adj.* neutral, unparteiisch; **-ity** *n.* Neutralität; **-ize** *v.* neutralisieren, unwirksam machen; für neutral erklären

neutron *n.* Neutron

never *adv.* nie(mals), durchaus nicht, gar nicht; **— mind!** das hat nichts zu sagen!

macht nichts!

nevermore *adv.* nimmermehr

nevertheless *adv.* nichtsdestoweniger, dessenungeachtet, dennoch

new *adj.* neu, frisch; unerfahren; **New Year** Neujahr; **New Year's Eve** Silvester(abend); — *adv.* neulich, soeben, seit kurzem; **-ness** *n.* Neuheit, Neuerung; (fig.) Unerfahrenheit; — *n. pl.* Neuigkeit, Nachricht; **-sy** *adj.* voller Neuigkeiten

newborn *n.* Neugeborene; — *adj.* neugeboren

newcomer *n.* Ankömmling, Neuling

newfangled *adj.* neumodisch

new-found *adj.* neu erfunden (*or* gefunden)

Newfoundland *n.* Neufundland

newlywed *n.* Neuvermählte; — *adj.* neuvermählt

newsboy *n.* Zeitungsjunge

newscast *n.* Nachrichtensendung

newspaper *n.* Zeitung; — **clipping** Zeitungsausschnitt

newsprint *n.* Zeitungspapier

newsreel *n.* Wochenschau

newsstand *n.* Zeitungsstand, Zeitungskiosk

next *adj.* nächst, folgend; — **door** nebenan; — **time** ein anderes Mal; **the — day** am nächsten Tag; — *adv.* zunächst, gleich darauf; dann; — **to** neben; — **to nothing** fast gar nichts; — *prep.* nächst, bei, an

nib *n.* Nadelspitze

nibble *v.* (be)nagen, (be)knabbern

nice *adj.* nett, hübsch; fein, zart, zierlich; empfindlich, sorgfältig; **-ly** *adv.* nett, lieblich, sanft; genau, richtig, regelrecht; **-ty** *n.* Feinheit, Zartheit, Zierlichkeit; Genauigkeit; Schärfe

niche *n.* Nische; (fig.) Versteck

nick *n.* Kerbe, Einschnitt; **in the — of time** zur rechten Zeit, wie gerufen; — *v.* (ein-)kerben, einschneiden

nickel *n.* Nickel, Fünfcentstück

nickel-plated *adj.* vernickelt

nickname *n.* Spitzname, Kosename; — *v.* mit Spitznamen (*or* Kosenamen) rufen

nicotine *n.* Nikotin

niece *n.* Nichte

night *n.* Nacht; Abend; **by —** nachts, bei Nacht; **— club** Nachtklub, Nachtlokal; **— letter** verbilligtes Brieftelegramm (ausserhalb der Geschäftsstunden); — **school** Abendschule, Fortbildungsschule; **-ly** *adj.* nächtlich, Nacht-; **-ly** *adv.* jede Nacht, allnächtlich

nightcap *n.* Schlafmütze; (coll.) Schlaftrunk

nightfall *n.* Einbruch der Nacht

nightgown *n.* Schlafrock; Nachthemd, Nachtgewand

nightingale *n.* Nachtigall

nightmare *n.* Alp(drücken), Nachtmahr

nightshade *n.* Nachtschatten

nightshirt *n.* Nachthemd

nihilism *n.* Nihilismus

nimble *adj.* flink, hurtig; gewandt, behend

nine *adj.* neun; — *n.* Neun(er); **-fold** *adj.*

neunfach; **-teen** *adj.* neunzehn; **-teen** *n.* Neunzehn(er); **-teenth** *adj.* neunzehnt; **-teenth** *n.* Neunzehnte; Neunzehntel; **-tieth** *adj.* neunzigst; **-tieth** *n.* Neunzigste; Neunzigstel; **-ty** *adj.* neunzig; **-ty** *n.* Neunzig(er)

ninny *n.* Tropf, Dummkopf

ninth *adj.* neunt; — *n.* Neunte; Neuntel

nip *n.* Schlückchen; — *v.* nippen; kneifen, zwicken; (cold) schneiden; — **in the bud** im Keime ersticken; **-ping** *adj.* scharf, streng; beissend, schneidend

nipple *n.* Brustwarze, Zitze; Sauger, Nuckel

niter, nitre *n.* Salpeter

nitrate *n.* Nitrat, salpetersaures Salz

nitrogen *n.* Stickstoff; Nitrogen

no *adv.* nein, nicht; — *adj.* kein; **by — means** durchaus nicht; **in — way** keineswegs; **— man's land** Niemandsland; **— one** niemand, kein; **there is — such thing** nichts dergleichen, so etwas gibt es nicht; — *n.* Nein; Absage

nobility *n.* Adel(stand)

noble *n.* Adlige; — *adj.* edel, vornehm, grossmütig; **-ness** *n.* Adel, Würde; Edelmut

nobleman *n.* Edelmann

nobody *pron.* niemand; — *n.* unbedeutende Person

nocturnal *adj.* nächtlich, Nacht-

nod *n.* Nicken, Wink; — *v.* nicken, winken; (fig.) schlafen, träumen

noise *n.* Lärm, Geräusch; **make —** lärmen, Aufsehen machen; **-less** *adj.* geräuschlos, still

noisy *adj.* lärmend, geräuschvoll; aufdringlich

nomad *n.* Nomade; **-ic** *adj.* nomadisch; unstet

nominal *adj.* nominell, namentlich; Namen-; angeblich

nominate *v.* aufstellen, zur Wahl vorschlagen; ernennen; nominieren

nomination *n.* Aufstellung, Ernennung

nominative *n.* Nominativ, Nennfall

nominee *n.* Vorgeschlagene

nonacceptance *n.* Nichtannahme, Annahmeverweigerung

nonaggression *n.* Nichtangriff

nonalcoholic *adj.* alkoholfrei

nonchalant *adj.* nonchalant, nachlässig

noncombatant *n.* Nichtkämpfer, Zivilist

noncommissioned *adj.* nicht bevollmächtigt; **— officer** Unteroffizier

noncommittal *adj.* (sich) nicht bindend; reserviert

nonconformist *n.* Dissident

none *pron.* kein, niemand; — *adv.* nichts, keineswegs

nonentity *n.* Null, Nichts; Unding, Erdichtung

nonessential *adj.* unwesentlich

nonobservance *n.* Nichtbeobachtung

nonpartisan *n.* Parteilose; — *adj.* unparteiisch, parteilos

nonpayment *n.* Nicht(be)zahlung

nonproductive *adj.* unproduktiv, nichts erzeugend

nonsectarian *adj.* nicht sektiererisch

nonsense n. Unsinn

nonsensical adj. unsinnig, sinnlos, albern

nonskid adj. nicht rutschend; Gleitschutz-

nonstop adj. ununterbrochen, ohne Pause; Nonstop-

noodle n. Nudel

nook n. Ecke, Winkel; Schlupfwinkel

noon n. Mittag

noonday n. Mittag(szeit)

noontide n. Mittagszeit

noose n. Schleife, Schlinge; Fallstrick, Falle

nor conj. noch; auch nicht; **neither . . . — weder . . . noch**

norm n. Norm, Regel, Muster; **-al** adj. normal, regelrecht, vorschriftsmässig; **-al school** Berufsschule; Lehrerseminar; **-alize** v. normalisieren

north n. Nord(en); Nordstaaten; **— Pole** Nordpol; **— adj. and adv.** nördlich; **-ern** adj. nördlich, Nord; **-erly** adj. and adv. nördlich; **-ward** adj. nördlich; **-wards** adv. nordwärts, nach (or von) Norden

northeast n. Nordosten; **— adj. and adv.** nordöstlich; **-ern** adj. nordöstlich

north-northeast n. Nordnordost; **— adj. and adv.** nordnordöstlich

north-northwest n. Nordnordwest; **— adj. and adv.** nordnordwestlich

North Pole n. Nordpol

northwest n. Nordwesten; **— adj. and adv.** nordwestlich; **-ern** adj. nordwestlich

Norway n. Norwegen

nose n. Nase; Schnauze; **blow one's — sich die Nase schnauben; bridge of the — Nasenrücken; lead by the — nasführen, an der Nase herumführen; pay through the — übermässig bezahlen; — dive** Sturzflug

nosebag n. Futterbeutel

nosebleed n. Nasenbluten

nostalgia n. Heimweh; Nostalgie

nostril n. Nasenloch; Nüster

not adv. nicht; **— any gar kein; — (as) yet** noch nicht; **— at all** keineswegs; **even** nicht einmal

notable n. Standesperson; **— adj.** merkwürdig, bemerkenswert; ansehnlich, beträchtlich

notary n. Notar

notation n. Aufzeichnung; (math. and mus.) Bezeichnung

notch n. Kerbe, Einschnitt, Scharte; Kimme; (geol.) Engpass; **— v.** kerben, einschneiden

note n. Notiz, Anmerkung; Note; Ruf, Ansehen; Nachricht, Kunde; (com.) Rechnung, Schuldschein; (mus.) Note, Ton; **take — pl.** sich Aufzeichnungen machen; **— v.** notieren, anzeigen, bezeichnen; beachten; **-d** adj. berühmt, bekannt; berüchtigt

notebook n. Notizbuch

noteworthy adj. beachtenswert merkwürdig

nothing n. Nichts, Null; Unbedeutenheit, Nichtigkeit; **for — umsonst; next to — fast nichts; — but nichts als; — adv.**

durchaus nicht

notice n. Notiz, Nachricht, Anzeige; Ankündigung, Bekanntmachung; Beachtung, Aufmerksamkeit; Kündigung; **at a moment's — jeden Augenblick; at short — kurzfristig; give — (to)** kündigen; **until further — bis auf** weiteres; **— v.** bemerken, beachten; **-able.** adj. wahrnehmbar, bemerkbar; bemerkenswert, beachtlich

notification n. Anzeige, Bekanntmachung; Vorladung

notify v. anzeigen; vorladen

notion n. Begriff, Idee; Ahnung; Absicht; pl. Kleinigkeiten, Kindereien, Luftschlösser; Kurzwaren

notoriety n. Offenkundigkeit

notorious adj. berüchtigt, offenkundig

notwithstanding conj. obgleich, trotzdem; **— prep.** ungeachtet, trotz; **— adv.** nichtsdestoweniger, dennoch, trotzdem

nought n. Null, Nichts

noun n. Hauptwort, Substantiv; **proper — Eigenname**

nourish v. (er)nähren; erhalten, hegen, pflegen, unterhalten; nahrhaft sein; **-ment** n. Nahrung(smittel)

novel n. Roman; **— adj.** neu, ungewöhnlich, überraschend; **-ist** n. Romanschriftsteller; **-ty** n. Neuheit; Ungewöhnlichkeit

Novocain n. Novokain

now adv. nun, jetzt; eben, kürzlich; bald, dann; **by — schon jetzt; just — soeben; — and then dann und wann, hier und** da; **till — bis jetzt; — interj.** nun aber! jetzt! **— conj.** nun da

nowadays adv. heutzutage

nowhere adv. nirgend(wo)

nozzle n. Düse; Mundstück, Tülle; (zool.) Schnauze, Rüssel

nuclear adj. kernförmig; Kern-; **— fission** Kernspaltung; **— war** Kernwaffenkrieg

nucleus n. Kern

nude n. Nackte; **— adj.** nackt, bloss

nudge n. leichtes Anstossen, Rippenstoss; **— v.** leicht (or heimlich) anstossen

nudist n. Nudist, Anhänger der Nacktkultur

nudity n. Nacktheit, Blösse

nugget n. Goldklumpen

nuisance n. Plage, Schaden; Unfug, Verdruss, Ärgernis

null adj. nichtig, ungültig; null; fehlend; **-ify** v. ungültig machen (or erklären)

numb adj. starr, erstarrt; betäubt; **— v.** erstarren, betäuben

number n. Zahl; Nummer, Ziffer; Menge, Anzahl; (gram.) Zahl; **back — alte** Ausgabe; **round — runde Summe; — v.** numerieren, zählen, rechnen; **-less** adj. zahllos, unzählig

numeral n. Zahl(zeichen), Ziffer; (gram.) Zahlwort; **— adj.** Zahl-

numerator n. Zähler

numerous adj. zahlreich, sehr viele

numismatics n. Münzkunde

nun n. Nonne; **-nery** n. Nonnenkloster

nuptial adj. hochzeitlich, ehelich; Hochzeits-, Ehe-, Braut-; **— n. pl.** Hochzeit,

Trauung
Nuremberg n. Nürnberg
nurse n. Schwester, Krankenschwester,
Pflegerin; Kindermädchen; **male —**
Pfleger, Wärter; **wet — Amme; —** v.
pflegen; grossziehen; nähren, stillen;
–ry n. Kinderstube; (agr.) Baumschule,
Pflanzschule, Schonung; **–ry school**
Kindergarten; **–ry rhymes** Kinderlieder
nursemaid n. Kindermädchen
nursing n. Krankenpflege; Kinderpflege;
— bottle Milchflasche, Saugflasche
nut n. Nuss; (mech.) Schraubenmutter;
(coll.) **be –s** verrückt sein
nutcracker n. Nussknacker
nutmeg n. Muskatnuss
nutriment n. Nahrung; Futter
nutrition n. Ernährung, Nahrung; Nähr-
wert
nutritious, nutritive adj. nährend, nahrhaft; Ernährungs-
nutshell n. Nusschale; (fig.) Kleinigkeit:
in a — kurz und bündig, in wenigen
Worten, in aller Kürze
nylon n. Nylon
nymph n. Nymphe

O

oaf n. Dummkopf, Einfaltspinsel, Tölpel
oak n. Eiche; Eichenholz; **–en** adj. eichen-
oar n. Ruder, Riemen
oarsman n. Ruderer
oasis n. Oase
oat n. Hafer
oath n. Eid, Schwur; Verwünschung,
Fluch
oatmeal n. Haferflocken, Hafermehl;
Haferschleim
obdurate adj. verhärtet, verstockt; hartherzig; halsstarrig
obedience n. Gehorsam, Unterwerfung
obedient adj. gehorsam, unterwürfig
obese adj. feist, fett(leibig)
obesity n. Fettleibigkeit, Feistheit
obey v. gehorchen, befolgen
obituary n. Todesanzeige; Totenliste;
Nachruf, Nekrolog
object n. Gegenstand, Objekt; Ziel.
Zweck; **–ive** n. (gram.) Objektsfall:
(mil.) Operationsziel; (phot.) Objektiv;
(fig.) Endziel; **–ive** adj. objektiv, gegenständlich, sachlich; **–ivity** n. Objektivität, Sachlichkeit
object v. Einspruch erheben, einwenden;
entgegenstellen, vorhalten; **–ion** n.
Einwand, Einspruch, Einwurf; **raise
an –ion** einen Einwand erheben;
–ionable adj. anrüchig, nicht einwandfrei
obligation n. Verpflichtung; Verbindlichkeit; (com.) Schuldschein; **be under —**
verpflichtet (or verbunden) sein
obligatory adj. verbindlich, bindend,
verpflichtend, obligatorisch
oblige v. zwingen; verpflichten, bewegen,
nötigen
obliging adj. gefällig, verbindlich
oblique adj. schräg, schief; indirekt, mittelbar; unaufrichtig

oblivion n. Vergessenheit; Vergesslichkeit
oblivious adj. vergesslich, vergessend
oblong adj. länglich; **—** n. Rechteck
obnoxious adj. anstössig, widerwärtig,
verhasst
oboe n. Oboe
obscene adj. obszön, unanständig,
schlüpfrig, zotig
obscenity n. Obszönität, Unanständigkeit; Schlüpfrigkeit, Zote
obscure adj. dunkel, unbekannt; unklar
obskur; **—** v. verdunkeln, verkleinern
obscurity n. Dunkelheit, Unbekannte,
Unklarheit, Obskurität
obsequious adj. kriechend, unterwürfig,
servil, willfährig
observance n. Befolgung, Innehaltung;
Brauch; (eccl.) Observanz
observant adj. beobachtend, befolgend;
achtsam
observation n. Beobachtung; Befolgung;
Bemerkung; **— car** Aussichtswagen
observatory n. Sternwarte, Observatorium
observe v. beobachten, wahrnehmen;
bemerken; beachten, halten; **–r** n.
Beobachter; Zuschauer; Befolger
observing adj. aufmerksam, sorgfältig
obstacle n. Hindernis
obstetrician n. Geburtshelfer
obstetrics n. Geburtshilfe
obstinacy n. Hartnäckigkeit, Halsstarrigkeit, Eigensinn
obstinate adj. hartnäckig, halsstarrig,
eigensinnig
obstruct v. verstopfen, versperren; hemmen, verzögern; **–ion** n. Verstopfung;
Hindernis, Hemmung; Verzögerung
obtain v. bekommen, erhalten, erlangen;
–able adj. erhältlich, erreichbar
obvious adj. klar, deutlich; augenscheinlich, unverkennbar
occasion n. Gelegenheit, Anlass, Veranlassung; **—** v. veranlassen, verursachen,
bewirken; **–al** adj. gelegentlich, zufällig;
Gelegenheits-
occident n. Westen, Abendland; Okzident; **–al** adj. westlich, abendländisch
occult adj. okkult, verborgen, geheim;
–ism n. Okkultismus, Geheimwissen-
schaft
occupant n. Besitzer, Inhaber; Bewohner
occupation n. Beruf, Beschäftigung; Besetzung; **— army** Besatzungstruppen
occupy v. besitzen, innehaben, einnehmen;
bewohnen; in Besitz nehmen, besetzen;
beschäftigen; **be occupied with** arbeiten
an
occur v. geschehen, vorkommen, sich
ereignen; einfallen; **–rence** n. Ereignis,
Vorkommnis; Vorfall
ocean n. Ozean, Weltmeer; **–ic** adj.
Meeres-, See-
o'clock adv. pünktlich; genau; **two —**
genau zwei Uhr
octagon n. Achteck; Oktagon
octane n. Oktan; **— rating** Oktanzahl
octave n. Oktave
octopus n. Achtfüssler; Polyp, Krake
ocular adj. okular; Augen-

oculist *n.* Augenarzt
odd *adj.* seltsam, sonderbar; ungerade; einzeln; etwaig; **—ity** *n.* Seltsamkeit, Sonderbarkeit; **—s** *n.* (*pl.*) Vorgabe, Vorteil; Unterschied; Wahrscheinlichkeit; ungleiche Wette (*or* Partie); **—s and ends** Reste, Überbleibsel, Abfälle
ode *n.* Ode
odo(u)r *n.* Geruch; Duft, Wohlgeruch
of *prep.* von, aus, unter, über, an, bei, in, nach, vor, durch
off *adv.* ab, weg, fort, davon, herunter; entlegen, entfernt, weit, fern; aus dahin; verloren, zu Ende; flott, frei; **— and on** ab und an, ab und zu, hin und her; **—** *prep.* von . . . weg; von . . . her; fort von; (naut.) auf der Höhe von; **—** *adj.* entferntest; Seiten-, Neben-; **—l** *interj.* weg! fort! **hands —l** Hände weg!
off-color *adj.* schlüpfrig, unanständig; verfärbt
offend *v.* beleidigen, ärgern; sich vergehen, verstossen; **-er** *n.* Beleidiger, Verletzer; Missetäter
offense *n.* Beleidigung, Verstoss; Übertretung; (law) Vergehen; **take —** übelnehmen
offensive *n.* Angriff, Offensive; **—** *adj.* offensiv, angreifend; Angriffs-; beleidigend, anstössig
offer *n.* Angebot; Offerte; Anerbieten; **—** *v.* offerieren, (an)bieten; sich darbieten (*or* zeigen); **— one's service** seine Dienste anbieten; **-ing** *n.* Anerbieten; Opfer(ung)
offertory *n.* Kollekte, Opfergabe
offhand *adj.* and *adv.* auf der Stelle, aus dem Stegreif; ungezwungen, frei
office *n.* Amt, Büro, Geschäft, Lokal; Dienst, Funktion, Pflicht; **— boy** Laufbursche; **— hours** Geschäftsstunden, Dienststunden; **— supplies** Büroartikel; **-r** *n.* Beamte; Offizier; Polizist
official *n.* Beamte; **—** *adj.* offiziell, amtlich, Amts-
officiate *v.* amtieren; (eccl.) den Gottesdienst leiten
offset *n.* (bot. and zool.) Sprössling, Ableger, Seitenzweig; (com.) Gegenforderung, Gegenrechnung; (typ.) Offsetdruck; **—** *v.* ausgleichen, kompensieren
offshoot *n.* Ausläufer, Spross; (fig.) Abzweigung
offshore *adv.* von der Küste ab (*or* her); vom Lande entfernt
offside *adj.* abseitig; **—** *adv.* abseits
offspring *n.* Nachkömmling, Abkömmling; Spross
oft(en) *adv.* oft, öfters, oftmals; häufig, wiederholt
ogle *v.* beäugeln, liebäugeln
ogre *n.* Menschenfresser, Ungeheuer
oil *n.* Öl; Petroleum; **crude —** Rohpetroleum; **drying —** rasch trocknendes Öl; **heavy —** Schweröl; **mineral —** Mineralöl; **vegetable —** Pflanzenöl; **— color** Ölfarbe; **— field** Ölfeld; **— painting**

Ölgemälde; **— well** Petroleumquelle; **—** *v.* (ein)ölen, einfetten, (ein)schmieren; **-y** *adj.* ölig, ölhaltig; (fig.) glatt, geschmeidig; salbungsvoll
oilcan *n.* Ölkanne
oilcloth *n.* Wachstuch
oilskin *n.* Ölzeug
ointment *n.* Salbe
okay, o.k. *n.* Zustimmung, Bestätigung; **—** *adj.* richtig, billigend; **—** *v.* billigen, zustimmen; **—l** *interj.* stimmt! richtig! in Ordnung!
okra *n.* Eibisch
old *adj.* alt, altbekannt, altbewährt; verbraucht, abgenutzt; veraltet, altmodisch; **become** (*or* grow) **—** alt werden, altern; of **—** von jeher, ehemals; **— age** hohes Alter, Greisenalter; **— hand** alter Praktikus; **— maid** alte Jungfer; **— timer** Alte; Altmodische; **Old World** alte Welt, östliche Hemisphäre
old-age pension *n.* Altersrente
old-fashioned *adj.* altmodisch
old-time *adj.* aus alter Zeit
oleomargarine *n.* Margarine, Kunstbutter
olfactory *adj.* Geruchs-
olive *n.* Olive; Olivengrün; **— branch** Olivenzweig, Ölzweig; **— drab** Graugrün; **— grove** Olivenhain, Olivenpflanzung; **— oil** Olivenöl; **— tree** Olivenbaum, Ölbaum; **—** *adj.* olivengrün
omelet(te) *n.* Omelett(e), Eierkuchen
omen *n.* Vorzeichen, Omen
ominous *adj.* unhe lvoll; ominös
omission *n.* Auslassung, Weglassung, Unterlassung
omit *v.* auslassen, unterlassen; übersehen, versäumen
omnibus *n.* Omnibus; Sammelband, Sammlung; (lit.) Allumfassend
omnipotent *adj.* allmächtig
omniscience *n.* Allwissenheit
on *prep.* auf, an, zu, in, über; von, unter; vor, hinter; bei, mit, nach; **—** *adv.* darauf, fort, vorwärts, weiter; ferner; **and so —** und so weiter; **— and —** immer weiter; **—l** *interj.* vorwärts!
once *adv.* einmal, einst; vormals, dereinst; **at —** (so)gleich, auf einmal; **for — diesmal; — (and) for all** ein für allemal; **— more** noch einmal, wieder; **— upon a time** es war einmal; **—** *conj.* sobald
one *adj.* ein; einzig; **— and the same** einerlei; **— day** eines Tages; **—** *pron.* ein; man; **— and all** alle und jeder; **— another** einander, sich; **— by —** einer nach dem anderen, einzeln; **—** *n.* Eins, Einser
oneself *pron.* (man) selbst, sich; **by —** aus eigenem Antriebe, von selbst; **with —** mit sich selbst
one-sided *adj.* einseitig
onetime *adj.* einstmalig, einmalig
one-track *adj.* eingleisig; **— mind** beschränkter Verstand
one-way *adj.* einbahnig; **— street** Einbahnstrasse; **— trip** einfache Fahrt; **— ticket** Fahrkarte für den Hinweg

onion n. Zwiebel

onionskin n. seidig-glänzendes Durch-schlagpapier

onlooker n. Zuschauer

only adj. einzig; — yesterday erst gestern; — adv. nur, bloss; allein; erst

onset n. Angriff, Sturm; Anfang, Beginn

onto prep. nach . . . hin; auf

onward adv. nach vorne, vorwärts; weiter fort; — adj. fortschreitend; vorgeschritten; vorgerückt; -s adv. nach vorne, vorwärts

onyx n. Onyx

opal n. Opal

open adj. offen, auf; frei, geöffnet, öffentlich; offenbar, aufrichtig, offenherzig, freigebig; unentschieden; in the — air unter freiem Himmel, im Freien; — house offenes Haus; — letter offener Brief; — question offene (or offenstehende) Frage; — season Jagdzeit; — secret offenes Geheimnis; — shop Unternehmen für organisierte und unorganisierte Arbeiter; — v. öffnen, aufmachen; aufgehen; aufschlagen; freimachen, entfalten; eröffnen, beginnen; aufschliessen; -ing n. Öffnung, Eröffnung; freier Platz, offene Stelle; Anfang, Beginn; -ing adj. eröffnend, beginnend; Eröffnungs-

open-air adj. im Freien befindlich; Freilicht-

openhanded adj. freigebig, mildtätig

openhearted adj. offenherzig, aufrichtig

open-minded adj. offenherzig, aufrichtig; vorurteilslos, unbefangen

openmouthed adj. mit offenem Munde; gaffend

opera n. Oper; — glass(es) Opernglas; — hat Klapphut; — house Opernhaus; -tic adj. zur Oper gehörig, opernhaft

operate v. (ein)wirken, tätig sein; (com.) leiten, betreiben; (mech.) in Gang setzen; (med.) operieren

operation n. Wirkung; Verfahren, Verrichtung; (com.) Leitung, Unternehmen; (mech.) Betrieb; Bewegung, Gang; (med. and mil.) Operation; have an — operiert werden

operator n. Wirkende, Bewirkende; Maschinenarbeiter; (com.) Betriebsleiter, Geschäftsleiter; (med.) Operateur; (tel.) Telefonist(in); (coll.) Spekulant

operetta n. Operette

opiate n. Schlafmittel, Opiat

opinion n. Meinung, Ansicht; Gutachten; (law) Gerichtsbeschluss; give an — seine Meinung sagen, ein Gutachten abgeben; in my — meiner Ansicht nach; public — öffentliche Meinung

opossum n. Beutelratte, Opossum

opponent n. Gegner, Opponent

opportune adj. gelegen, passend, günstig; rechtzeitig

opportunity n. (günstige) Gelegenheit

oppose v. entgegensetzen, entgegenstellen; opponieren; (sich) widersetzen

opposite n. Gegenteil, Gegensatz; Gegner; — adj. gegenüberliegend, gegenüberstehend; entgegengesetzt; take the —

side Partei für die andere (or gegnerische) Seite ergreifen; — adv. and prep. gegenüber

opposition n. Gegenseite; Widerstand, Hindernis, Widerspruch; (ast. and pol.) Opposition

oppress n. bedrücken, unterdrücken; überwältigen; -ion n. Druck, Unterdrückung; Überwältigung; -ive adj. (be)drückend, tyrannisch; -or n. Bedrücker, Unterdrücker; Tyrann

optic adj. Augen-, Seh; -al adj. optisch; -ian n. Optiker; -s n. Optik

optimism n. Optimismus

optimist n. Optimist; -ic adj. optimistisch

option n. Wahl, Wahlrecht; -al adj. freigestellt, unverbindlich

optometrist n. Augenfachmann, Optiker

optometry n. Messung der Sehschärfe

or conj. oder; either . . . — entweder . . . oder; — else sonst, wo nicht, oder andrenfalls

oral adj. mündlich, Mund-

orange n. Apfelsine; Orange; — juice Orangensaft; — tree Orangenbaum; — adj. orangenfarben

oration n. Rede, Standrede

orator n. Redner, Sprecher; -y n. Redekunst, Beredsamkeit

orb n. Himmelskörper; (med.) Augapfel

orbit n. Augenhöhle; Bahn; Kreisbahn; Erdkreisbahn; — v. die Erde umkreisen

orbital decay n. allmähliche Verkleinerung der Eklipse durch Luftwiderstand

orchard n. Obstgarten

orchestra n. Orchester; -te v. orchestrieren

ordain v. anordnen, verordnen; ordinieren, die Priesterweihe geben (or nehmen)

ordeal n. Gottesurteil; (fig.) Feuerprobe

order n. Befehl, Verordnung, Verfügung; Ordnung; Orden(szeichen); Klasse, Rang; (com.) Auftrag, Bestellung, Order; (math.) Grad, Reihe; pl. Weihegrade; by — of im Auftrag von; in — in Ordnung; angebracht; in — to um . . . zu, damit; make to — nach Mass machen; on — in Auftrag; — of battle Schlachtordnung; out of — in Unordnung; nicht bei der Sache; rush — Eilauftrag; standing — Geschäftsordnung; — v. befehlen; verordnen; (an)ordnen; (com.) bestellen; — around herumkommandieren; -ly n. Ordonnanz, Offizier vom Dienst; Lazarettgehilfe, Wärter; -ly adj. ordentlich, wohlgeordnet, regelmässig; fügsam, gesittet; Ordonnanz-

ordinance n. Verordnung, Verfügung; Satzung, Gesetz

ordinary adj. gewöhnlich, üblich, gebräuchlich; gemein, niedrig

ordnance n. Artillerie, schweres Geschütz

ore n. Erz, Metall; — deposit Erzlager

organ n. Organ, Stimme; Werkzeug; (mus.) Orgel, Harmonium; — stop Orgelregister; internal — (pl.) innere Organe; -ic adj. organisch; -ism n. Organismus; -ist n. Organist

organdy n. Organdy

organ-grinder *n.* Leierkastenmann

organization *n.* Organisation, Organisierung; Bildung, Errichtung

organize *v.* organisieren

orgy *n.* Orgie

orient *n.* Orient, Morgenland, Osten; — *v.* orientieren; **-al** *adj.* orientalisch, morgenländisch; östlich; **-ation** *n.* Orientierung

orifice *n.* Öffnung, Mündung

origin *n.* Ursprung; Herkunft, Abstammung; **-al** *n.* Original, Urbild, Urschrift; **-al** *adj.* ursprünglich, originell; **-ality** *n.* Originalität; **-ate** *v.* entspringen; erzeugen, hervorbringen

oriole *n.* Pirol, Goldamsel

ornament *n.* Verzierung, Ornament; — *v.* verzieren, (aus)schmücken; **-al** *adj.* ornamental, ornamentartig; zierend, Zier-

ornithologist *n.* Ornithologe, Vogelkenner

orphan *n.* Waise; — *adj.* verwaist; **-age** *n.* Waisenhaus

orthodox *adj.* orthodox, strenggläubig, rechtgläubig

orthography *n.* Orthographie, Rechtschreibung

oscillate *v.* schwingen, pendeln; schwanken

oscillator *n.* (elec.) Schwingungserreger; (rad.) Frequenzgenerator

osmosis *n.* Osmose, Durchtritt

ossify *v.* verknöchern

ostensible *adj.* scheinbar, angeblich

ostentation *n.* Gepränge, Prahlerei

ostentatious *adj.* prangend, prahlerisch

osteopathy *n.* Knochenheilkunde; Osteopathie

ostrich *n.* Strauss

other *adj.* ander; **each —** einander; **every — day** einen Tag um den anderen; **the — day** dieser Tage, neulich; **—** *pron.* andere

otherwise *adv.* anders, sonst

otter *n.* Otter, Fischotter

ought *v.* sollte, müsste

ounce *n.* Unze

our *pron.* unser; **-s** *pron.* unsere

ourselves *pron. pl.* selbst, uns (selbst)

oust *v.* verdrängen, vertreiben; entsetzen, entheben

out *adv.* aus; draussen; heraus, hinaus; nicht zu Hause; fort, weg; offenkundig, bekannt, entdeckt; ausser Amt, nicht im Dienst; erschöpft, verbraucht; (sports) aus, nicht mehr im Spiel; — *prep.* aus, draussen, ausser; **—!** *interj.* heraus! hinaus! fort! weg! — *n.* Aus; **-er** *adj.* äusser; äusserst, fernst, Aussen-; **-ing** *n.* Spaziergang, Ausflug; Landpartie

out-and-out *adj.* durch und durch, völlig

outbid *v.* überbieten

outbreak *n.* Ausbruch, Aufruhr

outbuilding *n.* Nebengebäude

outburst *n.* Ausbruch, Explosion

outcast *n.* Ausgestossene, Verbannte; — *adj.* weggeworfen, ausgestossen; verbannt

outcome *n.* Ergebnis, Resultat

outcry *n.* Aufschrei; Geschrei

outdated *adj.* veraltet, überholt

outdo *v.* übertreffen, zuvortun

outdoor *adj.* ausser dem Haus; Aussen-; **— exercise** Freiübungen; **-s** *adv.* draussen, im Freien; nicht im Hause

outermost *adj.* äusserst

outfield *n.* Aussenfeld; **-er** *n.* Aussenspieler

outfit *n.* Ausstattung, Ausrüstung

outgrow *v.* herauswachsen, überwuchern; verwachsen; **-th** *n.* Auswuchs, Sprössling

outhouse *n.* Nebengebäude, Hinterhaus

outlandish *adj.* ausländisch, fremd(artig), seltsam

outlast *v.* überdauern

outlaw *n.* Geächtete, Vogelfreie; Verbrecher; — *v.* ächten, für vogelfrei erklären

outlay *n.* Auslage, Ausgabe; Betriebskosten

outlet *n.* Ausfluss, Abfluss; Ausweg; Absatzgebiet

outline *n.* Umriss, Skizze; — *v.* entwerfen, skizzieren, umreissen

outlive *v.* überleben, überdauern

outlook *n.* Ausblick, Aussicht; Ausguck

outlying *adj.* auswärtig; ausserhalb (*or* entfernt, abseits) liegend

outmoded *adj.* unmodern, aus der Mode gekommen

outmost *adj.* äusserst

outnumber *v.* zahlenmässig übertreffen

out-of-date *adj.* unzeitgemäss, veraltet

out-of-door(s) *adj.* ausserhalb des Hauses; im Freien stattfindend (*or* wachsend)

out-of-the-way *adj.* abgelegen, abgesondert; versteckt

outpatient *n.* Patient in ambulanter Behandlung

outpost *n.* Vorposten

output *n.* Ausbeute, Ertrag; (com.) Produktion; (min.) Förderung

outrage *n.* Ausschreitung, Gewalttätigkeit; Frevel; — *v.* beleidigen, schändlich behandeln; **-ous** *adj.* zügellos, gewalttätig; schimpflich; übermässig

outrank *v.* den höheren Rang haben; rangieren über

outright *adj. and adv.* gerade heraus; offen, ohne Vorbehalt; völlig

outset *n.* Anfang, Beginn

outside *n.* Aussenseite; Äussere; — *adj.* äusser, äusserst; Aussen-; — *adv.* (dr)aussen; — *prep.* — (of) ausserhalb; **-r** *n.* Aussenseiter

outskirts *n. pl.* Grenze, Saum, Peripherie

outspoken *adj.* ausgesprochen; ehrlich, freimütig; offen

outstanding *adj.* hervorragend; **— debts** Aussenstände

outstretch *v.* ausstrecken; weit öffnen

outward *adj.* äusser; äusserlich; nach aussen; — *adv.* auswärts, nach (dr)aussen; **-ly** *adv.* äusserlich

outweigh *v.* das Übergewicht haben; überwiegen

outwit *v.* an Einsicht übertreffen; überlisten

outworn adj. abgenutzt, verbraucht; abgetragen

oval n. Oval; — adj. oval

ovary n. Eierstock; (bot.) Fruchtknoten

ovation n. Ovation

oven n. Ofen

over prep. über; jenseits; an, auf; bei, vor; — adv. hinüber, herüber; darüber; übrig; vorbei, vorüber; wieder, nochmals; übermässig, zu sehr; all — überall, ganz fertig; — again noch einmal; — and above ausserdem, über und über; — and — (again) immer wieder; — there da (or dort) drüben; — adj. ober

overage adj. zu alt, veraltet

over-all adj. überall, allgemein

overalls n. pl. Overalls, arbeitsanzug

overbearing adj. anmassend, hochfahrend

overboard adv. über Bord

overburden v. überladen, überlasten

overcharge n. Überteuerung; — v. überteuern, überfordern; überladen

overcoat n. Überrock, Überzieher

overcome v. überwinden, überwältigen; be — hingerissen sein

overcooked adj. ausgekocht, zu lange gekocht

overcrowd v. überfüllen

overdo v. übertreiben, überanstrengen; zu stark (or weit) treiben; zu viel tun; -ne adj. übertrieben; überanstrengt; zu stark gekocht

overdose n. Überdosis

overdrive n. Geschwindigkeitsregler

overdue adj. überfällig; verfallen; verspätet

overeat v. sich überessen

overestimate v. überschätzen

overexposure n. Überbelichtung

overflow n. Überschwemmung; Überfluss; — v. überfluten, überschwemmen; überfliessen

overgrown adj. übermässig gross; überwachsen

overhaul v. überholen, einholen; völlig ausbessern; gründlich nachsehen

overhead n. Unkosten, Geschäftskosten; — adv. ober; (dr.)oben; im oberen Stock

overhear v. belauschen

overheat v. überhitzen, überheizen; (mech.) heiss laufen lassen

overjoyed adj. übermässig entzückt (or erfreut)

overland adj. zu Lande; Überland-; — adv. auf dem Lande, über Land

overlap v. überragen; überschneiden, übereinandergreifen, übereinanderliegen; überlappen

overload n. Über(be)lastung; — v. überladen, überlasten

overlook v. übersehen, überblicken, überschauen; hinabblicken auf; hervorragen; überlesen

overlord n. Ober(lehens)herr

overnight adj. and adv. über Nacht

overpass n. Übergang, Überführung

overpower v. überwältigen, unterdrücken

overproduction n. Produktionsüberschuss

overrate v. überschätzen; zu hoch veranschlagen (or veranlagen)

overrule v. verwerfen, zurückweisen; überstimmen

overrun v. überholen, übertreffen; überlaufen, überrennen; überwachsen

oversea adj. überseeisch; -s adv. über See

oversee v. beaufsichtigen, überwachen; -r n. Aufseher, Inspektor

overshadow v. überschatten, beschatten, verdunkeln

overshoe n. Überschuh

oversight n. Versehen, Auslassung

oversleep v. verschlafen

overstep v. überschreiten

overstuffed adj. völlig (aus)gepolstert

oversupply n. Überangebot, Überfluss; überreiche Versorgung (or Zufuhr)

overtake v. einholen, überholen; überraschen, überfallen

overtax v. zu hoch besteuern; überschätzen

overthrow n. Umsturz, Niederwerfung; — v. umstürzen, umwerfen, umstossen

overtime n. Überstunden

overture n. Vorschlag, Angebot; (mus.) Ouvertüre

overturn r. umwerfen, umkehren, umschlagen

overview n. Überblick, Übersicht; Inspektion

overweight n. Übergewicht; — adj. überladen

overwhelm v. überwältigen, zerschmettern; überschütten; -ing adj. überwältigend, erdrückend

overwork n. Überarbeitung; — v. (sich) überarbeiten (or übermüden)

ovum n. Ei

owe v. schuldig sein, schulden, verdanken

owl n. Eule; Kauz

own adj. eigen; einzig; my — self ich selbst; of one's — für sich allein; of one's — accord aus eigenem Antrieb, von selbst; — v. besitzen; -er n. Besitzer, Inhaber; Eigentümer; -ership n. Eigentum(srecht); Besitz

ox n. Ochse

oxalic acid n. Oxalsäure, Kleesäure

oxide n. Oxyd

oxidize v. oxydieren

oxygen n. Sauerstoff; — tent Sauerstoffzelt

oyster n. Auster

P

pace n. Schritt, Tritt; Gang; (mus.) Tempo, Geschwindigkeit; keep — Schritt halten; — v. (einher)schreiten, gehen; (sports) Schrittmacher sein; — off abschreiten

Pacific Ocean n. Stiller Ozean

pacifist n. Pazifist

pacify v. beruhigen, besänftigen, befriedigen

pack n. Pack, Paket; Bündel; Menge, Fülle; Last, Bürde; Meute, Rotte,

Rudel; Bande; (cards) Spiel; — **animal Packesel**, Lasttier; — **train** Lastzug; — v. (zusammen) packen, bepacken, zusammendrängen; parteiisch zusammensetzen; — **up** einpacken; **-age** n. Paket, Ballen; Verpackung; **-er** n. Packer, Verpacker; Packmaschine; **-et** n. Paket; **-ing** n. Packen, Verpacken; Verpackung, Packmaterial; (mech.) Dichtung; **-ing house** Fleischkonservenfabrik; Packhaus

pact n. Vertrag, Pakt

pad n. Kissen, Polster; Wulst, Bausch; Block; (zool.) Ballen; Fährte; — **of paper** Papierblock; — v. auspolstern; wattieren; **-ding** n. Polsterung, Wattierung; Polstermaterial

paddle v. paddeln; (coll.) tätscheln; — **wheel** Schaufelrad; — n. Paddel

padlock n. Vorhängeschloss; — v. mit einem Vorhängeschloss versehen (or verschliessen)

pagan n. Heide; — adj. heidnisch; **-ism** n. Heidentum

page n. Page; Botenjunge, Amtsdiener; Blatt, Seite; — v. paginieren, mit Seitenzahlen versehen; durch Namensaufruf herausfinden

pageant n. Festspiel, Aufzug; Schaustück; **-ry** n. Schaugepränge, Prunkaufzug

pail n. Eimer, Kübel

pain n. Schmerz, Pein, Qual; Sorge, Kummer; pl. Mühe, Leiden; Wehen; — v. quälen, peinigen; Schmerz verursachen; **-ful** adj. schmerzhaft, schmerzlich; peinlich, quälend; **-less** adj. schmerzlos

painstaking adj. arbeitsam, gewissenhaft; peinlich, sorgfältig

paint n. Farbe; Anstrich; Schminke; — v. malen; anstreichen; (sich) schminken; **-er** n. Maler; Anstreicher; **-ing** n. Gemälde; Malen, Malerei

paintbrush n. Malerpinsel; Antreicherpinsel

pair n. Paar; — v. (sich) paaren, vereinigen; sich verbinden

pajamas n. pl. Pyjama, Schlafanzug

pal n. Gefährte, Kamerad

palace n. Palast

palatable adj. schmackhaft, wohlschmeckend

palate n. Gaumen; (fig.) Geschmack

palatial adj. palastartig

Palatinate n. Pfalz

pale v. (er)bleichen, erblassen; — adj. bleich, blass; (fig.) matt; **-ness** n. Blässe, Farblosigkeit

paleface n. Bleichgesicht

palette n. Palette

palisade n. Palisade

pall n. Bahrtuch, Leichentuch; — v. langweilen, schal werden, den Reiz verlieren

pallbearer n. Bahrtuchhalter

pallet n. Strohlager, Strohsack

palm n. Handfläche, Handteller; (bot.) Palme, Palmbaum; (fig.) Sieg; **Palm Sunday** Palmsonntag; — v. in der Handfläche verbergen; — **off a thing on someone** jemandem etwas andrehen;

-etto n. Palmetto

palpitate v. klopfen, schlagen; zittern, zucken

palpitation n. Klopfen, Schlag(en); Herzklopfen

palsied adj. gelähmt, gichtbrüchig, wackelig

palsy n. Lähmung; (fig.) Ohnmacht

pamper v. verzärteln

pamphlet n. Broschüre, Prospekt, Flugschrift, Pamphlet

pan n. Pfanne, Tiegel

panacea n. Allheilmittel, Wundermittel

Panama hat n. Panamahut

pancake n. Pfannkuchen, Eierkuchen

pancreas n. Bauchspeicheldrüse

panda n. Panda, Katzenbär; **giant —** Riesenpanda, Bambusbär

pandemonium n. Höllenlärm

pane n. Scheibe, Platte; Fach, Füllung

panel n. (arch.) Füllung, Fach; Tafel; (law) Geschworenenliste, Geschworenenbank; (fig.) Sachverständigengruppe; — **discussion** Sachverständigengespräch

pang n. plötzlicher Schmerz, Stich; Angst, Qual

panhandler n. Bettler

panic n. Panik, panischer Schrecken; — adj. panisch; **-ky** adj. beunruhigt; beunruhigend

panic-stricken adj. von Schrecken ergriffen (or gelähmt)

panorama n. Panorama

pansy n. Stiefmütterchen

pant n. Keuchen, Herzklopfen; pl. Hosen, Unterhosen; — v. keuchen, nach Luft schnappen; (heart) pochen; (fig.) verlangen, streben; **-aloons** n. pl. Beinkleider; **-ies** n. pl. Schlüpfer

pantheism n. Pantheismus

panther n. Panther

pantomime n. Pantomime, Gebärdenspiel

pantry n. Speisekammer, Vorratskammer

papa n. Papa

papacy n. Papsttum

papal adj. päpstlich

pa(w)paw n. Papaya

paper n. Papier; Zeitung; Blatt, Zettel; Tapete; Vortrag, Vorlesung; (educ.) schriftliche Arbeit, Fragebogen; pl. Briefschaften, Dokumente, Akten; **blotting —** Löschpapier; **carbon —** Kohlepapier; **toilet —** Toilettenpapier; **papieren; — bag** Papiertüte; — **boy** Zeitungsjunge; — **chase** Schnitzeljagd; — **clip** Büroklammer, Heftklammer; — **cutter** Papierschneider, Papierschneidemaschine; — **knife** Papiermesser; **money** Papiergeld; — v. tapezieren

paperweight n. Briefbeschwerer

par n. Gleichheit, gleicher Wert; Pari; **at —** auf Pari, gleich an Wert; — adj. **value** Gleichwertigkeit, Pariwert; — prep. **excellence** par excellence, vorzugsweise

parable n. Parabel, Gleichnis

parachute n. Fallschirm

parade n. Parade; Prunk(aufzug), Gepränge; — v. paradieren; in Parade auf-

marschieren; prunken; (mil.) defilieren,
vorbeiziehen

paradise n. Paradies

paraffin n. Paraffin

paragon n. Vorbild, Muster

paragraph n. Paragraph, Absatz, Abschnitt

parakeet n. Wellensittich, Sittich

parallel n. Parallele, Parallellinie; (geog.) Parallelkreis; — adj. parallel, gleichlaufend; — v. parallel machen (or laufen)

paralysis n. Lähmung, Paralyse; **infantile — Kinderlähmung**

paralyze v. lähmen, lahmlegen

paramedics n. (mil.) Fallschirm-Sanitätspersonal

paramilitary n. pseudomilitärisch, halbmilitärisch

paramount adj. höchst, unumschränkt

paraphernalia n. Ausstaffierung

paraphrase n. Umschreibung, Paraphrase; — v. umschreiben, paraphrasieren

parasite n. Parasit, Schmarotzer

paratroops n. pl. Fallschirmtruppen

parcel n. Paket, Ballen; Teil, Stück; Parzelle; Menge, Masse; **small — Päckchen; — post** Paketpost; — v. parzellieren, abteilen

parch v. austrocknen, verdorren; rösten, dörren

parchment n. Pergament

pardon n. Verzeihung, Vergebung; Pardon; (law) Begnadigung; — v. entschuldigen, verzeihen, vergeben; begnadigen; **-able** adj. verzeihlich

pare v. schälen; (ab)schneiden, beschneiden

parent n. Vater, Mutter; pl. Eltern; **-age** n. Familie, Abstammung, Herkunft; Elternschaft; (fig.) Urheberschaft; **-al** adj. elterlich; väterlich, mütterlich; **-hood** n. Elternschaft

parenthesis n. Parenthese, Einschaltung; (typ.) Klammer

paring knife n. Schälmesser

parings n. pl. Schale, Späne, Abfall

Paris green n. Pariser Grün

parish n. Gemeinde, Kirchspiel; **-ioner** n. Gemeindemitglied, Pfarrkind

parity n. Gleichheit, Gleichstellung. Gleichberechtigung; (agr.) Preisabkommen

park n. Park, Anlage(n); Garten; — v. parken; **-ing** n. Parken; **-ing place** Parkplatz

parkway n. Parkstrasse; schöngelegene Autostrasse; Allee

parley n. Unterhandlung, Unterredung; — v. unterhandeln

parliament n. Parlament; **-ary** adj. parlamentarisch

parlor n. Salon, Empfangszimmer; Gästzimmer; **funeral —** Begräbnishalle; — **car** Salonwagen

parochial adj. Pfarr-, Gemeinde-

parole n. Parole, Losungswort; Ehrenwort; **on —** auf Ehrenwort (entlassen); — v. bedingt entlassen

paroxysm n. Paroxysmus, Anfall

parquet n. Parkett

parrot n. Papagei; (fig.) Nachschwätzer; — v. nachplappern

parsley n. Petersilie

parsnip n. Pastinakwurzel

parson n. Pfarrer, Pastor; **-age** n. Pfarrhaus

part n. Teil, Anteil; Bestandteil, Stück, Glied; Stadtteil, Gegend; Lieferung; Seite, Partei; Pflicht; (hair) Scheitel; (mus.) Stimme, Partie; (theat.) Rolle; pl. Anlagen, Talente, Fähigkeiten; **do one's —** seine Schuldigkeit tun; **for my —** meinerseits; **for the most —** grösstenteils; **in —** teilweise; **— of speech** Redeteil; **take —** in teilnehmen an; **take someone's —** für jemand Partei ergreifen; **— payment** Teilzahlung; — v. (sich) trennen, aufgeben, scheiden; (hair) scheiteln; **-ing** n. Trennung, Abschied; Teilung, Scheidung; Scheiteln; **-ly** adv. teils, zum Teil; in gewissem Grade

partake v. teilhaben, teilnehmen; mitessen

partial adj. teilweise, Teil-; parteiisch, einseitig, eingenommen; **-ity** n. Parteilichkeit, Vorliebe

participant n. Teilnehmer; — adj. teilnehmend

participate v. teilnehmen, teilhaben

participation n. Teilnahme

participle n. Partizip, Mittelwort

particle n. Stückchen, Teilchen; (gram.) unbeugbares Wort (Verhältnis-, Binde- oder Umstandswort); (phys.) Partikelchen

particular adj. besonder, einzeln; wählerisch; sonderbar; — n. Einzelheit; **in —** insbesondere, besonders

partisan n. Partisan, Parteigänger; Partisane; **-ship** n. Parteigängertum, Parteigeist

partition n. Einteilung, Teilung; (arch.) Scheidewand; — v. (ein)teilen, verteilen

partner n. Partner, Teilhaber, Teilnehmer; Gefährte, Gesellschafter; Tänzer, Mitspieler; **silent —** stiller Teilhaber; **-ship** n. Teilhaberschaft, Gemeinschaft; Handelsgesellschaft; **general -ship** Gesellschaft mit unbeschränkter Haftung; **limited -ship** Gesellschaft mit beschränkter Haftung; **silent -ship** stille Teilhaberschaft

partridge n. Rebhuhn

part-time job n. Nebenbeschäftigung

party n. Partei; Gesellschaft; Partie; Teilhaber, Teilnehmer; Interessent; Beteiligte; (mil.) Abteilung; **— line** Gemeinschaftstelefon

pass n. Pass, Engpass; Zugang, Durchfahrt; Reisepass, Passierschein; (mil.) Urlaubsschein; (sports) Zuspielen, Ausfall; (theat.) Freikarte; — v. (vorüber) gehen; einholen, überholen; passieren; genehmigen; (über)reichen; bestehen. annehmen; (cards) passen; **come to —** geschehen; **— away** sterben; **— by** vorübergehen; **— for** gelten für; **— judg-**

ment (*oder* **sentence**) ein Urteil fällen; — **off** ausgeben; — **on** weitersagen; weitergeben; — **out** ohnmächtig werden; — **over** übersehen, übergehen; **-able** *adj.* gangbar, leidlich; passierbar; **-age** *n.* Korridor, Gang; Passage; Durchreise, Überfahrt; (book) Absatz. Abschnitt; (mus.) Lauf; (pol.) Annahme; **-é** *adj.* passé, veraltet, altmodisch; **-enger** *n.* Reisende, Fahrgast, Passagier; **-ing** *n.* Vorbeigehen, Hinübergehen; Durchgang; (pol.) Durchbringen; in **-ing** im Vorbeigehen; **-ing** *adj.* vorübergehend; genwärtig, jeweilig; dahineilend, flüchtig; **-ing grade** (educ.) Versetzungsnote **to make a** — *v.* Avancen machen; (avi.) den Flugplatz anfliegen

passer-by *n.* Vorübergehende

passion *n.* Leidenschaft, Liebe, Verlangen; Wut, Ärger, Zorn; Passion; **-ate** *adj.* leidenschaftlich, begeistert, passioniert

passive *adj.* passiv, leidend, untätig

passkey *n.* Hauptschlüssel, Drücker

Passover *n.* Passah(fest)

passport *n.* Pass, Reisepass; (mil.) Passierschein, Geleitbrief

password *n.* Parole, Losung(swort)

past *n.* Vergangenheit, Vergangene; — *adj.* vergangen, verflossen; vorbei, ehemalig; vorüber, hin; vorig, früher; — **master** Altmeister; — **participle** Partizip der Vergangenheit; — **perfect** Plusquamperfekt; — **tense** Zeitform der Vergangenheit; — *prep.* vorbei an; über; nach; **a quarter** — **nine** viertel Zehn, Viertel nach Neun; **at half** — **seven** um halb acht; — **all belief** unglaublich; — **comparison** unvergleichlich; — *adv.* vorbei, vorüber

paste *n.* Paste, Teig; Kleister, Klebstoff; Pappe; — *v.* pappen, kleistern; (auf)kleben

pasteboard *n.* Pappdeckel, Pappe

pasteurize *v.* pasteurisieren, keimfrei machen

pastime *n.* Zeitvertreib, Kurzweil

pastor *n.* Pastor

pastoral *adj.* pastoral, seelsorgerisch; Hirten-

pastry *n.* Gebäck; Pastete, Torte; Konditorware; — **shop** Konditorei

pasture *n.* Weide, Weideland, Futter; — *v.* (ab)weiden, grasen; auf die Weide treiben

pasty *adj.* teig(art)ig; bleich

pat *n.* Schlag, Klaps; — *adv.* and *adj.* eben recht, passend; bequem, treffend; **stand** — seinen Standpunkt verteidigen; — *v.* tappen, patschen, tätschein; — **on the back** beglückwünschen

patch *n.* Fleck, Flicken, Lappen; — *v.* flicken, ausbessern; — **up** flicken, zusammenstoppeln

patchwork *n.* Flickwerk, Flickerei

patent *n.* Patent, Privilegien, Freibrief; — *adj.* offen(bar); — **fastener** Druckknopf; — **leather** Lackleder; — **medicine** Markenmedizin; — *v.* patentieren

paternal *adj.* väterlich

paternity *n.* Vaterschaft

path *n.* Pfad, Weg; **-less** *adj.* pfadlos, unwegsam

pathetic *adj.* rührend, pathetisch

pathfinder *n.* Pfadfinder

pathological *adj.* pathologisch

pathology *n.* Pathologie, Krankheitslehre

pathos *n.* Pathos

pathway *n.* Pfad, Weg, Fussteig

patience *n.* Geduld, Ausdauer; (cards) Patience

patient *n.* Patient, Kranke; — *adj.* geduldig; ausdauernd, beharrlich

patio *n.* Patio, spanischer Innenhof

patriarch *n.* Patriarch

patriot *n.* Patriot; **-ic** *adj.* patriotisch; **-ism** *n.* Patriotismus, Vaterlandsliebe

patrol *n.* Patrouille, Runde; — *v.* patrouillieren

patrolman *n.* Schutzmann auf Streife

patron *n.* Patron, Schutzherr; Gönner; Kunde; — **saint** Schutzheilige; **-age** *n.* Protektion, Gönnerschaft; Schutz; **-ize** *v.* beschützen, begünstigen; gönnerhaft behandeln; besuchen

patter *n.* Klapper, Platschen; Getrappe; — *v.* klappern, plappern, trappeln

pattern *n.* Muster, Modell, Probe; Vorbild

patty *n.* Pastetchen

paunch *n.* Bauch, Wanst

pauper *n.* Arme, Almosenempfänger

pause *n.* Pause, Unterbrechung; (mus.) Fermate; — *v.* pausieren, innehalten, verweilen

pave *v.* pflastern; (fig.) bedecken; — **the way** den Weg bahnen (or ebnen); **-ment** *n.* Pflaster(ung), Pflastermaterial

pavilion *n.* Pavillon, Lusthaus; Zelt

paving *n.* Pflaster

paw *n.* Pfote, Klaue, Tatze; — *v.* mit den Pfoten stossen (or schlagen, stampfen, scharren); (be)patschen

pawn *n.* Pfand; (chess) Bauer; — *v.* verpfänden, versetzen

pawnbroker *n.* Pfandleiher

pawnshop *n.* Pfandleihe, Leihhaus

pay *n.* Zahlung, Bezahlung, Auszahlung; Lohn, Gehalt; **half** — Halbsold; **in the** — **of** im Dienste von; — **roll** Gehaltsliste; — *v.* (be)zahlen, auszahlen; belohnen, vergelten; erweisen, entrichten; — **a visit** einen Besuch abstatten; — **attention** achtgeben; — **back** zurückzahlen; — **no attention** keine Aufmerksamkeit schenken; — **off** abzahlen; — **one's way** seinen Verbindlichkeiten nachkommen; — **up** vollständig auszahlen; **-able** *adj.* zahlbar; schuldig; fällig; **-ing** *adj.* zahlend; **-ing teller** Kassierer (am Auszahlungsschalter); **-ment** *n.* Zahlung, Bezahlung; Lohn, Belohnung; **cash -ment** Barzahlung; **deferred -ment** verspätete (or aufgeschobene) Zahlung; **-ment in advance** Vorauszahlung; **-ment in full** volle Auszahlung; **-ment in part** Teilzahlung; **-ment on account** (oder **by installment**) Ab(schlags)zahlung; **stop -ment** die Zahlungen einstellen; **terms of -ment**

Zahlungsbedingungen
payday *n.* Zahltag
payload *n.* Nutzlast
paymaster *n.* Auszahler; (mil. and naut.) Zahlmeister
payoff *n.* Ergebnis; Auszahlung
pea *n.* Erbse; — **green** Erbsengrün
peace *n.* Friede(n), Sicherheit, Ruhe, Eintracht; **-able** *adj.* friedfertig, friedliebend; **-ful** *adj.* friedlich; ungestört
peacemaker *n.* Friedenstifter
peach *n.* Pfirsich; — **tree** Pfirsichbaum
peacock *n.* Pfau
peak *n.* Spitze, Gipfel; — *adj.* — **performance** Spitzenleistung; **-ed** *adj.* spitz; kränklich aussehend
peal *n.* Geläute, Glockenspiel; Gekrach, Schall, Schlag, Geschmetter; — *v.* läuten; schallen, schmettern; krachen, dröhnen
peanut *n.* Erdnuss; — **brittle** Erdnussnougatstücken; — **butter** Erdnussbutter
pear *n.* Birne; — **tree** Birn(en)baum
pearl *n.* Perle; **-y** *adj.* perlartig, perlmutterartig; perlenfarben; perlenreich
peasant *n.* Bauer, Landmann
peat *n.* Torf
pebble *n.* Kiesel(stein)
pecan *n.* Hickorynuss; — **tree** Hickorybaum
peck *n.* Doppelgallone, Viertelscheffel; Schnabelschlag, Schnappen; — *v.* picken, hacken
picture window *n.* Aussichtsfenster
peculiar *adj.* eigentümlich, besonder; seltsam; **-ity** *n.* Eigentümlichkeit, Besonderheit; Seltsamkeit
pecuniary *adj.* geldlich, pekuniär; Geld-; — **difficulties** Zahlungsschwierigkeiten
pedal *n.* Pedal; Fusshebel; *v.* treten
peddle *v.* hausieren; **-r** *n.* Hausierer
pedestal *n.* Fussgestell; Piedestal, Säulenfuss; **large** — Postament
pedestrian *n.* Fussgänger
pediatrician *n.* Kinderarzt
pedigree *n.* Stammbaum; Herkunft; **-d** *adj.* mit Stammbaum versehen
peek *n.* Blick, Blinzeln; — *v.* spähen, blinzeln
peel *n.* Schale, Rinde, Haut; — *v.* (ab)schälen, abhäuten; sich schälen
peep *n.* heimlicher (or verstohlener) Blick; — *v.* neugierig (or heimlich, verstohlen) blicken
peephole *n.* Guckloch
peer *n.* Pair; Ebenbürtige, Gleiche; — *v.* schauen, spähen, lugen; **-less** *adj.* unvergleichlich, einzig
peevish *adj.* launisch, verdriesslich, mürrisch
peg *n.* Pflock, Holznagel; Dübel, Spund; Klammer; Haken; (mus.) Wirbel; — *v.* festpflöcken, abstecken
pelican *n.* Pelikan
pellagra *n.* Hautflechte
pellet *n.* Kügelchen; Schrotkorn
pell-mell *adv.* durcheinander, ganz verworren; blindlings
pelt *n.* Pelz, Fell; — *v.* bewerfen; nieder-

stürzen, niederprasseln
pelvis *n.* Becken
pen *n.* Feder; Schreibfeder; Hürde, Verschlag; **stroke of the** — Federzug; — **name** Schriftstellername; — *v.* schreiben, abfassen; einpferchen
penal *adj.* Straf-, strafbar, sträflich; **-ize** *v.* mit Strafe belegen; strafen; **-ty** *n.* Strafe, Busse; Strafpunkt
penance *n.* Busse, Büssung
pencil *n.* Bleistift, Zeichenstift; — **of rays** Strahlenbündel; — **protector** Bleistifthülse; — **sharpener** Bleistiftanspitzer; — *v.* zeichnen, entwerfen; (eyebrow) nachziehen
pendant *n.* Anhänger; Gehänge; Gegenstück, Pendant
pending *adj.* schwebend, noch anhängig, unentschieden
pendulum *n.* Pendel, Perpendikel
penetrate *v.* durchdringen
penetration *n.* Durchdringung, Eindringen; Scharfsinn
penguin *n.* Pinguin
penholder *n.* Federhalter
penicillin *n.* Penicillin
peninsula *n.* Halbinsel
penis *n.* Penis, männliches Glied
penitence *n.* Busse, Reue, Zerknirschung
penitent *adj.* bussfertig, reuig; zerknirscht; **-iary** *n.* Zuchthaus; Besserungsanstalt
penknife *n.* Federmesser
penmanship *n.* Schreibkunst; Schönschreiben; Schrift
pennant *n.* Wimpel, Fähnchen
penniless *adj.* ohne Geld, dürftig, arm
penny *n.* Penny; Pfennig
pension *n.* Pension, Rente, Ruhegehalt; **widow's** — Witwenrente; — *v.* pensionieren; **-er** *n.* Pensionär, Rentenempfänger
pentagon *n.* Fünfeck, Pentagon
pentameter *n.* Pentameter, fünffüssiger Vers
penthouse *n.* Luxuswohnung im obersten Stock; Schutzdach
pent-up *adj.* beschränkt, verhalten
penurious *adj.* karg, geizig
peony *n.* Päonie, Pfingstrose
people *n.* Volk, Nation; Leute, Menschen; Verwandte; — *v.* bevölkern
pep *n.* Energie, Initiative, Mut; — **talk** anfeuernde Rede
pepper *n.* Pfeffer; **green** — grüne Paprikaschote; **red** — roter (or spanischer) Pfeffer; Paprika, Piment; — *v.* pfeffern; **-y** *adj.* pfeffer(art)ig; (fig.) scharf, heftig, hitzig
pepper-and-salt *adj.* pfeffer- und salzfarben; grau meliert
peppermint *n.* Pfefferminz(e); — **drops** Pfefferminzplätzchen
pepsin *n.* Pepsin
peptic *adj.* Verdauungs-
per *prep.* per, durch, für, mit, laut; — **annum** pro Jahr, jährlich; — **capita** pro Kopf; — **cent** Prozent; — **diem** pro Tag, täglich
perambulator *n.* Kinderwagen
percale *n.* Perkal, feinfädiger Baumwoll-

stoff

perceive v. (be)merken, wahrnehmen; erlangen, empfinden

percentage n. Prozentsatz

perceptible adj. wahrnehmbar, bemerkbar; vernehmlich

perception n. Wahrnehmung, Empfindung(svermögen); Anschauung, Vorstellung

perch n. Stange; (ichth.) Barsch; — v. sitzen; sich setzen

perchance adv. vielleicht; von ungefähr

percolator n. Perkolator, Kaffeemaschine

percussion n. Erschütterung, Stoss; — cap Zündhütchen; — instrument Schlaginstrument

perdition n. Verdammnis, Verderben

perfect adj. vollkommen, vollendet, perfekt; gültig; — n. Perfekt; — v. vervollkommen, vollenden, ausbilden; -ion n. Vollkommenheit, Vervollkommnung; Vollendung; Perfektion

perfidious adj. treulos, verräterisch, perfid

perforate v. durchbohren, durchlöchern, perforieren

perforation n. Perforation, Lochung

perforce adj. gewaltsam; notgedrungen

perform v. vollziehen, ausführen; erfüllen, verrichten; (mus. and theat.) spielen, vortragen; aufführen, darstellen; -ance n. Ausführung, Verrichtung, Vollendung, Erfüllung; (mus. and theat.) Spiel, Vortrag; Aufführung; Vorstellung; Darstellung; first -ance Erstaufführung; -er n. Ausführende, Vollbringer; (mus. and theat.) Künstler, Vortragende; Schauspieler, Darsteller

perfume n. Parfüm; Duft, Wohlgeruch; — bottle Parfümflasche; — v. parfümieren

perfunctory adj. gewohnheitsmässig, mechanisch; oberflächlich, gedankenlos

perhaps adv. vielleicht, etwa; möglicherweise

peril n. Gefahr; -ous adj. gefährlich, gefahrvoll

perimeter n. Umfang; Umkreis

period n. Periode, Zeitraum, Zeitpunkt; Ziel, Ende; (typ.) Punkt; — of grace letzte Frist, -ic adj. periodisch; -ical n. Zeitschrift, Revue; -ical adj. periodisch, wiederkehrend

periscope n. Sehrohr, Periskop

perish v. umkommen, zugrundegehen, -able adj. vergänglich, verderblich; hinfällig

peritonitis n. Bauchfellentzündung

perjure v. — oneself falsch schwören, einen Meineid leisten

perjury n. Meineid

perk v. — up sich aufmuntern (or herausputzen, recken, aufrichten); — up one's ears die Ohren spitzen; -y adj. schmuck, geputzt; keck, übermütig, selbstbewusst

permanence n. Fortdauer, Ständigkeit

permanent adj. ständig, dauernd, anhaltend; — wave Dauerwelle

permissible adj. zulässig

permission n. Erlaubnis

permit n. Erlaubnis; Erlaubnisschein, Passierschein; — v. erlauben, gestatten

pernicious adj. verderblich, schädlich; gefährlich, nachteilig

peroxide n. Superoxyd; — blonde Wasserstoffblondine

perpendicular adj. senkrecht; aufrecht, steil; — n. Senkrechte; Perpendikel

perpetrate v. begehen, verüben, verbrechen

perpetual adj. beständig, fortwährend, ewig

perplex v. verwirren, bestürzen; -ity n. Verwirrung, Bestürzung; Verworrenheit

persecute v. verfolgen; quälen, drangsalieren

persecution n. Verfolgung, Belästigung

perseverance n. Beharrlichkeit, Standhaftigkeit; Ausdauer

persevere v. beharren, ausdauern

persimmon n. Dattelpflaume

persist v. beharren, verharren; hartnäckig bestehen; -ence n., -ency n. Beharrlichkeit; Hartnäckigkeit, Eigensinn; Dauer; -ent adj. beharrlich, hartnäckig, eigensinnig

person n. Person, Mensch; (theat.) Rolle; in — selbst, in eigener Person; -able adj. hübsch, ansehnlich, wohlgebildet; -age n. Persönlichkeit, Standesperson; -al adj. persönlich; (fig.) anzüglich; -al property persönlicher Besitz, persönliches Vermögen; -ality n. Persönlichkeit; (fig.) Anzüglichkeit; -ification n. Verkörperung, Personifizierung; -ify v. verkörpern, personifizieren; -nel n. Personal, Belegschaft

perspective n. Perspektive, Ausblick; — adj. perspektivisch

perspiration n. Schweiss, Ausdünstung

perspire v. (aus)schwitzen

persuade v. überzeugen, überreden; einreden

persuasion n. Überzeugung, Überredung; Meinung

persuasive adj. überredend, überzeugend

pert adj. keck, vorlaut; naseweis; unverschämt

pertain v. (an)gehören; gebühren, betreffen

pertinence n. Angemessenheit, Schicklichkeit; Geeignetheit

pertinent adj. angemessen, schicklich, passend; zweckdienlich

perusal n. Durchlesen, Durchsicht

pervade v. durchdringen; durchziehen

perverse adj. widernatürlich, pervers; verkehrt; (fig.) verdreht

perversion n. Verdrehung, Abkehr

pervert v. verdrehen, verkehren, umkehren; fälschen; verführen

pessimism n. Pessimismus

pessimist n. Pessimist, Schwarzseher; -ic adj. pessimistisch

pest n. Pest, Seuche; (fig.) Plage; -er v. belästigen, beunruhigen, plagen; -ilence n. Seuche, Pestilenz

pet n. Liebling, Lieblingstier; Schosskind, Schosstier; Schoss-, Lieblings-; zahm;

— name Kosename; — v. (ver)hätscheln; **-ting** n. Verzärteln, Liebkosen, Betasten

petal n. Blumenblatt, Blütenblatt

petition n. Bitte, Bittschrift, Gesuch; (pol.) Protest; **make a** — ein Gesuch einreichen; — v. bitten, ersuchen

petrel n. Sturmvogel

petrify v. versteinern

petrol n. Benzin; **-eum** n. Petroleum, Erdöl; **-eum** adj. **-eum jelly** Vaseline

petticoat n. Unterrock

pettiness n. Geringfügigkeit, Unbedeutenheit; Kleinlichkeit

petty adj. klein, geringfügig, unbedeutend; kleinlich; — **cash** Portokasse; — **larceny** (kleiner) Diebstahl; — **officer** Obermaat; — **thief** kleiner Dieb

petulant adj. übellaunig, verdriesslich; launenhaft, empfindlich

petunia n. Petunie

pew n. Kirchenstuhl, Kirchenbank

pewter n. Zinn

phantom n. Phantom; Gespenst

pharmaceutic(al) adj. pharmazeutisch

pharmacist n. Apotheker, Pharmazeut

pharmacy n. Apotheke

pharynx n. Rachenhöhle

phase n. Phase, Wandlung, Stadium

pheasant n. Fasan

phenol n. Phenol, Karbolsäure

phenomenal adj. phänomenal

phenomenon n. Phänomen, Erscheinung, Wunder

philander v. eine Liebelei haben

philanthropist n. Philantrop, Menschenfreund

philanthropy n. Philanthropie, Menschenliebe

philatelist n. Philatelist, Briefmarkensammler

philharmonic adj. philharmonisch

philology n. Philologie, Sprachwissenschaft

philosopher n. Philosoph

philosophic(al) adj. philosophisch

philosophize v. philosophieren

philosophy n. Philosophie

phlegm m. Schleim; Phlegma; **-atic** adj. phlegmatisch

phobia n. Phobie, krankhafte Angst

phone n. Telefon; **-tic** adj. phonetisch; **-tics** n. Phonetik, Lautbildungslehre

phonograph n. Grammofon

phosphate n. Phosphat

phosphorescent adj. phosphoreszierend

phosphorus n. Phosphor

photo n. Foto; — **finish** Sieg durch Zielfotografie; **-genic** adj. fotogen

photoelectric adj. fotoelektrisch

photoengraving n. Hochdruckätzung

photograph n. Fotografie; — v. fotografieren; **be -ed** fotografiert werden (or sein) **-er** n. Fotograf; **-ic** adj. fotografisch; **-y** n. Fotografie

photogravure n. Lichtkupferätzung

photoplay n. Filmdrama

photostat n. Fotostat, Fotokopiermaschine

phrase n. Phrase, Redensart, Ausdruck;

Satz; — v. ausdrücken, phrasieren; **-ology** n. Ausdrucksweise, Phraseologie

physic n. Arznei, Heilmittel; Abführmittel; **-al** n. Körperübung; Untersuchung; **-al** adj. physisch, körperlich; **-al education** körperliche Ausbildung; **-al geography** physikalische Geographie; **-al sciences** Naturwissenschaften; **-ian** n. Arzt; **attending -ian** behandelnder Arzt; **-ist** n. Physiker, Naturforscher; **-s** n. Physik, Naturlehre

physiognomy n. Gesichtsbildung; Physiognomie

physiological adj. physiologisch

physiology n. Physiologie

physique n. Figur, Körperbau

pianist n. Pianist

piano n. Klavier, Piano; **grand** — Flügel; **player** — Pianola

piazza n. Platz; (arch.) Säulengang, Veranda

pica type n. Ciceroschrift

piccalilli n. scharf gewürztes Gemüse

piccolo n. Piccoloflöte, Oktavflöte

pick n. Picke, Haue, Spitzhacke; (fig.) Auswahl, Beste; — v. picken, hacken; aussuchen, auswählen; lesen, pflücken; **— a pocket** eine Taschendiebstahl begehen; **— out** auswählen; **— up** aufheben, aufnehmen; (auf)picken, aufgabeln

pickaninny n. kleines Kind (or Negerkind)

pickax(e) n. Picke; Hacke

pickerel n. Hecht(art)

picket n. Pfahl, Pflock; (mil.) Pikett, Vorposten; Streikposten; **— fence** Pfahlzaun; — v. einpfählen

pickle n. Eingepökelte; Essiggurke; — v. (ein)pökeln, in Essig einmachen

pickpocket n. Taschendieb, Langfinger

pickup n. Beschleunigung; (phonograph) Tonarm, Tonabnehmer; (coll.) Aufgabeln; (—**truck**) offener Lieferwagen

picnic n. Picknick; — v. picknicken

pictorial adj. malerisch; illustriert; Maler-

picture n. Bild(nis), Gemälde, Zeichnung, Fotografie; Schilderung, Beschreibung; **— puzzle** Vexierbild; **— window** Bildfenster, Fenster mit einem schönen Ausblick; — v. malen, abbilden; schildern, beschreiben; **-sque** adj. malerisch

pie n. Pastete

piece n. Stück; (chess) Figur; (mil.) Geschütz; **give someone a — of one's mind** jemand die Meinung sagen; **go to -s** entzwei gehen; — v. stücke(l)n, flicken, ausbessern, ansetzen

piecemeal adv. stückweise; — adj. einzeln

piecework n. Akkordarbeit, Stückarbeit

pier n. Landungsplatz, Hafendamm, Mole; (arch.) Pfeiler

pierce v. durchstechen, durchbohren, eindringen; (fig.) durchblicken, durchschauen

piercing adj. durchdringend; schneidend; scharf; (fig.) rührend

piety n. Frömmigkeit; Pietät

pig n. Schwein, Ferkel; (min.) Mulde; **-gish** adj. schweinisch, unflätig

pigeon n. Taube; **clay** — Tontaube; **cock**

— Täuberich; **homing —** Brieftaube
pigeonhole n. kleiner Taubenschlag; (fig.) kleines Schreibtischfach
piggyback n. Huckepack
pigpen, pigsty n. Schweinekoben, Schweinestall
pike n. (ichth.) Hecht; (mil.) Pike
pile n. Haufen; Pfahl; (elec.) galvanische Säule; (fabric) Flor; pl. Hämorrhoiden; — **driver** Ramme; — v. aufschichten, aufhäufen, aufstapeln
pilgrim n. Pilger, Wallfahrer; **-age** n. Wallfahrt, Pilgerfahrt
pill n. Pille
pillar n. Pfeiler, Träger, Säule; Stütze
pillory n. Pranger; — v. an den Pranger stellen
pillow n. Kopfkissen, Kissen, Polster
pillowcase, pillowslip n. Kissenüberzug, Polsterüberzug
pilot n. (avi.) Pilot, Flieger; (naut.) Lotse, Steuermann; (fig.) Führer; — **burner** Sparbrenner; — **light** Kontrollampe; — v. (avi.) fliegen; (naut.) lotsen, steuern; (fig.) führen
pim(i)ento n. Jamaikapfeffer
pimpel n. Pickel, Pustel
pin n. Nadel; Anstecknadel; (bowling) Kegel; (mech.) Stift, Pflock, Nagel; (mus.) Wirbel; (fig.) Kleinigkeit; (sl.) Bein; **safety —** Sicherheitsnadel; — v. anstecken, anheften
pinafore n. Lätzchen, Kinderschürze
pincers n. pl. Kneifzange, Beisszange; (zool.) Scheren
pinch n. Kneifen; Kniff; Prise; (coll.) Klemme; — v. kneifen, zwicken, klemmen
pine n. Kiefer, Föhre; — v. sich abhärmen; schmachten; — **for** sich sehnen nach
pineapple n. Ananas
pinfeather n. Stoppelfeder
pingpong n. Pingpong, Tischtennis
pink n. Rosa; (bot.) Nelke; (fig.) Gipfel; **in the — of condition** in bester Verfassung; — adj. blassrot, rosa
pinpoint v. präzise angreifen (or festlegen)
pint n. Pinte (0,57 Liter)
pin-up n. Schönheitsfotografie; — adj. Schönheits-
pioneer n. Pionier; (fig.) Bahnbrecher
pious adj. fromm, gottesfürchtig
pipe n. Rohr; Röhre, Röhrenleitung; Tabakspfeife; (mus.) Pfeife; — v. pfeifen. Flöte spielen; durch Röhren leiten; **-r** n. Pfeifer
pipeline n. Rohrnetz; Leitungsnetz
piping n. Pfeifen, Pfiff; Röhrensystem; (dress) Paspel; — adj. pfeifend; siedend; (fig.) sanft, ruhevoll
piquant adj. pikant
pique n. Groll, Pikiertheit; — v. beleidigen, kränken, reizen
piracy n. Seeräuberei; (fig.) Raub geistigen Eigentums; unbefugtes Nachdrucken; Plagiat
pirate n. Pirat, Seeräuber; (fig.) Plagiator; — v. Seeräuberei treiben; unbefugt nachdrucken; (rad.) schwarzhören

pistil n. Stempel, Griffel
pistol n. Pistole
piston n. (mech.) Kolben; (mus.) Klappe, Ventil; — **engine** Kolbenmotor; — **rod** Kolbenstange
pit n. Grube; Höhle; (agr.) Miete; (bot.) Stein; (com.) Börse; (med.) Narbe; (theat.) Parterre; (fig.) Grab; — v. in einer Grube fangen (or vergraben); gegeneinander hetzen; entgegenstellen
pitch n. Wurf; Grad, Höhe, Neigung; (chem.) Pech; (mech.) Zahneinteilung, Schraubenganghöhe; (mus.) Tonlage; (naut.) Stampfen; — v. werfen; aufstellen, aufschlagen; verpichen; (mus.) den Grundton angeben, stimmen; (naut.) stampfen; **-er** n. Krug; (baseball) Werfer; **-ing** n. (naut.) Stampfen
pitchfork n. Heugabel
pitfall n. Fallgrube; (fig.) Falle
pith n. (bot.) Mark; (fig.) Kern, Kraft, Energie; **-y** adj. mark(art)ig; kernig, kräftig
pitiful adj. mitleiderregend; erbärmlich, jämmerlich
pitiless adj. mitleidslos, unbarmherzig
pituitary adj. schleimig, Schleim; — **gland** Hirnanhang
pity n. Mitleid, Erbarmen; — v. bemitleiden, bedauern
pivot n. Zapfen, Angel; (fig.) Drehpunkt
placard n. Plakat, Anschlagzettel
place n. Platz, Stätte, Ort, Stelle; Ortschaft, Stadt; Wohnort, Wohnsitz; Stellung, Rang, Amt; (theat.) Sitz; — v. stellen, setzen, legen; herrichten; einordnen, unterbringen; **-ment** n. Unterbringung
plagiarize v. plagiieren, abschreiben, ausschreiben
plague n. Pest, Seuche; Plage; — v. heimsuchen, plagen
plain adj. einfach, schlicht; deutlich, klar, verständlich; offenbar; unumwunden, offen, redlich, aufrichtig; ungekünstelt; unansehnlich; ungemustert, einfarbig; — n. Ebene, Prärie; **-ness** n. Einfachheit, Schlichtheit; Klarheit, Deutlichkeit, Verständlichkeit; Unansehnlichkeit
plain-clothes man n. Geheimpolizist, Detektiv
plaint n. Beschwerde, Einspruch; Klage(schrift); (poet.) Wehklage; **-iff** n. Kläger; **-ive** adj. jammernd, kläglich
plait n. Falte; Flechte; Zopf; — v. falten, (ver)flechten
plan n. Plan, Entwurf; Grundriss; Projekt; — v. planen, beabsichtigen; entwerfen
plane n. Ebene, Fläche; (mech.) Hobel; Flugzeug, Tragfläche; — v. hobeln; ebnen, glätten; — adj. flach, eben; — **tree** Platane
planet n. Planet; **-arium** n. Planetarium
plank n. Planke, Bohle; (pol.) Programmpunkt; — v. dielen, verschalen
plant n. Pflanze, Gewächs; Setzling, Steckling; (com.) Betriebsanlage, Fabrik; (coll.) Kniff, Schwindel; Irrefüh-

rung, Falle; — v. (an)pflanzen, einpflanzen; anlegen, ansiedeln; aufpflanzen; aufstellen, errichten; -er n. Pflanzer; Plantagenbeisitzer

plantation n. Pflanzung; Plantage

plaque n. Plakette

plasma n. (phys.) Plasma

plaster n. Gips, Stuck; Bewurf, Tünche; (med.) Pflaster; — v. bewerfen, tünchen; überkleben; (med.) bepflastern; (fig.) bedecken; **sticking —** Heftpflaster; **— cast** Gipsverband; -er n. Stukkateur; Gipsarbeiter; -ing n. Stuck; Bewerfen mit Mörtel; Tünchen

plastic adj. plastisch; bildend, formend; bildungsfähig, formbar; Kunststoff-; -s n. Plastik; Kunststoff

plate n. Platte, Tafel; Teller; Tafelgeschirr, Tafelsilber; — v. plattieren, versilbern; **— glass** Tafelglas, Spiegelglas

plateau n. Hochebene, Plateau

platform n. Tribüne; (pol.) Parteiprogramm; (rail.) Bahnsteig

platinum n. Platin

platitude n. Plattheit

platonic adj. platonisch

platoon n. Zug

platter n. grosse, flache Schüssel

plausible adj. plausibel, glaubwürdig, einleuchtend, überzeugend

play n. Spiel(erei); Spielraum; Handlungsweise; (mech.) Gang; (theat.) Schauspiel; Vorstellung, Aufführung; **keep in —** in Gang halten; — v. spielen; tändeln; (cards) ausspielen; (mus.) aufspielen; (theat.) aufführen; darstellen; **— a joke** einen Streich spielen; **— up to** sich aufspielen; -er n. Spieler; (theat.) Schauspieler; **-er piano** Pianola; -ful adj. spielend, spielerisch; scherzhaft, lustig; -ing adj. spielend; -ing card Spielkarte

playboy n. Lebemann

playfellow, playmate n. Spielkamerad, Gefährte

playground n. Spielplatz, Tummelplatz; Schulhof

playhouse n. Schauspielhaus, Theater

playpen n. Laufstall

plaything n. Spielzeug

playwright n. Schauspielauthor

plea n. Beweisgrund; Rechtfertigung, Verteidigung; Entschuldigung, Vorwand, Ausrede; **put in a —** einen Einwand vorbringen; -d v. plädieren, vor Gericht reden; sich entschuldigen (or rechtfertigen); als Beweis anführen; einwenden; -d guilty sich schuldig bekennen; -ding n. Plädieren; Schriftsatz; -dings n. pl. Prozessakten; Gerichtsverhandlungen

pleasant adj. angenehm; munter, vergnügt, heiter; -ry n. Munterkeit, Fröhlichkeit; Scherz, Witz

please v. belieben, geruhen; vergnügen, ergötzen; (jemanden) gefallen, angenehm sein, befriedigen; **do as you — tu**, was Dir gefällt, mach, was du willst; **if you —** bitte; **— be seated** bitte, nehmen Sie Platz; **-d to meet you** ich bin erfreut, Sie kennenzulernen

pleasing adj. gefällig, angenehm

pleasure n. Vergnügen, Gefallen; Freude. Lust; **at —** nach Belieben

pleat n. Falte; Flechte; — v. falten; flechten; -ing n. Falten; Flechten

plebiscite n. Volksentscheid, Plebiszit

pledge n. Pfand, Unterpfand; Bürgschaft, Sicherheit; Gelübde; — v. verpfänden, versetzen; (sich) verpflichten, versichern

plenteous, plentiful adj. voll, reichlich; ergiebig, fruchtbar

plenty n. Fülle, Überfluss; Menge; — adj. reichlich

pleurisy n. Rippenfellentzündung, Brustfellentzündung

pliable, pliant adj. biegsam, geschmeidig; nachgiebig; passend

pliers n. pl. Drahtzange, Flachzange

plight n. Zwangslage; Zustand; — v. versprechen, verpfänden

plod v. mühsam (or schwerfällig) gehen; schuften, sich mühen (or plagen); (educ.) büffeln; -der n. angestrengt Arbeitender; (educ.) Büffler

plot n. Parzelle, Flecken; Entwurf, Grundriss, Plan; Anschlag, Komplott, Verschwörung; (lit.) Handlung, Knoten; — v. entwerfen, planen; anzetteln; sich verschwören; -ter n. Entwerfer, Urheber; Anstifter, Verschwörer

plow, plough n. Pflug; Pflügen, Ackerbau; — v. pflügen, ackern; durchfurchen; (naut.) durchschiffen; **gang —** Mehrscharpflug; **rotary —** Wendepflug, Kippflug; -ing n. Pflügen

plowboy n. Ackerknecht

plowman n. Pflüger, Landmann

plowshare n. Pflugschar

pluck n. Zupfen, Ruck; Mut, Schneid; — v. pflücken, zupfen; rupfen; -y adj. mutig, tollkühn; (phot.) scharf, klar

plug n. Pflock, Pfropfen; Zapfen, Stöpsel; Verschlussstück; (elec.) Stecker; Steckdose; **spark —** Zündkerze; **water —** Wasserhahn; — v. verstopfen, zustopfen; (ein)stöpseln

plum n. Pflaume, Zwetschge; **— pudding** Plumpudding, Rosinenpudding; **— tree** Pflaumenbaum

plumage n. Gefieder, Federkleid

plumb n. Lot, Senkblei; — adj. lotrecht, senkrecht, gerade; (coll.) vollkommen; **— line** Lotleine, Senkschnur; senkrechte Linie; — v. richten, loten; löten; -er n. Klempner, Rohrleger, Installateur; Bleigiesser; -ing n. Rohrlegerarbeit, Installationsarbeit; Bleigiesserei

plump adj. plump, drall, feist; derb, grob; — v. aufschwellen, dick werden; plumpsen; herausplatzen; — adv. geradezu, glatt, offen; rundweg; plötzlich, mit einem Ruck; **—!** interj. plumps!

plunder n. Raub, Diebstahl; Beute; — r. berauben, (aus)plündern

plunge n. Untertauchen, Bad; Sturz, Sprung; (coll.) Patsche; — v. (unter)-tauchen; fallen, stürzen, sinken; spekulieren; –r n. Taucher; (mech.) Kolben; Tauchkolben; (coll.) Spekulant

plural n. Plural, Mehrzahl; — adj. mehr(fach), –ity n. Mehrheit, Vielheit, Mehrzahl; (pol.) Majorität

plus prep. plus, mehr

plush n. Plüsch

plutocrat n. Plutokrat

plutonium n. Plutonium

ply n. Falte; Flechte; Windung; — v. falten, biegen; winden; betreiben; bedrängen, zusetzen; (naut.) lavieren, regelmässig fahren

plywood n. Sperrholz

pneumatic adj. pneumatisch; — **brake** Luftdruckbremse

pneumonia n. Lungenentzündung

poach v. zertreten; matschig sein (or werden); (hunting) wildern, –ed adj. –ed eggs verlorene Eier; –er n. Wilddieb, Wilderer

pock n. Pocke, Blatter

pocket n. Tasche, Beutel, Sack; (billiards) Loch; (min.) Erznest; — v. einstecken, heimlich nehmen; — **money** Taschengeld; — **veto** die Annahme eines Gesetzesentwurfes durch Nichtunterschreiben verzögern

pocketbook n. Taschenbuch; Brieftasche

pocketful n. Taschevoll

pocketknife n. Taschenmesser

pock-marked adj. pockennarbig

pod n. Hülse, Schale, Schote; (zool.) Herde, Schwarm, Zug

poem n. Gedicht, Dichtung

poet n. Poet, Dichter; –ic(al) adj. poetisch, dichterisch; –ic license dichterische Freiheit; –ry n. Poesie, Dichtkunst; pastoral –ry Hirtengedicht, Idylle; write –ry dichten, Verse schreiben

poinsettia n. Poinsettia

point n. Punkt; Spitze; Strich, Kante; Frage, Sache; Pointe; Schärfe; Hinsicht, Rücksicht; (art) Graviernadel, Radiernadel; (cards) Auge; (geol.) Vorgebirge, Landspitze; (hunting) Geweihsprosse; Stehen, Anzeigen; (law) Streitpunkt; (lit.) Hauptpunkt, Nachdruck; (mil.) Anweisung, Befehl; (naut.) Kompasstrich; Besteck; (sports) Punkt, Treffer; (time) Zeitpunkt, Augenblick; pl. Weichen; (gram.) Vokalzeichen; **at all –s** ganz und gar; **boiling —** Siedepunkt; **bring to a —** zu Ende bringen; **come to the —** zur Sache kommen; **decimal —** Komma, Dezimalstelle; **freezing —** Gefrierpunkt; **gain one's —** sein Ziel erreichen; **get the —** die Sache verstehen (or begreifen); **in —** of in Hinsicht auf; **main —** Hauptpunkt, Hauptsache; **make a — of** auf etwas bestehen (or drängen); **— of honor** Ehrenpunkt, Ehrensache; **— of order** Punkt der Geschäftsordnung; **— of view** Gesichtspunkt; **speak to the —** zur Sache sprechen; **strain a —** eine Ausnahme machen, es nicht genau nehmen; **that's the —** das ist es, darum geht es; **that's not the —** das gehört

nicht hierher; **to the —** genau, gänzlich; **turning —** Wendepunkt; — v. punktieren; spitzen, schärfen; zeigen, hinweisen; (hunting) stehen; (mil.) anlegen, richten, zielen; –ed adj. spitz; zugespitzt; punktiert; (fig.) anzüglich, scharf; –er n. Zeiger, Weiser; Zeigestock; (hunting) Hühnerhund, Vorstehhund; –less adj. stumpf; (fig.) witzlos

point-blank adv. (schnur)gerade; unverhohlen; — adj. unumwunden, rundweg, offen

poise n. Gewicht, Gleichgewicht; Haltung; — v. (ab)wägen, balanzieren; im Gleichgewicht halten

poison n. Gift; Gifttrank; — v. vergiften; (fig.) verführen; — adj. — **gas** Giftgas; —**ivy** giftiger Efeu; –**ing** n. Vergiftung; –**ous** adj. giftig; (fig.) verderblich, schädlich

poke n. Schlag, Stoss; — v. stossen; stochern, stöbern; fühlen, tasten; — **fun at** sich lustig machen über; — **one's nose into other people's affairs** seine Nase in andrer Leute Angelegenheiten stecken; –r n. Feuerhaken, Schüreisen; (cards) Poker(spiel)

polar adj. Polar-; — **bear** Eisbär; –ity n. Polarität; –**ize** v. polarisieren

pole n. Pfahl, Pfosten, Stange; (ast., phys. and fig.) Pol; — **vault** Stabhochsprung

polestar n. Polarstern; (fig.) Leitstern

police n. Polizei; — **court** Polizeigericht; — **dog** Polizeihund; — **headquarters** Polizeipräsidium; Polizeidirektion; — **state** Polizeistaat; — **trap** Autofalle; — v. überwachen

policeman n. Polizist, Schutzmann, Wachmann

policewoman n. Polizistin, Polizeiagentin

policy n. Politik; Police; **insurance —** Versicherungspolice

policyholder n. Policeninhaber

polio(myelitis) n. Poliomyelitis, spinale Kinderlähmung

polish n. Politur; Polieren; (fig.) Glätte, Schliff; — v. polieren, glätten; (fig.) verfeinern; –ed adj. poliert, glänzend, glatt; (fig.) gesittet

polite adj. höflich, gefällig; –**ness** n. Höflichkeit, Gefälligkeit

political adj. politisch; — **economy** Volkswirtschaft; — **group** Interessenverband; — **science** Staatswissenschaft

politician n. Staatsmann, Politiker

politics n. (pl.) Politik

polka n. Polka; — adj. — **dot** Punktmuster

poll n. Wahl, Abstimmung; Stimmenzählung; (fig.) Kopf, Schädel; pl. Wahllisten; Wahllokal; — **tax** Kopfsteuer; — v. kappen, stutzen; abschneiden; registrieren, eintragen; abstimmen, seine Stimme abgeben; (Wähler) befragen; (sports) besiegen; –**ing** n. Wählen, Abstimmen; Wahlakt, Wahlbeteiligung; –**ing** adj. –**ing booth** Wahlbude; –**ing place** Wahllokal

ollen n. Pollen, Blütenstaub

ollinate v. bestäuben

ollination n. Bestäubung

ollute v. beflecken, entweihen; schänden

ollution n. Befleckung, Verunreinigung: Entweihung

lo n. Polo

lygamist n. Polygamist

lygamy n. Polygamie, Vielweiberei

lymerization n. Polymerisierung

omerania n. Pommern

ommel n. Knopf, Knauf

omp n. Pomp, Pracht, Gepränge; **–ous** adj. pompös, prunkvoll, hochtrabend

ompadour n. hochgekämmtes Haar

ond n. Teich, Weiher

onder v. erwägen, überlegen; nachsinnen; **–ous** adj. schwer, gewichtig; schwerfällig

ontiff n. Pontifex, Papst; Hohepriester

ontoon n. Ponton, Brückenkahn; **— bridge** Pontonbrücke

ony n. Pony; (educ.) Eselsbrücke

oodle n. Pudel

ool n. Pfuhl, Teich, Lache; (billiards) Poule(spiel); (cards) Spieleinsatz; (com.) Ring, Trust, Kartell; gemeinsame Kasse; (race) Totalisator; **—** v. einen Ring (or Konzern, Interessengemeinschaft) bilden; sich zusammenschliessen

oolroom n. Wettlokal; Billardzimmer

oor adj. arm, (be)dürftig; ärmlich, armselig; schlecht; (agr.) mager, dürr, unfruchtbar; **— farm** Armenkolonie; **— health** schwache Gesundheit; **— law** Armenrecht

oorhouse n. Armenhaus

oor-spirited adj. bösartig, gemein, feige

op n. Knall, Klatsch; Sekt; **—** v. knallen, puffen; (coll.) anhalten; **—** in hineinplatzen; **—** off entwischen; **— the question** einen Heiratsantrag machen; **—!** interj. paff! puff! **—goes the weasel** weg war es! **-per** n. Maisröster

opcorn n. Puffmais, gerösteter Mais

ope n. Papst

oplar n. Pappel

oppy n. Mohn

opulace n. Pöbel, gemeines Volk

opular adj. populär, volkstümlich, Volks-; **-ity** n. Popularität, Volkstümlichkeit; **-ize** v. popularisieren, volkstümlich machen; gemeinverständlich darstellen

opulation n. Bevölkerung

opulous adj. volkreich, stark bevölkert

orcelain n. Porzellan

orch n. Vorhalle; Veranda, Vorbau

orcupine n. Stachelschwein

ore n. Pore; (bot.) Staubbeutel

ork n. Schweinefleisch; **— chop** Schweinekotelett; **— sausage** Bratwurst (aus Schweinefleisch)

orous adj. porös, löcherig

orpoise n. Tümmler, Meerschwein

orridge n. Hafergrütze, Haferschleim

ort n. Hafen, Ankerplatz; Backbord; Tor, Pforte; Luke, Öffnung; Haltung, Anstand; Portwein

portable adj. tragbar; **— typewriter** Reiseschreibmaschine

portage n. Tragen, Transport; Ladung, Fracht, Gepäck; Trägerlohn, Zustellungsgebühr

portal n. Portal, Haupttor; **— vein** Pfortader

portend v. vorbedeuten, verkünd(ig)en

porter n. Portier, Pförtner; Träger, Dienstmann; Porter(bier)

porterhouse steak n. Ochsenrostbraten

portfolio n. Mappe; (pol.) Portefeuille

porthole n. Luke, Öffnung; (mil.) Schiezscharte

portiere n. Portiere, Türvorhang

portion n. Portion, Anteil; Erbteil, Heiratsgut; Ration; (fig.) Schicksal; **—** v. (ver)teilen, austeilen; ausstatten

portly adj. stattlich, ansehnlich; (coll.) beleibt

portrait n. Porträt, Bild(nis)

portray v. porträtieren, (ab)malen, schildern

pose n. Pose, Positur; **—** v. posieren, in Positur stellen, aufstellen, aufwerfen

position n. Position, Haltung; Stellung, Stand, Lage; Grundsatz, Behauptung

positive adj. positiv; bestimmt, ausdrücklich; **—** n. (gram. and phot.) Positiv

posse n. Aufgebot, bewaffnete Macht; (coll.) Schar, Haufen, Masse

possess v. besitzen; beherrschen; **— oneself** of in Besitz nehmen, sich einer Sache bemächtigen; **-ion** n. Besitz; **be in -ion** of innehaben; **get -ion** of sich bemächtigen; **take -ion** of Besitz ergreifen von; **-ive** adj. besitzanzeigend; **-or** n. Besitzer, Eigentümer

possibility n. Möglichkeit

possible adj. möglich

possibly adv. möglicherweise, vielleicht

post n. Post; Botschaft; (arch.) Pfosten, Pfahl; (com.) Stelle, Amt, Posten; Stellung; (mil.) Posten; **— card** Postkarte; **— office** Postamt, Postverwaltung; **—** v. postieren; anschlagen; eintragen; ernennen; zur Post geben, einstecken; **— no bills!** Plakate ankleben verboten! **-age** n. Porto; **-age stamp** Briefmarke; **-al** adj. postalisch; **-al order** Postanweisung; **-er** n. Kurier, Eilbote; Plakat

post: **-erior** adj. nachkommend, später, nachherig; hinter, Hinter-; **-erity** n. Nachkommenschaft; Nachwelt; **-pone** v. aufschieben, verschieben; vernachlässigen; unterordnen; **-ponement** n. Aufschub, Verzug; Unterordnung; **-humous** nachgeboren, nachgelassen, hinterlassen; posthum; **-ure** n. Stellung; Gestalt, Haltung; Zustand

postgraduate n. (nach Erlangung eines Grades) Weiterstudierende; **—** adj. (nach Erlangung eines Grades) weiterstudierend

postman n. Briefträger, Postbote; **rural —** Landbriefträger

postmark n. Poststempel

postmaster n. Postmeister, Postdirektor

post-mortem n. Leichenschau; **—** adj.

nach dem Tode geschehend
post-office box n. Postfach
postpaid adj. frankiert; portofrei, franko
postscript n. Nachschrift, Nachtrag
postwar adj. Nachkriegs-
posy n. Motto, Denkspruch; Blumenstrauss
pot n. Topf, Tiegel; Krug, Kanne; (cards) Einsatz; (mech.) Schmelztiegel; — v. im Topf aufbewahren; einkochen, einmachen; eintopfen; — roast Schmorfleisch; **-ter** n. Töpfer; **-tery** n. Tongeschirr, Steingut; Töpferei
potato n. Kartoffel, Erdapfel; **baked -es** überbackene Kartoffeln; **fried -es** Bratkartoffeln; **mashed -es** Quetschkartoffel, Kartoffelpüree; **sweet —** Batate, süsse Kartoffel; — **beetle**, — **bug** Kartoffelkäfer; — **blight** Kartoffelmehltau
potbellied adj. dickbäuchig
potboiler n. Brotverdienst
potency n. Kraft, Macht, Stärke; Potenz;
potent adj. mächtig, vermögend, stark; potent; **-ate** n. Machthaber, Potentat; **-ial** adj. möglich; potentiell, mächtig; **-ial mood** Möglichkeitsform; **-iality** n. Möglichkeit, Wirkungsvermögen; Potenzial; (elec.) Spannung
potherbs n. Küchenkräuter, Suppengrün
pothole n. (geol.) Gletscherloch; (mech.) Schlagloch
potion n. Arzneitrank
potluck n. **take —** fürlieb nehmen mit dem, was die Küche gibt
pouch n. Beutel, Tasche; (mil.) Patronentasche; (orn.) Kropf; (coll.) Dickbauch; — v. einstecken; beschenken
poultice n. Breiumschlag
poultry n. Geflügel, Federvieh; — **yard** Geflügelhof
pounce n. Stoss, Sprung; (art.) Pause; (orn.) Klaue, Kralle; — v. durchlöchern, durchbohren; krallen, klauen; pausen; herabstossen, sich stürzen auf
pound n. Pfund; Einzäunung; Fischsammelbecken; — **sterling** englisches Pfund (20 shillings); — v. pfänden; einsperren; zerstampfen, zerstossen
pour v. giessen, schütten; strömen, rinnen; sich ergiessen
pout n. Schmollen; — v. schmollen, (Lippen) aufwerfen
poverty n. Armut, Mangel
poverty-stricken adj. verarmt, dürftig
powder n. Pulver, Puder, Staub; (mil.) Schiesspulver; — **case** Puderdose; — **magazine** Pulvermagazin; — **puff** Puderquaste; — v. pulverisieren; (sich) pudern, bepudern; bestäuben, bestreuen; (fig.) übersäen; **-ed** adj. pulverisiert; gepudert, bestreut; fein gemustert
power n. Kraft, Stärke, Macht; Vermögen; (law) Vollmacht; Zurechnungsfähigkeit; (math.) Potenz; (mech.) Kraft, Last; (mil.) Heeresmacht; (naut.) Seemacht; (pol.) Autorität, Regierung, Staat; Gewalt; **horse —** Pferdestärke; **in —** an der Macht; —

of attorney Anwaltsvollmacht; **the -s that be** die höheren Mächte; **reasoning -s** Urteilskraft; — **dive** (avi.) Sturzflug; — **drill** Kraftbohrer; — **plant** Kraftwerk, Kraftanlage; **-ful** adj. kräftig, mächtig; einflussreich; **-less** adj. kraftlos, machtlos, ohnmächtig
powerhouse n. Kraftwerk; (sports) spielstarke Mannschaft
powwow n. laute politische Versammlung; Indianerversammlung; lärmende Krankheitsbeschwörung, Kriegstanz; — v. laute (politische) Versammlungen abhalten
pox n. Syphilis; **chicken —** Windpocken; **cow —** Kuhpocken; **small —** Pocken, Blattern
practicability n. Ausführbarkeit
practicable adj. ausführbar, gangbar, brauchbar; fahrbar
practical adj. praktisch, tatsächlich, wirklich; geschickt; — **joke** handgreiflicher Spass; — **nurse** ausgebildete Krankenpflegerin
practice n. Praxis, Ausübung; Anwendung, Ausführung; Brauch, Gewohnheit; Übung, Training; pl. Kunstgriffe, Schliche, Kniffe; —, **practise** v. praktizieren, ausüben; anwenden, ausführen, betreiben; üben, trainieren
practitioner n. Praktiker, geschickter Mensch; Gesundbeter; **general —** praktischer Arzt
pragmatic(al) adj. pragmatisch; gemeinnützig; geschäftig, wichtigtuerisch
Prague n. Prag
prairie n. Prärie; — **chicken** Präriehuhn; — **dog** Präriehund
praise n. Preis, Lob; Anerkennung, Danksagung; — v. preisen, loben; anerkennen, rühmen, verherrlichen
praiseworthy adj. preiswürdig, lobenswert
prance v. paradieren, einherstolzieren; (horse) sich bäumen
prank n. Possen, Streich; Schelmerei, Schabernack
prattle n. Geplapper; — v. schwatzen, plappern
pray v. beten; (er)bitten, ersuchen; **-er** n. Gebet, Andacht; Bitte, Gesuch; **the Lord's Prayer** das Vaterunser; **-er book** Gebetbuch; **-er meeting** Betstunde; Gebetsversammlung; **-er wheel** Gebetsmühle
preach v. predigen; lehren, verkünden; **-er** n. Prediger; **-ing** n. Predigen, Predigt; Lehre; (coll.) Strafpredigt
preamble n. Vorrede, Einleitung; Präambel
prearrange v. vorher anordnen, vorbereiten
precarious adj. widerruflich, kündbar; prekär, zweifelhaft, unsicher
precaution n. Vorsicht(smassregel); Behutsamkeit; **-ary** adj. vorsichtig, vorbeugend; Vorsichts-, Warnungs-
precede v. vor(an)gehen, vorausgehen; den Vorrang haben; einführen; **-nce** n. Vorausgehen; Vorrang, Vortritt, Vorzug; **-nt** n. Präzedenzfall, Rechtsbei-

spiel; **-nt** adj. vor(an)gehend, vorausgehend; früher

preceding adj. vorhergehend

precept n. Vorschrift, Regel; Gebot, Unterweisung; (law) Vorladung, Verordnung

precinct n. Distrikt, Bezirk, Bereich, Gebiet; Grenze; Gehege

precious adj. kostbar, teuer; geziert; **— stone** Edelstein

precipice n. Klippe, Abgrund; (fig.) kritische Lage

precipitate v. (herab)stürzen; (chem.) fällen; (fig.) überstürzen, beschleunigen; **—** adj. überstürzt, übereilt; voreilig, vorschnell; plötzlich; **—** n. (chem.) Niederschlag

precipitation n. Sturz; Hast; (chem.) Niederschlag

precise adj. präzis; bestimmt, genau; (fig.) pedantisch

precision n. Präzision, Genauigkeit

predecessor n. Vorgänger

predestination n. Prädestination, Vorherbestimmung

predicament n. Kategorie, Ordnung; (coll.) Verlegenheit, missliche Lage

predicate n. Prädikat, Aussage; **—** v. behaupten, aussagen; begründen

predict v. vorhersagen, verkünd(ig)en; prophezeien; **-ion** n. Prophezeiung, Weissagung

predisposed adj. vorbereitend; geneigt (or empfänglich) machend

predominant adj. vorherrschend, überwiegend

predominate v. vorherrschen; beherrschen, die Oberhand haben

pre-eminence n. Hervorragen, Hervorstechen; Vorrang, Vorzug

pre-eminent adj. hervorragend, hervorstechend; ausgezeichnet

pre-existence n. früheres Dasein, Präexistenz

preface n. Vorrede, Vorwort; Einleitung; **—** v. einleiten

prefect n. Präfekt

prefer v. vorziehen; vorbringen, einen Antrag stellen; **-able** adj. vorzuziehend, vorzüglicher (als); **-ence** n. Vorziehen; Bevorzugung; Vorliebe; Präferenz, Vorzugsrecht; **-ential** adj. Vorzugs-, bevorzugt; **-red** adj. bevorzugt; **-red stock** Prioritätsaktien, Vorzugsaktien

prefix n. Vorsilbe; **—** v. vor(an)setzen

pregnancy n. Schwangerschaft; (zool.) Trächtigkeit; (fig.) Fruchtbarkeit

pregnant adj. schwanger; (zool.) trächtig; (fig.) fruchtbar, inhaltvoll

preheat v. vorwärmen, vorheizen

prehistoric adj. prähistorisch

prejudice n. Voreingenommenheit, Vorurteil; Schaden; **—** v. vorher einnehmen, Abbruch tun

prelate n. Prälat

preliminary adj. vorläufig; einleitend, Vor-

prelude n. Einleitung, Vorspiel; **—** v. präludieren; einleiten

premature adj. frühreif; vorzeitig; (fig.) übereilt, vorschnell

premedical adj. vormedizinisch

premeditate v. vorher bedenken (or überlegen); **-d** adj. **-d murder** vorbedachter (or geplanter) Mord

premier n. Ministerpräsident, Premierminister

première n. Première, Uraufführung, Erstaufführung; Debüt

premise n. Voraussetzung; pl. vorerwähnte Punkte; Grundstück, Haus und Nebengebäude; **—** v. vorausschicken

premium n. Prämie, Preis; Zinsen; Belohnung; **at a —** pari, sehr gesucht

premonition n. Warnung; Vorahnung

preoccupation n. Vorwegnahme; Voreingenommenheit, Vorurteil

prepaid adj. vorher bezahlt, frankiert

preparation n. Vorbereitung, Zubereitung; (chem.) Präparat

preparatory adj. präpariert, vorbereitet, zubereitet; vorbereitend

prepare v. vorbereiten, zubereiten; präparieren

prepay v. voraus bezahlen; frankieren, freimachen; **-ment** n. Vorausbezahlung; Frankieren

preponderance n. Übergewicht

preposition n. Präposition, Verhältniswort

preposterous adj. verkehrt, widersinnig; unnatürlich, albern

prerequisite n. Vorbedingung; **—** adj. vorher erforderlich, zuerst nötig

prerogative n. Vorrecht; **—** adj. vorgehend, bevorrechtigt

prescribe v. vorschreiben, befehlen; (law) verjähren; (med.) verordnen, verschreiben

prescription n. Vorschrift, Verordnung; (law) Verjährung; (med.) Rezept

presence n. Gegenwart, Anwesenheit, Vorhandensein; Erscheinung, Gespenst; **in —** gegenwärtig; **in — of** im Beisein (or in Gegenwart) von, angesichts; **— of mind** Geistesgegenwart

present n. Geschenk; (gram.) Gegenwart, Präsens; pl. Dokumente, Schriftstücke; **at —** gegenwärtig; **be —** at beiwohnen; **by the —** hierdurch, beigefügt; **for the —** vorläufig, im Augenblick; **—** adj. gegenwärtig, anwesend, vorhanden; laufend, sofort, augenblicklich; fertig, bereit; **all —** alle Anwesenden; **in the —** case im vorliegenden Falle; **— company excepted** die Anwesenden ausgeschlossen; **— crisis** gegenwärtige Krise; **— money** bares Geld; **— participle** Partizip des Präsens; **— value** Gegenwartswert; **this —** jetzt; **—** v. präsentieren, vorstellen, vorführen, zeigen; darstellen, schenken, geben; (theat.) darstellen, darbieten; **— a draft** einen Wechsel vorzeigen; **— arms** das Gewehr präsentieren; **— itself** es zeigt sich von selbst; **— oneself** sich selbst vorstellen; **— oneself to view** persönlich erscheinen; **-able** adj. vorstellbar, präsentierbar; **-ation** n. Darstellung, Vorstellung; Vorlage

present-day adj. heutig

presentiment n. Vorgefühl, Ahnung

preservation n. Bewahrung, Erhaltung; Konservierung

preserve n. Konserve, Eingemachte; Wildpark, Gehege; pl. Eingemachte; Schutzbrille; — v. bewahren, erhalten; retten, schützen, hegen; konservieren, einmachen; — **timber** Holz imprägnieren

preside v. präsidieren, den Vorsitz (or die Aufsicht) führen; **-ncy** n. Präsidium, Präsidentschaft; **-nt** n. Präsident; Vorsitzende, Vorsteher; **-ntial** adj. präsidial; Präsidenten-

press n. Pressen, Druck; Gedränge, Andrang; Dringlichkeit; Bedrängnis, Verlegenheit; Presse, Kelter; Zeitungswesen, Journalismus; Druckgewerbe; — v. pressen, drücken, auspressen, keltern; (be)drängen, treiben, nötigen, beschleunigen; aufzwingen; **be -ed for** in Verlegenheit (or Bedrängnis) sein wegen; **-ing** adj. pressend; drängend, dringend; **-ure** n. Druck, Spannung; **-ure cooker** Dampfkochtopf; — **-gauge** Druckmesser; **-ure suit** n. Druckkombination; **-urize** v. (avi.) den Luftdruck regulieren; **-urized cabin** n. Druckkabine

presswork n. Druckarbeit

prestige n. Prestige, Nimbus, Ansehen

presume v. annehmen, vermuten

presuppose v. voraussetzen

pretend v. vorgeben, heucheln; **-er** n. Heuchler

pretense, pretence n. Vorwand, Scheingrund; Anspruch; **false —** Vorspiegelung falscher Tatsachen

pretentious adj. anspruchsvoll, anmassend

pretext n. Vorwand; **on —** unter dem Vorwand

prettiness n. Niedlichkeit, Nettigkeit; Geziertheit

pretty adj. hübsch, niedlich; artig, nett; fein, sauber

pretzel n. Bre(t)zel

prevail v. überhandnehmen; vorherrschen; die Oberhand gewinnen (or haben); **-ing** adj. vorherrschend; allgemein geltend; häufig

prevalent adj. vorherrschend, geltend, weit verbreitet; mächtig, überlegen

prevent v. zuvorkommen, verhüten, verhindern; vorbeugen, vorbauen; **-able** adj. verhütbar; **-ion** n. Vorbeugung, Verhütung; Verhinderung; **-ive** adj. vorbeugend, Schutz-; **-ive** n. Präservativ

preview n. Vorschau

previous adj. vorhergehend; vorläufig; **— payment** Vorschusszahlung

prewar adj. Vorkriegs-

prey n. Raub, Beute; **beast of —** Raubtier; **bird of —** Raubvogel; — v. rauben, plündern; erbeuten; (fig.) nagen

price n. Preis; Lohn, Belohnung; (fig.) Wert; **above —** unschätzbar; **at any — um** jeden Preis; **best —** günstigster Preis; **cost —** Einkaufspreis; **fall in -s** Preissturz; **fixed —** fester Preis; **high**

-s hohe Preise; **lowest —** niedrigster Preis; **sale —** Verkaufspreis; **trade —** Engrospreis, Handelspreis; — **control** Preiskontrolle; **— list** Preisliste, Kursliste; — **mark** Preisangabe; — v. den Preis festsetzen, auszeichnen; **-less** adj. unschätzbar, unbezahlbar

prick n. Stachel, Dorn, Spitze; Ahle, Pfrieme; Stich, Biss; Punkt, Ziel; **-s of conscience** Gewissensbisse; — v. (durch)stechen; anspornen, anstacheln, antreiben; punktieren; foltern; prikkeln; — **a card** eine Spielkarte markieren; — **up one's ears** die Ohren spitzen; **-ly** adj. stachelig, dornig, juckend, stechend; prickelnd; **-ly heat** Hitzepickel; **-ly pear** Feigenkaktus

pride n. Stolz; Hochmut, Überhebung; (fig.) Pracht, Gepränge; — **will have a fall** Hochmut kommt vor dem Fall; **in the —** of his years in der Blüte seiner Jahre; **take —** in auf etwas stolz sein; — v. stolz sein, sich gross tun; — **oneself** on sich brüsten mit

priest n. Priester, Geistliche; **-hood** n. Priesteramt, Priesterwürde; Priesterschaft

prim adj. schmuck, sauber, fein; geziert, gekünstelt, steif

primacy n. Vorrang, Vortritt

primarily adv. zuerst, ursprünglich, anfänglich; insbesonders

primary n. Hauptsache; (ast.) Hauptplanet; (pol.) Vorwahl; — adj. primär; erst, hauptsächlich, höchst; ursprünglich, primitiv; Ur-, Anfangs-, Grund-, Haupt-, Elementar-; — **accent** Hauptbetonung; — **coil** Hauptspule; — **colors** Grundfarben; — **education** Volksschulbildung; — **election** Urwahl; — **school** Elementarschule, Volksschule, Grundschule

prime n. Anfang, Ursprung; Erste, Beste; Kern, Blüte; (com.) beste Qualität; (math.) Primzahl; (mus.) Grundton, Prime; (fig.) Frühling, Jugend; Lebenskraft; — adj. erst, vorzüglichst, vornehmst; (math.) unteilbar, einfach; (fig.) jugendlich, blühend; ursprünglich; — **creation** Urschöpfung; — **minister** Ministerpräsident; — v. grundieren; vorbereiten; anstiften; **-r** n. Fibel, Abebuch; Elementarbuch; Zündapparat; **-val** adj. ursprünglich, urzeitlich

priming n. Grundierung; (mil.) Zündung; — adj. — **coat** Grundanstrich

primitive n. (gram.) Stammwort; — adj. primitiv, ursprünglich, anfänglich; einfach, roh; Stamm-, Grund-; — **rock** Urgestein

primrose n. Primel, Schlüsselblume; (color) Rötlichgelb

prince n. Prinz, Fürst; — **consort** Prinzgemahl; **-ly** adj. prinzlich, fürstlich; **-ss** n. Prinzessin, Fürstin

principal n. Hauptperson; Chef, Prinzipal, Lehrherr; Rektor, Direktor; — adj. vornehmst, hauptsächlich, Haupt-; **-ity** n. Fürstentum, Fürstenwürde; **-ly** adv.

vornehmlich, besonders
principle n. Prinzip, Grundsatz; (chem.) Grundbestandteil
print n. Druck; Abdruck, Kopie; Kupferstich, Holzstich; Druckschrift; (phot.) Abzug; (fig.) Eindruck, Mal, Form; **in — im Druck, gedruckt; out of —** vergriffen; **—** v. (ab)drucken, bedrucken; kopieren; mustern; (phot.) abziehen; (fig.) einprägen; **-ed** adj. gedruckt, bedruckt; **-ed cotton** bedruckter Baumwollstoff; **-ed matter** Drucksache; **-er** n. Drucker, Buchdrucker; **-er's devil** Druckfehlerteufel; **-er's ink** Druckerschwärze; **-ing** n. Drucken, Bedrucken; **art of -ing** Buchdruckerkunst; **-ing office** Druckerei; **-ing press** Druckmaschine, Druckerpresse
printshop n. Druckerei
prior n. Prior; **—** adj. früher, älter; **—** adv. **— to** vor; **-ity** n. Priorität; Vorrang, Vorzug(srecht)
prism n. Prisma
prison n. Gefängnis, Kerker; **—** v. einkerkern; **-er** n. Gefangene; **— of war** Kriegsgefangene
privacy n. Abgeschiedenheit, Zurückgezogenheit, Stille; Heimlichkeit
private n. (mil.) Gemeine; **in — unter vier Augen; —** adj. privat, Privat-; geheim, heimlich, verborgen; vertraulich; nicht amtlich (or öffentlich); eigen, persönlich
privation n. Entbehrung, Entblössung, Mangel
privilege n. Privileg, Vorrecht, Sonderrecht; **—** v. privilegieren, bevorrechten
prize n. Preis, Prämie, Lohn, Belohnung; Vorteil, Gewinn; (naut.) Prise; **— fight** Boxkampf, Ringkampf; **— question** Preisfrage; **— ring** Ring für Preiskämpfe; **—** v. gewinnen; belohnen; schätzen, taxieren; wegnehmen; (naut.) aufbringen
prizefighter n. Berufsboxer, Berufsringer
pro prep. pro, für; **—** adv. vor(wärts): anstatt; **—** n. (pol.) Jasager; (sports) Berufsspieler; **the -s and cons** das Für und Wider, die Ja- und Neinstimmen
probability n. Wahrscheinlichkeit
probable adj. wahrscheinlich, mutmasslich
probation n. Beweisführung, Prüfung; (eccl.) Noviziat; (law) bedingte Freisprechung, Bewährungsfrist; Probezeit; **-er** n. Prüfling; (eccl.) Novize; (law) unter Bewährungsfrist Stehende
probe n. Sonde; **—** v. sondieren, gründlich untersuchen
problem n. Problem, Aufgabe
procedure n. Prozedur, Verfahren; Handlungsweise
proceed v. vor(wärts)gehen, fortschreiten, fortfahren; hervorkommen, vonstatten gehen; (law) gerichtlich belangen, einschreiten; **-ing** n. Verfahren; **-ings** pl. Rechtsgang, Rechtsverfahren; Akten, Protokolle; Verhandlungen; **-s** n. pl. Ertrag, Gewinn; **gross -s** Bruttoertrag; **net -s** Reinertrag, Nettogewinn

process n. Prozess; Fortschreiten, Fortschritt; Verlauf, Vorgang; (anat. and bot.) Fortsatz, Verlängerung; (chem. and law) Verfahren; (phot.) Entwicklung; **—** v. prozessieren, vorladen, belangen; behandeln; reproduzieren, entwickeln; **-ion** n. Prozession, Umzug
proclaim v. proklamieren, bekanntgeben, verkünden
proclamation n. Proklamation, Bekanntmachung
procrastinate v. verschieben, aufschieben; (ver)zögern, zaudern
procure v. anschaffen, besorgen, verschaffen; erhalten, erlangen; erwerben; bewirken
prod n. Stachelstock; Ahle; Stich; **—** v. stechen; anspornen
prodigal n. Verschwender; **—** adj. verschwenderisch; **the — son** (bibl.) der verlorene Sohn
prodigy n. Wunder; Monstrum, Missgeburt
produce n. Erzeugnis, Produkt; Ertrag; **—** v. produzieren, erzeugen; einbringen, hervorbringen; (theat.) inszenieren; **-r** n. Produzent, Erzeuger; (theat.) Regisseur
product n. Produkt, Werk; Schöpfung, Frucht; **-ion** n. Produktion, Erzeugung; Beibringung, Vorlegung; (theat.) Regie; **-ion cost** Gestehungskosten; **-ive** adj. produktiv, schöpferisch; ertragreich, fruchtbar
profane adj. profan, weltlich; gottlos, lästerlich; **—** v. profanieren, entweihen
profanity n. Ruchlosigkeit, Gottlosigkeit; Entweihung, Profanierung
profess v. bekennen, gestehen; behaupten, ausüben, betreiben; **-edly** adv. ausgesprochen, unverhohlen; unleugbar; **-ion** n. Beruf, Handwerk; Bekenntnis; **-ional** adj. berufsmässig, professionell, Berufs-; **-or** n. Professor
proficiency n. Tüchtigkeit, Fertigkeit
proficient adj. tüchtig, geschickt; bewandert
profile n. Profil, Seitenansicht
profit n. Profit, Gewinn, Nutzen, Ertrag; **net — Reingewinn; — and loss** Verdienst und Verlust; **— sharing** Gewinnbeteiligung; **—** v. profitieren, gewinnen; **— by** Nutzen ziehen aus; **-able** adj. einträglich, vorteilhaft, gewinnbringend; **-eer** n. Profitmacher, Schieber; **-eer** v. Profite machen, schieben, Schiebergeschäfte betreiben
profligate adj. liederlich, verschwenderisch
profound adj. tief(gehend), gründlich; scharfsinnig, tiefgründig
profuse adj. übervoll, übermässig; verschwenderisch
profusion n. Überfluss; Verschwendung
progenitor n. Vorfahr, Ahn
prognosis n. Prognose
prognostication n. Voraussage; (med.) Prognose
program(me) n. Programm
progress n. Fortschritt; Fortschreiten; **—**

v. Fortschritte machen, fortschreiten; **-ive** adj. progressiv, fortschreitend, zunehmend; fortschrittlich

prohibit v. verbieten, untersagen; verhindern; **-ion** n. Prohibition; Verhinderung, Verbot, Einhalt

project n. Projekt, Plan, Entwurf; — v. vorspringen; entwerfen, planen, vorhaben; **-ile** n. Geschoss, Projektil; **-ion** n. Entwurf; Vorsprung; (film) Projektion; **-or** n. Erfinder, Entwerfer; (film) Projektionsapparat

proletarian n. Proletarier; — adj. proletarisch

proletariat n. Proletariat

prologue n. Prolog; Einleitung, Vorwort

prolong v. verlängern, dehnen; prolongieren

promenade n. Promenade; Spaziergang; — v. promenieren, spazierengehen

prominence n. Prominenz, Berühmtheit; Vorsprung

prominent adj. prominent, hervorragend; **be** — berühmt (or bekannt) sein

promiscuous adj. vermengt, vermischt; verworren; unterschiedslos

promise n. Versprechen, Zusage; (fig.) Erwartung; — v. versprechen

promising adj. viel versprechend, verheissungsvoll

promissory adj. versprechend; — **note** Eigenwechsel, Promesse

promote v. (be)fördern; gründen; **-r** n. Förderer, Gönner; Gründer; Anstifter

promotion n. Förderung, Begünstigung; Beförderung

prompt adj. prompt, unverzüglich, sofortig; pünktlich; bereit; — v. antreiben, veranlassen; (theat.) soufflieren

prone adj. geneigt, gesenkt; hingestreckt

prong n. Spitze; Zacke, Zinke

pronoun n. Fürwort, Pronomen

pronounce v. aussprechen, betonen; verkünden, erklären; entscheiden; **-d** adj. ausgesprochen, entschieden; **-ment** n. Erklärung, Äusserung

pronunciation n. Aussprache

proof n. Beweis, Probe; — adj. standhaft, undurchdringlich, fest; bewährt

proofread v. Korrektur lesen; **-er** n. Korrektor, Korrekturleser

prop n. Stütze, Strebe; — v. stützen, tragen

propaganda n. Propaganda

propagate v. propagieren, verbreiten

propel v. vorwärtstreiben; fortbewegen; **-ler** n. Propeller; **-ler blade** Propellerflügel

propensity n. Vorahnung

proper adj. eigen, eigentlich, eigentümlich; geeignet; proper, anständig, sauber, nett; gründlich; — **name** Eigenname; — **fraction** (math.) echter Bruch; **in — form** in passender Form; **-ly** adv. eigentlich, richtig

property n. Eigentum, Vermögen; Eigenschaft; Grundstück, Grundbesitz

prophecy n. Prophezeiung, Weissagung

prophesy v. prophezeien, weissagen

prophet n. Prophet; **-ic** adj. prophetisch

prophylactic adj. prophylaktisch, vorbeugend; — n. Vorbeugungsmittel, Gegenmittel

propitious adj. geneigt, gnädig; günstig, gütig; glücklich

proportion n. Proportion, Verhältnis; Gleichmass; Anteil; (math.) Proportionale; — v. in ein Verhältnis bringen; **-al** adj. proportional, verhältnismässig; gleichmässig; **-ate** adj. angemessen, im richtigen Verhältnis stehend; **-ed** adj. proportioniert, im richtigen Verhältnis stehend

proposal n. Vorschlag; — **of marriage** Heiratsantrag

propose v. vorschlagen, beantragen; beabsichtigen; anhalten

proposition n. Vorschlag, Antrag; (gram., math. and phil.) Behauptung; Lehrsatz

proprietor n. Eigentümer, Inhaber, Besitzer

propriety n. Genauigkeit, Richtigkeit; Schicklichkeit

propulsion n. Antrieb, Fortbewegung

prorate v. gleichmässig verteilen

prosaic adj. prosaisch, alltäglich

prose n. Prosa; — **writer** Prosaschriftsteller, Prosaiker

prosecute v. verfolgen; fortsetzen, betreiben; (law) anklagen, einklagen

prosecution n. Verfolgung, Durchführung; (law) Anklage, gerichtliche Verfolgung

prosecutor n. Verfolger, Durchführende; (law) Kläger, Ankläger; Staatsanwalt

prospect n. Ansicht; Aussicht, Erwartung; **-ive** adj. zukünftig, voraussichtlich; vorausblickend; **-or** n. Schürfer, Goldgräber; (fig.) Spekulant; **-us** n. Prospekt; Ankündigung, Voranzeige

prosper v. gedeihen, gelingen; **-ity** n. Wohlstand; Gedeihen, Wohlfahrt; **-ous** adj. glücklich, günstig

prostitute n. Prostituierte; — v. prostituieren; preisgeben, entwürdigen

prostitution n. Prostitution

prostration n. Niederwerfung, Demütigung; Erschöpfung; Fussfall

prosy adj. langweilig, prosaisch

protect v. (be)schützen, sichern; (chess) decken; **-ion** n. Schutz; **-ive** adj. schützend, Schutz-; **-ive coloring** Schutzfärbung; **-or** n. Schützer; **-orate** n. Protektorat

protégé n. Schützling

protein n. Protein, Eiweisstoff

protest n. Protest, Einspruch, Widerspruch; — v. protestieren, sich verwahren, Einspruch erheben

Protestant n. Protestant

protocol n. Protokoll; — v. protokollieren

proton n. Proton

prototype n. Urbild, Vorbild

protract v. aufschieben, verzögern, in die Länge ziehen

protrude v. (her)vortreten; hervorstehen, überhängen; ausstrecken

proud adj. stolz, trotzig; hochmütig; froh; — **flesh** wildes Fleisch

prove v. prüfen, beweisen, dartun; probieren, erproben; sich ergeben (or erweisen); (law) beglaubigen

proverb n. Sprichwort; **-ial** adj. sprichwörtlich

provide v. anschaffen, verschaffen; besorgen; bereithalten; versehen, versorgen; (law) vorsehen, festsetzen; **-ed** conj. **-ed that** vorausgesetzt, dass; wofern nur, wenn anders; **-ed** adj. angeschafft, verschafft; besorgt, versorgt, unterhalten; bereithaltend; **-nce** n. Vorsehung; Vor(aus)sicht, Vorsorge; **-nt** adj. fürsorglich; vorsichtig; haushälterisch; **-ntial** adj. durch die Vorsehung bestimmt; glücklich, gelegen; **-r** n. Fürsorgende, Versorger; Lieferant

province n. Provinz; Bezirk, Gebiet; (fig.) Wirkungskreis

provincial n. Provinzler, Provinzbewohner; **—** adj. provinziell, kleinstädtisch

provision n. Beschaffung, Fürsorge; Vorrat; Provision. Maklerlohn; pl. Proviant, Vorrat; Nahrungsmittel, Lebensmittel; Mundvorrat; **-al** adj. provisorisch, vorläufig

provocation n. Provokation, Herausforderung

provocative n. Reizmittel, Reizung; **—** adj. provokatorisch, aufreizend, herausfordernd

provoke v. provozieren, herausfordern; aufreizen

provoking adj. herausfordernd, empörend; erbitternd, ärgerlich

prow n. Bug

prowess n. Tapferkeit, Heldenmut

prowl v. herumstöbern, umherstreichen; **-er** n. Plünderer, Räuber; Einbrecher; Bummler

proximity n. Nähe, Nachbarschaft

proxy n. Stellvertretung; Stellvertreter, Bevollmächtigte; Vollmacht

prude n. Prüde, Spröde; **-ry** n. Prüderie, Zimperlichkeit

prudence n. Klugheit, Vorsicht, Bedachtsamkeit

prudent adj. klug, vorsichtig; bedachtsam; sparsam

prudish adj. prüde, spröde; zimperlich; steif

prune n. Backpflaume; **—** v. stutzen, beschneiden

pruning n. Beschneiden, Stutzen; pl. Reisigholz; **— hook** Gartensichel; **knife** Gartenmesser; **— shears** Baumschere

pry v. spähen, gucken; (coll.) die Nase hineinstecken

psalm n. Psalm

pseudonym n. Pseudonym, Deckname

psychiatrist n. Psychiater

psychiatry n. Psychiatrie

psychic adj. psychisch, seelisch

psychoanalysis n. Psychoanalyse

psychologic(al) adj. psychologisch

psychologist n. Psychologe

psychopathic adj. psychopathisch, geistig

psychrometer n. Feuchtemesser für Atmosphären

ptomain(e) n. Ptomain, Leichenalkaloid; **— poison** Leichengift; **— poisoning**

Leichenvergiftung

public n. Publikum; Offentlichkeit; Gemeinwohl; **in —** vor aller Welt; **make — öffentlich** bekanntmachen; **—** adj. öffentlich; publik; offenkundig; gemeinnützig; Staats-; **— appointment** Staatsstellung; **— auction** öffentliche Versteigerung; **— debt** Staatsschuld; **— enemy** Staatsfeind; **— function** öffentliches Amt; **— library** Volksbücherei; **— official** Staatsbeamte; **— opinion** öffentliche Meinung; **— property** Staatseigentum; **— relations** Meinungsforschung; Propagandaabteilung; **— spirit** Gemeinsinn; **— utilities** öffentliche Betriebe (Elektrizität, Gas, Wasser; Verkehrswesen); **— works** öffentliche Bauten; **-ation** n. Herausgabe; Bekanntmachung, Veröffentlichung; **-ist** n. Publizist; **-ity** n. Öffentlichkeit; Reklame, Propaganda; **-ize** v. veröffentlichen, publizieren

publish v. veröffentlichen; verlegen, herausgeben; **-er** n. Verleger, Herausgeber; **-ing** n. Verlegen, Herausgeben; **-ing company** Verlag(sgesellschaft); **-ing house** Verlag(shaus)

puck n. Elf, Kobold, Puck

pucker n. Falte, Bausch; **—** v. (sich) falten, runzeln; zusammenziehen

pudding n. Pudding

puddle n. Pfuhl, Pfütze, Lache; **—** v. verschlämmen, besudeln; plantschen

pudgy adj. fleischig; untersetzt

puff n. Hauch, Windstoss; Paff; (baking) Windbeutel; (coll.) Lobhudelei; Schwindelreklame; **powder —** Puderquaste; **—** v. blasen; rauchen, paffen; aufblasen, aufbauschen; anpreisen; **-y** adj. aufgeblasen, geschwollen; bauschig; (naut.) böig; (fig.) schwülstig

pug n. Mops; Knetlehm; **—** v. (Lehm) kneten; (mit Lehm) verschmieren; **—** adj. **— nose** Stupsnase

pugilism n. Boxkunst

pugilist n. Faustkämpfer, Boxer

pull n. Ziehen, Reissen; Zug, Ruck; (pol.) Einfluss; (sl.) Vorteil; **—** v. ziehen, reissen, zerren; rupfen, zupfen; (naut.) rudern; **— off** aufbrechen, abreissen; **— out** ausziehen, ausreissen; **— through** durchbringen; durchkommen; **— up** weggehen; heraufziehen, ausrotten; anziehen; anhalten; **-er** n. Reisser, Raufer; **nail -er** Kistenöffner

pulley n. Rolle, Scheibe; Treibrad; Flaschenzug

pulmonary, pulmonic adj. Lungen-

pulmotor n. Atemgerät, Sauerstoffapparat

pulp n. Fruchtmark, Fruchtfleisch; (mech.) Lumpenbrei; **—** adj. **— magazine** Sensationsblatt

pulpit n. Kanzel, Katheder

pulpwood n. Holz zur Papierbereitung

pulsate v. pulsieren; pochen, schlagen

pulse n. Puls(schlag)

pulsejet n. Antriebsrakete; **— engine** Raketenmotor

pulverize v. pulverisieren; zu Staub werden (or machen)

puma n. Puma, Kuguar, Berglöwe

pump n. Pumpe; air — Luftpumpe; feed — Speisepumpe; — room Trinkhalle; — v. (aus)pumpen; aufblasen; (coll.) ausforschen, ausfragen; -er n. Pumper; Petroleumbrunnen; (sports) Niederlage

pumpkin n. Kürbis

pun n. Wortspiel, Wortwitz; — v. witzeln, mit Worten spielen

punch n. Puff, Stoss, Schlag; (beverage) Punsch; (mech.) Stanze, Locheisen; Pfrieme; **Punch** Hanswurst, Kasperle; — v. puffen, stossen, schlagen; (mech.) lochen, (aus)stanzen, durchschlagen

punctual adj. pünktlich, prompt; -ity n. Pünktlichkeit, Promptheit; Genauigkeit

punctuate v. mit Satzzeichen versehen

punctuation n. Interpunktion

puncture n. Stich; (tire) Loch; — v. perforieren, (durch)stechen; ein Loch bekommen; (med.) punktieren

pundit n. Gelehrter; Pandit

pungent adj. scharf, stechend; **schmerz-** haft; (fig.) beissend

punish v. (be)straten, züchtigen; -able adj. strafbar, straffällig; -ment n. Strafe, Bestrafung

punk n. Zunderholz; (sl.) Gauner

punt n. (cards) Punkt; (football) Treten, bevor der Ball den Boden berührt; — v. (football) den Ball, bevor er den Boden berührt, treten; (game) setzen

puny adj. winzig; schwächlich

pup n. Welpe, kleiner Hund; — v. werfen; -py n. Welpe, junger Hund, junge Robbe; (coll.) Grünschnabel

pupa n. Puppe, Larve

pupil n. Schüler, Zögling; (anat.) Pupille

puppet n. Puppe, Marionette; — show Puppenspiel, Marionettentheater

purchase n. Kauf, Ankauf, Erwerbung; (mech.) Hebevorrichtung; — v. kaufen, erwerben, erhandeln, erstehen; aufwinden; -r n. Käufer, Abnehmer

pure adj. rein, unverfälscht, lauter; (min.) echt, gediegen

purée n. Püree, Brei

purgatory n. Fegefeuer

purge n. Reinigung, Säuberung; (med.) Abführmittel; (pol.) Säuberungsaktion; — v. reinigen, säubern; (med.) abführen

purifier n. Reiniger; Reinigungsmittel; Reinigungsapparat

purify v. reinigen, läutern; (chem.) raffinieren, klären, desinfizieren

Puritan n. Puritaner

purity n. Reinheit, Lauterkeit

purple n. Purpur; — adj. purpurn, purpurrot; — v. (sich) purpurrot färben

purport n. Inhalt, Sinn; — v. enthalten, bedeuten; meinen

purpose n. Vorsatz, Absicht; Zweck, Ziel; Wirkung, Erfolg; on — absichtlich, vorsätzlich; to no — zwecklos, vergebens; to the — zweckentsprechend; — v. beabsichtigen, bezwecken, vorhaben

purr v. schnurren

purse n. Tasche; Geldbeutel, Portemonnaie; — v. einstecken; -r n. Zahlmeister,

Proviantmeister

pursuance n. Verfolgung, Fortsetzung

pursue v. verfolgen, nachsetzen; fortsetzen, fortfahren

pursuit n. Verfolgung; Nachstellung

push n. Stoss, Schub; Vorstoss, Angriff; Hieb, Stich; — **button** Kontaktknopf; — v. stossen, schieben, treiben, drücken, drängen, antreiben; betreiben, befördern; verfolgen, bedrängen; — **ahead** vorwärtsstossen; — **back** zurücktreiben; — **through** durchstossen, durchdrücken; **-ing** adj. drängend, strebsam; unternehmend, energisch; kühn, zudringlich

pushover n. leichtes Spiel; einfache Sache; Schwächling

puss(y) n. Kätzchen

put v. Stoss, Wurf; — v. stossen, werfen, schleudern; zwingen, nötigen; bewegen, bereden; setzen, stellen, legen; — **aside** beiseite setzen; — **away** weglegen, fortschicken; — **down** niedersetzen; niederschreiben; unterdrücken, zum Schweigen bringen; — **forth** herausstellen, ausstrecken; (bot.) treiben, keimen; — **in order** in Ordnung bringen, aufräumen; — **off** aufschieben, hinhalten; — **on** (dress, shoes) anziehen, (hat) aufsetzen; — **out** auslöschen, verwirren; — **out of action** ausser Gefecht setzen; — **over** verschieben, überweisen; beschwindeln; — **together** zusammenstellen, zusammensetzen; — **up** aufstellen, aufschlagen, aufspannen; — **up with** dulden, sich gefallen lassen; -t v. einlochen, putten; -ter n. Steller, Setzer; (min.) Karrenschlepper

putrid adj. faul, verfault; verdorben; — fever Faulfieber

putt n. (golf) Schlag; -er (golf) Ballkelle

putty n. Kitt; — v. kitten

puzzle n. Rätsel; Verlegenheit, Verwirrung; jigsaw — Zusammensetzspiel, Puzzle(spiel); — v. verwirren; in Verlegenheit sein (or bringen)

pyrex n. Pyrex, Jenaer Glas

pyrometer n. Hitzegradmesser

python n. Python, Riesenschlange

Q

quack n. Quacksalber; Marktschreier; — adj. quacksalberisch; prahlend; — v. quacksalbern; prahlen; quacken, schnattern

quadrangle n. Viereck; (arch.) viereckiger Hof, Häuserblock

quadrant n. Quadrant, Viertelkreis

quadrilateral adj. vierseitig

quadroon n. Viertelneger; Kind eines Mulatten und einer Weissen (or umgekehrt)

quadruped n. Vierfüssler; — adj. vierfüssig

quadruple adj. vierfältig, vierfach; — v. (sich) vervierfachen; -ts n. pl. Vierlinge

quail n. Wachtel; — v. verzagen

quaint adj. wunderlich, seltsam; altmodisch

quake *n.* Erdbeben; Zittern, Beben; — *v.* zittern, beben

Quaker *n.* Quäker

qualification *n.* Qualifikation, Befähigung, Tauglichkeit

qualify *v.* qualifizieren, befähigen; mässigen, mildern; benennen, näher bestimmen

quality *n.* Qualität, Güte; Eigenschaft, Beschaffenheit

qualm *n.* Anfall; Übelkeit, Schwäche, Ohnmacht; (fig.) Skrupel, Bedenken

quandary *n.* Verlegenheit, verdriessliche Lage

quantity *n.* Quantität, Menge; Länge, Grösse

quarantine *n.* Quarantäne; Isolierung; — *v.* unter Quarantäne stellen; — **a nation** eine Nation in Schranken halten

quarrel *n.* Zank, Streit, Zwist; — *v.* (sich) zanken, streiten

quarrelsome *adj.* zänkisch, streitsüchtig

quarry *n.* Steinbruch; (hunting) Beute; (fig.) Fundgrube

quart *n.* Quart; (mus.) Quarte

quarter *n.* Viertel, Quartal; Stadtviertel; Himmelsrichtung, Windrichtung; Fünfundzwanzigcentstück; — **of an hour** Viertelstunde; — *s pl.* Quartier, Logis; Wohnung; Gnade, Pardon; — *v.* vierteilen; (mil.) einquartieren, unterbringen; **-ly** *adj.* quartalsweise, vierteljährig

quarterback *n.* (football) ausserhalb der Gruppe stehender Ballfänger; (fig.) Spielleiter

quarter-deck *n.* (naut.) Achterdeck

quartermaster *n.* Quartiermeister; (naut.) Steuermannsmaat

quartet *n.* Quartett

quartz *n.* Quarz

quay *n.* Kai, Uferstrasse

queen *n.* Königin; (chess and cards) Dame; — **bee** Bienenkönigin, Weisel; **-ly** *adj.* königlich, wie eine Königin

queer *adj.* wunderlich, seltsam, sonderbar

quell *v.* überwältigen, unterdrücken, bezwingen

quench *v.* (aus)löschen, stillen; unterdrücken

quest *n.* Suchen, Nachforschen, Untersuchung, Prüfung

question *n.* Frage; Befragung, Untersuchung; Streitfrage, Sache, Angelegenheit; (law) Verhör; (math.) Aufgabe; (pol.) Verhandlungsgegenstand; **be out of —** nicht in Betracht kommen; **beyond —** ohne Frage; **in —** fraglich; vorliegend; **put a —** eine Frage stellen; — *v.* befragen; streiten; (law) untersuchen, verhören; (fig.) bezweifeln, misstrauen; **-able** *adj.* fraglich, zweifelhaft; bedenklich, fragwürdig; **-naire** *n.* Fragebogen

quibble *n.* Ausflucht, Vorwand; — *v.* ausweichen, Ausflüchte machen

quick *adj.* schnell, rasch, hurtig; beweglich, behend; lebendig, lebhaft; heftig, stark; **be —!** schnell! beeil dich! — **ear** feines Ohr; — **eye** scharfes Auge; —

fire Schnellfeuer; — **returns** schneller Umsatz; — **time** (mil.) Schnellschritt; — *n.* Lebende; empfindliches Fleisch; **cut to the —** auf das Empfindlichste kränken; **-en** *v.* beleben, beschleunigen; aufleben; sich regen; **-ness** *n.* Schnelligkeit, Geschwindigkeit; Lebhaftigkeit

quick-freezing *n.* Schnellgefrierung; schnellarbeitende Gefriermaschine

quicklime *n.* ungelöschter Kalk, Ätzkalk

quicksand *n.* Flugsand, Treibsand

quicksilver *n.* Quecksilber

quick-tempered *adj.* leidenschaftlich, reizbar

quick-witted *adj.* schlagfertig, scharfsinnig

quiescent *adj.* ruhig, still; ruhend

quiet *n.* Stille, Ruhe; Ungestörtheit; (fig.) Frieden, Seelenruhe; — *adj.* still, ruhig; gelassen, friedlich; gemütlich, harmlos; — *v.* (sich) beruhigen, stillen, besänftigen; (law) in Ruhe lassen; **-ness** *n.*, **-ude** *n.* Ruhe, Stille; Friedfertigkeit, Gemütsruhe, Gleichmut

quill *n.* Feder; Federkiel; (mech.) Weberspule; (mus.) Rohrpfeife; (spices) Rindenrolle; (zool.) Stachel

quilt *n.* Steppdecke; **crazy —** Flickendecke

quince *n.* Quitte; — **tree** Quittenbaum

quinine *n.* Chinin

quinsy *n.* Halsbräune

quintet *n.* Quintett

quip *n.* Witz, Stichelei; Kniff; Spitzfindigkeit

quit *v.* verlassen, aufgeben; quittieren; zurückzahlen; — *adj.* quitt; frei, los; **-ter** *n.* Weggehende, Drückeberger

quite *adv.* ganz, gänzlich; völlig, durchaus; (coll.) ziemlich

quiver *n.* Schauer, Zittern; Köcher; — *v.* zittern, beben

quiz *n.* Rätselfrage, Quiz; Prüfung; Neckerei, Spöttelei; — *v.* (aus)fragen, prüfen; aufziehen, necken

quorum *n.* beschlussfähige Mitgliederzahl

quota *n.* Quote, Anteil, Kontingent; Beitrag

quotation *n.* Anführung, Zitierung; Zitat; (com.) Preisnotierung; **— marks** Anführungszeichen; Gänsefüsschen

quote *n.* Zitat; — *v.* zitieren, anführen, angeben; (com.) notieren; — **a price** ein Preisangebot machen

quotient *n.* Quotient; Teilzahl, Teilwert; **intelligence —** Intelligenzberechnungswert

R

rabbet *n.* Falz, Fuge, Nut; — *v.* falzen; einfügen

rabbi *n.* Rabbi(ner)

rabbit *n.* Kaninchen

rabble *n.* Pöbel, Haufen

rabid *adj.* wütend, rasend, toll

rabies *n.* Tollwut, Hundswut; Wasserscheu

rac(c)oon *n.* Waschbär

race *n.* Rasse, Geschlecht, Volksstamm; Wettrennen, Wettlauf; Strömung, Lauf; Strom, Rinne; — **horse** Rennpferd; — **track** Rennbahn; — *v.* rennen, wettlaufen, wettfahren, wettreiten; **-r** *n.* Wettläufer; Rennpferd, Rennboot, Rennwagen; (mech.) Laufschiene

racecourse *n.* Rennbahn

racial *adj.* rassenmässig; Rassen-

racism *n.* Rassenvorurteil

rack *n.* Gestell, Ständer, Stativ; Reck; Raufe; (mech.) Zahnstange; (rail.) Gepäcknetz; — **railway** Zahnradbahn; — *v.* recken, strecken; foltern, quälen; — **one's brains** sich den Kopf zerbrechen

racket *n.* Lärm, Getöse, Tumult; (tennis) Schläger; (sl.) Erpressergeschäft; **-eer** *n.* Schieber, Erpresser; **-eer** *v.* schieben, erpressen

radar *n.* Radar

radiance *n.* Strahlen, Glanz; (geom.) Strahl

radiant *adj.* strahlend, leuchtend; strahlenförmig; — *n.* (opt.) Radiationspunkt

radiator *n.* Heizkörper; Kühler

radical *adj.* radikal, gründlich; wesentlich; — *n.* (chem.) Grundstoff; (gram.) Stammwort; (pol.) Radikale; **-ism** *n.* Radikalismus

radio *n.* Radio, Rundfunk, directional — Funkpeilgerät; — **amplifier** Verstärkerröhre; — **announcer** Rundfunkansager; — **beacon** Stationszeichen; Peilturm; — **beam** Richtstrahl; — **homing** Radiopeilung; — **hookup** Ringsendung; Übertragung; — **listener** Rundfunkhörer; — **message** Funkspruch, Rundfunkmeldung; — **operator** Funker; — **receiver** Rundfunkempfänger; — **set** Rundfunkapparat; — **transcription** Schallplattensendung; — *v.* funken, senden

radioactive *adj.* radioaktiv

radioactivity *n.* Radioaktivität

radiobroadcasting *n.* Rundfunksendung; — **station** Sender, Rundfunksender

radio(tele)gram *n.* Funkspruch

radiotherapy *n.* Radiotherapie

radish *n.* Rettich; **little** — Radieschen

radium *n.* Radium

radius *n.* Radius, Halbmesser; (anat. und mech.) Speiche

raffle *n.* Auswürfeln, Auslosen; (coll.) Gerümpel, Abfall; — *v.* (aus)losen, (aus)würfeln

raft *n.* Floss; — *v.* flössen

rafter *n.* Sparren, Dachsparren; Flösser

rag *n.* Lumpen, Lappen, Fetzen; *pl.* Putzwolle; **-amuffin** *n.* Lump(enkerl); **-ged** *adj.* uneben, rauh; zottig; zackig; abgerissen, zerlumpt, schäbig

rage *n.* Wut, Raserei; Ekstase; Sucht, Manie, Gier; — *v.* wüten, rasen, toben; **fly into a** — wütend (*or* rasend) werden; — **oneself out** sich austoben

raging *adj.* wütend, rasend, tobend

ragtime *n.* groteske Negermusik

ragweed *n.* Klette, wilde Aster; **European** — Kreuzkraut

raid *n.* Überfall, Streifzug; Raubzug; (police) Razzia; — *v.* überfallen; **-er** *n.* Angreifer; (avi.) Jagdflugzeug, Bom-

benflugzeug; (naut.) Kaperschiff; Nahkämpfer

rail *n.* Riegel, Querholz; Geländer; (orn.) Ralle; (rail.) Schiene, Schienenstrang; *pl.* Eisenbahnaktien; **by** — per Eisenbahn; **third** — Stromschiene; — *v.* umzäunen, mit einem Geländer versehen; schimpfen, schelten; **-ing** *n.* Geländer, Brustwehr; Gitter; **-ing** *adj.* spottend, schmähend; **-lery** *n.* Spötterei, Stichelei

railroad *n.* Eisenbahn; **belt** — Ringbahn; **electric** — elektrischer Zug; **elevated** — Hochbahn; **narrow-gauge** — Schmalspurbahn; **standard-gauge** — Normalspurbahn; — **crossing** Bahnkreuzung; — **stock** Eisenbahnkapital; — **track** Schienenstrang; — *v.* per Eisenbahn befördern; (sl.) durch Verleumdung ins Unglück (*or* Gefängnis) bringen

railway *n.* Schienenweg; **cable** —, **funicular** — Drahtseilbahn

raiment *n.* Kleidung

rain *n.* Regen; — **gauge** Regenmesse; — *v.* regnen; **it never -s but it pours** ein Unglück kommt selten allein; **it -s cats and dogs** es regnet in Strömen; **-y** *adj.* regnerisch

rainbow *n.* Regenbogen

raincheck *n.* Eintrittskartenabschnitt (falls wegen schlechten Wetters umdisponiert wird); (coll.) Rückversicherung

raindrop *n.* Regentropfen

rainfall *n.* Niederschlag; Regenmenge

rainproof *adj.* wasserdicht, regenfest

raise *n.* Gehaltserhöhung; — *v.* (auf)heben, erhöhen; errichten, aufrichten; erheben, hervorrufen, erregen; züchten; aufziehen; beschwören; (mil.) ausheben, werben; (min.) fördern, gewinnen; (pol.) aufwerfen, vorbringen; (tax) eintreiben, einkassieren; — **an objection** einen Einwurf machen

raisin *n.* Rosine

rake *n.* Rechen, Harke; (naut.) Überhängen, Neigung; (coll.) Müssiggänger, Wüstling; — *v.* rechen, harken; zusammenscharren, zusammenraffen; durchstöbern; (mil.) bestreichen; (fig.) überblicken, betrachten; (coll.) liederlich leben

rally *n.* Sammeln, Sammelsignal; (med.) Erholung; (pol.) Massenversammlung; — *v.* (sich) wieder sammeln; (med.) sich erholen; (fig.) anfeuern; scherzen; spotten

ram *n.* Widder; (mech.) Ramme; **battering** — Sturmbock, Mauerbrecher; — **jet** Vorstossrakete; — *v.* (ein)rammen; ansetzen

ramble *n.* Streifzug, Ausflug; — *v.* umherstreifen, abschweifen; (bot.) ranken, wuchern; **-r** *n.* Umherstreicher, Nachtschwärmer; (bot.) Kletterrose

ramification *n.* Verzweigung, Abzweigung

ramp *n.* Rampe, Auffahrt; — *v.* sich zum Sprung erheben; tollen; **-ant** *adj.* wuchernd; (fig.) zügellos, ausgelassen

ramshackle *adj.* wackelig, baufällig; (fig.) verworren

ranch *n.* Farm; Viehwirtschaft; **-er** *n.* Farmer, Viehzüchter

rancid *adj.* ranzig; (fig.) widerlich

random *n.* Zufall; **at —** blindlings, aufs Geratewohl

range *n.* Reihe, Kette, Raum, Umfang; Bereich, Reichweite, Tragweite, Ausdehnung, Spielraum; Bezirk; (cooking) Kochherd; (mil.) Schussweite; Schiessplatz; (mus.) Stimmumfang; **— finder** Entfernungsmesser; **—** *v.* (ein)reihen, ordnen; durchstreifen, durchwandern; sich erstrecken, reichen; (mil.) die Schussweite bestimmen; (naut.) entlang fahren; (rail.) rangieren; **-r** *n.* Umherstreifer; Förster; (mil.) Jäger

rank *n.* Reihe, Linie, Glied; Rang, Stand, Klasse, Dienstgrad; **— and file** Reihe und Glied; gemeine Soldaten; **rise from the -s** von der Pike auf dienen; **—** *adj.* stark, rein, richtig; ranzig; üppig, übermässig, fruchtbar; **—** *v.* rangieren, rechnen zu; (sich) ordnen

ransack *v.* durchsuchen, durchstöbern; plündern

ransom *n.* Lösegeld, Loskauf; **—** *v.* loskaufen, auslösen; (rel.) erlösen

rap *n.* Schlag, Klopfen; Heller; (sl.) unverdiente Strafe; **—** *v.* schlagen, klopfen; raffen, fortreissen; verweisen

rapacious *adj.* raubgierig, räuberisch; habgierig, unverschämt

rape *n.* Raub, Entführung; (bot.) Raps, Rübsen; (law) Notzucht, Vergewaltigung; **—** *v.* rauben; (law) vergewaltigen, notzüchten

rapid *adj.* schnell, rasch; reissend; rapid; **— consumption** (med.) galoppierende Schwindsucht; **— fire** Schnellfeuer; **— march** (mil.) Laufschritt; **-s** *n. pl.* Stromschnellen, Strudel; **-ity** *n.* Schnelligkeit, Geschwindigkeit; Ungestüm

rapine *n.* Raub, Plünderung

rapt *adj.* geraubt, entführt; (fig.) entrückt, hingerissen, entzückt; versunken; **-ure** *n.* Entrückung; Verzükkung, Ekstase; **-urous** *adj.* hinreissend, entzückend; leidenschaftlich

rare *adj.* selten, rar; dünn, fein; locker, porös; **-fied** *adj.* verdünnt

rarity *n.* Rarität, Seltenheit

rascal *n.* Spitzbube, Halunke, Schuft; **-ly** *adj.* gemein, schuftig, erbärmlich

rash *n.* Hautausschlag; **—** *adj.* hastig, übereilt; unvorsichtig, vorschnell; **-ness** *n.* Hastigkeit, Übereiltheit, Unbesonnenheit; Ungestüm

rasp *n.* Raspel, Reibeisen; **—** *v.* reiben, raspeln, kratzen; (mus.) krächzen; (fig.) kränken, verletzen

raspberry *n.* Himbeere

rat *n.* Ratte; (sl.) Überläufer; Streikbrecher; **—** *v.* Ratten fangen; (sl.) verraten, überlaufen

rate *n.* Rate, Anteil; Mass, Verhältnis; Preis, Betrag; Dosis; Veranschlagung; Abgabe, Steuer; Geschwindigkeit; **at a low —** wohlfeil; **at any —** auf jeden

Fall, um jeden Preis; **— of discount** Diskontsatz; **— of exchange** Wechselkurs; **— of interest** Zinsfuss; **—** *v.* schätzen; taxieren; ansehen, bestimmen; besteuern; regulieren; ausschelten

rather *adv.* eher, lieber; ziemlich; vielmehr

ratification *n.* Ratifizierung, Bestätigung

ratify *v.* ratifizieren, bestätigen

rating *n.* Schätzung; Rang, Klasse; Verweis

ratio *n.* Verhältnis

ration *n.* Ration, Anteil, Bedarf; **-ing** *n.* Rationierung

rational *adj.* vernunftgemäss, vernünftig; rational

Ratisbon *n.* Regensburg

rattle *n.* Gerassel; Klapper, Knarre; **—** *v.* rasseln, klirren; klappern, knarren; röcheln; (fig.) verwirren

rattlesnake *n.* Klapperschlange

ravage *n.* Verwüstung, Verheerung; **—** *v.* verwüsten, verheeren

rave *v.* rasen, toben; schwärmen, faseln

ravel *v.* verwirren; (sich) auftrennen, ausfasern

raven *n.* Rabe; **-ous** *adj.* gefrässig, heisshungrig

ravine *n.* Hohlweg; Bergschlucht

ravish *v.* rauben, entführen; schänden; (fig.) hinreissen; **-ing** *adj.* entzückend, hinreissend

raw *adj.* roh, ungekocht; rauh; unerfahren; unreif; unbearbeitet; (med.) wund(gerieben); **— materials** Rohstoffe, Rohmaterial

rawhide *n.* ungegerbtes Leder; Reitpeitsche

ray *n.* Strahl; (ichth.) Roche

rayon *n.* Rayon, Kunstseide

razor *n.* Rasiermesser, Rasierapparat; **— blade** Rasierklinge; **— strop** Streichriemen; **electric —** Trockenrasierer

reach *n.* Bereich, Strecke; Hörweite, Schussweite, Reichweite; Ausdehnung; **—** *v.* (er)reichen; erlangen, greifen; ausstrecken; (sich) erstrecken

react *v.* reagieren, rückwirken; entgegenwirken; **-ion** *n.* Rückwirkung, Gegenwirkung; Reaktion; **-ionary** *n.* Reaktionär; **-ionary** *adj.* reaktionär; **-ivate** *v.* reaktivieren

read *v.* (ab)lesen; (an)zeigen; auslegen; studieren; **—** *adj.* belesen, bewandert (in); **-able** *adj.* lesbar, lesenswert; **-er** *n.* Leser, Vorleser; Erklärer; Lesebuch; **-ing** *n.* Lesen, Lesung; Vorlesung; Lektüre, Lesestoff; Lesart, Auffassung; Belesenheit; Durchsicht, Korrektur; **-ing room** Lesezimmer

readily *adv.* bereitwillig; gleich; leicht; gern

readiness *n.* Schnelligkeit, Raschheit; Bereitwilligkeit; Bereitschaft

ready *adj.* bereit, fertig; schnell, gewandt; (com.) bar, prompt; (naut.) klar

ready-made *adj.* (gebrauchs)fertig; **— clothes** Konfektionskleidung

real *adj.* wirklich, tatsächlich, real; wahr, echt; (law) unbeweglich; **— estate** Grundbesitz; **— wages** Reallöhne;

–sim n. Realismus; **–ist** n. Realist; **–istic** adj. realistisch; **–ity** n. Wirklichkeit, Realität; **–ization** n. Verwirklichung, Realisierung; (com.) Geldanlage; **–ize** v. verwirklichen, ausführen, realisieren; sich vorstellen, erkennen; (com.) anlegen, verwerten; einbringen, erzielen; zu Geld machen; **–ly** adv. wirklich, in der Tat

realm n. Reich; Gebiet

ream n. Ries; — v. erweitern

reap v. schneiden, mähen; ernten; **–er** n. Schnitter; Mähmaschine

rear n. Hinterseite, Hintergrund; Rückseite; (mil.) Nachhut, Nachtrab; — adj. Hinter-, Rück-; — **admiral** Konteradmiral; — v. aufheben, aufrichten; errichten; aufziehen, grossziehen; sich bäumen

rearmament n. Wiederbewaffung, Wiederaufrüstung

rearrange v. neu ordnen

rearview n. Rückansicht

rear-vision mirror n. Rückspiegel

reason n. Vernunft, Verstand; Grund, Ursache; Recht, Billigkeit; Einsicht, Überlegung; by — of wegen; for this — aus diesem Grunde; in — massvoll; it is against all — es ist gegen alle Vernunft; it stands to — es ist vernünftig; listen to — Vernunft annehmen; without — ohne Grund; **–able** adj. vernünftig, verständig; billig, mässig; **–ing** n. Urteil(en); Beweisführung

reassurance n. wiederholte Versicherung, Beruhigung; (com.) Rückversicherung

rebate n. Rabatt, Abzug; (arch.) Kannelierung; Falz

rebel n. Rebell, Aufrührer, Empörer; — adj. rebellisch, aufrührerisch; — v. rebellieren, sich empören (or auflehnen); **–lion** n. Aufruhr, Empörung, Widerspenstigkeit; **–lious** adj. aufständisch, widerspenstig

rebirth n. Wiedergeburt

rebound n. Rückprall; Rückstoss; Widerhall; — v. zurückspringen, zurückprallen, abprallen; widerhallen

rebroadcast n. wiederholte Rundfunksendung

rebuild v. wieder aufbauen, wiederherstellen; **–ing** n. Umbau

rebuke n. Tadel, Vorwurf; — v. tadeln, schelten, zurechtweisen

rebut v. (law) widerlegen

recall n. Zurückrufung; Widerruf; Hervorruf; — v. zurückrufen; wieder wachrufen; widerrufen

recap n. (tire) neuer Belag; — v. neu vulkanisieren; **–itulate** v. rekapitulieren, kurz wiederholen

recapture n. Wiedereinnahme, Wiederfestnahme; — v. wieder einnehmen (or festnehmen)

recast v. umgiessen, umformen

recede v. zurücktreten, zurückweichen; abstehen

receipt n. Annahme; Quittung, Empfangsschein; (med.) Rezept; pl. Eingänge; **acknowledge** — den Empfang

bestätigen; — v. quittieren, bestätigen

receivable adj. annehmbar; — **bills** offenstehende Rechnungen

receive v. empfangen, erhalten; einnehmen; aufnehmen; annehmen; anerkennen; **–r** n. Empfänger; Einnehmer; (chem.) Rezipient; (mech.) Behälter, Sammelgefäss; (tel.) Hörer; **–r in bankruptcy** Konkursverwalter; **–r of stolen goods** Hehler; **–rship** n. Konkursverwaltung

recent adj. neu, frisch; **–ly** adv. kürzlich, vor kurzem, unlängst

receptacle n. Behälter; (anat.) Gefäss; (coll.) Schlupfwinkel

reception n. Empfang; Annahme; Aufnahme; **–ist** n. Empfangsdame

receptive adj. aufnahmefähig, empfänglich

recess n. Unterbrechung, Ferien; (arch.) Nische, Vertiefung; (fig.) Winkel; **–ion** n. wirtschaftlicher Stillstand

recipe n. Rezept

recipient n. Empfänger

reciprocal adj. wechselseitig, gegenseitig; reziprok

reciprocate v. austauschen, erwidern; abwechseln(d wirken)

reciprocity n. Gegenseitigkeit

recital n. Vortrag, Vorlesung; (mus.) Konzert

recitation n. Rezitation, Deklamation; Vortrag

recitative n. (mus.) Rezitativ

recite v. rezitieren, vortragen, deklamieren, aufsagen

reckless adj. tollkühn, verwegen; rücksichtslos; leichtsinnig, unbekümmert

reckon v. rechnen, zählen; schätzen, meinen, vermuten; **–ing** n. Berechnung, Abrechnung; Zählung; Schätzung

reclaim v. reklamieren, rückfordern; bessern, zivilisieren; (agr.) urbarmachen, abgewinnen; (law) protestieren; (zool.) zähmen

reclamation n. Reklamation, Rückforderung; Besserung; (agr.) Urbarmachung, Gewinnung; (law) Protest, Einspruch

recline v. (sich) lehnen, ausruhen

recognition n. Anerkennung, Beglaubigung; Erkennen

recognize v. anerkennen, beglaubigen; wiedererkennen

recoil n. Rückstoss, Rücklauf; — v. zurückfahren, zurückweichen, zurückstossen, zurückschaudern; sich zurückziehen

recollect v. sich fassen (or wieder sammeln); sich erinnern; **–ion** n. Erinnerung, Gedächtnis

recommend v. empfehlen; **–ation** n. Empfehlung

recommission v. wieder in Dienst stellen

recompense n. Entschädigung, Ersatz; Belohnung

reconcile v. versöhnen, schlichten; in Einklang bringen

reconciliation n. Versöhnung, Aussöhnung

recondition n. Wiederinstandsetzung, Reparatur; — *v.* wieder instandsetzen, reparieren

reconnaissance *n.* Aufklärung

reconsider *v.* von neuem betrachten (*or* erwägen)

reconstruct *v.* wieder aufbauen (*or* herstellen)

record *n.* Bericht, Aufzeichnung; Urkunde, Dokument; Verzeichnis, Protokoll, Register; Schallplatte; (pol.) Vergangenheit, Ruf; (sports) Rekord, Höchstleistung; *pl.* Archiv, Papiere; Geschichtsbücher; **off the —** im Vertrauen, ohne Aufzeichnungen zu machen; — *v.* eintragen, registrieren; verzeichnen, aufzeichnen, protokollieren; überliefern; (sports) einen Rekord aufstellen; **-er** *n.* Registrator, Protokollführer; Archivar; Geschichtsschreiber; (mech.) Zähler; Aufnahmeapparat; (sports) Zeitnehmer

record-breaking *adj.* rekordbrechend

recount *v.* wieder erzählen

re-count *v.* wieder zählen, nochmals berechnen

recoup *v.* schadlos halten, ersetzen

recourse *n.* Zuflucht; Regressrecht

recover *v.* wieder erlangen (*or* erobern); wiederfinden; wiedergutmachen; einholen, nachholen; herauskommen; sich erholen; — **one's senses** wieder zum Bewusstsein (*or* zu Verstand) kommen; — **property** Eigentum zurückerhalten; **-y** *n.* Wiedererlangung, Wiedereroberung; (law) Schadenersatz; (med.) Wiederherstellung, Genesung, Rekonvaleszenz

recreate *v.* sich erholen; erfrischen; neu gestalten, umschaffen

recreation *n.* Erholung, Erfrischung; Neugestaltung

recruit *n.* Rekrut, Neuling; — *v.* rekrutieren, ergänzen, wiederherstellen; erneuern; **-ing** *n.* Rekrutierung; — **office** Bezirkskommando, Werbebüro

rectangle *n.* Rechteck

rectangular *adj.* rechteckig, rechtwinkelig

rectifier *n.* Entzerrungsgerät, Gleichrichter

rectify *v.* berichtigen, verbessern; (rad.) gleichrichten, entzerren

rector *n.* Rektor; Pfarrer; **-y** *n.* Rektorat; Pfarre, Pfarrhaus

recuperate *v.* sich erholen; wieder herstellen (*or* kräftigen)

recur *v.* zurückkommen; wieder einfallen; periodisch wiederkehren; **-rence** *n.* Wiederkehr, Rückkehr; Zurückfliessen; **-rent** *adj.* wiederkehrend; rückläufig, zurückfliessend

red *n.* Rot; (art.) Rötel; — *adj.* rot; (pol.) rot, kommunistisch; (fig.) blutig, blutgefärbt; — **herring** getrockneter Hering; (coll.) Vorspiegelung, Finte; — **lead** Mennig; — **man** Rothaut, Indianer; — **pepper** Piment, Paprika, roter (*or* spanischer) Pfeffer; — **tape** Bürokratie, Amtsschimmel; **-den** *v.* röten, rot färben (*or* werden); erröten; **-dish** *adj.* rötlich; **-ness** *n.* Röte,

Rötung

redbird *n.* Kardinal

red-blooded *adj.* vital, mutig; (coll.) waschecht

redbreast *n.* Rotkehlchen

redcap *n.* Gepäckträger; (orn.) Stieglitz, Distelfink

redeem *v.* auslösen, zurückkaufen; tilgen; wiedergutmachen, wieder einbringen, ersetzen; befreien, erlösen; **-er** *n.* Einlösende; **Redeemer** Erlöser, Heiland

redemption *n.* Rückkauf; Auslösung; Wiedergutmachung; (rel.) Erlösung

red-haired *adj.* rothaarig

redhead *n.* Rotkopf

red-hot *adj.* rotglühend; (coll.) heftig, hitzig; (news) neuste

red-letter day *n.* Festtag, Glückstag, Freudentag

redskin *n.* Rothaut, Indianer

red-tape *adj.* bürokratisch

reduce *v.* verkleinern, vermindern; herabsetzen, abschwächen; zurückführen (auf); (chem.) reduzieren; (med.) entfetten

reducing agent *n.* Reduktionsmittel; (med.) Entfettungsmittel

reduction *n.* Verringerung, Verminderung, Abschwächung; (med.) Entfettung

redundant *adj.* überfliessend; übermässig, üppig; weitschweifig; (fig.) überflüssig

redwing *n.* Rotdrossel

redwood *n.* Rotholz

reed *n.* (arch.) Kannelierung; (bot.) Ried, Rohr; (mech.) Weberkamm; (mus.) Mundstück, Zunge; Rohrflöte

reef *n.* Riff, Klippe; — *v.* raffen, einziehen

reek *n.* Rauch, Dunst; — *v.* rauchen, dampfen; räuchern, ausdunsten

reel *n.* Haspel, Rolle, Spule; (coll.) Taumel, Wirbel; — *v.* haspeln, rollen; taumeln, wirbeln; — **off** herunterleiern

re-elect *v.* wiederwählen; **-ion** *n.* Wiederwahl

re-enforce *v.* (sich) verstärken; wieder inkraftsetzen

re-enter *v.* wieder eintreten (*or* eindringen, eintragen)

re-establish *v.* wiederherstellen

refer *v.* verweisen, hinweisen; — **to** hinweisen auf, sich beziehen auf; **-ee** *n.* Schiedsrichter, Unparteiische; (law) Sachverständige; **-ee** *v.* als Schiedsrichter tätig sein; **-ence** *n.* Referenz, Verweisung; Empfehlung; Auskunft; Erwähnung, Anspielung; **works of -ence** Nachschlagewerke; **-endum** *n.* Volksentscheid

refill *n.* Nachfüllung; Ersatzbatterie; — *v.* neu füllen, auffüllen, nachfüllen

refine *v.* verfeinern, reinigen, läutern; (mech.) raffinieren; **-ment** *n.* Verfeinerung, Veredlung; Feinheit; (mech.) Raffinierung; **-ry** *n.* Raffinerie

reflect *v.* zurückwerfen, reflektieren, widerspiegeln, zurückstrahlen; **-ion** *n.* Reflexion, Zurückstrahlung; Reflex; (fig.) Überlegung; Tadel; **-or** *n.* Reflektor; Rückstrahler

reflex n. Reflex, Widerschein; — adj. reflektiert, zurückgebogen; Reflex-

reforest v. wiederaufforsten

reform n. Reform, Verbesserung; — v. verbessern; (eccl.) reformieren; -ation n. Umgestaltung; (eccl.) Reformation; -atory n. Besserungsanstalt; -atory adj. bessernd, reformatorisch; -er n. Verbesserer; (eccl.) Reformator

refrain n. Refrain, Kehrreim; — v. sich enthalten, zurückhalten, bezähmen, zügeln

refresh v. (sich) erfrischen, auffrischen; erquicken; -e n. Erfrischung; Auffrischung; (law) Zuschlagshonorar; -er adj. erfrischend, auffrischend; -er course Wiederholungskurs; -ment n. Erfrischung

refrigeration n. Abkühlung, Kühlung

refrigerator n. Kühlschrank, Eisschrank; Kühlapparat

refuel v. tanken; wieder füllen

refuge n. Zuflucht; Ausflucht, Ausweg; Schutzinsel; -e n. Flüchtling

refund n. Ersatz, Zurückzahlung; — v. zurückzahlen, zurückerstatten, ersetzen

refusal n. Weigerung, Verweigerung; Ablehnung; Vorkaufsrecht

refuse n. Abfall, Kehricht, Müll; (fig.) Abschaum, Ausschuss; — v. verweigern, ablehnen, abschlagen, zurückweisen

refute v. widerlegen

regain v. wiedergewinnen, wiedererreichen

regal adj. königlich, fürstlich; -ia n. Abzeichen; Krönungsschmuck

regard n. Achtung, Ansehen; Aufmerksamkeit, Rücksicht; Hinsicht; pl. Grüsse, Empfehlungen; give -s Grüsse übermitteln; in — to hinsichtlich, was mich betrifft; with — to mit Rücksicht auf; — v. achten, ansehen, betrachten; beachten; betreffen; -ing prep. betreffs; in Anbetracht, hinsichtlich; -less adj. unachtsam, unaufmerksam; unbekümmert; rücksichtslos; -less adv. -less of ohne Rücksicht auf

regency n. Regierung, Regentschaft

regenerate v. (sich) erneuern; nachladen

regeneration n. Regenerierung, Wiederherstellung; Wiedergeburt

regent n. Regent, Herrscher, Reichsverweser

regime n. Regime, Regierung(sform); -n n. Regierung; (gram.) Rektion

regiment n. Regiment; (pol.) Herrschaft; — v. in Regimente einteilen; organisieren; -ation n. Einteilung in Regimente; Organisation; Disziplinierung

region n. Region, Gegend, Bezirk; (anat.) Stelle; -al adj. regional, örtlich, strichweise

register n. Register, Verzeichnis; (mech.) Registriervorrichtung, Schieber; (mus.) Register; cash — Registrierkasse; — v. einschreiben, registrieren, verzeichnen; eintragen, aufzeichnen, buchen; -ed adj. registriert, eingeschrieben; -ed letter Einschreibebrief, Einschreiben

registrar n. Registrator

registration n. Registrierung, Eintragung

registry n. Registratur; Register; Eintragung

regret n. Bedauern, Schmerz; pl. Ablehnung, Absage; — v. bedauern; vermissen; -ful adj. bedauernd; kummervoll; -table adj. bedauerlich

regular n. aktiver Soldat; (eccl.) Ordensgeistliche; (coll.) Stammkunde, Stammgast; — adj. regulär, regelmässig; pünktlich, richtig, ordentlich; (geom.) normal, symmetrisch; — army aktives Heer; -ity n. Regelmässigkeit; Richtigkeit, Ordnung

regulate v. regulieren; ordnen, regeln; einrichten, stellen

regulation n. Regulierung, Regelung; Anordnung

rehabilitate v. rehabilitieren; wiedereinsetzen

rehabilitation n. Rehabilitierung; Wiedereinsetzung

rehash v. wiederkäuen, aufwärmen

rehearsal n. Wiederholung; Vortrag; (theat.) Probe

rehearse v. wiederholen, rezitieren; (theat.) proben

reign n. Regierung(sdauer); (fig.) Macht, Herrschaft; — v. regieren, herrschen

reimburse v. wiedererstatten, entschädigen; -ment n. Wiedererstattung; Deckung, Entschädigung

rein n. Zügel; give — to die Zügel schiessen lassen; — v. zügeln, zurückhalten

reincarnation n. Reinkarnation, Wiederverkörperung

reindeer n. Renntier

reinforce v. verstärken; -d adj. verstärkt; -d concrete Eisenbeton; -ment n. Verstärkung

reinstate v. wiedereinsetzen, wiederherstellen, wiederinstandsetzen

reiterate v. (dauernd) wiederholen

reject v. ablehnen, zurückweisen; ausmustern; verwerfen, verschmähen; -ion n. Ablehnung, Abweisung; Ausmusterung

rejoice v. erfreuen, sich freuen (über)

rejoicing n. Freude; pl. Freudenbezeigungen, Lustbarkeiten; — adj. erfreulich, freudig

rejuvenate v. verjüngen

relapse n. Rückfall; — v. zurückfallen; rückfällig werden, einen Rückfall bekommen

relate v. erzählen, berichten; sich beziehen, in Verbindung bringen; -d adj. berichtet, erzählt; verwandt

relation n. Bericht, Erzählung; Verhältnis, Bezug; Verwandtschaft, Verwandte; -ship n. Verwandtschaft

relative n. Verwandte; (gram.) Relativpronomen; — adj. relativ, verhältnismässig, bedingt; bezüglich; verwandt

relativity n. Relativität

relax v. lockern, schwächen; erschlaffen, nachlassen; entspannen, zerstreuen, erheitern; -ation n. Lockerung, Nachlassen, Erlass; Entspannung, Zerstreuung, Erholung

relay n. Wechsel, Ablösung; (sports) Stafette; (tel.) Relais; **— race** Stafettenlauf

release n. Entlassung, Freilassung, Freigabe, Befreiung; Ausklinken; **—** v. entlassen, freilassen; freigeben; auslösen; erlösen

relent v. nachgeben; sich erweichen lassen; **-less** adj. unnachgiebig, unerbittlich; unbarmherzig

relevant adj. erheblich; angemessen; einschlägig

reliability n. Zuverlässlichkeit, Verlässlichkeit

reliable adj. zuverlässlich, verlässlich

reliance n. Verlass, Vertrauen, Zutrauen

reliant adj. vertrauensvoll, zuversichtlich

relic n. Reliquie; Andenken; Überrest; pl. sterbliche Hülle

relief n. Erleichterung, Linderung; Abhilfe; Unterstützung; (art) Relief; (mil.) Ablösung, Entsatz; (fig.) Hervorhebung; **— map** Reliefkarte

relieve v. erleichtern, lindern; helfen, unterstützen; ablösen, ersetzen

religion n. Religion

religious adj. religiös; **— instruction** Religionsunterricht

relinquish v. verlassen, aufgeben, verzichten auf, überlassen

relish n. Geschmack, Wohlgefallen; Beigeschmack, Würze; **—** v. gerne essen; schmackhaft machen; schmecken, munden; würzen

reload v. wieder beladen

reluctance n. Widerstreben, Widerstand; Abneigung

reluctant adj. widerstrebend, widerwillig; unwillig; zögernd

rely v. sich verlassen; bauen auf

remain v. (ver)bleiben, übrigbleiben; dauern; **-der** n. Rest; (books) Restauflage; (com.) Rückstand, Saldo; (law) Anwartschaft; **-s** n. pl. Überreste, sterbliche Reste; (lit.) hinterlassene Werke

remake v. wiedermachen, erneuern

remark n. Bemerkung, Anmerkung; **—** v. bemerken, beobachten; äussern; **-able** adj. bemerkenswert, merkwürdig; auffallend

remedy n. Heilmittel: Hilfsmittel, Gegenmittel; Rechtsmittel; **—** v. heilen; (ab)helfen

remember v. sich erinnern, eingedenk sein, behalten

remembrance n. Erinnerung, Andenken; Gedächtnis

remind v. erinnern, mahnen; **-er** n. Verweis, Mahnung; Wink

remit v. übersenden; verzeihen; erlassen, nachlassen; **-tance** n. Sendung; Verzeihung; **-ter** n. Absender, Übersender

remnant n. Überbleibsel, Rest

remodel v. umbilden

remonstrance n. Einwand, Vorstellung, Einspruch

remonstrate v. einwenden, Vorstellungen machen

remorse n. Gewissensbiss, Zerknirschung;

-ful adj. reuevoll, reumütig; **-less** adj. reuelos, gefühllos, hartherzig

remote adj. entfernt, entlegen; **-ness** n. Entfernung, Entlegenheit

removable adj. fortschaffbar; abnehmbar, auswechselbar; absetzbar

removal n. Beseitigung, Wegräumen; Entfernung, Entlassung

remove v. wegschaffen, wegräumen; beseitigen, entfernen; absetzen, entlassen; **-r** n. Spediteur; **spot -r** Fleckenentferner

remunerate v. belohnen, entlohnen

remuneration n. Belohnung, Entschädigung

rend v. (zer)reissen; spalten, bersten

render v. zurückgeben, vergelten; abstatten, leisten; einreichen; übersetzen; (lit.) vortragen; (mech.) ausschmelzen

rendezvous n. Rendezvous, Stelldichein; Treffpunkt

rendition n. Übergabe, Ergebung; Auslieferung; (theat.) Vortrag

renew v. erneuern; **-al** n. Erneuerung

renounce v. entsagen, verzichten auf; verleugnen; (cards) nicht bedienen

renovate v. renovieren, erneuern

renown n. Ruhm, Ruf; Name; **-ed** adj. berühmt, namhaft

rent n. Miete, Pacht; (geol.) Riss, Spalte, Kluft; **—** v. mieten; (ver)pachten; **-al** n. Rentenverzeichnis, Zinsregister; Miete; **-al** adj. Miets-, Pachts-; **-er** n. Mieter, Pächter

renunciation n. Verzichtleistung, Entsagung

reopen v. wieder(er)öffnen

reorder v. neuordnen; erneut bestellen

reorganize v. reorganisieren, neugestalten

repair n. Reparatur, Ausbesserung, Instandsetzung; **—** v. reparieren, ausbessern, instandsetzen; wiedergutmachen; **— shop** Reparaturwerkstatt; **-ed** adj. repariert, ausgebessert

reparable adj. wiederherstellbar; wiedergutzumachen

reparation n. Wiederherstellung; Ersatz, Entschädigung; (pol.) Reparation

repast n. Mahl(zeit)

repatriate v. repatriieren, in die Heimat zurückbringen

repay v. zurückzahlen, entschädigen; belohnen, vergelten

repeal n. Widerruf, Aufhebung; **—** v. widerrufen, aufheben

repeat v. (sich) wiederholen; **-ed** adj. wiederholt; **-er** n. Wiederholer; (law) Vorbestrafte; (pol.) Doppelwähler

repeating decimal n. periodischer Dezimalbruch

repel v. zurücktreiben, zurückstossen, abstossen; **-lent** adj. abstossend; zurückstossend

repent v. bereuen; **-ance** n. Reue; **-ant** adj. reuig; bussfertig

repercussion n. Rückprall; (fig.) Widerhall, Rückwirkung

repertoire n. Repertoire, Spielplan

repetition n. Wiederholung; Vortrag

replace v. ersetzen; wieder hinstellen (or

einsetzen); **-ment** n. Ersatz
replenish v. ergänzen; wieder füllen
reply n. Antwort, Entgegnung; Erwiderung; — v. antworten, entgegnen
report n. Bericht; Schulzeugnis; Gericht; Knall; — v. (sich) melden, berichten, Bericht erstatten; **-er** n. Reporter, Berichterstatter
repose n. Ruhe, Schlaf; — v. (sich) ausruhen, schlafen; ruhen; vertrauen; beruhen
represent v. darstellen, vorstellen; vertreten; **-ation** n. Schilderung, Darstellung; Vorstellung; Vertretung; **-ative** n. Repräsentant, Vertreter; Stellvertreter; **House of Representatives** Abgeordnetenhaus; **-ative** adj. bezeichnend, vorstellend; (stell)vertretend
repress v. unterdrücken, einschränken
reprimand n. Tadel, Verweis; — v. tadeln, einen Verweis erteilen
reprint n. Neudruck, Nachdruck; — v. neudrucken, neuauflegen
reproach n. Vorwurf, Tadel; Schande; — v. vorwerfen, tadeln; schelten
reprobate n. Verworfene, Schuft; — adj. verworfen, ruchlos, verdammt; — v. verwerfen, missbilligen; (rel.) verdammen
reproduce v. reproduzieren, nachbilden
reproduction n. Reproduktion, Nachbildung
reproof n. Vorwurf, Verweis
reprove v. missbilligen, tadeln, rügen
reptile n. Reptil
republic n. Republik; **-an** n. Republikaner; **-an** adj. republikanisch
repudiate v. verwerfen, zurückweisen; verstossen
repudiation n. Verwerfung; Nichtanerkennung; Verstossung
repugnant adj. widersprechend, zuwider; widerstrebend
repulse n. Zurücktreiben; Zurückweisung; — v. zurückschlagen; zurücktreiben; zurückweisen, abschlagen
repulsion n. Zurücktreibung; (phy.) Abstossung; (fig.) Abscheu, Widerwille
repulsive adj. abstossend; widerwärtig
reputable adj. achtbar, anständig; angesehen
reputation n. Ansehen, Ruf
repute v. halten für, hochschätzen
request n. Bitte, Gesuch; Anspruch, Forderung; (com.) Nachfrage; **on** — auf Verlangen; — v. bitten, ersuchen
require v. verlangen, (er)fordern; nötig haben; **-ment** n. Forderung, Bedürfnis; Erfordernis; **-ments** pl. Ansprüche
requisite n. Werkzeug, Zubehör; (fig.) Notwendigkeit; — adj. erforderlich, notwendig
requisition n. Anforderung; (mil.) Requirierung
resale n. Wiederverkauf, Weiterverkauf
rescind v. aufheben, umstossen; für ungültig erklären
rescue n. Rettung, Befreiung; — v. retten, befreien; (law) gewaltsam befreien
research n. Forschung; Nachforschung

resemblance n. Ähnlichkeit
resemble v. ähneln, ähnlich sein, gleichen
resent v. übelnehmen; **-ful** adj. empfindlich; grollend, rachsüchtig; **-ment** n. Empfindlichkeit; Unwille, Rachsucht
reservation n. Vorbehalt; Naturschutzgebiet, Reservat
reserve n. Reserve, Vorrat; Vorsicht, Zurückhaltung; — v. reservieren, aufsparen, aufbewahren; zurückhalten, belegen; **-d** adj. reserviert, vorsichtig; zurückhaltend; belegt, vorgemerkt
reservoir n. Reservoir, Behälter
reset v. wiedereinsetzen; (typ.) neu setzen
reside v. wohnen, ansässig sein, residieren; **-nce** n. Wohnsitz; Aufenthaltsort; Residenz; **-nt** n. Bewohner, Ortsansässige; **-nt** adj. wohnhaft, ansässig; sich aufhaltend; **-ntial** adj. wohnend; Wohn-
residue n. Überrest, Abfall; (chem.) Rückstand; (com.) Restbestand
resign v. entsagen, verzichten; aufgeben, niederlegen; sich abfinden; **-ation** n. Amtsniederlegung, Rücktritt; Ergebung; **-ed** adj. ergeben, resignierend, resigniert
resin n. Harz; **-ous** adj. harz(art)ig; (elec.) negativ
resist v. widerstehen, sich widersetzen; **-ance** n. Widerstand; **-ance coil** Widerstandsspule; **-ant** adj. widerstehend, gegnerisch
resolute adj. resolut, entschlossen, entschieden
resolution n. Auflösung; Entschluss; (pol.) Resolution, Beschluss
resolve n. Entschluss; Beschluss; — v. beschliessen; (auf)lösen; **-d** adj. entschlossen, fest
resonance n. Resonanz; Widerhall
resonant adj. nachklingend, widerhallend
resort n. Zuflucht; Badeort, Kurort; **summer** — Sommerfrische
resource n. Hilfsquelle, Hilfsmittel; Zuflucht; pl. Geldmittel; **-ful** adj. reich an Hilfsquellen; findig
respect n. Respekt, Achtung, Ehrfurcht; Rücksicht, Hinsicht; Beziehung; pl. Grüsse, Empfehlungen; — v. verehren, schätzen, respektieren, achten; betreffen, sich beziehen; berücksichtigen; **-ability** n. Achtbarkeit, Ansehnlichkeit; **-able** adj. achtbar, ansehnlich; (com.) solid, reell; **-ed** adj. angesehen; **-ful** adj. respektvoll, ehrerbietig; **-ing** prep. in Bezug auf, hinsichtlich; **-ive** adj. jedesmalig, jeweilig; **-ively** adv. beziehungsweise
respiration n. Atmen, Atemzug
respond v. antworten, erwidern; reagieren; (law) haften
response n. Antwort, Erwiderung; Reaktion, Erfolg
responsibility n. Verantwortlichkeit, Verantwortung; Verpflichtung
responsible adj. verantwortlich, vertrauenswürdig
responsive adj. empfänglich, entsprechend; beantwortend; Antwort-

rest n. Rest; Stütze, Gestell; Rast, Ruhe, Schlaf; (fig.) Friede, Tod; **— room** Toilette; **— cure** Liegekur; **— v.** rasten, ruhen; liegen, schlafen; (sich) stützen, (sich) lehnen; **-ful** adj. ruhig; beruhigend; **-ive** adj. widerspenstig, störrisch; **-less** adj. rastlos, ruhelos; schlaflos, unruhig; **-lessness** n. Rastlosigkeit; Unruhe

restaurant n. Restaurant

restitution n. Wiederherstellung, Wiedererstattung

restoration n. Wiederherstellung; Wiedereinsetzung; (art) Restaurierung, Erneuerung

restore v. wiederherstellen, wiedereinsetzen; (art) restaurieren, erneuern; (med.) heilen, gesund machen

restrain v. abhalten, zurückhalten, in Schranken halten; unterdrücken, hemmen, hindern; **-t** n. Zurückhaltung; Hindernis, Hemmung, Zwang; Einschränkung; Haft, Gefangenschaft

restrict v. beschränken, einschränken; **-ion** n. Verbot, Einschränkung, Vorbehalt

result n. Resultat, Ergebnis, Folge; **— v.** folgen, sich ergeben

resume v. wiederaufnehmen, wieder anfangen

resurrect v. wiedererwecken; **-ion** n. Auferstehung

resuscitate v. wiederbeleben (durch künstliche Atmung)

retail n. Kleinhandel; Einzelhandel; **at —** im kleinen (or Detail); einzeln; **— v.** im Einzelhandel verkaufen; (coll.) umständlich erzählen; **-er** n. Kleinhändler, Einzelhändler

retain v. zurück(be)halten; festhalten, beibehalten; **-er** n. Anhänger, Dienstmann; Vorschuss; (law) Prozessvollmacht, Anwaltshonorar

retaliate v. vergelten, Vergeltung üben

retaliation n. Wiedervergeltung

retard v. verzögern, verspäten; aufhalten

retention n. Zurückhalten; Beibehaltung

retina n. Retina, Netzhaut

retire v. (sich) zurückziehen; pensionieren; (sports) ausscheiden; **-ment** n. Rücktritt, Ausscheiden; Pensionierung; Zurückgehen

retiring adj. zurückhaltend, bescheiden

retort n. Erwiderung, Entgegnung; (chem.) Retorte; **— v.** zurückgeben, erwidern

retrace v. zurückverfolgen, zurückführen

retract v. zurückziehen, widerrufen; (med.) zusammenziehen, verkürzen; **-able** adj. einziehbar, zurückziehbar

retread n. (tire) neuer Belag; **— v.** neu vulkanisieren; wieder betreten, zurückschreiten

retreat n. Rückzug; Zapfenstreich; Zufluchtsort, Zurückgezogenheit; **— v.** zurücktreten, sich zurückziehen; sich zur Ruhe setzen

retrench v. beschneiden, verkürzen; auslassen; (sich) einschränken; (mil.) sich verschanzen

retrieve v. wiedererlangen, wiederherstellen; ersetzen, gutmachen; (dog) apportieren

retroactive adj. rückwirkend

retrogression n. Rückgang, Rückwärtsgehen; rückläufige Bewegung

return n. Rückkehr, Wiederkehr; Antwort, Erwiderung; (arch.) Seitenflügel; (com.) Rückgabe, Rückzahlung; (law) Wiedervorladung; (med.) Rückfall; (mil.) Bericht, Meldung; (pol.) Wiederwahl; pl. Einnahmen, Gewinne; Statistiken; Wahlberichte, Wahlergebnisse; **in — als** Vergeltung; **in — for** als Ersatz für; **without —** unentgeltlich, umsonst; **by — mail** postwendend; **— match** Revanchepartie; **— ticket** Rückfahrkarte; **— trip** Rückfahrt, Rückreise; **— visit** Gegenbesuch; **— v.** zurückkommen, wiederkehren; antworten, erwidern; (cards) nachspielen; (com.) zurückzahlen, zurückerstatten; (fencing) zurückschlagen; (law) wieder vorladen; (med.) rückfällig sein (or werden); (mil.) berichten, melden; (pol.) wählen; **-able** adj. zurückzugebend

reunion n. Wiedervereinigung; Gesellschaft

reunite v. wiedervereinigen, wieder versöhnen

revaluation n. Aufwertung, Umwertung

reveal v. aufdecken, enthüllen, offenbaren

revel n. Trinkgelage, Schwelgerei; **— v.** schwelgen, schwärmen; **-(l)er** n. Schwärmer; Nachtschwärmer; **-ry** n. lärmende Festlichkeit

revelation n. Enthüllung, Offenbarung

revenge n. Rache, Revanche; Genugtuung; **— v.** rächen, revanchieren; **-ful** adj. rachsüchtig, rächend

revenue n. Einkommen; Zoll; pl. Einkünfte; **— cutter** Zollkutter; **— stamp** Steuermarke, Banderole

revere v. verehren; **-nce** n. Verehrung; Verbeugung; **-nce** v. hochachten, ehrerbietig grüssen; **-nd** adj. ehrwürdig, hochwürdig; Reverend n. Hochwürden; **-nt(ial)** adj. ehrerbietig, ehrfurchtsvoll

reverie, revery n. Träumerei, Schwärmerei

reversal n. Umkehrung, Umstossung; (mech.) Umsteuerung

reverse n. Umkehrung; Rückseite; (fig.) Rückschlag, Schicksalsschlag; Gegenteil; **— adj.** umgekehrt, verkehrt, entgegengesetzt; **— v.** umkehren, umstellen; umstossen; (mech.) umsteuern

revert v. umkehren; zurückkommen; wenden; (law) heimfallen

review n. Durchsicht, Prüfung; Rückblick, Überblick; (educ.) Wiederholung; (law) Revision; (lit.) Kritik, Rezension; (kritische) Zeitschrift, Rundschau; (mil.) Parade, Truppenschau; (theat.) Revue; **— v.** durchsehen, prüfen; zurückblicken auf; (law) revidieren; (lit.) rezensieren, kritisieren; (mil.) mustern, Parade abhalten; **-er** n. Kritiker, Rezensent

revile v. schmähen, verunglimpfen

revise n. nochmalige Durchsicht, Revision; — v. revidieren, nochmals durchsehen

revision n. Revision, nochmalige Durchsicht

revival n. Wiederbelebung, Wiederaufleben; Erneuerung; (law) Wiederinkrafttreten; (rel.) Erweckung; Wiedergeburt; (theat.) Wiederaufführung

revive v. wiederbeleben; erneuern, wieder einführen; wieder aufleben; erwecken

revoke v. widerrufen, aufheben, zurücknehmen; abschwören; (cards) nicht bedienen

revolt n. Revolte, Empörung, Aufruhr; — v. revoltieren, (sich) empören; -ing adj. aufrührerisch; (fig.) empörend, abstossend

revolution n. Revolution, Umsturz, Umbruch, Umschwung; Umdrehung; (ast.) Umlauf, Kreislauf; -ary n. Revolutionär; -ary adj. revolutionär, Umsturz-; -ist n. Revolutionär; -ize v. revolutionieren, aufwiegeln; umgestalten

revolve v. sich drehen um, rotieren, kreisen; (fig.) erwägen, überlegen

revolver n. Revolver

revolving adj. sich drehend, Dreh-

revue n. Revue

reward n. Belohnung, Vergeltung; Preis; — v. belohnen, vergelten

rewrite v. nochmals schreiben, umschreiben

rhapsody n. Rhapsodie

Rhenish Palatinate n. Rheinpfalz

rhetoric n. Rhetorik; -al adj. rhetorisch

rheumatic adj. rheumatisch

rheumatism n. Rheumatismus

RH-factor n. (med.) Rhesusfaktor

rhinoceros n. Rhinozeros, Nashorn

rhubarb n. Rhabarber

rhyme n. Reim, Vers, Gedicht; — v. (sich) reimen, dichten; -ster n. Verseschmied

rhythm n. Rhythmus; -ic(al) adj. rhythmisch

rib n. Rippe; (naut.) Spant; — v. rippen; (coll.) spotten; -bed adj. gerippt, geriffelt

ribbon n. Band, Borte; Streifen; -s pl. Zügel; Fetzen; **typewriter** — Farbband; — v. bebändern

rice n. Reis; — **paper** Reispapier

rich adj. reich; nahrhaft, kräftig, fett; ergiebig, fruchtbar; (mus.) voll.; (coll.) gepfeffert, gelungen; -es n. pl. Reichtümer, Vermögen; -ness n. Reichtum; Reichhaltigkeit, Gehalt; Pracht

rickety adj. rachitisch; (fig.) gebrechlich, hinfällig, schwach

rid v. befreien, freimachen; **get — of** loswerden; **-dance** n. Befreiung

riddle n. Rätsel; Sieb; — v. enträtseln, erraten; sieben

ride n. Ritt, Fahrt; — v. reiten, fahren; — **a bicycle** radfahren; — **at anchor** vor Anker liegen; **-r** n. Reiter; Fahrer, Fahrende; (arch.) Strebe; (com.) Beiblatt; (law) Zusatz

ridge n. Rückgrat, Rücken; (agr.) Furche, Rain; (arch.) First; (geol.) Kamm, Grat; Kette; — v. (sich) furchen

ridgepole n. Dachfosten

ridicule n. Lächerliches; Spott, Hohn; — v. lächerlich machen, bespötteln

ridiculous adj. lächerlich

riding n. Reiten; Fahren; reitend, fahrend; — **boot** Reitstiefel; — **breeches** Reithose; — **master** Reitlehrer, Stallmeister; — **school** Reitbahn

riffraff n. Abfall, Ausschuss; (coll.) Gesindel

rifle n. Gewehr, Büchse, Stutzen; — **barrel** Gewehrlauf; — **corps** Schützenabteilung; — **range** Schiessplatz, Scheibenstand; Schussweite; — v. rauben, plündern

rifleman n. Scharfschütze; (mil.) Jäger

rift n. Riss, Spalte, Ritze, Sprung

rig n. Takelung; — v. aufputzen; ausrüsten; (naut.) auftakeln; -ging n. Takelage

right n. Recht; Richtige; Rechte, rechte Seite; Anrecht, Vorrecht, Anspruch; **all -s reserved** alle Rechte vorbehalten; **by -s** von Rechts wegen, eigentlich; — **and wrong** Gutes und Böses; **to the** — nach rechts; — adj. recht, richtig; gerade; (law) rechtmässig, gesetzmässig, gerecht; — **angle** rechter Winkel; — adv. ganz, gänzlich; gerade, genau; augenblicklich; geradesweg; richtig; **all** — schon gut, einverstanden; **be** — recht haben; übereinstimmen; **it serves him** — es geschieht ihm recht; **against** gerade gegenüber; — **ahead** geradeaus; — **away** sofort, sogleich; — **off** gleich (fort), gleich davon; — **on** geradezu, **set** — berichtigen, zurechtweisen; reparieren; —! interj. recht! gut! richtig! — v. (avi.) abfangen, abschiessen; (law) Recht verschaffen; (naut.) aufrichten; -eous adj. rechtschaffen, redlich; gerecht; -ist n. Rechtsradikale

rightabout n. Rechtswendung

right-angled adj. rechtwinklig

right-hand adj. rechtshändig; recht, rechtschaffen; **to the — side** nach rechts, zur rechten Seite (or Hand)

rigid adj. starr, steif; unbeugsam, nachsichtslos; -ity n. Starrheit, Steifheit; Festigkeit, Strenge, Härte; Unbeugsamkeit

rigmarole n. Geschwätz, Salbaderei

rigor n. Strenge, Härte; (med.) Schüttelfrost; — **mortis** Leichenstarre, Totenstarre; -ous adj. streng, hart; scharf, genau

rim n. Rand, Krempe; Radkranz, Felge

rime n. Reif, Rauhfrost

rind n. Rinde, Borke; Schale

ring n. Ring; Kreis; Reif; Öse, Öhr; (mus.) Schall, Klang; Geläute; — **finger** Ringfinger; — v. beringen; umringen; kreisen; klingen, klingeln, läuten; — **in** einläuten; — **out** ausläuten; — **the bell** die Glocke läuten; (coll.) Lärm schlagen; — **up** anrufen; -ing n. Klingeln;

-ing *adj.* klingelnd; brausend
ringleader *n.* Rädelsführer, Anführer
ringworm *n.* Ringelflechte
rink *n.* Eisbahn; Rollschuhbahn
rinse *v.* (aus)spülen, ausschwenken
riot *n.* Aufstand, Aufruhr; Lärm, Tumult; — *v.* Aufruhr stiften; lärmen, toben; schwelgen; **-er** *n.* Aufrührer, Meuterer; Schwelger; **-ous** *adj.* aufrührerisch; lärmend, schwelgerisch; liederlich
rip *n.* Riss; (coll.) Kerl; — **cord** Reissleine; — *v.* (zer)reissen; auftrennen; **-ping** *adj.* aufreissend; (sl.) famos
ripe *adj.* reif; **-n** *v.* reifen
ripple *n.* kleine Welle; Kräuselung; Geriesel; — *v.* (sich) kräuseln; plätschern, rieseln
rise *n.* Aufstehen; Aufsteigen; Aufstieg; Erhöhung, Steigung; Zuwachs, Zunahme; Steigerung; Ursprung; (arch.) Bogenhöhe, Durchgang; (com.) Steigen, Aufschlag; (mus.) Anschwellen; (sun) Sonnenaufgang; — *v.* aufstehen, sich erheben, aufsteigen; emporkommen, heraufkommen; aufgehen; entstehen, wachsen, zunehmen; (mus.) anschwellen; — **above** übertreffen; **-r** *n.* Aufstehende; Frühaufsteher; Aufständische
risk *n.* Risiko, Gefahr, Wagnis; — *v.* riskieren, wagen, aufs Spiel setzen; **-y** *adj.* riskant, gefährlich, gewagt
ritual *n.* Ritual; — *adj.* rituell, feierlich
rival *n.* Rivale, Nebenbuhler, Konkurrent; — *adj.* wetteifernd, nebenbuhlerisch, Konkurrenz-; — *v.* rivalisieren, wetteifern, konkurrieren; **-ry** *n.* Rivalität, Konkurrenz; Wetteifer
river *n.* Fluss, Strom; — **bed** Flussbett; — **horse** Flusspferd
riverside *n.* Flussufer; Flusseite
rivet *n.* Niet(e); — *v.* (ver)nieten; befestigen, heften
roach *n.* Küchenschabe; (ichth.) Plötze, Rotauge
road *n.* Strasse, Weg; Fahrbahn; (min.) Strecke; (naut.) Reede; (coll.) Eisenbahn; **main** — Hauptstrasse; **paved** — Pflasterstrasse; **metal** Schotter; **-ster** *n.* Tourenwagen
roadblock *n.* Strassensperre; Hindernis
roadway *n.* Fahrdamm; Strassendamm; (min.) Förderbahn
roam *v.* umherstreifen, durchstreifen
roar *n.* Gebrüll; Brausen, Krachen; Rollen, Donnern; — *v.* brüllen; brausen, krachen; rollen, donnern; **-ing** *adj.* brüllend; geräuschvoll; (coll.) kolossal
roast *n.* Braten; — *adj.* — **beef** Roastbeef, Rinderbraten; — *v.* braten, rösten; (mech.) brennen, backen; **-er** *n.* Röster; Bratrost; Spanferkel, Brathuhn
rob *v.* (be)rauben; **-ber** *n.* Räuber; **-bery** *n.* Raub; **highway -bery** Strassenraub
robe *n.* Robe, Staatskleid; Talar, Amtskleid; — *v.* (sich) kleiden; schmücken
robin *n.* Rotkehlchen
robot *n.* Robot; Maschinenmensch
robust *adj.* robust, derb, kräftig
rock *n.* Fels; Stein; Klippe; (coll.)

Schaukel; — **bottom** Urboden; Wirklichkeit; — **crystal** Bergkristall; — **garden** Steingarten; — **salt** Steinsalz; — *v.* schwanken, wiegen, schaukeln; **-er** *n.* Kufe; **-er** *adj.*, **-er arm** Kipphebel; **-ing** *adj.* schaukelnd, wiegend; **-ing chair** Schaukelstuhl; **-y** *adj.* felsig
rocket *n.* Rakete; — **base** *n.* Raketenbasis; **circumlunar** — Mondrakete; **ferry** — Raketenfähre; **multi-stage** — Vielstufenrakete; **retro** — Rückfeuerungsrakete; Bremsrakete; **secondary** — Landerakete
rocket-propelled *adj.* raketengetrieben; — **plane** Raketenflugzeug
rod *n.* Rute, Stab, Stange; **connecting** — Verbindungsstange
rodent *n.* Nagetier
Roger! *interj.* (avi.) Viktor-Viktor!
rogue *n.* Landstreicher; Schurke, Spitzbube
roll *n.* Rolle; Walze, Welle; Semmel, Brötchen; Verzeichnis, Liste; Rollen; Wirbel; (naut.) Schlingern; **call the** — namentlich aufrufen; — **call** Namensaufruf; (mil.) Appell; — *v.* rollen, walzen; wälzen; wirbeln; (naut.) schlingern; — **the drum** Trommelwirbel schlagen; **-er** *n.* Rollende, Walzer; Walze, Rolle; (naut.) Sturzsee; (orn.) Roller; Tümmlertaube; **-er bearing** Rollager; **-er coaster** Fahruntersatz; Berg- und Talbahn; **-er skate** Rollschuh; **-er towel** endloses Handtuch; **-ing** *adj.* rollend; wellenförmig; **-ing mill** Walzwerk; **-ing pin** Nudelholz; **-ing stock** rollendes Material, Wagenpark
rollicking *adj.* ausgelassen, übermütig
roll-top desk *n.* Rollschreibtisch
roly-poly *n.* Teigrolle; (coll.) rundliche Person; — *adj.* kugelrund
Roman *n.* Römer; — *adj.* römisch; — **type** Antiquaschrift
romance *n.* Romanze; Erdichtung, Erzählung; Romantik; **Romance** *adj.* romanisch; — *v.* erdichten; aufschneiden
romantic *adj.* romantisch; **-ism** *n.* Romantik
romp *n.* Balgerei; (coll.) Range; — *v.* tollen, toben; sich balgen; **-ers** *n. pl.* Spielanzug
roof *n.* Dach, First; — **of the mouth** Gaumen; — **garden** Dachgarten; — *v.* bedachen, überdachen; (fig.) bergen, schützen; **-ing** *n.* Dachdeckerarbeit; Bedachung; Dachmaterial
rook *n.* (chess) Turm; (orn.) Saatkrähe; (coll.) Bauernfänger, Betrüger; — *v.* (chess) rochieren; (coll.) betrügen
rookie *n.* Neuling, Anfänger
room *n.* Raum, Platz; Zimmer, Stube; (fig.) Gelegenheit, Spielraum; **-er** *n.* Mieter, Mitbewohner; **-y** *adj.* geräumig, weitläufig
roommate *n.* Stubengenosse
roost *n.* Hühnerstange; Hühnerstall; (coll.) Ruheplatz; — *v.* (wie Hühner auf der Stange) sitzen (*or* schlafen);

–er n. Hahn

root n. Wurzel; (gram.) Stammwort; (mus.) Grundton; (fig.) Quelle, Ursache, Ursprung; **take —** Wurzel fassen (or schlagen); **—** v. (ein)wurzeln; (um)wühlen; (fig.) einprägen; **— out** ausroden, ausjäten; vertilgen; **–ed** adj. eingewurzelt, verwurzelt; eingebettet, eingelagert; **–er** n. Ausrotter, Vertilger; (sl.) Anhänger

rope n. Tau, Seil, Strick, Strang, Schnur; (naut.) Reep; **—** v. mit einem Seil zusammenschnüren (or fangen); anseilen

ropedancer, ropewalker n. Seiltänzer

rosary n. Rosengarten, Rosenbeet; (eccl.) Rosenkranz

rose n. Rose; Rosa, Rosenfarbe; Windrose; Rosette; (mech.) Brause; **–tte** n. Rosette

rosebud n. Rosenknospe

rosebush n. Rosenstock, Rosenstrauch

rosewood n. Rosenholz

rosin n. Geigenharz, Kolophonium; **—** v. mit Harz einreiben (or überziehen); harzen

roster n. Verzeichnis, Liste; (mil.) Diensttabelle

rostrum n. Tribüne, Rednerpult; Schnabel

rosy adj. rosig, rosenrot; (fig.) blühend

rot n. Fäule, Fäulnis; Verwesung; (sl.) Unsinn, Gewäsch; **—** v. (ver)faulen, verwesen, vermodern, verrotten; (coll.) verkommen; **–ten** adj. faul(ig), verfault; stinkend; mürbe; morsch, verfallen; (coll.) verdorben, niederträchtig

rotary adj. rotierend, kreisend; sich drehend; **— press** Rotationsmaschine

rotate v. rotieren, sich drehen, kreisen; (ab)wechseln

rotation n. Rotation, Umdrehung; Abwechslung, Folge

rote n. Routine; **by —** durch blosse Übung, rein mechanisch

rotogravure n. Fotogravüre

rotor n. drehender Zylinder

rotund adj. rund, kreisförmig; abgerundet; (mus.) volltönend

rouge n. rote Farbe (or Schminke), Rouge; (mech.) Polierrot, Englischrot

rough n. Rohe, Unbearbeitete, Grobe; **—** adj. roh, erstmalig; rauh, holprig, uneben; ungebildet; (naut.) stürmisch; **— draft** erster Überschlag (or Entwurf); **–en** v. rauhen; rauh machen (or werden); (fig.) verwildern; **–ness** n. Rauheit, Roheit; Heftigkeit

rough-and-ready adj. grob aber zuverlässig; gerade recht

round n. Runde; Kreis; Kreislauf, Umlauf; (arch.) Rundgang; (mil.) Salve, Ladung; (mus.) Rundgesang; **—** adj. rund, kreisförmig; abgerundet; voll, ganz; beträchtlich; offen; gründlich; **make —** abrunden; **— number** runde Zahl; **— steak** rundes Steak (vom Rindsschenkel); **— table** grüner Tisch; Forum; Diskussionsgruppe; **— trip** Rundreise; **—** adv. ringsumher, in der Runde; **all the year —** das ganze Jahr hindurch; **—** v. (ab)runden; umgeben, einfassen; umfahren, umbiegen; (naut.) umsegeln; **— up** zusammentreiben, einkreisen; **–ness** n. Rundung, Rundheit; (fig.) Geradheit, Offenheit

roundabout adj. weitläufig, umständlich; (fig.) umfassend, weitschauend

roundhouse n. (rail.) Lokomotivenschuppen; (naut.) Hinterdeckkajüte

roundup n. Zusammentreiben, Einkreisung

rouse v. (auf)wecken, aufwachen; (hunting) aufjagen, aufstöbern; (fig.) erregen, anregen

roustabout n. Dockarbeiter; Gelegenheitsarbeiter; Handlanger

rout n. Bande, Rotte; Rudel; Flucht; **—** v. aufstöbern; in die Flucht schlagen, vernichten

route n. Route, Strasse; Strecke

rove v. umherstreifen, umherwandern; **–r** n. Landstreicher, Vagabund

row n. Rudern; Reihe, Linie; Lärm, Prügelei; **—** v. rudern; (auf)reihen, anreihen; lärmen, prügeln; (coll.) ausschelten; verderben; **–dy** n. Rowdy, Raufbold, Strolch; **–dy** adj. lärmend, händelsüchtig; gewalttätig, roh

rowboat n. Ruderboot

royal adj. königlich; (fig.) fürstlich, prächtig; **–ist** n. Royalist; **–ty** n. Königtum; Königshaus; Mitglied der königlichen Familie; (lit.) Tantieme

rub n. Reiben, Abreibung; (coll.) Klemme; Stichelei; **—** v. reiben; (ab)wischen, einreiben; (ab)scheuern, putzen; **— against** anstossen, anstreifen; **— down** abreiben, striegeln; (coll.) ausschimpfen; **–ber** n. Reiber; Waschlappen

rubber n. Gummi; Gummireifen; **–s** n. pl. Gummischuhe; **hard —** Hartgummi; **— band** Gummiband; **— cement** Klebestoff; **— gasket** Gummidichtung; **— plant** Gummipflanze; (mech.) Kautschukfabrik; **— stamp** Gummistempel; (coll.) automatische Zustimmung; **–ize** v. gummieren, mit Gummi beziehen

rubbish n. Schutt, Kehricht; Plunder, Schund; Wirrwarr; (coll.) Unsinn

rubble n. Geschiebe, Geröll; Trümmergestein

rubdown n. Abreibung; **—** v. abreiben

ruby n. Rubin; Rubinrot

rudder n. Ruder; Steuerruder; (avi.) Seitensteuer

rude adj. grob, unhöflich, roh; wild, heftig; rauh; (fig.) ungebildet, kunstlos; **–ness** n. Grobheit, Roheit; Rauheit

rudiment n. Rudiment, Ansatz

ruffian n. Grobian, Raufbold; Schuft, Lump; **—** adj. roh, wüst, rauflustig

ruffle n. Manschette; Halskrause; Kräuseln; (mil.) Trommelwirbel; (fig.) Unruhe, Aufregung; **—** v. falten, kräuseln; zerknittern, zerdrücken; (fig.) beunruhigen

rug n. Decke, Teppich; Vorleger; **—** v. zerren

rugged *adj.* rauh; zottig; zerzaust; uneben, gefurcht

ruin *n.* Ruin; Zusammenbruch, Untergang, Verderben; *pl.* Ruinen; — *v.* ruinieren, verderben; zerstören, verheeren; **-ous** *adj.* verfallen, baufällig, schadhaft; verderblich

rule *n.* Lineal; Masstab; Regel, Verordnung, Verfügung, Vorschrift; Norm, Richtschnur; (law) Rechtsgrundsatz; (pol.) Regierung, Geschäftsordnung; **as a — in der Regel; — of three** Regeldetri; **standard —** Normalmass; — *v.* linieren; regeln, anordnen, festsetzen; leiten, regieren, beherrschen; entscheiden, verfügen; **-r** *n.* Lineal; Herrscher

ruling *n.* Regelung; (law) Entscheidung; — *adj.* herrschend; vorherrschend

rum *n.* Rum; — *adj.* seltsam, wunderlich

rumba *n.* Rumba; — *v.* Rumba tanzen

rumble *v.* rumpeln, rasseln

ruminant *n.* Wiederkäuer; — *adj.* wiederkäuend; (coll.) nachdenklich

ruminate *v.* wiederkäuen; (coll.) grübeln, nachdenken

rummage *n.* Durchsuchen, Kramen; Umwälzung; **— sale** Ramschverkauf; — *v.* durchsuchen, durchstöbern; wühlen

rumor *n.* Gerücht, Gerede; — *v.* Gerüchte verbreiten (*or* aussprengen)

rump *n.* Rumpf; Rest; (orn.) Bürzel; (zool.) Hinterteil, Kreuz, Steiss

run *n.* Lauf; Laufen, Rennen; Verlauf, Gang; Ausflug, Reise; Bach, Fluss; (com.) Sorte; Andrang, Zulauf, Nachfrage; (mech.) Betrieb, Leistung; (mus.) Lauf; (naut.) Route; Geschwindigkeit; (theat.) Aufführungsserie; **in the long —** auf die Dauer; **am Ende;** — *v.* rennen, laufen, eilen; fliessen, strömen, rinnen; umlaufen, zirkulieren; leiten, betreiben; lauten; **— across** zufällig treffen, in die Quere kommen; **— aground** auflaufen, scheitern; **— away** durchgehen, davonlaufen; **— down** (her)ablaufen; abhetzen; (naut.) auf Grund setzen; (coll.) schlecht machen; **— for office** sich um ein Amt bewerben; **— into** sich belaufen; treffen; **— off** davonlaufen, durchgehen; **— over** überfahren; überlaufen; **— out of** sich ausgeben, sich erschöpfen; **— the risk** Gefahr laufen, riskieren; **-ner** *n.* Renner, Läufer; (bot.) Ausläufer; (mech.) Schieber; Kufe; **-ning** *n.* Rennen; Lauf, Gang; **-ning** *adj.* laufend, rennend, fliessend; ununterbrochen; **-ning board** Trittbrett; **-ning gear** Getriebe; **-ning mate** (pol.) Nebenkandidat; (race) Schrittmacher; **-ning water** fliessendes Wasser

runaway *n.* Flüchtling, Ausreisser; Durchgänger

run-down *adj.* abfliessend, ablaufend; erschöpft, heruntergebracht

rung *n.* Sprosse

runner-up *n.* Zweite (im Endkampf)

runway *n.* Lauf; Tierpfad; (avi.) Rollbahn

rupture *n.* Bruch; — *v.* brechen; sprengen

rural *adj.* ländlich; bäuerlich; Land-

ruse *n.* List, Kunstgriff

rush *n.* Anstrum, Andrang; (bot.) Binse; **— hours** Hauptverkehrsstunden, Hauptgeschäftsstunden; **— order** Eilauftrag; — *v.* (sich) stürzen, drängen; eilen, jagen, stürmen; schiessen, rauschen

Russia *n.* Russland

Russian *n.* Russe; — *adj.* russisch

rust *n.* Rost, Moderfleck; (bot.) Brand; (fig.) Untätigkeit; — *v.* (ver)rosten; modern; **-y** *adj.* rostig, verrostet; moderfleckig; (bot.) brandig; (fig.) rostfarben, abgetragen, verschossen

rustic *n.* Landmann; (arch.) Bossenwerk; — *adj.* ländlich, bäuerisch

rustle *n.* Rascheln, Rauschen; — *v.* rascheln, rauschen; (coll.) sich rühren (*or* dranhalten)

rustproof *adj.* rostsicher

rut *n.* Geleise; (zool.) Brunst, Brunft; — *v.* furchen; brunsten, brunften

rutabaga *n.* Kohlrübe

ruthless *adj.* unbarmherzig, grausam

rye *n.* Roggen; **— field** Roggenfeld

S

sabbath *n.* Sabbat; (fig.) Ruhetag

saber, sabre *n.* Säbel, Schwert

sable *n.* Zobel; Zobelfell

sabotage *n.* Sabotage

saboteur *n.* Saboteur

SAC (Strategic Air Command) *n.* Strategisches Luftkommando

saccharine *n.* Sacharin

sack *n.* Sack, Tasche; (mil.) Plünderung; (coll.) Laufpass, Entlassung; — *v.* einsacken; plündern; entlassen

sackcloth *n.* Sackleinen

sacrament *n.* Sakrament

sacred *adj.* heilig; geweiht; sakral, geistlich

sacrifice *n.* Opfer; — *v.* opfern, aufs Spiel setzen; mit Verlust verkaufen; **— oneself** sich aufopfern

sacrilege *n.* Sakrileg, Kirchenschändung

sad *adj.* traurig, kläglich, jämmerlich; schlimm; dunkel; **— sack** (sl.) nasser Sack, trübe Tasse, Kaczmarek; **-den** *v.* (sich) betrüben; schwärzen; **-ness** *n.* Traurigkeit, Schwermut

saddle *n.* Sattel; **— horse** Reitpferd; — *v.* satteln

saddlebag *n.* Satteltasche

safari *n.* Safari, Expedition

safe *n.* Safe, Bankfach; Geldschrank; — *adj.* sicher, unversehrt; ausser Gefahr; gesund; zuverlässig; **— and sound** frisch und gesund; **-ty** *n.* Sicherheit; **-ty belt** Rettungsgürtel; (avi.) Anschnallgurt; **-ty catch** Sicherheitskette; **-ty island** Schutzinsel; **-ty pin** Sicherheitsnadel; **-ty valve** Sicherheitsventil

safebreaker *n.* Geldschrankknacker

safe-conduct *n.* sicheres Geleit; Schutzbrief

safe-deposit *adj.* gesichert; **— box** einbruchssicherer Schrank

safeguard n. Schutz; Eskorte, Konvoy; — v. beschützen, schirmen

safelight n. Farbfilter; Dunkelkammerlampe

saffron n. Safran

sag n. Senkung; — v. sacken, sich senken, durchhängen, nachgeben; (naut.) nach Lee treiben

saga n. Sage

sage n. Weise; (bot.) Salbei; — adj. weise, verständig

sagebrush n. Wermut, Edelraute

Sagittarius n. Schütze

sail n. Segel; Segelfahrt; — v. segeln; fahren, durchsegeln; -ing n. Segeln; Segelschiffahrt; -ings n. pl. Schiffsabfahrtzeiten; -ing adj. segelnd; -or n. Matrose, Seemann

sailboat n. Segelboot

sailfish n. fliegender Fisch

saint n. Heilige; **guardian —** Schutzheilige; **Saint** adj. Sankt, Heilige; — v. heiligsprechen; -ly adj. heilig, geheiligt; fromm

sake n. for God's — um Gottes willen; for my — meinetwegen

salad n. Salat; — bowl Salatschüssel; — dressing Salatsosse

salamander n. Salamander, Molch

salary n. Gehalt, Besoldung

sale n. Verkauf, Absatz; Umsatz; Auktion; **clearance —** Räumungsausverkauf; **-s tax** Verkaufssteuer; — **price** Verkaufspreis

salesclerk n. Verkäufer(in)

salesman n. Vertreter; **traveling —** Geschäftsreisende; **-ship** n. Verkaufsgewandtheit, Kunst des Verkaufens

salesroom n. Verkaufsraum

saliva n. Speichel

sallow adj. blass, gleich, gelblich

salmon n. Salm, Lachs; Lachsfarbe; — adj. lachsfarben; — **trout** Lachsforelle

saloon n. Salon, Empfangszimmer; Saal; (coll.) Kneipe

salt n. Salz; (fig.) Würze, Witz; — adj. salzig, gesalzen, gepökelt; — **mine** Saline; — **water** Salzwasser, Seewasser; — v. (ein) salzen, pökeln; -y adj. salzig; pikant

saltpeter, saltpetre n. Salpeter

saltshaker n. Salzstreuer

salutation n. Begrüssung; Gruss

salute n. Gruss; (mil.) Salut, Salutieren; — v. grüssen, salutieren

salvation n. Erlösung; Rettung

salve n. Salbe, Heilmittel; — v. salben, heilen; beruhigen; retten

same adj. nämlich, gleich; ebenerwähnt, vorerwähnt, besagt; derselbe, dieselbe, dasselbe; (fig.) einförmig, eintönig; **all the —** dessenungeachtet, gleichwohl; **it's all the —** to me es ist mir einerlei (or ganz gleich); **-ness** n. Gleichheit, Identität; Eintönigkeit

sample n. Probe, Muster; — v. (aus)probieren, kosten; Proben zeigen (or nehmen); **-r** n. Probennehmer; Mustersticktuch

sanatorium n. Sanatorium, Heilanstalt

sanctify v. weihen; heiligen

sanctimonious adj. frömmelnd, scheinheilig

sanction n. Sanktion, Sühnemassnahme; Genehmigung, Bestätigung; Gesetz; — v. sanktionieren, gutheissen, bestätigen

sanctuary n. Heiligtum, Freistätte; Tempel

sanctum n. heilige Stätte; (fig.) Privatgemach

sand n. Sand; — **pit** Sandgrube; **-y** adj. sand(art)ig

sandal n. Sandale

sandalwood n. Sandelbaum, Sandelholz

sandbag n. Sandsack; — v. mit Sandsäcken verstopfen (or niederschlagen)

sandblast n. Sandstrahlgebläse

sandbox n. Sandkiste; (rail.) Sandstreuer

sandpaper n. Sandpapier

sandstone n. Sandstein

sandstorm n. Sandsturm

sandwich n. Sandwich; belegtes Brot; — **man** Plakatträger; — v. zusammenklappen, aufeinanderlegen; einlegen

sane adj. geistig gesund, vernünftig

San Francisco n. San Francisco

sanguine adj. vollblütig, blutreich; (fig.) sanguinisch, zuversichtlich

sanitary adj. sanitär; Gesundheits-

sanitation n. Gesundheitswesen

sanity n. geistige Gesundheit

sap n. Saft; (mil.) Sappe, Laufgraben; (fig.) Lebenskraft, Mark; (coll.) Schwachkopf; — v. untergraben; -ling n. junger Baum; (coll.) Grünschnabel

sapphire n. Saphir; Saphirblau

sarcasm n. Sarkasmus, bitterer Spott

sarcastic adj. sarkastisch

sardine n. Sardine

sash n. Fensterrahmen; (mil.) Feldbinde, Schärpe

Satan n. Satan

satanic adj. satanisch

satchel n. Schulmappe; Umhängetasche

sateen n. Satin

satelite n. Satellit, Trabant

satin n. Atlas

satire n. Satire

satiric(al) adj. satirisch

satirize v. verspotten, bespötteln

satisfaction n. Genugtuung, Befriedigung; Zufriedenheit; Bezahlung, Tilgung

satisfactory adj. befriedigend, zufriedenstellend; genügend

satisfy v. genügen, befriedigen; zufrieden stellen; bezahlen; sühnen; überzeugen

saturate v. sättigen, völlig durchdringen

Saturday n. Sonnabend, Samstag

satyr n. Satyr

sauce n. Sosse, Tunke; (coll.) Würze; — v. mit einer Sosse versehen, würzen; (coll.) unverschämt sein

saucer n. Untertasse; Untersatz

saucy adj. frech, unverschämt; (coll.) pikant

sauerkraut n. Sauerkraut

sausage n. Wurst; **pork —** Bratwurst aus Schweinefleisch

savage n. Wilde, Barbar; — adj. wild, wüst; roh, barbarisch; **-ry** n. Wildheit,

Roheit; Barbarei

save v. retten, bergen; aufbewahren; erlösen; (er)sparen, schonen; — prep. ausser, ausgenommen; unbeschadet, ohne; -r n. Retter; Sparer

saving n. Rettung; pl. Ersparnisse; -s **bank** Sparkasse; — adj. rettend; sparsam, haushälterisch; vorbehaltend

savio(u)r n. Retter, Erlöser; **Savior** Heiland

saw n. Säge; — v. sägen

sawdust n. Sägespäne, Sägemehl

sawmill n. Sägemühle, Schneidemühle

Saxony n. Sachsen

saxophone n. Saxophon

say n. Rede, Meinung, Wort; — v. sagen, sprechen; berichten; aufsagen, vortragen; anführen, erwähnen; entscheiden; widersprechen, bestreiten; meinen; — **mass** Messe lesen; **that is to** — das heisst; **-ing** n. Redensart, Ausspruch; Gerede; Sprichwort

scab n. Schorf, Räude; (coll.) Lump; (sl.) Streikbrecher

scabbard n. Scheide

scaffold n. Schaffott; (arch.) Gerüst; (theat.) Schaubühne, Zuschauertribüne; **-ing** n. Gerüst; Rüstmaterial

scald v. Verbrennung, Brandwunde; — v. verbrennen, verbrühen; abkochen, ausbrühen

scale n. Schuppe; (math.) Gradeinteilung, Masstab, Zahlensystem; (mech.) Waage, Waagschale; (mus.) Tonleiter, Skala; (fig.) Stufenleiter, Abstufung; **platform** — Brückenwaage; — v. schuppen, abschaben, abscharren; (ab)wiegen, wägen; (art) richtig darstellen; (mil.) erstürmen, ersteigen; (fig.) prüfen

scallop n. Kammuschel; Muschelform; Langette, Auszackung; — v. in der Schale (or mit geriebener Semmel) zubereiten

scalp n. Skalp, Kopfhaut; (coll.) Perücke; — v. skalpieren; (com.) schwarzhandeln, spekulieren, schachern; **-er** n. Skalpierende; Spekulant; **ticket -er** Schwarzhändler für Eintrittskarten

scamp n. Schuft; Taugenichts; **-er** n. Pfuscher; Ausreisser

scandal n. Skandal; **-ize** v. Ärgernis geben; **-ous** adj. skandalös

Scandinavian n. Skandinavier; — adj. skandinavisch

scant(y) adj. knapp, kärglich, dürftig; beschränkt

scapegoat n. Sündenbock

scar n. Narbe, Schramme; Klippe, Steilhang; — v. schrammen; vernarben

scarab(aeous) n. Mistkäfer; Skarabäus

scarce adj. selten, rar; spärlich, knapp; **-ly** adv. kaum

scarcity n. Seltenheit; Teuerung, Mangel

scare n. Schrecken, Panik; — v. erschrecken, scheuchen

scarecrow n. Vogelscheuche; Schreckbild

scarf n. Schal, Halstuch; Schärpe; (mech.) Lasche

scarfpin n. Schalnadel; Krawattennadel

scarlet n. Scharlach, Scharlachrot; — adj.

scharlachrot, scharlachfarben; — **fever** Scharlachfieber

scatter v. (sich) zerstreuen, verbreiten; ausstreuen

scatterbrained adj. flatterhaft, zerstreut, faselig

scavenger n. Strassenkehrer; (enth.) Aaskäfer; Mistkäfer; (zool.) Aasgeier

scenario n. Drehbuch, Filmmanuskript

scenarist n. Drehbuchautor

scene n. Szene, Auftritt; Schauplatz; pl. Kulissen, Dekoration; **-ry** n. Szenerie, Gegend. Bild; (theat.) Dekoration

scenic(al) adj. szenisch, dramatisch; malerisch

scent n. Geruch; Duft, Wohlgeruch; (hunting) Witterung, Fährte; — v. riechen; durchduften; wittern

scepter, sceptre n. Zepter

sceptic(al) adj. skeptisch, zweifelnd

schedule n. Zettel; Verzeichnis, Tabelle; Fahrplan; — v. aufzeichnen, festlegen; anhängen

schematic adj. schematisch

scheme n. Schema; Plan, System; — v. schematisieren, planen, entwerfen; (coll.) Ränke schmieden; **-r** n. Plänemacher, Projektemacher; (coll.) Ränkeschmied

schism n. Schisma

scholar n. Schüler; Gelehrte; (educ.) Stipendiat; **-ly** adj. gelehrt; **-ship** n. Gelehrsamkeit; (educ.) Stipendium

school n. Schule; (ichth.) Zug; (whales) Herde; **high** — Mittelschule, höhere Schule: — v. schulen, unterrichten, bilden; **-ing** n. Schulunterricht; Schulzucht

schoolhouse n. Schulhaus, Schulgebäude

schoolteacher n. Schullehrer

schooner n. Schoner

science n. Wissenschaft; Kenntnis, Kunst

scientific adj. wissenschaftlich, gelehrt; systematisch

scientist n. Gelehrte, Wissenschaftler; Forscher

scissors n. pl. Schere

sclerosis n. Sklerose, Verkalkung; Geweberverhärtung

scold n. Schelter; — v. schelten, zanken, keifen; **-ing** n. Schelte

scoop n. Schaufel; Schippe; Schöpfkelle; (geol.) Höhlung, Vertiefung; (med.) Spatel; (newspaper sl.) Sensationsnachricht; (coll.) Gewinn; — v. (aus)schaufeln; (aus)schöpfen; aushöhlen; (coll.) zusammenscharren

scooter n. Segelschlitten; (toy) Roller

scope n. Ausdehnung, Reichweite, Spielraum; Gesichtskreis; Absicht, Zweck, Ziel

scorch v. rösten, versengen, verbrennen; (coll.) spotten; (sl.) dahinsausen

score n. Kerbe; Rechnung, Zeche; Schuld, Posten; zwanzig Stück; (mus.) Partitur; (sports) Spielstand **what's the —?** wie steht das Spiel? — v. kerben; aufschreiben; (mus.) instrumentieren; (sports) Spielstand verzeichnen, Punkte gewinnen

scorn n. Verachtung; Hohn, Spott; — v. geringschätzen, verachten; verhöhnen; **-ful** adj. verächtlich; höhnisch, spöttisch

scorpion n. Skorpion

Scot n. Schotte; **-ch** adj., **-tish** adj. schottisch

scoundrel n. Schurke, Schuft, Lump

scour v. scheuern, reinigen; entfetten; eilen, jagen; durchstöbern; **-ge** n. Geissel; Peitsche, Rute; **-ge** v. geisseln, peitschen; strafen

scout n. Späher, Kundschafter; Aufklärer; **boy** — Pfadfinder; **girl** — Pfandfinderin; — v. spähen, kundschaften; aufklären

scoutmaster n. Pfadfinderführer

scowl n. mürrischer Blick, finsteres Aussehen; — v. finster (or mürrisch) blicken

scramble v. strampeln; klettern, sich reissen (um); — n. (mil.) Alarmstart; **-d** adj., **-d eggs** Rührei

scrap n. Stückchen, Brocken; Bruchstück; Bild, Ausschnitt; pl. Grieben; Abfall; — **heap** Abfallhaufen; — **iron** Abfalleisen, Alteisen; — v. kämpfen; boxen; sich prügeln

scrape n. Schaben, Kratzen, Scharren; Kratzfuss; (coll.) Klemme, Patsche; — v. (ab)schaben, (ab)kratzen, (ab)scharren; (mus.) fiedeln; **-r** n. Kratzer; Schaber; Fussabtreter; (mus.) Fiedler

scratch n. Ritz, Riss, Schramme; Ausganspunkt; (sports) Strich, Linie; — **paper** Schmierpapier; — v. (zer)-kratzen, ritzen, schrammen; (aus)-streichen; (coll.) kritzeln, schmieren

scrawl n. Gekritzel; — v. (be)kritzeln

scrawny adj. dünn, mager, knochig

scream n. Geschrei, Gekreisch; — v. schreien, kreischen

screech n. Schrei, Gekreisch; — v. kreischen, schrillen, schreien

screen n. Schirm; Schutz(wand); (arch.) Lettner, Schranke; (film) Leinwand, Bildfläche; (mech.) Sieb; — v. beschirmen, (be)schützen; decken; geheimhalten; (film) verfilmen; abblenden; (mech.) (durch)sieben

screw n. Schraube; Schraubengewinde; Korkenzieher; (fig.) Druck; — **driver** Schraubenzieher; — **propeller** Schiffsschraube; — v. (fest)schrauben; (fig.) verdrehen, verzerren, verziehen; bedrängen, drücken; klemmen

scribble n. Gekritzel, Geschmiere; — v. kritzeln, beschmieren

scribe n. Schreiber, Sekretär; (mech.) Markierinstrument; — v. schreiben; markieren

scrimmage n. Gedränge; Handgemenge, Getümmel

scrip n. Zettel; (com.) Interimsaktie; (coll.) Papiergeld; **-t** n. Schrift; Handschrift; Manuskript; (film) Drehbuch; (law) Originaldokument; (theat.) Rollenbuch, Textbuch; **-tural** adj. schriftmässig, biblisch

Scripture n. Heilige Schrift, Bibel; Bibel-stelle

scroll n. Pergamentrolle; Papierrolle; Liste, Entwurf; (arch.) Spirale, Schnecke, Schnörkel; — **saw** Bogensäge; — v. eintragen; entwerfen, auf-setzen; (auf)rollen

scrollwork n. Verschnörkelung

scrub n. Gestrüpp, Busch(werk); (coll.) Packesel; — v. schrubben, scheuern; (coll.) sich plagen; **-ber** n. Schrubber, Scheuerbürste

scruple n. Skrupel, Zweifel, Bedenklichkeit; (fig.) Kleinigkeit; — v. Bedenken haben; Anstand nehmen

scrupulous adj. allzu bedenklich, ängstlich; gewissenhaft, peinlich

scrutinize v. erforschen, prüfen, untersuchen

scrutiny n. Nachprüfung; Forschen, genaue Untersuchung

scuff n. watschelnder Gang, Schlurfen; — v. schlurfen, schlorren; abnutzen; **-le** n. Balgerei, Handgemenge, Getümmel; **-le** v. sich balgen, raufen, handgemein werden

sculptor n. Bildhauer; Bildschnitzer

sculpture n. Bildhauerarbeit, Skulptur; Bildhauerkunst, Holzschnitzkunst; — v. meisseln, aushauen; modellieren

scum n. Schaum; (mech.) Schlacke; (coll.) Abschaum; — v. abschäumen; (mech.) entschlacken

scurrilous adj. gemein, pöbelhaft, zotig

scurvy n. Skorbut; — adj. schändlich, niederträchtig

scuttle n. Kohlenkiste, Kohleneimer; rascher Schritt; (arch.) Luke; (naut.) Bullauge; — v. eilen; (naut.) versenken, anbohren

scuttlebutt n. (naut.) Trinkwasserbrunnen; (sl.) Latrinengerücht

scythe n. Sense, Sichel

sea n. See; Meer; Seegang; **heavy** (or **rough**) — hochgehende See; — **breeze** Seewind; — **food** Seefische; — **gull** Seemöve; — **horse** Seepferdchen; — **level** Meeresspiegel; — **urchin** Seeigel; — **wall** Uferdamm, Mole

seaboard n. Meeresufer, Seeküste; — adj. am Meer gelegen

seacoast n. Meeresküste

seagoing adj. die offene See befahrend; — **vessel** Ozeanschiff

seal n. Siegel, Stempel; (mech.) Verschluss; (zool.) Seehund, Robbe; — v. versiegeln, verschliessen; (fig.) besiegeln bestätigen; **-ing** n. Siegeln; **-ing adj -ing wax** Siegellack

sealskin n. Seehundsfell; Seal

seam n. Saum, Naht; (geol.) Schicht, Flöz; (med.) Narbe; Falte; — v. säumen, zusammennähen; schrammen, furchen; **-less** adj. nahtlos; **-stress** n. Näherin

seaplane n. Seeflugzeug

seaport n. Seehafen, Hafenstadt

sear v. brennen, versengen; (fig.) brandmarken

search n. Suche; Untersuchung, Durchsuchung; Forschung, Nachforschung;

in — of auf der Suche nach; — v.
suchen; untersuchen, durchsuchen;
(nach)forschen; sondieren
searchlight n. Scheinwerfer
seashore n. Seeküste
seaside n. Strand; Meeresküste
season n. Jahreszeit; Saison; — **ticket**
Dauerkarte, Abonnementskarte; — v.
würzen; trocknen; gewöhnen, akklima-
tisieren; **-able** adj. zeigemäss, passend;
-al adj. der Jahreszeit entsprechend;
Saison-; **-ed** adj. gewürzt; getrocknet
seat n. Sitz, Stuhl; Platz; Wohnsitz;
Schauplatz; Gesäss; **front** — Vordersitz; — **cover** Sitzüberzug; — v. (hin)-
setzen; (pol.) einsetzen, anstellen; be
-ed sitzen; sich setzen; **-ing** n. Bestuh-
lung; **-ing** adj. **-ing capacity** Zahl der
Sitzplätze
seaward adj. seewärts gerichtet; **-s** adv.
seewärts
seaweed n. Tang; Alge
seaworthy adj. seefest, seetüchtig; **seeklar**
secede v. abfallen, ausscheiden; sich
trennen
secession n. Abfall, Absonderung; Spaltung
seclude v. absondern; ausschliessen
seclusion n. Zurückgezogenheit, Abgeschiedenheit
second n. Sekunde; Sekundant, Beistand;
Zweite; — adj. zweite; nächst, folgend,
nachstehend, untergeordnet; — **childhood** zweite Kindheit. Altersschwach-
sinn; — **hand** Sekundenzeiger; —
lieutenant Leutnant; — v. sekundieren,
beistehen, unterstützen; **-ly** adv. zwei-
tens, zum zweitenmal; **-ary** adj. sekundär, nächstfolgend; untergeordnet;
Neben-, Hilfs-; — **school** höhere Schule
secondhand adj. aus zweiter Hand, gebraucht; antiquarisch; — **dealer** Alt-
warenhändler; Antiquar; — **shop** Alt-
warenhandlung; (books) Antiquariat
second-rate adj. zweitrangig, minderwertig
secrecy n. Verschwiegenheit, Heimlichkeit; Verborgenheit
secret n. Geheimnis; **in** — insgeheim, im
Vertrauen; — adj. geheim, heimlich;
verborgen; — **service** Geheimdienst;
-ly adv. im geheimen, im verborgenen;
-ive adj. verschwiegen, geheimtuerisch;
(med.) ausscheidend
secretariat n. Sekretariat; Kanzlei
secretary n. Sekretär; Schriftführer;
(orn.) Sekretärvogel; (pol.) Minister;
private — Privatsekretär
secrete v. verstecken, verbergen; (med.)
ausscheiden, absondern
secretion n. Absonderung, Ausscheidung
sect n. Sekte; **-arian** n., **-ary** n. Sektierer;
-arian adj. sektiererisch
section n. Sektion; Schnitt, Durchschnitt;
Abschnitt, Abteilung; (med.) Sezie-
rung; (mil.) Zug; (rail.) Strecke
sector n. Sektor; (mil.) Abschnitt
secular adj. hundertjährig; (fig.) weltlich,
säkular
secure adj. sicher, gewiss; gesichert, befe-

stigt; — v. sichern; befestigen, festmachen; sicherstellen; sich verschaffen
security n. Sicherheit, Gewissheit; Schutz;
Bürgschaft; — **risk** n. Sicherheitsrisiko;
(pol.) unzuverlässiger Regierungsbe-
amte
sedan n. (auto.) Sedan
sedate adj. gelassen, gesetzt; ruhig
sedative n. Beruhigungsmittel
sediment n. Sediment; Bodensatz, Niederschlag; (geol.) Ablagerung; **-ary** adj.
sedimentär; Ablagerungs-
sedition n. Aufruhr, Aufstand, Empörung
seduce v. verführen, verlocken, verleiten
seductive adj. verführerisch
see n. erzbischöflicher Stuhl, Erzbistum;
Holy See päpstlicher Stuhl, Papsttum;
— v. sehen, ansehen; wahrnehmen, erblicken, beobachten; einsehen, begreifen; besuchen, empfangen; **I don't**
— **it** ich sehe das nicht ein; **live to** —
erleben; — **to it** dafür sorgen (or
achten); — **to the door** zur Tür begleiten; **—I** interj. schau! sieh da! **-ing**
n. Sehen, Sehvermögen; **-ing** conj. **-ing**
that angesichts; da ja; **-ing** adj. **worth**
-ing sehenswert; **-r** n. Seher, Prophet
seed n. Same, Saat; (ichth.) Milch,
Rogen; (fig.) Geschlecht, Abkunft, Ursprung; — v. säen, Samen ausstreuen;
besäen; entkernen; (bot.) Samen tragen, in Samen schiessen; **-ling** n. Säm-
ling, Steckling; **-y** adv. voller Samen,
in Samen schiessend; (coll.) schäbig
seek v. suchen; durchsuchen, durchforschen; begehren, verlangen; trachten, streben
seem v. (er)scheinen; **-ing** n. Anschein;
-ingly adj. anscheinend, scheinbar;
-ingly adv. zum Schein, dem Anschein
nach; **-ly** adj. anständig, geziemend,
schicklich
seep v. durchlaufen, durchsickern
seersucker n. kreppartiger Leinendruck
(or Baumwolldruck)
seesaw n. Schaukel, Wippe; — v. schaukeln, wippen
seethe v. sieden, kochen; einweichen, aufweichen
segment n. Segment, Abschnitt
segregate adj. abgesondert; — v. trennen;
(sich) absondern
segregation n. Absonderung, Trennung
seismograph n. Seismograph, Erdbeben-
messer
seize v. ergreifen, fassen, packen; festnehmen; beschlagnahmen; sich bemächtigen, in Beschlag nehmen
seizure n. Ergreifung, Festnahme; Be-
schlagnahme; (med.) plötzlicher Anfall
seldom adv. selten
select v. auswählen, auslesen; — adj.
auserlesen, auserwählt; **-ion** n. Auswahl; **-ive** adj. wahlweise, auswählend;
Auswahl-
selenium n. Selen
self adj. derselbe, dieselbe, dasselbe; —
pron. selbst; — n. Selbst; Ich
self-acting adj. selbsttätig, automatisch
self-addressed adj. mit Anschrift ver-

sehen

self-confident *adj.* selbstvertrauend, sich auf sich selbst verlassend

self-conscious *adj.* selbstbewusst; befangen

self-contained *adj.* zurückhaltend, verschlossen; beherrscht; (mech.) unabhängig

self-control *n.* Selbstbeherrschung

self-defense *n.* Selbstverteidigung; (law) Notwehr

self-denial *n.* Selbstverleugnung

self-evident *adj.* selbstverständlich, augenscheinlich

self-explanatory *adj.* sich selbst erklärend; selbstverständlich

self-expression *n.* (art) Ausdruck der Persönlichkeit, ˙Persönlichkeitsstempel

self-governing *adj.* sich selbst regierend; selbständig

self-help *n.* Selbsthilfe

self-indulgence *n.* Nachsicht gegen sich selbst; zügellose Genußsucht

selfish *adj.* selbstsüchtig, eigennützig; egoistisch; **-ness** *n.* Selbstsucht, Eigennutz; Egoismus

self-made *adj.* selbstgemacht; — **man** Selfmademan; durch eigene Kraft emporgestiegener Mann

self-possession *n.* Selbstbeherrschung, Geistesgegenwart; Fassung

self-preservation *n.* Selbsterhaltung; Selbstschutz

self-propelling *adj.* Selbstfahr-, Selbstantrieb-

self-protection *n.* Selbstschutz

self-reliance *n.* Selbstvertrauen

self-reliant *adj.* selbstvertrauend, selbstsicher

self-respect *n.* Selbstachtung

self-righteous *adj.* selbstgerecht; pharisäisch

self-sacrifice *n.* Selbstaufopferung

selfsame *adj.* ebenderselbe, ebendieselbe, ebendasselbe

self-satisfied *adj.* selbstzufrieden

self-seeking *adj.* selbstsüchtig, eigennützig

self-service *n.* Selbstbedienung

self-starter *n.* Selbstanlasser

self-stopping *n.* Selbstsperrung

self-sufficient *adj.* selbstgenügsam; selbstversorgend, dünkelhaft

self-support *n.* Selbsterhaltung; Selbstversorgung

self-taught *adj.* autodidaktisch

sell *n.* (coll.) Betrug, Täuschung; — *v.* verkaufen, veräussern, absetzen; sich verkaufen, gehen; verraten; (coll.) täuschen, betrügen; — **out** ausverkaufen, Lager räumen; **-er** *n.* Verkäufer

seltzer *n.* Selters, Selterwasser

selvage *n.* Kante, Borte; Webekante

semantics *n. pl.* Semantik, Wortbedeutungslehre

semaphore *n.* Zeichentelegraf; Flaggenwinken

semblance *n.* Ähnlichkeit; Ebenbild, Gestalt, Erscheinung; Anschein

semester *n.* Semester

semiannual *adj.* halbjährig

semicircle *n.* Halbkreis

semicircular *adj.* halbkreisförmig, halbrund

semicolon *n.* Semikolon; Strichpunkt

semifinal *adj.* halbbeendet; **-s** *pl.* Vorschlussrunde, Vorschlussspiele

seminar *n.* Seminar, Arbeitsgruppe; **-y** *n.* Seminar, Erziehungsanstalt; (bot.) Pflanzenschule

semiofficial *adj.* halbamtlich

semiweekly *adj.* halbwöchentlich, zweimal wöchentlich

semiyearly *adj.* halbjährlich

senate *n.* Senat

senator *n.* Senator; **-ial** *adj.* senatorisch

send *v.* senden; aussenden, entsenden; schicken; — **for** holen lassen; **-er** *n.* Absender; (mech.) Taste; (rad.) Sender; **-ing** *n.* Sendung, Senden

senile *adj.* senil, altersschwach

senior *n.* Senior, Ältere, Rangältere; — *adj.* älter; Senior-, Ober-; **-ity** *n.* höheres Alter (or Dienstalter)

sensation *n.* Empfindung, Eindruck; (fig.) Sensation, Aufsehen; **-al** *adj.* sensationell, aufsehenerregend; Empfindungs-

sense *n.* Sinn; Gefühl; Bedeutung; Vernunft; **common** — gesunder Menschenverstand; — **of sight** Gesichtssinn; **talk** — vernünftig reden; — *v.* wahrnehmen, empfinden; (coll.) verstehen; **-less** *adj.* besinnungslos; unempfindlich, gefühllos, leblos; sinnlos, unvernünftig

sensibility *n.* Sensibilität, Empfindungsvermögen, Empfindlichkeit

sensible *adj.* fühlbar, empfänglich; verständig

sensitive *adj.* empfindlich, sensitiv; empfänglich, feinfühlig; — **plant** Mimose

sensitization *n.* (phot.) Lichtempfindlichmachen

sensitize *v.* empfindlich machen

sensory *adj.* Empfindungs-, Sinnes-

sensual *adj.* sinnlich, fleischlich; **-ity** *n.* Sinnlichkeit

sensuous *adj.* sinnlich, sinnenfreudig

sentence *n.* Spruch; (gram. and mus.) Satz; (law) Rechtsspruch, Urteil, Entscheidung; — *v.* (ver)urteilen; (fig.) verdammen

sentiment *n.* Empfindung, Gefühl; Meinung; **-al** *adj.* sentimental, gefühlvoll, empfindsam; **-ality** *n.* Sentimentalität, Rührseligkeit

sentinel *n.* Wachthabende, Posten

sentry *n.* Wache, Wachposten; Schildwache

separable *adj.* trennbar, ablösbar

separate *v.* (sich) trennen, (sich) scheiden, (sich) absondern, auseinandergehen, sortieren; — *adj.* getrennt, abgesondert, einzeln; separat; geschieden; **under** — **cover** (com.) mit derselben Post; **-ly** *adv.* einzeln, besonders

separation *n.* Trennung, Scheidung

separator *n.* Scheidemaschine; **cream** —

Zentrifuge, Entsahner
September n. September
septic adj. septisch, Fäulnis erregend; —
poisoning Blutvergiftung; — **tank** Klär-
becken
sepulchre n. Grab, Grabstätte, Gruft
sequel n. Folge, Fortsetzung; Ergebnis
sequence n. Reihenfolge, Anordnung
sequoia n. Rotholzbaum, Sequoia
seraph n. Seraph
Serbia n. Serbien
serenade n. Serenade, Ständchen; — v.
ein Ständchen bringen
serene adj. hell, klar, heiter; ungetrübt,
ruhig
serf n. Sklave, Leibeigene
sergeant, serjeant n. Sergeant, Feld-
webel, Wachtmeister
serial n. Fortsetzungsroman; Serienauf-
führung; Sendereihe; — adj. reihen-
weise, periodisch, serienweise
series n. pl. Reihe; Reihenfolge, Serie
serious adj. ernst(haft), seriös; feierlich,
wichtig, schwer
sermon n. Predigt; Sermon
serpent n. Schlange; — ine n. Serpentine,
Schlangenlinie; (min.) Serpentin; -ine
adj. schlangenartig, schlangenförmig;
schlängelnd
serum n. Serum: Blutwasser
servant n. Diener, Bediente; Magd;
public — Staatsbeamte
serve v. dienen; servieren, bedienen, aufwarten, auftragen; verwalten, genügen;
verbüssen; (tennis) anspielen; — **a**
warrant die Klageschrift (or Vorladung)
zustellen; **that** -**s him right** das geschieht ihm recht
service n. Dienst; Arbeitsleistung, Bedienung; Stellung; Gehorsam, Unterwerfung; Service, Tafelgeschirr; (com.)
Nutzen, Vorteil; (eccl.) Gottesdienst;
(law) Zustellung; (mil.) Dienstpflicht,
Heeresdienst; (rail.) Verkehr; (tennis)
Aufschlag, Anspiel; **at your** — zu Ihrer
Verfügung; **be of** — zu Diensten
stehen; **night** — Nachtdienst, Nacht-
verkehr; — **station** Tankstelle; -**able**
adj. zweckdienlich, nützlich; dienst-
tauglich, brauchbar, dienstbereit
servitude n. Dienstbarkeit, Knechtschaft
servomotor n. Hilfsmotor; Kraftver-
stärker; Stellmotor
sesame n. Sesam
session n. Tagung, Sitzung; Sitzungsperiode
set n. Satz; Garnitur, Service, Besteck;
Reihe, Folge; Richtung; (ast.) Sinken,
Untergang; (film) Standfoto; (horses)
Gespann; (rad.) Apparat; (tennis)
Partie; (sl.) Pack, Bande; — v. (hin)-
setzen, (hin)stellen, legen; wenden;
(ein)richten, ordnen, zurechtmachen;
befestigen; (agr.) pflanzen; (ast.)
sinken, untergehen; (hunting) (vor)-
stehen, hetzen; (jewels) fassen; (med.)
einrenken; (mus.) schärfen; (mus.)
komponieren, in Noten setzen; — **aside**
beiseitesetzen; verwerfen; — **back** zu-
rücksetzen, zurückstossen; — **on fire**

anzünden; — **the table** den Tisch
decken; — **up** aufsetzen, aufstellen;
erheben, erwecken; einrichten; -**ter** n.
Setzer; (zool.) Setter, Vorstehhund;
-**ting** n. Setzen, Stellen; Umgebung,
Umrahmung; (ast.) Untergang; (chem.)
Erstarrung, Gerinnung; (jewels) Fassung; (mech.) Erhärten; Einstellung;
(naut.) Richtung; (theat.) Inszenierung
setback n. Rückschlag; Gegenströmung
Zurückverlegung
setscrew n. Stellschraube
settle n. Ruhebank; — v. bestimmen,
entscheiden; bezahlen; beilegen,
schlichten; abmachen; sich niederlassen
(or ansiedeln); sich senken, sich setzen;
nachlassen, sich legen; -**ment** n. Regelung, Abmachung, Verabredung; An-
siedlung, Niederlassung; -**r** n. Ansiedler, Kolonist
setup n. Haltung, Aufmachung; (sl.) ab-
gekartetes Spiel
seven n. Sieben(er); — adj. sieben; -**teen**
n. Siebzehn(er); -**teen** adj. siebzehn;
-**teenth** n. Siebzehnte, Siebzehntel;
-**teenth** adj. siebzehnt; -**th** n. Siebente;
Siebentel; -**th** adj. siebent; -**ty** n.
Siebzig(er); -**ty** adj. siebzig
sever v. (ab)trennen, absondern; abhauen, zerschneiden, aufbrechen, aus-
einanderreissen; -**ance** n. Trennung,
Scheidung
several adj. getrennt, gesondert; einzeln,
besonder, verschiedene, mehrere; -**ly**
adv. getrennt; besonders, einzeln;
jointly and — samt und sonders
severe adj. streng, nachsichtslos; ernst;
hart, heftig; rauh
severity n. Strenge, Härte; Genauigkeit
sew v. nähen, heften; -**er** n. Näher; -**ing**
n. Nähen, Näherei
sewage n. Abwasser
sewer n. Abzugskanal, Siel, Kloake
sex n. Geschlecht; -**ual** adj. sexuell, ge-
schlechtlich; Geschlechts-
sextant n. Sextant
sexton n. Küster
shabby adj. schäbig, abgetragen; (coll.)
gemein
shack n. Bretterbude, Hütte
shackle n. Fessel; -**s** n. pl. Handschellen;
— v. fesseln, anketten
shade n. Schatten, Schattierung; Schirm;
(fig.) Kleinigkeit; — v. beschatten, verdunkeln; schützen; (art) abstufen,
schattieren
shadow n. Schatten(bild); Schutz; — v.
verdunkeln, beschatten, andeuten; bergen, schützen; heimlich beobachten;
-**y** adj. schattig, dunkel; wesenlos
shadowboxing n. Trainings boxen (ohne
Gegner)
shady adj. schattig; zweifelhaft, anrüchig
shaft n. Schaft, Stiel; Pfeil, Speer; (mech.)
Achse, Spindel, Welle; (min.) Schacht,
Grube
shaggy adj. zottig, langhaarig; rauh
shake n. Schütteln, Erschütterung;
(mus.) Triller; pl. Zittern, Schüttelfrost; — v. schütteln, rütteln; erschüt-

tern; zittern, beben; (mus.) trillern; — hands die Hand schütteln (or geben); zu einem Abkommen gelangen; -r n. Schüttler, Zitterer; Streuer; **cocktail** -r Mixbecher; **salt** -r Salzstreuer

shakedown n. Notbett, Notlager; (coll.) Erpressung

shake-up n. Aufruhr, Erregung; (coll.) Reorganisierung, Personalwechsel

shaky adj. zitternd, unsicher; wackelig, hinfällig; unzuverlässlich

shale n. Schiefer(ton)

shall v. werden, sollen; — **we go for a walk?** wollen wir spazieren gehen?

shallow adj. seicht, flach; (fig.) oberflächlich

sham n. Imitation, Schein, Täuschung; Überzug; — **battle** Scheingefecht; — **jewelry** Talmischmuck; — v. vortäuschen, betrügen, hintergehen; sich verstellen, simulieren

shame n. Scham; Schande, Schmach; — v. sich schämen; beschämen; schänden, verunehren; -**ful** adj. schändlich, schimpflich, schmachvoll; -**less** adj. schamlos; unverschämt

shamefaced adj. schamhaft, schüchtern

shampoo n. Kopfwäsche; — v. den Kopf waschen, schampunieren

shamrock n. Feldklee; (fig.) Kleeblatt

shank n. Schenkel, Unterschenkel; (bot.) Stiel, Stengel; (mech.) Schaft, Rohr

shanty n. Hütte, Bude

shape n. Gestalt, Form; (coll.) Zustand, Verfassung; — v. bilden gestalten; formen, anpassen, einrichten; ersinnen; -**less** adj. formlos, ungestalt; -**ly** adj. wohlgestaltet, ebenmässig; -r n. (mech.) Fräsmaschine

share n. Teil, Anteil; Beitrag; (com.) Aktie, Anteilschein; Kux; Kontingent, Quote; — v. teilen; verteilen, austeilen; gemeinsam geniessen (or erdulden); teilhaben, teilnehmen; -r n. Teiler, Teilhaber

shareholder n. Aktienbesitzer, Aktionär

shark n. Hai(fisch); (sl.) Gauner

sharp n. (mus.) Kreuz; (sl.) Gauner, Bauernfänger; (sports sl.) Eingeweihte; — adj. scharf, schneidend, spitz; hitzig; hart, hell; streng, bitter, beissend; rasch, heftig; (coll.) spitzfindig, verschlagen; **two o'clock** — genau zwei Uhr; -**en** v. (ver)schärfen, spitzen; reizen; (mus.) erhöhen; -**ener** n. Schärfer; **pencil** -**ener** Bleistiftanspitzer; -**er** n. Gauner, Schwindler; -**ness** n. Schärfe, Strenge, Härte; Heftigkeit; (fig.) Scharfsinn

sharpshooter n. Scharfschütze

shatter n. Bruchstück, Scherbe; — v. zerbrechen, zerschmettern, zerrütten

shatterproof adj. bruchsicher

shave n. Rasieren; **close** — knappes Entkommen; — v. (sich) rasieren; -r n. Rasierer; Leuteschinder, Wucherer; (coll.) Grünschnabel

shawl n. Schal, Umschlagetuch

she pron. sie

sheaf n. Garbe, Bündel; — v. in Garben binden, bündeln

shear n. Schur; (mech.) Schneidemaschine; — v. scheren, abschneiden; (coll.) rupfen, übervorteilen

sheath n. Scheide, Futteral; (ent.) Flügeldecke; -**e** v. in die Scheide stecken; einhüllen, bedecken

shed n. Schuppen; Hütte; — v. vergiessen; verbreiten; verlieren, abwerfen

sheen n. Schein, Glanz

sheep n. Schaf; (coll.) Schafskopf; -**ish** adj. schafsmässig; einfältig, blöde

sheepman n. Schafzüchter

sheepskin n. Schaffell, Schafleder; (coll.) Diplom

sheer adj. rein, lauter; bloss; dünn, zart; steil, senkrecht; — adv. gänzlich, völlig; — v. (naut.) scheren

sheet n. Bettuch, Laken; Blatt, Platte, Bogen; Fläche; **blank** — unbeschriebener Bogen (or Wahlzettel); — **anchor** Notanker; — **glass** Tafelglas; — **iron** Eisenblech, Weissblech; — **lightning** Wetterleuchten; — **metal** Blech; — **music** Notenblatt; — v. überziehen, einhüllen; -**ing** n. blattweise Anordnung; Laken

shelf n. Brett; Regal, Fach; Gestell; (geol.) Felsvorsprung; (naut.) Riff; **corner** — Eckregal; **on the** — (coll.) ausrangiert

shell n. (bot.) Schale, Hülse, Schote; (ent.) Flügeldecke; (mech.) Mantel, Gerippe, Gerüst; (mil.) Granate, Bombe; (zool.) Muschel, Schale, Schild, Panzer; (fig.) Gehäuse; **cartridge** — Patronenhülse; **turtle** — Schildkrötenschale, Schildpatt; — **room** (naut.) Granatenmagazin; — **shock** (mil.) Nervenerschütterung (nach einer Granatenexplosion); — v. schälen, enthülsen; (ichth.) abschuppen; (mil.) bombardieren, beschiessen

shellproof adj. bombensicher

shelter n. Schutzraum; Schuppen; Schutz, Obdach, Unterschlupf; **air-raid** — Luftschutzkeller; — v. (be)schützen; (be)schirmen

shelve v. mit Brettern (or Regalen) versehen; auf ein Brett (or Regal) stellen; sich neigen, abschüssig sein; (coll.) ausrangieren, unberücksichtigt lassen

shepherd n. Schäfer, Schafhirt; (bibl.) Seelenhirt

sherbet n. Scherbett, Sorbett

sheriff n. Sheriff, Bezirkspolizeibeamte

shield n. Schild; Schirm, Schutz; Beschützer; Schutzdach; — v. (be)schirmen, (be)schützen; bedecken, behüten

shift n. Schicht; Veränderung, Wechsel; Behelf; Auskunftsmittel; Notlüge, List, Kniff; — v. (ver)schieben; wechseln, verändern; sich davonmachen; sich heraushelfen, sich herauslügen; sich durchschlagen; sich umziehen; (naut.) wenden, umspringen; -**less** adj. hilflos; ungewandt; faul; -**lessly** adv. unzuverlässig; -**y** adj. schlau, verschlagen

shimmer n. Schimmer; — v. schimmern, flimmern

shin(bone) n. Schienbein
shine n. Schein, Glanz; (coll.) Neigung; — v. scheinen, leuchten; (coll.) putzen; (fig.) glänzen
shingle n. Schindel; (coll.) Praxistafel; pl. (med.) Gürtelrose; — v. mit Schindeln decken; kurz schneiden
shining n. Scheinen, Glänzen; — adj. scheinend, glänzend
shiny adj. blank; schimmernd; hell
ship n. Schiff; —'s papers Schiffspapiere; — v. schiffen; an Bord bringen (or nehmen); verladen, verschiffen, versenden; anheuern; —ment n. Verladung, Vorschiffung; Warensendung; (naut.) Schiffsladung; —per n. Verschiffer, Verlader; (com.) Absender; —ping n. Verschiffung, Verladung; (com.) Versand; (naut.) Schiffe, Flotte; Gesamttonnenzahl; —ping clerk Versandabteilungsangestellte; —ping room Versandabteilung, Versandraum
shipboard n. Bord, Schiff(sseite); on — an Bord
shipbuilding n. Schiffbau, Schiffsbaukunst
shipmate n. Schiffskamerad; Mitreisende
shipowner n. Reeder, Schiffsbesitzer
shipwreck n. Schiffbruch; Wrack; —ed adj. gestrandet, gescheitert; schiffbrüchig; —ed person Schiffbrüchige, Gestrandete
shipyard n. Schiffswerft
shirk n. Drückeberger; — v. sich drücken; (educ.) schwänzen
shirr v. Gummifäden einziehen; kräuseln
shirt n. Hemd; — cuff Manschette; — sleeve Hemdsärmel; — stud Manschettenknopf
shiver n. Splitter, Bruchstück; Schauer, Erzittern; pl. Fieberschauer, Schüttelfrost; — v. zerbrechen, zersplittern; schau(d)ern, zittern; —ing adj. erzitternd, schaudernd
shoal n. Menge, Masse, Schwarm; (naut.) Untiefe, Sandbank; — of fish Fischzug, Fischschwarm; — v. flacher werden; wimmeln, sich drängen
shock n. Stoss, Zusammenstoss, Erschütterung; (geol.) Erdstoss; (med.) Schock, Nervenerschütterung; (mil.) Angriff, Anfall; electric — elektrischer Schlag; — absorber Stossdämpfer; — wave Stosswelle; — v. (an)stossen; zusammenstossen, erschüttern; Anstoss geben, beleidigen; —ing adj. anstössig, verletzend; unangenehm, empörend
shockproof adj. stossfest, stossicher
shoe n. Schuh; Hufeisen; Beschlag; Hemmschuh; rubber — Gummischuh; — polish Schuhkrem, Schuhwichse; — v. beschuhen; beschlagen
shoeblack n. Schuhputzer, Stiefelputzer
shoehorn n. Schuhanzieher
shoemaker n. Schuhmacher
shoestring, shoelace n. Schnürsenkel
shoot n. Schuss; Schiessen; Gleitbahn; Abladestelle; Stromschnelle; (bot.) Schössling; (min.) Erzlager, Rutsche; — v. schiessen; fliegen, stürzen, strömen; (bot.) keimen, treiben; (film)

aufnehmen, drehen; (mil.) (ab)schiessen, (ab)feuern; —ing adj. —ing gallery Schiesstand; —ing star Sternschnuppe
shop n. Laden, Geschäft; Werkstatt, Betrieb; (fig.) Fach, Beruf; pastry —, confectionery — Konditorei; talk — fachsimpeln; — v. einkaufen; —per n. Käufer, Kunde; Einkäufer; —ping n. Einkaufen, Besorgung; go —ping Einkäufe machen, Geschäfte besuchen
shopkeeper n. Ladeninhaber, Geschäftsbesitzer
shoplifter n. Ladendieb
shopwindow n. Schaufenster
shore n. Strand, Ufer, Küste; Gestade; (arch.) Stütze, Strebe; — leave Landurlaub; — line Küstenstrich
short adj. klein, kurz; beschränkt, knapp; sparsam; trocken, barsch; (cake) mürbig, knusprig; (sl.) unverdünnt; a — while ago vor kurzem; for — abgekürzt; on — notice in kurzer Zeit, kurzfristig; run — knapp werden, ausgehen; — circuit Kurzschluss; — sale schneller Absatz; Baissespekulation; — temper Ungeduld, Reizbarkeit; — wave Kurzwelle; — n. Kürze; kurze Silbe, kurzer Vokal; pl. Shorts kurze Hosen; —age n. Mangel, Knappheit; Fehlbetrag, Abgang, Gewichtsverlust; —en v. (ab)kürzen, vermindern, verringern; abnehmen; (bot.) beschneiden; —ening n. Verkürzung; Backfett; —ly adv. kürzlich; kurz, bald
shortcake n. Mürbekuchen,
shortchange v. zu wenig herausgeben
short-circuit v. kurzschliessen
shortcoming n. Unzulänglichkeit, Pflichtversäumnis; Mangel, Schwäche
shorthand n. Stenografie, Kurzschrift; — adj. stenografisch; — v. stenografieren
shortsighted adj. kurzsichtig; —ness n. Kurzsichtigkeit
shortstop n. Innenspieler zwischen zweitem und drittem Mal
short-term adj. kurzfristig
shot n. Schuss; Geschoss, Kugel; Schütze; Stoss, Schlag, Wurf; (sl.) Spritze; bird — Schrot
shotgun n. Jagdflinte, Schrotflinte
should v. sollte, würde
shoulder n. Schulter, Achsel; (meat) Kamm, Bug; — blade Schulterblatt; — knot, — loop, — mark Achselstück, Achselklappe; — strap Schulterriemen; — v. schultern; drängen; (fig.) auf sich nehmen
shout n. Geschrei, Gejauchze; Ruf; — v. rufen, schreien, jauchzen
shove n. Schub, Stoss; — v. schieben, stossen; drängen; — off abstossen, absetzen
shovel n. Schaufel, Schippe, Spaten; — v. schaufeln, häufeln
show n. Schau(stellung); Ausstellung; (theat.) Schauspiel, Aufführung; (fig.) Angabe, Prunk; — bill Plakat; — card Musterkarte; — window Schaufenster, Auslage; — v. zeigen; bekanntmachen, erklären, deuten; ausstellen, darstellen;

beweisen, erscheinen; — off hervorstechen, sich grosstun; — oneself superior to sich überlegen zeigen; — one's
true colors sein wahres Gesicht zeigen;
— up blosstellen, entlarven; –y adj.
prächtig, prunkvoll, glänzend; auffällig

showboat n. Theaterschiff

showcase n. Schaukasten, Glaskasten

shower n. Schauer; (fig.) Erguss, Fülle,
Menge; — bath Brause, Dusche; — v.
(sich) ergiessen, hageln, regnen

showman n. Schausteller, Austeller;
(theat.) Komödiant; –ship n. Darstel-
lungskunst

showroom n. Ausstellungsraum, Vorführ-
raum

shred n. Schnitzel; Fetzen, Streifen; —
v. zerschneiden, zerfetzen, zerreissen

shrewd adj. scharfsinnig; klug, schlau;
–ness n. Scharfsinn, Schlauheit; Verschlagenheit

shriek n. Gekreisch, Angstschrei; — v.
kreischen, schreien

shrill adj. schrill, gellend, durchdringend

shrimp n. Garnele, Krabbe; (coll.) Knirps

shrine n. Schrein, Heiligtum; Kapelle

shrink v. schrumpfen, einlaufen, sich zusammenziehen; abnehmen, schwinden;
(fig.) zurückschrecken; –age n. Einlaufen, Schrumpfen; Abnahme,
Schwund

shrivel v. einschrumpfen, runzeln; falten,
zerknittern; (fig.) vergehen

shroud n. Leichentuch, Sterbehemd;
(naut.) Want(tau); (fig.) Gewand, Kleidung; pl. (naut.) Wanten; — v. einhüllen; verbergen

shrub n. Strauch, Busch, Staude; –bery
n. Gebüsch, Gesträuch, Buschwerk

shrug n. Achselzucken; — v. schaudern,
mit der Achsel zucken

shudder n. Erzittern; Schauder; — v.
(er)beben, erzittern, schaudern

shuffle n. Schieben, Stossen; Ausflucht;
Schiebung; (cards) Mischen; (walk)
schleppender Gang; — v. schieben,
stossen; verwirren, durcheinanderbrin-
gen; (cards) mischen; (walk) schwerfällig gehen, schlürfen, scharren

shuffling adj. schiebend, mischend;
schleppend; (fig.) unredlich, ausweich-
end

shun v. (ver)meiden, ausweichen; beiseite
schieben (or drängen)

shut v. (ver)schliessen, zumachen; zuziehen; ausschliessen, aussperren; –ter
n. Schliesser; Deckel, Klappe, Schieber;
Rolladen, Jalousie, Fensterladen; Schalter; (mech.) Verschluss

shutdown n. Stillstand, Arbeitsnieder-
legung

shut-in n. Patient, Bettlägrige

shuttle n. Weberschiffchen; — service
Zubringerverkehr, Pendelverkehr

shy adj. scheu, schüchtern, zurückhaltend; behutsam; argwöhnisch, misstrauisch; –ness n. Scheu, Schüchternheit, Zurückhaltung; Behutsamkeit;
Argwohn

sick adj. krank; unwohl, übel; schwach,
kraftlos; überdrüssig; –en v. kränkeln,
erkranken, dahinsiechen; krank machen, anekeln; –ly adj. schwächlich,
kränklich; unpässlich, krankhaft, ungesund; blass; schmerzlich; widerlich;
–ness n. Krankheit; Übelkeit, Schwäche

sickbed n. Krankenbett

sickle n. Sichel

side n. Seite; Rand, Ufer, Grenze; (geol.)
Abhang; (geom.) Schenkel; (pol.) Partei, Bezirk; — by — dichtbeieinander,
nebeneinander; — adj. seitlich, indirekt; Seiten-, Neben-; — aisle Seitenschiff; — arms Seitenwehr; — dish
Nebengericht, Vorspeise, Nachspeise;
— issue Nebensache, Nebenpunkt; —
light Seitenlicht; Streiflicht; — line
Nebenerwerb, Nebenberuf; — show
Nebenschau; — view Seitenansicht; —
v. Partei ergreifen; beiseitelegen

sideboard n. Anrichte(tisch), Büffet

sideburns n. Kotelette, Backenbart

sidecar n. Beiwagen

sidesaddle n. Damensattel

side-step v. beiseitetreten, ausweichen

sidetrack n. Nebengeleis(e); — v. verschieben; (rail.) rangieren

sidewalk n. Bürgersteig, Trottoir

sidewards, sideways, sidewise adv. seitwärts

siding n. (rail.) Nebengeleis; Weiche

siege n. Belagerung

sierra n. Sierra, Gebirgskette

siesta n. Siesta, Mittagsruhe

sieve n. Sieb; — v. (durch)sieben, sichten

sift v. sieben, sichten; aussondern, auslesen; prüfen, untersuchen

sigh n. Seufzer; — v. seufzen (nach)

sight n. Sehen, Gesicht; Sehkraft; Blick,
Anblick; Einsicht; (gun) Visier, Korn;
(fig.) Menge, Masse, Schauspiel, Erscheinung, Merkwürdigkeit, Sehenswürdigkeit; at first — im ersten Augenblick; at — sogleich, augenblicklich;
bomb — Bombenzielgerät; by — vom
Sehen; bei Vorlage; on — bei Sicht (or
Vorlage); out of — ausser Sicht; aus
den Augen; play at — vom Blatt
spielen; — draft Sichtwechsel; –less
adj. blind; unsichtbar; –ly adj. ansehnlich, stattlich

sight-seeing n. Besichtigung der Sehenswürdigkeiten; — adj. schaulustig; —
car Rundfahrtenwagen

sight-seer n. Schaulustige, Besucher der
Sehenswürdigkeiten, Tourist

sign n. Zeichen, Gebärde, Wink;
Anzeichen, Kennzeichen, Merkmal;
Schild; (ast.) Tierkreiszeichen; (com.)
Firmenzeichen, Unterschrift; (med.)
Symptom; (mus.) Vorzeichen; —
language Zeichensprache; — v. unter-
zeichnen, unterschreiben; Zeichen geben, winken; –al n. Signal; busy –al
Besetztzeichen; –al box Feuermelder;
(rail.) Stellwerk; –al code Signalcode;
–al light Signallicht, Signalfeuer; –al
mast Signalmast; –alize v. deutlich
machen, auszeichnen; –atory adj. unter-

zeichnend; **-ature** *n.* Unterschrift, Namenszug; (mus.) Vorzeichen; **-et** *n.* Siegel, Handzeichen

signalman *n.* (rail.) Weichensteller; (naut.) Signalgast

signboard *n.* Aushängeschild, Firmenschild

significant *adj.* bedeutsam, bezeichnend

signify *v.* bezeichnen, bedeuten, andeuten; bekanntmachen

signpost *n.* Schilderpfosten, Wegweiser

silence *n.* Schweigen, Stille, Ruhe; Schweigsamkeit, Verschwiegenheit; — *v.* beruhigen, beschwichtigen; zur Ruhe bringen; **-r** *n.* Schalldämpfer; (auto.) Auspufftopf

silent *adj.* still, ruhig, schweigend; schweigsam, verschwiegen; (gram.) stumm; — **partner** stiller Teilhaber

Silesia *n.* Schlesien

silica, silex *n.* Kieselerde

silk *n.* Seide; Seidenstoff; Seidenzeug; — **stockings** Seidenstrümpfe; **-en** *adj.* seiden, seidig; **-iness** *n.* Seid(enart)ige; **-y** *adj.* seid(enart)ig; (fig.) weich, zart

silkworm *n.* Seidenraupe

sill *n.* Schwelle; Fensterbrett

silliness *n.* Torheit; Albernheit

silly *adj.* einfältig, dumm; albern, töricht

silo *n.* Speicher; (mil.) Raketenbunker

silver *n.* Silber; Silbergeld; Silbergerät; — *adj.* silbern; silberhell; — **fir** Silbertanne, Edeltanne; **-foil** *—* **leaf** Blattsilber; — **fox** Silberfuchs; — **glance** Silberglanz, Schwefelsilber; — **grey** Silbergrau; — **paper** Silberpapier, Staniolpapier; — **plating** Silberplattierung; — **thistle** Bärenklau; — **wedding** silberne Hochzeit; — *v.* versilbern; **-y** *adj.* silbern, silberglänzend; silberhell; Silber-

silversmith *n.* Silberschmied, Silberarbeiter

silverware *n.* Silberwaren, Silberzeug

similar *adj.* ähnlich, gleich(artig); **-ity** *n.* Gleichartigkeit, Ähnlichkeit

simile *n.* Gleichnis, Vergleich

simmer *v.* sieden, brodeln, wallen

simple *adj.* einfach, schlicht; einfältig, arglos, simpel; **-ton** *n.* Einfaltspinsel, Tropf

simplicity *n.* Einfachheit, Schlichtheit; Unbefangenheit, Einfalt

simplify *v.* vereinfachen, erleichtern

simply *adv.* einfach, schlicht, klar; bloss, nur; schlechthin

simultaneous *adj.* gleichzeitig, simultan

sin *n.* Sünde; — *v.* sündigen; sich versündigen; **-ful** *adj.* sündig, sündhaft; **-ner** *n.* Sünder

since *adv.* seitdem, vorher; — *prep.* seit; — *conj.* da, weil, seit(dem)

sincere *adj.* aufrichtig; lauter, wahr; ernst; **-ly** *adv.* gänzlich; **-ly yours** Ihr (sehr) ergebener, hochachtungsvoll

sincerity *n.* Aufrichtigkeit, Redlichkeit

sine *n.* (math.) Sinus

sinew *n.* Sehne; (fig.) Stärke, Stütze; **-y** *adj.* sehnig; nervig, kräftig

sing *v.* singen, klingen; summen; (lit.)

besingen; **-er** *n.* Sänger; **-ing** *n.* Singen, Gesang

singe *n.* leichte Verbrennung; — *v.* (ver)sengen

single *adj.* einzig, einzeln, einfach; unverheiratet, ledig; **bookkeeping by — entry** einfache Buchführung; — **fight** Zweikampf; — **file** Gänsemarsch; **-ness** *n.* Alleinsein; Einfachheit

single-breasted *adj.* einreihig

singlehanded *adj.* einhändig; allein, eigenhändig, selbständig

single-minded *adj.* aufrichtig, grundehrlich, ohne Falsch

single-track *adj.* eingleisig, einspurig

singly *adv.* einzeln, allein; besonders

singular *adj.* einzigartig, sonderbar, ungewöhnlich; (gram.) Singular-; — *n.* Einzahl, Singular

sinister *adj.* unheilvoll, finster; böse, schlecht, unrecht

sink *n.* Ausguss; Abzugskanal, Senkgrube, Kloake; (theat.) Versenkung; — *v.* sinken, untertauchen, untergehen; einfallen, sich senken; abnehmen, erliegen, entarten; verfallen; graben; (naut.) versenken; **-er** *n.* Schachtarbeiter; (naut.) Senkblei; **-ing** *adj.* **-ing fund** Tilgungsfonds

sinus *n.* Krümmung, Höhlung; Bucht; (anat.) Höhle; (math.) Sinus

sip *n.* Schluck; Nippen, Schlürfen; — *v.* nippen, schlürfen

siphon *n.* Siphon, Saugheber

sir *n.* Herr; **dear** — sehr geehrter Herr

siren *n.* Sirene

sirloin *n.* Lendenstück

sissy *n.* Weichling; femininer Junge (*or* Mann)

sister *n.* Schwester; (eccl.) Nonne; **-hood** *n.* Schwesternschaft; **-ly** *adj.* schwesterlich

sister-in-law *n.* Schwägerin

sit *v.* sitzen, sich setzen; (pol.) tagen; **-ting** *n.* Sitzung, Tagung; (orn.) Brüten; **-ting room** Wohnzimmer

site *n.* Lage, Platz; Sitz; Schauplatz

situate *v.* unterbringen; **-d** *adj.* untergebracht, gelegen

situation *n.* Situation, Lage, Stellung, Zustand, Umstand

six *n.* Sechs(er); — *adj.* sechs; **-fold** *adj.* sechsfach; **-teen** *n.* Sechzehn(er); **-teen** *adj.* sechzehn; **-teenth** *n.* Sechzehnte; Sechzehntel; **-teenth** *adj.* sechzehnt; **-th** *n.* Sechste; Sechstel; (mus.) Sexte; **-th** *adj.* sechst; **-tieth** *n.* Sechzigste, Sechzigstel; **-tieth** *adj.* sechzigst; **-ty** *n.* Sechzig(er); **-ty** *adj.* sechzig

six-shooter *n.* sechsläufiger Revolver

size *n.* Grösse, Gestalt; Format, Umfang; (com.) Nummer, Mass; (mil.) Kaliber; (min.) Mächtigkeit; — *v.* einordnen, sortieren; Mass nehmen; (coll.) beurteilen; **-d** *adj.* angemessen, in der Grösse von; geleimt

sizzle *n.* Zischen; — *v.* zischen

skate *n.* Schlittschuh, Rollschuh; (ichth.) Glattroche; **roller** — Rollschuh; — *v.* Schlittschuh (*or* Rollschuh) laufen;

—r n. Schlittschuhläufer, Rollschuhläufer

skating rink n. Kunsteisbahn; Rollschuhbahn

skeleton n. Skelett, Gerippe; Rahmen, Gestell

skeptic n. Skeptiker; — adj. skeptisch

sketch n. Skizze, Entwurf, Handzeichnung; (theat.) Sketch; — v. skizzieren, entwerfen

skewer n. Speiler, Fleischspiess; — v. aufspiessen

ski n. Ski; — **jump** Sprungschanze; Skisprung; — v. skilaufen

skid n. Ausrutschen; (avi.) Kufe; (mech.) Hemmschuh, Hemmkette; (naut.) Ladebord; — v. hemmen, bremsen; ausrutschen, abrutschen; gleiten, schleudern

skilful adj. geschickt, gewandt, bewandert

skill n. Geschicklichkeit, Fertigkeit, Gewandtheit; **-ed** adj. geschickt, erfahren; kundig, geübt

skillet n. Bratpfanne

skim n. Abschäumen; Dahingleiten; — adj. — **milk** Magermilch; — v. abschöpfen, absahnen; flüchtig durchsehen (or durchlesen); dahingleiten; **-mer** n. Schaumlöffel

skimp v. knapp halten, knausern; **-y** adj. knauserig, sparsam

skin n. Haut, Fell, Pelz; (bot.) Schale, Hülse; (mech.) Leder, Decke; — v. bedecken, überziehen; häuten, abbalgen; abschälen; (sl.) filzen, prellen; **-ny** adj. hautartig; fleischlos, mager

skin-deep adj. oberflächlich

skintight adj. dicht anliegend, prall

skip n. Sprung; — v. springen, hüpfen; überspringen, auslassen

skipper n. (avi.) Flugzeugkommandant; (naut.) Schiffer, Kapitän

skirmish n. Scharmützel, Geplänkel; — v. plänkeln

skirt n. Frauenrock; Rand, Saum; — v. umsäumen; umgeben; (sich) entlangziehen

skull n. Schädel, Hirnschale; (coll.) Kopf

skullcap n. Hausmütze; (bot.) Helmkraut; (mil.) Sturmhaube

skunk n. Skunk, Stinktier; Skunkpelz; (sl.) Schuft

sky n. Himmel; Luftraum; — **blue** himmelblau

skylark n. Feldlerche; — v. Unfug treiben, Dummheiten machen

skylight n. Oberlicht, Lichthof; (naut.) Deckfenster

skyline n. Horizontlinie; Silhouette; Wolkenkratzerkette

skyrocket n. Raumrakete; — v. raketengleich aufsteigen, in die Höhe schiessen

skyscraper n. Wolkenkratzer, Hochhaus

slab n. Platte, Fliese; Schalbrett

slack n. Flaute; (min.) Grus; (naut.) loses Tauende; pl. Slacks; lange, weite Hosen; — adj. schlaff, lose, locker; matt; (nach)lässig; (com.) flau; **-en** v. erschlaffen, ermatten, nachlassen, (sich) verlangsamen; entspannen; **-er** n.

Drückeberger, Schlappschwanz

slag n. Schlacke

slam n. Schlag, Knall; (cards) Schlemm, Durchmarsch; — v. zuschlagen, zuknallen; (cards) Schlemm bieten (or machen)

slander n. Verleumdung; — v. verleumden, schmähen; **-er** n. Verleumder

slang n. Slang; Jargon; Berufssprache

slant n. Abhang, Schräge; Neigung, Richtung; — v. sich neigen, abfallen; schräg liegen (or legen), abschrägen; (coll.) angleichen; **-ing** adj. schief, schräg; quer, geneigt; abschüssig

slap n. Klaps, Schlag; — adv. stracks; — v. klapsen, schlagen

slash n. Hieb, Schlitz, Schmarre, Schnitt; — v. hauen, schlitzen, schneiden

slat n. Querholz, Leiste, Schiene

slate n. Schiefer; (educ.) Schiefertafel; (pol.) Kandidatenliste; — adj. schieferfarbig, blaugrau; — v. mit Schiefer decken; (pol.) auf die Kandidatenliste setzen

slaughter n. Schlachten; Gemetzel, Blutbad; Ermordung; — v. (ab)schlachten; niedermetzeln

slaughterhouse n. Schlachthaus

slave n. Sklave; — v. sich schinden (or plagen), **-ry** n. Sklaverei, Knechtschaft; Schinderei; **white -ry** Mädchenhandel

slaw n. Krautsalat

slay v. erschlagen, umbringen; vernichten; **-er** n. Totschläger, Mörder

sled(ge) n. Schlitten, Schleife

sledge (**hammer**) n. Schmiedehammer, Vorschlaghammer

sleek adj. glatt, blank; geschmeidig; — v. glätten, putzen; gleiten

sleep n. Schlaf; — v. schlafen; — **soundly** fest schlafen; **-er** n. Schläfer; (rail.) Schlafwagen; Querträger, Schwelle; **-iness** n. Schläfrigkeit; (fig.) Trägheit; **-ing** n. Schlafen; Ruhen; **-ing** adj. schlafend; **-ing bag** Schlafsack; **-ing room** Schlafzimmer; **-ing sickness** Schlafkrankheit; **-less** adj. schlaflos; (fig.) ruhelos; **-y** adj. schläfrig, verschlafen, träge

sleepwalker n. Nachtwandler, Somnambule

sleepyhead n. (orn.) Ruderente; (fig.) Schlafmütze

sleet n. Schlossen, Graupeln; Hagelschauer; — v. graupeln, hageln

sleeve n. Ärmel; (mech.) Muffe; **laugh in one's** — sich ins Fäustchen lachen; **-less** adj. ärmellos

sleigh n. Schlitten

sleight n. Kunststück, Taschenspielerei

slender adj. schlank, dünn, mager; schwach, dürftig

Sleswick-Holstein n. Schleswick-Holstein

sleuth n. Spürhund; (coll.) Detektiv

slice n. Schnitte, Scheibe; — v. abschneiden, in Scheiben schneiden

slick adj. gewandt, glattzüngig; glatt, geölt; — v. glätten, polieren; **-er** n. wasserdichter Mantel; (coll.) gerissener

Gauner

slide *n.* Gleiten; Gleitbahn; (film) Diapositiv; (geol.) Erdrutsch; (mech.) Gleitbacke, Läufer, Schieber; — **rule** Rechenschieber; — **valve** Schieberventil; — *v.* (aus)gleiten, rutschen, schlittern; einschieben, laufen lassen; (fig.) hinübergleiten

sliding scale *n.* bewegliche Lohnskale (*or* Preisskala)

slight *n.* Nichtachtung, Geringschätzung; — *adj.* verächtlich, geringschätzig; gering, unbedeutend; dünn, schwach, leicht; — *v.* geringschätzig behandeln, vernachlässigen; **-ness** *n.* Geringfügigkeit, Nachlässigkeit; Schwäche, Dünnheit

slim *adj.* schlank, schmächtig; unbedeutend, unwesentlich; gerissen; **-ness** *n.* Schlankheit

slime *n.* Schleim, Schlamm

sling *n.* Schleuder; Tragriemen, Gewehrriemen; Wurf, Stoss; (med.) Schlinge, Binde; — *v.* schleudern; überhängen, umschlingen; (mil.) schultern

slingshot *n.* Schleuder

slink *v.* schleichen

slip *n.* Gleiten, Rutschen; Entschlüpfen, Entwischen; Unterrock; Kissenbezug; (bot.) Spross, Steckling; (naut.) Helling; (fig.) Fehler, Versehen; — **of paper** Zettel; — **of the tongue** Versprechen; — *v.* gleiten, rutschen; ausgleiten; schleudern; entwischen, entschlüpfen; (fig.) sich irren (*or* versprechen); **-pery** *adj.* schlüpfrig, glitschig, glatt; (fig.) unzuverlässlich, veränderlich

slipcover *n.* Möbelüberzug; Schutzumschlag

slipper *n.* Pantoffel, Hausschuhe

slipshod *adj.* latschig, nachlässig; unordentlich

slit *n.* Schlitz, Spalte; — *v.* (zer)schlitzen, spalten

sliver *n.* Splitter; — *v.* abreissen, abspalten, splittern

slobber *n.* Geifer; — *v.* geifern, sabbern

slogan *n.* Schlagwort, Reklametext

sloop *n.* Schaluppe, Korvette

slop *n.* Pfuhl, Pfütze; Schmutzfleck; *pl.* Spülwasser; Gesöff; Krankensuppe; fertiggekaufte Kleidungsstücke; — **pail** Spüleimer; **-py** *adj.* nass, wässrig; (coll.) schmutzig, nachlässig

slope *n.* Abhang, Neigung, Böschung; Abschrägung, Fall; — *v.* abfallen; (sich) neigen (*or* abschrägen)

slot *n.* Öffnung, Einwurf, Schlitz; (mech.) Kerbe, Nut; — **machine** Automat

slouch *n.* schlaffe Haltung; Müssiggänger; — *adj.* **hat** Schlapphut; — *v.* schlottern, schlendern; (coll.) latschen

slough *n.* Sumpf, Pfütze; (mech.) Schlauch, Balg; (med.) Schorf; (zool.) abgeworfene Schlangenhaut; (fig.) Niedergeschlagenheit

slovenly *adj.* schmutzig, schlampig, liederlich

slow *adj.* langsam, träge; spät, nachgehend; schwerfällig, bedächtig; faul, nachlässig; — **motion** Zeitlupe; — *v.* verlangsamen, hinziehen; — **down** langsamer fahren, sich mehr Zeit lassen; **-ness** *n.* Langsamkeit; Nachlässigkeit; Begriffsstutzigkeit

sludge *n.* Schlamm; Eisscholle

slug *n.* Schlag; (mech.) Hackblei, Metallstück; (zool.) Wegschnecke; — *v.* einen Schlag versetzen; **-gard** *n.* Faulenzer, Müssiggänger; **-gish** *adj.* träge, schwerfällig, faul; albern, dumm; (agr.) unfruchtbar; **-gishness** *n.* Trägheit, Schwerfälligkeit

sluice *n.* Schleuse, Siel; durchgeschleuste Wasser; — *v.* schleusen; überschwemmen, berieseln; waschen

slum *n.* Hintergasse; *pl.* Elendsviertel, Verbrechergegend; — *v.* Elendsquartiere besuchen, im Armenviertel arbeiten

slumber *n.* Schlummer; — *v.* schlummern

slump *n.* Preissturz, Nachlassen

slur *n.* Fleck, Makel; Vorwurf, Verleumdung; (mus.) Bindezeichen; — *v.* beschmutzen, beflecken; verleumden; vertuschen, übergehen; (mus.) binden, schleifen

slush *n.* Matsch, Schlamm; (mech.) Schmiere

small *n.* Kleine; Kurzwaren, Kleingebäck; — **of the back** Kreuz, Lendengegend; — *adj.* klein, schmal, gering, dünn, schlank; (fig.) kleinlich, beschränkt; — **arms** Handwaffen; — **change** Kleingeld; — **fry** kleines Gemüse, Kinder; — **hours** erste Morgenstunden; — **intestine** Dünndarm; — **talk** Plauderei; **-ish** *adj.* winzig, schmächtig; **-ness** *n.* Kleinheit, Schmalheit; Unbedeutenheit

smallpox *n.* Pocken, Blattern

smart *n.* Schmerz, Stich; — *adj.* gewandt, gerissen, schlau, pfiffig; elegant, fein; schmerzhaft, heftig, stechend, schneidend; — **money** Schmerzensgeld; **-ness** *n.* Schlauheit, Gescheitheit; Eleganz; Schneidigkeit

smash *n.* Zerschmettern; Krach; Zerstörung; (tennis) Schmetterball; (sl.) Zusammenbruch, Bankrott; — *v.* zerschmeissen, zertrümmern, (zer)schmettern

smashup *n.* schrecklicher Zusammenstoss (*or* Zusammenbruch)

smattering *n.* oberflächliche Kenntnis

smear *n.* Schmiere; Schmiererei; (coll.) Verleumdung; — *v.* schmieren; beschmieren, besudeln; (coll.) anschwärzen

smell *n.* Geruch; Duft; **sense of** — Geruchssinn; — *v.* riechen; duften; (coll.) aufspüren

smile *n.* Lächeln; — *v.* lächeln, schmunzeln

smirch *v.* beschmieren, besudeln

smite *v.* (er)schlagen, treffen, eindringen; heimsuchen, vernichten

smith *n.* Schmied; **black-** Grobschmied, Hufschmied; **-(er)y** *n.* Schmiede; Schmiedehandwerk smock n. Frauenhemd; Kittel; — frock Staubmantel. Arbeitskittel

smog n. Rauchschleier, Dunstschleier; russige Atmosphäre

smoke n. Rauch, Qualm, Dunst; (coll.) Rauchware; — consumer Rauchverzehrer; — pipe Abzugsrohr; — screen Rauchvorhang; künstlicher Nebelschleier; — v. rauchen, räuchern; qualmen, dampfen; (mil.) einnebeln; —less adj. rauchlos; —less powder rauchschwaches Pulver; —r n. Raucher; Räucherer; (coll.) Raucherabteil

smokehouse n. Räucherhaus

smokestack n. Schornstein, Rauchfang

smoking n. Rauchen; Räuchern; — adj. rauchend, räuchernd; — car Raucherabteil; no —! Rauchen verboten!

smoky adj. rauchig, qualmig; dampfend, nebelig

smolder n. Qualm; — v. schwelen, qualmen; glimmen

smooth adj. glatt; mild, schlicht, sanft; poliert; (fig.) fliessend, geschmeidig, schmeichlerisch; — v. glätten, polieren, ebnen; plätten; (fig.) mildern, schlichten; —ly adv. sanft, weich; geschoren; klumpenfrei; fliessend; —ness n. Glätte, Ebenheit; (fig.) Sanftheit, Freundlichkeit

smother n. Qualm, Dunst; — v. ersticken; dämpfen, schmoren

smudge n. Fleck, Schmutz; — v. (be)schmieren, beschmutzen

smug adj. schmuck, sauber; (fig.) eitel, selbstzufrieden

smuggle v. schmuggeln; —r n. Schmuggler

smuggling n. Schmuggel

smut n. Russ(fleck); Schmutz; Zote; (agr.) Brand; — v. berussen, beschmutzen; (agr.) den Brand bekommen; —ty adj. russig, schmutzig; (agr.) brandig; (fig.) schlüpfrig, zotig

snack n. Bissen, Imbiss; Anteil; go —s teilnehmen, teilhaben

snag n. Knoten, Knorren; Baumstumpf; (zool.) Geweihsprosse; Raffzahn

snail n. Schnecke

snake n. Schlange, Natter; — v. schlängeln, winden

snap n. Zuschnappen, Schnapper; Knall, Knack(s); Bruch, Sprung; (coll.) etwas Leichtes; — v. schnappen, zuschnappen; (zer)springen, abbrechen; (coll.) anschnauzen; — one's fingers at someone jemandem ein Schnippchen schlagen; —per n. Schnapper; —py adj. schnippig, bissig; beissend; (coll.) lebhaft, elegant

snapdragon n. Löwenmaul

snapshot n. Schnappschuss, Momentaufnahme

snare n. Schlinge, Fallstrick; — v. verstricken, umgarnen; mit einer Schlinge fangen

snarl n. Knurren; — v. knurren, brummen

snatch n. schneller Griff, Ruck; Stückchen, Bissen; Augenblick; — v. schnell ergreifen, erhaschen, erschnappen; an sich reissen

sneak n. Schleicher, Kriecher; Duckmäuser; — v. schleichen, kriechen; stibitzen; angeben

sneer n. Hohnlächeln, Naserümpfen; Stichelei; — v. hohnlächeln, spötteln, die Nase rümpfen

sneeze n. Niesen; — v. niesen

snicker n. Gekicher; — v. kichern

sniff n. Schnüffeln, Naserümpfen; — n. schnüffeln, schnuppern, riechen; die Nase rümpfen; (fig.) spionieren, wittern; —le n. Näseln; —le v. näseln; schnupfen, triefen; wimmern

snip n. Schnippen; Schnitzel; — v. schnippen; schnipseln, schneiden

snipe n. Schnepfe, Bekassine; — v. Schnepfen schiessen; (mil.) aus dem Hinterhalt (or grosser Entfernung) schiessen; —r n. Scharfschütze

snivel n. Nasenschleim, Rotz; — v. Schluchzen, wehleidig tun; —ly adj. triefnasig, schnüffelnd

snob n. Snob, Grosstuer, Protz; —bish adj. snobistisch, eingebildet; protzig

snood n. Haarband, Haarnetz

snoop n. Schnüffler; (coll.) Detektiv; — v. schnüffeln, aufspüren; (coll.) spionieren

snooze n. Schlummer, Schläfchen; — r. schlummern, ein Schläfchen tun

snore n. Schnarchen; — v. schnarchen

snorkel n. Schnorchel; Feuerleiter

snout n. Schnauze, Maul; Rüssel; (mech.) Mundstück, Tülle; (coll.) Nase

snow n. Schnee; — line Schneegrenze; — owl Schneeule; — v. schneien; —y adj. schneeig, beschneit; schneeweiss

snowball n. Schneeball; — tree Schneeballstrauch

snowbound adj. eingeschneit

snowdrift n. Schneewehe

snowdrop n. Schneeglöckchen

snowflake n. Schneeflocke

snowplow n. Schneepflug

snowshed n. Lawinenschutzwand

snowslide n. Lawine

snowstorm n. Schneesturm

snowsweeper n. Schneepflug

snow-white adj. schneeweiss; Snow-white n. Schneewittchen

snub n. Zurechtweisung, Rüge, Verweis; — v. rügen, verweisen, schelten, anfahren

snub-nosed adj. stumpfnasig

snuff n. Schnupftabak; Schnauben; — v. schnauben, schnüffeln, schnupfen; näseln, verschnupft sein; —er n. Tabakschnupfer; Lichtputzschere; —le v. schnuppern, beschnüffeln; näseln; —les n. pl. (med.) festsitzender Schnupfen

snuffbox n. Schnupftabakdose

snug adj. schmuck, nett; eng; behaglich, wohnlich; —gle v. (sich) anschmiegen, liebkosen

so adv. so, also; derartig, indem; wie, auch; and — forth und so weiter; I hope — ich hoffe es; — as solange als; — much (gerade) soviel; — much more um so mehr; — then darum, daher

soak n. Einweichen; (coll.) Kneiperei,

Sauferei; — v. einweichen, einsaugen, durchnässen; (coll.) sich vollaufen lassen

soap n. Seife; (sl.) Schmus; Bestechungsgeld; — **bubble** Seifenblase; — **opera** Schmalzoper, schmalziges Programm; (rad.) Schauspielserie für Hausfrauen; — **works** Seifenfabrik; — v. (ein)seifen; (sl.) schmeicheln, bestechen; **-less** adj. seifenlos; (coll.) ungewaschen; **-y** adj. seifig; (coll.) glatt(züngig)

soapbox n. Seifenkiste; (coll.) improvisierte Plattform

soapstone n. Speckstein

soapsuds n. pl. Seifenlauge, Seifenwasser

soar v. sich erheben (or aufschwingen); **-ing** n. Aufstieg; **-ing** adj. hochfliegend, erhaben

sob n. Schluchzen, Schluchzer; — v. schluchzen

sober adj. nüchtern, mässig; ernst, besonnen

so-called adj. sogenannt

soccer n. Rugbyart

sociability n. Geselligkeit

sociable adj. gesellig

social adj. sozial; gesellschaftlich, gesellig; — **science** Sozialwissenschaft, Soziologie; — **security** Sozialversicherung; — **services** soziale Einrichtungen; — **work** Fürsorge; — **worker** Fürsorger; **-ism** n. Sozialismus; **-ist** n. Sozialist; **-istic** adj. sozialistisch; **-ize** v. sozialisieren

society n. Gesellschaft; Verein, Bund

sociological adj. soziologisch

sociology n. Soziologie, Sozialwissenschaft

sock n. Socke; Einlegesohle; (sl.) Prügel

socket n. (anat.) Höhle, Pfanne; (elec.) Fassung; (mech.) Röhre

sod n. Rasen(decke); — v. mit Rasen belegen

soda n. Soda, kohlensaures Natron; **baking —** Backpulver; — **bicarbonate** doppelkohlensaures Natron; — **cracker** Salzkeks; — **fountain** Siphon; — **water** Selterwasser

sodium n. Natrium; — **chloride** Chlornatrium, Kochsalz

sofa n. Sofa, Ruhebett

soft adj. weich, sanft; mild, zart; zärtlich; (coll.) einfältig; — **coal** Braunkohle; — **drink** alkoholfreies Getränk; — v. erweichen; mildern, lindern; (fig.) besänftigen; **-ening** n. Erweichen; **-ening of the brain** Gehirnerweichung; **-ness** n. Weichheit, Sanftmut, Milde

softball n. Baseballart

soft-boiled adj. weichgekocht; — **eggs** weich(gekocht)e Eier

soft-pedal v. zurücknehmen, leiser treten

soft-spoken adj. leise sprechend; (fig.) sanft, mild

soggy adj. durchweicht, nass, feucht; sumpfig

soil n. Boden, Erde; Suhle; Schmutz, Fleck; (agr.) Dünger; — v. beschmutzen, besudeln, beflecken; (agr.) düngen, Grünfutter geben; **-ed** adj. beschmutzt, besudelt, befleckt

solace n. Trost, Erquickung; — v. trösten, erquicken, aufheitern; beruhigen

solar adj. solar; Sonnen-; — **plexus** Sonnengeflecht; — **system** Sonnensystem; **-ium** n. sonniger Raum, Glasveranda

solder n. Lot; Lötzinn; Kitt, Bindemittel; — v. löten, kitten; (fig.) verbinden, zusammenfügen; **-ing** n. Löten; **-ing iron** Lötkolben

soldier n. Soldat; **-ly** adj. soldatisch, militärisch; Soldaten-

sole n. Sohle; (ichth.) Seezunge; — adj. allein, einzig; (law) ledig, unverheiratet; — v. besohlen

solemn adj. feierlich, würdevoll; **-ity** n. Ernst, Feierlichkeit, Würde; Festlichkeit; **-ize** v. feiern, festlich begehen; feierlich stimmen

solicit v. nachsuchen, ersuchen; (dringend) bitten, sich bewerben; erfordern; ansprechen, belästigen; **-ation** n. Ersuchen, dringende Bitte; **-or** n. Antragsteller; Bittsteller; (law) Anwalt; **-ous** adj. besorgt, bekümmert; **-ude** n. Besorgnis, Sorge; Sorgfalt

solid adj. fest, dicht, massiv, dauerhaft; echt, gediegen, stark, gesund; (com.) kreditfähig, solide; (geom.) körperlich; kubisch; (pol.) einstimmig, einhellig; (fig.) zuverlässig; in — **color** einfarbig; — **geometry** Stereometrie; **-n** n. (fester) Körper; **-arity** n. Solidarität; **-ify** v. (sich) verdichten, verhärten; **-ity** n. Solidität; Festigkeit, Gediegenheit

soliloquist n. Monologisierende

soliloquy n. Monolog, Selbstgespräch

solitary n. Einsiedler, Eremit; — adj. allein, einsam, abgesondert, einzig; lerisch; öde, abgelegen; zurückgezogen; einzeln

solitude n. Einsamkeit, Öde

solstice n. Sonnenwende

solution n. Lösung

solve v. (auf)lösen; **-ncy** n. Zahlungsfähigkeit; **-nt** adj. (auf)lösend; zahlungsfähig; **-nt** n. Lösungsmittel

some adj. and pron. irgendein, ein gewisser; etwas; einige, etliche, manche; etwa, ungefähr; — adv. etwas, sehr

somebody n. jemand; — adj. and pron. jemand, irgendein

somehow adv. irgendwie, auf irgendeine Art

someone pron. irgendjemand, irgendein

somersault, somerset n. Purzelbaum; — v. einen Purzelbaum (or Kobolz) schiessen

something n. etwas; — adv. etwas, ein wenig; ziemlich; — **else** etwas anderes

sometime adv. einmal, einst; ehemals; — adj. ehemalig, früher; **-s** adv. zuweilen, manchmal

somewhat n. etwas Bedeutendes; — adv. etwas, ein wenig; einigermassen, ziemlich

somewhere adv. irgendwo(hin); — **else** anderswo

somnambulism n. Nachtwandeln, Somnambulismus

son n. Sohn

sonar n. Sonar-Gerät (ein speziell amerikanisches Gerät, eine Verbesserung des Echolot)

song n. Lied; Gesang; (lit.) Gedicht; **buy for a** — spottbillig kaufen; **Song of Solomon** Hohe Lied Salomons; — **sparrow** Rohrsperling; — **thrush** Singdrossel; — **writer** Liederdichter, Liederkomponist; **-ster** n. Sänger; Singvogel

songbook n. Liederbuch, Gesangbuch

sonic adj. mit Schallgeschwindigkeit; — **barrier** Schallgrenze; — **boom** Schallexplosion

son-in-law n. Schwiegersohn

sonorous adj. klangvoll, wohltönend

soon adv. bald, schnell; früh(zeitig); **as** — **as** sobald wie; **-er** adv. eher, früher; lieber; **no -er than kaum .. als; -er or later** früher oder später

soot n. Russ; — v. (be)russen; **-y** adj. russig, berusst; russend; (fig.) düster

soothe v. beruhigen, besänftigen, lindern

soothsayer n. Wahrsager

sophism n. Sophismus; Trugschluss

sophist n. Sophist; **-ic(al)** adj. sophistisch; **-icate** v. unnatürlich (or gekünstelt) werden; aufklären; anders darstellen; **-icate(d)** adj. gekünstelt, unnatürlich; anspruchsvoll, weltklug; **-ication** n. Sophisterei, Trugschluss; Verfälschung; **-ry** n. Sophistik, Spitzfindigkeit

sophomore n. Student (im zweiten Jahr)

sopping adj. durchweicht; — **wet** klatschnass

soprano n. Sopran; — **singer** Sopranistin

sorcerer n. Zauberer, Hexenmeister

sorceress n. Zauberin, Hexe

sorcery n. Zauberei, Zauberkunst; Hexerei, Magie

sordid adj. schmutzig; gemein; geizig

sore n. wunde Stelle; Übel; — adj. wund, schmerzhaft, entzündet; empfindlich; schlimm; — **throat** Halsschmerzen, Halsweh

sorehead n. Sauertopf, Missvergnügte

sorghum n. chinesisches Zuckerrohr

sorority n. Schwesternschaft; Mädchenclub, Frauenclub

sorrel n. Sauerampfer; (zool.) Rotfuchs; — adj. rotbraun, fuchsrot

sorrow n. Sorge, Trübsal; Gram, Kummer, Leid; — v. trauern, sich grämen (or grämen, betrüben); **-ful** adj. sorgenvoll, kummervoll; betrübt, jämmerlich

sorry adj. traurig, bekümmert, betrübt; **be** — etwas bedauern; **I am very** — es tut mir leid; entschuldigen Sie, bitte

sort n. Sorte, Art, Gattung, Qualität; **in some** — of gewissermassen, Weise; **out of** **-s** unpässlich, verdriesslich; **something of the** —, **that** — of **thing** etwas Derartiges; — v. sortieren, aussuchen; klassifizieren, aussondern; übereinstimmen

so-so adv. soso, leidlich, einigermassen

sot n. Trunkenbold; **-tish** adj. versoffen, dumm

soul n. Seele; **-ful** adj. seelenvoll

sound n. Ton, Laut, Schall, Klang; (ichth.) Schwimmblase; (med.) Sonde;

(naut.) Sund, Meerenge; — adj. gesund, unversehrt, unbeschädigt; unverdorben; tadellos; stark, tüchtig, gründlich; (sleep) fest; — **track** Tonspur; — **wave** Schallwelle; — v. (er)tönen, (er)schallen, (er)klingen; erschallen lassen; (med.) sondieren; abhorchen; (naut.) loten; **-ing** n. Lotung; **-ing** adj. tönend, klingend, klangvoll, wohlklingend; (er)schallend; (gram.) stimmhaft, (fig.) bombastisch; **-ing line** Lotleine, Senkschnur; **-ness** n. Gesundheit, Unversehrtheit; Stärke; Gründlichkeit, Zuverlässigkeit, Richtigkeit

soundboard n. Resonanzboden

sounder key n. Morsetaste

soundproof adj. schalldicht; — v. schalldicht machen

soup n. Suppe, Brühe; (avi.) Milchsuppe, Nebel

sour n. Säure, Saure; — adj. sauer; scharf, bitter, geronnen; (agr.) kalt, nass; (fig.) sauertöpfig, mürrisch; — v. säuern; (fig.) erbittern, erzürnen, versauern

source n. Quelle, Ursprung; Urheber

souse n. Salzlake, Pökelbrühe; — v. einsalzen, einpökeln, durchnässen

south n. Süden; Südseite; Südwind; — adj. südlich, Süd-; **-ern** adj. südlich; **-erner** n. Südländer, Südstaatler

southernmost adj. südlichst

South Pole n. Südpol

southward adv. südwärts

southwest n. Südwest(en); **-(ern)** adj. südwestlich; **-er** n. Südwestwind; (hat) Südwester

souvenir n. Souvenir, Andenken

sovereign n. Souverän, Herrscher; Sovereign, Pfund Sterling; — adj. souverän, unumschränkt; höchst, vornehmst; unübertrefflich, unfehlbar; **-ty** n. Souveränität, Oberherrschaft

Soviet n. Sowjet

sow n. Sau, Bache, Mutterschwein; (mech.) Mulde; — v. (aus)säen, ausstreuen; **-er** n. Säemann, Säemaschine; **-ing** n. Aussaat; Saatkorn

soybean n. Sojabohne

spa n. Heilbad, Kurort

space n. Raum, Platz; Zwischenraum; Zeitraum; Flächeninhalt; — **capsule** Kapsel des Astronauten; Weltraumschiff; — **command** Fernlenkung, Fernsteuerung; — **control** Photogrametrie; — **suit** Überdruckkombination, Raumanzug des Astronauten; — v. einteilen, in Zwischenräume setzen; (typ.) durchschiessen, sperren

spaceship n. Raumschiff

spacious adj. geräumig, umfassend; weit

spade n. Spaten; (cards) Pik; **call a** — **a** — das Kind beim richtigen Namen nennen; — v. graben; umgraben

span n. Spanne; (agr.) Gespann; (arch.) Spannweite; — **of a bridge** Brückenweite, Brückenbogen; — v. (um)spannen, überspannen; (naut.) zurren

spangle n. Flitter; — v. mit Flitter be-

setzen; flimmern, funkeln; (fig.) übersäen

spaniel n. Spaniel, Wachtelhund

spank n. Schlag, Klaps; — v. klapsen;
eilen, flitzen

spar n. Sparren; (min.) Spat; (naut.)
Spiere; (fig.) Finte; — v. Scheinhiebe
machen; (boxing) trainieren; (fig.) sich
streiten

spare v. (er)sparen, schonen; erübrigen;
entbehren; — adj. sparsam, spärlich;
mager, karg; verfügbar; — **anchor**
Reserveanker; — **bed** Gastbett; —
money Sparpfennig, Notgroschen; —
parts Ersatzteile; — **time** Freizeit,
Mussezeit; — **tire** Ersatzreifen; -**ly**
adv. sparsam, spärlich; kaum

sparerib n. Rippespeer, Rippenstück

sparing n. Sparen, Sparsamkeit; — adj.
sparsam, karg; spärlich, knapp; voraussehend

spark n. Funke(n); — **plug** Zündkerze;
-**le** n. Funke(n); -**le** v. funkeln, blitzen,
sprühen; (wine) schäumen

sparrow n. Sperling, Spatz; — **hawk**
Sperber

spasm n. Krampf; -**odic** adj. krampfhaft

spastic adj. zuckend

spatial adj. räumlich

spatter n. Spritzer; Geknatter; — v.
(be)spritzen

spatula n. Spatel; (orn.) Löffelente

spawn n. Laich, Rogen, Fischbrut; — v.
laichen; (coll.) aushecken; -**ing** n.
Laichen

speak v. sprechen, reden; äussern; (mus.)
erschallen, erklingen; (naut.) anpreien;
so to — sozusagen; — **for** bitten, ein
Wort einlegen für; — **for oneself** sich
verteidigen; — **in torrents** sich in einem
Wortschwall ergiessen; — **out** laut
sprechen; offen reden, aussprechen; —
plainly freiheraus sprechen; — **to** anreden, ins Gewissen reden; — **up!**
heraus mit der Sprache! -**er** n. Sprecher,
Redner; Vorsitzende; -**ing** n. Sprechen,
Reden; -**ing** adj. sprechend, ausdrucksvoll; -**ing trumpet**, -**ing tube** Sprachrohr

spear n. Speer, Spiess, Lange; — v. durchbohren, (auf)spiessen

spearhead n. Speerspitze, Lanzenspitze;
(mil.) Vortrupp, Spitze

special adj. speziell; besonder, eigen, ausserordentlich; Spezial-; — **delivery**
Eilzustellung; -**ist** n. Spezialist, Fachmann, Facharzt; -**ize** v. spezialisieren;
einzeln anführen; besonders ausbilden;
-(**i**)**ty** n. Spezialität; (law) besiegelte
Urkunde

special-delivery letter n. Eilbrief

species n. pl. Art, Gattung, Sorte

specific adj. spezifisch; eigen(tümlich), besonder; — **gravity** spezifisches Gewicht;
— n. (med.) besonderes Heilmittel;
-**ation** n. Spezifizierung; Einzelangabe,
Beschreibung; -**ations** pl. Bestimmungen

specify v. einzeln angeben (or benennen);
spezifizieren

specimen n. Probe(stück), Muster, Exemplar

spectacle n. Anblick; Schauspiel, Schau;
pl. Brille, Augengläser

spectacular adj. schauspielerisch; lärmend;
— n. (TV) Fernsehgrossprogramm

spectator n. Zuschauer, Beobachter

spectral adj. geisterhaft, gespenstisch;
(phy.) Spektral-

spectroscope n. Spektroskop, Spektra-
lapparat

spectrum n. Spektrum, Farbenbild; **solar**
— Sonnenspektrum

speculate v. spekulieren

speculation n. Spekulation

speech n. Sprache; Rede, Vortrag; Unterredung, Unterhaltung; -**less** adj.
sprachlos, stumm

speed n. Eile, Schnelligkeit, Geschwindigkeit; (mech.) Gang, Lauf; (fig.) Beschleunigung, Fortgang, Erfolg; **average** — Durchschnittsgeschwindigkeit;
good —! viel Glück! (or Erfolg!); **initial**
— Anfangsgeschwindigkeit; — **limit**
(zulässige) Höchstgeschwindigkeit; —
v. (be)eilen; beschleunigen, fördern;
(fig.) glücken, gelingen; -**ily** adv.
schnellfüssig; eilfertig; rasch bereit;
baldig; förderlich; -**y** adj. eilig, schnell,
rasch; (fig.) glücklich

speedboat n. Rennboot; Schnellboot

speedometer n. Tachometer, Geschwin-
digkeitsanzeiger

speed-up n. Beschleunigung

speedway n. Schnellstrasse

spell n. Zauber; Zauberformel; Ablösung;
(med.) Anfall; (coll.) Unterbrechung,
Atempause; — v. bezaubern; ablösen;
ausrufen; (gram.) buchstabieren, richtig schreiben; (fig.) entziffern, ergründen; -**er** n. Fibel; Buchstabierer;
-**ing** n. Buchstabieren; Orthographie,
Rechtschreibung; -**ing bee** Buchstabierwettbewerb

spellbound adj. (fest)gebannt, bezaubert

spend v. spenden, ausgeben, verwenden;
erschöpfen, verschwenden; (time) verbringen

spendthrift n. Verschwender; — adj. verschwenderisch

spent adj. verausgabt, verbraucht; erschöpft, entkräftet; matt

sperm n. (männlicher) Same

spew v. (aus)speihen; (coll.) sich erbrechen

sphere n. Sphäre, Wirkungskreis; Kugel,
Erdkugel, Himmelskugel

spice n. Gewürz; (fig.) Würze, Beigeschmack; — v. würzen

spick-and-span adj. blitzblank; funkel-
nagelneu; schmuck

spicy adj. würzig, aromatisch; gewürzt;
(coll.) pikant

spider n. Spinne; (mech.) Dreifuss

spigot n. Zapfen, Hahn

spike n. Nagel, Stift; (bot.) Ähre; Kolben;
Dorn, Stachel; (zool.) Geweihsprosse;
pl. (sports) Spikes

spill n. Umwerfen, Abfluss; Fidibus;
(coll.) Sturz; — v. verschütten,

verspritzen, vergiessen; (naut.) brassen; (coll.) abwerfen

spin n. Wirbeln; Drehung; rasche Fahrt; — v. wirbeln, kreiseln, trudeln, drehen; spinnen; **-dle** n. Spindel, Spule; **-ning** n. Spinnerei; Gespinst; **-ning adj. -ning frame** Spinnmaschine; **-ning jenny** Mehrspulmaschine; **-ning mill** Spinnerei; **-ning wheel** Spinnrad

spinach n. Spinat

spinal adj. spinal, Rücken-; — **column** Rückgrat, Wirbelsäule; — **cord** Rückenmark

spine n. (anat.) Rückgrat; (bot.) Dorn, Stachel; (geol.) Grat; (ichth.) Stachel

spinster n. alte Jungfer

spiral adj. Spiral-; schneckenförmig, schraubenförmig; — **stairs** Wendeltreppe; — n. Spirale, Schneckenlinie

spire n. Spitze, Gipfel; (arch.) Turmspitze; Kirchturm

spirit n. Geist; Gespenst; Genie; Sinn, Mut; Seele, Gemütsart; pl. Spiritus; Spirituosen; **in high -s** guter Laune; — v. begeistern, aufmuntern; — **away** verschwinden lassen, wegzaubern; entführen; **-ed** adj. geistvoll, lebhaft, feurig; mutig; **-ism** n. Spiritismus, Geisterglaube; **-ual** adj. geistig, geistlich; geistreich; **-ualism** n. Spiritualismus; Spiritismus; **-ualist** n. Spiritualist; Spiritist

spirit v. (hervor)spritzen; (hervor)strömen

spit n. Speichel, Spucke; Sprühregen; (geol.) Landzunge; (mech.) Spiess; — v. spucken, speien; (auf)spiessen; **-tle** n. Speichel; (coll.) Spucke; **-toon** n. Spucknapf

spite n. Groll, Ärger, Verdruss; Bosheit; **in — of** trotz, ungeachtet; **out of spite** aus Groll, zum Ärger; — v. grollen, ärgern; kränken; **-ful** adj. boshaft, gehässig; feindselig

spitfire n. Hitzkopf

spitz n. (dog) Spitz

splash n. Fleck, Spritzer; — v. (be)spritzen, platschen

splayfoot n. Spreizfuss

spleen n. Spleen, Verschrobenheit, üble Laune; (anat.) Milz

splendid adj. glänzend, prächtig, herrlich

splendo(u)r n. Glanz, Pracht, Herrlichkeit

splice n. Verbinden, Einfügen; (naut.) Spleissen; (sl.) Heirat; — v. verbinden, einfügen; verweben; (naut.) spleissen; (sl.) verheiraten

splint n. Splitter, Span; (mech.) Splint; (med.) Schiene; — v. schienen; **-er** n. Span, Splitter; **-er** v. (zer)splittern, zerspalten

split n. Spalt, Riss, Bruch; Spaltung; — adj. gespalten, gespaltet; — v. spalten, zereissen; bersten; (sich) entzweien; — **one's sides with laughter** sich totlachen; **-ting** adj. spaltend; sehr heftig, schnell; **-ting headache** rasende Kopfschmerzen

spoil n. Raub; (mech.) Schlacke; pl.

Beute, — v. (be)rauben, plündern; verderben; verwöhnen; stören; **-er** n. Räuber, Plünderer; Verderber; Störenfried

spoke n. Speiche, Sprosse; (mech.) Hemmvorrichtung

spokesman n. Wortführer, Fürsprecher

sponge n. Schwamm; (coll.) Schmarotzer; **throw up the —** (sports) sich für besiegt erklären; — v. abwischen, auslöschen; reiben; aufsaugen; (coll.) schmarotzen; — **up** sich vollsaugen; **-r** n. Wischer; Anfeuchter; (naut.) Schwammfischer; (coll.) Schmarotzer

spongecake n. Biskuitkuchen

spongy adj. schwammig, porös

sponsor n. Förderer, Gönner; Bürge; Pate; (rad.) reklamemachende Firma

spontaneity n. Spontaneität; Freiwilligkeit

spontaneous adj. spontan, freiwillig; Selbst-; — **combustion** Selbstverbrennung

spook n. Spuken; — v. spuken

spool n. Spule; — v. (auf)spulen

spoon n. Löffel; — v. (aus)löffeln; **-ful** n. Löffelvoll

spore n. Spore

sport n. Sport; Spiel, Unterhaltung; — **shirt** Sporthemd; — v. spielen, sich belustigen, scherzen; Sport treiben; **-ing** adj. spielend; sporttreibend; Sport-; **-ive** adj. lustig, scherzhaft; kurzweilig; sportlich

sportsman n. Sportler; Sportliebhaber; Weidmann; **-ship** n. Sportlichkeit

spot n. Fleck(en), Klecks; Tupfen, Punkt; Stelle, Ort; (cards and dice) Auge; — **cash** Bargeld; — **remover** Fleckenentferner; — v. (be)flecken; tüpfeln, sprenkeln; feststellen; **-ting** adj. **-ting system** Meldesystem; **-less** adj. fleckenlos; unbefleckt; **-ted** adj., **-ty** adj. gefleckt, fleckig; gesprenkelt, getupft; (fig.) befleckt, besudelt; **-ted fever** Flecktyphus

spotlight n. Scheinwerfer(licht)

spouse n. Gemahl; Gatte; Gattin

spout n. Wasserstrahl; Ausguss, Traufe; Tülle, Schnabel; (naut.) Wasserhose; — v. hervorspritzen, hervorquellen, herausprudeln, herausspringen; (fig.) deklamieren, vortragen

sprain n. Verrenkung; — v. verrenken

sprawl v. sich spreizen (or rekeln)

spray n. Sprühregen; (bot.) Zweig, Reis; (mech.) Zerstäuber, Spritze; (naut.) Gischt; — **gun** Spritzpistole, Zerstäuber; — v. bestäuben, (be)sprühen, zerstieben; (med.) ausspritzen

spread n. Verbreitung; Ausdehnung, Umfang, Fläche; Bettdecke; Tischtuch; (mil.) Streuung; — adj. ausgebreitet, breit; — v. (aus)breiten, verbreiten, entfalten, ausspannen, ausdehen; (be)decken; bestreichen

spree n. Spass, Streich, Jux; Zechgelage, Bummel

sprig n. Spross, Schössling; (mech.) Zwecke, Stift; (fig.) Sprössling

sprightly *adj.* lebhaft, heiter, munter; mutig

spring *n.* Frühling; Frühjahr; (geol.) Quelle; (mech.) Feder; Federkraft; (fig.) Triebfeder, Ursprung; **— balance** Federwage; **— gun** Selbstschuss; **— mattress** Sprungfedermatratze; **—** *v.* springen; emporschiessen; sprudeln; (fig.) entspringen, entstehen; befreien; **— back** zurückspringen; **— from** entspringen von (*or* aus); **-er** *n.* Springer; (arch.) Gewölbetragstein; (zool.) Springbock; **-like** *adj.* frühlingshaft; **-y** *adj.* elastisch, federnd

springboard *n.* Sprungbrett

sprinkle *n.* Sprühregen; Sprenkelmuster; **—** *v.* (be)sprengen; bespritzen, sprühen; sprenkeln; **-r** *n.* Rasensprenger; Giesskanne; Sprengwagen

sprinkling *n.* Sprengen, Spritzen; (coll.) Anflug, Anstrich

sprint *n.* Sprint; kurzer, scharfer Wettlauf; **—** *v.* sprinten

sprite *n.* Geist, Kobold

sprocket *n.* Radkranzstift; **— wheel** Kettenrad

sprout *n.* Spross(e), Sprössling, Keim; **—** *v.* spriessen, wachsen, keimen

spruce *n.* Fichte; **—** *adj.* nett, sauber, schmuck; geputzt; **—** *v.* herausputzen

spry *adj.* flink, hurtig, munter; rüstig

spun glass *n.* gesponnenes Glas

spur *n.* Sporn; Steigeisen; Antrieb; (geol.) Ausläufer; **on the — of the moment** ohne Überlegung, spornstreichs; **win one's —s** sich die Sporen verdienen; **— stone** Prellstein; **— wheel** Kammrad

spurn *v.* mit dem Fuss wegstossen; verschmähen

spurt *n.* Strahl; Ausbruch; Ruck; plötzliche Anstrengung; Spurt; **—** *v.* herausspritzen; spurten

sputter *n.* Gesprudel; (fig.) Getue, Lärm; **—** *v.* spritzen, sprühen; hervorsprudeln

sputum *n.* Auswurf, Speichel

spy *n.* Spion, Späher, Kundschafter; *v.* spionieren, spähen; kundschaften

spyglass *n.* Fernglas, Fernrohr

squabble *n.* Zank, Streit; **—** *v.* (sich) zanken, streiten

squad *n.* Trupp, Rotte; Mannschaft; **-car** Funkwagen; **-ron** *n.* Schwadron; (avi.) Staffel; (naut.) Geschwader

squalid *adj.* schmutzig, abstossend; armselig

squall *n.* Schrei; (naut.) Bö, Windstoss; **—** *v.* aufschreien; plötzlich wehen

squalor *n.* Schmutz, Unflat

squander *v.* verschwenden, verschleudern; umherschweifen; **—** *n.* Verschwendung

square *n.* Platz, Viereck, Quadrat; (chess) Feld; (mech.) Winkelmass; Reisschiene; **—** *adj.* viereckig, quadratisch; redlich, rechtschaffen; passend; **be quitt** sein; **— dance** Quadrille; **— deal** faires Spiel; **— inch** Quadratzoll; **— foot** Quadratfuss; **— mile** Quadratmeile; **— number** Quadratzahl; **— root** Quadratwurzel; **—** *v.* ausgleichen, abrechnen; (geom.) abmessen, anpassen;

(math.) ins Quadrat erheben

square-built *adj.* vierschrötig

squash *n.* Brei; Ausgepresstes; Platsch, Fall; Gedränge; (bot.) Kürbis; **lemon — ** Zitronenlimonade; **—** *v.* zerquetschen, zerdrücken; (fig.) unterdrücken

squat *n.* Hocken, Kauern; (min.) Erznest; **—** *adj.* kauernd; plattgedrückt; untersetzt; **—** *v.* sich ohne Rechtstitel ansiedeln; **-ter** *n.* Hockende, Kauernde; (fig.) Ansiedler ohne Rechtstitel

squaw *n.* Squaw, Indianerfrau; Frau

squawk *n.* schriller Aufschrei; **—** *v.* schrill aufschreien

squeak *n.* Gequiek; **—** *v.* quieken, quietschen

squeal *v.* quieken, quäken, schreien; (coll.) protestieren; verraten, ausplaudern

squeeze *n.* Druck; Quetschen; Gedränge; **—** *v.* (sich) drücken, pressen, quetschen, drängen; **-r** *n.* Presse

squelch *n.* heftiger Schlag (*or* Fall); **—** *v.* zerdrücken, zermalmen; (fig.) unterdrücken

squint *n.* Schielen; Neigung, Hang; **—** *adj.* schielend; schräg, schief; **—** *v.* schielen; schräg (*or* verstohlen) anblicken

squire *n.* Gutsherr; (fig.) Begleiter; **—** *v.* begleiten

squirm *v.* sich krümmen (*or* winden)

squirrel *n.* Eichhörnchen

squirt *n.* Spritze; Strahl; (coll.) Emporkömmling, Wichtigtuer; **—** *v.* spritzen

stab *n.* Stich, Stoss; Stichwunde; (fig.) Streich; **—** *v.* (er)stechen; verwunden

stability *n.* Stabilität, Dauerhaftigkeit, Festigkeit; Standfestigkeit, Beständigkeit

stabilize *v.* stabilisieren

stable *n.* Stall; **—** *adj.* stabil, dauerhaft, beständig; **—** *v.* (ein) stallen

stack *n.* Haufen, Schober; Meiler; Stapel. Stoss; Schornstein; (mil.) Gewehrpyramide; **—** *v.* schichten, stapeln; aufstellen

stadium *n.* Stadium, Kampfbahn

staff *n.* Stab; Stock, Knüttel, Pfahl; (mech.) Stange, Welle; (fig.) Stab, Personal, Mitarbeiter; **editorial —** Redaktionspersonal; **music —** Notensystem, Notenlinien; **— officer** Stabsoffizier

stag *n.* Hirsch; (coll.) Strohwitwer; **-party** Herrengesellschaft

stage *n.* Gerüst, Gestell; Bühne, Schauplatz; (fig.) Stadium, Station, Stufe; **— landing** — Landungsbrücke; **— box** Proszeniumsloge; **— direction** Inszenierung; **— effect** Bühnenwirkung; **— fright** Lampenfieber; **— scenery, — setting** Bühnendekoration; **— whisper** Bühnengeflüster; **—** *v.* auf die Bühne bringen, inszenieren

stagger *n.* Schwanken, Taumeln; **-s** *pl.* Schwindel Drehkrankheit; **—** *v.* taumeln, schwanken; verblüffen; stutzig werden

staging *n.* (theat.) Inszenierung

stagnancy *n.*, **stagnation** *n.* Stagnierung, Stockung, Stillstand

stagnant adj. stagnierend, stillstehend, stokkend

stagnate v. stagnieren, stillstehen, stocken

stain n. Fleck; Beize; (fig.) Makel, Schandfleck; — v. (be)flecken; färben; **-less** adj. fleckenlos, unbefleckt; (fig.) tadellos; **-less steel** rostfreier Stahl

stair n. Stufe; pl. Treppe; **back –s** Hintertreppe

staircase, stairway n. Treppenhaus

stake n. Pfahl, Stange; Marterpfahl; (bet) Einsatz, Preis; **be at** — auf dem Spiel stehen; — v. pfählen; einsetzen, aufs Spiel setzen, wagen, wetten; — **out** (or **off**) abstecken

standpoint n. Standpunkt, Gesichtspunkt

stale n. Urin, Harn; — adj. schal, matt, abgestanden, fade; altbacken, abgenutzt; (sports) übertrainiert; — v. schal werden, verflauen; wertlos machen; urinieren; **-ness** n. Schalheit, Abgestandenheit; Plattheit, Abgenutztheit

stalemate n. Unentschieden, Stillstand; (chess) Patt; — v. zum Stillstand bringen, lähmen; (chess) Patt setzen

stall n. Abteilung, Stand; Bude; Chorstuhl; (theat.) Sperrsitz; — v. einstallen; festfahren, festsitzen; steckenbleiben; (avi.) sacken

stallion n. Hengst, Zuchthengst

stalwart adj. standhaft; stark, kräftig, handfest

stamen n. (bot.) Staubfaden

stamina n. Ausdauer, Widerstandskraft

stammer n. Stottern, Stammeln; — v. stottern, stammeln; **-er** n. Stotterer, Stammler

stamp n. Stampfen; (mail) Briefmarke, Poststempel; (mech.) Stampfer, Stanze, Stempel; **postage** — Briefmarke, Postwertzeichen; **revenue** — Zollstempel, Zollmarke; — v. (auf)stampfen; zerstossen; (mail) frankieren, abstempeln; (mech.) prägen; lochen, stanzen, stempeln; eichen

stampede n. Panik, wilde Flucht; — v. in wilder Flucht davonjagen, durchgehen

stand n. Stand, Stehen; Stillstand, Widerstand; Standpunkt. Höhepunkt; Halteplatz; Stativ, Ständer. Gestell; Lesepult; Tribüne; — v. stehen, sich befinden; stillstehen; anhalten, aushalten, ausstehen, ertragen; bestehen; stellen; — **aside** beiseitestehen, beiseitetreten; — **back** zurückstehen; — **by** aufhelfen, bereitstehen; — **in** vertreten; — **in line** in der Reihe stehen; — **off** abstehen, zurücktreten; — **one's ground** sich behaupten; — **out** hervorragen; widerstehen; — **still** stillstehen; — **treat** die Zeche bezahlen; — **up** aufstehen, sich erheben; **-ing** n. Stand, Stellung; Rang, Ruf; Dauer; **-ing** adj. stehend; fest, dauernd; **-ing room** Stehplatz

standard n. Standard, Muster, Masstab, Norm, Durchschnitt; Ständer, Pfosten; (mil.) Standarte; (orn.) Blütenblatt; Stamm; **gold** — Goldwährung; — **of**

living Lebenshaltung; — adj. massgebend; aufrecht, gerade; hochstämmig; Normal-, Muster-; — **measure** Standardmass; — **time** Normalzeit; Durchschnittszeit; — **works** klassische Werke; **-ization** n. Normung; **-ize** v. normen, vereinheitlichen

standard-gauge adj. Normalspur

standstill n. Stillstand, Pause

stanza n. Stanze, Strophe

staple n. Stapelung; Stapelplatz; Haupterzeugnis, Rohstoff; Heftklammer; — adj. stapelnd, heftend; — v. stapeln, heften; **-r** n. Heftmaschine

star n. Stern, Gestirn; (film) Star; **–'s and stripes** Sternenbanner; — v. besäen; mit einem Stern versehen; (theat.) glänzen, in der Hauptrolle auftreten; gastieren; **-let** n. Sternchen, kleiner Star; **-red** adj., **-ry** adj. sternenbesät; gestirnt; Stern(en)-

starboard n. Steuerbord

starch n. Stärke; (fig.) Steifheit; — adj. gestärkt; (fig.) steif, förmlich; — v. stärken

stare n. Starren; — v. (an)starren

stark-naked adj. splitter(faser)nackt

starlight n. Sternenlicht; (fig.) schwächliches Licht; — adj. sternenhell

star-spangled adj. sternenbesät

start n. Sprung, Satz, Ruck, Stoss; Aufschrekken, Zusammenfahren, Stutzen; Start, Anfang, Aufbruch, Abfahrt, Abflug; **get a** — einen Anfang machen, einen Vorsprung erhalten; **make a new** — ein neues Leben beginnen; — v. aufspringen, aufschrecken, stutzen, zusammenfahren; aufbrechen, abfahren, abfliegen, starten; (mech.) anlassen, in Gang setzen; — **a business** ein Geschäft anfangen (or errichten); — **an objection** einen Einwand machen; — **off**, — **out** abfahren, aufbrechen; abweichen; **-er** n. Starter, Anlasser, Erreger; **-ing** n. Anlassen, Starten; Ablauf; **-ing point** Ausgangspunkt; Startlinie; **-le** n. Bestürzung, Schreck; **-le** r. erschrecken, bestürzt sein; **-ling** adj. erschreckend, ergreifend, aufsehenerregend; bestürzt

starvation n. Hungerleiden, Verhungern; (med.) Hungertod

starve v. verhungern, aushungern; (mech.) stehenbleiben; (fig.) verkümmern

state n. Stand, Zustand, Beschaffenheit; (pol.) Staat, Macht; **–'s evidence** Zeuge (or Beweismaterial) für den Staatsanwalt; — v. angeben, darlegen, feststellen; **-ly** adj. staatlich, prächtig, erhaben; pomphaft; **-ment** n. Darlegung, Angabe, Aussage; Vermögensstand; (com.) Voranschlag, Überschlag; Aufstellung, Auszug

Statehouse n. Regierungsgebäude, Parlament

stateroom n. Staatszimmer; (naut.) Luxuskajüte; (rail.) Luxuswagen

statesman n. Staatsmann, Politiker; **-ship** n. Staatskunst, Regierungskunst

static *adj.* statisch; (rad.) störend; — *n.* (rad.) Sendestörung; **-s** *n.* Statik, Gleichgewichtslehre

station *n.* Standort, Standpunkt; Stelle, Rang, Stand, Stellung; Geschäft, Posten; Station; — **agent** Stationsbeamte; — **hall** Bahnhofshalle; — **house** Polizeiwache; — **wagon** Tourenwagen; **-ary** *adj.* stationär, stillstehend, beständig, fest

stationery *n.* Papierwaren, Schreibwaren

statistic *adj.* **-al** *adj.* statistisch; **-ian** *n.* Statistiker; **-s** *n. pl.* Statistik

statue *n.* Statue, Standbild, Bildsäule

stature *n.* Statur, Wuchs

status *n.* Status, Zustand; Stellung, Rang

stave *n.* Daube; (lit.) Stanze, Strophe; (naut.) Steven; — *v.* ein Loch einschlagen; verdichten; brechen; — **off** abwehren

stay *n.* Aufenthalt, Stockung; Träger, Stütze, Strebe; (naut.) Stag; *pl.* Korsett; — *v.* bleiben, verweilen, sich aufhalten; hindern, hemmen; stützen; (naut.) stagen; **-er** *n.* Steher

stay-at-home *n.* (mil.) Heimatkrieger

stead *n.* Statt, Stelle; Nutzen, Vorteil; — *v.* nutzen, dienen

steadfast *adj.* unentwegt, standhaft; unverwandt, unerschütterlich

steady *adj.* fest, unerschütterlich, sicher; regelmässig, stetig; zuverlässig, beständig; — *v.* festmachen, festhalten; sich behaupten

steak *n.* Fleischscheibe, Steak

steal *n.* Diebstahl; — *v.* stehlen, entwenden; — **away** sich fortschleichen

stealth *n.* Heimlichkeit; **by** — heimlich(erweise); **-y** *adj.* verstohlen, heimlich

steam *n.* Dampf, Dunst; Ausdünstung; — *adj.* dampfend, dunstend; — **bath** Schwitzbad; — **boiler** Dampfkessel; — **cooker** Dampfkochapparat; — **engine** Dampfmaschine, Lokomotive; — **gauge** Manometer; — **heating** Dampfheizung; — **pressure** Dampfdruck; — **roller** Dampfwalze; — *v.* dampfen, ausdunsten; dünsten; (coll.) schnauben, rasen; **-er** *n.* Dampfer; Dämpfer

steamboat *n.* Dampfschiff, Dampfer

stearin(e) *n.* Stearin

steed *n.* (lit.) Schlachtross; (coll.) Stahlross

steel *n.* Stahl; — *adj.* stählern; — **filings** Stahlstaub; — **helmet** Stahlhelm; — **plate** Stahlblech; — **wool** Stahlspäne; — *v.* stählen; stahlhart machen; (ver)härten

steel-clad *adj.* stahlgepanzert

steel-colored *adj.* stahlfarben, stahlblau

steelworks *n. pl.* Stahlhütte, Stahlhammer

steelyard *n.* Schnellwaage

steep *n.* Steilhang; Eintauchen; Lauge; — *adj.* steil, jäh, abschüssig; (coll.) schwierig, sehr gross; — *v.* eintauchen, einweichen, tränken, imprägnieren

steeple *n.* spitzer Turm; Kirchturm; — **jack** Turmdecker

steeplechase *n.* Hindernisrennen

steer *n.* Steuern; (zool.) Stier; — *v.* steuern, lenken; **-age** *n.* Steuerung; Kurs; **-ing** *n.* Steuerung; Steuermannskunst; **-ing** *adj.* steuernd, lenkend; — **whee** Steuer(rad)

stein *n.* Bierglas, Masskrug, Humpen

stem *n.* Stamm; Stengel, Stiel; — *v.* von Stengeln befreien; stemmen; eindämmen, stauen

stench *n.* Gestank, übler Geruch

stencil *n.* Schablone, Matritze; — *v.* mit einer Schablone (*or* Matrize) arbeiten

stenographer *n.* Stenograf

stenography *n.* Stenografie, Kurzschrift

stenotyping *n.* Druck in Kurzschrift

step *n.* Schritt, Tritt; Fusstapfe; Stufe; **be in** — Schritt halten; **by** **-s** Schritt für Schritt, stufenweise; **false** — Fehltritt; — *v.* schreiten, treten, gehen; fortschreiten; abschreiten, ausmessen; — **aside** ausweichen; — **in** einsteigen; einen Besuch machen; — **out** austreten, aussteigen; — **up** hinaufgehen

stepbrother *n.* Stiefbruder

stepdaughter *n.* Stieftochter

stepfather *n.* Stiefvater

stepladder *n.* Stehleiter

stepmother *n.* Stiefmutter

stepsister *n.* Stiefschwester

stepson *n.* Stiefsohn

stereophonic *adj.* volltönend; sterephonisch

stereoscope *n.* Stereoskop

stereotype *n.* Stereotypie, Plattendruck; — *adj.* stereotyp; feststehend, unveränderlich; — *v.* abdrucken; (fig.) eine bleibende Form geben

sterile *adj.* steril, unfruchtbar

sterility *n.* Sterilität, Unfruchtbarkeit

sterilize *v.* sterilisieren, unfruchtbar machen

sterling *n.* Sterling; — *adj.* echt, hochgradig; hervorragend; zuverlässig

stern *n.* Heck; — *adj.* finster, ernst, streng; unnachgiebig

stet *v.* (typ.) stehenlassen

stethoscope *n.* Stethoskop

stevedor *n.* Staumeister; Lader, Stauer

stew *n.* Gedämpfte, Geschmorte; (coll.) Verwirrung, Aufregung; — *v.* dämpfen, schmoren; (educ. sl.) büffeln

steward *n.* Verwalter; (avi. and naut.) Steward; **-ess** *n.* Stewardess, Aufwärterin

stick *n.* Stock, Stange, Stab; (avi.) Steuerknüppel; Bombenabzug; — *v.* stecken; kleben, heften; ertragen; stocken, (stehen)bleiben; — **to** festhalten an, bleiben bei; anstecken, ankleben; — **together** zusammenhalten; **-er** *n.* Stecker, Stecher; Ankleber; (com.) Ladenhüter; Klebezettel; **-y** *adj.* klebrig, zäh; feucht, dunstig

stickle *v.* hartnäckig streiten; **-r** *n.* Eiferer, Verfechter; **-r for ceremony** Formenmensch

stickpin *n.* Krawattennadel

stiff *adj.* steif, starr; dicht; schwierig, hartnäckig; stark; **-en** *v.* steif werden; verhärten, versteigen; erstarren (lassen); stärken; **-ness** n. Steifheit; Widerstandsfähigkeit; Halsstarrigkeit; Gezwungenheit

stifle v. ersticken, unterdrücken; vertuschen

stifling adj. erstickend

stigma n. Stigma

still n. Stille, Ruhe; (chem.) Destillierapparat; — adj. still, ruhig, regunglos; — adv. noch (immer); — conj. (je)doch, dennoch; — v. destillieren; stillen; **-ness** n. Stille, Ruhe

stillborn adj. totgeboren

stilt n. Stelze; (orn.) Stelzvogel; **-ed** adj. gestelzt; (fig.) gespreizt, hochtrabend

stimulant n. Reizmittel; — adj. stimulierend

stimulate v. (an)reizen

stimulation n. Reizung; Antrieb

stimulus n. Reizmittel

sting n. Stachel; Stich, Biss; (fig.) Schärfe. Spitze; Antrieb; — **ray** Stachelrochen; — v. stechen; (fig.) schmerzen; verwunden; anstacheln; **-iness** n. Geiz; Kargheit; **-ing** adj. stechend; scharf. schmerzhaft; **-ing nettle** Brennessel; **-y** adj. geizig; kärglich, knapp

stink n. Gestank; — adj. — **bomb** Stinkbombe; — v. stinken; verstänkern

stipulate v. (aus)bedingen, festsetzen

stipulation n. Abmachung; Festsetzung; Klausel

stir n. Bewegung, Aufregung; Getümmel. Auflauf; — v. rühren; anschüren, bewegen, aufstören; sich rühren; — **up** aufrühren, reizen; **-ring** adj. anregend, aufregend; belebend, begeisternd

stirrup n. Steigbügel; (arch.) Steigeisen

stitch n. Stich, Masche; — v. stechen; nähen, sticken, heften; häkeln; (agr.) furchen

stock n. Stamm, Stock; Block, Klotz; (agr.) Vieh(stand); (bot.) Stengel. Strunk; (com.) Vorrat, Lager, Stammkapital; pl. Inventar; Barvermögen; Aktien, Staatspapiere, Effekten; Stapel; in — lagernd, vorrätig; **rolling —** (rail.) Betriebsmaterial; — **on hand** Warenbestand; — adj. lagernd, (bereit) stehend, ständig; — **book** Aktienverzeichnis; Zuchtregister; — **company** Aktiengesellschaft; — **dove** Holztaube; — **exchange** Börse; — **list** Kurszettel; — **market** Effektenbörse; Viehmarkt; — **play** (theat.) Repertoirestück; — **raiser** Viehzüchter; — v. lagern, aufspeichern; vorrätig haben, versorgen; (cards) betrügerisch mischen; **-ade** n. Staket, Einpfählung, Palisaden; **-y** adj. stämmig, untersetzt

stock-blind adj. stockblind

stockbroker n. Börsenmakler

stockholder n. Aktionär

stocking n. Strumpf

stockpile n. Materialreserve, Vorratshaufen; **atomic —** Atomkernreserve; — v. Rohmaterial aufspeichern

stockroom n. Lagerraum

stockyard n. Viehhof

stoke v. schüren, stochern; **-r** n. Heizer;

Schürhaken

stole n. Stola

stolid adj. unerschütterlich, gleichmütig

stomach n. Magen; (fig.) Appetit, Neigung; — v. verdauen; vertragen, (fig.) sich gefallen lassen

stone n. Stein; (bot.) Kern; (min.) Edelstein; — adj. steinern, steinig; Stein-; — **coal** Steinkohle, Anthrazit; — **falcon** (orn.) Merlin; — **fruit** Kernobst; — **marten** Steinmarder; — **pit** Steinbruch; — v. steinigen; mit Steinen einfassen; entkernen; (fig.) versteinern, verhärten

stone-broke adj. bankrott, vollkommen abgebrannt

stonecutter n. Steinhauer, Steinklopfer; Steinschleifer

stone-dead adj. mausetot

stone-deaf adj. stocktaub

stonemason n. Steinmetz

stony adj. steinig, steinern; versteinert

stooge n. Stichwortbringer, Double; Schreiberseele; Neuling in der Unterwelt

stool n. Schemel; Stuhl; (med.) Stuhlgang; — **pigeon** Lockspitzel, Zeichengeber; (orn.) Locktaube

stoop n. gebeugte Haltung; Demütigung; (arch.) Verande; — v. sich beugen (or herablassen); neigen; demütigen; (orn.) herabstossen

stop n. Halt; Einhalt, Stillstand, Pause, Unterbrechung; Haltestelle; Hemmung, Hindernis; (mus.) Klappe, Ventil; Register; Griff; — **light** Bremslicht; — **order** begrenzter Auftrag; — **signal** Haltesignal, Haltezeichen; — **watch** Stoppuhr; — v. (ver)stopfen, (ver)sperren; aufhalten, einhalten, einstellen; (stehen)bleiben, anhalten, ruhen; unterbrechen; hemmen, hindern; (bot.) beschneiden; (med.) stillen; (mus.) greifen; **-page** n. Hemmung, Einstellung, Anhalten, Stockung; Verstopfung; **-per** n. Stöpsel, Pfropfen; Aufhalter; Hemmung, Versperrung; **-per** v. verstopfen, zustöpseln; **-ping** n. Halt, Anhalten; (dent.) Plombe, Füllung; **-ping** adj. **-ping place** Haltestelle

stopover n. Zwischenaufenthalt

storage n. Lagerung, Aufspeichern; Lagergeld, Lagermiete; — **battery** Akkumulator

store n. Geschäft, Laden; Lager, Magazin, Speicher; Vorrat, Menge; **department —** Kaufhaus; — v. aufhäufen, aufspeichern; einlagern; versehen, versorgen

storehouse n. Lagerhaus; Warenniederlage; (fig.) Schatzkammer

storekeeper n. Magazinverwalter; Geschäftsbesitzer; (naut.) Proviantmeister

storeroom n. Vorratskammer, Lagerraum

stork n. Storch; **-'s bill** Storchenschnabel

storm n. Sturm; Gewitter; — **center** Sturmzentrum; — **door** Doppeltür; — **troops** Sturmtruppen; — **window** Doppelfenster; — v. stürmen; toben, wüten; **-y** adj. stürmisch

story n. Geschichte, Erzählung; Handlung; (arch.) Stock(werk), Geschoss; (fig.) Flunkerei; **short** — Novelle; — v. erzählen, erfinden; (fig.) flunkern

stout n. Dickwanst; Porterbier; — adj. dick, beleibt; stämmig, kräftig; derb; (fig.) standhaft, mannhaft

stove n. Ofen; Kochherd

stowaway n. (naut.) blinder Passagier

straddle n. Spreizen; (pol.) Schwanken; — adv. rittlings; — v. spreizen, grätschen; (pol.) schwanken

straggle v. umherstreifen; abweichen; zerstreut liegen; -r n. Herumstreicher, Nachzügler, Versprengte; (bot.) Schössling

straight n. Gerade; — adj. gerade, direkt; vollständig, rückhaltlos; — **line** Gerade, gerade Linie; — adv. gerade-(swegs); sogleich; **-en** v. gerade machen, glatt ziehen; straffen; (fig.) in Ordnung bringen

straightaway adj. gerade, gradlinig

straightedge n. Lineal; Richtscheit

straightforward adj. geradsinnig; ehrlich, redlich; — adv. geradeaus

straightway adv. geradeswegs, auf der Stelle

strain n. Spannung, Anstrengung; Verdrehung, Formveränderung; (biol.) Geschlecht; (med.) Verrenkung; (mus.) Ton, Weise; — v. (an)spannen, straffen; ausdehnen, strecken; anstrengen, überanstrengen; verrenken; verdrehen; (mech.) durchpressen; filtrieren; — **to one's breast** umarmen; **-er** n. Durchschlag, Seiher, Filter

strait n. Meerenge, Strasse; (fig.) Zwangslage; — adj. eng, knapp, schmal, begrenzt; — **jacket** Zwangsjacke; **-en** v. verengen, einengen, beschränken

strand n. Strand, Ufer; Strähne, Strang; — v. stranden

strange adj. fremd; ungewöhnlich, seltsam; auffallend; **-r** n. Fremde, Ausländer; (law) Unbeteiligte; (fig.) Neuling

strangle v. erdrosseln, erwürgen, strangulieren; (fig.) ersticken; (pol.) zu Fall bringen; — adj. — **hold** Würgegriff

strap n. Riemen, Gurt; (mech.) Treibriemen, Tragriemen; (mil.) Achselschnur; — v. mit Riemen befestigen, festschnallen, verschnüren; züchtigen; **-ping** adj. stämmig, robust

strategic adj. strategisch

stratified adj. aufgeschichtet, schichtförmig

stratocruiser n. Stratosphärenflugzeug

stratosphere n. Stratosphäre

straw n. Stroh; Strohhalm; (fig.) Belanglosigkeit; — adj. strohig; Stroh-; (fig.) wertlos, leer; falsch; — **hat** Strohhut; — **vote** Probeabstimmung

strawberry n. Erdbeere

stray n. Verirrte; — adj. irre, verirrt, verlaufen; — v. irregehen, abirren; umherschweifen

streak n. Strich, Streifen; (min.) Ader; (fig.) Anflug, Anwandlung; — v. streifen

stream n. Strom, Fluss; Bach, Wasserlauf; Strömung; — v. strömen, fliessen; **-er** n. Wimpel, Fahne; Strahl

streamline n. Stromlinie(nform); — v. in Stromlinienform bauen; modernisieren; **-d** adj. stromlinienförmig, schnittig, modernisiert

street n. Strasse; Gasse

streetcar n. Strassenbahn, Elektrische

strength n. Stärke, Kraft, Festigkeit; Widerstandsfähigkeit; (mil.) Mannschaftsbestand; **gain** — wieder zu Kräften kommen; **-en** v. (ver)stärken, kräftigen; (fig.) bekräftigen

strenuous adj. tätig, eifrig; anstrengend

streptococcus n. (med.) Streptokokkus

streptomycin n. Streptomyzin

stress n. Druck, Gewicht, Nachdruck; Betonung; Heftigkeit; — v. betonen, unterstreichen

stretch n. Ausdehnung; Spannung; Strecke, Weite, Umfang; Anstrengung; (fig.) Übertreibung; — v. strecken, dehnen, spannen; recken, weiten; sich ausdehnen, sich anstrengen; (fig.) überschreiten, übertreiben; **-er** n. Strecker; (med.) Tragbahre; (naut.) Rippe, Spant; Fussbrett; (sl.) Flunkerei; **-ing** adj. **-ing course** (arch.) durchgehende Schicht

strict adj. strikt, streng; genau, pünktlich; — **order** ausdrücklicher Befehl; **-ly** adv. strenggenommen, ausschliesslich

stride n. langer Schritt; Schrittweite; (fig.) Fortschritt; — v. schreiten; durchschreiten

strife n. Streben; Wettbewerb; Streit

strike n. Streik, Aufstand; (baseball) Nichttreffer; — v. streiken, die Arbeit einstellen; treffen, schlagen, stossen; abschliessen; anzünden; (flag) streichen; (min.) schürfen; — **a balance** eine Bilanz ziehen; **-r** n. Streikende; (sports) Schläger

strikebreaker n. Streikbrecher

striking adj. Schlag-; streikend; überraschend, auffallend; treffend; (bot.) wurzelschlagend

string n. Schnur, Band, Bindfaden; (anat.) Nerv, Sehne; (bot.) Rippe, Ader, Faser; (mus.) Saite; — adj. — **bean** grüne Bohne; — v. aufreihen, aufziehen; verschnüren; anspannen, überanstrengen; bespannen; **-ed** adj. geschnürt, angebunden; (mus.) Saiten-; — **instrument** Streichinstrument; — **quartet** Streichquartett; **-y** adj. faserig, sehnig; saitenartig; klebrig, zäh

strip n. Streifen; Zerstörung, Abbruch; Entkleidung; — v. abstreifen, abziehen, abschälen; entkleiden, entblössen; auseinandernehmen

striptease n. Auskleideakt

stripe n. Streifen, Strich; Strieme; — v. streifen, streifig machen; **-d** adj. streifig, gestreift

strive v. streben, sich bemühen (or anstrengen); sich sträuben; streiten

stroke n. Schlag, Streich, Hieb, Stoss;

Strich; (mech.) Hub; (med.) Schlagan-
fall; — of a pen Federstrich

stroll n. Schlendern; Spaziergang; — v.
umherziehen, schlendern, bummeln;
-er n. Umherstreifende; Landstreicher,
Strolch

strong adj. stark, kräftig, tüchtig; fest,
schwer; überzeugend, gewaltig; energisch, lebhaft; — room Stahlkammer;
-ly adv. sehr; durchaus; stark

strongbox n. Geldschrank

struck adj. betroffen, ergriffen

structural adj. organisch, baulich; — iron
Gusseisen, Schmiedeeisen

structure n. Bau, Struktur, Gefüge;
Aufbau

struggle n. Ringen, Kampf; Anstrengung;
— v. ringen, streiten, kämpfen; sich
abmühen

strychnine n. Strychnin

stub n. Stumpf, Stubben; Abschnitt; —
v. anstossen; (agr.) roden; -ble n.
Stoppel; -by adj. stämmig, untersetzt;
borstig, stachelig

stubborn adj. widerspenstig, halsstarrig;
hartnäckig

stucco n. Stuck, Stukkatur

stuck-up adj. hochnäsig, hochmütig

stud n. Nagel, Stift; Knopf; Buckel,
Knauf; (arch.) Pfosten, Eckpfeiler;
(zool.) Gestüt; — book Zuchtbuch;
— mare Zuchtstute; — v. verzieren,
besetzen, besäen

student n. Student, Studierende; Gelehrte

studied adj. einstudiert, vorsätzlich

studio n. Studio, Atelier

studious adj. fleissig; bemüht, beflissen

study n. Studium, Studieren; Untersuchung; Studierzimmer; (art.) Studie;
— v. studieren; (er)forschen; (theat.)
einstudieren

stuff n. Stoff; Zeug; (com.) Ware; —!
interj. dummes Zeug! — v. (voll)stop-
fen, ausstopfen; polstern; (cooking)
füllen, spicken; (fig.) vorflunkern, weis-
machen; — up verstopfen; -ing n.
Füllung; Polsterung; -y adj. dick;
dumpf, schwül; (fig.) eigensinnig

stumble n. Stolpern, Straucheln; Fehltritt; — v. stolpern, straucheln

stumbling block n. Hindernis; Stein des
Anstosses

stump n. Stumpf, Stummel, Strunk; (pol.)
Plattform; — speech Wahlrede; — v.
stampfen; abstumpfen, stutzen; roden

stun v. betäuben; verblüffen; -ning adj.
betäubend; verblüffend, famos

stunt n. Kunststück, Bravourstück, Trick,
Sensation; (biol.) Verkümmerung; —
v. Sensationen vollbringen; (avi.) kunst-
fliegen; (biol.) verkümmern

stupendous adj. erstaunlich, riesig

stupid adj. dumm, beschränkt, stupid;
langweilig; -ity n. Stupidität, Dummheit

stupor n. Erstarrung, Betäubung;
Stumpfsinn

sturdily adv. handfest, derb, kräftig;
standhaft

sturdy adj. stark, derb; starr, hart

sturgeon n. Stör

stutter n. Stottern, Stammeln; — v. stottern, stammeln

sty n. Schweinestall; (med.) Gerstenkorn

style n. Stichel, Griffel; (med.) Sonde;
(fig.) Stil, Ausdrucksweise; Mode; in
— stilvoll; modisch; — v. (be)nennen,
betiteln

stylish adj. stilgerecht, modisch, elegant

stylist n. Stilist

stylographic adj. stylografisch; — pen
Füllfeder(halter)

sub n. Vorschuss; (coll.) Ersatz; Untergebene; U-boot

subcommittee n. Unterausschuss

subconscious n. Unterbewusstsein; —
adj. unterbewusst

subdivide v. unterteilen

subdivision n. Unterabteilung

subdue v. unterwerfen, überwältigen;
unterdrücken; dämpfen

subhead n. Untertitel

subject n. Gegenstand, Thema, Vorwurf;
Untertan; (gram.) Subjekt; — adj.
untergeben, untertan, unterworfen;
ausgesetzt; — matter Gegenstand,
Hauptinhalt; — v. unterwerfen; aussetzen; -ion n. Unterwerfung; Abhängigkeit; -ive adj. subjektiv, persönlich, einseitig, voreingenommen

subjunctive n. Konjunktiv; — adj. Kon-
junktiv-

sublease n. Untermiete; — v. unterver-
mieten

sublet v. unterverpachten

sublime n. Erhabene; — adj. erhaben,
grossartig; — v. sublimieren, läutern,
veredeln

submarine n. Unterseeboot; — adj. unterseeisch; — v. (coll.) versenken, torpedieren

submerge, submerse v. überschwemmen;
(naut.) untertauchen, versenken

submission n. Unterwerfung, Ehrerbietung

submissive adj. ehrerbietig, unterwürfig

submit v. unterwerfen, unterbreiten, vorlegen; anheimstellen; sich fügen

subnormal adj. unternormal

subordinate n. Untergebene; — adj.
untergeordnet; Neben-; — v. unterordnen, abstufen

subordination n. Unterordnung, Subordination

suborn v. verleiten, anstiften

subpoena n. Vorladung unter Strafandrohung; — v. unter Strafandrohung vorladen

subscribe v. abonnieren; unterschreiben,
zeichnen; anerkennen; -r n. Abonnent;
Unterzeichner; (tel.) Teilnehmer

subscription n. Abonnement; Unterschrift, Unterzeichnung

subsequent adj. (nach)folgend, nachherig, später

subservient adj. dienlich, nützlich, förderlich; unterwürfig

subside v. sinken; sich senken; abnehmen, nachlassen

subsidiary n. Hilfe, Beistand; — adj. behilflich, mitwirkend; Hilfs-; Neben-

subsidize v. subventionieren, mit Geld unterstützen

subsidy n. Unterstützung, Subvention

subsist v. bestehen; sich ernähren, auskommen; erhalten; **-ence** n. Dasein, Bestand; Unterhalt

substance n. Substanz, Stoff, Wesen; Vermögen

substantial adj. wesentlich; kräftig, nahrhaft; vermögend

substantiate v. verwirklichen; beweisen; beglaubigen

substitute n. Stellvertreter; Ersatz; — v. ersetzen, vertreten

substitution n. Einsetzung; Stellvertretung, Ersetzung; Unterschiebung

substructure n. Unterbau

subterranean adj. unterirdisch

subtilize v. verfeinern; ausklügeln

subt(i)le adj. subtil, fein, zart; spitzfindig

subtitle n. Untertitel, Nebentitel

subtract v. subtrahieren, abziehen; **-ion** n. Abnahme, Wegnahme, Entziehung; (math.) Subtraktion, Abziehen

suburb n. Vorstadt; pl. Vororte, Umgebung; **-an** adj. vorstädtisch; (fig.) unfein; **-anite** n. Vorstädter

subvention n. Subvention, Beihilfe, Unterstützung

subversive adj. subversiv, umstürzlerisch, unterminierend, zerstörend

subway n. Tunnel, unterirdischer Gang; Unterführung; Untergrundbahn

succeed v. gelingen, glücken; (nach)folgen

success n. Erfolg, Gelingen; Fortgang, Ausgang; **-ful** adj. erfolgreich, glücklich; **-ion** n. Folge, Nachfolge, Reihenfolge; Thronfolge, Erbfolge; **-ive** adj. aufeinanderfolgend, ununterbrochen; (law) erbberechtigt; **-or** n. Nachfolger; Thronfolger

succor n. Hilfe, Beistand, Unterstützung; (mil.) Entsatz; — v. helfen, beistehen, unterstützen; (mil.) entsetzen

succotash n. junger Mais mit Bohnen

succulent adj. saftig; strotzend

succumb v. unterliegen, erliegen

such pron. and adj. solch; so ein; derartig; **no — thing** nichts dergleichen, mitnichten; **— as** diejenigen, welche; **— like** dergleichen; **—** adv. auf diese Art (or Weise)

suck n. Saugen; — v. saugen, säugen; aufsaugen; (fig.) aussaugen; **-er** n. Sauger; Säugling; (bot.) Saugwurzel; (ichth.) Lumpfisch; (coll.) Gimpel, Einfaltspinsel; **-ing** adj. saugend, Saug-; **-le** v. säugen, nähren, stillen

suction n. Ansaugen; **— pump** Saugpumpe

sudden adj. plötzlich, unerwartet, unvermutet

suds n. pl. Sud; Seifenwasser, Seifenlauge

sue v. (ver)klagen, nachsuchen

suede n. Wildleder

suet n. Talg, Nierenfett

suffer v. (er)leiden, (er)dulden; ertragen, ausstehen; erlauben; **-ing** n. Leiden; **-ing** adj. leidend, duldend

suffice v. genügen, befriedigen

sufficient adj. genügend, ausreichend; fähig

suffocate v. ersticken

suffocation n. Erstickung

suffrage n. Stimmrecht, Wahlrecht

sugar n. Zucker; (coll.) Süsse; Geld; **— beet** Zuckerrübe; **— bowl** Zuckerdose; **— cane** Zuckerrohr; **— mill** Zuckerpresse; **—** v. zuckern; verzuckern, versüssen; **-y** adj. zuckersüss, zuckerig

sugar-cane adj. Rohrzucker-

sugar-coated adj. überzuckert, verzuckert

suggest v. vorschlagen; anregen, eingeben; **-ion** n. Anregung, Vorschlag, Wink, Rat; Suggestion; **-ive** adj. andeutend, inhaltvoll; suggestiv

suicidal adj. selbstmörderisch

suicide n. Selbstmord; Selbstmörder

suit n. Anzug; Kostüm; (cards) Farbe; (law) Prozess; (fig.) Bewerbung; **—** v. passen, kleiden, stehen; anpassen, einrichten; entsprechen; zufriedenstellen; **-or** n. Bewerber; Bittsteller; (law) Prozessierende

suitability n. Geeignetheit, Angemessenheit

suitable adj. passend, geeignet; schicklich

suitcase n. Handkoffer

suite n. Gefolge; Reihe, Folge; **— of rooms** Zimmerflucht

sulfa drugs n. pl. Sulfanomiden

sulk n. Schmollen, mürrische Laune; — v. schmollen, verdriesslich sein; **-y** adj. verdriesslich, ärgerlich, launisch; trotzig

sullen adj. mürrisch, unfreundlich; feindselig

sulphur n. Schwefel; **— dioxide** Schwefelsauerstoff

sultry adj. schwül, drückend

sum n. Summe; Betrag; (math.) Exempel; (fig.) Inhalt, Inbegriff, Vollendung; **— total** Gesamtsumme, Endsumme; **—** v. summieren, zusammenrechnen, zusammenzählen; **-marize** v. (kurz) zusammenfassen; **-mary** n. Zusammenfassung, Übersicht; Inhaltsangabe; Auszug; **-mary** adj. summarisch, kurz zusammengefasst; **-mation** n. Summierung, Zusammenfassung

summer n. Sommer; **—** adj. sommerlich; **— house** Sommerhaus, Landhaus; **— resort** Sommerfrische; **— sausage** getrocknete Wurst

summertime n. Sommerzeit

summit n. Gipfel, Höhe, Spitze

summit conference n. Gipfelkonferenz

summon v. auffordern; (be)rufen, zitieren; aufbieten; (law) vorladen; **-s** n. pl. Aufforderung, Mahnung; (law) Vorladung

sumptuous adj. kostbar, prächtig

sun n. Sonne; **— bath** Sonnenbad; **— parlor** Glasveranda; **— porch** Veranda; **— visor** Sonnenschutz; **—** v. (sich) sonnen; **-less** adj. sonnenlos, schattig; **-ny** adj. sonnig; strahlend, freundlich; **-ny side** Sonnenseite

sunbeam n. Sonnenstrahl

sunbonnet n. leichter Frauenhut

sunburn n. Sonnenbrand; **-t** adj. sonn-

(en)verbrannt
sundae n. Fruchtspeiseeis
Sunday n. Sonntag; Sonntags-
sunder v. absondern; (sich) trennen
sundial n. Sonnenuhr
sundown n. Sonnenuntergang
sundries n. pl. Verschiedenes; Diverse; Kleinigkeiten
sundry adj. mannigfaltig; allerlei; verschiedene, mehrere
sunfast adj. lichtecht
sunfish n. Sonnenfisch
sunflower n. Sonnenblume
sunglass n. Brennglas; pl. Sonnenbrille
sunlamp n. Höhensonne
sunlight n. Sonnenlicht
sunproof adj. gegen Sonnenbestrahlung geschützt
sunrise n. Sonnenaufgang
sunroom n. sonniger Raum; Glasveranda
sunset n. Sonnenuntergang
sunshade n. Sonnenschirm; Markise
sunshine n. Sonnenschein; (fig.) Frohsinn, Heiterkeit
sunshiny adj. sonnig, heiter
sunspot n. Sonnenfleck
sunstroke n. Sonnenstich
sup n. Schluck, Mundvoll; — v. schlucken; (ein)schlürfen; auskosten
superabundant adj. überreichlich, überschwenglich
superb adj. prächtig, vorzüglich, herrlich
supercilious adj. hochmütig, arrogant, anmassend
supererogatory adj. überflüssig
superficial adj. oberflächlich
superfluous adj. überflüssig, unnötig
superhighway n. Autostrasse
superhuman adj. übermenschlich
superimpose v. darüberlegen; überlagern
superintend v. beaufsichtigen, überwachen; verwalten; -ent n. Oberaufseher, Inspektor; Vorsteher, Verwalter
superior n. Vorgesetzte, Höherstehende; — adj. ober, höher; vorzüglich, überlegen; -ity n. Überlegenheit, Vorrecht
superlative n. Superlativ; — adj. unübertrefflich, höchst
superman n. Übermensch
supermarket n. Selbstbedienungsladen
supernatural adj. übernatürlich
supersede v. verdrängen, ersetzen; absetzen; (law) für ungültig erklären
supersonic adj. Überschall-
superstition n. Aberglaube
superstitious adj. abergläubisch
superstructure n. Überbau, Oberbau, Hochbau
supervise v. beaufsichtigen, überwachen
supervision n. Beaufsichtigung, Aufsicht, Oberaufsicht
supervisor n. Aufseher, Inspektor, Kontrolleur; Vorsteher
supper n. Abendessen, Abendmahl; Nachtmahl; **Lord's Supper** das Heilige Abendmahl
supplant v. verdrängen, vertreiben; ausstechen
supplement n. Ergänzung, Nachtrag, Anhang; Beilage; — v. ergänzen; bei-

legen; -al adj., -ary adj. nachträglich; Ergänzungs-, Nachtrags-
supply n. Vorrat, Versorgung; Proviant; — and demand Angebot und Nachfrage; — r. ergänzen, ersetzen, abhelfen; versorgen, liefern
support n. Stütze, Unterlage; Stativ, Gestell; Träger; (mus.) Begleitung; (fig.) Unterstützung, Unterhalt; — v. (unter)stützen; unterhalten, beistehen; (chess) decken; (mus.) begleiten; (fig.) auskommen; -er n. Unterstützer, Beistand, Gönner; (pol.) Anhänger; (med.) Träger
suppose v. voraussetzen, vermuten, annehmen; -d adj. vorausgesetzt, mutmasslich; scheinbar, vermeintlich
supposing conj. unter der Voraussetzung; — that für den Fall, dass
supposition n. Voraussetzung, Vermutung
suppress v. unterdrücken, verheimlichen; -ion n. Unterdrückung
supremacy n. Obergewalt, Vorrang
supreme adj. höchst, vornehmst; oberst, grösst
surcharge n. Zuschlag, Verteuerung; — v. überladen, verteuern; mehr berechnen; mit einer Geldstrafe belegen
sure adj. sicher, gewiss; **make** — sich vergewissern; **to be** — allerdings, freilich; **-ly** adv. sicherlich, zuverlässlich; wahrhaftig; **-ty** n. Bürgschaft, Bürge; Sicherheit, Gewissheit
sure-footed adj. standfest; (fig.) zuverlässlich
surf n. Brandung; — **riding** Wellenreiten
surface n. Oberfläche, Aussenseite; (geom.) Fläche(ninhalt); (min.) Tag; — adj. oberflächlich; — **mining** Tagebau; — **tension** Oberflächenspannung; — v. auftauchen, emporkommen; (mech.) flachdrehen
surfboard n. Wellenreiter(brett)
surfboat n. besonders starkes Boot
surfeit n. Übersättigung, Überladung; Ekel; — v. (sich) überladen, übersättigen; sich ekeln
surge n. Aufwallung; (naut.) Woge, Sturzsee, Brandung; — v. wogen, wallen, branden; anschwellen
surgeon n. Chirurg
surgery n. Chirurgie
surly adj. mürrisch, unfreundlich, sauertöpfisch, finster
surmise n. Vermutung, Argwohn, Verdacht; — v. vermuten, argwöhnen, verdächtigen
surname n. Zuname, Familienname; — v. beim Zunamen nennen
surpass v. übersteigen, überschreiten
surplice n. Chorhemd, Stola
surplus n. Überschuss; Überfluss; Überrest
surprise n. Überraschung; (mil.) Überrumplung; — v. überraschen, erschrecken; (mil.) überrumpeln, überfallen
surprising adj. überraschend, erstaunlich
surrender n. Auslieferung, Übergabe, Ergebung; (law) Abtretung; — v. ausliefern, übergeben; sich ergeben; ab-

treten

surrogate n. Surrogat, Ersatzstoff; Stellvertreter; (law) Nachlassverwalter

surround v. umgeben; (mil.) umzingeln; **-ing** n. Einschliessung; **-ings** pl. Umgegend, Umgebung, Nachbarschaft; **-ing** adj. umgebend

surtax n. Steuerzuschlag

surveillance n. Überwachung; Aufsicht

survey n. Überblick, Übersicht; Besichtigung; Vermessung; — v. überblicken, übersehen; besichtigen; vermessen, ausmessen; **-ing** n. Inspektion, Verwaltung; Ausmessung; Feldmesskunst; **-or** n. Aufseher, Inspektor, Verwalter; Feldmesser, Landmesser

survival n. Überleben; Fortleben; Überrest

survive v. überleben, fortleben; übrig bleiben

surviving adj. überlebend, fortlebend; übrig bleibend

survivor n. Überlebende; (law) Hinterbliebene

susceptible adj. empfänglich, empfindlich; erregbar; fähig

suspect n. Verdächtige, Beargwöhnte; — adj. verdächtig; — v. verdächtigen, (be)argwöhnen, vermuten

suspend v. aufhängen; entlassen, entheben, suspendieren; aufschieben; (com.) einstellen; (mus.) anhalten; (pol.) vertagen; **-er** n. Aufschiebende; **-ers** pl. Hosenträger

suspense n. Aufschub, Unterbrechung; Spannung; Unentschiedenheit, Ungewissheit; (law) Urteilsaussetzung

suspension n. Einstellung, Aufschub; (einstweilige) Amtsentsetzung; Aufhebung; (mech.) Aufhängen; — **bridge** Hängebrücke

suspicion n. Verdacht, Argwohn

suspicious adj. verdächtig, argwöhnisch, misstrauisch

sustain v. stützen, tragen; aufrechterhalten, unterhalten; **-ing** adj. beistehend; **-ing program** (rad.) nicht kommerzielles Programm

sustenance n. Lebensunterhalt, Nahrung; (coll.) Lebensmittel

suture n. Naht; — v. nähen

swab n. Scheuerlappen, Kehrwisch; Schwamm; (med.) Abstrich; — v. aufwischen

Swabia n. Schwaben

swaddling clothes n. pl. Windeln

swagger n. Grosstun, Prahlen; — adj. — **stick** kurzer Offiziersstab; — v. stolzieren; grosstun, prahlen; **-er** n. Grosstuer, Renommist

swain n. Schäfer; Liebhaber

swallow n. Schlund, Kehle; Schluck, Trunk; (orn.) Schwalbe; — v. verschlingen, (ver-)schlucken; zurücknehmen

swallow-tailed adj. schwalbenschwänzig; — **coat** Frack; (coll.) Schwalbenschwanz

swamp n. Sumpf, Morast, Moor; — v.

überschwemmen; unterdrücken; (naut.) versenken

swan n. Schwan; — **song** Schwanengesang; — **dive** Auerbachsprung

swank n. Aufschneiderei, Spiegelfechterei; — adj. prahlerisch, schick, fesch; — v. renommieren, aufschneiden; **-y** adj. elegant, luxuriös

swap n. Tausch, Handel; — v. tauschen; umsetzen, losschlagen

swarm n. Schwarm, Haufen, Gewimmel; — v. schwärmen, wimmeln

swart(hy) adj. schwärzlich, dunkelfarbig

swastika n. Hakenkreuz

swath(e) n. Binde, Wickelband; (agr.) Schwaden, Sensenhieb; — v. (ein)-wicken, einhüllen

sway n. Schwingen, Schwung; Ausschlag, Übergewicht; Einfluss, Macht; — v. schwingen, schwanken, schwanken; herrschen; beeinflussen

swear v. (be)schwören; fluchen; — **in** vereidigen

sweat n. Schweiss; — v. schwitzen; sich abmühen; (coll.) ausbeuten

sweater n. Sweater

sweatshop n. Ausbeutungsbetrieb

Sweden n. Schweden

sweep n. Fegen, Kehren; Schwung; Krümmung, Windung; Bereich, Spielraum; Schornsteinfeger, Strassenkehrer; (mil.) Schussweite; **make a clean** — **reinen Tisch machen**; — v. fegen, kehren; schleppen; krümmen, winden; (mil.) bestreichen; **-er** n. Feger, Kehrer; **-ing** n. Ausfegen; **-ings** pl. Kehricht, Abfall; **-ing** adj. ausgedehnt, schwungvoll; umfassend, durchgreifend

sweepstake(s) n. Wettrennen (Prämie aus Wetteinsätzen)

sweet adj. süss, lieblich, hübsch; frisch, rein; sanft, freundlich; — **alyssum** (bot.) Lobelie; — **basil** Basilikum; — **potato** Batate, süsse Kartoffel; **have a** — **tooth** ein Leckermaul (or eine Naschkatze) sein; — n. Süsse; (fig.) Annehmlichkeit; pl. Süssigkeiten, Leckereien, Zuckerwerk; **-en** v. (ver-)süssen; angenehm machen; **-ness** n. Süssigkeit, Wohlgeschmack; Lieblichkeit, Freundlichkeit; Annehmlichkeit

sweetbread n. Thymusdrüse; Bauchspeicheldrüse; (meat) Kalbsmilch

sweetbrier, sweetbriar n. Heckenrose

sweetheart n. Geliebte, Liebchen, Schatz

sweetmeats n. pl. Zuckerwerk, Süssigkeiten; Eingemachtes

swell n. Anschwellung; (geol.) Anhöhe; (mech.) Ausschweifung; (med.) Geschwulst; (mus.) Crescendo; (fig.) Anwachsen; (coll.) Hauptkerl; — adj. flott, famos; — v. (an)schwellen, aufwallen; sich blähen (or aufbauschen); aufblasen; vergrössern; **-ing** n. Schwellen; (med.) Beule

swelter v. verschmachten, hinschmelzen, versengen

swept adj. gefegt, gekehrt

swerve n. Seitenbewegung, Abweichung; — v. abweichen, abschweifen, ablenken

swift n. (mech.) Haspel; (orn.) Mauerschwalbe, Turmsegler; — adj. schnell, eilig; geschwind, flüchtig; voreilig

swig n. Schluck; — v. schlucken, zechen

swim n. Schwimmen; — **bladder** Schwimmblase; — v. schwimmen: gleiten, schweben; schwindlig sein; schwemmen; **-mer** n. Schwimmer; **-ming** n. Schwimmen, Gleiten; **-ing** adj. schwimmend, gleitend, schwebend; — **pool** Schwimmbassin, Schwimmbad

swindle n. Schwindel(ei); — v. (be)schwindeln; **-r** n. Schwindler

swine n. Schwein; (coll.) Schweinigel, Schweinehund

swing n. Schwung; Schaukel; (boxing) Schwinger; (mech.) Freilauf, Spielraum; (mus.) Swing; — v. schwingen, schaukeln, schwanken, baumeln; sich drehen; **-ing** n. Schwingen, Schaukeln; Schwankung; **-ing** adj. schwingend, schaukelnd

swipe n. Schlag, Stoss; (mech.) Schwengel; (coll.) Schluck; — v. schlagen, stossen; (coll.) stehlen; heruntergiessen

swirl n. Strudel, Wirbel; — v. (herum)wirbeln

switch n. Gerte, Rute; (elec.) Schalter; **ignition** — Zündschalter; — **box** Schaltkasten; (rail.) Weichenbock; — v. peitschen; (elec.) umschalten, schalten; — **off** ausschalten, ausknipsen; umschalten

switchboard n. Klappenschrank, Schalttafel, Schaltbrett

switchman n. (rail.) Weichensteller

Switzerland n. die Schweiz

swivel n. Drehring, Drehzapfen; (mil.) Karabinerhaken; — **chair** Drehstuhl; — v. sich drehen

swollen adj. angeschwollen

swoon n. Ohnmacht; (coll.) Begeisterungsdusel; — v. in Ohnmacht fallen; vor Begeisterung die Sinne verlieren

swoop n. Stoss, Sturz; — v. (herab)stossen

sword n. Schwert; Degen, Säbel; — **belt** Degengehenk, Säbelkoppel

swordfish n. Schwertfisch

sycamore n. Sykomore; Maulbeerfeigenbaum

syllable n. Silbe

symbol n. Symbol, Sinnbild; **-ic(al)** adj. symbolisch, sinnbildlich; **-ism** n. Symbolik; **-ize** v. symbolisieren, sinnbildlich darstellen

symmetric(al) adj. symmetrisch, gleichmässig, ebenmässig

symmetry n. Symmetrie, Ebenmass

sympathetic adj. sympathisch, mitfühlend; harmonierend, seelenverwandt

sympathize v. sympathisieren; — **with** übereinstimmen mit; mitfühlen, mitempfinden; **-r** n. Sympathisierende, Mitfühlende; Anhänger

sympathy n. Sympathie; Mitgefühl

symphony n. Symphonie, Sinfonie

symposium n. Gastmahl; Symposium

symptom n. Symptom, Anzeichen

synagogue n. Synagoge

synchronize v. synchronisieren; (watch) gleichgehend machen; gleichzeitig sein

syncopation n. Synkopieren; Verkürzung

syndicate n. Syndikat, Konsortium, Konzern; — v. zu einem Syndikat zusammenschliessen

synonym n. Synonym; sinnverwandtes Wort; **-ous** adj. synonym, sinnverwandt

synopsis n. Übersicht, Zusammenfassung; Synopsis

synthetic adj. synthetisch, künstlich

syphilis n. Syphilis

Syria n. Syrien

syringe n. Spritze, Injektionsnadel; — v. (aus)spritzen, einspritzen

syrup n. Sirup

system n. System; Verfahren; **-atic** adj. systematisch, planmässig

T

tab n. Streifen; Riemen, Aufhänger; Klappe; (coll.) Anweisung, Scheck

tabernacle n. Tabernakel; (Jewish) Stiftshütte

table n. Tisch; Tafel, Platte; Tabelle, Register; Tischgesellschaft; **folding** — Klapptisch; **round** — Tafelrunde; **side** — Seitentisch; **set the** — den Tisch decken; — **d'hôte** Hoteltafel; feste Speisenfolge; — **of contents** Inhaltsverzeichnis; **turn the -s** den Tisch umdrehen; **wait at the** — aufwarten, servieren; — **cover** Tischdecke; — **linen** Tischzeug; — **manners** Tischmanieren; — **service** Tafelaufsatz; Tischbedienung; — **tennis** Tischtennis; — v. verzeichnen, katalogisieren; auf den Tisch legen; vorschlagen

tableau n. Gemälde; Bild

tablecloth n. Tischtuch

tablespoon n. Esslöffel; **-ful** n. Esslöffelvoll

tablet n. Tablette, Pastille; Täfelchen

tableware n. Tischgeschirr

Tabloid n. Tablette; Zeitung im Halbformat, Sensationsblatt

taboo, tabu n. Tabu, Verbot; — adj. tabu, verboten, verrufen; — v. verbieten, untersagen, in Verruf bringen

tabular adj. tafelförmig; blättrig; tabellarisch

tabulate v. katalogisieren; zusammenfassen

tabulation n. Tabellarisierung

tachometer n. Tachometer

tacit adj. stillschweigend

tack n. Stift, Zwecke, Reissnagel; — v. (an-)heften; (naut.) lavieren, wenden

tackle n. Gerät, Geschirr; (football) Griff; (mech.) Flaschenzug; (naut.) Takel, Tauwerk; — v. befestigen; packen, festhalten

tact n. Takt, Feinfühligkeit; **-ful** adj. taktvoll; **-less** adj. taktlos

tactics n. Taktik

tadpole n. Kaulquappe

taffeta n. Taf(fe)t

tag n. Ende, Stück; Stift; Etikett, Preisschild; Troddel, Quaste; — v. etikettieren; auszeichnen; (coll.) anheften

tail n. Schwanz, Schweif; Rute, Wedel; Ende, Schluss, Anhang; Kehrseite

taillight n. Schlusslicht

tailor n. Schneider; **-ing** n. Schneidern, Schneiderei

tailor-made adj. vom Schneider angefertigt

taint n. Fleck(en), Makel; (med.) Ansteckung; (fig.) Verderbnis; — v. beflecken, verderben, vergiften; (med.) anstecken

take n. Einnahme; (film) Szene; (typ.) Manuscript; — v. (an)nehmen, abnehmen, aufnehmen, einnehmen, mitnehmen, übernehmen, wegnehmen; ergreifen; machen; erfordern; verstehen, ansehen; — **aback** verwirren, erstaunen; — **after** ähneln, nacharten; — **apart** auseinandernehmen; — **a walk** spazierengehen; — **away** wegnehmen, entfernen; — **care of** in Verwahrung nehmen; sorgen für; — **charge of** Verantwortung übernehmen für; — **effect** in Kraft treten; gelingen; — **fire** Feuer fangen; — **for granted** als selbstverständlich annehmen; — **heart** Mut fassen; — **it easy** es sich leicht machen; — **off** abnehmen, ausziehen; kopieren; (avi.) abfliegen; — **out** herausnehmen; — **place** stattfinden; — **the liberty** sich die Freiheit nehmen; — **to it** sich angewöhnen, liebgewinnen; — **upon oneself** sich anmassen; aufsichnehmen; **-r** n. Abnehmer

take-home adj., — **pay** n. Nettogehalt

take-in n. (coll.) Einnahme; Betrug

take-off n. Nachahmung, Karikatur; (avi.) Abflug; Start

taking adj. einnehmend, reizend; (med.) ansteckend; — n. Einnahme; (phot.) Aufnahme; pl. Gesamteinnahme, Gewinn

talc(um) n. Talk; — **powder** Körperpuder

tale n. Erzählung, Geschichte; Märchen; **tell** ~ s aus der Schule plaudern

talebearer n. Zuträger, Angeber

talent n. Talent, Begabung; **-ed** adj. talentiert, begabt

talk n. Gespräch; Geschwätz, Gerücht; — v. reden, sprechen, plaudern, klatschen; sich unterhalten; **-ative** adj. geschwätzig, gesprächig, redselig; **-er** n. Redner, Sprecher; Schwätzer; **-ie** n. (coll.) Sprechfilm, Tonfilm; **-ing** n. Unterhaltung, Geplauder; **-ing** adj. redend, sprechend; plaudernd; geschwätzig; **-ing machine** Sprechmaschine, Grammofon; **-ing picture** Sprechfilm, Tonfilm

tall adj. gross, hoch, lang; ausserordentlich; (coll.) fabelhaft

tallow n. Talg; (mech.) Schmiere; — v. einfetten; schmieren

tally n. Abrechnung; (fig.) Kerbholz, Gegenstück; — adj. — **sheet** Abrechnungsbogen; — v. abrechnen, nachzählen; übereinstimmen, einkerben

talon n. Kralle, Klaue; (cards) Talon

tambourine n. Tamburin

tame adj. zahm; (fig.) matt, schal, eindruckslos; — v. (be)zähmen, bändigen; mildern; (fig.) demütigen

taming n. Zähmung, Bändigung

tamper v. sich vergreifen, hineinpfuschen; intrigieren

tan n. Lohe; Gelbbraun; Sonnenbräune; — adj. lohfarben, gelbbraun; — v. gerben; bräunen; (coll.) durchwalken; **-ned** adj. lohfarben; sonnenverbrannt; **-ner** n. Gerber; **-nery** n. Gerberei; **-nic** adj. gerbend, Gerb-; **-nin** n. Tannin, Gerbsäure; **-ning** n. Gerberei; (coll.) Prügel

tandem n. Tandem; — adv. hintereinander

tangerine n. Mandarine

tangible adj. greifbar, fühlbar; körperlich

tangle n. Verwicklung, Gewirr; Knoten; (bot.) Riementang; — v. (sich) verwirren, verwickeln

tango n. Tango

tank n. Behälter; (mil.) Tank; **water** — Zisterne; — **car** Tankwagen, Kesselwagen; — v. tanken, füllen

tantrum n. üble Laune, Rappel, Koller

tap n. Zapfen, Spund; Hahn; Gewindebohrer; Pochen; pl. (mil.) Zapfenstreich; — **dance** Steptanz; — v. anzapfen, anstecken, anbohren; anschliessen, abzweigen; pochen, klopfen

tape n. Band, Streifen, Schnur; (sl.) Branntwein; **adhesive** — Leukoplast; **red** — Bürokratismus; — **recording** Tonbandaufnahme; — v. bebändern, binden, heften

tapeline n. Bandmass

taper n. Wachskerze; (geom.) Verjüngung; — adj. spitz zulaufend; konisch, verjüngt; — v. spitz zulaufen, sich verringern; (sich) zuspitzen

tapestry n. Wandteppich, Gobelin

tapeworm n. Bandwurm

tapioca n. Tapioka

taproom n. Schenkstube, Bar

tar n. Teer; (sl.) Teerjacke, Matrose; — v. teeren; **-ry** adj. teerig

tarantula n. Tarantel(spinne)

tardiness n. Langsamkeit, Verspätung

tardy adj. langsam, säumig, spät

target n. Ziel(scheibe)

tariff n. Tarif

tarnish n. Trübung, Anlaufen; Belag; — v. trüben, beflecken; anlaufen, matt werden

tarpaulin n.. (geteerte) Wagendecke; (naut.) Persenning, Ölzeug

tarry v. zögern, säumen, warten; — adj. zögernd, wartend

tart n. Fruchttörtchen; Pastete; — adj. scharf, sauer, herb; schroff

tartar n. Weinstein, Zahnstein

task n. Aufgabe; Tagewerk; (educ.) Arbeit; — v. beschäftigen, anstrengen

tassel n. Quaste, Troddel; — v. mit Quasten (or Troddeln) verzieren

taste n. Geschmack, Kostprobe; (fig.) Neigung, Lust; — v. kosten, probieren, schmecken; (fig.) empfinden, geniessen; — **of** schmecken nach; einen Nachgeschmack haben; –ful *adj.* schmackhaft; (fig.) geschmackvoll; –less *adj.* unschmackhaft; geschmacklos

tasty *adj.* köstlich; appetitlich; (fig.) stilvoll, modisch

tatter *n.* Lumpen, Fetzen; –ed *adj.* zerlumpt, zerfetzt

tatting *n.* Spitzenarbeit

tattle *n.* Geschwätz, Plauderei; — *v.* schwatzen, plaudern

tattletale *n.* Klatschgeschichte

tattoo *n.* Tätowierung; (mil.) Zapfenstreich; — *v.* tätowieren; (fig.) trommeln

taunt *n.* Hohn, Spott; Stichelei; — *v.* verhöhnen, spotten; sticheln

taupe *n.* Mausgrau; — *adj.* mausgrau

Tauris *n.* Tauris

taut *adj.* steif, straff; stramm; (fig.) herausgeputzt

tavern *n.* Taverne, Schenke, Wirtshaus; **roadside —** Wegschenke, Rasthaus

tawdry *adj.* auffallend, prahlerisch, aufgeputzt, billig

tax *n.* Steuer, Gebühr, Abgabe, Zoll; (fig.) Bürde, Last; **additional —** Steuerzuschlag; **— collector** Steuereinnehmer; **— rate** Steuerbetrag; — *v.* taxieren, abschätzen, veranschlagen; besteuern; (fig.) in Anspruch nehmen; beschuldigen; –able *adj.* steuerbar, steuerpflichtig; zollpflichtig, verzollbar; –ation *n.* Besteuerung, Steuer(n); (law) Schätzung

tax-exempt *adj.* steuerfrei, nicht steuerpflichtig

taxi *n.* Taxe; — *v.* mit einer Taxe fahren; (avi.) anrollen, entlangrollen

taxicab *n.* Taxe

taximeter *n.* Taxameter, Fahrpreisanzeiger

taxpayer *n.* Steuerzahler

tea *n.* Tee; Teestrauch; **— ball** Teei

teacart *n.* Teewagen

teach *v.* lehren, unterrichten, unterweisen; –er *n.* Lehrer; –ing *n.* Lehren, Unterricht; Lehre; –ing *adj.* belehrend, unterrichtend; –ing **staff** Lehrkörper

teacup *n.* Teetasse, Teeschale

teakettle *n.* Teekessel; Teemaschine

team *n.* Team; Mannschaft, Partei; Gespann

teamwork *n.* Zusammenarbeit; (sports) Zusammenspiel

teapot *n.* Teekanne, Teetopf

tear *n.* Träne, Tropfen; Riss; Abnutzung; **— bomb** Tränengasbombe; **— gas** Tränengas; — *v.* tränen, tropfen; (zer)reissen, zerfleischen; dahinrasen, dahinstürmen; –ful *adj.* tränenvoll; (fig.) beklagenswert

teardrop *n.* Träne

tearoom *n.* Teestube, Teeraum

tease *v.* plagen, quälen; necken, hänseln; (mech.) kämmen, zupfen

teaspoon *n.* Teelöffel; –ful *n.* Teelöffelvoll

technical *adj.* technisch, gewerblich; fachlich; –ity *n.* technische Eigentümlichkeit; Fachausdruck

technician *n.* Techniker

technicolor *n.* Technicolor; Farbfilmtechnik

technics, technique *n.* Technik, Kunstfertigkeit

technology *n.* Technologie, Gewerbekunde

tedious *adj.* langweilig, weitschweifig; lästig; –ness *n.*, **tedium** *n.* Langeweile; Langweiligkeit, Weitläufigkeit; Abneigung

tee *n.* Mal, Marke, Ziel; (golf) Erdhaufen; **— off** (golf) wegschlagen, das Spiel eröffnen

teem *v.* erzeugen; wimmeln, übervoll sein

teen-age *n.* Entwicklungszeit; Flegeljahre; — *adj.* teen-age-, halbwüchsig; **–r** *n.* Backfisch; Halbwüchsige

teens *n.* *pl.* Entwicklungsalter; (math.) Zehner (von 10 bis 19)

teeth *n.* *pl.* Zähne; **set of —** Gebiss; –ing *n.* Zahnen; –ing **ring** Beissring

teetotaler *n.* Abstinenzler, Temperenzler, Enthaltsame

telautogram *n.* Bildtelegramm

telecast *v.* (tv.) Fernsehsendungen übertragen

telegram *n.* Telegramm, Depesche

telegraph *n.* Telegraf; — **operator** Telegrafist(in); — *v.* telegrafieren

telepathy *n.* Telepathie

telephone *n.* Telefon, Fernsprecher; **dial —** Selbstanschlusstelefon; — **booth** Fernsprechzelle; — **directory** Telefonbuch; — **exchange** Fernsprechamt; — **operator** Telefonist(in); — **receiver** Telefonhörer

telescope *n.* Teleskop, Fernrohr

teletype *n.* Fernschreiber, Fernschreiben; — *v.* fernschreiben

television *n.* Fernseher

tell *v.* erzählen, sagen, mitteilen; benachrichtigen; unterscheiden; herausfinden, erkennen; zählen; befehlen; –er *n.* Erzähler; Zähler; (com.) Kassengehilfe; **paying –er** Kassierer am Auszahlungsschalter; **receiving –er** Kassierer am Einzahlungsschalter; –ing *adj.* wirkungsvoll, eindrucksvoll

telltale *n.* Ausplauderer, Zuträger

temper *n.* Stimmung, Laune; Gemüt(sart); Wut, Ärger; (mech.) Mischung, Härtegrad; **lose one's —** die Geduld verlieren, heftig werden; — *v.* mässigen, mildern; anpassen; (mech.) härten, mischen; –ament *n.* Temperament; Art; –amental *adj.* temperamentvoll; (fig.) launenhaft; –ance *n.* Mässigkeit, Enthaltsamkeit; –ate *adj.* mässig, massvoll, gemässigt, ruhig; –ate **zone** gemässigte Zone; –ature *n.* Temperatur; –ed *adj.* gestimmt, gelaunt; gleichmütig, gelassen; (mech.) gehärtet

tempest *n.* Sturm; Gewitter; –uous *adj.* stürmisch, ungestüm

temple *n.* Tempel, Gotteshaus; (anat.) Schläfe

tempo *n.* Tempo; Zeitmass

temporal *adj.* zeitlich; weltlich; (anat.) Schläfen-

temporary *adj.* zeitweilig, vorläufig; vor-

übergehend
temporize v. hinhalten; zaudern, zögern
tempt v. versuchen, verlocken; (fig.) herausfordern; **-ation** n. Versuchung, Reiz; (fig.) Herausforderung; **-ing** adj. versuchend, verführerisch, verlockend; reizend
ten n. Zehn(er); — adj. zehn
tenacious adj. festhaltend, treu, beharrlich, zäh, hartnäckig
tenant n. Mieter, Insasse; Pächter; — v. mieten, pachten; bewohnen
tend v. (be)dienen, pflegen; (be)hüten; (fig.) neigen, gerichtet sein, abzielen; **-ency** n. Richtung, Tendenz, Neigung; Zweck; **-er** n. (naut. and rail.) Tender
tender adj. zart, zärtlich; weich, schwach; empfindlich; — n. Angebot; **legal —** gesetzliches Zahlungsmittel; — v. hochschätzen, hochachten; anbieten; **-ness** n. Zartheit, Weichheit; Zärtlichkeit
tenderfoot n. Neuling, Anfänger
tenderhearted adj. weichherzig, kleinmütig
tenderloin n. Lendenstück, Filet
tendon n. Sehne
tendril n. Ranke
tenement n. Haus; Wohnung; **— house** Mietshaus
tenet n. Grundsatz, Lehrsatz
tennis n. Tennisspiel; **— court** Tennisplatz; **— player** Tennisspieler
tenor n. (law) Inhalt, Abschrift; (mus.) Tenor; (fig.) Wesen, Beschaffenheit, Fortgang, Verlauf
tense n. (gram.) Zeitform; **past —** Vergangenheit; — adj. straff, gespannt; **-ness** n. Straffheit, Spannung
tension n. Spannung; Gespanntheit; (phys.) Expansion, Spannkraft; **high — Hochspannung**
tent n. Zelt; **oxygen — Sauerstoffzelt;** — v. zelten
tentacle n. Fühler, Fühlhorn
tentative adj. versuchend, Versuchs-
tenth n. Zehnte; Zehntel; (mus.) Dezime; — adj. zehnt; **-ly** adv. zehntens
tenuous adj. dünn, fein, zart; geringfügig, dürftig
tenure n. Besitz(anspruch); Amtszeit
tepid adj. lau(warm); **-ity** n. Lauheit
term n. Termin, Frist; Zeitdauer; (educ.) Semester, Studienjahr; (gram.) Ausdruck, Wort; (law) Sitzungsperiode; (math.) Glied; pl. Bestimmungen, Bedingungen; Preise; Honorare, Schulgeld; Beziehungen; **be on good -s** auf gutem Fusse stehen; **come to -s** sich einigen (or vergleichen); **-s of payment** Zahlungsbedingungen; — v. benennen; **-inal** n. Grenze, Spitze, Ende; (rail.) Endstation; **-inal** adj. End-, Termin-; letzt; (bot.) gipfelständig; **-inate** v. beendigen, schliessen; begrenzen; beilegen; **-ination** n. Ausgang, Grenze; Ende; (gram.) Endung; **-inology** n. Terminologie, Fachsprache; **-inus** n. Grenze, Endpunkt; (rail.) Endstation
termite n. Termite

terrace n. Terrasse; — v. (terassenförmig) aufsteigen
terrestrial adj. irdisch; Erden-
terrible adj. schrecklich, furchtbar
terrier n. Terrier
terrific adj. fürchterlich, schreckenerregend; (coll.) ungeheuer, kolossal
terrify v. erschrecken, entsetzen
territory n. Gebiet, Bezirk; Territorium
terror n. Terror, Schrecken, Entsetzen; **-ism** n. Gewaltherrschaft; **-ist** n. Terrorist; **-ize** v. terrorisieren
terror-stricken adj. von Schrecken ergriffen
terse adj. bündig, kurz, markig
test n. Test, Probe; Prüfung, Untersuchung; (chem.) Reagens; (fig.) Prüfstein; **— case** Schulbeispiel, Präzedenzfall; **— pilot** Testpilot; **— tube** Probierröhre; Reagensglas; **-ament** n., Testament (bibl.) Testament; **-er** n. Prüfer; (arch.) Baldachin, Himmel; **-ify** v. (be)zeugen; **-imonial** n. Zeugnis, Attest; **-imonial** adj. beglaubigend, bezeugend; **-imony** n. Zeugnis, Beweis; Zeugenaussage; **-ing** n. Versuch; Kennzeichen, Merkmal; **-y** adj. eigensinnig, mürrisch; reizbar
tetanus n. Tetanus, Wundstarrkrampf
tether n. Spannseil; (fig.) Spielraum; — v. kurz halten, anbinden, begrenzen
text n. Text; (rel.) Bibelstelle; **-ual** adj. textmässig, textlich, Text-
textbook n. Lehrbuch, Schulbuch; Leitfaden; (mus.) Textbuch
textile adj. gesponnen, gewabt; webbar; Textil-, Web-; **-s** n. pl. Textilien, Webwaren
texture n. Struktur, Gewebe
than conj. als, denn; damals, darauf
thank n. Dank; pl. Danke! — v. danken, verdanken; **-ful** adj. dankbar, erkenntlich; **-fulness** n. Dankbarkeit, Erkenntlichkeit; **-less** adj. undankbar
thanksgiving n. Danksagung; (rel.) Dankgebet; **Thanksgiving (Day)** Dankfest; Erntedankfest
that adj. and pron. jene, diese, solche, welche; der, die, das; — conj. dass, damit, weil, da; — adv. dermassen; so
thatch n. Dachstroh; — v. mit Stroh decken; **-ed** adj. strohgedeckt; **-ed roof** Strohdach
thaw n. Tau; Tauwetter; — v. (auf)tauen
the art. der, die, das; pl. die; — adv. desto, um so, nur noch
theater n. Theater; **— of war** Kriegsschauplatz
theatrical adj. theatralisch, bühnenmässig; Theater-
thee pron. dich, dir, deiner
theft n. Diebstahl
their pron. ihr; pl. ihre; der (or die, das) ihrige
them n. pron. sie; ihnen; **-selves** pron. sie (or sich) selbst; allein
theme n. Thema, Gegenstand; (gram.) Stamm; (mus.) Motiv
then adv. darauf, (als)dann; damals, da; nun; denn, daher, darum, also, folglich;

doch, freilich; **every now and —** alle
Augenblicke; **now and —** dann und
wann, hier und da
thence *adv.* von dort, dorther; daher,
daraus; seitdem; **-forth** *adv.* seitdem,
von da ab
theocracy *n.* Gottesherrschaft, Theokratie
theologian *n.* Theologe
theologic(al) *adj.* theologisch
theology *n.* Theologie
theorem *n.* Lehrsatz
theoretical *adj.* theoretisch
theory *n.* Theorie
theosophy *n.* Theosophie
therapeutics *n.* Therapeutik, praktische
Heilkunde
therapy *n.* Therapie, Heilverfahren
there *adv.* da, dort; darin; dorthin; —!
interj. so ist's recht! schon gut!
thereabouts *adv.* da herum; ungefähr
(soviel)
thereafter *adv.* danach, demgemäss
thereby *adv.* dadurch, damit, dabei, daran
therefore *adv.* deswegen, deshalb, darum,
folglich
therefrom *adv.* davon, daran, daraus
therein *adv.* darin, dadurch; in dieser
Beziehung
thereof *adv.* davon, dessen, deren
thereon *adv.* darauf, daran, darüber
there(un)to *adv.* dazu, noch dazu; ausserdem
thereupon *adv.* darauf(hin), hierauf; dem-
zufolge
therewith *adv.* damit, darauf; im gleichen
Augenblick
thermal, thermic *adj.* Thermal-, Wärme-,
Heiz-; **— waters** heisse Quellen
thermite *n.* Thermit
thermometer *n.* Thermometer
thermonuclear *adj.* thermonuklear
Thermos bottle *n.* Thermosflasche
thermostat *n.* Thermostat
thesaurus *n.* Wörterbuch
these *pron.* diese
thesis *n.* These, Leitsatz
they *pron.* sie, die(jenigen), solche; man
thiamin *n.* Vitamin B1
thick *n.* Dicke, Mitte; (coll.) Dummkopf;
— *adj.* dick, gross, dicht; trübe, undeutlich; vertraut; (voice) heiser; **-ly**
adv. oft, häufig; schnell hintereinander;
schwerfällig; **-en** *v.* verdicken, (sich)
verdichten (or trüben); verstärken; **-et**
n. Dickicht; **-ness** *n.* Dicke, Stärke;
Dichtheit
thickheaded *adj.* dickköpfig
thick-skinned *adj.* dickhäutig, dickscha-
lig; (coll.) dickfellig
thief *n.* Dieb; (fig.) Schelm, Spitzbube
thievish *adj.* diebisch; spitzbübisch; hein-
lich
thigh *n.* Schenkel, Oberschenkel
thighbone *n.* Schenkelknochen
thimble *n.* Fingerhut; **-ful** *n.* Fingerhut-
voll
thin *adj.* dünn, mager; spärlich, schwach,
leicht; **—** *v.* verdünnen, lichten, vermindern; abnehmen; **-ness** *n.* Dünne,
Dünnheit; Zartheit; (coll.) Seichtheit

thine *pron.* dein; der (or die, das) deinige
thing *n.* Ding, Sache; Wesen, Geschöpf;
pl. Kleider, Gepäck; Angelegenheiten
think *v.* denken, meinen, glauben; gedenken; sich besinnen; **-er** *n.* Denker; **-ing**
n. Denken, Nachdenken; Denkver-
mögen; Meinung
thin-skinned *adj.* dünnhäutig; (fig.)
feinfühlend, empfindlich
third *n.* Dritte; Drittel; (mus.) Terz; **—**
adj. dritt
thirst *n.* Durst; (fig.) Begierde, Verlangen;
— *v.* dürsten; (fig.) verlangen; **-y** *adj.*
durstig; (agr.) dürr, versengt; (fig.)
gierig
thirteen *n.* Dreizehn(er); **—** *adj.* dreizehn;
-th *n.* Dreizehnte, Dreizehntel; **-th** *adj.*
dreizehnt
thirtieth *n.* Dreissigste, Dreissigstel; **—**
adj. dreissigst
thirty *n.* Dreissig(er); **—** *adj.* dreissig
this *adj.* and *pron.* dies, das; laufend,
gegenwärtig; heutig, letzt; hier(her)
thistle *n.* Distel
thither *adv.* dorthin, dahin
thong *n.* Riemen, Peitschenschnur
thorn *n.* Dorn; (mech.) Stachel; **— in the
side** der Dorn im Auge, der Pfahl im
Fleisch; **-y** *adj.* dornig, stach(e)lig;
(fig.) beschwerlich
thorough *adj.* gründlich, vollkommen,
vollendet, vollständig, gänzlich, völlig;
-ly *adv.* durchgreifend, durch und
durch; **-bred** *n.* Vollblut; **-bred** *adj.*
vollblütig, reinblütig; **-ness** *n.* Gründlichkeit, Vollständigkeit
thoroughfare *n.* Durchgang, Durchfahrt;
no —! Durchfahrt verboten!
those *adj.* and *pron.* jene, die(jenigen),
solche
thou *pron.* du; **—** *v.* duzen
though *conj.* obgleich, obschon, obwohl,
wenn auch; **—** *adv.* allerdings, freilich,
immerhin, übrigens, doch
thought *n.* Gedanke, Einfall; Nachdenken; **-ful** *adj.* gedankenvoll; nachdenklich; aufmerksam, rücksichtsvoll;
-fulness *n.* tiefes Nachdenken; Aufmerksamkeit, Rücksichtsnahme, Sorgfalt; **-less** *adj.* gedankenlos; achtlos,
sorglos, rücksichtslos
thousand *n.* Tausend; **—** *adj.* tausend;
-th *n.* Tausendste, Tausendstel; **-th**
adj. tausendst
thrash *n.* Dreschen; **—** *v.* dreschen; (coll.)
verdreschen; **-er** *n.* Drescher; Dresch-
maschine; **-ing** *n.* Dreschen; (coll.)
Prügel
thread *n.* Faden; Zwirn, Garn; Faser,
Fiber; (mech.) Gewinde; (min.) Ader;
-bare *adj.* fadenscheinig, abgetragen,
schäbig
threat *n.* Drohung; **-en** *v.* (be)drohen,
androhen; **-ening** *adj.* drohend
three *n.* Drei(er); **—** *adj.* drei; **-fold** *adj.*
dreifach
three-legged *adj.* dreibeinig; **— stool**
Dreifuss; dreibeiniger Stuhl
thresh *v.* dreschen; **-er** *n.* Drescher; **-ing**
adj. dreschend; **-ing machine** Dresch-

maschine
threshold n. Schwelle
thrice adv. dreimal
thrift n. Wirtschaftlichkeit, Sparsamkeit
Gedeihen; (bot.) Grasnelke; **-less** n.
verschwenderisch; **-y** adj. sparsam,
haushälterisch; gedeihend
thrill n. Schauer, Zittern, Erbeben; — v.
durchbohren, durchdringen, durch-
schauern, erschüttern; packen, aufregen; **-er** n. Schauergeschichte; **-ing**
adj. erregend, spannend; sensationell
thrive v. gedeihen, geraten, wachsen;
Glück (or Erfolg' haben
throat n. Kehle, Gurgel, Schlund; Hals;
Rinne; **clear one's** — sich räuspern;
sore — Halsschmerzen, Halsweh
throb n. Pochen, Klopfen, Schlagen;
Pulsschlag; — v. pochen, klopfen,
schlagen
throne n. Thron; (fig.) Herrschaft; — v.
thronen; an der Macht sein; auf den
Thron setzen; erheben
throng n. Gedränge, Menge, Schar; — v.
drängen, strömen; bedrängen
throttle n. (anat.) Luftröhre; (mech.)
Hals; Drosselklappe; Drosselung; — v.
(er)drosseln, abdrosseln
through prep. durch; aus, vor; mittels;
überall in; während; — adv. hindurch;
durchaus, ganz und gar; — adj. offen,
frei; durch(gehend)
throughout prep. ganz, hindurch; während; — adv. in jeder Beziehung,
durchaus, überall
throw n. Wurf; Wurfweite; (geol.) Verwerfung; (mech.) Kolbenhub; — v.
werfen, schleudern; giessen, schütten;
(chem.) fällen; (dice) würfeln; (mech.)
einschalten, ausschalten; — **down**
niederwerfen, unterdrücken, zerstören;
— **into gear** den Gang einschalten, in
Gang bringen; — **out of gear** den Gang
ausschalten
thrush n. Drossel; (med.) Mundfäule
thrust n. Stoss, Schub, Stich; Angriff.
Anfall; (mech.) Druck; — v. stossen,
stechen; (ein)drängen, einwerfen
thud n. Dröhnen; — v. (er)dröhnen
thug n. Meuchelmörder
thumb n. Daumen; (mech.) Zapfen; —
notches Daumenabdrücke, Fingerab-
drücke; — v. beschmutzen, abgreifen;
durchblättern; (mus.) klimpern, leiern;
— **a ride** durch Fingerzeichen eine
Mitfahrt erbitten
thumbnail n. Daumennagel; — adj.
haargenau
thumbscrew n. Flügelschraube, Flügel-
mutter; Daumenschraube
thumbtack n. Reissnagel
thump n. Schlag, Puff; (coll.) Plumps,
Bums; — v. schlagen, puffen; (coll.)
hämmern; plumpsen, knuffen; schwerfällig gehen
thunder n. Donner; — v. donnern, toben;
-ing adj. donnernd, tobend; **-ous** adj.,
-y adj. donnernd; gewitterschwül;
gewaltig
thunderbolt n. Donnerkeil; Blitz(strahl)

thunderclap n. Donnerschlag
thundershower n. Gewitterschauer, Ge-
witterregen
thunderstorm n. Gewitter(sturm)
thunderstruck adj. vom Blitz getroffen;
(fig.) wie vom Donner gerührt
Thuringia n. Thüringen
Thursday n. Donnerstag
thus adv. so, also; daher, so sehr; auf diese
Weise
thwack n. derber Schlag; — v. schlagen;
prügeln
thwart n. (naut.) Ducht, Ruderbank; —
v. durchkreuzen, vereiteln
thy pron. dein; **-self** pron. du selbst; dir,
dich (selbst)
thyme n. Thymian
thyroid n. Schilddrüse
tick n. Ticken; Punkt, Haken; (ent.)
Zecke; (coll.) Tick; Pump; Klaps; — v.
ticken; punktieren; anhaken; (coll.)
borgen, pumpen klapsen; **-er** n.
Börsentelegraf; (coll.) Herz, Uhr; **-er**
tape Papierstreifen des Börsentele-
grafen (or Zeitungstelegrafen); **-ing** n.
Ticken; Drillich, Drell
ticket n. Zettel; Schein; Eintrittskarte;
Billet, Fahrkarte; Pfandschein; (com.)
Etikette, Preiszettel; (pol.) Kandidatenliste, Wahlzettel; (police) Straf-
mandat; **roundtrip** — Hin- und Rückfahrkarte; **season** — Dauerkarte,
Abonnement; — **collector** Fahrkartenkontrolleur; — **office** Fahrkartenaus-
gabe; — **scalper** Schwarzhändler mit
Eintrittskarten; — **seller** Billettver-
käufer; — **window** Fahrkartenschalter
tickle n. Kitzel(n); — v. kitzeln; reizen,
schmeicheln
tickling adj. kitzelnd; reizend
ticklish adj. kitzlig; (fig.) wankelmütig,
unzuverlässig, heikel
tidal adj. flutartig; Flut-; — **wave** Flut-
welle, Springflut
tidbit n. Leckerbissen
tide n. Gezeiten; Ebbe, Flut; (fig.)
Strömung; **high** — Hochwasser; Flut;
— v. fluten; (mit dem Strom) treiben;
glücklich überwinden
tidewater n. Flut(wasser)
tidings n. pl. Nachrichten; Neuigkeiten
tidy adj. nett, reinlich; schmuck; — v. —
up wegräumen, aufräumen; zurechtmachen
tie n. Band, Schleife, Knoten; Krawatte;
Verbindung, Bindung; (rail.) Schwelle;
(sports) Unentschieden; — **beam** Ver-
bindungsbalken; — v. (ver)binden,
(ver)knüpfen; vereinigen; (med.) unter-
binden; (rail.) mit Schwellen versehen;
(sports) gleich stehen
tier n. Reihe, Lage; (theat.) Sitzreihe,
Rang
tie-up n. Verkehrsstörung; Geschäfts-
störung; Maschinenstörung
tiger n. Tiger; — **lily** Tigerlilie; — **moth**
Bärenspinner
tight adj. dicht, fest; straff, gespannt, eng,
knapp, prall; undurchlässig; energisch,
fähig; schwierig; (sl.) beschwipst; —

squeeze Klemme; **-s** n. pl. Trikot; knapp anliegende Hosen; **-en** v. straff spannen (or festziehen); zusammenziehen, verengen; **-ness** n. Festigkeit, Dichtheit

tightrope n. straffgespanntes Seil; Seiltänzerseil

tigress n. Tigerin

tile n. Ziegel, Kachel, Fliese; (coll.) Zylinderhut; — v. mit Ziegeln decken, kacheln, Fliesen legen

till prep. bis zu (or auf); — **now** bis jetzt; — conj. bis; — n. Ladenkasse, Schalterkasse; — v. bestellen, ackern, pflügen; **-er** n. (agr.) Pflüger

tiller n. (bot.) Wurzelspross; (naut.) Pinne; — adj. — **rope** (naut.) Steuerleine

tilt n. Neigung, Kippe; Auseinandersetzung; Stoss; Geschwindigkeit; — v. neigen, kippen; überdecken; stossen; streiten

timber n. Holz, Baumbestand; **building** — Bauholz; — **line** Baumgrenze; — **wolf** grauer Wolf; — v. zimmern, bauen

timberland n. Nutzwald

timberwork n. Zimmerwerk; Holzbau

timbre n. Timbre, Klangfarbe

time n. Zeit; Zeitpunkt, Zeitabschnitt, Zeitalter; Lebenszeit; Frist; Mal; (mus.) Takt, Tempo; Zeitmass; **at all -s** stets, immer; **at no** — niemals; **at some** — or other irgendwann; **at the same** — zur gleichen Zeit; **at -s** hin und wieder manchmal; **before one's** — verfrüht; **behind** — hinter der Zeit, veraltet; verspätet; **for the** — being für den Augenblick; unter den Umständen; **from** — **to** — gelegentlich; **in no** — im Nu; **in** — im Takt (or Schritt); rechtzeitig; **keep** — pünktlich ankommen; Takt halten; die Zeit kontrollieren; **on** — pünktlich; **out of** — zur Unzeit; **spare** — Mussestunden; **take** — sich Zeit nehmen; **what is the** — wie spät ist es? — adj. — **and again** wieder und wieder; — **ball** (naut.) Zeitball; — **bomb** Zeitbombe; — **clock** Kontrolluhr; — **exposure** Zeitaufnahme; — **fuse** Zeitzünder; — **lens** Zeitlupe; — **limit** Frist; — **sheet** Kontrollblatt (für geleistete Arbeitsstunden); — **signal** Zeitzeichen; — v. die Zeit abmessen (or einteilen, bestimmen); (mus.) Takt halten (or angeben); **-less** adj. zeitlos, ewig; **-liness** n. Rechtzeitigkeit; **-ly** adj. (recht)zeitig, frühzeitig; passend; aktuell; **-r** n. Zeitnehmer, Unparteiische; (mech.) Stoppuhr

timecard n. Kontrollkarte

timekeeper n. Uhr; (mus.) Metronom; (sports) Stoppuhr

timepiece n. Zeitmesser, Uhr

timesaver n. Zeitersparer

timetable n. Zeittabelle; (educ.) Stundenplan; (rail.) Fahrplan

timeworn adj. abgenutzt, veraltet

timid adj. furchtsam, schüchtern; **-ity** n. Furchtsamkeit, Schüchternheit

timing n. Zeiteinteilung, Einstellung

timothy n. Timotheusgras

tin n. Zinn; Weissblech; Zinngerät; — **can** Konservendose; — **foil** Zinnfolie, Staniol; — **plate** verzinntes Eisenblech; — v. verzinnen; **-ned** adj. verzinnt; **-ner** n. Zinngiesser, Verzinner; Klempner; **-ny** adj. blechern

tine n. Zinke, Zacken

tinge n. Tünche; Färbung, Anstrich; — v. tünchen, einen Anstrich geben, färben

tingle n. Prickeln, Kribbeln; — v. klingen; prickeln, kribbeln

tinker n. Kesselflicker; — v. Kessel flicken; herumflicken

tinsel n. Rauschgold, Rauschsilber; Flitter; falscher Glanz; — adj. flitternd, glänzend; — v. mit Flitterwerk schmücken

tinsmith n. Blechschmied

tint n. Farbe, Tönung, Schattierung; — v. färben; abtönen, schattieren

tiny adj. winzig, sehr klein

tip n. Spitze, Ende, Zwinge; Mundstück; Trinkgeld; leichter Stoss, leichte Neigung; Wink, Rat; **have at the** — **of one's fingers** aus dem Handgelenk schütteln; — v. beschlagen, bekleiden; tippen, kippen, umwerfen, umstürzen; Winke (or Ratschläge) geben; Trinkgeld geben; **-ple** n. Getränk; — v. zechen, picheln; **-sy** adj. berauscht, angeheitert; benebelt

tiptoe n. Zehenspitze

tirade n. Tirade; Wortschwall

tire n. Ermüdung, Abspannung; (mech.) Reifen; (rail.) Radkranz; pl. Bereifung; **flat** — Reifenpanne; **spare** — Ersatzreifen; — v. erschöpfen, ermüden, (über)anstrengen; (mech.) bereifen, beschienen; **-d** adj. müde, verbraucht; (fig.) überdrüssig; **-less** adj. unermüdlich; **-some** adj. ermüdend, langweilig; verdriesslich

tissue n. Gewebe; — **paper** Seidenpapier

tit n. Kleine; (anat.) Zitze; — **for tat** wie du mir, so ich dir; Wurst wider Wurst

titanic adj. titanisch, riesenhaft

tithe n. Zehnte; Zehntel; (fig.) unbedeutender Teil

title n. Titel; Überschrift, Aufschrift; (law) Rechtstitel, Anspruch; — **deed** Besitztitel, Eigentumsurkunde; — **page** Titelseite; — **role** Titelrolle

titmouse n. (orn.) Kohlmeise

tittle n. Pünktchen, Tüttelchen

to prep. and adv. an, in, nach, zu; auf, gegen, für; bis, bis auf (or zu); damit; um zu; vorwärts, weiter; dazu, deswegen; — **and fro** hin und her, auf und ab

toad n. Kröte

toadstool n. Giftpilz

toast n. Toast, geröstetes Brot; Trinkspruch; — v. toasten, Brot rösten; trinken auf; **-ed** adj. geröstet; **-er** n. Brotröster

toastmaster n. Toastleiter

tobacco n. Tabak(pflanze); **cut** — Schnittabak; — **pouch** Tabaksbeutel

toboggan n. flacher Schlitten; — v. rodeln;

(com.) fallen

today adv. heute, heutiger Tag; **a week from** — heute in einer Woche; — adv. heute, heutigentages

toddy n. Grog

to-do n. Geschäftigkeit, Lärm, Aufsehen

toe n. Zehe; Spitze; — **dancer** Spitzentänzer; — v. mit den Zehen berühren; — **the line** sich am Start aufstellen; die Regeln (or seine Verpflichtungen) einhalten

toenail n. Zehennagel

tog n. Kleidung; — v. (coll.) sich fein machen

together adv. zusammen, miteinander; beisammen, beieinander; zugleich, gleichzeitig; nacheinander, hintereinander

toil n. Mühsal, Plackerei, Schererei; — v. sich abmühen (or plagen); -**ful** adj., -**some** adj. mühsam

toilet n. Toilette; (med.) Säuberung; — **paper** Toilettenpapier; — **water** Gesichtswasser

token n. Zeichen, Merkmal; Andenken; Münze; — **payment** Anzahlung

tolerable adj. erträglich, leidlich

tolerance n. Toleranz, Duldung, Duldsamkeit

tolerant adj. tolerant

tolerate v. dulden, leiden, tolerieren

toleration n. Duldung, Nachsicht

toll n. Zoll; Wegegeld, Brückengeld; — **bridge** Zollbrücke; — **call** Ferngespräch; — v. Zoll (or Steuern) erheben; läuten; (fig.) ködern; -**ing** n. Geläute

tollgate n. Schlagbaum

tomato n. Tomate

tomb n. Grab(mal); — v. bestatten, begraben

tomboy n. Range, Wildfang

tombstone n. Grabstein, Leichenstein

tomcat n. Kater

tome n. Band, Buch

tomfoolery n. Narretei

tomorrow adv. morgen; **day after** — übermorgen; — adj. — **morning** morgen früh; — adv. morgen

tom-tom n. Tamtam

ton n. Tonne; (fig.) Ton; -**nage** n. Tonnage, Tonnengehalt, Lastigkeit

tone n. Ton, Klang, Laut; Sprechweise; Betonung; Tönung, Färbung; (med.) Spannkraft; — v. tönen, klingen; (art) abtönen, färben; (mus.) stimmen; erschallen; (phot.) tonen; — **down** herabstimmen; — **up** höher stimmen

tongs n. pl. Zange

tongue n. Zunge; (geol.) Landzunge; (mech.) Klöppel; (fig.) Sprache; **hold one's** — den Mund halten, schweigen; **slip of the** — Sprachfehler; Versprechen

tongue-tied adj. sprachlos; mundfaul

tonic n. (med.) Stärkungsmittel, Tonikum; (mus.) Grundton, Tonika; — adj. tonisch; stärkend

tonight adv. heute nacht; (fig.) heute abend

tonsil n. Mandel; -**lectomy** n. Mandeloperation; -**litis** n. Mandelentzündung

too adv. zu, allzu; auch, noch, dazu, ebenfalls, gleichfalls; überdies

tool n. Werkzeug, Gerät, Instrument; — **bag** Werkzeugtasche; — **chest** Werkzeugkasten; — v. mit Werkzeugen arbeiten

toot n. Tuten; Hornstoss; — v. tuten, blasen; -**le** v. dudeln; schwatzen

tooth n. Zahn; **molar** — Backenzahn; — **paste** Zahnpaste, Zahnpasta; — **powder** Zahnpulver; -**ed** adj. gezahnt; -**less** adj. zahnlos

toothache n. Zahnschmerzen, Zahnweh

toothbrush n. Zahnbürste

toothpick n. Zahnstocher

top n. Spitze, Höhe; (head) Scheitel, Schopf; Haupt; (house) Giebel, First; (mech.) Kappe, Deckel; (mountain) Gipfel, Kuppe; (naut.) Topp, Mars; (toy) Kreisel; (tree) Wipfel, Krone; — adj. oberst, vornehmst; grösst, höchst, äusserst; — **hat** Zylinderhut; — v. bedecken; übertreffen, überragen; kappen; -**ple** v. (um)kippen, umstürzen; überhängen, vorstehen

topaz n. Topas; **smoky** — Rauchtopas; **yellow** — Goldtopas

topcoat n. Überrock, Überzieher; leichter Mantel

toper n. (coll.) Säufer, Trinker

topflight adj. hervorragend, vorzüglich; erstklassig, prima

top-heavy adj. oberlastig

topic n. Thema, Gegenstand; -**al** adj. örtlich, lokal; aktuell

topknot n. Haarknoten; (orn.) Haube

topmost adj. höchst, oberst

topnotch adj. erstklassig, ausgezeichnet, prima

top-secret adj. streng geheim

topsoil n. Ackerkrume, Humusboden

topsy-turvy adv. kopfüber, halsüberkopf; — adj. umgestürzt, verkehrt, verdreht

torch n. Fackel

torchbearer n. Fackelträger

torchlight n. Fackelschein; — **procession** Fackelzug

toreador n. Torero, Stierkämpfer

torment n. Folter, Qual, Marter; — v. foltern, quälen, peinigen, martern; -**or** n., -**er** n. Peiniger, Quälgeist; Folterknecht

torn adj. zerrissen, zerfetzt, geschlitzt

tornado n. Tornado, Wirbelsturm

torpedo n. Torpedo; (ichth.) Zitterrochen; — **boat** Torpedoboot; — **tube** Torpedorohr; — v. torpedieren; (fig.) unwirksam machen

torque n. Drehung

torrent n. Wolkenbruch; Sturzbach; (fig.) Wortschwall; -**ial** adj. strömend, reissend; (fig.) wortreich

torrid adj. verdorrt, verbrannt; heiss; — **zone** heisse Zone

torso n. Torso, Rumpf

tort n. Unrecht; -**ure** n. Tortur, Folter; — v. foltern, martern

tortoise n. Schildkröte; — **shell** Schildpatt, Schildkrötenpanzer

tortoise-shell adj. Schildpatt-

Tory *n.* Tory; Loyalist; — *adj.* toryistisch; loyalistisch

toss *n.* Werfen; Wurf, Stoss; Würfeln, Losen; — *v.* bewegen; (herum)werfen, stossen; würfeln, losen

tossup *n.* Hochwerfen; (fig.) Ungewissheit

tot *n.* Kleine; -ter *v.* wanken, wackeln, schwanken; -tering *adj.* wankend, wackelnd, schwankend

total *adj.* total, ganz gänzlich; — **loss** Totalverlust; — **war** totaler Krieg; — **weight** Gesamtgewicht; — *n.* Gesamtbetrag; — *v.* sich belaufen auf; -**itarian** *adj.* totalitär

touch *n.* Berührung; Tastsinn, Gefühl; Anflug; (art) Pinselstrich; (mus.) Anschlag; — *v.* berühren, anrühren; anstossen; erreichen; betreffen; spielen; färben, angreifen; sich berühren; -**able** *adj.* berührbar, fühlbar; -**ing** *adj.* (be)rührend, ergreifend; -**ing** *prep.* in betreff, wegen, betreffend; -**y** *adj.* empfindlich, reizbar

touch-and-go *adj.* leicht hingeworfen, oberflächlich, flüchtig

touchback *n.* (football) Ball hinter der eigenen Ziellinie

touchdown *n.* (football) Ball an (*or* hinter) der feindlichen Ziellinie

touchiness *n.* Empfindlichkeit

touch-me-not *n.* Rührmichnichtan

touchstone *n.* (mech.) Probierstein; (mech.) Kieselschiefer; (fig.) Prüfstein

tough *n.* Raufbold; — *adj.* zäh, fest, hart; robust; unnachgiebig; schwierig; -**en** *v.* zäh machen (*or* werden)

toupee, toupet *n.* Toupet; unechtes Haar

tour *n.* Tour; Reise, Rundreise; Reihenfolge; — *v.* durchreisen, bereisen; an einer Tour teilnehmen; -**ing** *n.* Reisen; -**ist** *n.* Tourist

tourist court *n.* Motorhotel; Zeltplatz

tournament *n.* Turnier, Wettkampf, Wettspiel

tourniquet *n.* (med.) Abbindematerial

tousle *v.* zerzausen, verwirren

tow *n.* Tau; Schleppen; Werg; — *v.* (ab)schleppen

toward(s) *prep.* and *adv.* gegen, nach, zu, betreffend; gegenüber; fast, ungefähr; bevorstehend

towel *n.* Handtuch; **roller** — endloses Handtuch

tower *n.* Turm; — *v.* sich emportürmen (*or* erheben, hervorragen, aufschwingen)

towline *n.* Schlepptau, Bugsiertau

town *n.* Stadt; **home** — Heimatstadt; Stadt; städtisch; — **council** Stadtverordnetenversammlung; — **crier** Ausrufer; — **hall** Rathaus; — **planning** Städtebau

townsman *n.* Bürger, Stadtbewohner

toxin *n.* Giftstoff, Toxin

toy *n.* Spielzeug; Tand; — *v.* spielen; tändeln, liebäugeln

trace *n.* Spur, Fährte; Grundriss; Strang, Zugseil; **kick over the —s** über die Stränge schlagen; — *v.* nachspüren, verfolgen; herausfinden; zeichnen,

durchpausen; abstecken; anspannen; -**able** *adj.* auffindbar; nachweisbar; zurückzuverfolgen(d); -**r** *n.* Verfolger; (mech.) Vorzeichner, Pauser

trachea *n.* Luftröhre; (bot.) Spiralgefäss

tracing *n.* Durchzeichnen; Pauszeichnung; — *adj.* — **paper** Pauspapier

track *n.* Spur; Bahn; Geleis(e); Fährte, Pfad; **race** — Rennbahn; -**less** *adj.* spurlos, pfadlos

tract *n.* Strecke, Gegend; Ausdehnung; (lit.) Traktat, Abhandlung; -**able** *adj.* handlich, lenksam, folgsam; -**ion** *n.* Zug(kraft); Spannung; (med.) Zusammenziehung; -**or** *n.* Zugmaschine, Trecker; Schlepper

trade *n.* Handel; Handwerk, Gewerbe; Geschäft; Verkehr; **board of** — Handelsamt; — **price** Engrospreis, Grosshandelspreis; — **school** Handelsschule, Gewerbeschule; — **union** Gewerkschaft; — **winds** Passatwinde; -**r** *n.* Händler, Handelsmann; (naut.) Handelsschiff

trade-in *n.* Eintauschobjekt

trademark *n.* Schutzmarke; Fabrikzeichen

tradesman *n.* Geschäftsmann, Kleinhändler

tradespeople *n. pl.* Geschäftsleute, Kleinhändler

trade-unionism *n.* Gewerkschaftswesen

trading *n.* Handel(n)

tradition *n.* Tradition, Überlieferung; -**al** *adj.* traditionell, überliefert, herkömmlich

traffic *n.* Verkehr, Handel; **heavy** — starker Verkehr; — **lane** Autoreihe; Fahrbahn; — **light** Verkehrslicht; — **sign** Verkehrszeichen; — *v.* handeln; (coll.) verschachern

tragedy *n.* Tragödie, Trauerspiel

tragic *adj.* tragisch

trail *n.* Spur, Fährte; Schwanz, Schweif; Schleppe; — *v.* verfolgen, nachspüren; (nach) schleppen, (nach)schleifen; hinziehen, nachfolgen; -**er** *n.* (bot.) Kriechpflanze, Ranke; (car) Wohnwagen; Anhänger; (film) Vorschau, Beiprogramm; (mech.) Hemmstange; (coll.) Spürnase; -**ing** *adj.* nachschleppend, verfolgend, nachfolgend; -**ing arbutus** (bot.) kriechender Grindelstrauch

train *n.* Zug; (dress) Schleppe; (mech.) Kette, Räderwerk; (fig.) Reihe, Folge; (mil.) Train; Lafettenschwanz; (fig.) Reihe, Folge; Gefolge; — **conductor** Zugführer; — **oil** Tran; — *v.* ziehen; (nach)schleppen; schulen, erziehen, ausbilden, trainieren; dressieren; (mil.) exerzieren, drillen; (mus.) harmonieren; -**er** *n.* Trainer, Ausbilder; Erzieher; Dompteur; -**ing** *n.* Training, Übung, Ausbildung; Erziehung; Dressur; (bot.) Spalierzucht; (mil.) Exerzieren, Drillen

trainload *n.* Zugladung

trainman *n.* Mitglied des Zugpersonals

trait *n.* Strich, Zug; Umriss

traitor *n.* Verräter; -**ous** *adj.* verräterisch,

treulos

trajectory *n.* Flugbahn, Fallkurve; Geschossbahn

tramp *n.* Landstreicher, Vagabund; Getrampel; (fig.) Wanderung; — **steamer** unfahrplanmässiger Frachter; — *v.* wandern, vagabondieren; trampeln; **-le** *n.* Getrampel; **-le** *v.* trampeln

trance *n.* Trance, Traumzustand; Verzückung

tranquil *adj.* ruhig, gelassen; **-lity** *n.* Ruhe

tranquilizer *n.* medizinisches Beruhigungsmittel

transact *v.* verrichten, durchführen, abwickeln; (ab)machen; **-ion** *n.* Transaktion, Geschäft

transatlantic *adj.* transatlantisch; Ozean-

transcontinental *adj.* transkontinental

transcribe *v.* abschreiben, kopieren; (rad.) Schallplatten (or Tonbandaufnahmen) senden

transcript *n.* Abschrift, Umschrift; Übertragung; **-ion** *n.* Abschreiben; Umsetzen; (rad.) Bandaufnahme, Schallplattenwiedergabe; Umschnitt

transept *n.* Querschiff

transfer *n.* Übertragung, Transfer; Verlegung, Versetzung; Abzug, Umdruck; (mil.) Transferierung; (rail.) Umsteiger; — *v.* übertragen, versetzen; verlegen; umdrucken; transferieren; (rail.) umsteigen; **-able** *adj.* übertragbar; **-ence** *n.* Übertragung, Versetzung

transfiguration *n.* Umgestaltung; (rel.) Verklärung

transfigure *v.* umgestalten, umbilden; (rel.) verklären

transfix *v.* durchstechen, durchbohren

transform *v.* umwandeln, umformen; sich umbilden; **-ation** *n.* Verwandlung, Umformung; Umgestaltung; **-er** *n.* Transformator, Umformer

transgress *v.* überschreiten, übertreten; sich vergehen; **-ion** *n.* Überschreitung, Übertretung; Vergehen; **-or** *n.* Übertreter, Schuldige, Missetäter; Sünder

transient *n.* Durchreisende; — *adj.* vorübergehend, vergänglich, flüchtig

transistor *n.* Transistor; Verstärker (Elektronensystem)

transit *n.* Transport; Durchgang, Durchfuhr; Transit; Verkehrsstrasse; — *v.* passieren; **-ion** *n.* Übergang; **-ional** *adj.* Übergangs-; **-ive** *adj.* transitiv; **-ory** *adj.* vergänglich, flüchtig

translate *v.* übersetzen, übertragen; auslegen, umsetzen, versetzen

translation *n.* Übersetzung

translator *n.* Übersetzer

transmission *n.* Übertragung, Übermittlung; Vererbung, Fortpflanzung; (mech.) Transmission; (rad.) Sendung

transmit *v.* übermitteln, übertragen; senden; **-ter** *n.* Sender; Übermittler

transmute *v.* verwandeln; umgestalten

transoceanic *adj.* überseeisch, Ozean-

transom *n.* Querholz; Oberfenster

transparency *n.* Durchsichtigkeit; Transparent

transparent *adj.* transparent, durchsichtig

transpiration *n.* Ausdünstung, Schweiss; Transpirieren

transpire *v.* ausdunsten, transpirieren, ausschwitzen; (fig.) ruchbar werden, geschehen

transplant *v.* verpflanzen

transport *n.* Transport, Beförderung; Spedition; (naut.) Transportschiff; — *v.* transportieren, befördern; **-ation** *n.* Transport, Beförderung, Versendung

transpose *v.* transponieren, versetzen; (gram.) umstellen

transposition *n.* Transponierung, Umstellung

transship *v.* umladen

transubstantiate *v.* stofflich umwandeln

trap *n.* Falle, Fussangel; Klappe; *pl.* Siebensachen; — **door** Falltür; (theat.) Versenkung; — *v.* Fallen stellen, in einer Falle fangen; (fig.) ertappen; **-per** *n.* Trapper, Fallensteller; **-pings** *n. pl.* Schmuck, Staat, Putz

trapeze *n.* Trapez

trash *n.* Abfall, Plunder; (coll.) Unsinn, Blech; **-y** *adj.* wertlos, unnütz; kitschig

travail *n.* mühevolle Arbeit; (med.) Wehen; — *v.* sich abarbeiten; (med.) in den Wehen liegen

travel *n.* Reise; (mech.) Bewegung, Lauf, Hub; — *v.* reisen; durchwandern; **-er** *n.* Reisende; (mech.) Laufvorrichtung; **-ing** *adj.* reisend, fahrend, wandernd; (mech.) Lauf-; **-ing companion** Reisegefährte; **-ing expenses** Reisespesen; **-ing salesman** Handelsreisende; **-og(ue)** *n.* Reisevortrag mit Illustrationen

traveler's check *n.* Reisescheck

traverse *n.* Durchquerung; Querbalken, Quergang, Querträger; — *adj.* kreuzweise, quer; — *v.* durchqueren, durchgehen; durchforschen; (fig.) durchkreuzen

trawl *n.* Schleppnetz; Grundnetz; — *v.* mit Schleppnetz fischen; **-er** *n.* Schleppnetzfischer; Schleppnetzboot

tray *n.* Servierbrett, Tablett; Schale

treacherous *adj.* verräterisch, treulos, unzuverlässig

treachery *n.* Verrat, Treulosigkeit; Untreue

tread *n.* Tritt, Schritt; Gangart; — *v.* treten, gehen, schreiten; betreten, begehen; **-le** *n.* Pedal

treason *n.* Verrat, Treubruch; **high —** Hochverrat

treasure *n.* Schatz; — *v.* (Schätze) sammeln, aufhäufen; (fig.) hochschätzen; **-r** *n.* Schatzmeister, Zahlmeister; Kassierer

treasury *n.* Schatzkammer; (pol.) Finanzministerium; — **note** Schatzanweisung

treat *n.* Bewirtung, Schmaus; Hochgenuss; Runde, Lage; — *v.* behandeln; bewirten, freihalten; — **a patient** einen Patienten behandeln; — **of** handeln von; **-ise** *n.* Abhandlung; **-ment** *n.* Behandlung, Verfahren; **-y** *n.* Vertrag

tree n. Baum; (mech.) Schaft, Stamm; (fig.) Galgen; **family** — Familienstammbaum; — **frog** Laubfrosch; **-less** adj. baumlos

trek n. Treck; — v. trecken, im Ochsenwagen reisen

trellis n. Spalier, Gitter; — v. vergittern, verflechten; (bot.) am Spalier ziehen

tremble n. Zittern; — v. zittern

tremendous adj. furchtbar, schrecklich; kolossal

tremor n. Zittern, Beben

trench n. Graben; — v. umgraben, Gräben ziehen

trend n. Neigung, Richtung, Lauf; Tendenz; — v. sich neigen (or erstrecken, richten); streben

trespass n. Vergehen; Übertretung, Verletzen, Eingriff; — v. sich vergehen; übertreten; unbefugt eindringen; über Gebühr in Anspruch nehmen; **-er** n. Übertreter, Rechtsverletzer; unbefugt Eindringende

tress n. Locke, Haarflechte, Haarsträhne

Treves n. Trier

triad n. Dreiheit, Dreizahl; (mus.) Dreiklang

trial n. Versuch, Probe, Prüfung; Experiment; (law) Untersuchung, Verhör, Verhandlung; (fig.) Versuchung; Heimsuchung; — **balance** Rohbilanz; — **order** Probebestellung

triangle n. Dreieck; (mus.) Triangel

triangular adj. dreieckig

tribal adj. den Stamm betreffend; Stammes-

tribe n. Stamm, Geschlecht, Sippe

tribulation n. Trübsal, Drangsal, Quälerei

tribunal n. Tribunal, Gericht(shof); Richterstuhl

tribune n. Tribüne; Rednerbühne

tributary n. Tributpflichtige; (geol.) Nebenfluss; — adj. tributpflichtig; steuerbar; untergeordnet; (geol.) zufliessend; (fig.) helfend

tribute n. Tribut, Zins, Abgabe; Beitrag; (fig.) Bezeugung

trick n. Trick, Kniff, Kunstgriff, Streich; (cards) Stich; — v. überlisten, betrügen, hereinlegen, zum besten haben; verleiten; (cards) stechen; **-ery** n. Betrügerei, Gaunerei; **-iness** n. Mutwilligkeit; **-ster** n. Betrüger, Gauner; Taschenspieler; **-y** adj. heikel, verwickelt; (hinter)listig

trickle n. Tröpfeln; — v. tröpfeln, träufeln, rieseln

tricycle n. Dreirad

tried adj. erprobt, treu, zuverlässig

triennial adj. dreijährig, dreijährlich

trifle n. Kleinigkeit, Lappalie; (cooking) Auflauf; — v. scherzen, spassen, tändeln

trifling adj. tändelnd; geringfügig, unbedeutend, wertlos

trigger n. Drücker, Abzug; (phot.) Auslöser

trigonometry n. Trigonometrie

trillion n. Trillion; (USA) 1.000.000.000.000; (Europe) 1.000.000.000.000.000

trilogy n. Trilogie

trim adj. geputzt, gepflegt, ordentlich, nett; — v. in Ordnung (or ins Gleichgewicht) bringen, zurechtmachen, ausrüsten; pflegen, putzen, schmücken; garnieren; trimmen; — n. Ordnung, Zustand, Ausrüstung, Putz; **-ming** n. Putzen; Garnieren; Ausarbeitung; **-mings** pl. Besatz; Garnierung; Ausstaffierung

trinity n. Dreiheit; (ec.) Dreieinigkeit

trinket n. Schmuckstück; (fig.) Kram, Tand

trio n. Trio

trip n. Trippeln, Stolpern; Fehltritt, Fehler; Ausflug, Reise, Fahrt; **one way** — einfache Fahrt; **return** — Rückfahrt; **round** — Rundreise, Hin- und Rückfahrt; — v. trippeln, stolpern, straucheln; einen Fehler machen; einen Ausflug machen; loslassen, losmachen; **-ping** n. Trippeln, Hüpfen; — adj. trippelnd; munter, flink

triphase current n. Drehstrom

triple adj. dreifach, dreimaltig; — v. (sich) verdreifachen; **-t** n. drei Dinge (or Personen) derselben Art; (mus.) Triole, Trio; **-ts** pl. Drillinge

triplicate adj. dreifach; — v. dreifach ausfertigen

tripod n. Dreifuss; Stativ

trisyllable n. dreisilbiges Wort

trite adj. abgenutzt, abgedroschen; alltäglich

triumph n. Triumph; — v. triumphieren, frohlocken; **-ant** adj. triumphierend

trivial adj. trivial, alltäglich, gewöhnlich; **-ity** n. Trivialität, Plattheit

troll v. rollen, (sich) drehen; vor sich hin trällern

trolley n. Rollwagen, Draisine; — **bus** Oberleitungsbus; — **car** Oberleitungswagen

trombone n. Posaune

troop n. Trupp(e), Schar, Haufen; — v. sich sammeln (or scharen); haufenweise ziehen; **-er** n. Kavallerist; (theat.) Schauspieler

troopship n. Truppentransporter

trophy n. Trophäe, Siegeszeichen

tropic n. Wendekreis; pl. Tropen; — adj. Wendekreis-; **-(al)** adj. tropisch

trot n. Trott, Trab; — v. trotten, traben; **-ter** n. Traber; (coll.) Fuss, Treter; **-ting** adj. trottend, trabend

trouble n. Unruhe, Störung; Verdruss, Belästigung, Beschwerde, Plage; Unannehmlichkeit; **be in** — in Verlegenheit (or Sorge) sein; — **shooter** Störungssucher; — v. beunruhigen, stören; verdriessen, belästigen; Kummer verursachen, quälen, ängstigen; **-ed** adj. gestört, betrübt, beunruhigt; **-some** adj. lästig, beschwerlich, störend

troublemaker n. Störenfriend

trough n. Trog, Mulde, Wanne; Kanal; Strombett; — **of a wave** Wellental

troupe n. (theat.) Truppe

trousers n. pl. Hosen, Beinkleider

trousseau n. Brautausstattung

trout n. Forelle
trowel n. Maurerkelle, Hohlspatel
troy (weight) n. Goldgewicht
Troy n. Troja
truant n. Müssiggänger, Faulenzer; (educ.) Schwänzer; — adj. träge, müssig, bummelnd; (educ.) schwänzend
truce n. Waffenstillstand, Ruhe
truck n. Lastwagen, Güterwagen; Tausch-(handel); (sl.) Plunder; **small** — Handwagen; — **farm** Gemüsefarm; — **frame** Lokomotivrahmen, Waggonrahmen; — v. in Lastwagen (or Güterwagen versenden; tauschen, handeln); **-age** n. Lastwagenbeförderung; Güterwagenverkehr; Fuhrlohn
truckman n. Tauschhändler; Lastwagenfahrer
trudge n. Fusswanderung; — v. wandern, gehen; sich fortschleppen
true adj. wahr, echt, wirklich; treu; genau, (regel)recht; **come** — sich bewahrheiten; — **bill** (law) Anklagebestätigung; — v. in die richtige Form (or Lage) bringen, berichtigen
truehearted adj. treuherzig
truelove n. Herzliebste
truism n. Binsenwahrheit, Binsenweisheit
truly adv. aufrichtig, wahrhaftig, wirklich
trump n. Trumpf; (mus.) Trompete; (fig.) Prachtmensch; — v. auftrumpfen; übertrumpfen; — **up** erdichten; überstechen; **-et** n. Trompete; (mil.) Signalhorn; (coll.) Ausposauner; **-et** v. trompeten, die Trompete blasen; (coll.) ausposaunen; **-eter** n. Trompeter; (mil.) Hornist; (orn.) Trompetertaube
truncate v. stutzen, verstümmeln; (math.) abstumpfen; — adj. gestutzt, verstümmelt; stumpf
trunk n. Stamm, Stumpf; (anat.) Rumpf; (arch.) Säulenschaft; (zool.) Rüssel; (coll.) Schrankkoffer; — adj. Stamm-, Rüssel-; — **line** (rail.) Hauptlinie; (tel.) Fernleitung
trunnion n. Drehzapfen
truss n. Bund, Bündel; (arch.) Kragstein, Stütze; (bot.) Büschel; (med.) Bruchband; — adj. untersetzt, stämmig; — v. schnüren, bündeln; stützen
trust n. Trust, Unternehmerverband; Vertrauen, Glauben; Verwahrung, Pflegschaft, Pfand; **in** — in treuen Händen; **on** — auf Kredit; — v. (ver)trauen, anvertrauen; glauben; **-ee** n. Sachverwalter, Treuhänder, Kurator; **-eeship** n. Treuhandverwaltung, Kuratorium; **-ful** adj. vertrauend, zutraulich; **-iness** n. Zuverlässigkeit, Glaubwürdigkeit; Redlichkeit; **-ing** adj. vertrauensvoll, vertrauensselig; **-y** adj. treu, redlich; sicher, beharrlich
trustworthy adj. vertrauenswürdig, zuverlässig, glaubwürdig
truth n. Wahrheit, Wahrhaftigkeit; Wirklichkeit, Genauigkeit; **-ful** adj. wahrhaft(ig); **-fulness** n. Wahrhaftigkeit
try n. Versuch, Probe; — v. versuchen, probieren; prüfen; anprobieren; sich bemühen; **-ing** adj. prüfend; (fig.)

kritisch, peinlich
try-on n. Anprobe; (sl.) Versuch
tryout n. Ausprobieren; Ausscheidungsspiel
tub n. Bad(ewanne), Kübel, Zuber; — v. ein Wannenbad nehmen, baden; (bot.) in Kübel pflanzen; (sl.) im Rudern unterrichten; **-bing** n. Wannenmaterial, Wannenfabrikation; Rudertraining
tuba n. Tuba, Bombardon
tube n. Tube; Rohr, Röhre; Pfeife; (med.) Kanüle; (rail.) Tunnel; **amplifying** — Verstärkerröhre; **electronic** — Elektronenröhre; **inner** — Luftschlauch; **test** — Probierröhre, Reagensglas; **vacuum** — Vakuumröhre; — v. in Tuben (or Röhren) füllen
tuber n. Knoten, Schwellung; (bot.) Knolle; (sl.) Kartoffel
tubercle n. Tuberkel, Knötchen; Warze, Höcker
tuberculosis n. Tuberkulose
tubing n. Röhrenmaterial; Röhrenanlage
tubular adj. röhrenförmig; Röhren-
tuck n. Falte, Einschlag, Umschlag; (sl.) Näscherei; — v. falten, einschlagen, umschlagen; umkrempeln; einwickeln
Tuesday n. Dienstag
tuft n. Büschel; Quaste, Franse; (orn.) Haube, Schopf; — v. mit Büscheln (or Quasten, etc.) schmücken; **-ed** adj. buschig, buschreich; mit Büscheln (or Quasten) geschmückt; Hauben-
tug n. Ruck; Mühe, Anstrengung; — **of war** Tauziehen; — v. ziehen, zerren, zausen, zupfen; schleppen; (sich) abmühen
tugboat n. Schlepper, Schleppdampfer
tuition n. Unterricht, Anleitung, Belehrung
tulip n. Tulpe
tulle n. Tüll
tumble n. Sturz, Fall; (fig.) Wirrwarr; — v. stürzen, fallen, purzeln; taumeln; umstürzen, umwerfen; durchwühlen, stopfen, zerknüllen; **-r** n. Gaukler; Wasserglas; (mech.) Gewehrverschluss; (orn.) Tümmler; (toy) Stehaufmännchen
tumble-down adj. hinfällig, verfallen
tummy n. (coll.) Bauch
tumor n. Tumor
tumult n. Tumult, Lärm, Aufruhr; **-uous** adj. lärmend, stürmisch, ungestüm
tuna n. (bot.) Fackeldistel, indianische Feige; (ichth.) Thunfisch
tune n. Melodie, Lied; Tonstück; Stimmung; — v. (ab)stimmen; tönen, klingen; anstimmen; — **in** (rad.) einstellen; **-ful** adj. wohlklingend, lieblich; melodisch; **-r** n. Stimmer; (rad.) Abstimmskala
tungsten n. Wolfram
tuning n. Stimmen; — adj. — **dial** Stationsskala; — **fork** Stimmgabel
tunnel n. Tunnel; Stollen; — v. durchbohren, einen Tunnel anlegen
turban n. Turban
turbid adj. trübe, wolkig, schmutzig; (fig.) verworren

turbine n. Turbine; **blast —** Gebläse-turbine
turbojet n. Turbinen-Luftstrahlmotor
turboprop n. Propeller-Turbinenmotor
turbulent adj. turbulent, stürmisch
tureen n. Terrine
turf n. Turf, Rennbahn, Rennsport; Rasen(narbe); Torf; — v. mit Rasen belegen; Torf stechen
turkey n. Truthahn; — **buzzard** amerikanischer Geier
Turkey n. die Türkei
Turkish n. Türkisch; — adj. türkisch; — **bath** Dampfbad; — **towel** Frottiertuch
turmoil n. Aufruhr, Unruhe; Getümmel
turn n. Umdrehung; Krümmung, Kurve; Richtung, Wendung; Neigung, Hang; Veränderung; Art, Gestalt; Reihenfolge; Dienst(leistung); Wechsel; (com.) Turnus, Geschäftsgang; (min.) Schicht; (mus.) Doppelschlag; (coll.) Schock, Schreck; **a good —** eine gute Wendung; **by —s** der Reihe nach, abwechselnd; **it is his —** er ist an der Reihe; **sharp —** scharfe Biegung; — v. (um)drehen, (um)wenden, umkehren; lenken, richten; neigen, formen, verändern, gestalten; abwechseln; an der Reihe sein; trudeln; drechseln; — **against** aufbringen gegen; sich wenden gegen; — **away** abwenden, abweisen, wegjagen; — **back** zurückdrehen; umwenden, umkehren; (sich) abwenden; — **down** herunterschrauben, kleinstellen; ablehnen; — **off** ableiten, abwenden, ablenken, ausdrehen, abschalten; — **on** anleiten; anstellen, aufdrehen; sich wenden (or richten) auf; — **out** wegjagen; (sich) nach aussen wenden; ausfallen, sich herausstellen; — **over** umwenden, umschlagen; überdenken; übertragen, übergeben; umsetzen; übergehen; purzeln; — **pale** erbleichen, erblassen; — **the corner** um die Ecke biegen; — **to** (sich) wenden an; lenken (or richten) auf; umwandeln in; sich verwandeln in; hinauslaufen auf; **-ing** n. Umwenden; Drehung, Biegung, Krümmung, Ecke; Abweichung; **-ing** adj. drehend, drehbar; **-ing point** Wendepunkt, Entscheidung
turnbridge n. Drehbrücke
turndown n. Umlegekragen; Zurückweisung; — adj. umgelegt
turnip n. weisse Rübe, Steckrübe
turnout n. Versammlung; Ausstaffierung, Aufputz; (com.) Gesamtproduktion; Aussperrung; (mil.) Ausrücken; (rail.) Ausweichstelle
turnover n. Umwerfen; Umschlag; (com.) Umsatz; — adj. umgeschlagen
turnpike n. Schlagbaum; Strasse, deren Benutzung bezahlt werden muss
turnstile n. Drehkreuz
turntable n. Drehscheibe; Plattenteller
turnup adj. umklappbar
turpentine n. Terpentin
turquoise n. Türkis
turret n. Türmchen; (mil.) Panzerturm; (rail.) Ventilationsaufsatz

turtle n. Schildkröte
turtledove n. Turteltaube
tusk n. Fangzahn, Stosszahn, Eckzahn
tussle n. Rauferei, Zank; — v. raufen, sich balgen; zanken
tutelage n. Vormundschaft; (educ.) Unterricht
tutor n. Hauslehrer, Privatlehrer; Vormund; — v. unterrichten, belehren; nachhelfen; zurechtweisen
tuxedo n. Smoking; — **coat** Gesellschaftsanzug
twaddle n. Geschwätz, Geplapper; — v. schwatzen, plappern
twang n. Singsang; Schwirren; — v. schwirren; (mus.) klimpern
tweak n. Zwicken, Kniff; — v. zwicken, kneifen
tweed n. Tweed
tweezers n. pl. Pinzette
twelfth n. Zwölfte; Zwölftel; — adj. zwölft
Twelfth-night n. Dreikönigsabend
twelve n. Zwölf; — adj. zwölf
twelvemonth n. Jahr; **this day —** heute in einem Jahr
twentieth n. Zwanzigste; Zwanzigstel; — adj. zwanzigst
twenty n. Zwanzig(er); — **odd** zwanzig und darüber; — adj. zwanzig; **-fold** adj. zwanzigfach
twice adv. zweimal, zweifach, doppelt
twice-told adj. nacherzählt; abgedroschen
twiddle n. Drehen; — v. drehen; tändeln; vibrieren
twig n. Zweig, Rute; Wünschelrute; — v. (coll.) beachten, bemerken, verstehen
twilight n. Zwielicht, Dämmerung; — adj. dämmern, dämmerig; Dämmerungs-
twill n. Köper; — v. köpern
twin n. Zwilling; — adj. doppelt, Zwillings-; — **screw** Doppelschraube; — v. paaren; Zwillinge gebären
twine n. Zwirn, Schnur, Bindfaden, Garn; Windung, Geflecht, Gewirr; (bot.) Ranke; — v. zwirnen, zusammendrehen; schnüren, weben, schlingen; (sich) winden; verflechten; (bot.) ranken
twin-engined adj. zweimotorig
twinkle n. Flimmern, Funkeln, Glitzern; Blinzeln, Zwinkern; — v. flimmern, funkeln, glitzern; blinzeln, zwinkern
twinkling n. Augenblick; **in the — of an eye** im Nu
twirl n. Wirbel; (dance) Pirouette; — v. wirbeln
twist n. Drehung, Windung; Verdrehung, Verrenkung; (mech.) Geflecht, Maschinengarn, Twist; (mil.) Drall; (fig.) Verwicklung; — v. drehen, winden; verdrehen, verrenken; wickeln, spinnen, (ver)flechten; **-ed** adj. gewunden
twitch n. Zupfen, Ruck; Zwicken, Kneifen; (med.) Zuckung; — v. zupfen, zerren, kneifen, zwicken; (med.) zucken
twitter n. Gezwitscher, Gezirpe; (fig.) Aufregung; — v. zwitschern, zirpen; (fig.) zittern
two n. Zwei(er); Paar; — adj. zwei; **-fold** adj. zweifach, doppelt

two-by-four n. Brett (zwei zu vier Zoll)
two-cycle adj. Zweitakt; — n. Zweitakt
two-faced adj. doppelzüngig, falsch
two-fisted adj. (coll.) kräftig, handfest
two-handed adj. zweihändig; für zwei Personen
two-piece adj. zweiteilig
two-seater n. Zweisitzer
two-step n. Twostep, Zweierschritt
tycoon n. Industriemagnat
type n. Typ(us), Urbild, Vorbild, Muster; Art, Gestalt, Charakter, Persönlichkeit; Merkmal; (typ.) Type, Druckbuchstabe; — bar Schreibmaschinentaste; — founder Schriftgiesser; — v. Schreibmaschine schreiben, tippen
typesetter n. Schriftsetzer; Setzmaschine
typesetting n. Schriftsetzen
typewrite v. Schreibmaschine schreiben, tippen; -r n. Schreibmaschine; portable -r Reiseschreibmaschine; -r ribbon Farbband
typhoid adj. typhös; — fever Unterleibstyphus
typhoon n. Taifun
typhus n. Flecktyphus
typic(al) adj. typisch, charakteristisch
typify v. typisieren, (vor)bildlich darstellen
typing n. Maschineschreiben, Tippen
typist n. Maschineschreiber(in)
typographer n. Buchdrucker
typography n. Buchdruckerkunst, Typographie
tyrannic(al), tyrannous adj. tyrannisch, grausam, ungerecht, streng
tyrannize v. als Tyrann herrschen; — over tyrannisieren
tyrant n. Tyrann
Tyrol n. Tirol

U

ubiquitous adj. allgegenwärtig
udder n. Euter
ugliness n. Hässlichkeit, Widerwärtigkeit
ugly adj. hässlich, widerwärtig; ekelhaft
ukase n. Ukas; Edikt, Befehl
ukulele n. Ukulele; Hawaiiguitarre
ulcer n. Geschwür; -ate v. schwären
ulster n. Ulster
ulterior adj. jenseitig; weiter, anderweitig
ultimate n. Endgültige, Grundsätzliche; — adj. endlich, (aller)letzt; -ly adv. zu guter Letzt
ultimatum n. Ultimatum
ultimo n. Ultimo; — adj. im letzten (or vorigen) Monat
ultramodern adj. übermodern
ultrasonic adj. in Überschallgeschwindigkeit
ultraviolet adj. ultraviolett, infrarot
umber n. Umbra, Umbererde; (art.) Bergbraun; — adj. dunkelbraun
umbilical adj. Nabel-; — cord Nabelschnur
umbra n. Kernschatten, Schlagschatten; -ge n. Schatten, Anstoss, Verdacht; take -ge Anstoss nehmen, übelnehmen
umbrella n. Schirm; (pol.) Kompromiss;

— stand Schirmständer
umlaut n. Umlaut; — v. den Selbstlaut verändern
umpire n. Schiedsrichter, Unparteiische; — v. Schiedsrichter (or Unparteiischer) sein
unabashed adj. unverschämt, unverfroren
unabated adj. unvermindert; -ly adv. unablässig
unable adj. unfähig; be — ausserstande sein
unabridged adj. unverkürzt
unaccented adj. unbetont
unacceptable adj. unannehmbar
unaccomodating adj. unnachgiebig, ungefällig
unaccountable adj. unverantwortlich; unerklärlich, sonderbar
unaccustomed adj. ungewohnt; ungewöhnlich
unacquainted adj. unbekannt, unkundig, unerfahren
unadulterated adj. unverfälscht, rein
unadvised adj. unbedacht, unbesonnen
unaffected adj. unberührt, ungerührt; unbefangen, ungekünstelt; natürlich, einfach
unaided adj. ohne Unterstützung; unbewaffnet, bloss
unaltered adj. unverändert
unanimity n. Einstimmigkeit, Einmütigkeit
unanimous adj. einstimmig, einmütig
unapproachable adj. unzugänglich; unvergleichlich
unapt adj. untauglich, ungeeignet
unarmed adj. unbewaffnet; wehrlos
unassailable adj. unangreifbar; unerschütterlich
unassisted adj. ohne Beistand (or Unterstützung)
unassuming adj. anspruchslos, bescheiden
unattached adj. ungebunden, lose; (educ.) extern; (law) herrenlos; (mil.) zur Verfügung
unattainable adj. unerreichbar
unattended adj. unbegleitet; ungepflegt, vernachlässigt, verwahrlost
unattractive adj. nicht anziehend, reizlos
unavailing adj. nutzlos, vergeblich
unavoidable adj. unvermeidlich, unumgänglich; (law) ununstösslich
unawares adv. unvermutet, plötzlich, unversehens
unbalanced adj. unausgeglichen; aus dem Gleichgewicht gebracht
unbearable adj. unerträglich
unbecoming adj. unpassend; unkleidsam
unbelief n. Unglaube; Misstrauen
unbeliever n. Ungläubige
unbeloved adj. ungeliebt
unbend v. (sich) entspannen; nachlassen; -ing adj. unbiegsam; unbeugsam
unbiased adj. unbefangen, vorurteilsfrei; unparteiisch
unbid(den) adj. ungeheissen, ungeladen, ungebeten; (cards) nicht angesagt
unbind v. abbinden; entbinden, befreien
unblemished adj. unbefleckt, makellos; rein

unbolt v. aufriegeln; **-ed** adj. unverriegelt, offen; (fig.) rauh, grob

unborn n. ungeboren; zukünftig

unbosom v. sich offenbaren

unbound adj. ungebunden; (book) geheftet; **-ed** adj. unbegrenzt, schrankenlos, zügellos

unbreakable adj. unzerbrechlich

unbroken adj. ungebrochen, ungebändigt; ununterbrochen

unbuckle v. losschnallen, abschnallen

unburden v. entladen; entlasten; erleichtern

unbutton v. aufknöpfen

uncalled-for adj. ungerufen, unaufgefordert; nicht verlangt (or gerechtfertigt)

uncanny adj. unheimlich, nicht geheuer; (fig.) ungeschickt

unceasing adj. unaufhörlich

uncertain adj. ungewiss, unsicher; unbestimmt; unbeständig, unzuverlässig; unentschlossen; **-ty** n. Ungewissheit; Unzuverlässigkeit

unchangeable adj. unveränderlich

unclaimed adj. nicht beansprucht (or gefordert); **— letters** unbestellbare Briefe

uncle n. Onkel

unclean adj. unrein, unsauber; unkeusch

unclouded adj. unbewölkt, wolkenlos; heiter

uncomfortable adj. unbequem, unbehaglich, ungemütlich; unerfreulich

uncommon adj. ungewöhnlich, ungemein; selten

uncommunicative adj. verschlossen

uncompromising adj. unnachgiebig; (fig.) unleugbar

unconcern n. Gleichgültigkeit; **-ed** adj. gleichgültig sorglos; unbekümmert, unbeteiligt, unbetroffen

unconditional adj. unbedingt, bedingungslos

unconfined adj. ungehindert, unbegrenzt

unconscientious adj. gewissenlos

unconscious adj. unbewusst, unwissend; (med.) bewusstlos

unconstitutional adj. verfassungswidrig

uncontested adj. unbestritten

uncontrollable adj. unkontrollierbar; unumschränkt, zügellos

unconventional adj. unkonventionell; formlos, zwanglos; natürlich

uncork v. entkorken

uncorrupt adj. unverdorben; unbestochen

uncouple v. loskoppeln; (aus)lösen

uncouth adj. ungeschlacht, roh, linkisch; wunderlich, seltsam

uncover v. enthüllen, aufdecken; entblössen

unction n. Salbe, Einreibung; **extreme —** letzte Ölung

uncultured adj. unkultiviert, ungebildet

uncut adj. un(auf)geschnitten, unbehauen

undamaged adj. unbeschädigt

undated adj. nicht datiert; ohne Datum

undecided adj. unentschieden; unschlüssig

undefined adj. unbegrenzt; unbestimmt

undeniable, adj. unleugbar, unbestreitbar

under prep. unter(halb), weniger; **— adv.** unten; darunter; **— adj.** niedrig, untergeordnet; Unter-

underage adj. unmündig, minderjährig

underbid v. unterbieten

underbrush n. Unterholz, Gesträuch

undercarriage n. Fahrgestell

undercharge v. nicht genügend berechnen (or beladen)

underclothes n. pl., **underclothing** n. Unterkleidung, Leibwäsche

undercurrent n. Unterströmung, Gegenströmung

undercut n. Unterhöhlung; (meat) Filet; **— v.** unterhöhlen; unterbieten

underdog n. Benachteiligte; Unterliegende

underdone adj. nicht gar, halb roh

underestimate v. unterschätzen

underexposure n. (phot.) Unterbelichtung

underfed adj. unterernährt

underfoot adv. unter den Füssen; von unten

undergo v. erdulden, ertragen; sich unterziehen

undergraduate n. Student (ohne Universitätsgrad)

underground n. Untergrund; **— adj.** unterirdisch; Untergrund-

underhand(ed) adj. unter der Hand; heimlich, versteckt; hinterlistig, unehrlich

underline v. unterstreichen

underling n. Untergebene; Kriecher

underlying adj. zugrundeliegend; Grund-

undermine v. unterminieren, untergraben

underneath prep. unter; **— adv.** unten; unterwärts, unterhalb, darunter

undernourished adj. unterernährt

underpass n. Unterführung

underpay v. ungenügend (or schlecht) bezahlen

underpin v. unterlegen, unterbauen, stützen

underrate v. unterschätzen; herabsetzen; zu niedrig ansetzen

underscore v. unterstreichen

undersell v. verschleudern, unter dem Wert verkaufen

undershirt n. Unterhemd

underside n. Unterseite

undersigned n. Unterzeichnete; **— adj.** unterzeichnet

understand v. verstehen, begreifen; vernehmen; annehmen; sich verstehen auf; **that is understood** das ist selbstverständlich; **-ing** n. Verstand, Verständigung; Einvernehmen, Einverständnis; Voraussetzung; **-ing** adj. verständig, einsichtsvoll

understatement n. Unterschätzung; zu geringe Angabe

understudy n. (theat.) zweite Besetzung; Ersatzschauspieler; **— v.** einstudieren (or einspringen) für

undertake v. unternehmen, übernehmen; **-r** n. Leichenbestatter; Unternehmer

undertaking n. Leichenbestattung; Unternehmen, Unterfangen; Unternehmung

undertone n. Unterton; Flüsterton

undervalue v. unterschätzen; geringschätzen

underwater adj. Unterwasser-

underwear n. Unterzeug, Leibwäsche

underweight n. Untergewicht

underwood n. Unterholz, Gestrüpp

underworld n. Unterwelt

underwrite v. unterschreiben; versichern; —r n. Versicherer

undeserved adj. unverdient

undeserving adj. unwürdig

undesirable adj. unerwünscht

undeveloped adj. unentwickelt; — country unterentwickeltes (or unerschlossenes) Land

undiluted adj. unverdünnt, unverfälscht

undiminished adj. unvermindert

undismayed adj. unverzagt, unerschrocken

undisputed adj. unbestritten

undisturbed adj. ungestört; unerschüttert

undivided adj. ungeteilt; nicht verteilt

undo v. aufmachen, aufbinden, aufdecken, auftrennen, aufknöpfen; ungeschehen machen, aufheben; —ing n. Aufmachen; (fig.) Verderben

undoubted adj. unbestritten; zweifellos

undress n. Hauskleid, Negligé, Morgenrock; (mil.) Halbuniform; — v. (sich) entkleiden, ausziehen, ablegen

undue adj. ungebührlich; unangemessen, unverhältnismässig; (com.) noch nicht fällig

undulant fever n. Mittelmeerfieber, subtropisches Wechselfieber

undulate v. sich wellenförmig bewegen, wogen, wallen; — adj. wellenförmig, gewellt

unduly adv. unziemlich, ungehörig; übertrieben

undying adj. unsterblich, unvergänglich

unearth v. ausgraben, aufstöbern; ans Licht bringen

unearthly adj. unheimlich; überirdisch

uneasiness n. Unruhe, Unbehagen; Unbequemlichkeit

uneasy adj. unruhig, unbehaglich; unbequem

uneducated adj. unerzogen, ungebildet

unemotional adj. leidenschaftslos, passiv

unemployed adj. arbeitslos, erwerbslos; unbeschäftigt; — capital totes (or brachliegendes) Kapital

unemployment n. Arbeitslosigkeit, Erwerbslosigkeit

unending adj. endlos, unendlich

unequal adj. ungleich(mässig), unverhältnismässig; —ed adj. unvergleichlich, unübertroffen, unerreicht

unerring adj. unfehlbar, untrüglich

unessential adj. unwesentlich

uneven adj. uneben, ungleich; ungerade

unexampled adj. beispiellos

unexceptionable adj. untad(e)lig, vortrefflich

unexpected adj. unerwartet, unvermutet; unvorhergesehen

unexplored adj. unerforscht

unfading adj. unverwelkbar; (color) echt

unfailing adj. unfehlbar, untrüglich; unerschöpflich

unfair adj. unfair; unehrlich, unbillig

unfaithful adj. ungetreu, treulos; wortbrüchig; nicht wortgetreu

unfaltering adj. nicht schwankend; unerschrocken

unfamiliar adj. unbekannt, ungewohnt, ungewöhnlich

unfavorable adj. ungünstig, unvorteilhaft

unfeigned adj. unverhohlen

unfinished adj. unvollendet

unfit adj. untauglich, ungeeignet, unfähig; — v. untüchtig (or untauglich) machen

unfold v. (sich) entfalten; ausbreiten, aufschlagen; enthüllen

unforeseen adj. unvorhergesehen

unforgettable adj. unvergesslich

unforgiving adj. unversöhnlich

unfortunate adj. unglücklich, unglückselig

unfounded adj. unbegründet, grundlos

unfrequented adj. unbesucht; einsam, verlassen

unfurl v. entfalten, aufspannen, ausspannen; (naut.) losmachen

unfurnished adj. nicht ausgerüstet; unmöbliert

ungainly adj. ungeschickt, linkisch, plump

ungodly adj. gottlos; verrucht

ungrateful adj. undankbar

ungratified adj. unbefriedigt

ungrounded adj. unbegründet, grundlos

unhandy adj. ungeschickt, unbequem

unhappy adj. unglücklich, un(glück)selig, elend

unharmed adj. unbeschädigt, unverletzt, unversehrt; ungekränkt

unhealthy adj. ungesund, schädlich; krankhaft

unheard-of adj. ungehört, unerhört; unbekannt

unheeded adj. unbeachtet, unbemerkt; unerwogen

unhesitating adj. ohne Zögern

unhinge v. aus den Angeln heben; zerrütten

unhook v. aufhaken, aushaken

unhurt adj. unbeschädigt, unverletzt, unversehrt

unification n. Vereinheitlichung, Vereinigung

uniform n. Uniform; — adj. einförmig, einheitlich; Einheits-; — v. uniformieren; —ity n. Gleichförmigkeit, Gleichmässigkeit; Einheitlichkeit, Übereinstimmung

unify v. verein(ig)en, vereinheitlichen

unilateral adj. einseitig

unimpaired adj. unvermindert, ungeschwächt

unimpeachable adj. vorurteilsfrei; unanfechtbar

unimpeded adj. ungehindert

unimportant adj. unwichtig

uninformed adj. ununterrichtet

uninjured adj. unbeschädigt, unverletzt, unversehrt; ungekränkt; unverdorben

unintelligible adj. unverständlich

unintentional adj. unabsichtlich

uninterrupted adj. ununterbrochen

uninviting adj. wenig einladend

union n. Einheit, Eintracht, Übereinstimmung; Vereinigung, Verbindung, Verein; (pol.) Gewerkschaft; **–ism** n. Gewerkschaftswesen; **–ist** n. Gewerkschaftler; **–ize** v. eine Gewerkschaft bilden; einer Gewerkschaft zuführen

unique adj. einzig(artig), ungewöhnlich

unison n. Einklang, Gleichklang; Übereinstimmung; in — unisono, einstimmig

unit n. Einheit; Abteilung; **–ary** adj. Einheits-, Einer-; **–y** n. Einheit, Einigkeit, Eintracht

unite v. (sich) vereinigen, verbinden; **–d** adj. vereinigt; einig; **United States** Vereinigte Staaten

Univac n. Elektronengehirn

universal adj. allgemein, allumfassend; Universal-; **–ity** n. Vielseitigkeit

universe n. Universum, Weltall

university n. Universität

unjust adj. ungerecht, unbillig; **–ifiable** adj. unverantwortlich; nicht zu rechtfertigen

unkempt adj. ungekämmt; ungepflegt, roh

unkind adj. unfreundlich; lieblos

unknowingly adv. unwissentlich, unbewusst

unknown n. Unbekannte; — adj. unbekannt; unerkannt; unbewusst, ungewöhnlich

unlace v. aufschnüren, aufbinden; lösen

unlaid adj. ungelegt; ungestillt

unlawful adj. ungesetzlich; unerlaubt

unleash v. losbinden, loskoppeln; entfesseln

unless conj. wenn nicht; ausser, ausgenommen; es sei denn, dass

unlettered adj. unbelesen, ungelehrt; unwissend; (lit.) nicht mit Buchstaben bezeichnet

unlicensed adj. nicht konzessioniert; unberechtigt

unlike adj. ungleich, unähnlich; — adv. anders als; nicht wie

unlikely adj. unwahrscheinlich; ungeeignet; aussichtslos

unlimited adj. unbegrenzt, grenzenlos; unbeschränkt, schrankenlos

unload v. abladen, entladen, ausladen; erleichtern; (com.) massenhaft auf den Markt werfen; (naut.) löschen, ausschiffen

unlock v. aufschliessen; (fig.) aufdecken

unloose v. (auf)lösen, losmachen, loslassen

unlovable adj. unliebenswürdig

unlovely adj. reizlos, abstossend

unlucky adj. unglücklich, unheilbringend, verhängnisvoll

unmanageable adj. unlenksam; unfolgsam, widerspenstig; unhandlich

unmannerly adj. unmanierlich, ungezogen, unartig

unmarked adj. unbezeichnet; unbemerkt

unmarried adj. unverheiratet, ledig

unmask v. (sich) demaskieren, entlarven

unmatched adj. ungepaart; unvergleichlich

unmentionable adj. unaussprechlich;

nicht zu erwähnen, unnennbar

unmerciful adj. unbarmherzig

unmindful adj. unbedacht, ohne Rücksicht, sorglos

unmistakable adj. unverkennbar

unmixed adj. unvermischt, unverfälscht; rein

unmodified adj. unverändert

unmoved adj. unbewegt, ungerührt

unnamed adj. ungenannt

unnatural adj. unnatürlich

unnavigable adj. nicht schiffbar

unnecessary adj. unnötig, überflüssig

unnerve v. entnerven, entmutigen

unnot(ic)ed adj. unbemerkt, unbeachtet

unnumbered adj. ungezählt, unzählig, zahllos; unnummeriert

unobjectionable adj. einwandfrei

unobserved adj. unbe(ob)achtet, unbemerkt; unbefolgt

unobtainable adj. unerreichbar

unobtrusive adj. unaufdringlich, bescheiden

unoccupied adj. unbesetzt, unbenutzt; unbeschäftigt

unofficial adj. unoffiziell, nicht amtlich

unorthodox adj. unorthodox; nicht (recht) gläubig

unpack v. auspacken; entlasten, entladen

unpaid adj. unbezahlt, unbelohnt; (letter) unfrankiert

unpalatable adj. unschmackhaft, ungeniessbar

unparalleled adj. beispiellos

unpleasant adj. unangenehm

unpolished adj. unpoliert; (fig.) ungebildet

unpopular adj. unpopulär, unbeliebt

unpractical adj. unpraktisch

unprecedented adj. beispiellos, unerhört; noch nie dagewesen

unprejudiced adj. unbefangen, vorurteilsfrei

unpremeditated adj. unüberlegt, unvorbereitet; aus dem Stegreif; (law) unvorbedacht

unpretending, unpretentious adj. anspruchslos, bescheiden

unprincipled adj. skrupellos, gewissenlos; unsittlich, gottlos

unproductive adj. unproduktiv, unfruchtbar, unergiebig

unprofessional adj. nicht berufsmässig, laienhaft

unprofitable adj. uneinträglich, unvorteilhaft; nutzlos, vergeblich

unprotected adj. ungeschützt, unbeschützt; schutzlos

unprovided adj. nicht vorgesehen, unvorbereitet

unpunished adj. ungestraft, straflos

unqualified adj. ungeeignet, unberechtigt; unbeschränkt

unquenchable adj. un(aus)löschbar; unersättlich

unquestionable adj. unbestreitbar, unzweifelhaft

unravel v. entwirren, aufräufeln; lösen

unreadable adj. unleserlich

unready adj. nicht fertig; unentschlossen

unreal *adj.* unwirklich, wesenlos

unreasonable *adj.* unvernünftig; grundlos; unmässig

unrecognizable *adj.* nicht wiederzuerkennen

unreconciled *adj.* unversöhnt

unrelenting *adj.* unerbittlich

unreliable *adj.* unzuverlässig

unremitting *adj.* unablässig, unaufhörlich

unremunerative *adj.* nicht lohnend

unrequited *adj.* unerwidert

unreserved *adj.* unnummeriert, nicht reserviert; vorbehaltlos, rückhaltlos, unbeschränkt

unresponsive *adj.* unempfänglich

unrest *n.* Unruhe, Ruhelosigkeit; —ing *adj.* rastlos, ruhelos

unrestrained *adj.* ungehemmt, uneingeschränkt; unbeherrscht

unripe *adj.* unreif, unzeitig, unfertig

unrivaled *adj.* ohne Nebenbuhler; unvergleichlich

unroll *v.* abrollen, entrollen; entfalten

unruled *adj.* unbeherrscht; (paper) unliniiert

unruly *adj.* unbändig, ungestüm; widerspenstig, störrisch; ausgelassen, stürmisch

unsafe *adj.* unsicher, gefährlich

unsanitary *adj.* unhygienisch

unsatisfactory *adj.* unbefriedigend

unsavory *adj.* unschmackhaft, geschmacklos; widerwärtig, widerlich

unscathed *adj.* unbeschädigt, unverletzt

unschooled *adj.* ungeschult

unscientific *adj.* unwissenschaftlich

unscrew *v.* abschrauben, aufschrauben, losschrauben

unscrupulous *adj.* gewissenlos, bedenkenlos

unseasonable *adj.* unzeitig; (fig.) ungelegen

unseat *v.* vom Sitz heben, aus dem Sattel werfen; (pol.) absetzen; für ungültig erklären

unseemly *adj.* unziemlich, unschicklich, unpassend

unseen *adj.* ungesehen, unbemerkt; unsichtbar

unselfish *adj.* selbstlos, uneigennützig

unsettled *adj.* ungeordnet, ungeregelt, unbestimmt; unbeständig, schwankend; unbesiedelt; — accounts unbezahlte Rechnungen, unbeglichene Konten

unshakable *adj.* unerschütterlich; standhaft

unsightly *adj.* unansehnlich; hässlich

unskilful *adj.* ungeschickt

unskilled *adj.* unerfahren, ungeschult, ungelernt

unsociable *adj.* ungesellig

unsolved *adj.* ungelöst, ungeklärt

unsophisticated *adj.* unverfälscht, ungekünstelt; natürlich, schlicht

unsound *adj.* ungesund, kränklich; angegangen, verdorben, faul; brüchig, wurmstichig

unsparing *adj.* freigebig, reichlich; schonungslos, unbarmherzig, streng, hart

unspeakable *adj.* unaussprechlich, unsagbar; unsäglich

unspoken *adj.* ungesagt, unerwähnt

unstable *adj.* unbeständig, unstet schwankend; labil

unsteady *adj.* unstet, unbeständig, unsolide

unstressed *adj.* unbetont

unsubdued *adj.* unbesiegt, unbezwungen

unsubstantial *adj.* unkörperlich, wesenlos; unsolide

unsuccessful *adj.* erfolglos

unsuitable *adj.* unpassend, ungeeignet, unziemlich, unstatthaft, unschicklich; untauglich, unfähig

unsullied *adj.* unbeschmutzt, unbesudelt, unbefleckt; lauter, rein

unsurpassable *adj.* unübertrefflich

unsuspected *adj.* unverdächtig

unswerving *adj.* standhaft, fest

untamed *adj.* ungezähmt, ungebändigt

untangle *v.* entwirren

untarnished *adj.* ungetrübt, glänzend

untaught *adj.* ungelehrt, unwissend

untenable *adj.* unhaltbar

unthinkable *adj.* undenkbar

unthinking *adj.* gedankenlos, sorglos, unachtsam

untidy *adj.* unordentlich

untie *v.* aufbinden, aufknoten, auflösen; aufknüpfen; (er)lösen

until *prep.* bis; — *conj.* bis (dass)

untilled *adj.* unbebaut

untimely *adj.* unzeitig, unpassend, ungelegen, ungünstig; frühzeitig

untiring *adj.* unermüdlich

unto *prep.* (poet.) zu, an, nach; für, auf, gegen

untold *adj.* ungesagt, unerzählt; unerwähnt, ungezählt, unermesslich; unbeschreiblich

untouched *adj.* unberührt, unangetastet; ungerührt

untoward *adj.* ungünstig, widrig; widerspenstig; ungeschickt, verkehrt

untried *adj.* unversucht; ungeprüft, unerprobt; unerfahren; unerledigt; (law) noch nicht verhört

untrod(den) *adj.* unbetreten

untroubled *adj.* ungestört, unbelästigt; ungetrübt

untrue *adj.* unwahr; untreu

untrustworthy *adj.* unzuverlässig

untruth *n.* Unwahrheit

untutored *adj.* ununterrichtet, ungebildet

unused *adj.* ungebraucht, unbenutzt; ungewohnt

unusual *adj.* ungewöhnlich, ungebräuchlich; ungewohnt

unvarying *adj.* unveränderlich, unwandelbar

unveil *v.* (sich) entschleiern, enthüllen

unversed *adj.* unbewandert, unerfahren

unwanted *adj.* unerwünscht

unwarranted *adj.* unberechtigt; unverbürgt

unwelcome *adj.* unwillkommen

unwholesome *adj.* ungesund, schädlich

unwieldy *adj.* unbeholfen, ungelenk; unhandlich, sperrig

unwilling *adj.* unwillig, abgeneigt, widerwillig

unwind *v.* loswinden, loswickeln; (sich) abwickeln, aufgehen; lösen

unwise *adj.* unklug, töricht

unwittingly *adv.* unwissentlich, unbeabsichtigt

unwonted *adj.* ungewohnt, ungewöhnlich

unworkable *adj.* unpraktisch; unbrauchbar

unworthy *adj.* unwürdig

unwounded *adj.* unverwundet, unverletzt

unwrap *v.* aufwickeln, auswickeln; auspacken

unwritten *adj.* ungeschrieben, unbeschrieben; mündlich überliefert; — **law** Gewohnheitsrecht

unyielding *adj.* unnachgiebig, unbeugsam; unergiebing

up *adv.* auf, hinauf, in die Höhe, empor, aufwärts; herauf; oben; aufgestanden, aufgegangen, aufgestiegen; angeschwollen; aufgeregt; aus, vorbei; **be — to something** einer Sache gewachsen sein; **it is — to me** es hängt von mir ab, es liegt bei mir; — *prep.* herauf, hinauf; — **to bis auf** (*or* an); —**l** *interj.* auf! herauf! hinauf! — *n. pl.* **the — and downs of life** die Wechselfälle des Lebens

upbraid *v.* vorwerfen, vorhalten; **-ing** *adj.* vorwurfsvoll, tadelnd, scheltend

upbringing *n.* Erziehung; Aufziehen, Grossziehen

upbuild *v.* aufbauen, errichten

upgrade *n.* Abstufung; Aufstieg, Steigung; — *v.* abstufen, abteilen

upheaval *n.* Erhebung; Umwälzung

uphill *adj.* bergan, bergauf; (fig.) mühsam

uphold *v.* hochhalten; aufrecht(er)halten, stützen

upholster *v.* dekorieren; (auf)polstern; ausstatten; **-er** *n.* Polsterer, Dekorateur; **-y** *n.* Dekorierung; Polsterung; Möbelbezüge

upkeep *n.* Instandhaltung; Unterhaltungskosten

upland *n.* Hochland; — *adj.* Hochlands-; hochgelegen

uplift *v.* emporheben; erheben

upon *prep.* an, auf, in, über, zu; aus, durch, nach, unter, von; gemäss, zufolge; — *adv.* darauf, hinterher; beinahe

upper *adj.* höher, ober, Ober-; — **end** Kopfende; — **deck** Oberdeck; — **hand** Oberhand; — **jaw** Oberkiefer; — **lip** Oberlippe

upper-case *adj.* (typ.) gross gedruckt

upper-class *adj.* den oberen Gesellschaftsschichten angehörend

uppermost *adj.* oberst, höchst; vorherrschend, hauptsächlich

uppish *adj.* (coll.) anmassend, arrogant

upright *adj.* aufrecht, gerade; aufrichtig, rechtschaffen

uprising *n.* Erhebung, Aufstand; Aufstehen, Aufsteigen; Entstehen

uproar *n.* Getümmel, Lärm, Unruhe; Aufruhr; **-ious** *adj.* aufrührerisch, lärmend, tobend

uproot *v.* entwurzeln, ausreissen; vertilgen

upset *n.* Umwerfen, Umsturz; Misserfolg, Fehlschlag; Streit; — *adj.* festgesetzt, angesetzt; — *v.* umstürzen; in Unordnung (*or* aus der Fassung) bringen; aufregen, stören

upshot *n.* Ausgang, Ende; Beschluss; Ergebnis

upside-down *adj.* auf den Kopf stellend; verkehrt, umgekehrt; — *adv.* drunter und drüber; auf dem Kopf

upstairs *adv.* oben; nach oben; hinauf

upstanding *adj.* gerade, aufrichtig; (coll.) vorzüglich

upstart *n.* Emporkömmling, Neureiche

upstream *adv.* stromauf(wärts); gegen den Strom

up-to-date *adj.* zeitgemäss, modern, modisch

uptown *n.* Wohnbezirk (vom Zentrum entfernt); obere Stadtteile

upturn *n.* Umsturz; (com.) Heraufschnellen; — *v.* aufwerfen, hochwerfen; umstürzen

upward *adv.* aufwärts, steigend, in die Höhe; darüber

uranium *n.* Uran

urban *adj.* städtisch, Stadt-; **-ite** *n.* Grosstädter; **-ization** *n.* Verstädterung

urbane *adj.* artig, höflich, gebildet

urbanity *n.* Höflichkeit; Urbanität

urchin *n.* (zool.) Igel; (coll.) Schlingel, Schelm

uremia *n.* Harnvergiftung

urethra *n.* Harnröhre

urge *n.* Trieb; — *v.* drängen, (an)treiben; dringen, nötigen, zusetzen; **-ncy** *n.* Dringlichkeit; **-nt** *adj.* dringend, dringlich

urinal *n.* Harnglas, Ente; (coll.) Pissoir

urinate *v.* urinieren, harnen; Urin lassen

urine *n.* Urin, Harn

urn *n.* Urne; Gefäss

us *pron.* uns; **of —** unser

usable *adj.* brauchbar, benutzbar

usage *n.* Gebrauch; Brauch, Herkommen; Behandlung

use *n.* Gebrauch, Benutzung, Anwendung, Verwendung; Nutzen; Gewohnheit; — *v.* anwenden, verwenden, gebrauchen, (ver)brauchen; (be)nutzen; ausüben, betreiben; **she -d to do** sie pflegte zu tun, sie tat gewöhnlich: **-d** *adj.* gewohnt; gebräuchlich; üblich; verbraucht, abgenutzt; **-ful** *adj.* nützlich, dienlich, brauchbar; **-fulness** *n.* Nützlichkeit; **-less** *adj.* nutzlos, unnütz, unbrauchbar; fruchtlos, vergeblich; **-lessness** *n.* Nutzlosigkeit; **-r** *n.* Benutzer, Gebraucher

usher *n.* Türhüter; (law) Gerichtsdiener; (theat.) Platzanweiser; — *v.* einführen, ankündigen, anmelden; (theat.) Plätze anweisen; **-ette** *v.* Platzanweiserin

usual *adj.* üblich, gewöhnlich

usurer *n.* Wucherer

usurp *v.* sich aneignen, an sich reissen; usurpieren; **-ation** *n.* widerrechtliche Aneignung usury *n.* Wucher; **practise** — Wucher treiben

utensil *n.* Gerät; Werkzeug; *pl.* Utensilien, Gerätschaften

uterus *n.* Gebärmutter, Uterus

utility *n.* Nützlichkeit, Nutzen; **public utilities** gemeinnützige Betriebe

utilization *n.* Nutzbarmachung, Nutzanwendung, Verwertung

utilize *v.* verwerten, nutzbar machen

utmost *adj.* äusserst, fernst, höchst, grösst

Utopian *n.* Utopist; — *adj.* utopisch

utter *adj.* äusserst, gänzlich; — *v.* äussern, aussprechen, ausstossen; **-ance** *n.* Äusserung, Ausdruck, Ausspruch, Wort; Aussprache

uttermost *adj.* äusserst, fernst, höchst, grösst

uvula *n.* Zäpfchen

V

vacancy *n.* freie Stelle, Vakanz; Leere, Lücke

vacant *adj.* frei, offen, unbesetzt, vakant; leer, unbewohnt

vacate *v.* leeren, räumen, freimachen; aufgeben; aufheben

vacation *n.* Ferien, Urlaub

vaccinate *v.* impfen

vaccination *n.* Impfung

vaccine *n.* Impfstoff, Lymphe

vacillate *v.* schwanken, wanken; unschlüssig sein

vacuous *adj.* leer, ausdruckslos

vacuum *n.* Vakuum; (luft)leerer Raum; — **bottle** Thermosflasche; — **cleaner** Staubsauger; — **filter** Vakuumfilter; — **tube** Vakuumröhre, Geisslersche Röhre

vagabond *n.* Vagabund, Landstreicher; — *adj.* umherstreifend, vagabundierend; — *v.* vagabundieren

vagina *n.* (nat.) Scheide

vagrancy *n.* Landstreicherei

vagrant *adj.* unstet, ziellos, wandernd

vague *adj.* vag, unbestimmt, ungewiss; schwankend

vain *adj.* eitel; nichtig, leer, vergeblich; **in** — vergebens, umsonst

valance *n.* kurzer Vorhang; (fabric) halbseidener Damast

valence *n.* Wertigkeit

valentine *n.* am St. Valentinstag gewählter Schatz (*or* gesandter Gruss)

valet *n.* Kammerdiener

valiant *adj.* tapfer, mutig

valid *adj.* wirksam, triftig; rechtsgültig; **-ate** *v.* legalisieren, für rechtsgültig erklären; **-ity** *n.* Gültigkeit

valise *n.* Reisetasche

valley *n.* Tal; (arch.) Dachkehle

valor *n.* Wert, Gehalt; Tapferkeit, Mut; **-ous** *adj.* tapfer, kühn

valuable *adj.* wertvoll, hochwertig, kostbar; — *n. pl.* Kostbarkeiten, Schmucksachen, Wertsachen

valuation *n.* Abschätzung, Wertbestimmung, Veranschlagung; (fig.) Wertschätzung, Würdigung

value *n.* Wert, Preis; (com.) Valuta; **face** — Nennwert; **real** — Realwert; — *v.* (ab)schätzen, veranschlagen; (fig.) schätzen, achten; **-less** *adj.* wertlos

valve *n.* Ventil, Klappe; **air** — Luftventil; **exhaust** — Auslassventil

vamp *n.* (shoe) Oberleder; (sl.) Vamp; — *v.* zurechtflicken; (mus.) improvisieren

vampire *n.* Vampir

van *n.* Möbelwagen; Gepäckwagen; (agr.) Getreideschwinge; (min.) Erzschwinge; **cattle** — Viehtransportwagen

Van Allen Radiation Belt *n.* Van Allens Radiationsgürtel

vandal *n.* Vandale; **-ism** *n.* Vandalismus

vane *n.* Wetterfahne, (mech.) Flügel

vanguard *n.* Vorhut, Vortrab

vanilla *n.* Vanille

vanish *v.* (ver)schwinden, vergehen; **-ing** *adj.* verschwindend; **-ing line** Fluchtlinie

vanity *n.* Eitelkeit, Nichtigkeit, Vergeblichkeit; — **case** Puderdose

vanquish *v.* besiegen, überwältigen

vapid *adj.* abgestanden, schal; matt, geistlos

vapor *n.* Dunst, Dampf; — *v.* (ver)dunsten, (ver)dampfen; (coll.) prahlen; **-ize** *v.* (ver)dampfen, (ver)dunsten; **-ous** *adj.* dunstig, dampfartig; (fig.) nebelhaft, duftig

variable *adj.* veränderlich, veränderbar; verstellbar

variance *n.* Veränderung; Uneinigkeit

variant *adj.* verschieden, veränderlich; unbeständig

variation *n.* Variation, Abweichung; Abänderung; Abwechslung, Unterschied

varicose *adj.* krampfadrig; — **vein** Krampfader

varied *adj.* variiert, verändert; verschiedenartig, mannigfaltig

variety *n.* Mannigfaltigkeit, Auswahl, Menge; Spielart

various *adj.* mannigfaltig, verschieden(artig); abwechslungsreich

varnish *n.* Firnis, Lack; Anstrich; — *v.* firnissen, lackieren; (fig.) beschönigen

varsity *n.* (coll.) Universität; — **crew** Rudermannschaft der Universität

vary *v.* variieren, (ver)ändern, (ab)wechseln, abweichen; veränderlich sein; **-ing** *adj.* variiert; abwechselnd; veränderlich

vase *n.* Vase

Vaseline *n.* Vaseline

vassal *n.* Vasall, Lehnsmann

vast *adj.* ungeheuer, gewaltig, riesig, unermesslich

vat *n.* Fass; Bottich, Kufe

vaudeville *n.* Schlager; Vaudeville, Varieté

vault *n.* Sprung; (arch.) Stahlkammer; Gewölbe, Wölbung; — *v.* (über)wölben; springen, hinwegspringen über

veal *n.* Kalbfleisch; — **chop** Kalbskotelett

vector *n.* (avi.) Winkel der Luftverdrängung beim Fliegen

veer *v.* (sich) drehen, wenden; (naut.)

halsen, fieren

vegetable n. Gemüse; — adj. Pflanzen-, Gemüse

vegetarian n. Vegetarier; — adj. vegetarisch

vegetate v. vegetieren

vegetation n. Vegetation

vehemence n. Vehemenz, Heftigkeit, Leidenschaft

vehement adj. vehement, heftig, leidenschaftlich

vehicle n. Fuhrwerk, Fahrzeug; (fig.) Träger, Ausdrucksmittel

veil n. Schleier, Hülle; — v. (sich) verschleiern, verhüllen; bemänteln

vein n. Ader; — v. ädern, marmorieren; -ed adj., -y adj. geädert; marmoriert, gemasert

vellum n. Pergament

velocity n. Geschwindigkeit

velvet n. Samt; — adj. samten, samtweich; -y adj. Samt-; (fig.) sanft, mild

venal adj. käuflich, feil

vend v. verkaufen, feilbieten; -or n. Verkäufer, Händler; Verkaufsautomat

veneer n. Furnier; Anstrich, Tünche; — v. furnieren, einlegen, auslegen; (fig.) umkleiden; den Anstrich geben

venerable adj. ehrwürdig, verehrungswürdig

veneration n. Verehrung

venereal adj. wollüstig; Liebes-, Geschlechts-; (med.) venerisch

Venetian n. Venezianer; Venezianisch; — adj. venezianisch; — blind Jalousie

vengeance n. Rache; Strafe

venial adj. verzeihlich, entschuldbar

venison n. Wildbret

venom n. Gift; -ous adj. giftig, vergiftet

vent n. Öffnung, Loch; Abzug, Ausweg; (mil.) Zündloch; (zool.) After; give — sich Luft machen (or aussprechen); — v. lüften; ziehen; auslassen

ventilate v. ventilieren, lüften; (fig.) erörtern

ventilation n. Ventilation, Lüftung(sanlage); (fig.) Erörterung

ventilator n. Ventilator

ventriloquist n. Bauchredner

venture n. Wagnis, Risiko; Einsatz; Spekulation; — v. wagen, aufs Spiel setzen, riskieren; spekulieren; -some adj. unternehmend, wagend, verwegen

veracious adj. wahrhaftig, wahrheitsliebend; glaubwürdig

veracity n. Wahrhaftigkeit, Wahrheit

veranda(h) n. Veranda

verb n. Verb, Zeitwort; -al adj. wörtlich, mündlich; buchstäblich; Wort-, Verbal-; -atim adv. wörtlich, wortgetreu; -iage n. Wortschwall; Ausdruck- (sweise); -ose adj. wortreich; weitschweifig

verdant adj. grün(end), blühend; (coll.) unreif

verdict n. Urteil, Meinung; (law) Geschworenenspruch

verdigris n. Grünspan

verdure n. Grün; Frische

verge n. Rand, Einfassung; Stab; (mech.)

Spindel; — v. sich neigen, streifen, übergehen; begrenzen

verification n. Nachprüfung, Bestätigung

verify v. (nach)prüfen, beweisen, bestätigen

verily adv. wahrlich, wahrhaftig, wirklich; vollkommen

veritable adj. wahr(haftig), wirklich, echt

verity n. Wahrheit, Wirklichkeit

vermicelli n. Fadennudeln

vermicide n. Wurmmittel

vermilion n. Zinnober(rot); — adj. hochrot; — v. zinnoberrot färben

vermin n. Schädling, Ungeziefer

vermouth n. Wermuth

vernacular adj. einheimisch; Landes-

vernal adj. Frühlings-

versatile adj. veränderlich, beweglich; vielseitig, gewandt

versatility n. Beweglichkeit, Gewandtheit; Wandelbarkeit

verse n. Vers; Strophe; **blank** — Blankvers; -d adj. versiert, bewandert, erfahren

versify v. Verse machen; dichten, reimen; in Verse bringen

version n. Version, Fassung, Darstellung; Lesart; Übersetzung

versus prep. kontra, gegen

vertebra n. Wirbel; pl. Rückgrat, Wirbelsäule; -l adj., -te adj. Wirbel-; -te n. Wirbeltier

vertex n. Spitze, Scheitel

vertical adj. vertikal, senkrecht; Scheitel-; — fin (avi.) Seitenflosse; — line Senkrechte; Lot(rechte)

vertigo n. Schwindel

very adv. sehr; — adj. derselbe; **the —** thing gerade das; **the —** thought schon der Gedanke; **to the — bone** bis auf den Knochen; **Very light** Leuchtkugel

vespers n. pl. Vesper; Abendgottesdienst

vessel n. Gefäss; (naut.) Schiff

vest n. Weste, Jacket

vest v. bekleiden, bedecken, einkleiden; einsetzen; verleihen

vested adj. festbegründet, festgesetzt; erworben

vestibule n. Vestibül, Vorhof, Vorhalle; Hausflur

vestige n. Spur; Merkmal, Überbleibsel

vestment n. Amtsgewand; Messgewand; Kleid

vest-pocket edition n. Taschenausgabe

vestry n. Sakristei

vestryman n. Kirchenälteste

veteran n. Veteran; — adj ausgedient; erfahren

veterinary n. Tierarzt; Veterinär; — adj. tierärztlich

veto n. Veto; — v. sein Veto einlegen; verbieten

vex v. schikanieren, quälen, ärgern; necken; -ation n. Verdruss, Ärger, Sorge, Schikane; -atious adj. quälend, ärgerlich, verdriesslich; neckend

via prep. via, über, bei

viaduct n. Viadukt, Überführung

vial n. Phiole, Flasche

vibrant adj. vibrierend

v. abnehmen, sinken; (fig.) verfallen
want *n.* Mangel, Bedürfnis, Armut; — *v.* (er)mangeln, bedürfen; verlangen, wünschen; —ing *adj.* fehlend, (er)mangelnd
wanton *n.* Schelm; (fig.) Wüstling; liederliches Frauenzimmer; — *adj.* mutwillig, ausgelassen; frevelhaft, ausschweifend; wollüstig, geil
war *n.* Krieg; — *v.* Krieg führen; streiten; — **like** *adj.* kriegerisch, Kriegs-; — **fare** *n.* Kriegsführung; Kampf
warble *n.* Getriller, Schmettern, Schlagen; — *v.* trillern, schmettern, schlagen; —r *n.* Sänger; Singvogel
ward *n.* Wache; Krankensaal; Gefängnisabteilung; (law) Vormundschaft, Mündel; (pol.) Wahlkreis, Bezirk; — *v.* behüten, bewahren; — **off** abwehren, abwenden; parieren
warden *n.* Wärter, Wächter, Aufseher; Vormund, Pfleger; Vorsteher
wardrobe *n.* Garderobe; Kleiderschrank, Kleiderkammer
ware *n.* Ware
warehouse *n.* Warenlager, Lager; Speicher
warehouseman *n.* Lagerverwalter
warily *adv.* vorsichtig, behutsam, bedächtig
warm *adj.* warm, heiss; feurig, leidenschaftlich; — *v.* wärmen; (sich) erwärmen; —ing *adj.* erwärmend; —ing pan Wärmflasche, Anwärmer; —ing *n.* Erwärmung; —th *n.* Wärme; Herzlichkeit; Lebhaftigkeit, Feuer, Eifer
warm-blooded *adj.* heissblütig; (zool.) warmblütig
warmhearted *adj.* warmherzig, herzlich, teilnehmend
warmonger *n.* Kriegshetzer
warn *v.* warnen; ermahnen; benachrichtigen; —ing *n.* Warnung; Mahnung; Benachrichtigung; Kündigung; air-raid —ing Fliegeralarm, Luftwarnung
warp *n.* Kette, Aufzug; (naut.) Bugsiertau; (wood) Verwerfung; — *v.* sich verziehen (or werfen); verzerren; (naut.) verholen, bugsieren
warrant *n.* Vollmacht; Berechtigung, Erlaubnis; (law) Haftbefehl; Haussuchungsbefehl; Vollstreckungsbefehl; — *v.* bevollmächtigen, berechtigen; verbürgen, garantieren; rechtfertigen; —y *n.* Garantie, Gewähr; Bürgschaft(sschein); Berechtigung
warrior *n.* Krieger
warship *n.* Kriegsschiff
wart *n.* Warze, Auswuchs; —y *adj.* warzig
wartime *n.* Kriegszeit
wary *adj.* bedachtsam, vorsichtig, wachsam; sparsam
wash *n.* Wäsche; Abwaschen; Spülwasser; Wellenschlag; Tünche, Anstrich; (geol.) Schwemmland; (naut.) Kielwasser, Ruderblatt; — *v.* waschen; (be)spülen; reinigen; schwemmen; schlämmen; waschecht sein; —able *adj.* waschbar, waschecht; —er *n.* Wäscher; Waschmaschine; Spülmaschine; (mech.) Dichtungsscheibe, Man-

schette; —ing *n.* Wäsche, Waschung; (mech.) Plattierung; (phot.) Wässern; —ing *adj.* waschend; —ing **machine** Waschmaschine
washbowl *n.* Waschbecken, Waschschüssel
washerwoman *n.* Wäscherin, Waschfrau
washout *n.* (geol.) Auswaschung; (coll.) Reinfall, Durchfall
washstand *n.* Waschständer, Waschschüssel
wasp *n.* Wespe
waste *n.* Abfall, Schwund, Verlust; Verwüstung, Verödung; Vergeudung, Verschwendung; Abnutzung; (law) Vernachlässigung, Verfall; — pipe Abzugsrohr; Abflussrohr; — *adj.* wüst, öde, unbebaut; unnütz, unbrauchbar; überflüssig; — *v.* verwüsten, verheeren, veröden; vergeuden, verschwenden; — **away** hinschwinden, sich verzehren, verfallen; —ful *adj.* verheerend; verschwenderisch; —r *n.* Verschwender; Verwüster; Ausschuss; (coll.) Tunichtgut
wastebasket *n.* Papierkorb
wastepaper *n.* Altpapier, Makkulatur
watch *n.* Wache; Wachsamkeit; Taschenuhr; (mil.) Posten; **night** — Nachtwache; **stop** — Stoppuhr; **wrist** — Armbanduhr; — *v.* wachen, bewachen; achtgeben, beobachten; — **out!** *interj.* Achtung! gib acht! —ful *adj.* wachsam, aufmerksam, achtsam; (fig.) schlaflos
watchdog *n.* Hofhund, Kettenhund; (fig.) Zerberus
watchmaker *n.* Uhrmacher
watchman *n.* Wächter, Nachtwächter; (rail.) Bahnwärter
watchtower *n.* Wachtturm, Warte
watchword *n.* Parole, Losung
water *n.* Wasser; Gewässer; **be in low** — auf dem Trockenen sitzen; — **bird** Wasservogel; — **cask** Wasserfass; — **closet** Wasserklosett; — **color** Aquarellfarbe, Wasserfarbe; — **cress** Brunnenkresse; — **cure** Wasserkur; — **front** Hafengegend; — **gap** Felsbachspalte; — **gas** Wassergas; — **gate** Schleusentor; — **gauge** Wasserstandsanzeiger, Pegel; — **glass** Wasseruhr; (chem.) Wasserglas; — **level** Wasserstand(slinie); (mech.) Wasserwaage; — **lily** Seerose, Teichrose; — **main** Hauptwasserrohr; — **meter** Wassermesser; — **moccasin** Mokassinwasserschlange; — **polo** Wasserpolo, Wasserball; — **power** Wasserkraft; — **tower** Wasserturm; — **wing** Brückenmauer; Schwimmgürtel; — *v.* (be)wässern, berieseln; begiessen, besprengen; verwässern, verdünnen; tränken; tränen; —ing *n.* Wässern, Bewässern, Begiessen; —ing **place** Schwemme, Tränke; —ing **pot** Giesskanne; —y *adj.* wässerig, feucht, nass; Wasser-; wasserreich
water-cooled *adj.* wassergekühlt
waterfall *n.* Wasserfall
waterlogged *adj.* wassergefüllt; sinkend, leck

watermark n. Wassermarke, Wasserzeichen

watermelon n. Wassermelone

waterproof adj. wasserdicht, imprägniert

watershed n. Wasserscheide

waterspout n. Wasserhose; Wasserstrahl; (arch.) Speiröhre, Traufe

waterworks n. pl. Wasserwerk(e); Wasserkünste; (sl.) Tränenschleusen

watt n. Watt

wave n. Welle, Woge; Wellenlinie; Schwenken, Wink(en); short — Kurzwelle; sound — Schallwelle; — length Wellenlänge; — v. wellig machen, wellen; wogen; wehen, flattern; winken, schwenken; -d adj. gewellt, wellenförmig; -r p. wanken, schwanken; zaudern, unschlüssig sein; flackern

waving adj. wankend, schwankend; unschlüssig

wavy adj. wogig, wogend; wellig, gewellt

wax n. Wachs; — adj. wächsern; — candle Wachskerze; — paper Wachspapier; — v. wachsen, bohnen, polieren; wichsen; pichen; -en adj. wächsern, wachsfarben; (fig.) nachgiebig; -y adj. wachsartig, weich; (med.) wachsbleich

waxwork n. Wachsfigur

way n. Weg, Strasse; Bahn, Kurs, Richtung, Strecke; Fahrt; Weite, Entfernung; Wandel, Benehmen; Zustand; Mittel, Methode, Art und Weise, Verfahren; by the — nebenbei, beiläufig; by — of über; force one's — sich gewaltsam eindrängen; give — aus dem Wege gehen, weichen; in no — keineswegs; on the — unterwegs, auf dem Wege; out of the — ungewöhnlich; entlegen; -s and means Mittel und Wege

wayfarer n. Reisende, Wanderer; Hotelpächter

waylay v. auflauern, nachstellen

wayside n. Strassenrand, Wegseite; by the — an der Strasse (or am Wege) gelegen

wayward adj. launisch, eigensinnig, widerspenstig; unregelmässig

we pron. wir

weak adj. schwach; kränklich; -en r. schwächen; schwach werden; verdünnen; entkräften; nachlassen; -ling n. Schwächling; -ness n. Schwäche, Schwächlichkeit; Schlaffheit

weak-minded adj. schwachsinnig; charakterschwach

wealth n. Wohlstand, Reichtum; (fig.) Fülle, Überfluss; -y adj. reich, vermögend, begütert, wohlhabend

wean n. entwöhnen; abgewöhnen, abbringen von

weapon n. Waffe; Wehr

wear n. Tragen; Tracht, Mode; Abnutzung; — v. tragen, anhaben, aufhaben; abtragen, abnutzen, erschöpfen; — out a person jemanden ermüden (or langweilen); -ing adj. -ing apparel n. Kleidung(sstücke)

weariness n. Müdigkeit, Ermüdung; (fig.) Überdruss

wearisome adj. mühsam, beschwerlich, ermüdend; (fig.) langweilig, belästigend

weary adj. müde, matt; (fig.) überdrüssig; ermüdend, lästig

weasel n. Wiesel

weather n. Wetter, Witterung; (naut.) Luv; — forecast Wettervoraussage; — report Wetterbericht; — strip Dichtungsleiste, Dichtungsstreifen; — v. lüften; dem Wetter aussetzen, verwittern; (arch.) abschrägen; (naut.) luvwärts umschiffen; (fig.) widerstehen, wetterfest sein

weather-beaten adj. wettergebräunt, abgehärtet, wetterfest; mitgenommen

weathercock n. Wetterhahn, Wetterfahne

weatherman n. Wetterberichterstatter, Meteorologe

weather-strip v. (gegen Wettereinflüsse) abdichten

weather-tight adj. wetterdicht

weave n. Gewebe; Weberei; — v. weben, wirken; flechten; (fig.) ersinnen; -r n. Weber

web n. Gewebe, Netz; (orn. and zool.) Schwimmhaut; — v. weben, wirken; (zool.) einspinnen; -bed adj. (orn. and zool.) mit Schwimmhäuten versehen

web-footed adj. schwimmfüssig

wed v. heiraten, ehelichen; verheiraten, trauen; -ded adj. verheiratet, angetraut, ehelich; (fig.) ergeben, eng verbunden; -ding n. Heirat, Hochzeit, Trauung; -ding cake Hochzeitskuchen; -ding ring Trauring

wedge n. Keil; — v. (ver)keilen, spalten

wedlock n. Ehe(stand)

Wednesday n. Mittwoch

wee adj. klein, winzig

weed n. Unkraut; (coll.) Kraut, Tabak; widow's — Witwentrauer; — v. jäten; säubern, auslesen; -y adj. unkrautartig, verkrautet

week n. Woche; by the — wochenweise, wöchentlich; — end Wochenende; -ly adj. wöchentlich; -ly publication Wochenschrift

weep v. (be)weinen, beklagen; feucht sein, tröpfeln; -ing adj. weinend; Trauer-; -ing willow Trauerweide; -ing n. Weinen, Klagen

weigh v. (ab)wiegen; (ab)wägen, erwägen; gelten, den Ausschlag geben; (naut.) lichten; -t n. Gewicht; Wucht, Schwere, Last, Druck; Bedeutung; inspector of -ts and measures Eichamtsinspektor; -ty adj. gewichtig, schwer(wiegend); erheblich; drückend

weightlessness n. Schwerelosigkeit

weird adj. unheimlich, geisterhaft, überirdisch; merkwürdig; Schicksals-; the Weird Sisters die Parzen

welcome n. Willkommen(en); — adj. willkommen, angenehm; — v. willkommen heissen, bewillkommnen; you are — es ist gern geschehen; —! interj. herzlich willkommen!

weld r. (zusammen)schweissen; — n. Schweissnaht; -er n. Schweisser; -ing *n.* Schweissen

welfare *n.* Wohlfahrt, Wohlergehen, Wohlstand; — **society** Fürsorgeverein; — **state** Nation mit verstaatlichter Fürsorge; — **work** Wohlfahrtspflege, Fürsorgewerk

well *n.* Brunnen, Quelle; Schacht; — *adj.* wohl

well *adj.* gut, schön, richtig; wohl; gänzlich, völlig; **as** — **as** so gut wie, sowohl als auch; **very** —! sehr gut! — **then!** nun gut! wohlan!; — *adj.* wohl, gesund; —! *interj.* gut! schön! richtig! nun!

well-behaved *adj.* wohlerzogen, anständig

well-being *n.* Wohlergehen, Wohlstand, Wohlfahrt

wellborn *adj.* hochgeboren, von guter Herkunft

well-bred *adj.* wohlerzogen; artig, manierlich; (zool.) von guter Abstammung

well-defined *adj.* gut definiert

well-disposed *adj.* wohlgesinnt, wohlmeinend

well-done *adj.* gut gemacht; (cooking) gar, gut gebraten

well-groomed *adj.* gut gepflegt; elegant

well-intentioned *adj.* wohlmeinend, wohlgemeint

well-known *adj.* wohlbekannt

well-nigh *adv.* beinahe, fast

well-off *adj.* gut situiert, wohlhabend

well-timed *adj.* rechtzeitig; angebracht

well-to-do *adj.* wohlhabend, begütert

well-wisher *n.* Gönner, Freund

welter *n.* Rollen; Wälzen; (fig.) Aufruhr; — *v.* rollen, sich wälzen; schwimmen

welterweight *n.* Weltergewicht

wench *n.* Mädchen, Frauenzimmer; Strassenmädchen

wend *v.* (sich) wenden, lenken

west *n.* West(en); (fig.) Abendland; — *adj.* westlich, westwärts; (fig.) abendländisch; **West-**; **-erly** *adj.*, **-ern** *adj.* westlich, West-; (fig.) abendlich; **-ward** *adv.* westwärts

Westphalia *n.* Westfalen

West Prussia *n.* Westpreussen

wet *n.* Nässe, Feuchtigkeit; — **blanket** *adj.* feuchtes Tuch; (coll.) Spielverderber; — **nurse** Amme; — *adj.* nass, feucht; (coll.) benebelt; — *v.* nass machen, durchnässen; benetzen, anfeuchten; begiessen

wether *n.* Hammel

whack *n.* Schlag, Stoss; (sl.) Versuch; Anteil; Zustand; — *v.* (coll.) durchschlagen; (sl.) verteilen; prügeln; —! *interj.* klaps! schwaps!

whale *n.* Wal(fisch); — **oil** Tran

whalebone *n.* Fischbein

wharf *n.* Kai; Landeplatz; — *v.* löschen

what *pron.* was (für ein), wer; wie(viel); welch; — **is the matter?** was ist los?

what(so)ever *pron.* and *adj.* was auch (immer); welch auch (immer); was nur

wheat *n.* Weizen; **winter** — Winterweizen

wheatear *n.* Weizenähre

wheel *n.* Rad; Getriebe; Umdrehung; **driving** — Triebrad; **gambling** — Glücksrad; **paddle** — Schaufelrad; **potter's** — Töpferscheibe; **spinning** — Spinnrad; **steering** — Steuerrad; — **base** Radstand; — **chair** Rollstuhl; — **rope** (naut.) Steuerreep; — *v.* rollen, (sich) drehen; (mil.) schwenken

wheelbarrow *n.* Schubkarren

wheeze *v.* keuchen, schnauben, röcheln

whelm *v.* bedecken, verschütten; (fig.) erdrücken

when *adv.* wann, zu welcher Zeit; — *pron.* seit wann, wie lange; — *conj.* wenn, während, als; sobald

whence *adv.* von wo, woher; woraus, weshalb

when(so)ever *adv.* wann auch immer, so oft als

where *adv.* wo(hin), woher, da

whereabouts *n.* Aufenthalt, Wohnort; — *adv.* woherum, worüber, weswegen; wo ungefähr

whereas *conj.* da nun, während doch; wohingegen

whereat *adv.* worüber, wobei, worauf; woran

whereby *adv.* wobei, wodurch, wovon, womit

wherefore *adv.* warum, weshalb, weswegen, wozu

wherein *adv.* worin (auch immer)

whereof *adv.* wovon; dessen, deren

where(up)on *adv.* worauf(hin), wonach

wherever *adv.* wo auch (immer); wohin auch (immer)

wherewith *adv.* womit, mit wem; **-al** *adv.* and *pron.* womit; nötig; **-al** *n.* Erforderliche, Mittel

whet *v.* wetzen, schärfen, schleifen

whether *conj.* ob

whetstone *n.* Schleifstein, Wetzstein

whey *n.* Molke

which *pron.* welch; der, die, das

which(so)ever *pron.* and *adj.* welch (or was) auch immer

whiff *n.* Zug, Paff; Hauch; (coll.) Nu

while *n.* Weile, Zeitraum; — *conj.* während, indem, so lange (wie)

whim *n.* Einfall, Laune, Grille; **-sical** *adj.* grillenhaft, launenhaft; wunderlich; **-sy** *n.* Laune; Grille(nhaftigkeit)

whimper *n.* Gewimmer, Winseln; — *v.* wimmern, winseln

whine *n.* Gewimmer, Gewinsel; — *v.* weinen, wimmern, winseln; jaulen, jammern

whinny *n.* Gewieher; — *v.* wiehern

whip *n.* Peitsche; Geissel; (pol.) Einpeitscher; — **hand** Oberhand; — *v.* peitschen; schlagen, geisseln; (pol.) einpeitschen, durchpeitschen; **-ped** geschlagen, gepeitscht; **-ped cream** Schlagsahne

whippoorwill *n.* Ziegenmelker

whirl *n.* Wirbel, Strudel; (bot.) Quirl; (zool.) Gewinde; — *v.* (sich) drehen, wirbeln; kreisen

whirlpool *n.* Wirbel, Strudel

whirlwind *n.* Wirbelwind, Windhose

whisk *n.* Wedel; kleiner Besen, Handfeger; Schneeschläger; — *v.* wischen, fegen, kehren; abstauben; schwingen, wirbeln; schlagen

whisker n. Wischer, Feger; — pl. Backenbart

whisk(e)y n. Whisky

whisper n. Wispern, Geflüster; — v. wispern, flüstern, raunen

whistle n. Pfiff, Pfeifen; Pfeife, Flöte; — v. pfeifen

whit n. Jota, Punkt; Bisschen

white n. Weiss(e); Eiweiss(körper); (fig.) Reinheit, Wahrheit; — adj. weiss; farblos; (fig.) rein, unbefleckt; — **ant** Termite; — **feather** weisse Feder; Feigheitszeichen; — **gold** Weissgold; — **heat** Weissglut; — **lead** Bleiweiss; — **lie** Notlüge; — **matter** (anat.) Gehirnhaut; Rückenmark; — **oak** Silbereiche; — **pine** Silberkiefer; — **poplar** Silberpappel; — **sauce** Mehlschwitze, Einbrenne; — **slavery** Mädchenhandel; **-n** v. weissen, tünchen; weiss machen; weiss (or grau, blass) werden, ergrauen; bleichen; **-ness** n. Weisse, Blässe; (fig.) Reinheit

white-collar worker n. Büroangestellte

white-haired adj. weisshaarig

white-hot adj. weissglühend

whitewash n. Tünche; — v. tünchen, weissen; (fig.) rein waschen, übertünchen

whither adv. wohin

whittle v. schnitze(l)n; — **away** (or **down**) beschneiden

whiz n. Zischen, Sausen; — v. zischen, sausen

who pron. wer; welch; der, die, das

whodunit n. (coll.) Kriminalroman, Detektivgeschichte

who(so)ever pron. wer auch (immer); ein jeder, der

whole n. Ganze, Gesamtheit; — adj. ganz, ungeteilt; voll(ständig); heil, unversehrt

wholehearted adj. aufrichtig, ernst

whole-meal bread n. Vollkornbrot, Schrotbrot

wholesale n. Grosshandel; (fig.) in Bausch und Bogen; — adj. Gross-, en gros; **-r** n. Grosshändler, Engroshändler

wholesome adj. heilsam, zuträglich, bekömmlich; gesund; nützlich

whole-wheat adj. Weizenschrot

wholly adv. ganz, gänzlich; ganz und gar; vollkommen, völlig

whoop n. Schrei, Geschrei; — v. (auf)schreien; **-ing cough** Keuchhusten

whop v. vertobaken, prügeln

whore n. Hure

whose pron. wessen; dessen, deren

why adv. warum, weshalb, weswegen; **that is** — deshalb, darum

wick n. Docht

wicked adj. böse, schlecht; gottlos; verrucht, lasterhaft

wide adj. weit, breit, fern; umfassend, abweichend; **far and** — weit und breit; **-n** v. erweitern, (aus)weiten; verbreitern; verbreiten

wide-awake adj. hell wach; (fig.) aufmerksam, schlau

wide-eyed adj. mit weitgeöffneten Augen

widespread adj. weit verbreitet (or ausgebreitet)

widow n. Witwe; **-ed** adj. verwitwet; verwaist: **-er** n. Witwer; **-hood** n. Witwenstand

width n. Weite, Breite

wield v. handhaben, schwingen, führen; beherrschen, leiten; ausüben; (er)tragen

wife n. Weib, Ehefrau, Gattin, Gemahlin

wig n. Perücke; — v. (coll.) schelten, ausschimpfen

wiggle n. Schwänzeln, Schlängeln; — v. schwänzeln, schlängeln

wild n. Wildnis, Wüste, Einöde; — adj. wild, stürmisch; toll, zügellos, ausschweifend; ziellos; abenteuerlich; ungezähmt, verwildert; (bot.) wild wuchernd (or wachsend); — **boar** Wildschwein, Keiler; — **oats** (coll.) Jugendstreich; **-erness** n. Wildnis, Wüste, Einöde; (fig.) Unmenge

wildcat n. Wildkatze; (com.) unsolides (or ungesetzliches) Unternehmen; (rail.) führerlose Lokomotive; — adj. planlos; schwindelhaft; (com.) unsolid, ungesetzlich; (rail.) nicht fahrplanmässig, unkontrolliert

wildfire n. Feuersbrunst; **spread like** — sich wie ein Lauffeuer verbreiten

wild-goose chase n. vergebliche Bemühung (or Jagd); Querfeldeinritt

wile n. List, Tücke; Kniff

wilful adj. eigensinnig, eigenwillig; (law) vorsätzlich

will n. Wille, Wunsch; Macht, Willkür; (law) letzter Wille, Testament; **at** — nach Belieben, ohne Einschränkung; — v. wollen, wünschen, verlangen; (law) letztwillig verfügen, hinterlassen; **-ing** adj. (bereit)willig; willens; **-ingness** n. Bereitwilligkeit, Geneigtheit

willow n. Weide

will-o'-the-wisp n. Irrlicht

willy-nilly adv. wohl oder übel

win n. Gewinn, Sieg; — v. gewinnen, siegen, den Sieg davontragen; erlangen; (mil.) erobern, einnehmen; **-ner** n. Gewinner, Sieger; **-ning** n. Gewinn, Nutzen, Ausbeute; **-ning** adj. gewinnend, einnehmend

winch n. Winde, Kran, Kurbel

wind n. Wind; Luftzug; Hauch, Atem; — **instrument** Blasinstrument; — **tunnel** (avi.) Windkanal; — v. ausser Atem sein (or bringen); **-ed** adj. ausser Atem; **short -ed** kurzatmig; **-ward** n. Windseite, Luv(seite); **-ward** adv. windwärts, luvwärts; **-y** adj. windig, stürmisch; (med.) blähend; (fig.) aufgeblasen, prahlerisch

wind v. (sich) winden, wickeln; (bot.) ranken; — **up** schliessen. end(ig)en; aufwickeln; (watch) aufziehen; (fig.) abwickeln; (com.) liquidieren; **-ing** n. Windung, Krümmung; Wicklung; Gewinde; **-ing** adj. sich windend; **-ing sheet** Leichentuch, Sterbehemd; **-ing stairs** Wendeltreppe

windbag n. Blasebalg; (coll.) Windbeutel

windfall n. Fallobst; Windbruch; (fig.) Glücksfall, unerwarteter Gewinn

windlass n. Winde; Kran

windmill n. Windmühle

window n. Fenster; (com.) Schaufenster, Auslage; Schalter; — **blind**, — **shade** Jalousie. Rouleau; — **shutter** Fensterladen; — **sill** Fenstersims, Fensterbrett; **French** — Flügelfenster

windowpane n. Fensterscheibe

windpipe n. Luftröhre

windshield n. Windschutzscheibe; — **wiper** Scheibenwischer

wine n. Wein; — **bag** Weinschlauch

wing n. Flügel; Seite; (arch.) Seitenflügel; (avi.) Tragfläche; Staffel; (football) Aussenstürmer; (mil.) Flanke; pl. (theat.) Kulissen, Seitendekoration; — **case** (ent.) Flügeldecke; — **spread** Flügelweite; — **stroke** Flügelschlag; — v. mit Flügeln versehen, beflügeln, beschwingen; durchfliegen, überfliegen

wink n. Wink; Blinzeln, Blinken; (fig.) Augenblick; **not get a** — **of sleep kein Auge zutun**; — v. winken, blinzeln, blinken

winsome adj. gefällig, angenehm; anziehend

winter n. Winter; — **wheat** Winterweizen; — v. überwintern, Winterquartiere beziehen

wintry adj. winterlich; kalt, frostig

wipe v. Wischen, Putzen; (sl.) Schlag, Hieb; — v. (ab)wischen, putzen; auswischen, reinigen; (ab)trocknen; (sl.) prügeln; — **out** (coll.) ausrotten

wire n. Draht; (coll.) Telegramm; **barbed** — Stacheldraht; **conducting** — Leitungsdraht; **live** — geladener Draht; **screen** — Netzdraht; — **bridge** Hängebrücke; — **fence** Drahtzaun, Drahtgitter; — **gauge** Drahtmass; — **photo** Bildtelegramm; — **rope** Drahtseil; — **screen** Drahtnetz, Drahtsieb; — **tapping** Anzapfen (der Leitung); Abhören (telefonischer or telegrafischer Mitteilungen); — v. mit Draht versehen (or befestigen); (mech.) Leitungen legen; (coll.) drahten; -**less** adj. drahtlos; Funk-

wirepuller n. Drahtzieher

wiring n. Leitung, elektrische Anlage

wiry adj. drahtig; sehnig, zäh

wisdom n. Weisheit, Klugheit; Einsicht; Gelehrsamkeit, Wissen; — **tooth** Weisheitszahn

wise n. Weise; — adj. weise, klug; verständig, einsichtig; erfahren; gelehrt

wisecrack n. witzige Bemerkung; — v. witzige Bemerkungen machen

wish n. Wunsch. Verlangen; Glückwunsch; — v. wünschen, verlangen, wollen; beglückwünschen; -**ful** adj. sehnsüchtig, verlangend

wishbone n. (orn.) Brustbein

wishy-washy adj. wässrig, schwach; gegenstandslos, kraftlos

wisp n. Wisch; Strähne; Irrlicht

wistful adj. sehnsüchtig, sehnlich; gedankenvoll

wit n. Witz; Verstand, Geist; Witzbold; **be at one's** — **'s end** sich nicht mehr zu helfen wissen; **to** — nämlich, das heisst; -**less** adj. witzlos, geistlos; gedankenlos; -**tingly** adv. wissentlich, geflissentlich; -**ty** adj. witzig, geistreich; (fig.) beissend

witch n. Hexe, Zauberin; — v. verhexen, verzaubern; -**ery** n. Zauberei; Entzücken

witchcraft n. Hexerei; Zauberkunst, Zauberei

with prep. mit; bei, nebst, durch, von, über

withdraw v. (sich) zurückziehen, wegziehen, abziehen; herausziehen, herausnehmen; entfernen, abwenden; (law) zurücknehmen, widerrufen; -**al** n. Zurückziehung, Abhebung; Zurücknahme; Entziehung; (law) Widerruf; (mil.) Rückzug

wither v. (ver)welken; austrocknen, verdorren; (fig.) vergehen

withhold v. zurückhalten, abhalten, vorenthalten

within prep. innerhalb, binnen, in; — adv. im Innern, drin(nen), darin; inwendig; daheim, zu Hause; — **bounds** (mil.) erlaubt, gestattet

without prep. ohne; ausserhalb, ausser; — adv. aussen, draussen; äusserlich; auswendig; nicht daheim (or zu Hause); **that goes** — **saying das versteht sich** von selbst

withstand v. widerstehen, widersetzen, widerstreben

witness n. Zeuge; Zeugnis; — v. bezeugen; Zeuge sein; zugegen sein

wizard n. Zauberer, Hexenmeister, Magier

wobble n. Schlottern, Torkeln; — v. schlottern, torkeln; schwanken, wackeln

wobbly adj. wackelnd, wackelig; torkelnd, schlotternd

woe n. Leid, Elend; Pein, Weh; -**ful** adj. kummervoll, elend, jämmerlich; bedauernswert, leiderfüllt

wolf n. Wolf; **cry** — blinden Alarm schlagen

woman n. Frau, Weib; (coll.) Weibsbild; —'**s rights** Frauenrechte; -**hood** n. Weiblichkeit; (coll.) Frauenwelt; -**kind** n. weibliches Geschlecht, Frauen(welt); -**ly** adj. weiblich, fraulich; (coll.) weibisch

womb n. Leib, Schoss; (anat.) Gebärmutter

wonder n. Wunder; Verwunderung; — v. (sich) wundern, bewundern, verwundern, staunen; gern wissen wollen, neugierig sein; -**ful** adj. wundervoll, wunderbar, wunderschön; erstaunlich

wonderland n. Wunderland

wont n. Gewohnheit, Gebrauch; -**ed** adj. gewöhnlich, gewohnt

woo v. freien, werben, anhalten; (fig.) suchen; locken; drängen

wood n. Holz; Wald(ung), Forst, Gehölz; Brennholz; (typ.) Holzblock; — **alcohol**

Holzalkohol; — **anemone** Waldane-mone, Windröschen; — **louse** Holz-wurm, Assel; — **pigeon** Holztaube; — **pulp** Holzschliff, Zellulose; — **wind** (mus.) Holzblasinstrument; — v. auf-forsten; mit Brennholz versehen; -ed adj. waldig, bewaldet; -en adj. hölzern; Holz-; -y adj. waldig; holzig; Wald-, Holz-

woodbine n. Geissblatt

woodchuck n. Murmeltier

woodcraft n. Weidwerk, Jägerei

woodcut n. Holzschnitt; -ter n. Holz-fäller; Holzschnitzer

woodland n. Waldland, Waldung

wood(s)man n. Waldbewohner; Förster

woodpecker n. Specht; **spotted** — Bunt-specht

woodpile n. Holzhaufen, Holzstoss

woodruff n. Waldmeister

woodshed n. Holzschuppen

woodwork n. Holzwerk; Holzarbeit

wool n. Wolle; -en adj. wollen; Woll-; -y adj. wollig; Woll-; (coll.) verschwom-men, verschleiert

word n. Wort; Nachricht, Bescheid, Meldung, Botschaft; Rede; Spruch; Zusage, Versprechen; (mil.) Losungs-wort; Kommando; pl. Wörter, Worte; Wortwechsel, Rede; Text; **by — of mouth** mündlich; -**iness** n. Wortfülle, Wortschwall; -**ing** n. Ausdruck(sweise), Stil; Wortlaut; -y adj. wortreich, weit-schweifig

work n. Werk, Arbeit; Tat, Tätigkeit; Beruf, Beschäftigung; Leistung, Er-zeugnis; (mech.) Gang, Getriebe; pl. Fabrik, Anlage, Betrieb; Werke; — v. arbeiten, bearbeiten; wirken; in Gang bringen (or setzen), bewirken; -**able** adj. ausführbar, brauchbar; schmieg-sam, bearbeitbar; -**er** n. Arbeiter; Urheber; -**ers** pl. Arbeiterschaft; -**ing** n. Arbeit, Wirken; Bewegung; Arbeits-prozess, Bearbeitung; (chem.) Gärung; -**ing day** Werktag, Arbeitstag; -**ing** adj. arbeitend

workbench n. Werkbank, Arbeitstisch

workhouse n. Besserungsanstalt, Arbeits-haus

work(ing)man n. Arbeiter; Handwerker

workmanship n. Geschicklichkeit, Kunst-fertigkeit

workout n. Geschicklichkeitsprobe; (sports) Training; Leistungsprüfung

workshop n. Werkstatt, Werkstätte

world n. Welt; Erde; (fig.) Menge; -**ly** adj. weltlich, irdisch, Welt-; zeitlich

world-wide adj. weltberühmt, allgemein anerkannt, weitverbreitet

worm n. Wurm; (mech.) Gewinde; — **gear** Schneckengetriebe; — **powder** Wurmpulver; — v. sich krümmen (or winden); kriechen; nach Würmer graben; Würmer entfernen; -y adj. wurmig, madig, wurmstichig, von Würmern befallen; (fig.) kriechend

worm-eaten adj. wurmstichig, vermottet

wormwood n. Wermut

worn(-out) adj. abgenutzt, abgetragen; verbraucht

worry n. Sorge; Quälerei, Plage; — v. (sich) sorgen; plagen, quälen; zerren

worse adj. schlechter, schlimmer, übler, ärger; **so much the** — umso schlimmer

worship n. Anbetung, Verehrung; Gottes-dienst; — v. verehren, anbeten

worst n. Schlimmste, Ärgste; **at (the)** — im schlimmsten Falle (or Zustand); — adj. schlechtest, schlimmst, ärgst; — adv. am schlechtesten (or schlimmsten, ärgsten)

worsted n. (fabric) Kammgarn, Wollgarn

worth n. Wert; — adj. wert, würdig; **be** — wert sein, gelten, kosten; -**iness** n. Würdigkeit, Verdienst; -**less** adj. wert-los; unwürdig, nichtswürdig; -y n. Ehrenmann, Würdenträger; -y adj. würdig; verdienstvoll, trefflich; ehrbar; schätzbar, rühmlich

worth-while adj. **be** — sich lohnen, der Mühe wert sein

would-be adj. angeblich, vermeintlich, scheinbar, sogenannt; Schein-

wound n. Wunde; Verwundung, Verlet-zung; (fig.) Kränkung; — v. verwun-den, verletzen; (fig.) kränken

wrangle n. Zank, Streit; — v. zanken, streiten

wrap v. (ein)wickeln, einschlagen, ein-hüllen; verpacken; -**per** n. Packer; Hülle, Überzug, Umschlag; Packpa-pier; Umhüllung; Morgenrock; -**ping** n. Hülle, Mantel; Packmaterial

wrath n. Zorn, Grimm, Wut; -**ful** adj. zornig, grimmig, wütend

wreath n. Kranz; Girlande; Gewinde; -e v. winden, flechten; bekränzen, um-winden; sich ringeln

wreck n. Wrack; Schiffbruch; (fig.) Ruin, Verfall, Untergang; — v. zum Scheitern bringen; zerstören, zertrümmern; zu-grunde richten; **be** -**ed** scheitern; -**age** n. Schiffstrümmer, Strandgut; (fig.) Trümmer, Reste; -**er** n. Strandräuber; (fig.) Abbrucharbeiter

wren n. Zaunkönig

wrench n. Drehung, Verrenkung; (mech.) Schraubenschlüssel; — v. winden, drehen; verdrehen, verrenken

wrest v. zerren; entwinden, entreissen

wrestle n. Ringen; — v. ringen, kämpfen; (coll.) sich herumbalgen; -r n. Ringer

wrestling n. Ringkampf

wretch n. Unglückliche, Elende; **poor** —! armer Teufel! -**ed** adj. unglücklich, armselig, erbärmlich; nichtswürdig, verächtlich

wriggle v. sich winden (or schlängeln), sich hin und her drehen

wring v. (aus)ringen; (aus)pressen; (um)-drehen; entreissen; (hands) ringen; -**er** n. Auswringer; (mech.) Wringma-schine; (coll.) Erpresser

wrinkle n. Runzel, Falte; Kniff; — v. (sich) runzeln; falten

wrist n. Handgelenk; — **watch** Arm-banduhr

wristband n. Manschette; Armband

writ n. Schrift; (law) gerichtlicher Befehl,

Vorladung, Klageschrift; (pol.) be-
hördlicher Erlass

write v. schreiben; — **down** niederschreiben, aufschreiben; — **off** abschreiben;
— **poetry** Verse schreiben, dichten; —
up (coll.) anpreisen, herausstreichen;
-r n. Schreiber; Schriftsteller

write-up n. (coll.) Anpreisung, lobender
Artikel

writhe v. sich winden (or krümmen)

writing n. Schreiben; Schrift; Handschrift; Aufsatz, Werk; Schreibart,
Stil; Schriftstellerei; (law) Urkunde,
Dokument; **in** — schriftlich: **the
present** — das vorliegende Schreiben;
— **desk** Schreibtisch, Schreibpult;
Schreibmappe; — **paper** Schreibpapier

wrong n. Unrecht; Kränkung, Beleidigung; Irrtum; Schaden; — adj. unrecht,
falsch; verkehrt, unrichtig, irrig; unbillig; — v. Unrecht tun, benachteiligen,
Schaden zufügen; kränken, beleidigen;
-ful adj. ungerecht; beleidigend, kränkend; nachteilig; **-ly** adv. mit Unrecht,
fälschlich, versehentlich, auf ungerechte (or verkehrte, falsche) Weise

wrongdoer n. Missetäter, Übeltäter;
Beleidiger

wrong-sided adj. (phot.) seitenverkehrt

wrought adj. bearbeitet, verarbeitet; —
iron Schmiedeeisen

wry adj. schief, krumm; verdreht; — **face**
schiefes Gesicht, Grimasse

Wurtemberg n. Württemberg

X

Xanthippe n. Xanthippe; (fig.) zänkisches
Weib

Xmas, Christmas n. Weihnachten, Weihnachtsfest

X ray n. Röntgenstrahl; Röntgenbild,
Röntgenplatte; **X-ray** adj. Röntgen-;
— **specialist** Röntgenologe; — v.
röntgen, durchleuchten

xylograph n. Holzschnitt

xylophone n. Xylofon

Y

yacht n. Jacht, Segelboot

yam n. Yamswurzel

yank v. (coll.) zerren, wegreissen; fort-
schnellen

Yankee n. Yankee, Nordamerikaner; —
adj. yankeemässig

yap n. Gekläff; — v. kläffen

yard n. Hof(raum); (agr.) Viehhof; (measure) Elle; (rail.) Rangierbahnhof

yardmaster n. (naut.) Werftaufseher;
(rail.) Rangiermeister

yardstick n. Zollstock; (fig.) Masstab

yarn n. Garn; (naut.) Kabelgarn, Ducht

yaw n. & r. Kursabweichung; abtreiben;
wenden; gieren

yawing n. Seitenbewegung

yawl n. Jolle

yawn n. Gähnen; — v. gähnen, klaffen

yea adv. ja, gewiss; — **or nay** ja oder nein;
the -s have it die Jastimmen sind in der

Mehrheit

year n. Jahr; pl. Jahre; Alter; **all** —
around das ganze Jahr (hindurch);
many -s ago vor vielen Jahren; **-ling**
n. Jährling, einjähriges Tier; **-ly** adj.
jährlich, jährig; ein Jahr dauernd

yearbook n. Jahrbuch

yearn v. sich sehen, verlangen, schmachten; **-ing** n. Verlangen, Sehnsucht

yeast n. Hefe; (water) Gischt, Schaum

yell n. gellender Schrei, Geheul; Erken-
nungsruf; — v. gellen, schreien, heulen

yellow n. Gelb; Eigelb; — adj. gelb; —
fever gelbes Fieber; — **jacket** (ent.)
gelbe Wespe, — **press** Hetzpresse,
Schundpresse; — v. gelb werden; ver-
gilben; **-ish** adj. gelblich, fahlgelb

yelp n. Gekläff; — v. kläffen, bellen

yen n. (Japanese coin) Yen; (coll.) Sehnsucht, Verlangen

yes adv. ja; — **indeed** ja wahrhaftig; —
truly ja freilich; — **man** Jasager

yesterday n. gestriger Tag; — adv.
gestern; **day before** — vorgestern; **I
was not born** — ich bin nicht von
gestern

yet adv. noch; jetzt (noch), bis jetzt;
nunmehr, schon, selbst, sogar; — conj.
doch, dennoch, obwohl, obgleich,
gleichwohl, trotzdem

yield n. Ertrag, Ausbeute, Ernte; — v.
einbringen, tragen, abwerfen; überlassen, aufgeben, übergeben; gewähren,
zugeben; sich fügen, nachgeben; (mil.)
sich ergeben; **-ing** adj. ergiebig, einträglich; nachgiebig, dehnbar; willfährig

yodel n. Jodler; — v. jodeln

yoke n. Joch; — v. ins Joch spannen;
(fig.) unterjochen

yokel n. Tölpel

yolk n. Eidotter, Eigelb

yon(der) adv. dort, drüben; jenseits; an
jener Stelle; — adj. jene, jenseitig

yore adv. — **of** ehemals, vormals, ehedem

you pron. du, Sie, man, ihr

young adj. jung; frisch, neu; unerfahren;
**Young Men's Christian Association,
Y.M.C.A.** Christlicher Verein junger
Männer; **Young Women's Christian
Association, Y.W.C.A.** Christlicher Ve-
rein junger Mädchen; **-ster** n. Junge,
Bursche; Kind

your pron. dein, Ihr, euer; **-s** pron. der
(or die, das) deinige (or Ihrige, eurige);
sincerely -s Ihr ganz ergebener; **-s
truly** Ihr ergebener; **-self, -selves** (pl.)
(du, Sie, ihr, sich) selbst; (dich, Sie,
euch) selbst

youth n. Jugend; Jüngling, junger
Bursche; junge Leute; — **hostel**
Jugendherberge; **-ful** adj. jugendlich,
jung

yucca n. Yukka, Palmlilie

Yule n. Weihnacht(en), Julfest

Yuletide n. Weihnachtszeit

Z

zeal n. Eifer; Wärme; **-ous** adj. eifrig;

warm, innig, herzlich
zebra *n.* Zebra
zephyr *n.* Zephir
zero *n.* Null; Nullpunkt; (phys.) Gefrierpunkt; — **hour** Entscheidungsstunde
zest *n.* Behagen, Wohlgefallen; Würze, Beigeschmack
zigzag *n.* Zickzack; — *adj.* zickzackförmig; — *v.* im Zickzack laufen
zinc *n.* Zink; — *v.* verzinken
zipgun *n.* selbsthergestelltes, primitives Gewehr
zipper *n.* Reissverschluss
zither *n.* Zither
zodiac *n.* Tierkreis
zone *n.* Zone; Gebiet; Bezirk, Bereich
zoo *n.* Zoo, zoologischer Garten; **–logic(al)** *adj.* zoologisch; **–logy** *n.* Zoologie, Tierkunde
zoom *r.* (avi.) senkrecht in die Höhe steigen, hochreissen
zyme *n.* Gärungsstoff, Ferment

STRONG AND IRREGULAR VERBS

In the following table compound verbs are included only where the corresponding simple verb does not occur, or where it is very uncommon. Where the stem vowel changes in the present indicative, the change is indicated in parentheses following the infinitive. When the auxiliary of the perfect is a form of *sein*, it is indicated by the word *ist*. When transitive forms using *haben* also occur, *ist* is enclosed in parentheses (*ist*). Verbs marked with an asterisk (*) sometimes have weak forms.

Infinitive	Past	Past Participle
backen (ä)	buk	gebacken
befehlen (ie)	befahl	befohlen
befleissen	befliss	beflissen
beginnen	begann	begonnen
beissen	biss	gebissen
bergen (i)	barg	geborgen
*bersten (i)	barst	ist geborsten
*bewegen	bewog	bewogen
biegen	bog	gebogen
bieten	bot	geboten
binden	band	gebunden
bitten	bat	gebeten
blasen (ä)	blies	geblasen
bleiben	blieb	ist geblieben
braten	briet	gebraten
brechen (i)	brach	gebrochen
brennen	brannte	gebrannt
bringen	brachte	gebracht
denken	dachte	gedacht
*dingen	dang	gedungen
dreschen (i)	drasch, drosch	gedroschen
dringen	drang	gedrungen
dürfen	durfte	gedurft
empfehlen (ie)	empfahl	empfohlen
erbleichen	erblich	ist erblichen
erlöschen (i)	erlosch	ist erloschen
*erschrecken (i)	erschrak	ist erschrocken
essen (i)	ass	gegessen
fahren (ä)	fuhr	ist gefahren
fallen (ä)	fiel	ist gefallen
fangen (ä)	fing	gefangen
fechten (i)	focht	gefochten
finden	fand	gefunden
flechten (i)	flocht	geflochten
fliegen	flog	ist geflogen
fliehen	floh	ist geflohen
fliessen	floss	ist geflossen
fressen (i)	frass	gefressen
frieren	fror	gefroren
gären	gor	gegoren
gebären (ie)	gebar	geboren
geben (i)	gab	gegeben
gedeihen	gedieh	ist gediehen
gehen	ging	ist gegangen
gelingen	gelang	ist gelungen
gelten (i)	galt	gegolten
genesen	genas	ist genesen
geniessen	genoss	genossen
geschehen (ie)	geschah	ist geschehen
gewinnen	gewann	gewonnen
giessen	goss	gegossen
gleichen	glich	geglichen
*gleissen	gliss	geglissen
*gleiten	glitt	ist geglitten

Infinitive	Past	Past Participle
*glimmen	glomm	geglommen
graben (ä)	grub	gegraben
greifen	griff	gegriffen
haben (hat)	hatte	gehabt
halten (ä)	hielt	gehalten
hangen (ä)	hing	gehangen
hauen	hieb	gehauen
heben	hob	gehoben
heissen	hiess	geheissen
helfen (i)	half	geholfen
kennen	kannte	gekannt
kiesen	kor	gekoren
*klimmen	klomm	ist geklommen
klingen	klang	geklungen
kneifen	kniff	gekniffen
kommen	kam	ist gekommen
können (kann)	konnte	gekonnt
kriechen	kroch	ist gekrochen
küren	kor	gekoren
*laden (ä)	lud	geladen
lassen (ä)	liess	gelassen
laufen (äu)	lief	ist gelaufen
leiden	litt	gelitten
leihen	lieh	geliehen
lesen (ie)	las	gelesen
liegen	lag	gelegen
lügen	log	gelogen
mahlen	mahlte	gemahlen
meiden	mied	gemieden
*melken (i)	molk	gemolken
messen (i)	mass	gemessen
misslingen	misslang	ist misslungen
mögen (mag)	mochte	gemocht
müssen (muss)	musste	gemusst
nehmen (nimmt)	nahm	genommen
nennen	nannte	genannt
pfeifen	pfiff	gepfiffen
*pflegen	pflog	gepflogen
preisen	pries	gepriesen
quellen (i)	quoll	ist gequollen
raten (ä)	riet	geraten
reiben	rieb	gerieben
reissen	riss	gerissen
reiten	ritt	ist geritten
rennen	rannte	ist gerannt
riechen	roch	gerochen
ringen	rang	gerungen
rinnen	rann	ist geronnen
rufen	rief	gerufen
salzen	salzte	gesalzen
saufen (äu)	soff	gesoffen
saugen	sog	gesogen
*schaffen	schuf	geschaffen
*schallen	scholl	geschollen
scheiden	schied	ist geschieden
scheinen	schien	geschienen
schelten (i)	schalt	gescholten
schieben	schob	geschoben
schiessen	schoss	geschossen
schinden	schund	geschunden
schlafen (ä)	schlief	geschlafen
schlagen (ä)	schlug	geschlagen
schleichen	schlich	ist geschlichen
*schleifen	schliff	geschliffen
schleissen	schliss	geschlissen
schliefen	schloff	ist geschloffen
schliessen	schloss	geschlossen
schlingen	schlang	geschlungen
schmeissen	schmiss	geschmissen
*schmelzen (i)	schmolz	ist geschmolzen

Infinitive	Past	Past Participle
schneiden	schnitt	geschnitten
*schrauben	schrob	geschroben
*schrecken (i)	schrak	ist erschrocken
schreiben	schrieb	geschrieben
schreien	schrie	geschrieen
schreiten	schritt	ist geschritten
schweigen	schwieg	geschwiegen
*schwellen (i)	schwoll	ist geschwollen
schwimmen	schwamm	ist geschwommen
schwinden	schwand	ist geschwunden
schwören	schwur	geschworen
sehen (ie)	sah	gesehen
sein	war	ist gewesen
senden	sandte	gesandt
	sendete	gesendet
*sieden	sott	gesotten
singen	sang	gesungen
sinken	sank	ist gesunken
sinnen	sann	gesonnen
sitzen	sass	gesessen
sollen (soll)	sollte	gesollt
speien	spie	gespieen
spinnen	spann	gesponnen
sprechen (i)	sprach	gesprochen
spriessen	spross	ist gesprossen
springen	sprang	ist gesprungen
stechen (i)	stach	gestochen
*stecken (i)	stak	gesteckt
stehen	stand, stund	gestanden
stehlen (ie)	stahl	gestohlen
steigen	stieg	ist gestiegen
sterben (i)	starb	ist gestorben

Infinitive	Past	Past Participle
stieben	stob	(ist) gestoben
stinken	stank	gestunken
stossen (ö)	stiess	gestossen
streichen	strich	gestrichen
streiten	stritt	gestritten
tragen (ä)	trug	getragen
treffen (i)	traf	getroffen
treiben	trieb	getrieben
treten	trat	(ist) getreten
*triefen	troff	getroffen
trinken	trank	getrunken
trügen	trog	getrogen
tun	tat	getan
*verderben	verdarb	(ist) verdorben
vergessen (i)	vergass	vergessen
verlieren	verlor	verloren
wägen	wog	gewogen
waschen (ä)	wusch	gewaschen
weben	wob	gewoben
weisen	wies	gewiesen
wenden	wandte	gewandt
	wendete	gewendet
werben (i)	warb	geworben
werden (i)	wurde, ward	ist geworden
werfen (i)	warf	geworfen
wiegen	wog	gewogen
winden	wand	gewunden
wissen (weiss)	wusste	gewusst
wollen (will)	wollte	gewollt
zeihen	zieh	geziehen
ziehen	zog	(ist) gezogen
zwingen	zwang	gezwungen

* The following verbs are always weak when used in the meanings indicated: bewegen (move physically); pflegen (be accustomed to); schaffen (to work, do); schleifen (drag); schmelzen (melt something); schrecken (frighten); schwellen (make larger); sieden (seethe); stecken (stick, put).

TRAVELER'S CONVERSATION GUIDE

ENGLISH-GERMAN

STATION OR AIRPORT
DER BAHNHOF ODER DER FLUGHAFEN

Here is my passport.
Hier ist mein Pass.

Here is my baggage.
Da ist mein Gepäck.

Here are the checks.
Hier sind die Scheine.

Where is the porter?
Wo ist de Träger?

Please put my bags in a taxi.
Bitte, schaffen Sie die Koffer in einen Taxi.

I have nothing to declare.
Ich habe nichts zu verzollen.

Must I pay duty on this?
Ist das zollpflichtig?

How much?
Wieviel?

How many pieces of baggage?
Wieviel Stück Gepäck?

Where is the baggage room?
Wo ist die Gepäckaufbewahrung?

I want to check my baggage.
Ich möchte mein Gepäck aufgeben.

Where is the ticket office?
Wo ist der Fahrkartenschalter?

I want a ticket to _____.
Ich möchte eine Fahrkarte nach ____ haben.

Where can I get change money?
Wo kann ich Geld wechseln?

Please give me Deutsche Marks.
Bitte, geben Sie mir Deutsche Mark.

Where is the men's room? (ladies' room?)
Wo ist die Herrentoilette? (Damentoilette?)

Here is a tip.
Heir ist ein Trinkgeld.

Is that all?
Ist das alles?

That is all.
Das ist alles.

TAXI
TAXI

Porter, please take my luggage to a taxi.
Träger, laden Sie mein Gepäck in ein Taxi, bitte.

What is your rate to _____?
Was ist der Preis nach ————?

Take the shortest way.
Bitte, fahren Sie den kürzesten Weg.

Where is the shopping district?
Wo ist das Geschäftsviertel?

Stop here.
Halten Sie hier.

Please wait for me.
Bitte, warten Sie auf mich.

Drive more slowly (faster).
Bitte, fahren Sie langsamer (schneller).

To the Hotel _____.
Zum Hotel _____.

Where is a good hotel?
Wo gibt es ein gutes Hotel?

Is it expensive?
Ist es teuer?

Is there a good restaurant?
Gibt es ein gutes Gasthaus?

TRAIN
DER ZUG

Where is the railroad station?
Wo ist der Bahnhof?

What is the fare to _____?
Was kostet die Fahrt nach _____?

I want a ticket to _____.
Ich möchte eine Fahrkarte nach _____?

One way.
Hinfahrt.

Round trip.
Hin-und Rückfahrt.

Where are the first- (second-) class cars?	Wo sind die Wagen erster (zweiter) Klasse?
Please put my baggage on the train (in my compartment).	Bitte, tragen Sie mein Gepäck in den Zug (in mein Abteil).
At what time does the train for _____ leave?	Um wieviel Uhr fährt der Zug nach _____ ab?
On what track does the train leave?	Von welchem Bahnsteig fährt der Zug?
Is there a dining-car on this train?	Hat dieser Zug einen Speisewagen?
Is there a sleeping-car on this train?	Hat dieser Zug einen Schlafwagen?
Does the train stop at _____?	Hält der Zug in _____?
All aboard!	Alle einsteigen!
Are you the conductor?	Sind Sie der Kondukteur?
Where is the dining-car?	Wo ist der Speisewagen?
Is there time to get something to eat?	Habe ich genug Zeit um etwas zu essen?
Where is the smoking compartment?	Wo ist das Raucherabteil?
Is the train on time?	Ist der Zug pünktlich?
Why are we stopping?	Warum halten wir?

AIRPLANE / DAS FLUGZEUG

I am flying to _____.	Ich fliege nach _____.
Is there motor service to the airport?	Gibt's einen Zubringerdienst?
Here is the airport.	Hier ist der Flugplatz.
What planes are there to ——?	Wann gehen Flugzeuge nach ——?
How much luggage is each passenger allowed?	Wieviel Gepäck darf jeder Passagier mitnehmen?
What is the charge for extra luggage?	Wieviel kostet weiteres Gepäck?
Please put my luggage on the plane for _____.	Bitte laden Sie mein Gepäck in das Flugzeug nach _____.
At what time do we leave (arrive)?	Um wieviel Uhr fahren wir ab (kommen wir an)?
Which is the plane to ——?	Welches ist das Flugzeug nach —?
The plane leaves on runway No. _____.	Das Flugzeug fliegt von Position Nummer _____ ab.
Here is the waiting room.	Hier ist der Wartesaal.
Where is the stewardess (hostess)?	Wo ist die Stewardess (Aufwärterin)?
Wait for me at the gate.	Warten Sie auf mich bei der Schranke.
How high are we flying?	Wie hoch fliegen wir?
How fast are we flying?	Wie schnell fliegen wir?
I feel sick.	Mir ist schlecht.
We are thirty minutes late.	Wir haben dreissig Minuten Verspätung.
When do we arrive at _____?	Wann kommen wir in _____ an?
Where is the airline office?	Wo ist das Fluglinienbüro?

BUS OR STREETCAR / DER AUTOBUS ODER DIE STRASSENBAHN

Does this streetcar (bus) go to _____?	Geht diese Strassenbahn (dieser Autobus) nach _____?
Wait at the car (bus) stop.	Warten Sie bei der Strassenbahn (Autobus) Haltestelle.
How much is the fare, please?	Was kostet die Fahrt, bitte?
Will you please tell me where to get off?	Sagen Sie mir, bitte, wo ich aussteigen muss.
I want to go to _____.	Ich möchte nach _____ gehen.
Do I need a transfer?	Brauche ich ein Umsteigebillet?
When does this car (bus) return?	Wann fährt diese Strassenbahn (dieser Autobus) zurück?

SHIP	DAS SCHIFF
Which way to the quay?	Wie kommt man zu der Landestelle?
When does the ship sail?	Um wieviel Uhr geht das Schiff ab?
May visitors come on board?	Können Besucher on Bord kommen?
I am going to my stateroom.	Ich gehe in meine Kabine.
I am going on deck.	Ich gehe auf Deck.
I want to rent a deck chair.	Ich möchte einen Liegestuhl mieten.
I want to speak to the purser (deck steward).	Ich möchte gern mit dem Zahlmeister (Decksteward) sprechen.
Where are the lifeboats (life preservers)?	Wo sind die Rettungsbote (Rettungsgürtel)?
Where is the dining salon?	Wo ist der Speisesalon?
When are meals served?	Wann wird serviert?
I am seasick.	Ich bin seekrank.
Have you a remedy for seasickness?	Haben Sie ein Mittel gegen Seekrankheit?
We are landing at _____.	Wir gehen in _____ an Land.

AUTOMOBILE — DAS AUTO

AUTOMOBILE	DAS AUTO
Do you have a road map?	Haben Sie eine Autokarte?
Can you draw me a map?	Können Sie mir eine Zeichnung machen?
Which is the road to _____?	Welche Strasse führt nach _____?
How far is _____?	Wie weit ist es bis _____?
Is the road good?	Ist die Strasse gut?
Is there a good restaurant (hotel) in _____?	Gibt es ein gutes Gasthaus (Hotel) in _____?
Where is the garage?	Wo ist die Garage?
Fill her up.	Machen Sie den Tank voll.
Do I need oil (water, air)?	Brauche ich Öl (Wasser, Luft)?
How much is a liter?	Was kostet ein Liter?
Give me thirty liters.	Geben Sei mir dreissig Liter.
Please check the tires (the oil, the battery, the water, the spark plugs).	Bitte, sehen Sie die Reifen (das Öl, die Batterie, das Wasser, die Zündkerzen) nach.
Please wash the car.	Bitte, waschen Sie den Wagen.
Please grease the car.	Bitte, schmieren Sie die Maschine ab.
Please tighten the brakes.	Bitte, ziehen Sie die Bremse an.
Is there a mechanic here?	Ist ein Mechaniker hier?
The engine overheats (stalls).	Der Motor überhitzt (bleibt stehen).
Can you tow me?	Können Sie mich ziehen?
Where may I park?	Wo kann ich parken?

ROAD SIGNS — DIE STRASSENZEICHEN

ROAD SIGNS	DIE STRASSENZEICHEN
Stop	Halt!
Slow	Langsam!
Caution	Vorsicht!
Detour	Umleitung
Danger	Gefahr
Notice	Achtung!
Road closed (open)	Strasse geschlossen (offen)
Crossroads	Kreuzung
One way	Einbahnstrasse
(Dangerous) curve	(Gefährliche) Kurve
Speed limit 30 km. an hour	Geschwindigkeitsgrenze 30 Km.
Ladies	Damen

Gentlemen	Herren
lavatory	der Waschraum
Entrance	Eingang
Exit	Ausgang
No smoking (admittance, parking, spitting).	Rauchen (Eintritt, Parken, Spucken) verboten.
Tourist Information Office	(Touristen) Auskunfsstelle
Extreme caution	Ausserste Vorsicht
Keep right (left)	Rechts (links) fahren
Grade crossing	Bahnübergang
Watch out for trains	Vorsicht auf den Zug
Narrow bridge	Enge Brücke
No thoroughfare	Keine Durchfahrt
No right (left) turn	Nicht rechts (links) einbiegen
Steep grade (up)	Starke Steigung
Steep grade (down)	Starkes Gefälle
No trespassing	Unbefugtes Betreten verboten
School	Schule

HOTEL

DAS HOTEL

Where is a good hotel?	Wo gibt es ein gutes Hotel?
Is it expensive?	Ist es teuer?
I want a room.	Ich wünsche ein Zimmer.
Have you a room with bath?	Haben Sie ein Zimmer mit Bad?
I made a reservation.	Ich habe eine Vorbestellung gemacht.
Have you a single (double) room with bath (with shower)?	Haben Sie ein Einzel- (Doppel-) zimmer mit Bad (mit Brause)?
How much is it by the day (week, month)?	Wieviel kostet es täglich (wöchentlich, monatlich)?
I should like to see the room.	Ich möchte das Zimmer sehen.
It is too small (large, noisy, hot, cold).	Es ist zu klein (gross, laut, heiss, kalt).
Are meals included?	Sind Mahlzeiten einbegriffen?
Where is the bathroom (the telephone, the lavatory, the dining room)?	Wo ist das Badezimmer (das Telephon, die Toilette, der Speisesaal)?
What is the room number?	Was ist die Zimmernummer?
Open the window.	Machen Sie das Fenster auf.
Close the door.	Machen Sie die Tür zu.
Please bring towels (soap).	Bringen Sie Handtücher (Seife), bitte.
Please send the chambermaid (the valet, the waiter).	Bitte, schicken Sie das Zimmermädchen (den Hausdiener, den Kellner).
I want these shoes shined.	Ich möchte diese Schuhe putzen lassen.
I want it pressed.	Ich will ihn nur bügeln lassen.
Please take these suits (these dresses) to be cleaned.	Lassen Sie diese Anzüge (diese Kleider) bitte reinigen
Is there any mail for me?	Ist Post für mich da?
Please mail these letters for me.	Bitte, senden Sie diese Briefe für mich ab.
Some stamps.	Einige Briefmarken.
Some writing paper.	Etwas Schreibpapier.
An envelope.	Einen Briefumschlag.
Please change the sheets (pillow cases, towels).	Bitte, wechseln Sie die Leintücher (die Kissenbezüge, die Handtücher).
Call me at 6 a.m.	Wecken Sie mich um sechs Uhr morgens.
Who is there?	Wer ist es?
Wait a minute.	Bitte, warten Sie eine Minute!

Do not disturb.	Bitte, nicht stören!
I want an interpreter (guide, secretary) who speaks English.	Ich möchte einen Dolmetscher (einen Führer, eine Sekretärin) der (die) Englisch spricht.
Prepare my bill, please.	Meine Rechnung, bitte.

RESTAURANT

DAS RESTAURANT

Where is a good restaurant?	Wo ist ein gutes Restaurant?
A table for two, please, (near the window).	Ein Tisch für zwei, bitte, (nah dem Fenster).
Let me have the menu (wine list).	Bitte geben Sie mir die Speisekarte (Weinkarte).
What do you recommend?	Was empfehlen Sie?
Do you have a table d'hôte dinner (lunch, breakfast)?	Haben Sie ein Table d'Hôte Abendessen (Mittagessen, Frühstück)?
What wine do you recommend?	Welchen Wein empfehlen Sie?
Give us an aperitif (whiskey, gin, liqueur).	Geben Sie uns ein Aperitif (Whisky, Wacholderbranntwein, einen Likör).
Bring us this, please.	Bringen Sie uns das, bitte.
Bring us two orders of soup.	Bringen Sie uns zwei Portionen Suppe.
We should like to have dinner (lunch) German style.	Wir möchten gern Abendessen (Mittagessen) auf deutsche Art haben.
Bring us orders of _____.	Bringen Sie uns Portionen ____.
eggs	Eier
toast	Toast
chops	Koteletten
omelet	Omeletten
chicken	Huhn
duck	Ente
oysters	Austern
shrimps	Krabben
salad	Salat
liver	Leber
beans	Bohnen
roast beef	Rostbraten
roast pork	Schweinebraten
pork chops	Schweinekotelett
steak (rare, medium, well done)	Englisch, halb durchgebraten, gut durchgebraten)
fish	Fisch
lobster	Hummer
lamb	Lamm
radishes	Radieschen
carrots	Karotten
peas	Erbsen
lettuce	Kopfsalat
spinach	Spinat
rice	Reis
potatoes (fried, mashed)	Kartoffeln (gebraten, Püree)
tomatoes	Tomaten
cucumber	Gurke

cabbage	Kohl
stringbeans	Schnittbohnen
onion	Zwieblen

Please bring _____:	Bitte, bringen Sie mir _____
milk and cream	Milch und Sahne
vinegar and oil	Essig und Öl
lemon	Zitrone
salt and pepper	Salz und Pfeffer
cheese	Käse
tea	Tee
coffee	Kaffee
a napkin	eine Serviette
fork	Gabel
knife	Messer
teaspoon	Teelöffel
What have you for dessert?	Was haben Sie zum Nachtisch?
ice cream	Eis
pastry	Backwerk
fruit	Obst
cake	Kuchen
pie	Torte
I should like a cup of tea (black coffee, coffee with milk)	Ich möchte eine Tasse Tee (schwarzen Kaffe, Milchkaffee).
The check, please.	Die Rechnung, bitte!

THE MARKET   DER MARKT

I should like to go shopping.	Ich möchte einkaufen gehen.
Can you tell me where I can buy _____?	Können Sie mir sagen wo ich _____ kaufen kann?
I should like to go to a department store.	Ich möchte gern zu einem Warenhaus gehen.
a shoeshop	einem Schuhladen
a bookstore	einer Buchhandlung
a cigar store	einem Tabakladen
a stationer's	einem Papiergeschäft
I should like to see _____.	Ich möchte gern _____ sehen.
How much is this?	Wieviel kostet dies?
What size (color)?	Welche Grösse (Farbe)?
Do you have it in white? (black, red, brown, green, blue, yellow)	Haben Sie das in weiss? (schwarz, rot, braun, grün, blau, gelb)
Do you have something larger (smaller)?	Haben Sie etwas Grösseres (Kleineres)?
May I try this on?	Kann ich dies anprobieren?
Have you a better quality?	Haben Sie eine bessere Qualität?
This is too expensive.	Es ist zu teuer.
I like this one.	Mir gefällt dies hier.
Sale	Verkauf
Bargain sale	Ausverkauf
It does not fit.	Es passt nicht.
I shall take it with me.	Ich werde es mitnehmen.
Send it to the Hotel _____, please.	Senden Sie es zum Hotel _____, bitte.

THE POST OFFICE   DAS POSTAMT

Can you direct me to the post office?	Können Sie mir den Weg zum nächsten Postamt zeigen?
Where can I get some stamps?	Wo kann ich Briefmarken bekommen?
How much is the postage?	Was ist die Gebühr?
What is the local postage here?	Was kostet ein einfacher Brief?

What is the regular postage to the U.S.A.?	Was kostet ein einfacher Brief nach U.S.A.?
What is the airmail postage to the U.S.A.?	Was kostet Luftpost nach U.S.A.?
I want to send this package.	Ich möchte dieses Paket absenden.
I want it insured.	Ich möchte es versichern.
Here is the (my) address.	Hier ist die (meine) Adresse.

PHOTOGRAPHER — DER PHOTOGRAPH

I should like some camera film No. _____. (a roll of color film)	Ich möchte Kamerafilm Nummer _____. (eine Rolle Farbfilm)
Please develop the films (plates).	Bitte, entwickeln Sie diese Filme (Platten).
How much does it cost to develop a roll?	Wieviel kostet est eine Rolle zu entwickeln?
I want one print (enlargement) of each.	Ich möchte einen Abzug (Vergrösserung) von jedem.
I want these pictures developed for tomorrow.	Ich möchte diese Bilder für morgen entwickeln lassen.
When will it be ready?	Wann wird es fertig sein?

EVERYDAY EXPRESSIONS — ALLTÄGLICHE AUSDRUCKE

Good morning.	Guten Morgen.
Good day.	Guten Tag.
Good afternoon.	Guten Tag.
How are you?	Wie geht est Ihnen?
Good evening.	Guten Abend.
Goodbye.	Auf Wiedersehen.
Well, thank you.	Danke, gut.
And you?	Und Ihnen?
Pleased to meet you.	Sehr angenehm.
Yes.	Ja.
No.	Nein.
Please.	Bitte.
Thank you.	Danke schön.
All right.	Sehr gut.
Don't mention it.	Nichts zu danken.
Pardon me.	Entschuldigen Sie.
Not at all.	Sicher nicht.
O.K.	Schön! (or Machen wir!)
I am sorry.	Et tut mir leid.
Isn't it so?	Nicht wahr?
I'm glad.	Es freut mich.
Perhaps.	Vielleicht.
I agree.	Ich bin einverstanden.
I (don't) think so.	Ich glaube ja (nicht).
You're right (wrong).	Sie haben recht (unrecht).
Would you like _____?	Möchten Sie gern _____?
Do you like _____?	Gefällt Ihnen _____?
Do you want _____?	Wünschen Sie _____?
I (do not) understand.	Ich verstehe (nicht).
Can anyone here speak _____?	Kann hier jemand _____ sprechen?
Please speak slowly.	Bitte sprechen Sie langsam.
Not so fast.	Nicht so schnell.
I see.	Ich verstehe.
I (don't) know.	Ich weiss (nicht).
I am glad.	Es freut mich.
I am ready.	Ich bin fertig.
Don't forget.	Vergessen Sie nicht.
Gladly.	Gerne.
Certainly.	Gewiss.
Of course.	Natürlich.

I am most grateful.	Ich bin sehr dankbar.
The pleasure is mine.	Gleichfalls.
May I introduce you to _____?	Darf ich Ihnen _____ vorstellen?
My name is _____.	Ich heisse _____.
Here is my card.	Hier ist meine Karte.
Give my regards to _____.	Besten Gruss an _____.
Please sit down.	Bitte setzen Sie sich.
Make yourself at home.	Machen Sie sich bequem.
What time is it?	Wieviel Uhr ist es?
Do you mind my smoking?	Stört es Sie, wenn ich rauche?
May I open (close) the window (the door)?	Darf ich das Fenster (die Türe) öffnen?
Bring me _____.	Bringen Sie mir _____.
Take this away.	Nehmen Sie das weg.
I am tired.	Ich bin müde.
I am hungry.	Ich habe Hunger.
I am thirsty.	Ich habe Durst.
Please send for a doctor.	Bitte rufen Sie einen Arzt.
I am going out.	Ich gehe aus.
I shall return at _____ o'clock.	Ich komme um _____ Uhr zurück.
Has anyone asked for me?	Hat jemand nach mir gefragt?
Where are we (you) going?	Wohin gehen wir (Sie)?
Which way?	Welche Richtung?
To the right (left).	Nach rechts (links).
This way.	Diese Richtung.
That way.	Dorthin.
Notice!	Achtung!
Entrance.	Eingang.
Exit.	Ausgang.
Pedestrians.	Fussgänger
Knock.	(An)klopfen.
Ring the bell.	(An)läuten.
Can you tell me _____?	Können Sie mir _____ sagen?
I am looking for _____.	Ich suche _____.
Push.	Drücken!
Pull!	Ziehen!
Quiet.	Ruhig.
Free.	Frei.
Occupied.	Besetzt.
A pleasant stay.	Angenehmen Aufenthalt!
As quickly as possible.	So schnell wie möglich.
How long have you been waiting?	Wie lang warten Sie schon?
You have been very kind.	Sie waren äusserst gütig.
A pleasant journey.	Glückliche Reise.
Let me hear from you.	Lassen Sie von sich hören!
I want an interpreter.	Ich möchte einen Dolmetscher haben!

THE WEATHER   DAS WETTER

What is the weather like today?	Wie ist das Wetter heute?
It is a fine day.	Es ist ein schöner Tag.
It is (very) warm (cold).	Es ist (sehr) warm (kalt).
It is raining (snowing).	Es regnet (es schneit).
The wind is blowing from the north (south, east, west).	Der Wind bläst von Norden (Süden, Osten, Westen).
What is the weather likely to be tomorrow?	Wie wird das Wetter morgen sein?

TIME   DIE ZEIT

What time is it?	Wieviel Uhr ist es?
It is five o'clock.	Es ist fünf Uhr.
It is a quarter past six.	Es ist viertel nach sechs.

It is half-past seven.	Es ist halb acht.
It is a quarter to eight.	Es ist viertel vor acht.
It is twenty past nine.	Es ist zwanzig nach neun.
It is ten to ten.	Es ist zehn vor zehn.
Midday	Mittag
Midnight	Mitternacht
Sunday	Sonntag
Monday	Montag
Tuesday	Dienstag
Wednesday	Mittwoch
Thursday	Donnerstag
Friday	Freitag
Saturday	Samstag
Spring	Frühling
Summer	Sommer
Autumn	Herbst
Winter	Winter
January	Januar
February	Februar
March	März
April	April
May	Mai
June	Juni
July	Juli
August	August
September	September
October	Oktober
November	November
December	Dezember

THE NUMERALS   DIE ZAHLEN

nought	null
one	eins
two	zwei
three	drei
four	vier
five	fünf
six	sechs
seven	sieben
eight	acht
nine	neun
ten	zehn
eleven	elf
twelve	zwölf
thirteen	dreizehn
fourteen	vierzehn
fifteen	fünfzehn
sixteen	sechzehn
seventeen	siebzehn
eighteen	achtzehn
nineteen	neunzehn
twenty	zwanzig
twenty-one	einundzwanzig
thirty	dreissig
forty	vierzig
fifty	fünfzig
sixty	sechzig
seventy	siebzig
eighty	achtzig
ninety	neunzig
one hundred	hundert
one thousand	tausend
one million	eine Million